ISBN 978-0-484-40694-9
PIBN 10797999

Contents:

PRICE· ONE COPY, ₽ 50, TWO COPIES, $ .75, FOUR, $1.00, SIX, ₸1.25, EIGHT, $1.50, TEN, $1.75, TWELVE, $2.00.

A

DESCRIPTIVE LIST

OF

NOVELS AND TALES

DEALING WITH

AMERICAN COUNTRY LIFE.

COMPILED BY

W: M. GRISWOLD, A. B. (HARVARD.)

EDITOR OF "THE MONOGRAPH", A COLLECTION OF FIFTY-FOUR HISTORICAL AND
BIOGRAPHICAL ESSAYS; AND OF "TRAVEL", A SIMILAR SERIES
DEVOTED TO PLACES.

CAMBRIDGE, MASS:
W: M. GRISWOLD, PUBLISHER.
1890.

[*From the "School Bulletin," Aug.*, 1892.]

We hope teachers will not fail tŏ recognize the work **W. M. Griswold** is dŏing in his classified bibliography. He sends us a DESCRIPTIVE LIST OF NOVELS AND TALES DEALING WITH LIFE IN FRANCE (Cambridge, Mass., 1892, 8vo, pp. 94, $1.00), which is of immediate practical use tŏ the teacher of French history as well as of French literature.

• [*From the "Central Christian Advocate."*]

Mr. Griswold has dŏne an excellent work, which will be appreciated by all librarians, and by many people of cultivated taste whŏ wish tŏ get on the track of the best French fiction, or at least tŏ secure sŏme guidance and information in regard tŏ its qualities and characteristics. His former "lists" have dealt with American City and Country Life, with Life in England, etc . . . Life in city and country, peasant life and soldier life, the reckless and adventurous career of the free and easy student in Paris, and the rude rustic amŏng the mountains,—all these phases of French life pass in review in the books which Mr. Griswold has here catalogued. A guide like this would be invaluable tŏ a student of French literature, telling as well what tŏ avoid, as what tŏ secure and read.

[*From the "Boston Commonwealth,"* 13 *Aug.*, 1892.]

If all libraries wer generously equipped with these Lists, the long-suffering curator of books would find more pleasure in life. The compilation and selection ar made with rare skill. The poor book drops into deservd oblivion, while the worthy but neglected and forgotten good book is restored tŏ the eye of the world.

Sŏme not too busy people make note of the name of a novel recommended by a trustworthy critic, but when the time for use cŏmes the note seldom is at hand, and, if ready, generally givs the mere title and no idea of the contents. But here is a series of brochures that contain excerpts from the fairest critical notices, often from several sources, and ŏne is enabled tŏ form a sort of judgment of choice without actually glancing at the book itself. Of course, those dealing with foreign lands must for the grêater part be translations, since with few exceptions the most truthful and vivid characterizations cŏme from the compatriot whŏ has summered and wintered his fellows. Few people realize the patience, skill, and labor involvd in such an undertaking as the publication of these successiv lists, but those whŏ dŏ should urge upon ŏthers the use of so valuable a means of education and pleasure. As a series of 'condensed novels' they ar interesting, too.

NOVELS OF AMERICAN COUNTRY LIFE.

The object of this list is to direct readers, such as would enjoy the kind of books here described, to a number of novels, easily obtainable, but which, in many cases, have been forgotten within a year or two after publication. That the existence of works of fiction is remembered so short a time is a pity, since, for every new book of merit, there are, in most libraries, a hundred as good or better, unknown to the majority of readers. It is hoped that the publication of this and similar lists will lessen, in some measure, the disposition to read an inferior NEW *book when superior* OLD *books, equally fresh to most readers, are at hand.*

This list will be followed by others describing fiction dealing with American City Life, and with lists of "International" and Romantic novels. The compiler would be pleased to have his attention called to any works deserving a place which have escaped his attention. It may be observed that, while excluding all which do not deal with country life, he has tried to include among these only such as are well-written, interesting, and free from sensationalism, sentimentality, and pretense.

The selected "notices" here given are generally abridged.

ACHSAH [by W. M. F. ROUND: *Lee & Shepard*, 1876.] "There is a certain smartness about 'Achsah' which may make it popular in those rustic communities where living examples of the models portrayed in its pages are to be found. The heroine, Achsah, is a country girl, the danter of Deacon Sterne. This deacon is the best-drawn character of the book; his cunning, hypocrisy, and meanness make him an amusing caricature of certain Yankee faults. He bears the mark of being drawn from life by a very bitter enemy, who does not always hold his hand when he is expressing his scorn. The hero, Owen Rood, who accumulates money by writing magazine articles—one of them on Luther!—is a creature of the imagination rather than of flesh and blood. His troubles are of a familiar sort, and are easily cleared away as we approach the end of the story. What is good in all this is the account of the unadulterated **New England** people; less good is the romantic part, and the plot is too light to bear the superstructure." [Nation. 1

ADIRONDACK STORIES [by PHIL-ANDER DEMING, *Houghton*, 1880.] "Geographically, the Adirondacks are at no great distance from the Atlantic, but for literary purposes they are very far west indeed, and Mr. Deming's style and method show him to be distinctly related to that group of writers who have their head-quarters beyond the Rocky Mountains. His subjects, chosen from a common, even rude life, are poetic and pitched in a low key, consisting mostly of some bit of elemental pathos simply and suggestively rendered. The most original and striking feature of Mr. Deming's work is his adherence to pure narrative,

ALL ABOARD. [by "OLIVER OP-
TIC," i. e., W: T. ADAMS: Boston,
Brown, Bazin & Co., 1856.] The author
"writes in the plain and direct style which
suits those whom he addresses, and accomplishes with great tact a task by no
means easy. We mean that he stimulates
the natural relish of the boy for out-door
exerçises and hardy sports, whilst he
inculcates the advantage of obedience,
disciplin, and good conduct. The little
tale is of home life. The boys of a large
school, near a lake, get up a boat club,
under the superintendence of a retired
Captain. Boating is thêir chief delight;
and the incidents which gro out of it ar
more varied and more amusing than you
might suppose, whilst thêy ar skilfully
made tŏ furnish ample occasion for moral
lessons. The admission of ŏne blac sheep
—admitted under kindly promptings—
brings with it a train of evils, ending in a
very wel-described adventure of juvenile
piracy. A gang of young rowdies carry
off all the boats, and defiantly enc· ·p o..
an island. In due course of time, however, the scamps ar routed, after having a
most dolorous time of it, and the happy
youngsters ar taut the difference between
lawless and lawful pleasures. Mr. Adams

has handled a difficult theme with great
credit." [Albion.   2 m
ALONE [by "MARION HARLAND," i.
e., M .. Virginia (Hawes) Terhune: Richmond, Va., 1855.] "is a tale of Southern
domestic life—not negro life—but the life
of cultivated, wel-meaning, suffering and
striving white folk. It must hav sŏme
local truth in it, for it is in its "fifth edition"; yet we can not recognise anything
peculiar tŏ the South in its characters and
inçidents. It shŏs, however, a sharp
insight intŏ motivs, marking the niçest
distinctions and shades of character with
a keen, firm touch, and without those
strong and exaggerated contrasts which
ar too often evidençes of confused conçep-
tions and imperfect execution. The heroin is not exactly an original creation,
but is a wel-defined and skilfully develop-
character, and "Charley" and Mr. Lacy ar
agreeably drawn, while Miss Josephine is
almost too much of a vixen for the refined
society in which she is allowed tŏ circulate. Thêre is more mutual complaçency
and admiration, too, among the leading
friends than is compatible with a true
social intercourse. But the tone of the
work is subdued, and the religious spirit
healthful and liberal." [Putnam's Mag. 2 q

and the strong, often dramatic effects gained by discarding entirely the dramatic form. We recall no other writer who has attempted to express so much in this way. The story is told almost without aid from the characters, who unburden themselves mainly throu the medium of the author, in the "oratio obliqua." Sometimes they are not allowed to speak at all; *Lida Ann*, the subject of a very true and tender sketch, does not utter a word while her sad little life history is unfolded. The reader is not called upon to be present at the scene, but merely to listen to a relation of what has taken place; yet such is the vigor and truth of Mr. Deming's narrative that we are transported thither despite the prohibition, and only afterwards begin to wonder how characters whose speech we have not heard, whose actions are by no means elaborately dwelt upon, have been made so real and vivid to us. Mr. Deming possesses the art of turning at once to the most effective point of his story and setting it in a strong light. He writes in a repressed, trenchant style, so weeded of redundances that the few words which remain seem doubly charged with meaning. It is not often that a book made up of fragmentary publications exhibits such unity as we find in these Adirondack stories. Not only is the scene the same throuçôt, but a certain steadfastness of literary purpose is everywhere apparent. There is no unevenness, or shifting of styles; the aim raised in the beginning is pursued to the end. It is a book which distinctly gains in value by being read as a whole. It is only in that way that its full significance as a picture of an out-of-the-way life can be measured. Each sketch is the story of a single character or incident; the whole book is the history of a community. The entire action takes place within "the neighborhood," a term including, apparently, about 20 miles of Adirondack forest, and the individual most carefully studied is the public sentiment of this district. Every event is viewed not alone by itself, but in reference to how the world, that is the knot of men at a country-shop, regard it; and Mr. Deming has learned the inconsistencies, the harsh cruelty and warm, capricious kindliness, of this omnipotent jury, as he has noted the shifting aspects of the **Adirondack** scenery, which forms a variant frame-work for his dramas. His landscape is caut by a few instantaneous strokes, and is set before us full of moisture, atmosphere, and movement." [Atlantic. **2**

AMONG THE LAKES [by W: O. STODDARD, *Scribner*, 1883.] "A narrative of life at a delightful country home, where city cousins and country cousins are reunited during the summer. It is quiet and healthful in tone, and full of mirth and cheerfulness. Piney Hunter, the country boy, is a remarkably fine fellow. Bi, the city youth, has also points of excellence, tho he does not especially rouse our admiration. Any boy or girl from 8 to 14, ôt to enjoy the book thoroly." [Nation. **3**

ANNIE KILBURN [by W: D. HOWELLS, *Harper*, 1888.] There is more satire than pathos in this story, yet the account of the domestic life of the clever and generous, and (in spite of his one "bad habit") attractive lawyer, is full of pathos. It is a case of dipsomania rather than habitual drunkenness which is here presented, and no one who has lived in a **New England** town can fail to recognize the truth of this picture of a man, well-born, well-educated, of unusual ability and deeply interested in his profession, yet ruined by drink. We have spoken first of this character not because he is, by any means, of the first importance in the novel, but for the reason that his prototype is appallingly frequent in New England life, and has rarely been treated in literature except in publications avowedly tracts, whose descriptions, if read at all by the cultivated public, would of course be subject to discount.—The other characters are nearly all equally good;—the clergyman, able, earnest, self-sacrificing, inclined to take the teachings of Jesus literally and seriously, (therein reminding one of "Joshua Davidson"), and hence inevitably falling out with his satisfied and selfish parishioners, whose chief representative is the typical smart business man of a small town, here admirably drawn. The life of the summer colony, again (the geography of the place suggests Beverly) is brôt out, especially in their relations to the towns-people, in a delightfully humorous fashion. It may be added that tho the motives of the story are serious they are handled with so much humor that the narrative is as entertaining and amusing as it is true to life. **4**

APRIL HOPES [by W: D. HOWELLS. *Harper*, 1887.] "Mr. Howells shows a light and exquisite touch in "April Hopes," a novel, it is safe to say, in which all his finer qualities are seen at their best. The story is for all the world like a spring day when showers and sunshine gracefully intermingle. Story, we say, while in reality there is no story at all. Only an account of how two young things fell in love with one another and quarrelled and made up, and quarrelled again, and made up again, and broke off the engagement once more, and finally made up for good and were married. And how charmingly the affair is put before us —all the foolish, silly, entrancing details are there, and never does the author exceed the limits of probability or the canons of good taste. It is like a pretty play, for the narrative in the book is a poor penny-worth of bread to an infinite deal of sack in shape of bright and sparkling dialog. We sit and watch Dan and Alice at their love meetings and their love quarrels, hear them exchange their bits of romantic non-sense, see them go throu their little deceits and flights of tragedy and playing at broken hearts, and listen while they utter protestations of undying affection and vows of unwavering faith. It is all very pretty, very dainty, very touching, and every one who assists at the performance must feel that here at any rate is a bit of reality. The doctrine of elective affinities has no place in the world of "April Hopes." "Girlhood," in the author's view, "is often a turmoil of wild impulses, ignorant exaltations, mistaken ideals, which really represent no intelligent pur-pose, and come from disordered nerves, ill-advised reading, and the erroneous per-spective of inexperience." When two creatures thus constituted indulge in the frantic effort of trying to reconcile their ideals the comedy and tragedy of court-ship begin, for, as Mr. Howells says once more, "the difficulty in life is to bring ex-perience to the level of expectation, to match our real emotions in view of any great occasion with the ideal emotions which we have taut ourselves that we aut to feel." The novel is truly a charming production." [Boston "Literary World."] Much of the action is at **Cam-pobello**, and the descriptions of the scen-ery are charming. **5**

BEAUTY AND THE BEAST [by BAYARD TAYLOR, *Putnam*, 1872.] "In the 4 stories we have named, and es-pecially in 'Jacob Flint's Journey,' and 'Friend Eli's Dauter,' we find a native charm and a fine local flavor that we should not know where to match outside of Auer-bach's tales. There is, with an utter difference of material, a natural similarity of atmosphere in these **Pennsylvania** and German stories. They are alike in rusticity of event and character, and in the country sweetness which hangs about them like an odor of fields and woods, as well as the unpatronizing spirit in which simple people's life is regarded." [At-lantic. **6**

BETTY LEICESTER [by S.. O. JEW-ETT, *Houghton*, 1889.] "Possesses the vital touch without which no incident can impress itself; with which the sim-plest details are imbued with a real life of their own. The descriptions of country life and scenes are exquisite. There are good suggestions to those whose lives have become so fixed in a narrow and unchanging routine that even the sim-plest form of entertaining seems moment-ous and overpowering. Everything is invested with a simple and health-

ARDIS CLAVERDEN. [by FRANK
R: STOCKTON: N.-Y., Dodd, 1890.]
"Jack Surry and Ardis keep the stage
throuóut the play; but it is with Dr.
Lester, whŏse fine manners, pure affection, and persistent nobility of character
ar most effectivly delineated, that the
author makes us linger. Dr. Lester is
clearly the true hero of the story, and from
the moment when he 'let down his long
legs preparatory tŏ slipping from the
fençe' until, at the end, 'Ardis stepped tŏ
his side, and, stooping, kissed him,' he
wil hav the sympathy and lŏve of the
'gentle' reader. He is most delicately and
justly conçeived and consistently portrayed. The reader knoes how it is tŏ be with
him from the start, and from the start understands Ardis' feeling and how it must
all cŏme out; and yet with a hopeless eagerness he catches every promis which for
a moment britens the doctor's outlook.
Dr. Lester's relation tŏ the heroin is not
a new ōne in novels, but it is made closely
individual by its peculiar shading ... Tŏ
us the best episode is that in which the
heroin turns up in the Chiverleys' studio
in New-York. If thĕre is a brĕak in the
interest of the story anywhĕre, possibly it
preceded the introduction of the Chiverleys; but with them came a fresh infusion
of life and inçident, a new grouping of
parts—a strong 'spurt,' if we may so speak
of it, which carries us tŏ the winning post.
The Chiverleys ar delightful and wholesōme; picked up, ōne would say, out of
life, and cōme tŏ stay in the mind. Thĕre
ar many persons on the stage whŏ cōme
and go, filling the background with a rich
Virginia life, and about it all a wholesōme atmosphere." [Critic.   **5 h**

ARTEMUS WARD, HIS TRAVELS. C: FARRAR BROWNE (1834-67) : N.-Y., *Carleton*, 1865.] "Half the book consists of miscellaneous narrativs and brief romançes : the ŏther half is made up of humorous reminisçençes of travel tŏ "California and Bac." Our columns hav sŏmetimes profited by floating waifs of the eminent shoman's humor—such as the romance of "William Barker, the Young Patriot." In this wel-knŏn bit of burlesque, we recognize the motiv of Artemus Ward's humor, and the reason of his popularity. He appeals directly tŏ common-sense, under a garb of absurdity. Thêre is much plain, homely truth in what he says so extravagantly, and his blunt satire touches sensibilities which ar utterly invulnerable tŏ more delicate sarcasm. His knoledge of the American character, too, is peculiarly comprehensiv and accurate, and his habit of observation of social life is keen and always activ. These latter points ar espeçially shŏn in the chapters headed *"Affairs Round the Village Green,"* and "Agriculture," and in the accounts of local dŏings at "Baldinsville." But this clever writer is successful not ŏnly in hitting ŏff the prominent characteristics of the groser phases of American civilization, he displays equal feliçity of touch and keenness of wit in occasional sallies at polished soçiety and at the follies of current literature and journalism. The chapters on Boston, New-York, and Richmond, and the romançe of "Only a Mechanic" illustrate his talent in these particulars. The latter, which fils scarçely twŏ pages, is a remarkably pungent satire, and is much better calculated than any serious revue, however bitter in telling, tŏ purge silly story-writers of thêir ridiculous conçeit. Tŏ conçeit, indeed, and tŏ puerility and imposture of all sorts, Artemus Ward displays a heârty enmity which is rooted in hī prinçiples and a good heârt. His writings hav thêir moral, no less than thêir comic bearing." [Albion. **5 j**

AS IT MAY HAPPEN [**Pennsylvania**] = No. 192.

ASCHENBROEDEL = No. 193.

ASCUTNEY STREET. [by ADELINE
DUTTON (TRAIN) WHITNEY: London,
Ward & Lock, 1890.] "Mrs. Whitney
has had a grêat deal of practiçe sinçe she
wrote 'Faith Gartney's Girlhood' [No.
30 m] but her readers wil probably agree
for the most part in plaçing that meritorious little story abŏve all its successors.
'Ascutney Street' is no rival tŏ it. Traçes
of morbidity and sentimentality, affectations of style and moral tall talk wer
observable in the former work; thêy ar
common in the new ŏne. And yet when
the author allows herself tŏ tel her quite
simple and pretty story straitforwardly,
forgetting self-consciousness and mannerism, thêre is again the genuin ring with
which her readers ar acquainted. Unfortunately this is too seldom the case,
and in trying tŏ be pithy or profound she
is oftener than not tiresŏme and incomprehensible." [Athenæum. 5 k

ASPENDALE = No. 194.

BERENICE, [by M.. HAYDEN
(GREEN) PIKE: Boston, *Phillips*, 1856.]
"a tale of the Passamaquoddy [**Maine**]
region, has unusual merit. It is simple
and unpretending, but is marked, throuóût, by grêat good sense, quic perceptions, poetic sensibility, and considerable
artistic skil." [Putnam's.   **6 r**

BERTIE [Phil'a, *Hart*, 1851.] "is a
North-Carolina story, the hero of which
is a knoing Yankee, self-styled a Professor, whŏ manufactures hydraulic cement
and constructs cisterns. His adventures
in the old North State ar made the means
of giving a lively and entertaining account
of the habits and character of its people."
[Southern Literary Messenger.   **6 t**

ful but constant interest, from the beginning, where Betty starts alone, with some misgiving, for Tideshead, to the very last page, when she and her father are leaving the quaint little village with real regret, albeit to take up their wider life once more." [Nation. 7

BETWEEN WHILES [by H.. (F.) (H.) JACKSON, *Roberts*, 1887.] "Is a collection of tales which, with the exception of the first and longest, have already been printed. And they very well stand the test of being half forgotten after a hasty reading in some magazine, and then, years afterward, being read again. In every case the memory of the story, almost as soon as the first sentence is read, comes back in all its entirety, the characters seem like old friends, and there is genuine pleasure in listening to their simple talk and breathing the wholesome odor of their surroundings. The first story, "The Inn of the Golden Pear," was left incomplete at the author's death, and one regretfully wonders what she would have made of the lives of Willan and Victorine. The few chapters which but finish what might be called the first episode are filled at once with strength and subtlety quite beyond anything else in the volume. In spite of the sudden infatuation of Willan, and the quaint romance of a bygone time that would serve ordinarily to give such a tale a tinge of unreality, there is a naturalness, a pervading sense of being close to life and nature, a vigor and grasp, that compels one's interest and admiration. But it is chiefly the purity, the elevation and gentle fervor which throuout these stories disclose their author at her best, and win the hearts of her warmest admirers." [Nation. 8

BLUFFTON [by M. J. SAVAGE, *Lee & Shepard*, 1878.] "Is one of many books of the same kind which are to be written, and the public who see in it a partial description of what the public thots and speculations are and have been, will be grateful if the books that are to come are as good-humored, as sincere, and no more inconclusive than

this one. The story is simple. The Rev. M: Trafton goes from the East to take charge of a church in the **West.** He has no doubt of the orthodoxy of his creed or of the firmness of his belief; and full of hope and youth he means to live his life strait out in the place where his work is appointed. At first he is eminently successful. The sermons, which come from his heart, touch the hearts of his hearers. He finds the one woman for him; she accepts his offer, and life looks full of the best and happiest promises. Gradually he is found less than orthodox. A council is called to consider his heresies, and before it assembles, questions as to his personal character and the purity of his life furnish further food for inquiry. These, of course, are triumphantly vindicated, but his misbeliefs are manifest, and his betrothed counts him an infidel and refuses to break her father's heart by marrying him. So far all is natural and coherent........Job's asses and oxen are here represented by travels in Europe for Mr. Trafton, after which he meets his former love in a summer-house in a gentleman's place in California. They make it up at once; her father is dead—we believe he left a competent fortune—and soon after Mr. Trafton receives a call from a certain number of people in New York who desires to hear whatever he may have to say, and with this nimbus neatly fitted round his head the book closes." [Nation. 9

BOSCOBEL [N. Y.: *W. B. Smith & Co.*] "Shows not very much skill in contrivance of plot or portraiture of character; but it is worth an hour's reading for the pretty sketching of **Florida** scenery and of the life there of the winter sojourners." [Nation. 10

CAPE COD AND ALL ALONG SHORE [by CHARLES NORDHOFF, *Harper*, 1869.] "The editors of this Magazine [Atlantic] remember with pleasure "*Elkanah Brewster's Temptation*;" and we fancy that there are others who will be glad to read it a second time in this collection. It is no dispraise of them to say that Mr. Nordhoff's stories are all light—

BROUGHTON HOUSE = No. 203.
BURKETTS LOCK. [by M.. GREEN-
WAY McCLELLAND: N.-Y., *Cassell*,
1889.] "The scene is laid amŏng humble
folk on the banks of the James River
[Virginia], and in a hilly city easily
recognizable as Lynchburg. Without
Miss Murfree's verboseness and continual digressions intŏ irrelevant descriptions
of natural beauties unnotiçed by her actor's, Miss McClelland's command of
mountaineer dialect is equal tŏ the Tennessee writer's, and she dŏes not wearv
us with it. The story is sad, simple, and
too short. Grannie and Polly ar strong
and piquante; Rob Redd, a representativ
of the class whŏ win the lŏve of everybody and deserv nobody's. Hester is
pure, fine and hī; an artistic contrast tŏ
her weak, vain, unfortunate sister."
[Homemaker.]—"The entire tone is
strong, unaffected, and sympathetic. The
miserable tragedy of Delia is touched
with pathos and quiet force; the character
of Hester is admirable in simple and sinçere outlines; while the life of the section
is portrayed with many clever strokes.
The scenes whêre Hester listens tŏ the
counçil of the relativs of Delia, planning
the doom of the betrayer, and the final
discŏvery of the double falsity of Rob
Redd, ar truly dramatic, and excelleut in
proportion and in mŏvement." [Boston
"Literary World." **10 p**

BURR-CLIFF [by "Paul Creyton," i.e.,
J: TOWNSEND TROWBRIDGE: Boston,
Phillips, 1854.] "is an amusing, raçy
little volume, consisting of a series of fam-

ily pictures, wel and truthfully drawn, in
which clouds and sunshine alternate, but
the latter predominates. It presents, in
lively contrast, twŏ families, the ŏne living
in the country, independent, intelligent,
and wel-ordered, with a desire for self-
culture, and taste tŏ enjoy nature's perfect works as spread out before them in
"Hil and verdant slope, woodland and
vale, and sparkling stream." Tho ŏther
in a city, with scanty means, straining
every nerv tŏ keep up appearançes, the
soul cramped by the shackles of artifiçial
life, the natural affections deadened. The
characters ar wel sustained; the conversations lively and spirited. The book contains sŏme profitable hints in relation tŏ
the treatment due tŏ ŏur superiors in age,
quite apropos at the present time, when
the child may almost literally be said tŏ be
Father of the man." [National Era.]—
It "tels the pleasant story of the people
whŏ livd thêre and the people whŏ went
thither tŏ liv, the honest farmer of the
genuin New-England stamp, and his
sturdy sŏns and smiling dauters, the old
grandparents, Joyful and Hopeful by
name, just tottering down the hil of life,
the broken-down merchant seeking tŏ hide
his disgraçe in retirement, the fine city
lady, poor and dependent, yet scorning tŏ
labor with her hands, the good clergyman,
the pedantic schoolmaster, the good children and the nauty ŏnes—all characters
which we ar sure must hav been sketched
from life, so truthful ar thêir outlines."
[Norton's Lit. Gazette. **10 s**

BUTTONS INN = No. 206.

"easy things to understand,"—aim to please and entertain folk, and do not grapple with problems of any kind, unless perhaps the doubtful wisdom of forsaking simple Cape Cod and country-town ways, for the materializing and corrupting career of newspaper men and artists in New York. Elkanah Brewester barely overcomes his temptation, and returns to the Cape just in time to be true to Hepsy Ann, while Stoffle McGurdigan actually succumbs, becomes a great editor, and breaks faith with pretty Lucy Jones. Tho the interest of these and the other stories of the book is not complex, the satire is wholesome and just, and the reader will scarcely escape being touched by the pathos. The character in them is good enuf to be true of the scenes of most of tales which take us among places and people seldom touched by magazine fiction, and not here exhausted. It seems to us that *Mehitabel Roger's Cranberry Swamp* is the best of all." **11**

CAPE COD FOLKS [by SALLY P. McLEAN, Boston, *Williams*, 1881.] "The author is so successful in her sketches of real life that it is a pity she has not confined herself to them. It is only a new illustration of the fact that the power of reproduction is quite other than that of creation. What she saw or knew she has given with vivid force. A note from the publishers implies that some offense has been taken at the frankness of the portraiture of local manners, but surely not by the delightful, impossible, actual "Cedar Swampers" themselves, for the tone of the book as a whole is one of hearty appreciation : for one example, the recognition of the beauty and power of their singing, and the part played by such music in a simple, primitive community—their one fine art. The impression of the book that will linger longest may be the refrain of the hymns swelling and dying above the monotone of the surf." [Nation. **12**

CAPTAIN POLLY [by SOPHIE SWETT,' *Harper*, 1889.] "Is a fine tale of a wise and courageous girl, who may serve as a good model for other girls to grow like, and also as a lesson in shamefacedness to boys for their silly airs of superiority over their sisters. Nothing shows more plainly the greater nearness of boys to their savage ancestry than the fiction which still holds among them that it is they who hold the reins of government. The Captain Polly of this book was the natural and actual ruler of her family, but that did not in the least shake the confidence of her brothers that both their organization and their stock of ideas were in every way superior to hers." [Nation. **13**

CHANCE ACQUAINTANCE, A. [by W: D. HOWELLS, Boston, 1873]. " 'A Chance Acquaintance' introduces some of the people who had figured briefly in 'Their Wedding Journey,' and weaves for them a love story on **Canadian** ground, in a way that shows that one need not be an Arbuton to prefer the half-European flavor of that unamericanized part of the country to the less romantic scenery of the United States. But if the setting is partly foreign, the story does not lose in interest on that account, and the people who are brôt before us are taken as types of two very different kinds of Americans. The heroine, Kitty Ellison, is a Western girl who has had none of the advantages of finishing schools, symphony concerts, and Lowell lectures, but has been reared among sensible people who have had their work to do and who, besides attending to that, had been sturdy Abolitionists at a time when slavery had more defenders than it has now. From the glimpse we get of her life it is easy to see how well it encouraged the independence and individuality of her character, and the humor which is so prominent an American trait. The other actor in the play is Mr. Miles Arbuton, of Boston, who has had bestowed on him all that the heart of man could desire—wealth, good family, personal attractiveness of a certain sort, education, foreign travel, so that if young people had nothing better to do than to serve as examples of the truth of proverbs it would seem as if here were a romance ready to break forth between two such different people. The lack of resemblance lies, too, much deeper than this. Kitty has all the charm which must belong to a young, pretty, kindly, sympathetic girl, while Arbuton has all the narrowness, coldness, and exclusiveness which are disagreeable when they are found in contrast with what one would naturally expect from all the advantages he possesses, and, it must be said, with what one sees of such people in the flesh. With Kitty, Mr. Howells has been remarkably successful; he has drawn a really charming girl, and how difficult and rare a thing that is to do every novel-reader can testify. All her part in the love-making, her innocence, her readiness to be pleased, her kindness towards Arbuton's foibles, her sensitive dignity, her charming humor, belong to a real human being, not to the familar lay-figure which, one day practical, the next sentimental, goes throu the conventional process of love-making with dull uniformity in the writings of the majority of novelists. The plot of the story is simply that of the wooing of this lovely girl by the cold Boston man, whose blue blood freezes in his veins at any reference to the South End of his native city. The story is very prettily told, with its conclusion successfully hidden till the last from the prying wonder of the reader. The many little touches of humor which every reader of Mr. Howells has learned to expect in his works, and which have given him his place as the best of the younger generation of American humorists, are to be found continually in this novel. The descriptions of the scenery, which must be familiar to many, are well done." [Nation.   14

CIRCUIT RIDER, THE [by E: EGGLESTON; N. Y., *Ford*, 1874.] "Mr. E: Eggleston's stories have had from the beginning a great popularity with a large circle of readers, and it has been in many ways well deserved. They are full of incident; all of these rapid events occur amid scenes almost entirely new to the Eastern reader and the new generation of Westerners; and they have, in a high degree, the element of dialectic

speech, which intrinsically for itself is a popular element, and which, delusively perhaps as often as really, confers upon the personages of the story that appearance of reality and individuality for which the novel-writer has to watch so keenly and work so hard. Another important quality of Mr. Eggleston's books, and one which does much to hold fast the sort of readers whom his novelty and liveliness attract, is his good nature, which never fails to make him always kind to his characters and keeps for him a constant supply of a practical poetic justice which ensures the marriage of the almshouse girl to the hero of the tale, and makes out of the hero the sheriff of the self-same county where the regulators had nearly had him convicted for horse-stealing." [Nation.   15

COUNTRY BY-WAYS [by S.. O. JEW-ETT, *Houghton*, 1881.] "Miss Jewett herself seems sure only of catching and holding some flitting movement of life, some fragment of experience which has demanded her sympathy. One of the stories, indeed, *Andrew's Fortune* has a more deliberate intention, and we are led on with some interest to pursue the slight turns of the narrative; yet in this the best work is in the successive pictures of the village groups in the kitchen and at the funeral. It would be difficult to find a formal story which made less draft upon one's curiosity than *Miss Becky's Pilgrimage*, yet one easily acquires a personal regard for Miss Becky herself. Miss Jewett's sketches have all the value and interest of delicately executed water-color landscapes; they are restful, they are truthful, and one is never asked to expend criticism upon them, but to take them with their necessary limitations as household pleasures. The sketches and stories which make up the volume vary in value, but they are all marked by grace and fine feeling; they are thŏroly wholesome; they have a gentle frankness and reverence which are inexpressibly winning, when one thinks of the knowingness and selfconsciousness and restlessness which by turns characterize so many of the cou-

CLOCKMAKER (The), or the Sayings and Dŏings of Sam Slick of Slickville. [by T: CHANDLER HALIBURTON (1797-1865): N.-Y., 3 vols., 1837-40.] "It is 30 years sinçe Mr. Haliburton attracted the attention of a colonial public by writing a series of letters recording the observations, humors, and oddities of a traveling Yankee cloc-maker, whŏ looked at life with a shrewd, penetrating, yet not unkindly eye. Those whŏ ar old enuf tŏ recollect the period in question wil remember that for a long while 'Sam Slick' was 'the rage.' His sayings wer quoted in every newspaper, and became incorporated in the popular slang. He achieved a popularity almost equalling that of 'Mrs Caudle', sŏme years later; and he was soon gonorally accepted by the English public as a type of 'the Yankee' pure and unadulterated. The book was, in truth, a production of marked ability. Sam Slick is ŏne of those fictitious characters which may really be termd creations . . . Of course "the Clocmaker" dŏes not giv a complete idea of American character, in which thêre ar larger and nobler elements; but (allowing for the inevitable exaggeration of a caricature) he is true tŏ a certain phase of transatlantic life. Sam is the regular Yankee trader —'cute,' wary, dodgy, humbugging, inconçeivably audaçious, abounding in self-reliançe under all possible çircumstançes, as little troubled with a 'nice conscience' as the sailor in Chaucer, and yet in sŏme respects a good fello after all. In his way, Sam is a genius. His impudençe alone is an inspiration. With little education, and with a slimy accumulation of slang cŏvering his speech as mud and ooze cŏver the bottom of an old ship, his nativ New-England shrewdness makes him almost a philosopher. His vue of life may be narro, but it is all the sharper for its narroness, and thêre ar not wanting touches of pathos in the midst of the humor." [London Review, 1865.]— " 'Sam Slick' deservs tŏ be entered on ŏur list of friends containing the names of Tristram Shandy, the Shepherd of the 'Noctes Ambrosianæ,' and ŏther rhapsodical discoursers on time and change, whŏ, beside the delights of thêir discourse, possess also the charm of individuality. Apart from all the worth of Sam's revelations, the man is preçious tŏ us as a queer creature—knoing, impudent, sensible, sagacious, vulgar, yet not without a certain tact: and overfloing with a humor as peculiar in its way as the humors of Andrew Fairservice." [Athenæum.]— "We can distinguish the real from the counterfeit Yankee at the first sound of the voiçe, and by the turn of a single sentence; and we hav no hesitation in declaring that Sam Slick is not what he pretends tŏ be; that thêre is no organic life in him; that he is an imposter, an impossibility, a nonentity. A writer of genius, even if he write from imperfect knoledge, wil, as it wer, breathe the breath of life intŏ his creations. Sam Slick is an awkward and hily infeliçitous attempt tŏ make a character, by heaping tŏgether, without discrimination, selection, arrangement, or taste, every vulgarity which a vulgar imagination can conçeive, and every knavery which a man blinded by national and political prejudice can charge upon nêbors whŏm he dislikes." [C. C. FELTON.

15 h

CLOVERNOOK, or Recollections of our Neighborhood in the West. [by ALICE CARY (1822-71): N.-Y., *Redfield*, 1854.] "The writer has depicted Western scenes and characters, Western homes and manners, with a fidelity and accuracy of which those only whŏ hav livd amŏng them ar capable. The old-fashioned "Quilting Party," so common and so indispensable in the days of our grandmŏthers, is painted tŏ the life; and as we read her humorous description we almost sĭ for the simple, unartifiçial life of the country, with its true heârts and honest purposes. "My Visit tŏ Randolph" reminds us of sŏme of Dickens' lively sketches; and Miss Matilda Hamersley might pass for a second Mrs. Skewton. The simple but beautiful pictures of life amŏng the poor, with its patient enduraņçe for lŏve's sake, and sacrifiçe of selfish wishes for the comfort of the whole, ar written with touching pathos, which reaches the heart and calls forth its better feelings." [National Era. **15 m**

COL. DUNWOODIE = No. 214.

COUNTER CURRENTS [**So. California**] = No. 219.

tributions by women to our literature."
[Atlantic. **16**
COUNTRY DOCTOR, A. [by S.. O.
JEWETT, *Houghton*, 1884.] "It is a
positive pleasure to think how many
young voices will be reading aloud,
this summer, Miss Jewett's delightful
sketch of 'A Country Doctor.' We say
sketch, for tho the book has been heralded
as a novel, it is as strictly a sketch as any
of those which have won for her a now
most enviable fame. Miss Jewett's work
is as purely and finely **New England** as
Whittier's poetry. Her instinctive refinement, her graceful workmanship, place
her second only to Mrs. A.. (Thackeray)
Ritchie. Her country doctor is unmistakably a loving portrait from life. We like
him and his friend all the better for a reminiscence of the Doctor May and the Doctor Spencer of 30 years ago. Not that they
are in the least copies—only examples of
the same type. By the side of Doctor Leslie is a most gracious figure, first a wayward
child, then a girl of eager heart and steady
will. So far as the story follows the
thread of her fortune, and develops her
character, it might be called a novel; but
plot in the ordinary sense it has none. . .At
the close, the heroine, looks forward to no
happiness of wife or mother, but to the
profession—still unusual, tho no longer isolated—for which she had patiently trained
herself in medical school and hospital."
[Nation. **17**
COUPON BONDS, [by J: T. TROW-
BRIDGE, Boston: 1873.] "We think the
best of Mr. Trowbridge's stories, in the
new volume of them just published, is
The Man Who Stole a Meeting-House,
which we suppose our readers have not
forgotten. It deals, like all the others,
with the rustic character of **New England,** bringing out here and there its lurking kindness and delicacy, but impressing
you chiefly with a certain sardonic hardness in it,—a humorous, wrong-headed
recklessness, which Mr. Trowbridge has
succeeded in embodying wonderfully well
in old Jedworth. The story is as good as
the best in this sort of study, and in struc-

ture it is as much more artistic as it is less
mechanical. In some of the other tales
the coming coincidence and surprise may
be calculated altogether too accurately:
all is plotted as exactly as if for the effects
of a comedy. This is true in a degree of
Coupon Bonds, which is such a capital
story, and so full of human nature; and it
is almost embarrassingly true of *Archi-
bald Blossom,* and of *Preaching for Selwyn.* Mr. *Blazay's Experience, The
Romance of a Glove, Nancy Blynn's
Lovers,* and *In the Ice,* are better; but
none are so good as *The Man Who Stole
A Meeting House,* which for a kind of
poise of desirable qualities—humorous conception, ingenious plot, well-drawn character and a naturally envolved moral in old
Jedwort's disaster and reform—is one of
the best New England stories ever written,
to our thinking. They are all inviting
stories; they all read easily." [Atlantic. **18**
COUSIN POLLY'S GOLD MINE, [by
A.. E. ( ) PORTER: *Harper,* 1879.]
...."The brothers loved the same sweet
girl, Alice Leigh, and the more favored won
her; but the fortune which she brôt her
husband melted away. Their orphaned
children became the wards of their patient
and large-hearted uncle; and there is admirable poetic justice and a really artistic
convergence of different lines of destiny
in the end, where poor, miserly Polly
finds death in her fulfilled desires by falling into the pit excavated by the first
miners on her old farm, and the wealth
which she had clutched so blindly comes
by natural inheritance to Alice's children
and their adoptive father, and comes just
in time to lift from the brave shoulders of
the true hero of the tale the burden which
must soon have crushed them. It must be
confessed, however, that this plot looks
better in outline than with the author's
filling. There is absolutely no action in
the book, and the conversations, especially
of the more refined characters, are as priggish and impossible as the situations are
simple and veracious." [Atlantic. **19**
DEEPHAVEN [by S.. O. JEWETT,
Boston, 1877.] "The gentle reader of

this magazine [Atlantic] cannot fail to have liked, for their very fresh and delicate quality, certain sketches of an old New England seaport, which have from time to time appeared here during the last 4 years. The first was 'Shore House,' and then came 'Deephaven Cronies' and 'Deephaven Excursions.' These sketches, with many more studies of the same sort of life, as finely and faithfully done, are now collected into a pretty little book called 'Deephaven,' which must, we think, find favor with all who appreciate the simple treatment of the near-at-hand quaint and picturesq. No doubt some particular seaport sat for 'Deephaven,' but the picture is true to a whole class of old shore towns, in any one of which you might confidently look to find the 'Deephaven' types. It is supposed that two young girls—whose younggirlhood charmingly perfumes the thôt and observation of the whole book—are spending the summer at 'Deephaven,' Miss Denis, the narrator, being the guest of her adored ideal, Miss Kate Lancaster, whose people have an ancestral house there; but their sojourn is used only as a background on which to paint the local life: the 3 or 4 aristocratic families, severally dwindled to 3 or 4 old maiden ladies; the numbers of ancient sea-captains cast ashore by the decaying traffic; the queer sailor and fisher folk; the widow and old wife gossips of the place, and some of the people of the neighboring country. These are all touched with a hand which holds itself far from every trick of exaggeration, and which subtly delights in the very tint and form of reality; we could not express too strongly the sense of conscientious fidelity which the art of the book gives, while over the whole is cast a light of the sweetest and gentlest humor, and of a sympathy as tender as it is intelligent..... Bits of **New England** landscape and characteristic marine effects scattered throuoût these studies of life vividly localize them, and the talk of the people is rendered with a delicious fidelity." **20**

DESMOND HUNDRED, THE [by J.

(G.) AUSTIN, B'n, 1882.] "It is hard to say whether this is intended as a novel of American life or a religious novel, or both. So far as the plot goes, it might be of almost any country; but the scene is laid partly in **New England,** and most of the characters are New England people, and the author has a high estimation of New England. Still, the hero of the book is a clergyman, who renounces the woman he loves and allows his brother to marry her, and there is a great deal about religion in the course of the story. Several of the characters, again, are English, and there is something in the tone of the religion and of the love which is not American. The author is evidently very much at home in New England, and the more commonplace New England characters and dialog in the book are very good. The story opens with the preparations for the reception in a New England village of the popular Dr. Manoah Sampson, who is bringing home his wife. The novel, altogether, is above the average in the drawing of character, but in plot is rather weak, and in places vague." [Nation. **21**

DAVAULT'S MILLS [by C : H : JONES; *Lippincott,* 1876.] "This novel is well-written, and displays here and there pleasant touches of humor and intelligent observation, but it lacks the compactness which is needed for the successful treatment of a story. The development of the plot runs on too calmly, and the conversations of the characters, altho natural enuf in themselves, sometimes give too little aid in bringing matters to the necessary crisis, so that the eager reader of novels, accustomed to more fiery drafts, will perhaps find this tale pall upon his taste." [Nation. **22**

DOCTOR OF DEANE, THE [by M.. (TOWLE) PALMER, *Lothrop,* 1888.] "A bright and well-written little book. Within its modest limits it holds an uncommonly distinct and agreeable group of portraits. Uncommon, too, is the perceptive quality which has taken note of innumerable subtleties of thôt and feeling

DEACON'S WEEK = No. 225.
DEVIL'S HAT [Peun.] = No. 229.
DI CARY [Virginia] = No. 230.
DISTRICT SCHOOL AS IT WAS
(The). [by WARREN BURTON (1800-66) :
Boston, *Carter, Hendee & Co.*, 1833;
N.-Y., *Taylor*, 1838.] "The author of
this little book, if he does not relate what
he has seen, and that of which he has been
a part, is no careless observer of men and
women, boys and girls, matters and
things. He givs a lively description of
the 'Old Schoolhouse,' on the summit of
a bald hil, of its external appearance and
internal arrangement, of the female teachers in summer and the male teachers in
winter, of the urchins and youth who attended, of the various kinds of disciplin,
of the things taut and how they wer taut,
of the winter sports, &c. All this is conducted with a good deal of dramatic effect.

At one time we ar moved by indignatiou
or pity; and at another we ar excited to
lafter, as the scene changes. There is
abundance of action, comic, tragi-comic,
and farçical; and our interest increases in
it, as it advançes. The author groes upon
us as he proceeds, becoming more and
more natural and lively in his humor,
more true to life in his descriptions."
[American Monthly Review.]—"The author is an artist of no ordinary power.
His descriptions, tho confined to the humble sphere of the village school, ar interesting from their wonderful fidelity to
nature. We ar reminded by them of
Mount's Barnfloor Sketches, which in gra-
phick (sic) truth and expressiv simplicity
we hav rarely seen surpassed." [N.-Y.
Mirror, 1838.] Compare No. 127. 22 m
DR. HEIDENHOFF, = No. 232.
DOCTQR JOHNS = No. 233.

under the conditions of daily life, and set them down with a faithfulness that is in touch with nature, yet which never becomes odious by over-analyzing. We are not perfectly sure that every feminine reader will agree with the author in writing down modesty as Dr. West's most impressive trait, but we are sure that there will be found in the book a happy alternation of the thots which sparkle and those which softly shine." [Nation. **23**

DR. BREEN'S PRACTICE [by W: D. HOWELLS, Boston, 1881.] ."Is a novel of New England life, in which Mr. Howells shows his usual skill and humor, and more than an ordinary amount of ingenuity. The plot is founded on an idea which has, so far as we know, not been utilized in fiction before. Dr. Grace Breen is a young New England girl, who represents what Mr. Howells seems to think the modern form of Puritanism, this ancient faith taking in her a moral rather than a religious form, and making her conscience sensitive as regards all her relations with fellow-creatures to a degree unknown in parts of the world unaffected by Puritan traditions. The scene of the story is laid in a seaside "resort" known as "Jocelyn's," where may be found the usual **New England** summer boarding-house, with its visitors from all quarters. Grace Breen having had some years before an unfortunate love affair, in which she had been badly treated by her lover, has adopted the practice of medicine, much as other women enter convents or go out as missionaries—tho Mr. Howells intimates that this is putting the case in rather an exaggerated way; but at any rate, she has chosen this work with the intention of giving her life to it and supporting herself by it....." [Nation. **25**

EARNEST TRIFLER, AN [by M.. A. SPRAGUE, Houghton, 1879.] "This is a clever little love-story of a sort that a clever woman knows best how to tell. Rachel Guerrin, the heroine, is a New England girl, living in a secluded village, throu which a railroad has been laid out. Two engineers come to the

place, representing two types familiar to novel readers—one the strong, earnest man, given to deep and overwhelming feelings, but poor at the expression of them; the other a gay young butterfly, charming in conversation, agreeable to women from his gayety and society, but more given to expression than to emotion. Both of these gentlemen fall in love with Rachel, and of course, the strong, earnest man married her. Rachel Guerrin is an attractive picture of a girl, brôt up, as so many girls are brôt up nowadays, in a remote and sequestered corner of the world, but admitted, throu literature of all kinds, to a vicarious knowledge of men and cities. Her relations with her two lovers are well described, and her conversation is always bright. Indeed, it is in her dialog that Miss Sprague is at her best. Her conversations are always lively, if possibly a little too witty for real life. The other characters are not good. The strong, earnest man does not justify the intense interest he excites in Rachel's breast, and tho Halstead is much better, it is really Halstead in the act of flirting with Rachel which makes up most of his character as we see it. These flirtations are certainly admirable, but flirtation does not alone make a novel." [Nation. **25**

EAST ANGELS [by C. F. WOOLSON, Harper, 1886.] In this there is nothing so fresh or remarkable as are the opening scenes of Miss Woolson's Anne.' The movement is intentionally languid, fitted to the surrounding. Evert Winthrop and Margaret Harold, the people to whom Miss Woolson devotes most space, are presented full blown, past the period of growth, and the period of decay still remote. Their completeness is immediately recognized, their stability taken for granted, and it is impossible to stimulate concern about what they do or think or feel. They are so essentially those to whom life brings no severe tests, no moments when character reels before temptation, that the emotional crisis to which they are subjected in the later chapters provokes neither fear nor

DOCTOR'S DAUGHTER (The) = No. 236.

DOUGLAS FARM (The) [by MARY EMILY (NEELEY) BRADLEY: *Appleton*, 1856.] "is a pleasant sketch of life in **Virginia**. The author writes fluently and gracefully, and shŏş considerable skil in constructing a plot. Thêre ar no startling events, and striking characters in her story, which is a simple episode of ordinary family life; but happily thêy ar not needed. The best things in the book ar the bits of talk amōng the farm negroes. Thêy ar lâfably characteristic." [Albion. **24 r**

EASTFORD [by "Wesley Brooke," i. e., G: LUNT (1803-85) : Boston, *Crocker*, 1855.] "is the exhibition of the life of a New-England town throu the characters of its prominent people. We hav nŏthing like it for fidelity tŏ the facts of Yankee life. The characters, tho strongly individualized, ar stil representativ. The author has happily seized the traits both of the past and the present generation, and the interest of the volume depends in no small degree on the exhibition of the struggle, now going on in every **New England** village, between old and . new fashioned opinions, practiçes and people. The clergyman, the physician, the lawyer, the politiçian, the trader, all hav tŏ meet the champions of new vues in theology, in mediçin, in law, in politics, in reform, in social life. The author leans tŏard the conservativs—lŏves tŏ giv them the best of the joke and the argument, and is more thŏroly genial in depicting them, than in portraying thêir opponents; but he stil represents the latter, not as mere embodied opinions, but as men and women, and sŏme of the scenes in which thêy appear, and carry on the duel of controversy, ar quite dramatic ... The style of the volume is pure, sweet, graçeful and vigorous. It is equal tŏ all the demands of description, narration, conversation, and discussion, varying with unobtrusiv and flexible ease with the variations in the writer's moods, and with the changes in his inçidents. The power of description is quite notiçeable. The account of the shipwrec, and the scenes in the woods of **Maine**, ar especially vivid and true." [Graham's Magazine.   **27**

ENDURA = No. 242.

9 h

doubt. We know they will come out without damage, and bloom on serenely for many a day.......Garda Thorne is the perpetual bud. On first acquaintance she piques curiosity; even if the matter does not suggest possibilities of development, the reader instinctively looks ahead with expectation. But Garda passes throu the fires of life, her selfishness unimpaired, her capacity for sleep undiminished, and, tho it is not mentioned, probably fulfills the only possibility of young girlhood which we all scorn to contemplate—grows fat. In the delineation of these characters, it is clear that Miss Woolson understands what she means to do, and the fault is comparative worthlessness of design, not defective execution. In representing the passionless, shallow, selfish Garda, as a child of the South and of Nature, she is perhaps at fault; aside from her habit of dozing in the sun, Garda is a dauter of the long-conventionalized North. The numerous passages descriptive of **Florida** are the most agreeable and valuable in the book. They are faithful, often vivid, and occasionally reproduce the fantastic impression made upon the imagination by the most unreal and elusive of landscapes." [Nation.   **26**

EASTFORD [by G: LUNT, *Putnam*, 1855.] **New England.**   **27**

ECHO OF PASSION, AN. [by G: P. LATHROP, *Houghton*, 1882.]..."There are passages of strong dramatic power, which move one by the very slightness of the means employed; and the conversations, while charged with meaning, are not of the teasing character of those in the former book, because they come from a more real and intense feeling. But the strength of the work is in its masterly development of the central 'motif'; its unhesitating disclosure of the subtle self-deceit of Fenn, making the lie tell itself throu the story; its fine rendering of the noble wife and of the half-willing temptress, whom we may honorably love and admire if we do not happen to be in Fenn's situation. The ebb and flow of the passion, its apparent checks yet real accumulation of power,

are true to nature, and the whole story is remarkable for the skill with which very natural and probable incidents are made to present a spiritual conflict." [Atlantic.**28**

ELSIE VENNER [by O. W. HOLMES, Boston: 1861.]...."There is no need of our analyzing "Elsie Venner," for all our readers know it as well as we do. But we cannot help saying that Dr. Holmes has struck a new vein of New England romance, and the character of the heroine has in it an element of mystery; yet the materials are gathered from every-day **New England** life, and that weird border-land between science and speculation where psychology and physiology exercise mixed jurisdiction, and which rims New England as it does all other lands. The character of Elsie is exceptional, but not purely ideal. In Dr. Kittredge and his "hired man," and in the principal of the "Apollinean Instituut," Dr. Holmes has shown his ability to draw those typical characters which represent the higher and lower grades of average human nature; and in calling his work a romance he quietly justifies himself for mingling other elements in the composition of Elsie and her cousin. Apart from the merit of the book as a story, it is full of wit, and of sound thot that sometimes hiding behind a mask of humor. Admirably conceived are the two clergymen, gradually changing sides almost without knowing it, and having that persuasion of consistency which men feel, because they must always bring their creed into some sort of agreement with their dispositions." [Atlantic. **29**

END OF THE WORLD, THE [by E: EGGLESTON, N. Y., *Judd*, 1872.] "It is a pleasure to turn to so simple-minded and innocent a story as Mr. Eggleston's "End of the World," which is announced on the title-page to be a love story, but which is much more and much better in its way than that. There are the young man and the young woman who are persecuted and separated by heartless parents; they also add to their sufferings by misunderstanding one another; there is the fever, which is epidemic with heroes;

ENGLISH ORPHANS (The). [by M .. J .. (HAWES) HOLMES: *Appleton*, 1855.] "A certain English gentleman is the happy father of three dauters, twŏ of whŏm emigrate tŏ America before the opening of the tale, leaving him with the third. The young lady, poor thing, takes it intŏ her head tŏ marry her music-teacher; whêreat papa discards her and the consequent babies. Hard times cōme upon the young couple, and thêy too ar compelled tŏ emigrate. Arrived in this new world, after a time, death enters thêir circle. First the father dies, then the mōther, and a brave little boy, named Frank; while Mary, Ella, and Alice remain, the latter a mere infant. A certain Mrs. Campbell, whŏ in the end turns out tŏ be her ânt, adopts Ella, a pretty dol and as selfish as she is pretty; but Mary, whŏ isn't a bit interesting, and little Alice go tŏ the Poor-house l—This American Poor-house and its inmates ar admirably described. Thêre ar the keeper, whŏse wife is always sic; Miss Grundy, a sort of general factotum whŏ keeps the paupers in order; Mrs. Sal Furbish, a crazed gentlewoman and widoᵗ whŏse ruling passion is correct grammar; and Uncle Peter, a simple-minded old fello, whŏ plays doleful tunes on a bad violin. Thêre ar ōther personages and ōther inçidents; but these make the cream of the work. Of course Mary dōesn't remain in the Poor-house all her days. She makes friends by the score; has the benefit of a good education; becōmes the mistress of a village-school, and finally marries a Mr. George Morcland, whŏ came over in the ship with her—a merry-hêarted chap, whŏ teased her as a boy, and lōved her as a man. Not much of a plot, perhaps; but thêre is much merit in the handling of it." [Albion. **30 h**

FAITH GARTNEY'S GIRLHOOD [by
ADELINE DUTTON (TRAIN) WHITNEY:
London, *Low*, 1866.] "is a story which
every girl wil be the better for reading.
Free from the sicly sentimentalism and
dreary dulness which characterises so
many moral stories, it teaches an admirable lesson without becŏming distasteful
or tedious. Much of the same humor is
visible in it which enlivened "The Gayworthys" [No. 258], and the same quic-
ness of observation which enabled its
author tŏ draw such pleasant pictures of
the quiet life of **New England.** Faith
Gartney is the dauter of a man of business whŏ suffers losses, and the story of
her girlhood tels how her character is
refined and tempered by adversity. At
first, her life mŏves rather monotonously,
and she finds herself wishing "that sŏmething would happen" tŏ giv free scope tŏ
her energy; but time brings with it suffiçient occasions for her tŏ exert herself.
She is able tŏ assist and nurse her father
during the troubles which cŏmc upon him
and the ilness tŏ which thêy giv rise, and
she finds in a number of ŏther cases of
affliction and suffering fresh opportunities
for dŏing good. Life, which at first appears purposles‹, gradually reveals its
true meaning tŏ her as she groes older,
and, as the fançies of her childhood's days
giv plaçe tŏ the realities which cŏme with
the years in which she groes tŏ womanhood, she recognises the true priveleges
aud duties by which her position in society is attended." [London Review. **30 m**
FAMOUS VICTORY = No. 245.

FAR IN THE FOREST [**Penn**] =
No. 690.

FAR-AWAY MELODY (A). [by
M.. ELINOR WILKINS: Edinburgh, *Douglas*, 1890.] "Mr. Douglas has dŏne wel
tŏ republish these excellent little stories.
The stories wer written, tŏ quote the author's words, "about the village people of
New England." Thêy ar studies of the
descendants of the Massachusetts Bay
colonists, in whŏm can stil be seen traçes
of those features of wil and conscience, so
strong as tŏ be almost exaggerations and
deformities, which characterized thêir ancestors. The author has a keen sense of
heroism and all which is heroic, and she
presents it tŏ us in various pleasing
shapes. · Fidelity tŏ conscience characterizes all the heroes and heroins of her
stories, however poor or ignorant or stupid thêy may be. If a complaint must be
made it is that we ar not told cnuf about
the people whŏ ar introduced. Thêre is
no elaboration; no attempt tŏ traçe the
grŏth of character or tŏ exhibit the variety of its manifestations. Each story is
just an inçident. The vail is lifted for the
moment from sŏme commonplace life tŏ
reveal the divinity which dwels thêrein,
and then immediately it is drawn down
again. We dŏ not ask ôur author tŏ giv
us more elaborate stories. Probably she
knoes her powers best; and many writers
would find it easier tŏ compose elaborate
stories than tŏ exercise the severe self-
repression which is necessary tŏ keep the
sketches within these narro bounds.
Thêre ar 14 stories in each volume, and it
would be a difficult task tŏ determin which
is the best. Nŏne certainly is more beautiful than that of Lois in "*Robins and*

Hammers," and nŏne more pathetic than
the little tragedy of "*An Honest Soul.*"
Thêre is fine humor in "*An Object of
Love*" and in "*An Unwilling Guest.*"
Persons of philanthropic' tendençies whŏ
busy themselvs with trying tŏ dŏ good tŏ
people against thêir wil might with advantage take tŏ heart the lesson taut in the
last-named story, and in the really touching inçident recorded in "*A Mistaken
Charity.*" However purchasers may wel
be left tŏ themselvs; thêy ar not likely tŏ
leave any part of the books unread.
Grêat literary power may be disçerned
throuôut; indeed ŏnly a true artist in
letters could hav presented such subjects
as these effectually." [Academy.]—"The
poetry of homely things receives good
illustration here. The breath of country
life cŏmes refreshingly from its pages;
lilacs, "apple-blŏs," "cherry-biŏs," balsam
and phlŏx breathe thêir perfume for us;
green country lanes invite us tŏ a ramble,
and many a gray, unpainted cottage opens
hospitable doors. The people ar, for the
most part, lanky, angular, middle-aged,
innoçent and narro-minded; the women
predominate, and thêy wêar il-fitting, old-
fashioned calico and muslin gowns and
rule thêir lives with almost morbid conscientiousness. The men ar ruf and exacting and extremely "sot" in thêir ways;
but in men and women alike unsuspected
delicaçy of sentiment springs up throu the
unpromising exterior, as the blue bel
peers out throu the creviçes of New-
Hampshire granit. The sketches sho the
unbending pride, the strength of purpos,
and the hatred of hypocrisy which mark
the true rural New Englander." [Epoch.] See, also, No. 55. **30 w**

and finally, of course, they are married. This is all told pleasantly enuf, and in a way which every one will be glad to see in a story which does not pretend to any deep searching of the human heart, but which will, we have no doubt, be very popular among people who do not read most of the best and a multitude of the worst novels every year. But better than that, to our thinking, is the greater novelty of the scene to which the author introduces us, and the amusing people—Second Adventists, **Western Methodist** exhorters, confidence-men, and so forth—whom he has sketched in a very lifelike way. The plot of the story is certainly hackneyed, but there is considerable freshness in the telling of it, and, above all, the author deserves praise for the good-nature and cheerfulness, and the lack of false sentiment, which together make the story better than would its literary merits alone.' [Nation. **30**

FARNELL'S FOLLY [by J : T. TROW-BRIDGE, *Lee & Shepard*, 1885.] "The facility with which Mr. Trowbridge always writes is as apparent as ever in his latest novel. The 400 and more pages which are required to tell the story of 'Farnell's Folly' were, we may be sure, not written painfully, nor yet carelessly; but there is a rapidity about the style that makes the movement of the story seem tedious by contrast. As now and then happens with facile writers, the points are often so much insisted on that the characters, while not seemingly exaggerated, still fail to seem natural. Then, a reader objects even to the apparent assumption that he has no discernment whatever. The story is essentially American in its qualities. The people of Waybrook, their environment and traditions, are all in keeping with a village of **Western New York**. Ward Farnell, whose magnificent house was to have been his pride and became his folly, is a type of the successful American, led on to financial ruin by love of display; and some of the minor characters are excellent from the way in which the limitations of their birth and

nurture are portrayed, while their real worth and honesty are not sunk out of sight. Tho the story is American, it is not new; both the incidents and the characters have an exasperating way of seeming to have been already encountered somewhere. This is ordinarily a mark of commonplaceness: yet it may not be disagreeable to many who have grown tired of the strained effort for novelty in much of the current fiction—the painful search for queer types and unused material—to read a novel in which imaginations are not asked to leave the earth, nor even to dwell in strange places." [Nation. **31**

FIRST LOVE IS BEST [by "GAIL HAMILTON," *Estes & Lauriat*, 1877.] "The thesis of the title is established by the record of the life of a young girl who, after being disappointed by finding one betrothed lover worthless, marries a much better man, and in time learns to love him. The story is told with considerable skill and, of course, with abundant humor. It is surprising to see how a writer whose shrewishness—if we may be allowed the term—has become notorious, should be able to write a story so full of good-humored satire and real sentiment. It is, of course, not a great novel, but it is bright and readable." [Nation. **32**

FIVE HUNDRED DOLLARS [by H. W. CHAPLIN, *Little & Brown*, 1888.] "The time is not lost which is spent in making the acquaintance of the characters in these 'Stories of **New England** Life,' They may be plain people, without romance or legends of any sort, without any tendency towards introspection or fine discrimination in the matter of motives or spirituality; but they have a firm hold on the essentially worthy things in life and character. It is a hold which they maintain by faith, and which serves them thro every-day trials and keeps them up to a high level of truth and right. The stories are excellent as stories; they are fine in the simplicity and quietness of their tone. Their interest is unstrained and natural as can be, yet it is always sufficient. They

FARMINGDALE. [by "Caroline Thomas," i. e., JULIA CAROLINE (RIPLEY) DORR: *Appleton*, 1854.] "If this be a first book, it is a most promising ŏne. We took it up listlessly, a little alarmed at its bulk; but we had hardly read a page, before we felt assured that it was sŏmething beyond the common run. Beginning, middle, and end, it is welsustained.—The tale is a simple ŏne; ŏnly the life-history of a couple of orphans, a narrativ of trials and final triumphs. But it is powerfully and beautifully told, now rousing you tŏ a bitter but just indignation, and now waking the tears and smiles of pathos and mirth. As a picture of life and manners "Down East," it seems tŏ us tŏ be life itself. Towns like "Farmingdale" ar, we believe, scattered all over **New-England**; and men and women like uncle and ânt Graham, (how cordial ŏ̂ur detestation of the latter) ar not rare. Cruel step-fathers, hard-heârted ânts, and the gardians of the children of the dead generally, should read "Farmingdale" and profit by it; it holds the mirror up tŏ Nature fearfully. And the young folk should read it also, espeçially the orphans; for it shŏs how God raises friends for the helpless and unprotected, and how much even the weakest can accomplish, when thêy work with earnest and willing heârts." [Albion. **30 w**

FLUSH TIMES OF ALABAMA AND MISSISSIPPI. [by Jo. G. BALDWIN: *Appleton*, 1853.] "In the department of humor we think it can not be questioned that Southern writers hav excelled. The Georgia Scenes [No. 37 d]—Major Jones' Courtship by Thompson, and Simon Suggs by Hooper, constitute an aggregate of fun the like of which it would be difficult tŏ find in óur literature, and here we hav a new humorist, whŏ, in óur judgment, surpasses them all. The drōlery of the writer is irresistible, but apart from this, thêre ar graçes of style which belong peculiarly tŏ him, and ar always appearing in the most delightful manner." [Southern Literary Messenger. **33 k** are subdued without being dull; they are telling and sincere." [Nation. 33

FOE IN THE HOUSEHOLD, THE [by CAROLINE CHESEBRO; Boston; 1871.] "To those who read Miss Chesebro's beautiful story as it appeared from month to month in these [Atlantic's] pages, we need not say much in its praise; for its charm must have been felt already. To one thinking, it deserves to rank with the very best of American fictions, and is surpassed only by Hawthorne's romances and Mrs. Stowe's greatest work. It has a certain advantage over other stories in the freshness of the life and character with which it is employed; but it required all the more skill to place us in intelligent sympathy with the people of the quaint sect from whom most of its persons are drawn. It is so very quietly and decently wrôt, that perhaps the veteran novel-reader, in whom the chords of feeling have been rasped and twanged like fiddle-strings by the hysterical performance of some of our authoresses, may not be at once moved by it; but we believe that those who feel realities will be deeply touched. Delia Holcombe, in her lifelong expiation of her girlish error, is a creation as truthful as she is original; and in her sufferings throu her own regrets, the doubts of her unacknowledged dauter, the persecutions of Father Frost, the unsuspicious tenderness of her second husband, all the high ends of tragedy are attained; and the tragedy is the more powerful since in time it has become a duty rather to hide than to confess her deceit. No book of our time has combined so high qualities of art and morals with greater success than "The Foe in the Household," for which, in the interest of pure taste and sentiment. we could not desire too wide a currency." 34

FOR THE MAJOR [by C. F. WOOLSON, Harper, 1883.]...."We do, however, feel very well acquainted with Mrs. Carroll and the Major, who are the chief personages of the book, living in a mountain village, presumably in North or South Carolina. Mrs. Carroll is a woman well on in years, who masquerades as a young and childlike wife...It is not very difficult for his wife to support the character, which she does with great adroitness. The reader might imagine that her disguise was to be stripped from her finally, and that she was to be turned out of the story in her true character, whereas all the disillusionizing is done deliberately by herself, and it is seen that the one cause for the deception is its justification; for love was at the bottom of it: the love first of a woman grateful to the man who came forward to the relief of her and her child, and then the same love and gratitude taking the form of devotion to the failing husband. The deception, in which the dauter joins, is all for the Major, and when the Major dies the mask falls." [Atlantic.] The charm of the story,—the quiet, placid, refined village life, is hardly indicated in the foregoing extract. 35

FROM FOURTEEN TO FOURSCORE [by MRS. SUSAN W. JEWETT, Hurd & Houghton, 1871.]—In the "introduction" to this interesting story, the author informs us that she wrote it "to please herself,"—an assertion well sustained throuôut the book, in the character which she has chosen to personate. It might easily pass for the transcript of an old lady's journal and reminiscences, written "with no view to publication," but to gratify a favorite grandchild. We do not mean to imply that it is not also likely to please others, but simply that it is not written in the interest of any theory, or party, or sect—that it is not didactic—that it cannot properly be classed among the "religious" novels, tho there is a good deal of religion in it—that it can hardly be called even a "love story," if that means following the checkered fortunes of two persons throu many fears and joys, doubts and hopes, to the inevitable conclusion. It is rather a collection of several love-passages, with quite the usual amount of cross-purposes, united, however, by the author's personality, to whose own story the main interest of course belongs. It belongs rather to the "quiet" class of novels than the exciting, yet it never degenerates into dulness. The

12

GAYWORTHYS (The). [by ADE-LINE DUTTON (TRAIN) WHITNEY: Bos-ton, *Loring*, 1865.] "Stories of New-England life hav a singular charm about them, which every reader must feel, but which it is not easy tŏ analyze. In thêir descriptions of the scenery on which thêir characters ar accustomed tŏ gaze, and of the old-fashioned homesteads belonging tŏ thêir farmers, we seem tŏ recognize sŏme-thing of the sense of quiet enjoyment which steals over the mind when the eye takes in the tranquil beauty of an English landscape, on a stîl Sunday afternoon in Autumn. All which we see appears tŏ speak of security and content; all nature seems to rest, and sŏmething in the sun-light, and the balmy air, and the seldom-broken silençe touches the nobler feelings of the heârt with its mute appeal. Throu-ôût 'The Gayworthys,' we ar conscious of this charm. The story of the chequered lives of a few unimportant and undistin-guished New-Englanders is so admirably told, and thêir characters ar depicted with so much vigor, cŏlor, and humor, that the book is ône which it is a real pleasure tŏ read, and having read, tŏ remember. It is interesting, if not exciting, as a story, and as a moral lesson it is admirable. Its effect can not be ôther than beneficial, and its teaching is as superior tŏ that of most sermons as its technical merit is tŏ that of the grêat majority of novels. Stories with a moral ar apt tŏ be dul; but this is as bright and sparkling as if it made no pretensions tŏ be imprŏving . . . Very pleasant indeed ar the pictures of country life contained in the story, and of the quiet **New-England** home in which the Gayworthys dwel. Very sweet and touching, too, ar .the family portraits, from that of the father, old **Dr.** Gay-worthy, the kind-heârted, simple-minded patriarch, tŏ those of Hulda and Ebene-zer, the servants of the establishment. The romance in the lives of twŏ of the dauters, Rebecca and Joanna, is portrayed with true feeling and in very beautiful language." [London Review.] See, also, No. 258. **36 p** mere scenery of the narrative is of the slightest kind, and somewhat too vague, perhaps; but this is far from being the case with the sketches of character, which really form the true and permanent value of the book, and are positive additions to our spiritual portrait-gallery. Prominent among these are "Aunt Rebecca," and "Aunt Content"—the two most interesting persons in the book, unless the narrator herself be an exception. Both of these have had their lifelong trials, arising in each instance from disappointed love. But in the one case the lover's death brot the disappointment, and in the other his mariage. There is also a similarity in the two cases, in that both have sisters for rivals; but with the difference that the sister of Aunt Rebecca is a successful rival, and the sister of Aunt Content a disappointed one. Yet the former could be called successful only in a very literal and worldly sense. She is aware that her husband has given her but "a divided heart," the unmarried sister being still the most deeply loved. And in her treatment of this very difficult relation, the author seems to us to have shown rare delicacy and truth of sentiment." [Nation. **36**

GEMINI, [*Roberts*, 1878.] "....An extremely simple and sorrowful little story, [Scene in **New Hampshire**] evidently by a new author, but bearing a stamp of quiet veracity which is allied more nearly than we sometimes think to the highest art. It is the humblest of tragedies, and has nothing to do with "terror," and little with passion; but it does purify the heart by "pity," as we read. The style reveals, on every page, that deep and ample but hardly conscious culture, still oftenest attained in solitary places by those who go much to books for their own sake only, and not because the demands of conversation or the customs of a social clique require it." [Atlantic.] "It is a singularly touching and realistic picture of village life. Along with the bare, barren, narrow, and forbidding side of New England life and character, it depicts

the homely domestic virtues, the high sense of duty, the loyalty to conviction, the quiet persistence, the tireless struggle against opposing circumstance, which have given New England its moral grandeur and intellectual præeminence." [Appleton's. **37**

GIRL GRADUATE, (A) [by *C. P.* WOOLLEY, Boston, 1889.] "Is a product of New England culture unimpaired. Everything is decorous and honest and uplifting, and there is either no grammar at all, or a great deal of it, very inflexible and stately. The girl graduate has the grammar, while her family and friends have it not; and one of the problems which, at 18, confront her is how she may gain an entrance into those charming circles where it is believed to be pretty evenly distributed. Maggie Dean is the dauter of an illiterate machinist, and would be described by an Englishman as "a young person educated above her station." To Maggie's father, as to thousands of American fathers of the same class, the English phrase is meaningless. They are accustomed to knowing that their women are finer than they, and in their hearts, are proudest when "one of the girls" is like unto the owl for wisdom and the bird of paradise for plumage. To those fond and guileless men she cannot have been educated above her station, for does not her education makes her equal with the best? It is left to the girl herself to find out that it does not, and then comes the bitter hour. In the story of the 'Bread-winners', the worst consequences to a girl's nature of recognition of this dissappointing truth are described with a stern disregard of popular sentiment. It would be pleasant to be able to believe that the Maggie of that famous story is exceptional and Mrs. Woolley's Maggie typical; but we fear that the anonymous author generalized from the wider experience, and that his views about the effect of high-school education upon the multitude were less rosy. Still, it is cheerful to have Maggie Dean purged of vulgar ambitions by the fire of social snubbing, and developing a refinement which does not always accom-

GEORGIA SCENES [by A: BALDWIN
LONGSTREET (1790-1870): Augusta,
Georgia, 1836.] 'is most heârtily wel-
côme. The author, whoever he is, is a
clever fello, imbued with a spirit of the
truest humor, and endowed, moreover,
with an exquisitly discriminativ and penetrating understanding of character in
general, and of Southern character in
particular . . . Seldom hav we lâfed as im-
moderately over any book as over this . . .
The second Article is "The Dance, a Personal Adventure of the Author" in which
the oddities of a bacwoods reel ar depicted
with inimitable forçe, fidelity and picturesque effect. "The Horse-swap" is a vivid
narration of an encounter between the
wits of twŏ Georgian jockies. This is
exçellent in every respect—but espeçially
in its delineations of Southern bravado,
and the keen sense of the ludicrous evinçed
in the portraiture of the steeds." [South-
ern Literary Messenger.   **37 d**

pany the knowledge gained from books."
[Nation.   38

GOOD INVESTMENT, (A) [by W: J.
FLAGG, *Harper*, 1872.] "Is an account
of life in Southern **Ohio**, apropos of the
rise in the world of a bright young boy.
The story is unaffectedly written, the romance is pleasant, if not madly exciting,
no more are the ordinary flirtatious of
other people, and we are glad to recommend the book as a good step in the right
direction on the part of an American novel-writer. There is a good deal of truth of
local coloring in the figure of the old man
whose lands were the subject of the investment. Not so good is the love-story, with
its haps and changes; and perhaps the
novel tries to contain too much, but, as
we say, it may be awarded a word of
praise." [Nation.   39

GRAYSONS,(THE) [by E: EGGLESTON,
Century Co., 1888.] "Mr. Eggleston's
pictures of western life are always worth
reading. In 'The Graysons' he has introduced as one of his characters A'braham
Lincoln—the main incident of the story
being the acquittal of the hero of a charge
of murder throu Lincoln's dramatic exposure, on the trial, of the perjury of the
principal witness for the prosecution. The
plot of the story is simple enuf, and is
made the means of introducing us to **Illinois** life of a generation ago or more.
The dialect is carefully given, and most of
the characters drawn with distinct individuality and interest. The Graysons themselves, Tom, Barbara, and the old mother,
are very well portrayed, and the attempts
to lynch Tom furnish lively reading. Mr.
Eggleston would probably disclaim all intention to idealize, nevertheless he contrives to infuse a dash of romance into
early Western life which possibly is not
true to nature, yet is not on that account
necessarily reprehensible." [Nation.   40

GREAT DOCTOR, (THE) [by ALICE
CARY] "is one of the best stories of life
in the middle West ever written."
[Howells.   41

GREAT MATCH, (THE) [by M.. P.

(WELLS) SMITH, *Roberts*, 1877.] "This
book is full of spring and summer coloring,
apt to the approaching season on the eve of
which it appears,and it drops from the press
with an inspiring click as of the first base-
ball which flies from the bat, announcing
the end of winter. It is in fine, a bright,
attractive story of base-ball matches, and
matches of a more gentle sort, agreeably
peppered with villainy in small quantities,
so as to sustain the relish. But there is so
much clever observation of character,such
charming description of nature, such excellent humor hightened by refinement,
that the book—dealing with a popular
American theme hitherto untouched—is a
notable triumph of current story-writing."
[Atlantic.   42

GUARDIAN ANGEL, (THE) [by O.
W. HOLMES, *Fields*, 1867.]   43

HANNAH THURSTON [by BAYARD
TAYLOR, *Putnam*, 1864.] '...'.a very
remarkable book, a really original story
admirably told, crowded with lifelike character, full of delicate and subtle sympathy,
with ideas the most opposite to the author's, and lighted throuout with that playful humor which suggests always wisdom,
rather than mere fun.......Yet there are
a dozen characters interwoven into the
plot of this book, everyone of whom is to
the reader as a remembered friend, a living
and moving figure, whom he can recognize
as if he were in the flesh, whose action he
can study, and in whom the slightest incoherence would startle him as incoherences
in actual life might do.....Hannah Thurston takes as her part the advocacy of
woman's rights, becomes a lecturer so
like, and yet so different from, the Dinah
of "Adam Bede," and at 30 renounces
mariage in favor of the mission she fancies herself called to perform. She is at
the hight of her village influence, recognized by all as a woman whom it is possible for men to love, yet with something in
her beyond womanhood, when she meets
Maxwell Woodbury, Mr. Taylor's type of
a man, who may be shortly described as a
good "Rochester," and finds her theories

imperfect. The plot consists in the gradual victory of earthly love over Hannah's
dreamy imagination, the slow recognition,
worked out with exquisite art, of the great
truth that woman desires a place in the
world which is not that of man's equal
ally." [Spectator.   **44**

HARMONIA [byM.. A.OLNEY, *Macmillan*, 1888.] "The most salient feature
of 'Harmonia' is its length, but, after enduring for a season, one learns to pity, and
in a mild degree embrace, even as a sojourner in some dull village passes from
apathy to observation, and thence to interest in the prosy annals of the place. 'Harmonia' disarms criticism by styling itself
a chronicle; wisely, for there is no plot, no
construction, no climax, but day upon day
of little doings. The persons are chiefly
English settlers of to-day in a wholly unre-
constructed Southern State [Virginia]
who are trying to build a town, farm the
land, and make their fortunes. The juxtaposition of English and the native blacks
makes a contrast in races effective and new.
The few white Americans who appear are
mainly "poor trash," or swindling land-
agents, or shirking clergymen. The exceptions are one or two American women
who, spite of the inevitable English appointments for American women of hobbies and divorces, are meant to be, and are,
attractive characters. In other words, it
is an English view of life on American
soil; the livers being English, under the
not unpicturesq phase of a new settlement
in a region comparatively old. It is observable that this gives the English a capital chance to make the best of it, and we
must own to sharing the wicked American
land-agent's regret that the foreign settlers
should buy the land, obtain influence, and
yet despise the privileges of citizenship.
The wicked land-agent's revenge even
Americans must deplore, but it is well to
allude to it, that those intending to read
the book may perceive that it is not wholly
without the scent of battle. There is burglary, there is kidnapping, there are
snakes, but not to any uncomfortable ex-

tent. Naturally arise the discussions of a
thousand topics—personal, social, and political—which are treated with honesty
and spirit. The negro portraits are especially lifelike, tho not from most agreeable originals. The English colony, as
hinted, absorbs most of the merit and the
spoils. Among its numbers are some very
real persons, and the chronicle of their
very real doings, told with humor and zest,
will have an attraction for those who like
pictures of life and manners rather than
form and dramatic quality—pictures, let it
be added, nearly coequal in extent with
the original occurrences." [Nation.   **45**

HIGH-LIGHTS [by C. (WHITNEY)
FIELD, *Houghton*, 1886.] "It is rather a
pretty idyl, narracing how a neat-handed
Phyllis, of rare domestic and intellectual
accomplishments, ensnared the heart of a
wandering knight of the pen and brush.
It is very nice to know that intellectual
giants on a holiday become as babes. The
melancholy 'Jaques' doing 'Silvius' unbe-
known would not offer a more refreshing
spectacle. The sophisticated intelligence
has some difficulty in accepting the probability of such transformation, but to the
author of 'High-lights' it is evidently as
natural, easy, and positive a process as
breathing." [Nation.   **46**

HILLSBORO' FARMS [by S. D. COBB,
1868.]   **47**

HIS GRANDMOTHERS [by H.. (S.)
CAMPBELL, *Putnams*, 1877.] "In this
book (which surely has not a title suggestive
of amorous frenzy) we find the grandson's
wife's friend becoming engaged to the husband's partner. While this concession is
made to the tastes of the inveterate reader
of novels, there is also a good deal that is
really entertaining in the poor wife's story
of the two grandmothers-in-law who planted themselves in her home. One was an
amiable, silly creature, while the other
was a domestic tyrant of the most virulent
kind. She bullied her granddauter and
petted her easily-beguiled grandson; she
bôt a pig and cow, and then put the family, excepting the grandson, on short allow-

HILLS OF THE SHATEMUC [by Su-
SAN WARNER (1819-85): *Putnam*, 1856.]
"has many of the characteristics of 'Queechy,' [No. 117 s] but fewer of the faults.
Like that, it is diffuse, and in parts dul;
but like that, also, it betrays marked originality, vigor of conception, lively dialog,
and, occasionally, beautiful description.
Nor dŏ we find in this work what was a
recommendation tŏ sōme, but an offense
tŏ us, in her former work—a too frequent
and even violent introduction of peculiar
religious sentiments. The piety of it is
just as deçided, but more lovely; the characters hav more breadth and variety, and
the inçidents, we think, är managed with
greater artistic skil." [Putnam's. 46 r

ance of skimmed milk, making insufficient butter from the cream, while she sold two quarts of good milk to a neighbor for her own emolument. In a word, she exhausted nearly all the methods of refined cruelty which have such frequent and crushing effect in the enforced intimacy of family life. The story ends with the curtness of one of Mother Goose'e melodies; but there is a good deal of humor in this amusing sketch which could find better employment in a real story. The writer has the unfortunate gift of clear-sightedness, and at times she shows considerable cleverness, as in her description of her own character." [Nation. **48**

HIS LITTLE ROYAL HIGHNESS [by RUTH OGDEN, *E. P. Dutton & Co.*, 1887.] "Is a story of our **New Jersey** coast In the vicinity of New York. We recommend it as truthful, wholesome, and entertaining, and helpful in the cultivation not only of good morals, but of literary taste." [Nation. **49**

HIS SECOND CAMPAIGN [by M. THOMPSON : *Osgood*, 1883.] "Its opening description of a secluded mountain valley, in Northern **Georgia**, and its residents and belongings, is a prose idyl of exquisite beauty, rich in the poetry and color of rural life, and framing a figure of perfect maiden loveliness. The story is told with spirit and vivacity, and it is affluent of striking situations and incidents illustrative of contrasted phases of the social life of the South and North." [Harper's. **50**

HONORABLE SURRENDER, (AN) [by M.. ADAMS, *Scribner*, 1883.] "...... The heroine is living in the village of Unity, beating the wings of her desires and expectations against the bars of a narrow and monotonous fate. Until the age of 16 she has taken the ups and downs of life with her father, a rather discreditable and wholly shifty Irishman, till, finding a grown dauter an encumbrance, he has let her take up her abode with her mother's **New England** kinsfolk, and here Mr. Kenneth Lawrence finds her. The story offers excellent opportunities, and the sit-uations are well chosen. The chief fault of the book lies in the character of Alice, who proves incapable of duty, love, or passion, and has little interest or sympathy with life except for its value and consequences to herself." [Lippincott's. **51**

HOOSIER SCHOOLMASTER, (THE) [by E: EGGLESTON, *Judd & Co.*, 1872.] "The scene of the story is in Hoopole County, **Indiana**, a locality which we hope. the traveler would now have some difficulty in finding, and in a neighborhood settled, apparently, by poor whites from V'a and K'y, sordid Pennsylvania Germans, and a sprinkling of 'cute, dishonest Yankees. The plot is very simple and of easy prevision from the first, being the struggles of Ralph Hartsook with the young idea in the district school on Flat Creek, where the twig was early bent to thrash the schoolmaster. He boards round among the farmers, starting with "old Jack Means," the school trustee, whose son Bud, the most formidable bully among his pupils, he wins to his own side, and whose dauter, with her mother's connivance, falls in love with him and resolves to marry him. But the schoolmaster loves their bound-girl Hannah, and makes enemies of the mother and dauter; and they are not slow to aid in the persecution which rises against him, and ends in his arrest for a burglary committed by the gang of the neighborhood, including some of the principal citizens of Flat Creek. Of course it comes out all right, tho the reader is none the less eager because he foresees the fortunate end. The story is very well told in a plain fashion, without finely studied points." [Atlantic. **52**

HOPE'S HEART-BELLS [by SARA LOUISA OBERHOLTZER, *Lippincott*, 1884.] "in spite of its romantic title, is a very pretty and sensible story of a rural **Quaker** family, and, besides the pleasant diction of the Friends, preserves their just and kindly spirit and their quiet ways. Now that the Puritan girl has had her turn in literature and almost vanished, no heroine quite so well fulfils the Novelist's ideal of

HOMESPUN [by "T: Lackland," i. e. G: CANNING HILL: N.-Y., *Hurd*, 1867.] "is a very pleasant and sketchy book, full of quiet pictures from the **New-England** life of the past generation, redolent with the sights and pleasures and experiençes of the country. The articles on Sunday in the Country, the Town Meeting, the Country Minister, and the District School ar extremely suggestiv." [Church Monthly. **50 s**

HOMEWARD BOUND [by JA. FENIMORE COOPER (†, 1851): Phil'a, *Lea*, 1838.] "is exclusivly a 'tale of the sea,' of which element the reader never lŏses sight. Thére is no naval fight or chauçe of a fight; and, with the exçeption of the romantick (sic) and bily wrŏt scenes with the children of the desert, the author has prinçipally relied for his effects on the delineation and contrast of character amŏng his dramatis personæ. The narrativ is chiefly carried on by way of dialog; relieved whére necessary by description; and bý means of those characteristick (sic) and conversational sketches, and the occasional 'stage directions' of the author, the reader rapidly becŏmes as intimate with Eve Effingham, her family, and her lŏvers; with Captain Truck, his mate, his steward, aud théir subordinates; with Mr. Monday, an English commercial traveler; and Mr. Dodge, an American rank-lŏving and mob-worshipping provinçial editor, as if he had himself traversed the Atlantick (sic) and combated the Arabs in théir cŏmpany. Collectivly these personages form an admirable gallery of portraits, illustrating each his class. The author-artist is, we think, ent:tled tŏ hī commendation, not ŏnly for his skil, but for his impartiality. The portraits ar distinguished not merely as interesting and effectiv speçimens of Americans art; but as faithful and spirited resemblançes of théir European and American archetypes. The most or g nal and effectiv, the most character stick (s c), edifying, and from its very exçess of excellence, offensiv, is that of Steadfast Dodge, Esq. This portrait alone would entitle Mr. Cooper tŏ a place amŏng the first-rate literary portrait-painters of his or of any age." [N.-Y. Mirror, 1838. **466** an *ingénue* as the Quaker maiden, for her very limitations are an added charm, making her remain forever in great part an umsophisticated child, seeing with the pure, clear eyes of wonder, reverence, and faith. Hope herself is a very attractive creation, and we are glad to have her retain the pretty "thee" and "thy" in her speech to the end of her history." [Lippincott's.   53

HOUSE OF YORKE, (THE) [by M.. AGNES TINCKER: *Catholic Publishing Society.*, 1872.] "This rather curious story has in it much good feeling, much good thinking, some pretty poetry in prose, some clever tho slight sketching of character, some very unreal and clumsily constructed simulacra of living human beings, some humor, much refinement, which seems to have been at one time pained, but which attracts. As a novel, the "House of Yorke" is not at all or very little, skilful or interesting, tho there are some good scenes and situations. Notably there is a love scene between Miss Clara and her lover which a very old novel-reader will enjoy, as, indeed, he will enjoy most which that young lady is and does and says, as well as most which is said and done and been by her father before her. Those two figures stand quite lifelike, especially when the young lady's notion of a "Dick" is about, or the hero Carl—a most virginal conception, who being alive would be meritorious of instant death. All the Yorke family, in fact, are apparently taken from the life, and if they are hardly a well-composed and well-painted group, they make a very good photographic group, well colored. We must praise also for its interest some portions of the story which seem to us very good as transcripts of the thôts and feelings of a child under certain circumstances. Fresh, sincere, and interesting this part of the book seems to us, tho here and there marked by a crudeness and want of reserve which speak of youth in the artist, and of an untrained hand, but which will not prevent her conciliating the good-will of those who make her ac-

quaintance. There is, however, good reading in this poor novel. One may read it with great pleasure if one is an enthusiastic Roman Catholic; or even if one's self is not an enthusiastic Roman Catholic, but likes to observe the "flame of sacred vehemence" and little sense in other people; and one may read it with a pleasant and laudable triumph and indignation, if one is a well-grounded protestant, and either thinks the Pope of Rome a very designing personage or a much misguided old man. Our readers will find, besides these things, some things that are good and pleasant, and for the sake of these they will readily forgive the writer her violence of anti-Protestantism. As she would perhaps tell us in like case—she may very well be forgiven, because she evidently must have personally experienced a very poor sort of Protestantism or she would never have turned Papist. With which piece of abuse in return for all that we have endured from her in going throu her book, and with an invocation of the glorious and immortal memory of the last King William but one, the Dutch traitor, namely, who won the battle of the Boyne, we take leave of our agreeable author." [Nation.   54

HUMBLE ROMANCE, (A) [by M.. E. WILKINS, *Harper*, 1887.] "These stories of **New England** country people are written with a power of characterization that is unusually effective. The author has seized upon a number of well-defined types—the poor girl who has "lived out" all her life and finally runs away with the peddler; the old woman who pieces quilts for a living, and, fearing she has defrauded her employers, rips them up and does her work all over by mixing the pieces again; the girl who promised her dying father to pay the mortgage, and does it, going without adornments and losing her betrothed; two old women taken from their poor dwelling by well-meaning friends to the "Old Ladies' Home," and languishing in homesickness there till they finally desert their luxurious quarters by stealth and make their way back to their previous

HUCKLEBERRIES. [by ROSE (TERRY) COOKE (†, 1802): *Houghton.* 1891.] "Whŏever has tasted the delight of gathering and eating huckleberries on sŏme rocky New-England hilside, or in sweetfern-scented pasture, wil appreciate the fitness of this title. All lŏvers of human nature relish the peculiar flavor of the old **New-England** character-product of stern and rugged natural surroundings, ruled over by a capricious climate and sŏmewhat twisted by the force of spiritual winds, prevalently easterly—and Mrs. Cooke has portrayed many differing types of this character with all thĕir delightful inconsistencies. *"Grit"* and *"Odd Miss Todd"* illustrate that unexpectedness in human nature which relieves the monotony of existence everywhĕre, and causes the narro horizon of village life tŏ broaden out illimitably; while certain ŏther stories in the collection sho forth the steadfast courage, the shamefaced tenderness, and the dogged obstinacy (sŏmetimes called "pure cussedness") which, in combination, produce the full-flavored human fruit of New England soil. Mrs. Cooke herself possesses the gift which she ascribes tŏ sŏme of her characters, of seeing beauty in its humblest manifestations, and she also possesses a rarer gift—the power of unsealing the eyes of ŏthers tŏ behold this beauty." [Nation. **54 r** abode; the little old maid devoted to her cat, and doubting the existence of a beneficent Providence when he is lost—these are a few of the themes upon which Miss Wilkins employs her talent; and simple as they are, she casts them into forms which impress us by their faithfulness, their careful reproduction of rustic traits, and their recognition of the human attributes of love, devotion, forbearance, patience, and honesty, which underlie the scant, pitiful, narrow lives whose experiences and conditions she describes so well. Miss Wilkins has a realistic touch that is singularly effective, and at the same time her comprehension of inner motives is inspired by the revelations of a refined imagination. The simplicity, purity, and quaintness of her stories set them apart from the outpouring of current fiction in a niche of distinction where they have no [?] rivals." [Boston "Literary World." 55

IN THE CLOUDS [by "C: E. CRADDOCK," *Houghton*, 1887.] "The author's power of realizing the ruf native types with which she deals is known to all readers, as well as that subtlety by which she discerns the core of sweetness and goodness that is in them… To be sure, the heroine, the beautiful, bewildered, faithful, loving, fearless Alethea, with that quaint and fleeting charm which we have learned to know in her and in her sister heroines, goes quietly mad, in the pathetic and attractive guise which insanity so often assumes in fiction. But we do not greatly object to this; young girls involved in such tragical coils do sometimes go mad. A truer character than either of these is the country lawyer Harshaw, who is ascertained with extraordinary accuracy, and who lives in mind and person before us…. But the various groups in the mountaineers' cabins and moonshiners' caves, in the county court-room, and the "settlement" groceries, as well as in the mirrored vestibules of the Nashville hotels and the marble halls of legislation, are forcibly and faithfully done." [Howells. 56

IN THE DISTANCE [by G: P.

LATHROP, *Osgood*, 1882.] "It is Monadnoc which is 'In the Distance,' dominating the lives of the personages of the story, tho the author, aware that this is not the effect of mountains upon the immediate dwellers thereby, imports his dramatis personæ, the keepers of a summer holiday and the young new clergyman of the village. This New England story is not uninteresting, and some of the situations are almost thrilling; but there was a subtlety in the original conception which only a stronger imaginative power could realize. The hero has a force and a nobility which compel belief in him; but we could wish that he had been left to himself to discover the folly and selfishness of his very self-denial. Proofs of keen and delicate observation are not wanting." [Nation. 57

IN THE GRAY GOTH] "Of Miss E.. S. Phelps' short stories we like most "In the Gray Goth," an incident of life among the lumbermen of the Maine woods, very simple, powerful, and affecting, and of an unstrained human quality which the gifted author too seldom consents to give us." [Howells] See "Men, Women and Ghosts."

IN THE TENNESSEE MOUNTAINS [by "C: E. CRADDOCK," *Houghton*, 1884.] "A collection of detached stories not unfrequently produces upon the mind the rather unfortunate impression that any one of them is more and better than all taken together as a whole. Not so with Mr. Craddock's. True, he needed to tell but one story to prove his power as a simple narrator, who can catch a single incident, sketch in strong lines the few characters involved, and throw it all in high relief against a broad background with a power of conception and of execution almost simultaneous. But the 8 stories now grouped under the title of 'In the Tennessee Mountains' present in their total effect something much more than mere short stories. We have not only one mountain valley, but a whole country of hills—not a man and a woman here and there, but the people of a whole district— not merely a day of winter or of summer, but all the year.... A like felicity has fallen to Mr. Craddock. His vivid pictures of the rufness and loneliness of a wild country are not painted for their own sake, but because if we know them our hearts will be stirred by the sorrow and the joy of the life that is spent there. It is a hard life: the men are uncouth and stern, at the best; at the worst, wicked as only borderers can be. The women are gaunt and melancholy: "holding out wasted hands to the years as they pass; holding them out always, and always empty." But side by side with them is that strange miracle of young girlhood. We find it again and again as we find the wild rose lending tender beauty to the grim story. It may be rather the result of the grouping of the stories than of any plan of the writer, but he has enforced anew that saying of George Eliot's: "In these delicate vessels is borne onward throu the ages the treasure of human affections." The reader cannot forget them, for they remain in his thôt as a saving grace to those lawless communities. It is hardly needful to add that the style is admirable, with marked characteristics of its own which extend beyond the mere expression, and produce at times an effect of rhythm, not of words, but of thôt—if such a thing is possible. "The 'harnt' that walked Chillowhee" has all the power of a pathetic refrain in music." [Nation.   59

INSIDE OUR GATE [by C. (CHAPLIN) BRUSH, *Roberts*, 1889.] "A book by the author of 'The Colonel's Opera Cloak' is sure of a public, and those who venture 'Inside Our Gate' will find wholesome cheer. The book is not a story like the former one—in fact, it is not a story at all, but a chronicle of home life, such as must appeal nearly to all who are set in families, and must give to the solitary a sense of domesticity. One would like, provided one had not maltreated an animal, to be shriven at the hands of so gentle and so humorous a priestess as presides over this home altar. The story of her housekeeping, her children, her maid-ser-

vants and their lovers, her cats and dogs and birds, is full of naturalness and charm. A humorous realism gives the book its leading motive, altho pathos is not wanting. The chapter describing the scene between the Scotch servant, Tibbie, and her braw wooer, the baker, is as amusing a presentment of Caledonianism as has found its way into print." [Nation.   60

IS THAT ALL? [by HARRIET W. PRESTON, *Roberts*, 1877.] "Is as slight as possible, altho, in a very innocent and gentle way, it approaches the amusing. It reads like the work of an inexperienced hand, of some one who is not overburdened with the results of long observation and study, and who yet in time may be able to fill out substantially the wavering outlines of figures introduced as human beings. The characters are as unsubstantial as paper dolls, they are visible only when one looks directly at them; when they are not just before the reader, there is only a faint line to denote their presence, whereas in some books, one feels conscious of the people he reads about almost as if he were in the same room with them. A despairing sense of this feebleness of touch would seem to have inspired the author with the appropriate title of the story, which describes the social complications of a winter in an old-fashioned **New England** village. The plot, altho as transparent as an enigma in a jest-book, manages to be the means of introducing some mild social satire." [Nation.   61

JOHN BRENT [by THEODORE WINTHROP, *Ticknor*, 1864.] "The scene is placed in the wild **Western plains,** among men entirely free from the restraints of conventional life; and the book has a buoyancy and brisk vitality, a dashing, daring, and jubilant vigor, such as we are not accustomed to in ordinary romance of American life. ......Helen, the heroine of the story, is a more puzzling character to the critic; but, on the whole, we are bound to say that she is a new development of womanhood. The Author exhausts all his resources in giving "a local

ISLAND NEIGHBORS [Martin's Vineyard] = No. 276.

JACOB SCHUYLER'S MILLIONS [New-Jersey] = No. 759.

JAMES MOUNTJOY. [by AZEL STEVENS ROE (†, 1886): *Appleton*, 1850.] "The scene, characters, and plot ąr all purely American. No locality is named, but it is evident tŏ anyŏne at all acquainted with the country that it must be sōmewhêre in the [New] Jersey Pines. It should șeem improbable that such a state of society should exist within a day's sail of so prosperous a city as Philadelphia, but it is nevertheless true, and as far as we hav examined the work we hav no doubt that it is a truthful representation of what life in the Pines is, and what by industry and enterprize it may becōme." [National Era. **61 f**

JOHN ANDRQSS [Pennsylvania] = No. 279.

JOHN BODEWIN'S TESTIMONY = [Idaho] = No. 766.

habitation and a name" to this fond creation of his imagination, and he has succeeded. Helen Clitheroe promises to be one of those "beings of the mind" which will be permanently remembered." [Atlantic. **62**

JOHN WARD, PREACHER [by MARGARET (CAMPBELL) DELAND, *Houghton*, 1888.] "The author has here given a picture of that 'rara avis' a logical Calvinist. Any real Calvinist is at this hour rare; one who accepts the full consequences of his faith always has been. J: Ward believed in the damnation of the heathen, and more, in the damnation of all who disbelieved in damnation—of all who, to quote one of his elders, were not "grounded on hell." This is also professedly the belief of thousands to-day, who yet eat, drink, and are merry. J: Ward believed, suffered, crucified himself, and fell a martyr to his faith at his own hands, in a fashion logical, but hardly natural. One must admire the sublime acquiescence and loyalty of his wife; yet, in following her course, it is impossible not to feel that the alloy of a little natural self-assertion furnishes a necessary working quality in the imperfect affairs of humanity, and that Helen Ward was nearly as great a foe to domestic peace from one extreme, as were, from the other, Psyche and Elsa of Brabant. J: Ward's concerns, however, are not the only, perhaps not the main, interest of the book. The village of Ashurst supplies some charming scenes of country life, drawn with the tender grace and quaintness in which the poet of 'The Old Garden' dipped an earlier pen. Dr. Howe's figure is an especially individual one. He is the genial rector of the village, whose theology is wholly perfunctory, whose kindness of heart is wholly real. It is as impossible not to be fond of him as it is to feel that in any crisis he would prove a stronghold. Mammon has no temptations for him, but common sense has, in situations where common sense is a blunder, or at least a crime. About the village spinsters and the elderly village bachelor, and the loves and rivalries and

incompleted lives of Asnurst, hangs an old-time fragrance, as of a grandmother's rose-jar; but only a modern novelist (or a Greek poet) could have stated and left unsolved so many questions touching on tragedy." [Nation. **63**

JOLLY GOOD TIMES [by "P. THORNE," *Roberts*, 1875.] "Not only deserves its title, but the further praise of being pronounced a jolly good book. We took it up without much expectation of reward, because country life has been a hard-worked theme, and many of the stories about it have had nothing whatever to recommend them beyond the natural attraction of the subject for city children. On this occasion, however, the author has something definite to tell. The Kendall children and their neighbors and playmates live in the Connecticut Valley, not far from Deerfield, and we are given a sketch of their life during one period from the breaking-up of winter till the appearance of snow just after Thanksgiving. The merit of the story lies in its evident biographical truth. It is very plain that "P. Thorne" writes from memory and observation, and not from pure fancy. The result is a charming local picture, quite worth the attention of English boys and girls, as showing what New England life is in a respectable farmer's family—plain folk, who do their own work, but entirely free from the low-comic variety of Yankee talk and manners too often deemed essential to the success of a New England story." [Nation. **64**

JOSEPH AND HIS FRIEND [by BAYARD TAYLOR, *Putnam*, 1870.] "is a book of a different kind, addressed to a less numerous class of readers—those who prefer the pleasing manner in which a story is told to ingenuity of plot or extravagance in incident. It is a very quiet story, indeed, of simple country Pennsylvania life, but it never relapses into dullness, and it will teach the ethical purpose of the writer more effectually than a highly wrôt romance could do, tho it were it ever so exciting." [Scribner's

Monthly. **65**

KAVANAGH, A TALE [by H: W. LONGFELLOW, Boston, 1849.] "... as far as it goes, Kavanagh is an exact daguerreotype of **New England** life. We say daguerreotype, because we are conscious of a certain absence of motion and color, which detracts somewhat from the vivacity, tho not from the truth, of the representation. From Mr. Pendexter with his horse and chaise, to Miss Manchester painting the front of her house, the figures are faithfully after nature. The story, too, is remarkably sweet and touching. The two friends, with their carrier-dove correspondence, give us a pretty glimpse into the trans-boarding-school disposition of the maiden mind, which will contrive to carry every day life to romance, since romance will not come to it." [J. R. Lowell, in North American Review. **66**

KING OF FOLLY ISLAND, (THE) [by S.. O. JEWETT, *Houghton*, 1888.] Miss Jewett "....is more touched by what is cheery and lovely in them than by what is gloomy and stern. They come to her in idyllic shapes, if it be not a contradiction in terms to call the homely little dramas in which they figure idyllic. Her knowledge of **New England**, reveals the letter as well as the spirit of what is most characteristic therein, but somehow, as she reveals it, the letter is illuminated with the spirit. She has drawn no character which is not true to his or her environment and temperament, which is not vital and individual, and which does not think, feel, and talk as the same person would in life. If her readers do not feel this, it is because they are ignorant of the people who, and the manners which, are the subjects of her art, not because her art is defective. It is affectionate, pathetic, exquisite. Nothing more exquisite than "Miss Tempy's Watchers" was ever written. [R: H: Stoddard. **67**

LAD'S LOVE, (A) [by ARLO BATES, *Roberts*, 1887.] This is a summer story, and in its way, is perfect. The scenic back-ground is given with admirable distinctness, the characters are all refined, the incidents natural, the talk, of which there is much, clever and amusing in a high degree. It is moreover, as befits a thoroly cheerful story, the chaff and humor of youth, rather than the wit and sarcasm of middle age, which, even when best deserved, are apt to leave a somewhat melancholy impression. "There is a good deal of what artists term 'atmosphere' in 'A Lad's Love'—— —a tale of summer life at **Campobello.** [Compare "April Hopes"]. The wonderful panorama of sea and sky, with a charm of color that always sets one dreaming of Mr. Black's descriptions of the Hebrides, are mirrored in these pages, and the usual social drama of watering-place life is graphically pictured.... The story is furthered developed in the arrival of Mrs. Van Orden's dauter, a young lady of 17 with the aplomb of 25, to whom in time the "lad's" love is dexterously transferred by the elder lady. The usual excursions and picnics diversify the progress of the love-making (of which there is an abundance), and the analysis of the emotional nature of a young man of 20, of fine temperament, ardent feeling, and deprived of a mother's love, is perhaps, the finest thing in the book, and is so subtly and delicately told as to be quite worthy of Mr. Bates." [Boston "Traveller." **68**

LADY OF THE AROOSTOOK, (THE) [by W: D. HOWELLS, *Houghton*, 1879.] "The demure "Lady" with her unconscious, wild-rose freshness, has made friends on all sides : the book has been already handed over to Art, and its good things not merely enjoyed, but enjoyed in the fastidious and epicurean way in which Mr. Howells's writings always insist upon being read. It is a style that does not aim at large effects, but in which a "point" is made in every other sentence, and every point tells. And there is something more than realism in these pictures. Never perhaps have the **New England** provincialisms been rendered in so attractive and truly artistic a manner as in the delineation

LANMERE. [by JULIA CAROLINE (RIPLEY) DORR: N.-Y., *Mason*, 1856.] "Mrs. Dorr's second novel justifies the praise we bestoed upon her first, "Farmingdale" [No. 30 w]. It is a truthful, but by no means flattering, picture of certain phases of life and thôt in New-England. The hard practicality and narro sehse of duty which is said tŏ petrify many ŏtherwise estimable persons Down-East, and represses or maddens all whŏ cŏme in contact with them, could scarcely be more strikingly and consistently drawn. Mrs. Dorr's mind is a clear and calm ŏne; she thŏroly understands the evĭl she satirĭzes, and knocs how tŏ be just, even whêre she condemns." [Albion. **70 f**

LAST ASSEMBLY BALL (**Idaho**) = No. 786.

of the heroine, where they impart an individuality and a quaint half-awkward grace such as some British novelists have drawn from a use of the Scotch dialect or of a foreign accent. Lydia is a rare and charming personation, a heroine who is distinctly and honestly countrified without a tinge of vulgarity, and who, tho taking but a modest share in the conversation of which the book is full, never for a moment loses her individuality or incurs the reproach of tameness." [Lippincott's. **69**

LAND OF THE SKY, (THE) [by "CHRISTIAN REID," *Appleton*, 1876.] 'trifling as it is, is pleasant reading, tho more as a guide-book than as a novel. The little band of southern youths and maidens, who have already seen good service in this author's stories, here rest from their more serious labors and take a trip together throu the mountains in and about the western part of **North-Carolina.** This comparatively unknown region must be full of interest to those who are not afraid of ruf fare, and it is well described, with all the attendant incidents of swollen streams, slippery rocks, and steep climbs, in this book. For the sentimental reader there is a full supply of harmless flirtations." [Nation. **70**

LATE MRS. NULL, (THE) [by F. R: STOCKTON, *Scribner*, 1886.] "The book is delightfully unmoral. The characters go their several ways, undetermined by any noble ends or high designs; they behave like ordinary mortals in a world which is not troubled by strainings of conscience; there are dilemmas, but they are not the dilemmas of a moral universe; there is a logic, but it is the logic of circumstance, and rewards and punishments are served out by a justice so blind as not to know her left hand from her right.... So we follow the ins and outs of the late Mrs. Null and her fellow characters with scarcely any incredulity or sense of the absurdity of their relation to each other, chiefly because Mr. Stockton, with his innocent air, never seems to be aware of any incongruity in their conduct.....It is,

however, when dealing with **negro life** that Mr. Stockton shows himself at his best. He fairly revels in this side-show of the world's circus, and takes an almost childish delight in the exhibition of negro character and life. We suspect that the figure in the book which will linger longest in the reader's mind is that of Aunt Patsy; and the description of the Jerusalem Jump with Aunt Patsy's exit from the world upon that occasion, is one of the most carefully written, as it is one of the most effective, passages in the book. It is not strange that Mr. Stockton should feel at home with the negroes. They offer him precisely that happy-go-lucky type of character which suits the world of his imagination. They save him the necessity of invention, and he can abandon with them that extreme gravity of demeanor which he is obliged to assume in order to give an air of reasonableness to his white characters." [Atlantic. **71**

LIKE UNTO LIKE [by "SHERWOOD BONNER," *Harper*, 1878.] "'Sherwood Bonner' in this, her first novel, has touched upon a period in the struggle between North and South which has been little treated by novelists. The antagonists are represented not in the smoke of battle, but at that critical and awkward moment when the first steps towards reconciliation are being made. A proud but sociable little **Mississippi** town is shown in the act of half-reluctantly opening its doors to the officers of a couple of Federal regiments stationed within its bounds...... Plot there is none, and of incident very little. Light, often sparkling, conversations and charming bits of description follow in ready succession like beads upon a string. Lack of incident is atoned for by charm of writing, and in the vivacity of the scenes the reader disregards the slenderness of the connecting thread, or perhaps forgets to look for it." [Lippincott's.**72**

LITTLE COUNTRY GIRL, (A) [*Roberts*, 1885.] "'SUSAN COOLIDGE' being the author, it is not surprising to find this an easy, natural, refined little story, inter-

LEDHORSE CLAIM [**Idaho**] = No. 786.

LIFE IN THE NEW WORLD [**Arkansas**] = No. 291.

LIKE AND UNLIKE [by AZEL STEVENS ROE (†, 1886): *Peterson,* 1862.] "We wonder how a book so tedious as this ever found its way intŏ print. We confess tŏ having read it throu, and tho its morality is unimpeachable, it is a book which we can not praise. The hero enters the scene at the age of 16 or 17, and from first tŏ last he is represented as a pattern of goodness. He dŏes nŏthing improper, exhibits no frailties, makes no mistakes such as the best of youth must sŏmetimes commit, and is a model and a teacher tŏ all around him. Such a character is most certainly misrepresented; and tho the motiv in its production may hav been a good ŏne, it wil hav no effect. Books, tŏ dŏ good, must make thêir characters hu- , man, subject to the same temptations, trials and failings as living humanity. Then let them attain perfection if thêy wil, but let it be by struggles such as we all must undergo in the same road." [Godey's. 71 v

LITTLE MEN [by LOUISA MAY AL-
COTT (†, 1888): *Roberts*, 1871.] "is
really a most charming book, on a subject
of the first importançe. We hav many
exçellent works on the training of children, but few which cŏme tŏ the level of
the masses. Here, however, the subject
is ably put in the form of a narrativ which
can not fail tŏ becŏme popular ... The
'little men' ar the pupils at Plumfield, a
school kept by Mr. Bhaer and his wife—
Uncle Fritz and Ant Jo—as thêir little
friends lŏvingly call them. The pupils
ar few, but these few form a sŏmewhat
heteroġeneous mixture. We hav boys
whŏse parents ar wel-tŏ-dŏ alŏng with the
twŏ heroes of the story—Nat, whŏ used
tŏ go 'fiddling round the streets,' and
Dan, 'the boy whŏ sold the papers'—'a
regular bad lot,' as he described himself.
This wil perhaps shoc English ideas of
what a select boarding-school ôt tŏ be,
but fortunately Plumfield is in America,
whêre, of course, 'ŏne man is as good as
anŏther.' Nat is sent tŏ the Bhaers by an
old friend of thêirs, Uncle Laurie; and,
after remaining sŏme time at Plumfield,
thêy ar induçed by Nat tŏ receive Dan.
The latter, when he makes his appearançe, is deçidedly 'a bad lot;' and, perhaps, the most interesting part of the
book is the account of the way Uncle
Fritz and Aunt Jo went tŏ work tŏ drive
out of him the spirit of mischief and disorder, and fil him with a lŏve of honor
and honesty. Kindness and sympathy ar
the means whêreby the boys ar ruled at
Plumfield. Thêy lŏve and respect thêir
teachers, and fear tŏ giv them pain by
dŏing wrŏng. The lads ar put upon thêir
honor, thêy feel this, and act accordingly.
Thêir peculiar likings ar carefully observed by thêir gardians, and suitably
encouraġed and directed. Every care is
taken tŏ make Plumfield a happy home.
In summer the lessons ar short, the holidays lŏng; all sorts of outdoor work and
amusements ar devised, and thêy becŏme
such a 'rosy, heârty, sunburnt set of boys'
as ŏne could desire tŏ see. Aunt Jo takes
it intŏ her head that it would imprŏve the
tone of the boys if she had sŏme girls
among them, and accordingly this new
element is introduçed. After giving it a
fair trial, she has the satisfaction of prŏving tŏ Uncle Laurie that her plan has not
been a failure, as he predicted it would
be ... Mrs. (sic) Alcott writes in a graçeful, easy, and fluent style, has a grêat lŏve
of her subject, and knoes thŏroly what
she is writing about. The result is that
she has produçed a book which wil be
pleasant reading tŏ old and young, while
tŏ parents, and ŏthers having the care of
children, it wil be of grêat value. The
children's amusements ar capitally described, and thêir talk is thŏroly natural."
[Examiner.   **73 h**

LITTLE NORSK (A) [by HAMLIN GARLAND: *Appleton*, 1892.] "The "Little Norsk," Elga by name, ŏtherwise called "Flaxen," ĭs a child whŏm twŏ bachelor settlers on the Dakota plateau undertake tŏ rear. She is found in a nĕbor's hut, her mŏther lying frozen tŏ death by her side, while her father had perished in the sno trying tŏ get help. The situation, delightful enuf while "Flaxen" ĭs a child, and produçing complications when she groes intŏ a woman, is described both humorously and pathetically. The story, in fact, ĭs distinctly good; but perhaps the most striking thing in it is the picture of the pitiless winter, and of the delights of returning spring, proportionately grêat tŏ the horrors tŏ which thêy succeed." [Spectator.]— "Thêre is sŏmething quaint, old-fashioned and very sweet about the story. These twŏ men, living all alone in a cabin on the dreary plains of Dakota, ar very amusing and at times very pathetic when fate has forçed them intŏ the orphan-asylum business, as thêy express it. One of them brings this little dauter of Norwegian parents home throu a terrific blizzard, nearly lŏsing his life in the effort tŏ dŏ so, and his companion's heârts go out in lŏve towards the helpless little creature whŏse dead mŏther lay in a cold and deserted shanty miles away, and whŏse father was lying buried in the sno in sŏme ravine beside his patient oxen. As long as she wished tŏ stay she would be his Flaxen and he would be her 'pap,' the elder man said, and the younger could content himself with the less honorable position of uncle. She is thêir joy and thêir inçentiv, until she is old enuf tŏ becŏme a problem the solution of which groes tŏ be a very serious matter tŏ the twŏ honest fellŏs whŏ hav undertaken it." [Critic.   **73 m** esting without being exciting. The various descriptions of **Newport** scenery are graphic and charming; the graceful refinements of wealth and taste are pleasantly sketched. The books tends rather to make the reader feel that life without all these softer adjuncts is hardly desirable Perhaps to counteract this tendency, the author has given to "The Little Country Girl," a stronger 'morale' than to her wealthy cousins, aud makes the happy ending of the story turn on her clear-sighted rectitude of thôt." [Nation. 73

LITTLE WOMEN [by LOUISA M. ALCOTT, *Roberts*, 1869.] "Miss Alcott's book is just such a hearty, unaffected, and "genial" description of family life as will appeal to the majority of average readers and is as certain to attain a kind of success." [Nation.] "These dear "Little Women," Meg, Jo, Beth, and Amy. are already bosom friends to hundreds of other little women, who find in their experiences the very mirror of their own lives. In Part First we find them 4 natural, sweet girls, with well-defined characters, which, in Part Second, are developed to womanhood throu such truthful and lifelike scenes as prove Miss Alcott to be a faithful student of nature. It isn't 'à la mode' now to be moved over stories, but we pity the reader who can repress a few tears as well as many hearty lâfs over the lives of these little women." [Galaxy. 74

LOUISIANA [by F.. (HODGSON) BURNETT, *Scribner*, 1880.] "A lady from New York, whose surroundings have been those chiefly of literature and art, is alone at a **North Carolina** watering-place, and amuses herself with a new and interesting type of Southern native humanity, a young girl of great beauty and simplicity, but utterly ignorant of the world in which Miss Olivia Ferrol has lived.... The pathos of the story, while there is a touch of unreality about it, is fine and pervading, while the special charm is in the pictures of mountain life in **North-Carolina.** The book is graceful, and if the plot is a

trifle artificial the execution is so skillfully and affectionately done that we are almost ready to forgive the author for limiting herself as she has." [Atlantic. 75

LOVE AND THEOLOGY [by C. P. WOOLLEY, *Osgood*, 1888. "Mrs. Woolley's novel has a very large infusion of theology. The theology is of the "liberal" order, but the manner in which it is presented should not repel anyone, for the author plainly knows very well that religion is more than theology, and the spirit in which she writes is one of candor and reverence for all faiths sincerely held. The hero, Arthur Forbes, has graduated from the divinity school and finds himself no longer able to preach the Calvinistic creed in which he was reared. If this is not exactly an uncommon experience now-a-days, it is hardly less common a thing that such a divinity student should be engaged to a deacon's dauter. But substance and character are given to Mrs. Woolley's story by the fact that Rachel Armstrong does not, as so many do in common life, accept her lover and tolerate his heresy until mariage shall have brôt them into essential unity of belief. She deems him an apostate : shut in as she has been from the larger movements of thôt, which have borne him away, she believes it her duty to harden her heart against him, and if nature and destiny had not been too strong for her resolution, neither she nor her lover would have maried. This strenuous pair, who, tho they cannot live apart, never come to think alike, find a more common counterpart in the genial Chase Howard, the rector of St. Andrew's, and the lively Miss Fairfax. whose "advanced" ideas on woman's lot find no difficulty in mingling with her Broad-Church liberality. The curious picture Mrs. Woolley gives of the western church over which Arthur Forbes is settled bears all the marks of life. The author perceives the deficiencies of crude "liberalism," as well as of strict Calvinism, and offers an expression of the vital faith to which both must come in the convictions to which Rachel at last ad-

LONG LOOK AHEAD (A) [by AZEL STEVENS ROE (†, 1886): N.-Y., *Derby*, 1855.] "is the latest addition tŏ a class of books which hav rapidly cŏme intŏ fashion on this side of the water. For want of a better name, let us call them American Novels. Unlike the fictions of Cooper or any previous American novelist, thêy deal with men and manners, purely American; ŏne set with the South and Slavery, anŏther with prim and puritanic New-England. "Tempest and Sunshine" [No. 154 t] and "Farmingdale" [No. 30 w], ar respectivly fair samples of each. In the same list with "Farmingdale," but far belo it in point of individuality and power, cŏmes the "Long Look Ahead." The scene is laid in **Connecticut**, and the characters ar mostly indigenous tŏ that region. The entire worldly all of twŏ young men, C : and A : Vincent, consists of a dilapidated farm; and the object of the book is tŏ sho how thêy rejuvenated it, by working early and late, and taking long looks ahead. Other matters ar intermingled; but the gist of the affair is a description of the every-day life of a farmer, and a laudation of it as the most independent life which a man can lead. In the course of the narrativ a good many personages ar introduçed, but nŏne which ar likely tŏ leave a ma:k on the reader's mind. Thêy ar not drawn from life, but ar the traditionary characters of fiction. Thêre ar a moral and energetic hero, 2 or 3 model young women, a Good-Samaritan of a Colonel, and the requisit number of "Chores" in the shape of nêbors, etc. Thêy talk a grêat deal, but not remarkably wel. We learn nothing from thêir endless chat, except a few farming memoranda; how the old barn looks, newly painted, what the colt is worth, and the probable amount of the wheat crop! And all this in the stiffest and properest English." [Albion. **74 m** heres." [Boston "Lit. World." **76**

LOVE IN IDLENESS [by E. W. OL-NEY [KIRK], *Lippincott*, 1877.] "A number of people, young and middle-aged, are gathered for the summer in the beautiful **Connecticut** country house of one of them—a wealthy young bachelor. There they all fall in love. We can hardly say that everybody falls it love with everybody else; but it is pretty nearly that. Everybody is in love with some one; and the consequence, after a good deal of cross-purposing and some suffering, is half a dozen marriages........It is absolutely without plot, has hardly enuf coherence to be called a story, is entirely without incident. And yet it is very interesting from the first page to the last.....The book is strongly American; but its Americans are of the most cultivated classes." [Galaxy. **77**

MALBONE [by T: W. HIGGINSON: *Fields*, 1869.] "is a story which reveals in every page the charm of a scholarly and polished style. The characters are drawn with firmness and delicacy; many of the scenes are unusual and poetic, and the best of them are powerfully elaborated. "Hope" is a good ideal of a whole-souled, noble woman, strong, true, earnest, loving and winning love, as the sun attracts its planets to resolve about it. "Malboue," so confidently balancing upon the extreme verge where unscrupulous selfishness becomes acknowledged villainy, and so constantly saved from the worst consequences of his faults by a harmonious temperament and kindly nature, is delineated with the delicacy and skill which so subtle a character demands. "Aunt Jane," with her sound judgment and spicy, invigorating wit, is a good offset to "Malbone's" soft seductiveness, while poor little "Emilia," so capricious, so passionate, and so beautiful, whom the author shields from the indignation of her friends and of his readers—and shows his poetic feeling and his art in doing so—by casting over her a double shield of mysterious unconsciousness and of perfect loveliness, is a tropical

flower planted in an ungenial clime, who soon throbs away her passionate, misplaced life, and finds repose in death." [Galaxy. **78**

MAN OF HONOR. (A) [by G: C. EGGLESTON, *Judd*, 1874.] "The scene is laid principally on a **Virginia** family homestead. The tale relates the adventures of a gentleman who, among other things, loses and recovers a large sum of money, and very nearly loses his character, throu no fault of his, at the same time. He is arrested for debt in New York; he takes part in a fox-hunt in Virginia; he is jilted by a designing Northern girl, and loves and maries a true-hearted Virginian, turns out a born journalist, and altogether gets himself into and out of difficulties in a very creditable manner." [Galaxy. **79**

MARGARET, [by SYLVESTER JUDD, *Roberts*.] "We do not propose to add anything to the stormy and controversial criticism excited by this book 25 years ago. American it certainly is. A fair, impartial portrait of American society it certainly is not. Quaint, queer, original, minutely accurate in its descriptions, but often false in sentiment and philosophy, and crude and uncouth in expression, it well deserves a permanent place in American literature; but we should be sorry to believe it, with all its glaring defects of both thôt and manner, to be 'the most thoroly American book ever written'." [Harper's. **80**

MARSH ISLAND, (A) [by S.. O. JEWETT, *Houghton*, 1885.] "....Her feeling for rural life and her clear comprehension of rural people were never better displayed than in this little story. A generous play of late summer and autumn radiance lights up its every nook and corner; it is mellow with warm color and odorous of late fruits and flowers.....But all the inhabitants of Marsh Island are human and attractive, and the untiring industries of the well-ordered household soothe one like the rhythm of a song.....The more impassioned side of life does not suit Miss Jewett so well as the humorous and pastoral; but each detail about her heroine is attract-

MANITOU ISLAND [by M.. GREEN-WAY McCLELLAND: *Holt*, 1892.] "The title suggests Canadian rather than Caro-linian associations... Immediate disil-lusion folloes, however, as soon as ŏne reads a few lines: the green, drizzly, slug-gish swamps and lagoons of the middle Atlantic coast open their foliaged vistas; the flight of water-fowl whirrs throu the pages; a humid, heavy atmosphere hangs in the distançe, and a dilapidated Southern mansion reveals itself with all its ançestral belŏngings as the centre of the romançe. Here a family circle is gathered upon whŏm a blight or a mildew has fallen: a spent and fallen raçe inhabits the manor, which seems like tŏ be engulfed by the encroaching swamp; the land is lo; the water and the marsh envelop everything in thêir haze and ooze; a primitiv popu-lation of fishermen and shingle-splitters flit about on the canals and tarns of the end-less water-waste and render the uncanny spot uncannier stil. The author's pen is powerfully descriptiv in its reproduction of these landscape vicissitudes: too pow-erfully, indeed, for the pleasure of the reader, for ŏne has a sense of suffocation under her dramatic interpretation of the stil as wel as the 'live' and wriggling life of the multitudinous swamp: her long delineations ar so real, so vivid, so pictur-esque that thêy overshado the personal element in the story and dwarf it; the sombre surroundings thro even intenser gloom on the gloomy plot, and the artistic balançe of things is upset by the insistent dominançe of dark over bright. The story is ŏne essentially sad. Is it any wŏnder that people go mad, that raçes attenuate, that emotional transcend intellectual ex-periençes in such an environment? The Alpine valleys ar full of 'crétins' whŏse reason has ebbed from them under the sinister influençes of isolation, gloom and morbid physical conditions. The Atlantic wastes, in thêir dismal constançy, thêir uninterrupted monotony, produçe similar pathological effects, which Miss McClelland seizes for a vigorous but painful narrativ, in which human suffering plays far too prominent a part tŏ be agreeable. Dr. Irène, Trigg, the idiot, Javan Anselm ar definable people, with features which ŏne cannot help rememberiug, but the remem-brançe is hardly pleasureable, except in the case of the first. Miss McClelland paints insanity admirably; her dialog, too, is good; but her lengthened descriptions hardly leave her space enuf tŏ develop character; it is a diminutiv picture in a very large frame." [Critic. **79 f**

LOVE OF A LIFETIME = No. 299.
LUCY ARLYN [New-York] = No. 300.

LUCY HOWARD'S JOURNAL [by LYDIA (HUNTLEY) SIGOURNEY (1791-1865): *Harper*, 1858.] "is the imaginary record of the daily life of a young woman of 40 years ago, in which all her thôts, feelings and emotions ar nôted down with equal grace and simplicity. She passes throu the disciplin of school, travels about the country, marries, becômes a môther, enters upon housekeeping, and writes reçipes in verse, and generally commends herself to ôûr liking as a sensible and exemplary person. She dôes not weary us with theories concerning thę sphere of woman, nor project fantastical schemes of reform. Altôgether she may be commended tô the acquaintançe of her sex most cordially—the men, we think, would not generally appreçiate her humdrum amiability." [Southern Literary Messenger. **77 s**

MARRIED NOT MATED [by ALICE CARY (1822-71): N.-Y., *Derby*, 1857.] "is by far Miss Cary's best book, and it affords us pleasure tŏ praise it. We hav several times had occasion tŏ notice this lady, sŏmetimes a little severely, for what we deemed her chief fault—the melancholy monotony of her writings. We hav nothing of the sort tŏ harp at in "Married not Mated." Bating the moral of the story, which is implied rather than distinctly stated, it is a pleasant and in many respects a merry book. It is impossible tŏ read sŏme chapters without lăfing heártily. Miss Cary has a rich vêin of quiet humor, which shŏs itself in the creation of twŏ really comic characters, characters of which any modern novelist might wel be proud—Rache, an impudent, free-and-easy domestic, and Uncle Peter, or as his cards hav it, Mr. Samuel P. J. T. Throckmorton, a second edition of Pecksniff with original variations.

Both ar exçellently drawn." [Albion.] —It "is a lively and agreeable story, told with much freshness of feeling, a keen insight intŏ common life, and not a little humor." [Putnam's Mag.   80 p

MARTIN MERRIVALE X HIS MARK. [by J: TOWNSEND TROWBRIDGE: Boston, *Phillips*, 1854.] "Thêre is a freshness about the humor, a depth tŏ the pathos, a detail in the description, an intimate acquaintançe with human nature, and an originality throuóüt, which, in these days of professional bookmaking it is a satisfaction tŏ meet . . . The Ïmpulsiv, hopeful Martin, in lŏve with literature, but long unable tŏ discŏver or experiençe any of its "amenities," is a character worthy of story. His treatment at the hands pf Boston publishers and editors wil strike a sympathetic chord in the memory of many a fledgeling in authorship." [Norton's Lit. Gazette.   81 h ive, and nothing in recent fiction is more true, touching, and womanly than Doris' journey to Westmarket in the autumnal dawn to keep her lover at home from the fishing-banks." [Lippincott's. 81

MATE OF THE 'DAYLIGHT' [by S.. O. JEWETT, *Houghton*, 1884.] "Miss Jewett's stories need no commendation, but we delay a moment to mark them as another example, of which there are so few among the works of women, of that careful study which finds and brings out what we have to call the negative side of life. The world is accustomed to such positiveness and downrightness of fact and motive that it does not often realize the force of what does not happen—the meaning of *not doing*. Of the stories before us, "The New Parishioner" and "The Only Son" are striking illustrations, and, at the same time, are by far the most interesting. Miss Jewett, moreover, has a style, in the true sense, a manner of expression, fitting and beautiful, and her own." [Nation. 82

MEN, WOMEN AND GHOSTS [by E.. S. PHELPS [WARD] : *Fields*, 1869.] "These stories possess that peculiar quality which touches the heart, the quality to which we refer when we say of a singer that she has "a tear in her voice." Sympathetic and full of human kindness, there is scarcely one of them, however simple it may be, which does not contain thrilling or really pathetic passages. The author has a keen sense of humor also, and her style is delightfully fresh, unstudied and attractive. "*Kentucky's Ghost*" is one of the most vivid and thrilling ghost stories we have read for many a day. "*In the Gray Goth,*" "*One of the Elect,*" "*Calico,*" "*No News,*" "*The Tenth of January,*" are also excellent." [Galaxy. 83

MERCY PHILBRICK'S CHOICE [by H.. F. JACKSON, *Roberts*, 1877.] "The style of this book is a model for study. It is quiet and clear and strong. Everywhere there is a calm and just selection of words, moderation and delicacy of epithet; in the pictures, whether of **New England**

scenery or manners, a kind of gentle and unstudied fidelity. It is not and does not pretend to be a typical love story. It is merely the simple recital of a strange heart experience, and a strangely sad one. A woman of the richest capacities, both mental and affectional, meets in her early, artless youth a man upon whom she somewhat eagerly bestows her heart, and who proves only half worthy of it." [Atlantic. 84

MIDSUMMER MADNESS, (A) [by E. [W.] (OLNEY) KIRK: *Osgood*, 1885.] "This book is most refreshing. The scene of the story is laid on the banks of the great river **Delaware,** and a delicious sense of open air, of trees and flowers, of the many tinted lights of sunset, tinging the broad river and the sky above, pervades the book.....The author limits herself strictly to the possible; but she gives us the bright side of nature—the sunshine, the warmth, the color which we love..... And very pleasant it is, and very grateful to Miss Kirk we feel for so much that is delightful. The lawns of the two large country houses whose inhabitants form the 'dramatis personæ' of the tale, slope down to the banks of the great river; the time, as the title indicates, is mid-summer, and the weather is perfect. The story is, of course, the old, old story; of plot and incident it contains the minimum, and of analysis of character the minimum also; just enuf to account for the actions of the different persons where they are not perfectly self-evident, and no more. But, altho almost without plot or incident, the interest of the story never flags from the first page to the last." [Spectator. 85

MISS GILBERT'S CAREER [by J. G. HOLLAND, *Scribner*, 1860.] "....What the moral loses the story gains. Our author has lost nothing of that genuine love of Nature, of that quick perception of the comic element in men and things, of that delightful freshness and liveliness, which threw such a charm about the former writings of Timothy Titcomb. No story can be pronounced a failure which has vivacity and interest; and the volume

MERRIMACK [by DAY KELLOGG
LEE (1816-69): N.-Y., *Redfield*, 1854.]
"is distinguished for naturalness of style,
easy flo of narrativ, and peculiarly interesting revelations of the life and spiritual
experiençes of a factory girl." [National
Era.]—"In many respects it is a unique
volume. As a picture of certain phases
of manners it is entitled tŏ hi praise.
Mr. Lee is evidently wel acquainted with
the home and factory life of **New-
England**, and the reader fully shares his
knoledge when he has dŏne with him.
During the composition of his tale he
seems indeed tŏ hav subjected his mind
tŏ an exhausting proçess, for he leaves
absolutely nŏthing tŏ be imagind. A
grêat literary artist, like De Foe, may contrive tŏ hiten his general effect by a
Flemish fidelity tŏ truth; but this in lesser
hands is apt tŏ becŏme tedious and uninteresting. This is not entirely the case
with Mr. Lee, for altho his narrativ
suffers from this defect, it has stil many
points of interest and is wel worth the
reading. He is clear, simple, even elegant in style. with a certain freshness and
breadth, and a cordial sympathy for the
good and true." [Albion.   **84 k**

MILLIONAIRE OF ROUGH AND READY = No. 839.

MINISTER'S WOOING = No. 840.

MISS BAGGS' SECRETARY [by CLARA L.. (ROOT) BURNHAM: *Hough-ton*, 1892.] "is as pretty and bright a little tale as ŏne would care tŏ fil an idle hŏ͞ur with. It boasts little originality of plot, since the unexpected inheritançe of a grêat fortune by a quiet, rustic little body, whŏ has but scant notion how tŏ use or enjoy it, is by no means a new situation in fiction. Its character-drawing has but few subtle shades; for its good people ar inclined tŏ be very, very good, and its bad people tŏ be horrid. But it is told with so much freshness and so much wholesŏm humor; its ethics ar so sound and sweet; it has so much unmarred youth and honest lŏve and genuin sunshine in it, that ŏne folloes it throuŏ͞ut with a warmth of hea͞rt which lasts intŏ memory; and what better praise need the little story ask? Moreŏver it boasts, despite ŏ͞ur too sweeping assertion, ŏne hīly original character, in the 'Joodge,' a delightful elderly parrot, of a pessimistic and satirical turn of mind. The story of a few summer weeks at **West Point**, during which twŏ youthful lŏve stories cŏme tŏ harmonious adjustment, is charmingly told. We hav endless and most fasçinating glimpses of cadet life. from which the most stoical reader can scarçely fail tŏ gather at least a flush of the 'cadet fever' which we ar assured few sojourners at West Point altŏgether escape. And the little lŏve-scene upon the wind-blŏn, daisy-carpeted hilside is as fresh and tender and fetching a bit of youthful sentiment as we hav chançed upon in many a day. [Commonwealth.]—It is "ŏne of the freshest and most interesting stories which hav cŏme from the press in a long while. Thêre is nothing espeçially startling or original in the plot, nŏthing particularly novel or grêat about the characters: thêy ar ordinary men and women dŏing and saying the commonplaçe things which make the sum of existence in the everyday world. Herein lies the cleverness of its author, that she should hav taken hold of such a story and invested it with so much humor, so much sweetness, and an interest so intensely human, that ŏne finishes the book, closes it, and puts it away with the same feeling of regret he might hav in parting from a delightful companion with whŏm he has spent an afternoon. Its sub-title describes it as a West-Point romance, and the description of a cadet's life is so good as tŏ impress officers with the idea that the manuscript, in such particulars, was corrected by ŏne of thêir number. The action takes plaçe quite as much in New-York as at West-Point, however." [Critic.   **86 t** before us adds to vivacity and interest vigorous sketches of character and scenery, droll conversation and incidents, a frequent and kindly humor, and, underlying all, a true, earnest purpose, which claims not only approval for the author, but respect for the man." [Atlantic. **86**

MISS TEMPY'S WATCHERS, ☞ "King of Folly Island" or "Tales of New England."

MISS VAN KORTLAND [by F. L. BENEDICT: *Harper*, 1870.] "is a most entertaining novel. Just in what particular the charm lies, it is difficult to tell—altho, perhaps, it owes much to the happily chosen language in which the story is told. The reader is carried along so pleasantly, by the current of daily affairs, that he forgets, until the book is laid down, that there are some things in it which were trivial, not much that was unusual, and nothing sensational. There was no plot to goad us on, but, instead of the conventional stage-effect, there was a pleasantly told story of genuine men and women. It is a tale of American society; and our National characteristics and customs are drawn with unusual fidelity. · · · There is a good deal of sentiment, and here it is honest and refreshing because there is no suspicion of affectation or shamefacedness about it. The scene is laid in the region of the coal-mines of **Pennsylvania**, and the descriptions of mountain scenery—which are never tedious, form not the least interesting part of the book." [Overland. **88**

MRS. BEAUCHAMP BROWN [by J.. (G.) AUSTIN, *Roberts*, 1880.] "Unless we had read it here we should never have believed that life on the coast of **Maine** could be so exciting, so cosmopolitan in its scope, so thrilling in its incidents. There is a jumble of notabilities—leaders of Boston and Washington society, a Jesuit father, an English peer, a brilliant diplomatist on the point of setting out on a foreign mission, a Circe the magic of whose voice and eyes is responsible for most of the mischief which goes on, Anglican priests, a college professor, collegiates, at least one raving maniac, beautiful young girls and Yankee men and women. From the company, Mrs. Beauchamp Brown alone emerges with a distinct identity. ....The Yankees are capitally done, and the local color is excellent. There is not much to be said for the other characters." [Lippincott's. **89**

MODERN INSTANCE, (A) by W: D. HOWELLS, *Osgood:* 1882.] "....The sketches of country town life in Equity, [**Maine**] the portraits of the old squire and his faded wife, of the humorous philosopher in the logging camp, of Mr. Witherby the journalist, whose conscience is kept in the counting-room; the touches which reveal the veneering of culture bestowed by a small college on a mean man; the rapid outlines of a lank Western village,—these, and many more which recur as one thinks of the story, remind one that the hand has not lost its cunning. The familiar glimpses of a woman's mind, also, when that mind is like the upper drawer in her bureau, reappear in the case of Marcia; and the passages between her and her husband are new readings from the old story, which Mr. Howells tells so well. ....If Marcia is more than an individual, eccentric woman; if she is the product of a life where religion has run to seed, and men and women are living by traditions which have faded into a copy-book morality, Bartley Hubbard represents a larger and more positive constituency." [Atlantic]. "....We suggest that perhaps every reader, however good or refined, feels in himself or herself a resemblance to some one of the common American types with which it is filled. .....As a work of moral fiction 'A Modern Instance' is unequalled. It is a picture of the career of a rascal of the most frequent American pattern. He is neither cruel nor a slave of his passions, nor has he any desire to sacrifice others to himself. On the contrary, he is very good-natured and amiable, and likes to see everybody happy about him. But of honor or principle he has no idea whatever

27

MOODS. [by LOUISA MAY ALCOTT: Boston, *Loring*, 1865.] " 'From oŭr necessities of lŏve arise oŭr keenest heârt-aches and oŭr miseries.' Trite tho it be, this truth is rarely realized, save in actual sorro, or in the sympathetic perusal of sŏme sorroful tale. Such a tale is *Moods* whêrein the poet's thôt finds graphic and touching illustration. We hav rarely met a lŏve-story in which power and pathos ar so impressivly combined. In details, as wel as in general effect, it deservs earnest praise. Conçeived in an ideal atmosphere, which is consistently preservd, the story yet rests upon the solid basis of life. Its inçidents, if not espeçially novel in themselvs, ar sufficiently novel in thêir combination tŏ arouse and sustain the reader's interest. But its chief and characteristic merit is sŏmething hier than vitality in the reçital of inçident or the portrayal of action. Its delineation of character and its analysis of emotional experiençe ar the elements of its intellectual power. Its scene is laid in **New-England**, and its narrativ deṣcribes the fortunes and the moods of 3 persons, a woman and twŏ men, the former lŏved by both the latter. Unless we grêatly err, the reader wil find that "Moods" is ŏne of the best lŏve-stories yet produçed in America. While no less delicate than truthful in its delineation of the workings of the master passion, it is instinct with a hi purpos. It teaches a lesson. important tŏ youth, and not insignificant tŏ maturity —that, altho its neçessity of lŏve be not satisfied, the heârt should yet be true tŏ itself, nor seek tŏ escape suffering by any compromise with fate . . . In the way of special beauties, we might praise the simpliçity and naturalness of Miss Alcott's style: the feliçity of pictorial tints, the fidelity, and the heârty home feeling of her account of a "golden wedding;" the delicate, tender, profound sympathy of her analysis of Sylvia's sorro and Geoffrey's anguish; the tragic pathos and the dramatic art of her chapter entitled "Asleep and Awake;" and, finally, the the brief picture of the death of Warwick, which ŏne sees dimly throu a mist of tears. The faults of the story ar a certain prolixity in the earlier chapters, superfluous explanation in the last ŏne, and lac of comprehensiv thŏroness in the portrayal of characters." [Albion. **90 t**

In fact, for the oldfashioned notion of principle he has substituted a new idea—that of the primary importance of "smartness"—i. e., of that quality which enables a man to get ahead of his fellows by short cuts, dodges, tricks, and devices of all kinds which just fall short of crime." [Nation.   90

MORTAL ANTIPATHY,(A) [by O.W. HOLMES; *Houghton*, 1886.] "....Humor and kindly satire abound, and the study of a strange idiosyncrasy enables the novelist to make use of much curious knowledge. Maurice Kirkwood, a young man who is brave, accomplished, and good-looking, owing to a remarkable accident in infancy, has such a repugnance to the near presence of young women, that any sudden contact with them causes a violent derangement of the heart's action, and endangers life. ....He cherishes the hope that, as like cures like, some lovely woman may lift the curse from his life. And the curse is removed at last in an American village which he has chosen for a temporary abode. ....The chief attractions of the narrative are to be found in humorous incident, and in the delineation of character. In Arrowhead village, the Pansophian Society is in great favor among the students of the college and the young ladies of the institute. Two of these girls stand out prominent. . . The book is full of passages touching on the follies of the day, in which the geniality of the writer conceals in large measure the the severity of his satire." [Spectator. 91

MYSTERY OF METROPOLISVILLE (THE) [by E: EGGLESTON; N. Y., O. *Judd*, 1873] "is very good.....Any one who cares for a simple story well told, for characters who are genuine people and whose talk is always amusing, will get satisfaction at the hands of Mr. Eggleston. The book is full of humor, observation, and a healthy spirit which is sure to leave a good impression. [Nation.] Scene is in **Minnesota** in 1857.   92

NEIGHBOR JACKWOOD. [by J: T. TROWBRIDGE. *Sheldon & Co.* 1858.] "Parts of "Neighbor Jackwood" we read with sincere relish and admiration; they showed so true an eye for Nature and so thoro an appreciation of the truly humorous elements of **New-England** character, as distinguished from the vulgar and lāfable ones. The domestic interior of the Jackwood family was drawn with remarkable truth and spirit, and all the working characters of the book on a certain average level of well-to-do rusticity were made to think and talk naturally, and were as full of honest human nature as those of the conventional modern novels are empty of it. An author who puts us in the way to form some just notion of the style of thôt proper to so large a class as our New England country-people, and of the motives likely to influence their social and political conduct, does us greater service than we are apt to admit." [J. R. Lowell in "Atlantic."   93

NEW ENGLAND BYGONES [by "E. H. ARR"[i. e., ROLLINS] : *Lippincott*, 1880.] This little volume is a record of life in a typical New-England farm-house 50 years ago. The scenes and incidents are treated with the tenderness which haunts all remembered childhood in a pleasant and long-forsaken home. The aspect of the country throu the varied seasons, the routine of the in-door work, the character of the village worthies, the peculiarities of the village institutions, and the special experiences and delights of childhood are dwelt upon minutely and faithfully. The whole forms a true picture of **New England** life in the more remote districts, with its stern and unamiable features unsoftened, and its strong, hardy characteristics unhightened. It stirs a feeling of respect even while it fails to attract admiration, or to waken any regret that the ideal it illustrates has passed away." [Nation.   94

NEW SCHOOLMA'AM (THE) [by H. ALGER: *Loring*, 1878.] "has some real humor in it. It is the slightest of sketches, describing the adventures of a rich young girl who becomes tired of fashionable life in the city and takes the place of school-mistress in a village among the mountains. She meets the gifted and penniless artist and they marry. The author's little hits at the country people and the city people who spend the summer in the country are amusing." [Nation. **95**

NEWPORT [by G: P. LATHROP, *Scribner*, 1884.] "There is much careful study of individualities and much felicity of description in "Newport." It is not so much a story as a picture, in which all the component parts must be seen at once in order to blend with, modify, set off, and subdue each other. The author has a very good command of his subject, and sees **Newport** in its different aspects and phases, with its pageants, its amusements, its faults, follies, and crimes,—"set about by its dark purple spheres of sea," and arched over by its lovely skies..... Mr. Lathrop has succeeded in producing characters who, without faults of art or taste, go throu their parts, informing them with a spirit at once graceful and frivolous, petty and generous. He has avoided both the grotesque and the heroic." [Scribner's. **96**

NEXT DOOR [by CLARA L.. BURNHAM: *Ticknor*, 1886.] "The excellences of 'Next Door' are not of the highest sort, but they are as refreshing—in the general lack of excellences of any sort—as a morning rain in a dry season. The tone is airy and light, but never flippant, while the story keeps unflagging pace with the style. All throu, one is entertained rather than interested; and it is very good entertainment, too, following the adventures of Aunt Ann and her cat, and the development of her nieces' love affairs. It would be hard to find two more pleasant, lovable girls than Kate and Margery, in the first place, or more worthy, suitable husbands for them than J: Exton and Ray Ingalls, in the second. Then it is pleasant to accompany such characters throu scenes so naturally and admirably done as the girls' boarding-house life and their vacation in the country. It is a great satisfaction to read on in confidence to the end,

with a tolerably safe assurance that you will find no straining for effect, no posing, nor, in fact, anything but straitforward, genuine work. The book is noticeable, equally with its other good qualities, for its freshness." [Nation. **97**

NIMPORT [by E. L. BYNNER: Boston, *Lockwood*, 1877.] "In many ways this belongs to the better class of light stories. .... It is the record of a family who lose their money at their father's death. One girl goes off to be a governess, another stays at home with her brother; and their adventures make the story, or at least they would have made a very readable story if all sorts of superfluous tragedy had not been lugged in. .... But where this fault does not exist the book is full of cleverness. The humor throuout is natural and easy; the people are described as a clever woman sees them. In a word, it must be said that the author has certainly shown considerable ability in writing this readable novel." [Nation. **98**

NORWOOD. [by H: W. BEECHER: *Scribner*, 1868] "We have felt, in reading this novel, that the author had a faculty which might be turned to pleasant account in writing for the stage. This notion was suggested less by dramatic management of situations, or by sustained dialog, than by a certain felicity in expressing the flavor and color of **New England** life in the talk. The range is narrow, and the grade is not that of the highest comedy; but here is representation, not mere study, of character, &, so far, drama. We should be sorry to yield this point; for it is one of the few to be made in favor of the present novel as a work of fiction···· · Yet all this is not to the exclusion of thot and feeling, which give delight in their play amongst the ins and outs of Yankee nature and over the varied picturesqueness of village neighbors and neighborhoods. It would be a loss not to have read that description of a Sunday in Norwood, or the night-fishing or the nutting-party, or going to Commencement at Amherst; and one could ill afford not to know the charm of Quaker farm-life in Pennsylvania, as it appears here after the fatigues of one of the most wearisome and exhausting of stories." [Atlantic.] Norwood was burlesqued in "Gnaw-wood, or New England life in a Village, by H: W. B. Cher." 99

OLD BATTLE-GROUND, (THE) [by J: T. TROWBRIDGE, Sheldon, 1860.] "whose name bears but an accidental relation to the story, is an interesting and well-constructed tale, in which Mr. Trowbridge has introduced what we believe is a new element in American fiction, the French Canadian. The plot is simple and not too improbable, and the characters are well individualized. There is a good deal of pathos in the book, marred here and there with the sentimental extract of Dickens flowers, but it is in his more ordinary characters that Mr. Trowbridge fairly shows himself as an original and delightful author. His boys are always masterly. Nothing could be truer to Nature, more nicely distinguished as to idiosyncrasy, while alike in expression and in limited range of ideas—or more truly comic, than the two who figure in this story." [J. R. Lowell in Atlantic. 100

OLD FRIENDS AND NEW [by S.. O. JEWETT; Houghton, 1879.] "is a collection of stories, all gracefully done, and The Lost Lover and Madame Ferry may be especially commended for the delicate fancy they illustrate." [Nation. 101

OLD HOUSE BY THE RIVER (THE) [by W: C. PRIME: Harper, 1853.] "is the title of a charming volume, full of sweet pictures of rural life, overflowing with tender and delicate sentiment, tho free from sentimentality, and written in a style of exquisite purity and grace, not unworthy of Irving or "Ik. Marvel." ....With its justly colored portraitures of nature, its simplicity and truthfulness of feeling, and its rare appreciation of silvan life, it can not fail to be welcomed as a beautiful addition to rural literature." [Harper's. 102

OLD MAID'S PARADISE, (AN) [by E.. S. PHELPS [WARD] Houghton, 1885.] "The old maid's paradise is a $500 house which Carona Somebody, spinster, has built on the cliffs overlooking Fairharbor, and where she spends a memorable summer. The trials she has with house plans and carpenters, the perplexities of incipient housekeeping, the idiosyncrasies of the Pomona-like maid-of-all-work, the blundering kindness of brother Tom, the cheerful and unconscious ignorance of sister Sue, the vagaries of a black-and-tan-terrier—these elements of fun are all used to advantage, and as a background there are glowing descriptions of sea and shore in sunshine and storm, bits of pathetic 'genre' from the lives of a fisher folk, charming presentations of fascinating "types." The book is perhaps no more than a trifle, but it is a trifle that could come only from the practised pen of an adept. The book has in it the zest of sea breezes, the light and color of summer days. Its humor is exquisite; its pathos is the pathos of simplicity." [Boston "Literary World." 103

OLD NEW-ENGLAND DAYS [by SOPHIA M. DAMON, Boston, 1888.] "The insight which one gets of a phase of civilization in America which has now nearly passed away, throu such books as 'Old New England Days' and 'Uncle 'Lisha's Shop', is well worth having. Even tho the stories, as such, are without literary form or finish, and could more properly be called a collection of anecdotes, there is about them the spirit of the sturdy, honest simplicity which has for so long characterized the rural population of New England and which makes one regret its decadence and gradual absorption, while the realist novel-writer is describing its demoralization by the march of progress and city boarders." [Nation. 104

OLD SALEM. [by "ELEANOR PUT-NAM": Houghton, 1886.] "Not a few of our readers will remember a short series of charming papers in the Atlantic, upon the cupboards and shops of Salem, and

30

upon a "dame-school" there, which were distinguished by simplicity and freshness of touch, and seemed really to have absorbed into their sentiment the not too oppressive odor of antiquity which still lingers about the streets and wharves of that sleepy city. It would be difficult to write about "Old Salem" without entertainment: but the author of these papers had so delicate a touch, so womanly a tenderness for associations, and yet humor and fancy, and alertness in catching the artistic outlines of character, together with such loving acquaintance with the scene, that the pictures of 'Old Salem' which she promised would have been a rare treat. Of these but one new one, and that a fragment, is added to those already published—a sketch: 'My Cousin the Captain." [Nation. **105**

OLDTOWN FOLKS [by H. (B.) STOWE, *Fields*, 1869.] "The story is slight and unsensational, but the characters are admirably sketched, and the various scenes present a picture of **New England** life during the past century, in which the charm of fiction is combined with the reality of history. The good, warm-hearted grandmother, who presides with such genuine kindliness over her charitable home, a beacon of light to the unfortunate; Aunt Lois, so severe and well disciplined; Miss Mehitable, with her large, loving nature somewhat repressed by sorrow and untoward circumstances, but only the more deepened and refined, it may be, upon that account; "Lady" Lathrop and her dignified husband Parson Lathrop; Sam Lawson, the village do-nothing, the terrible Miss Asphyxia—and indeed, all the characters of the book, are as real and living as any of the people, still clothed in flesh, whom we may chance to meet." [Galaxy. **106**

OLDTOWN FIRESIDE STORIES [by H. (BEECHER) STOWE, *Osgood*, 1872.] "Sam Lawson, who tells these stories, is doubtless the most worthless person in Oldtown; but compare his amusing streaks of God-fearing piety, his reverence for magistracies and dignities, his law-abiding-

ness, his shrewdness, his readiness, with the stolid wickedness, the indifference and contempt of those back-woods ruffians for everyone else, and you will have some conception of the variety of the brood which the bird of freedom has gathered under her wings. To be sure, the back woods have long been turned into railroad-ties and cord-wood, and Oldtown is no more, but this only adds to the interest and value of true pictures of them. Mrs. Stowe, we think, has hardly done better work than in these tales, which have lured us to read them again and again by their racy quaintness, and the charm of the shiftless Lawson's character and manner. The material is slight and common enuf, ghosts, Indians, British, and clergymen lending their threadbare interest to most of them; but round these familiar protagonists moves a whole Yankee village world, the least important figure of which savors of the soil and "breathes full East." The virtues of 50 years and more ago, the little local narrowness and intolerance, the lurking pathos, the hidden tenderness of a rapidly obsolescent life, are all here, with the charm of romance in their transitory aspects,—which, we wonder, will the Hibernian Massachusetts of future times appreciate? At least this American generation can, keenly, profoundly, and for ourselves, we have a pleasure in the mere talk of Sam Lawson which can come only from the naturalness of first-rate art." [Atlantic. **107**

ONE SUMMER. [by BLANCHE W. HOWARD: *Osgood*, 1875.] "The word "charming hardly expresses with sufficient emphasis the pleasure we have taken in reading it; it is simply delightful, unique in method and manner, and with a peculiarly piquant flavor of humorous observation. The plot, indeed, is commonplace: a city young lady meets a city gentleman while summering in a **New England** village, with results dear to the heart of novel writers and readers. . . These defeets, however, as well as others that might be pointed out, are of small moment in comparison with those sterling qualities which we have already mentioned as belonging to the book, and with the genuine humor which pervades it like an atmosphere. This humor is of rare quality—delicate and yet hearty, and racy without being in the slightest degree vulgar." [Appleton's. **108**

ONLY AN INCIDENT [by G... D. LITCHFIELD, *Putnam*, 1884.] has the virtue of modesty which its title implies. The author is quite at home among the favored people of Joppa, [**New York**] and touches their blind self-sufficiency with a vivacity which is in no way allied to spitefulness. This thoro familiarity with the manners and habits of a small community may perhaps account for an unconscious use in narrative of colloquialisms which are often vulgar and not infrequently ungrammatical." [Nation. **109**

OUR COUSIN VERONICA [by M.. E.. WORMLEY [LATIMER]: *N. Y.*, *Bunce*, 1856.] "The scene is chiefly among the mountains of **Virginia**, and the characters are taken from the aristocracy of the Old Dominion. In the unfolding of the plot, we are, however, taken both to England and the Northern States, giving the writer an opportunity for several contrasts of scenery and character, which she uses with excellent artistic effect." [Harper's. **110**

PASTORAL DAYS [by W: HAMILTON GIBSON: *Harper*, 1880.] "deserves and will hold a distinct place in the literature of rural **New England.** His point of view is not that of the philosopher, nor even of the full-grown man humoring himself with reminiscence; it is that of the boy who has never ceased to be a boy, who does not call up old scenes, but still lives in them, and whose portraiture of country life a generation ago is no more an effort than to tell the exact name of "Hometown" or the real name of "Amos Shoopegg." This happy continuity of feeling determines the style of the narrative. Its character-painting is excellent, and all the changes and circumstances of the New England year are truthfully described." [Nation. **111**

PATTY'S PERVERSITIES.[by ARLO BATES: *Osgood*, 1881.] "Extravagances of every description pervade this story. "Patty" is, of course, the heroine of the tale, and her "perversities" consist chiefly in encouraging all the lovers she dislikes, and snubbing systematically the one she does love, for no reason that can be set forth more concisely than the author has done it. The successful lover is projected as a softened Rochester, but appears to the reader as a humdrum lawyer, resentful of no ill-treatment and meekly in-lined to accept the matrimonial yoke when his mistress's perversities finally suggest that consummation. There is a sharp young lady with dyspepsia, who deals in epigrams and is addicted to a constant consumption of popcorn, a bowl of which she always carries with her; a matron of extreme silliness, who directs her life by the aid of proverbs; a comic servant, and, finally, a most extravagant mystery, whose complications are so intricate and the elucidation of which leads to so little that it is really difficult to tell what it is all about." [Nation. **112**

PEARL OF ORR'S ISLAND (THE) [by H. (B.) STOWE, *Ticknor*, 1862.] "Mrs. Stowe is never more in her element than in depicting unsophisticated New England life, especially in those localities where there is practical social equality among the different classes of the population. "The Pearl of Orr's Island", the scene of which is laid in one of those localities [the **Maine** coast] is every way worthy of her genius. Without deriving much interest from its plot, it fastens the pleased attention of the reader by the freshness, clearness, and truth of its representations, both of Nature and persons. The author transports us at once to the place she has chosen as the scene of her story, makes us as familiarly acquainted with all its surroundings as if we had been born and bred there, introduces us to all the principal inhabitants in a thoroly "neighborly" way,

PEOPLE AT PISGAH. [by EDWIN
W. SANBORN: *Appleton*, 1892.] "To
those whŏ desire a touch of the good old-
fashiond comic-almanac humor, such as
charmd the boyhood of persons now 55
years old, we can confidently recommend
this little book. Thêre ar in it traçes of
later and very reçent knoledge—passages
which recall the trials for heresy, past,
or future, in which many take a lively
interest; but the staple of the booklet is of
the Sam Slick and Davy Crockett period.
Drŏl inçidents, with no conçeivable purpos in life except tŏ raise a lâf, ar set in
lively motion, ŏne after anŏther, with
breathless haste, until the misadventures
of the Rev. Dr. Van Nuynthlee of New-
York, whŏ is the hero of the story, gets so
complicated that the reader wŏnders how
he wil ever escape from thêir snaky coils.
Nor in fact dŏes he, for the last page
leaves him at the mercy of Miss Prudençu
Winthrop of Boston, whŏ has set what she
is pleased tŏ call her heârt on marrying
Dr. Van Nuynthlee, but whŏ has been
supplanted in his affections by the Widow
Suydam. His future torment may therefore be imagind. The first chapters of
the book ar in a quiet, grave tone, not
without seriousness, but all this vanishes
as the plot reveals itself, and the fun of
the situations becōmes too much for the
moderation of the author. He then lays
the rêins of his judgment on the mane of
his drŏl fançy, and away we go, throu all
sorts of rustic dilemmas, quite out of keeping with the grave outset of the tale.
Thêre is a genuin humor in it, and much
skil and graçe of style." [Springfield
Republican. **113 s**

and contrives to impress us with a sense of the substantial reality of what she makes us mentally see, even when an occasional improbability in the story almost wakes us up to a perception that the whole is a delightful illusion......In the rest of the population of Orr's Island the reader cannot fail to take a great interest, "Cap'n" Kittredge and his wife, Miss Roxy and Miss Zephania Pennel, are incomparably good. Each affords matter enuf for a long dissertation on **New England** and human character. Miss Roxy, especially, is the typical old maid of Yankee-land, and is so thoroly loveable, in spite of her idiom, her crusty manners and eccentricities, that the only wonder is that she should have been allowed to remain single. But the same wonder is often expressed, in actual life, in regard to old maids superior in education, accomplishments, and beauty, and her equals in vital self sacrifice and tenderness of heart." [Atlantic.   **113**

PETER CARRADINE [by CAROLINE CHESEBRO', *Sheldon & Co:* 1863.] "The second title of this novel, "The Martindale Pastoral," indicates its design and scope. We think that there is no female writer in America, who equals her in the power of unfolding character. In this work she has made a great advance upon any of her previous efforts. She has a story to tell— interesting, if not exciting to those who have been accustomed to "thrilling" plots. Her characters are here persons who might really have lived in this world, and the phases of their development are wrôt with the conscientious care of a genuine artist. Without attempting to give an analysis of the story and characters, we content ourselves by saying that the cultivated reader will deem "Peter Carradine" the best American novel which has been written for years." [Harper's.   **114**

PILOT FORTUNE [by MARIAN C. L. REEVES and EMILY READ, *Houghton*, 1885.] "cannot be said to be strikingly original either in plot or situation, but the **Nova Scotia** fishing-village which makes the background of the novel is so well touched off, the local color so fresh **an** unmistakable, and the narrative so easily and lightly given, that the book becomes vivid and effective. There is little mere description, but a few strokes of the pen draw the picture for us so clearly that we seem to breathe the crisp air of those high latitudes all throu the story of Milicent and her lovers." [Lippincott's.   **115**

POGANUC PEOPLE [by H. (B.) STOWE, *Fords*, 1878.] "The old New England rural life can hardly be too fully and too minutely illustrated for those who came too late to behold it, for the significance of that life in the fast-cumulating story of this nation is inestimable.' [Atlantic.   **116**

PRICE SHE PAID (THE) [by F. L. BENEDICT: *Lippincott*, 1883.] "is one of the author's best, with the same ease in delineation of character, the same vivacions and sparkling talk, which made "St. Simon's Niece" a popular book. The little drama here is played out in the picturesque highlands of **Pennsylvania**, and the story chiefly concerns the heroine's dilemma about her lovers. There are, indeed, two heroines, and the effect created is of endless coquetries and prettinesses and all the irresistible array of feminine caprices. But the best character in the story is Denis Bourke, a young Irishman who carries off the honors as hero with unusual dignity and reality. Mr. Benedict has not been carried away by admiration of the analytical novel of the period, and his characters are developed by their own expression of themselves." [Lippincott's.   **117**

QUEEN HILDEGARDE [by L. E. (HOWE) RICHARDS: *Estes & Lauriat*, 1889.] "is sweet and wholesome, with a distinct purpose, yet without the appearance of "preaching". Hildegardis Graham, the petted only dauter of wealthy parents, finds to her dismay that they are for the first time to leave her behind when they take a journey. Her sensible mamma, fearing that Hilda is getting frivolous and shallow in her artificial city life, decides

PETER GOTT. [by J. REYNOLDS: Boston, *Jewett*, 1856.] "There is a homely simplicity in this story, added tŏ a vigorous, manly strength. Narrating the life of Peter Gott, whŏ as a "**Cape Ann** fisherman" by good sense and persevering industry accumulated a fortune without forfeiting the respect and affection of his acquaintances, the book describes with much minuteness the manner in which the fisheries ar carried on. Written sŏmewhat in the Robinson Crusoe style, entirely devoid of pretentiousness, aiming ŏnly at a plain reçital of facts without rhetorical flourishes, it wil, by that class which can appreçiate it, be read with grêat pleasure. Thêre is no plot, no remarkable adventures or hair-breadth escapes. We find it difficult tŏ determin in what particular such books hav thêir especial charm—it must be in thêir truthfulness." [Criterion. **114 d**

PETTIBONE NAME = No. 338.

PICTURES OF COUNTRY LIFE [by
ALICE CARY (1822-71): N.-Y., *Derby*,
1859.] "includes a series of tales and
sketches of villagers, and incidents of
their lives—felicitous in description, with
frequent pathos and tenderness." [Century.] It "is a not unfit companion for
the record of 'Our Village' (No. 1657).
It is healthful, entertaining reading, and
the pleasure it is able to giv is as pure and
honest as it is great." [Nation. **114 m.**

PRUE AND I [by G : W : CURTIS (†, 1892) : N.-Y., *Dix*, 1856.] is "not large in bulk nor pretentious in subject, yet genial and gentle tŏ the full, and written with so cunning carelessness that as you saunter along from page tŏ page you ar scarçely conscious of the rich soil which lies beneath the surfaçe. We dŏ not mean that in these pleasant glimpses at the social world you shal find a treatis on the whole duty of man or a homily for every day of the week. We aver ŏnly that, tingd tho it be with epicureanism, Mr. Curtis' philosophy is wholesŏme and kindly ; that he counsels a good use of the world, not a deadly crusade against those whŏ abuse it ; that he is too wise tŏ dream of extinguishing ostentation and folly, by penned or spoken satire, contenting himself with the more practical object of reduçing them tŏ thĕir proper value in the eyes of lookers-on. Herein he succeeds. "Prue and I," a lŏving and contented couple, form a connecting link for the half-dozen papers here gathered, tho each is able tŏ stand alone. Our favorit is "My Châteaux," for whŏ is so poor in hopes, so beggared in imagination, as not tŏ ŏn a castle in Spain? Very delightfully, and with sŏme profit withal, ar the tenures of these Spanish estates investigated, and the varied rŏll of thĕir possessors called over. If you hav not seen this amendment on the Peerage Book, we advise you tŏ get it. Sŏme ŏther good things too, you wil find appended—sŏme in which the style may remind you of "The Sketch Book," and the tone of the "Essays of Elia." " [Albion. **117 k**

QUALITY OF MERCY (The) [by W: DEAN HOWELLS: *Harper*, 1892.] "is a tract for the times. It is purely realistic, and propounds a common problem of the day, tŏ whŏse solution the author offers no aid. One meets again nearly every character whŏ figured in "Annie Kilburn" [No. 189]; Annie herself appears but ŏnce or twice, and then for a moment only; but Putney, the Northwicks, the Hilarys, Mr. Gerrish, ar personages of the new chapters of life in Hatboro. The frequent tale of the defaulter is told. Northwick, whŏ has long been the treasurer of a grêat corporation of which Hilary is president, has for years, tŏ use his self-considerate phrase, been borroing the funds of the company tŏ speculate with. The story begins just as this has been found out. The president, because he is an old friend of the family, givs Northwick 3 days in which tŏ replaçe the the stolen mōney. We hardly need say that Northwick makes for Canada that night. But he is not made of so strong a stuff as he had thôt. Exile often brêaks down the stoutest, and Northwick weakens mentally and physically until he would prefer an American jail tŏ freedom in Canada, and he voluntarily returns tŏ Hatboro, ōnly tŏ die on the way. In the mean time his family hav stripped themselvs of all thêy held, and his old friend Hilary has robbed himself tŏ make good the speculations of Northwick. Disaster, shame and obloquy hav been the result of greed; it is true the virtues of the Hilarys and the firmly-rooted prinçiples of the defaulter's dauter shine more brightly by contrast, but thêy dŏ not ôffset the misery caused by ōne man's sin. Nor dōes the punishment of exile and ignominy better Northwick; he pities himself and hugs the hope that he may compromise,—that with his previous record the world wil not press him too hardly, that mercy wil be granted; and he dies in this conviction." [Springfield Republican.]—"It is a better novel than "A Modern Instance," because the author keeps more closely tŏ the story and indulges in fewer philosophical digressions. It is a study of a respectable bank defaulter. [San Francisco Chronicle.]—"Northwick seems tŏ be a type of men of his kind as true tŏ life as ar Silas Lapham [No. 357] and Bartley Hubbard [No. 90]. The pleasure tŏ be derived from reading this study is a purely literary ōne, and, grêat as that is, it can not dispel the depression caused by the subject's intrinsic pain. The author has, however, dōne his best tŏ liten inseparable gloom. Notiçeably inspiriting is the reporter,—genial, light-hêarted, and kind in almost every relation of life, yet perfectly unscrupulous when animated by a desire tŏ make a 'beat' in the interest of his paper. The perusal of the book must increase the admiration of the author's constant readers for the fidelity with which he has pursued his chosen way,—tŏ present a series of pictures of common American life. Thêy must also be impressed by that steady advançe in knoledge which is helping him in his later works tŏ represent his people as, after all, more human than American. And, without loss of brilliancy, his style has gained urbanity, even tenderness, and thus compels a personal affection throu which intellectual admiration suffers no detraction." [Nation.   **117 p**

QUAKER GIRL OF NANTUCKET =
No. 351.
QUAKER HOME (A). [by G: FOX
TUCKER: Boston, *Russell*, 1890.] "The
wil point involvd is ōne of grêat interest.
The book is pleasantly written, the anecdotes and scenes ar largely taken from
life, the descriptiv passages wil be readily
recognized by visitors tŏ **New Bedford**,
and the volume is of exceptional value in
that, unlike ōther novels written about
Quakers, it givs a graphic and extremely
interesting portrayal of the home-life,
habits, customs, vues and religious convictions, as wel as the beautiful traits of
that "peculiar people." [Boston Transcript. **117 m**
QUEECHY [by SUSAN WARNER (1819-
85): *Putnam*, 1854.] "is a book without
a parallel, except in the "Wide Wide
World" (No. 0401); and it is very hī
praise tŏ say of it, as we can, that the
natural refinement and beauty of sōme
of the characters renders the book readable in spite of the surprising vulgarity of
most of them. Unless we ar very much
in error in ōŭr inferençes from her writings, this author has spent her days in a
quiet country life.—the happiest and best

of all modes of life, but ōne which is not
the best preparation for the painter of
fashionable manners. Her country people ar all true and forçible—coarse, but
never vulgar; and had all the characters
been made of such persons, the work
would hav been unexçeptionable. But
when the Author attempts, as with the
grêatest confidence she dōes, tŏ describe
the best society of New-York, Paris, and
London, her failure is too grêat tŏ be
absurd; it is melancholy tŏ behold the
working of a so ruinous mistake. Had
Dickens written many of this lady's hi-
society scenes, and introduced them as
exposures of the vulgarities intŏ which
the loest çity shopkeepers and thêir wives
and dauters fall by endeavoring tŏ assume
the 'haut ton,' the satire would hav been
acçepted as a masterpiece . . . Tŏ an English reader, the effect of many portions of
"Queechy" must be particularly ludicrous
and painful in this regard. For example,
Mr. Carleton, a man of ançient and noble
family, is not ōnly a Methodist, but he
carries his religion intŏ the ball-room, and
discourses of the ōne thing needful tŏ his
partner in the dance." [North British
Review. **117 s**

to leave her in the country for 3 months with her own old nurse, now the wife of a well-to-do farmer. The girl, called the queen of her fastidious set at home, goes to the farm, and finds all her high breeding severely strained not to express openly her disdain at her homely surroundings. Preparing herself to be thoroly wretched, she overhears a conversation between the farmer and his wife, in which Dame Lucy tries to explain the dear mother's plan; and the girl's wish to be some time what her mother wishes, grows into a resolve. The change comes almost too suddenly to be artistic, but it is very welcome, and the book goes on with interesting accounts of her life and occupations at the farm. An agreeable humor pervades the book without in the least jarring upon the sense of fitness." [Nation. **118**

QUEER PRINCESS. (A) [by F.. EATON, *Lothrop*, 1888.] "A bright, quaint story. "The Princess" is a motherless little girl reared by an adoring circle of elders. Queer and precocious she is, but also sweet and lovable. Her playmate and housemate, Dick, a poor boy educated and cared for by Miss Minerva, an eccentric aunt of the "Princess," is a noble little fellow, but too refined for his antecedents. Various other child-figures add to the drollery and charm of the book, among whom Miss Flora is the greatest oddity. The story seems long-drawn-out, being a succession of scenes rather than a brisk narrative, and the style is peculiar; but the humor, good sense, and warm-hearted feeling make us forget the faults of the book." [Nation. **119**

RACHEL ARMSTRONG, ☞ "LOVE AND THEOLOGY."

RACHEL'S SHARE OF THE ROAD. [by KATE W. HAMILTON : *Osgood*, 1882] "The dauter of a railway king, wrapped in all luxury, Rachel's heart is loving and her foot and hand ready. ....Rachel's opportunity lies among the few workmen upon the road with whom she comes in contact; and it is the skilful management of incidents, essentially melodramatic,

such as railroad strikes, shop-burnings, and the like, that the great merit of the book is shown. To use so much of them, and no more, as shall bring out the individual characteristics of the personages of the story, requires a power of reserve not often found out of the foremost rank of novelists. The story is not much more than a sketch, but the firm, delicate outlines, and clear, pure color, prove a hand which might succeed in more elaborate work." [Nation. **120**

RALEIGH WESTGATE [by H.. (K.) JOHNSON : *Appleton*, 1889.] "The writer has evidently lived long enuf in **New England** to become thoroly conversant with the peculiarities of the people. She displays a familiarity with their habits of mind, their modes of speech and of living that gives evidence of careful research. The romance which connects these character-pictures is of an unusual type and has a mystery interwoven with it which lifts the book out of the commonplace. The hero himself is an interesting study of individuality equally impressed by heredity and by circumstances. The evolution of a practical man from a dreamer is skillfully delineated." [Homemaker. **121**

RAYMOND KERSHAW [by MARIA M. COX, *Roberts*, 1888.] "This story will surely meet with the success it well deserves. It is entertaining, it is helpful, it is sweet and wholesome; its influence is all for the gentle courtesies and amenities of life, for a wide charity and good will towards one's fellow beings; it is written in a clear and pleasing style; and the story, as a story, is engaging and of unflagging interest...To relate how this young man, aided by Alison, had the change made to a farm which had been the father's costly "hobby," how the two formed and carried out a plan of laborious, self-sacrificing life there, how each of the household worked in his or her own way for the common good, how they found time and means to give holidays to the mill hands, who had loved their father, how everything prospered in the end—this seems to have been the author's purpose." [Boston "Literary World." **122**

RECOLLECTIONS OF AUTON HOUSE. [by "C. AUTON:" *Houghton*, 1876.] "Children of a larger growth, as the author admits in his preface, were the immediate audience for which these reminiscences were intended...It would be an injustice to this little book to pass it by among the ephemeral juvenile productions of the year. It is more than an irresistibly droll family history; it is a true picture of the domestic life of a period dating two generations back." [Nation. **123**

REVEREND IDOL (A) [by LUCRETIA NOBLE: *Osgood*, 1882.] "is a study of summer life, which will better repay reading than critical examination. The scene of the story is laid on **Cape Cod** in vacation time, when the Rev. Kenyon Leigh and Miss Monny Rivers have got nicely domiciled in a quiet boarding-house —the one to work on his next winter's sermons, the other to pursue her rather solitary art-studies. The minister, tho a discreet and earnest man, has been hopelessly and helplessly a "reverend idol" among the women of the congregation, and has fled to 'the Cape' for a few summer weeks to possess his soul in peace and have the "usual half-holiday." He dreams, poor man, that, so far as female idolatry is concerned, he is safely "out of the business." Miss Monny Rivers, who has been more or less a reverend idol among the young men, and is certainly a piquant and charming girl, has come for a similar purpose. That is, she, too, would like a half-holiday from lovers.....The plot being thus simple and old-fashioned, the scenery is plain and easily moved, seldom shifted. The reverend hero is drawn not as a reverend, but as a hero.....Given a lively spirit, a saucy tung, but a good heart, an artistic temperament, and an unbounded capacity of worship for the unknown and unknowable qualities of the heroic in man, and we have the ever old, ever new, and ever delightful woman whom it is always a pleasure to see fall to the lot of a worthy man." [Scribner's. **124**

RICHARD EDNEY. [by S. JUDD: *Phillips, Sampson & Co.*, 1850.] "With not a few faults, this is a capital book. For the most part, it is fresh, vigorous, and healthful; it is generally simple and natural; its domestic scenes are drawn to the life; and the reader sees at once that the whole is the result of real observation and of true feeling...It is 'a tale, simple and popular, yet cultured and noble, of morals, sentiments and life,' pratically treated and pleasantly illustrated; and its hints on being good and doing good are such as will commend themselves to the intellect and heart of the heedful reader. The scene is laid in the neighborhood of an interior town in far-off **Maine**, upon the borders of one of its broad rivers, and in the midst of a vast timber region, the characteristics of which are depicted with great power." [Knickerbocker. **125**

ROCKY FORK [by M.. (H.) CATHERWOOD, *Lothrop*, 1882.] "tells the story of a few summer days in a little neighborhood of farmhouses of central **Ohio** long ago. The children are the central figures, but there is a due background of older people. The book has simplicity and sweet homeliness. Very rarely has plain country life been so faithfully described. It seems usually impossible to do it without a tinge of vulgarity, which is just what true American country-life escapes. Some fine fibre in American nature, when close to fields and woods and sky, keeps it always noble, however rude the exterior. If there is a hint, towards the end of the book, that refined manners are of their nature insincere, it is evidently a tribute to some supposed prejudice of the sort, not out of the writer's own conviction. Her people are all graciously attractive.....It is useless to try to transplant the children. They must be known in their own woods and meadows. Theirs was a blessed world of happy "make-believes" where simple pleasures yet had charm." [Nation. **126**

RODERICK HUME [by C. W. BARDEEN, Syracuse, N. Y., 1879.] "Somewhere in the early part of this century was published a book, half humorous, half descriptive, called 'The District School as It Was.' It was in striking contrast to this "Story of a New-York Teacher." The scene was laid in New England, which gave a local quality to be allowed for; but, all allowance made, there is a mighty change in 50 years between the two stories. Then literature was cultivated, if not "on a little oatmeal," yet under the sternest conditions. Short sessions, scant salaries, severe discipline necessary to induce the refractory flock to begin the ascent to Parnassus, were the rule, and the teacher's place was supposed to be held by stress of necessity. The times change however, and we change with them, and trust-funds, endowments, and shrewd speculation play a prominent part in the more recent story. To furnish a marketable article is the object of the school management, and the reputation and capacities of the teacher are points to be scored in the game. The under-teachers are a powerful and well-connected body, and school events are also village events. The book is vivacious, and the Author knows the ground he describes. ....Mr. Bardeen, carrying his hero throu hope, disappointment, folly, and despair, brings him out with flying colors at the close of the book." [Nation. **127**

RODMAN THE KEEPER. [by CONSTANCE F. WOOLSON: Appleton, 1880.] "The writer of these sketches, living in the South for several years, has acquired a just appreciation of the present state of society in that region, and in her graceful way she tells these stories of southern life and manners, exercising her subtle humor upon its faults and follies, and dwelling with pathos upon its sorrows and regrets. A woman's sympathetic heart ever guides the pen of this charming writer, who is always natural, but never commonplace, and who will win an admirer in every reader of "Rodman the Keeper." [Penn. Monthly.] Each of the sketches has that breath of life in it which belongs alone to what is called human interest. In each the sympathy is awakened and takes hold upon the life of some human being with vital intensity. In each a human life passes throu its ordeal, and if the endings of the tales are for the most part unconventional, they are not the less true, not the less artistic, not the less dramatic on that account.....Miss Woolson's art is superb, and she is lovingly faithful to it." [N. Y. Eve. Post. **128**

ROSE CLARK. [by "FANNY FERN:" Mason Brothers, 1856.] "The plot of the story is of an unpretending character, free from extravagant incidents and artificial complications, and deriving its interest from the natural pictures of life in the experience of the heroine. Left an orphan in infancy, and exposed to the usual trials of adverse fate, Rose Clark develops a sweet feminine nature, and wins both sympathy and admiration by her noble womanly bearing in the most perplexing circumstances. Several striking episodes are woven into the principal narrative, highly spiced with the pungent satire for which the authoress possesses a so remarkable gift." [Harper's. **129**

ROSE IN BLOOM, By L. M. ALCOTT, Roberts, 1876.

ROSECROFT. [by W: M. F. ROUND. Lee & Shepard, 1881.] "The plot of the story is based on such harsh unkindness that we are glad to take refuge in its improbability; but the village oddities are worth knowing, and Mrs. Stowe herself has done nothing better than the old negress, unlettered Rachel, and her Bible reading." [Nation. **130**

ROXY [by E: EGGLESTON, Scribner, 1878.] "....Were it possible for a man to have offered him the choice of his place and epoch in the world, it is not to be supposed that any sane person would select a town in Southern Indiana at the date of the Tippecanoe campaign.....Yet such things Dr. Eggleston saw in his youth, and in such participated. We are no less sure, after reading his vigorous, humorous, and (the theme considered) marvelously picturesque narrative, that he met them like a man, than that he afterward grasped them like a philosopher, and has now portrayed them like a genuine artist. The book is appropriately named after the heroine, who is the centre of all its action, and on whom, as on his worthiest subject, the author has shed the strongest light and bestowed the most careful study. The remarkable character of Roxy Adams is not only clearly conceived, but thoroly and admirably developed." [Atlantic. **131**

RUDDER GRANGE [by F. R: STOCKTON, *Scribner*, 1880.] "We would believe that we are telling most of our readers what they know when we remind them that Rudder Grange is the fit name of an abandoned canal-boat, which the reporter of the story, his wife, servant Pomona, and a boarder took possession of and transformed into a floating hut; that when the canal-boat went under, in a sudden storm, the Grangers transferred the title to a less unique house, which they hired and finally bôt, in the country; and that about these two houses, the water house and the land house, most of the adventures of these babes in worldliness gathered..... Pomona, with her taste for violent reading, her ingenuity in devices, and her experience as a newly maried bride, is a positive contribution to the characters of humorous literature. Indeed, the faithfulness with which the characters are drawn gives the book a position much above that of most contemporaneous fun. There is conscientious literary work in it and an unfailing healthfulness of play." [Atlantic. **132**

SAM SHIRK [by G: H. DEVEREUX: *Hurd & Houghton*, 1871] "is a very interesting and vivid picture of adventure [in the **Maine** woods] in hunting, logging, fighting with Indians, with enuf of a love story interwoven with it to add the necessary human zest. The descriptions of scenery are evidently the work of a lover of nature, and the characteristic scenes of the book, have the unmistakable flavor of

the woods, and show that the author is intimately conversant with the free, wholesome life of adventure which he describes." [Monthly Relig. Mag. **133**

SAXE HOLM'S STORIES [2nd. Series, by H.. (FISKE) JACKSON, *Scribner*, 1878.] "in this instance, are 5 short love-stories, the anonymous writer evidently being convinced that no other subject is much worth treating. The book might bear for motto the old doggerel:

"Oh ! 'tis love, 'tis love, 'tis love
That makes the world go round."

Two of these stories are good—"*Farmer Bassett's Romance*" and "*Joe Hale's Red Stockings*"—but the others float in an atmosphere of unreality. "*Joe Hale's Red Stockings*" might be true, every word of it, and has pleasant pictures of sea and shore, light-house and. hospital, and of human beings leading lives therein which make it the more remarkable that the same author should write such stuff as 'My Tourmaline.' [Nation. **134**

SEALED ORDERS [by E.. S. PHELPS [WARD], *Roberts*, 1880.] "Miss Phelps excels in stories of kindly and lonely women, for the most part single, warped into an eccentricity, which is quaint and amiable, by a narrow life, withdrawn from all the realities and activities of the world, save the important exception of charity. The best of these stories is of such a woman, a poor dressmaker without friends, who becomes, throu her goodness to all who need a helping hand at the boarding-house where she lives, the central figure and main-stay of them all, albeit quite unconsciously. '*The True Story of Guinever*' has nothing to do with anything real, but is prettily fanciful. Queen Guinever, who is in this case the charming little wife of a master carpenter, is saved just on the brink of the catastrophe, and, with her sorrowful lesson learned, brôt back to happiness. A somewhat similar but less successfully told story, is '*The Lady of Shalott*.' The remaining tales produce an unpleasant effect of what we may paradoxically call the eccentricity of commonplace." [Nation. 135

SHADY SIDE, OR LIFE IN A COUNTRY PARSONAGE, (THE) [by MARTHA (S.) HUBBELL: *Jewett*, 1853.] "This is a new edition of a book too widely known to ask for criticism. We are told that, at its first appearance, no fewer than 50,000 copies were required to satisfy the demand. If the circulation of the book serves, in any degree, to waken our rural community to a sense of their frequent injustice touching the ministers of religion,—what to give them and what to expect from them, we hope the last edition may find as many readers as the first." [Church Monthly. 136

SIMPLY A LOVE STORY. [by P. ORNE, *Cupples*, 1885.] "The scenes are in a New England fishing-town, and are described with all the invigorating interest that comes of the peculiar life on its shore and on its adjacent waters. The leading actor is a sea-captain's daughter. . . . The action is lively and holding, deriving particular interest from its opposition of character and its counterplots. It is well managed to lead up to an unexpected finale." [Boston "Globe." 137

SIX TO ONE [by E: BELLAMY, *Putnam*, 1878.] "is as bright as any one could wish. The One is a broken-down New York editor who goes to Nantucket to recruit; the Six are the maidens unto whose mercies he falls, and they begin his torture by promising one another not to hold any private tête-à-têtes with him. Nevertheless, the end is seen from the beginning. Two of them fall in love with him, and he falls in love with only one, the gentlest and shyest of all, whose pleasures and emotions have hitherto been associated only with the sea. This life-long, intimate inweaving of her moods with the changing ocean-view makes the transition to a life centred in human relations a difficult experience, and the conflict is the most refined conception in the book, and is pleasing until the dénouement comes. . . . . Except for some melodrama and extremely bad taste like this, and some remarkable

sallies of wit, the book has much merit." [Nation. 138

SNOWBOUND AT EAGLE'S [by BRET HARTE: *Houghton*, 1886.] "is of as little value as anything he has written. Regarded as a story, it is worthless. Regarded in detail, for its bits of description, keen conversations, witty sayings, it has the excellences found in everything from the same strong hand. Harte never makes a slip in turning a sentence, or a paragraph, or a brief episode; but when the story is nothing, and when in his excellent handling of details he still does not make any strikingly brilliant or humorous points, readers will not care much for the book; there is nothing in it but the technique, and that interests only the specialist in literary criticism. As in everything of Harte's, the external sincerity, the careful truth to nature, as far as her sights and sounds go, is constantly marred by an unreality, a theatrical insincerity, even a defect of observation, in dealing with human nature." [Overland.] "The characters are well drawn: J: Hale, the transplanted gentleman of culture; his weak and slightly faded wife; his shallow-minded but positive mother-in-law; Colonel Clinch, who strives to hit the happy mean between law and lawlessness; Zeenie, the coarse backwoods beauty; and even Falkner, the mysterious and moustached villain pro tempore. George Lee, and Kate, the heroine, so far as the story has a heroine, are more feebly drawn; the former is the familiar noble-hearted rascal and rake, who never 'went back' on a friend or insulted a respectable woman. The blemish in the story is the unpleasant flirtation of Lee and Mrs. Hale, and the gratuitous soupçon of a similiar fault on the part of Hale towards Zeenie. The conclusion is mildly dramatic; we seem to be transported to the theatre, and hear the ladies adjusting their wraps and the gentlemen hunting for their hats, in the uneasy 5 minutes before the curtain falls." [Critic. 139

SOMEBODY'S NEIGHBORS. [by

SHOEPAC RECOLLECTIONS [by "Walter March," i. e., ORLANDO BOLIVAR WILLCOX: N.-Y., Bunce, 1856.] "is a fine, delightful story. It is fine in every sense, not stained by a single attempt at fine writing. The scene of the story is Detroit. "Ours was a little antiquated city. Its inhabitants wer mostly French. At the time I came upon the stage, the transition to a modern American town had scarcely begun. The body of the population was stil of the 'ancien régime.' The few Americans wer officers, or ex-officers, of either the general or the territorial government, and their families, relativs, dependents, and friends, whom they had persuaded to venture beyond the "jumping-off place," as Buffalo was then termed. The spirit of emigration had not been fully aroused, and the spirit of speculation, if felt at all, was confined to the fur-traders, a class made up of all nations.' The book pictures Detroit as a small Paradise in those days. Living in this pleasant place, misfortune comes upon the March family. The father dies, and the mother, with her three boys and a girl, ar left to their ōn resources. The account of their struggles and their triumphs make up this exquisit story, this fine and faithful history of a family." [Criterion.]—It is "a delightful picture of life upon the Canadian frontier; full of pictures delicately limned; of humor exquisitly touched; of character finely shaded—a fresh, spirited, true, and almost perfect book." [Mrs. Stephens' Mag.: **136 k**

ROSE (TERRY) COOKE: *Osgood*, 1881.]
"....Connecticut is seen once or twice in
the stories which follow, which all relate
to quaint **New England** life of the "Sam
Lawson" order, with much dialect, local
slang, and other familiar coloring, One of
the best is "*Cal Culver and the Devil.*"
Cal was the village do-nothing, with his
mind "nigh about made up" on an all important question :. . . .The titles of Mrs.
Cooke's stories are as suggestive as anything further we can say of them—such
as "*Dely's Cow,*" "*Miss Beulah's Bon-
net,*" "*Polly Mariner, Tailoress,*"
"*Squire Paine's Conversion,*" and "*Mrs.
Flint's Maried Experience.*" [Boston
"Literary World." **140**
SOUTH COUNTY NEIGHBORS [by
ESTHER B. CARPENTER, *Roberts*, 1888.]
"By "South County" is meant the Narra-
gansett region in **Rhode-Island**, which
has more people of peculiar character than
one would be likely to find anywhere else
in New England, unless it might be in
some out-of-the-way corner where an
aboriginal element still lingers. A collection of country folk with more individuality, more oddities, is seldom found
between the covers of a book. The
sketches are bright, racy, with plenty of
mother wit, and each character as original
as if he or she were the only specimen of
the kind, yet all are vital with the humanity which makes the whole race kin.
"Bucolic and seafaring types" the author
designates them, and asserts that they are
"simply types, rather than likenesses" but
the reader will feel sure that they are
excellent dashes, at least, at portraiture."
[Boston "Literary World." **141**
SPHINX'S CHILDREN, (THE) [by
ROSE (TERRY) COOKE, *Ticknor*, 1886.]
"Every page of Mrs. Cooke's work shows
thôtful painstaking. 'The Sphinx's Children' is but the name of a rather fantastic
[and almost unreadable] sketch which is
prefixed to a collection of the stories. One
One of them, "The Deacon's Week," with
the sweet sobriety of its working-day piety,
has long ago made its way round the

world. The stories all contribute to the
impression of careful observation with
much loving sympathy, and of a constant
aim after the simplest and most effective
expression. So many of them are in a
minor key that the sadness becomes a
burden. In some shape or other, the ever-
recurring subject is the forbidding aspect
of New England [**Connecticut**] life, one
or two generations ago, and the revolt of
the younger or more ardent spirits against
it. The total effect is to make it duller,
colder, harder, than it really was. One
drive along the old Connecticut turnpikes
will show proof enuf of the existence of
a large and generous life, side by side with
such homes as Mrs. Cooke has preferred
for her chief study. Her picture to be
complete should more fully include both.
At least, the apple blossoms come once a
year in New England." [Nation. **142**
STEADFAST; [by ROSE (TERRY)
COOKE: *Ticknor*, 1889.] "Whatever
Mrs. Cooke writes is eagerly accepted by
her public, which is large and intelligent.
Her stories of New England life are the
best in the language, none excepted.
"Steadfast," her first novel, is the successor of "Somebody's Neighbors." The
scene is laid in a hill township in **Connecticut**.....The studies of New England
character and manners of 150 years ago
are able and conscientious.....Indisputa-
bly the finest part of the book is the episode
—it is hardly more—of Rachel Mather's
love and sufferings. Her mariage, her
long martyrdom and her beautiful mission
to husband and parish are depicted with
equal strength and delicacy. Esther, pas-
sion-driven, undisciplined, and tossed between alternate sinnings and repentings,
is an artistic contrast. What may be
called the second-class characters are, as
usual, in Mrs. Cooke's hands, inimitable.
She has done nothing better than Deacon
Ammi and Miss Tempy." [Home-
maker. **143**
STILLWATER TRAGEDY, (THE)
[by T: B. ALDRICH: *Houghton*, 1880.]
"The motive of the story is a murder. The

SPARROWGRASS PAPERS (The) [by F⁚ SWARTWOUT COZZENS (1818-69): N.-Y., *Derby*, 1856.] is "a very charming book, redolent of geniality, gentleness, quaint humor, and sound philosophy; and if this praise appear at first sight too hî, it wil, we think, be borne out by careful examination. For the moral lessons (which ar insinuated, rather than inculcated by these playful effusions) ar exçellent and greatly needed. You hav lâfed probably, from month tŏ month, over the mishaps and disappointments of the Sparrowgrasses in their efforts at perfect rural bliss. But hav you nothing noted of the contented, good-͵empered, and lŏving spirit which under- the general tone of badinage? If so, you hav read carelessly and unprofitably, and wil dŏ wel tŏ read again. Depend upon it, thére ar not a few of us whŏ hav mentally "got the heaves, got 'em bad, too," and go fuming and fussing throu life tŏ the annoyance of ŏurselvs and ŏthers, because town and country, men, women, public affairs and private, won't cŏme out preçisely as we wish. In the way of books, it might be advisable for such vain searchers after the philosopher's stone tŏ try dieting for a while on (C⁚) Lamb and Sparrowgrass." [Albion.]—"Mr. Cozzens is a true humorist.

He unites the exuberance of fun, the simple pathos, and the quic sympathy and perception which make that most delightful quality which has been claimed by a competent critic tŏ be almost peculiar, in its fullness, tŏ modern literature. Delicate sarcasm, truthful painting, picturesque description, and gushing geniality ar so harmoniously combined in the Sparrowgrass Papers, that they seem tŏ us tŏ be a most valuable addition tŏ ŏur literature, and tŏ plaçe the author amŏngst the most promising of ŏur younger writers. The sketches ar éntirely free from caricature; they ar full of nature and familiar life, and they sho in so sparkling detail, and ar a so lively and carefully studied commentary upon the amusing episodes of country or suburban experiençe, that we can not dismiss them merely as gay magazine papers. We ar essentially a serious people. Satire which has a sting, and a moral drift, is not uncommon in ŏur literature. But pure fun and sweet sarcasm ar not tŏ be easily çited, except from Irving. The Sparrowgrass Papers ar of that graçeful, humane, and genial school; and we shal easily be pardoned ŏur natural pride that Mr. Sparrowgrass first told in ŏur pages his story of "Living in the Country." [Putnam's. **141 p**

SQUIBOB PAPERS (The) [by G: HORATIO DERBY (1823-61): N.-Y., *Carleton*, 1865.] "Ten years ago was published a volume entitled "Phœnixiana, or Sketches and Burlesques, by John Phœnix," which reçeived a cordial and general welcŏme. It was composed of miscellaneous articles of a humorous character, which had first seen the light in California . . . The spirit of this book was spontaneous, exuberant, and uncontrolable fun. That spirit stil wins applause for "Phœnixiana." Mr. Derby has been dead several years, and new humorists hav sprung up, in this prolific American soil—humorists of diverse gifts and of singular talents. Yet "John Phœnix" retains his supremacy in this particular department of letters, sharing his kingdom ŏnly, perhaps, with "Artemus Ward." We believe, too, that his reputation is destind tŏ endure. His humor cropped out of a substratum of truth, and it pictured, as wel as lâfed at, peculiar phases of American manners and social life. Sŏmetimes, too, it went a little deeper, and curiously lit-up human nature. This is seen as wel in *The Squibob Papers*, as in its better knŏn predeçessor. This new volume has been made up of selections from the unpublished writings left by Captain Derby, 27 in number." [Albion. **142 h**

SQUIRREL INN (The). [by FRANK R: STOCKTON: N.-Y., *Century Co.*, 1891.] "The friskiness of the name of the inn fits wel the story, which is as nimble as ŏne could desire. All the figures ar on the alert, and succeed in plaçing themselvs in the most unexpected situations at every turn. In this, as in ŏther of Mr. Stockton's stories, thére is an od efłect produced by the old-fashioned address indulged in by the men toard the women. It really seems as if, in this author's eyes, a woman wer a most unaccountable creature." [Atlantic.]—It is "sŏmething like a Jonsonian comedy of "humors," modern and Stocktonian, of course, yet as fantastic in creation as anything in the elder master's work. The world of the ecçentric persons whŏ ar met incongruously in the "Squirrel" is the world of nŏne of us, whatever ŏur nationality, and peopled of strange creatures. The landlord of the inn reçeives summer boarders, conditionally. Thêy must be friends of that irreproachable family, the Rockmores of Germantown. No ŏthers need apply. You may kno everybody else in Philadelphia; but unless the Rockmores kno you the "Squirrel" wil not reçeive you . . . A wild and genial Irishman, a quaint spinster from a nêboring village, a young lady of studious tastes whŏ acts as nurse to a pleasing and useful baby, and the mŏther of this baby help tŏ cheer the landlord and his wife by their company. Lastly, thére is a literary young man whŏ dŏes not kno the Rockmores of Germantown, but is introduced by a stratagem thrŏu the arts of a charming young widŏ, the mŏther of the baby. The lŏve-making and match-making, the plotting and counter-plotting, which ensue beggar description. It is a maze of pleasant devices, an imbroglio which is excellently diverting." [Saturday Review. **142 j** first thing to be said about the author's treatment of it is that it is not sensational. The author has realized exactly how such a tragedy would affect a New England village. And yet there is nothing in the story in the nature of a police report. The affair is idealized cnuf to remove it from that. · · ·Mr. Aldrich knows the New England girl. With a real and yet poetic hand Margaret appears on the scene, with the mingled sweetness and strength of her class. The love scenes between Richard and Margaret are tender and engaging. · · ·In his treatment of the labor problem, is shown an insight and strength, in regard to practical questions, which might not have been demanded of a poet and a romancer. We do not know anywhere a more admirable description than he gives us of a "strike." All its illogical passion and futility are sketched to the life. Nor will the reader find elsewhere a better portrait of a manufacturing village, with all the grime of it revealed and nothing overdrawn. Such pictures are apt to give the reader a horror, and convince him that living in them would be impossible for a cleanly disposed person. But the author gives the compensating aspects of the place, and we see that residence in Stillwater would not be a martyrdom. The whole book, in short, is sane and sensible. [Hartford (Conn.) Courant.　**144**

STORY OF A BAD BOY, (THE) [by T: B. ALDRICH, *Fields*, 1869.]　"·····
Much of Master Tom's "badness" was comparative, and, perhaps, thrown into unfair relief by the puritanic austerity of the quaint **New England** town [Portsmouth, N. H.] where he lived, whose inhabitants, "were many of them pure Christians every day of the seven, except the seventh." But Master Tom has his faults, besides his disposition to evade the Sunday School. He assisted in adding an old stage-coach to a Fourth-of-July bonfire; he joined a secret society of young losels, yclept "The Centipedes," the walk of whose various feet was ungodly; he aided and abetted in the setting off of an

ancient and decayed battery, to the midnight alarm of the people of Rivermouth; he changed the signs in the Rivermouth streets; he ran away to go to sea. All of which is picturesquely, and, we fear, fascinatingly set forth, with some account of his loves for a wonderful pony, who returned his affection, and a grown-up lady, who didn't. The characters are well drawn, tho not so well as to divide the interest with the hero, who is, in fact, himself a subordinate figure to the incidents. There is good taste, as well as good sense, in the treatment of the "fight with Conway," and the ingenious elision of merely coarse details. The love-scene, where Tom's grown up Dulcinea characteristically evades his passion, and settles his *status* by "rumbling his hair all over his forehead," is natural and half pathetic. Taken altogether, Mr. Aldrich's little friend stands a much better chance of living in literature than many grown-up heroes." [Overland.　**145**

STORY OF A COUNTRY TOWN. (THE) [by E. W. HOWE: *Osgood, 1884*.] "The author has described a community which feeds its higher life with a faith no longer held as an aspiration, but as a warning; the people, meanwhile, have been dislocated from the conditions which brôt them into healthy association with the world. They are engaged in a sordid struggle for existence; they have lost their ideals, and the world seems to mock at them. A more dreary waste than the country town which Mr. Howe describes could not well be imagined. It appears to have no traditions, even, of beauty, and certainly no anticipations of hope. It is degraded spiritually and mentally, and nature itself seems to take on the prevailing gray hue, and to shut in upon the narrowing circle of life. The circumstances of this life are recorded with a pitiless fidelity. ·It is a **Western** [Kansas] town,—that is all we know. He uses a merciless frankness of speech, and there is a remarkable candor in his manner; it is only when the reader has separated him-

STORY OF A CHILD (THE) [by MA. WADE (CAMPBELL) DELAND: *Houghton*, 1892.] "is a book of singular power and charm. It is a study of imaginativ childhood, with its wŏnderful capaçity of self-torture, its infinit refinements of self-pity, its restless creativ faculty, its wild enigmatic yearnings for the unspeakable, and its impatient scorning of material limitations. The revelation of these things is effected as with a master-key. The sympathy and insight ar so delicate, penetrativ, and intense as tŏ suggest an intuitiv proçess. The Chaucerian phrase "subtle-piercing" is the ŏne adequate term which expresses the peculiar quality of the charm. It is a fine circumstançe of irony that the imaginativ child of the story should hav a precoçious, sballo little worldling for her chosen companion. Tŏ Effie the serious and passionate attempts of Ellen tŏ realize her imaģinativ ideas appear tŏ be nŏthing but play. Ellen is just simply the "funniest girl" of her acquaintançe. The association of the twŏ is deeply pathetic and humorous as presented, the humor and the pathos of it being suģģested with admirable art, blended indefinitly as the joys and sorrŏs of childhood ar ... Thêre is not a touch of excess in the treatment of the extremely delicate and complex situation. One such touch, indeed, would suffiçe tŏ imperil the foundations of the work, but we find nothing of the sort in this remarkable little book." [Saturday Review.]—"Not ŏnly has the author of John Ward [No. 63] exçelled any of her previous works—so far as style is conçerned—in this volume; she has produced the most remarkable and most intimate study of a child's mind we kno ... But the book is quite as much

a study of surroundings and heredity as of the mind of a child with pagan instincts, and a grandmŏther whŏ seeks too severely tŏ curb them. It is easy tŏ take iu Old-Chester, a hundred years behind the times, in the opinion of such of its nativs as hav left it for what thêy account as the "grêat world." One can easily picture it as it "lies amŏng the roling hils of Western **Pennsylvania,**—hils which hav never echoed with the scream of the locomotiv, but ar folded in a beautiful green silençe, broken ŏnly by the silken ripple of little streams which run across the meadŏs, or throu the dappled shadŏs of the woods." In Old-Chester everybody knoes everybody else, and livs like everybody else. It is a puritanic community. Thêy mark time by the notable transgressions of ŏthers. A particular period is remembered thus: "Henry Temple"—he is the ambitions worldling of the village—"voted the wrong ticket the year thêre was a snostorm when the apple-trees wer in bloom." You can with perfect ease take in all the characters which figure in the story. Thêre is Mrs. Dale whŏse life with the brilliant, weak old man, her husband, has ossified her conduct intŏ a too stern rectitude. Thêre ar the Temples,—Henry, the worldling, whŏ livs but little in Old-Chester; his invalid wife; and his sister Jane, whŏ nurses that wife and, still more, an affection for Tommy Dove, the mild apothecary, whŏm, however, her brother has driven from his house as not good enuf tŏ be her husband. Thêre is Mrs. Wright, Mrs. Dale's nêbor, whŏ, "despite her 45 years, was stil in the bubbling inconsequençe of youth." Abŏve all, thêre ar the twŏ children,—Effie Temple, the dauter of the worldling, and Ellen Dale, whŏ has in her more of her pagan grandfather than of her severely Christian grandmŏther. Effie it is whŏ, being a child of (comparativ) luxury, teaches Ellen discontent with her surroundings and her grandmŏther's system of education. But Effie has not the imagination or the resolution of her playmate. Ellen is confined tŏ her house because she has strue the servant, Betsy Thomas, and has declined tŏ apologise for the blo. Effie suġġests that thêy shal run away tŏgether. Ellen agrees, but Effie turns coward at the last moment. So Ellen runs away alone, saying tŏ her faithless companion:—"I'll write tŏ you, tho I don't think you ar a very good friend." But besides the marked influençe of heredity and surroundings on Ellen Dale, it is that mysterious sŏmething apart from both which means originality of character, which constitutes her speçial fasçination. She is a Wordsworthian child, and yet, also, a Shelleyan ŏne,—inasmuch as her imaġination is always seeking tŏ overleap itself. We hav said enuf tŏ sho that thêre is no child in reçent fiction better worth making the acquaintançe of than Ellen Dale." [Spectator.]—"Miss Deland has given a charming picture of life in a New-England (sic!) villaġe. Here time passes quicly—the inhabitants, thêir houses, thêir trim-bordered gardens, ar all much alike—equally polite, reservd, and ġently critical of ŏne anŏther. But the little town has its character. Thêre the young person finds no scope: is, in fact, kept in exemplary subjection. He is taut that when he is iu the company of his elders and betters, it is tŏ profit by example, and be grateful for adviçe. But intŏ this little prim world is born a child full of imaġination and impulse, whŏse

grandfather had been deemed a blac sheep in Old Chester. This child, being easily influençed, fel under the sway of a minx in short dresses—dauter of a nêbor whŏ livd usually in New-York. Now this precoçious young person soon persuaded her friend that submission tŏ the Old Chester ideal was absurd. And after several attempts at rebellion—which brôt dismay and grief tŏ the grandmŏther and household—the children made up thêir minds tŏ run away. When the fateful moment came, Ellen was steadfast, but the ŏther's couraġe failed her, and thus Mrs. Dale's granddauter went alone intŏ the wide world. How she wandered and suffered fatigue, fear and hunger, is very prettily and naturally described, and long before the 24 hoûrs absençe ended the poor little wanderer had realized the folly of her escapade. Also the lŏve-story of twŏ elderly persons is described with much tenderness and sympathy. Altŏgether the book is a wholesŏme and faithful picture of child-life—with a bacground of grave experiençes, graçefully touched." [National Observer.]—"Not alone tŏ the author's earlier characters is little Ellen Dale a happy foil, but tŏ many latter-day writings from ŏther pens, in which a preposterous raçe of nondescripts pass for real children. No ŏne can read of this child and not be touched tŏ the inmost consciousness by the living, breathing reality of the little maid. Her head is half in the clouds, half upon the affairs of her elders; her warm little heârt is full, not of schemes of reforming her grandmŏther or of elevating the masses, but of childish play and the reproduction in her games of the delightful fairies, prinçesses or martyrs of her reading." [Nation. **145 p** self from the fascination of the style that he. perceives how completely the whole book is spun from the brain of the writer. ....Nature is as cheerless as human life, and the book is a nightmare without the customary self-conviction of the nightmare." [Atlantic. · **146**

SUMMER IDYL (A) [by "CHRISTIAN REID," *Appleton*, 1878.] "is a tranquil and well-told story of summer leisure and pleasant family life in the beautiful scenery of the mountains of North Carolina. In it one may find various and quiet pleasure." [Nation. **147**

SUMMER IN A CANON. (A) [by KATE D. WIGGIN, *Houghton*, 1889.] "Pleasanter far is Mrs. Wiggin's "A Summer in a Canon." And this not only to Western readers familiar with the sort of life pictured, but probably even more to those to whom the outdoor summer, with no postponements on account of the weather, is first made real in these pages. It is a simple story of the life of a party of bright young people, guided by one or two wise older ones, in a camping trip in Southern California. Their fun and their mishaps and their amusements and adventures, and most of all their merry talks and spicy letters, are made very interesting. There is no sentimentality in the book, and the one girl who tries to introduce a little coquetry is vigorously disapproved by these healthy young folk. This breezy, outdoors life, with its moral and physical healthfulness, its sparkling wit and kindly fun, will cause the book to be loved by young people, and by all older people, too, whose hearts are still young." [Overland. **148**

SUMMER IN LESLIE GOLDTHWAITE'S LIFE. (A) [by A. D. (T.) WHITNEY: *Ticknor*, 1867.] "The story of the "Summer" is told in a charming style, and abounds in happy hits and suggestive thôts at home and in the mountains, and has many a capital lesson." [Radical.] "Simple, natural, and homely, thôtful, earnest, and 'human,' we find on these pages one of the best stories for young people,—and for old, too, which was ever written.....Thus passing her holiday time among the mountains, rattling over the stony roads or playing croquet upon the lawn, climbing rocky hillsides, or darning stockings and making children's dresses. And when she went to her home it was with a fuller heart and a riper soul than that with which she had left it, and you who go with her to the story's end will feel yourself a debtor to this young life. Leslie Goldthwaite is the figment of a novelist's brain perhaps, but the humanity in her appeals to that in your heart and ours, which recognizes it as akin to itself." [Friend. **149**

SUMMER IN OLDPORT HARBOR, (A) [by W. H. METCALF: *Lippincott*, 1887.] "A breezy novel, full of the flavor of out-door life, just the book to take up at the sea-shore for an idle hour on the veranda. It concerns principally the experiences of a young doctor and his artist chum, who come to Cup Island, near the Connecticut shore, to pass their vacation, and who are joined by the sister of one of the young men and her nearest friend, who bring with them Bid, a maid-of-all-work, to superintend the cooking arrangements of a very primitive cottage. The descriptions of natural scenery are clever and realistic, the character-drawing is generally very good, and Mr. Sandy, the village postmaster and shop-keeper of Oldport, is sketched with a good deal of humor." [Boston "Gazette." **150**

SUZETTE [by M.. S. (N.) TIERNAN: *Holt*, 1886.] "is not exactly a picture of Richmond [Va.] in the forties, being rather a chronicle of pleasant family life. The old city, with its generous homes and its traditions, fills in the edges and the corners of the canvas much after the fashion in which the garden is introduced, or the hills, in the pictures which artists describe as figures with landscape. Miss Tiernan follows very closely the method of grouping by contrasts—the lonely little heroine, almost a waif, in the chill grandeur of the great house, and the beloved dauter and

SUT LOVINGOOD'S YARNS. [by G: WASHINGTON HARRIS (1814-69) : N.-Y., *De Witt*, 1867.] ' Of this mythical personage, the last of the band of American Humorists, so called, we hardly kno what tŏ say, except that he has amused us sŏme, wearied us more, and disgusted us not a little. As bad spelling is now deemed ōne of the essentials of humor, we wer prepared tŏ encounter it here, but we wer not prepared, we confess, for the entire absence of humor by which it is thêrein characterized. The fault may lie in the writer, whŏ seems tŏ hav no genius in that direc_ tion, or it may lie in the dialect which he attempts tŏ reproduçe. What this dialect really is, we kno not, but we should say at a venture that it was the mixed speech of the "mean whites" of Tennessee and Kentucky. The hero, Sut Lovingood, describes himself as a "durn'd fool," but is in reality anything else, being a smart, tho ignorant country youth, with a long pair of legs and a grêat talent for running fast, a strong passion for cheap whiskey, and, if possible, a stronger passion for " selling" his nêbors, and being "sold" by them in turn, as in "Parson Bullen's Lizards," "A Razor Grinder in a Thunder Storm," "Sicily Burns's Wedding," "Old Burns' Bull Ride," the whole volume, in fact, being a glorification of the "sell," or practical joke. Many of Sut's jokes ar amusing, but most ar open tŏ the charge of coarseness. The coarseness in question is partly in conçeption, and partly in execution. An element of farçe in its loosest sense, meaning thêreby inçidents of the most lâfable description, strung tŏgether without regard tŏ probability or possibility, is, in ôur way of thinking, about the ōnly merit which Mr. Harris' volume possesses." [Albion. 150 w sister in the bustling life of a home which affection makes glad in spite of slender means; two men, the one growing into a lonely recluse, the other frank-hearted, giving and winning confidence. The types are none of them new, but they are saved from being conventional by the freshness of the author's fancy and the ingenuity and originality of the incidents. The surroundings, too, are novel, for all **Southern** cities are still very remote from us, and life in them as it was forty years ago is utterly different from the hurried rush of city life today. A small circle, living on, generation after generation, without change, develops a community of interest known nowhere else. The life was certainly narrow, yet its sympathies were thereby the deeper. It is easy to call it indifferent, idle, or by a harsher term, but in it all there was a charm of placid leisure such as survives in the pages of 'Sir Charles Grandison.'" [Nation. **151**

SWALLOW-BARN [by J: P. KENNEDY: *Putnam*, 1851.] "Its quiet yet forcible pictures are of that class which live in the memory, because they are true sketches of homely, every-day life. It really does one's heart good to follow the author in his limnings of country-life in the 'Old Dominion' some 30 years ago; the portraits of the characters who made up her quiet and happy neighborhoods; 'the mellow, bland, and amiable luxuriance of her old-time society;' the good fellowship of 'Old **Virginia**;' its hearty and constitutional companionableness, the thriftless gayety of the people, their dogged but amiable invincibility of opinion, and that overflowing hospitality which 'knew no retiring ebb'." [Knickerbocker. **152**

TALES OF NEW-ENGLAND [by S.. O. JEWETT: *Houghton*, 1890.] "Eight of Miss Jewett's stories, selected from her previous volumes, make a group of quiet pictures of quaint, homely people living everyday lives in uneventful places. The most delicate art gives interest to apparently barren material. Without an effort

at creating an effect, the author presents real life with reverential truthfulness, and shows how even the most unprepossessing people have their "history," worthy of contemplation. Many of the characters are **New England** "old maids," but most of these cherish the memory of some romance. The men are plain speaking folk, and are not without their own important life services. For a piece of exquisite literary art, there has been nothing published lately in short stories more perfect than "*Miss Tempy's Watchers*." Other stories have their own charm." [Boston (Mass.) "Journal." **153**

TALLAHASSEE GIRL (A) [by MAURICE THOMPSON: *Osgood*, 1882.] "abounds in crudities of thôt and absurdities of expression at which it is impossible not to smile; yet, it is quite the best of the "Round-Robin Series." Its sketches are broken, but one catches from them the charm of the faded dignity, the drowsy afternoon calm of the old **Southern** capital. Lucie, the heroine, is a gracious figure, and it is in her portrait and in the conception of the relations of the three men of the story to her and to each other, that the marked merit of the book lies. The delicacy and reserve of handling with which the main idea is developed, even in the extravagance of style, suggest a musician who can compose a sweet and tender harmony and yet knows not quite how to manage the pedals. The surmise is obvions that the book is a first effort. If so, it is either a chance hit of unusual felicity, or else it is the evident promise of something better." [Nation. **154**

TENTING AT STONY BEACH [by M.. L. POOL: *Houghton*, 1888.] "Humor here occasionally degenerates into smartness; nevertheless it is for the most part genuine humor, and it includes a lively sense of character both among the South Shore [**Cape Cod**] natives and the summer folk. The pretty girl of our civilization, who pushes into the canvas homes of the tenters, is caut with much of Mr. James's neatness, while Yates, the "shif'-

less toot," and his beautiful energetic wife, and Randy Rankin and her husband, are verities beyond his range. It is a pity that Miss Pool does not hold her hand altogether from caricature and melodrama, but it must be owned she does not." [Howells. **155**

THEIR WEDDING JOURNEY [by W: D. HOWELLS: *Osgood*, 1872.] "....Basil and Isabel March, after a broken engagement, have maried, and, some weeks afterward, start upon their wedding journey, having a horror of being looked upon as a bridal pair.....Their journey is up the Hudson, across New York to Niagara, then to Canada, and thence home. Any extracts we might make would give little sense of the exquisite flavor of the whole, and our readers will find content only in reading the volume. It is a pleasant book when you are tired, and when you are not; and, while it will entertain your hour of leisure, it will assert its worth even in your busier moments." [Overland. **156**

THEOPHILUS AND OTHERS [by M.. (M.) DODGE: *Scribner*, 1876.] "is not fairly a novel: it is a collection of short sketches. It is full of humor, and altho there are at times signs of watering the jokes, there is hardly one of the sketches which is not entertaining. The first and longest one, 'Dobb's Horse,' is a fair sample of Mrs. Dodge's humor in its derision of the seeker after pleasure in the country. But perhaps the best is 'Miss Malony on the Chinese Question.' 'Our Debating Society Skeleton' also shows how a good story can be well told. The book is not one of great importance, and the humor is of an irresponsible kind which does not strike very deep, but it is always innocent and agreeable." [Nation. **157**

THOUSAND A YEAR (A) [by MRS. E. M. BRUCE: *Lee & Shepard*, 1866.] "is a romance full of reality. It describes the trials of a clergyman and his family, living, or rather starving, on inadequate salaries: tho it belongs to the "Shady-Side" literature, it is written in a genial mood, and abounds in wit and humor. If you would

know something of the unrequited toil of a class of men (and of their overworked and patient wives) to whom American civilization owes a debt which can never be paid, get the book and read it, and do something to lift their heavy burdens." [Monthly Rel. Mag. **158**

THREE GENERATIONS. [by SARAH A. EMERY: *Lee & Shepard*, 1872.] "It is a view of country life in **Massachusetts** in the closing years of the last; and first of the present, centuries—a series of sketches, it may be called, connected by a story. In point of literary merit it is far inferior to Mrs. Stowe's work; but in minuteness and fidelity of description, and a certain realism which it is not easy to analyze, it must rank higher.....Its scene is laid, for the most part, in and near Newburyport, and many of its incidents seem to be facts, or founded on facts. For those who live, or have lived, in that ancient city, the book will possess an interest that we should in vain try to define; and all who have reverence for the past, and care to know what life was in the early days of the nation—every day life, in one of the most notable communities of New England—will find it an entertaining, and, we believe, accurate report." [Boston "Literary World." **159**

TOMPKINS AND OTHER FOLKS [by P. DEMING, *Houghton*, 1885.] "Readers of the magazines have already met ' *Tompkins and Other Folks.*' However, the stories lose nothing by being grouped, and any one who enjoys encountering an old acquaintance in good company will take up the volume with pleasure. The chief charm of the stories is their quietness; after that, perhaps, in their suggestiveness, tho they owe not a little to their tone of kindly humor and mildness. Mr. Deming avoids the disagreeable things in life; his stories show a disposition to be lively—not from animal spirits, but from that genial attitude of mind induced by looking on the bright side. That Tompkins should lose his illusions, and turn from the enthusiastic hopes of his college days to auctioneering in Chicago, might be made to seem a genuine tragedy. Yet most young men are enthusiastic, their hopes have some such ending as Tompkins'; and Mr. Deming prefers to dwell, in his pleasant, half-pathetic way, on the auctioneer's unromantic love affair and his warm-hearted remembrances of early days. One or two of the stories are hardly more than sketches. "The Court in Schoharie" is nothing but the description of court week in a slumberous, old-fashioned village among the Catskills; but it is done with such a touch of sympathy—the influence of the simple people and their humble, picturesque surroundings on the old Judge's remaining bit of sentiment is so delicately suggested—that the piece is better than a story would have been. This sketch and "*Mr. Toby's Wedding Journey*" make the best of the book: but throughout there is an evenness both in matter and in style that makes a choice almost entirely a matter of taste." [Nation. **160**

TWO COLLEGE GIRLS [by H.. D. BROWN: *Ticknor*. 1888.] "is an attempt at a "Tom Brown" for a girls' college,—presumably Vassar. Without succeeding to the fullest extent, the book is an interesting and amusing story of the life of the girl undergraduate. The characteristics of the New England girl are bröt into sharp contrast with the Chicago girl, her room-mate; yet the differences are shown to be more of early association and education than inherent in the real characters of the girls. The demure maiden whose home is "seventy miles from Boston" never had the chance to develop a frivolous liking for frizzes and ribbons, and the Chicago girl is not without her serious aspirations, in spite of her giggling and fondness for pickles. The influence of these two on each other, mutual repulsion, gradually disappearing on closer knowledge, is well shown. Of course, the quiet girl captures the brother of her room-mate, and at the end is borne off to married felicity in Chicago." [Overland]. "The heroine—a singularly unattractive and provincial

young woman, of that narrow experience and rigid integrity of nature typical of the better class of New England farmers—made her first exit from her village to take her examinations for what was really her entrance, not only to college, but to a broad and healthful life. There she met the hundred different types of people which make up the great world. Intellectual girls, rich and fashionable girls, girls of all kinds, some of them immeasurably her inferiors in acquirements, and yet possessed of that nameless attraction which made them beloved by everybody, and which she herself so conspicuously lacked. To her chagrin, she discovered that good scholarship was not the one standard of judgment, and that to be loved and honored it was not enuf to have entered as a sophomore. For some months she nursed the natural pride which in her little New England village had seemed to her a pledge of her superiority, until her isolation became unbearable. Then she came to recognize the truth that without the grains of sweetness and humanity, learning will make neither a wise nor a happy woman. Her college-life was thus truly an education." [Critic. **161**

TWO COMPTON BOYS [by A: HOPPIN: *Houghton*, 1884.] "The audience, of young and old, whom Mr. Hoppin captivated with his 'Auton House'—may their number never grow less—will experience no disappointment on reading 'Two Compton Boys.' We have again a graphic picture of Providence (and, to a considerable extent, of New England) life in the youth of men now just past the middle age. and one which the historian may accept as trustfully as any chronicle he is likely to depend upon. But whereas in 'Auton House' we were made acquainted with the 'vie intime' of a single family, in 'Two Compton Boys' the scenes are mostly away from home, (not the same home if one may guess), at school and afield, and there is something like the evolution of a plot with half a tragedy. The humor remains, the comical illustrations are renewed, and an hour of profitable relaxation can be promised any one who follows the fortunes of Dick Reydon and his sable 'alter ego' Peez Fittz." [Nation. **162**

TWO RUNAWAYS. [by H. S. ED-WARDS· *Century Co.*, 1889.] "Mr. Edwards has a rare and charming talent: he reproduces the negro in his multifarious 'funniness' and tenderness and dramatic tendencies with a completeness, a sympathy, never before compassed by a **South-ern** writer : his pathos brings instant tears ; his humor is as spontaneous as it is human ; and beneath both lies the most intricate knowledge of negro character—grown from life-long association,—loving appreciation, and a power of throwing himself into the 'mêlée' of the rather mixed negro nature which we have not before seen in a writer of his 'section.' It is not the negro alone, however, with whom he deals: he is equally felicitous in his delineations of 'cracker' experience. 'Elder Brown's Backslide' is a capital tidbit of this kind, and 'A Born Inventor' is the most amusing skit imaginable. There are three Negro tales in this collection that show real genius: 'Two Runaways,' 'Ole Miss and Sweetheart,' and 'De valley an' de Shadder.' The middle story is as exquisite as anything in Daudet: while all show an uncommon dramatic power, which crops out, too (decked with wreathing smiles and fast following tears), in 'An Idyll of Sinkin' Mount'in.' This is a thin volume, but it is thick with suggestiveness and promise." [Critic. **163**

UNCLE JACK'S EXECUTORS. [by ANNETTE L. NOBLE, *Putnam*, 1880.] "Uncle Jack was a country doctor, dead before the book begins, and his executors are 3 young women living together on the old place with their aunt. A more cheerful, optimistic collection of women it would be hard to find. One is an artist, with proclivities for surgery and medicine; another is a writer; and the third the general utility member. They have little money besides what the two professional sisters earn, but their life is a free and unconstrained one. The aunt is a cleverly sketched, inconsecutive old lady, with a little echo in her of Mrs. Nickleby, but more refined and less of a caricature. Three men are introduced, one of whom, Jerry Scudder, a well-to-do farmer, wishes to marry the housekeeperly Dorothy, but is easily persuaded by her to keep his affections till she finds a wife for him, which she does in Molly Howells. A second is a young clergyman of sense and spirit, and the third an editor....We can promise our readers a very agreeable hour over the book. It is not, Heaven be praised, in the highest style of art, but it is full of good nature and kindliness; some of the scenes are sketched with real humor, and if the book seems amateurish, it has at any rate a refinement and quality of freshness which we wish were more common in professional work." [Atlantic. **164**

UPON A CAST [by C.. DUNNING [WOOD] : *Harper*, 1885.] "is a very amusing little story, and turns on the experiences of a couple of ladies who, with a longing for a quiet life, "The world forgetting, by the world forgot," settle in "New-broek" [**Poughkeepsie**.] Little counting upon this niche outside the world becoming a centre of interest or a theatre of events, the necessity of presenting their credentials to the social magnates of the place does not occur to these ladies,—one the widow of a Prussian officer, and the other her niece. They prefer to remain, as it were, incognito; and, pried into as the seclusion of the new-comers is by all the curious, this reticence soon causes misconstructions and scandals. The petty gossip, the solemnities of self-importance, and the Phariseeism of a country neighborhood are very well portrayed, and, we fear, without any especial exaggeration. The story is told with unflagging spirit, and shows quick perceptions and a lively feeling for situations." [Lippincott's.] "A novel quite fit and proper for summer reading; it is light and pleasant and extremely entertaining. The action, which embraces but the brief space of a summer, is rapid, ·

and, if never absorbing, is still never entirely devoid of interest." [Nation. **165**

VACATION IN A BUGGY. (A) [by MARIA L.. POOL, *Putnam*, 1887.] "A very sparkling, entertaining narrative of the adventures of two ladies who started with a buggy and a horse 'warranted sound and kind in all harness,' for a trip throu Berkshire [**Massachusetts.**] The weather was intensely hot when they started, they had a variety of amusing adventures, and the description of scenes and towns is very life-like. It is witty and humorous, but very natural as well. The two women were very courageous and had a good time, as they surely deserved it." [Hartford "Religious Herald." **166**

VASSALL MORTON [by FRANCIS PARKMAN: *Phillips, Sampson, & Co.*, 1856.] "is honorably distinguished from most American novels by its hearty manhood, its simple and honest strength. It never lags, is nowhere tedious, but presses to its purpose without halt or bend or any book-making inflations.....The main action of the piece is carried on in places most familiar to us. New York and Boston and dear old Cambridge [Mass.] interchange on its broad stage with the Alps, and the Lake of Como. We hear the peculiar talk of our streets and country folk, together with slight sounds of the languages across the sea, but none of them to excess. There is but a touch and a hint, and enuf is suggested. The volume, tho soon read, comprises great variety, and ministers to many kinds of emotion. It has strokes of genial humor and of deepest passion, tones of the most ordinary life and the tramp of romantic adventure.....We commend the book to the public for a wholesome book, as well as a most engaging one." [Christ. Examiner. **167**

VILLAGE PHOTOGRAPHS. (by AUGUSTA LARNED, *Holt*, 1887.] "This volume illustrates the fact that a village offers as good opportunities for the observation of human nature, within limits, as does the city, with the added advantage of a country sincerity and hardiness of cha-

raeter. This particular village is of the **New England** type. Its inhabitants have a familiar look as they come before us in turn. There are the judge, the jack-of-all-trades, the young man of genius without an occupation, the recluse with a dark romance, the ne'er-do-well, and the good doctor, who belongs to the group in which Holmes delights, and who is drawn with a skill not inferior to his own. There are women of all varieties of weakness and strength of mind, schoolmistresses, old maids, flirts, widows, in an abundance that accurately indicates, one thinks, the surplus of the sex. It is a long story which the author tells. She has exhausted the field, not in the sense of telling all that is to be known, but in leaving out no detail that belongs to the general impression. A good many life-histories are related, not as the novelist writes them, but in the way in which they are really known to the people of the town. One lives in the place, as he reads, and finds out that there is no secrecy possible for any of its inhabitants. Sooner or later even the passing stranger learns their affairs from start to finish. The description of these human matters makes the bulk of the book, tho the course of the seasons and the natural features of the woods and mountains and "the pine barrens" are utilized to keep a country atmosphere always present. The rustics are true rustics, true Yankees; and whoever likes the "simple annals of the poor" will find this volume full of reality, and sometimes touched with homely pathos." [Nation. **168**

WALTER THORNLEY [by SUSAN R. SEDGWICK, 1859.] "Altho wearing the garb of a fictitious work, this charming domestic story is too rich in natural incidents and familiar characters not to have been founded in personal experience. Its scenes have a singular air of reality, while brightened with a true glow of imagination and romance. In just and expressive delineations of character, and in a high tone of moral sympathy, the present volume fully sustains the reputation of the

WANDERINGS AND FORTUNES OF SOME GERMAN EMIGRANTS (The). [by F: GERSTACKER (1816-72) : *Appleton*, 1848, 216 p.] "The substançe of this entertaining book is evidently no fiction, tho the author has added certain romantic flourishes tŏ the main outline of his story, which very sucçessfully fulfils the usual conditions of a novel. But it is impossible tŏ read mâñy pages without perçeiving that he is telling what he must hav seen, knŏn, and suffered—so minute and çircumstantial is the narrativ : and as he is gifted with considerable powers of observing and describing, the reality of his work renders it extremely life-like and engaging . . . At Bremen we ar first introduçed tŏ the party. Thêy ar of all ranks—sŏme merchants, a barrister, a "Von" of the landed class, a clergyman with wife and twŏ fair dauters, sundry mechanics and workmen of various trades, and sŏme dozen peasants—gathered from different parts of Germany . . . How the lŏve affair of Bertha and Werner ended, and in what manner the survivors of the colony became fixçd in a more happy settlement, it is needless tŏ relate. Suffiçe it tŏ say, that the fortunes of those whŏm we hav learned tŏ lŏve in this history take, on the whole, a satisfactory turn : and that what we learn of the ŏther adventurers,—sŏme of whŏm fall intŏ sad conditions and nŏne of whŏm grêatly prosper,—seems tŏ be quite as good as thêy had at all deservd. Mr. Gerstäcker seems tŏ be a genial observer of the humors and ways of men, as wel as apt in the business of daily life—with sŏme readiness in portraying both in a simple, dramatic fashion." [Athenæum.]—"We ar not sure how much of this book is truth and how much fiction; but be that as it may, it carries with it an air of grêat probability, and for aut we can see, may be true tŏ the letter . . . It is full of interesting inçident, and the man whŏ can read 10 pages of it without wishing tŏ keep on, must hav the organs of both curiosity and sympathy but very imperfectly developed." [American Literary Magazine. 557 m

writer." [Harper's.   **169**
WAY DOWN EAST [by Seba Smith,
Derby, 1855.] "The author's brain is
overflowing with Yankee traditions, local
anecdotes, and personal recollections,
which he reproduces with a freshness and
point, which always protect the reader
from satiety. The force of his descriptions
consists in their perfect naturalness.
They are never overcharged—never distorted, for the sake of grotesque effect,
never spiced too highly for the healthy
palate—but read almost like literal transcripts of **New England** country life,
before the age of railroads and telegraphs
had brushed away its piquant individuality." [Harper's.   **170**
WHAT-TO-DO-CLUB (The) [*Rob-
erts,* 1885.] "is a work of collaboration
by H.. Campbell and Mrs. Poole, the
former telling a pleasant, if not very original, story of **New England** life, the latter writing the letters in which the doings
of the "Busy-Bodies," a New Jersey club,
are related for the instruction of the
"What-to-Do's." Both clubs are in search
of employment which shall be at once
interesting and profitable. The assurance
of the writers that each experiment is an
actual one, truthfully described, makes
the book a valuable storehouse of information. The tone of it is admirable, sweet,
and healthful, making gentle household
things and home affections of the first importance, and then trying to show what
occupations are not incompatible with
them, either in fact or in spirit." [Nation.   **171**
WHITE HERON. (A) [by S.. O.
Jewett: *Houghton,* 1886.] "Of Miss
Jewett's stories little can ever be said, except to remark afresh on their beauty,
their straitforward simplicity, and above
all, their loving truth to the life of rural
New England not merely in its external
aspects, but in its very heart and spirit.
....In view of the current misconceptions
of the Puritan temper which threaten to
fasten themselves upon history, such
authentic records of its rugged kindliness,

its intensity of personal affections, its
capacity for liberality, are invaluable.
Nor can one doubt that these 'bona-fide'
Yankees, yet lingering among the remote
farms, are the true descendants in character as well as blood of the original colonists, if he will compare them with 'G:
Eliot's' studies of the farmer folk from
among whom they came. The community
of essential character, modified by 200
years of greater independence, more liberal
thôt, and harder effort. is unmistakable.
"A White Heron" contains 2 or 3 stories
which are among the author's best, tho the
average of the collection is scarcely equal
to previous ones. The first story, "A
White Heron," however, is perfect in its
way—a tiny classic." [Overland.   **172**
WIND OF DESTINY (The) [by A.
S. Hardy, *Houghton,* 1886.] "is far
from being a bad novel. One cannot, of
course, expect every story which "turns
out the wrong way" to be a genuinely
powerful tragedy; but, for the absence of
intense dramatic interest, one expects compensation in the way of pathos or surprise, and this Mr. Hardy has managed to
give. In spite of a shadowy uncertainty
which vails the chief characters, there is a
genuineness about honest Jack Temple
which, just in time, saves the story from
seeming unreal. His is indeed the pathetic
figure of the tale, tho the lonely Schönberg,
with his sad memories, seems to have been
meant for the part. And it is to Jack also
that one's sympathies go out, rather than
to Rowan Ferguson, the painter, when the
happiness of both is destroyed by the weak
woman who had loved Rowan and married Jack. There is a quiet nobleness
sometimes in the aspect of an every-day
man of business who is capable of deep
feeling, and of showing it without ostentation, which is dear to the American
heart; and tho Mr. Hardy depends largely
upon his fatalism to replace natural motives, the misery of Jack Temple is plainly
apparent and very touching." [Nation. **173**
WOMAN'S INHERITANCE (A) [by
Amanda M. Douglas: *Lee & Shepard,*

WIDOW BEDOTT PAPERS (The).
[by F.. MIRIAM (BERRY) WHITCHER:
N.-Y., *Derby*, 1855.] "Tŏ all whŏ lŏve
pure scandal, gossip, and caricature, this
grotesque volume wil be bily acceptable...
If the keen, tho broad, satire of the book
be merited by ŏur rural friends, then the
less said by "countryfolk" against the
absurdities and selfishness of city life and
city manners the better. The "poitry"
in the volume wil produce many a hearty
lâf, and on the whole, we feel gratified at
making the humorous acquaintance of the
Widow Bedott." [Criterion.]—"It shŏs
the peculiarities of ŏur New-England [?]
nébors, especially those of the Widow
Bedott. Most books of this sort overdŏ
the yankee vernacular. But the Widow
Bedott is perfect in her parts of speech, a'
model woman of the class tŏ which she
belongs. She is ignorant and prejudiced,
mean, malicious, and quarrelsŏme, a
slanderer, and abŏve all, an unwearied
fisher of men. The end of her being is tŏ
entrap sŏme fool intŏ marrying her. Her
schemes and manœuvres ar baffled for a
long time, thêy ar so profoundly transparent; but she finally catches a burning,and
a shining light—Elder Sniffles, a Baptist
clergyman. If the 'materiel' of the
"Widow Bedott Papers" had been worked
intŏ a consistent story, with a proper
surrounding of characters, scenery and
inçidents, thêy might sŏme day hav filled
a curious niche in the history of American literature. As it is, thêy wil be
widely read, largely lâfed over, and then
forgotten. No permanent business can
be dŏne on so small a capital as ŏne character, even tho that ŏne be the Widow
Bedott." [Albion.]—"Mrs. Bedott is a
vulgar, inconsolable wido, the centre of a
village sewing and literary çircle, herself
gifted with the art of writing "poitry" of
which we hav here sŏme most admirable
speçimens. Sinçe the famous Caudle
Lectures, nŏthing like them has appeared
til Widow Bedott began tŏ pour forth her
lamentations in "poitry," and tŏ tel the
various methods she took tŏ regain her

standing as a married woman ... The
village society of the rural districts of
New-York ar pictured tŏ the life.
Nŏthing can better evidençe the fidelity
and graphic power of these pen and ink
sketches than the çensure inflicted upon
the poor artist, from the çircles of soçiety
in which she livd." [National Era. **0401 p**
WIDOW SPRIGGINS (The) [by F..
M. (BERRY) WHITCHER: N.-Y., *Carleton*, 1867.] is "anŏther contribution tŏ
American Humor, and, considering the
time when it was written, a creditable
ŏne. It is not equal tŏ the *Widow Bedott
Papers* [No. 0401 p], and it is much inferior tŏ the effusions of "Artemus
Ward," "John Phœnix," "Josh Billings,"
and the rest of the later American humorists. Mrs. Whitcher was a woman of
talent, whŏ might hav dŏne good things,
had she livd longer, and learned the art
of writing; as it was, her compositions
hav a decidedly amateurish air, such as
we expect tŏ find in the columns of country journals. The Widow Spriggins, whŏ,
by the way, is not a wido til after the
conclusion of her reminisçençes, is a sentimental country girl, of cheap education
and acquirements, whŏse head, such as it
is, had been turned by novel-reading.
Refusing a good match in her nativ village
of Podunk, she flies tŏ an adjacent town,
whêre she opens a seminary, and meets
lots of adventures amŏng the young men,
whŏ ar attracted by her superior charms
and intelligençe. She repels thêir advançes with scorn, as becŏmes a reader of
the "Children of the Abbey," and similar
hi-flŏn fictions, but finally capitulates tŏ
Spriggins, whŏse relict she soon becŏmes.
Thêre is not much originality in all this,
nor, we conçeive, much humor; if thêre
be, it is so clumsy that it escapes us: in a
word it is mere horse-play. That writing
of this sort should make a "sensation" in
country town, whêre everybody knoes
everybody else, and gossip is ready tŏ
put the cap of the satirist on the nearest
head, we can believe; but further than
this, we can not go." [Albion. **0402 q**

WOLFSDEN. [by J. B.; Boston,
Phillips, 1856,] "The author givs evidençe of possessing the true Yankee eye
and brain. His descriptions of the rural
life and character of **New-England** ar
fresh, accurate, and life-like, shōing that
certainty of grasp which proceeds from
experiençe as wel as observation. The
scenes in New-York and "down South"
ar comparativly failures. The pathos,
the passion, the dry, quaint, drŏll humor,
often verging on extravagançe, ar all of
the peculiar New-England type. The
vigor and variety of power displayed in
representation of character, the feliçity of
its separate scenes, and its easy mastery
of language and illustration, indicate that
it was not a first attempt." [Graham's
Magazine.]—"As a work of art, it is
manifestly open tŏ criticism; the plot is
not particularly ingenious, and the style,
often vigorous, terse, and picturesque, is
sŏmetimes careless and in bad taste, altho
never dul or commonplaçe. Vued, however, as a picture of New-England rural
life, it has, in ŏůr opinion, few equals.
The story of the child-hunt in the wild
Maine woods, the slêigh-rides and singing parties and path-brêakings, the in-
tensely-wrŏt tragedy of the blacsmith
and his tempter, and the tender pathos
and simple beauty of sŏme of the descriptions of life and Nature indicate the
ability of the author." [J: G. Whittier. **173 s**

WOMAN IN SPITE OF HERSELF =
No. 0406.

1886.] "is one of the books which the critic's feeling would lead him to speak of more impatiently than his judgment would sanction; for the book is well-meant, it is not without a respectable degree of pure story interest, is free from coarseness, and has a sensible moral. In fact, its defect is is the same as that of the typical Sunday-school book (save for the sentimentalizing of religion, of which it is not guilty)—that is, a pervasive atmosphere of the second rate in intellect and taste. It is hard to say how this comes in. The author makes a very great point of good society, and does not palpably break with the facts in describing it; perhaps it is more by what she fails to put in, that she succeeds in being hopelessly second-rate. Her heroines are admirable compounds of loveliness and excellence, her heroes, Bayards; and they carry out their parts with reasonable correctness; but while they move on briskly throu the action of the piece (for Miss Douglas has a very fair idea of the construction and motion of a narrative), they never *live*—they are merely embodied ideas." [Overland. **174**

YEAR IN EDEN (A) [by HARRIET W. PRESTON, *Roberts*, 1887.] "is saved by the presence of 2 or 3 genuine and natural characters. They are not those to whom most care is given, and who, in the action, are most important. One is Professor Griswold, clever, pushing, plausible, and untrustworthy; the others are two old maids, the fine drawing of whose insignificance contrasts curiously with the woodenness and conventionality of those who ôt to be significant. Women like the Misses Midleton—dignified, content, serene, for all their material poverty—are to be found in every small community, but very seldom have they been so delightfully shown to the world as by Miss Preston. The only excuse for the intrigue, an exceptionally disgraceful one even outside of Eden, is that it brings out the finest points of these sweet old gentlewomen. The disgrace of their niece's flight with a "married, middle-aged man" was needed

even to suggest to them that such a thing could be: how it could be in their own set, among their own flesh and blood, they would never understand. Nor, from the author's delineation, does the reader understand; he can only accept, with the fulness of worldly knowledge, the possibility. The passion which might impel a man of fashion to a socially destructive step does not exist in the well-dressed stick which came as the serpent into Eden. For the woman's part in the affair there is no reason, excepting that an Italian-Yankee may be expected to be unbalanced, and that the name "Monza" may impose an obligation to be shocking." [Nation. **175**

YOUNG MAIDS AND OLD: [by C. L.. (ROOT) BURNHAM: *Ticknor*, 1888.] ."This is another example of how well an honest-hearted and modest woman may amuse and entertain readers of her own sex. Without one approach to dangerous ground she has drawn the picture of a good-hearted but flirty girl for one of her heroines, and without one trace of prudishness delineated extreme modesty, refinement, and reserve in the other, while involving both of them in cordial, honest, happily terminated love-making. And on that achievement we are heartily glad to congratulate her. She is never dull, and she never preaches, but her story leaves a thoroly pleasant and desirable impression on the reader's mind." [Catholic World. **176**

ZEPH. [by H..(F.) JACKSON: *Roberts*, 1886.] ."So careful a student of her art was Mrs. Jackson, and so much knowledge had she of how to study it wisely, that in the few years between her beginning to to write fiction and her death, she had already so far overcome the more superficial natural defects in her fiction, that few readers would notice them at all in Zeph. The plot of the story seems to us incongruous, artistically speaking. It begins with one motive, and seems to be ending with another. Zeph's devotion to his wife is the theme at the outset, and it foreshadows a story of tragic loyalty, unchangeable to the end. Yet soon we find this wife passing very easily out of his life, and after his divorce, his relation to Miss Sophy becomes the theme; nor does the assurance given by the sketch of the intended close, that the story was to be brôt back to its original theme by the death of the first wife, entirely meet this objection. One cannot quite avoid the suspicion that some tender-heartedness on the author's part towards her characters interfered with the carrying out of the tragedy to its legitimate end." [Overland. **177**

ZURY. [by Jo. KIRKLAND : *Houghton*, 1887.] "We cannot recall any fiction worth mention before "Zury" dealing with the middle **West**, except E: Eggleston's stories, and Howe's two gloomy novels. Mr. Kirkland in some respects excels either of these authors. He writes with a more assured pen, a more even and firm literary training. He is never crude, and

is thoroly original, in the sense of never depending on conventional types in character or incident, and copying nothing but life. Nevertheless, he is not very individual, and either Mr. Howe's or Mr. Eggleston's stories leave a much more distinct mark on the mind than his. Perhaps by his crude devices, perhaps in spite of them, Mr. Eggleston did attain "go;" and perhaps by his unconscionable imitation and ghastly sensationalism, perhaps in spite of them, Mr. Howe is impressive. "Zury" is full of excellences, yet it hardly impresses itself on the reader. This is chiefly, we should say, because the plot is not pleasant, and the unpleasant element in it does not make itself seem necessary and inevitable, as it should in an artistic book; partly, too, because the style, admirable tho it is—plain, direct, and full of intelligence and quiet humor—has not that highly readable quality which may be called brightness." [Overland. **178**

INDEX.

PRICE. ONE COPY, I.60;¹ TWO COPIES. $ .75; THREE, $1.00; FOUR, $1.25; FIVE, $1.50; TEN, $2.50; FIFTEEN, $3.00.

A

DESCRIPTIVE LIST

OF

NOVELS AND TALES

DEALING WITH

AMERICAN CITY LIFE,

INCLUDING SOME WORKS DESCRIPTIVE OF COUNTRY LIFE OMITTED FROM PREVIOUS LIST.

COMPILED BY
W: M. GRISWOLD, A. B.
EDITOR OF "THE MONOGRAPH", A COLLECTION OF FIFTY-FOUR HISTORICAL AND
BIOGRAPHICAL ESSAYS; AND OF "TRAVEL," A SIMILAR SERIES
DEVOTED TO PLACES.

CAMBRIDGE, MASS:
W: M. GRISWOLD, PUBLISHER.
1891.

NOVELS OF AMERICAN CITY LIFE.

The object of this list is to direct readers, such as would enjoy the kind of books here described, to a number of novels, easily obtainable, but which, in many cases, have been forgotten within a year or two after publication. That the existence of works of fiction is remembered so short a time is a pity, since, for every new book of merit, there are, in most libraries, a hundred as good or better, unknown to the majority of readers. It is hoped that the publication of this and similar lists will lessen, in some measure, the disposition to read an inferior NEW book when superior OLD books, equally fresh to most readers, are at hand.

This list will be followed by others describing INTERNATIONAL, ROMANTIC, ECCENTRIC and FANCIFUL novels and tales. The compiler would be pleased to have his attention called to any works deserving a place which have escaped his attention. It may be observed that the compiler has tried to include only such works as are well-written, interesting, and free from sensationalism, sentimentality, and pretense. But in a few cases, books have been noticed on account of the reputation of their authors, or their great popularity, rather than their merit.

The selected "notices" here given are generally abridged.

ABRAHAM PAGE, ESQ. [by J: SAUNDERS HOLT: *Lippincott*, 1869.] "To read them is to get much the same kind of pleasure that one finds in listening to the talk of a shrewd, sensible old man, such as one occasionally meets in out-of-the-way country places, who, having spent all his days in one spot, has been colored by his surroundings to the very marrow, and whose judgments on men and things, if they have the defect of being provincial and narrow, have also the virtue of resulting fairly from his own observations . . . But usually he confines himself closely to the matter he has in hand. That matter is description of life and manners in the little Southern village where he was born, and where he lived all his days in the comfortable assurance that life had nothing better or pleasanter to offer than what could be found within its limits. Content-

ment is certainly a virtue, and it is hard to say who could practise it with greater hopes of success than a man situated as "Mr. Page" describes himself to have been, who felt the pleasant conviction that to be a gentleman was the chief end of man, and that only a Southerner, the owner of slaves, could ever hope to attain it. Under such circumstances, a cheerful serenity and a calm confidence in surveying and analyzing the meaner works of God's hand could hardly fail to be engendered in any bosom. Such was the result, at all events, in "Mr. Page's" case; and, considering the 2 unaffectedly pleasant books which, but for this satisfaction with himself and this thōro persuasion of the soundness of all his positions, would certainly have been less peculiarly pleasant, we find in ourselves not the least disposition to quarrel with it. Mr. Page has looked at life with

50

eyes of a shrewd, humorous, and quasi-filosofical observer, and has told in an easy and natural way what he has seen and what he has thôt about it." [Nation. **179**

ACROSS THE CHASM. [by JULIA MAGRUDER: *Scribner*.1885.] "This is done throu the personality of Margaret Treven-non, an exceptionally charming and unprejudiced Southern girl, who acquires her first experience of Northern character during a winter spent in **Washington**· This is not a Hyperborean latitude for studying Northern character, but even here Margaret finds such a change from the social customs and minor morals to which she has been accustomed that it can only be wondered what she would have found in a chillier region—Boston, for instance. The chief subject of her wonder and of her animadversions is the careful anxiety with which 'Northerners' choose their acquaintances, shielding themselves from social derogation and desirous to be intimate only in 'the best circles'. She cannot understand why 'a lady born and reared should even have to think of anything like that'; and is of opinion that it is too disagreeable a puzzle 'to decide whom to treat civilly and whom to snub'; an idea which is derided by her Washington cousin as a 'hi-flown Southern notion' of too general hospitality. This discriminating Margaret is the centre of many pleasing pictures of the liter aspects of social life, and sits in serene judgment upon the conflicting claims of 3 lovers—an amiable but indolent and 'shiftless' Carolinian, an energetic and ambitious New-Yorker, and a polished cosmopolitan who has outgrown any special sympathy with either section." [American. **180**

ADVENTURES OF A WIDOW. The [by EDGAR FAWCETT: *Osgood*, 1884.] "In this social study, or rather satire, the well known censor of fashionable life in **New-York** assumes to wê and judge the different elements of society thêre, to contrast the merits and demerits of various cliques and to pronounce upon their comparative claims to respect, the chief types chosen being ultra-fashionable and LITER-

ARY New-York. The connecting link between these diverse elements is the widow of promised adventures, Pauline Varick, young, rich, of bluest Knickerbocker blood, who has gained dearly bôt experience from a short but unhappy mercenary mariage. Disgusted with the emptiness, frivolity, meaness of aim, and poverty of achievement of the social circle in which she had been trained to her matrimonial bargain and sale, the aim of her riper rears is to make herself the centre of a new and better form of society of which the members shall be 'men and women of intellectual calibre, workers, not drones; thinkers, writers, artists, poets, scholars.' Aided by the versatile and fascinating Irish-American journalist, Kindelon, and a literary Mrs. Dares and her 2 dauters, she succeeds in establishing her 'salon' and assembles in her luxurious mansion the best which can be gathered of literary and artistic workers. Fresh from contact with Mrs. Poughkeepsie's circle of aristocratic pretension and idealess vacuity, she hopes to interest herself in the society of historians, novelists, essayists, poets, sculptors and painters. But the experiment is not a success. Her assemblage of lions snap, snarl, and lacerate each other and their hostess. Rude things are said and done, egotists prate of themselves and theorists romp ôn their hobby-horses unchecked." [American]—"We should not wonder if some of Mr. Fawcett's portraits—perhaps all of them—had been furtively done from life, and if he mit lâf at the success with which he has set a few obnoxious individuals in the pillory of type. It is hard to feel, for example, that in the company assembled at Mrs. Varick's first salon—in Mr. Prawle, Mr. Trevor, and Mr. Corson, the poets, and in Mr. Bedloe, [Roe ?], the pietistic novelist, 'who wrote 'The Christian Knight in Armour,' we do not see caricatures of authors familiar to us all. The appearance of these figures is the signal for a good deal of debate and criticism on books, authors. reading, and the general intellectual and literary life." [Bost."Lit.World." **181**

ADVENTURES OF TOM SAWYER.
The [by 'M: TWAIN:' *American Publishing Co.*, 1876.] "... The tale is very dramatically wrôt, and the subordinate characters are treated with the same grafic force which sets Tom alive before us. The worthless vagabond, Huck Finn, is entirely delitful throuout, and in his promised reform, his identity is respected; he will lead a decent life in order that he may one day be thôt worthy to become a member of that gang of robbers which Tom is to organize. Tom's aunt is excellent, with her kind heart's sorrow and secret pride in Tom; and so is his sister Mary, one of those good girls who are born to usefulness and charity and forbearance and unvarying rectitude. Many village people and local notables are introduced in well conceived character; the whole little town lives in the reader's sense, with its religiousness, its lawlessness, its droll social distinctions, its civilization qualified by its slave-holding and its traditions of the wilder West which has passed away. The picture will be instructive to those who have fancied the whole **Southwest** a sort of vast Pike County, and have not conceived of a sober and serious and orderly contrast to the sort of life that has come to represent the Southwest in literature." [Atlantic. **182**

ALICE BRAND. [by ALBERT GALLATIN RIDDLE: *Appleton*, 1875.] "The author is very much in earnest about reproducing the life of a given place and period [**Washington**, 1865-9] as it passed under his eyes, and has done well to give us portraits instead of purely typical figures. . . . The perspective and finish of the book are unsatisfactory; background and foreground are interchangeable; and the love-story of Col. Mason and Ellen Berwick far outstrips in interest that of Frank and Alice. Mason's Congressional experiences give rise to some rather interesting passages, which, with the scenic and somewhat questionable glimpses of lobbying and pardon-broking operations, suggest regions of research from which a master mît draw something worthy the pains. . . . But, with all its faults and its

weakness, 'Alice Brand' has vigor in it; the study of the mischievous, honest, impetuous American youth, Grayson Vane, is not bad; and among American novels which make a point of being water-marked with their nationality, it will stand above the average." [Nation. **183**

AMBITIOUS WOMAN. An [by EDGAR FAWCETT: *Houghton*, 1883.] "This novel deals with the career of Claire Twining, who from an early age has set before herself the ambition of mounting from a very humble station to a hi position in society, and finally accomplishes her aim by unscruplous efforts and the aid of her exceptional beauty and charm,— a charm which is strong enuf to beguile the reader of her history into a sort of sympathy with her, in spite of the crass selfishness with which she avows and follows sordid and intrinsically vulgar aims. . . . The success of Claire in gaining a position in this carefully defended oligarchy [in **N. Y.**], her trials, and hazards, and losses, and the manner in which she finally snatches victory from defeat, must not be forestalled for the reader. The aim of the author is professedly to show the vanity and worthlessness of her ambition, its barren fertility, and the shallowness of its selfish joys; but in his desire to excuse his heroine and render her worthy of the reader's sympathies, Mr. Fawcett makes his point too well. The pomps and vanities which are Claire's allurements are depicted in too attractive colors. The ginger is too hot in the mouth, and the cakes and ale too savory, to be given up without reluctance. The sad shadow of satiety which infallibly follows the sun-glare of such worldly joys and successes is not allowed to be seen at all. Claire loses her fortune, to be sure, and concludes to comfort herself with family affection; but the reader may imagine that with a return of her former wealth would come former ambitions. Altogether there may be reasonable doubts of Mr. Fawcett's success in inculcating his moral, but there can be none about the entertaining qualities of his book. It is not only readable but charming." [American.]—"It is the story of a penniless girl, who, understanding clearly what she wishes in life, understands the time to seize and hold every opportunity and make every step in her career promote her ambition. The story is in no respect a pleasing one, the characters being not only unlovely in themselves, but with false tendencies which permit no illusions. The heroine, Claire, strikes us as a somewhat wooden and conventional person, limited and hindered by sordid and prosaic ideas. Quite untouched by the passion she inspires in her husband, she finds nothing in his single-hearted devotion which she is not ready to throw away when reverses come. This is the weakest place in the book, and at the same time offers Mr. Fawcett his best opportunity, for the wronged husband's nobility and goodness at this crisis go far to retrieve the story from commonplace. The reality of Claire's final repentance and atonement impresses us but feebly. Worldliness is not a temporary folly, which may be assumed or dismissed at pleasure, but is the result of deficient insīt, narrow sympathies, and a barren heart." [Lippincott's.　　　　　　　　　184

AMERICAN POLITICIAN. An [by F. M. CRAWFORD: *Houghton*, 1884.] A clever, amusing, and interesting sketch of **Boston** society, with some political scenes truthfully and entertainingly done. Most of the political matter however, is dull, and a part is so preposterous,—not to say childish—as to form a political "Alice's Adventures."　　　　　185

ANGLOMANIACS. The [by CONSTANCE (CARY) HARRISON: *Cassell*, 1890.] Tho only half as long as is usual, this is a nearer approach to a successful novel of american [**New-York**] society than anything previously published. It is full of shrewd observation and clever talk, without sacrificing to these features its interest as a story. In the first three-quarters of the book there is no occasion for unfavorable criticism, except, perhaps, as to the title, which is at least inadequate. The struggle in which the heroine is involved

and her mother exclusively engaged is not, except incidentally, the aping of english manners;—it is rather an example of the constant effort, always going on in a wealthy society, of the newly-enriched to conquer a position among leading families. The possibility of winning a title into the bargain—may, or may not, add new interest to the game. In this story, the use of the english connection appears to be to serve as a fulcrum for Archimedes' lever. —Towards the close of the story the author appears to have spent her force, and lost her interest, so that she cuts the knot of the story instead of untwisting it, which would have produced a more satisfactory, tho a more laborious conclusion.　　186

ANNALS OF BROOKDALE. [by F.. (BOOTT) GREENOUGH: *Lippincott*, 1881.] "A pleasant idyllic picture of the **New-England** village of 25 or 30 years ago." [Atlantic.　　　　　　187

ANNE. [by C. F. WOOLSON: *Harper*, 1882.] "If Miss Woolson has stood easily at the head of American women novelists, it is less because she has given us the best than because she has given us little but the best. In Miss Phelps we have to forgive some superfluous sentiment; in Mrs. Davis an extreme degree of the uncanny element; in Mrs. Burnett, the impossible refinement of her 'lower class' characters; in Mrs. Spofford, a Disraelish tendency to mother-of-pearl bedsteads and diamond studded thimbles. Miss Woolson makes no demands of this sort upon our clemency. Her longest sustained effort, the novel 'Anne', promised, for 400 pages, to be all that we had learned to expect from her. When, therefore, toward the close we find that Miss Woolson resorts to melodramatic clap-trap of the cheapest variety to unite her lovers—that there is to be not only a plot but a climax, and that they are all to live happily ever after, the artistic mistake is so colossal, so incongruous, so incredible, that we are not merely disappointed; we lâf. . . . The story divides itself easily into 3 parts; the first, a series of clear, exquisite etchings. giving in distinct tho colorless outlines a picture of the pallid winters on the great northern lakes; the second, a water-color, giving a picture of society, as illustrated by summer boarders, with all the fidelity of a fotograf, but with a lit and color which are the author's own;—the third, a chromo—such a mixture of murder and mariage, of heliotrope and orange blossoms, that perhaps the less said of it the better." . . . [Critic. 188

ANNIE KILBURN. [by W: D. HOWELLS: *Harper*, 1889.] "For the story of her attempts, her failures, and her successes—in which last she is not rich—readers must go to the pages of what seems to us the best book Mr. Howells has written. He has certainly never given us in one novel so many portraits of intrinsic interest. Annie Kilburn herself is a masterpiece of quietly veracious art,—the art which depends for its effect on unswerving fidelity to the truth of nature; but because she is painted in low tones, she stands out from the canvas a little less distinct than 1 or 2 of the other figures. Mr. Peck, the minister, is a striking character, a sort of Savonarola in homespun. He is as enthusiastic in his way as Miss Kilburn is in hers: tho while her enthusiasm is sanguine, his is sombre, and he has a finer grasp of the facts of life, because he sets his face like a flint against pleasant illusions. If the portrait of Mr. Peek be notably impressive, that of the clever, superficially cynical, but essentially kindly Bohemian, Ralph Putney, is as notably brilliant. The defect of the ordinary clever man of fiction is that we do not hear his cleverness, we only hear about it; but Putney's clear sited, biting persiflage sparkles and corns-cates for Mr. Howells' readers, and is not left to be accepted by them on vague report. Above all, we feel that he is a human being, not a mere costumed machine for the turning out of epigrams; indeed the main charm of 'Annie Kilburn' lies in the fact that it arouses and maintains our interest in the wholesome commonplaces of human nature and human experience of which we can never tire." [Spectator.] See also notice in "Novels of Country Life." **189**

ANTONY BRADE. [by ROBERT [T. S.] LOWELL: *Roberts*, 1874.] "This story, 'lovingly written for all who have been boys or are boys or like boys,' is wholesome, hearty, human. It gives pictures of life at a boy's school under Episcopal influences ["St. Marks"] in a **New England** country town, [Southboro, Mass.] and of society in that little gossiping world. The pivot of interest round which the story revolves is the mystery concerning the history of Antony Brade, who is a charming yet thoroly boylike figure, and whose companions are described to the life in their studies, their mischief, their play. Mr. Parmenter, [Burnett] the fussy, meddlesome trustee of the school, whose wealth, acquired in the sale of perfumery, gives him the airs of a lord of the manor, is drawn with special felicity. Mr. Lowell's 'New Priest at Conception Bay' proved that he had rare power of giving genuine pictures out of fresh and unwonted scenes for men and women; his present book is successful in making picturesque fases of life which are familiar to us, and without formally inculcating any 'morals,' is leavened with hi principles and Christian spirit." [Unitarian Review. **190**

ARTHUR BONNICASTLE. [by J. G. HOLLAND: *Scribner*, 1873.] "The moral is well pointed therein, but conventional verbiage, threadbare platitudes, feeble clatter, and decorous inanity are wont to be resented by resolute, impetuous souls who are eager for the retarded dénouement. . . . Whatever be the verdict in regard to the literary merit of "Arthur Bonnicastle," it is safe to predict for it a genial, generous reception from those who entertain a harmless, enthusiastic sort of respect for florid simplicity, almost suffocating propriety, and the most patient and faithful indoctrination of moral lessons. Over such the work will diffuse a cheering caloric, and a mildly pleasant radiance. [Overland. **191**

AS IT MAY HAPPEN [by "TREBOR" (RO. S. DAVIS): *Porter & Coates*, 1879.] "first challenges attention by the claim to be a novel of American life and character. It is a novel of rather low life and generally worthless character; and it is to be hoped that this does not make it more distinctively American, tho the author evidently thinks it does. . . .There is an abundance of disagreeable incident in the story, and no luck, from the outset, of action; but toward its close, surprises come tumbling down; the author breaks into a kind of war-dance, and there is something so broadly farcical in his distribution of princely fortunes and assignment of brownstone fronts to the (comparatively) virtuous upon the last page that one wonders if, after all, he may not have written this book upon a wager as to how preposterous a farrago the public would accept in the way of domestic fiction. There are certain involuntary vulgarisms in the style, however,—like the incessant use of 'transpire' for occur,—which forbid the supposition of deliberate mockery. It is particularly hard to take a book of this sort seriously and consider it with patience. Yet, concluding it to have been written in good faith, we are resolved to dwell on it for a little, because, curiously bad as much of the present performance is, it is yet haunted by a strange kind of amorfous possibility of merit. In the first place, it has the indubitable advantage of a scene laid in the **Middle States.** The very quietude and indifference of that region, its neutrality amid the stress of effort and the storms of faction which have raged on either side of it for a hundred years, have allowed the deposit of a soil, the exhalation of a certain dreamy atmosfere. favorable, or at least possible, for romance. . . . **Pennsylvania,** the paradise of the lazy and the byword of the progressive. whose long drawn name, even, is compounded of Quaker flegm & rustic monotony and ends in a yawn.—Pennsylvania furnished scenery for all those intense and original studies of Mrs. (Harding) Davis, and for Bayard Taylor's most powerful and symmetrical novel, the Story of Kennett; and, thanks to the fact that its antic action passes precisely thêre, even 'As it May Happen' is thŏroly invested with an atmosfere and equipped

with a landscape. It is also—what is yet more unusual—equipped with a plot, which the author is somewhat too impatient to unravel, but which is ingenious if not new; and thêre is real humor." [Atlantic. **192**

ASCHENBROEDEL, [by K.. CARRINGTON: *Roberts*, 1882.] "The Aschenbrödel of this volume lived in an old-fashioned house in an old-fashioned **New-England** town. She had good books and a sparkling mind; a fun-loving, nature-loving, girlish spirit, in a vigorous, elastic body, with no petty pride yet quite enuf of the nobler sort; ambition is as natural to such a spirit as it is to that of the robust boy who has his fortune to make. Alice had the mental training and some of the luxuries of the educated and refined, but the locus of the stranded. For, tho she remembered better days,—a brother in college and college friends of his, one of whom still existed in her mind as the ideal youth, —yet the fortune of the family was not large and her social mates, including the brother and the ideal youth, were gone. Books and magazines were hers, and the echoes of a distant intellectual life, an exhilarating sense of the possibilities of her own nature; but a depressing sense of the probabilities of her future." [Century. **193**

ASPENDALE. [by HARRIET WATERS PRESTON: *Roberts*, 1871.] "The quiet currant of this tale follows 2 friends, Christine and Zoe, who have retired to a **New-England** village; and its main interest, as is usual in retired lives, is chiefly derived from the conversations and thôts which are set in the outer framework of the story." [Religious Magazine. **194**

AT DAYBREAK, [by "A. Stirling," i.e., ANNIE LYDIA (MCPHAIL) KIMBALL: *Osgood*, 1884.] "is a decidedly pleasant little novel—somewhat faulty in construction, but still containing nice people and written in agreeable language. It does not caricature, and exaggerates very little; it is thŏroly unpretentious: and it has an agreeable air of freshnesss and originality. The heroine is both sweet and natural and the story ends well." [Overland. **195**

AUTOBIOGRAPHY OF A NEW-ENGLAND FARM-HOUSE, The [by N. H. CHAMBERLAIN: *Carleton*, 1865.] "The value of this portraiture of **New-England** life and associations lies in the charm of old romance, which Mr. Chamberlain, a late convert from Unitarianism, and the rector of a Connecticut parish, has thrown into stern Puritanism. What Kingsley has done to throw a fascination around the Puritan maiden, he has done to soften the hardness with which we regard life in New-England. It is a less skilful pen he holds than Hawthorne's, but the delineation is often as exquisite. Mr. Chamberlain has done in prose what Longfellow has done in the 'Courtship of Miles Standish.' He has not attempted the impossible thing, as did Sylvester Judd in his 'Margaret;' but he has painted the familiar scenes and incidents of the country life of to-day, and of a century ago, with poetical feeling and a delicate religious touch. He lacks just the indescribable something to make him a poet, but his prose is all the better because he is not a poet. The book has its limitations, and a large class of persons—the realists—will be entirely disappointed in it; the other class—who like the home-touches of Whittier and the dreaminess of Longfellow—will be delited with it. The volume is open, too, to severe criticism; it is much disjointed; it tends to mannerism in style; the story is incomplete and unsatisfactory." [Church Monthly. **196**

BASSETT CLAIM, The, [by H: RUTHERFORD ELLIOT: *Putnam*, 1884.] "is a story of Washington life with the usual setting of legislative intrigues kept well in the background, while the real interest depends upon the loves of young men and women, and the struggles of the former to get on in the world. The story is very simple and very natural, with just a dash of mystery at the end to give it a romantic flavor. The people one meets in its pages make no pretence of being anything more than ordinary human beings, with some knowledge and cultivation, and as a consequence turn out to be very pleasant acquaintances. The most pleasant one of all, perhaps, is old Tom Bassett. This kindly old gentleman's influence is seen here and there throuout, tho he dies almost at the opening of the story, with the title of his bill, 'for the relief of old Tom Bassett,' upon his lips. His long life had been spent mainly in efforts to have his and the other French-Spoliation claims paid, and the brevity of the few touches with which the genial impression of him is given adds to its distinctness The whole story, in fact, is told with a directness, with now and then a vein of spritly humor. which relieve a somewhat open and ineffective plot. With more sombre treatment it would have proved wearisome; for there is nothing absorbing in the fact that old Tom's great-nefew should go to **Washington** to help forward the claim; nor that his mother and sister should follow him; nor that he should fancy himself in love with a pretty girl, be jilted, and forget her; nor even in the fact that his college chum should have been all along in love with Miss Bassett, and finally mary her. But these simple elements are so well developed that, with the frequency of lively conversation and epigrams, and the slit air of mystery, and the charm about Miss Sheffield, the story is never dull. [Nation. **197**

BETTER TIMES, [by ELLEN [WARNER] (OLNEY) KIRK: *Ticknor*, 1889.] "One of the best is 'The Story of a Silk Dress.'—It has so much variety of incident, such fertility of invention, so free an infusion of humor and humorous situations, and so happy a sketching of quaint characters, that it would bear, we think, to be arranged as a 'parlor comedy', and would be very much more lively and interesting than many offered us in that guise. The one which gives title to the volume, 'Better Times,' is full of dramatic situations, a strong, earnest story. 'These Tales,' the author says in a brief Prefatory Note, "were written in the better times when she was younger, and when stories made themselves out of instinct and sympathy, rather than from experience or observation, and when painstaking realism was not thôt of';

but it must not be supposed from this that they have not been carefully constructed, or that they lack a true art." [Amer. **198**

BONNYBOROUGH [by ADELINE DUTTON (TRAIN) WHITNEY: *Houghton*, 1886.] "is a worthy successor to 'The Wide, Wide World' and other 'talky' books, in which the characters made muffins, invented new readings of Bible texts injected into New-England slang, and were generally harmless idiots with a mania." [Catholic World.] "Four people in it are eventually maried; but besides courtships, with the usual amount of allegory baffling the intelligence of even quite sentimental critics, there seems singularly little for one, in the slang of the day, 'to catch on' to. There is page after page, chapter after chapter, of village gossip, or picnics, or nice little meals, or heart-rending analysis of motive, and quite incomprehensible metafor and simile; but there seems much less of the charm which Mrs. Whitney used to infuse even into her wildest soarings into the Infinite or divings into the Eternal."—[Critic.] "It contains the usual exasperating quantity of affectations, epigrams, ejaculations, clasping of hands dramatically over small matters, which have been long destroying, in the esteem of critical people, the work of a writer who once promised so well. There is thôt underneath all this, and Mrs. Whitney's people are always alive; but the growth of this disastrous sentimentalism and mannerism upon her have sadly alienated many who started in hopefully with her in the day of 'Faith Gartney' and 'Leslie Goldthwaite'." (No. 149) [Overland. **199**

BOSTONIANS, The, [by H: JAMES: *Macmillan*, 1886.] "To speak after the manner of Mr. James' distressingly conscientious characters, I am not sure that it is quite rit for anyone to read 'The Bostonians' throu, so long as anything useful or entertaining remains to be done on earth. An anomalous young Southerner gradually falls in love with a young girl of uncanny, sibylline eloquence and charlatanic parentage. He has for his chief rival an unwholesome Boston spinster of disordered nerves who turns tragical over the fear that her friend of friends may make common cause with the tyrant-man. A featureless collector of bric-à-brac would rather like to mary the heroine himself. The inevitable Europeanized young widow makes rather more ardent love to the hero. He fails in a very interesting way as a lawyer, a magazinist, and a child's tutor. He proses, she proses, all prose. At last there is an altogether superfluous elopement, with hints that the happy couple will starve before long, unless they can live on her inspiration and his political recalcitrancy. That is about all, except elaborate pictures of corner groceries, cheap lodging-houses, and other things of like interest." [Lippincott's] "Another chapter of 'The Bostonians' is kindly supplied by "HENRIETTA JAMES," in a tiny pamflet [Bloomfield, N. J.: *S. M. Hulin*.] The author is quite rit in feeling that the true interest of the Tarrant-Ransom affair lay, not in how Ransom won Miss Tarrant, but in how they 'got on' after he had won her. It is not impossible that the author is also rit in thinking that they did not 'get on' at all; that Mr. Ransom finally ran away with Mrs. Luna, leaving Mrs. Ransom to go back with her baby to Olive Chancellor, take up her life-work again, and finally mary Burrage." [Critic. **200**

BREAD-WINNERS, The [by J: HAY: *Harper*, 1884.] "Altho 'The Bread-Winners' is called a 'social study' the writer seems to have brôt to his task strong preconceptions, not to say prejudices, and adhered to them throuôut the story with a rigid consistency which does not belong to actual life. He shows everywhere the careful observation not of a humorist, or even of a man of the world to whom class-differences, all outside manifestations of human beings, are characteristic and suggestive, but of a man of fastidious taste who has been forced into over-close contact with coarse habits and ruf talk and shrunk back from them in disgust. Were this an every-day story, the author's prepossessions would be a matter of little importance. His all-conquering hero,

Farnham, gifted with every distinction and charm, wit, all unchallenged, put his foot on the neck of the dragon he so easily destroys, and win the plaudits of his admirers. But, dealing as he does with a serious problem like that which the labor question presents, one is surprised to find a clever author, whose wit is accurate and whose experience seems to have been something actual, apparently slighting the claims of his subject." [Lippincott's.] "But the most vital contribution to the social study, if not the central figure in the whole composition, is the carpenter's dauter, Maud Matchin. To the gallery of national types—thus far a very limited one, she forms a distinct and significant addition. Those who have noticed the type will recognize at once the veracity of this representation; and those who are not familiar with it will understand, from the decision with which she is modeled, that Maud is no make-believe creature. A beautiful, hard, sordid, and commonplace girl, whose mind is warped by wild desires for social advancement, she is the exponent as well as the victim of a badly regulated education in the public schools. In this instance, the author has suggested unflinchingly, and with a great deal of discernment, one of the most curious and perplexing fenomena in that condition of things which is known as American civilization. Maud is not a pleasant person to contemplate, but she is alarmingly real; and her destiny, in marying a falsely acquitted murderer, very likely intimates only the tithe of the evil which development of that sort of character is accomplishing. Against the discouraging and possibly exaggerated background in which these coarser personages move, the author sets his hero, Farnham, and his heroine, Alice Belding, with her worldly, well-disposed but somewhat blunt-minded mother, surrounded by a group of outlined figures who stand for society in [Cleveland.] It may be said in passing that the tone and characteristics of a town or 'city' of that description are conveyed by this novelist almost to perfection,—a thing

which, so far as we remember, no one has even attempted to do before." [Atlantic.   **201**

BRETON MILLS, The, [by C: Jo. BELLAMY: *Putnam*, 1879.] "comes near being a really powerful story. The author calls it a romance, and therefore disallows being called to a strict account for knowledge of human nature or probable succession of events; but it is a pity, since he has experience and ability to do as well as he does in the earlier part of the book, that he should not have bestirred himself to do a really good piece of work. As it is, the story is like a chimera, which begins with a human figure and ends with arabesque. The Breton Mills are apparently woolen mills, owned by one man. There are 1000 work-people in these mills, and the interest of the book consists in the exposition of the poverty of the operatives and the imperious will of the owner—one aspect of the strife between labor and capital. There are powerful pieces of description. The burning of the mill, with the varying instincts and influences acting on the operatives, who could have saved it but do not, is very dramatic, and the cautious endeavor on the part of Philip Breton to deal justly and kindly, when he inherits the mill property, with the early gratitude and subsequent discontent of 'the hands' is well described; but the heroine of the love-story is an impossible creature, who elopes with an eloquent 'workingman's orator,' lives with him for more than a year, and then returns to her father's house to be as much as ever the 'idol and the fancy's queen' of Philip Breton. He maries her with enthusiasm, in spite of the gravest doubts as to her reputation, and presently flings up all his plans, gets rid of his mills, and flees with his wife to Europe, since the speech and the looks of those around express contempt for her. This is a lame and impotent conclusion, resembling the fall rather than the rise of the rocket. Nevertheless the book is worth reading for its insit into the life of the workers with their hands. There is exaggeration and incoherence in the style, but there is also some knowledge and some sympathy." [Nation. **202**

BROUGHTON HOUSE, The [by BLISS PERRY: *Scribner*, 1890.] "is one of the least ambitious of stories——almost without plot or movement of the usual kind, and yet full of the interest which character always inspires. It is a bit of genre painting—quiet and delicate like 'Cranford,' with humor and pathos just rippling the placid surface. The Village of Broughton is in **New-England** [Berkshire county] far enuf from the railway to preserve its rural simplicity. There is 'a level half-mile of elm-arched street,' with the great white Congregational church at one end, and the Academy building at the other. Midway between them, the broad, grassy street widens into a gravelled space in front of the village inn, The Broughton House." [Life. **203**

BROWNS, The, [by M.. PRUDENCE (WELLS) SMITH: *Roberts*, 1884.] "is the simple and pretty story of some brit. pleasant and sensible people, not too brit and good for human nature's daily food. It is by the author of 'Jolly Good Times,' [No. 64] and if not exactly 'jolly' itself, is 'good' and pleasing." [Critic. **204**

BURGLARS IN PARADISE [by E.. S. (PHELPS) WARD: *Houghton*, 1886.] "is a continuation of 'An Old Maid's Paradise' [☞ No. **103**] that having been an idyl, while this is mostly comedy. The author mixes burlesque with realism, so that in the midst of reading what Corona, or Puelvir, or Matthew Launcelot, really did, related with delicate truth to character, you are told with an unchanged air of simple veracity of something which of course they did not do, but only approximated. There is no danger of deceiving the unwary, but there is of mixing flavors incongruously." [Overland. **205**

BUTTON'S INN. [by A. W. TOURGEE: *Roberts*, 1887.] "The story of itself really has a genuine and wholesome interest, and one follows the fortunes of Dolly Button and her two worthy, generous lovers with a feeling which grows to be personal and warm-hearted. The success

in life of the hero is not fenomenal nor undeserved, and there is not one who has the true american spirit who will think any the less of him for attempting and achieving it. In fact, the modern spirit all over the world deems the man who does not want money as materially defective, and would vote Plutarch's words in praise of Coriolanus, that 'it is the hier accomplishment to use money well than arms; but not to need it is more noble than to use it' entirely obsolete." [Nation. **206**

CARPET KNIGHT, A. [by "HARFORD FLEMMING" i. e., HARRIET (HARE) MCCLELLAN: *Houghton*, 1885.] "The charm of the book,—for charm it has,—is in its reproduction of refined manners and those slit shades of difference in personality which our modern conventional life affords. The story is slit,—we are bound to say that it is no more bewildering than the streets of the city [**Philadelphia**] in which its scenes are laid; but as he reads one grows lazily indifferent to the mere plot, and finds himself taking a cheerful interest in the several persons of the story. It is something to have a story of American society which is as amiable and smooth as much of our urban society is. In its way it reinforces one's confidence in good manners. One is reminded that the ordinary amenities of life are not disregarded. He may know this well enuf from his experience, but he will scarcely know it from current fiction; and so, while 'A Carpet Knight' will not stir his soul or take him into a hily analyzed circle of human beings, it will leave him with the comfortable feeling that he has passed an agreeable evening in society without the necessity of dressing his tired body and bracing his mind for the purpose." [Atlantic.]—"In the 'Carpet Knight' not a trace of rational purpose is discoverable. It is made up of chatter: to call it conversation were profanity. This chatter is pretty evenly distributed among a dozen or so of people who live in Philadelphia, and one or two who go thither occasionally from Boston and New-Rochelle, whence they were doubtless temporarily exiled by nebors having a share of that irascibility which accompanies moderate intelligence. It is barely possible that the author had an inspiring idea—no other than to sing again the joys and splendors of the 'Assembly,' a sacred institution for which, as is well known in polite circles, Philadelphia exists." [Nation. **207**

CECIL DREEME, [by THEO. WINTHROP: *Ticknor*, 1861.] "The incidents of the novel occur in some of the best known localities of **New-York**. Nobody can mistake Chuzzlewit Hotel and Chrysalis College. Every traveler has put up at the first and visited some literary or artistic friend at the second. Indeed, Winthrop seems to have deliberately chosen the localities of his story with the special purpose of showing that passions almost as terrible as those which are celebrated in the tragedies of Aiskulos and Sophokles may rage in the ordinary lodging-houses of New-York. He has succeeded in throwing an atmosfere of mystery over places which are essentially commonplace; and he has done it by the intensity with which he has conceived and represented the eternal thôts, struggles, and emotions of the men and women by whom these edifices are inhabited." [Atlantic. **208**

CHANTICLEER: A THANKSGIVING STORY. [by CORNELIUS MATHEWS: Boston, *Munsey & Co.*, 1850.] "That a period which—apart from its hier purposes—is consecrated to good eating and drinking should be likewise celebrated by an appropriate literary offering, is a very happy idea. which Mr. Mathews has pleasantly carried out. Our yearly festival of Thanksgiving is connected with all those cherished recollections of youth which neither grow dim with age nor become obliterated by the ceaseless turmoil of this anxious life. It serves to recall the home of early days, the faces and haunts and cheerful gatherings of childhood; the friends and relatives who sat around the festive board in bygone times, whose memory is held in effectionate reverence now. 'Chanticleer' is not exactly what may be called a child's book, and yet it is intended

to appeal to the hearts of the young; to teach a lesson which shall penetrate deeply, and make a lasting impressing; to enlist their sympathies in the cause of truth and justice, and to lead them, by identifying themselves with the personages of the story, to make a suitable application. The characters in this interesting little narrative are all evidently drawn from nature, and faithfully portray a class in **New-England** which has existed since its early settlement, and which we trust may be fairly represented for many long years to come." [Round Table. **209**

CHEZZLES, The. [by LUCY GIBBONS MORSE: *Houghton*, 1888.] "This is one of the freshest and in every way most delitful books for young people, or rather about young people,—for it will be read with equal delit by persons of all ages,—which we have seen in a long time. It is in brief the history of a very agreeable family of **New-England** folk, some of them located for the time in France, the chief characters being certain children whose intelligence and vivacity give a bubbling charm to the volume from the first page to the last. As in the best works of this nature, 'The Chezzles' has a not too intricate yet definite story to tell. The character drawing is touched with really hi art." [American. **210**

CHILDREN OF OLD PARK'S TAVERN, The [by F.. A. HUMPHREY: *Harper*, 1886.] "is a very pleasant story of the 'South Shore' of **Massachusetts** as it was in the stage-coach days, when Webster was a member of political conventions, and children with old-fashioned names played old-fashioned games and held their elders in due respect. Dolly and Ned will delit the hearts of all rit thinking young people. Their youthful adventures about the quaint old tavern and among the woods and marshes will interest young readers whose tastes have not been vitiated." [Nation. **211**

CHILD OF THE CENTURY, A [by J: T. WHEELWRIGHT: *Scribner*, 1887.] "This clever story is full of genuine humor, and not without several portentous morals. The child of the century is a Boston lawyer, who, at the age of 30, after a life of seclusion and hard work, resolves on an outing, and in the transatlantic passage finds his plans for the study of Dante seriously interfered with by the presence of a certain black-eyed dauter of a Cincinnati clothing dealer. Sewell falls in with various types of the traveling american, and they are all admirably depicted. When he comes back he 'runs for Congress' in a contest which many readers will regard as historical. Political life in **Washington**, as well as the social features of that city, are skillfully treated." [Boston "Lit. World." **212**

CHILDREN OF THE EARTH, [by ANNIE ROBERTSON (MACFARLANE) LOGAN: *Holt*, 1886.] "is a very original and deeply interesting novel, full of plot, incident, spirited talk and character, and never too improbable for belief. It deals with that question—decidedly of the earth, earthy—which novelists would much better leave entirely alone unless they can treat it as well as it has been treated here: the old, old problem of confused love and duty, passion and law. . . . The extreme cleverness, and the innate nobleness of this conception, are hardly appreciated on the first reading, when the reader is absorbed in the interest of the book as a mere story; but the fineness of it, as a study of human nature, makes it really a striking study of the conflict between good and evil." [Critic. **213**

COLONEL DUNWODDIE, MILLIONAIRE [by W: MUMFORD BAKER: *Harper*, 1878.] "is a story of **Southern** life since the war, and it is Southern in spirit to heart's core; but we cannot imagine anything better fitted to warm the best hearts among us towards that devoted region than this revelation of what is in the best of theirs. . . . We are introduced to a hero who presently becomes as real to us as Col. Newcome, and hardly less dear; a chivalrous, fiery, faulty, tender soul, the outlines of whose character are so finely and firmly drawn for us, at the very outset, that all his previous

and all his subsequent career, every act, word, project, chimera, blunder, and triumf, become logical, natural, necessary." [Atlantic. **214**

COLONEL'S OPERA CLOAK, The, [by CHRISTINE (CHAPLIN) BRUSH: *Roberts*, 1879.] "is simple and direct, using an odd garment in the possession of a hand-to-mouth Southern family as a leading thread, and setting out neither to instruct nor to astonish, but simply to amuse. It is also a character-sketch of shiftless Southern people in Northern cities. . . . Leslie St. John, the heroine, sets out to be nothing more than a sweet, affectionate little maid, and, in being that, satisfies the reader, as well as Tom Douglas." [Scribner's. **215**

COLOR STUDIES [by T: ALLIBONE JANVIER: *Scribner*, 1885.] "Piquant, novel and ingenious, these little stories, with all their simplicity, have excited a wide interest. The best of them, 'Jaune d'Antimoine' is a little wonder in its dramatic effect, its ingenious construction, its happy combination of exquisite comedy with the intensity which touches the deepest springs of sympathy. The touch is at once so delicate and so funny, so intellectual, and so lâfable, that to read the story is to give one's self an hour of very keen enjoyment." [Critic.] "While each story is complete in itself there is an ingenious dovetailing of interest and character which makes it almost a continuous work. 'Rose' and her delitful old father, and 'Vandyke Brown,' whom she maries, and several others, appear throughout the series, taking, after their own adventures have been given in detail, an appropriately lower place to the fresh characters introduced. The lucky title expresses the idea exactly. The stories are all illustrative of american artist life, and we risk nothing in saying that the theme has never been touched with a surer, neater hand. The trials of young painters in their hard period of obtaining recognition, the easy-going life of the studios, the air of the picture galleries and the bohemian living rooms, are all litly yet pointedly indicated by Mr. Janvier, with that other insistence upon honest love, which makes the world go round for painters as for meaner folk. There is very pleasant humor; the dialog is so good that we wish there was more of it. In work of this kind everything should be sharp, quick, rit on the spot. It is a delitful little book." [American.] "It is refreshing to be able to say a word of hearty, thankful praise about a volume containing 4 short stories by Mr. Janvier. Novelists and critics are continually bewailing the dearth of materials for romance in America, most conspicuously in **New-York**. Mr. Janvier convinces us that the needful matter is all about us, and that only the eye to see, the heart to feel, and the tung to express have been lacking. His simple, kindly stories are fragments of the romance of Greenwich Village, of Fourth Street and crooked Tenth Street, and of all the region about Jefferson Market. His characters are chiefly toiling disciples of art, and in their delineation the ideal and real are very skilfully blended." [Nation.] "'These 'Color Studies' are cleverly written, quaintly humorous, and unaffected in style. Notwithstanding their unpretentiousness they introduce us to real people of the sort whom it is a pleasure to know, and whose lives and surroundings are invested with a more than fleeting interest." [Boston "Lit. World." **216**

CONECUT CORNERS. [N. Y., *Mason*, 1855.] "A novel of **New-England** life, in which DR. LYMAN ABBOTT joined hands with his brothers B: V. and Austin." [Boston "Lit. World." **217**

CONVENTIONAL BOHEMIAN, A, [by EDMUND PENDLETON: *Appleton*, 1886.] "is a society novel, but the average society novel is many things which it is not. . . The only suggestion of the antique is in the leading lady, who is introduced at the advanced age of 30. . . The old girl has long suffered the neglect or contempt of novelists. She is between the young-girl and the old-maid. She never had the ingenuousness of the one; she never can have the inflexibility of the other. The moral severity common to both is impossible to her. If she had maried young, she would still be 'young Mrs. So-and-So'. If she ever does mary, she is virtually the old girl still. So the old girl whom the conventional bohemian takes to illumine the domestic hearth remains the reckless, whimsical, unscrupulous Angèle Wentworth. He realized, too late, that perhaps the only situation in life where the old girl cannot rally her forces and shine is by the domestic hearth. There is no good in trying to depict the old girl as a lovable person in life, or a person who, in fiction, can attract the sympathies of rit-minded persons. The author has not tried so to depict Angèle. . . Except in the glibness of their talk, none of the people are literary figures. They are real. . . But, on the whole, the novel is clever and entertaining. It is so singularly free from cant that it may be deemed immoral by the multitude who still confound freedom from cant and hypocrisy with immorality. The author's range of thôt and, perhaps, of sympathy has been limited by his horizon of observation; but, as far as the thôt and the sympathy go, they are clear and warm. In the balance of judgment, the courage of opinion, the passion and conviction of some chapters, lies the promise of work of wider scope and more catholic application." [Nation. **218**

COUNTER-CURRENTS [by SOPHIE WINTHROP WEITZEL: *Roberts*, 1889.] "is a brit, piquant little book whose scene opens in **Southern California,** and the life of tourists and health-seekers in that favorite region of the fruit, the flower, and the vine is agreeably described. Along with these travel sketches is developed a lively love story, four young people are thrown together, whose fates their friends and families have already allotted. This admirable arrangement is upset by the spontaneous awakening in the mind of each of the four of a genuine passion. Change about is fair play, and Dorothy and Sidney find their destinies each in the other, and Fletcher and Elinor ultimately come together. But there is more in the well-told story than this. Both Fletcher and Elinor fail to find in their daily lives an outlet for their best energies, and an answer to their deepest problems. How Fletcher rejects the too-easy, over-pleasant existence which is urged upon him, and after suffering, aspiration, and struggle makes a career for himself in which he feels that he can do good, is well worth a perusal. In fact, 'Counter Currents' is a brave, honest, little book with ideas in it, and ôt to find many readers." [American] "A pleasant story of contemporaneous life, in which simplicity of style, good taste, and an agreeable optimism render one for a while not very exacting of the author." [Atlantic. **219**

CRANSTON HOUSE. [by HANNAH ANDERSON ROPES: Boston, Otis Clapp, 1859.] "A touching story of suffering, struggle, and triumf over difficulties. Sallie and Peter, around whom the interest of the story gathers intensely as it proceeds, are two beautiful characters drawn with admirable skill. We are stronger and better for having known and loved 'Aunt Mary', even in idea. The book has the rare merit of being a novel whose interest is unflagging from the opening chapter to the close, and of illustrating at the same time the hïest spiritual truths, as shown in practical life. You may read it for recreation in a leisure hour, or for cheer and comfort in the path of duty, or of both together; and there are not many books of the class which will perform a more beneficent use." [Religious Magazine. **220**

CRAQUE-O'-DOOM. [by M.. (HART-WELL) CATHERWOOD: Lippincott, 1881.] "A capital story ... quite uncommonplace, following the social fortunes of a young girl who is lifted out of the lowest conditions of birth and intelligence into a fine character and hï station, all throu the notice, the insït, and the love of a rich and cultivated man, a cripple, who sees 'the angel in the marble.' The scene and characters are thoroly american, and the treatment fresh and original." [Boston "Lit. World." **221**

DAISY. [Continuation of "Melbourne House"; Lippincott, 1868.] "Daisy Randolph, like her predecessors, Ellen Montgomery, Elfleda Ringgau, and the rest of them, is a too good little girl, who makes a triumful passage from infancy to maidenhood, discomfiting sinners, fascinating and confounding the ungodly with sit of so much saintliness in so small a space, and not only only earning a title to the goods of the next world, but gaining a more than tolerably fair share of those distributed in this. Most people who read novels know what and how Miss Warner writes ... With a sweet pathos she recounts her sorrow at finding her father not quite up to her standard of goodness, her trials and prayers over the multiplication table, the yearnings of her spirit over her 700 slaves, and the good effects on them of the prayer-meeting which she established in her kitchen, presiding herself at the mature age of 11 years, and, as she says, impressing them with the keenest sense of her immeasurable superiority." [Nation. **222**

DARKNESS AND DAYLIGHT [by M.. J.. (HAWES) HOLMES: Derby, 1850?] "It is hard to understand how Mrs. Holmes ever came to be ranked among those authors whose rit to a place on the shelves of public libraries has been disputed. She has written somewhat of Southern life. but most of her scenes are in New-England. There is, however, very little local coloring to them, and the dramatic interest is slit. In spite of her literary failings, there is a certain smoothness of narration and lïtness of plot which have made her a very popular writer, particularly with girls and young women. The aggregate sale of all her books is stated to be about half a million, some reaching a sale of more than 50.000 each. Her own words furnish the truest commentary on what she has done or tried to do. She says: 'I try to avoid the sensational, and never deal in murders, or robberies, or ruined young girls; but rather in domestic life as I know it to exist. I mean always to write a good, pure, natural story, such as mothers are willing their dauters should read, and such as will do good instead of harm.' Among her best are 'Lena Rivers,' 'Meadow Brook,' 'Darkness and Daylight,' and 'Edith Lyle.' We notice that her name is on the tabooed list sent out by the American Library Association. [Boston "Lit. World." **223**

DAUGHTER OF BOHEMIA. [by "CHRISTIAN REID:" i. e., F.. E. (FISHER) TIERNAN: *Appleton*, 1874.] "The scene is laid in the **South.** The characters are for the most part Southerners—the young woman engaged to the young man, the chattering widow, the peaceful Mr. and Mrs. Middleton: not that there is anything specially Southern about them; they are like well-bred people the world over. The other characters are Captain Max Tyndale and Miss Norah Desmond; the last named is the dauter of Bohemia. We shall give no analysis of the story: it well deserves reading, not only for its plot, but also for the clever manner in which it is told, and, in great measure, for the excellent way in which the characters, and particularly the women, are drawn: Leslie Graham, with her amiable, affectionate, honest nature, is well described, and in excellent contrast is Norah—good, too, but in another way." [Atlantic.] "Like all "Christian Reid's" books, this is a strained, exaggerated picture of unreal life. Its personages are in a state of chronic nervous tension, loving or hating—usually hating—with a vehemence which must ultimately injure their fysical health . . . Miss Reid's personages are singularly devoid of originality and vivacity, and resemble well-dressed and decorous puppets, manipulated by a not too skilful hand." [Boston "Lit. World." **224**

DEACON'S WEEK. The. [by ROSE (TERRY) COOKE: *Putnam*, 1884.] "This small, paper-covered volume, contains one of the best of Mrs. Cooke's stories, illustrated. All people who love the old ways in **New-England,** and who have ever "been to meetin" there—especially to "protracted meetin",—will appreciate Deacon Emmons' Christian fortitude in relating his week's experience, and Mrs. Cooke's fine sense of New-England humor in re-

porting the protracted "meeting". The characters are well drawn and r icy. The illustrations, moreover, are quite as good in their way as the story." [Critic.] See, also, No. 142. **225**

DEARLY BOUGHT [by CLARA L.. (ROOT) BURNHAM: *Sumner*, 1884.] "is a love story, of course, and there are 2 or 3 lines of love-making running throu it side by side; but they do not blur the effect, and the individuality of the characters and the separateness of their action are well preserved. The central interest is furnished by the relations between Lenore Fayette and her aunt Deborah Belden, with whom she has come to live in quiet Alderley, an elm-shaded town, 2 hours' ride or so from **Philadelphia.** .. Lenore has a hard time with Aunt Deborah, but a pleasant time in Alderley, where there is an agreeable set of people, including several persons who become favorites, and 1 or 2 curiosities. Among the latter is Hepsy Nash, who lived as 'help' at Elmdale from the time she was 14; and chief of the former is Dr. Lemist, who attends Lenore in more than a merely professional capacity, and gives her at last a prescription which she is glad to take. . . The writing is good. It is neither soft, stiff, affected, nor artificial. The dialog is lifelike and natural. There is an unconsciousness and simplicity about the style which are quite refreshing; a composure and reserve of power which belong to real ability." [Boston "Lit. World." **226**

DEBUTANTE IN NEW-YORK SOCIETY, A. [by RACHAEL BUCHANAN: *Appleton*, 1888.] "Yet the heroine, altho she has a nice sense of the minor refinements of life, is neither frivolous nor altogether worldly. She has a keen perception of the real meaning of life,—cares for the what as well as the how, for realities as well as the shining varnish. Thus with these intimations of her possessing a really firm character, we are a little surprised at the worldly prudence she exhibits in throwing over the 'lover who half wins her heart because he is poor. She is, in fact, a very good type of the modern **New-York** girl, who distrusts traditions of love in a cottage, and likes to have a steam yacht and a cottage at Newport. What strikes us painfully in this rose-colored account of fashionable society, is that such well-bred people, in spite of their elegance and fastidiousness, are compelled to live on the perilous verge of vulgarity and to consort with vulgar people. From the necessity of making rich mariages there seems to be no way to avoid familiarity with people who murder the queen's english." [American.]—"There is no kind of fiction so silly or so profitless as this. Most of the kind are at once offensive and ridiculous, but the Débutante is only tiresome, crude and very 'fresh.'" [Nation. **227**

DEMOCRACY. [*Holt*, 1880.] "Its aim, which is not well represented by its title, is to depict the political society of **Washington**, the characteristics of the class which cabals and manœuvres for the possession of office and power. These characteristics are all embodied in the person of senator Ratcliffe, the other figures of the same class, including the newly-elected president, being either his tools.or his victims, are much more faintly delineated. The heroine, Mrs. Lee. is a widow, rich, refined and intellectual, whose absorbed interest as a spectator brings her into close intercourse with Ratcliffe, and who is alternately fascinated and repelled by his bold, astute and unscrupulous course. Her own conduct, and the danger of her marrying Ratcliffe and becoming an instrument of his ambition, arouses the solicitude of her sister and of a chivalrous friend, a Virginian of the old school, who cherishes a secret and hopeless love for her; and the combined efforts of the two to save her from Ratcliffe's designs form the undercurrent of the action and bring about the dénouement. Among the minor characters having little or nothing to do with the plot are a couple of forein envoys, lord Skye and baron Jacobi, whose comments serve as a kind of chorus, and Miss Virginia Dare, who typifies the peculiarities of the american young lady as

displayed in society. These are sufficiently good elements for a story distinctively and charactistically american, and they are handled with considerable skill. There is no lack of continuity in the action, no dullness in the description, no sign of languor, indecision, or want of clear perception in the management of the story or in the writing. The style is crisp and pointed, the conversations are generally entertaining, there are many vigorous sketches of characters and scenes, and many touches, if not of humor, of a piquancy that may pass for wit. . . . 'Democracy' is at once a more brilliant and a more realistic novel than "Through One Administration"; it was, in fact written with a more distinct purpose. The writer had a clear vision, and seized the most salient types of American political men and presented them with a swift smiting word. . . . 'Democracy' is, however, full of epigrammatic touches which suggest humor without being exactly humorous, and show an enjoyment of the subject itself, besides a racy appreciation of the author's cleverness in treating it. There is, too, a delicate literary aroma in 'Democracy' not to be found in an equal degree in 'The Bread Winners.' But the two books are not without many points in common, and the writer of each has the advantage of a clear perception of what he has to say and the wit to make others understand it as clearly." [Lippincott's.]—"It will be remembered that the point on which 'Democracy' turns is the discovery that the heroine that the Secretary and ex-Senator had accepted a bribe, and that she came to this knowledge throu the revelation of "Carrington," who was the confidant of "Mrs. Samuel Baker," to whom as his widow, the said "Baker," a notorious lobbyist, had left his papers, among which were some that told the story of the Senator's rascality. The latter is aware that this secret of his is known to "Carrington" and therefore interests himself in getting him out of the way, and succeeds in inducing a brother Secretary to send him to Mexico. Now for the coincidence, which can be verified by any one who will consult the Springfield *Republican* of April 13, 1880, page 4, the period referred to being that of the District of Columbia ring; "He (Huntington) died, and left in his wife's hands a lot of papers, among which were some which interested Mr. Blaine. These papers were passed by Mrs. Huntington to a young man named Frank Gassaway. Mr. Blaine became greatly interested in Mr. Gassaway's welfare, and sôt numerous important appointments successfully for him. He finally obtained for him a Government position in California." [Corres. "Nation," 1884. **228**

DEVIL'S HAT, The [by MELVILLE PHILIPS: *Ticknor*, 1887] "is a story of the **Pennsylvania** oil regions, overflowing with local color; indeed the story—which is slit enuf, but told with intelligence and good-breeding, and quite out of the ordinary line in plot—seems used chiefly as an excuse for descriptions of the oilmining. The title does not indicate any Satanic legend in the story, the 'Devil's Hat' was only the name given to a hatshaped hill, in which the hero of the story sunk his well." [Overland. **229**

DI CARY. [by M. JACQUELINE THORNTON: *Appleton*, 1879.] "We have here a delineation of the fortunes, or misfortunes, of Southern life at the close of the war, during the period of reconstruction. The scenes are natural and life-like, and the general effect is good. We have said Southern life; we mit better have said Virginian, for it is the Old Dominion which mostly furnishes the material. The tone of the author is enthusiastically loyal to the genius of **Virginia,** but the spirit and temper of the work are excellent throuôut. Its literary merit is above the average." [Boston "Lit. World." **230**

DIVORCE [by MARGARET LEE: *Lovell*, 1883.] "is a study of certain fâses of contemporary american life which is Trollopean in its abject, literal fidelity. The 'milieu' she has chosen is intensely respectable. Her people are rich, but not too rich. They mingle in 'good' society and live on Fifth Avenue, tho none of them

enter that **New-York** empyrean composed of 'the 400' best families. They are all christians—even the villain of the piece "is a member of our church, he is in a good business, he sings exquisitely." There is nowhere throuôut the volume any attempt made after brilliancy in conversation or what is called cleverness in narrative or description. The conversations, nevertheless, have, besides the very great merit of naturalness, that of continuously forwarding the progress of the story at the same time that they elucidate and bring out character. . . . Constance, while a most charming character, is yet not so rare a type. On a solid foundation of the virtues natural to the élite of her sex, purity, sincerity, lovingness, there has been reared a solid superstructure of the supernatural virtues. She maries a man whom she wholly admires, and loves intensely and unselfishly. He gives her in return the biest feelings of which he is capable. Even in betraying her confidence, in squandering her fortune, in descending at the last to vulgar brutality and the long deceit involved in getting a 'Connecticut divorce' from her, he never loses his consciousness of her superiority nor his absolute trust in her undying love for him. What he does is simply to live out his own nature, as she does hers." [Catholic World. **231**

DR. HEIDENHOFF'S PROCESS. [by E: BELLAMY: *Appleton*, 1880.] "The story opens with a realistic sketch of a village prayer-meeting, at which a young man who was known as a penitent thief and a sincerely reformed sinner, but who had apparently never forgiven himself, rises at the last moment to relate a fâse of his experience. The confession of which this is the end makes the little congregation uncomfortable, but they pass out into the air, and among them go a young man named Henry Burr and a young woman, the village coquette, Madeline Brand. . . The village tragedy changes for a time the course of youthful life, but soon that is resumed in its customary form, and in the frolic of the summer Henry and Madeline are brôt to the verge of betrothal. Just at this point, however, a disturbing element appears in the arrival from the city of a young clerk, who brings a supposed hier degree of civility, and the coquette begins her arts upon him. Henry is driven to despair, and leaves the village for the city where he tries to take up a fresh life. He is drawn back by his sincere love only to find that the clerk has achieved a base victory over the coquette, has deserted her, and that she has fled to the city in her shame. He returns at once and after a long search finds her, and then begins his heroic effort to reinstate her. He gives her his love still, but she in her dullness has nothing but a miserable gratitude to offer him. She allows him to remain her friend, and she has no love left for her betrayer. His calm persistence makes Henry a pure and unattainable saint in her eyes, and at length her indifference and her dull languor give place to a sense of her own unworthiness, and because she loves him she resolves to destroy herself. . . So skillfully has the author managed the dream, suppressing the grotesqueness in the conception of Dr. Heidenhoff, that, in spite of the somewhat uncanny nature of the subject, one has only to be thoroly interested in Madeline to go along with the story in simple credulity. Scarcely, however, has his mind become adjusted to the situation, before it is again rudely pained by the brief conclusion. A letter is at this moment brôt to Henry. It is Madeline's real good-by, before, like George Bayley, she seeks to plunge into the river of Lethe. The painfulness of the story is genuine. There remains in the reader's mind a tenderness for the girl, a profound sadness. The figure of Madeline throuoût the narrative is admirably sketched, and the change in her life is firmly and not sentimentally presented. Praise belongs also to the truthfulness of the picture which Mr. Bellamy draws of commonplace village life. There is no caricature and no sentimentalizing, but the rude love-making and limited intellectual life are given with a true touch. It often happens that a citi-

zen writing from recollection or observation of country life almost unconsciously offers some comparison between the two modes: there is nothing of that here. Mr. Bellamy writes like one of the villagers, yet with an intellectual power of selection which one only so bred would not have. We do not observe a false note in the realism of the story, and there is an abundance of felicitous touches." [Atlantic. **232**

DOCTOR JOHNS [by DONALD GRANT MITCHELL: *Scribner*, 1866.] "The period dates from the war of 1812 and reaches to 20 years ago. Mr. Mitchell draws upon memory, not imagination, for his materials. He has attempted to give the story of 'certain events in the life of an Orthodox minister of **Connecticut.**' It is not exactly a narrative of parish life, nor of public service; but starting from the humble parsonage in Ashfield, where Dr. Johns is the central figure, he weaves into the story from time to time such elements as set forth that home in all its features, and at the same time throws upon it enuf of the outside world to give a good background for his portraits. There are the Puritan minister in his austere theology; the Puritan spinster in her worldly primness; the goodnatured sinner called the Squire; the sharp, shrewd deacons; the aristocratic families; the headquarters of Satan at the village tavern; the factotum of a country doctor; the sharp-visaged, dyspeptic clerical brethren of néboring towns; the varying beauty and pleasant quiet of a New-England home. The author paints all this so that it stands before you in his pages. Then he introduces forein elements to contrast with the Puritan education. The unfortunate child of a college friend is taken to the parsonage to be brôt-up. This Adèle becomes the heroine of the book; she is one of those hasty, sensitive girls who can be found only in France, and her brit, quick, passionate life shows in all its hideous deformity the narrowness and imperfection of the Puritan kind of Christian nurture. There is also a glimpse of city scenes There are the delicate touches of life abroad. . . It is first the quiet village; then the breath of the world; then, the old village again where all are going to live and die. It is only a Connecticut village, not different 'for better for worse' from a hundred others; but in it there is life enuf to make a passionate story of 600 pages without even then using one half its materials. As for its characters, the great figure of Dr. Johns is foremost and central. He imposes the iron grasp of Puritanism upon every one; but he has a good heart nevertheless, and in spite of his religion there is a great soul of goodness in him, and men and women love him; and the little Adèle finds her way to his heart and she becomes to him as a daunter. Mr. Mitchell paints all these Congregational ministers with full allowance for the influence of what now seems a most arbitrary. severe, and soulless religious system. They were all men of whom more mit have been made, men who, thinking only of duty, made life a gloomy warfare with the Devil." [Church Monthly. **233**

DOCTOR SEVIER. [by G: W. CABLE: *Osgood*, 1884.] "The story of the book may be true, and so far reasonable—we make no point of that—but in its almost unrelieved pain it is disagreeably true, if true at all. . . It is depressing from first to last. It has no plot, and it is solely concerned with telling the pitiful story of 2 earnest young souls,—a husband and wife —who, by no amount or exercise of virtue, of labor and of self-denial, can get so much as standing place in this prosperous land, or not until the unequal struggle has resulted in a success as hard as defeat. . . The sketches of scenery, street life and manners in **New-Orleans** are wonderfully vivid. The time is the 5 years or so "befoh de wah"; and the period of the great struggle, and the feeling of that epoch is deftly indicated. . . But we fear Mr. Cable's love of dialect is forcing him to unpleasant extremes. There are irish, germans and italians in this book, who talk varieties of brogue." [American. **234**

DOCTOR WILMER'S LOVE [by

MARGARET· LEE: *Appleton*, 1868.]· "is a story which cannot fail to be attractive to the general reader. It contains enuf action to prevent weariness, a plot which is never intricate nor involved, and a range of characters of which each one possesses a distinct and individual interest. It is a simple but well-sustained narrative of the joys and sorrows, the aspirations and disappointments. the struggles and temptations, of which our present society furnishes daily examples. . . Altho the doctor is, of course, the principal personage in the book, he fairly divides the interest with the pure and gentle girl whose history commands our warmest sympathies. The main incidents of the story are such as mit readily come within the experience of a fysician. and the family may be congratulated whose members, from choice or accident. are enabled to rely for mental and bodily aid upon so conscientious and sympathetic a friend as Dr. Wilmer." [Round Table. **235**

DOCTOR'S DAUGHTER (The) [by "SOPHIE MAY," i. e. Rebecca Sophia Clarke: *Lee & Shepard*, 1872.] "is a little story of **New-England** country people. It does not call for rapturous applause, but it is certainly innocently and good-naturedly written." [Nation. **236**

DRONES' HONEY. [by "SOPHIE MAY," i.e., R.. S. Clarke: *Lee & Shepard*, 1887.] "The title of this pleasant little story is taken from a passage in Plato: 'When a young man has tasted drones' honey . . . then he returns into the country of the lotus-eaters.' But altho there is an idle and luxurious fellow, he is even at his climax of epicureanism a worthy and exemplary hero. He spends his summer in a quiet New-England village and plays not only an ornamental but a useful part at picnics and other social gatherings. So far from eating 'drones' honey,' he is a fair sample of a working bee so far as all polite obligations are concerned. There are few startling incidents in the book; but a vast amount of talking is done." [American.]—"It limps a little in plot perhaps; but it is good enuf to leave the reader touched and made thôtful as he lays it down, and for some time afterward. Two sweet and noble young women—the one beloved, the other not; the friendship existing between such women: these are the main figures, and the main topic; for the young man whom love leads him to abjure 'drones' honey' and become a worker in the world, is rather a figurehead, tho an appropriate and effective one. Narransane, the **Maine** village, is delitfully sketched." [Overland. **237**

EBB-TIDE. [by "CHRISTIAN REID," i. e., F.. E. (Fisher) Tiernan: *Appleton*, 1872.] "Iu spite of a little flash of horror iu one of the shorter tales, Miss Reid deals with nothing more deadly than the flash of beauteous eyes. Her novel is decidedly a 'novel of society,' and is very readable as such novels go. She has certainly the merit of making her men and women talk like people of good breeding, altho it must be said that they all lack the cool composure which is supposed to belong exclusively to the worldling; but then it is only beneath the mîty impulse of the tender passion that they ever speak at all. The longer story from which the volume takes its name is, perhaps, the best; but there is no one of the shorter tales which is without merit. If this author would look to something bier than the flirtatious on hotel verandas, there would seem to be no reason why she should not write something better, something of more real interest. She has the merit of avoiding many of the errors which are made by the majority of novelists upon such themes, and, apparently, she is capable of seeing and describing much more genuine passion than the rather trivial manifestations of it which form the only subjects of this volume. At any rate one is justified in hoping for something better, for this is good of its kind." [Nation. **238**

EDITH LYLE, see DARKNESS AND DAYLIGHT.

EIGHT COUSINS. [by LOUISA M. ALCOTT: *Roberts*, 1875.] "There are the same vigor, discrimination, character-portraiture, and racy dialog which characterize all her writings. It is no mean artist who can skilfully group a score or more of prominent figures, and still bring his hero or heroine into bold relief, at the same time preserving the distinct individuality of every leading character. This Miss Alcott achieves with rare genius and ability. She marshals her battalion of uncles, aunts, cousins, **nefews**, and nieces with the dexterity of a general, and every one of them steps forth with military precision at the word of command. It would be impossible to mistake the beautiful and meek Aunt Peace, with hair as white as snow and cheeks which never bloomed, but ever cheerful, busy, and full of interest in all that went on in the family, especially the joys and sorrows of the young girls growing up about her, to whom she was adviser, confidante, and friend in all their tender trials and delits. Equally impossible would it be to fail to discern instantly the striking individuality of Aunt Plenty—the stout, brisk old lady, with a sharp eye, a lively tung, and a face like a winter-apple, always trotting, chatting, and bustling amid a great commotion of stiff loops of purple ribbon that bristled all over her cap, like crocus-buds." [Overland] see sequel "ROSE IN BLOOM." **239**

ELLEN STORY [by EDGAR FAWCETT: *E. J. Hale*, 1876.] "is a pure love tale. We do not remember a novel in which the attention is more exclusively occupied with the hero and heroine, and with the circumstances attendant upon the development of their love. .. The scene is entirely at a great watering place, **Newpo**rt being plainly the one which the author had in mind. The hero, a young man of fine appearance. great wealth, and well connected, is of course furiously the fashion. [The heroine is] the poor cousin of some newly rich and ultra fashionable people, who are passing the summer at the great hotel, to which they have brôt Miss Story almost in charity, she being convalescent from a severe illness. The choice proves to be not a very severe test of Mr. Howard's power of conferring distinction; for she is really the handsomest woman, both in face and figure, at the hotel, and a very hi-spirited, intelligent girl withal... Mr. Howard and Miss Story fall in love with each other, and she does become the belle of the summer. The incidents of their wooing are quite original; but they are nevertheless not at all forced, and they are managed very skilfully." [Galaxy. **240**

EMILY CHESTER [by A.. MONCURE (CRANE) SEEMÜLLER: *Ticknor*, 1864.] "is more than an ordinary novel. Its excellences and faults are peculiar, and show the writer to be a person of unquestionable genius and insit. The interest of the story grows out of the singular psychological relations of the principal characters. There is no relief of by-play; no lesser personages move across the stage and interrupt the painful progress of the drama; no gay flash of wit, no repartie, lits the sombre picture; there is not even the form of a plot; nothing happens unexpectedly, in fact nothing happens at all, yet the story is one of absorbing interest. The only important event is the mariage of the heroine, and the desolation and despair which follow are inevitable,—inevitable, because they do not result from outward circumstances, but from the conflict of natures inherently inharmonious. Emily Chester is a girl of vigorous intellect, great clearness of perception, and delicate but healthy nervous organization. Like all heroines, she is beautiful,—of a grand and lofty beauty, according with her character. It is her misfortune to become, in early life, an object of passionate devotion to a man with whom she has great intellectual sympathy, but from whom she experiences an absolute fysical repulsion. At a time of great weakness and prostration she maries him, but with renewed fysical strength this feeling of repulsion returns with added force, and continues until her death. Frederick Hastings, the only other character of importance, is a friend of Emily's early and happy years, and an entire contrast to her husband. Graceful, accomplished and

amiable, a perfect gentleman in spirit and life, he is entirely agreeable to her, and her nature gladdens in his presence like a flower in the sunshine. Crampton, the husband, meets her intellectual needs; Frederick Hastings fulfils the cravings of her heart... Emily's aversion to her husband never becomes hatred, and never prevents a grateful, admiring regard for him. His stormy passions and iron will never tempt him to take revenge for his disappointment in any unworthy act. His love and tenderness for his wife strengthen and briten to the end. And Hastings, whose affection for Emily exceeds in devotion and warmth what most men call love, is, after her mariage, always the friend, never the lover." [Christian Examiner. **241**

ENDURA [by B. P. MOORE: *San Francisco*, 1885.] "is a story of 3 generations of a New-England family, who beginning in the first as poor and rugged pioneers, prospered, and in the third found themselves heirs to an enormous forein estate. The story is very naive and sincere, and (1 or 2 points excepted) excites rather friendly feeling in the critic by its spirit. It rambles on with little reference to its plot, and an evident determination to put in about all the author remembers of **New-England,** whether it comes into the story or not. The New-England that appears in it is evidently drawn from boyhood memories; but the mere fact that the village remembered is a Baptist and Methodist village, shows that it is not to be deemed a typical one. A great deal of stress is laid upon the decay of the New-England village, which is credited largely to bigotry; but in view of the way in which many towns in the middle West thrive upon this same bigotry, it is not worth while to join issue upon the point." [Overland. **242**

FAIR PHILOSOPHER. (A) [by "HENRI DAUGÉ:" i. e., MRS. HAMMOND: *Harlan*, 1882.] "We find this a pleasing book, and one which recommends itself for truth and good taste. The filoso-fizing, the familiarity with serious authors, and the like, turns out to be no pedantry, but simply the unaffected habit of thôt and speech of that society which is in a true sense the best. As a story it is nothing: it is gracefully constructed, and the narrative does not lag; still it makes no point of what is technically known as 'narrative interest,' nor has it any special originality. What we value it for is the picture, at once charming and true to nature, of the sisters Drosée and Jo,—of the tone of thôt and feeling and the attitude toward the world in which they lived. We do not remember ever to have read a novel which kept its scene entirely inside one of those little groups of american life which lie—and are glad to lie— entirely outside the world of fashion; the groups where books are read and written, where the words of filosofical discussion are commonplaces of chat, and all without any sense of importance or effort to stand on intellectual tip-toes. The charm of this intellectual life, its freedom from conventioualities, its character of sweetness and purity, its unanxious earnestness, its liability to unnecessary, painful contact with a society of different standards:— these are all well brôt out. . . Not the least of the virtues of 'A Fair Philosopher' is this hi conception of love,—a relief, indeed, to the reader after the monotony of caprice and passion which make up love in most novels. It cannot be said that there are not in this novel slips of taste; but these lapses do not seriously mar the gentle, lit seriousness of the whole picture." [Californian. **243**

FAITH GARTNEY'S GIRLHOOD [by ADELINE DUTTON (TRAIN) WHITNEY: *Loring*, 1863.] "is a quiet, simple story, noticeable for purity of tone and delicacy of feeling rather than for vigor. The style is admirable. If not a great book, it is something better—a good one." [Harper's.]—"I should not dare to tell how many times my copy has been read. The secret of its interest is that a girl's nature is here pictured so truthfully and sympathetically that every girl just leaving childhood behind her finds here some

image of herself, and something, too, which thrills and awakens her whole inner life. The story is full of sentiment. It is gushing, and tender, and innocent, and probably all true in any young girl. It is a book which every such person should read. It will stir and direct her sleeping energies. Glory McWhirk is a beautiful creation. The story is chiefly a series of pictures of character; it is not artistically or very carefully written; but the author is a woman of genius, and she has a true sympathy with the life she describes. . . . The author has constructed a clever plot, and developed it throu a very interesting succession of scenes, with natural characters; tho most of the Faith Gartneys whom we have heard speak of it seem to think the heroine is maried to the wrông man after all. And, we must confess, the hearty lay lover appears to us to have decided advantages over the slitly lackadaisical young clergyman." [Church Monthly. **244**

FAMOUS VICTORY (A) [*Jansen, McClurg & Co.*, 1880.] tho it has "a love story running throu it, is really a satire upon american politics, and as such has made us lâf here and there . . . Much of the story's action goes on in a **Connecticut** village, where the president has his mills, where several suitors make **love** to his pretty danters, and where a labor-reform agitation ends in a riot and destruction of the great capitalist's property. There is profanity in the book, of course, and a good deal of loud and slangy talk—for does not such belong to the subjeet? But it is written with much truth to nature, and its sharp hits at certain weaknesses of the national character are effective in no small degree. It is vigorous if not powerful, and racy if not always refined " [Boston "Literary World." **245**

FATHER BRIGHTHOPES. [by "PAUL CREYTON," i. e., J: TOWNSEND TROWBRIDGE :[*Phillips, Sampson & Co.*, 1853.] "Paul Creyton tells a capital story; draws his characters with a firm hand; has a deal of lurking fun in his composition: and never fails to inculcate a good moral lesson." [Church Review. **246**

FIGS AND THISTLES. [by ALBION
WINEGAR TOURGÉE · *Fords*, 1879.]
"Readers who have enjoyed E: Eggleston's
excursions into the land of Roxys and
Hoosier Schoolmasters will like Judge
Tourgée's 'Figs and Thistles', which is a
story of life in the Western Reserve
[**Ohio**], told with quite as much careful
attention to realistic detail and faithful
reflection of ruf and rollicking character
as works of this class are usually to be
credited with, and with rather more literary ability. And we must confess that it
has often made us lâf, in spite of our tastes
and principles, which are steadily set
against slang and profaneness and coarse
dialect, however true such touches may be.
Such books have a function in preserving
local traits which are fast disappearing
with the changing landscape; and they
are choice food, we very well know, for
certain palates: tho for our part we prefer fiction of a different quality." [Boston
"Literary World."]—"The story is of the
temptation of a conscientious hero who,
from obscure beginnings, has pushed himself throu college, into business success,
and into Congress; this is made particularly trying, but his wife, who does excellent
duty as a 'dea ex machinâ', steps in and
rescues her husband in a melodramatic
scene. The details are unimportant, and
the actual historical properties are used
exclusively as properties and have no
political interest. The merit of the book
consists in its showing of the conjunction
of self-reliance and humorous tolerance in
american character, the origin and peculiarities of which form the puzzle that so
many forein travelers set themselves to
solve." [Nation. **247**

FOOLISH VIRGIN (A) [by ELLA
WEED: *Harper*, 1883.] "is a young lady
just out of college, 'with a liberal education
on her hands', and ready to devote herself
to 'frills', as her school girl vocabulary
designates polite accomplishments. She
takes to china-painting, since 'in Cincinnati one must do something'. The story
is only what the author herself would call

a ·skit'; and as to plot, nothing but a petty
vivacity makes it worth a half-hour's reading. The **Cincinnati** setting is a novelty.
It is drolly given, with a good deal of
'vraisemblance'—a sort of mean proportional between ancient Boston and the true
West, wherever that may be. There is
seldom found in the class to which the
book belongs a better bit of delicate satire
than the account of the Boston lady's art-
lecture and the audience thereat."
[Nation. **248**

FOOLS OF NATURE. [by ALICE
BROWN: *Ticknor*, 1887.] "The intrinsic
evidence of this clever story is that the
author has had limited opportunities for
observation. Sarah Ellis is the ideal, and
far from a low one, of the New-England
woman novelist: she is a creature prone to
distort into caricature the divine faces of
duty, and love and truth. The young man
who maries Sarah is another ideal, far too
elegant a person ever to make a boarding
house his habitat. The **New-England**
village people, on the other hand, are
realistic studies, well characterized and
amusing, while the sketch of Linora, tho
verging on burlesque, hits hard at a feminine propensity for providing one's self
with a romantic background." [Nation. **249**

FOR A WOMAN. [by NORA PERRY:
Ticknor, 1885.] "From Mr. Hawthorne's
pretensions undertakings and weak com-
pletions, we turn with real relief to Nora
Perry's modest and charming little story.
It is among novels what her verses are
among poetry. It is fresh, healthful, and
refined, has plenty of feeling, yet nothing
dramatic, and is, we think, correct and
wise in its reading of life and love. Its
very completeness within its degree ex-
cludes much comment. It is not one of
the books which everyone should read;
but it is one which a great many people
should." [Overland. **250**

FOR SUMMER AFTERNOONS. [by
"SUSAN COOLIDGE," i. e., S.. CHAUNCEY
WOOLSEY: *Roberts*, 1876.] "A charming collection of stories about New-England people and things, in time of peace
and war,—parted from each other by

lovely bits of verse. 'Martin' in the hospital brings freshly back the terrible earnest of those days so far away, yet so near to all of us who have lived throu them; the 'Camp-Meeting Idyl' is very racy; 'Under the Sea' is full of the color of **Mt. Desert.** The dainty little volume is a very charming companion for these days when 'summer taints in the sky.'" [Unitarian Review. 251

FOR THE MAJOR. [by C. F. WOOLSON: *Harper*, 1883.] "It is a very clever, a very dramatic, and a very interesting book. It is woven in one piece, firmly, evenly, beautifully; there are no seams or thin places, (save one defect in the beginning) of its construction... There are beautiful touches in the book. Very daintily is the society of 'Far Edgerly' sketched in; we can almost see Miss Dalley, who was so devoted to Tasso; and we smile whenever we think of poor Miss Corinna. It ends beautifully, sweetly,— we had almost said softly. We feel as one sometimes does on leaving the theatre. The curtain is down, the stage is empty, the lits are out, and we pick up the burden of life again; but for a little while the music of the last act rings in our ears, and our thôts are with the people we have watched so closely. We hate to leave 'Far Edgerly', and the Major, and those two women and little Star. If the mission of a novel be to interest and entertain, to give us new and delitful friends, and to be a pleasant spot to think of and to go back to, then it is the greatest success we have had for many a day." [American] see No. 35. 252

FOUR OAKS. [by "Kamba Thorpe," i. e., E.. WHITFIELD (CROOM) BELLAMY: *Carleton*, 1867.] "This is a story of everyday life in which all the incidents are probable, and, what is yet more rare, the characters are all perfectly natural. A number of men and women, differing in age tho not in station, are brôt together on terms of pleasant acquaintance, and there is a more liberal allowance than usual of intelligent men and brainless nonentities, of sensible women and those

torments of modern society, women of an uncertain age on the look-out for husbands; and altho there are no villains, there are mischief-makers enuf to occasion unpleasant complications, which, together with mysterious miniatures and family secrets, combine to sustain an interest which the events of the story would not otherwise suffice to keep alive. The scene opens in the pleasant town of Netherford, where, after a severe round of introductions to the forefathers and relatives of the heroine, we are presented to a charming, good-hearted, and beautiful girl,—a little spoiled, rather self-willed, and somewhat too self-reliant, but so true and honest, so free from all the vices which attach to the fashionable and fast young lady, that we are grateful to the author who awakens our interest for a woman equally endowed with vitality, modesty, and common-sense. There is an absence of all romance about a life passed among such restless and ill-assorted people as form the society of Netherford, but the author has refrained from giving us any exaggerated or extravagant scenes; he is throuôut consistent and natural, and his imagination has evidently been greatly assisted by personal observation." [Round Table. 253

FRIENDS [by E.. S. (PHELPS) WARD: *Houghton*, 1881.] "is simply the story of a beautiful, tender, true-hearted young woman, who loses a husband whom she loves with her whole nature, and who after a long widowhood, maries his most intimate friend, a life-long acquaintance of her own too... The interest of the book is in the way the end is reached. It is a study of 'the patient renewals of life, the slow gathering of wasted forces, the gradual restoration of landmarks and symptoms of content, the gravely rebuilt fire-sides, by which forever ears must listen for the footsteps of the flood'. These are traced with much delicacy in the woman's case, and the growth and development of love with much truth to nature in the man's. From the moment when he thinks that to be the comfort of a dead friend's widow is the most thankless position in the world and wishes, 'honestly enuf. that John were there to do his own consoling,' until the last sentence,—'It was heaven on earth to him at least. If to her it was earth after heaven, what cared he,"—the sequence of emotions and events is perfectly logical. There is no plot or action, there are instead successive fäses of feeling as various and infallible as the fenomena of stars or tides." [Atlantic. **254**

FROM MADGE TO MARGARET [by "CARROLL WINCHESTER," i. e., Caroline G. (Cary) Curtis: *Lee*, 1880.] "is a history of development of character. Madge is a girl 'born and bred in a farmhouse' who marries young, and goes to a life wholly new to her and full of temptations. The struggle is how to bring a volatile but brit and lovable wife to sympathize with her husband and be truly his helpmeet. The tone is excellent, the pictures of home life, the parental and sisterly feeling, are beautiful; and it is altogether a sweet and wholesome book." [Boston "Literary World." **255**

FROM HAND TO MOUTH [by AMANDA MINNIE. DOUGLAS: *Lee*, 1877.] "is a thoroly good, true, pure, sweet and touching story. It covers precisely those fäses of domestic life which are of the most common experience. and will take many of its readers just where they have been themselves. The style is admirable for its nervous compactness, naturalness, is nowhere sacrificed for effect, and the whole current runs with the spontaneity and freshness of a mountain brook. There is trouble 'in it, and sorrow, and pain and parting, but the sunset glorifies the clouds of the varied day, and the peace which passes understanding pervades all. For young women whose lives are just opening into wifehood and maternity, we have read nothing better for many a day." [Boston "Literary World." **256**

GALLANT FIGHT, A [by "MARION HARLAND," i. e., M.. Virginia (Hawes) Terhune: *Dodd*, 1888.] "is a most lady-like production, and may be recommended as certain not to bring the blush of

shame to the cheek of the most innocent. And yet the 'gallant fit' intended by the title we take to be the long struggle kept up by Mrs. Richard Phelps not to 'let on' to him, or to anybody, that she knows her husband has once been on the verge of unfaithfulness to her. . . . Mrs. Terhune has told her story in an interesting way. But there is, as usual in her work, a cookbook sort of flavor in it, an atmosfere of tatting and tatling, and crochet work, and æsthetic chromos, and general primness, prosperity and prettiness, which makes 'ladylike' at once the most comprehensive and descriptive of adjectives for it." [Catholic World. **257**

GAYWORTHYS (The) A Story of Threads and Thrums. [by A. D. (T.) WHITNEY: *Loring,—Low*, 1865.] "is a story with pleasant delineations of american rural life in the village of Hillbury, and of the more pretentious society of the seaport town of Selport. There is a pleasant, racy flavor in the tale, but the style would be better if it were quieter; it is too staccato, and disturbs the reader. . . . The episode of Gabriel Hartshorne, the unspoken, 'kindness' between him , and Joanna Gayworthy, is excellent, and written with quiet power, which fills the heart of the reader with reverence for the simple heroism of the young man who could put aside all his hopes to do a son's duty by his poor old crazed father. The disappointment of the two sisters, neither of them knowing how the clouding of their life had come to pass, is touching. The character of the sailor is the picture of a real hero; indeed, the whole story gives a glimpse of the lives of self-renunciation which we may thank God are not rare in the world. In the end, some of the thrums and threads are woven into a comfortable result: but only after much tribulation. . . 'The Gayworthy's is not a lively novel; but it is a book which no one can read without feeling the better for it, for it appeals to the best sympathies and instincts of human nature." [Athenæum. **258**

GENTLEMAN OF LEISURE (A) [by EDGAR FAWCETT: *Houghton*, 1881.]

is an "admirable social satire. 'A Hopeless
Case' prepared us to think well of his work
in this direction, but here he is perhaps
more happy than in the former book.
Clinton Wainwright, an american by birth
but a european by education, is called by
business from London to New-York, and
is there introduced into 'society.' Expecting to find a democracy, he finds
an aristocracy, founded upon birth,
lineage, and other considerations, which
he supposed were entirely disregarded in
the politics and social life of America.
This is the key-note of the book, and it
enables Mr. Fawcett to do some clever
writing in a line in which he is particularly clever. The story is not without a well
arranged plot, but the chief charm is the
admirable vein of satire which runs throu
it." [Californian.   259
  GLEN LUNA. [by "AMY LOTHROP,"
i. e., Anna B. Warner: N.-Y., and London,
1852.] "This lengthy, but well-meant and
well-executed story may pair off with
'Queechy'. Like that novel, it is devoted
to the downward progress of gentility
towards poverty:—an argument, by the
way, of strange frequency in the domestic
fiction of America. In 'Glen Luna' too,
as in 'Queechy,' poverty is deprived of its
sting, and sacrifice of its difficulty, by the
angelic nature of some among the suffering
and struggling parties. If there be not
more of Arcady than of America in the
sweet-tempered, cheerful and graceful
heroines portrayed in these tales, the New
World has great occasion to be proud of
its dauters. If their 'favor and prettiness'
be somewhat flattered, the moral of books
like 'Glen Luna' is not much the worse for
the flattery. Meanwhile, they are agreeable to read; and this last of the flock not
the least agreeable." [Athenæum. 260
  GRANDISON MATHER. [by H: HAR-
LAND: Cassell, 1889.] "But nothing can
be more attractive than such a study of
newly maried life as the author makes in
'Grandison Mather'. The scene is in New-
York, and the history is that of a young
literary man who maries a lovely girl, loses
his fortune throu the rascality of his agent

and retrieves. himself throu his powers
and the inspiration of her faith and affection. Their adversity will have thrills
and pangs enuf for the reader, who will
make acquaintance throu them with the
facts of a LITERARY struggle as they
are; there are times for holding the breath,
times of poignant defeat and disappointment, when one must look at the last page
to reassure oneself. Mr. Harland is a born
story-teller; he attracts you from the first
word, and goes on to the end with a cum-
ulative interest." [Howells.   261
  GRANDISSIMES, see ROMANTIC NOV-
ELS.
  GUARDIANS (The) [by HARRIET W.
PRESTON and L.. DODGE: Houghton,
1888.] "is a rather remarkable novel; the
studies of character are elaborate and
varied, the incidents are admirably arranged, the style is graceful and sparkling.
Some of the events in the story, such as a
clandestine mariage, a midnit conflagration
and a fatal ride, partake of the sensational,
but they are not treated at all in a sensational way. 'The Guardians' is a novel far
above the average." [Boston "Lit. World."]
"In a certain balance between strength
and grace, between feeling and ration-
ality, between intensity and moderation,
the book not only bespeaks its double
authorship, but proclaims an authorship
of opposite sexes, if we surmise correctly."
[Critic.]—"The interest is not dependent
on plot, but on the careful character study,
and the remarkably crisp and natural conversations. The scene where the boy
lover proposes a secret mariage to the
younger sister, to save himself from being
forced to mary the elder sister in accordance with the plans of the masterful Mrs.
Rothery, is exquisitely droll. The action
also of the same two when a real passion
makes the girl regret the childish and
clandestine vows is well and spiritedly
drawn. A love affair of a very different
sort is that of the elder sister and her
gardian. The book is not a great one,
and probably was not written in expectation that it would be; it lacks the force,
scope, and depth, requisite to a great book:

but it certainly is a very pleasant book, one that holds its readers unwearied, and even stands the test of a second reading. It bears no internal evidence of the *dual authorship*, and the style is uniformly brit, clear, and intelligent." [Overland. **262**

HAZARD OF NEW FORTUNES, (A) [by W: D. HOWELLS: *Harper*, 1890.] "Looking on New-York from an outsider's point of vue, he has wisely chosen his characters from the heterogeneous body of new residents. This method gives him striking contrasts of character. . . . Head and shoulders above them all is Fulkerson —the syndicate-man turned magazine manager. He is a delit from the first page to the last, tho one can imagine him very trying to a sensitive and proper man in life. He is the flower of Western audacity, shrewdness and optimism transplanted to New-York. Daring schemes are his inspiration. There is just the touch of charlatanism about him which, in the rit environment, would make him a show-man. But you are not offended, because he has a fine, genial way of taking you into his confidence and showing you the beauties of the joke.—In the Dryfoos family there is an echo of the Laphams, tho the characters are sufficiently different to overthrow any charge of repetition. The elder Dryfoos is a genuine study of the traits of a Pennsylvania german in unusual surroundings.—But the subtilest bit of work in the book is Beaton,—selfish and mean, weak-willed, narrow-minded, and hard-hearted; and aimless with all his talent! He represents a not uncommon fäse of the artistic temperament which many fascinating good fellows exhibit in varying degrees." [Life.]—"Indeed, the author is so much impressed with the mity flow of human life in the world of New York that he is scarcely conscious, as so genuine a humorist would be, of the whimsical nature of the enterprise which forms the apparent cause of the story. (Basil March moves to New-York for the purpose of taking charge of a literary journal, which is to be conducted upon a rather vaguely described plan of co-operation.) . . . He is

much more successful in his conveyance of Lindau's german-silver english, and it is when we come to Lindau himself, and to Dryfoos, with his untamed dauters, his pathetically conceived wife, and his martyr son, that we find ourselves in the heart of the story and in the secret of Mr. Howells' great gain as a novelist. We cannot say that these figures are handled more deftly than others which he has fashioned, but they mean more. They ally themselves distinctly with greater problems, with deeper insit of life, and our confidence in Mr. Howells is increased because of the wise reserve which he has used. They are not instruments in his hand for breaking the false gods of the Philistines; they are men and women into whom he has breathed the breath of life; but that breath comes from a profounder inspiration than he was wont to draw." [Atlantic. **263**

HEART STORIES [by T. BARTLETT: *Putnam*, 1889.] "The author's literary record was a brief one, but reading these exquisitely tender and pathetic little stories, one cannot help a feeling of deep regret that a life which promised so much should have been cut off at 26." [Boston "Literary World." **264**

HELEN TROY [by C. (C.) HARRISON: *Harper*, 1881.] "is an advance upon 'Golden Rod.' The author has more material and handles it better. The scenes of the little drama are prettily set, whether in the New-York drawing-room or on the hillside at **Lenox.** The heroine we all know—gay, too careless perhaps, but true at heart, and strong and steady when trial comes." [Nation. **265**

HEPHZIBAH GUINNESS [by SILAS WEIR MITCHELL: *Lippincott*, 1880.] "gives the title to a volume of 3 well-told stories. The scenes of the first two are laid in **Philadelphia,** and they deal with the straitest sect of the Quakers. The devices which these find allowable in their relations with the people of the world, and their jealous watchfulness lest one of their number should slip from the fold, form a good background to 2 pleasant little love-stories, which are, however, in so low a key that the tragic element of the second seems a little incongruous. The third story, 'A Draft on the Bank of Spain' is more ordinary." [Nation. **266**

HERMAN. [by "E. FOXTON," i. e., S.. HAMMOND PALFREY: *Lee*, 1866.] "The true power and pathos of the book rise ever hi and hier, and all minor defects are flooded out of sit. It is no small happiness that we have to do from the beginning with a family hitherto wellni unknown in American noveldom,—a family rich and not vulgar, beautiful and not frivolous, hily educated and fastidious, yet neither bitter nor disdainful,—refined, honorable, serene, affectionate. We are not merely told that they are so. We mingle with them, we *see* it, and are refreshed and revived thereby. It is pleasant to miss for once the worldly mother, the empty danter, the glare and glitter of shoddy, the low rivalry, the degrading strife, which can hardly be held up even to our reprobation without debasing us. Whether or not the best mode of inculcating virtue is that which gives us an example to imitate rather than a vice to shun, we are sure it is the most agreeable. It is infinitely sweeter to be attracted by the fragrance of Paradise than to be repelled by the sulfurous fumes of Pandemonium. The contemplation of such a home as this book opens to us is pleasant to the eyes and good for the heart's food, and to be desired to make one wise. A pure domestic love shines throu it, tender, tranquil, and intense. Its inmates are daintily, delicately, yet distinctly drawn. They are courteous without being cold, playful without rudeness, serious yet sensible, reticent or demonstrative as the case may be, yet in all things natural. It is not a book, it is life. Each is a type of character matchless in its way, but each is also a living soul, whose outward elegance and grace are but the fit adjuncts of its inward purity and peace. Even if such a home never existed, we should still defend its portrayal, as the Vicar of Wakefield wrote his wife's epitaf during her life that she mit have a chance to become

worthy of its praise. . . . We know no work of fiction so full as this of beauty and wisdom, so free from folly, so resplendent with intellectual life. and with moral purity, so apt to teach, so graceful in the teaching. We follow it with admiration and sympathy, from its gay beginning, throu all the pain, the passion. and the peace, to the heartache of its closing pages, —that close, supremely sad, yet strangely beautiful. 'She sang to him, and he slept; she spoke, and he did not awaken.' " [Atlantic. **267**

HESTER STANLEY AT ST. MARKS. [by H. [E..] (PRESCOTT) SPOFFORD: *Roberts*, 1882.] "Mrs. Spofford in her delitful story of 'Hester Stanley,' has given us a surprise in demonstrating her ability, under stern necessity, to do without bric-à-brae. The dormitories of the boarding-school where the scene is laid are as bare as they would have been in life; not a single mother-of-pearl bedstead dares to raise a silken canopy; and the garden is an actual old-fashioned garden, instead of the literary conservatory, only adapted to the movements of a Tennyson's Maud, into which Mrs. Spofford usually leads us. She surprises us again by showing a decided gift for humor. We recommend the book to everybody," [Critic. **268**

HOMESPUN YARNS [by A. D. (T.) WHITNEY: *Houghton*, 1887.) "are all twisted to one issue—that is, to display her intimate knowledge of the vues and ways of Divine Providence. That a young girl's cloth is sufficient for her coat; that a housewife's pickles are saited to taste; that lovers unite or separate,—all these interesting mundane matters are referred to the direct interposition of God. Mrs. Whitney no more means to be irreverent than she means to be funny. She has been writing in this fashion for so many years that she doubtless feels herself familiar with Deity without any diminution of awe. . . Her constant devotion to a literal 'deus ex machina' burdens her stories with an artificiality which is intensified by the studied affectation of her style. The people who read them are still bound to the dark ages of our fiction. They want the supernatural and the unnatural." [Nation. **269**

HONEST JOHN VANE. [by J : W: DE FOREST: New Haven: *Richmond & Patten*, 1875.] "In this country, there has never been so good a political satire as this; but its excellence as such is only one of many. The malleable, blubberly good-intention of the hero, who weakens by stress of circumstances into a prosperous rogue, is very keenly appreciated, with all the man's dim, dull remorse, his simple reverence for men better than himself, his vulgar but efficient cunning with men as bad or worse. You more than half pity him, feeling that if such a soul as his had been properly trained, it would by no means have gone to the devil. Olympia Vane, for some reasons, we should be inclined to think a still better work of art. Her gradual expansion from the vulgar belleship she has enjoyed among her mother's boarders, from her 'tuf flirtations' with the undergraduates of a college town, into the sort of unhappy social success of her **Washington** life, is grafically traced. Her sort of rich, undelicate handsomeness affects you like something you have seen." [Atlantic. **270**

HONOR MAY. [by M.. BARTOL: *Ticknor*, 1866.] "A book without slang and vulgarism is singularly refreshing. Hi-toned, gracefully written, bearing the impress of New-England without being provincial, quiet and quieting, 'Honor May' will win and hold readers of whom a writer may well be proud." [Religious Magazine. **271**

HOPELESS CASE. (A) [by EDGAR FAWCETT: *Houghton*, 1880.] "When we look for a picture of American society we are offered Mr. Fawcett's A Hopeless Case and think ourselves well off with so entertaining a story. As a portraiture of one fase of **New-York** society, it seems to us exceptionally clever. Mrs. Leroy, Rivington Van Corlear; Oscar Schuyler, Mr. Gascoigne, and other ladies and gentlemen are positively present, and the success is attained by no elaborateness of touch, but by a simple and truthful display of char-

acters needed to present a full group of society figures. The placidity of their unemotional life is made apparent to the reader, and he does not feel that it is insipid. The subtle grace and charm of the do-nothing world has been reproduced to a shade, and the petty ambition and discontent of the unfortunate aspirants to fame in it are not allowed to disturb the even tone of the picture. Yet Mr. Fawcett knew very well that this flat background, however exquisitely painted, would not of itself make a picture, and he has projected from it; as a contrasting object, the figure of Agnes Wolverton, representing a life and society more in earnest and moved by hier impulses. If the society was good, Miss Wolverton, shot into it from another sfere, was to reveal its insufficiency and to supply a standard which should measure its shortcomings. It is perhaps the misfortune of the contrast that Miss Wolverton is less a hi-spirited, ingenuous and noble girl, making the lit in which the other life is read, than a somewhat angular, aggressive and self-sufficient maiden, who enters the arena not only with a misconception of what lies before her, but with a misapprehension of what really constitutes the best society. We are to be persuaded that it was a hopeless case when Mrs. Leroy attempted to transform her cousin into a charming girl of society, and we grant that the venture was not successful: but there is implied in all this that Agnes was rit and loyal to an ideal, while Mrs. Leroy was the delicate slave of a petted conventionalism. Now we are not prepared to accept Miss Wolverton's reading of the case. We think the Van Corlear set were better to her than she deserved, and that instead of going off into blankness after undertaking to arrange society to her mind, it would have been more becoming if she had shown a little humility, and—we are almost ready to add,—modesty,—and disappeared from the story hand in hand with Mr. Livingston Maxwell. Her society friends were really forbearing toward this inharmonious creature."

[Atlantic. **272**
HOUSE AT HIGH BRIDGE (The)
[by Edgar Fawcett: Ticknor, 1886.]
"seems to us quite the most successful
work of fiction that he has produced. It
has, in the first place, the advantage of
having an interesting story to tell, concerning itself with a situation arranged with
ingenuity, and lending itself to dramatic
treatment naturally. The characters employed to enact the story have been
chosen from everyday types, with the
loyalty to native and simple materials
which Mr. Fawcett has consistently
maintained in his essays in novel-writing;
and in this instance he has returned, for
his background, at least, to the common
folk treated with intelligence in 'An Ambitions Woman'[No. 184]. These people are
shown without palliation, in the practice of
their small economies, the exercise of their
doubtful tastes, and the pursuit of their
cheap ambitions,—the women living in
the fear of a social code derived from 'The
Complete Book of Etiquette,' and skilled
in shifts by which to make a show on very
little; the men faithful machines for turning out the very little. . . The similarity of
the germ thôt of this novel to that of Mr.
"Anstey's" admirable 'Giant's Robe' will
have struck all who may have read both
books. But the subject—that of the theft
of a manuscript and the publication of it
under the name of the thief, is an extremely interesting one, and we are glad to see
it treated once more and from another
point of vue; and, again, the new treatment is in many ways very clever and
original. It is the young girl's lover in
Mr. Anstey's work who commits the
wrong, and he fails in his suit throu her
discovery of his baseness. This is a simple
and powerful way of using the idea; Mr.
Fawcett has involved it more, both his way
too has force and meaning." [Church
Review. **273**
HOUSE OF A MERCHANT PRINCE
(The). [by W: H: Bishop: Houghton,
1883.] "The most generous critics of Mr.
Bishop's novel will probably confess that
it is a little dull; the most conscientious

will find themselves obliged to state that it
is very, very dull. The motive is good;
for altho the sudden disgrace of merchant
princes has long been a favorite theme with
novelists, Mr. Bishop's prince is not merely denounced as a forger, but proved not
to have been a forger, and yet shown to
have been very near to becoming a forger.
There is double point here, and the theme
could have been worked into a striking
short story, but the 400 pages into which
Mr. Bishop has lengthened it, and which
James Payn, or the author of 'Val Strange',
or Mrs. Riddell, or almost any French
writer, after choosing such a title, would
have filled with ingenious and mysterious
mercantile transactions, are padded with
the material which gives the sub-title to
the book—'A Novel of New-York'; in
other words, with society gossip, hardly
above the level of what mit be gleaned
from the morning papers, and with the
latest information as to the decorative art
of fashionable rooms, even down to the
ruby-velvet mat and open-work table-cloth
of the dinner-table." [Critic. **274**
HUNDREDTH MAN. (The) [by Fr.
R: Stockton: Scribner, 1887.] "Two
almost distinct stories here march side by
side. One of these motives is a wildly
farcical 'strike' in a New-York restaurant,
on the basis of a demand of the waiters
that they be allowed to wear dress-coats
instead of aprons and jackets. The restaurant is owned by a pompous bank president who makes the best part of his living
by selling oyster stews, but who is ashamed
to have the business known, and conducts
it throu a 'manager'. There is much broad
fun in the incidents bearing on this part
of the scheme, but there is subtlety about
it, too. When we come to what may be
called the second story we find a social filosofer who deliberately sets himself to
break an engagement of mariage, because
he thinks the young man in question is not
worthy of the young woman in question.
He does this, heedless of the fact that the
natural consequence of a forcible taking
away of underpinning of that nature means
only one thing—the change of the young

woman's affections from the unworthy object to the agent which makes her realize the unworthiness. Yet our filosofer consistently maintains that he does not want this bily attractive girl for himself, and, in fact, he does his questionable work as he laid out to do and then leaves the heroine to go into a 'decline' without stretching out a helping finger, she being, in the end, snatched from the decline by an honest fellow in whose protestations of devotion she cannot but believe. The admirers of Mr. Stockton will find much to jog their curiosity in these vivacious, picturesque, and not seldom deeply moving pages." [American. **275**

ISLAND NEIGHBORS (The) [by ANTOINETTE B. BLACKWELL: *Harper*, 1871.] "is a novel of american life; but of life within the limited sfere whose boundaries correspond to the coast-lines of **Martha's Vineyard**. . . . It is so quiet and unobtrusive a story, the period of its action is so brief, its characters are so few, and its incidents so homely and unsensational, that the reader will often pause and wonder why he likes it so well. For there is certainly a very potent charm in its pages—a charm which one parts with regretfully at the end. Perhaps it is the salty flavor that exhales from it—a fresh and bracing emanation that acts upon the blasé literary appetite like sea-air upon the fysical. This hypothesis harmonizes so well with the ardent admiration of sea-side nature which glows on every page—every one of which is saturated with briny love and lore—that it is pleasantest to accept it. The Warren family, rich Bostonians, hired a furnished cottage on the island for the summer. . . We have given only the thread of the love-plot, without hinting at the wealth of fresh and piquant entertainment which is found in its descriptions of the island amusements—of the ride to Painted Cliffs, of the camp-meeting, the fishing parties, the drawing of the great seine, the daily peregrinations and simple pleasures of the children, and the thrilling sketch of their peril in the great storm. All these must be read to be appreciated;

and we can truthfully say that we have never seen more cheerful and pleasing pictures of a quiet summer life than they present." [Boston "Literary World." **276**

JACOB SCHUYLER'S MILLIONS, see ROMANTIC NOVELS.

JEAN MONTEITH, [by M.. GREENWAY McCLELLAND: *Holt*, 1887.] "Its scene is a little settlement at the foot of the Cumberland range, its motif the loyal devotion of a young girl to her father's memory. It is a brave little story, of a sort to help and not hinder the growth in character of anyone who reads it: and, which must be counted for riteousness in these days of 'dialect', its characters as a general thing speak a language which we can read without the aid of a special lexicon of mispronunciations and verbal oddities." [Boston "Literary World." **277**

JESSAMINE [by "MARION HARLAND," i. e., M.. V. (H.) Terhune: *Carleton*, 1873.] "is rather better than such persons as have let 13 of her novels go by unread mit think. It gives us an account of the misery that may be wrôt in the female heart by the hideous wiles of the male flirt. No one who takes up the book will expect to find it a formidable rival of "Middlemarch." It will be found, however, perfectly free from the questionable morality and the uneasy examination of a morbid heart which go so far towards spoiling what should be an innocent form of amusement. The machinations of the flirt are well described, as well as the heroine's perturbations; and if the story is not a great one, it is yet a good one." [Nation. **278**

JOHN ANDROSS [by REBECCA [BLAINE] (HARDING) DAVIS: N.-Y., *Judd*, 1874.] "is certainly a very readable novel. Mrs. Davis writes well; with all her grimness she has a very agreeable humor, and if about all the men there is a certain exaggeration of their prominent qualities, the women—both the serious and sensible one whom the men of the story deem dull, and the frivolous and pretty one whom they with equal unanimity take for charming and loving—are very well described. The scene of the story is laid in western **Pennsylvania**, in the coal and oil region, and in Philadelphia and Harrisburg, and the local color is very well given. ... The plot turns on the sufferings of an amiable but weak man, who, partly by his own fault and partly by force of circumstances, has fallen into the power of a 'ring', which needs his glib tung and ready manners for aid in doing its dirty work in buying members of the legislature. ... One should remember, however, that even in works of fiction it would be very hard to exaggerate the evil doings of Pennsylvania legislators and rings." [Atlantic. **279**

JOHN BODEWIN'S TESTIMONY, see ROMANTIC NOVELS.

JOHN GODFREY'S FORTUNES. [by BAYARD TAYLOR: *Putnam,—Low*, 1864.] "The first volume, in which we have the hero's childhood, is full of clear, lit, transparent sketches, full too of humor, and a genuine artistic pathos. The sketches of the **Pennsylvania** village life of the child with his mother, of his school experience, of his mother's death, of his apprenticeship to his uncle, and the religious revival in his uncle's church, of his literary ambitions, of his first start in life on his own account 'to teach school,' of the romping girl who wishes him to make love to her and thereby fritens him out of his wits, and of the composed young lady who accepts his hi-flown devotion with so sly an acquiescence, are all clear, brit, and fascinating. . . When Mr. Taylor gets his hero fairly embarked in literary life in **New-York** the sketches become more blurred, and the more brilliant scenes are somewhat irrelevant to the story,—being introduced more for their intrinsic humor or point than for their bearing on the principal character. But some of these are still very clever and piquant,—one especially of a transcendental poetess being at least as good as any of the similar sketches in 'Martin Chuzzlewit'. . . The Mr. Brandagee mentioned in this paragraf is a literary Bohemian, whose conversation,—quick, rattling, full of real insit and viv-

acity,—is admirably sketched." [Spectator. **280**

JOHN THORN'S FOLKS. [by ANGELINE (GRUEY) TEAL: *Lee*, 1884.] "The 'Western life' of the present study is not so very far West; no further, indeed, than the section so well portrayed in Eggleston's novels; but the **Indiana** of 'John Thorn's Folks', is not that of the 'Circuit Rider' and the 'Hoosier Schoolmaster'; the northern part of the state is more clearly allied to the East, from which most of its inhabitants have emigrated, than are the older settlements in the more southern portions, and offers less bizarre and eccentric types of character. The level and serene aspects of the scenery have no doubt their effect upon the residents. In this little study of Western life there is certainly nothing thrilling or sensational. The narrative flows throu a rather uneventful course of matrimonial misunderstandings, entanglements, and threatened misfortunes to a peaceful and pleasant termination. The story is, in fact, rather thin, yet in its very moderation and modesty gives promise." [American.]—"This book deserves a better name. Something in the very word 'folks' suggests a hopeless combination of poor dialect and still poorer story; but the little tale, tho very simple and unpretending, is well written and interesting. The 'folks' are limited to John Thorn and Mrs. Thorn. popularly described as 'odder'n odd.' The best of the book is in its quiet pictures of homely country life, relying for interest, not on absurd methods of speech, but on quaint habits of thôt and judgment." [Critic. **281**

JUST ONE DAY. [by J : HABBERTON: *Lockwood*, 1879.] "This clever 'jeu d' esprit' puts, in a capital way, the old question of 'Which has the harder lot, the mother who stays at home with unceasing worry from the care of children and the household, or the father, who spends his working hours and much of his leisure away?' The answer is given in no uncertain strain, and the contrast of the struggle on the part of the affectionate wife to bear her heavy burden, and the cool assumption of the husband that he does his whole duty in providing the means of living, without any care as to how it is used, so that his comfort is secured,—is admirably put. The story rises to a much hier plane than that of 'Helen's Babies' and its numerous progeny, unless this be counted the last of that long line." [Penn. **282**

JUSTINA [by SOPHY (WINTHROP) (SHEPIERD) WEITZEL: *Roberts*, 1886.] "is a novel of rather unusual merit. It is at once imaginative and realistic, and the story is related with a sort of sympathetic vigor which is very attractive. . . The plot is concerned with the honorable love of a woman for a man who has been shamefully trapped into an early and unhappy mariage. The interest turns upon the strength of character shown by the lovers, and their successful determination to do their full duty to themselves and to society. The struggle lasts years; it is painful but it is ennobling. . . It is a powerful little tale." [American.]—'Justina' has a moral. It is a study of that delicate, but, to the pens of women, evidently attractive question—the extent to which the obligation of mariage is binding, on account of the legal tie, when for any reason the moral claim of husband or wife has ceased to exist. . . The author, with some daring, yet with perfect purity, takes it as the straitforward and common-sense vue, that where a third person stands legally between the hands of lovers, yet for any reason has forfeited the rit to interpose between their hearts, the situation should be accepted just as it stands—the legal barrier respected, the freedom for avowed friendship and affection taken. . . Passing by this main point, we must add that the social background of the study is well drawn, refined and intelligent. The life and manners of wealthy and somewhat cosmopolitan people of intellect and station in an aristocratic New-England village, the tranquil charm of the place, the serenity and sweetness of manners, the influences which produce, as their final and typical result, such a 'nice girl' as Mary

Beverly—all these are well caut." [Overland. **283**

JUSTINE'S LOVERS [by J: W: DE FOREST: *Harper*, 1878.] "is an exceedingly clever story . . . It contains the cleverest characterization, the keenest insit into motives, and the most delicate discrimination of human varieties. . . It is, in fact, a noticeably well-bred book. We tremble when the scene is shifted to Washington, but even the seemingly compulsory search for a place under government cannot make Justine vulgar. We respect the author so unféinedly that we feel as if it would be almost impertinent to hint that she is telling her own experience; but we may at least affirm that she has contrived to inform her tale with an intense reality, and that it fixes our attention and absorbs our sympathies very much as the true story of an extremely engaging young woman would do." [Atlantic.]—"That at least a considerable portion of it is true is evident—for in the **Washington** episode several very prominent personages barely escape being named, and personal feeling unmistakably enters into the clever portrayal of that 'insolence of office' with which office-seekers at Washington are apt to become bitterly familiar. From any point of vue, 'Justine's Lovers' is piquant, and we should add pleasing, if we knew how its feminine readers would regard its naively frank revelations of the motives and reasons which determine the average woman's attitude towards mariage. Never, we think, have these determining reasons been exhibited quite so bare of the customary vestures of sentiment. . . Yet the tone of the book is not at ail cynical, nor does it awaken a feeling of cynicism in the reader. On the contrary, it has the effect, which Burke said his experience of life had had upon him, of making us think better of mankind; and it is a conclusive tribute either to the author's skill or to the essential ritness and verity of her heroine's character, that, in spite of Justine's pliancy toward lovers, she retains not only our sympathy but our respect to the last. One thing concerning the story may be affirmed with confidence, and that is that it is thŏroly readable." [Appleton's.]— "'Justine's Lovers' was an attempt to imitate the ordinary "woman's novel." Not a critic in the U. S. questioned the sex of the writer; I looked over all the reviews sent to Harpers in order to see if this would be so." [Author's note to compiler. **284**

KATHARINE EARLE. [by ADELINE (TRAFTON) KNOX: *Lee*, 1874.] "The best part is the account of the heroine's childhood, which was spent in Poplar Street, in Boston, a place venerable with the antiquity of 25 years. . . This is by no means a wonderful novel, but the frank, honest character of the heroine is not at all badly drawn, and there are no violent and unnatural incidents." [Atlantic. **285**

KITTY'S CLASS DAY [by LOUISA M. ALCOTT: *Loring*, 1865;—Also in "Proverb Stories."] "is a gracefully-told story which relates the mishaps which befell a little girl on the Harvard class-day in consequence of her neglecting to sew the facing on her dress, and trusting to basting-threads and pins. The results of her negligence were hardly so serious as they should have been made in the interests of sound morality, since, by means of her small troubles, she discovered the general good-for-nothingness of the youth with whom she fancied herself about to fall in love, and surrendered her heart instead, before class-day was over, to a much more satisfactory person: which seems as if Kitty were rather to be congratulated on her laziness." [Nation. **286**

LAKEVILLE. [by M.. (HEALY) BIGOT: *Appleton*, 1873.] "This not very clever book has an interest and a present value which ŏt to bring it into notice, because its chief merit, an admirable picture of the garish life of one of our great Western cities, is too delicately done to be appreciated by a foreiner, who sees, when he sees at all, only broad characteristics, while the story is too completely native in its tone to be anything but ignored by an american. Lakeville is **Chicago**. . . The reckless, comfortless existence of a com-

munity mad in the pursuit of sudden wealth; its bald, hard, almost dreary aspect; its narrow range of feeling, its coarse excitement and its indescribable vulgarity—'Lakeville' sets forth with a fidelity which one cannot altogether understand, so unshrinking is it. And here ends what is in reality the only valuable part of the book. The rest of the story is laid abroad; a provincial french household, and the character of one of its inmates, 'une jeune fille bieu elevée,' are cleverly sketched." [Penn. **287**

LAST ASSEMBLY BALL, see ROMANTIC NOVELS.

LAW UNTO HERSELF. [by R.. [B.] (H.) DAVIS: *Lippincott*, 1878.] "Mrs. Davis writes stories which can hardly be called pleasant, and which frequently, as here, deal with most unpleasant persons; but there is an undercurrent of recognized rectitude and a capacity for calling a spade a spade which sets her writings in a category far removed from french morality. She is often worse than careless in her language; but tho she shows bad taste in various ways, or perhaps because of this, she succeeds in giving a truer impression of american conditions than any writer we know except Mr. Howells, while there is a vast difference between his delicately illuminated presentations of our social absurdities and Mrs. Davis' grim and powerful etchings. Somehow she contrives to get the american atmosfere, its vague excitement, its strife of effort, its varying possibilities. Add to this a certain intensity, a veiled indignation at prosperity, and doubt of the honesty of success, and we get qualities which make Mrs. Davis' books individual and interesting if not agreeable." [Nation. **288**

LENA RIVERS, see DARKNESS AND DAYLIGHT.

LENOX DARE [by VIRGINIA F.. TOWNSEND: *Lee*, 1881.] "is a fresh and vigorous story. It is a portrayal of a character which may perhaps not often be found in the quiet, out-of-the-way nooks and corners of our american country life, but, when found, is to be bily prized as a national possession, for no-where except in our own country do we find existing just those condition which are necessary for its development." [Penn. **289**

LESSON IN LOVE (A) [by E. [W.] (O.) KIRK: Osgood, 1881.] "is a very good story. It is, besides, an american novel in the strictest sense, that is to say not only are its characters, incidents, and situations american, but it is direct, without color, hardly romantic, and almost bleak. . . . Accordingly, in the fruits of her observation we have a very natural and credible story. The hero is a busy lawyer, whose distinguished abilities are abundantly recognized and make him a good catch. His industry, however, has had the effect of making him a good deal of a bear, and he is rarely seen in society. Engaged as counsel by the family attorney of Mrs. K.. Warrington, he nevertheless finds his imagination touched by his fair client, and before he really knows it he is engaged to her. . . On his side there is little sentiment, and he has to ask himself whether he is really in love or not, until he meets the plaintiff in the suit to break his fiancée's late husband's will, when he promptly falls in love with her in earnest. It perfectly fits with his character that he should not perceive this, and, without much thôt of infidelity, he continues to discharge his duties to Katherine while he enjoys himself with little Doris, who is considerably under 20 and exactly cut out for him. His engagement is kept a secret throu his fear of ridicule, and he has therefore, plenty of opportunity for bily reprehensible conduct, which he indulges with the serene, or at least only vaguely troubled, conscience of a man absolutely selfish, healthy, and active-minded. Doris reciprocates his feeling at once. This state of things finally collapses throu its discovery by Katherine, who bestows herself upon a cousin (who has worshiped her for year), and Truax hies him to Doris and probably has made her a miserable woman ever since." [Nation. **290**

LIFE IN THE NEW WORLD [by "C:

SEALSFIELD," i. e, Carl Postl : New-York, 1842.] "The only novelist who has shown the manners of this country in at all the rit spirit was a German [Austrian] whose stories, published under the pseudonym of Charles Sealsfield, at intervals from 1828 to 1842, attracted, it is said, a great many readers; tho they have now passed into deep obscurity. Sealsfield's supreme advantage was that of an impartial and very impressible mind, to which the immense and varied stretches of our many-chambered life were suddenly revealed. The vast range, the richness of the material, awoke an exhaustless enthusiasm in him, and his life was passed in journeying throu every part of the States, and into the outlying wilderness, and in reporting, throu the medium of novels, his curious and almost limitless discoveries. Nothing escaped him; he did not close his eyes to a single foible or error, and all which he has to tell us of our manners is based on a frame of fact as unyielding and coldly certain as iron. Yet, withal, he possessed a comprehension of our entire system and the quality of our national being which would be rare in a native american. His 'Life in the New World' is a series of novels opening one into another with a continuousness which he must have caut from the Mississippi and the Red River, along whose shores the scenery of the stories is unfolded; and ruf, diffuse, ragged in plan as they are, they give a panoramic vue of american character which is surely one of the most singular things in literature. I say literature; yet you are haunted, in reading him, by a suspicion that it is not fiction, but hugely agglomerated fact, which you have before you. And this is partly true. . . In this story, or rather enormous fragment,—all his books are more or less such, —he uses a Philadelphian magnate with the scarcely masked name of Stephen G—d. In Rambleton, he tries the case of family pride, and of american flirtation ; for there is something judicial in his whole treatment of his themes. We have elsewhere planter-life depicted, and slavery discussed. 'The Squatter Chief' is a bold, bloody, and yet vigorous story with a deep pathos about it. Yet there is a rawness, a lingering exaggeration, in these powerful frescoes. Sealsfield, tho a profound genius, missed being an artist." [G: P. Lathrop in Atlantic.]—"German critics,—H. Ethé, —for example, have long held up Sealsfield as a first-rate genius, and we now find that Dr. Kapp, tho looking at him from a different standpoint, concurs in this vue. 'With what extraordinary success,' he writes, 'did Sealsfield study and observe these people. Even now americans can learn certain features of their character better from him than from the best of *their* writers.' His works form so many chapters 'of the history of civilization, which he paints in truly seductive colors. But their greatest attraction is due to the fact that this modern history is typical for the development of humanity at large, and suggests many wéty points with respect to its oldest history.' In Germany, these works 'were literally devoured, and were a regular topic of students' conversation, both among themselves and with ladies.' In the United States, 'on the most favorable reckoning, he can have had only a few hundred readers, and they forgot his books as soon as read. At present he is here known 'not even by name.' In the Boston Public Library Dr. Kapp could find only one of his works, and 'no american literary history even mentions his name.' This is hardly a fair statement, for Allibone gives him fitting notice, and refers to Griswold, tho the list of his books, compared with Dr. Kapp's, is defective." [Nation. **291**

LITTLE JOANNA. (The) [by E.. W. (C.) BELLAMY: *Appleton*, 1875.] "'Little Joanna' is a story of **Southern** rural life, very quiet and barren of incident, but praiseworthy for refinement in thôt and style and for skilful sketches of character. The heroine is a girl of 15, the granddauter of Judge Basil, with whose widow she lives. Another inmate of the house is a middle-aged lady, known as Pamela, a hard-working, hi-minded, but grim and

rather repulsive person. The widow herself, of lily aristocratic antecedents, leads an easy life in comparative poverty, dreaming of past grandeur. The closing pages, in which the drama hastens to its close, are more entertaining than their predecessors, and the dénouement is satisfactory." [Boston "Literary World." **292**

LITTLE JOURNEY IN THE WORLD. (A) [by C: D. WARNER: *Harper*, 1890.] "Mr. Warner, also, appears to have been struck by New-York as a mirror of modern life, but his attention has been concentrated on a single fase,—the insidiousness with which wealth quickly acquired eats into the finer nature. His theme is a very simple one, but is played in many variations. The reader is introduced to a girl of noble qualities and sensitiveness to impressions, and is asked to witness how her nature is slowly undermined by the silent approaches of the enemy of all spiritual things, the unriteous Mammon. He will observe no marked changes in the superficial nature of the woman. She remains throuôut the book as gracious, as kind, as beautiful, as when she first appears to the little chorus of the story, the néboring circle in a town [**Hartford**], which discusses from time to time the problems suggested by the tale. Her circumstances change: she passes from this seclusion and this little society of cultivated men and women into the very conspicuous circles of **New-York** society; she exchanges a moderate living for one of steadily increasing munificence, and, step by step, rises in the scale of splendor, until she has what, in the eyes of the world, is a commanding position, the wife of one of the richest men in New-York, the mistress of a superb establishment, in possession of all which refined taste can buy, and unstained by any breath of scandal. The task which Mr. Warner set himself was to indicate the slow but steady deterioration of the woman herself at the core, the gradual creeping in of the paralysis of her spiritual faculties, the dying out of that fire-on-the-hearth which was kindled and kept alive in the sweet sobriety of her maidenhood."

85

[Atlantic. **293**
LITTLE PUSSY WILLOW. [by H. [E..] (B.) STOWE: *Fields*, 1871.] "This also is charmingly illustrated, and is a sweet wholesome story for girls, full of the best flavor of the **New-England** country-life, which no one describes so well as Mrs. Stowe. The little maid who is born in the back-country among the hills, to whom Mother Fern and little Mistress Liverworth and Pussy Willow give their gifts like the fairies of old,—the last the 'gift of always seeing the brit side of every-thing,'—grows up with helpful hands and sunny heart, a cheery example of the best thing that grows in this happy corner of the earth. Meantime, little Emily Proudie in New York is fiting the losing battle for health and happiness, under the disadvant-age of too many so-called advantages. It is a good day for the wilted city damsel when she is sent for recovery to the country farm-house, where she learns from little Pussy Willow how to make butter and to look at nature, and to live for other people and not for herself alone." [Relig-ious Magazine. **294**
LITTLE SISTER. [by JANE (WOOLSEY) YARDLEY: *Roberts*, 1882.] "That it is still possible to produce a fiction of the old-fashioned type, simple, pure, probable, and entertaining, the appearance now and again of a book like 'Little Sister' agreeably proves. Honor Armytage, the Little Sister of the story, is a young widow, with two little children, and a pretty, will-ful step-dauter, not many years her junior. Poor, clever, proud with that self-respect-ing pride which has in it no tinge of self-love or self-seeking, full of sweet traits and of inconsistencies no less sweet, loyal to her heart's core to all old ties, but most loyal of all to truth, this Little Sister strikes us as being as good a picture as has often been given of what is distinctive and best in american womanhood. For tho Honor has Scotch blood in her veins, she is essentially, american, too in the common sense which underlies her kindliness; and while she has all the grace and refinement of an english or french lady, there is about

her that flexibility, that gift of adapting herself to circumstances, of living and helping to live, which seems the peculiar endowment of our country-women at their best. She is individual as well. Not every american woman has the clear honesty of soul which characterizes Hon-or, and which leads her to take off her widow's cap and lay it on the fire, the very hour she realizes that her heart has opened to a second love. . . To those who have learned to demand pungent flavor and hi coloring in fiction, this little story, with its simplicity in plot, may seem tame. We commend it to those readers whose palates are more fastidious or less vitiated, who can discriminate between pink and scarlet, and still enjoy in a book freshness, refine-ment, and delicacy of handling." [Bos-ton "Literary World." **295**
LITTLE UPSTART (A) [by W: H: RIDEING: *Cupples*, 1885.] "is a brit and clever novel. Its title is a grain off-color, for the tinge of severity attaching to that epithet does not deservedly character-ize our judgment of the young lady whose personal history and literary fortunes are the subject of the tale. A literary novel, the book mit be called. **Boston** is its scene, and Boston people, mostly, are its characters. Its action is a sort of masquer-ade. Throu a thin veil of fiction we dis-cern a company of men and women, many of whom, notwithstanding their disguises, we are sure we know. . . The heroine is a Vermont girl, barely out of her teens, who from a journal she had furtively kept has written a book, the publication of which has made her famous and brôt her to Boston to be lionized. Here she falls into the hands of a fat, coarse, loud Mrs. Ames, a shoddy poet and social parvenue, with an unctuous and occasionally tipsy husband. Mrs. Ames, recognizing the gifts and graces of Miss Belknap, clutches at her and sets out to utilize her as a means for her own advancement. Meantime, of course, the much-talked-of young author finds a lover, a member of an ancient and honorable family, and in due time he and Miriam mary, and settle down in an apart-

ment on Beacon Hill, much to the disgust of his lofty mother and sisters, who have a great contempt for Mrs. Ames, and no kindness towards any 'little upstart' whom she may be chaperoning. Mrs. Ames' struggles to get into the Denbigh set are frantic, subtile, and amusing. She is a character, a caricature of her kind, and broadly but effectively drawn." [Boston "Literary World." ✦ **296**

LONG LOOK AHEAD. (A) [by AZEL STEVENS ROE: *Derby*, 1855.] "There is much in this book which may by impatient readers be deemed 'long-winded,' but the book is a good book notwithstanding. It has a healthy, hearty, out-of-doors, country air about it, and the details of real american farm life are charming in their natural homely delineations. There are some long conversations in which different religious sects are made to talk to one another, but it is managed in so kindly and pious a spirit, and the results are so full of pleasant incident and good feeling that to lay the good counsel to heart would more profit the reader than to be critical and find fault because the action of the story is somewhat delayed. The character of the hero, who goes about his work 'rit off,' is drawn with spirit. The book has a decidedly american accent, but it is that of a healthy nationality and not a vulgar provincialism; and as a genuine picture of american country life we recommend it to our readers." [Athenæum. **297**

LOVE IN THE NINETEENTH CENTURY [by HARRIET W. PRESTON: *Roberts,* 1873.] is "a very pleasant, brit, happy story with nothing morbid or sensational about it. The narrative flows on in a clear and healthful stream, interrupted by discussions which are natural and sensible. This story calls itself a fragment, and we trust the author will complete it when the 2 young people have had a few years more of experience. Early mariages, made desirable by skillful, economical habits, inexpensive tastes, rational modes of enjoyment and reasonable wishes, will do much to check the feverish ambition and foolish extravagance which are under-

mining the purity and happiness of our domestic relations. The influence of this little book with its cheerful vues and anticipations is all in the rit direction." [Religious Magazine. **298**

LOVE OF A LIFETIME. The [by CAROLINE G. (C.) CURTIS: *Cupples,* 1884.] "Its value lies less in its plot and action than in its grafic, natural, and lifelike delineation of **New-England** village scenes and experiences of a certain type a quarter of a century ago; not caricaturing quaintness and oddity of figure and temper and speech, but holding them up to speak for themselves." [Boston "Literary World." **299**

LUCY ARLYN. [by J: T. TROWBRIDGE: *Ticknor,* 1866.] "The scene of the story is Northern **New-York**: the date is recent. Lucy Arlyn, the heroine, is a girl of unusual intellect, quick sensibility, and a deep, passionate nature. Full of irrepressible longings after the unimaginable and the infinite, her restless maiden fancy sis for she knows not what, and nowhere finds it. Left without a mother at an early age, and her father absent, she is resigned to the care of a widowed aunt with a mariageable dauter, who does not si for the infinite but distinctly wishes to be maried, and is, perhaps, a little envious of the superior graces of her cousin. In this uncongenial air our heroine, still seeking and finding not. meets the son of a néboring squire of hi degree, who is the deadly enemy of Lucy's father. The young man, too, is no common youth; of vehement passions and a powerful imagination, he has been nursed in luxury and is ignorant of self-control. He, likewise, has a weakness for the infinite; but with a genuinely masculine liking for a tangible substratum for his imaginings, he accepts this girl as a temporary equivalent; and after some gentle but pardonable attempts at opposition on her part, an elopement and secret mariage follow. He places her in a néboring farmhouse and pays her stolen visits; but, to deceive his father, who has forbidden the mariage on pain of disinheritance, keeps up the forms of filial duty. Meanwhile the young man grows weary; longings for the infinite begin again to show themselves, and he becomes the leader of a body of spiritists then in the néborhood, who are searching for hidden treasure under the guidance of a half-crazy girl, one of their number, who, lead by spiritual mentors, has left an uncongenial mariage, to fall deeply in love with our hero. While these 2 pursue, hand in hand, their search for things below the earth by means of powers above it, poor Lucy is left alone; her child is born, and she endures at once the ignominy of what the world believes an unhallowed maternity and the anguish of forsaken love. So we are led on from episode to episode, from tragedy to tragedy, till, at last, from Iliad on Iliad of woes—from despair, murder and sudden death—we rest with grateful hearts in the Fortunate Islands." [Round T. 300

MABEL VAUGHAN [by MARIA SUSANNA CUMMINS: Phillips,—Low, 1857.] "is a quiet and intensely good story, about a model heroine of the Queechy school, who after doing her duty as a sister and a dauter, finds at last her reward in a model senator, whose declaration of love reads like a maiden-speech. The book is carefully written; and the story keeps 'within its banks' like the most órderly Thames; but there is a lack of all freshness and spirit. 'Aunt Sabiah' is the only character who seems like a sketch from life. Her sad, patient, shadowy existence is well indicated, and the little reviving sparkle in her old age of the one romance of her life is very well put in, and touches the reader like a strain of an old melody 'played in tune', and is far better than the more labored and ambitious intentions of the other portions." [Athenæum.   301

MC VEYS (The) [by JO. KIRKLAND: Houghton, 1888.] "is a very good novel. The present story is a sort of sequel to Zury: [No. 178.] But "The McVeys" stands sufficiently on its feet to prevent one's ignorance of its predecessor from being a great misfortune. Possibly if the mistiness surrounding Zury's relation to

Anne and her twins were cleared away more fully than it is by the allusions to her editing a Fourierite newspaper in her youth, and the not very explicit hints by which she evaded Dr. Strafford's amusing importunities, it would be less pleasant reading. As it stands, it may be recomended safely. It is full of wholesome lessons on a good many adverse points, and they have the merit of being given without the least touch of didacticism. The talk, let the speakers be who they may, is uniformly interesting and characteristic, and almost always amusing into the bargain." [Catholic World.]—"The life here drawn has taken some steps in civilization beyond the pioneer days of the thirties and forties of the Illinois farming community; for the railroad has come and towns are rising, and there is hint of the coming greatness of Chicago. But in its essence there is but little difference; it is still the extremely provincial life of the fresh water community, sunk in filistinism, out of touch with all the world, and flat as its prairies, yet capable of producing strong and able men, whose rugged virtues and familiarity with overcoming obstacles saved the Union in the days when a great idea moved the whole land, and even the prairies felt the common impulse. This life Mr. Kirkland choose for his study. Pleasing he does not make it,—that would require a false coloring of his picture,—but it is certainly interesting as a study of the great shaping forces, albeit somewhat in the ruf, that make an american commonwealth. As such it is full of hope for the future." [Overland.   302

MADAME LUCAS [by—( ) Wells: Osgood, 1882.] "is a St. Louis story, [disguised as St. Leon,] and with a beautiful and clever Parisian widow for heroine, who has come to the Mississippi Valley capital to live on her fortune, loses it, loses also her heart to a man who secretly has a wife living: and finally, going back to France with a bruised heart, buries herself in a sisterhood. Madame Lucas is the center of a lotos-eating set of ARTISTS, musical and other, whose dialog is reported with some skill; and the discovery of her lover's half-breed wife on the shore of one of the great lakes is managed with some dramatic effect." [Boston "Literary World." **303**

MADONNA OF THE TUBS (The) [by E.. S. (PHELPS) WARD: *Houghton*, 1886.] "is a very delitful little book from the hand of a lady who has done some fine and some doubtful things. It is the story of a fisherman and his family, and of his loss and recovery, and all the little tragedy of a temporary quarrel nearly turned into a great one. But for the interposition of a 'summer boarder'that curiously and vulgarly fine, banal, and unmeaning person, who so often comes in to spoil the natural scene in american romances, the story of the hard-working wife, so tender and true, but with her spark of temper and quick impatience, and the ruf but loving sailor-husband and all their brood, is at once charmingly told and full of pathos and humor. The ruf little house, so clean and brit when all is well, so forlorn under the pressure of sorrow; the mother with her children. so faulty, and tender, and human; the big fisherman, with his ruf ways and superstitions; the salt, keen atmosfere of the sea, and even the special americanism of 'the instrument,'—are all delitful. natural and true. We should have preferred to escape the inevitable fine lady, so superior to the other summer boarders in the ineffable fineness of Beacon Street; but that, perhaps, was too much to be hoped. We do not pretend that Miss Phelps' little book is a masterpiece, but it is very pretty, natural and true." [Blackwood's. **304**

MAN PROPOSES. [*Lee*, 1880.] "Mr. Hugh Prescott is a business man in **Boston**, whomh is partner is about to ruin. In his counting-house he has a nefew, Robert, a theological student, acting as his secretary; and there is a very original person among the clerks, named Amory. In the end Amory proves the hero, having the best material for the making of one. He it is who enriches Mr. Prescott as well as himself by buying stock in a copper mine. He is a very original character; and

the fatherly music-master, who goes to Italy to find out about Phœbe's parentage, is another. The girl herself is unique but not impossible, and very attractive; we like her; with her sincere spirit, her rare voice and beauty as we first meet her; she 'wears well' tho her unusualness is manifested in her clairvoyant experiences; and we are glad that she brings her fortune, nobility, and love to the rit man at last." [Boston "Literary World." **305**

MAN STORY. A [by EDGAR WATSON HOWE: *Ticknor*, 1886.] "'The Story of a Country Town' [No. 146] won hi praise from two critics who did not derive their knowledge of **Western** life solely from books. When Mr. Howells and 'M: Twain' both certify that they have been struck by such a picture, we may be sure that it is worth looking at, at least, especially when there is more agreement than we are wont to expect from critics as to what the features of the picture are. 'Amid the prevailing harshness and aridity,' says one of them, 'there are episodes of tenderness and self-devotion that are like springs of water out of the ground.' "Your pictures of the arid village life.' says the other, 'and the insides and outsides of its people, are vivid, and. what is more, true. I know. for I have seen it all and lived it all." The aridity, it should be noticed, is inherent in the life described, and not in the author. . . The scene is laid in the very heart of the great Western divorce country—that is, somewhere where divorce is regarded as a natural consequence of any ill-assorted mariage, and where at the same time this does not interfere with a hi development of fidelity and affection between those fortunately constituted mates who are designed for each other by nature. Combined with a good deal of literary cleverness, there is what an artist would complain of as a total lack of background. We feel that we are in a new place, in a society without any past, without any associations, in which (apart from the eternal passion which keeps the world going) there is nothing left of all which has made life interesting and attractive except railroads as a means of locomotion and 'dry-goods' as its object. The very language of the story is not the english of literature, but a curious mixture, in which a literary flavor contends with a strong disposition towards bad grammar. Altogether, is this a new species of literature, or is it merely a poor and outlandish species? Heaven forbid that we should find any fault with it as being Western. But what is it?" [Nation. **306**

MAN'S WILL (A) [by EDGAR FAWCETT: *Funk*, 1888.] "is a novel which would serve as a tractate for the teetotalers. It is the story of a man's struggle with an inherited taste for drink, a battle lost time and again, until delirium tremens scares the poor fellow into a resolve which holds. The drunkard's course from the first glass of beer at a Columbia students' mock burial to the fearful end is told with painful particularity. Columbia men, by the way, will not be pleased at the picture of student life given by Mr. Fawcett, and New-York society people will doubtless find their own portraits somewhat too black in the drawing. As in all of the author's work, however, there is a distinct falling short of the object aimed at, and the reader is all the time conscious of this, tho he may not be able to analyze the feeling. The characters are distinct enuf, but not real enuf, and the minute details of how and why the hero drinks every glass of liquor, from one schooner of beer to many sips of absinthe, are wearisome rather than instructive. The effect on his sister of the father's murder in a bar-room, in making her a temperance fanatic, and her relations with her easy-going husband, are better told." [Overland. **307**

MARGARET. [by "LYNDON," i. e., Matilda A. Bright: *Scribner*, 1868.] "Simply and sympathetically told, with entire freedom from straining after effect, and with unfailing good taste, this is almost a model of our idea of a pleasant book. It deliberately relinquishes intensity for naturalness, and, we think, with excellent effect. It is not wine, but cool water fresh from the spring. Without a single absorbing situation, it is also without a single false note. Yet it is far from tame. The story of a sound, gentle, generous woman, and of a noble, earnest, refined man, who lose years of youth and love by the treachery of others, is surely no dull episode, when all the characters are life-like and all the conceptions are clear and true." [Round Table. **308**

MARTIN CHUZZLEWIT. [by C: DICKENS, 1844.] "Here are all our old friends, Jefferson Brick, Col. Diver, Elijah Pogram, Chollop, and the rest of them in a new dress, indeed, but as quaint and impudent and as impossible to survey without lâfter as ever. For our part, we think that all our english censors, from Basil Hall and Mrs. Trollope down to Lowe and Ruskin, have served and do serve a most useful purpose for the country they criticise. There are still plenty of americans who may be benefited by reading 'Martin Chuzzlewit." [Round T'le **309**

MARTIN'S VINEYARD [by AGNES HARRISON: *Low*, 1872.] "is a very clever novel, done in that 'low toue' which artists love and lovers of art appreciate. It is not a little curious that a tale so thoroly american. so full of local lit and shade, should come to us with an english imprimatur, and the name of a writer known to us only by some contributions to english magazines. Quaker life in a New-England village was no doubt striking enuf to make a lasting impression on a traveler alive to novel effects, and to this we perhaps owe the book, which, in the shape of a romance, reproduces, very effectively, the 'interior' of a Quaker household on the Massachusetts coast, with all its contrasts of that quiet exterior to which all outward exhibition of feeling is subdued, and of that depth of passion which works with the more force because it is long concealed. But better even than the Quaker love-story, better, too, than the clever sketches of nature as seen in a New-England coast village, is the life of the village: the various types are well-chosen, and made to play their parts naturally and to the full development of the story." [Penn.]—"A domestic tale, not encumbered by too many characters, unsullied by interludes of crime, and exciting a deep, yet quiet interest, not by the book-maker's tricks, but by the skill of a writer who has evidently studied closely, and to some purpose the workings of the heart, it is a novel which we can heartily commend. We are taken far away from the scenes and circles which have become so hackneyed, and are introduced to a little island called Martin's [**Martha's**] Vineyard, situated some 5 miles from the coast of New England. . . In fact, the story is composed in an artistic, yet natural manner. Milly herself is a charming creation. She is simply an unselfish, good-looking girl, who, romantic tho she be, is an admirable house-wife, and is unconscious of her charms." [Athenæum. **310**

MASTER. (The) [by M.. (ANDREWS) DENISON: Boston, *Walker*, 1862.] "Among the lesser tales of the day is a volume very interesting in its incidents, und very charming in its spirit,—a tale of a music-master, his household and his friends. The charms. trials and perils of the profession are sketched with great felicity and beauty. The story is well developed, easily winning and retaining the reader's attention,—tho it hinges on a quite unnecessary and painful mystery, which is resolved at the end in a somewhat theatrical tableau. Each of the characters, with a curious skill. and without any duplicating, is endowed with some specialty of musical genius; and the serene, noble figure of the Master, large-hearted, gentle, and touched by great griefs. is well worthy to be the central figure. The contrast of the maidens, the brilliancy of the younger man, the half-cynic wisdom and tragic experience of the elder, the crazed tenant of the 'den,' the proud, fond, jealous wife, with the background of humbler life, and the picturesque suggestion of Southern landscape as a foil to the **New-England** city, make a great wealth of material for so small a compass." [Christian Examiner. **311**

MEADOW BROOK, see DARKNESS AND DAYLIGHT.

MELBOURNE HOUSE. [by SUSAN WARNER: *Putnam,—Nisbet*, 1865.] "Daisy wishes to be religious, and having read the commandment about the 'Sabbath-day' she refuses to sing a song out of an opera when desired to do so by her mother, because she does not feel it to be rit. . . Now Daisy acted up to her lit, and showed a hi sense of principle—we do not complain of her; but we do complain against the author for putting the father and mother hopelessly in the wrong—setting them in a cruel and persecuting lit and making a child rise in judgment against them:— it is bad teaching. Mrs. Randolph, the mother, is utterly disagreeable and worldly in all she says and does: the father is a little better, but the aunt is vulgar. Daisy alone is the preacher of goodness and the exemplar for everybody. It is not a good moral to teach children. The office of a parent is sacred. At the age of 6 a spirit of reverent obedience to parents, pastors and masters is better than any amount of doctrinal accuracy." [Athenæum. **312**

MIDGE. (The) [by H : CUYLER BUNNER: *Scribner*, 1886.] "Dr. Evert Peters lives in the French quarter of **New-York**, and by his generous services to a dying woman, friendless in a strange country, wins the affection of her little dauter. In fact, the child is so devoted to him that in spite of his first embarrassment at the situation, he cannot bring himself to part with her. Accordingly, 'the Midge', as he calls the little foreiner, grows-up under his protection, britening with her young life his dim old rooms in Washington Square. They enjoy the ease and freedom of a harmless bohemianism, and are in a way indifferent to social codes. Heroes and heroine's always display a sort of moral somnambulism which enables them to walk over slippery places utterly unconscious of the dangers that lurk beneath, hence it is not until 'the Midge' is 18 that the good doctor begins in logical order to put 2 and 2 together, and makes the delitful discovery that the next thing in order for himself and 'the Midge' to do is to be maried. Unluckily he is just a little late: an entirely superfluous and uninteresting youth of 20 odd has jumped at the conclusion that the young girl has been brôt up by the benevolent minded doctor, at infinite expense and pains, to contribute to *his* happiness, and while our favorite hero is chuckling over his own prospective felicity, he suddenly awakes to the fact that the young people are engaged and wish to mary immediately and go to housekeeping. There is nothing especially original in all this, but Mr. Bunner has told the little story so pleasantly, with entire fidelity to nature, and a little dash of humor without exaggeration, that it makes one of the most readable novels of the season." [American. **313**

MILLY [by LUCY ELLEN GUERNSEY: *Loring*, 1866.] "is an interesting and unpretending little book, in which certain fāses of school-girl life are truthfully depicted, and the various thôts, feelings, and motives of action incident to that period of youth carefully analyzed. The story, tho very simple, has a good purpose, and the moral is inculcated with as little sermonizing as possible. . . We believe, however, that the reader's favorite will be the energetic, honest, and hopeful Priscilla. She and her mother are by far the most sensible and worthy persons in the book; there is a healthy moral tone about them, an absence of all that is morbid or unreal, and a cheerful submission to the crosses of life truly refreshing. . . We cheerfully commend 'Milly' to the perusal of all young people; they will not only be deeply interested in the simple story, but greatly benefited by its wholesome influence." [Round Table. **314**

MINISTER'S CHARGE. (The) [by W : D. HOWELLS, *Ticknor*, 1887.] "Lemuel Barker, the young New-England rustic who goes to Boston, falls into temptation, but into no temptation of the grosser sort in which the true follower of the realists would delit to wallow. The truth is that Mr. Howells, tho he professes to be a real-

ist and to describe life as it is, is not one. He paints the life around him as he chooses to see it. He fits his human beings for presentation in the pages of a family magazine and in novels which may be read by every young girl. He impresses us as a sincere and pure-minded gentleman who arranges his groups, carefully chosen, each member with his working clothes on, and then fotografs them. . . Statira and Manda Greer, the giggling working-girls of 'The Minister's Charge,' are known by certain tricks of manner and speech common to the most frivolous class of **Boston** working-girls. But we learn nothing of their inner lives—if they have any. Lemuel's love-making in the boarding-house room is innocent enuf; but we feel that it is not Lemuel's tender New-England conscience or Statira's principles which make it innocent, but the fact that Mr. Howells (tho invisible, and with an eye to the fact that he writes for american families) is a most careful chaperon.—The Rev. Mr. Sewell, the minister whose amiable habit of telling pleasant fibs has brôt Lemuel to Boston, is a charming character. He is true to life, and, we must admit, something more than a fotograf. He ministers to a very respectable Boston flock; he is sincere in spite of his amiable fibs; he wishes to do rit and to be father-confessor to his people, without the faintest knowledge of moral theology or any training for the work, except a good heart and some experience of the human race in general, and the Bostonians in particular." [Catholic World.]—"It is lit with the most pervasive yet most delicate and elusive spirit of fun. Even that awful nitmare, the New-England conscience, loses all its grimness in the person of Mr. Sewell, and becomes conscious of its incongruity, despite the monitions of the self-constituted gardian angel, Mr. Sewell's wife. It is this spirit of humor that makes it possible to preserve the friendliness of the reader towards such every-day characters as Manda Grier and Statira, and makes one follow with interest all the scenes in the police court, in the Wayfarer's Lodge, and in the street cars, which have excited the ire of more than one critic. But the best character in the book is that of Lemuel. The author has, to be sure, forsworn his own literary tenets even when he seems most anxious to conform to them, for Lemuel is quite as much an ideal, an improbability, as if he had been drawn less awkward and countrified. It is a sort of accepted convention to praise the homely virtues of the country at the expense of the city; but people who know their world would not look very confidently towards the rural districts for any marked examples of purity and simplicity. —Many of us, however, can find it in our hearts to pardon Mr. Howells for cherishing old ideals, and he certainly has succeeded in presenting a very captivating picture of young, unspoiled, untrained manhood, strong and uprit, yet painfully conscious of its own gaucherie. And one of the most admirable effects is produced by the way in which the character of Lemuel defines itself in the reader's mind not so much by what he himself says and does, as by the impression he makes upon others." [Lippincott's. **315**

MISS MARGERY'S ROSES. [by R. C. MEYERS: *Peterson*, 1879.] "A simply and sweetly told little story is 'Miss Margery's Roses,' with only 4 people in it, 2 sisters and their lovers, with a rich and fragrant garden round them, in the midst of whose perfume acquaintance ripens into friendship, and friendship into love; and love makes a strange mistake, and one disappointed but faithful heart is left long to wait for its reward. The receiving by one woman of an oral declaration of love intended for another, with a happy marriage growing out of it, is not a common device in fiction, and we are not sure that it would work smoothly in real life; but here it is made to answer very well." [Boston "Literary World." **316**

MISS NANCY [by IDA RAHM: Phil'a: *McKay*, 1884.] "is an amusing little story; the britness occasionally degenerates into mere smartness, but it is on the whole entertaining. It paints the struggles in society of a pretty country girl who spends a winter in **Philadelphia**, and who is pretty and brit enuf to enslave the royal notice of the most desirable young gentleman in society until she crosses the Rubicon and goes to visit relatives on the wrong side of Market Street." [Critic. **317**

MR. TANGIER'S VACATIONS. [by E: E. HALE: *Roberts*, 1888.] "Mr. Tangier is a city lawyer who stops his brain in the city just in time to prevent it from running away with his life, and flees to parts unknown for rest. The rest is quickly resolved into a lively interest in the country community about him, and thus the story goes on with a hop, skip, and a jump, taking in all sorts of brit situations, and giving an opportunity for a great variety of entertaining social schemes. Mr. Hale's ingenuity never deserts him, and his rattle is a most diverting compound of sense and nonsense. Before one knows it one has pulled the string and gasped under a shower-bath of refreshing, stimulating ideas." [Atlantic. **318**

MRS. MAYBURN'S TWINS [Phil'a, 1882] = JUST ONE DAY.

MRS. PEIXADA [by "SIDNEY LUSKA." i. e., H : Harland: *Cassell*, 1886.] "is a very good story, thoroly thôt-out, well put together, and not painfully melodramatic even in its most striking situations. One cannot overlook the fact that a story made up of telling incidents, strange coincidences, crimes, and casualties, is of but little value; yet much may be forgiven a writer who can throw such an atmosfere of reality over the uncommon happenings he tells about, and whose characters are so distinct and interesting in their personality. Arthur Ripley and his chum, Julian Hetzel, are very pleasant acquaintances. Mrs. Berle, their landlady—whose husband is a commercial traveler and seldom at home—with her host of relatives at their informal gatherings, makes a unique setting for Mrs. Lehmyl. The inevitable cakes and wine which are passed in Mrs. Berle's parlor, the breezy mingling of english and german in the conversation, the music and talk, and cigars, are all touches which count. The peerless Mrs. Lehmyl, however, is the one for whom all the rest is spread out as a background. The vue of the river from Beekman Place is for her approval; all the music and discussion of Wagner is apropos of her magnificent voice, and leads to her singing 'Lehn deine Wang.' The chief objection to characters like Mrs. Lehmyl—in whom, long before she becomes Mrs. Arthur Ripley, the habitual novel-reader easily recognizes Mrs. Peixada—is that as a set-off to some evil-appearing fact of their lives, they must be endowed with so many and so hi excellences. They are apt to seem extravagantly painted. It is an inevitable drawback, however, to any novel which has its tragedy at the wrong end, that there must always be a shadow over the lives of some of the actors. We hope that "Sidney Luska" will use his undoubted faculty for story-telling in a way that will bring his readers closer to humanity, and lead both him and them entirely away from melodrama and sensationalism." [Nation. **319**

MODERN FISHERS OF MEN. [*Appleton*, 1879.] "The experience of a young, untried clergyman among the "Various Sexes, Sects and Sets of Chartville Church and Community" are depicted with a lively pen, some typical characters are presented and natural incidents occur. . . The interest of the story is sustained and satisfactory." [Penn. **320**

MORGESONS (The) [by E.. D. (B.) STODDARD: *Carleton*, 1863.] "is worth reprinting after more than 20 years since its first publication. It is an intensely New-England story. The life depicted is narrow, provincial, and uninteresting, but the characters have some of the stuff in them which makes them worth drawing. Technically, the best thing in the story is its vigorous, condensed dialog.— Sociologists have led us to believe that the type of New-England woman depicted in this story is almost obsolete; that life is daily becoming for her a little gayer and more reasonable." [Life.]—"I was particularly impressed with the childhood of the heroine, and the whole of the first part of the book. It seemed to me as genuine and life-like as anything which pen and ink can do. The latter part showed much power, but struck me as neither so new or so true. There are very few books of which I retain any memory, so long after reading them, as I do of 'The Morgesons.' I hope you will not trouble yourself too much about the morals of your next work —they may be safely left to take care of themselves." [Letter of N. Hawthorne, 1864. **321**

MY DAUGHTER ELINOR [by F. L. BENEDICT: *Harper*, 1869.] "deserves the credit of being an ambitious, and in some measure successful, effort to delineate a kind of social life which american novelists have seldom undertaken, and in which they have still seldomer achieved any appreciable successes. . . It is something to have perceived that, for the purposes of a society novel, the life of the wealthier classes of **New-York** and **Washington**, as being less provincial and less given to notions and 'isms' than New-England life, either in city or village, offered some promising material, and that political and financial crises afforded a newer and more suggestive field for lively writing than theological dogmas, the burden of which is no longer very severely felt, or than social questions which are rapidly settling themselves without attracting overmuch attention from 'society.' . . . It suffers, however, in some degree from its excessive length, and to a much greater one from the author's desire to be always lively, effective, and brilliant in his style. Brilliant, however, he never is, but, on the contrary, often slipshod, always self-conscious, and sometimes even boisterously loud." [Nation. **322**

MY WIFE AND I [by HARRIET [E..] (B.) STOWE: *Ford*, 1871.] "may have been meant to be more a lesson than a delit, and possibly should not be deemed a novel, tho it is hard to consider it in any other way. The plot is meagerly this: A young country-bred college-graduate, who goes to **New-York** and lives by literature, maries, in spite of Mrs. Grundy, a young girl of wealth and fashion, and they set up housekeeping on one of the back streets; and in a little house which the artistic feeling and domestic genius of the wife have made beautiful, they live happily upon a pittance of $7,000 a year. Some toilers in Grub Street would not think this poverty; but Mrs. Stowe achieves for her young people all the social hardship of penury without its discomforts and privations... The purposes of the book are good, and we suppose the sketches of the women-reformers and she-Bohemians are not too luly colored: but it seems to want all fineness of touch and mellowness of tone." [Atlantic.]—"The opening chapters are, by all odds, the most agreeable. There are few more charming pictures of life in a country parsonage than that in which she introduces her hero; and if all his affectional experiences were as delitful as his earliest, we should find this book to be almost peerless in modern fiction. The transition is indeed painful from the innocent bliss of his boyish courtship to the conceited young-mannishness of his college career, and later to the meretricious glitter of New-York fashionable life... The career of Henry Henderson is more interesting than himself. He is a 'newspaper man,' and in his acquaintance we enjoy opportunities of seeing the inside workings of journalism. We hope Mrs. Stowe exaggerates in her description of "The Great Democracy," but her account, no doubt, has a basis of fact, and is interesting. We were specially amused by her reference to the literary part of editorial labor... In addition to its general merit as a treatise on the woman question. there are many admirable things in this book, such as only Mrs. Stowe could do. The author's observations on fashionable life, and on our periodical literature, are shrewd and forcible; and the general filosofy of the work is vigorous and sound." [Boston "Literary World."] See *WE AND OUR NEIGHBORS.* **323**

NELLY OF TRURO [by Mrs. Hornblower: N. Y.,—*Low*, 1857.] "is a really pretty, natural story, containing pictures of american country life and society, which are clever without pretence; and there is throuôut a tone of refined good sense which we are glad to notice." [Athenæum. **324**

NEXT DOOR, see COUNTRY NOVELS.

NO GENTLEMEN. [by C L.. (Root) Burnham: Chicago, *Sumner*, 1881.] "Miss Hopeful Bounce, in the solitude of her Pineland farm-house. conceived the happy idea of advertising for summer boarders. with the proviso that they were to be wholly of her sex. Her modest announcement, attracted the attention of a party of Boston girls just graduated from school and desirous of storing strength against the trials and fatigues of their first winter., They accordingly engaged board at Red Farm and walked. talked, rode and climbed fences in maiden independence, until they came to a proper sense of the utility of the male element in human society. Need it be said that the author was all this time slyly engaged in providing for the introduction of this very element? It beamed on Red Farm, and, by degrees, changed acid to sweet, the green rind to the ruddy; and when the party returned to Boston, the winter's battle was, for some of its members, already won." [Critic. **325**

NO. 40 [by Nannie W. Tunstall: Richmond, *McCarty*, 1884.] "is anonymous, but capitally written. without a trace of effort or art, and with clear verisimilitude to facts. It tells of a loveable young girl, a stranger at the Hygeia. who fires the affections of two gentlemen there, one a Bostonian who loses the prize. the other an old friend of her mother's, who wins it. It is a pleasing little tale, with a fresh piquant taste to it." [Boston "Literary World." **326**

OLD-FASHIONED GIRL, (An) [by Louisa M. Alcott: *Roberts*, 1870.] "And yet it is a pretty story, a very pretty story; and almost inexplicably pleasing, since it is made of such plain material, and helped with no sort of adventure or sensation. It is nothing, in fact, but the story of a little girl from the country. who comes to visit a gay city [**Boston**] family, where there is a fashionable little lady of her age, with a snubbed younger sister, a gruff, good-hearted, mischievous brother,—as well as a staid, sensible papa, a silly, sickly mamma, and an old-time grandmother. In this family Polly makes herself ever so lovely and useful, so that all adore her, tho her clothes are not of the latest fashion, nor her ideas, nor her principles; and by and by, after 6 years, when she returns to the city to give music-lessons and send her brother to college, Mr. Shaw fails, and the heartlessness of fashionable life, which his children had begun to suspect, is plain to them, and Tom's modish fiancée jilts him, and Polly maries him, and Fanny Shaw gets the good and rich and elegant Sydney, who never cared for her money, and did not make love to her till she was poor. That is about all; and as none of these people or their doings are strange or remarkable, we rather wonder where the power of the story lies. There's some humor in it, and as little pathos as possible, and a great deal of good sense, but also some poor writing, and some bad grammar. One enjoys the simple tone, the unsentimentalized facts of common experience, and the truthfulness of many of the pictures of manners and persons. Besides, people always like to read of kindly self-sacrifice, and sweetness, and purity, and naturalness; and this is what Polly is, and what her character teaches in a friendly and unobtrusive way to everybody about her. The story thus mirrors the reader's good-will in her well-doing, and that is perhaps what, more than any other thing, makes it so charming and comfortable; but, if it is not, pleasing the little book remains, nevertheless." [Atlantic. **327**

OLD FRIENDS AND NEW. [by S.. O. JEWETT: *Houghton*, 1879.] "It is a rare gift to be able to use the materials which lie close at everybody's hand. To do this requires tact and skill, as well as an observing eye and nicety of discrimination, and, moreover, such breadth of sympathy, such a 'fellow-feeling' for one's

kind, that the events of the most common, matter-of-fact life seem worth the telling; and all this Miss Jewett has. She is not only one of the sweetest and most charming of writers, but her pages have all along suggestions helpful towards a kindlier and hier way of living; not tacked on in the shape of a moral at the end, but running throu them like a golden thread." [Boston "Literary World."]—"Miss Jewett will have an audience somewhat less numerous than some of the other story tellers, but she will have one whose quality will be of the finest, and whose admiration will be of the heartiest. The purity of her sentiment, the unstrained felicity and naturalness of her style, the thoro likableness of all the people to whom she introduces us, all conspire to render her stories about as nearly perfect in their way as anything can be. With which uncompromising sentiment the critic may as well take himself off, before he is tempted to some other enthusiastic utterance." [Good Company. **328**

OLIVIA DELAPLAINE. [by EDGAR FAWCETT: *Ticknor*, 1888.] "The scene is in **New-York**, and the dominant note is the love of wealth and the subordination of every instinct to the necessity of pushing on to secure a good place in the world. But Mr. Fawcett's picture of fashionable life is not an attractive one. His heroine, a young girl reared in affluence, is cajoled into marying a rich man, vastly her senior, whom she supposes to be at the point of death. He recovers and allows her to find out that he gained a young and beautiful wife by a successful ruse... The story is unpleasant in the extreme, and the only touch of humor to be found in the book is in a scene at an 8th Avenue boarding-house. This is extremely vulgar, but it is broad, natural vulgarity, with an ease and instantaneousness about it which gives the characters reality. We do not believe in being so nice that we cannot bear the vulgarest of people when they are acting naturally. But the vulgarity of some of Mr. Fawcett's fine people is too odious to be borne." [American. **329**

ONLY AN INCIDENT [by G.. DENIO LITCHFIELD: *Putnam*, 1884.] "is one of the most charming stories we have read lately. At first it seems only an amusing study of village [i. e., **Cazenovia, N. Y.**] life, but we soon see that both the humor and the study are such as Miss Woolson mit have given us—and we could hardly give it hier praise. When the story begins to develop, tho it is only the hackneyed plot of a beautiful city girl with her fine clothes bewitching the heart of a little country girl's lover, the treatment is most original, and managed with power as well as tenderness. For the city girl is no idle flirt; she never knows that she has captivated the lover—never tries for him, never wants him, never accepts him. . . She suggests capabilities, and altho she seldom proves them, one is so conscious of her perfect purity and candor that there is charm in spite of selfishness. The story, like the heroine, is unassuming, but full of interest." [Critic. **330**

OPERETTA IN PROFILE (An) [by "CZEIKA," i. e., L.. E. Furniss: *Ticknor*, 1887.] "is one of the cleverest and most entertaining skits we have had for many a day. It purports to be the history of an attempt in a small suburban town to raise money for the church by an original operetta, full of local hits. The subject is suggestive enuf as a target for sarcasm. but the treatment lifts the little theme quite out of the range of ordinary burlesque, into the sfere of really brilliant satire." [Critic. **331**

ORIGINAL BELLE. (An) [by E: P. ROE: *Dodd*, 1885.] "Mr. Roe has scarcely any of the qualities which go to make a first-rate novelist. His imagination is thin and slow, his ability to create natural people is not large, the conversations which he finds for them are such as never could be held outside a book, and his style is one of undiluted commonplace. That his books sell more widely than those of any american novelist is nothing to his credit. There will always be a larger audience for such work as his than there

can be for the delicate art of Howells." [Church Review. **332**

OSBORNE OF ARROCHAR. [by A. M. DOUGLAS: *Lee*, 1890.] "Miss Douglas has here attempted more and achieved more than in the last book of hers before it. That was a story of domestic economy, and dealt with chickens and roses rather than with feeling and character. The present book offers a picture of **Maryland** society in the transition stage. when the traditions of aristocracy are fading, and the practical spirit of the New South has not obtained complete ascendency. The heroine, one of a group of sisters dispossessed of a family estate by an inconvenient kinsman, becomes a clerk in a mercantile house, in spite of the protest of her incapable mother. She has overheard certain uncomplimentary remarks made by the inconvenient kinsman mentioned, in regard to the condition of the estate on his unexpected return from the dead, or rather from years of travel. These make her cherish a bitter hatred for him, which furnishes the proper 'motive' for the regulation love tale between them, wherein her anger is conquered gradually by his force and magnanimity. He is the stereotyped woman's hero, dark, oriental, masterful, Rochester-like. Two of the sisters also have their love histories, and each is so different from their elder sister, and from each other, that the principle of heredity seems to find little credence in Miss Douglas' eyes. Nevertheless, the characters, principal and subordinate, are well drawn, and the movement not more monotonous than girl's stories of domestic life have to be. As a result it is pleasant reading, without in any way being a powerful book, and is read with something like interest throu its four and a half hundred pages to the inevitable result." [Overland. **333**

OTHER GIRLS. (The) [by A. D. (T.) WHITNEY: *Osgood,—Low*, 1873.] "In this little book there is plenty of sorrow and trial. but they are never depressing. The details of the narrative about 'the other girls,' what they did, what they said, what they thôt, desired, suffered and

NOVELS OF AMERICAN CITY LIFE.

accomplished, have more analogy with american manners and customs than with english ones. The history of Bell Bree and Kate Sencer who went out to service, and made such a paradise of their kitchen as to tempt one to prefer it, for living in, to the finest drawing-room that upholsterer ever furnished, would not be possible as a literal experience in England; but the spirit which animated the 2 girls, the brit, cheery, helpful spirit, that makes all their work, in kitchen and parlor, quite a beautiful piece of life-work,—the spirit which would make 'drudgery divine, if we would only let it,' and which would help to drive away the dulness and commonplace which makes this world so weary to our lives,—is possible everywhere. We had marked a great many passages for extract; but it is better that people should buy and read for themselves this most charming and helpful little work, which is filled with thôts which will give rise to kindred thôts and put ideas into the minds of those who read it, which may result in the practice of unthôt-of ways of showing help and kindness to all, far or near. It is a most suggestive little book, and, tho rather rambling, if judged merely as a story, it takes in so many pleasant things and people, and tells of so many different interests, that few would wish it different from what it is." [Athenæum. **334**

OUR UNCLE AND OUR AUNT. [by AMARALA (ARTER) MARTIN: *Putnam*, 1889.] "Of all the books which have been written with the purpose of ameliorating the condition of women, there are few which will prove more effective upon the mind of the average voter, than 'Our Uncle and Our Aunt.' The dry bones of argument and fact are thrown into the form of a lively tale, in which Uncle Sam and his wife play a conspicuous part; and the nearly impossible feat is accomplished of awakening an interest in characters which exist for the purpose of carrying on a discussion." [Nation. **335**

OUT OF THE QUESTION. [by W: D. HOWELLS: *Osgood*, 1877.] "Had

this little comedy been launched upon the 'No Name' sea of literature, the wise public would doubtless have declared that there was the unmistakable touch of a woman's hand in it; that it was quite 'out of the question' for any man to have so subtle an intuition of feminine character. But what is the proof of true genius, if not the possession of this very 'double-nature?'" [Boston "Literary World." **336**

PAGANS (The) [by ARLO BATES: *Holt*, 1884.] "is very clever and suggestive. It describes the doings and opinions of a knot of **Boston** artists and writers,— Bohemians in freedom from conventionalism and contempt for the standards of uncultured respectability,—not as regards personal morality or exclusive devotion to "wein, weib, gesang." To the common canons of morality they add another which they deem of at least equal wêt,—that no honest man may do artistically poor work because it is pecuniarily profitable. They preach the virtue of living up to one's ideals, even when these are not approved by society, and when popularity and luxury are thereby forfeited. The talk, of which there is much, is always interesting and sometimes brilliant. The book is worth reading more than once, tho we fancy that we owe its 'milieu' to the imagination rather than the observation of the author.—See, also, Notice of sequel, "The Philistines." **337**

PETTIBONE NAME (The) [by "MARGARET SIDNEY,". i. e., Harriet Mulford (Stone) Lothrop: *Lothrop*, 1886.] "is a really unique and entertaining story even for one of the long-familiar type known as the 'tale of **New-England**.' The plot turns on the foolishness of an old man who has left all his property to his son, and later to his dauter with heroic sacrifice on the part of the dauter, for the sake of preserving the Pettibone name. All this part of it is very weak, and decidedly not New England like; but incidentally a great deal of genuine humor is woven in, and the story as a whole is well worth reading." [Critic. **338**

PHILISTINES (The). [by ARLO

98

BATES: *Ticknor*, 1889.] "Despite the difficulty of depicting the spiritual deterioration of character, Mr. Bates has been successful in his further delineation of the decline of Arthur Fenton, who, as the reader of 'The Pagans' will remember, on his mariage with Edith Caldwell eschewed Pagan principles for Philistine patronage. Just whether the Bartley Hubbards of humanity, even in dress coats, are inspiriting studies, is perhaps another question. The people of this new book are very much those of 'The Pagans', with some inferior additions; notably Mrs. Amanda Welsh Sampson and her small coterie. There is a broader field of action; we have human nature on a larger scale, brilliant social pictures, and talk on more varied subjects. One cannot but ask, however, is it wise in Mr. Bates, after so artistic a success as that of 'The Pagans' to give us a series of variations on the theme? All knew that Grant Herman's mariage must be a failure; that Edith Fenton would be called upon to go throu the test of fire in trying to live up to her creed of the obligation of maried love; that Fenton himself would easily decend into every Avernus which temptation could afford; that Ninette could never fulfil the complex requirements imposed upon her; and while we are sensible of the skill with which the author has traced the subtle law of development of each of their natures, we wish we had not been invited to drink this cup to its dregs. The book is full of clever situations, of masterful handling of material, of finesse, of brilliancy of style, and of epigrams which excite our warmest admiration." [Critic **339**

PHŒBE. [by MIRIAM (COLES) HARRIS: *Houghton*, 1884.] "'Rutledge', we have heard, still survives in successive small circles which have more youth than literary experience. For their sake, 'Phœbe' should be distinctly condemned. The early incidents are wantonly shocking, and all the rest would be possible only in a world where neither logic nor morals exist." [Nation. **340**

PINK AND WHITE TYRANNY [by HARRIET [E..] (B.) STOWE: *Roberts,—*

Low, 1871.] "is a short novel, showing the beguiling ways of a pretty american girl, whose sober-minded husband, having begun by thinking her an angel, allows her to spend his money, and makes no complaint of 'the inflammation of his weekly bills;' but his eves are opened when he falls into misfortune, and sees her as she really is, and indeed, rather worse. Yet he magnanimously carries out Mrs. Stowe's moral, and, instead of complaining or deserting his wife, makes the best of her, and loves her loyally to the day of her death, and actually creates a loving heart in her frivolous bosom. The pictures of american fine ladies and the frenchified ideas of life and manners are amusing, but the story is very slit, and shows a state of society which is not healthful or pleasant." [Athenæum. **341**

PLAYING THE MISCHIEF [by J: W: DE FOREST: *Harper*, 1875.] "maintains an aspect of consistency and truth which puzzles us even if it does not convince. No doubt it is rather trying to the patience to concentrate our attention throu every page of a long novel upon a woman who, while she is, as the author describes her 'beautiful, graceful, clever, entertaining, and amiable,' is also a most incorrigible and heartless flirt, whose only persistent motive in life is selfish greed, and whose sole purpose, during our acquaintance with her, is to swindle the government... In spite of all defects, however, whether of structure or of style, 'Playing the Mischief' is one of the liveliest and most entertaining of recent novels, and we are confident that no one who reads it (unless it be a Congressman, who mit perhaps find it depressing) will find fault with us for recommending it." [Appleton's. **342**

POLITICIAN'S DAUGHTER. (A) [by MYRA (S.) HAMLIN, *Appleton*, 1886.] "Mrs. Hamlin has introduced us to new scenes. She takes us to a Massachusetts [Gardiner, Maine] town. A Boston snob who fancies that the fact that his great grand-father worked hard to live around Plymouth Rock gives him a patent of nobility, walks home with Miss Harcourt (the politician's dauter) from church. ... Miss Harcourt bears herself in a spirited manner throuóut the novel, rejects a typical politician's son, and maries Bradley. After this she was, we presume, translated alive to the hits where the Boston Brahmins sit on hī and meditate on their great merits. 'A Politician's Daughter' is a clever story, 'sketched rather than filled out. There are some good satirical hits, and some speeches worth remembering. The style is interesting but careless: it is evidently the work of a woman of refinement whose observation of life is quick but not far-reaching." [Catholic World.]—"The qualities of this first essay lie in streaks,— some good and some poor. On the whole the average is in favor of the author, who should be encouraged to try again, and they are not against the reader, who may find an afternoon's entertainment in the story. The 'politician' is of the true Maine stamp, which has not proved of the biest quality of late; he has a shady past and a lovely dauter; and the problem of the book is whether this dauter shall mary the man she loves. or Irving Chipman, who belongs to her father's political set, and who by knowledge of the father's secrets is capable of ruining him. The dialog is weak in spots, and becomes stilted and melodramatic; the descriptive passages are strong, sometimes even brilliant, and have the true touch of talent. ... This book is just to the virtues of old **New-England** towns, alive to the beanties of old New-England homes, appreciative (with satirical asides) of 'Boston culture,' espouses the cause of the scholar in politics and, in the case of the Maine politician, holds the mirror up to nature." [Boston "Literary World."]—"A Politician's Daughter is written by a person who appears to have seen politicians in processions, perhaps, and their dauters in galleries, but scarcely to have had a nearer and more intimate acquaintance." [Atlantic.] The author's father was a senator and ass't secretary of the Treasury;

her husband's father was governor, envoy, senator, and vice-president. [Boston "Literary World." **343**

POOR MR. PONSONBY. [by "DOROTHY FORSTER" in: *New-England Mag.*, Nov. 1890.] This story, by a (to us,) unknown writer, combines enuf good qualities to make successful a much longer work of fiction. It is interesting, and well written; it shows perfect familiarity with society without descending to personal allusions or upholstery; the characters are described not only with knowledge but with sympathy, and above all, the motive is original, and the device of the plot well concealed to the end. There is, too, a serious side to the tale in that the heroine, —a fine girl—who finds herself, unexpectedly, and undeservedly, in a painful situation, rits herself without allowing her ill-luck to spoil her temper or affect her future. **344**

PRINCESS. [by M.. G. MCCLELLAND, *Holt*, 1886.] "It is a pleasure to find a new story by Miss McClelland, whose 'Oblivion', was so interesting and artistic. 'Princess' has the same clear-cut style, artistic finish, and piquant coloring, and is filled with the same shrewd observation, comment, and picturing. The story is the old one of an unhappily maried man wooing an unsuspecting girl, and the treatment at first bids fair to be so satisfactory, that it is a disappointment to find that in the opinion of the author love is enuf." [Critic. **345**

PRIVATE THEATRICALS. [by W: D. HOWELLS: *Ticknor*, 1880?] "There was not much seriousness about 'Out of the Question' or 'Private Theatricals'; if there was a problem concealed in either it was, as one mit say, a society problem rather than a social one. But there was unstinted sweetness and lit, a happy filosofy, a subtle, delicate, unapproachable humor, a style which touched all these qualities with its charm, and was itself the best of charms. It may seem wrongheaded and whimsical to wish that Mr. Howells had gone on producing work of this character, for clearly we should, in that case, have lost 'Silas Lapham' and perhaps even 'The Undiscovered Country.' But the wish is born of the sincere conviction that such work is most congenial to his talent." [Church Review. **346**

PRUDENCE PALFREY [by T: B. ALDRICH: *Osgood*, 1874.] "is a slit sketch of New-England life, with numerous bits of satire and humor. The story opens with the young hero, John Dent, penniless, and madly in love with his uncle's ward, Prudence. Since he is anxious to make a sudden fortune before marrying, he leaves for the West in search of gold-mines, but without any formal engagement. In this new region he makes his fortune, and loses it again by the treachery of his partner, 'Nevins.' Meanwhile, Miss Prudence hears nothing from him for a long time after his first letter, and lends a not wholly unwilling ear to the love-making of a Mr. James Dillingham, a young clergyman who had lately come to the place where she lived. News is brôt to the uncle (who favors Dillingham) that John is dead. Dent returns, however, and it turns out that Dillingham, the clergyman, is really Mr. 'Nevins' himself. . . In this case his course has occasioned the turning at the last of a sketchy tale of sentiment and **New-England** character into a tale of clumsy incident, and this is a rudimentary artistic blunder." Scene: **Portsmouth, N. H.** [Nation. **347**

PRUE AND I [by G: W: CURTIS: N.-Y.. *Dix*, 1856.] "is an american imitation of C: .Lamb—brit, sparkling, and humorous. It is written with a good-natured, self-complacent affability, which disarms criticism. It chronicles only the smallest possible beer,—but the beer is sweet and wholesome. It is chirping, cheerful, and inoffensive." [Athenæ. **348**

PURE SOULED LIAR (A) [Chicago: *Kerr*, 1888,] "is a story of some merit. At least it deserves notice for its choice of locale, in that it takes us out of the round of drawing-room and tennis-court life and makes a bold stroke for something more picturesque. The characters have a *BO-*

HEMIAN flavor, being mainly students in an art school, and the whole air and movement of the little tale may be said to be unusual. . . There is nothing unworthy here, either in morals or art." [Amer. **349**

QUAKER CITY. (The) [by G: LIPPARD: *Phil'a*, 1846.] "This novel was a weird and awful book,—an attack on society, in which Lippard spoke with the frankness of a frenchman, and the venom of an insane man. Society in **Philadelphia** was divided into factions. The laboring class was on the author's side, but the press generally condemned the story as vicious and unnatural, and people in hi places, who were said to have appeared as characters in the book, were outraged. . . More than 100,000 copies of 'The Quaker City' were sold, and it was re-published in London, and also in Germany, where it was issued over the name of F: Gerstäcker." [American. **350**

QUAKER GIRL OF NANTUCKET (A) [by M.. K.. [CONGDON] (JENKINS) LEE: *Houghton*, 1889.] "is the old and hackneyed tale of the child cast up by the sea, and the babies who are 'mixed,' but the dress of the old plot redeems it; for **Nantucket** is a picturesque setting for a story, and this, tho it is almost a child's story in its simplicity, yet takes the reader pleasantly into the company of the amfibious dwellers on the venturesome sand heap which braves the Atlantic. The study of Quaker character, both of the strict and the liberal types, is very good. Of course the story winds up all rit, the mystery is cleared away, and both the waifs come to their own at last, but not before the reader has learned to like both boys and little women, quaker and butterfly, whom he has seen grow to be brides for them." [Overland.]— "Charming, idyllic, dreamy, with the unworldly purity of that isolated island, the book is full of incident, of delitful fancy, of clear characterization, and of a reserve force which makes us hope the author will in her next story try for deeper truths." [Critic. **351**

QUEEN MONEY. [by E. [W.] (O.)

NOVELS OF AMERICAN CITY LIFE.

KIRK: *Ticknor*, 1888.] "The author describes this life just as it is, any exaggeration being due to misconception, not to wilful or stupid misrepresentation. His regret that it is not better or more is plain, and the feeling urges him to make the most of the ardor, honesty, and good aspiration which the country boy, Otto March, brings to town with him, and of the refinement and gentleness of that home where he finds his sweetheart. He perceives, as the unhappy Mr. Charnock says, that half heartedness is a fault of the age—a convenient absolution for Mr. Charnock and the rest of us, if we were not obliged to reflect that men and women make the age, and that, therefore, each individual is responsible for his share of its defects and virtues. For artistic purposes the author might have preferred that the indefatigable Arria White should have had a more moving grievance against her husband than his disapproval of her salad dressing, and he does faintly suggest one. If he had carried the suggestion further, he would have slandered his society. It is the american's naturally respectful attitude towards women, his innate respectability, which saves our enormously wealthy, notoriously unspiritual communities from moral corruption. It is the bad taste, the fysical beauty and vivacity, the mental superficiality and idleness of the Fanny Brockways, which lead foreiners and hasty native tourists to very unjust and false conclusions." [Nation.   352
QUEEN OF SHEBA. (The) [by T: B. ALDRICH: *Osgood*, 1878.] "Mr. A's books take one into good company, put him at his ease, and provide for him an entertainment which, if it be not bily stimulating to his moral nature is, at least, entirely free from every suggestion of evil. This last novelette is perhaps the best that he has written. John Flemming, the impetuous lover of Marjorie Daw, reappears in this story, without strongly reminding us of his former self. The episode of the New Hampshire village into which the hero entered just as the inmates of the insane asylum had escaped, after having

locked in their keepers, is sufficiently humorous; and the sentiment of the story which takes its rise from this incident is cleverly and artistically managed." [Sunday Afternoon.   353
RALEIGH WESTGATE [by H.. (KENDRICK) JOHNSON: *Appleton*, 1889.] is "a rather pleasing and original story. The hero is a young man of hi antecedents and reduced fortune, he becomes—a book agent. The mingling of comedy and ideality makes the book entertaining, not only in the vicinity of York and Kittery [Maine]—the scene of the romance—but wherever leisure invites to the reading of lit literature." [Bos. "Lit. World." 354
REAL FOLKS. [by A. D. (T.) WHITNEY: *Osgood*. 1872.] "There is too much preaching in Mrs. Whitney's book, that is the truth. If it were to be read as a homily, there would be no fault to find, for it teaches sincerity, charity, and all active Christian usefulness. There is no objection to religion in novels, we suppose, even on the part of the ideally heartless critic whom Mrs. Whitney takes to task: and certainly we all desire novels to be pictures of human experience. The trouble with bily moralized novels is apt to be that they are not pictures of human experience, but the experience of preternatural automata, and that the only real foiks in them are the bad ones,—the awful examples to be avoided." [Atlantic.   355
RESPECTABLE FAMILY (A) [by RAY THOMPSON: Chicago, *Donnelly*, 1880.] "conforms to the conditions required of a good, readable, and useful story, and is indeed all of that. The 'family' in question is one living in the outskirts of New-York city, the young and hopeful member of which forms an honorable attachment for a worthy but plebeian girl of the néborhood; a step which is regarded with great horror by his aristocratic parents. Both the young man and young woman behave, however, with great good sense and discretion, and in the end conquer the natural but unwise prejudice against their union, and are happily maried; the 'respectable family' entering into

102

the festivities of the occasion with very good grace." [Boston "Lit. World." **356**

RISE OF SILAS LAPHAM. (The). [by W: D. HOWELLS: *Ticknor*, 1885.] "It is very gratifying to be able to say, after all the wonderful work Mr. Howells has done, that perhaps his last book is the best of all. It is always possible to criticise Howells: to say that he sometimes oversteps the line of good taste; that he is at bottom cynical and never heartily sympathizes with his characters, and so fails to catch in his stories the final glow of secret fire which would make them great and very great. But it is much better to appreciate what Mr. Howells is, than to seek out the few things that he is not. He is the most significant person in american literature to-day, and still on the up-grade; he is the man who has given american novel-writing its standing; who has achieved some virtues of insit and of expression that are new to literature. It is impossible to do justice to the precision and perfection with which he 'takes off' every-day life and speech; and more than that, he has only to turn his scrutiny upon the most bare and unromantic fase of life, and the reader sees it in its true lit, as it appears to the one that is living it. When was the romance of business—the anxiety and pain and desire that do, in fact, make business life almost as full of human emotion as love affairs—so brot out as in 'The Rise of Silas Lapham'? Moreover, there is a warmer quality in this story than in any previous book—a movement toward the hier plane yet, that his admirers have always longed to see him rise to. . . But waiving criticisms it remains that both the love-romance and business romance are carried throu with an almost unparalleled comprehension of character and feeling, and perfection in expressing them. Lapham himself is, of course, the central figure, and nothing could be more perfect than the ruf man of success, all whose gentlemanly virtues at bottom cannot make him agreeable. No social study has ever made so clear the inevitable differentiations which create themselves in even

a democratic society." [Overland.]— "Silas strikes us as an admirable characterization. If he is in certain respects a less original presentation than Bartley Hubbard, he is at least a hero who draws more strongly upon the reader's sympathics and takes surer hold of the popular heart. In fact, Silas, with his big, hairy fist, his ease in his shirt-sleeves, his boatful belief in himself, his conscience, his ambition, and his failure, makes, if we include his sensible wife, the success of the novel. . . While the Coreys try faithfully to compass the best which is known and thôt in the world, the Laphams go to the other extreme, and touch depths of ignorance and vulgarity almost incredible for a family living in Boston with eyes to see, ears to hear, and, above all, money to spend. . . But putting aside the humor and comedy, the book has other points of value, and as a study of a business-man whom success floats to the crest of the wave only to let him be overwhelmed by disaster as the surge retreats, presents a striking similitude to 'César Birotteau'. . . Each man, broken and bankrupt, displays in his feebleness a moral strength he had not shown in his days of power: thus the name 'The rise of Silas Lapham' means his initiation into a clearer and more exalted knowledge of his obligations to himself and to his kind." [Lippincott's.] —"His portraiture of 'Silas' as a 'self-made' man, ignorant in many ways, yet keen, quick and intelligent in all directions, a pushing, energetic striver after money, yet one who in the sorest pinch refuses to do a dishonest act, a coarse-grained man who yet possesses a fine sense of the point where honor sets its limit, a thick-skinned man who is yet sensitive to the voice of conscience,—this portraiture, we say, is entirely successful, and the whole story, designed to develope this character, and to present it as one type of american men, has artistic unity and completeness." [American. **357**

ROGER BERKELEY'S PROBATION. [by H.. (STUART) CAMPBELL: *Roberts*, 1888.] "This story is on the scale of a cabinet picture. It presents interesting figures, natural situations, and warm colors. Written in a quiet key, it is yet moving, and the letter describing the fortunate sale of Roger's painting sends a tear of sympathetic joy to the reader's eye. Roger Berkely was a young american art student in Paris, called home by the mortal sickness of his mother, and detained at home by the spendthriftness of his father and the embarrassment which had thereby overtaken the family affairs. Roger is obliged for the time to abandon his art work, and takes a situation in a mill, and this trying diversion from his purpose is his 'probation.' How he profits by this loss is shown in the result. The mill-life gives Mrs. Campbell opportunity to express herself characteristically in behalf of down-trodden 'labor.' The whole story is simple, natural, sweet, and tender." [Boston "Literary World." **358**

ROLAND BLAKE. [by SILAS W. MITCHELL: *Houghton*, 1886.] "The real interest of the story is to be found toward the end, in the uncommonly sweet and idyllic love-story, with its touch of melodrama. If it were not for Dr. Mitchell's firm grasp upon character, and the true and discriminating hand with which he paints it, together with his ability to interest the reader in that process of character _growth which interests him, all of the story that precedes Blake's wooing by the seaside (save the war-scenes) would drag, —the milieu being thin, the 'dramatis personæ' scanty, and the action slow. But, as we have said, the studies of character are capital, and they would compensate for much. Olivia is one of the purest girl figures presented in fiction for a long time; she is not less well understood than the grosser and more worldly people of the book, nor less solidly bodied-forth, but an elusive and tender perfume hovers about her, and for once we understand as well as the author why the hero falls in love with the heroine. . . And when we say that Roland Blake is good, but hearty; hi-minded, but not morbid; inflexibly true, just, and uprit, but not a prig, and as

much alive as if he were the villain of the book instead of the hero, the reader will understand that Dr. Mitchell has done something worth while. In seeing such an excellent fellow safely maried to so lovely a girl we have a hearty pleasure, which we should not know how to justify by canons of criticism. We must not neglect to say that, tho Dr. Mitchell is as true to real life as we could ask, he surrounds all his story, and especially the courtship between these two, with a tender, poetic atmosfere, which is the final charm of a charming novel." [Church Review. **359**

ROOT-BOUND [etc.] by ROSE(TERRY) COOKE: *Congregational Pub. Society*, 1885.

ROSE IN BLOOM [by LOUISA M. ALCOTT: *Roberts*, 1877.] "is the sequel to 'Eight Cousins' [No. 239]. and begins with the return of Rose, Uncle Alic and Phœbe from their travels in Europe. The cousins are united as before, with this difference only, that during the 2 years passed abroad, the indescribable change between childhood and youth and maidenhood has taken place, and those who parted as boys and girls meet as men and women, and see each other with different eyes. Rose, the heroine, is an excellent girl, who gains the hearty admiration of the reader for her filanthropic plans, and his hearty sympathy as well, in her doubts and disappointments. The book is præeminently a love-story, and one in which both young people and their elders will find interest. Its tone is thoroly sweet and wholesome, bringing to mind in many ways 'Little Women,' [No. 74] and like that it is full of brit and funny sayings and doings, often so intermingled with pathetic and tender touches that we feel uncertain whether it behooves us most to lâf or to wipe our eyes." [Library Table. **360**

ROSES OF SHADOW. [by T: RUSSELL SULLIVAN: *Scribner*, 1885.] "A piece of amateur water-color may easily produce an agreeable sensation, despite the absence of professional skill and confidence. There is a quality of refinement about such work, the out-come of good-breeding and good taste, which one accepts with satisfaction as a genuinely good thing. This is what makes Mr. Sullivan's timid novel, with its faint strokes, a book better worth reading than some which can more surely stand the test of criticism. The quality of refinement which pervades it is an agreeable quality. Even the club scenes take a harmless impropriety; there is no swagger about them, and one feels that a man of the world does not necessarily smell of brandy. More than this, there is a disposition to depend for interest upon real sentiment. One is honestly asked to care for a man who has been disappointed in love, and to be glad that a woman has escaped an unhappy mariage. We do not know that any great thing is to be expected from this writer, but if he will develop from a decorative into a constructive artist and retain all his fineness of tone, one has reason to hope for fiction of a quiet sort which may be genuinely good and interesting." [Atlantic.]—"There is a certain ingenuity in the story of 'Roses of Shadow.' It is not a pretty, or wise, or particularly entertaining story; but a mere will-o'-the wisp of a plot keeps the reader reading, from sheer curiosity as to what it can all be about. The sequel hardly proves worthy of the curiosity, but the book is unique in its ability to keep you reading what you don't particularly like." [Critic.]—"Granting all these defeats, the book is still very entertaining, and does not in the end leave the impression of sadness threatened by the Niagara episode. The style is at once easy and refined, conveying most happily that atmosfere of good breeding and polite society which is indispensable to the novel of manners, but which so many of them lamentably fail of. The descriptions have the pleasant quality of not too much, except perhaps the scenes at Niagara, and those are fine in themselves, only they over-wêt the story. The bits of **Boston** are picturesque and original, and this last means the more that they come after Mr. James and Mr. Howells. Of characters

we find far more interesting than any of the leading personages an Italian artist and his New-England wife, of an incongruity and a sympathy each equally delitful. The book unquestionably promises a future." [Nation. **361**

RUBINA [N.-Y., *Gregory*, 1864.] "is a close and detailed picture of **New-England** life and character. The poor young orfans have a dismal time of it among their hard and coarse relatives. The sterner forms of Puritanism are well depicted. The scene at the funeral of poor Denis, with its harrowing and denunciatory sermon over the corpse of the innocent girl, is powerful and true. The character of the 'help,' Debby, is drawn from life and is admirably conceived and sustained. The book is, however, melancholy and monotonous. So many young and generous hearts beating themselves forever against the sharp stones of the baldest utilitarianism; so many brit minds drifting into despair in the surrounding chaos of obstinate, stolid, and perverse ignorance! It is a sadder book than 'The Mill on the Floss,' of which it reminds us. How the aspiring and imaginative must suffer in an atmosfere so cold and bliting!" [Continental. **362**

RUTLEDGE, see *PHŒBE.*

SAY AND SEAL. [by SUSAN & ANNA B. WARNER: *Lippincott*, 1860.] "The scenes of this clever novel—for it has great merit, notwithstanding its faults of style,—are laid in the very unromantic state of **Connecticut.** Not in a forsaken and neglected hamlet, but near a brit, thriving village, full of school committees, bustling spinsters, busy workmen, and money-making shop-keepers, all unsofisticated, but very shrewd. There is the busy old housekeeper and her bustling danter, both bubbling over with simplicity and activity. The inquisitive old maid, of staid manners, and bily moral, is painted to the very life. There is also a Mr. Linden, an eccentric schoolmaster, who is everybody's guest, talks learnedly on all manner of subjects, and contrives not to make himself understood on any. Mr.

Linden is an excessively dull gentleman, but our authors have succeeded in making him perform well an interesting part in the story. The book is a clever and well-drawn picture of life in the country, and our fair authors have succeeded in investing it with a deep interest, notwithstanding the ruf quality of the materials they had to work with. It may be objected by some, that the dialog is at times heavy, and perhaps too diffuse." [Crayon. **363**

SEA ISLAND ROMANCE (A). [by WM. PERRY BROWN, New York: *Alden*, 1888.] "It is with considerable delicacy of touch that the character of the Southern heroine is drawn. The texture of the whole story is dainty and graceful. Its outline is simple; merely that of a youth and maiden who would fall in love with each other, absolutely ignoring the fact that there had been a war before they were born in which their fathers had been on opposite sides. By turns one finds himself in sympathy with the angry fathers and with the young culprits. with the Southern planter and ex-colonel who despises his thrifty Northern ex-general nébor for making money out of fosfate rock, and with the Northerner's scorn for the ex-Confederate's hauteur and overbearing pride. The escape of the lovers is the ease of Lord Ullin's dauter dualized, for in this modern instance the two fathers stand on the shore and beseech the storm to spare each his child, which it happily does, and they come back very securely united and forgive their fathers for having tried to separate them." [Critic. **364**

SEACLIFF [by J: W: DE FOREST: Boston, *Phillips*, 1859.] "is a very readable novel, artful in plot, effective in characterization, and brilliant in style. 'The Mystery of the Westervelts' is a mystery which excites the reader's curiosity at the outset and holds his pleased attention to the end. The incidents are so contrived that the secret is not anticipated until it is unveiled, and then the explanation is itself a surprise. The characters are generally strongly conceived, skilfully discriminated, and happily combined. The

delineation of Mr. Westervelt, the father of the heroine, is especially good. Irresolute in thôt, impotent in will, and only occasionally fretted by circumstances into a feeble activity, he is an almost painfully accurate representation of a class of men who drift throu life without any power of self-direction. Mrs. Westervelt has equal moral feebleness with less brain, and her character is a study in practical psychology. Somerville, the villain of the piece, who unites the disposition of Domitianus to the manners of Chesterfield, is the pitiless master of this female slave. The coquettish Mrs. Van Leer is a prominent personage of the story; and her shallow malice and pretty deviltries are most effectively represented. She is not only a flirt in outward actions, but a flirt in soul, and her perfection in impertinence almost rises to genius. All these characters betray patient meditation, and the author's hold on them is rarely relaxed. A novel evincing so much intellectual labor, written in a style of careful elaboration, and exhibiting so much skill in the development of the story, can scarcely fail of a success commensurate with its merits." [Atlantic. **365**

SIDNEY. [by MA. [WADE] (CAMPBELL) DELAND: *Houghton*, 1890.] A beautifully told story, whose pathos is relieved from painfulness by the frequent interposition of delitfully humorous scenes. Its only fault is the unreal seeming of the "milieu" which, tho charming, has the effect of being a study after british novels rather than from observation at home. "In "Sidney," Mrs. Deland asks In a world where death is inevitable, is it worth the while to love? So far as one can reach her conclusion throu the characteristic and curious impersonality and impartiality of her style it is the Tennysonian. rather than the Dantean view,—that " 'Tis better to have loved and lost than never to have loved at all," rather than that "it is truth the poet sings That a sorrow's crown of sorrow is remembering happier things." "Sidney" is painted with a touch as firm and as delicate as that which gave us "John

Ward". The canvas is larger, and more crowded with figures, and it is not the characters who embody and present the purpose who are most real, and therefore artistically successful, but the collateral and subordinate characters, who, being in the background, have nothing to do but be comfortably natural and human. Sidney herself has almost as little hold on our apprehension as has Undine: while Mrs. Paul and Kate, and even pathetically colorless little Miss Sally, come instantly into our acceptance with a step that rings healthily clear on every day ground. The tale is of a man whose whole interest in existence is so centred in his wife that on her death he becomes a pessimist. Sidney is his only child, and from her infancy he makes it his care to rear her in his own beliefs: chief among them that love is the most monstrous mistake and irony in the universe, and is to be shunned as the most dreadful pestilence of life. [The following is from a review of "Margaret Jermine", London, 1886:—"A peculiar father is responsible for the peculiar infancy, education, and subsequent fortunes of the heroine. In despair at the loss of his wife, he rushes from the worship of love to an opposite extreme, in which he discovers, declares, and would fain propagate a filosofy which shall exclude love, and herewith suffering, from the human race. He is mad enuf to try the experiment in sober earnest on his only child."] The purpose of the tale is to show how Sidney exchanged these beliefs for others, more hopeful, if scarcely more usual, and how she bore the tests imposed on her by this literal change of heart. As we have said, the dependent plots and subordinate characters are very delitfully done, and are very living and instant in their appeal to our human interest. The scenes between Mrs. Paul and her son, and her son's very brilliant and very human wife, the Kate who is emfatically the most signal success of the book, are something quite wonderful in their grafic truth and pungent humor. Little Miss Sally, and her exasperating lover, in whose final entrance into a mon-

astery we fervently acquiesce, are also admirable types, tho we cannot, with Mrs. Deland, deprecate the natural and wholesome contempt of healthy minds, for the man who, to the continual hurt of his fellows, pauses to wê a strained and morbid scruple against his obvious and honorable duty. Despite the somewhat gray atmosfere of the book, there are no tears in it. It moves throuôut in the dry lit of earnest purpose and well-wrôt art; it takes its place without challenge in the ranks of thôroly good literature; and it adds a fresh leaf to the enduring laurels won by the author of "John Ward." [Boston Transcript.]—"It is so curiously destitute of local color, so painstakingly supplied with english frases, habits and names, that not until after reading many chapters, and turning back to satisfy speculation on this point, is it found that Mercer, where the scene is laid, is a manufacturing town somewhere in Pennsylvania. True, the american cloven foot peeps out, here and there, in incidental allusions to 'ice-cream', 'the Perryville plank-road', and 'eggs at 35 cents a dozen', but in chief part, the tone of the story is so denationalized as to suggest affectation in the author... Little is there beyond an occasional hum from the world of workaday, a whiff of factory smoke drifting across a paragraf, to suggest that Mrs. Deland's men and women are of our time and land." [Critic. 366

SILVER PITCHERS. [by Louisa M. Alcott: Roberts,—Low, 1876.] "The first story in Miss Alcott's volume is a pretty temperance tale. It tells how three beautiful young girls made a league to induce the young men of their acquaintance to forswear the use of wine or stimulants. The young ladies in Miss Alcott's tale are americans, and the conditions of american society are somewhat different from ours, so that english girls, whilst adopting the spirit, must carry out the details according to their own sense of ingenuity and propriety." [Athenæum.367

SIMPLE HEART (A) [by S.. Barnwell Elliott: N.-Y., Ireland, 1887.] "is the story of a man who failed—always a pathetic subject,—and it is made more pathetic because it was the man's success which wrôt his failure. A simple-hearted carpenter in one of the ruf towns of **Texas**, he became a preacher, and raised the people to a level above his own, until they cried out for finer manners, a handsome church, and all which goes therewith. The humor in the little tale is as marked as the pathos, and while the whole is told realistically, with no attempt at rhetoric or analysis, it forms an imaginative bit of insit into character and life that redeems it from being a mere fotograf of the commonplace and makes it a valuable study as well as a beautiful and touching story." [Critic. **368**

SOCIAL EXPERIMENT (A) [by ANNIE ELIZA (PIDGEON) SEARING: *Putnam*, 1885.] "is a quiet, refined, elevated story, a little thn perhaps in its portrayal of personality, a little lacking in color, somewhat too insistent of ethical theories, but a pure, womanly, helpful story, creditable alike to the author's mind and heart. The influence of 'George Eliot' is distinctly perceptible; rather, however, in the governing motives of the tale than in the method of its expression. The social experiment consists in the transplanting of a pretty and intelligent village girl to a home of wealth in **New-York**, where with native intuition she soons adapts herself to her new surroundings, and becomes a social success. 'She had a way of pushing unwelcome thôts behind her at all times, and without distinctly planning to be selfish, took 'the goods the gods provide, nor asked the reason why.' How the ties of her early years titened when she thôt them severed forever, how at length she hears the message that no real happiness can come to her unless she takes up her burden, and by self-sacrifice makes reparation for her selfish neglect of duty; and how she returns to the crude, hard conditions of her girlhood, to work out that self-sacrifice, and how at last she finds peace—this the author relates with sincerity and enthusiasm, appealing always to the better side of

human nature, and not often appealing in vain." [Boston "Literary World." **369**

SONS AND DAUGHTERS. [by "H Hayes," i. e., E. [W.] (O.) KIRK: *Ticknor*, 1887.] "There is, however, no such reward in store for those who wearily plod along with the 'Sons and Daughters' of a suburb of **Philadelphia**. The impossible creatures of the vanishing romance fulfilled their mission, such as it was, much more satisfactorily than do these dreary and insipid misrepresentations of actual life and thôt." [Nation. **370**

STEP ASIDE (A) [by C.. DUNNING [WOOD]: *Houghton*, 1886.] "is a lovestory, with the old fashioned theme of love versus luxury. We can hardly agree with the morality of the conclusion, that a man should mary his sweetheart before he sees his way clear to support her, lest a richer may steal her meanwhile; but the lesson with reasonable limits—that is, that with youth and health, love and a very simple householding should be enuf for honest hearts, and desire for luxury should never stand in the way—is undoubtedly a sound one. 'A Step Aside' has throu all its first part quite an idyllic touch, with the fine old french father, the pretty Pauline, and the excellent Hugh. After the father's death it darkens to a threat of the tragic, in which the writer evidently feels uncomfortable, tho she does not allow her hand to tremble till she has carried the lovers safe throu to a somewhat shorn and tempered 'happiness ever after'." [Overland.] —"It is no lit thing to have done with so firm a hand. To depict nice shades of character and action without quibbling; to present the commonplaces of life without dwelling unnecessarily upon ignoble details; to be natural without being loose, and real without using an H H H pencil; to disclose the foundation of character without eternally fumbling at the roots of life; to be sturdily moral without being goody-goody; to draw people who are perfectly distinct without exaggeration of their characteristics,—to do all this is to do what belongs to a strong artist working in severely plain materials: and this Miss

Dunning has accomplished with a success which excites our admiration, and leads us to praise with scarcely a reservation a book which is throu and throu an honest piece of work." [Atlantic. **371**

STORY OF A WALL-FLOWER [by "DOROTHY PRESCOTT", in *New-England Magazine*, Jan. 1891.] deserves as much praise, and for the same merits, as was given to "Poor Mr. Ponsonby." These tales are almost unique in that, being stories of society, they show no traces of imitation, conscious or unconscious, of english models, and in the striking originality of the central situation. **372**

STORY OF AN OLD NEW-ENGLAND TOWN, [*Cupples*, 1884] = No. 187.

STORY OF HELEN TROY see HELEN TROY.

STORY OF MARGARET KENT (The) [by "H: Hayes," i. e., E. [W.] (O.) KIRK: *Ticknor*, 1886.] "is neither a new nor a pleasant one. It is told with a certain degree of facility, however, which gives it the air of a commonplace, clever piece of fiction-writing. There is no lack of incidents or situations, nor of characters not well enuf drawn to be worthy of praise, nor yet poorly enuf drawn to deserve unqualified censure. The novel, in a word, is commonplace throuôut. . . From the character of the book as a whole, however, one is inclined to think that the author has tolerably succeeded in what he set out to do, and one remembers that 'Not failure, but low aim is crime'." [Nation.]—"Its interest is the more striking ·because it depends, in one direction, only upon perfect simplicity of detail, and in another upon the somewhat hackneyed sensationalism of severe illnesses with remarkable cures of the people whom it is desirable to cure and the death of uncomfortable people who are better out of the way. It is a pity that it dwells upon a divorce, even tho the husband and wife are not divorced after all, and there are rather too many lovers in the story for belief, and the successful one is apparently the result of being obliged to have a hero of some kind. . .

For a society novel it gives the graceful worldliness of fashionable New-York with piquant vividness." [Critic. **373**

STRANGERS AND WAYFARERS. [by S.. O. JEWETT: *Houghton*, 1890.] "Every such volume of her work is sure to be delitful, and this well maintains the regard we have given to those gone before. In the hour of her biest success she can hardly have surpassed 'The Town Poor,' or 'A Winter Courtship' or 'By the Morning Boat.' In these,—as in all others, indeed,—there is acute observation, deep sympathy, a delitful humor, and a fine literary art. No one, we think, writes such short stories as Miss Jewett. Others equal her at some points—may, at single points, even surpass her; but the complete result of her labor is a cameo, carved, polished, and finished, which bears study and yields pleasure at every point. She has worked her New-England field well, and has drawn so many characters from it that one mit fear repetition, yet there is no appearance of this. As human character is so different the real artist can draw it in a thousand different forms without repeating. And to our view Miss Jewett is a true artist." [American. **374**

SUCCESSFUL MAN (A). [by·JULIEN GORDON", i. e., Julia (Storrow) Cruger: *Lippincott*, 1890.] "Daniel Lawton, at the age of 45, after having led a studious life among books, a progressive one among men and affairs, and a negative domestic existence as the husband of a worthy ̦but uninspiring woman and the father of happy children, finds himself, by his enthusiastic nomination for the governorship of his state, the hero of the hour. All society is open to him. His entrance into that social stratum where living has become one of the fine arts is throu the guidance of one of those seductive women whose very fascination for men of character often consists in their superiority to the 'beau monde.' Constance Gresham was an 'elegante' both by environment and temperament; but she had the desire for fuller life, and she was dangerous to Daniel Lawton for just that reason. She recognized the force and the original feeling of the man; and these she wished to turn to account for her glory: so she made him the fashion in her world. But the nicety of the question is not the sincerity of the love between Mrs. Gresham and Dan Lawton; it is the recognition of the situation by Mrs. Lawton, and by the reader, who, more clearly than that stunned and groping woman, realizes that this is one of the irrefutable facts of life, especially of american political life. The question is psychic, not ethical; even Mrs. Lawton in her dull pain saw clearly that while she had settled into an absorbed and routine domesticity, hardly interesting herself in her husband's career, he had gone on doubling the 5 talents which had been given him until he was catching into that reward which worldly capacity commands. It is here, when husband and wife are driving together, when she speaks, when he remembers all she has been to him, that the story closes—how we shall not divulge." [Critic. **375**

SUPERIOR WOMAN (A). [by JANE (WOOLSEY) YARDLEY: *Roberts*, 1885.] "The style of the work is easy, unaffected, and lucidly simple; its incidents, tho by no means startling or even striking, are such as are well adapted to the end of developing the character of the heroine. . . The scene is laid in the city of New-York and its environs, and the fact that there is no exhaustive study of the fashionable life of that city is one which calls for grateful praise." [American. **376**

SUSY L—'S DIARY [by ELIZA J.. CATE.] "had a wide and deserved popularity because of its purity of style and delicate delineation of character. The scene is laid in a New-Hampshire village, and the story embodies much of what was best and truest in New England country life half a century since." [Boston "Literary World." **377**

SWORD OF DAMOCLES (The). [by ANNA K.. (GREEN) ROHLFS: *Putnam*. 1881.] "On the whole the influence of the work is not bracing; there is the smell of the lamp about it; it is morbid, sensational, hysterical: it lacks repose, humor,

pronounced articulation and anatomy. The style is wearisomely prolix, and the conversation of the characters has uniformly a school-girl formality and Johnsonian pomposity which is both tedious and comic. As a study of New-York life, however, the work deserves to meet success." [American. **378**

TAKEN BY SIEGE [*Lippincott*. 1887.] "tells the story of a country boy who goes to New-York to try his fortune as a journalist. Finally becomes managing editor, and maries the prima donna. There is an air of ingenuousness about the book which half redeems it, but it is an innocent story enuf." [Atlantic. **379**

TENDER RECOLLECTIONS OF IRENE MACGILLICUDDY (THE) [by LAURENCE OLIPHANT: *Blackwood*,—*Harper*, 1878.] "is worth noticing as an attempt, which has evidently made a hit, to portray from a foreign point of view the manners of New-York. It is interesting to notice what it is that has struck the author as the leading characteristics of the society which chiefly congregates in that expensive quarter. The freedom and the "smartness" of the young ladies, and the part played by maried men of a certain age in bringing them out, guiding their first steps in society, presiding at their début in the "german," entertaining them at evening repasts at Delmonico's—these points had been already more or less successfully touched upon. But the great feature of New-York fashion is the eagerness and energy displayed by mariageable maidens in what is vulgarly called "hooking" a member of the English aristocracy." [Nation. **380**

THEIR PILGRIMAGE [by C: D. WARNER: *Harper*, 1886.] "is the fruit of a happy idea, brilliantly conceived and well carried out. The idea of twisting together a love story and a panorama of travel is indeed not new. . . Mr. Warner's story, if such it may be called, has however, a much wider range of scenery for its accommodation, and is rather more a series of watering-place sketches than a novel. As such it is delitful. His fresh humor, his keen eye for the traits which distinguish the commonplace from its brother commonplace, and his well-defined but equally well-restrained sympathetic quality, always dashed with just a touch of cynicism, and sometimes, it must be admitted, yielding to fits of fastidiousness. Nevertheless few men could have tasted the changing fases of summer life at all leading eastern watering-places with a more just appreciation of all, and it is instructive as well as delitful to follow him." [American.   **381**

THIEF IN THE NIGHT (THE). [by H. [E..] (P.) SPOFFORD: *Roberts*, 1872.] "The impression which this novel makes is a very curious one. The author sins against reality both by improbabilities of fact and impossibilities of sentiment. There is a misplaced splendor about it, a tawdry elegance, in which our New-England 'Ouida' delits, which is as incongruous as a masquerade dress in a horse-car. The characters flaunt about in brocades and silks and satins; they dine off gold, and never speak without alliteration. They are as elegant as the ladies and gentlemen on tailors' pattern sheets, but look to see what they really are, and you find something equally offensive by reason of its silliness and its wickedness." [Nation. **382**

THROUGH ONE ADMINISTRATION [by F.. [E..] (H.) BURNETT: *Osgood*, 1883.] "is the story, in its main lines, of a young woman entering Washington society just as a young officer in the army—who if he had staid longer in Washington would doubtless have won the young woman—left for the frontier. After 8 years, Col. Tredennis returns to find Bertha the wife of a man who is lit-minded and selfish. She has apparently thrown herself into society from a love of power and a pursuit of happiness, but the return of the friend of her youth is the occasion for a better knowledge of her. She has secretly retained her love of him, which has grown more intense with the decline of her respect for her husband. Throu one administration we are allowed to see the torture of this unhappy woman. Outwardly she is the britèst, the gayest, of mortals, and little

by little these arts are made use of by her husband to accomplish corrupt ends. Col. Tredennis looks on in anguish. He refuses to abandon his faith in her, but that faith must rest upon recollection and occasional glimpses of her real nature; the sit which is offered him is of a heartless, restless woman. . . It is plain that **Washington** society has given Mrs. Burnett much food for reflexion, and the lives of the men and women who draw their bread from official patronage are depicted with power and earnestness. There is much that is in protest against corruption, and there are glimpses of political life as seen from the interior." [Atlantic.]—"The book is full of charm and intelligence. . . It is exquisitely feminine,—full of the soft frou-frou of silken gowns, the odor of heliotrope, the sparkle of jewels on pretty hands, and the flutter of gracefully wielded fans. In fact, the interest of the book centres in Bertha, who is one of the prettiest figures in recent fiction: she fills the stage, and the men, who are subordinate characters, fall into appropriate positions, —the professor, the fact of whose paternity surprises himself, and who studies Bertha,—Richard Amory, who is Bertha's husband and the father of her children, but who, wrapped in love of himself and his objects, allows her to become 'une femme incomprise,'—Col. Tredennis, who loved Bertha from the first, but did not speak at the rit time, hence is silent and faithful,—Arbuthnot, in love with Bertha, senators, etc., all admiring Bertha and revolving about her.—The Westoria Land Scheme, which gradually absorbs Amory, makes him use every effort in his power to promote its success, and he puts his wife into doubtful positions.—compelling her to do a little lobbying for him with her circle of admiring senators. But Bertha fits her way throu her difficulties valiently to the end, and we could wish her better rewarded at the last. The final solution of the problem the incidents of the story have created is pathetic and hopeless." [Lippincott's.   **383**

THROUGH WINDING WAYS. [by

ELLEN W. OLNEY [KIRK] : *Lippincott*, 1879.] "There is always a catastrophe in Miss Olney's stories, but in this the ending is better than common. The interest does not flag at all, tho we have found ourselves giving a si of relief at its turning out so well. There are some unhappy things in it, but the characters generally are noble." [Boston "Literary World." **384**

TINKLING CYMBALS [by EDGAR FAWCETT : *Osgood*, 1884.] "is designed to show the hollowness of modern fashion as contrasted with that land of ideals and ideas which borders on the coast of that other land called Bohemia. Leah Romilly, its heroine, is the dauter of a lady who, in her ardent youth, had scaled the lecturer's platform at a time when to do so involved grave things. . . The end of this experience is to leave Mrs. Romilly stigmatized for life as a person of eccentric or immoral notions. Her young and beautiful dauter, bred among reformers and 'earnest thinkers,' hankers, with a perfectly natural reaction, after that other world where people are content to be beautiful and well mannered and well dressed, to take things litly, amuse themselves easily and constantly, and not worry about 'subjects'. This world she finds in Newport, and she maries one of its denizens, a pet of society, charming and accomplished, who, with a rapidity of decadence known only to the theater, becomes within a twelvemonth an unmitigated, drunken brute; and poor Leah arrives at her real happiness only after his opportune death further in the story." [Boston "Literary World." **385**

TRANSPLANTED ROSE (A) [by M.. E.. (WILSON) SHERWOOD : *Harper*, 1882.] "carries its own scented atmosfere and the britness of its coloring along with it, and gives a detailed account of the splendors of New York life, which, if material and prosaic, has at least the merit of intense realism. . . The society we enter is not alone fashionable, it is correct; and it is the author's function not only to show the privileges and delits of the few, but to moralize upon the weaknesses of human nature in not keeping itself wholesome

under the temptations of wealth and position. The heroine, Rose, a breezy Western girl, comes to visit her aunt in New-York, and meets successes which are in themselves troubles, since she is raw, untutored, undisciplined either by experience or good taste in the code of polite manners. Her progress is, however, rapid and the climax of her success (mariage to an englishman of rank), shows, no doubt, the fitting reward of virtue for all american girls. If a thread of sensationalism and melodrama had been excluded from the little book, it would better have presented the ideas which the writer wished to convey, besides being pleasanter and more rendable." [Lippincott's. **386**

TRITONS [by E. L. BYNNER : Boston, *Lockwood*, 1878.] "is a wholesome and good humored tale of New-York life. . . Both stories are above the average, and impress one as being the facile work of a clever and agreeable man. There is real humor in each, especially in the too rare appearances of the gentleman in Tritons with a mania for china and interior decoration. 'Our drawing-room', he remarks casually at breakfast, 'is commonplace and inartistic. My design is to have the floor laid in 'Marqueterie' of different varieties of irish oak: to have the walls covered with japanese stamped leather, with a dado of ebonized cherry carved in cameo, after a mediæval design of hunting scenes and insignia for which I have drawings. The cieling I shall have painted in panels and cross-hatched with ebonized moldings, while for the frieze I am going to have a fac-simile cast of the Parthenon frieze actually set in the wall. What do you think of that, my dear?'—'I think it will be a jumble of an early english castle, a japanese palace, and a grecian temple, all shaken up and poured into a yankee parlor: and it will be fritful; but then you know I have no intuitive perception."—It is the legitimate function of Mr. Bynner's raillery to touch off the follies of respectable society. When he essays to irradiate with a glare of unnatural cheerfulness the lodgings of a crippled fireman, and to reduce to a series of jingling rimes the 'short and simple annals of the poor,' he fails." [Atlantic. **387**

TRUE TO A TYPE. [by Ro. CLELAND: *Blackwood*, 1887.] "The hero of Mr. Cleland's story of unpolished american life is not an exact replica of Enoch Arden, tho there are several points of resemblance in the 2 characters. Joseph Maylor is true to a type in a more tragical fashion than the Laureate's hero, but the pathos excited by his misfortunes is not so pure and tender as that which is created by the poem. . . The gifts displayed by the author of 'True to a Type' are well suited to the telling of a humorous narrative of provincial existence in **New England**, and it is a pity that Mr. Cleland was not satisfied with a more commonplace plot. As for humor, there is plenty of a kind." [Athenæum. **388**

TRUMPS. [by G: W: CURTIS, *Harper*, —*Low*, 1861.] "The materials are drawn from the many-colored exhibitions of fashionable and commercial life in New York; and they are wröt into a cabinet of portraitures which vividly reflect the familiar traits of the original." [Harper's]—"If this novel be, as it professes, a picture of american town life, America in general, and **New-York** in particular, must be a dreadfully vulgar place. The vulgarity is not on the surface,—not a vulgarity of mere manner, dress, or accent,—but a vulgarity which is innate, that oozes out at every pore; a vulgarity which seems to be congenital, as naturalists say, and to have been, moreover, handed down throu many generations. The vulgarity of worldliness pervades every page of this picture of New-York society; it is as tho the universe were suddenly changed into one great stock-exchange, where to make money and to spend it upon fine upholstery, fine dinners, and fine dress are the being's end and aim of all human creatures,—the chief end of man and his whole duty. There is no ideal, no disguise of science, art, fame, or antiquity; it is all being in business and making money in order to live in the abundance of material luxury; or else,

being in business, to fail and become poor, to live in a small house, and to wear a limp white cravat, which, in this novel, at least, is always the outward and visible sign of having been unfortunate in business. If this novel be a picture of the manners of the day, all we can say is that America must be a dreadful place to be obliged to live in,—one great provincial town, with no metropolis in the distance, where better things mit at least be hoped for, whether to be realized or not." [Athenæum. **389**

TULIP PLACE [by VIRGINIA W. JOHNSON: *Harper*, 1886] "even if it does not strike one as a remarkably good portrait of New-York, is nevertheless full of a grateful vitality and vividness which make it an extremely interesting story. It has a little air of quaintness which seems decidedly of forein influence, and all its situations are too strained to be in the least like Mr. Howells' realism; yet it is all entertaining and suggestive, and combines so much humor, pathos, and thôtfulness, that the reader is sure to be delited with it." [Critic. **390**

TWICE MARRIED [by CALVIN W. PHILLEO: N.-Y., *Dix & Edwards*, 1855.] is "a well-told rural story with carefully studied descriptions of character and scenes 'in the steady old state of **Connecticut**. [Crayon.]—"Has two extremely good points about it,—a short racy preface and the quality of not pretending to be more than it is,—viz., a lively, readable, amusing story of american rural life. The incidents cannot be called very probable, but when a reader is amused he does not care to be critical. The hero's character is well drawn." [Athenæum. **391**

TWO MEN. [by E.. D. (B.) STODDARD: *Bunce*, 1865.] "The reader will find that he has lited upon no ordinary novel. He will read it eagerly for its interest, slowly for its fullness, and he will lend it to those among his friends who have a sense for the uncommon, an ear for rare and fine melody, an eye for nature's scale of color, a soul to which nothing human is forein. By a majority of readers Mrs. Stoddard's book will be called queer and nothing more;

and, truly, nothing is easier than to find fault with its angularities, its abruptness, its needlessly sphinx-like wording . . . Is it a Muse, this practical New-England woman whose story lies equally in the woods and in the kitchen, whose cake-making goes on at the same time with the plucking-out of men's and women's souls and holding them to the lit? It is precisely this mingling of the homely and the awful which gives 'Two Men' its quality. The rude **New-England** sea-coast life, with all its austerities, bears the relation to the character of the book which the moors of Yorkshire do to C.. Brontë's genius." [Nation, 1888,—by Emma Norton Ireland] —"In plot, in character and treatment, 'Two Men' is one of the most original books written by an american woman; it is original in its goodness and in its badness; the author's faults, like her merits, are almost wholly her own, and not Miss Shepherd's, as in the works of Miss Prescott [Spofford], nor C.. Brontë's, as in the works of Miss Harding [Davis]... Apart from this intensity, the literature of the book is excellent. The style is exquisitely clear and sharp-cut: the reader is hurried to the end with a tireless succession of events, and there is a peculiar pleasure and repose to the interest in being made to rest at last solely on the fortune of Philippa and Jason. Altogether the novel must be accepted as an original expression of american feeling, and its characters, however exceptional, as veritable american types." [Nation, 1865, —by W: D. Howells. **392**

UNCLE 'LISHA'S SHOP. [by Row-LAND E. ROBINSON: *Forest & Stream Pub. Co.*, 1887.] "Twenty-two sketches of homely life in **Vermont**, as it was a generation ago. The sketches are continuous in so far that they deal with the same characters, who meet for the most part in the shoe-shop of 'Lisha Peggs . . . So much for the mere external features of the sketches. It would be a mistake to think that the book belonged in the category of thread-bare New-England dialect fiction. Mr. Robinson has the art of a story-teller, and the gift of portrait-painting; and ,when

now and then he touches upon the tender-er side of this homely life, he does it with a sure hand. The compactness of his style is remarkable, and his eye for picturesqueness in nature is keen and sympathetic. The book is racy, but very close to the soil. It is long since we have seen so masculine a treatment, and in spite of the extreme Yankeeism of speech and frase, the book impresses one as singularly fresh and genuine." [Atlantic. **393**

UP FROM THE CAPE. [by HEZEKI-AH BUTTERWORTH: *Estes*, 1883.] "The plea is presented in the form of a pictured contrast between a Boston family and a Cape Cod family, the two heads of which are brothers. The story is told by Jefferson, the son of the **Boston** father. The latter is 41, gray, careworn, sleepless, and dragging himself into an early grave with stocks, per cents, and chloral. The mother is given to Newport, another son is enjoying himself abroad, and the father is slaving his life away in the effort to feed the tastes of an ambitious, idle, and pleasure-loving family. Jefferson is the single exception, and his father's solitary comfort. Uncle Eben, down on the Cape, where Jefferson goes to visit, is 65, but looks younger than his city brother: has lived a quiet and peaceable life, in all godliness and honesty, is content with such things as he has on the old farm, and exhibits a simple, homely character. Aunt Desire, his partner, is offered as the quaint and original figure of the book, and makes some amusement with her clam bakes, her unfortunate investments in the Rev. Dr. Gamm's Colorado mines, and her visits to Boston doctors." [Boston "Literary World." **394**

UPS AND DOWNS. [by E: E. HALE: *Roberts,—Low*, 1873.] "This story, dealing with the ruf and ready vicissitudes of practical life, contains greater variety of incident and character. Without revealing the mechanism of his plot, we may say that Mr. Hale traces the fortunes of a young american from his college days, in which he enjoys the advantage of inherited wealth, to the time when, having lost all by an adverse stroke of fortune, he succeeds in re-establishing himself in a position of independence, and shares his well-earned prosperity with a charming bride... The two heroines, Jasper's Bertha and Oscar's charming Ruth, are simply delitful. Self-reliant, as are all their country-women, and plucky to the verge of rashness in their battles with adverse circumstances, they never lose the essential gentleness which is so often mistakenly associated with fysical or moral weakness. It is notable, too, that, having fôt their own way most resolutely where the conflict was needed, they do not disdain to find the best reward of their success in the retirement of domestic love." [Athenæum.   **395**

VIRGINIA INHERITANCE, A. [by E: PENDLETON : *Appleton*, 1888.]   "Mr. W: Chatterton, of New-York, is the ritful owner of the Virginia plantation concerned in this little story, but in order to claim his inheritance he is obliged to dispossess a poor, proud family of southern cousins who have lived all their lives on the estate in the full belief that it belongs to them. Accordingly Felix Perry, a New-York lawyer, is sent to Virginia to acquaint the southern Chattertons with the fact that they have no legal rits to the place, and that they must renounce their sentimental ones. The lawyer does not find this task easy. Accident leads him to the Chatterton house and he becomes, against his will, domesticated with the very people he has come to put out of possession. He makes his mission known and tries to find quarters elsewhere but is treated with such magnificent courtesy, and it is made so clear to him that his presence on the spot is wholly desirable, that he settles down more or less contentedly to study the Virginia Chattertons. They are one of the typical southern families with which novels have made us familiar. In fact our northern story-writers go to the South for picturesque examples and contrasts, just as english novelists seek them in Ireland. From this imaginative point of vue, the South is an Ireland, unconquered and unconquerable,—swelling with pride, prejudice and

discontent; thriftless, impracticable, talking of millions without a penny in its pocket, piquing itself on superior gentility and dining off a potato. What the South lacks, however, (in order to maintain the parallel) is the irish spirit of humor. These Virginia Chattertons, dilapidated and out-at-elbows as they are, strike us as too dull and solemn to be interesting... The scene soon changes from Virginia to **New-York**, where the southern Chattertons arrive to establish themselves. From this point the interest of the story seems to us submerged in the wider stream of character and events. Mr. Pendleton's study of his New-York people is not so successful as of his rather well-worn southern types. Mrs. Denvers, for example, altho given a striking part, does not play it in a way to engage the reader's sympathy. And indeed the general dénoument is rather too unpleasant for a story which has made no pretension to soar hi or penetrate deep into character and motive. Its purpose would have been better carried out had it contained more lit and cheerful effects." [American.   **396**

WAR OF THE BACHELORS (The) [by G: F. WHARTON: New-Orleans, *Wharton*, 1883.]   "is a comedy, but it is of an elevated tone; it is clean and free from coarseness; it is written with a good deal of vivacity and bonhommie; it shows really considerable wit and conversational brilliancy, and as a mirror of a fâse of **New-Orleans** life, we cannot doubt that it is accurate and vivid. As a composition it lacks background, but its figures balance well, and its dialog is well maintained. As a book there is too much of it. Condensation would improve it." [Boston "Literary World."   **397**

WASHINGTON SQUARE. [by H: JAMES: *Harper*, 1881.]   "Here the author pushes his acceptance of the commonplace almost to the length of audacity, and the story is painfully devoid of life, or color, or movement, or any salient points whatever. The heroine is the embodiment of all that is common-place and flegmatic, and pages of exhaustive analysis are expended in defining and explaining this perfectly uninteresting and ordinary young woman, who is laboriously shown to be not wholly without the feelings common to humanity. The substance of the matter seems to be that no girl is too stupid or inert to fall in love if any man should undertake to make love to her, even from interested motives. In the character of Dr. Penniman a good deal of clever insit is shown, and there are plenty of well-turned, slitly cynical remarks on the general order of things; but the story drags sensibly from a lack of the dramatic sense which enables an author to show, not that the common-place is common-place, but that beneath the common-place often lie the elements of drama which are unperceived by the ordinary observer." [American. **398**

WATCHMAN (The) [by JA. A. MAITLAND: N.-Y.,—; *Routledge*, 1855.] "is an interesting story of american life, full of incidents which are put together like a child's puzzle. No events in real life were ever so clean cut and so well fitted. The people who at the beginning of the book were apparently without either name or country find, in the last hundred pages, not only friends and relatives of the biest respectability, but titles, estates, husbands, wives, and all the various rewards which in moral stories it is customary to bestow upon deserving virtue, and which, being always consoling to the reader's sense of poetical justice, is perhaps the reason why such stories continue to be read by rational beings." [Athenæum. **399**

WE AND OUR NEIGHBORS. [by H. (E..) (B.) STOWE: New-York, *Ford*, 1875.] "'This book brings us back to the circle of friends we meet in 'My Wife and I', and is superior to the earlier work. . . Intellectual strength and beauty of style are not to be found in this book; but one great merit it has: it is the record of quiet, unobtrusive, every-day life, which by thötfulness make many share in the britness of a little home in a back street. It shows the beauty and power of little acts of self-sacrifice and love, for which every

life has ample opportunity, and which novelists are apt to overlook in straining after great deeds of heroism, which can enter into but few lives." [Penn Monthly.]—"When a pet dog 'ticks' across the room, and puts his nose between the 'sluts'; when one young lady 'chippers', another 'snickers', [Mr. W: Black frequently uses "suiggers" in the same sense.—W: M. G.] and a third has 'mifis and tiffs', we know not whether we are studying a new and enlarged english language, or merely a dialect chequered with expressive but local flowers of speech. Of grammar, however, we think we do know something; and we should be a little surprised to hear a lady of good position, on either side of the Atlantic, say, 'I don't see as he has the least intention,' or, 'I don't see what's to object to'. . . Mrs. Stowe seems to advocate that kind of intersexual friendship, which, in some parts of our colonial empire, is called 'Muffining'. Muffining, in itself, is a pleasant amusement; at least, we have been told so by experts; but it is objected to by stern and experienced mammas as not conducing to the stern and serious business of matrimony. Indeed, it is said that muffins are seldom known to get engaged to one another, tho of course there may be exceptions. A male muffin is consequently looked upon by mammas as a noxious person, who is of no use himself, and fritens away those who mit be turned to good account. It must be observed, too, that a muffin is not by law or custom compelled to limit his patronage to one young lady at a time; and there have been cases known in which a large-hearted male muffin has kept a whole charming family single for several years, and has at last 'discovered the state of his feelings' for an unknown chit of a girl in an adjoining parish." [Athenæum. **400**

WIDE-WIDE WORLD (The) [by SUSAN WARNER: *Putnam*, 1851.] "appears to have been written by an american lady of the evangelical school; and its special object is to show that human happiness depends less on the discharge of social and moral obligations than on the observance of certain conventional codes of worship. As a work of art, we can say but little in its favor; yet there are in it such descriptions of american scenery and so nice portraiture of character—especially female—as suggest the idea that the writer is capable of better things." [Ath. **0401**

WIDOW GOLDSMITH'S DAUGHTER. [by JULIE P. SMITH: Hartford, *Brown & Gross*, 1870.] "Writing this novel seems to have been a labor of love to its author. To her, at least, her imaginary world and its people have been convincingly real, and she has painted them with a brisk confidence in her subject, and in her ability to do it justice. which is far from unpleasant. . . She holds up vulgar and commonplace people to ridicule in a way which, to say the least of it, is not suggestive of over-refinement on her part. Her heroine, too, belongs to a type which seems to be fatally prevalent in our native novels —such of them, at least, as are written by women—the young woman who is tormented by a thirst for knowledge, who studies german while she washes her dishes, has a french grammar surreptitiously hidden in her mending-basket, and confounds her enemies and moves her lovers with fond pride by coming out at critical moments with pleasing facts in history or the last new thing in science. Still, much of Miss Smith's work is rather effectively done, and the way in which she displays her characters is often suggestive. Oddly enuf too, it is her faults which are her virtues; and with a more restrained vivacity and a keener sense of what ôt to be omitted in making her studies from life, tho she mit produce more unexceptionable work, we doubt if she would be half so amusing as she is at present." [Nation. **0402**

WIDOW WYSE (The) [by H.. MARR BEAN: Boston, *Cupples*, 1884.] "is an entertaining little book, good for its brevity, its swift movement, and its frequently clever bits of character. It is stated that Mr. Apthorpe is supposed to be the portrait of a well-known **Boston** wit [T: Appleton], but there is little to suggest the trenchant sayings of the gentleman who wished someone would be kind enuf to tether a shorn lamb at the corner of Winter and Tremont Streets during the winter and spring. . . The real art of the book— slit and careless art, but none the less ingenious and clever—is in the delineation of the Widow Wyse: the fair young widow with that supreme art of fascination which is merely the ability to flatter—to make everyone, from the butcher's boy, almost, to Mr. Apthorpe, believe when he meets her that for the first time in his life he is appreciated. The skill, of course, lies in the subtlety of the flattery, and this, so difficult to reproduce in fiction, has been very cleverly given. We are not told in long paragrafs the woman's motives and her successes, but we see her at work. She flits from page to page. from friend to friend, from plot to plot, from airy speech to deliberate intrigue, with a capacity to foresee what may be useful to her, perhaps tomorrow, perhaps 5 years hence, which is exceedingly well reproduced by the author." [Critic. **0403**

WILLIAM HENRY AND HIS FRIENDS [by ABBY (MORTON) DIAZ: *Osgood*, 1871.] "will have a cordial welcome from all the readers of the 'William-Henry Letters.' The new book has, in greater degree, the merits of the first,— surprising unaffectedness, and singular fidelity to nature. . . The material of the book is of the simplest kind: it is merely the diversions and adventures at the farm during the summer in which Mr. Fry boards there with William-Henry's grandmother. William-Henry has been home some years from school, and throuôut this volume is seeking that place in a great wholesale business which he gets at last. He is a veritable young man, as he was a true boy; and we believe there never were more genuine persons in literature than his cousins Lucy-Maria and Matilda, his Aunt Phebe and his Uncle Jacob. The sweetest moral is implied by the whole course of the story,—tho it is scarcely a story,—and it is full of a perfectly delitful humor. Indeed, as a humorist, Mrs. Diaz must be recognized among the first who amiably and profitably please." [Atlantic. **0404**

WOLF AT THE DOOR, (The) [*Roberts*, 1877.] "is a **Boston** story throu and throu. Without great pretensions to either originality, strength, or sharpness of outline, it is free from the commoner faults, and after detaining the reader for its hour will suffer him to go on his way with a pleasant impression. The interest turns on the love-fortunes of a young heiress, whose figure is very cleverly sketched, and toward whom one finds a pleasant feeling growing in his mind. By the 'wolf at the door' is meant the loss of her large property throu the manipulation of a pair of scamps; a disaster from which relief comes to her in the person of a faithful and worthy lover, whom she had nearly lost throu a misunderstanding caused by the treachery of an acquaintance." [Boston "Literary World." **0405**

WOMAN IN SPITE OF HERSELF (A.) [by J: CORDY JEAFFRESON: *Hurst*, 1871.] "This powerfully-written and exciting tale possesses several claims to public attention. In the first place the scene is laid in **Canada**, the oldest and most picturesque of british colonies. Every one who feels an interest in that hospitable land will read with eagerness and sympathy the excellent descriptions of life in the old dominion—english and french 'society', old-world habitans and fresh importations from the green and enthusiastic island, clerical and legal notabilities, garrison loungers, and colonial belles, are all presented to us in grafic and well-ordered groups. The scenery of the **St. Lawrence** affords a theme for Mr. Jeaffreson's descriptive power. In the character of Felicia Avalon, masculine in her accomplishments and her spirit of independent integrity, womanly in her enthusiasm and tenderness, her indignation and despair, our author has given good evidence of his creative originality. Not less admirable is the generous simplicity, the priestliness without arrogance or guile, which characterize her brother Felix; as

charming, tho less original, is the rare nature of the hapless Jemmy, a type of those femininely gentle spirits occasionally to be found combined with intellectual vigor beyond the average of boyhood. When we add to these merits that our author is never dull, that his narrative never flags or fails in continuous energy, we have said enuf to indicate the general excellence of his work." [Athenæum. **0406**

WOMAN'S REASON (A) [by W: D. HOWELLS: *Osgood*, 1883.] "is an interesting contribution to the discussion of self-help by women, in the form of a narrative of Miss Helen Harkness' experience from the time when she lost her father, her lover, and her money until she recovered her lover and was relieved from the predicament in which she found herself. Not until she has sounded the gamut from decorating pottery to serving behind the counter in a fotograf shop is her lover allowed to come to her rescue. He is kept away by an ingenious series of disasters, but the reader awaits his final return with a calm confidence in the upritness of the story-teller. . . Yet how thoroly enjoyable this story is to anyone who knows the originals! We are not certain that a familiar acquaintance with **Boston** and Cambridgeport and the Beverly shore can be dispensed with in a satisfactory appreciation of the characters and situations." [Atlantic. **0407**

WOMEN'S HUSBANDS. [*Lippincott*, 1879.] "Of three good stories here republished the first is 'The Barber of Midas', in which the course of true love is obstructed by the curiosity and meddlesome fussiness of a man who is intended to show that these traits are not exclusively feminine ones, and who fulfils the mission not too obtrusively. 'The False Prince' portrays the struggles of a snobbish man to hide his vulgar antecedents. In 'Narcissus', the third and best, the hero alienates by his self-worship the woman whom he loves, and maries her who only reflects his image. The latter dies but he loses his second chance from the same cause, and passes his life in unsatisfied longing for he knows not what." [Nation. **0408**

WORK. [by LOUISA M. ALCOTT: *Roberts*, 1873.] "The plan of the story is simple. The heroine, an orfan, whose father has been a scholarly and refined man, leaves, at 21, the roof of the rather hard and coarse maternal uncle who had grudgingly cared for her so far, and 'seeks her fortune'. She becomes in succession a housemaid. an actress, a governess, a seamstress, a companion, a copyist, and—after due complications, of course.—a wife, and illustrates in every one of these capacities what is never once loftily asserted,—the real dignity of work. In the qualities which we usually associate with hi-breeding. when we admire it most sincerely,—courage, magnanimity, and delicate honor, first of all in money matters,—Christie's character is peculiarly rich: and he who has proved that these qualities are quite as often found in the obscure as in the splendid walks of life, has done much to bind together the best of every class. Christie, —honest, unfastidious, generous, brilliant, affectionate Christie, is a lady everywhere; and following the checkered path we have indicated, has worked out at 40 a rather shadowed, but sweet and significant destiny. She is but a ruf crayon sketch beside the exquisite cabinet picture of Kitty Ellison, in 'A Chance Acquaintance,' but the motif of both portraits is the same, the grace and the glory of the same order of womanhood is celebrated in both, vehemently by the woman, chivalrously by the man." [Boston "Literary World."]—"This book, which covers a larger field than her other stories, fully sustains Miss Alcott's reputation. Vivacity, clearness, a straitforward directness and earnestness of purpose, pathos, with much skill in filling out the details, are among the hi qualities which carry us throu the story, with increasing interest." [Relig. Magazine. **0409**

YESTERDAY. [by E.. WINTHROP JOHNSON: *Holt*, 1882.] "The book has a positive moral interest as a picture of what life may be made, or more, how a life may even be redeemed; how one mistake, one great sin it may be, need not bring utter ruin, tho a man had no better faith in him than this. The story leads over delicate, even dangerous ground, but, throuốut, conduct is judged with a temperance and justice which commands respect in spite of the lower motives. The rattling pace of the opening chapters should not repel the reader, and he will find himself repaid by the picture of an actor's life from a novel point of vue. Grace Delahay, the heroine, is an ennobling example of the restraining influence of a fine-souled woman even when her direct efforts are thwarted, and her only opportunity is the silent witness of steady pure-living." [Nation. **0410**

YOKE OF THE THORAH (The). [by "SIDNEY LUSKA": *Cassell*, 1887.] "A Jewish artist of repute in his native city, **New-York**, meets and falls in love with the dauter of a yankee customer. Before declaring himself he has a mental struggle over the commandments in the Thorah which forbid under pain of dire penalities the mariage of a jew and a christian. But the man conquers the jew and the day for the wedding is fixed. Elias then confides his secret to his uncle, the rabbi, who calmly tells him that the Lord will interfere, and that the mariage will never take place, and in apparent conformity with the profecy Elias, in the midst of the ceremony, is stricken with a epileptic fit. The disease so affects his character that he readily succumbs to his uncle's influence, renounces Christine, and maries a jewess. ... Mr. Harland has created several life-like personages, notably the rabbi and old Redwood, the rude, uncultivated, straitforward father of Christine. Altogether the best part of the book is that describing the manners and customs of the german jews, who are one and all depicted with grafic power. Nothing could be better in their way than Mr. and Mrs. Blum and Mr. Koch, with their free and easy vulgarity and warm hearts, or Tillie Morgenthau, with her prosaic, flashy demeanor and musical genius." [Boston "Literary World." **0411**

YOUNG GIRL'S WOOING (A) [by E: P. ROE: *Dodd*, 1884.] "throws no lit on the problem of his unquestionable popularity. The large annual circulation of such unqualified trash may be an encouraging sign of the times to the sentimental moralist, than whom no human being has less faculty for looking facts in the face, for seeing life as it is, or for properly conceiving what it should or mit be. The thôt that it is read at all must depress those who believe that the average literary taste is some measure of average intelligence, of national soundness, mental and moral." [Nation. **0412**

ZACHARIAH THE CONGRESSMAN. [by GILBERT ASHVILLE PIERCE: Chicago, Donnelley, 1880.] "Its theme is commonplace, and its workmanship is of the cheap and salable grade. Zachariah is a sensible Westerner, whose head—and we may add whose heart—is turned by political flattery and preferment, and whose misfortunes begin with his election to office and his removal to **Washington**. He there forgets his old and worthy friends, and forms new and dangerous ones, and becomes a wiser man only by first being made a sadder one. A certain verisimilitude underlies parts of the story, and there is a quaint truthfulness in much of the dialect which is woven into it; but its purpose hardly goes further than mere amusement, and in that respect it cannot afford satisfaction to a very hi order of taste. Some things in it are rather silly." [Boston "Literary World." **0413**

A revue, after all, is often in a strange language to every one not acquainted with the book under discussion; but if this has been read the comments of the revuer have more significance, his points are understood, and his praise or dispraise more keenly relished or disrelished. There is always great pleasure in comparing opinions, and no doubt immense satisfaction in finding one's own discernment confirmed. So much greater is the interest in reading a revue after, rather than before, reading the book, that I often wonder whether this is not the best purpose of criticism. If I may judge by my experience and personal likings, a revue is of little interest unless the book is already, in some measure, at least, familiar. But, if that is true, what, again, becomes of the cash value of the revue? Leaving this narrow monetary side of the question, it is certain, I think, that the aggregate influence of book-revues is an aid to literature. It may be difficult to trace this influence in many instances; it may often glance without effect, and sometimes repress rather than help deserving productions; but as a whole, it no doubt widens the knowledge of literature and nourishes the taste for it. It is not, indeed, certain that literature would be possible to any large extent if there were no heralds to proclaim and no chorus to celebrate it. [O. B. Bunce.

PRICE: ONE COPY, $ .50; TWO COPIES. $ .75; THREE, $1.00; FOUR, $1.25; FIVE, $1.50; TEN, $2.50; FIFTEEN, $3.00.

A

DESCRIPTIVE LIST

OF

INTERNATIONAL

NOVELS

COMPILED BY
W: M. GRISWOLD, A. B.

EDITOR OF "THE MONOGRAPH", A COLLECTION OF FIFTY-FOUR HISTORICAL AND
BIOGRAPHICAL ESSAYS; AND OF "TRAVEL," A SIMILAR SERIES
DEVOTED TO PLACES.

CAMBRIDGE, MASS:
W: M. GRISWOLD, PUBLISHER.
1891.

INTERNATIONAL NOVELS.

The object of this list is to direct readers, such as would enjoy the kind of books here described, to a number of novels, easily obtainable, but which, in many cases, have been forgotten within a year or two after publication. That the existence of works of fiction is remembered so short a time is a pity, since, for every new book of merit, there are, in most libraries, a hundred as good or better, unknown to the majority of readers. It is hoped that the publication of this and similar lists will lessen, in some measure, the disposition to read an inferior NEW book when superior OLD books, equally fresh to most readers, are at hand.

This list will be followed by others describing EUROPEAN, ROMANTIC, ECCENTRIC and FANCIFUL novels and tales. The compiler would be pleased to have his attention called to any works deserving a place which have escaped his attention. It may be observed that the compiler has tried to include only such works as are well-written, interesting, and free from sensationalism, sentimentality, and pretense. But in a few cases, books have been noticed on account of the reputation of their authors, or their great popularity, rather than their merit.

The selected "notices" here given are generally abridged.

ABBÉ CONSTANTIN. [by LUDOVIC HALEVY: *Munro,—Putnam*, 1882, *Dodd*, 1888-9.] "All american readers of "Abbé Constantin" will believe that this success is well deserved, for it is due to the charming portraits of 2 american girls. One of the authors of that personification of feminine Parisianism, Froufrou, has now attempted to draw a cousin of Lydia Blood and Daisy Miller. Strange to say, the attempt is a complete success. Mrs. Scott and her sister, Miss Bettina Percival, are true americans—and they are true ladies. It is perhaps a tribute to the purity of the american character that the story in which these ladies play the principal part is not only altogether delītful, but as innocent as it is interesting." [Nation. 401

ACCOMPLISHED GENTLEMAN, An. [by JULIAN STURGIS: *Appleton*, 1879.] "The scene of the story is laid

in Venice, and the descriptions of the town and its sea and sky are charming; sunshine and moonlīt illumine the pages, and there is the līt touch of the man who, however strong his sensations may be, dreads above all things to be 'heavy in hand.' There is a piratical countess, a stout female devotee of art, a boyish, knowing young british peer, a foolish society man for whose mariage we predict no good, and then an enchanted island, a youthful divinity and a gallant wooer, a friendly friend and a maestro full of good intent; these last and the Venetian setting make the charm of the book. There are many felicities of frase." [Nation. 402

ADELE [by JULIA KAVANAGH: *Hurst*, 1857.] "is a charming novel, full of delicate character-painting. The workmanship is good throuout, and the interest kindled in the first

111

chapter burns britly to the close."
[Athenæum. **403**

ADRIAN LYLE, Phil'a, 1889, =
GRETCHEN. **404**

AFTERGLOW. [by G: P. LATH-
ROP: *Roberts*, 1877.] "The subject is
found in the relations and experiences
of a set of americans resident in
Dresden, among whom mingle a
saxon and a prussian officer, an englishman, and 1 or 2 other people. As
a love-story it is thoroly pure and
wholesome, but in its analysis and
delineation of conflicting passions it
goes far deeper than ordinary works."
[Boston "Lit. World." **405**

AGATHA PAGE, [by I: HENDER-
SON: *Ticknor*, 1888.] "The scene is
in **Rome**. The theme is an old one:
the virtuous man who maries a noble
woman for love, but who entertains,
later, a passing fancy for an ignoble
woman who conceives a passion for
him. Both women suffer greatly, the
man not very much, and the wife
comes out victorious and happy in the
end. The wife, Agatha Page, is half-
american, and has been bred at home;
her cousin and rival, a full-blood
Italian, has on the contrary, been educated in a convent." [Cath. World. **406**

ALMOST A DUCHESS [by
OLGA DE LONGUEIUL: *Roberts*,
1884.] "is a very well told story ...
not only distinctly foreign, but showing on many pages the knowledge of
French life with which few english
people are likely to be acquainted.
The plot turns upon the legality of a
mariage contracted by a frenchman in
England against the will of his parents
before he is 25. . . . Independently of
this plot, it possesses much interest
and gives with much ease and naturalness pictures of an english country
nêborhood and glimpses of house-

hold life in France." [Lippincott's. **407**

ALMOST AN ENGLISHMAN. [by
MOSES LEWIS SCUDDER: *Putnam*,
1878.] "A lawyer and a Bostonian
who have been college classmates,
cross the Atlantic in company with a
father and dauter returning to England, and a husband and wife from Chicago. The lawyer, Ketchum, is a rabid
american. The Bostonian, Hill, is an
abject english admirer and copyist.
Ketchum's character is drawn sympathetically, Hill's theoretically, but
there is a certain brute ability in the
way they are developed and discriminated. . . . Nevertheless, Ketchum is
the 'deus ex machina' who by his energy and shrewdness unravels all the
plots, detects the criminals, and prepares the way for the reward of virtue.
At the last, Hill receives his english
bride from the hands of relatives,
whose hearts thrill with joyful relief
when they find that the Bostonian does
not expectorate upon their carpets,
while Ketchum appropriately maries
the widow of the Chicago defaulter, to
whom he had prudently proposed
before her husband's release from the
body. Mr. Scudder makes a rather
good point when he represents the
english bride as reproving her husband
for despising his country, and bracing
him to patriotism; but his prevailing
purpose seems to have been to make
both his britons and his yankees as
unpleasant as possible." [Atlantic. **408**

ALTIORA PETO, [by LAURENCE
OLIPHANT: *Harper*, 1883.] "There
are 2 American girls, one of whom is
a great heiress, and both of whom
represent our glorious country by
great freedom of manner and language, combined with that purity of
heart which in Mr. Oliphant's vue of
the world, the absence of convention-

ality tends to produce. They have with them a terrible old companion or chaperon named Hannah, who talks like something between a Maine Yankee and Buffalo Bill. Her conversation, masculine as it is, does not interfere with her having an excellent heart. . . . Americans who feel sore over the way english writers misrepresent american girls, may derive a good deal of consolation from the way in which Mr. Oliphant treats english society. As depicted by him, it is a combination of Bohemia and Botany-Bay. It is of course closely connected with the world of finance, Altiora herself being the victim of a stupendous fraud perpetrated by her financial gardians. We say the book is an extravaganza, partly because of the burlesque character of the situations; but the author calls it a novel, and perhaps it is as an international novel that it will have to be judged." [Nation,   **409**

AMERICAN, The [by H: JAMES: *Osgood*, 1877.] "The hero, Christopher Newman, a self-made Yankee who has gathered a great fortune before the age of 35, and gone to **Paris** to spend it, naively resolves to take him a wife out of the Faubourg St.Germain, gets the entrée in a sufficiently unlikely manner to that difficult stronghold and very nearly succeeds in carrying out his project. His wife is in fact promised him by her hi-bred and fastidious family. But when these potentates see an unexpected chance of marying her to an imbecile Irish lord they break their pledge. The passive bride, whose heart had really been won, has just spirit enuf to baffle them by going into a convent." [Atlantic.] "The story is naif in the extreme— almost what a Frenchman would call brutal in its simplicity. A rich, pros-

perous, ignorant, wandering american, fresh from San-Francisco and potential money-making, and entirely unacquainted with fine society, finds himself in Paris; and after a few adventures . . . he announces, with the utmost frankness and sincerity, his intentions in a more important matter. . . . His confidence in himself, tho so unjustifiable, has always a certain nobleness in it; and he is never vulgar, nor commonplace, nor petty, but has in him a large and magnanimous nature—something princely and fine, notwithstanding the sharp limitations of his experience, his ignorance and false security. The Old World crushes the representative of the New. It erects before him a cruel, incomprehensible barrier, and sucks the soul out of him, and remorselessly cuts off all his hopes. He is no match for it, tho he thinks at first that he is far more than a match. This is the way in which aristocratic France deals with the American. It baffles him, confounds him, cuts off his ambition and his ideal, and makes an end of what was to have been so good—his future, the reward of his exertions, the fine dream upon which he had concentrated all his hopes." [Blackwood's.   **410**

ANDROMEDA, [by "G: FLEMING,"i.e., Julia [Constance] Fletcher): *Roberts*, 1885.] "The story opens in Tirol where, at the homely whitewashed inn, are staying a frank, careless, keen-witted young Englishman; his life-long friend and confidant, the marquis of San-Donato; the elderly, winning Agatha Dillon, and her hi-bred, undemonstrative, beautiful young half-sister, Clara Dillon, who is supposed by the marquis to represent 'a modern Andromeda, chained to the rack of an impossible engagement, and dependent altogether upon the intervention of hĭ Heaven, and a Perseus for release.' But the first few chapters involve a singnificant change of parts. Clare rejects the suit of the handsome, vacuous Clayton, and becomes the affianced of the marquis, not because she loves him, but because of her womanly admiration for his noble character, and pity, perhaps, for his lonely fate. . . . One always feels sure of Lord Irwin's rollicking good-nature and of the cold, proud, stately Gina's innate selfishness and incapacity for affection. And then there are clever bits of portraiture like that of the emancipated governess, 'a short, compact, active, little englishwoman of 45, with brĭt eyes and smooth sandy hair and a very red face and throat,' who had come abroad 'to digest her liberty.' . . . And as a back-ground to all these human interests we have luminous pictures of scenery among the mountains of **Tirol**, or on the sun-scorched shores of Italy. 'Andromeda' may not be a great novel, but it vindicates thŏroly the author's aim, and is a work varied in motive, fresh and original in conception, strong and finely finished in style." [Boston "Lit. World."] "If Andromeda has more of pure narrative and less of drama than the author has accustomed us to expect from her, it is still a very touching story of self-sacrifice, wrôt with great delicacy. . . . The tale is romantic, if one pleases to use the frase ; but so long as there is any ideal left to human consciousness, hearts will thrill with the admiration of hĭ-heartedness. Besides, "George Fleming" knows the power of a wise restraint. To it she owes the artistic perfection of her

pictures, and from it no less comes her fine discrimination in moral forces. The healthful atmosfere of the book gives it an importance apart from its literary merit. The chief situation is the same that has oftenest been used for evil example—a woman betrothed to one man, but loving his friend, who in turn loves her. That the author has chosen to show how pure and noble souls may save themselves in such peril, is another welcome witness against the theory that a story cannot be vivid or exciting without the appeal to the passions of sense." [Nation. **411**

ARCHIE LOVELL, [by ANNIE EDWARDS: Church, 1867.] "'We all love Archie, and our sympathies spontaneously adapt themselves to every situation of the fresh, unconventional, venturesome, and innocent girl, whose wilfulness gives so much zest to her personality. . . . What grace, what playfulness, what nautiness, what freshness in her character! What a charming and fresh personality, what lively naturalness, what pointed protest against coarseness and awkwardness do you discover in the development of her nature ! . . . 'Archie Lovell' is a faithful, a brilliant, a varied picture of English men and women, modified by Continental [**French**] experience." [Galaxy. **412**

AT CAPRI, [by "CARL DETLEF," i. e., Clara Bauer: Porter & Coates, 1875.] "'is remarkable for its skillful portraiture of character. The hero, a sober and learned professor, is thrown into the society of a young widow, the baroness Valmont, who is described, with little exaggeration, as 'the most bewitching woman in the world'. Despite his infatuation, he clings to his studies, comforting himself with the belief that his passion is reciprocated. Indeed, it seems to be, for the baroness lavishes upon him the wealth of a seemingly boundless affection. At last comes to him a terrible blow; he learns that she is betrothed and soon to be married... The little baroness is certainly one of the most original characters we have met in fiction, and the history of her career, if not instructive, is singularly entertaining. The sketches of life at **Capri** —in the little colony of artists, and among the peasants—are well drawn, and the account of the tarantella is a remarkable specimen of grafic description." [Boston "Lit. World." **413**

AT THE ELEVENTH HOUR [*Putnam*, 1882] = BALLROOM REPENTANCE. **414**

AT THE RED GLOVE. [by K,. S. MACQUOID: *Harper*, 1885.] Altho the scene is laid in Bern, it is a typical french story of french people with french ideas and characteristics, and it is french as well in the symmetry of its arrangements and effects and its admirable technique... Everything is progressing to Madame's content, when a little convent-girl, Marie Peyrolles, comes to Bern to live with her aunt, a glove-seller, whose sign in the Spitalgasse gives the name to the story. It would be a difficult matter to find a prettier piece of comedy than that which ensues upon Marie's advent. It is all simple, spontaneous, and, on the part of the actors, entirely serious, yet the effect is delitfully humorous. **Bern,** with its quaint, arcaded streets, its Alpine vues, and its suburban resorts, makes a capital background, and gives the group free play to meet all sorts of picturesque opportunities. The story is told without any straining after climaxes, but

with many felicitous touches which enhance the effect of every picture and incident." [Lippincott's.] "In skilful simplicity of the plot-construction, in litness of artistic touch as exhibited in the delineation of character, and in general literary excellence, this is the most perfect and enjoyable of Mrs. Macquoid's works. . . . Madame Carouge is sometimes the object of pity, and sometimes a subject of amusement, but never altogether repellant. One's sympathy is, indeed, enlisted on the side of the heroine of the story—for such she is, in spite of the rivalry of the timid, pretty shop-girl—in the opening chapters, in which she is found united in a loveless mariage of convenience to Carouge. He dies when she is but 28. 'Ah! but after all, I do not owe him much,' the beautiful woman said; 'he has wasted my youth. I am 28, and I have not yet begun to live.' But she has read and dreamed; and an ideal lover is one of the inhabitants of her dreamland. . . . But Mrs. Macquoid may be forgiven any weakness in her portrait of Madame Carouge, for having given us Captain Loigerot, so ridiculous in love, so pompous in manner, and yet withal so magnanimous a gentleman. When he discovers how the land lies between Rudolf and Marie, he not only retires from the field with dignity, but he becomes the chief agent in promoting their happiness. One is pleased to see him, in the last chapter, taking so kindly to the rôle of god-father to the children of the woman he loved sincerely after his fashion, If 'At the Red Glove' were merely a good comedy, it would merit very hi praise. But it is something more and better."[Spectator.**415**

AUNT SERENA [by B. W.

(HOWARD) TEUFEL: *Osgood*, 1881.]
"is a story of very unequal merit. In
'Aunt Serena' we have a picture of a
very sweet. woman. . . . She takes her
beautiful niece to Europe. There, in
[Stuttgart], Rose meets the hero,
a man of talent, handsome and rich.
It is a very natural, straitforward love-
story to its climax while listening to
'Lohengrin.' It would have been far
better if that had been the end, for
what comes after is as unnatural as it
is unpleasant. A lady whom Sidney
Bruce had once known. if not loved,
presents herself upon her own invitation. at Aunt Serena's party for Rose's
birthday. She is a figure now familiar
to commonplace, the Circe of the Cleo-
patra pattern. The author endows
her with every charm of person and
manner, especially the latter, and
yet on the next page she does that for
which 'repulsive' is only the mildest
word that can be used. Speaking
generally of the book, the fine New
England types in it did not need as a
foil the narrow walls of a German
pension, with its petty, gossiping
life, and occupants not only mean but
stupid." [Nation. **416**

BABYLON.[by [C:]GRANT[BLAIR-
FINDEL] ALLEN: *Appleton*, 1885.]
"His theme is simple and manageable
—a farmer's boy in Western New-
York. and a peasant boy in England,
one of whom has a native genius for
painting and the other for sculpture;
and the steps by which they escape the
bonds of circumstance. get to Rome,
where they meet, and win fame and
their sweethearts. In an affectionate
and somewhat naive way, which beguiles the reader to lay aside critical
judgment and enter into the spirit of
the thing with him, he follows his 2
lads along, as also the little peasant

girl whom he has destined for the young
sculptor." [Overland. **417**

BALLROOM REPENTANCE, A
[by ANNIE EDWARDS: *Bentley* and
Tauchnitz, 1882.] "Whoever has the
patience to persevere beyond the first
100 pages will find himself, to his surprise, rewarded. The component
parts of the novel—scheming mothers,
weak dauters. dissipated heroes, gamblers and gaming-tables—are so essentially poor, and the style at first so
low in tone, that it is surprising to
find how good a story is developed
from the material. Perhaps the main
point to be noted is that it is interesting: but the novelist is certainly not
devoid of power who can create a hero
with glaring faults and a heroine with
decided weaknesses. yet interest us in
both and prevent us from despising
either." [Critic.] See "At the
Eleventh Hour." **418**

BEATRICE [by JULIA KAVA-
NAGH: *Appleton*, 1865.] "is spirited,
full of incident, written with correctness and grace, and ornamented with
tasteful pen-and-ink sketches of lovely scenery." [Nation. **419**

BELINDA. [by RHODA BROUGH-
TON: *Appleton*, 1883.] Scene in
Dresden. "The author can be refreshingly funny, and the spritly sallies of the shrewd, good-natured,
coarsely-ironical Sarah almost always
excite spontaneous lâfter. In the
range of current lit literature, it would
be hard to find truer sketches from
nature than Sarah, her grandmother,
and her dogs. Here Miss Broughton
forgets to try to be wise and deep,
and is genuinely trivial, genuinely
worldly, almost as genuinely vulgar.
And on comparing 'Belinda' with the
author's earlier productions, it will be
seen that she has reached that stage

of growth which recognizes self-limitations, and has confined her attempts at wisdom and profundity to occasional abstract reflections, for originating which the most spiteful of us will not hold her responsible, She has cultivated a fine feeling for nature, too, and sets her scenes effectively." [Nation. **420**

BEYOND RECALL. [by ADELINE SERGEANT: *Holt*, 1883.] "Another novel of the refined and agreeable sort. It has eminently the air of unaffectedly good society. Its ladies are all more or less winning, its gentlemen are gentlemen in spite of the weaknesses of the lover. . . . The locality of the story is Ramleh, a suburban village a few miles from Alexandria, whither the gentlemen go to business and the ladies shopping, by a little local train. There is something really fascinating in the little english colony, with its social gayeties. its friendly, informal spirit. its sensible business men, its tropical gardens, and its desert—more beautiful than dreary—stretching around it. The inexhaustible quaintness of the contrasting life of ancient **Egypt**, so harmoniously flowing together, supplies one source of unfailing interest throuout the book; however other points fail to interest, one feels that he knows Ramleh; it remains among his mental pictures; he even feels attached to the village, as its people did. The Egyptian politics, too, and the culmination of the narrative in the Alexandrian massacre, are interesting, and free from the sensational—as also, it must be admitted, from the thrilling." [Overland. **421**

BLEDISLOE [by ADA M. TROTTER: *Cupples*. 1887.] "is an attractive story of the invasion of a sleepy english village by 2 brĭt 'american girls, who win friends and lovers, find a great deal to criticise. institute some piquant comparisons and on the whole have a thŏroly good time. Aunt Pen, a charming old maid; Bet, a quaint serving-woman; the handsome, selfish, sport-loving rector, who wishes to clear himself of debts by marrying his beautiful dauter; Keith, a proud. austere. athletic artist in love with Effie; Kent Beresford, a gruff, good-hearted, many-sided lawyer; these are among the leading characters. The author has an easy style; and her humor is fresh and invigorating." [Boston "Lit. World." **422**

BLUE-STOCKING. A [by ANNIE EDWARDS: *Sheldon*, 1877.] "The heroine of the story is Daphne Chester, a young widow with a child, who, living a secluded life in **Jersey**, was in her extreme youth led into mariage with a good-for-naut, who deserted her, and died miserably, relieving her of an intolerable burden. She lives with 3 maiden aunts at an old farm, and is oppressed by the monotony of her existence. . . For Daphne is very beautiful in the fair, golden-haired, Venus style. Rarely have the personal charms of a fair woman been more deftly set forth—rather indicated than described—in any of the many novels of the day. We feel rather than see that she must have been enchanting." [Galaxy. **423**

BOURBON LILIES [by E.. [J—] (WILLIAMS) CHAMPNEY: *Lockwood, Brooks & Co.*. 1878.] "is a particularly graceful and finished little story, showing much tenderness of feeling and liveliness of mind. The scenery and characters are almost exclusively **french**." [Atlantic.] "With the best side of artist life in Paris, Mrs. Champney is familiar; and her story, which is rather a sketch than a romance, presents an agreeable picture of some fases of that life. . . . The narrative is enriched by legendary tales of the locality. [Sunday Afternoon. **424**

BUNDLE OF LETTERS, A. [by H: JAMES.] . . . "In 'The Europeans,' 'A Bundle of Letters' and 'The Pension Beaurepas' one and the same attempt is made to exhibit the wholesome simplicity, the fresh, instinctive, native virtue, of the american types in contrast with the satisfaction, conventionality, and lower moral ideas and standards of the european. And that these qualities are represented as co-existing with other less desirable and admirable characteristics—with the narrow-mindedness of a Puritan family and the vulgarity of nouveaux-riches tourists—merely proves the fidelity of Mr. James' observation, and gives to his creations the stamp of genuine reality. The failure of the Wentworth family to comprehend the baroness Eugenia is a testimony to their simple-minded purity of thôt; and the ineffectual endeavor of Miss Aurora Church to conduct herself like one american-born tho european-bred brings into relief the sincerity and straitforwardness as well as the plebeian breeding of Miss Sophie Ruck. The fact that this purity and sincerity of nature are attributed to persons whom we recognize as 'common', low-placed in the social scale, is what makes Mr. James' compliment to his country the more significant: these virtues, he implies, are every-day virtues among us americans; we take them as matters-of-course, unaware how precious they are and how far from being the current of social life in other countries." [Corres. Boston

"Lit. World." **425**

BY THE TIBER, see ROMANTIC NOVELS.

CABIN AND GONDOLA [by C.. DUNNING [WOOD]: *Harper*, 1886.] "contains several short stories, which all show originality and versatility, and strength both of conception and style. They are of every variety, and all are good." [Critic.] "It takes 11 tales to fill out the 200 pages, and, as a rule, they are quite short, airy, and lit; yet they strike one as being more than sketches, after all. Whatever may be the facts in the case, one feels in reading them that they were not dashed off with recklessness; they seem to show the finishing marks of a careful hand. It is entirely to this finish of form and an engaging delicacy of style that the stories owe their charm, for there is nothing strikingly original about them. . . . The author's fondness for making a plot of the simplest materials and for turning the story on the very slitest incidents is noticeable throuout, and one finds one's self wondering, when the volume is put aside, what there was in it that interested him; but the interest is there, nevertheless." [Nation. **426**

CAPTAIN MANSANA, [by BJÖRNSON: *Houghton*, 1882.] "In 'Captain Mansana' the most considerable and by far the most powerful story of the 3, Mr. Björnson takes an Italian subject, the love history of a man whose presence of mind, courage, love of honor, whose fysical strength and energy, dexterity and shrewdness, rouse to the hiest pitch our expectations as to his future possibilities, but at the same time fill us with solicitude. The central scene in this singularly simple but intensely dramatic narrative is Mansana's conquest of the affections of the princess Theresa Leaney under the advantage of a terrible railway accident, in which the lover's strength and prowess completely vanquish the lady's heart. . . . Mansana's is a wild and tumultuous nature, and after this his heart is touched for a moment throu sympathy, by a young girl. But Theresa follows him, recovers him to loyalty. and the story leaves them happily maried in Hungary." [Boston "Lit. World." **427**

CARLINO [by GIOVANNI [DOMENICO] RUFFINI: *Lippincott.* 1870.] "is nothing but the story of how a simple and affectionate young italian, in the quality of servant. subdues the pride of an aristocratic master. and becomes, in the baron's despite, his sole support and most loved and valued friend. . . . When the Baron is thrown from his horse and made a cripple for life, he remembers with meekness and longing this despised friend. and for the rest the story is the account of their affectionate association. But it is full of charming sketches of French and Italian characters and manners; and tho it is brief, yet if it is really the business of an author to make his reader happier and desirous of being better, then Mr. Ruffini has here achieved success not surpassed by that of any other of his very delitful books. We do not mean to hint that the little story is artistically defective; on the contrary it is the best literature, and of a kind of fiction,—simple, direct, and confident, like that of Auerbach, Björnson, and Erckmann-Chatrian,—which no one born to speak english has yet had the courage to attempt, tho it is evident that nothing pleases english-readers better." [Atlantic. **428**

CHOISY. [by JAMES P. STORY: *Osgood*, 1872.] "The chief charm of this story is in its representations of Parisian life. which surpass in spirit and realism anything we have lately read. The reader finds it hard to believe that they are not the work of a Parisian. The picture of Paris on race-day is marvellously vivid: and, in a dozen sentences, the author makes us at home in the Latin Quarter. To the opera, the famous cafés, the Jockey Club, the Mabille—indeed, to almost every theatre of 'fast' life in Paris—he is a cicerone of few but sufficient words. who knows whereof he speaks, and is never tedious. The two best characters in the book are Jack Somers and Nina Choisy; Charley Wales represents the average 'fast' young man, and Huntley is cast in a mold that has been worn out in fiction. Somers is a spring of perennial delit; he never opens his mouth but to amuse the reader, and his character is a problem which one never grows weary in studying. Of Nina Choisy we can say only that her loveliness of person and manner go as far toward excusing Charley's sin as any merely human considerations could do; the reader admires while he blames her, and pities the fair young girl whom cruel fate has made the wife of an imbecile old man. and whose untutored heart yields itself at the first masterful summons. We have read many better american novels. but not one of more absorbing interest. It deals, as we have said. with very prepossessing varieties of vice; but thotful readers. who apprehend the real significance of Charley's sufferings and of Nina's melancholy career, will find in it a moral lesson which gains impressiveness from the medium in

CHEVALIER OF PENSIERI-VANI (The). [by H: B. FULLER: Boston, Cupples, 1891.] "It is always pleasant tŏ wander in spirit over a land so full of beauty and so replete with historical and artistic interest as **Italy** with an author whŏ knoes and appreçiates it thŏroly. The book is a record of the wanderings of a dilettante in the fine arts in pursuit of rare expressions of genius. He searches for relics in Etruscan tŏmbs ŏnly tŏ be ashamed of his vandalism in remŏving them; he pursues a Perugino all over Italy, ŏnly tŏ find at Pisa that it is not a Perugino at all but sŏmething rarer stil—a Sodoma; he looks for traçes of the Goths in Ravenna, and cŏmes away content with bits of mosaic; and he rummages in musty bookstalls in Venice in the hope of finding an Aldine which might hav been overlooked by the connoisseurs. The topics ar all handled in a very graçeful manner, touched by lŏving fingers trained tŏ a perfect appreçiation of the happiness tŏ be obtaiued in and throu them. Any ŏne tŏ whŏm the beauty and interest in such things appeal wil derive considerable enjoyment from this little book, which cŏvers grŏund he has probably gŏne over himself and tŏ which he is never loath tŏ return." [Critic.]—"The Chevalier's emotions ar of the kind which should stir responsiv thrills in the breast of the sentimental traveler whŏse tastes tend tŏ art and archæology, and Aldine imprints, and the like. The author's descriptiv art is pleasantly revealed in these sketches, tho the persons introduçed in a sŏmewhat discursiv narrativ ar closely vailed and make a vague sho. The Prorege of Arcopia, the Duke of Avon, the agreeable Contessa, Pensieri-Vani himself, ar mysterious, possibly illustrious Incogniti. But most of us hav met Occident, the young untraveled American." [Saturday Review.]—"The appearance of the book with an additional chapter is very welcŏme tŏ those whŏ hav made the chevalier's acquaintançe, and affords a fit occasion for recommending him tŏ those whŏ dŏ not yet kno him as a charming traveling companion; ŏne traverses with him a country too wel knŏn tŏ be regarded as a sho, but so lŏved that its every road is fruitful of pleasure. Yet delightful as the Italian atmosphere is, and accomplished an interpreter as Mr. Fuller is, his delicate satire so insinuates itself throu the reader's mind that the very marked style which challenges, and gets his continual admiration alŏng the way, finally seems tŏ exist in order tŏ emphasize the significançe of the cavaliere's title. It is true that we ar warned against taking things too seriously; we ar advised tŏ aççept the cavaliere "as he is." And indeed thére is no ŏther way tŏ take him; notwithstanding which ŏne feels a half humorous pity as ŏne leaves the lonely little dilettante with nŏthing in particular tŏ justify his existençe, and the sense of the fact irretrievably lodged beneath the sensations of his passing hŏur. And then on the ŏther hand, young Mr. Occident and the extraordinary young woman whŏ givs up a public singer's cause tŏ go home with him tŏ Shelby county,—thêy, too, may hav thêir vain regrets later, and the possible prima donna wil be almost sure tŏ. The book is an exquisit bit of literary work." [Springfield Republican. **428 s**

COSMOPOLIS. [by PAUL BOURGET: N.-Y., *M. J. Ivers*, 341 pp., *Tait & Co.*, 343 pp., *Waverly Co.*, 341 pp., 1893.] The soçiety described "is a group comprising several nationalities, and abiding in **Rome**. It is the very best society, so far as birth and wealth and the cultivation of the world can make the best. The author's serious motiv is tŏ prŏve the permanençe of race; his hypothesis being that, in moments of passion, when a man's nature is deeply touched, raçial traits wil sho . . . But thêre ar many moments when his grêat creativ skil relegates theory tŏ oblivion, and these ar the moments when, having reflected, we find that the theory has been most cleverly eluçidated. The Countess Steno, and the wife of Boleslas Gorka, ar drawn with extraordinary forçe and finish . . . Twŏ such characters giv a novel literary distinction; and a half dozen more, dŏne with almost equal understanding, truth, and particularity, confer fame." [Nation.] —"By laying the scene in **Rome**, Mr. Bourget is enabled tŏ bring intŏ close relations a group of men and women whŏ differ widely both in thêir characteristics and in thêir artistic value. Sŏme of them strike us as old acquaintançes; the clever and unscrupulous Jewish finançier whŏ has set his heårt on marrying his angelic dauter tŏ a ŏnce rich Roman noble, reduçed tŏ trading on a grêat name; the good-natured and cynical French writer whŏ wil dŏ anything for his friends exçept put himself tŏ inconveniençe; the American brother and sister with a faint tinġe of negro blood and the traditional virtues and viçes of the slave,—all these,

altho thêy play important parts, ar in themselvs but supernumeraries. Four people, however, take the stage by right— the Countess Steno, the Marquis de Montfanon, Boleslas Gorka and his English wife. Caterina Steno, the descendant of a long line of noble Venetians, reverts directly tŏ a type familiar tŏ those whŏ kno anything of the social life of Venice in the last century. She has many virtues, few meannesses, and no morals in our sense. She is ġenerous, affectionate after her fashion, brave enuf tŏ play for hi stakes, and loyal while she lŏves. She dŏes not cheat herself, nor lie, from choiçe, tŏ ŏthers, and her nervs ar as strŏng as her passions. From a moral point of vue she is, of course, wholly tŏ be condemned, but looked at artistically, she givs a degree of the same pleasure which ŏne feels before a portrait by Tiziano of sŏme woman whŏ may hav wrung heårts and ruined lives in her day, but whŏse beauty is immortal and irresponsible. The character of Maud Gorka is much simpler. Married tŏ a Pole whŏm she dearly lŏves, her honest English nature has always suffered vaguely from the subtle and tortuous element inherent in the Slavonic raçes, and when the tragedy cŏmes which wrecs her happiness, she behaves with a strict justiçe and sŏmewhat hard nobility which we feel tŏ be the ŏnly course possible tŏ her. The contrast of these twŏ women is immensely effectiv, and not too much insisted upon, for Bourget has a keen sense of what is called, in the slang of anŏther art, "values." " [Critic. **431 p**

which it is conveyed." [Boston "Lit. World." **429**

CHRIS. [by W: E: NORRIS: *Macmillan*, 1888.] "Here are emotional incidents in plenty, but all is sweet and brīt, and, as we may say, aboveboard. No shame either to character or intelligence to have this pretty tale on one's table, or to put it in the hands of one's growing dauter. 'Chris' is delītful." [American.]—"Mr. Norris has written another entertaining story, fresH, clean and readable. It is all about a young english girl left an orfan at **Cannes,** and sent to live with an eccentric and miserly old aunt in London. Three lovers gather round her, two for her worth and one for her money, and the course of the story finds its interest in her parries and thrusts in dealing with these lovers, only one of whom deserves her. Mr. Norris is a līt and pleasant writer, with a vein of humor and a knack for character drawing." Boston "Literary World." **430**

CONFIDENCE. [by H: JAMES: *Houghton*, 1880.] "As a bit of what may be called social imagination, the story is deserving of hī praise. From very slender materials Mr. James has woven a complicated plot about the distinctly defined heroes and heroines, and the ins and outs of the game form as entertaining a book as one can care to read. The main hero, Bernard Longueville, is the thôtful, clever fellow, the observer, who is not uncommonly found in Mr. James' stories; and we have, too, a new specimen of the large class of chattering American girls, one Blanche Evers, whose artless prattle is capitally given. The other heroine is of sterner stuff, a really serious character, and her mother is the well-known American matron, who when well on in years does her hair in as complicated involutions as if she were a girl in her teens. The relations in which these people stand to one another are sufficiently intricate, and their social skirmishing does them credit. The chief heroine. Angela, plays her part with especial skill; her swift comprehension of the position in which she is placed in regard to the two men— which should serve against those unhealthy alliances—and her handling of the tangled threads at the end of the book are certainly entertaining reading." Scene: **Siena & Baden.** [Atlantic. **431**

DAISY MILLER. [by H: JAMES: *Harper*. 1879.] "The story of Daisy Miller has a different motif from the others. It is a purely american picture; and the strange, beautiful, dainty, innocent, and very foolish little american girl, with her ignorant defiance of all rules, is criticised and condemned by americans abroad, not by the society native to the places which she scandalises. The wonderful mother, and still more wonderful little boy. are figures which must be quite familiar to every frequenter of forein hotels; but we never met anything so daring as Daisy herself. The end of the story is unnecessarily tragic. The poor little pretty trifler mīt surely have been shipped home to Schenectady. and let off with her life." [Blackwood's. **432**

DANGEROUS GUEST. A [by H: JACKSON: *Harper*, 1870.] "is a very entertaining novel, the 'dangerous guest' being a charming young french girl, and the danger a wedding, which despite the gardian care of some officious intermeddlers, is consummated at the end of the story.

The experiences of the french family in **England** are very happily sketched, and the character of Josephine is a very fascinating one." [Harper's. **433**

DIANA WENTWORTH. [by CARO-LINE FOTHERGILL: *Harper*, 1888.] "What would the english lady novelist do without the english governess, her woes, her trials, and her triumfs? 'Diana Wentworth' is but a new variation on the old theme. Jacewo, a dull little town in **Posen**, is her Villette, and John Garthwaite, an english civil-engineer employed on a new railroad between Jacewo and Berg, takes the rôle of the burly young fysician of C.. Brontë's books. That this book suggests the comparison is certainly a point in its favor. The characters are well-drawn, and the country, we believe, is virgin soil in english fiction. The fact that everyone except the heroine and her lover are 'just hateful' is, of course, quite in the style of this sort of novel, and rather adds to the interest." [Critic. **434**

DOCTOR ANTONIO. [by GIOVAN-NI [D.] RUFFINI: Edinburgh, *Constable*,—N.-Y., *Rudd*, 1860.] "But the true and touching interest of the story would carry a reader throu a much heavier medium; indeed, except that they interrupt the flow of the narrative. the details are not devoid of an interest of their own. Lucy is one of the most charming impersonations of an english girl we have met in the course of many novels. The outline of the story is simple; it derives its charm from the grace and delicacy with which the details are filled in, and the strong individuality inpressed upon every point of character. scenery or incident. The character of Sir John Davenne is an admirable little bit of comedy, and there is a dash of

genuine, graceful fun about it, that could scarcely have been given from an english point of vue. The gradual melting away of all the dear, proud, stiff old baronet's prejudices, and the consequent fair play that is given to his best qualities, and his gradual conversion to his dauter's faith in Doctor Antonio, is charming.—and so is the happy pastoral life they all lead during Lucy's convalescence." [Athenæum. **435**

DR. JACOB [by MATILDA [BAR-BARA] BETHAM EDWARDS: London, 1864; *Roberts*, 1868.] "is a story which partakes somewhat of the style of the German novelists without their extreme tediousness. It represents certain fases of life which afford but little scope for novelty or adventure, but which nevertheless call out whatever there is of good or bad, of passionate or enthusiastic, in the nature of every one. ... Dr. Jacob is the central figure to which all the others are subordinate; one of the most skillfully drawn, original, and unsatisfactory characters we have ever met. A man of brilliant attainments, not bad at heart. but seemingly devoid of principle, with a profound appreciation of all that is good in others, and trusting to his intellectual strength to keep him from the consequences of his errors. Tho 60 years of age, his attractions are so great that he wins the love of a very young girl, whose affection is displayed with such artless simplicity and yet with such earnestness that we can scarcely blame the doctor for lacking courage to resist the temptation of loving in return. ... The scenes with poor little Kätchen are drawn with much delicacy and are very touching. There is no display of remarkable power in any portion of the book, but the interest never flags, and altho it is not what may be called a story with a bad ending, yet the close of it is very unsatisfactory." Scene is **Frankfurt.** [Round Table. **436**

DOCTOR'S DILEMMA. The [by "HESBA STRETTON," i. e., Hannah Smith: *Appleton*, 1872.] "There is a pleasing freshness in the plot of the story, and its locale is comparatively unfamiliar. It is well tho not brilliantly written ... The French episode is exceptionally well told. Olivia, in her second flit, obtains in London a position as teacher in a school in **France.** Going thither, she finds that she has been deceived.—that the pension is a myth, and she is left penniless and friendless. Making her way on foot toward the coast, she falls into the hands of a kind curé, remains with him and his sister while a fever desolates the town, nurses the sick, and endears herself to all the villagers. There her husband finds her, and there he presently dies. This curé is one of the most beautiful characters we have met in fiction. But Tardiff, the ruf fisherman, loving Olivia with an absorbed and undying love, yet recognizing his unworthiness, and content to serve her for no reward beyond a smile or a kind word,—Tardif is the britest gem. The peculiarities of life in the **Channel Islands** are felicitously set forth, and the grand scenery of that region receives appropriate recognition. The book is pure in tone and elevating in its influence." [Boston "Lit. World." **437**

DORA. [by JULIA KAVANAGH: *Appleton*, 1868.] "Reverse of fortune induced the family to seek retirement and economy at **Rouen,** where Dora's life began in earnest. . . . The quiet

life of a mediæval lady was not for Dora; she set about work in earnest, and in the pursuit of artistic labor she encountered one who was to become the arbiter of her future destiny . . . Richard Templemore, a widower, is a finely-drawn character; his intellectual superiority, fine taste and hi moral tone are not inconsistent with the weakness he displays in matters of the heart. The situation of a man bound to one woman by gratitude and to another by love—under obligations to the superior, but attracted to the inferior by an uncontrollable passion—is not uncommon in life." [Round Table. **438**

ELEANOR MAITLAND [by CLARA (ERSKINE) (CLEMENT) WATERS: *Osgood*, 1881.] "brings home an american woman traveling in Germany, followed by a titled german, who wooes her amid diplomatic scenes in **Washington,** finally to win her in the face of his mother the countess. The heroine, a widow whose only mistake in life was her first mariage to a man she did not love, approaches very near to being that rare character—the perfect woman . . . It is a work full of thôt, wit, beauty, and refinement; the pen has scarcely made one false stroke in it throuout; and the book will give almost unalloyed enjoyment to a wide circle of readers." [Boston "Lit. World." **439**

ELIANE [by PAULINE (LA FERRONNAYS) CRAVEN: *Gottsberger*, 1882.] "is a quiet story of french country life with a number of interesting characters, with pleasant sketches of social ways, and with just enuf incident to sustain the somewhat undue tendency to sentimentality which crops up now and then, but is generally repressed before great harm is done to the reader's sensibilities ... Eliane is made unhappy, and Raynold de Limings led to a mésalliance by the obstinacy of the latter's mother, on the other hand Blanche takes the man chosen for her and is more than content." [Boston "Lit. World." **440**

ERLACH COURT [by "Ossip Schubin," i. e. Lola Kürschner: *Lippincott*, 1889.] "is an excellent spot for two of the subordinate characters, a husband and wife who have been indifferent to each other during nine years of maried life, to fall deeply in love with one another; but the fortunes of the pretty little heroine are luckily soon transplanted to Paris. and the proper sentimental climax is reached, after a due number of obstacles have been overcome. The brisk, gay Parisian atmosfere makes a very pleasant antidote to german sentiment, and several of the characters who are involved in the history of Stella's fortunes are sketched with humor and vivacity. The hero is somewhat less terrible than most german heroes. He is 35, and of course gray, and has the interesting temperament which seems to be always associated with premature grayness. Without, he is all indifference, within, all ardor, and we leave the pretty young heroine at last in his hands with entire confidence. The telling of the tale goes easily and smoothly, and we are sure that most girls under 20 and women over 50 will pronounce it 'a very pretty story'. [American. **441**

ERNEST CARROLL [by H: Greenough: *Ticknor*, 1859.] "is not so much a novel as a narrative, pleasantly unfolded. with much anecdote, many choice bits of art-gossip and descriptions of life and scenery in Italy

and Austria." [Religious Mag.. **442**

ESAU RUNSWICK. [*Putnam*, 1882.] An abridged and altered edition of A Faithful Lover. **443**

ESTELLE RUSSELL [by M.. A. Olney: *Harper*. 1870.) "is a uniformly readable novel. Its scene is laid, for the most part, in Toulouse, and the author gives us some delitful pictures of society among the french Protestants of that famous town. [Boston "Lit. World." **444**

ESTHER'S FORTUNE. [by Lucy Cecilia (White) (Lillie) Harte: *Porter & Coates*, 1889.] "Our sympathies are awakened at the outset in favor of the dejected-looking american girl of 18, left alone in a Munich apartment with a hired piano, a porcelain stove, a small bed with a suffocating coverlet, a single roll of bread, and empty pockets. This is Esther Bradford; the story is of 'Esther's Fortune.' Miss Esther finds friends in need among the Munich professors. good-hearted fellows soaked in music, beer, and human kindness. A Miss Lisle takes her to London as 'companion'. Here she makes the acquaintance of many pleasant people and places. is lionized as a singer and discovers hitherto unknown relatives. She helps to start homes for poor girls in the metropolis, falls in love with and maries a celebrated scientist, and bids us adieu in a fine, old-fashioned garden, holding our sympathy to the last." [Critic. **445**

EUNICE LATHROP, SPINSTER [by Annette Lucille Noble: *Putnam*, 1882.] "is clever and amusing. The spinster heroine is a jolly little woman. kindly affectioned towards most of the human race. and as unlike the typical 'old maid' as possible. . .

A good story. told in an unusually brīt and pleasant manner." [Penn Monthly.] "Eunice Lathrop has some incidents so sensational that we should have passed it by but for the very pretty sketching in the earlier chapters. The pictures of the life of the country minister and his dauter are very delicate." [Nation.] "It has a Massachusetts beginning and end; a London middle; an Atlantic voyage; a selfish man between 2 lovely women. who could be happy with either were t'other dear charmer away; a silent lover. who comes into his inheritance only on the last page, and an english widow who dies abruptly of a pistol shot under circumstances which point to a murder and nearly get the halter around an innocent man's neck. There is also the 'widow's' whimsical foundling, a very amusing creation with old-fashioned ideas, blunt talk. and Papistical devotions; and Eunice Lathrop. a knowing spinster of the true New England type. The story has originality. wit, vivacity. and well drawn characters, The style is careless, however... There is nothing better in the book than the chapters describing Mrs. Cudlip's London boarding-house, which are written feelingly. The author's individuality is marked; a twinkle in her eye and a droll inflection to her voice bring the reader at once into a merry mood. and she certainly amuses." [Boston "Lit. World." **446**

EUROPEANS. The [by H: JAMES: *Houghton*, 1878.] "We have here a brother and sister of mixed Swiss and American parentage, who have passed all their lives (they are both in the nêborhood of 30) on the Continent. The sister. Eugenia. has made a morganatic mariage with a German prince.

which the rēgning family desires to annul; and the brother, Felix, tho a pleasant fellow and a clever artist. is virtually a penniless adventurer; so the two come to seek their fortune among their american cousins. These prove to be people of wealth and the hīest respectability, living puritanically and yet with dignified abundance at a fine old country-seat. 7½ miles from Boston, and the equable currents of suburban life are of course terribly disturbed by this unlooked-for forein irruption. In the end, Felix wins and carries away to the Parisian heaven the younger and more enterprising of his pretty cousins; while Eugenia. after a course of the most finished coquetry with a gentleman retired from the India trade. returns as she came. [Atlantic.]—"The picture of the Wentworths, as a typical American family, is an achievement of genius, and is sufficient of itself to lift the story into the domain of genuine creative art . . . Equally skilful in the execution and much happier as a conception is the character of her brother, Felix Young—American by parentage. European by birth and nurture, and Bohemian by profession and practice. He is the apostle. exponent. type. and exemplar of happiness as a creed and as a standard of conduct; and his influence upon the story is similar to that of a joyous smile upon a beautiful human face. The contrast between european and american life on their moral side, as exemplified by the baroness, is only hinted at by the author; but we have reason to be grateful for the protest which Felix Young embodies against the ascetic ideals. the hyper-puritanic standards, the strained conscientiousness, and the distrust of everything which takes the semblance of pleasure for pleasure's sake, which make american life, in spite of a certain austere nobleness and purity, the most colorless, joyless, fysically wearing and mentally exhausting, in the world." [Appletons'. **447**

EXILES, The. [by 'Talvi', i. e., THERESE (VON JAKOB) ROBINSON: N. Y., 1854]=''The story describes the varied fortunes, in this country, of a couple of German emigrants, from the hïer walks of society, who after a series of painfully disastrous events, find a tragic winding-up of their history in a remote town of Vermont. The most striking merits of the book are its vivid and subtle delineations of passion. the admirable fidelity of its character-drawing, its frequent touches of pathos, its grafic and effective descriptions of nature. and its life-like, home-like pictures of american manners." [Harper's. **448**

FACE TO FACE [by Ro. GRANT: *Scribner*, 1886.] ''is an amusing story in which the surface characteristics of english and american life are played with; but does not the author americanize his young woman a little too deeply?" [Atlantic. **449**

FAIR BARBARIAN (A) [by F.. [ELIZA] (HODGSON) BURNETT: 1876? *Osgood*, 1881.] "begins with the surprise of Miss Belinda Bassett at the unexpected arrival of an unknown niece from 'Meriker', with 6 trunks. Five of these trunks were sent to the attic; there was room for one only in Miss Belinda's little spare chamber, of which the 'fair barbarian', Octavia Bassett, proceeded to take unconcerned possession. Octavia's father is Miss Belinda's brother, who had emigrated 30 years before 'to get a place

where a fellow could stretch himself', and she had not seen him since. Her mother was a San Francisco actress, who died when she was born. Octavia has learned that she was a great favorite and 'awfully pretty', and herself wears diamonds, silken trains and satin furbelows, as it were, in memory of her. With her finery, her history, and her freedom of speech and manner, she overwhelms Aunt Belinda. But the aunt is quite as much fascinated as stunned, and listens to Octavia's stories of her father's silver mines. with a degree of interest approaching awe. In fact, her experiences with Octavia amount to a succession of shocks, which in turn communicate themselves to the nêbors, until Slowbridge is shaken to its foundations. Miss Pilcher's select seminary for young ladies is set on fire with the tung of gossip. The public curiosity, criticism, and censure find a general leader in Lady Theobald, a gíantess of the social world, with a pretty grand-dauter, Lucia. Lucia's destiny is mariage with Mr. Burmistone, the much detested agent of the Slowbridge Mills; while in the end Octavia caps the climax of Her original and independent career by marying one Jack Belasys." [Boston "Literary World." **450**

FAITHFUL LOVER (A) [by K.. S. MACQUOID: *Hurst*, 1882.] ''is a tale half French, half English, of an old man cramped and embittered by early disappointment, but won back to forgiveness and charity at last by the loving tenderness of his niece. Mrs. Macquoid has plenty of materials with which to fill in the details of her work." [Nation] *See No.* 443. **451**

FATE OF MANSFIELD HUMPHREYS (The) [by R: GRANT WHITE:

Houghton, 1884.] "is altogether the most direct and aggressive comparison of english and american society yet published in fiction. It exists merely for the sake of the comparison; the 'story' is well-nī as completely an excuse as in the conversations of 'Evenings at Home', or similar instructive literature. The character-drawing, however, is much more ambitious; and while not in the least a work of genius, is conscientious and consistent, and bears the appearance of truthfulness in the main traits. It must not be inferred from our calling this the most direct and aggressive comparison of English and American society, that it is partial or intemperate; on the contrary, the vues expressed are eminently candid, temperate, and generous. . . The leading thesis is that the best class of thōro-bred americans are full as much gentlemen as the best class of english—whom they closely resemble, as by blood entitled to do. Now it certainly seems a little ignominious for a people, as for an individual, to enter into a discussion as to its good-breeding. Even misrepresentations seem to be met with more dignity by a serene indifference than by discussion. If every english novelist and critic should maintain that all americans are vulgar, it would seem the most gentlemanly rejoinder to say to ourselves 'So much the worse either for England's knowledge or its standards', and continue to produce men, and books, and journals that are not vulgar; if we do this long enuf, no misapprehension can possibly stand against the simple force of fact." [Overland.   **452**

FLEURANGE, see ROMANTIC NOVELS.

FOREGONE CONCLUSION, A.

[by W: D. HOWELLS: *Osgood*, 1875.] "Mr. Howells has lived in Venice till the melancholy beauty of its decay has so taken possession of him that he can describe all fāses of its lïfe more perfectly than any other english pen we know; and against a background of palaces and canals he creates a picture of the drama of love, ever old, yet ever new, which causes a soul to dwell among the shadows of that great past. The american mother and dauter wandering forlorn in forein lands, in quest of the health for the elder which is never found, the artist consul, the priest wearily going throu the round of offices which are a lie to him, and dreaming over his inventions till he wakes to find himself in love with the young girl to whom he has taut Italian, the group of lesser characters, from gondolier to canonico, briefly drawn, but instinct with life, are delineated with the subtle skill of portraiture, keen irony, and delicious style, which makes a new book of Mr. Howells' a literary event. The atmosfere of the 'Queen of the Sea' hangs over all. Those who know **Venice** inhale its unique beauty again from these pages, and those who have never floated on those still waters, away from the common world, can see its spirit reflected here, as the outlines of its buildings and the hues of its skies are imaged in the canals below them." [Unitarian Review.   **453**

FOUR MEETINGS. [by H: JAMES, 1879.] "There is another little sketch, which is wonderfully pretty and pathetic, and which he calls 'Four Meetings'. It is the story of a little New-England governess, whose 'dream of life' it has been, as with Bessie Alden, to go to 'Europe,' and who saves her money with a kind of passion

126

for this end. She comes to Europe, meets, and is immediately victimised by, an american cousin in France, to whom her money is needful, and goes back again penniless but uncomplaining, having spent but 13 hours in that Europe for which she had so longed. It is cruel. One instinctively puts one's hand in one's pocket, wondering would it not have been possible somehow to make up Miss Caroline Spencer's loss. . . The picture of the heroine, in its faint colors and delicate outline, is very touching and gives us a pang of sympathy, even tho we feel that the pain is unnecessary, and that surely the american lady at the hotel must have managed some way of making it up to the sufferer." [Blackwood's. **454**

FOREIGN MARRIAGE. A. [by VIRGINIA WALES JOHNSON: *Harper*, 1880?] "Some would call it a more powerful story of modern life at **Florence** than 'The Neptune Vase' is of Siena. It is a reproof of the false ambition of american girls for title-hunting abroad." [Boston "Literary World." **455**

FRERES (The) [by "MRS. ALEXANDER," i. e., Annie (French) Hector: *Holt*, 1882.] "is a novel of english life with a german episode, and it is not easy to say which is the better picture,—that of the reduced family in their cheap London lodgings, or the precise, quaint, hospitable, narrow household at Dalbersdorf, and the social and military dignities of the little town of **Zittau**. Grace Frere, the heroine of the story, is one of those lovable, womanly, possible women, whom "Mrs. Alexander" has the art of depicting and making real, without any insistent analysis or description. The family group of which she makes

a part is all admirably done." [Boston "Literary World." **456**

GABRIELLE DE BOURDAINE [by LILY (HEADLAND) SPENDER: *Harper*, 1882.] "is a prettily told story of life on one of the **Channel Islands**. A side episode of secret passages and mysterious chambers adds nothing to the interest of it, which centres in Gabrielle and her father. a frenchman of strangely fallen fortunes." [Nation. **457**

GENTLE BELLE (A) [by "CHRISTIAN REID". i. e., F.. E. (F.) Tiernan: *Appleton*, 1878.] "opens in **Florence** with an english gentleman dying, leaving a pet dauter behind him. Her life the story follows throu the usual variety of joys and sorrows, to a happy termination. She has, in some respects. a marked personality, with a strong mind. and very cultivated tastes, and the development of her character under discipline is the author's leading motive." [Boston "Literary World." **458**

GIRTON GIRL, A [by ANNIE EDWARDS: *Harper*, 1886.] "The title is a misnomer. 'A Would-be Girton Girl'. or 'Why Marjorie Bertrand did not go to Girton,' would have been more exact. Nevertheless. we have a pleasant story of the idling life of english people in the picturesque setting of a **Channel Island**. Tutor and pupils present almost too obvious a combination in the first chapter. but their fortunes are so closely and cleverly interwoven with those of another pair. an artist and the beautiful wife to whose charms he is absurdly blind, that the reader has the chance for a good deal of speculation before the happy ending . . . In point of style and still more of incident. the book is brīt and attractive." [Nation. **459**

GOLDEN DAYS. [by JEANIE HERING: *Cassell*, 1873.] "These 'Golden Days' are a pleasant record of a girl's recollections of her school life in a quiet, quaint german town. It is entertaining, from the first taste of 'the black bread' to the last page, when the narrator takes sorrowful leave of the excellent Frau Alsberg and her school companions. Some of the incidents are more romantic than would or could occur in an english boarding-school; but the tone of the book is good, and so pleasant, that it really proves its claim to be the remembrance of Golden Days." [Athenæum. **460**

GOLDEN MEDIOCRITY [by EUGÉNIE (GINDRIEZ) HAMERTON: *Roberts*, 1886.] "is a pleasant story, full of simple and natural feeling, and offers besides a striking picture of the contrast in domestic habits and ideas of french and english people of equal rank and means. Mrs. Pearce, her son (a London literary man), and her niece, spend an autumn holiday in a provincial town in **France**, and become intimate with the family of Mr. Molé, a savant, and a gentleman of some private fortune. Hélène, the pretty dauter of Mr. Molé, is the cleverest of housekeepers and the most skilful of cooks. Nowhere is seen affectation, false pride, anything which fosters extravagant habits: all the members of the french family unite in a thrift and good sense which makes the large, difficult, expensive methods by which english people try to ensure domestic comfort seem the most absurd and unnecessary outlay of time and money. Just enuf of a love-story winds in and out of the narrative to set off the diversities of interests and characters. The book is pleasant

to read, besides being full of animating hints and facts, which, coming as they do from the french wife of one of England's most graceful and suggestive writers, make it well worth reading." [American.]—"It is subdued in tone, but in admirable taste. The interest is gentle but well kept up. Mrs. Hamerton paints the inside of a home. . . A pure and interesting story, which will do much to dissipate american prejudice against the french and to teach american mothers that riches and extravagance are not necessary to elegant and contented lives." [Catholic World. **461**

GRETCHEN [by "RITA." i. e., — ( ) Booth: *Lippincott*, 1889.] "tells of a pretty german girl betrayed into a mock mariage by a young englishman with weak eyes, whose clerical friend, Adrian, after much ado, sets things rit. Scene in England, **Germany**, and **Rome**." [Critic.]—"Rita's heroine is suggestively named, but her Faust is no necromancer—only an impulsive, self-pleasing youth, who trifles with ingenuous simplicity, and finds the social consequences too hard to face. A very dainty spirit is that of Margaret von Waldstein, in spite of the passion which ruins her. The theme is sad, but the story is well told." [Athenæum. **462**

GUENN. [by B. W. (HOWARD) TEUFEL.] see *ROMANTIC NOVELS.*

HAND & GLOVE. [by AMELIA B. EDWARDS, see *FRENCH NOVELS.*

HEAPS OF MONEY [by W: E: NORRIS: *Holt*, 1882.] "must have been one of his earliest attempts at fiction; and a very charming attempt it is. The plot concerns the adventures of a very interesting young woman who not only desires, but obtains, 'heaps of money.' The scene is laid on the Continent [**Dresden**], in part and among the incidents is a cleverly managed affair of honor. in the narration of which Mr. Norris displays the same familiarity and sympathy with the weakness and pettiness of human nature which are the source of so much of the attraction in 'Matrimony', and while he undoubtedly understands its good as well as its bad sides it is over the latter that in his later book he lingers most lovingly . . . When he wrote 'Heaps of Money' he had observed and reflected less ; hence, as a love-story, the earlier is the better of the two. As novels. their positions have to be reversed."[Nation.**463**

HEART OF STEEL. (A) [by "CHRISTIAN REID: i. e., F.. E. (F.) Tiernan: *Appleton*, 1883.] "There is in•the book much agreeable life among pleasant-mannered people in **Paris** and **Rome,** tho they are never quite interesting, in spite of a good deal of guide-book information that is parcelled out between them. It is fair to say that the information is of much the choicer kind, and it will please a good many people who have not already seen it in Mr. Hare's various books." [Nation.   **464**

HECTOR [by FLORA L. SHAW, *Roberts*, 1881.] "may be described as an english flower grown on french soil, since Hector is a little orfan, who is sent to **France** for awhile, and has fine times at Saleret with the cousin Zélie who tells the story, with Grandmère, with Madelon the servant, with Esquebesse the hunter and his 2 dogs, with Baptiste the miller, and with Marie-Anne the miller's maid. There is always a charm in french landscape, character. and incident ; and this book has that charm in its most refined and delicate forms. It is altogether a

sweet and pretty tale, and girls of tender heart will be in love with the handsome Hector from the frontispiece on." [Boston "Lit. World." **465**

HER PICTURE [by P. G. HAMERTON (?): *Roberts*, 1883.] "is a french story, the action beginning at a château near **Pau**, and being transferred afterward to **Paris** and then to a country-house at Montrémy ; while there is a painter in it, and pictures, and sweet music, and a good many lines and tints which suggest Mr. Hamerton, without anything. however. which equals the fotografic distinctness and dramatic power of 'Marmorne'. . . There are a number of lively people in the book, of a Parisian sort ; there is an enfant terrible. who makes some amusement; there is a crusty old millionaire who dies at the rīt time and leaves his money in the rīt place ; there is a good deal of merry society incident and party conversation ; there are some pleasing pictures of french life; there is no villain or villainy. The story is refined and agreeable." [Boston "Lit. World."**466**

HOUSE DIVIDED AGAINST ITSELF. (A) [by MA. O. (W.) OLIPHANT: *Blackwood*, 1886.] "The contrast between the perfect simplicity of a refined life in the seclusion of a little town in Italy. and the artificial existence in the great world of London society, is very cleverly presented. . . Frances Waring is a young girl living in **Bordighera** with her father. who is a lonely scholar. She knows nothing of her past history. The few people she knows occasionally go 'home,'—and frequently talk of 'home;' but her father never goes home. and never talks of it either, and Frances dares not ask him. She devotes herself to her father's comforts.

He is not above being particular about his dinner, and, in fact, is a selfish man of the shy and sensitive type. In her spare time, she sketches and reads, somewhat aimlessly perhaps; but her life. if it is secluded, is a thŏroly healthful and natural one. Suddenly it changes entirely. . . And so it gradually dawns upon poor Frances that she has a mother and a sister of whom she had never heard. How gradually it dawns upon her throu the impatience of the stranger her sister, and the half-ashamed. half-ludicrous confessions of her father, is inimitably told and described. Equally good is the description of the consternation of the little english colony, for any one 'in such a small community' to have a wife alive and never let any one know, was 'not quite respectable.' 'Bless me!' says the general; 'if the wife's all rĭt, what does the man mean? Why can't they quarrel peaceably, and keep up appearances as we all do?" [Spectator.] This novel is a sequel to "A Country Gentleman," for notice of which see Descriptive List of English Novels. **467**

HYPERION. By H : WADSWORTH LONGFELLOW : Boston, 1839.

IN A WINTER CITY.[by "OUIDA," i. e. L.. de La Ramé: *Lippincott*, 1876.] "There is but little doubt that in the future this accomplished writer will be devoting her attention to tales with a distinct moral purpose. if not to the composition of tracts; at present, however, she employs herself in amassing material for future repentance. It would be superfluous to say that she writes like a rowdy who has a certain feeling for things pathetic. In this novel, with a great deal of more than useless filligree, she nar-

rates with some skill the love of an italian duke for an immensely wealthy english widow, who loses her fortune when she maries again. 'Ouida' manages, in spite of all her faults, to make the people seem at times like something more than dissipated dolls." [Nation. **468**

IN CHANGE UNCHANGED [by LINDA (WHITE) (MAZINI) VILLARI: *Holt*, 1877.] "is a graceful story. The author uses her advantage of double nationality with a taste and skill which reminds us of 'Quits' and 'The Initials'. The heroine is a lovely young english widow named Edith Henderson, who going abroad for a Roman winter, and drifting towards Florence in the spring. finds at Bellosguardo, first an art, next an aunt, and lastly a lover. We leave her made happy in these 3 discoveries. We are treated to a brĭt run into the **Dolomite** region, and there are telling bits of description here and there, but these are subordinated to the human interests, and the most picturesque part of the book lies in the tenderly sketched little home at **Bellosguardo,** and its sweet, helpful inmate; a picture which more than one Florence habitué will recognize with a sĭ and smile as being from life. We commend this pleasant story as full of interest." [Boston "Literary World." **469**

IN THE WRONG PARADISE. [by ANDREW LANG: *Harper*, 1887.] "It mĭt be difficult to persuade many good people that Mr. Lang ever had a serious thôt, except the unrĭteous one of ridiculing missionaries in the person of the Rev. Thomas Gowles and in his adventures among the Phæacians. The Rev. Gowles is indeed rather a caricature. but some measure of his cant, ignorance. and conceit is

unfortunately too frequently found in those who undertake to Christianize the heathen, whether at home or abroad." [Nation. 470
INDIAN SUMMER. [by W: DEAN HOWELLS: *Ticknor*, 1886.] "We do not know why the critic should hesitate to call this the most wholly charming thing which Mr. Howells has given us. It is true that he has written a considerable number of volumes which may stand as so many protests against such a judgment, but there is not an 'Indian Summer' among them. It is not a book to analyse; it is a book to enjoy. To inquire why this līt,. slenderly-plotted, gay, wise story satisfies every sense with which we taste good literature, would be as impertinent as to challenge the source of a flower's perfume. His hero is older than the conscientious, admirable young men of the early novels, and the writer's outlook upon life is that of a man older than the author of 'A Chance Acquaintance.' but the increased age of both is the reverse of a loss, and we fancy that, like Imogene, no one will like Colville the less for having lived past certain things, or even for his rheumatic twinges and his sleepiness after evening parties. Colville is, to our sense, one of the most thōroly likable figures in fiction. His humorous goodness, his serious honesty of purpose,—which for not the first time in history accomplishes its aims less straitforwardly than its owner intends,—his nobility of heart, his tireless amiability of spirit, above all, if we may venture to say it, his habit of taking life with all earnestness, yet with a drollery which gives to all living a pleasant savor,— these excellent qualities make such a man as any of us mīt be glad to

know. . . Mr. Howells' art in painting womankind had never ampler opportunity than in this volume. Mrs. Bowen, Imogene Graham, and that dainty little woman, Effie Bowen, are as complete and characteristic creations as he has given us. Imogene's romantic girlishness, her womanly self-abnegation, her ingenuousness. her simplicity, and her ignorant culture are mingled without confusion, and with the consent of the reader's understanding. in a thōroly real young girl. Mrs. Bowen is less directly rendered by a series of delicate touches, but she is not less successful; while Effie, after Colville, is the triumf of the book. She is a child of a sort not altogether common in America, unfortunately,—the very pink of propriety, of obedience, of all the childish virtues. Her friendship with Colville one would say is as prettily done as anything of the kind in fiction, if there were anything quite like it in fiction. The story ends as the old-fashioned reader would have it. That is the manner in which Mr. Howells sometimes refuses to have it; but when it is so it is because life too would not have had it so." [Church Review.]— "It may be called a demonstration of the difference between youth and middle age. Theodore Colville, the leading man, is. at 40, still young in spirit, and is rather than not disposed to vote himself as belonging among young people, until he forms an intimate relation with an undoubted young one, whereupon the emptiness of his claim to youth becomes apparent. Twenty years before the time of the tale Colville had had a serious affair of the heart, in which he was worsted; after this lapse of a double decade we find him at **Florence** again where the early romance had been acted, and thrown accidentally into the company of a widow of his age, who had been a friend of the girl who had jilted him, and who knew all the circumstances of that affair. Thus Mrs. Bowen and Colville, both being lonely and heart hungry, seem in a manner providentially brôt together, and they are very adequately matched; but the game becomes curiously crossed. With Mrs. Bowen comes also on the scene a charmer of tne young generation, and before long the luckless Colville is in the toils of a second Florence engagement, not however, with the results of anger, bitterness and disenchantment of the first. He is a lover throu circumstances rather than by intention, and, in the end, this romance, too, is violently closed; but to the satisfaction of all parties, and 'Colville' maries the widow, the woman who suits him, who is suitable for him, and whom, if he had but known it, he had loved from the first. As we have said, this seems sliter than it is. The art with which these conflicting passions, attractions, resentments, humors, are indicated is just as perfect as anything in the best of Mr. Howells' work. Especially engaging are Colville's easy-natured tolerance, as we may call it, of life; the intense enthusiasm of the girl, Imogene Graham; and the sweetness of the child Effie, who is the unconscious instrument, in the close, of arranging matters in their proper shape." [American. **471**

INGEMISCO. [by "Fadette," i. e. MARIAN COLHOUN LEGARÉ REEVES: *Blelock*, 1867.] "No one who knows anything of Southern literature will be surprised to hear that we took up this novel without great expectations

of pleasure or profit. We confess to an agreeable disappointment. There is, to be sure, one very reprehensible Yankee in it, whose feet are of enormous extent, who is extremely ill-mannered, who speaks throu his nose and refers to the battle of Lexington; but he has nothing to do with the story and he fills but a very small space. We must not begrudge the Southern patriot who encourages literature something for his money, and we get off easily if we are made to swallow the Yankee alone. We mît have had 'the true Southern gentleman'. The Baroness Tautphœus has been the examplar whom the author of 'Ingemisco' has followed, and she has learned something of that admirable writer's charm. The scene of her story is Switzerland and **Bavaria**; her characters are a wealthy Scotch family with two human dauters, and certain foreiners, counts and peasants, whom they meet abroad; and the story tells how the hī-spirited Margaret, betrothed to a good young gentleman whom she rather liked, fell in love with Count Zalkiewski and by him loved and maried. There is much pleasant-reading in the accounts, full of little details of Swiss and German life, of excursions which the party make in Switzerland and Bavaria; the love affairs of Margaret and Harry May and the counts Zalkiewski and Falkenstein are very well managed; the people who talk and act are living people; the author's style is good, and in dialog unusually good. The whole effect of the novel is healthful, cheerful, and every way pleasant. 'Fadette' is not the Baroness Tautphœus; but even the echo of a sweet sound is good." [Nation. **472**

INITIALS. (The) [by JEMIMA

(MONTGOMERY) VON TAUTPHÖUS: *Bentley,—Peterson*, 1850.] "We have seldom had occasion to welcome a reprint with more unqualified satisfaction; it comes to us like a friend who won the admiration of our earlier days, and the appreciation of whose worth the experience of maturer years confirms. At the time of its first publication this work was much read, and excited considerable interest and hī praise. The style is easy, fluent, and occasionally picturesque, and the variety of incident, minuteness of detail, fidelity of delineation, and marked individuality of the several characters prove the accurate observation of the authoress as well as her excellent powers of description.—'The Initials' is a narrative of events occurring in everyday life in **Bavaria,** and is at once interesting, amusing, and in all respects probable; young people can get nothing but good from reading it, while those of all ages may profit by some of its lessons. The plot of the story is very simple, and consists mainly of the experiences of a young englishman who travels in Germany for the purpose of acquiring the language and, at the same time, of gaining some worldly knowledge. And his ignorance of everything concerning the country he is visiting affords the author an opportunity of imparting information concerning the opinions, government, and domestic habits of the dwellers in that land.—That Hamilton, with his pride of family and great expectations, should fall in love with a handsome german girl without any social position may not seem to be improbable, but that his admiration should be enduring to the extent of sacrificing his prospects in life by marying her, would, at first

glance, appear doubtful, and yet the reader who has noted throuout the hī moral tone, the strength of Hildegarde's intellect, her refinement, accomplishments, and extreme beauty must feel that the character of Hamilton rises in dignity from his appreciation of hers, and cannot fail to recognize the sterling qualities which render him not only capable of self-sacrifice, but worthy of her devotion." [Round Table.]—"Miss Braddon may do her worst, and Victor Hugo in translation may do his; but while 'The Initials' holds its own, there need be little fear of an utter perversion of the taste of the fiction-loving public. We venture even to set the new edition of this charming story against the 1000-and-1 editions of Mrs. Southworth's novels, published by the same house, and to find a little balance to their credit as purveyors for american readers. Stronger testimony in favor of 'The Initials' will hardly be required of us; but we are free to add that few novels have remained at once so fresh and so delïtful in our memory, and that we do not know where to turn for a more pleasing love-story in a thōroly realistic setting. We like it better than any other of baroness Tautphœus' works, and we hope and expect to see our opinion of it confirmed by the latest generation of which we shall have cognizance." [Nation.   **473**

INTERNATIONAL   EPISODE. (An) [by H: JAMES: *Harper*, 1879.] "It is the turn of his countrymen to be specially pleased with his last performance, because in it he has drawn the best kind of american girl,—gentle, proud, hi-minded, beautifully bred, and fair to see, as a matter of course,—who cannot for her life love a british peer because he is a peer, tho most amiably disposed toward him, and keenly susceptible with regard to the picturesque accessories and historic dignity of his position. The comedy has two acts, the first of which takes place in New-York and Newport, where the marquis of Lambeth and his cousin, Mr. Percy Beaumont, arrive in August, 'the season for watermelons and Englishmen,' and are received and entertained with a lavish hospitality which is also uncalculating, altho the noble visitors cannot believe it so. . . . When the curtain rises upon them in **England,** they have undergone the most striking transformation. Mrs. Westgate has dropped her twaddle. and is full of spirit, finesse, epigram ; Miss Bessie has developed into a model of maidenly dignity. capable of leading the story to the dénoûement foreshadowed above." [Atlantic. **474**

JET [by ANNIE EDWARDS: *Appleton*, 1878.] "scrambles gaily throu the debatable land of shabby forein society. and carries a gleam of youth and innocence with her". . . [Nation. **475**

JOHN DORRIEN. [by JULIA KAVANAGH: *Appleton*. 1875.] "The many admirers of Miss Kavanagh's 'Nathalie' will welcome in advance her new novel. It is a French story, tho its principal personage is english. We cannot follow out the plot. which is fresh and interesting. All the principal personages are life-like and individual." [Boston "Lit. World." **476**

KICKLEBURYS ON THE RHINE. The [by W: M. THACKERAY: *Smith*, 1850.] "Everybody who has gone up the Rhein must have encountered Kickleburys by the score:—my lady the mother, steeped to the chin in worldly vulgarity—Mrs. Milliken her warlike. and the fair Fanny. her loving and lovely dauter.—not to speak of the courier, Hirsch. and the tall footman Bowman.—the last a figure as constant in Mr. Titmarsh's tale as a white horse is in a picture by Wouvermans. Not every one, however. who sees Kickleburys is able to describe them in all the length and breadth of their grandeur and of their smallness." [Athenæum. **477**

KINGS IN EXILE, see ROMANTIC NOVELS.

KISMET. [by "G : FLEMING," i.e., Julia [Constance] Fletcher: *Roberts*, 1877.] "As long as there are readers who care for a novel packed from cover to cover with interesting scenes,—a promising flirtation which ripens into enthusiastic love-making by which 3 persons are in turn made miserable. so long such books as 'Kismet' will be liked. The scene of the story is the Nile, the characters are for the most part voyagers on that river. and descriptions of the wonders which line its shores make an imposing background to the litness of the incidents. The setting of the story makes the book really impressive; the scenery is brôt before the reader not in the way a topografical map is constructed, but by dexterous touches which show that the anonymous author can rise above recording the vicissitudes of a more or less conventional courtship. But a good many writers have shipwrecked just at that,—which seems so easy and is really so hard. All the good scenery in the world will not make a dull novel entertaining; but when, as in the case here, the story is interesting, the reader can only be grateful for everything thrown in over measure."

[Lippincott's. **478**

KNIGHT ERRANT [by "EDNA LYALL," i. e., Ada Ellen Bayly : *Appleton*. 1888.] "while a somewhat hysterical performance, is a novel not without power. It has a very marked motive in the feeling of the leading part, and the narrative is fresh, varied, and picturesque. The hero sacrifices his love and hope of happiness to secure the reputation and prosperity of his sister. The sacrifice is made to appear not altogether unreasonable, while it has proper elevation and pathos. The story has, moreover, an art atmosfere, and 'musical people' may read it with interest. But when all is said it is not restful, as a really good book is sure to be, but feverish." Scene **Naples**.

[American. **479**

KNIGHT OF THE BLACK FOREST (The) [by G., DENIO LITCHFIELD : *Putnam*, 1885.] "is a pencil sketch, only, a piece of half-hour work, but it is drawn with dash and spirit, with firmness and vigor, and its life-likeness and animation go far toward condoning for a certain loudness of accent in the delineation of one of the characters... Two young american ladies are journeying with their Aunt Sarah by way of Cöln to Rippoldsau in the Black Forest... On reaching the hotel at Rippoldsau, the girls first are treated to the apparition of a real german count, and next are overtaken by an american friend, the lover of Lois, who has come all the way across the water to declare himself. Henceforth the story is a lit and amusing comedy between the count and the american on one side, and the girls on the other; Betty having a decided taste for a flirtation under these romantic circumstances,

the count being not at all averse to such an amusement for a passing hour, and Prentiss & Lois having a more serious time of it. Which of the two men proved to be the true Knight we will leave the book itself to tell." [Boston "Lit. World." **480**

LA BEATA [by T: ADOLPHUS TROLLOPE : *Chapman*, 1861.] "is a novel of which there is nothing to say but what is good. It is a charming story; and tho the theme is as old as the world, it has the eternal and ever-renewed freshness of life. The story required to be very skilfully handled; and in his management of poor Beata the author has shown himself an artist as well as a thōro gentleman. ... Poor Beata is not a lawful wife, nor has she been 'deceived,' as the frase is; but she is so young and unconscious of having done anything wrong, that she has not, even when abandoned, an idea that she has anything to repent of, but she sits down patiently and submissively, without a touch of bitterness, under desertion, privation, and misery. 'La Beata' is not perfect, poor darling! But her loyal, trusting affection, her uncomplaining gentleness, draw the heart of the reader to her more than if she had possessed hier qualities. Her ignorance is kept clear of every tinge of foolishness, and her sorrow is not in the least wearisome. She is, far away, the most touching heroine we have met with since 'Eva' in Maturin's novel of 'Pour et Contre'—a novel few of the present generation are likely to have read." [Athenæum.] —"It takes those familiar with its scene as completely into the life and moral atmosfere of **Florence**, as does 'The Vicar of Wakefield' into the rural life of England before the days of railways and cheap journalism. The streets, the dwellings, the people and incidents are so truly described. the perspective is so correct, and the foreground so elaborate, that with the faithful local coloring and naive truth of the characters, we seem, as we read, to be lost in a retrospective dream,—tho more so as there is an utter absence of the sensational and rhetorical in the style. which is that of direct and unpretending narrative. The heroine is a saintly model tho at the same time a thŏroly human girl,—such a one as the artistic, superstitious, frugal and simple experience of her class and of the place could alone have fostered; the artist-hero is no less characteristic.—a selfish, clever. amiable, ambitious, and superficial italian, while the old wax-candle manufacturer. with his domicile, dauter and church relations, is a genuine Florentine of his kind. . . An english family delineated without the least exaggeration, and with the striking contrasts such visitors always present to the native scene and people of Italy, adds to and emfasizes the salient traits of the story." [Atlantic. 481

LAKEVILLE, see NOVELS OF AMERICAN CITY LIFE.

LA MARCHESA. [by PAUL HEYSE: Stock, 1887.] "Everyone who knows anything of contemporary german literature is familiar with some, at least, of the 'Novellen' of Paul Heyse. They are the most finished works of art which have been produced in Germany during the lifetime of the present generation. In all of them the writer seeks to be true to the facts of life, but that does not mean—as it means in the case of so many writers who claim to be exceptionally faithful interpreters of reality

—that he devotes attention only to commonplace or disagreeable elements of human nature. His aim is to penetrate to the inmost recesses of striking types of character, and to give vivid representations of ideas which appeal powerfully to the imagination. No living writer, either in Germany or elsewhere, surpasses him in the skill with which he makes a short story an adequate medium for the expression of fresh and brilliant conceptions, and the variety of his tales is not less remarkable than the strength. grace, and purity of their style." Scene. the Riviera. [Athenæum. 482

LATIN QUARTER COURTSHIP, (A) [by "SIDNEY LUSKA." i. e., H: Harland: Cassell, 1889.] "Both books have the charm which can come only from a wholesome and generous talent dealing with the perennial interest of young love. They are very sweet; they are pure and fine. Perhaps the character in 'A Latin Quarter Courtship' is a little more delicately touched; after a year the young lady doctor and the very american painter in Paris survive in our thŏt as figures treated with subtle art to an effect of delitful humor."[Howells.483

LAVINIA [by G. [D.] RUFFINI: N. Y., Rudd, 1861.] "is extremely interesting. . . The narrative flows easily. and is sufficiently broken by dialog. diary, and epistle to secure variety. and prevent attention from flagging. The scene shifts frequently, and we are transferred from one place to another, and from one set of characters to another, but without unpleasant violence. . . The plot is intricate. without being annoying; and tho the general destiny of the hero and heroine, with the principal secondary characters. is fairly foreshadowed. yet the exact way in which justice is to be done, and the fates are to be compelled, is held in abeyance almost to the last. The characters are admirably sustained.—Paolo. the democratic Italian artist, Thornton, his friend and mentor, Du Genre, the French realist, Salvator Rosa and his betrothed. the Spanish Countess, and her dogs. the Bishop Rodiparni; the brace of Roman swindlers, the english Mr. Jones and his wife. and, above all, the charming. mercurial, romantic, and worldly Lavinia." [Christian Examiner. **484**

LEAH. [by ANNIE EDWARDS: *Sheldon*. 1875.["Mrs. Edwards has the advantage of being in her line decidedly clever. This line is the Continental english of damaged reputation —the adventurers. the gamblers and escaped debtors, the desperate economists, the separated wives, the young ladies without mammas who smoke cigarettes and 'compromise' themselves with moustachioed foreiners. . . Mrs. Edwards. as we say, is clever; she infuses a certain force of color into her picture of shabby gentility and anglo-forein Bohemia, She describes in these pages. with a good deal of eingnuity and vividness, an english boarding-house in the Rue Castiglione [Paris] and if Thackeray has been before her in 'Philip' this is hardly her fault. All women at heart, says the familiar axiom. love a rake; whether or no the author of Leah loves hers we cannot say, bnt she portrays them with a good deal of discretion. The distinguished. depraved. and impecunious Lord Stair is the best-drawn figure in the present volume." [Nation. **485**

LIKE SHIPS UPON THE SEA

[by F., E. (TERNAN) TROLLOPE: *Harper*, 1883.] "has a tragic incident. but deals mainly with commonplace people tho the latter set off very well english commonplace against italian or rather roman types, which. if exceptional from english standpoints. are ordinary enuf in so mixed a world as **Rome.** Nobody has any money to speak of; the burden of riches, the ostentation of wealth, the hard brutal force of it in the second-class novel, are repulsive." [Nation. **486**

LIL LORIMER. [by "THEO. GIFT," i. e., Dora Henrietta (Havers) Boulger: *Appleton*, 1887.] "A year or two ago we read this book with great pleasure; now we have re-read it with undiminished enjoyment. We have here plot, originality, picturesqueness, brilliancy, tenderness and humor. 'Lil' is the story of a poor little english Daisy Miller, bred by hand—by which we mean a father's hand, unguided by a mother's heart— in South-America. There is a touch of the author's skill in the mere title of the book. She gives, with the fine literary daring of one who means to interest you in her methods rather than in her ingenuity, the maried name of her heroine on the cover: so that you know, when you begin the story, that Lil Hardy is to mary not Melville, nor Pedro, but Max Lorimer. The whole story is as clever and entertaining as this bit of literary courage would lead us to expect. The local color of the home in **Uruguay** is delitful. the transition to England. with the same people set in new situations. gives admirable opportunity for study of character vs. environment; and the character drawing is very skilful. from the faulty but sweet little heroine and faulty but attractive hero, to the over-proud James Carnegie and the wonderfully sweet and womanly Alice." [Critic. **487**

LITTLE PETER, by "LUCAS MALET" see *List of French Novels.*

LOVE OR MARRIAGE by W: BLACK. see *List of English Novels.*

MABEL STANHOPE [by KATHLEEN O'MEARA: *Roberts,* 1886.] "is a story of life in a french boarding-school, and the consequences of this life. Charlotte Brontë made a morbid and over-colored study of the french [belgian?] pensionnat in 'Villette' but the ill-nature of it, and the false reasoning. make 'Villette' a sad book in spite of its genius . Miss O'Meara, having gotten nearer to truth and nature, paints her picture with the colors of life. . . Madame St. Simon is drawn with scrupulous truth to nature. This picture and another—that of Miss Jones. the starving english governess—are excellently done. . . . In contrast to the cold. calculating and merciless Madame St. Simon we are shown the unfortunate Miss Jones, an old maid, ugly. penniless, and homeless, but true. constant, and sincere. Miss Jones is hurried to the grave by madame's parsimonious manner of managing all parts of her establishment not seen by the public. She is a conscientious Protestant, and a pathetic example of invincible ignorance. . . The kindness of Mabel and the girls to her is a beautiful episode. She proves to be a true friend to the heroine when Madame St. Simon's true colors appear, Mabel, having left school, declares to her father her intention of becoming a Catholic; he, enraged. casts her off. She goes to **Paris,** hoping to find a chance to teach in Madame St. Simon's school. . . Miss Jones dies, not seeing the truth, but

belleving according to her lit, and Mabel struggles on alone with temptation and privation. The climax of the book—the discovery of the serpent under the roses of love—is managed without false and exaggerated coloring. Miss O'Meara has done a good thing in giving the world a novel which is pure, natural, and interesting." [Catholic World. **488**

MADAME DE MAUVES [in "*A PASSIONATE PILGRIM.*" by H: JAMES: *Osgood,* 1875.] "In "Madame de Mauves" the spring of the whole action is the idea of an american girl who will have none but a french nobleman for her husband. It is not, in her, a vulgar adoration of rank. but a girl's belief that ancient lineage, circumstances of the hiest civilization, and opportunities of the greatest refinement, must result in the noblest type of character. Grant the premises, and the effect of her emergence into the cruel daylit of facts is unquestionably tremendous: Baron de Mauves is frankly unfaithful to his american wife, and, finding her too dismal in her despair, advises her to take a lover. But 'Madame' is the strength of the story, and if Mr. James has not always painted the kind of women which women like to meet in fiction, he has richly atoned in her lovely nature for all default. She is the finally successful expression of an ideal woman which has always been a homage. perhaps not to all kinds of women, but certainly to the sex. We are thinking of the heroine of 'Poor Richard' of Miss Guest in 'Guest's Confession', of Gabrielle de Bergerac in the story of that name, and other gravely sweet girls of this author's imagining. Madame de Mauves is of the same race, and she is the finest,— as truly american as she is womanly;

and in a peculiar fragrance of character. in her purity. her courage. her inflexible hī-mindedness, wholly of our civilization and almost of our climate, so different are her virtues from the virtues of the women of any other nation." [Atlantic. **489**

MADAME DE PRESNEL. [by EMMA F.. POYNTER: *Holt*, 1885.] "Those who remember the nameless charm of 'My Little Lady' will welcome 'Madame de Presnel' by the same author; nor will it disappoint them. It is original in plot, graceful and refined in style. interesting throuout. It shows the kind of subtle cleverness which is its great attraction in the title, which is not the name of the heroine. but of the elderly lady who moves the various heroes and heroines to their proper positions on the chess-board. The mingled dignity and rashness of the true heroine are admirably set forth. She is an enthusiast who bears the consequences of ill-judged enthusiasm with the finest courage." [Critic.]—Scene is in **Rome**. "It is a fine example of what can be done to make a deeply interesting story• with no appeal to such motives. Hero and heroine are again an elderly man and a very young woman in italian surroundings. but the difficulties they encounter, the doubts which separate them, are of the kind which often recur in the course of virtuous lives. Youthful enthusiasm that gladly sacrifices itself, maturer judgment which will discharge honorable obligation at any cost, sanguine recklessness, more self-deceived than deceiving—out of these elements are evolved situations 'that are none the less stimulating because they are elevating. The balance of all the parts and the clearness of the

separate outlines gives a vivid effect to the whole. The side figures are not less attractive than the central group. The young Laure and her italian husband are delītful. There is no need to credit the author with deep intention of showing the results of mingling classes or races. Such as there is falls naturally into the course of the tale, and it is pleasant to find again that refined, hī-minded side of forein life. both french and italian, which had so admirable a presentation in 'Miss Bretherton." [Nation. **490**

M'LLE DE MERSAC [by W: E: NORRIS: *Holt.* 1880.] "is a story which. it is to be feared, will not be known so well as it deserves. The author is comparatively obscure, but he has written one of the best novels which has appeared for some time. The heroine is a french girl, living, at the time the novel opens, in **Algiers**, and her lovers are two: one a French officer, a man no longer young, who has no very savory reputation, to be sure, but is yet a man of the kindest heart and most tender nature; while the other is a young englishman, with certain attractive qualities, that by no means outwê his odious selfishness, conceit, and arrogance. The very skill with which the different characters are drawn acts adversely to the general popularity of the book; for the reader who is accustomed to poorer work and to a dishonest huddling aside of the hero's faults will find it hard to judge of people whose merits and defects are intermingled as they are in life. Cynics may have observed that all the engagements they hear about are those of faultlessly beautiful young women to perfect young men, and those are the people about whom novels are generally written. Here. however. we have very careful studies of character. and of the complications which depend for their existene on the nature of the persons who fate is described. Yet the problem is not complicated by a dead wêt of ethical considerations, as in George Eliot's later novels, over which morality hangs like a heavy pall; but the question simply is how these two men strike this simple, good. but somewhat cold and self-absorbed girl. The reader cannot avoid the suspicion that the author meant her to be more attractive than interesting, and no one can avoid curiosity about her fate. The termination of the story is disappointing. but it is, perhaps. the only one possible; and is it not. after all, less sad than either of the other alternative endings? Why a novel of the importance and excellence of this one should be less popular than White Wings—a commonplace novel diluted with salt water—it is not easy to say. In Mademoiselle de Mersac we find an admirable choice of opposite characters and a capital study of living people." [Atlantic. **491**

MADEMOISELLE MORI, see LIST OF ITALIAN NOVELS.

MAE MADDEN [by M.. MURDOCH MASON: Chicago,. *Jansen*, 1875.] "is a story of an american family in **Rome**. The heroine, 'Mae Madden.' is a volatile, wilful. hair-brained young creature, who finds delīt in the gravest social improprieties. and. in utter selfishness, gratifies her own longings at any cost. She talks slang, 'goes wild,' frequently 'makes a horse of herself. and sometimes a 'black-and-tan dog.' She receives the attentions of a Piedmontese officer. whom she encounters on the street, and

carries on a despesate flirtation with him; but is fortunately rescued by Norman Mann. who, possessing many good qualities. is yet weak enuf to mary her. The book belongs to a bad school. and is in bad taste; but there is much brītness about it." [Boston "Literary World." **492**

MAN'S A MAN FOR A' THAT. A [*Putnam*, 1879.] "Whatever may be the difference of opinion as to the interest of the story. there can be none as to its solidity, strength and clever workmanship. The material is the now rather common one of the adventures and experiences of an american family in Europe—chiefly in **Rome**. Out of this she has wrot another love story which. if it do not show the vivid color and the animation which have brilliantly distinguished some other recent ventures in this field. is at least wrôt with much grace and care." [Boston "Literary World." **493**

MARRYING AND GIVING IN MARRIAGE. [by M.. L.. (STEWART) MOLESWORTH: *Harper*, 1887.] "This author is one of the few english 'lady novelists' who would be greatly missed. She is safe; she writes well; she has lived among decent people with so much comfort that she does not find it necessary to run after indecent ones. Her 'Marrying and Giving in Marriage' is a pleasant story of the life of an english girl in **France**." [Catholic World. **494**

MICHELINE [by — ( ) BERSIER: *Dutton*, 1875.] "is a tale of french life. rather novel in character. From a vessel wrecked near Mont St. Michel, a little american girl is rescued. and is adopted. into the family of Bertrand. the jailer. She grows up with Ivon, his son. and the two become warmly attached. Together they effect the release of a prisoner,—a quite dramatic episode. Bertrand leaves his post and buys a farm, and thus Micheline is brôt into contact with an english family named Gordon. Ivon goes out to America to join Mr. Gordon's son, and there discovers Micheline's brother, who is reunited to his sister, and in due time Ivon returns to France, and maries Micheline. There are many pleasant sketches of life in rural **France** and in Jersey in the story, and a sweet tone characterizes it." [Boston "Literary World." **495**

MILLIONAIRE'S COUSIN (A) [by EMILY LAWLESS: *Holt*, 1885.] "is so slit an affair that we need not delay to do more than give it hearty commendation. The argument is by no means a trite one. That poverty should be no hindrance to true love is an old theme. Wealth too, has its rīts, and the author has made out her case very forcibly. The scene is **Algiers**, lītly but picturesquely sketched, and it still has the charm of novelty even after 'Mlle. de Mersao.'" [Nation.**496**

MISOGYNIST (The), [by POTH-ERO: in Tales from Blackwood, N. S., I.] "is an amusing record of the defeat of a bore by a paradoxical humorist he meets on his travels in **Normandie**." [Athenæum. **497**

MISS BAYLE'S ROMANCE [by W: FRASER RAE: *Holt*, 1887.] "has excited not a little interest in England, since most of the characters are not only taken from real life, but go throu their several parts under their names, so thinly disguised that they may easily be identified. The Prince of Wales figures conspicuously; Lord Randolph Churchill and Labouchère also appear in person; Mr. Yates is called Mr. Atlas, and E: King, the journalist and novelist, King Ed-

wards. Many others may easily be recognized, and it would not be a difficult matter to give the real name of the noble duke who has mines in Cornwall. Miss Chamberlain, of Cleveland, whose successes were so recently paragrafed, seems to have been the prototype of the heroine, Miss Alma Bayle, the dauter of a Chicago speculator, (called a banker in concession to english prejudices). This young and pretty american girl makes the acquaintance of the Prince of Wales at Monte-Carlo, then goes to England and enjoys all the brilliant and varied triumfs which belong to a beauty and great heiress who has been singled out for royal favor. As a study of americans abroad the book has no special originality. Miss Bayle conquers wherever she goes, her americanisms being deemed naive and charming. She is a healthy, sensible, commonplace girl with an aptitude of getting what she wishes out of life. Her father, the millionaire, is the bes drawn figure, and is so well put upon the scene that we see him in almost any relation of private and public life, even understand his very clear financial operations. He is, in fact, a distinct and significant addition to our gallery of national types." [American. **498**

MISS BRETHERTON, see ENGLISH NOVELS.

MISS ROVEL. [by V: CHFRBULIEZ: *Estes*, 1875.] "The heroine is one of the most original and striking characters we have met in fiction. She is a puzzle which it is at once pleasure and despair to study. The author indulges in a some violent assumptions as to english social usages in his account of Lady Rovel's status; but with this exception his work is nearly perfect. Raymond Ferray, a very learned and studious man, having been deceived by a woman in early life, becomes a hater of the sex, and retires, with his sister, to a quiet home in **Geneva.** By certain incredible chances, Meg Rovel, an untamed girl of 16, becomes an inmate of his house, and he gets entangled with her romantic fortunes. From hating her, he comes slowly to love her, and at last, having passed throu a labyrinth of bewilderments, becomes her husband. It is impossible to convey an idea of the piquancy of this story, of the distinctness and vigor with which the characteristics of the several personages are portrayed. A fine humor pervades the book, and there is a wicked bathos in the surrender of the magnificent voluptuary. Lady Rovel, to the magnetism of a Wesleyan missionary." [Boston "Lit. World." **499**

MRS. DYMOND. [by ANNE [ISABELLA] (THACKERAY) RITCHIE: *Harper*, 1886.] "Mrs. (Thackeray) Ritchie never needs to be commended. Her style has always the same graceful flow, and it has not lost one shade of its delicate refinement. In the midst of fiction so often painful, so often positively disagreeable, to open one of her books is like turning from a dusty hīway to a quiet garden softly līted and sweet in perfume. There is a life to be lived in the garden as well as in the dingy street, and it is good for us that once in a while some one is glad to portray it. Not that Mrs. Dymond always walked in flowery paths. She had her sorrows, and shared the sorrows of others, in a life not so different from the most in its experience as to make it worth the telling for the sake of its incidents alone. It is what she was in it that gives to it its charm. Her power was only that gentle power of a sweet and truthful spirit to impart its own quality to those about it. Under its influence injustice relents, the unwilling yield, the selfish are ashamed. This tender appeal for sympathy to all the hīer, more refined side of our mental and moral nature, which is always found in Mrs. Ritchie's stories, more than makes up for any lack in boldness of conception or in strength of grasp. Her descriptions have always had a unique value. Of mere wordpainting there has long been an excess in fiction. Her description is even more than a fit and fine setting for her personages. It opens our eyes to the life of inanimate things and the part they play in our human drama, sometimes only the part of sympathy taking on for our sake the colors of the spirit. Or if they defy us, defeat us, they win us and help us again by their calm, their friendliness of long companionship. She has drawn many pictures which no one forgets, and in this story there are many to remember with those in the 'Village on the Cliff.' It is **France** again, but France in the sad days of defeat,—of the siege of Paris, of the Commune. They are not pictures of battle-fields, not of blood or of flame, but of what the women saw as they sat with the children shivering on the edge of the storm." [Nation. **500**

MOSAIC-WORKER'S DAUGHTER (The) [by J. M. CAPES: *Bentley*, 1868.] "deals with an english family resident in **Rome**, and contains interesting pictures of Roman manners and society. The two english girls are very agreeable young ladies, but the Mosaic-Worker's dauter is the heroine. Roman politics are, of course, touched upon. There are spies and banditti, secret arrests, and a romantic mystery; also a priest. who is dreadfully in love with one of the english sisters. and suffers much in his mind in consequence. All, however, ends happily. There is an air of truthfulness and good feeling throuout the book. which makes it pleasant reading." [Athenæum. **501**

MY LITTLE LADY, see ROMANTIC NOVELS.

NEPTUNE VASE (The) [by VIRGINIA W. JOHNSON: *Harper*, 1881.] "is the charming story. charmingly told. of a young orfan girl at Siena. It gives a fascinating picture of italian life. and is. indeed, so saturated with the italian spirit that it is quite essential for the american element in it to be labelled. That it should be labelled distinctly. we insist upon, for Katy Osmond. adding to the dignity of the lady "of the Aroostook" a sweetness and gayety all her own. is quite too delitful a creation to be merged in her italian husband. agreeable as. we are willing to confess. is the young professor from Torino." [Critic. **502**

NEW HYPERION (The). [by E: STRAHAN. i. e., Earl Shinn: *Lippincott*, 1874.] "To a work of Saintine's we owe. with that sort of indebtedness which the french express by 'd'apres', 'The New Hyperion'. a clever story of which we have frequently had occasion to speak in praise. The preface honestly gives credit to Saintine. but there is much more originality in the work than the scrupulous adapter lets be supposed, and his brītness and wit will thõroly amuse his audience." [Nation. **503**

NORSEMAN'S PILGRIMAGE (A) [by H. H. BOYESEN: *Scribner*. 1875.] "Tho we recognize in the heroine traits that are characteristic of many american young women, they are combined with certain elements of character—a dignity, a grave sweetness. which, we think. are not apt to coexist with them. Especially, we should say. she lacks the accent of Boston girlhood. tho that is the city from which she hails. We must not. however. neglect to mention the many skillful touches of character. both in her portrait and in those of others. Mrs. Elder is excellent. Too much cannot be said in praise of the way in which Thora is rendered.—that delicate. dreamy snow-maiden of the north who seems like the ghost of Varberg's haunting love for his mother-land, and bears her disappointment with such sweet. pathetic silence. —The whole description of the norwegian homestead and the old grandparents is charming. Mr. Boyesen is. as yet. more harmonious in his pictures of Norway than in others." [Atlantic. **504**

NOT IN THE PROSPECTUS. [by "PARKE DANFORTH." i. e., Hannah Lincoln Talbot: *Houghton*, 1886.] "A brit, somewhat unskilful, but well-bred story. in which the humors of a personally conducted tour provide the incidents which the author seems hardly capable of inventing. The humor and gayety of the book are its sufficient excuse for being." [Atlantic.] "It has no especial mission, but is simply a story; and a pretty and refined one—unless it be deemed a mission to warn the unwary against the great European tourist excursions. The experiences of the tourist party are doubtless a little caricatured and Mr. Messer likewise; but on the whole. the lively account of both is doubtless a warning well worth heed-ing by the fastidious."[Overland. **505**

NOVEL WITH TWO HEROES (A) [by ELLIOTT GRAEME: *Griffin,* 1872.] "We congratulate the author on a decided success. The story is written in a lively and agreeable style, and, in tolerably idiomatic english. The scene is shifted from the university town of Städtlein [**Leipzig**] with its world-renowned conservatorium, to a town on the english coast. We are introduced to the hero on his way to Städtlein, there to be installed as secretary to Herr Bergmann, his father's friend. Arnold Müller is the son of a genius, of one, that is, whose love for science earned for him the contempt of his father, and the inheritance of a younger son. The simple life of the worthy director,—whose household consisted of his wife, his maiden sister, Mala, (his dauter,) and a mysterious old gentleman, known in his day as a famous violinist,—is charmingly told. Several of the portraits are evidently taken from life; in particular we feel convinced that there must have existed, if he does not exist now, the counterpart of Herr Alexis Wallraf, the brilliant musical critic, whose life is embittered by his absolute incapacity for original creation. The violent aversion conceived by Wallraf for the director's protégé is converted into the strongest liking when he discovers the unaffected modesty and genuine humility of the young composer. But the interest of the story is centred in Mala, the beautiful girl who has inherited her father's genius, and who, under different training, would have developed into an artist of the first rank, but who, thanks to Herr Bergmann and Frau Martha, is still, when on the threshold of womanhood, a simple german maiden, her

heart wholly given to her cousin Lucien." [Athenæum. **506**

ODD TRUMP (The) [by J. G. A. COULSON: N. Y., *Hale & Son,* 1875.] "is a tale of love, adventure and ghosts. It shows some cleverness, and seems to be written by an american who has lived a good deal in **England,** or, at any rate, is familiar with many peculiarities of english society. There are a good many characters, one of whom is an american, and he is better drawn on the whole than most americans are apt to be in novels of english authorship. The hero is the old-fashioned hero of novels of a generation ago—a strong, brave, tender-hearted, and honest young man, who opens the ball by rescuing the heroine from a watery grave and closes it by marrying her. The 'odd trump' is not a winning card held by one of the characters, but is the hero himself. We have seen better novels and we have seen worse. . . We do not mean to say that the 'Odd Trump' is a work of genius, but it shows a cleverness which is above belittling itself." [Nation. **507**

OLD BONIFACE [by G: H: PICARD: N. Y., *White,* 1886.] "is an entertaining, brit little story, quite unlike 'A Mission Flower' [see ROMANTIC NOVELS] but very delitful in a way of its own. It deals with a lovable little american in **England,** with 2 interesting lovers, and several charming old ladies. The book is full of amusing byplay,—old Boniface himself never appearing on the stage, but having a decided influence on the fortunes of the young people."[Critic.**508**

ON BOTH SIDES. [by F.. C. BAYLOR: *Lippincott,* 1886.] "It is as if the author wrote wrote her first story, "The Perfect Treasure" to sketch english social life as it appeared to a small party of americans who were domiciled at **Cheltenham**, and afterward had the happy thôt of bringing the english characters to America, with a roving commission to discover fäses of american social life, and incidentally to exhibit their own colors in stronger lĭt than it was possible to do at home. Many of the same persons appear in "The Perfect Treasure" and "On this Side," and to all intents and purposes the two stories may answer as one... There is an exuberance of good humor which keeps the reader entertained without any severe demand on his judgment, and it is long since we have had so clever caricature as is shown in Job Ketchum on the american side, and Sir Robert Heathcote and Mrs. Sykes on the english. Much is forgiven to one who makes us lâf honestly, and if on reflection we think that Miss Baylor has sometimes laid the color on rather thick,—that she has brôt together in Job Ketchum, for instance, too many incongruous virtues and linguistic felicities,—we are not prevented from asking our friends rĭt and left to amuse themselves with a book so brĭt as to create a sort of despair, as in the presence of literary prodigality. The little picture of the interior of a decayed Virginian household, dashed off almost at random, one may say, is so admirable that one cannot help wishing for the same kind of work carried out with sustained skill and the sort of structural ability which is essential to thôroly good work in fiction." [Atlantic. **509**

ONE YEAR. [by F.. M.. PEARD: *Roberts*, 1871.] "This story is very fresh and charming, with pleasant pictures both of french and english life. a good moral. and a happy ending." [Old and New. **510**

ONLY A CORAL GIRL. [by GERTRUDE FORD : *Harper*, 1888.] "The coral girl is Margherita, the beautiful dauter of a peasant women of Capri. When she goes with her coral to the hotel in Sorrento, Keith Ronaldson. a a dashing young englishman, sees and falls in love with her. She barely knows how to read and write (even this is improbable), but Keith maries her and in 2 years' time she appears in english society as a cultivated woman, possessed of all the social graces and capable of reading the works of Herbert Spencer and Carlyle. of course this is all absurd, but the reader who is content to take it for granted will have a strong, well-written story to reward him for his credulity. Margherita is a winning specimen of womanhood, and her devotion to her well-meaning but rather weak husband is beautifully expressed. Several society types are brôt in and depicted with vigor. The scene changes from **Capri** to England and back to Capri, with no attempt, however, at labored description. The interest is purely a human interest and does not depend on fine landscapes or bric-à-brac. It is a strong, simple, dramatic novel." [Boston "Literary World." **511**

ON THE SCENT. [by MA. MAJENDIE: *Hurst*, 1887.] "The success of the divining-rod in the hands of the medium is grafically described, and its best result is to bring the heroine into close terms of sympathy with her young english lover. Besides this leading incident, and the accurate description of peasant life in **France**, the author deserves some credit for the marked distinctness with which the various members of the ruined county family of Demstone are presented to the reader."[Athenæum.512 OUR OWN SET. i. e., "Unter Uns." [by "Ossip Schubin," i. e., Lola Kürschner: *Gottsberger*, 1884.] "This is a captivating little novel, liter and more dainty in touch than is usual in german fiction, and showing a good deal of skilful character painting. The scene of the story is Rome, but the story concerns only the group of hï-born austrian diplomats there who form 'Our Own Set', making intrusion into their aristocratic circle a difficult and dangerous thing to plebeians. The heroine, Zinka, who is admitted as an honorary member to this exclusive circle, is a charming character, innocently girlish, suspecting neither slīt nor evil. She suffers in discovering the innate worthlessness of Sempaly, who plays fast and loose with her affectious, but her healthy nature outgrows her grief without embitterment." [American.   513

PANDORA [in "The Author of Beltraflo", by H: James: *Osgood*, 1885.] "is by far the cleverest thing in a miscellaneous collection. Pandora is a representative of a new type, the self-made american girl. She had come from Utica, N. Y. and had taken her parents to Europe; and how count Otto Vogelstein of the german legation encounters her on her homeward voyage, and subsequently watches her career at the national capital, Mr. James relates with delītful humor. The count learned that the self-made girl was neither crude nor loud. She was simply very successful, and her success was entirely personal. She had not been born with the silver spoon of social opportunity, she had grasped it by honest exertion. You

knew her by many different signs, but chiefly, infallibly, by the appearance of her parents. . . But the general characteristics of the self-made girl was that, tho it was frequently understood that she was privately devoted to her kindred, she never attempted to impose them on society." [Boston "Literary World."   514

PASSIONATE PILGRIM. (A) [by H: James: *Osgood*, 1875.] "The tales are all freshly and vigorously conceived, and each is striking in a different way, while 'A Passionate Pilgrim' is the best of all. In this Mr. James has seized upon what seems a very common motive, in a hero with a claim to an english estate, but the character of the hero idealizes the situation; the sordid illusion of the ordinary american heir to english property becomes in him a poetic passion, and we are made to feel an instant tenderness for the gentle visionary who fancies himself to have been misborn in our hurried, eager world, but who owes to his american birth the very rapture he feels in gray England."[Atlantic.515

POINT OF VIEW (The) [in "The Siege of London," by H: James: *Osgood*, 1883.] "Mr. James' subtlety never appeared to better advantage than in this clever bundle of letters. When one considers that he has undertaken to make americans, who have been europeanized, return to America and report on the country, either to Europeans or to those of their own special kind, one sees what a feat is accomplished. These letters are so agile, so true to every wind of doctrine, so prospective, retrospective, and introspective, that the reader is lost in admiration. They are instantaneous mental fotografs, and among the freshest of Mr. James' witty decisions upon his country-men and women. He even abandons himself, in Marcellus Cockerel, to a certain luxury of praise of things american which has hardly a trace of irony, and shows, better than anything in the book, Mr. James' power of dramatic assumption. One generally feels that, however elaborately the various characters are dressed, the voice is always the voice of Mr. James, and that the blessing intended for the character falls upon the head of the spirited wit who has planned the disguise; but there is a downrit quality about Mr. Cockerel's speech. a vehemence of American assertion. which invests him with a singular individuality. [Atlantic. 516

PORTRAIT OF A LADY (The) [by H : JAMES: *Houghton*, 1881.] "is, as a whole, a hīly remarkable and moving tale, while in many of its parts it is marvelously dull, and while it is everywhere injured by the essential barrenness of the life depicted... Every reader of contemporary fiction ôt to find time for this book, in spite of its faults... The heroine sees and passionately desires the evil, and then flies like an arrow towards the hated and dreaded duty. One knows not whether to call it childish worship of convention, or womanly fear of rebellion against what had been fixed principles, or true moral insīt. In the result, these come, in such a case, to much the same thing. The contrast between this perfect submission to the guidance of the rīt in the case of the heroine, and the perfect if only momentary overthrow of the principles of a resolute and reflective man such as Caspar Goodwood, gives occasion for one of the finest scenes of the book. This young Goodwood, with his square jaw,

is a very tiresome figure all throu the early part of the book, and the outcome shows him to be merely one example of Mr. James' facility for making, in the beginning, a nuisance of what in time is seen to be a very respectable minor character, or even a character of the first importance. Warburton and Ralph Touchett are introduced as disagreeably as possible; but we grow to think hīly of them. The venerable banker shall receive our honor. But as for the other characters (excepting poor Pansey) it is with difficulty that one can speak politely of them. They are of various degrees of wearisomeness. Since they are rational animals, they in some sort keep our attention whenever we read of them. But they are of a miserable, puny, pigmy race; it really concerns us little to know what newspaper letters they write when they are well-meaning, or what dirt they eat when they are vicious." [Californian.]— "The heroine of the novel, after recklessly wasting her youth, maries a selfish creature of the type of "Grandcourt," and the book ends with the intimation that she may seek compensation with a lover for the wretchedness of a mistaken mariage. The story is told at interminable length; but that is the gist of it. It is a 'portrait' drawn without the least effort to show the noble, generous side of humanity; on the other hand it painfully vivisects a mass of unwholesome emotions, not worthy of attention for themselves. and whose demonstration leads to nothing in the way of warning and precept. The literary methods with which readers have grown familiar throu Mr. James' other books are extravagantly used in this novel. Such minute descriptions and suggestions. such cross-examinations of his puppets. our author has never before indulged in; the book is a bewildering series of inquiries into motives, and trains of obscure incentives leading into motives. And these motives are, very few of them. things which honest hearty souls care a fig about. The whole proceeding is abnormal. unreal, unhealthful. The humor is as abundant, the irony as perfect. as we are accustomed to expect from this quarter, and, if we could be satisfied with a series of pictures of human beings suggesting nothing of human sympathy, longing. belief, or hope, the peculiar manner of treatment mīt serve. We need only add that the characters are chiefly the anglo-americans to whose delineation Mr. James has so consistently devoted himself." [American. **517**

. PRELATE. (The) [by I: HENDERSON: *Ticknor*, 1886.] "Helen Rathbone. Mr. Henderson's heroine, is compelled to run the gauntlet of calumnies which leave her for awhile without a woman-friend in Rome. She has done no harm.—but has carried a message (a mysterious and bloodcurdling message, concerning which the reader's imagination is compelled to exercise itself in vain), from a Jesuit to the Prelate Altieri. who has left the Roman for the Old-Catholic communion, and her zeal cost her dear. Two ladies of hī rank see her enter the rooms of Altieri, from which she does not emerge until after dark. Being a heroine, and thus appointed to endure trying experiences, she behaves like the conventional heroine when her reputation is endangered. and utterly refuses to explain the reasons for this incomprehensible breach of propriety. Feeling herself

bound by a sacred promise she is silent. altho the worst motives are imputed to her, altho her closest friends are unequal to the ordeal of faith which her attitude of mystery imposes. Such Spartan firmness rouses our admiration. but a little yielding, a little rounding off of the sharp angles of Helen's perfection. would have endeared her to us more. Naturally, virtue like hers is not left unrecognized, and she is rehabilitated by the effort of a Roman lady of the hīest rank and social influence. who becomes her intimate friend. Helen is not however one of those heroines who are destined for the easy rewards of fate: she is finally engaged to mary the prelate, Altieri. but crossing each other in midocean the steamer on which Helen is a passenger runs down the vessel in which Altieri is returning, and he is drowned. The book is stiff, animated by little reality, rather dull, but it is not commonplace. and possesses among novels of its class distinct merits." [American. **518**

PROFESSOR (The) [by "Currer Bell," i. e., C.. (BRONTE) NICHOLLS : *Harper*, 1857.] "The heroine is a swiss girl, in humble but respectable life, who becomes acquainted with the Professor in a 'pensionat' in Bruxelles. Of a pure, unworldly nature—earning their daily bread by daily toil —with no taste for the pretentions and falsities of social life—and taut by the hard and bitter lessons of experience to sacrifice the idols of fancy to the worship of truth—these two unique personages are soon drawn into relations of unacknowledged sympathy with each other, and the ripening of this sentiment into a more exquisite passion forms the subject-matter of the story. The prominent characters in the scene are brôt into contrast with an unprincipled, conceited, and shallow frenchman. and an intriguing woman of the same nation, who conceals the spots of her nature beneath a shining vail of decorum and gentleness. A sturdy english humorist plays an important part in the drama, altho he is managed with less skill than the leading personages." [Harper's. **519**

QUEEN OF SHEBA (The) [by T: B. ALDRICH: *Osgood*, 1877.] "is a simple love-story, of which the scene is laid partly in New-Hampshire and partly in **Switzerland**. The author thus finds opportunity to compare 2 countries which, in some respects, are similar. and to draw some vivid word-pictures of scenery." [Unitarian Review. **520**

QUITS. [by JEMIMA (MONTGOMERY) von TAUTPHÖUS: *Lippincott*, 1866.] "Baroness Tautphœus writes easily, correctly, and elegantly. Her skill in description is remarkable, and her representation of externals, of manners and customs, of rural life. city life, and fashionable life, is minute and truthful. . . 'Quits' has merit. first, as a pleasant and good-humored sketch of the englishman at home and abroad. in London and on his travels,—and next, as a more rare picture of life in the mountain region of Southern Bavaria. In the scenes of the book there is a charming reality and distinctness." [Christian Examiner. **521**

REVERBERATOR (The) [by H: JAMES: *Macmillan*, 1888.] "was worth writing and is worth reading—two things which do not always seem to us true of the author's work. much as we invariably admire his technique. . . The heroine is very beautiful, with fine lines. delītful color, and graceful,

unaffected, girlish manners. Her manners, however, do not appear to be a great part of her charm for Gaston Probert, the only living son of a South Carolinian settled for many years in France. . . Gaston is not Francina Dosson's only admirer. He has been preceded by George M. Flack, whom the whole Dosson family regard as a great and elevated person on account of his supposed dignity as an editor. .. Fidelia has brôt the family abroad for the second time, knowing that rich american girls are said to do extremely well in the way of mariage 'over there', and she has no idea of giving her to an american even if an editor. Gaston meets Miss Dobson's entire approval and is not slow in gaining that of Francie also. His difficulty arises when he faces the thôt of presenting the socially unpresentable Dossons to his father and sisters. However, he gets over that without too much trouble. He is one of a most united and affectionate family, who appreciate the fact that his heart is irrevocably engaged, and who end by yielding, tho with some wry faces, graciously made in private for the most part. to Francie's innocent charm and striking beauty. She is taken into their interior, and Gaston's favorite sister, by way of proving to the little girl how fully they have adopted her as one of themselves, tells her quantities of family gossip. including the fact that one of their relatives 'had that disease—what do they call it?— that she used to steal things in shops'; now, all this, and a good deal of a still more scandalous nature, Francie innocently repeats to Mr. George M. Flack, whose disappointment with regard to herself she pities." [Catholic World.]—"The Proberts, father, son, and titled dauters, are all presented with Mr. James' utmost skill. Their mutual affection, their exquisite manners, their fastidiousness of reserve towards the public, and their graceful abandon when thrown together. They represent the very bloom of .french social culture and exotic civilization, and, naturally, when thrown into contrast with the Dossons, who have no manner, no reserves, no exclusiveness. no standards of taste,—whose whole idea of life is taking what comes easily, and letting all go easily,—the effect is striking.—The Proberts throw a veil over their dissatisfaction with the Dossons and summon all the charm of their fine manners to their aid. They pet Francie, talk to her freely, try to make her one of themselves by the tenderest intimacy. Francie accepts it, but the 'French ideas' do not easily assimilate with her vague american notions. Happening to be thrown into Mr. Flack's society, she confides to him that she is surprised at some of the complications of french life. Mr. Flack draws her out. and the whole revelation of what she has seen, heard, and divined about the Proberts is unreservedly poured forth for the edification of the journalist. Naturally, the whole account, exaggerated into monstrosity and made indecent with every sort of suggestion, is sent off to the Reverberator, and a fortnit or so later the Proberts find all their family history. atrociously garbled, in print. The situation is capitally handled when all the Proberts are arraigned against Francie, but we refer our readers to the story itself for the sequel. Mr. Flack had flashed his lantern into the privacy of a hī-minded family and had made a sensation.

The results of our obtrusive modern journalism are clearly set before us, and anybody may seize the moral. When Francie, with a crowd of unuttered regrets and repentances thinks of the mischief she has done. she wonders if all the lively, chatty letters, she reads in the papers means, like this about the Proberts, 'a violation of sanctities, a convulsion of homes, a burning of smitten faces, a rupture of girls' engagements.'" [American. 522

ROBIN [by LOUISA (TAYLOR) PARR : Holt. 1882.] "is agreeable and readable. and holds the reader's sympathies to the end. The story is not a new one. and the first half reminds one strikingly of 'Heaps of Money,' with a father and dauter living on the Continent, and a young englishman of good family established as 'ami de la maison.' Robin is a fresh and frank, purely girlish creation. and fulfils the first duty of a heroine by being charming. The idle, pleasure-taking. fictitious life at Venice is well described, and makes a picturesque background for the play of the 4 principal characters." [Lippincott's.]— "It is a beautiful story of resistance to temptation. and of the purification and elevation of character in both man and woman by such a struggle for self-conquest. It is essentially dramatic in the sense of action and reaction of the personages of the story upon each other." [Nation. 523

ROCK OF THE LEGION OF HONOR (Der Fels der Ehrenlegion) [by B. AUERBACH: in "Harper's Magazine." nov.-dec. 1870.] "tells of the love of a young german lady for a painter whom she meets in forein parts. There is considerable cleverness in the drawing of some of the people, especially of the heroine and her old schoolmates. The construction of the story is not its most admirable point; by the time the heroine is out walking near where the artist is painting [in **Switzerland**] the reader feels most marked premonitions of the impending spraining of her ankle a few pages further. This artist is painting a rock, and calls it the rock of the legion of honor because a picture of his, representing it, had won him that decoration." [Atlantic. 524

RODERICK HUDSON. [by H: JAMES: *Osgood*, 1875.] "The story is finely conceived, and the book has an indescribable charm. The history of a genius must always be fascinating and impressive, especially if it have 'vraisemblance', and the story of Roderick Hudson's rise and fall is almost terrible in its fidelity to psychological truth. But the great charm of the book lies in the atmosfere of **Rome** which pervades it—the very flavor of Italy. In no other work, except Hawthorne's 'Marble Faun', is the Eternal City made so familiar to our imaginations. It infects one irresistibly with the 'Roman fever,' and we feel as we read that, if all roads do not in fact lead to Rome, at least none is worth traveling which does not promise to lead there." [Appleton's.   525

SARCASM OF DESTINY (The) [by M.. E.. (W.) SHERWOOD: *Appleton*. 1878.] "is peculiar in one respect, as being a story of american society written by a person evidently a member of what in America is called society. The hero of this book is the son of a hungarian fysician and an english lady of rank. His wooing of Nina, an american lady of french descent and great wealth, is interfered with by the discovery that he has a wife living in the nêborhood; he dis-

appears, and Nina, after some delay, maries her kinsman, Vigée La Fontaine, and goes with him to Paris. She is established in the Faubourg, in the imposing and gloomy hotel of her mother-in-law, and her sister is at the same time an ornament of the American colony. The relations and differences of the two sisters are well described, and all the French part of the book is written with 'connaissance du fait.' Vigée becomes brutal, and the same woman who was the wife of Nina's lover turns up as Vigée's mistress, and dies, leaving a child whom Nina adopts and brings back to America with her. She loses her fortune, endures hardships of many kinds, her husband dies, and finally, of course, she maries her first love, whose career seems to be deemed peculiar and unfortunate, but not particularly blameworthy. The old lady, Miss Brown, who is supposed to tell most of the story, is cleverly sketched and quaint, and there is a good deal in the book besides what we have indicated— a description of Washington during the war, a lady traitor, a hī-toned lover, a dip into english society, and a subordinate love affair with suppression of letters, etc. Indeed, if we wished to be critical, we might say that the book is a little like a young minister's first sermon, beginning at the Deluge and telling all he knows. On the contrary, we do say that the book has much liveliness and "pace," and we have no doubt the author can write a much better one."[Nation.526

SEVEN YEARS. [by JULIA KAVANAGH: *Hurst*, 1859.] "Miss Kavanagh is always charming in her delineations of french provincial life and french interiors. She gives not only the outward form and features of things, but their internal meaning and significance. This makes all the difference betwixt wearisome trifling and sagacious indication of character. The first story, which gives its name to the book, is one of the best stories of the kind we ever read. As a work of art it is most skilfully contrived, and as a work of interest it is fascinating. Out of very homely details—with few incidents and no events—with scarcely any change of scene, and with characters which in their real existence were, without doubt, very trying to the patience of all who had to do with them, Miss Kavanagh has constructed a story of strong interest, and without any strain after effect, she has given to it a hī tone of true heroism—she has invested the simple 'continuance in well doing' with a dignity which is touching, because it is true." [Athenæum. **527**

SIEGE OF LONDON. (The) [by H: JAMES : *Osgood*. 1883.] "The story is of an american adventuress who, in her excessive power of adaption, reaches an admirably simulated respectability, and, having fascinated Sir Arthur Demesne, finally turns his defenses against himself. As a piece of warfare, Mrs. Headway's siege is conducted with admirable address. The reader is puzzled to know how a young woman, whose reported conversation, tho entertaining, is undeniably the expression of a hard, vulgar person, will succeed in making capture of the englishman, who, if slow-witted, has at any rate the sensibilities of a gentleman. Time, of so much consequences in most sieges, seems here a dangerous element, and one would suspect that Sir Arthur's wits would at last catch-up with his instincts. So they would, but Mrs. Headway

uses against him the very weapons upon which Sir Arthur must rely. He has an honor which has been wrôt out of poor material in a long series of generations, until now it has a nobility of temper, and thus far Sir Arthur Demesne has used it effectively. At the critical moment Mrs. Headway deftly wrests it from him, and points its blade another way. It is hardly worth while to look for any deep meaning in this brilliant little story. As a sketch of superficial manners it is vivacious and very intelligible. The humor in the study of the young diplomatist is capital, and one may take a grim satisfaction in seeing the very cautious Mr. Littlemore defeated by his own caution, and left to all the dissatisfaction which a too tardy resolution must have brôt him." [Atlantic. **528**

SIGNOR MONALDINI'S NIECE, see ROMANTIC NOVELS.

SIGHTS AND INSIGHTS: [by A. D. (T.) WHITNEY: *Osgood*. 1876.] "People who could talk in this way or listen to it with enjoyment could very well sit in their parlors at home and reason themselves to Europe or up the side of a house without inconvenience. When it is known that certainly a third of the book is made of this curious jumble of sentimentality, religion, transcendentalism, and stammering affectation, the reader may feel as inclined to fly from the novel as he would from these people in life, with their intense admiration for themselves and their ways, and contempt for people who do not boast of being sympathetic, and with their absolutely indecorous want of reserve. To outwê faults of this magnitude (and we have tried not to exaggerate them) there must be something in the novel of great merit, and what this is it is not hard to find. Mrs. Whitney has gone over the familiar track of **European** travel, and she has expressed anew and with considerable accuracy the impression made upon those who see it all for the first time. The little round Patience Strong made in Switzerland led her into no unknown byways, but the beauty of the scenery and its novelty really moved her, and the nonsense left her when she was not under the immediate influence of her traveling companions. Pictures, statues, ruins, and famous architecture found in her a warm admirer, who was sincere in her admiration even if at times a trifle incoherent. We have here something more genuine and better worth reading than the would-be mystical talk of Gen. Rushleigh and the rest. Another merit of the book is that these characters whom we have been abusing, have beneath all their absurdities and narrowness qualities which can only be admired." [Nation. 529

SILVIA. [by JULIA KAVANAGH: *Hurst*. 1870.] "Miss Kavanagh's heroine is charming. When we have said this, we have nearly exhausted our criticism; for tho there is much pleasant writing upon other points, and all the subordinate parts have a distinctness and originality of their own, it is on Silvia and her fortunes that our interest is concentrated, and tho secondary pictures are nowhere left incomplete, she stands out from the canvas naturally and undoubtedly predominant. We are first introduced to her. an italian orfan of noble roman parentage. as living at **Sorrento** under the gardianship of some distant relatives, whose friendly but retired villa she soon leaves for that of a

married friend in France, a change to which she looks forward with much girlish glee and curiosity. Having arrived at St. Rémy, she is thrown at first among a strangely assorted coterie of english. who garrison the house of Lady John Dory, one of those manœuvring women of the world, who for want of excitement, play chess with human pieces, and whose character and satellites are very amusingly described, and secondly finds a home less gay, but not less vitally interesting to her than she had anticipated, in the château of Madame de l'Epine, her early friend. That lady, having been deserted by her husband. a worthless spendthrift, is living with her father, a simple-hearted old french captain who speaks english with zealous intrepidity, and her half brother Charles Meredith, an engineer, and the hero of Silvia's first romance. .. How the good and bad of Silvia's complex tho honest nature are developed by this contact, till fickleness gives way to faith, and the eager girl becomes the loving woman, is a pretty story, and told with much subtle and delicate knowledge of humanity. The books abounds with humor of a quiet sort." [Athenæum.]—It is a story of Italian and French life, in sketching which the author manifests a charming aptness which could result only from an intimate acquaintance with their peculiarities. Some of her pictures of scenery and country life are delicious. Silvia is a winning character, and Dom Sabino Nardi is a quaint and interesting personage, whom it is a pleasure to know." [Boston "Literary World." 530

SOJOURNERS TOGETHER [by FRANK FRANKFORT MOORE: *Smith*, 1875.] "is a pleasant little story of a young man who comes to stay at a Swiss hotel where, a year before, he had met his fate. In the meantime he has been thrown over by the lady. . . . He returns to his old haunts, full of sweet and bitter fancies, and before long meets his fate again in the person of a young lady of charmingly simple manners, the dauter of a vulgar but good-hearted City man. . . This slit story is well told, and the various "sojourners together" in the Swiss pension are happily sketched. It is a pleasant little tale, which we can honestly recommend to our readers." [Athenæum.   **531**

SPIDERS AND FLIES. [by Percy Fendall: *Ward & Downey*, 1886.] "Mr. Fendall does not depend upon his plot in claiming our interest, and solves any difficulties that may occur in its development in a ruf-and-ready fashion. The final episode in particular is abruptly and crudely hurried throu. But in dialog and analysis he shows decided promise and is entirely at his ease in sketching that section of our society who by much residence abroad have divested themselves of their english reserve. And he has the artistic merit of effacing his own individuality and leaving the reader to judge entirely for himself as to the faults and virtues of his 'dramatis personæ'. The character of the heroine is well drawn and consistent, and commands our sympathies in spite of her many faults." [Athenæum.   **532**

SPRING FLOODS, by Ivan Turgenief, see *Romantic Novels*.

STORM DRIVEN   [by M.. (Healy) Bigot: *Lippincott*, 1877.] "is a book which any one may enjoy; altho it may not be strikingly new or original, the story is agreeably told. . . . Lil. John Bruce, and Leigh Ward

are all good types of the men and women of our world; and Issy, with her lofty enthusiasm for art, scorn of fashion, and short-cropped hair, is not the least delitful acquaintance we make. The pictures of **Paris** life are good." [Boston "Lit. World."**533**

STORY OF ELIZABETH (The). [by A.. [Isabella] (Thackeray) Ritchie: N. Y., *Gregory*, 1863.] "A more lovable or natural heroine than Elizabeth, it would be difficult to find. Even in her nautiness and petulance she is charming, and inspires the liveliest sympathy and regard. She is simple and unaffected, not hily endowed intellectually, not wise, but loving and lovely. And if sorrow teaches her at last to be heroic, hers is by no means a stilted heroism, for she learns the hard lesson in so artless and touching a way that it robs her of none of her childlike grace. . . This exquisite little story, when once read, can never be forgotten. It must ever be remembered with affectionate interest, inasmuch as it imparts its own warmth and glow to its readers, associating itself closely with all pleasant memories, such as 'song of bird and hue and odor of blossom,' which in its sweetness, freshness, and delicate coloring it much resembles." [Christian Examiner.]—"In Elly we have a heroine whom we cannot help grudging to the world of fiction; full of engaging beauties, and still more engaging faults; shining in so fresh and simple a loveliness; adorning and enjoying her beauty without vanity; artless and childlike, and yet not without the lustre of culture; loveable without any of the duly registered qualities which claim a fatigued admiration; at once trustful and wilful; pitying herself genuinely in her troubles, and yet pitying others more; with an innocent english mind and heart which are easy to enter into and yet bathed in a deep italian atmosfere; imaginative but not dreamy; with a golden cloud about her that neither dazzles nor overshadows, Elly has, on the whole, no rīt to belong to a novel, and it is the only thing which grieves us as we close the book." [Spectator. **534**

STRUGGLE (A). [by BARNET PHILLIPS: *Appleton*, 1878.] "Here we have at St. Eloi a château and a foundry; in the former a wealthy french ironfounder, and the heroine—his beautiful, impetuous, but hauty dauter, about to be betrothed to a man of the world, de Valbois. At the foundry a one-armed yankee, the hero, an ex-colonel, quiet, imperturbable, but valued by his employer as an admirable mechanic, a ready suggester of the rīt thing to make the iron quicker and better and the machinery to go when it is out of order. Then comes the franco-german war, the master is struck down with illness, de Valbois withdraws, Mr. Yankee runs the works, advises everybody, cares for his employer, and protects his dauter, whose respect and gratitude gradually deepens into love. But this man of perfect judgment gives no sign of his own affection until hauty mademoiselle quite pouts because it has not shown itself, and then the victory is complete." [Penn Monthly. **535**

SUMMER'S ROMANCE (A). [by M.. (HEALY) BIGOT: *Low*, 1877.] "The heroine is of unknown parentage, only moderately accomplished, and possessing a face which owes its chief attractions to the fact that it is expressive of a sensible mind and a loving heart. She is utterly without

adventitious advantages, and it is therefore no slīt evidence of talent that our sympathies, at first grudgingly given to the somewhat unpromising heroine, grow gradually warmer, and that at length we fall desperately in love with her. The hero is rather a poor creature for his position, but his defects are never exaggerated or untrue to nature; and, after all, how few perfect heroes are to be met in life! Again, the villain of the story is only unprincipled, and not a monster of crime. Of the subordinate characters, the young italian wife is a charming little sketch; while the aggressive preaching of Mrs. Cardwell is humorously, but not too humorously, described. Speaking of this book as a drama, we may congratulate the authoress on having given us most attractive scenery—so attractive, indeed, that we fancy many readers will feel a strong desire to visit **Capri**." [Athenæum. **536**

SUN-MAID (The) [by MARIA M. GRANT: *Harper*, 1877.] "is a very pleasant story, and a well written one; the style being clear, vigorous, and eloquent. The scene is mostly laid in **Spain**, but introduces spanish, english, french, and russian characters. The hero is an english nobleman; the heroine, the dauter of a russian poet,—an exile. Both are noble characters. Indeed, the whole tone of the book is superior, and its perusal leaves a sweet and beautiful impression."[Boston·Lit.World."**537**

SYBIL'S SECOND LOVE [by JULIA KAVANAGH: *Appleton*, 1867.] "is an old-fashioned novel, easily written, easy to read, not descending into tragic depths, but treating of the checks, changes, mortifications, and delīts which fall to the lot of a heroine cf 17. Sybil Kennedy is not remarkable in any way except for being truthful and straitforward, and she comes home from school at Brompton to her father's house on the western coast of **France** expecting to find everyone as honest as herself, and, of course goes throu the usual and sad process of attaining to worldly wisdom by bitter experience of falsehood. Her father is a mysterious irishman who has bôt a picturesque property on the wild sea coast in order to build mills and make rape oil; not a very romantic business in itself, but carried on by Mr. Kennedy in a dramatic way. . . Such a book, which leaves the deep waters of life untroubled, is not very interesting to young people, who desire to anticipate by their imaginations the strife and suffering which have not yet reached their hearts. But sometimes those who are passing throu the struggle, who are facing the realities of life, turn away from the writer who touches on them too closely, and seek rather repose and a gentle distraction from unquiet thôt. To such we recommend 'Sybil's Second Love.' " [Round T.**538**

TANGLED [by RACHEL CAREW: Chicago, *Griggs*, 1877.] "is an american production, of lît build. It is agreeably amusing, not by means of the noisy horse-play which has made the fame of some national humorists, but from the very absence of it. The sketch, too, has been carefully written and well deserves the half-hour's attention which would suffice for reading it." [Nation.]—"The double and twisted letters on the cover of this little volume appropriately represent the title. It is a humorous novelette of life at a **Swiss** watering-place, where the hero and heroine get into a 'maddening maze of things,' each

imagining the other to be insane—a supposition which succeeding chapters of accident confirm. This comedy of errors proves more entertaining to the reader than to the deluded tho not demented couple, who are kept from falling in love only by thôts of ineligibility for matrimony of persons in a non-compos-mentis condition. The villain of the piece is mildly personated by an english 'swell,' who tries to win the maiden for himself, while confirming her belief in the insanity of his rival. Riteous judgment, of course, overtakes him. The actual lunatic appears to claim his kingdom of foolishness, the mistake about the hero is cleared up, and all ends happily." [Library Table. **539**

TENTS OF SHEM [by [C:] GRANT [B.] ALLEN, *Chatto*, 1887.] "is romantic and picturesque in parts, and pleasant to read. The plot includes an intricate family complication, an absurd will, a forgery, and some love-making in **Algeria**. There are 2 heroes and 2 heroines, who, after a false start on the part of 2 of them, eventually pair off in a fit and proper manner. Mr. Allen has managed the necessary change in the affections of one of the young women most adroitly; and even when the incidents are most improbable they are nearly always clever. . . Indeed, there are few chapters in Mr. Allen's story which the reader will not find thôroly amusing." [Athenæum. **540**

THELMA. [by "MARIE CORELLI," i. e., Minnie Mackay: *Bentley*, 1887.] "Tho it is called a society novel, the first half, the best and most pleasant portion, deals with fell and fiord in **Norway**. Thelma is a beautiful and accomplished Norse girl, the motherless dauter of an honest farmer; she is discovered by a young english baronet, who after sundry adventures carries her off in his yacht. The incidents are not of a particularly novel kind. and indeed, the character and actions of the rascally clergyman who forces himself upon the heroine's notice are neither pleasant nor natural; but the local descriptions are good, and Thelma herself is fresh and lifelike. After her mariage the scene changes to London." [Athenæum. **541**

THROUGH LOVE TO LIFE. [by GILLAN VASE: *Harper*, 1889.] "In this novel, there is an almost confusing rapidity of movement. It is a work of great talent, impulsive, dramatic, and audacious, altho the audacity is well curbed. The writer has knowledge of the world, and also of literary effects; the contrasts of serious and amusing pages are well managed. It is not one of the novels which will be read and re-read with affection. but it is a brilliant, skilful, and exciting story of english and **continental** life." [Boston "Literary World." **542**

TO LEEWARD. [by FR. M. CRAWFORD: *Osgood*, 1882.] "The young lady who drifts 'to leeward' so easily and completely is the dauter of an english father and a russian mother, bred in **Rome**. Her lover is a dilettante englishman of unmingled race, but who has spent his life in roaming about the Continent, writing articles for magazines, and making love to whomsoever may offer. He is her lover, but not in the wholesome english sense. The whole 'mise en scène' is that, we have said, of a french novel—a thing which, fortunately, has never been adopted or adapted into english. Leonora maries, in the beginning of the book, a nat-

ural. genial, simple-minded italian ; so primitive a character, that little knowledge of the race is necessary to describe to us the kind, simple fellow, who is quite satisfied with his wife's very moderate affection for him. and who is utterly indisposed to poke under the surface, or make analytical investigations into her heart and thôts. She maries him for no particular reason except that he asks her, being herself rich, and in the enjoyment of all that society (in **Rome**) and the hĩer education can give. Evil fortune. however, throws in her way, when she begins to find her husband tiresome. a certain Julius Batiscombe, whom she had known and felt some interest in before—the english literary man 'à bonnes fórtunes.' 'He was known to be an englishman or irishman by birth.' we are informed : but in all ways he resembles much more the american of whom we have much previous knowledge in recent fiction." [Blackwood's. **543**

TONY THE MAID [by B. W. (HOWARD) TEUFEL: *Harper.—Low*, 1888.] "is a charming little story. Admitting that it is about nothing in particular. and that one of its 2 characters is glaringly inconsistent, nevertheless it is charming." Scene **Switzerland.** [Athenæum. **544**

TRAJAN. see ROMANTIC NOVELS.

TREASURE TOWER OF MALTA ('The) [by VIRGINIA W. JOHNSON: *Unwin*, 1890.] "is a pleasant summer story. in which hero and heroine are legitimately youthful. affectionate at sĩt, and artless in the expression of their mutual tendresse. This popular author has undoubtedly the artist's gift of conferring atmosfere. Her little love-idyl of **Malta** between Lieutenant Arthur Curzon, and

Dolores, granddauter of an english recluse long resident upon the island, is charmingly framed in descriptions of the place. One mĭt think that in no circumstances could the reader of frequent novels be roused to interest in the recital of a picnic; but there is refreshing novelty in a picnic of modern fashionable folk on the shores of St. Paul's Bay." [Critic. 545

'TWIXT WIFE AND FATHER-LAND [*Tinsley*, 1875.] is written "by some one who has caut the gift of the baroness Tautphöus of telling a charming story in the boldest manner, and of forcing us to take an interest in her characters which writers, far better from a literary- point of vue, can never approach. And the remarkable thing is that we hardly know why we feel an interest in the chief characters. For example, the heroine is like plenty of other english girls, as far as anything goes which we hear about her: she is well educated, impulsive, given to keeping a diary, and acting before she thinks; and yet the authoress has managed to give her an undefinable attraction which we are persuaded that no reader will resist. We cannot quite parallel her with that most charming of all the heroines of fiction. Hildegarde in the 'Initials'; but she mĭt almost be twin-sister to another favorite of ours, Nora in 'Quits,' and her mother will pair off very well with Mr. Nixon in the same story. The scene lies chiefly in South **Tirol**, first at Cortina (called in the story Zuel, but otherwise not disguised in the least) and afterwards at Meran; and the chief characters, after Camilla herself, are Austrians and Tyrolese." [Athenæum. 546

TWO CORONETS, see ROMANTIC NOVELS.

TWO GIRLS. [by F: WEDMORE: *King*, 1873.] "Welvertree, the hero, is a young man of the usual London type. . . who shows his moral vigor and something of intellectual self-reliance, in seeking the experiences of travel in so quiet a field as a remote country town in **Artois**. Here he meets two english residents, Beddingly Aucott and his dauter Cicely. There is much skill in the way in which our author enlists our sympathies with Aucott. . . Cicely is charming: 'Health had made nothing rude in her, and sensitiveness nothing weak. The whole face wore commonly a look fine and serene, which, even more than the beauty of the features, gave it distinction, because it said (to those who understood it) that she carried in her heart some happy secret which lĭtened all her ways'. Such is Welvertree's first love and better angel. . . Then Welvertree, between restlessness, pity, and admiration of her beauty, not unmixed with a sort of camaraderie in bohemianism, makes the false step of promising mariage in his turn. But Cicely, free, and loving, now re-appears upon the scene; Aucott dies; Welvertree has, of course, brain fever; Irma wages a fierce, tenacious struggle to retain the one man she has loved. She is too weak for the unequal contest. Failing, she falls back on 'mother Seine', the silent consoler of many such wrongs as hers; while Welvertree, who was never worthy of her ardor, finds acceptance too readily at the hands of one whose constancy is still more loftily above him." [Athenæum. 547

TWO LILIES. [by JULIA KAVANAGH: *Hurst*, 1877.) "This well-written story introduces us at the outset to the picturesque street architecture of an ancient **Norman** town. In such a scene, Edward Graham, the architect. is naturally entranced. But beauties of a more alluring type soon present themselves. The rival lilies are admirably contrasted. . . There are some strong minor characters. The aristocratic Mr. Bertram, who so felt his natural rīt to his position, that his true name of Jones seemed justly dropped as inadequate; simple Aunt Graham; Sarah, the Scots' loyal old servant; frivolous Mrs. Fay, and honest Merle the builder. are persons whom cne can remember. The weakest episode is that introducing the impossible Mortlocks, partisans of woman's rīts in their least attractive form, but even this has some humor of the farcial sort." [Athenæum. **548**

TWO OLD CATS. [by VIRGINIA W. JOHNSON: *Harper*, 1882.] "The scene is laid on the slopes of the Maritime Alps, at the borders of France and Italy. at **Monaco. Mentone.** and thereabout. The 'two old cats' are two old women. Miss Moir and Miss Sherewell; and the unfortunate mouse between them is dainty Annie Howard. The question at issue is whether Miss Annie. american. shall mary Arthur Cockburn. englishman; and the question is of course decided by the young people in the affirmative, notwithstanding the claws of the 'two old cats,' and the importunate rivalry of the fat and bald Mr. Belmes. The charm of the story— and it has a very positive charm—lies in its loving description of the Mediterranean background, the refinement of its materials and manner, and the skill of its characterization; little Jessica of pathetic fate, and Lord

Topover, being notable additions to the figures named above. Miss Johnson has intellect, feeling, an artist's sense for what strikes and pleases the eye, a gift of humor, sympathy with all the better instincts of human nature, and unusual literary skill. All these are in this book." [Boston "Literary World."]—"It is but a trifle of a story, and yet it is not trivial. The love-story and the lovers themselves are but secondary. We quite know beforehand the handsome and ingenuous pair who. after not too much adversity. happily walk off the stage hand in hand. The charm of the story is its setting—the shores of the Mediterranean. The cats are neither very old nor very bad—the one with paws of velvet, soft and beguiling; the other stern, repellant, always ready for scratches, but both equally selfish and self-seeking." [Nation. **549**

UGLY DUCKLING (AN). [by H: ERROLL: *Bentley*, 1887.] "In the remainder of the story the writer shows a lītness of touch and sense of humor which are in welcome relief to the sombre opening chapters. The school life at **Basel** and Kate's first romance are brītly told, tho there is a spice of caricature in the portraits of the various male visitors at Miss Schmidt's school. Here, too, we make the acquaintance of the good genius of the plot, the 'amurrican'. Miss Susie Miller, a frank and kind-hearted rattle. with a great belief in her powers of persuasion. who ultimately rescues 'the ugly duckling' from the persecutions of an unscrupulous admirer. . . A really pretty episode in the story is Kate's visit to a charming country house, where. after having hitherto always been bullied and oppressed elsewhere. she is made so much of that she can hardly believe in her good fortune. There is a good deal that touches one in 'An Ugly Duckling,' and the poetic justice of the dénoument is all the more welcome from having been so long deferred." [Athenæum. **550**

UNDER THE TRICOLOR. [by LUCY HAMILTON (JONES) HOOPER: *Lippincott*, 1880.] "The real object of the book is to give a sketch of the members of the american colony, who pass before us thinly disguised. First come the 'low americans' of Mme. Magne's boarding-house, utterly unable to appreciate any life beyond that of their homes, with their bad french. and their love of bargains at the Bon Marché. . . We are then taken to the quarter of the Arc de Triomphe and shown the american nobility. 'mortified at the fact that they were born under the stars and stripes,' 'the only foreiners in Paris who are ashamed of their nationality.' They adore fashion and rank and title, and try their best to live near the rose if they cannot quite be it, even turning Catholic sometimes to win the social heaven. Why not? As Henri IV. said: Paris vaut bien une messe! Another method—but more expensive —is to buy vicomtes and barons as husbands for their dauters. Some of them, however, prefer to adopt english manners and talk, and to prostrate themselves at the feet of english swells; this class is increasing. An interesting matter for observation is the position of this aristocratic american colony, as Mrs. Hooper describes it, encamped on the outskirts of french fashionable society. gazing longingly upon a promised land into which they cannot hope to enter, despised by the people·they most admire and despising each other." [Nation. **551**

UNFORESEEN (The). [by ALICE O'HANLON: *Harper*, 1885.] "The opening scenes are in a Canadian village. The French-Canadians are a comparatively unwritten people, and offer to the novelist a field where reality is almost one with romance and picturesqueness. Miss O'Hanlon begins very well, but abandons her fine opportunities for the attraction of a conventional background to her figures. Tho Mme. Vandeleur very soon loses her distinctive 'Canadienne' personality, she is a clever and brilliant adventuress, and her career is logically drawn. from its obscure beginning to its despairing end. She is by no means typical, but she is possible. Claudia Estcourt, the contrasting figure. is typical, and tho poetic justice may cry for the punishment of vanity. selfishness and cruelty, a wide experience of life will commend the author's inflexibility. The novel is overladen with characters, and spun out, but it is carefully constructed, guided by taste and fine intention, and, moreover. it is interesting and enjoyable." [Nation. **552**

VERA [by C.. L.. (HAWKINS) DEMPSTER: *Smith*, 1870.] "is one of those stories of which there is little to be said; that little. however, should be praise. It is remarkable chiefly for the agreeableness of its style, for its freedom from sensationalism—all its incidents being natural, and, to a large extent, historical.—for its glimpse of russian character, and for the strength and individuality of its hero and heroine. Col. St. John is not introduced to us as a prodigy in any respect; he is 'one of the simple great ones,' brave, manly, modest, and sincere; whose conduct is altogether consistent with his nature, as the author makes it appear. Véra is a really charming creation: no wonder Col. St. John, with his 40 years, and his maimed arm, fell in love with her. There is a womanly purity about her which is more rare in novels than it ôt to be; and while her character exhibits no notably positive features, it has a general effect of strength and symmetry most agreeable to contemplate." [Boston "Literary World."]— "Such is the first incident in the short but interesting tale, the thread of which is taken up again in **Rome**. There is a great deal of good description of russian and continental life, clear delineation of 2 gentle and yet decided characters, and a sufficiently exciting and happily concluded love-tale in store for those who care to learn the fortunes of the admirable Véra." [Athenæum. **553**

VICTIMS. [by "THEO. GIFT," i. e., D. H. (H.) Boulger: *Holt*, 1887.] "The charm lies wholly in the telling of the story. The story itself is made up from hackneyed material: a simple little french girl, a strong and manly englishman, cruel parents, a rich french count, an elopement, a frustration, a forced mariage, a duel, a brainfever, death of the innocent 'victim,' and final mariage of the hero to the strong fine english girl whom he ôt to have known enuf to mary in the first place. All this you are ready to declare you have read already a hundred times; but you haven't—at least, not told in the way this author tells it. The story is made singularly picturesque, chiefly with the local color of **Bretagne**, and there is great art in the way in which the author keeps our sympathy to the end for the al-

most. but never quite, ridiculous simplicity of the little french maiden. We are permitted to see that if she had had one-tenth the strength of the other heroine, she would have been spared half her woes; and yet we can never quite despise her lack of strength. Altogether the story is in its way original, entertaining and pretty, in spite of its sadness and tragedy." [Critic.]—"'Victims' is a story full of life and movement, and with no lack of plot. The contrivances are not at all badly managed and fitted together, . . . and the introduction of a jewish heroine and her relatives gives an opportunity for details of jewish life and character, which add a certain freshness of interest." [Athenæ. **554**

VILLAGE ON THE CLIFF (The). [by A.. [I.] (THACKERAY) RITCHIE : *Smith*, 1867.] "To a select proportion of novel-readers it is just possible that a story devoid of horrors and without an intricate plot may be an agreeable change; especially when such a story is related in good english, and in the natural and graceful style peculiar to the author of 'Elizabeth.' In 'The Village on the Cliff' we have a hero and a couple of heroines, all exceedingly like people we have known all our lives. . . The account of Catherine's maried life abounds in quaint and grafic touches of **Norman** life and manners. . . The great charm of the work lies, after all, not so much in the story, as in the pleasant, unaffected manner in which it is told, and the exquisite pictures which are everywhere presented to the reader in 2 or 3 well-chosen sentences." [Athenæum. **555**

VIRGINIA [by HENRIETTE A. DUFF: *Bentley*, 1877.] "is a rather pretty story. Since Hawthorne wrote 'Transformation,' the sculptor at **Rome** has been a favorite hero with ladies and others who, having spent a winter in the Eternal City and been free of a studio or two, like to convey their impressions in the form of fiction. Until the end of Papal times, there was always enuf of second-rate mystery and mild intrigue going on to prevent the introduction of such things from being as unnatural as it would seem if the scene were laid in any other capital. . . The story gets its name from a young Roman countess with whom the sculptor is in love, and also from a statue which he makes, representing the Virginia of the Republic and Macaulay's Lay. There is a rather puzzling connection between the two; for, tho the statue is not modelled from the lady, observers persist in detecting a likeness, which the artist will not acknowledge, tho ultimately he breaks the statue, rather than compromise the lady. However, he maries her at last, and all comes rīt. As we have said, the story is gracefully enuf told." [Athenæum.   **556**

VIVIAN THE BEAUTY. [by AN-NIE EDWARDS : *Appleton*, 1879.] "Nothing of Mrs. Edwards' has pleased us more than this. It is the simply told story of simple life in a german "schloss", with little Jeanne, her tutor and the houskeeper for chief figures. 'Vivian the Beauty' is an english actress, one of a party subsequently introduced upon the scene. We have discovered no special object in the book, beyond the pleasant, easy entertainment of the reader, and this is accomplished without too great a demand upon his faculties." [Boston "Literary World."   **557**

WEEK IN A FRENCH COUN-TRY-HOUSE (A). [by ADELAIDE (KEMBLE) SARTORIS : *Loring*, 1868.] "There are writers whose grace rather than their strength or beauty is their charm, and whose manner and tone qualify them for admission to the circle of the great ones and princes. Such surely is Mrs. Sartoris, the author of that delītful story 'A Week in a French Country-House',—with at least one character admirable and new in fiction—which no one ever read who would not wish he had not, and that it was still to read." [Nation. **558**

WHO   BREAKS—PAYS.   [by HENRIETTA   CAMILLA   (JACKSON) JENKIN : *Smith*, 1861.] "We have seldom found a story possessing so deep, absorbing, and well-sustained interest, combined with such apparent reality of incident, delicacy in perception and delineation of character, and such sympathetic analysis of emotion that it assumes throuout more the air of a true history than a mere work of fiction. Refinement and pure taste are everywhere present; the dialog is easy and flows with a smooth, life-like current; the descriptions of every-day life in **France**, **England**, and **Italy** are simple and truthful." [Round Table.]—"The story opens with the rather trite occurrence of a 'foreiner' poor yet noble, who gives italian lessons to support himself, falling in love with his rich and beautiful pupil, even as that model of the 'deeply, darkly, desperately' delītful Thaddeus of Warsaw, did before him, and under much the same circumstances as those in which Ruffini's Paolo falls in love with Miss Lavinia Jones. But it is pleasant to see what a nice judgment of the natural consequence of education and character and circumstances can make out of this romantic and hackneyed starting-point. It is a skilful biografer who can describe an entanglement throu all its fāses as justly, keenly, sympathetically, as the entanglement, in this book is described. No vulgar partizanship betrays an inward pique which the wounded novelist seeks to avenge by relating it to the world. The perusal of Lill's history would be a real balm to a girl—and many a one there is—who is or has been in Lill's predicament; i. e., pursued by a superior man whom she knows she ôt to love, but whom, somehow, she can not love. How tenderly, and yet with what unflinching insīt, are her weaknesses dealt with! How the delicate touches of humor līten the picture without ever rendering ridiculous the real suffering of the poor, young, thôtless, fashionable girl. This author dissects with gentleness and fellow-feeling, like a woman; not like a man who runs his sword throu the Gordian knot of feminine complexities, and holding up the ravelled cords, cries, 'There's your mental formation, madam!' But if our entertainer's sex is betrayed by her fineness, it never is by her femineity. She generalizes like a man. She is free from affectation. She does not permit one's feelings for either hero or heroine to conflict with the justice due to the other; one is forced to understand how there may be two sides to a story." [Nation. **559**

WINNIE'S HISTORY. [by M. C. M. (SENIOR) SIMPSON: *Hurst*, 1877.] "The scene is laid in **France**, and the description of french society seems drawn from experience. Tho Winnie's hero, an untruthful. histrionic roué, is widely different from the ideal she forms of her count, he has

the merit of being in love with her, as far as his nature will permit; and their attachment appears to raise the one from mere frivolity, and to enhance the unselfish simplicity of the other. As Émile dies in time to prevent further danger of unfaithfulness, Winnie preserves her ideal, and is happier in its possession than she would have been in the unromantic fruition of domestic happiness with sober Stephen Armstrong—a hero of a more genuine stamp. The character of this energetic young politician is līrly sketched, but is representative of many of the more conscientious of our rising public men; while in aunt Eunice, in the old french marquis, and the general and his wife, we find indications of appreciation of other types of character." [Athenæum. **560**

WITHIN AN ACE. [by H. C. (J.) JENKIN: *Smith*, 1869.] "A quiet little story, this is distinguished by the same gracefulness which we have before now commented on in the author's style. At the end of a tale like this it is, at first thôt, amusing to reflect, on looking back, how little of real plot has sufficed to keep one's attention wide awake. When we have said that a fine, sterling specimen of the genus gentleman (in the hīest sense of the word) maries a girl, good and clever at the core and perverse and foolish on the surface, and that they are 'within an ace' of separating for ever, till their good angel sets all things strait, we have, in fact, told all that the author has to tell. We need hardly remark, therefore, that her way of telling it is her chief merit: add to this that her faculty of portrait painting is of hī order; and the whole explanation of the author's success is unfolded. The dear old duke (the most flegmatic of his friends would hardly growl at that gush of enthusiasm), De Jencay, Chattie, and Yolande, are characters which do not stamp themselves on the reader's mind by jerks and blows, but by the same silent, gradual influence which forms true friendships in real life, stamp themselves even more effectively." Scene in **France**. [Athenæum. **561**

WOMAN-HATER (A). [by C: READE: *Harper*, 1877.] "Sanitary reform, the rit of women to become medical practitioners, the grandeur and beauty of noble music and the unutterable despicableness of that which is trivial—these are the burden and moral of the book, the 2 former being embodied in the person of Rhoda Gale, M. D., anglo-american, and the latter in La Klosking, great singer and anglo-dane. . . It has, what is rare nowadays, a complex, skilfully-constructed plot; it is full of life, and movement and vigor; it offers a favorable example of the trenchant and brilliant qualities of Mr. Reade's style; and the waywardness and mannerism which have marred much of his later work are far less conspicuous, chiefly, perhaps, because the story was written for anonymous publication. Readers may feel but scant interest in woman's rits, but when once they have begun the story they will be reluctant to lay it aside." [Appletons'. **562**

WON! [by —(LEUPOLD) BUXTON: *Bentley*, 1877.] "The quiet, happy, cultivated German home in which the good heroine is discovered by the characterless and under-bred hero, is remarkably well drawn. The manners and customs of the **Hamburgers**, the homely household routine, the simple pleasures, the half-stolid, half-sentimental ways of the men and women, the odd mingling of art and literature with pursuits which seem to us almost childish, and the enthusiasm about amusements which would be voted a rather severe form of boredom by our society, with its present hity peppered palate, are very well conveyed. This part of the narrative runs easily, and there is even some humor in the description of Claud Morel, the painter, who is in love with Pearl Gray, and of Lotta Steinmann, who is in love with him; of the solemnities of the betrothal-party, when the grand englishman and the pretty english governess are exhibited as the 'Brautpaar', and undergo all sorts of queen but kindly formalities; and of the 'ice-picnic' on the Alster." [Spectator. **563**

WOODHILL: *DeWitt*, 1856,= *THE EXILES*.

WORLD'S VERDICT (The) [by M: HOPKINS, *Ticknor*: 1888.] "is a readable, intelligently written story of dilettante americans living abroad and enjoying themselves in the society —apparently not too rigid in its standards—of similar unoccupied people. The author records a mild protest against this method of life by having his hero and heroine fall in love with earnest people outside their social lines, and throw the conventionalities over to wed and go to work; but it is all rather ineffective, and has a youthful sound." [Overland. **564**

Dear Mr. Griswold:

I am delighted with the notion of your list of Novels about Country Life in America and I think you have most charmingly realized it. The book will be useful to every book-lover, and critic, and librarian: now that it satisfies it, I know that I have always felt the need of just such a list.

W. D. Howells.

PRICE: ONE COPY, $1.00; TWO COPIES, $1.75; THREE, $2.25; FOUR, $3.00; FIVE, $3.25, SIX, $4.00; TEN, $6.00.

DESCRIPTIVE LIST

OF

ROMANTIC NOVELS.

COMPILED BY

W : M. GRISWOLD

EDITOR OF "THE MONOGRAPH", A COLLECTION OF FIFTY-FOUR HISTORICAL AND
BIOGRAPHICAL ESSAYS; AND OF "TRAVEL", A SIMILAR SERIES
DEVOTED TO PLACES.

CAMBRIDGE, MASS.:
W: M. GRISWOLD, PUBLISHER.
1890.

Romantic Novels are divided into two classes;—those which are and those which are not, historical. This list is devoted to the latter, but a few historical tales, in which history is at a minimum, have been included. An excellent bibliografy of Historical Fiction exists in the L. H. catalog of the Boston Public Library.

" No author without a trial can conceive of the difficulty of writing a romance about a country where there is no shadow, no antiquity, no mystery, no picturesque and gloomy wrong, nor anything but a commonplace prosperity in broad and simple daylit, as is happily the case with my dear native land. It will be very long, I trust, before romance-writers may find congenial and easily handled themes either in the annals of our stalwart republic, or in any characteristic and probable event of our individual lives. Romance and poetry, ivy, lichens, and wall flowers, need ruin to make them grow." [Nathaniel Hawthorne.

"Few things are more conclusively established in this commonplace day and practical land than the utter abolition of the romantic element of life. People who read Mrs. Radcliffe and the Ledger—and there are those besides ourselves, we are credibly informed, who are in the habit of reading both—must often heave a si of regret for the vanished and delitful mysteries commemorated in those obsolete but fascinating pages. Not the subtlest effort of imagination can again people the prosaic walks of daily life with the weird shapes that haunted every nook and corridor of Otranto's enchanted and enchanting castle. The lonely wayside inn which was wont to be the very nursery and stronghold of romance has become disgustingly commonplace and safe. No ingenious trapdoor opens to engulf the slumber of the unsuspecting traveler; no horrent spectre with flaming eyes and hollow voice emerges from the wall to menace and dismay; no lovely and compassionate barmaid clambers in at the window to warn of the murderous landlord and to save from his sanguinary toils; no foe the chance sojourner has to dread more deadly than the susurrant mosquito or the insidious cimex. The secret doors and hidden stairways and subterranean passages, the unbodied voices, the irresponsible skeletons, and unaccountable knits who made beautiful and thrilling the ways of a preternatural past, have forever disappeared. That whole charming web of mediæval romance the ruthless besom of modern enlitenment has swept into dust and oblivion. We are encompassed with an atmosfere of almost oppressive reality, and it is, a genuine relief when some unusually ingenious murder or flagrant fall of unsuspected respectability gives us a brief respite from the tyranny of the commonplace." [Round Table.

ROMANTIC NOVELS.

The object of this list is to direct readers, such as would enjoy the kind of books here described, to a number of novels, easily obtainable, but which, in many cases, have been forgotten within a year or two after publication. That the existence of works of fiction is remembered so short a time is a pity, since, for every new book of merit, there are, in most libraries, a hundred as good or better, unknown to the majority of readers. It is hoped that the publication of this and similar lists will lessen, in some measure, the disposition to read an inferior NEW *book when superior* OLD *books, equally fresh to most readers, are at hand.*

This list will be followed by others describing EUROPEAN, ECCENTRIC, *and* FANCIFUL *novels and tales. The compiler would be pleased to have his attention called to any works deserving a place which have escaped his attention. It may be observed that the compiler has tried to include only such works as are well-written, interesting, and are free from sensationalism, sentimentality, and pretense. But in a few cases, books have been noticed on account of the reputation of their authors, or their great popularity, rather than their merit.*

The selected "notices" here given are generally abridged.

ADAM AND EVE. [by LOUISA (TAYLOR) PARR: *Lippincott*, 1881.] "Eve and her mother live in decent poverty in London. Robert, a young watchmaker, is in love with Eve, and after the death of her mother tries to persuade her to remain with him instead of going to her paternal uncle in **Cornwall**. She has imagination, however and hi spirits, and Robert, who is a 'methody', has small attractions for her compared with the unknown cornish situation. Thither accordingly she repairs, and finds her relatives not only socially beneath her mother's station and education, but smugglers as well. They are, however. cordial and simple people, and she speedily domesticates herself. Her cousin Adam makes this easier to her by being a man of education and energy and hi temper, and by winning her affections. He is in turn beloved by his cousin Joan,

a true cornish girl, racy of the soil, and both the best character of the book and a character of which most novelists mit be proud. She deserves a better fate than she meets in the original Robert, who, having come to Cornwall to see how Eve is getting on, betrays the smugglers to the revenue officers, and, after being the cause of getting one of them hanged, is so attentive to him in his last hours as to captivate Joan." [*Nation.* **579**

ADVENTURES OF HARRY RICHMOND. [by G: MEREDITH: *Smith*, 1871.] "Any ouc... must have been struck with a story the thread of which was much harder to follow than is usually the case. Gipsies and german princes were perhaps the principal figures left on the mind of a chance reader; but there were also an irascible squire, an eccentric skipper, and a youth who was as perplexing as any one, for his name seemed at one time to be Richmond, at another Roy. Now that the book has appeared in a collected form, the connexion of these curious figures has become a little more distinct, and the whole story has taken as coherent shape as any story of Mr. Meredith is likely to do. His method of narrating in short staccato sentences, with an immense number of full stops, joined to his habit of constantly changing his scene, and favoring his readers with only the slitest possible intimation that a person who 3 lines back was in Hampshire is now in Germany, renders his novels by no means easy reading, if we would understand what is going on, and keep up with the progress of events. He is also fond of exercising his reader's ingenuity by giving only the very slitest hint at the real causes of some of the most important events. In the present book, for instance, we are left almost to our own resources to understand why Harry Richmond is set upon by 4 gipsies, at nit and beaten almost to death—an incident upon which hangs in a great measure the result of the story. We understand that there is a mistake; but we do not know who was the intended victim and what was his offense: we can say only, that altho we have an idea, we are by no means sure that it is a rit one. Not but what we are inclined to think that Mr. Meredith is rit in departing so far from the ordinary practice of novelists as to leave his mysteries unsolved, or at least not solved in that crude way which is prevalent, and which gives us only the same satisfaction that we gain from reading a book of riddles, and turning to the end to look at the answers. In the same way we never know exactly what was the parentage of Harry Richmond's father. He believes himself to be the legitimate son of a royal personage: his friends believe him to be the son, but illegitimate; but we have no intimation as to the truth of either theory, nor whether, if untrue, Mr. Richmond is a conscious swindler or a monomaniac. The author perhaps rather suggests the former; we incline to the latter and more charitable

vue. Such being Mr. Meredith's characteristics, it is not to be wondered at if we decline to give any sketch of the plot of this curious book. It is quite worth reading; but it is itself a sketch in 3 volumes. in spite of the extraordinary minuteness of description. Tho we know nothing about the gipsies, we feel certain that the girl Kiomi must be drawn from life. She is a wonderful creature, with her strange fierceness and affection; and we feel that Mr. Meredith has done us almost a personal wrong in bringing her to harm, which, moreover, from all we have ever heard or her race, seems an unnecessary stretch of probability. As to the other prominent characters, we must say that, while the most of them are of a class almost as strange to us as gipsies, and we suspect in some cases more imaginary, they are admirably consistent with themselves; and given the circumstances, which are perhaps hardly probable, would almost certainly have acted as they are made to do." [Athenæum. 580

AGNES SURRIAGE. [by E. L. BYNNER: Ticknor, 1887.] "There is a charm about this romance of colonial times which engages the reader's sympathies at the outset. The story is the familiar one of Sir Charles Henry Frankland's love for a beautiful girl whom he first saw busily scrubbing the stairs in the inn at Marblehead. He brôt her to Boston, had her educated, made her his mistress, and finally maried her, 10 years later, in Lisbon, in performance of a vow that he would do so if he escaped from the great earthquake, It is a story which offers fine opportunities to a writer endowed with an abundance of imagination. . . Up to the day of the elopement there is no criticism to make, and Agnes is. throuôut, an ideal character. . . But if the author does not always rise to the situation, his book is good, and possesses in a rare degree that quality of atmosfere of the period which is so difficult of attainment, in addition to an $a_{gr}eeab le$ style, which is suitably stately but never heavy." [Nation. 581

ALCESTIS [Holt, 1874.] "is a graceful, pleasing story, rather sad in tone, and is admirable mainly for its sketches of character. Its plot is slit, its personages few, and its incidents hardly better than commonplace. But the musical enthusiasm which pervades it, and the writer's remarkable power of delineating the operation of musical passion, give it a charm which all readers of delicate sensibilities, however ignorant of music they may be, will eagerly acknowledge. . . In the delineation of female character the author displays a masterly, or rather subtile power. Lisa is a grand woman; her self-sacrifice seems almost superhuman. But that she was only mortal we learn from the fact that, as Plauen's wife, she was peevish and unamiable. 'In small troubles we believe Lisa could vent her impatience: her deep grief she kept to herself, and her heart was not hardened.' But grand as she is, she is hardly lovable, tho, perhaps, her nature takes on a certain virility in sustained contrast with that of the sensitive and impulsive Sosquin, in whom the feminine element is very strong. Cécile perfectly realizes the common idea of a hauty, hiborn girl, to whom 'noblesse oblige' is more authoritative than the promptings of her heart. Faustina, the retired singer, is a well-drawn character, whom many readers would like to see more prominent. The book will find many admirers, not only among lovers of **music**, but among all who enjoy acute and refined analysis of character, and faithful interpretation of the passions. It is, in effect, an exhibition of the love of music and the love of woman in joint yet antagonistic possession of a fervid nature." [Boston "Lit. World." 582

ALCHEMIST (The). (Recherche de l'Absolu) [by HONORÉ DE BALZAC: N.-Y. *Rudd*, 1861.] "The wife and the dauter of Claës are among the finest portraits in story; and rarely indeed has love at its most spiritual, its most intellectual and yet its most passionate bits, been better analyzed than in that of Joséphine for her husband. Marguerite is more of a heroine, but she is less human, less real than her mother. For the alchemist himself we are

less able to feel admiration or sympathy because we believe less than Balzac probably did in the scientific basis of his mad search. . There may be a certain grandeur in the passion for scientific discovery which is willing to sacrifice not only self, wife and children, the respect of men, the honor of a family, upon the shrine; yet if to the moral weakness which accompanies this vast passion be added such intellectual defect as to make, in the 19th century, a semi-alchemist instead of a sober man of science, it is a poor shred of grandeur after all. Probably the scientific chemist of our day, as of Balzac's, would say that there was nothing intrinsically impossible in the substance of Claës' theories; but that as stated by him and as investigated, they were from the outside so vitiated, either by madness or ignorance that their victim has no more claim to our sympathies as a martyr of science than any other victim of an illusion. The picturesqueness and vividness of Balzac in all the 'properties' of his tale were never better than in the surroundings of this: the House of Claës is a flemish picture to remain fixed in the mind, not only by its external features, but by its expression, so to speak,—its significance as the embodiment of a race and a history." [Overland.]—"This, perhaps, more than any other work by Balzac, is distinguished by serenity of purpose, surety of touch, and magnitude of wisdom. The large utterances of a filosofer who had studied humanity to its depths and solved the problems of thôt and deeds, are here to be found gleaming like jewels on every page. We have said once before that to read Balzac at his best and understandingly is a liberal education. And we particularly commend the masterpieces of the 'Comédie Humaine' to all who would comprehend the true range and purport of fiction, and who, in the perplexing vagaries and flat unprofitableness of current literature, would have in constant vue a mountain range by which to take their bearings and guide their steps to the bits. We know of nothing more certain to disgust a thôtful person with the pettiness of the great mass of contemporary fiction than a systematic course of Balzac." [Boston "Literary World."]—"In this tale selfishness—or, call it self-occupation—takes its most ideal form. Balthazar is the amiable man of science; with that fanatical passion for speculation and experiment which spares nothing and no one, ... The science of Balthazar has in it something cruel. In real life, we fear, it would hardly encounter such a corrective as is here found in the Sage's provident dauter: the dauter of a mother murdered by the anxieties belonging to the Sage's wife.—The tale, however, is exçellently told." [Athenæum.   583

——, SAME ("Balthazar"), *Routledge*, 1859.

——, SAME ("Alkahest"), *Roberts*, 1887.

ALICE LORRAINE. [by R: DODDRIDGE BLACKMORE: *Low*, 1875.] "The incidents are rather more startling than artistic, and the poetical justice which straitens the tangled skeins of his story is a little far-fetched. The machinery by which the greek astrologer comes to the rescue of his descendants would be clumsy in most hands; but the romantic character of the tale. the period of which is laid in our last romantic epoch, that of the deadly duel with Napoleon in the great wars, renders such a device not quite incongruous. The disaster which befalls the old house of Lorraine is certainly a 'dignus vindice nodus'—nothing less than the loss by Hilary, the young staff-officer of Wellington, of £50.000 entrusted to his care for the payment of the army. Mischief so dire must needs have a woman's influence at the bottom of it; and it is not the litest part of Hilary's misfortune that it is the distracting beauty of a treacherous young spaniard which renders him false to his kentish love and careless of his military duty." [Athenæum.   584

ALKAHEST (The), *Roberts*, 1887, = THE ALCHEMIST.

ALL FOR LOVE. [by ELIZA A.. DUPUY:] "Duyckinck, in his comprehensive 'Cyclopedia of American Literature', [as well as Stedman, in his far more comprehensive 'Library'] has not seen fit to include the name of Miss Dupuy. If favor with her readers is a test of excellence, she is the equal of Mrs. Southworth · but let any one merely skim the many pages of one of her poorly-constructed, loose-jointed plots, and he shall echo the greek sentiment, "A big book is a big evil." The lack of spontaneous humor, or of anything approaching natural conversation, is, noticeable in all these writers, but in impenetrable dullness Miss Dupuy stands in the front. Perhaps this sombreness is needful as a fit setting for plots thick with the horrors of murder, bigamy, and poison. As a specimen of her careless style, there. is a scene in "The Discarded Wife"— a conversation between two housekeepers, which begins in the vernacular of the Middle States, develops into that of the South, and ends in the broad dialect of the plantation negro. Her best story is undoubtedly "The Huguenot Exiles," in which she relates the fortunes of her own family. " *The Discarded Wife*", " *The Cancelled Will*", "*The Hidden Sin*", and "*All for Love*", are the striking titles of her most prominent efforts. J. W. Davidson says of her "Planter's Daughter" that "it is redolent of murder, madness, tears, robbery, revolvers, corpses and confusion." Miss Dupuy was at one time under contract to furnish 1000 columns annually to the 'New-York Ledger'." [Boston "Literary World."] See also, notice of "How he did it."   585

ALMOST A DUCHESS. [by OLGA (GRANT) DE LONGUEIUL: *Roberts*, 1884.] "is a delitful and entertaining story without a single original element in it, yet charmingly original in its combination of hackneyed material. There is the ugly but devoted cousin; the fascinating young duke; the illegal mariage; the plain young relative with a dot, who becomes suddenly beautiful with years, and as she herself naively expresses it, by 'being extremely particular about her clothes'; the desertion; the managing mama; the repentance; the sick-bed; the death; and the final mariage with the devoted but homely cousin—with

168

all of which we have been familiar from youth. But the management of these details is entirely fresh and charming." [Critic.   586

AMONG ALIENS. [by F. E. (Ter-NAN) Trollope: *Blackett*, 1890.] "Given such time-honored ingredients as those which go towards the making of Mrs. Trollope's new story, it would be difficult indeed to produce any very original result. The experience of a pretty young english governess, belonging to the weakly amiable order of heroines, whose lot casts her into the hands of the usual noble roman family with patrician prejudice and inadequate material resources, scarcely possess the excitement of novelty. The hauty and ambitious princess Bastiani-Corleoni, her unusually unprincipled son, together with the priest full of orthodox priestly guile and sublety, and the inevitable brigand, are almost as familiar to the untraveled english reader as are roman churches, streets, peasants, ejaculations, and all the other properties, including the scenery of the italian landscape. These items are, however, none the less attractive for being old friends, and, indeed, Mrs. Trollope has succeeded in investing them with a freshness which is quite surprising. Catherine Wilson, the elder sister, of robust character and considerable determination, adds greatly to the merit of the story in her telling of it. She is by far the most successful and least conventional character in the book, and her simple personality sheds a pleasant atmosfere of wholesomeness and reality over all its situations, even the most well-worn," [Athenæum. 587

AMONG THE CHOSEN   [by M.. S. Emerson: *Holt*, 1884.] "is one of the well-written stories of which we cannot have too many, as a warning against whatever may be the attractiveness of life in 'communities' whose first law is the subversion of human nature. The uselessness, the suffering, the cruelty, the deceits and treacheries and hypocrisy, of such a life are well depicted; if the alluring charm that fascinates the victims even after trial, is made less evident, the

author is not to blame. Certainly the reader does not succumb easily to the magnetism of the unctuous Father John, but he knows that in real life there are people who do. The story is told with great vividness, the children being especially well managed, and the author has not forgotten that many converts to 'the chosen' are sincere and noble, whatever the leaders are. The bi-spirited girl who resents, even before she 'sees throu', the machinations of Father John is a fine creation. The interest in her fate is kept so intense that the author accomplishes the purpose of the book quite as well in letting her escape, as in making her a victim to the bitter end." (Critic.   588

ANTIQUARY (The) [by Sir Wa. Scott:] "is a tale of humble scottish life and manners, the scene chiefly in a small fishing town, the time the last 10 years of the 18th century, the connexion with historical events very slit." [Boston "Literary World."   589

ARGONAUTS OF NORTH LIBERTY. [by FR.] Bret Harte: *Houghton*, 1888.] There is 1 american story-writer who is bothered with no limitations of art or questions of ethics, but whose sole province is to tell his tale and have done with it. Mr. Bret Harte probably writes "out of his head" as much as any novelist except the purely imaginative or entirely sensational ones. His landscapes, naturally and completely as they are drawn, with all their briefness, are taken from only the most indistinct kind of memories, or from nothing at all, and his people come from anywhere and everywhere. It is true that they usually bring up on the Pacific Slope, and that they invariably have something interesting and amusing happening to them. There are enuf surprises and complications, for instance, turned off in the short tale '*A Phyllis of the Sierras*' to furnish many a writer with material for volumes. But we have seen nothing of late which can at all compare with '*The Argonauts of North Liberty*' for brief directness, for sustained and exciting interest, or for subtle, strong suggestiveness. The story "tells itself." and in an hour's reading one compasses the entire existence of 3 persons by simply knowing how they acted at 3 important periods of their lives. There is no need for minutiæ or details; the drama is played, the curtain is rung down promptly, and one's curiosity is satisfied. The last sentence of the book completes the first chapter of the story, and the circle is finished. The tale is too neatly told, the coincidences and contrasts are too effectively wrôt, and the action too rapid and culminating to bear marring by abridgment. But if one cares for a story that is just simply a story (for it is just simply a story), for characters which have nothing to recommend them but their human failings and passions, and can put up with a very small portion of wickedness which is never carried quite beyond the verge of respectability, one will surely read the history of Deacon Salisbury's dauter and her two husbands." [Nation. **590**

ARIADNE. [by "OUIDA," i. e., L.. de la Ramé: *Chatto*, 1877.] "When the first book, 'Held in Bondage,' appeared it was easy to see that Lawrence was her standard, but while the tone of "Guy Livingstone" was sufficiently low—as all must acknowledge—it had at least the merit of being original, while in her imitation everything that was objectional in his style was copied in so coarse a fashion as to become repulsive... Altho the 'haute noblesse' figure largely in her books, one never by any chance stumbles upon even the shadow of a lady or gentleman. Her men are never gentlemanly: her women are never womanly. There is a sort of fascination in her language, and a certain power which seizes on the fancy of boys and girls, and even of older persons, who demand a small excitement by way of amusement. There is almost always an interest in her stories, but it would be difficult to tell in what it consists, for the plots are never clever, the characters are not distinctly individualized and she has just her stock company. Each book contains the same people...'Ariadne,' her last, is by far the best in tone, is bet-

ter written, and contains some really charming descriptions of **Rome**, written with a loving, tender appreciation of nature and art that is quite astonishing. As a story, it is utterly unsatisfactory. The heroine—tho a genius, or because a genius—is an imbecile. The other characters do not amount to much, and tho there is not so bad a taste in the mouth as is generally left by her books, there is still the trail of the serpent." [Library Table.] —"On the one hand it is impossible for any competent critic not to notice, and in noticing not strongly to condemn, her fantastic folly of style, the preposterous pedantry, and withal inaccuracy, of her allusions, her hopelessly unreal moral atmosfere, the wearisome overstraining of her unnatural pathos, and the theatrical glare which distorts, sometimes very mischievously, her vues and representations of almost all subjects. There is consequently a temptation to indulge in mere sarcasm at these absurdities, and a danger of failing to do justice to her merits—,the merits of vivid presentation, of really skilful handling of her preposterous materials, and, especially in her later books, of true sympathy with humanity, as she understands it. These merits are not absent from 'Ariadne', and we may add that it is by no means badly constructed, and in matter of taste stands in favorable contrast to much of its author's earlier work. The plot, indeed, requires that the heroine should love more well than wisely, but this part of the story is dealt with inoffensively, and in a manner quite within the legitimate limits of art. Unfortunately, however, the book is decidedly dull; and it is needless to say that the last word of critical condemnation on a novel has been said when this fatal verdict has been pronounced. The book is dull—first, because of the unceasing strain of false sentiment and false pathos; secondly, because of its utter remoteness from familiar and probable human life; and, lastly, because of the almost superhuman folly of the allusions, casual disquisitions, and ornamentation generally... The hero is exactly the same artless creation whom Madcap Violet and every other schoolgirl who writes a novel at 16 imagines and always has imagined. Very beautiful, very rich, very clever, very wicked, with a mysterious fascination, and a total absence or heart, he is about as new as the Pyramids, and about as possible as the Chimæra: not to mention that he is much less interesting than either, and that his, inspired tirades upon subjects of literature and art are simply appalling. The story is not complicated. It is told by an old roman cobbler, a pleasant personage enuf, who strikes us as being one of the most successful of Ouida's creations. The cobbler finds a protégée in a young girl of wondrous beauty, who has been left an orfan, and has received from her father, a sculptor of more feeling than power, nothing but a multiplied portion of his artistic skill, and an enthusiastic love for antiquity." [Athenæum. **591**

ARTISTE. [by Maria M. Grant: *Hurst*, 1871.] "The friendship which arises between the accomplished frenchman and his favorite pupil proves of infinite service to Hazel when, maddened with jealousy, she leaves the house of her gardian and finds her way to London. Under old Dalcourt's training, her, genius, and with it her entire character, develops rapidly, and the woman succeeds in forgetting the great sorrow of the child. She makes her début at Paris, takes the Parisians by storm, and becomes the rage at every capital in Europe; supporting her friends the Dalcourts meanwhile out of her professional earnings. Her sudden disappearance from the house of her gardian was the occasion of a singular revolution in the habits of the indolent, dreamy artist who had in turn adopted, trained, and worshipped his orfan child-ward. It is not until he has lost her that he realizes the full force of his passion, and he spends years in vainly wandering over Europe in search of her. At last, when he has given up all hope of success, and has settled down to the prosaic duties of a landlord, chance throws her in his way at an italian

watering-place, where she is playing under her now famous pseudonym of 'La Listelle.' The two meet at the close of her performance, in the 'salle d'attente des artistes', and there Lennard learns that he has been loved and is loved still by this splendid actress, who is ready, at a word from him, to renounce her calling and her professional reputation to become his wife. As old Dalcourt remarked when he heard the news, Hazel Gray was 'artiste, mais pourtant femme.' They are maried then and there, and return to England to begin their new life. At this point the story appropriately ends." [Athenæum. **592**

AT ODDS. [by J. (M.) von Tautphöus: *Bentley*, 1863.] "The baroness Tautphöus properly belongs to a rather past away school of novelists, which she has refreshed and revived for us by variations derived from her large experience of Continental society,—we mean, the school which (whether involuntarily or didactically) sets forth a delicate and refined prudence as the basis of social life, and endeavors to measure characters and careers with reference to that standard... The author of 'The Initials' and 'Quits' constantly reminds us of that playful, secular school of fiction, so little now in vogue, which believed in the divinity of Good Sense, accepted without question the conventional morality, and found its stimulus less in warmth of feeling than in the keen edge of occasional repartie, and the sharp contrasts of the different schools of manners in different classes of life or different national characters. The proprieties are very different, of course, in the South German society to which the Baroness Tautphöus is accustomed, from those which were acknowledged more than 50 years ago by english and irish authoresses, —but they predominate in exactly the same way in the imagination of the writer, and give the same kind of advantages and disadvantages to her pictures... Still there are great merits in the book. The german counts are admirable pictures: the Director and Minna-Pallersburg are sliter sketches, equally life-like,—and the 2 half-sisters

and their mother, tho as we have said, too
much crusted over with anglo-german
decorum, or too intrinsically tame, correspond with their parts and are distinctly
enuf conceived. Then it is always delitful
to get into **Tirol** under the baroness Tant-
phöus' guidance, for it always brings back
memories of blended magnificence and
simplicity,—of a hearty, childlike, and
statuesque peasantry, living in scenes
which fill and thrill the imagination such
as no other country in Europe can yield
in equal measure." [Spectator. **593**

AT THE ALTAR. [by "E. WERNER,"
i. e., E.. Bürstenbinder: *Lippincott*, 1872.]
"The novels of E. Werner are always
above the average of german fiction, and
they further possess the rare merit of individuality. In the one before us, the
author has taken his subject from the
vexed question of Protestantism versus
Catholicism. The hero is a priest who has
been forced into this profession while an
infant. Family reasons make it desirable
he should not know the story of his birth,
namely that he is sprung from a Catholic
father and a Protestant mother. But the
Protestant blood makes itself felt. Tho
reared in all the traditions of his order, he
cannot wholly blind himself to its abuses.
His mental struggles are aggravated when
personal feelings come in contact with the
machinery of the Catholic Church. It is
vainly impressed upon him that he has
sworn allegiance at the altar. and that
before the priest and the Catholic every
human emotion must be trampled in the
dust. He cannot thus pacify his conscience, carefully trained tho it has been:
he revolts, and betrays some discreditable
monastic secrets, turns Protestant, and
maries. This in brief is the subject of the
novel, which is well constructed and well
sustained. and would beyond doubt be
perused with interest by english readers
but for the unsatisfactory manner in which
it [i. e., the Parker translation] is rendered into the language: all the german forms
and idioms are retained, and the novel is
simply and literally done, but not translated, into english... In short the book is

spoilt." [Athenæum.]—"The [Wister]
translation is a good one." [Nation. **594**
—, SAME, transl. by Parker, *Low*, 1878.
—, SAME, ("Sacred Vows") transl. by
Ness, *Remington*, 1877.
"These novels, thanks to Mrs. Wister,
are as well known in this country as
they are at home. Critics have often
praised this lady, not only for her literary
skill, but for the extraordinary tact displayed in the choice of tales for translation.
Praise for the latter, however, is due not
to her, but to' the lately deceased editor of
the 'Gartenlaube', who, as was some years
since pointed out, called into life a new
school of novelists, mostly women writing
pseudonymously, and some of whom—"E.
Marlitt', for instance, and "E. Werner"—
are to-day popular in every european language"... "With these facts in his mind, it
strikes a foreiner as singular enuf that
german critics should speak of these fictions with combined hatred and contempt.
A writer in a recent number of the Maga-
zin für die Litteratur cries out that they
are fit only for chambermaids and seam-
stresses, and otherwise describes them in
terms such as would be used in this country
only in reference to works beneath serious
criticism, such as those of Mrs. Holmes
and Mrs. Southworth." [Nation. **595**

ATELIER DU LYS (L'). [by MA.
ROBERTS: London, 1876.] "The scene
is laid in the time of the **Revolution**,
which has inspired so many novelists,
but. the history never impedes the action, and altho there is plenty of what is
called 'local color', it always seems to
have its place and not to be laid on with
any other object than to further the telling
of the tale. The general air of the time, the
alarm in everybody's heart, the way in
which the ordinary business of life went
on in spite of the manifold interruptions,
the certainty with which the different persons adapted themselves to new ways of
living and dying, in a word, all the different impressions one gets from the memoirs
of the time, are admirably recounted here
without overburdening the story with details. The plot is an ingenious one, and

158

the reader's attention never flags. The characters are drawn with great skill. A young girl, Edmée, is the heroine, and all sorts of dangers threaten her and her fortunes, and the reader knows no peace of mind, altho his anxiety is never really too great, until the babbling tung of her aunt and the clever machinations of the villain can at last do her no harm." [Nation. **596**

—. SAME ["Noblesse Oblige"], *Holt*. 1876.

AULNAY TOWER. [by B. W. (Howard) TEUFEL: *Ticknor*, 1885.] "There is a good situation in 'Aulnay Tower', but the book may be said to be all situation, with little movement, no development, and the very slitest free play of character and motive. The scene is laid at the château of the Marquis de Montauban, not far from Paris, at the moment in the francogerman war, when Sédan had been fôt, the emperor was a prisoner, and the Germans were investing the capital. . . The Countess Nathalie, a widow of 23, 'a beautiful woman, young, pale, fair-haired, stately, and forbidding,' confronts these invaders of her private peace and enemies of her country, intending to freeze them by her hautiness, her indifference, her disdain, but carries away from the first encounter a haunting and rankling recollection of a tall man in blue; while the tall man in blue, Adjutant von Nordenfels, 'from the moment she stood before the officers in her cold protest and unrelenting pride,' was madly in love with the countess." [Lippincott's.]—It is a "romance, almost one of the old-fashioned sort,—even the title is romantic,—and presents us the lovely and lonely chatelaine of an ancient tower in France, wooed by an ardent saxon lover, stalwart and pensively interesting, almost in the very midst of the bombardment of Paris. . . Manette, the maid of the countess, we find tedious and disagreeable. She belongs in one of the society plays, or in a variety show." [American. **597**

BALDINE. [by KARL ERDMANN EDLER: *Harper*, 1887.] "Nothing is lacking to render the charm of these simple yet profound stories supreme. Plot, dialog, description, are all that could be asked, and they are couched in exquisite prose. Without being in the least sketchy, they leave much for the reader to fill in from his heart and sympathies, and the delicate art of the writer is as convincingly displayed in this respect as in that portion of his tales which he has expressed in words. The reader instantly comprehends what is required of him, and it is only when he reaches the end of the volume that he realizes how much has lain between the lines, and what a triumf the author has scored in guiding him so deftly and imperceptibly to supply it out of the fulness of his nature, instead of himself giving utterance to it. An outline of the plots of these three life tragedies would convey but a feeble idea of their dramatic, poetic, and romantic worth, which the reader must obtain at first hand." [Nation. **598**

BALLET-DANCER'S HUSBAND (The). [by ERNEST FEYDEAU: Chicago, *Sumner*, 1880.] "Chapter second: the beautiful Barberine puts on a different dress, so to speak, assuming a character which we begin to respect. In due time the adored lover becomes her husband, and the others are remanded to a distance. But this time the story enchains attention, and we follow it to the end. It is the old and ever-pitiable story of woman's unselfish, unfaltering devotion to man, and of man's egotistical, brutal inhumanity to woman. . . These, of course, are the outlines of a powerful work, and for a french novel we cannot quarrel with it. Only it is inexpressibly painful. The fiendish cruelty of Saint Bertrand, the exquisite tortures endured by Barberine, the struggles of **Poland** under the clutch of Russia, the stern vengeance which has its way in the end,—all this makes a lurid picture, which we can only suffer ourselves to look upon for the masterly skill with which it is drawn. The fidelity of Barberine, the stern heroism of Eytmin, the honest friendliness of Gaskell, alone illuminate it. Those who have not nerve for a trying spectacle should pass it by." [Bos-

ton "Literary World." **599**
BALTHAZAR [London, 1859] = *THE
ALCHEMIST.*
BANNED AND BLESSED [by "E.
WERNER", i. e., E.. Bürstenbinder: *Lippincott*, 1884.] "is a vigorous and original story, excellently told, of one of the
great nobles, living in his 'schloss' among
the mountain-fastnesses, with a village
below him, of which all the inhabitants are
in a way his dependents, and at the same
time his enemies. Children shudder at his
name, all manner of evil deeds are imputed
to him, the priest has cut him off from the
church: in short, the lord of Werdenfels,
in spite of his great lineage and his princely wealth, is almost a pariah. He is, nevertheless, a victim rather than an oppressor
and the clearing up of the mystery which
encircles him is full of interest and animation. The setting of the story among the
glaciers and the snows, with the Ice-
Maiden lurking in the abysses to embrace
her prey, makes it weird and poetic. Nature works out the development of the
plot by sending down terrible spring floods
which threaten the village, and the working out of the story is very good. This
translation seems to us one of the best of
Mrs. Wister's, who always chooses [? see
No. 595] her work with discrimination."
[Lippincott's.] "It can be heartily recommended to the lovers of the old-fashioned
romantic story, if any such survive. It
has all the requisites, from the hereditary
feud between priest and baron to the
doting fidelity of the old retainer." [Na-
tion. **600**
——, SAME ("Enthralled & Released")
N.-Y., *Knox*, 1886.
BASIL. [by [W:] W. COLLINS].
"Mr. Collins can hide a secret better than
any man, he is a master of mystery; but
when once the secret is discovered, when
once the mystery is unravelled, his books
collapse at once, their interest perishes,
they are flat as conundrums to which you
have the answers. For to this writer plot
and incident are all in all, character
nothing. He has little spontaneity of humor, no reflexion, no aforistic wisdom, no

poetry, but little painting of scenery: and,
what there is, not of the best kind. He
relates his stories boldly and nakedly; he
pursues his plot with the directness and
pertinacity of a detective or a bloodhound.
From the beginning of the first chapter of
his work, he keeps his eye steadily fixed
on the last. So long as you have this book
open, you are spell-bound; whenever you
close it, you feel you have been existing in
a world of impossible incidents, and holding converse with monstrosities. The
touches which make the whole world kin,
the humor which is a perpetual delit, the
pathos which makes sacred, are not in
these books. Everything is tense, strained,
and unnatural." [North British Rev. **601**
BAY PATH (The). [by J. G. HOL-
LAND: *Putnam.* 1857.] "Stories about
the early settlers in **New-England** will always have an interest to the english reader.
It is the romance of american history.
'The Bay Path' is not a powerful tale, but
it is a very interesting one. John Wood-
cock is an excellent character, with his
shrewd, quaint, good sense, and intractable
nature. his false position among a decorous, orderly community, and their entire
inability to understand him or deal with
him. Mr. Moxon, the weak, foolish,
scrupulous, conscientious minister, with
his bewitched children, is a good character, well worked out. The pictures of
early settler life are well drawn, the whole
story is interesting, and has an air of truth
and reality which is bily to be commended.
The style, too, is good and simple; and the
english is not american, which will be a
recommendation to readers on this side of
the water." [Athenæum. **602**
BEAUTY OF AMALFI (The). [Lon-
don, 1852.] "We have here an italian tale
after the dear old romantic fashion,—compounded of gorgeous scenery, gay costume,
love wrecked by pride, political revolution,
and madness,—having the period of the
outbreak headed by Masaniello as its
date,—a peasant boy and girl for its lovers,—and among its actors the Zingara,
that inscrutable old sorceress, who, meet
her when, where, and how we will, is

always as acceptable as she is awful to old-fashioned readers of romance. We need say no more concerning 'The Beauty of Amalfi',—save and except that she is not the least engaging, tho she is the last, of her family." [Athenæum.　　**603**

BÉBÉE [by "OUIDA" i. e., L.. de la Ramé: *Lippincott*, 1874.] "is one of the most tenderly beautiful stories we ever read. The heroine is a girl, left friendless at a tender age, who supports herself by the sale of flowers in the streets of **Bruxelles.** She is a veritable child of nature, knowing nothing of the great world, but kind-hearted and simply good, it would seem instinctively. One day, the eyes of a famous painter fell upon her, attracted by her rare beauty. He becomes her friend, teaches her to read, gives her books, and thrusts back the horizon of life before her wondering gaze. Of course she learns to love him with all the strength of her vigorous nature. He is sorely tempted; but his better nature conquers. . ..This simple little plot is developed with exquisite delicacy and occasional passages of intense dramatic power." [Boston "Literary World."　　**604**

BEGGAR MY NEIGHBOR [by "E. D. GERARD," i. e., D. Gerard & E. (Gerard) Laszowska: *Blackwood*, 1882.] "can be most cordially praised. The authors made a decided success with 'Reata,' a book which many people held, not without reason, to be the best novel of its season. But their new book is really much better than 'Reata.' It is a well constructed story, quite interesting enuf to fix the reader's attention and stimulate his curiosity, without any mysteries, improbabilities, or horrors. But while the story would alone carry the reader along in spite of its simplicity, or rather by reason of the clearness with which it is worked out and the natural manner in which the events are made to follow each other, it is more particularly as a study of character that the novel will recommend itself. When the reader has once got before him the sketcher of the 3 brothers who play the chief men's parts and of the 2 cousins who

are the principal ladies, he is ready to pursue their history to the end, even tho it were far less ably invented and told than it is. The scene is in **Poland** except for a short time, during which one of the brothers, who is in the Austrian army, is followed to the disastrous campaign of 1859. This brother is an admirable study. In his noble character, where warm heartedness, spirit, devotion and truth, along with a fascinating unconsciousness of his merits, are yet mixed with a good deal of weakness and a want of intellectual vigor, the authors have presented a bit of human nature itself. . . Vizia has just missed being a beauty, and the ever-present consciousness of the contrast between herself and her cousin, whom she loves most warmly, has given a bitterness to her nature and hardened her features. But what she presents to the world only hides a character full of passion, self-denial, and devotion—a character which Balzac mit have been proud to draw. He would have done it more minutely, but he could not have made the picture more complete and striking. Kenia, the lovely cousin, is a child-like soulless creature, is also a true study, but she is a less uncommon type than Vizia. The same may be said of Lucyan, the polished scoundrel who has no conscience and no remorse—only selfishness almost without the excuse of passion. It should be added that the good taste and good sense of the authors combined with a remarkable knowledge of the world and a pleasant liking for fun, make their book no less agreeable as an amusement than their ability makes it interesting as a study." [Athenæum.　　**605**

BELLAH. [by OCTAVE FEUILLET: *Simms & M'Intyre*, 1850.] "For the french novelist the struggle in **Vendee** will always possess attractions similar to those held out to the Scot by the wanderings and wars of 'the Young Chevalier.' Mr. Feuillet has here given us ample proof of his ability to combine and work out the picturesque materials of history. Ambuscade — escape — irregular warfare — old houses divided against themselves—love

175

misunderstandings—peasant fidelity—and the affection of military comradeship—are well grouped and contrasted." [Athenæum. **606**

BERTHA'S ENGAGEMENT. [by A.. SOPHIA (WINTERBOTHAM) STE-PHENS.] "Readers of Mrs. Southworth are generally readers of Mrs. Stephens, whose works, filling at least 14 stout volumes, are thôt by some to be of too excitable a nature to supply to an eager public without restraint. Generally deemed a less desirable writer than Mrs. Southworth, she, like the latter, has relied for her successes upon the mis-doings of humanity—and humanity always likes to hear of its short-comings. Most sensationalism chooses for heroes and heroines the favorites of fortune, lords and ladies of hi degree, who live in manorial halls, sit on plush, dine off ancestral plate—all of which is pleasing to the populace: but Mrs. Stephens stoops a little lower than this, and does best when telling of domestic ways and humble people. Her ablest performance [is] '*Fashion and Famine*' [which see]. Other of her more readable stories are: '*The Rejected Wife,*' '*Bertha's Engagement,*' '*The Curse of Gold,*', '*Married in Haste,*' and '*The Old Countess.*' It is hardly necessary to say that titles like these decide the fate of sensational books, fully as much as any merit or demerit contained within the covers." [Boston "Literary World." **607**

BETROTHED (The). [by A. MANZONI: *Bentley,* 1845.] "The original is regarded as the best picture of the times, and the sweetest and most correct daguerrotype of italian life which has appeared in modern times. It at once gave its author fame. The scenes of this enchanting story lie amid the fairy shores of **Lake Como.** Among its characters is Carlo Borromeo, now the patron saint of Milano; and the sufferings of that city from famine and plague are vividly depicted. The sentiment of the tale is as unexceptionable as it is attractive and natural,—the characters ably developed, the language elegant—and over all broods the soft lit of the pleasant

south." [Democratic Review. **608** —, SAME ("Lucia the Betrothed"), N.-Y., *Dearborn,* 1834. —, SAME ("I Promessi Sposi"), *Lambert,* 1855.

BIMBI: [by "OUIDA", i. e., L.. de la Ramé: *Chatto,* 1882.] "Ouida is not, perhaps, exactly the writer whom one would select as a teller of stories for the young. It is not that her incidents are sometimes hardly suited 'virginibus puerisque;' it is not that she may lead the youthful mind astray by talking about 'Barabbi' or by disagreeing with the grammarians as to the syntax or accidence of ancient and modern languages, or even, as in the present volume, by leading them to suppose that the silver groschen is. or was. an Austrian coin. But there is in all her writings a sort of pessimistic tone, a tendency to make evil triumfant and good unfortunate, and to insist on the baser and more cruel elements of human nature, which if carried into children's books would soon leave very little heaven to lie about them in their infancy. On the whole, therefore, we were somewhat agreeably surprised by this book. Out of the 9 stories which it contains, 2, '*Moufflou*' and '*The Child of Urbino*' are really very pretty, tho in the case of the former the author has been unable to refrain from ending with one of those anecdotes of cruelty to a dog which seem to possess a morbid fascination for her. Of the remainder, 2 or 3 are clumsy imitations of Andersen, and the rest seem intended to show that all grown people are stupid or brutal. But even the best have the fault that nearly all stories for children have nowadays: they are not really children's stories, but studies of children, such as their elders may appreciate, but themselves never." [Athenæum. **609**

BLITHEDALE ROMANCE (The). [by NATHANIEL HAWTHORNE: *Ticknor,* —*Chapman,* 1852.] "The reader is not to imagine that 'The Blithedale Romance' is a cold or prosy essay, done after the fashion of a gilt pill, with a few incidents enabling the reader to swallow its wisdom.

Tho rich in thôt and suggestion, the tale is full of mystery, suspense, and passion, exciting the strongest interest. Besides Zenobia, Hollingsworth and the poet-narrator, the Blithedale [i. e., **Brook Farm**] community included the timid, pâle girl, Priscilla,—who appeared to have dropped into the midst of it from the clouds, and who joined the company with no or no more general idea than that of satisfying her heart's yearning for shelter and escape. Stern and self-engrossed as was Hollingsworth,—nay, because of his stern earnestness,—he contrived to fascinate both Zenobia and Priscilla: the former resolving to place her wealth at his disposal, —the other submitting her heart to him long ere she guessed that it was gone from her. The 2 women were thus brôt into unconscious rivalry; and excellently true to nature is the manner—as tender as it is real—in which Mr. Hawthorne manages to maintain the individuality of each. We do not remember any study of the passionate woman of genius, in which her whole heart-struggle is so distinctly portrayed, without the impression of what is unfeminine and repulsive being produced, as this of Zenobia." [Athenæum.] It "must not be deemed a literal history of life at Brook Farm, nor can the personages in the book be identified as actual residents there. Altho it has been said that "Zenobia" is a portrait of Margaret Fuller, Drake, the historian. denies the statement, and Georgiana Bruce Kirby says: "There was at the Farm a pretty, black-eyed girl who, before coming there. had been used as a clairvoyante for examining the patients of a Boston fysician. Young in knowledge, as in years, she yet gave the result of her clear-seeing in scientific terms. I never knew whether her powers gave out, or whether her confessor forbade her to pursue her profession. I think it was she who suggested 'Priscilla' to Hawthorne. 'Zenobia,' a friend of Miss [E.. P.] Peabody, was a resident at the farm." Was the latter Mrs. Biscacianti, the famous vocalist, then Eliza Ostinelli?" [C: M. Barrows. **610**

BLOCK HOUSE ON THE PRAIRIE (The). [by F: SPIELHAGEN: *London Pub. Co.*, 1882.] " 'Deutsche Pioniere,' one. of the most agreeable of Spielhagen's earlier stories, lies before us today in a fair and readable translation. The scene is laid in **America** about the middle of the last century, and describes the life led in those days by the german emigrants. The adventures of these pioneers on the outskirts of civilization, the hardships and difficulties with which they had to cope, are graficly told. In the course of the tale the wars of the french and english are introduced, as well as some account of the indian settlements and the sufferings that befell the german settlers from these nêbors. The whole story is healthier in tone, more probable, and more objective than is usual with Spielhagen. There is nothing exaggerated, nothing morbid . in these pages, and the characters are both agreeable and well drawn." [Athe. **611**

BLOODSTONE (The) [by DONALD MACLEOD: *Scribner*, 1854.] "is the title of an exciting story in the form of an imaginative autobiografy, relating a succession of wild scenes and adventures in german life, most of which are founded on the experience of the writer in one of the secret revolutionary societies of a german university, of which the symbol was a bloodstone cross. In spite of the essential incredibility of the incidents which compose the staple of the volume, it possesses a strange, weird attraction, and is written with undeniable originality and power. The introductory portions, describing several familiar scenes in the vicinity of New-York, contain frequent passages of quiet beauty, and will, we think, be most pleasing to the generality of readers." [Harper's. **612**

BLUE RIBBON (The) [by ELIZA TABOR: *Hurst*, 1873.] "deals primarily with the loves of an english farmer's son and a german factory girl (he eventually an inventor, she a singer) ; and. secondarily, by way of landscape and background. with life in an english cathedral town, sleepy and humdrum in its normal existence, but kindled periodically into life by its recurring musical festivals. The artistic enthusiasm of the heroine, and the scientific energy of the hero are aptly rendered, and the flitness of the former, tho a good deal overstrained (the mesmeric influence of the villain Notturino, who has power at a moment's notice to withdraw her completely from the pursuit of her art among the simple friends she has made in the cathedral town, and bind her to his chariot-wheels in the twofold capacity of an artist and a lover, appearing to us impossible in so simpleminded a dreamer as the gentle Gretchen), is at worst an exaggeration of a possibility in idealizing Germans." [Athenæum. **613**

BONAVENTURE. [by G: W. CABLE: *Scribner*, 1888.] "The noble simplicity of a life like Bonaventure's would be welcome from any hand. From Mr. Cable's it is doubly so; for, with the example of a worthy life full of sincerity, of elevation, and of sacrifice, made only the more lovely because of the unconsciousness with which it is given, one at the same time enjoys the pleasure of surrendering one's imagination to Mr. Cable's, and following the threads of his simple story, benefiting by his exquisite workmanship, his minute observation, and his artistic feeling, without a thôt behind. One cannot seriously find fault with the story of Bonaventure, or, rather, the cluster of stories growing out of his, and beautifully showing the breadth and power of influence which a simple, sincere, and hi-minded man may wield. They are so unpretentious, so devoid of the claptrap and sensationalism which the public demands—and generally gets, one must sorrowfully admit—that a sympathetic reader is not only pleased by reading them, but also elevated and made better. This not alone because the stories are unaffected in their simplicity, and free from the taint of melodrama, of course, but because at the same time they are pervaded with a spirit of faith, a faith in the nobility of truth, however homely, in the beauty of unselfishness, however simple." [Nation.] "The Grandissimes is one of

the great novels of our time, whereas Bonaventure is simply one of the gracefulest romances, in which hi motive, generous purpose, and picturesque material answer for the powerful realities of the other. The facts of the case—the aspiration and the heroic self-sacrifice of the young creole school-master among the Acadians of Louisiana are given by a species of indirection, a kind of tacking, which recalls Judd's method in his Margaret, a book which Mr. Cable could not have had in mind, but to which his work assimilates itself in the romantic atmosfere common to them both. It has its charm, but it also has a misty intangibility which baffles." [Harper's. **614**

BOUND BY HIS VOWS [*Lippincott's*, 1873] = *AT THE ALTAR.*

BOW OF ORANGE RIBBON (The) [by AMELIA EDITH (HUDDLESTON) BARR: *Dodd*, 1887.] "is a story of New-York in 1756, all alive with sturdy dutch men and women, and brilliantly set off with King George's soldiers. The antipathy of certain honest, godly Knickerbockers for the youthful english representatives of the flesh and the devil is discussed with a great deal of humor and vivacity, and the romance of the little dutch maiden with the giddiest of the offenders is as sweet and natural as tale of true love, not always running smooth, can be. The atmosfere of the story is thôroly old-time, and, whether the separate pictures are historically accurate or not, they make a pleasant combination. The end is happy, and that is pleasant, too, for to leave such whole-souled, friendly, nice people in permanent unhappiness would be positive grief." [Nation. **615**

BRAVE WOMAN, by "E. MARLITT": *Worthington*, 1891, = *SECOND WIFE.*

BRETON MAIDEN (A). [*Hurst*, 1888.] "Here the tale of the great revolution, as it affected the Breton peasants and their lords, is told in what—tho there is, of course, no lack of painfulness—is on the whole a pleasing and an interesting manner. There is a good deal which is human and simple, with less padding and grandiloquent writing than is natural to the common historical novel. The author has done wisely in confining the action of her story to one place, and in shunning Paris and direct contact with the greater and better-known events of the drama. Her knowledge of the time is sufficient to keep her clear of manifest errors, and, while she is by no means 'steeped in the literature of her subject,' or innocent of unassimilated history books, her manner is often the reverse of tedious. Her characters and incidents are interestingly and simply unfolded, and, instead of being merely a peg for history and local color, are the backbone of her story. The Breton maiden herself is a nice, natural, and rather modern young creature, and one has some sympathy for her three lovers, who are not without individuality. Finally, there are some touching scenes, and a good enuf suggestion of the 'general sentiment' of Bretagne and its people." [Athenæum. 616

BRIDE OF LAMMERMOOR (The) [by Wa. Scott, 1819.] "deals with Scotland during the reign of William and Mary, but making no use of public events." [Boston "Literary World."] It "has been described very justly as the most Shaksperian of all the Waverley novels. But there is a peculiar character stamped upon it,—the darkness of impending fate which broods over it from the first, which is never dissipated for a moment, and which is rather hitened than relieved by the absurdities of Caleb Balderstone. In 'Kenilworth', and in 'St. Ronan's Well,' we are often permitted to forget the tragic catastrofe which awaits us; the clouds alternate with sunshine, and the story is so told that a more favorable conclusion would have been nearly if not quite as consistent with its general tone and tenor as the one which takes place. But in 'The Bride of Lammermoor' it is impossible to shake off the consciousness of coming sorrow from the first moment to the last. If we did not know the end it would still be impossible to anticipate a happy one. In this respect it resembles rather the greek tragedy than

Shakspere. The haunting voice is never silent, and all the accessories of the plot contribute to hiten its effects. The first meeting of the future lovers in the forest-glade, whither Ravenswood had repaired to seek an intervue with the oppressor of his family, half contemplating a dreadful crime; the shot ringing from the thicket, and father and dauter saved from sudden death by the hand which mit otherwise have been raised for a far different purpose; the fountain with its ghastly legend, the gloomy oaks tenanted by the ominous raven who is sacred to the Lord of Ravenswood; the 2nd meeting of Lucy and Edgar in the midst of a raging tempest which breaks over them with redoubled fury as they enter the ruined castle of Wolfe's Crag, all that remains to Ravenswood of the property of his ancestors now in the hands of Lucy's family: all these elements of romance, mystery and terror unite to bring us into a frame of mind in harmony with the progress of the story, leading us to watch the downward course of the 2 devoted beings which form its central figure in profound and unremitting sympathy, but without the intervention of a ray of hope." [Macmillan's. 617

BRIDE'S FATE (The). [by Emma Dorothy Eliza (Nevitte) Southworth. "The austere reader, who of course is acquainted with the famous Mrs. Southworth only by hearsay, may object to see her name in a reputable journal of criticism. She is wont to be deprecated in public and devoured much in private, as the continual replenishing of all her books requisite in large libraries sufficiently attests. From 1849 to 1872 a complete set of her writings numbers 35 volumes, [in 1888 the number had reached 56]. To speak in detail of this female Lope de Vega is impossible,—indeed it is unnecessary, for her devoted admirers admit that to read one is to read all in substance; and yet they do read all, and little else apparently. How explain her remarkable popularity unless it is posited at once that admiration of this sort is worthless and counts for nothing? But this is unfair, and not quite the truth. [See No. 332.] Understanding well the craving for what is sensational and morbid in fiction, Mrs. Southworth, by a skilful use of the fascinations of crime, and by a systematic introduction of horror as an element of literary construction, has managed to cater so successfully to certain tastes that she stands easily at the head of this class of the trashy school. In her later works she seems to have regretted her earlier faults. ... Her style is clear, and she tells her story directly; but the reader must accustom himself to sudden breaks, as when, for instance, in "The Changed Bride," he finds an interval of 402 pages between one sentence and the next consecutive one. Judged by their popularity, Mrs. Southworth's principal stories are: "*The Changed Brides*", "*The Bride's Fate*", "*The Curse of Clifton*," ["*Fallen Pride*"], and "*The Gipsy's Prophecy*"— [Boston "Literary World."] See No. 473, and "Cruel." **618**

BRIGADIER FREDERICK. [by ERCKMANN-CHATRIAN: *Appleton*, 1875.] "We are introduced to an almost idyllic picture of the home of an old forester on the borders of the Vogesen; listen to the 'short and simple annals' of his family; watch the pretty love-making between the brigadier's pretty dauter and a handsome young forester who hopes to succeed him on his retirement; share their brit hopes and anticipations of the future; hear with incredulity the first vague rumors of war; and then the guns of Wörth and Phalzburg, the tramp of invading armies, the fierce rapacity of the soldiery, and the pains of exile, ending in death, and in desolation which is worse than death. All is told in such wonderfully simple, easy, and unpretentious style that the reader is apt to think slitingly of the achievement; and it is only when he contrasts it with the attempts of other writers in this field that he perceives that the apparent naturalness is simply the perfection of art." [Appleton's. **619**

BRIGAND'S BRIDE (The) [in "Fashionable Philosophy (etc.)" by

LAURENCE OLIPHANT: *Blackwood*, 1887. Also in "Tales from Blackwood," N. S., I.] "is by far the best thing in the book. From the beginning, where the narrator considers the question "whether I should enjoy myself most by joining the brigands, or the troops which were engaged in suppressing them," to the end, where he creates a panic in a small italian town by firing at the church bell with an air gun, it is quite in the fearless old 'Blackwood' fashion. No hier praise can be given to a short story". ... "The escape of the writer from the robber's clutches and the eccentric but effective manner in which he pays his debt of honor to the fair Valeria are excellently told. He went a little far, we think, but his love-making is capital." [Athenæum. **620**

BY SHORE AND SEDGE. [by FR. BRET HARTE: *Houghton*, 1885.] "... It is true that these later sketches have not all the dramatic force and beauty of the first ones; but it is not deterioration of power, so much as loss of novelty, that lessens the eagerness of the public for them. '*An Apostle of the Tules*', has more of the old quality than almost anything the author has lately done; '*Sarah Walker*' is well told, as everything from him is; and '*A Ship of '49*' is a very pretty story." [Overland. **621**

BY THE TIBER. [by M.. AGNES TINCKER: *Roberts*, 1881.] "The author has freely handled all the materials the situation affords, giving us picturesque sketches of Roman character, both of noble and peasant, and artistically mingling 2 plots, each of which lends meaning and interpretation to the other. The story opens among familiar romantic models: the southern moon shines, oleander and passion-flowers bloom, nitingales sing in the orange-scented groves. Our author has an ardent imagination, and can use all these resources eloquently and skillfully, seeing Italy not only with her eyes, but with a heart which beats passionately in response to all its enchantments. When one has read throu these opening chapters, which put the love of Vittorio before us, and begins the story of Valeria Ellsworth, the transition is almost as startling as leaving a play with all the adjuncts of music, rich scenery, foot-lits, etc., for the cool sunny daylit outside." [Lippincott's.]—"The italian landscape glows around us, the senses revel in its opulent bloom and perfume. . . The hero is the son of a nobleman, and his mother is a peasant. He is educated as a landscape gardener, and as he grows is distracted by the double nature of his destiny and the contrary tendencies of his nature. He becomes the gardener of a roman nobleman, and at once falls hopelessly in love with his dauter, a beautiful, but hauty and cruel girl. She is struck by his marvellous beauty, and tosses him a red rose. 'That rose burned on his heart with a fire never to be extinguished.' Donna Adelaide maries another, but intrigues with Vittorio; then causes his death at the hand of her emissaries, while a young lady artist from America becomes innocently entangled in the crime of the heroine, by unintentionally witnessing the assassination of the hero. It will be seen that there is a strong resemblance here to the plot of 'the Marble Faun.' Indeed the influence of that work upon the author is quite apparent. We miss entirely, however, the greek simplicity of style of Hawthorne. The author of 'By the Tiber' is often obscure and slovenly, and everywhere the style is too exuberant and unpruned." [American. **622**

·CAMILLA'S GIRLHOOD. [by LINDA (WHITE) (MAZINI) VILLARI: *Unwin*, 1886.] "This is a readable, if not a very exciting or intellectual production. A mawkish english girl maries a beautiful italian, and in the first chapter says goodby to him as he starts off shooting with an ill-looking dog of a brother. The ill-looking dog returns, having left the husband at the bottom of a precipice. He wishes to imprison the english wife, with a vue to pocketing her money; but the usual faithful english servant helps her mistress to escape with her little girl, and they get safely to England. . . An artist, a musician,

and 2 conspirators complete the dramatis personæ of a piece which has a fair amount of go." [Spectator. ` **623**

CANCELLED WILL, see *ALL FOR LOVE*.

CAPTAIN FRACASSE [by THÉOPHILE GAUTIER: *Holt*: 1880.] "presents the adventures of a company of strolling players of Louis XII's time—their vicissitudes, collective and individual, their miseries and gayeties, their loves and squabbles, and 'their final apportionment of worldly comfort—very much in the symmetrical fashion in which they have so often stood forth to receive it at the fall of the curtain. It is a fairy-tale of Bohemia, a triumf of the picturesque. . . The manners, the morals, and the language of the age of Louis XII. were much freer than those of our time even in France; and Gautier was not the artist to soften this feature in any picture of the time which he mit undertake to paint. . . All these episodes, without exception, the translator has remorselessly cut out, and has thereby mutilated the story irretrievably as a work of art." [Appleton's. **624**

—, SAME, *Putnam*, 1880.

CAPTAIN'S DAUGHTER (The) [in "Russian Romance", by A. S. PUSHKIN: *King*, 1875.] "narrates the adventures of a young officer and his sweetheart, during the troublous period in which Pougachef held at bay the forces of Catherine II. and ravaged so great a portion of Eastern Russia. The *Lady-Rustic* describes an interesting Russian flirtation; the "*Snow-Storm*" gives an account of an extraordinary incident, the mariage of a man without his consent to a young lady who thôt he was somebody else; the "*Pistol-Shot*" is an excellent story; the "*Moor of Peter the Great*" would have been more satisfactory had it possessed an end; the "*Undertaker*" is a somewhat flimsy sketch; but the "*Statton-Master*" is a touching story, simply and pathetically told, almost worthy of a place in Turgénief's 'Sportsman's Notes.' There is nothing very new in it for it merely tells how the pretty dauter of a provincial postmaster eloped with a passing hussar, but the way in which it is told is excellent. [Athenæum.] "This story does not concern itself with any lesson, or with showing how good or how bad people are, but is simply an unadorned record, told in the most charming way, of the adventures of a young russian officer who sees service against some rebels, and whose betrothal to the heroine forms the romantic part of the story. There is plenty of incident, and the narrative is so direct and simple that the reader becomes at once conscious of a master's hand. The hero's boyhood is described in two or three pages, and throughout the book there is no superfluity of expression; everything is set before us with two or three touches. The growth of the heroine's character from shy girlishness to mature strength and courage throu strange adventures is beautifully told. The mock czar, half cunning and half enthusiasm, the hero's grim servant—indeed, all the characters—are admirably drawn." [Nation. **625**

——, SAME, ["Marie"], transl. by M.. H. Zielinska: Chicago, *Jansen*, 1877.

——, SAME, transl. by J. Igelström: *City of London Pub. Co.*, 1883.

——, SAME, Calcutta, 1889. "Mr. Godfrey has translated Pushkin's charming novel in the belief that no other english version exists... It was translated together with some tales of Lermontof's, and published anonymously sometime before the Crimean War." [Athenæum.] Book referred to is "Sketches of Russian Life in the Caueasus, *Ingram*, 1853. **626**

CARDINAL'S DAUGHTER (The). [by CATHARINE A.. (WARE) WARFIELD.] Mrs. Warfield enjoys a steady popularity based upon her genuine ability, and somewhat, perhaps, upon the fact that all her stories are connected in plot. In spite of some objections made to her on the ground of a certain morbidness supposed to inhere in all she does, be it not overpraise to say that her gifts of a powerful imagination and considerable fancy are merits which outweigh her faults. If a still greater acquaintance with her would result in a

corresponding decrease in the reading of Mrs. Hentz or Miss Dupuy, it would be a gain." [Boston "Literary World." **627**

CARMELA. [by OLGA CANTACUZÈNE: *Tinsley*, 1880.] " 'Carmela' is a romance, tho its events are those of the present day. The heroine is without fault, and the sentiment is of the blest kind. The story is well contrived, and unblemished by any thing which is not fit for the most ingenuous minds. It was suited for translation into english, many of the characters and scenes in it being english. [Athenæum. **628**

CASTLE HOHENWALD (Die von Hohenwald) [by ADOLF STRECKFUSS: *Lippincott*, 1879.] "is a pleasant story, brit, readable, and full of the true german flavor. The most grafic point in the book is that relating to a midnit attack, during the war of 1870, and the escape of the Uhlan officers: materials so ably handled that we feel that the author has here struck a vein which she [!] will do well to develop more thoroly hereafter. The story has also the merit, and a great merit it is, of ending well." [Boston "Literary World." **629**

CASTLE OF OTRANTO. [by HORACE WALPOLE: 1764.] "To us of the present day this story is very nearly unreadable; it has more of the air of a caricature than of a genuine attempt to attract adult readers, and this feeling was shared by many of the author's contemporaries. What was absurd in its gigantic helmet and childish terrors seemed also absurd to them, but there were others who justified the writer's assertion: "I have not written the book for the present age, which will endure nothing but cold common sense.... I have composed it in defiance of rules, of critics, and of filosofers; and it seems to me just so much better for that very reason." In other words, Walpole, a delicate, fastidious man, familiar with what was going on in France as well as England, despised by his countrymen for what seemed like ridiculous affectation in his finical love for antiquities and gothic architecture, and for his indifference to the ruf amusements of a rude time, was, in fact, simply anticipating his age by his dissatisfaction with the meagre reasonableness of its vue of life. The success of his book and the enormous extent of his influence showed that he was on the rit path in his lâfable revolt. It was long before the ghost that left its gigantic helmet and sword about in his book was laid. It became a stock figure of romance, and even when, as in Mrs. Radcliffe's novels, the ghost itself evaporated into explicable feuomena, the grisly terror that his preseuce or nêborhood inspires remained a most useful source of entertainment." [T : S. Perry.] "The tale, with its supernatural horrors, which made the hair of the juveniles of our grandsires' age, "stand on end," is destined to perform the same feat to the present and to unborn generations. *The Castle of Otranto* is the putative parent of a popular and populous school of fiction. It has stood the test of time, it has maintained its original rank in the annals of fiction, and it would be "gilding refined gold" were we to waste space in superfluous laudation." [Leader 630

CATHERINE. [by JULES SANDEAU: *Routledge*, 1860.] "The central figure of the little society of Saint Sylvian is a priest possessed of all the excellencies of Chaucer's and Goldsmith's parsous. . . He has, however, one treasure in his niece Catherine, a girl of 17, called by all the country round sometimes La Petite Vierge, from a fancied resemblance to a picture of our lady, sometimes La Petite Fée, from her good deeds and her fairy-like appearance." [Saintsbury. 631

CECIL CASTLEMAINE'S GAGE. [by OUIDA: *Lippincott*, 1867.] "Notwithstanding the extravagance of this writer's style and her incorrigible passion for melodrama, there is a strength of imagination and a sustained vivacity about her stories which will always ensure their popularity and gain for them considerable acceptation even with the fastidious. Passion and copious flow of incident are valuable elements in fiction, and 'Ouida'

displays them with an affluence rivalled only by Miss Braddon. She belongs to a new and very odd school of romancists, who may be described as seeking to unite in their novels the dusty lore of a cyclopædist, the naive fervor of a child, and the interest of a fairy tale. . . The public seem 'for the moment to fancy this kind of writing, and if a mixture of Mother Goose and Dr. Johnson suits the general taste, it will of course be gratified. Some of the tales in this volume are, however, of a better stamp than mit be inferred from this description, and contain unmistakable evidences of power and artistic feeling. The story of '*Deadly Dash*,' for all its alliterative title and incredible plot, is excellent in its way, and there is comedy in '*Lady Marabout's Troubles*,' which few of 'Ouida's' female competitors can approach. Every one of these novelettes is hily interesting, which is, after all, perhaps, the best praise that can be offered." [Round Table. 632

CECIL DREEME, by TH. WINTHROP, = No. 208.

CHANGED BRIDES, see *BRIDE'S FATE.*

CHARLES AUCHESTER [by E.. S.. SHEPPARD: *Hurst*, 1853.] "is a novel illustrative of a life devoted to the enthusiastic cultivation of musical art. The characters are supposed to be taken from life, and to represent the romance in the history of several eminent composers and artists. Among those who are brôt upon the scene is Mendelssohn, whose rare, enthusiastic qualities are set forth in a brilliant and impressive lit. The novel contains many admirable specimens of character-drawing. Its narrative portions, altho unequal, are for the most part of a superior order of composition, and exercise a certain weird charm over the imagination of the reader." [Harper's.] "More than ordinary pains have been taken by the publishers to recommend this strange book on the score of the personal portraits which it has been alleged to contain. Week after week have lovers of music been invited to read about Mendelssohn, and Berlioz and Jenny Lind. Among those who care for the art, a considerable stir has been kept up with regard to the authorship of the half-crazy work, and gossip has been flung about respecting its truth, passion and beauty almost out-rhapsodizing the rhapsody with which its pages overflow... It is a strange, wild, affected, incongruous, mystical art-novel, —incomplete, incorrect, foolish, extravagant, still displaying feeling without discretion, power without learning, and a passion for music rather than a knowledge of it." [Athenæum. **633**

CHARLOTTE TEMPLE [by SUSANNA (HASWELL) ROWSON: 1790.] "written in the stilted, sentimental style of the day, still finds readers. In its main outlines it is a true story. The real name of Charlotte Temple was Charlotte Stanley, who was thrown on the streets of New-York by her betrayer, Colonel Montresor, the Colonel Montraville of Mrs. Rowson's novel. Like the villain of the story, Colonel Montresor afterwards maried in New-York. By a strange Nemesis, his eldest son became engaged to his dauter by Charlotte Stanley. This part of the story is told in the sequel to 'Charlotte Temple,' which was published after Mrs. Rowson's death under the title of 'Charlotte's Daughter.'" [Edinburgh Rev. **634**

CHATEAU LESCURE [New-York, *Dunigan*, 1855.] "is a pretty little story, told with grace and simplicity. The scene is laid in Vendée, at the period of the Revolution; the spirit and manners of the time have been well caut, and Colonel de Lescure, with his sorrows and brave silence, would do credit to a story of far more imposing proportions." [Athenæum. **635**

CHATEAU MORVILLE. [Philadelphia, *Claxton*, 1872.] "From the style and manner, it would seem intended for the amusement of girls of 14 or 15; but it would be about one of the last books we should offer to a rational being of any age for either amusement or instruction. A more foolish or romantic story could scarcely be put into the hands of a reader,

or one more calculated to furnish foolish thôts. The readers contemplated must be solely girls, for no boy under any dearth of literature would read a dozen lines of it." [Athenæum. **636**

CHILD OF THE REVOLUTION (A). [by MA. ROBERTS: *Hatchards*, 1887.] "A story by the author of 'Mademoiselle Mori' is always welcome, and in her last essay, tho confessedly addressed to a small circle, there is no falling-off in her characteristic qualities of refined thôtfulness and graceful portraiture. The scene is laid in France... As a foil to this passionate visionary, there is a delitful old chevalier. ... The chevalier's account of the fate of his tragedy is most amusing... So completely does this amiable old man insinuate himself into the affections of the reader, that it is quite a relief to learn at the end that his romance met the taste of the day, and was published with success. It seems to us, in conclusion, that the writer has very happily hit the mean between a mawkish romance of the Revolution and a needlessly realistic picture of its horrors. There is no shirking of the gloomy side of that epoch; but the effect is none the less impressive from the entire absence of sensationalism by which the story is marked." [Spectator. **637**

CHITA [by LAFCADIO HEARN: *Harper*, 1889.] "affords a text whereupon Mr. Howells mit exultantly discourse of the evils of "the romantic method." The author perpetrates almost every fault which that almost able writer avoids with repugnance; and even the qualities of fervid imagination and dramatic intensity which are undeniably displayed in Chita do not redeem it from its too obvious shortcomings of verbosity, rhetoric, and slurring of minor, but essential, details. Hysteria is not poetic force any more than convulsions are symptomatic of musculart strength; and Mr. Hearn is occasionally what admirers would call romantic, but what the unbiassed critic would term hysterical." [Academy. **638**

CHRISTIE JOHNSTONE. [by CHARLES READE: *Ticknor*, 1855]. "Perhaps his most remarkable triumf is the interest with which he invests the young fish-woman, Christie Johnstone. Raising her from all the low and disagreeable associations which every reader connects with the female vendor of fish, Mr. Reade has created a character whose native refinement, brit, clear intellect, and generous impulses make the reader almost forget amidst what scenes the beauty and strength of her moral and intellectual life were developed. Whether such a character could exist and grow more strong and more beautiful amidst such scenes is a question that we need not discuss. But Mr. Reade has drawn such a character and made it noble, true, and beautiful." [Christian Examiner. **639**

CHRISTINE [by ᴌOUIS ENAULT: *Roberts*, 1874.] '... 'In purity and delicacy is unexceptionable, and presents a picture of feminine loveliness, of ideal grace and fineness, we mean. it is a love-story, pure and simple; rather frenchy, as the saying is, in its filosofy and exuberance of sentiment, but exquisitely refined, piquant, and vivid. Rarely has woman received more delicate homage than the author offers her in the character of Christine. . . Without being dramatic or in any way startling, the story has a lively and unflagging action, and the interest of the reader, lited at the ball, where the hero and heroine meet for the first time, grows to a great flame which broadens to the end. The strength of the book is in sentiment; the two or three genuine love-making scenes are master-pieces,—the crossing of the lake, and the intervue in which the Count asks Christine to be his wife, for instance. But the shadows in this love-picture are even more lovely than the lit, soft and pure tho it is. . . Women will find in it a type of feminine loveliness which they may well imitate, and a worthy idol for their adoration in that noble gentleman, Baron de ʻVendel; and—but when we have said that it is a charming love story, need we use other arguments to commend it to the attention of our fair readers? It belongs to a class of novels

which, unfortunately, has gone out of fashion,—novels of pure sentiment. There is not a crime or a 'sensation' of any kind in it; a few readers, we are sure, will find in this deficiency a potent recommendation." [Boston "Literary World." **640**

CHRISTMAS FORTUNE [Boston: *Williams*, 1881] = Fortunes of Miss Follen.

CHRISTMAS ROSE (A) [by R. E. FRANCILLON: *Harper*, 1888.] "is a charming story. New and delitful in incident and in conception, quaint in treatment and felicitous in characterization, there breathes throuout it an ideal loyalty which seizes the reader and makes him, willy-nilly, a staunch Stuart. Nicholas Fenwick's courage and hopefulness after forty years of unsuccessful plotting in King James' behalf, Rupert Cleve's renunciation for his King, Hester's unflagging faith in her husband, even Mistress Parrott's service to Hester, all embody an ideal love and honor which quite befits the tide of Christmas, when all the world, throu some compelling influence, puts on its best thôts and does its worthiest deeds." [Critic. **641**

CHRISTOWELL. [by R: D. BLACKMORE: *Harper*, 1882.] "There is no danger that the reader will drop the book, or that he will skip the pages. Perhaps the author has nowhere brôt together stronger contrasts,—the quiet pleasure of the father and dauter among their vines in the garden, the wild life on the moor, the placid routine of village life, and the awful visitation of the litning and the flame. Yet once under the spell of the story-teller, we find it all true and real." [Nation. **642**

CIGARETTE MAKER'S ROMANCE (A). [by FR. MARION CRAWFORD: *Macmillan*, 1890.] "The cigarette maker and his companions in the little back shop of Herr Fischelowitz of Munich are only less forein than Turks and Chinese; they are Poles and Russians, and one of them is a Cossack. Whatever their vices may be, Mr. Crawford dwells most on their kindness towards a man of superior birth and gentle nature, whom misfortune has made their fellow-workman. The unhappy Count is a pathetic figure and really noble, verifying in his humble life the discredited adage: Blood will tell. The poor polish girl, Vera, revives another fast vanishing belief—that in the beauty and strength of woman's devotion. The happiness (which comes to her at last) is rarely the reward of the virtuous, it is occasionally, and there is no reason always to ignore the barely possible. There are warmth, sympathy, and sentiment in every chapter, and these things make joy, especially just after one has been mentally dwelling among miserable snobs, the best of whom has but the brain of a midge, a semblance of a human heart, and never suggest the possession of a possibly eternal soul." [Nation. **643**

CLARA MILITCH [by IVAN TURGÉNIEFF, 1884.] "will be published in the The Independent [1884.] "The publishers say: 'The tale has not, so far as known, appeared either in England or America; and if it has been translated at all it certainly is not accessible to any large portion of the reading public. The neglect of the translators is, perhaps, accounted for by the fact that this tale was not rendered into french by the author, according to his custom. [? See Critic, 8:100]. There are certain facts regarding the derivation of the characters in "Clara Militch" which are interesting. The princess of the story is an exact portrait of a parisian celebrity, a member of a french dynastic family. The consummate skill with which this lady's peculiarities are traced must render the character bfly humorous to those who have frequented her salon. The character of the heroine was, in all probability, suggested to the author by the young actress, Miss Feygbiné, whose tragic fate is remembered in the french capital." **644**

CLARISSA HARLOWE. [by S: RICHARDSON, 1748.] "That the heroine is one of the noblest, sweetest, and loveliest conceptions of woman ever drawn by the pen of man; that Lovelace, fiend as he is, so works upon our sympathies that, in spite of ourselves and our better nature, we can hardly blame—or at least can scarcely be surprised at—the fine ladies who entreated the author to reform and spare him; and the interest of the story, as it advances, makes the reader tremble in every nerve, while the catastrophe awakens almost insupportable feelings of pity and indignation and horror; that Clarissa herself, in her father's gloomy mansion, in all the weariness and grief and pain of her short life, appears like an angel walking throu the valley of the shadow of death, with only the sacred lit of her own purity around her;—all this is well known to the select few who have had the courage to venture upon the 8 volumes, and who, after a hundred temptations to throw them aside, have come at last to be fairly lost in admiration of the wonderful and resistless power of the writer. Yet to the great mass of modern readers the novels of Richardson are no more familiar than the sermons of Sherlock and Tillotson. The subject of 'Clarissa Harlowe' precludes even its mention in the polite circles of the decorous and profoundly moral age in which it is our privilege to live." [Lippincott's.] "No novel ever combined in a more striking degree deep realism and lofty idealism. The conception of Clarissa's noble self and Lovelace, the ignoble means by whose motive-means her history is turned from point to sadder points, is an antithetic conception of exquisite beauty and diabolical vice such as we must go far to equal and very far to surpass. . . It may be urged that, even if the average spirit were willing, the average flesh would be weak, for the perusal of a novel proverbially enormous in bulk and frêted with much moralizing in the spaces not devoted to the elaboration of a plot harrowingly tragical. But in the 2 recent editions of 'Clarissa' now under notice, the dimensions are moderate, and the direct moralizings reduced to a minimum, while the engrossing interest of the plot remains, and the exquisite insits into female character, with the bf implied teachings and tendencies of the book are unimpaired." [Contemporary Review. **645**

——, SAME, abridged, *Routledge, Tinsley*, 1868.

CLOISTER AND THE HEARTH (The) [by C: READE, 1860.] "is like a piece of medieval life transported bodily into the midst of us. It is in literature what Nürnberg is in art, a thing as real as the old city. . . We should say, putting aside Sir Walter and 'Notre Dame,' that there is no other such historical novel. To open Reade's masterpiece is to walk into a world of living folk, not in fictitious costume or charged with archæological detail, but at home among their natural surroundings, all individual, unconscious of our observation. . ." [Blackwood's.] See *A GOOD FIGHT.* **646**

CLOUDS AND SUNSHINE [by C: READE: *Ticknor*, 1855.] "is a well-told story. It mit be called a narrated play. . . There is a rapid movement, and a dramatic vigor about it which makes an impression we can liken only to an actual enjoyment of changing scenes, picturesque tableaux, and the presence of actors. We feel that some one is giving us a grafic description of a performance, seizing the salient points of character and situations, and reproducing them in a narrative form: speech and description glide into one another where each is most expressive. Every character in the story is well portrayed, and with comparatively few touches, so few indeed that we wonder how their individuality is so well expressed." [Crayon.] "Of all the writers of my day, he has seemed to me to understand literary honesty the least. On one occasion as he tells us, he bôt from a french author ["G: Sand"] the rit of using a plot taken from a play ["Claudie"] which he probably mit have used without such purchase, and also without infringing any international copyrit act. The french author not unnaturally praises him for the transaction, telling him that he is *"un vrai gentleman."* The plot was used by Reade in a novel ["Clouds and Sunshine"]; and a critic, discovering the adaptation, made known his discovery to the public. [See Athenæum, 7 nov. 1857]. Whereupon the nov-

elist became angry, called his critic a pseudonymuncle, and defended himself by stating the fact of his purchase. In all this he seems to me to ignore what we all mean when we talk of plagiarism and literary honesty. The sin of which the author is accused is not that of, taking another man's property, but of passing off as his own creation that which he does not himself create. When an author puts his name to a book he claims to have written all that there is therein, unless he makes direct signification to the contrary." [Anthony Trollope. **647**

COLLEEN BAWN (The), see *WILLY REILLY.*

COLOMBA. [by PROSPER MÉRIMÉE: transl. by A. R. Scoble, *Bentley*, 1853.] "A slit sketch of corsican manners, showing the retaliating vengeance of rival families, where murder takes the place of duelling according to custom. There is no intricacy or surprises of plot; but a peculiar fase of life on that island is presented in a well-translated sketch." [Crayon.] "For the lover of tales of adventure among strange scenes and curious passions this book will have its charm. The heroine—a young and romantic english lady and her father are not among the best drawn characters of the story; but they are not grossly wanting in national traits and triumfs. . . The Corsican however, is capital. Altogether, the tale has dash, energy and liveliness." [Athenæum. **648**

——, SAME, *Phillips, Sampson, & Co.*, 1856.]

CONSCRIPT (The) [by ERCKMANN-CHATRIAN: *Smith*, 1865.] "is an story of a conscript, drafted in that last conscription which was ordered after the retreat from Russia. It reads very much like a real story, and is told with a quaint simplicity and truthfulness which will win the reader's heart. All those soldiers were men once,' said a little boy, when taken to see a revue, and this story resolves at least one soldier back into the original man out of which he was made. Joseph, tho hero, is a good, honest alsacian lad, a watchmaker's apprentice, full of simplicity and goodness of heart; the little account of his everyday life, of his love for Catherine, how he worked over-hours to take her a watch on her fête-day, and their happiness on that occasion, reads like an idyl. Then the terrible news of the retreat, followed by the last conscription, when youths and boys were taken to fill the ranks which had been ravaged by death, is described with the quiet, grafic power of a fotograf. Poor Joseph tells how he, tho lame, was obliged to fulfil his lot, and how he was carried away, with despair in his heart, to join his regiment. The life of a young recruit of that period, the good comrades he met, the charms as well as hardships of the life, and, above all, how he became more manly in character, showing incidentally how war developes heroism as well as many horrors, are well given. Joseph is charming throuout. . . The little touches of german life in the towns where they were quartered, the hatred to the French which was on the eve of explosion, give a life and truth to the picture." [Athe. **649**

CONSUELO. [by "G: SAND", i. e., [Amantine Lucile Aurore (Dupin) Dudevant: transl. by Fr. G: Shaw, Boston, 1846; by F. Robinson, N. Y., 1851.] "Consuelo is not one of those voluptuous patrician beauties. The Venice she represents is that which toils and rows, and browns in the fierce sun,—not that which is lulled in the invisible seclusion of the gondola, by soft rocking of the waters, by drowsy chant of song, into all the dreams of idleness. The romance of her history is long, and mystical and strange, dealing with wonders and mysteries which we have no intention to enter into, and which injure the perfection of the tale in point of art, tho they never fail to carry on the reader in a strange trance of interest like the prolonged and endless stories of the 'Arabian Nights.' It is only its beginning which is Venetian; but that beginning is enuf for our purpose; and places permanently one of the most delitful figures in modern fiction within one of the most beautiful of scenes. Consuelo is a musi-

clan. She is a child of the streets, the dauter of a vagabond singer, who earned her bread by her guitar and her voice in cafés and public places, giving to her child neither training nor tradition beyond the very rudiments of such law and self-restraint as make existence possible. Consuelo has no reputation to gard, no prejudice of honor to get over, but has all the freedom of the lowest social class, and all the knowledge which is acquired unawares by children bred in the streets. . . She lives in her garret unguided, except by her own instincts, without support or gardian; and the reader feels nothing unnatural, nothing overstrained, in the simple goodness of the hi, yet lowly creature; nor even in her intercourse with her betrothed Anzoleto, who is not pure, as she is, but who, nevertheless, has so much of the cordial familiarity which a lad has for his friend, and of the habitual affection of a brother, mingled with the sentiment which they both call love, that even his youthful depravity is kept in check by the conjunction." [Blackwood's. **650**

COQUETTE (The) [by HANNAH (WEBSTER) FOSTER: 1802.] "is a novel written in letters, in the old fashion, and indeed its style is old fashioned, too, reminding one of Fanny Burney, Maria Regina Roche, and other writers, more talked of than read. The heroine, 'Eliza Wharton,' is stated to have been a Miss Elizabeth Whitman. Pierpont Edwards figures, not creditably, in the tale as 'Major Sanford.' Several real people are put into the book in different characters. He died in 1826, and she in 1788. The singularity of the book is its apparent truth. It makes not whether the narrative is true or false; or, if true, how much fiction is mixed with it." [Round Table. **651**

CORRESPONDENCE (A) [by I. TURGÉNIEF: in "Galaxy," dec. 1871.] "is one of his gloomiest and most tragical—a story to be shunned by those who have given up pathetic and mournful things, and even by some such as have not done so, but who will not read unrelieved tragedy. Still it is, as we say, very interesting as a study of character. The analysis is searching, and we should say that its results are perfectly in accord with truth. It is a simply told story: Four young people, who have known each other as children, are, as it happens, brôt together again in the first prime of their youth. They fall in love and become engaged to be maried, but the young men go away, and their love—partly a poetic dream, partly passion, partly luxurious trifling—early fades and cools and the girls are deserted. By-and-by Alexis writes to one of them; not to the one whom he has forsaken but to her sister, Maria Alexandrovna. Why he writes he does not know, he says, tho the reader sees why. And Alexis is not mistaken in the belief which he evidently half-cherishes that Maria will reply to him, and that soon her heart will be interested. We must not, however, tell the story on to its doubly tragical and ruinous castastrophe, tho we mît do so without interfering with its principal claims to attention, psychological truthfulness, and its excellence of finished workmanship. It is a kind of reading which one may perhaps feel a reluctance to recommend. Still its ability, at all events is not to be gainsaid, and its morbidness one may almost expect to find acting as its own antidote." [Nation.] "Two men had passed the summer in the country with two young girls, sisters, and had both fallen in love with them and become engaged. Neither engagement, however, came to any thing, one of the men was about to mary another girl, when the other wrote to her who had formerly been betrothed to his friend, giving this news and begging permission to correspond with her, which, after some reluctance she grants. Their letters are only 15 in number, but they picture wonderfully the state of the writers' mind. . But in spite of this flaw, the story is very extraordinary on account of the pathetic interest of the letters. We know hardly so faithful a description of failure and the disappointment it is sure to bring to others. There is not a superfluous word; we are not

shown how to grieve; we have given us merely the materials of grief, and no one can read the story unmoved." [Atlantic. **652**

COUNT KOSTIA. [by V: CHERBULIEZ: *Holt*, 1874.] "A russian nobleman, Count Kostia himself, is living in a castle on the Rhein, trying to hide his deep disgust for the fémale sex beneath an earnest devotion to byzantino history. His mariage had been an unhappy one, and he had doubts of the legitimacy of his only surviving child, a girl, whose resemblance to her mother is so hateful to him that he has dressed her as a boy. The hero of the story, Gilbert Savile, comes to the castle as secretary to the count, and soon finds himself growing interested in this young creature, whom he takes for a boy. He succeeds in overcoming her—apparently his—dislike, and finally, when he has discovered his mistake falls in love with her. At this juncture, by a series of most melodramatic incidents, the count's doubts are cleared, and he suddenly changes from a more than half-mad domestic tyrant to a most courteous and attentive father, and all ends happily. This is the outline of the novel, but it gives only a faint notion of the total impression. This framework is hidden by much that is distasteful, for the confusion of feeling about the boy who is really a girl is not an attractive thing, [compare Mrs. Jenkin's "Gain of a Loss"] and in order to clear all the complications it is necessary to stir some very turbid waters; but in spite of these defects there is so much imagination in parts of the story, so much ready invention, and so brilliant a wit, that the reader, even if inclined to condemn, must make large reserves of praise." [T: S. Perry.] "Melodrama is good after its kind, and novels after their kind; but in such a novel as 'Le Comte Kostia' or 'Le revanche de Joseph Noirel,' we feel as if we were almost before the foot-lits—as if the witty dialog and sensational scenes had been designed with reference to adaptation to the stage. His whole use of incidents is theatrical rather than literary; the author exaggerates the importance of the fysical facts at every crisis in his stories. In the theatre, the fact that everything is seen from a distance and under difficulties makes this admissible, but the same thing cannot be said of literature. At the theatre—or at any rate the melodrama—we are all children, and may be tickled with a straw or pleased with a rattle, particularly if there is a change of scene, and music to mark the points, when the rattle or the straw is brôt forward; but when we read, instead of seeing, we revolt at the childishness of the means used to excite our interest. Miduit walks among chimney-tops, swinging in mid-air over an abyss—even on a piece of new rope—struggling with savage dogs, and all such sports are cheap, well-worn incidents, which lend factitious importance to the story, in very much the same way as raising the voice in anger adds to the soundness of the argument. It is in the invention of scenes like these that Cherbuliez, when he is not at his best, delits. To this form of art he has lent much skill, so much indeed that it is easy to overlook the cheapness of some of these devices. Hugo has no sooner created an impossible situation than he is out among the audience leading the applause; but Cherbuliez wears an easier air of being amused at his ingenuity rather than profoundly convinced of its value." [Nation. 653

COUNT OF MONTE-CRISTO (The). [claimed by ALEX. DUMAS: Routledge.] "Whatever analytical criticism may say of the literary methods of the elder Dumas, his magnificent series of romances, 'Les Trois Mousquetaires' to 'Le Vicomte de Bragelonne,' remains an established fact, and it is difficult to imagine any epoch in the history of civilization when they will not be the delit of multitudes. Alexandre Dumas, with all his charlatanry, held the magician's wand, and evolved from the abodes of imagination and fancy shapes which, whether they inspire pleasure or terror, never fail to fascinate. The reader who surrenders to his spell is for the time lost to the sensations of every-day life, and in a world of dreams finds nepenthe for all sorrow. Such books arouse and stimulate while they soothe the wearied mind, and what a relief it is to turn from the commonplaces of contemporary realism to revel for a few hours in the creations of Dumas' fertile brain! They do not grow stale with age. To the man or woman of 30 they are as enticing as they are to the boy or girl of 16. There is much in them which in moments of stern reflection we mit wish away; but no healthy mind, we are sure, could be harmed by occasional contact with them. They carry their own antidotes, and one no more looks for a moral from them than from the tricks of a prestidigitateur. It is permitted sometimes in this valley of sorrow that the children of men shall be children and find amusement in childish things, and when the mood of pure enjoyment is uppermost none minister to it more effectually than the elder Dumas... Among the mountainous mass of volumes, good, bad and indifferent, upon which Alexandre Dumas stamped his name, 'The Count of Monte-Cristo' still stands in the world's estimation as the supreme efflux of his genius. Its unparalleled audacity of conception, its astonishing verisimilitude, its wonderful array of incident, its dramatic force in dialog, all combine to hold the attention captive. The death of Faria, the escape of Dantès, the nit on the barren island, the discovery of the hidden grotto, and the innumerable train of events which follow in the Chronicle of implacable hatred and studied revenge—who having once read, can forget them, or, unforgetting, cares not to read again and again?" [Boston "Literary World."] ."The 'Three Musketeers' for example, of which Mr. Thackeray was so fond, was written entirely by Auguste Maquet, whose acknowledged works prove that the claim advanced on his behalf is not unfounded, while 'The Count of Monte Cristo' was as notoriously the work of MR. FIORENTINO, of whom the same thing may be said." [Fr. Hitchman in National Review. 654

COUNT SILVIUS [by G: HORN: N.-Y.,

Harlan, 1882.] "takes us into the midst of a brilliant german city, and offers us widely differing groups of characters, and a plot intricate and almost exciting, except that it is overladen with incident and encumbered with some unreal and rather clumsy contrivances. It is the story of a noble who is reduced to the necessity of earning his bread, while in this book Count Silvius, having shown that he could gain a fortune after losing that which he inherited from his sires is rewarded by the discovery of hidden treasure of enormous value on the hereditary estate, which he has bôt back. Altho he is the title-character, the greatest interest of the story turns upon the experiences of Ada Turneyssen, which, if not exactly life-like, are exciting in a strange degree." [Lippincott's. **655**

COUNTERPARTS. [by E.. S.. SHEPPARD: *Smith*, 1854.] "There is not a page in it of truth or simplicity to suggest a doubt. We lay it down with a vague impression of glare and glitter,—a weariness as of interminable babble about nothing,—a sickening, half remorseful consciousness of time wasted in mere sensual frivolity. It is not, indeed, without occasional indications of ability; but they serve only to increase our disgust, by marking the author as one who "ôt to have known better;" and it cannot be denied that in his [sic] word-painting, he has plenty of brit colors at command, and blazes away with them in a style which puts daylit and sunshine to shame, and can be equalled only at Vauxhall." [Westminster. **656**

COUNTESS EVE (The) [by J: H: SHORTHOUSE: *Macmillan*, 1888.] "is a slit story, without any of the historical substance which, thŏroly penetrated as it was with a great power of imaginative vision, gave its chief interest to "John Inglesant." Nevertheless, it is a remarkable story, dealing with the mystical aspects of temptation in a manner which, tho pure and free from any kind of dangerous fascination, produces a profound impression on the reader's mind. . . Let us introduce the evil being who is, in

a sense, the chief character of the piece, a Mephistopheles, who is in general visible only to one of his victims, tho on one occasion at least he is half-perceived by the other, and is discerned in all his hideousness by the fine violinist to whom, characteristically enuf, Mr. Shorthouse entrusts the duty of a kind of earthly gardian angel. . . That picture of a tempter who pours all his direct inspirations of evil into the purer of the two natures which he desires to bring to destruction, while he only encourages the less pure nature to follow its impulses, and gives it a new sort of confidence in its powers, is originally conceived, and possesses a kind of subtlety which is wanting even in Goethe's Mephistopheles. But still more powerful, perhaps, is the picture of the effect which daily yielding to temptation of this sort has upon the naturally refined and fastidious but also selfish nature of La Vallière. As is usual with him, Mr. Shorthouse insists on the elevating influence of stateliness and historic associations. La Vallière finds the splendor, the ceremony, the stately associations of the count's château exerting over him a subduing influence which prevents him from being 'bold' in the sense in which the tempter wishes to make him bold." [Spectator.] "All the admirers of Mr. Shorthouse's works must find a peculiar charm in 'Countess Eve,' which may be called a mysterious prose poem rather than a romance. It is the old story told in a new way of Eve, Paradise, and the Serpent; but here good triumfs instead of evil, and Paradise is not lost. The 4 chief characters are presented in a way to seize and hold the imagination. The countess is a beautiful woman maried to a man much older, who lives in a world of his own, brooding over memories of a passionate youth of which his young wife has no part. Eve longs for sympathy and is eager to feel and know all that belongs to brit. hopeful youth; and when La Vallière, the actor, whispers to her 'the key to Paradise is love,' it is not so much a revelation as a confirmation of her beliefs.

191

La Vallière is a fascinating creation; an actor not only by profession but by instinct, finding in every situation a part and play and a stake to win by all the subtle forces of his striking personality. At the least opportunity which seems to promise enjoyment, he lets himself be carried away; and the Countess Eve possesses for him a mysterious attraction. The drama which is unfolded from this situation is not so much played by the human actors, as it is developed by the unseen presences within their hearts and souls, which tempt, warn, allure, and deny. Mr. Shorthouse's stories have a charm of suggestion, an atmosfere, a glamor, which moves the fancy and touches the heart with a sense of the strangeness, the pathetic mystery of life. It is not reality which he describes: his characters live, move, and have their being in a realm of fantasy, a world of beautiful but eerie lits. We feel as we read, obscurely, yet with a sense of its reality, the struggle of the soul with temptations, and its victory under the undying lits which faith has kindled. 'The Countess Eve,' in particular, is a mystical but charming allegory."
\ [American. 657

COUNTESS IRENE. [Blackwood, 1888.] "There is generally something to admire and still more to like in the novels of the author of 'Caterina;' and his 'Countess Irene' is pleasant reading. Over and above the charm of an uncommon britness and subtlety of insit, there is a general atmosfere of genial kindliness, which is affecting without being in the least maudlin. The mutual regard between the various characters is as agreeable as their author's esteem and affection for them; but there is the same lack of certainty, of balance, and of proportion as of old, and therewith the same looseness of ensemble and the same incoherence in the present-ment. Countess Irene is quite on another plan from pleasant Kate Harding or the sympathetic Caterina; but she is as likable as they, and her acquaintance is one to make, Perhaps to enjoy her story to the full one should have read 'Lauterdale' and followed

the fortunes of Caterina; such knowledge, indeed, in a reader is now and then assumed, but so modestly as quite to disarm the critic, and render the common reference to Balzac and Thackeray altogether unnecessary. The young countess is scarcely a creation; but her personality is distinctly fresh and piquant, and has something about it of the mystery and in-completeness of life. The author's knowl-edge is somewhat cosmopolitan, and his pictures of Viennese society are britly real. If anything drags it is the story of the polish singer and the sharks and harpies about her; they have their inter-est, but it is not sufficiently subordinated to the main features of the story." [Athe-næum. 658

COUNTESS OF RUDOLSTADT (Se-quel to CONSUELO) London, 1851.

COURTSHIP AND MARRIAGE. [by CAROLINE LEE (WHITING) HENTZ.] "Mrs. Hentz, who died in 1856, is now, tho still much read, wanting somewhat in public estimation. Of northern birth and education, she lived for many years in the south, and southern life has furnished material for her plots. It is amusing now to read her apologetics, invariably intro-duced, for the 'peculiar institution.' But at one time she had many admirers, who may remember the enthusiasm of callow youth over her. 'Linda,' or the 'Young pilot of the Belle Creole.' It is said that 93,000 copies of her writings were sold in 3 years; but at present it is hard to com-prehend this liking for her commonplaces, her romanticism of the Augusta J. Evans school, her now meaningless pictures of the beneficence of the patriarchal system, her heroines of 'aurora-borealian counte-nance,' as she has it somewhere, and her tiresome but spotless heroes, all of them 'sans peur, sans reproche,' sans everything in fact. Her merits are negative, for she is not ungrammatical, and there is nothing debasing in her plots. She may be fairly ranked below Mrs. Southworth and Mrs. Stephens, and put about on a par with Miss Dupuy. Girls of 16 and upwards still read her best remembered books:

192

‘*The Planter's Northern Bride,*' '*Ernest Linwood,*' 'Courtship and Marriage,' '*Love after Marriage,*' and '*Linda.*'" [Boston "Literary World."] See, also, notice of "Linda." **659**

COUSIN STELLA. (by H. C. (J.) JENKIN: *Smith,* 1859.] "We do not remember to have read a book which has charmed us more for a long time than 'Cousin Stella.' It is an excellent novel, written with great care; the interest is well sustained, the characters are life-like, and all act according to their nature, and not by the arbitrary rule of the author's will. Great subtlety is shown in the working of character; the incidents are subservient, or, rather, they are, as in life, more the consequence of the acts and motions of the human beings concerned in them than the causes of weal or woe. The story is well knit together; there are no weak joints or imperfect articulations; it is an extremely well-written, well-conceived story, with a degree of quiet power and precision of touch which makes us hope for a continuance of well doing. The scene is laid chiefly in **Jamaica,** at the time just previous to the passing of the Act of Emancipation. The scenes of planter life are grafic, and have the look of being done on the spot." [Atbe. **660**

CRADOCK NOWELL. [by R: D. BLACKMORE: *Harper,* 1866.] "The author seems to have set about his work with an oppressive sense of the duty of a novelist, and has labored assiduously to impart to his readers a vast amount of acquired knowledge, together with some original and peculiar specimens of filosofy, fraseology admirably adapted to justify Talleyrand's [?] saying that 'language was invented for the concealment of thôt'. The story of Cradock Nowell, not very new but nevertheless interesting, is awkwardly told and sadly involved; improbable situations are invented and family affairs unnecessarily complicated, but the character of the hero is well drawn, and the worthy parson John Rosedew and the eccentric Doctor Hutton mît leaven a much worse book. . . A storm, in which an indiaman

is wrecked, gives opportunity to Bull and his son to exercise their courage and intrepidity, and after a long contest with the waves 3 senseless bodies are washed ashore, Garnet's, his son Bob's, and a strange young woman, the latter proving to be the dauter of Sir Cradock's brother by an affghan woman. . . In describing a game of chess Mr. Blackmore finds the english language insufficient, and candidly, confesses: 'I am sorry and ashamed, but I can't express these things in english, for the language is rich in emotion but a pauper in filosofy.' The pedantry and ostentatious display of learning with which the volume abounds mît fairly be characterized as 'snobbish,' while the ponderous and abortive attempts at humor are even more tiresome than the greek and latin quotations." [Round Table. **661**

CREEDS. [by ANNIE EDWARDS: London, 1859.] "To this man, St. Just actually contrives, and even plots, to give the beautiful and noble girl whom he loves with all the passion of a young man's first fondness. . . but chiefly St. Just does this with the purpose of removing finally from his path the beautiful temptation which is the only obstacle to his ambitious schemes. Such a motive and such an action will seem to many readers quite unnatural and incredible. Unnatural it is; but incredible only to those who do not know the all-dominating power of what we call the priestly passion in such minds as those have who are attracted by the hierarchal power of the Roman Church. . . . St Just's power over Estelle is so great that she yields; and, loving him with the grand passion of her grand nature, she consents to be maried to the man whom she despises." [Galaxy. **662**

——, SAME ["Estelle"], *Sheldon,* 1874.

CRESSY. [by [Fr.] BRET HARTE: Boston: *Houghton,* 1888.] "Mr. Harte's stories are always charming, in spite of the improbabilities with which they are véined, and 'Cressy,' in which the element of improbability is a little more marked than usual, will hold the attention

193

to the end. The hero is a young school-master in **Southern California**, who be-comes e'ntangled with a fair but untutored pupil.' We must confess that we cannot see why the author does not allow them to mary and 'live happily ever afterwards,' but he probably had occult reasons for refusing his readers this consummation." [Dial.] "The more **Western stories** we read, the less we are tempted to advise others to read them. Most of the people written about are so irreclaimably vulgar in their language, ideas, and manners as to make association with them in literature as disagreeable as it would be in life. Such a sketch as 'Cressy' shows how diffi-cult it is for even a very clever writer to make sheer vulgarity interesting, for if 'Cressy' is not vulgar, she is nothing. Howells succeeds in doing it, but then he has a genius for this kind of writing, and would by this time have founded a school, except that he is inimitable. Mr. Harte, in his earlier stories, struck a new vein, which, while it lasted, was very rich. Now his literary ventures seem to be of a 'pros-pecting' turn, and the yield of 'pay-ore' to be less. The facility of narrative, the power of sympathy, the pathos and hu-mor are all there; but the incidents are improbable, the characters are invented and put together rather than created or drawn from nature, and the result is neither a fotograf nor a romance." [Na-tion. **663**

CRUEL AS THE GRAVE. [by E. D. E. (N.) SOUTHWORTH: *Peterson*, 1871.] Here, "Mrs. Southworth appears in her most oppressive and appalling aspect. She tells us how a number of sentimental people with sentimental names committed every variety of sentimental deeds, and how, after the villainous people had come to grief, the moral people maried each other and entered upon lives of sentimen-tal happiness. All this is told in a style which for weak sentimentality no one but Mrs. Southworth has ever attained.—The foregoing notice is one which applies with absolute propriety to any one of Mrs. Southworth's numerous works. They

differ from one another only in name, and to a slit extent, in incident. They are all weak, all sentimental, and all unworthy either of extended praise or condemna-tion." [Citizen. **664**

CRUSADE OF THE EXCELSIOR (The). [by [FR.] BRET HARTE: *Hough-ton*, 1887.] "The good ship Excelsior runs into a perennial fog bank off the coast of **Lower California**, and is borne by an ocean current into the harbor of Todos Santos. It is a harbor withdrawn from the world by the fog, so that for scores of years it has not been visited by any ship. The mystery is not explained why the people of Todos Santos did not sail out of the harbor, as they easily could, tho no ship would enter except by accident. Enuf that here is a Mexican 'gente de razon,' petrified in the customs of 90 years ago, and so content with their afternoon life as to care not at all for anything new. But they are surprised, and fraternize with the american officers of the Excelsior and her passengers. The ship is carried off by a mutiny, and for 8 months the pas-sengers are incorporated in various rela-tions with the people of Todos Santos. A bit of tragedy closes the variegated plot. Throu it all is recognized the familiar and pleasant cunning of the hand that holds the pen. One wishes it did not shake so often. It would be pleasanter if the con-tinual fog that shrouds Todos Santos had not so thoroly penetrated the story and made the characters seem larger than they were, moving in a misty way to do things which no one ever thinks to do under a clear sky. But of course this fringe of unreality makes for the author an oppor-tunity to dance his puppets in a more hu-morous way. This he does with a skill which inspires pleasure." [Overland.]— "Mr. Harte's stories invariably have the charm which is inseparable from a well-constructed narrative. He has always something interesting happening, gener-ally something amusing to note, and occa-sionally something so near to nature that it is beyond art. In spite of the uneven-ness of his work, one never can doubt the authorship of any page of it; and tho his may be in some respects a bad style, it is none the less style, and is entitled to the full ratio of influence which is accorded to that illusive and indefinable element in literature... The plot, while not at all impossible or unreal, is still fanciful enuf to admit of continual surprises and absorbing complications. Perhaps the conception of the Todos Santos community, would be too much for a devoted realist to forgive; but to the ordinary novel-reader, who seeks merely to be amused, the ludicrousness of the predicament into which the matter-of-fact passengers of the Excelsior are thrown when arrested by the Commandante of the Presidio as revolutionists, is too delitful to admit of cavil. Perhaps, too, an ardent admirer of the commonplace in art mit take objection to the figure of Senor Perkins, whose singular ambitions and queer conceits count for so much both in the machinery of the tale and in the amusement which it affords. But a just and deliberate estimate of the story in all its aspects must admit that Senor Perkins could not be spared, and further, that nothing in the book could be materially changed without its being spoiled." [Nation. **665**

CURSE OF CLIFTON, see *THE BRIDE'S FATE.*

CURSE OF GOLD, see *BERTHA'S ENGAGEMENT.*

CYRILLA [by J. (M) v. TAUTPHOEUS: *Hurst*, 1853.] "was a failure, for which the authoress of the "Initials" must deem herself indebted in one good novel to the english public. She can easily write one, if she will only give us a story of german life as she sees it,- not as she reads it in german novels.—Germans are no more able to write novels than the English to write diaries. A novel like "Cyrilla," with the interest all-centered on a case of bigamy, and at the end of which, the villain in a prisoner's van, meets the hero and heroine in a hearse—a story full of swooning, sudden death, clairvoyance, and duelling, is a good german novel, but of a kind which should be written in the ger-

man language, and confined to german readers." [Westminster. **666**

DANIRA [Chicago, *Rand*,] 1888 = *JUDGMENT OF GOD.*

DAPHNE [by "RITA", i. e.—( )Booth: *Lippincott*, 1880.] "is an original, and in some respects powerful, story, tho we do not like it over well. There is too much of willowy forms, and flushing cheeks, and long, long embraces, and clinging kisses, and that kind of thing——what the critics sometimes call, we believe, the 'warmth of the south.' It is a **musical** romance, with its scene laid mainly in **Florence** and **Bologna**, and with a young genius of a violinist for its leading character; the strange device being adopted of making two violins, an Amati and a Stradivarius, alternate in the recital of events. The point of the story is the separation of 2 fond lovers throu the treachery of a rival, who thereby succeeds in marrying the lady. The story is one of much passionate fervor, and is barely saved from being a painful one." [Boston "Literary World." **667**

DARK COLLEEN(The) [by HARRIETT (JAY) BUCHANAN: *Bentley*, 1887.] "is an interesting and romantic tale... Bisson, worthless as he is, has positive and peculiar characteristics, and tho totally unable to value his wild irish bride, mit have made his artificial little french woman a happy wife enuf. But it was a luckless day for Eagle Island when the too amiable Émile was cast upon its shores, and not again committed to the deep by its gloomy and superstitious inhabitants. Very original is the charm of the early days of poor Morna's romance, the rugged grandeur of her home, the picturesque habits and primitive ceremonies, the tenderness and ferocity of her melancholy keltic kindred, relieved now and then by the humor of irish visitors of a better-known type, such as Father Moy, the benevolent despot over the souls, and, within large limits, the bodies of his flock; Baron O'Cloaskey, the wandering piper, with his gentlemanly tho impoverished father, a 'cosherer' quite of the olden type, and his faithful ass, nearly as patrician in his instincts, and scarcely less dear to the affections of his owner. But these alleviations serve merely to enchance the tragedy of the tale, the exile and despair of Morna, and the long-suffering fidelity of her real lover, Truagh, who for her sake can forego even the vengeance on her betrayer which fortune offers him at last." [Athenæum. **668**

DAUGHTER OF THE MALEPEIRES (A) [*Remington*, 1885,] = *M'LLE DE MALEPEIRE*.

DEAD LAKE (The), and Other Tales. [by PAUL HEYSE: Leipzig: *Tauchnitz*, 1870.] "Heyse's stories are minute in details of emotions and feelings, but very vague as to facts, and it requires great attention to follow the thread, for they are all enveloped in a sort of mist, which breaks only at intervals, when the reader is allowed to catch a glimpse of what he is reading about, but he has to find his own way as well as he can from very brief indications: and this, to matter-of-fact english readers, who like to be told all about everything, is not satisfactory." [Athenæum.] The tales are '*The Dead Lake*,' '*Doomed*.''*Beatrice*' and '*The Beginning and End*.' **669**

DEAD MARQUISE (The) by [LEONARD KIP: *Putnam*, 1873.] "is the ill-chosen title of a tale of the french Revolution. It is in reality a pleasing little love-story, prettily told, which has the advantage of escaping from being horrible. With that terrible background one has to be careful to keep the tragedy from being too prominent, and this Mr. Kip has effected." [Nation. **670**

DEAD SECRET (The). [by [W:] W. COLLINS: *Bradbury & Evans*, 1857.] "We recommend all our readers to reread the story in its entire and perfect form; to possess themselves of these 2 volumes, as an english classic not excelled, we are bold enuf to say, in the whole range of fiction, for constructive art, for clear and ingenious narration, for chaste and vigorous style, for generous and healthful morality, not stuck upon its chapters (as in novels with a 'purpose')

like a fylactery, or a ticket on a blind imposter's waistcoat, but breathing throu the whole book an atmosfere of purity, of kindness, of piety to God and man .. The wild, vast, rambling old house on the desolate coast of **Cornwall**, flanked on the one side by bare sea, and on the other by bare moorland; the long range of deserted and moldering rooms in which 'the Secret' lies hidden, like guilt within the grave; the terror-stricken flit of the servant, Sarah Leeson, from the house where she has shut up, in the midst of ghostly dust and silence, the record of the tale which she would fain conceal; the weary misery with which, throu successive years, she wastes away in the consuming fire of her remorseful conscience and her superstitious dread; the strange yet natural manner in which the chief characters are brôt together, so that the plot may be unravelled; the opening of the deserted North Rooms, and the discovery of the Secret;—all these elements of romance produce a tale which Mrs. Radcliffe herself never surpassed for awful fascination, while, in other respects, the superiority of the living writer to the dead enchantress is too obvious to need pointing out. Beautiful is the capricious, womanly character of Rosamond Frankland, full of a pretty waywardness, yet steadfast as Heaven itself in her devotion to her blind husband. Most touching in *his* affections for his forlorn niece, Sarah Leeson, is the conception of the old German, Buschmann; and hère let us pause to remark that the way in which this simple, true-hearted old man relates certain matters in connexion with the history of his niece is singularly affecting, and powerful without any gross show of power—the occasional German idiom lending peculiar intensity to the language. We do not know any instance of gentle pathos more moving than the scene in which the weary wanderer, relieved of the tormenting secret, and lying in the embrace of her from whom she has been so long and cruelly separated, tells of her lonely desolation now past, and shows the

frail mementos with which she soothed it."
[Leader.] "He wrote one, a long time
since, that we did like very much—"The
Dead Secret." Only, even then, his love
of sensation, and mystery, and horror in
general, led him to give a simple story,
with a lovely heroine not a bit too brit and
good for human nature's daily food, a silly
title on account of which many people
whom the writer mīt have been glad to
have for readers, shut the book out of
their circle, and turned the key upon it."
[Scribner's. **671**

DEAF MUTE (The) by I. TURGÉNIEF,
= *MOUMOU.*

, **DEEMSTER** (The) [by T: HALL CAINE;
Appleton, 1888.] "imposes a standard for
criticism different from any by which the
mass of modern fiction may fairly be
measured. The novelists who deals with
primitive human passions, developing
them throu circumstances which lead inevitably to tragic action, challenges comparison with the creators of grand imaginative literature. The supreme virtue of
such literature lies in its power to lift people to the hīt of its theme, and to absorb
them in its action as absolutely as in
thrilling personal experience. The man
who achieves this effect with any sort of
completeness must have something in him
finer and rarer than literary talent, however brilliant and intelligently trained.
Mr. Caine invites the test and stands it
with honor. His subjective drama is the
old and awful one of good warring with
evil. There are moments in the conflict
when man's will and reason count for so
little, when he seems such a puppet of
passion and accident, that we can believe
he has no control of a game of dice played
by God and the Devil with human souls
for stakes. But the prevailing spirit is
stronger and more hopeful. No man is so
perfect that he may not fall into sin ; none
too bad for repentance and atonement.
The balance hangs trembling in suspense,
yet each man is responsible for its turning,
subject to no arbitary fate. In Dan Mylrea, the great figure of the novel, the fīt

rages most fiercely. Here is one of those
exceptional natures felt to be equal to a
hī destiny, seen with pain and horror to
be going strait down to the gates of Hell.
Nothing short of frītful calamity can stop
such a man, once he has taken the wrong
path, and he must know in his soul that
he alone is reponsible for the wrong before spiritual purgation becomes possible.
The antagonistic forces which rage in Dan
have less play in his father, the Bishop, and
in Ewan Mylrea. It is a fit of temporary
wrath, a maddening sense of final, unpardonable outrage to long suffering love,
which hurries Ewan on to his share in the
culminating tragedy. It is in a moment of
solitude for the fysical safety of his son that
the Bishop, with his faith in God's love and
mercy fallen away from him, wishes to do,
what would tarnish the whiteness of his
life and make his very rīteousness a reproach to him. The Deemster alone seems
to be irreclaimably evil, and his nature has
the least affinity with the universal, is
largely a product of one age, one locality,
and peculiar personal opportunities. Tho
tragedy is foreshadowed from the beginning, and sweeps along in a current of increasing force to the end, its sternness is
relieved by the form in which the novel is
cast, irregular, unstudied, abounding in
sharp contrasts of lāfter and of tears—the
form links literature inseparably with life.
The scene is the **Isle of Man,** in the beginning of the century. Time and place
permit rugged picturesqueness, a certain
fysical storminess, and add a romantic
element like that which the Venetian
coloring gives to *Othello's* consuming
jealousy." [Nation. **972**

DESPOT OF BROOMSEDGE COVE
(The). [by "C: E. CRADDOCK," i. e. M..
N. MURFREE: *Houghton*, 1889.] "The
scene is in the Tennessee mountains; the
persons are our old friends the mountaineers; but the characters are new, the situations are fresh, and the action has a
pristine vigor. The whole effect is that of
rugged strength; but there are passages,
episodes, incidents of surpassing delicacy
and beauty, and of a truth which delīts

and uplifts. The meeting of the hero and heroine while they take shelter from a shower under a way-side tree is one of these: it is simply perfect in its fidelity to nature and to their characters and social traditions. So far as we can recall, no fact or trait in the people is overstrained for the purpose of an effect; an admirable verity gives you the sense of its presence throuǒut. The Despot is imagined in the spirit of this; he is a poet who supposes himself a sort of profetic agent of the Almity because he is so filled with the splendid and awful beauty of the Bible; and the study of Marcella Strobe, good, shrewd, earthly, limited to fact by her affections and ambitions, but generous and fine all the same, is even more subtle. Her father and her grandmother—especially the latter, who is the bouffe element of the piece—are triumfs of a skill which we seldom find at fault in this book, with its large group of finely differentiated figures." [W : D. Howells. ·   **673**

DISCARDED WIFE, see *ALL FOR LOVE.*

DISOWNED (THE). [by BARON LYTTON (E: Bulwer), 1828.] "I left out Bulwer from my list,—perhaps you think I was too scrupulous,—but the very atmosfere of his early novels is corrupt, and I despise his sham filosofy and pretended profundity which looks so deep, and turns out to be nothing but a cloud of words. He is a vicious charlatan, whose company I should avoid as I would that of any plausible scoundrel in real life." [W : P. Atkinson, 1860.   **674**

DR. CLAUDIUS [by FR. MARION CRAWFORD: *Macmillan,* 1888.] "is a very simple story, with just enuf of mystery about the Doctor's true place and history to pique the reader's curiosity without irritating it; told with charming ease and vivacity, with clear insit to human nature, with grafic portraiture of character, with much intellectual power, and with a directness, force, and naturalness which never falter. The style sparkles, the book has many brit and brilliant things, the dialog is sharp and witty, and the persons stand out with great distinctness, and individuality. There is positively not an unpleasant thing about the story; it is as clean and fresh as a flower-garden; and, while having no very positive aim, it is refined and entertaining." [Boston "Literary World."]   "'Dr. Claudius' is a love-story of that good old-fashioned order which it requires some courage to adopt in these days of mental analysis, where the hero falls in love at first sit, and is in himself an embodiment of everything that is most heroic in man—a giant in strength and stature, a lion in courage, a lamb in gentleness. 'Dr. Claudius' is scarcely more probable than 'Mr Isaacs;' but the mystery is not so novel, is indeed one of the old and familiar mysteries which we accept as permissible in romance not yet grown too old to enjoy the perennial delit, dear to the primitive imagination of a prince in disguise. The hero bearing this fairy character, his friend and confidant was naturally an english duke—that being the condition of man which is most popular in the race to which Mr. Crawford belongs. But his Grace was so pleasant a fellow, and Dr Claudius himself, with all his perfections, so delitfully heroic, naif, as if brôt into being in the days of the Admirable Crichton, that to the simple reader the story will always be popular—more popular, probably, than its predecessor, which was not so easy to understand. The strange feature in it is the american—the only american Mr. Crawford has as yet contributed to our knowledge—the sybarite and millionaire banker, who is presented to us in the most genial lit, only to turn in the most unexpected and unaccountable manner into a villain—a step which it is evident occurred to the author as necessary only, after he had conceived the character in a totally different aspect." [Blackwood's.   **675**

DON QUIXOTE. [by CERVANTES.] "We shall begin with the renowned history of Don Quixote, who always presents something more stately, more romantic, and at the same time more real to our imagination, than any other hero upon record.

His lineaments, his accoutrements, his pasteboard visor, are as familiar to us as the recollections of our early home. The spare and uprit figure of the hero paces distinct before our eyes; and Mambrino's helmet still glitters in the sun! We not only feel the greatest love and veneration for the knit, but a certain respect for all those connected with him—the curate, and Master Nicolas the barber—Sancho and Dapple—and even for Rosinante's leanness and his errors! Perhaps there is no work which combines so much originality with such an air of truth. Its popularity is almost unexampled; and yet its real merits have not been sufficiently understood. The story is the least part of them; tho the blunders of Sancho, and the unlucky adventures of his master, are what naturally catch the attention of ordinary readers. The pathos and dignity of the sentiments are often disguised under the ludicrousuess and provoke lafter when they mit well draw tears. The character of Don Quixote is one of the most perfect disinterestedness. He is an enthusiast of the most amiable kind—of a naturé equally open, gentle, and generous; a lover of truth and justice, and one who had brooded over the fine dreams of chivalry and romance, till the dazzling visions cheated his brain into a belief of their reality." [Edinburgh Review. 676

DOUBLE WEDDING, see *THE CARDINAL'S DAUGHTER.*

DOVE IN THE EAGLE'S NEST (The). [by C.. M.. YONGE: *Macmillan,* 1866.] "This is one of Miss Yonge's prettiest and pleasantest stories. It is a tale of a young burger maiden of the free town of **Ulm**, in the middle of the 15th century, who is carried away to the castle of one of the robber barons of Suabia, situated on an eagle's crag, to nurse the sick dauter of their race. How she comforts and teaches the poor child, bringing a civilizing influence into the ruf, boorish lawlessness of the free-baron's household— how she is beloved by the young baron, who has been tamed by her gentleness and goodness,—how he maries her secretly,—

and how he is treacherously set upon and killed, with his father and their retainers, as they are on their road to make their submission to the emperor,—and how he spent his last breath in acknowledging his young wife and commending her to the care of the terrible old she-wolf, his mother, is charmingly told. Dame Kunigunde would gladly have burnt her for a witch, or put her into the oubliette, but she did not dare; and the gentle young widow becomes the mother of twin sons— Ebbo and Friedelmunde. The story of their youth and of their mother's training is the chief portion of the book. The struggle of the old Alderstein rule of robber violence and Faustrecht, the glory of being a free, independent baron, with the civilizing influence of religion and education, is very interesting. The difficulties and perils of poor Christina, who has no arms to meet them, except gentleness and great good sense,—her gradual triumf, and the transformation of the wild young eagle-like baron into a noble knit,—the death of the twin-brother, who is almost a saint,—the return of the long-lost father who had been reported dead, but who had endured a worse lot as a captive among the Turks,—and the final end and crowning of Christina's life-work, with her grandchildren around her, honor and prosperity in her domains, form altogether a good picture of german life in the 15th century." [Athenæum. 677

DRED. [by H. [E..] (BEECHER) STOWE: *Phillips, Sampson & Co.,* 1856.] "We can only say that we read it with an interest that held us steadily to the page, unwilling to skip a line,—except when the pages were occupied with describing the character or rehearsing the rant of 'Dred' himself... Bating only this nuisance in her pages, we offer our grateful thanks to her for their wisdom, their rich humor, their satire, and their indirect preaching of true humanity and true religion in place of fanaticism and stupid bigotry. It is very easy for the papers to say that the chief characters in the book are only reproductions of those in 'Uncle Tom's

Cabin.' But the assertion is not true. Old Tiff is not Uncle Tom; nor is Nina, Eva; nor is Tomtit, Topsy; nor are any of her characters duplicated. Fiction has no more striking or winning an embodiment than Old Tiff. He alone would stamp genius upon the work." [Christian Examiner. **678**

EBERHARDT, see *ELIZABETH*.

EKKEHARD [by Jo. V: VON SCHEFFEL: *Low*, 1872.] "is certainly a novel which well merited the pains taken in translating it, and the translation is excellent. Some readers, seeing on the title page that the book is a tale of the 10th century, may think that it must of necessity be stiff, and dull, and heavy; but 'Ekkehard' is exactly the reverse. It is full of interest; the incidents are quaint; the characters well drawn. The pictures of convent life and scholarship seem to be true, both to human nature in general and to the modifications of the period. The blandishments of the duchess, the ambitious love of Ekkehard, his disgrace and sorrows, and his final restoration to health of body and soul during his retreat at the hermitage among the Alps, are well told. The development of his sick fancies into the vigorous work of a real poet is set forth with masterly insit. The whole story reads like a true piece of biografy, and tho the characters lived a long time ago, and the names of the places are hard to english tungs, the substantial interest of the book will make it worth the reader's while to surmount those difficulties." [Athenæum. **679**

ELIZABETH. [by SOPHIE (RISTAUD) COTTIN: 1806; London, *Whittaker*, 1880.] "One takes up the new issue of this famous story with a curious desire to see whether it will reproduce the strong impression it made on a first reading. It seems a little less exciting, certainly, than it did in our youth, the difficulties being more quickly and more easily surmounted than the modern novelist permits; but there is the same sweetness and grace in the tenderly told story, and we may hand it over to the coming generation as a favor-

ite of our younger days without fear of being scoffed at for our enjoyment of it." [Critic.] ..."Elizabeth is called shortly after to another special intervue with her sovran (it is needless to say that this scene is laid in Germany), and, while waiting for him in the room where her mother's veiled portrait hangs, suddenly sees her own face in the glass, and is struck by a sudden resemblance which she has never remarked before, and which in a moment reveals to her the secret of her own life. The reader is scarcely told in so many words, but perceives at once that the father whom she has cursed is no other than this tender fatherly sovran, who has watched over her from her cradle with the most pathetic care, and who shows, in a double solicitude for her and her happiness his penitence for his early error. Perhaps this would scarcely be a moral fable for the use of princes—but it is a very pretty story, told with much tenderness and pathos, and with a touch of hier perception in that concluding scene"... [Blackwood's. **680**

——, SAME, *Gottesberger*, 1885.

ELIZABETH (ETC.) [by BEATRICE MAY BUTT: *Blackwood*, 1889.] "It is pleasant to receive another volume of tales from the graceful pen of Miss Butt. They have a strong family likeness, it is true, especially in all beginning with a description of landscape, and all being pitched in the minor key; but as the descriptions are good and the pathos does not deepen into tragedy, the book is readable... In 'Elizabeth' and 'Eberhardt' only the writer approaches tragedy. In the former story the lady of Schönfeld and the Prince involve their brit-spirited child in an awakening to surrounding evil which will affect her whole life, but not fatally, we are led to think; in the latter the passionate resentment which Leigh Curwen feels for her foster-brother's death is, finally allayed and replaced by a softer interest. Great and bitter are the disappointments incurred by the gentle heroines of these tales, but none sorrows without hope." [Athenæum. **681**

ELSA AND HER VULTURE, *Longmans*, 1876 = *VULTURE MAIDEN.*
ENDYMION. [by the EARL OF BEACONSFIELD: *Appleton*, 1880.] "An unconscious travesty of hi life runs throu the book, and the travesty follows not from the author's unfamiliarity with the details of this life, but from his importing into the whole conception his own essentially Cheap John estimate of life itself. There is something marvelous in the worship of Success which underlines Endymion. The hero of the book, at least the young man who gives the name to it, is an almost colorless effigy of humanity, who is moved on throu the pages by the alternate efforts of his sister and the woman whom he admires, and afterward maries, to the position of prime minister, a position utterly remote from the logical consequences of his intellect or will. He is the creature of accident, friendliness, and destiny, and as he is shoved along a step hier at each turn of the story, the reader comes to watch for his appearance a little hier up with curiosity, but without the least apprehension. The career of his twin, Myra, who finally becomes queen of a néboring country, is more distinctly the expression of her own will and determination, but the landing of these 2 characters at the summit of supposed human ambition is achieved with so mechanical a dexterity that the author's supreme satisfaction in the result appears positively childish. The figures are so unmistakably puppets, and the properties are so broadly theatrical, that when onc considers the place which the author has held in english political life it is impossible to resist the feeling that Endymion is a man's plaything, and by a converse proposition that the author, as head of the british cabinet, has the attitude of a showman. The unreality of the book is not the unreality of romance, but of the stage. The country, the characters, the historic events, and especially the morals and the sentiments are all fictitious. There is a false bottom to everything. It seems the easiest thing in the world to find the living counterparts of the several characters in the book, and one with only ordinary knowledge of modern England will readily name the persons who may be said to have sat to the author for their portrait. But in what does the truthfulness of the likeness consist? An author who has transplanted images from his observation into the imaginary field of his novel or romance pleases himself with the notion that his characters have their own life in the book, entirely independent of any life which their prototypes may have led in the actual world, and he is apt to resent the imputation of theft, or to deny that he has put his friends into his book. In Endymion one perceives that the likenesses are distorted tracings of actual persons: they bear to the originals the relation not of paintings, but of waxwork; there is a simulation of reality, and not an individual existance as imaginary creations studied from models in life. It must be added that the artist of this wax-work show has given some vicious little twists to features out of an apparent malice, and has treated his images somewhat as a pettish child sticks pins into her hapless doll. The figure of St. Barbe, for example, is a simulacrum of Thackeray, and the satire is amusing, but not very refined nor comprehensive." [Atlantic.] "The action of the novel begins with the throes of the reform movement, at the time when Canning is on his death-bed, and the Iron Duke is the hope of conservative England. Sidney Wilton, who represents Sidney Herbert, afterwards Lord Herbert of Lea, the well-known brother of the 12th Earl of Pembroke and Montgomery, opens the novel, emerging from White's Club, and coming at once into conversation with a friend, Mr. Ferrars, an imaginary character made to do duty as the father of Endymion Ferrars, under which name the Earl of Beaconsfield has clearly undertaken to describe certain features of the career of the Right Hon. B: Disraeli. Endymion Ferrars has a twin-sister Myra, another figment of the brain, who strikes the key-note of her brother's

character and career when she says to him, 'Power, and power alone should be your absorbing object, and all the accidents and incidents of life should only be considered with reference to that main result.' The boy himself when he is first introduced as a disdainful lad seven years old in a velvet jacket with silver buttons, announces that after going to Eton he is to go to Christchurch and then into parliament. Queen Hortense comes into the novel early, under the rather severe name of Agrippina, and Napoleon III., as Prince Florestan, with 'his graceful bow that always won a heart,' who sets forth from England in a yacht, and conquers his kingdom in ten days, after writing a pretty little note to Lady Palmerston, who figures in the book with her lord as Lord and Lady Roehampton. Lord Beaconsfield makes nothing of anachronisms in this curious production. He paints the Eglinton Tournament, and makes Prince Bismarck figure in it as the Count of Ferrol. Baron Lionel Rothschild appears as Baron Neuchâtel, Poole, the tailor, figures as Vigo. Cardinal Manning plays a part as Penruddocke, a prophet ordained in Mayfair, who regarded Lord Russell with well-bred honor. 'Soapy Sam' Wilberforce, bishop of Oxford, appears under the pseudonym of Dr. Comely. Lord Strangford is introduced first as Mr. and then as Lord Waldshire, Milner Gibson as Mr. Jorrocks, and Lord Melbourne as Lord Montford. One of the best pen-pictures in the book is that of Richard Cobden as Joe Thornberry, whose thin, clear voice was only less clear than his statements. Neither this, be it remembered, nor any other portrait in the book, can be regarded as a full length, and times, places, and persons are so tossed and tumbled together that the earl can confidently deny any given likeness to be the likeness of the person who sat for it in his mind." [L: J: Jennings. **682**

ENTHRALLED AND RELEASED [by "E. WERNER:" N.-Y., *Knox*, 1885.] "is simply a poorer translation of a very good story translated by Mrs. Wister

under the title of 'Banned and Blessed.'" —Which see. [Critic. **683**

——, SAME (Raymond's Atonement), *Bentley*, 1884.

EREMA. [by R: D. BLACKMORE: *Harper*, 1877.] "The scene is laid chiefly in **California**, while a considerable part of the action takes place there and in **New-York** and **Washington**. The principal characters, it is true, are without exception english or scotch, and even the minor personages are indian or mexican rather than american. . . The plot is more coherent, the incident upon which it turns is more moving, the solution is more skillfully withheld, and the interest is more continuously sustained, than in any other of Mr. Blackmore's works, with the possible exception of 'Lorna Doone'; and his peculiar skill in depicting rustic character throu the medium of the local vernacular seems to improve with practice. . . In vue of the extremely small part which love-making plays in 'Erema,' and the deep tragedy of its plot, it is surpassing to find that the impression which it leaves upon the mind, is, on the whole, agreeable—the story is not only exciting but enjoyable. A portion of this is due to the humorous flavor which the author contrives to impart to all his delineations of character, and the rest to the peculiar vividness and beauty of his descriptions of scenery." [Appleton's. **684**

ERNEST LINWOOD [1856], see *COURTSHIP & MARRIAGE.*

ERNEST MALTRAVERS. [by BARON LYTTON.] "Such, considerably softened, is the plot of what we deem a most objectionable book. However, our quarrel at this moment is not with its teaching, but with its extravagant pretentiousness. It is an ordinary novel,—neither more nor less, in execution not better than hundreds of novels, and in its idea much worse. Why it should be dedicated to the German people; why it should be called 'The Mysteries'; why it should be *an experiment in typical fiction', and have an aesthetic intention and a filosofical design, no human ingenuity can discover. . . The language is never bold, vigorous, or terse; it is sometimes eloquent, more rarely picturesque; very often it degenerates into mere bombast, or into a dilute mock-heroic. And there is througout a manner, more easily felt than described, which educated people in general most 'carefully eschew. This, which we may call the 'ever and a-non' style, would of itself prevent the author from being a great writer. We hardly like to call him vulgar; but he tries to be so superfine that he always reminds his readers of the 'Court Journal' and of tradesmen's circulars. Why, for example, need a man 'lave his face' instead of washing it? Why is a single servant 'a solitary domestic' and a cabman 'a ministrant of Trivia'? The last expression looks like a parody on Johnson, but there are several others of the same kind. Thus we have 'pomarian crudities' instead of apples; the vulgarism 'calligrafy' for writing, and 'somnambular accommodations' for bed-rooms." [Westminster Review. **685**

ERSILIA. [by EMMA F. POYNTER: *Holt*, 1876.] "For a pure, hi-toned, gracefully written story for summer holiday reading, full of true and noble thöt, tender and winning pathos, charming freshness and vividness of description, and refined and delicate fancy, and instinct with the life of a generous, idealized, self-forgetting tho passionate love, we can heartily recommend 'Ersilia'. . . It is but a story of life, a vivid presentation of the silent pathos and unobtrusive tragedy which is so constantly interwoven with the web of ordinary life. The characters stand before us in the reality of living and suffering human nature—tho 3 of them at least belong to its hier ranks; and Ersilia herself is as pure and sweet and ñobly conceived a female character as almost any in modern fiction. . . If the story is a little too sad in its course and its dénouement, this is to a great extent relieved by the noble patience, born of suffering, and the purification from selfishness which is the result of the sharp discipline of life—by the atmosfere of peace which broods over the close. . . . The scenery amidst which the events

of the story are laid is mainly that of the **Pyrenees**, southern France, and **Paris**—tho in the too short glimpses given us of the early life of Ersilia and Humphrey, and in the closing scenes of the tale, we are among english meadows and orchards. The romantic scenery of the Pyrénées—misty mountain and foaming waterfall, sunny valley and dark solemn ravine is given vividly." [Canadian Monthly. **686**

ESTELLE, by ANNIE EDWARDS; *Sheldon*, 1875, = *CREEDS*.

EXPIATION [by JULIA CAROLINE (RIPLEY) DORR: *Lippincott*, 1873.] "is an interesting american story, with a background of lonely woods which protect the rustic privacy of Altona, and a list of characters which combine city culture and country eccentricity. Patsy, the grim and self-sacrificing 'help'. . . is the best delineation in it, but the style is always lively, always feminine and pure, and the conception of a hi-bred, aristocratic family come to bury their mistakes and miseries in a forest seclusion, would have been thôt worthy of being worked by Emily Brontë. . . The novel is full of local american color, and entices the attention from the reader's first plunge to the end." [Lippincott's. **687**

EXCHANGE NO ROBBERY. [by MATILDA [BARBARA] BETHAM EDWARDS: *Harper*, 1882.] "is a very pretty and very improbable story, yet very 'vraisemblable'. It is of the sort which tempts a critic to tell it; but it would be a pity to reveal the secret of the mystification, innocent at first, but growing to a portentous and hazardous state secret. Grand kinsfolk are elated that the ducal house, 'so particularly unendowed in the female line, should produce such a paragon;' and, for once, confession becomes no duty, and, in the end, a pair of true lovers are happily 'fated by a jest'." [Nation. **688**

FALLEN PRIDE, see *BRIDE'S FATE.*

FAMILY FEUD (The). [by THOMAS COOPER: *Routledge*, 1855.] "This little book, bound in the devil's colors, black and brimstone—printed in a type as villainous as ever made the eyes of a patient reader ache—is for its freshness, vigor, and variety worth any half-dozen of the novels which come into the world with all the honors of binding and topography. Those who are not scared at the outset by its very unattractive appearance will find themselves well rewarded. The story is anything but probable; but there are such life-like descriptions, and the incidents are so romantic, that the reader is carried on to the end without delaying to criticise. The account of 'the feud between the Uphams and the Downhams,'—the origin of which nobody knows, except that it is a famous feud that began beyond the memory of man, and has been kept up ever since by succeeding generations in the town of Quarrelton,—is given with great drollery, and affords a curious insit into much parliamentary parish business, and relieves the more serious part of the story, which is also an hereditary feud, having its rise in bitter wrong and crime. There are, moreover, 2 villains of genuine dye, such as we have not often the pleasure of seeing circumvented and brôt to shame. Poetical justice is at last satisfactorily awarded, and all the feuds are assuaged, not exactly by brotherly love, but in a couple of happy mariages, such as one is always glad to hear about, whether in prose or verse, or in life. The short scene in which the two old men meet and are reconciled is admirable." [Athenæum. **689**

——, SAME, by J: GOTTFRIED KINKEL, in *Tales from Blackwood*, N. S., 21.

FAR IN THE FOREST. [by SILAS W. MITCHELL: *Lippincott*, 1889.] "The scene of the story liés in the forest countries of northern Pennsylvania where roads, if made at all, were so bad as to be almost impassable; where ways were unknown, and where the only human activities in the great woods were hunting and timber-cutting. Life under these conditions is necessarily of a rather heroic cast, involving dangers, privations, and a sustained battle against the forces of nature. But with all the drawbacks to the beauties and refinements of civilization Dr. Mitchell has yet given us in Bessy Preston,—who mit be called the heroine of the story, a character not often matched, in actual life or in fiction, for womanly force, sweetness, and that powerful radiating charm which is felt as much in this rude settlement in the woods as in city drawing-rooms. She is not a young woman; and when the story opens, she is watching by the bedside of her dying husband, a weak and self-indulgent man, whom she has brôt to these timber lands partly in the hope of removing him from temptation, and partly because the acres of forest she owns here are her last and only possession. While Preston lies dying, Bessy hears a moan outside the cabin, and going to the door finds an almost frozen man on the threshold. Thus destiny brings Riverius, a german hunter and scientist, into her life, just as she loses the husband for whom she has been forced to weep too many tears in life to have many left to mourn him now that he is gone. Riverius is, in his way, as fine a character as Bessy herself, but more narrow, more concentrated, impatient of inferiority, and obstinate in logic; judging his own requirements and those of others by the guage of intellect rather than of the heart. The plot of the story is delicate and intricate, and so naturally worked out that the various events,—acting and re-acting on the characters,—seem not to be events at all, but mere steps in the unfolding of the situation. . . . There is not a single loose thread in the story. Every character and every incident is needed to bring about the startling and admirable dénoument. Nothing better than the dramatic climax of the fire in the woods, the escape of Riverius, and Ance Vickers' expiation, is to be found in any fiction of the day. Not, however, that the author has striven for any sensational effects. The power of work lies wholly in its naturalness, its fidelity to everyday life, and the logic of events. The writer has been everywhere true, and the artistic value is nowhere spoiled by redundance and exaggeration."

[American. 690
FARINA. [by G: MEREDITH: *Smith*, 1857.] "Tho his tale has 'Farina' on its label, let none tap it expecting anything fragrant, or soft, or gentle. — Wild it is, on the contrary, and impudent and fierce: —full of a riotous, abundant fancy, such as we have not fallen in with of late. It is a masque of ravishers in steel,—of robber knits, who sat on their towers looking up and down the gorges of the Eifel to see what manner of prey mit be coming, of water-women more terribly fascinating than Loreley,—of monks nearly as sharp in dealing with the Great Toowell-known as St. Dunstan himself.——It has also a brave and tender deliverer and a heroine proper for a romance of Cöln." [Athenæum. 691

FASHION AND FAMINE [by A.. S. (W.) STEPHENS: *Bentley*, 1854.] "has great defects. In the first place, an american novel should be something out of the beaten track of the common-place contrasts of conventional society; and tho the scene of this romance is laid in or about the "Upper 10000" and the "Fifth Avenue" of the empire city, still the characters are all french, and the treatment is very english. In the next place, the plot is grotesquely impossible, the leading motives of the action are grandly incredible; and the novel, from first to last, is spoiled by an obtrusion of the flimsy filosofy in which some "females" indulge, when, having got pen in hand, they begin to point out how much better it is to be good than bad. These are startling faults, and yet the novel is far above the average, and is read with engrossing interest. This, we believe, is because Mrs. Stephens has a decided genius for telling and developing a story. There is power—dramatic power—here; and as it is, as she states in her preface, her first novel, we are inelined to anticipate a series of successes for her. The hero is a wholesale villain; a polished Yankee gentleman, who does all the men and undoes all the women; who commits forgeries, connives at embezzlement, occasionally crosses his mind

with murder, deserts his wife in order to leave room for a friendly débauché, who has bôt his rit in her, leaves his child to starve, commits bigamy, and dresses singularly well. He is a mixture of Don Juan and Iago, with Dumas' vue of life; and he looks to us remarkably out of place denned in the Astor House and immersed in dollars. The heroine is the deserted wife of this bold gentleman, who is incurably attached to him, but who allows the friendly débauché to complete the bargain; who goes with the débauché to Europe, where he dies, she obtaining all his wealth, which is boundless and accomplishes Monte-Cristo results, and who,' returning to New-York when her husband is arranging his bigamy, appeals to him for a redintegratio without disclosing her affluence, and being rejected, punishes him, *after* he has bigamised, by blazing on him in all her splendor at a dramatic ball, which she throws open to the whole Upper Ten Thousand. Result—suicide on his part, and eternal misery on hers; but a delitful ending in the secured happy future of her restored child, who is an angel —in a french way—a flower-girl who calls "f-r-r-ish r-r-oses" in the streets. This is the plot, which, as we have said, is rendered endurable by the vivid and vigorous way in which the story is told and the characters are arranged." [Leader. 692

FATAL MARKSMAN (The), [by J: A: APEL] "Prof. Masson says, 'seems to be from the german, tho it is not stated to be so.' It certainly does 'seem to be from the german,' if ever a story did. But are we really to believe that in these days, when even to a music lover the 'universal cultivation of music' is becoming more than sufficiently 'universal,'— when it is impossible for 6 people to meet and have 6 words of conversation uninterrupted by the bullets of the 'fatal marksman' at the piano-forte in the corner, —there exists among us an eminent scotch professor who is ignorant of the existence of a certain opera called 'Der Freischütz,' the story of which is told in DeQuincey's

'Fatal Marksman'? De Quincey, it must be admitted, did not 'state' that the 'Fatal Marksman' was a translation of the Story which Kind, by the addition of another character or two, turned into a libretto for Weber. De Quincey was an Opera-goer, and from its first appearance in 1821 'Der Freischütz' had been so famous that perhaps there could not possibly be a man, woman, or child who would not recognize and hail at once the story which the librettist had followed so closely. Among the english translations of this remarkable story—which Weber seems to have read in Apel's collection of ghost stories as early as 1810,—the best known, after De Quincey's, is that which appeared in a volume called ' *Tales of the Wild and Wonderful*,' published in 1852 by Hurst & Co. It is there called '*Der Freischutz, or the Magic Balls*,' and is stated to be 'from the german of A. Apel.' " [Th. Watts. **693**

FAUSTINE [by "RITA," i. e.,——(   ) Booth: *Lippincott*, 1882.] "is of the Ouida type of story, but distinctly without the badness. It is even remarkable for the reserve with which the material is handled. A scheming priest, a beautiful actress, an ardent youth, have many times figured in doubtful fiction, but in this book their adventures are wrôt into a tale which may safely be commended to lovers of thrilling incident." [Nation. **694**

FETISH CITY (The) [by F : BOYLE: In Tales from Blackwood, N. S., I.] "is a well-imagined story of the discovery of greek ruins beyond the Matabele territòry." [Athenæum. **695**

FICKLE FORTUNE [by "E. WERNER": *Bentley*, 1884.] = *WHAT THE SPRING BROUGHT.*

FIDDLER OF LUGAU (The). [by MA. ROBERTS: *Whittaker*, 1888.] " 'The Fiddler of Lugau' is a pleasing little story, tastefully written, as its authorship insures. The scene is laid for the most part in the saxon town of Lugau, during the early years of the century, affording a striking background for skillfully drawn pictures of life in **Germany** during the

Napoleonic wars. The presence of certain Netherlanders in the place, and that of a few Wends, lend variety to the personages, and furnish complications for the story, while the saxon hatred of Bonaparte, lacking completeness only by reason of another hatred of Prussia, the distant tramp of french troops, the suffering and uncertainty of the times, make a grimly effective setting for a tender little tale of love and loyalty, wherein **music** is the motive spring. The jealousies and revenges, professional and political, which run side by side, the peals of church chimes, and the eloquence of the violin, the alarms of war, and the home life in the families of Lugau, schoolboy tricks and faithful love, make up the story. Spite of the happy ending, it is a pathetic little history, shadowed by war and by the ever-touching tale of sensitive genius meeting no recognition except from a pair of loyal young hearts. All is told' with exquisite refinement. The vividness and charm of the local color make one feel the final change of scene to London and a merchant's household to be something of an anti-climax. One would rather have closed the book on the wooded moor which lay round Lugau, spirit-haunted, or at a saxon fireside with the grandmother knitting in the corner." [Nation. **696**

FIOR D' ALIZA. [by ALPHONSE DE LAMARTINE: *Houghton*, 1868.] "This new addition to the Riverside Classics is a fit companion to 'Undine' and 'Paul and Virginia.' The simple while eventful story of the love of the heroic Fior d' Aliza and her devotion, even to death if necessary, to her lover, was better adapted, perhaps, to the poetical form in which its author says it was originally his intention to embody it, than to the prose, unadorned tho not ungraceful, in which it appeared. . . . But there still remains for an hour's reading a very tender and touching story, romantic, picturesque, and nearly tragic." [Round Table **697**

FIRST LOVE, by I. TURGÉNIEF, *Allen & Co.*, 1884.

206

FIRST VIOLIN (The) [by JESSIE FOTHERGILL: *Holt*, 1864.] "possesses that nameless quality which redeems and excuses all defects, which animates and vivifies what would ordinarily be simply mechanical commonplace, which touches the feelings while stimulating the imagination, and which interests and pleases in a way that mere artifice can never achieve... The scene is laid in **Germany**, the hero being the leader of the orchestra in a small city [Düsseldorf] and the story as a whole gives a lively and probably trustworthy picture of professional musical life in the one country of the world where **Music** ranks in dignity and in the ardor which it arouses in its votaries with any of the other professions and pursuits. The character-drawing is particularly good; the incidents are cleverly managed if now and then involving rather too much of coincidence; and the local color is maintained by very delicate and artistic touches... It reads like the spontaneous record of an experience which had fired and inspired the author's whole nature." [Appleton's. **698**

FIVE-CHIMNEY FARM [by A. M. (HOPPUS) MARKS: *Low*, 1887.] "has a double plot, which does not cohere very obviously. The home life of the Copleys, an ancient landed stock in the Weald of Sussex, seems outraged by an erratic scion taking after his french mother, and spending his life among parisian factions. Both fases of existence are well described; the life of the farm and the country sounds and sits are presented to us with a minute vigor which invests them with an interest not less than attaches to the stormy scenes of french politics. The latter have evidently been thoroly studied, and the description of the 3 days of 1848 would form some striking chapters in a professedly historical book. Perhaps the novel is a little over-wéted by its discursiveness, but the matter discussed is so interesting that we are inclined, with the author, to let the story wait. Still there is considerable merit in the story; Katie Copley is a brit centre to the surrounding darkness of her parisian associates, and in Thrasybule the

posture-making yet passionate frenchman who thinks he honors her with his preference, she finds an admirable foil to her. self-forgetfulness and modesty." [Athenæum. **699**

FLEURANGE. [by PAULINE (LA F.) CRAVEN: *Holt*, 1873.] "The heroine, left an orfan by the death of her father, a french artist, finds a home with her uncle, Prof. Dornthal, a wealthy gentleman of Frankfurt, and her mother's brother. She is very happy among her new friends, for a time; and well she mit be, for their life as portrayed in these pages is paradisaic in its serenity of mutual trust, and activity of mutual sympathies. Suddenly a banking-house, in which nearly the whole of the professor's fortune was invested, goes to ruin, and the family are reduced to comparative poverty... Flenrange rejoins her uncle's family at Heidelberg, where some powerful scenes exhibit to the reader in his true prominence the hero of the book,—Clement Dornthal, who has loved his cousin with a steadily increasing fervor from the first...Thus Fleurange found herself the arbiter of his fate. She did not hesitate. She promised her rival she would return at once to Germany, and that the count should never know of her presence or her errand in Russia. Starting homeward next day, she saw the wedding party issuing from a church, and caut a glimpse of the man she loved, the husband of another woman. Two years passed by quietly at Heidelberg, and at last her eyes were opened to a knowledge of Clement's love; and recognition and reciprocation were simultaneous." [Boston "Literary World." **700**

FLIP (etc.) [by [FR.] BRET HARTE: *Chatto*, 1872.] "There is little or nothing new in Mr Harte's new volume. It is true that such stories as it contains are told more or less cleverly, and more or less for the first time. But they are told in the old way, with the old tricks and mannerisms; they take us over the old ground; they show us the old sort of characters; they exemplify the old faults and the old merits; and as we read we seem to have read them all before, and to have read them many times. The names are changed and the incidents have been shuffled and dealt anew. But the game is the same; and the pack and the players and the stakes are the same; and as we know exactly what is to happen and who is to win, our interest in the proceedings has evaporated." [Athenæum. **701**

FOR THE RIGHT. [by KARL EMIL FRANZOS; *Clarke*, 1888.]... " 'I have seldom, if ever,' says Mr. G: MacDonald, 'read a work of fiction which has moved me with such admiration;' and such an expression of feeling from such a man cannot fail to awaken hi expectations. Unless we are much in error, a great majority of the readers whose ethical and artistic perceptions are most trustworthy will feel that these expectations have been amply fulfilled, for the book of which Mr. Mac Donald speaks with so much enthusiasm is a story of exceptional beauty and elevation. In the ordinary sense of words which have never been very finely differentiated, 'For the Right' is a romance rather than a novel, tho the writer never relaxes his grasp of the real any more than he loses sit of the ideal. It is a picture of human nobleness contending with lonely and heroic courage against almost omnipotent ignoble forces... Taras Barabola is an utterly unlettered peasant, living upon his farm in the village of Zulawce, in the near presence of the great Carpathians. ... So the story ends, and it seems fitting that the dying words of a man who, however mistakenly, has lived for riteousness, should be words in which he does justice even to himself. We hope that what we have said has sufficed to make it clear that 'For the Right' is a singularly noble and beautiful book. To its purely artistic qualities we have done scant justice, but they are of a hi and commanding order. In his treatment of character, of incident, and of the wild landscape which forms a background for both, Mr. Franzos proves himself a master, tho his book is principally noteworthy not for these things, but for the portraiture of its central character,—a man of ideal nobleness who is betrayed into wrong by the mistake of supposing that he can transcend human limitations. We should say that the translation is a faithful rendering; as english, it is throuout admirable." [Spectator. **702**

FORTUNATE LOVERS (The). [by MARGUERITE OF NAVARRE: *Redway*, 1888.] "We have certainly no quarrel with the translation of certain of the novels of the 'Heptameron,' the reversion to their old title (not, it is true, either a very authentic or a very appropriate one) of 'The Fortunate Lovers,' and the issuing of them in a pretty volume. The Heptameron is an exceedingly pretty book— a much prettier book from the literary point of vue than Miss Robinson allowed in her monograf— a book the 'impropriety' of which has been grossly exaggerated by people who have never read it—a book of interesting and rather puzzling authorship, and lastly, one which strikes the key-note of a certain time better almost than any other single work. There has evidently been no difficulty in selecting rather more than a third of the whole collection, and the choice mit, if the translator and selector had pleased, have been larger... It is to degrade a really charming work of art and of literature to make its chief attraction consist in tittle-tattle about some real Emarsuittes and Nomerfides, or in the fact that some of the stories which Emarsuitte and Nomerfide told so prettily and so coolly were facts or gossip of the day. Books are not preserved for 300 years by such salt as this. It is because Marguerite, or the set of ladies and gentlemen and men of letters who clustered around her, managed to make this tittle-tattle illustrate a peculiar fase of society in a really literary, sometimes in a quasi-poetical fashion, that the 'Heptameron' is alive and charming." [Athenæum. **703**

FORTUNES OF MISS FOLLEN (The) [by HANNAH (   ) GOODWIN: *Appleton*, 1876.] "shows a marked improvement on her earlier books, which smacked of the school-room and the Sunday-school. In this she takes broader vues of life, and writes with the freedom derived from contact with the world. The story is simple yet fresh. The heroine is a german peasant girl, whose beauty and grace attract some american visitors at **Baden**, who learn to feel a deep interest in her fortunes. She is uneducated, but not ignorant, a superior musician, having had instructions from Conrad Klaist, who has learned to love her, but she is betrothed to one Ludwig, a fine young peasant, and is about to become his wife, when his mother and sister, who had opposed the match, contrived to break it off. She is a very lovely character, almost too lovely to be possible, and her refinement from rusticity to intelligence and elegance is a process quite too rapid and smooth to be credible. Conrad is rather pathetic, and one hears of his death in the army with regret." [Boston "Literary World."] A very charming story has been made of the life of a german peasant girl, who is born with a beauty of body and of soul which gradually lifts her into refined life." [Galaxy. **704**

——, SAME ("Christmas Fortune"), Boston, 1881.

FORTY-NINE [by "JOAQUIN" MILLER: *Funk*, 1884.] "as playgoers already know, is thrillingly interesting, and possesses more coherence, both of plot and style, than much of the author's other writing. It deals, of course, with those pathetic histories of early **California** when there was no telegraf to signal to the world the suffering of whole villages by cyclone or other general calamity and to bring back substantial sympathy; and when the individual sufferer, with the proverbial silence of the american hero, simply dropped out of line without a word. There is less of the coarseness and more of the ruf tenderness of Joaquin Miller than we are wont to find in his work, with much of that matchless power of vivid description which does not consist of mere adjectives, and which it is impossible to define, but equally impossible not to feel." [Critic. **705**

FOUR GHOST STORIES [by M.. L.. (STEWART) MOLESWORTH: *Macmillan*, 1888.] "are graceful and attractive. Ghost stories have always a certain charm, but these 4 are remarkable for the pretty setting which surrounds the thrilling part of the narrative. 'Lady Farquhar's Old Lady' is very touching; the scene lies in an old irish country house. '*Unexplained*,' is a weird tale of a remote german inn and an old cup and saucer." [Atbe. **706**

FOUR PHASES OF LOVE. [by PAUL HEYSE: *Routledge*, 1857.] "The tales have an impress of originality, and are agreeably moralized. Two of the titles are eccentric;—'Eye-Blindness and Soul-Blindness' and 'By the Banks of the Tiber.' The varieties of passion are forcibly suggested." [Leader. **707**

FREE JOE. [by J. C. HARRIS: *Scribner*, 1887.] "The stories bound under the title 'Free Joe' depict the life and characters with which he has already made us familiar. The georgian negro, bond and free, the poor white, and the mountaineer are given enduring life by his pen. It may be heresy to suggest it, but one feels that his portraits of the southern aristocrat, as he was before the war, are no less truthful. The rich young slave-owners with rather provincial tung, vues and clothes, who rejoice to sit by the hour in the corner grocery with their heels in the air, have a startling semblance of reality. The war undoubtedly deprived them of traditionally magnificent surroundings, but it can hardly be responsible for a total disappearance of the hauty mien tempered by infinite condescension, the unvarying elegance of diction, the chivalrous virtue, with which fancy loves to invest the old-time despot. In all his stories Mr. Harris prefers to describe the relation between master and slave as one of loving protection and graceful devotion, rather than one of brutal terrorism and craven fear. The master is always a hero to his valet, and the valet's love for the master passes that of a brother. Fortunately for those who like a pleasant tale, the author stands apart from the crusade to divorce the true and the beautiful." [Nation.] "Mr. Harris' southern sketches are always striking, from the genuineness of their humanity and their strong grasp of the deep realities of life. The pathos of such a story as 'Free Joe' would be almost too pitiful if it addressed itself to our hearts and consciences, and urged us to rit an existing wrong, instead of reviving thôtful reflexions upon the varied aspects of old times in the South. There is, however, just the difference between the fiction which puts meaning and inspiration into a great sweep of reform, as, for example, 'Uncle Tom's Cabin' or 'The Annals of a Sportsman,' —and picturesque, touching stories, like these—that there is between the worker who puts in the powerful yeast which is to leaven the whole loaf and the decorator who rounds it off and gilds it, afterward. Not but that tales like '*Little Compton*' and '*Free Joe*' are as strongly as gracefully told. But what they do is not to shape and mold existing facts, but to work up old traditions and revive and prolong the last faint echoes of our civil war. Full of sombre and terrible pictures as were the old days of slavery, they furnish a mass of picturesque material which no other fase of american life presents. The faithful slave—the lit of whose goodness and truth and faithfulness only serves to render his master's sins more visible in the surrounding darkness,—is dear to the heart of the romancer; and it is probable that he will for sometime continue to be a touching figure in our minor fiction. Mr. Harris does not, however, confine himself to pictures of bygone days. The last half of the book describes Georgia under the new régime." [American. **708**

FRESCOES. [by "OUIDA": *Lippincott*, 1884.] "The five stories in Ouida's new volume are all in dramatic form, and show the keen, pitiless hand of the author in customary exercise and power. The longer of the sketches lends its name to the book, and is the best of them. It is clever, powerful, harmless; brilliant with a certain brilliancy as is everything Ouida writes; and it is interesting. An english lady of family and property directs her agent in Italy to send her an artist capable of doing frescoes. . . The story is without bitterness or bad blood of any sort. '*Afternoon*,' one of the sketches which follow, is based on the improbability of a man's forgetting a girl whom he had maried and deserted; afterwards, when she has become a beautiful woman and a famous artist, falling in love with her; being denied by her and teased by the denial until bo has been punished long enuf; and then having the fact disclosed to him, and coming into possession of his own." [Boston "Literary World." **709**

GAIN OF A LOSS (The.) [by HENRIETTA CAMILLA (JACKSON) JENKIN: *Leypoldt*, 1869.] "It is some time since we have encountered "the Jesuit" in an english novel. He comes to lit again here, and we are glad to find not one of his typical and well known peculiarities wanting—he is as stealthy, as wily, and as unscrupulous as ever. As of old, his principal business is to "alienate into the coffers of the church" all the property belonging to other people which by hook or by crook he can lay his hands on; he is, in short, as immoral in private and as hypocritical in public as only the Jesuit of an english-woman's novel can ever hope to be. [Compare The Wellfields.] Poetical justice is meted out to him at last in a satisfactory manner, not simply in that his machinations come to naut,—that was to be expected—but his secret sins are discovered, and he is dogged throuôut Europe by a vindictive old woman whose meditated vengeance is grimly foreshadowed thus: "There are convent prisons where priests do penance for the crimes of having been found out." The novel contains, also, a number of other romantic and rather hi-strung personages—some of them remarkable for their beauty, some for their goodness; none, we think, for their superior intelligence—vueing them, that is, from an outsider's stand-point. As for the hero, it is hard to say whether his personal beauty, the mystery surrounding his birth, or his staunch Protestantism, which is of the muscular-christian type, endears him most to the heroine and to the reader. He is by no means a bad fellow, altho to the reader of many novels his character will not seem startlingly original. The story is pleasantly told, and will not, we suppose, be found the less readable because it contains plot and incident enuf for one of twice its length—not that it is itself short." [Nation. **710**

THE GALLANT LORDS OF BOIS DORÉE: ("Beaux Messieurs de Bois Dorée) [by G : SAND : *Dodd*, 1890.] "was one of her latest novels and one of the two or three which were successfully dramatized. It occupies a middle ground between her passionate romances and her pretty pastoral tales. Its time of action is in the early part of the seventeenth century, and it abounds in carefully drawn and picturesque description of the gentle manners, rude ways of living, and chivalrous ideas of the lesser nobility of that time. A tale of intrigue and fiting forms the connecting chain of these descriptions, and the romantic element is not missing." [Christ. Union. **711**

GARDEN OE ARMIDA (The). [by ANNE (SHELDON) COOMBS : *Cassell*, 1890.] "All that is most modern in vice, personified in an american gentleman, contrasted with the best approved antique virtues bound up in an italian nobleman, the two somehow brôt into harmony by the gentle widow, Rhoda Starr, who bitterly repents not being good enuf to sacrifice herself to the vicious and poetic Merriam, but who is quite good enuf to deserve the love of the saintly Di Loria—this makes 'The Garden of Armida' perhaps dangerous food for babes, but stimulating and wholesome for grown people. There is just enuf realism of the common sort to make it certain that the author is not fiting windmills; but the good Neapolitan is as real as the wicked New-Yorker. As is the case with all genuine antiques, he is perfectly simple and natural, there is not a trace of quaintness about him. The scene of the story is in Italy, and its

pines and precipices, its oranges and ices, get a fair share of attention ; but the reader is so occupied with the people in the book that he cannot weary of the scenery, and does not even remark the paucity of incident and the absence of plot. Even the wicked poet does something to justify our interest in him, at the end ; and tho he is held up as an awful example, it is with a mixture of strength, tact, and rit purpose, which secures just the proper degree of consideration for the creature, and no more." [Critic. **712**

GARDEN OF WOMEN (A). [by "SARAH TYTLER", i. e., Henrietta Keddie : *Smith*, 1875.] "Miss Tytler's rank hier than the run of magazine tales, and, in spite of her long sentences and occasionally involved forms of expression, they will be read with pleasure, We have two continental stories in *Lorlotte's* surrender to her Capitaine, and the tragic-comic love affairs between the much-enduring members of the princely house of *Kurzheim*. It is difficult to select special instances of the novelist's skill in so wide and various a field, but the tale of *Molly and Adam*, whose dour obstinacy works them so long a harvest of self-torture and discomfort, is, perhaps, the most masterly sketch of the peculiarities of scotch peasant character, while "*London Pride*" and "*Love lies Bleeding*" are the flowers we should choose from 'English Garden Plots.' The story, too, called appropriately *Rue*, of the fair young lady of quality who loses her lover throu the terrible misfortune of small pox, recalls several "over true" anecdotes of the plague, which caused many a domestic tragedy a century ago."] Athenæum. **713**

GEIER-WALLY [*Appleton*, 1876.]= *THE VULTURE MAIDEN.*

GERMAN LOVE [by F : MAX MULLER: *Chapman*, 1857.] "tho poetical and elegant in its confessions, is so prolix and so discursive, and the lovers talk so much like Quarterly Revuers about poetry, and matters of belief and resignation, more serious still, that we feel that the labor of a skilled translator has been somewhat thrown away in rendering what is so long, so learned, but so little like love-talk.— There is thôt in the book, but small reality; and the thôt will chiefly please those who would prefer to read the 'Papers of an Alien' in the original." [Athenæum.] "It relates in reminiscent form the love of a young man for an invalid princess, who who after much hesitation consented to marry him. The stress of emotion, however, put an end to her existence. There is little life in the book; but it has that distant prettiness which belongs by birth, one would say, to german writers of idyllic prose." [Nation.] "It is a 'fratras' of the most insipid and sickly sentimentality expressed in hyperbolical terms, and with 'a nice derangment of epitafs' worthy of Mrs. Malaprop." [Westminster Rev. **714**

——, SAME, ["Memories"] translated by G: P. Upton, Chicago, 1874.

——, SAME, translated by G. A. M., London, *Mullan*, 1877; *Sonnenschein*, 1884.

GIANNETTO [by MA. MAJENDIE: *Holt*, 1876.] "tho scarcely more than a novelette in dimensions, is a very strong and artistic piece of work. . . The story is of an italian fisher-boy, who, dumb from his birth, and passionately rebellious against the infliction, suddenly recovered his voice after a narrow escape from shipwreck in a storm. The strange character of this fenomenon, coupled with the boy's stranger mood, caused the superstitious villagers to believe that Giannetto, like Dr. Faustus of the legend, had entered into a compact with the evil-one. He appears to have shared this belief, and, tho he subsequently became a famous singer, he deemed himself inevitably given over to the Furies, and gradually degenerated into a gloomy, morose, and violent man. Finally, when on the verge of insanity or suicide, he was saved by the faithful ministrations of a priest, who had devoted himself for long years to this one object. The narrative is intensely, almost painfully interesting throuồut; and the author finds opportunities by the way to construct for us some exceedingly vivid and charming

pictures of italian scenery and social life." [Appleton's Journal. **715**

GLORIA VICTIS [by "Ossip Schubin": *Gottesberger*, 1886.] "is in every way as fine as 'Our Own Set' [No. 513], and in some ways finer. It goes deeper into the heart of human nature, with clear insit yet sympathetic comprehension, and is more powerful because more sad. The story of a sinning mother whose expiation lay in having to humiliate herself before the son she adored is most beautifully told; and the story of the son is not less strong and touching. Both stories are full of minor points of fine artistic value, and the final worth of the whole lies in the dignity, solemnity and sympathy with which a dangerous situation is dealt with." [Critic. **716**

GOLD ELSIE [by "E. MARLITT," i. e., Eugenie John: *Lippincott*, 1868,—*Strahan*. 1873.] "has much that is interesting and attractive. When we look critically at the characters and most of the framework of the plot, we find, indeed, that there is much exaggeration, and that idealism is carried to an excess—the good and charming being far too good and charming, while their opposites are systematically blackened. In spite of these faults, however, the story is pleasant and readable. We are interested in the heroine who gives her name to it, and we recognize the writer's claim to have such an overpowering regard for her chief character as makes it impossible that she should rest contented with merely natural attractions. The description of **Thuringian** forest scenery, of castle ruins, and of peaceful german households, add greatly to the charm of the story." [Athenæum.] "We have taken so much pleasure in reading this book that we really can not find it in our heart to comment ungratefully on the fact that in all essential details of plot and characterization it is an almost exact reproduction of its predecessor, 'The Old Mamsell's Secret.' ["Gold Elsie" was published 2 years before this "predecessor" but the order was reversed in the Wister translations.—W: M. G.] The author is still fiting vigorously against her ancient enemies, hypocrisy in religion and inordinate pride of birth and social position. We find our interest in the story—which is, however, quite well enuf managed—entirely subordinate to the amused admiration with which we regard its author. She is the heartiest of democrats, and much the best advocate of the woman's cause, as it appears in fiction, whom we have seen. The typical german woman, fair and rotund, who 'mends the papa's hose' and plays for him the part of a dutiful and overworked upper servant, and is fitly rewarded therefor by accompanying him to the family club and the festive beer-garden, has no recognized existence in Miss Marlitt's ideal world. Her heroines settle themselves firmly on the rock of their own individuality, and being unusually well provided with the weapons of personal beauty, innocence, and genuine love for truth, 'moral elevation and spiritual growth,' do most sturdy battle with cant and with the aristocratic prejudices of their lovers. They come out victorious, of course, and the heroes, who combine in a curious fashion the peculiarities of "Rochester" and "St. John Rivers," get in the end most loving and obedient wives. Really, both Elsiè in this story, and Felicitas in the former one, are altogether delitful characters—and none the worse for being idealizations rather than portraits, since the idealization is of a good kind, and will give young girls who may read the books an impulse in the rit direction. We commend them to all novel-readers—to many of whom the faults which interfere somewhat with our enjoyment of them—the author's over-fondness for dramatic situations, for instance, her love for ruined castles, buried treasures, and artistically unfortunate secrets, which finally provide the radical heroine with as aristocratic a lineage as that of her oppressor—will very likely not seem objectionable." [Nation. **717**

——, SAME, transl. by L. P. Palmer, in "Ladies Repository," march-nov., 1867.

GOLDSMITH'S WIFE (The) [by

HENRIETTE ETIENNETTE FANNY (ARNAUD) REYBAUD: *Appleton*, 1878.] "contains a charming brigand, melancholy, cultivated, devoted to his mother's portrait and another man's wife, a defender of helpless women, and a possessor of luxurious apartments in a lonely mountain pass; but his sins find him out and he dies at the block." [Nation. **718**

GOOD FIGHT (A). [by C. READE: *Harper*,1859.] "Mr. Reade has taken this little record, which would never have become historical but for the accidental consequences of the loves of Gerard and Margaret, and wrôt it into a story of exquisite grace and delicacy. A dead and half forgotten fact, he has warmed it into fresh life, and given it all the beauties which his brilliant imagination could endow it. Tho shorter and simpler than most, it is certainly inferior to none of his other works. Perhaps its simplicity is its first merit. The extravagant peculiarities of style which over-laid his two longest books have almost entirely disappeared in this. Here the narrative is for the most part as unostentatious as the events are natural. But its power is remarkable. Altho the regularity with which the incidents follow one another is such that they may all be anticipated, yet the interest in them never fades. There is nothing startlingly new in the whole story. On the contrary, it follows pretty closely the old formula of troubled true-love until the closing chapter, when triumfant virtue sets in. But this takes nothing from the effect. All is so clear and vivid in description, so glittering with gleams of wit, relieved by soft shadows of purest pathos, so full of the spirit of tender humanity, that the reader finds no reason to complain, except that the end is so speedily reached." [Atlantic. **719**

GRANDISSIMES (The) [by G: W. CABLE: *Scribner*, 1880.] "is a diversion in favor of the old romance. Nevertheless, in painting the old creole life of New-Orleans at the beginning of the century he has in effect broken new ground, and, as the soil is rich, one's first impression is that he has contented himself with merely overturning it. But, rich as it is, it needs an artist to exploit it with the success shown in 'The Grandissimes,' and Mr. Cable is a literary artist of unusual powers . . . The result is inevitably the happy one that the reader shares his enthusiasm before he suspects its existence, and— as we have admitted—is led into referring the merit of the book to its material. On the whole, one finally reflects, however, this is the homage a work of talent always exacts, and it is entirely probable that the actual creole milieu in 1802 was as prosaic as actuality always appears till the chronicler arrives with his magic lenses. The poetic vein in Mr. Cable is well developed and defined, and the picture he conjures from the Louisiana levees and swamps is steeped in sentiment. It has an atmosfere and fragrance quite its own throu which it communicates itself and its meaning palpably to the senses." [Nation.   720

GRAZIELLA [by A. DE LAMARTINE: translated by W. C. Urquhart: *Hotten*, 1871.] "purports to relate the author's experiences in early youth, while rusticating on the coast of Italy. He renders a service to a fisherman's family, and becomes installed in their cottage. With one of the inmates, a lovely girl named Graziella, he falls in love. Her parents propose to make her the wife of a wealthy cousin : but the girl objects, and runs away in the nit. Her young french lover finds her under remarkable circumstances ; but never returns, and soon afterwards hears of her death. The story is full of pathetic beauty, tinged with french filosofy and the enthusiasm of a young poet's imagination." [Boston "Literary World."   721

——, SAME, transl. by RUNNION, *Jansen*, 1875.

——, SAME, transl. by NORWOOD, *Charing Cross Pub. Co.*, 1876.

GREAT EXPECTATIONS. [by C: DICKENS: 1857.] "Pip, the hero of the book, is a youth suddenly promoted from the smithy of his brother-in-law, Joe Gargery, to the position of a young gentleman of great expectations. But neither Pip

nor the reader suspects, till they are told, whence these expectations are derived, and then Pip and the reader are equally surprised. Joe Gargery is one of the uncouth beings with a heart as huge as his body, of whom Dickens is so fond, whose simplicity of nature confounds the worldly sagacity of shrewd men. And Dickens makes his readers no less fond of him. The great blundering, ungrammatical, overgrown Joe, a kind of domestic Titan, helpless in speech, and of no education, is pathetic from his affectionate fidelity, and sublime throu the naked instinct of duty. . . Miss Havisham is the most emfatic sketch of character. She was the victim of some bitter nuptial disappointment, and in her grey age her crazed brain holds her the prisoner of that tragical moment. She lives in her chamber garnished for the bridal, wearing her nuptial veil and dress which have grown yellow with time, tottering upon her cane about the table upon which the bride cake molds and the ghastly candles burn the whole year round. The object of her life is to destroy the peace of men—to break their hearts in revenge for her own grief. She is old and withered, and can inflame no hearts with *her* beauty, so she cherishes a young and superb girl, whom she has educated to be her avenger. The convict is a hold picture is Dickens' most vigorous vein ; and Wemmick, the clerk of the criminal lawyer, who is a lawyer's clerk in town and a quaint, simple human being in the country, is one of those exquisitely humane touches which show the master of his art. Mr. Jaggers, the criminal lawyer, who knows all the evil doers and who seems capable of all their crimes, is curiously contrasted with his clerk." [G : W : Curtis.   722

GREAT LADY (A) [by "J : VAN DEWALL," i. e., A : Kühne: *Lippincott*, 1873]". . . is not unreadable, being a sombre tale of which the scene is laid in Poland, a country of which one hears willingly, in 1863." [Nation.   723

GREIFENSTEIN. [by FR. M. CRAWFORD: *Macmillan*, 1889.] "Mr. Crawford has written about people of many nationalities, but never, perhaps, has he been more imbued with the national spirit he infuses into his characters, nor more carried away by the fascination of the local coloring with which he enriches his canvas, than in 'Greifenstein.' It is a novel of german life; and he has made the book distinctively german by skillfully interpenetrating scenes, characters, and story with ideas, customs, traditions, which belong to germans and to germans alone. He is a brilliant painter, and likes large effects which waylay, startle, and dazzle the reader. The descriptions of german student life in the present novel are, in their way, the best part of the book. . . With less skillful treatment, and with less careful preparation of the reader's mind for some horrible dénoument, this scene would have been too revolting, too barbarous. As it is, the author has invested it with the stern majesty of the loftiest tragedy. The event has loomed behind the story from the beginning. There has been sin, and there must be expiation. Then the inherent qualities in the grim, stern old men; the acceptance of military necessity, their feeling of personal honor; their habit of indomitable courage; —all these characteristics render logical and possible· a brutal and materialistic punishment which suits the dark ages better than ours." [American.]—"The type of human nature depicted in this book, which is distinctly one for novel-readers to be thankful for, is that of the old-fashioned german country gentleman. And this requires to be drawn special attention to, because the story cannot be thoroly appreciated by any one who does not bear in mind the scrupulous respect for honor, both of families and individuals, which is characteristic of that type. . . . All the personages, save one, are of the heroic order,—knitly, brave, self-controlled, strong to do and to suffer, and unhesitating in choosing death rather than evil. Honor . is to them no myth, but a fact, a priceless possession, a household idol for which every other consideration is to be sacrificed, 'a law having rules, and

conditions, and penalties, and rewards, all defined in the heart, and all equally beyond the range of the intelligence'. . . And it is with a shuddering sense of inevitableness that one beholds them dealing out fierce justice (according' to their code) with a pitilessness which is rendered exeusable by the fact of their being every whit as pitiless for themselves as they are for others. Hilda von Sigmundskron is a maiden worthy of the knitly gentlemen amongst whom she moves as heroine. Beautiful, fearless, true, gracious, and unchanging, she is an attractive and unique figure, distinguished by a dominant strength of character that is really little short of sublime. [Spectator.   **724**

GUENN. [by B. W. (HOWARD) TEL- FEL: *Osgood*, 1883.] · The story of 'Guenn' is so brit and sympathetic, so well set off by a background of suggestive and charming pictures all tinged with delicate hues of sentiment, that few will hesitate to. pronounce it a very delitful book. Much of the freshness of reality is felt in every description, and so many fugitive and elusive traits of nature have been gathered at a happy moment of opportunity that it becomes evident that the author has been faithful in observation and study of some actual Plouvenec. . . She has given us the study of a girl, wild, passionate, and proud, untamable as the wind, whose exuberant and unexhausted feelings are all spent on a generous love for the artist who paints her picture. The artist Hamor is clearly a woman's hero,—beautiful with a 'tête de Christ,' cool, delicate, æsthetic, subordinating every faculty and every passion to his love for art." [Lippincott's.] "It is a brave venture to choose a subject so sad that only great merit in the telling of the story can ever bring the reader back to it. . . It is pleasant to give to the rest thoro and hearty praise. . . The story has in it all the possibilities of the tragedy that is at once the most sensational and the most commonplace in fiction. It is no ordinary power which makes such a story original in plot, and faithful to truth in the conditions in which it was imagined.

... 'Guenn,' the fairest and the shyest of girls among the fisher-folk in a little coast-village of **Bretagne**, is coveted and won by an artist for his model. Wakened to new life by contact with finer natures, the girl throws her whole soul into her hopes for the success of her picture, and into her devotion to the artist. The work done, he departs as litly as he came, and the poor child is broken-hearted, not dishonored; and therein appears the originality of the story." [Nation.   **725**

GUY LIVINGSTONE, see No. 591.

GUY MANNERING [by WA. SCOTT: 1815.] "is without historical connections other than those of social details; such as smugglers, gypsies, and the like. Scene in Scotland, and the time mlt be a generation later than that of 'Waverley.' Meg Merrilies is one of the characters." [Boston "Literary World."] "SIR WALTER SCOTT, that beloved writer, who, to quote George Eliot, 'has made a chief part in the happiness of many young lives,' had, as Goethe said, 'a wholly new art, with laws of its own.' No man knew better how to tell a story, or appreciated more keenly the value of a good plot. But the construction of a Waverley Novel, admirable tho it be, is not its chief distinction. The charm of these immortal tales is to be found in the vivid imagination, the quiet humor, the picturesque description, the keen sense of natural beauty, the recognition of what is noble as well as what is grotesque in human life, which inspires every page, The soul of Scott breathes throu them all, giving them unity, color, and poetical vitality. No modern writer has had such fame, not only in England, but on the Continent. 1,500,000 copies of his novels are said to have been sold in France before 1830, his popularity has not waned since, and no author has more richly deserved his fame. For Scott is one of the healthiest and purest of writers, as he was the most manly and lovable of men. It is his humanity, his large heartedness, which make him akin to Shakspere. In one sense, of course, there can be no comparison between these poets, but in the art

which elevates and sweetens human life, Shakspere and Scott are brothers." [Spectator.   **726**

GYPSY'S PROPHECY, see *BRIDE'S FATE.*

HARRY LORREQUER [by C: LÈVER: *Chapman*, 1847.] "was the first, and is in many respects the best, of Mr. Lever's stories. It displays all his excellence in perfection; it takes us completely into the marvellous land which he has made his, and throu which he travels, with so much ease and satisfaction. All the pleasures of life are spread before us; wit, wine, and women fitting and loving, daring leaps, absurd hoaxes, mad Irishmen. We are led from story to story, and have good things thrown before us in profusion; and it is all done so pleasantly. The monkeys who stay at home cannot help liking to hear the traveled monkey talk; and we are obliged to a writer who can almost persuade us that life painted in 'Harry Lorrequer' is a real or a possible life. What a passage throu the vale of tears we should make of it, if we could but come upon the land of this Mandeville of fiction, where every day we could get into a scrape and peril our life, only to emerge with greater glory and the securest safety; where men with the gayest irish songs and the best irish jokes were always gathered round the most sparkling bowls, and no one had ever anything to do, or suffer, or repent of!" [National Review.   **727**

HEART OF MIDLOTHIAN (The) [by SIR WA. SCOTT.] "is probably the best known of Scott's novels. G: Robertson is a young man of family who has taken to evil courses and is now the associate of smugglers and robbers. He is handsome, bold, reckless, and in his way generous; and having somehow made the acquaintance of Effie Deans, then living at home with her father, and her half-sister Jeanie, he falls sincerely in love with her, and tho he becomes her seducer is even at that time only dissuaded from marrying her by his companions. A child is born which mysteriously disappears; Effie is arrested on a charge of child-murder,

Missing Page

Missing Page

is the foundation whereon is constructed the exciting novel before us, which weaves the legend into the possible circumstances of a human being's life with remarkable skill, so as to make every detail of the life correspond exactly to what had been predicted, and yet not to introduce anything which is not explicable by natural causes. So cleverly is this done, that even when one has finished the book, one cannot say with certainty whether the heroine is meant to be a fulfilment and verification of the old tale, or merely a person whose career strangely lent itself to the impression that the legend had been something more than a legend. . . The book contains thrilling and novel situations, stirring adventures spiritedly told, and plenty of material to keep up the attention and interest, from beginning to end." [Spectator.] The same idea is used with great effect in a tale of absorbing interest (scene in Germany and Italy) called *The Portrait of Concitta P—*, by "E. Gerard" in "Longman's Magazine," Feb. 1891. **735**

HIDDEN SIN, see *ALL FOR LOVE*.

HIDDEN TREASURES [by F: HARDMAN, 1852.] "is an interesting tale of the prussian war against Bonaparte. It is neatly tho somewhat mechanically constructed, and is, we take it for granted, a translation from the german. There is good grouping of character in the story. It relates the fidelity of an old soldier to his colonel's family, who have been cheated out of their heritage by a wicked attorney, —and how the soldier buries in a forest a certain chest containing papers of consequence to the colonel's family. Young Sigismund is a spirited figure such as boys like to read about,—and there is enuf of the horrors of war in the tale to awaken love of peaceful life. The opening chapter, in which the french soldiers chase the old veteran and his old horse 'Ali,' is grafic and interesting, and in many parts of the story there are a freshness and a healthy vivacity which are very pleasing." [Athenæum. **736**

HIGHER THAN THE CHURCH [by W.. (BIRCH) v. HILLERN: *Gottesberger*,

1882.] "Hans loves Marie Ruppacher, but Marie's father despises an 'artist' and will not listen to his suit. At last, however, the stern parent consents, but only on the condition that Hans shall carve a new altar which shall be 'hier than the church.' Hans sets to work, and ingeniously crowns the new altar with an overbending mass of carved foliage, whose central branch touches the roof of the choir. 'Mr. Ruppacher', he calmly says, when his work is done, 'look above you, the altar here is exactly one foot hier than the church, and yet it stands within it. I have merely bent the top'. And so Hans wins his bride. The story is simply and sweetly told." [Boston "Literary World." **737**

HOHENSTEINS (The). [by F: SPIELHAGEN: *Leypoldt*, 1870.] "The story opens in the spring of 1848; and deals with 3 generations of the Hohenstein family then living, and variously affecting and affected by the political and revolutionary activity of that year and the following one... Munzer, an ardent patriot, and a revolutionary politician, is the real hero of the book, and is powerfully drawn... In the Hohenstein family, we have the usual rich and despotic head of the family, the usual interested and scheming heirs, and the female villain, who is rather a special possession of german novelists, but who in this instance is unusually genuine and coherent, tho decidedly improper; we have the good young man who is poor and wearisome, with the profligate favorites of fortune, his cousins—in short the usual dramatis personæ; but the life of the book is the incubation, the bursting forth and the collapse of a political movement, and here Spielhagen has been a true artist, and has focussed the lit on Munzer's figure. This man, variously gifted, influential, beloved, and sincere, whom we see first as the centre of a great and hopeful activity, we follow throu the tragic mistakes and failures of his life to its close (which, by the way, is the best managed thing in the book), and forgive him his long speeches for the sake of the earnestness in him." [Nation. **738**

HOMOSELLE [by M.. SPEAR (NICHO-LAS) TIERNAN: *Osgood*, 1881.] "is a charming addition to Southern literature. Dealing with life on the James River under the old régime, it is written with a tact and delicacy and cleverness which leave the fact of the author's Southern sympathies to be surmised merely from the abundance of local color . . . The conversation of the story, even to the love-making, is brít and pithy." [Critic. **739**

HONOR; or, The Slave Driver's Daughter. [by STEPHEN G. BULFINCH: *Spencer*, 1864.] "In this interesting volume, the sufferings and injustices caused by slavery find a vivid and yet a fair portraiture. There is no passion or partisanship in the colors; no extravagance or special pleading in the representation. Nor is there a single attempt at 'fine writing'. The plot is well-conceived and well brôt out. The interest deepens, with properly accumulating effect, to the close. Iu the development of character there is variety, united with distinct characterization, and a fine exhibition not only of the loftier and more delicate sense of 'honor' but of christian principle. We heartily wish this graceful work of an accomplished New England writer mit take the place of much of the heated, turgid, and tawdy composition which runs throu so many modern novels." [Church-Monthly. **740**

HOUR WILL COME (The). ["Und Sie kommt, doch!") by W.. (BIRCH) VON HILLERN: *Tauchnitz*, — *Gottesberger*, 1881.] "Historical in the sense that its scene is laid in a period 500 years back, is this 'Tale of an Alpine Cloister.' In truth, however, it belongs to no particular period or place, but it is one of those intense stories of passion and suffering, of sin and its expiation, which represent nothing which could have happened anywhere at any time, but which shake the soul and fire the imagination. Such a story has almost nothing in common with the modern novel, which aims to give a realistic and recognizable picture of life: its scale of portraiture is gigantesque, its characters are demigods or demons, the

emotions which it depicts are superbuman in their intensity, and its situations conform not to the probable or the possible, but to the dramatic unity of the author's conception." [Appleton's Jour. **741**

HOUSE OF PENARVAN (The). [by JULES SANDEAU: with "Notary's Daughter," by L. D'Aulney, *Bentley*, 1878.] "The picture of Renée de Penarvan, last of her race, burying her youth and beauty for years in the joint composition of a history of her house—her collaborator being a most admirably original copy [if the oxymoron be allowable] of Dominie Sampson—waking up to real life when she finds that there is still a Penarvan alive and in danger of the 2 unpardonable sins of liberalism and a mésalliance, captivating and marying him almost against his will, forcing him into the ranks of the Chouans, where he meets his death, bringing up her dauter, to whom she never forgives her sex, in stern seclusion, turning her off at once for marrying a bourgeois, and only at last melted into humanity by her grandchild, is in many ways an admirable one. . . . If 'La Maison de Penarvan' and its fellows are not acceptable to every mood of every mind, that is a drawback which they share with a good deal of literature. It may perhaps require a little time to adjust the eye to the subdued atmosfere of a region 'where the world is quiet', where there is passion enuf, but passion which rarely tears itself to tatters, and cán live, and sometimes die, without shrieking and attitudinising. But when the eye gets its focus it is apt to return to the spectacle, and to be greatly refreshed and delíted thereby. To use once more in an altered and happier form words which were applied to Mr. Sandeau by a greater than he in days long gone by. 'Quand on l'aura trouvé, on saura le garder'." [Saintsbury. **742**

——, SAME, in "Lilies of the Valley", *Tauchnitz*, 1879.

HOUSE OF THE SEVEN GABLES (The). [by NATHANIEL HAWTHORNE: *Tícknor*, 1851.] "While the story is regularly convergent to a dénoument, after

the manner of the novel proper, it is at the same time a perfect picture-gallery of scene and character. It is a most successful attempt to connect a bygone time with the very present that is flitting away from us. It is a legend, prolonging itself from an epoch now gray in the distance, down into our own broad day-lit, and bringing along with it some of its legendary mist; and the story has its moral, moreover, for it illustrates the truth that the wrong-doing of one generation lives into the successive ones, and divesting itself of every temporary advantage, becomes a pure and uncontrollable mischief... The sketch of the progress and final completion of the seven-gabled edifice is admirably artistic; and the weird picture of its founder, found dead in his apartment on the day of his 'house-warming' is worthy of the pen of Scott." [Knickerbocker.]—...
"The scene, which is laid in the old Puritanic town of Salem, extends from the period of the witchcraft excitement to the present time, connecting the legends of the ancient superstition with the recent marvels of animal magnetism; and affording full scope for the indulgence of the most weird and sombre fancies. Destitute of the hily-wrôt manifestations of passion which distinguished the 'Scarlet Letter,' it is more terrific in its conception, and not less intense in its execution, but exquisitely relieved by charming portraitures of character, and quaint and comic descriptions of social eccentricities." [Harper's. **743**

HOUSE ON THE MOOR (The) [by M. O. (W.) OLIPHANT: *Hurst*, 1860.] "is very interesting, and the interest deepens as the story proceeds. In the first volume the germ of hate, and the morbid brooding over a long past injury, are seen beginning their deadly growth. There is a quiet tragic power in the picture of the lonely house, the joyless fire-side, the unloving household, which is better than anything we remember by the same author." [Athenæum. **744**

HOUSEHOLD OF BOUVERIE [1860], see *CARDINAL'S DAUGHTER.*

HOW HE DID IT. [by E. A.. DUPUY: *Peterson*, 1871.] "Miss Dupuy is a southern lady who writes novels, in which there is a curious combination of all the faults and weaknesses which can well be contained in a work of fiction. 'How He Did It' may be taken as a fair sample of her skill as a novelist. Its plot is preposterous, its incidents absurd, its characters impossible, and its style utterly wretched. There may have been weaker novels written; but if so, we have never had the misfortune to meet them." [Citizen. **745**

HUGUENOT EXILES, see *ALL FOR LOVE.*

HUNCHBACK OF NOTRE DAME [*Bentley*, 1843; N.-Y., *Dick*, 1862] = *NOTRE DAME.*

IF, YES, AND PERHAPS. [by EDWARD E. HALE: *Ticknor*, 1868.] "So to write a fictitious narrative that you shall deceive even the very elect; to invent out of whole cloth a story which shall actually beguile numberless cool, sensible people, into fully believing every word you say—this requires such genius as few men besides Mr. Hale possess... It is not merely truthfulness to nature which marks Mr. Hale's works; that is too tame an expression; he absolutely takes you out of the domain of fancy, and compels you to believe that you are not only reading a record of what actually occurred, but a part of which you saw, or heard of, or read at the time; said point of time being, of course, years ago, but not so far off that your memory does not hold some trace of the story. You read more famous works of fiction than Mr. Hale's, with the flattering comment of 'How true to life this is!' But you read '*The Man without a Country*,' and '*My Double*,' with the feeling that this is life itself; it is a leaf out of the writer's own experience, and you enjoy being the first to whom he has confided the story. To cheat the sense into an involuntary belief that the imaginary persons were realities, and their haps and mishaps were actual occurrences —that is the audacity of genius... Nor is this peculiar charm of reality all which the author of these unpretending tales brings to his work. A wholesome lesson —not too prominent—points every tale, and throu the whole there gleams a thread of quaint humor which reminds one of some of the older english writers... There are 11 sketches or stories in the *book*, every one of which is good, and none containing a dull line." [Overland. **746**

IMMENSEE. [by TH. [WOLDSEN] STORM: Phil'a, *Leypoldt*, 1864.] "This little story is perhaps unrivalled in german fiction for its extreme simplicity and pathos. It opens with a sketch of an old man, in one of the quiet towns of the Rheinland, returning from his walk at the close of an autump day to his comfortable library, full of the books and pictures in the midst of which he had dwelt so long, and where, in the gathering darkness, he sits now to muse and to rest. And presently a moon-beam falls across the portrait of a well-remembered face, and he murmers 'Elizabeth' and dreams of the long-gone years,—of his merry childhood and happy home. The story which follows of the 2 children Reinhardt and Elizabeth,—how they grew up together, and strolled in the meadows, and were lost in the forest together,—is so very brief, and the event which parts them so very common, that one would be wholly at a loss to understand the fascination of the narrative from the mere statement of its incidents. While Reinhardt is absent at the university, Elizabeth is maried to another,—to his friend Eric, a very worthy person, preferred, of course, by the young lady's mother. Several years afterwards Reinhardt visits them; then suddenly tears himself away, and never sees again the child he had loved in his youth, or the maiden he loves still in age, but, buried in books, he masters his grief, and forgets the world. And there is as little in the thôt as in the style to make the story remarkable. The effect of it is rather in that touch of beauty and of sadness which we recognize in the conception of a life blited thus at the beginning, —in the mere suggestion of the void so

utter and so hopeless which is left for a time in every human heart by the disappointment of its early hope,—still more by the severing, as it were, of two beings so closely united in the memories of childhood that they seem to have been but the two-fold expression of a single life. It is a poem exquisite rather for what it suggests than for what it says. Like the faint murmur of music as it steals throu the leafy forests of a summer's day, it touches you in the dreamy stillness, not with a sense of its own melody, but of the ineffable sadness of the emotions it awakens. Life seems to grow stiller as you read. There is no tumult of the streets in it, no excitement of business, no struggle of ambition, no bitterness of hatred, nothing of the wrath of the world, as, with the noise of great rivers rushing on to the sea, it storms throu the congregations of men,—but only subdued voices and shadowy forms,—only the ghost of a buried hope, and the dismay of a vacant life. It unfolds no filosofical vue of love, analyzes none of its elements, determines none of its conditions. Yet the very sorrow it suggests so briefly and so simply is more eloquent than the best efforts of reasoning or of rhetoric." [Christian Examiner. **747**

IN HIS NAME. [by E: E. HALE: *Roberts*, 1871.] "The Rev. E. E. Hale's Waldensian story, 'In His Name,' is the best thing he ever wrote, and one of the best things ever written by anybody—a sweet and noble embodiment in romance of the truest christian life of the Middle Age, and truer christian life was never known." [Boston "Lit. World." **748**

IN OLE VIRGINIA. [by T: NELSON PAGE: *Scribner*, 1887.] "Collectively, Mr. Page's tales form an epic, historical and tragic. After reading them we see one figure with the certainty and distinctness of actual vision. Called by no matter what name, that figure is always the same —a young man, exquisitely fine of nature, gentle, chivalrous, hot-blooded, at once the pink of courtesy, courage incarnate, and honor's self. He can think no evil, much less do it. Born to lordship, his life-path cut strait throu gardens of roses that never fade. Almost before he comes to his own, his princedom is but an empty name; the roses are all thorns, he falls before the cannon's mouth, his dead fingers twined about his so-called country's flag. ' That is the beautiful figure by which, be it true to life or false, a capable story-teller has chosen to perpetuate the south which fôt and died. That is the figure which vivifies all the incidents, serious, melodramatic, and comic, and illumines every picture of family and plantation life. Mr. Page, like all who are notable in the rising host of southern writers of fiction, does not recite the epic impersonally as an outside observer, nor does he put it in the mouth of a survivor of the ruling class. The glory of the master is told by the lips and in the language of the slave. There is nothing more curious or interesting in this creative literature of the New South than the apparently spontaneous and almost uniform choice of the negro and his dialect as the mediums best fitted to lay bare the heart of the Old South. The obvious reasons for the selection, such as greater opportunities afforded by it for picturesqueness, for novelty, and for eccentric humor, are not sufficient wholly to account for it. Nor is it convincing to remark flippantly that all the gentlemen perished in the war, or to attribute to the authors a desire to correct a widespread belief in the horrors of the past conditions of servitude. The selection is not deliberate and calculated, but rather a strange general impulse, in obeying which probably not one of the authors perceived any singular significance. The thorogoing abolitionist may discover here the hand of fate, retributive and compensatory. The tradition of splendor and supreme distinction is handed down by those upon whose labor they were founded, and for whose sake they were annihilated . . . The only example in the volume of a character not drawn in dialect, yet full of life and free, is that of the Colonel in "Polly." The author has so thoroly imagined the hard-

drinking, hard-riding, freely profane old planter, that the words exactly descriptive come to him with perfect ease and naturalness." [Nation.   **749**

IN THE CARQUINEZ WOODS. [by [Fr.] Bret Harte: *Houghton*, 1888.] "is artistically perfect. The great forest takes possession of the imagination from the first, with its dim reaches, its many-voiced silences, its illimitable vastness, and makes a background against which the feverish human drama which invades it for a moment, and is swallowed in its destiny, impresses one with an effect of tragedy and pathos. The mysterious sounds and fantastic shadows of the gloom, the bear's dance, the strange torch-lited party, with its hideous interruption of the solitude, are excellently done. And at last the splendor and terror of the woods on fire, the stampede of the wild beasts, and the end of Teresa and Low, are described with both beauty and force. . . . 'In the Carquinez Woods' is a book to charm and move any reader." [Lippincott's.   **750**

IN THE ENEMY'S COUNTRY. [by Anna H. Drury: London, *Griffith*, 1891.] "We need not say much more in praise of this volume than that it takes for its subject much the same theme as that treated by Erckmann-Chatrian in their stories, and that it does not suffer from the comparison which is thus suggested. It is described on the title page as 'A Story of 1813,' and the scene is chiefly laid in the little town of Stenbrück, the hero and heroine being a young Parisian and the dauter of an english doctor. The bête noir of the tale is a Jew usurer, who makes himself generally odious. The story will well repay perusal." [Spectator.   **751**

INCURABLE. [by Paul Heyse: *Nutt*, 1890.] "The heroine is a hi-spirited girl, who has been sent to **Meran** for her health, and believes herself to be dying. At the same place there is an equally hi-spirited young man, who is also supposed to be on the verge of the grave. How they meet one another, and what comes of their discussions about life and death, the

223

heroine records in her diary, throu which alone the tale is told. The materials are rather slit, but the author displays his usual mastery of the principles of construction, and his striking power of revealing the essence of character without direct description. Altho less interesting than some of Heyse's more famous writings, the story gives a good idea of his method, and it is admirably translated." [Athenæum. **752**

INDIANA [by G: SAND: *Peterson*, 1850.] "may be said to be the first of her independent works, and it shows the first bloom of that freshness which never deserted her; yet it was written by a mature woman who had experienced, or suffered, or imagined she had suffered, all she expressed . . . Altho we dislike launching out in language which may pass for an affected imitation of the French, 'Indiana' was veritably the cry of a soul in anguish—the outbreak of an overstrung nature which finds relief in lamenting and denouncing its wrongs. Even when she is most morbid in her exaltation, when her hi-flown sentiments seem most false to common-sense and sound principles, there is an unmistakable air of conviction in them which persuades you of her earnestness. You feel you are being carried off your legs in spite of your better judgment. You cannot withhold your sympathy, altho you would fain invoke your convictions to help you to harden your heart . . . Indiana is nothing but sentiment and passion; altho of a more refined nature, and somewhat more hily educated, she is as little self-governed, and fully as capable of follies, as the unhappy Noun, her warm-blooded foster-sister. Like one of the volcanoes of her tropical latitudes, repressed emotions in subdued ebullitions have been wearing her fragile frame and wasting her delicate charms. She has a boundless yearning for sympathy and tenderness, and from her girlhood she has been accumulating treasures of love, which she sis for an opportunity of lavishing . . . Bred in the seclusion of a southern island, peopled by slaves and money-making

slaveholders, the chances of such a miracle are overwhelmingly against her. Her imaginative nature is altogether antagonistic to the interested motives of a hily practical society; she is inevitably predestined to point a moral as to the cruelty of those indissoluble marriages of 'convenance'. . . There is not a suggestion of grossness, or coarseness, and delicate and even dangerous topics are handled in the least objectionable way." [Blackwood's.] "Anyone now taking up 'Indiana', for example, would perhaps find it not quite easy to understand how the book produced such an effect. Our novel-writing women of to-day commonly feed us on more fiery stuff than this. Not to speak of such accomplished artists in impurity as the lady who calls herself Ouida, and one or two others of the same school, we have young women just promoted from pantalettes, who can throw you off such glowing chapters of passion and young desire as would make the rhapsodies of 'Indiana' seem very feeble milk-and-water brewage by comparison. Indeed, except for some of the descriptions in the opening chapters, I fail to see any extraordinary merit in 'Indiana'; and towards the end it seems to me to grow verbose, weak, and tiresome." [Justin McCarthy, in 1870. **753**

IRENE. [by OLGA CANTACUZÈNE-ALTIERI: *Warne*, 1887.] "'This story reminds us of 'Ouida' in her sober moods. The Marquis Miraldi, a roué who has little character or fortune left to him, maries, much against his will, a greek girl whom he has abducted. Her father has outwitted him. He leaves her for years at a ruined castle, which is the only fragment left of his hereditary possessions. There, under the old curé, she grows into an accomplished woman. The reader will, of course, guess the result. The Marquis falls in love with his wife, finds her, it seems, utterly indifferent to him, and torments himself with the fear that he has lost her love forever. The old curé, his nefew the artist (who, it may be supposed, entertains a hopeless passion for the deserted wife) and the Marquis' worldly mother, are described with great skill. 'Irene,' in short, is an interesting and wholesome story." [Spectator. **754**

ISHMAEL [by M.. E.. (BRADDON) MAXWELL: *Maxwell*, 1884.] "must take a place as one of the most remarkable of "Miss Braddon's" works. In it she has given a vivid picture of Paris under the Second Empire from its beginning to 1868. The extent of her intimate knowledge of every sort of detail of the period is really surprising, and it is hardly necessary to say that it is worked into her story with consummate skill. In passing touches she has admirably hit off the characteristics of most of the chief historical figures of the period, and she has succeeded equally well with some more elaborate studies. If her industry is surprising the vigor of her description is no less so. Her account of the coup d'état is as exciting a bit of narrative as any novel-reader could wish for, and is as vivacious, as if it had been by an eye-witness. Her picture is all the more interesting because it has been her object to give a picture and not so much to point a moral. She vues the whole from various standpoints, and she is no more inclined to indulge in too wild a condemnation of the crimes and recklessness of the rule of Louis Napoleon than she is to be dazzled by its splendor." [Athenæum. **755**

ITALIAN (The). [by A.. (WARD) RADCLIFFE: 1797.] "There are terrible scenes scattered with profusion in almost every chapter, relieved by vivid descriptions of italian scenery. The adventures of Vivaldi among the ruins of Paluzzo, possess the blest interest,—and the terrific scenes on the sea-coast in the ruined tower, where Schedoni, as he is about murdering Ellena, discovers her to be his dauter, are painted in the deepest tragic style." [American Review. **756**

IVANHOE. [by WA. SCOTT.] "England, nominally in the time of Richard I., but the scenes are really a make-up of the manners of more than one period, and are among the most grandly picturesque which Scott has drawn. Saxon and Norman are seen in contrast; old forest, bar-

onial hall, and tented field." [Boston "Literary World."]—"I am still a reader of Scott, and never appreciated the qualities of "Ivanhoe" so completely as on reading that master-piece last year. Of all authors, it is Scott who has given me the greatest sum of pleasure, and that of a very healthy kind." [P. G. Hamerton. **757**

IZA'S STORY. [by "G.. Ramsey," i. e., KATHLEEN O'MEARA: *Hurst*, 1870.] "The author of 'Iza's Story' has chosen a theme which has absolute novelty to recommend it, and she handles it with much power and skill, and with an intimate knowledge which impresses itself at once upon the reader. The intimate home-life of the Poles, the relations between the hier and lower ranks, and characteristic peculiarities of their 'ways', are all unknown to us. The political miseries, the national disasters and sufferings of the Poles, have occupied our attention, and obtained our sympathy, but of the people, in the same sense as we understand other foreiners set in the framework of fiction, we really do not know anything. Miss Ramsey's novel therefore instructs while it interests, and presents many a strangely fascinating picture of a people richly endowed with noble and romantic qualities, and with that essential grandeur of soul and of manners, which was the ideal of the old chivalry. 'Iza's Story' is a powerful and melancholy love-tale, in which the chief actors are hi-born and patriotic Poles, pursued by the vengeance of the Russian government, and ultimately falling under its stern, irresistible power. Prince Kasimir, a great Lithuanian noble, and his castle of Ramslaw in Podolia; his daughter, the Princess Iza, and her friends and servants; the néboring grandees; the peasants, so intensely feudal in their loyalty and affection, so ardently religious, so utterly unlike the peasantry we are all familiar with, are deeply interesting. In telling the sad, touching, heroic, dramatic story of their lives, Miss Ramsey illustrates it by fresh and vivacious pictures of national customs, festivals, and sentiments totally foreiu to our notions. The author introduces her readers to some truly hi, noble, and lovable types of polish character. . . . Nor is her work wanting in that quality which renders characteristic illustration most striking and true,—the quality of humor." [Contemporary Rev. **758**

JACOB SCHUYLER'S MILLIONS [by T: DUNN ENGLISH: *Appleton,* 1885.] "is an anonymous novel, evidently is a new [!] hand, which deserves favorable notice for the freshness of its scene, and leading characterization. It is devoted to an elaboration of the old dutch dwellers on the **Hudson**, about the Hackensack. The Hudson has been pretty well exploited by the fictionists, but this curious range of country seems to have hitherto escaped. The present author knows his ground well, and the sketches of character and environment are not without value. The story itself is to our taste flavorless, altho it is very sensational. 'Jacob Schuyler' died without making a will, or he secreted it so effectually that the heirs could not find it. At all events there is a tremendous and exciting hunt for the missing document, and therefrom grow the numerous incidents which form the body of the book. It is clever in a way, and the interest is certainly well sustained." [American. **759**

JACK HORNER. [by MARY S. (N.) TIERNAN: *Houghton, Mifflin & Co.,*] "How favorable are the chances of war to young women who take a wrong turn in the early stages of love-making is shown in Mrs. Mary Tiernan's 'Jack Horner'. Boadicea Disney, the little Confederate Treasury clerk, who so imprudently falls in love with a War Office clerk as poor as herself, is first helped to a rich and generous tho rather antiquated husband, and then rid of him by means of a cold caut on picket duty. And Madeline Key comfortably loses one husband and misses another in order that she may join hands with the rit one, who meets her last. Life in the Capital of the Confederacy in the final year of the War is the staple of the tale. Skirmishes with 'those people' beyond the Potomac and with that other enemy, Poverty, who had long before captured Richmond, are its principal incidents, The astonishing fashions at a Government reception, and the still more astonishing refreshments served at Bo' Disney's 'Ephemeral' Saloon, the junketing parties to drink spring water, the story of the 'family plate', lodted in happier days from a Mexican church, are among the comic ones. Among the more romantic happenings are the search for a yankee spy, and the cannonading which Madeline and her escort undergo all nit in a deserted village. All this coil of love and war and mistakes by the dozen goes on about the cradle of the Christmas waif, Jack Horner, whose secret we prefer that the reader should find out for himself. We assure him that if he 'sticks in his thumb' in the book, he will find it a 'plum' of lit literature, and will be well content to 'sit in a corner' until he has devoured it." [Critic. **760**

JAN VEDDER'S WIFE [by AMELIA E. (H.) BARR: *Dodd,* 1885.] "is a story of the shetland norsemen, homely and simple, but full of picturesqueness and vigor. The situation is a common one—a cold, riteous wife, quite the pattern saint, yet full of the narrow pride and vanity of a small, self-centred nature, driving a sweet tempered, unstable husband to the inn, to the fishing, anywhere away from home and her conscious correctness. Whether or not the habits of life and thôt among an isolated people be truthfully described, the reader gets the impression of truth, which is the essential. The handsome ne'er-do-well's fenomenal rise in the british navy recalls the legends of the Reformed Pirate, while the final measure of bliss is improbably full' and divided with a too careful impartiality. But for the sake of little Jan's welcome home to his heroic father, splendid in gold lace and buttons, what is feeble and tame may be over-looked; and, indeed, it is somewhat captious to refer to defects in a book so unpretentious and attractive." [Nation. **761**

JANE EYRE [by C.. (BRONTE) NICHOLLS: *Smith,* 1847.] "is, to our mind, the best of the Brontë novels in point of interest and of literary execution: it has the best story to tell, and it tells it in the most condensed and effective manner. In spite of some defects of conception, Rochester's character is not impossible or improbable. He lays himself open, in a measure, to be burlesqued, after the amusing fashion of Mr. Bret Harte's Condensed Novels; his 'grimness' is a trifle over-emfasized, it must be confessed; yet he is a flesh and blood man as the heroes of other novels are not. We must grant, moreover, that the author was not responsible for the feeble and flashy imitations of this character in the stories of succeeding writers." [Boston "Literary World."] " 'While groping, amid these empirical studies, 'Jane Eyre' drew me from deep to deep. The passion of that book, at once burning and purifying, was not then for me, nor was the ethical question it raised; but the miracle it wrôt was for me. (I was as if yielded to a mystical realm canopied by a strange firmament, whose meteors and comets, however weird, I understood and beheld without fear. The fulfilled dreams and presentations, the cry of lovers, heard and answered across long leagues, the vampire wife, were provided for in nature's new apparatus not disclosed in my law-book." [M. D. Conway.] "I know no interest more thrilling than that which she has been able to throw into the characters of Rochester and the governess, in the 2d volume of 'Jane Eyre'. She lived with those characters, and felt in every fibre of the heart, the longings of the one and the sufferings of the other. And therefore, tho the end of the book is weak, and the beginning not very good, I venture to predict that 'Jane Eyre' will be read among english novels when many whose names are now better known shall have been forgotten. 'Jane Eyre' and 'Esmond' and 'Adam Bede' will be in the hands of our grandchildren, when 'Pickwick', and 'Pelham' and 'Harry Lorrequer' are forgotten; because the men and women depicted are human in their aspirations, human in

their sympathies, and human in their actions." [Anthony Trollope.] This novel "possesses the charm of style, culture, and a breadth of thôt to which 'Jane Eyre' cannot make the slitest pretense. We have always deemed 'Jane Eyre' greatly overrated. It was a publisher's success, just as 'Romola' was a publisher's failure. Yet no one would dream of comparing the 2 novels. The success of 'Jane Eyre' was undoubtedly owing to its sensational scenes. The artist rejects the very passages which made the fortune of that tale. They offend against the first principles of art. The want of knowledge of the world and an absence of true character, as opposed to mere characterization offend even less critical readers." [Westminster Review. 762

JANUS. [by E: I, STEVENSON: Belford, 1889.] "We will not sketch the plot, which is one of character working throu incident, rather than of incident revealing character, except to say that the leading person, a young musical genius, is awakened temporarily to a sense of the power which exists in pure love, only to fall back and have his life blackened by the insidious encroachment on his nature of the power of evil resident in a false woman and responded to by his weakness. There is a little stiffness in some of the drawing, as in the case of Alexis, and not enuf is made of Johann Steins; but the book must be taken as a sketch, and with the limitations of a sketch conceded it is a strong piece of work. The mutations of Moritz Reisse's nature are not only truthful, they are portrayed with naturalness and without too much recourse to comment by the author. Nadine, the temptress, is well-conceived and consistent; the only fault one can find is rather a grave one, to be sure. The reader is scarcely bewitched by her, and has to take her power over Moritz too much on faith; but the depth of her intrigue is made very distinct; she is thôroly explained, and explained by the course of the story. We are especially pleased by the reserve which the author shows in dealing with the more specifically musical parts of the book. We are so accustomed to a moony treatment of **music** and musicians in fiction that it is a relief to find the subject used as an art, and not as a sentiment." [Atlantic. **763**

JESS. [by H: R. HAGGARD: *Smith*, 1887.] " 'King Solomon's Mines' deals with the marvelous, the incredible, we may say the impossible. 'Jess' deals with real life; nothing is narrated which mit not be strictly, literally true. It is the study of a strange and fascinating being, a story of noble love and devotion, not shrinking from crime and daring to face death. The tone of the book is decidedly sad; the central idea is that of an immense sacrifice, the background is the shame and dishonor of England. . . . Jess Croft and her sister Bessie are orfans and live with their uncle, Silas Croft, an englishman who has farmed in the Transvaal for 50 years. Bessie is the younger, a lovely, happy maid, untroubled by thôt; Jess, 3 years her sister's senior, is by no means an ordinary person. She is small, slit, and pale, with marvelous dark eyes, and an immense latent capacity for romantic love and devotion. . . We will not anticipate and deprive our readers of the harrowing pleasure of reading the story, told in Mr. Haggard's most striking manner, of how Jess laid down more than her life for her lover and her sister." [Athenæum. **764**

JEWS OF BARNOW (The) [by K: EMIL FRANZOS: *Appleton*, 1883.] "we recommend to all who seek in works of fiction, not the gratification of a passing moment, but that which alone gives real and permanent value, viz.: the artistic reproduction of life. The scene is laid in a Vodolian ghetto, and the personages are at first sit as unprepossessing—nay, repellant—as polish **Jews** are apt to be in reality. But a master-hand is revealed in the art wherewith we are subtly forced to recognize the humanity underlying these grotesque and uncouth externals, and to sympathize with human passion, suffering, and endurance in this outlandish environment. The sketches are all subdued and low in tone, and offer no sensational points; but

the author is a born story-teller, who never allows our interest to flag, and who displays genuine dramatic force in his handling of characters and situations." [Critic. **765**

JOHN BODEWIN'S TESTIMONY [by M.. [ANNA] (HALLOCK) FOOTE; *Ticknor*, 1886.] "well sustains the reputation won by the author. The story is one of a Western [U. S.] mining district where the rit of ownership in a lucrative mine is in litigation, and J: Bodewin is the witness on whose evidence the issue of the suit virtually turns. He has strong reasons for unwillingness to testify; and the merit of the story consists in the play of motives which sway him in contrary directions, and in the skillful adaption of the incidents of the tale to exhibit their working, as also the results which follow his final decision. There is less of directly local coloring and dialect than is usual in american stories dealing with the classes here represented; and the reader is to expect his satisfaction to arise from carefully drawn types of character, and dramatic fitness of detail—in which event he will not be disappointed." [Academy. **766**

JOHN INGLESANT [by J: H: SHORTHOUSE: *Macmillan*, 1882.] "will be one of the memorable books of the year. The author terms it—dreading, perhaps, to hear it called an historical novel—a filosofic romance; but whether considered as filosofy or as romance, it is alike remarkable. As filosofy, it is a wonderfully clear exposition not only of the catholic church, but of the differences of belief in a church which professes that it can have no difference of belief, as a romance it is thrillingly interesting; and as history, it illuminates the time in which the scene is laid —that of Charles I.—as fine acting illuminates a play of Shakspere. The author's power as a story-teller is shown in his tacitly saying to the reader, 'My hero is weak; but I defy you to despise him.' The hero is, indeed, the tool of a Jesuit, but so noble a tool that we forgive him for being one; he loves a woman not by any means above the average, but because he is true to her, we respect his marriage; and he is willing to die with a lie which disgraces him on his lips, that the lie may save the honor of a king whom he does not greatly love, and serve the purpose of a religious party to which he does not openly belong. ... It will be seen that the book is not one to be read litly. In style, it is admirable. Neither the interest of the story, the clearness of the theology, nor the vividness of the history owe anything to sensational event or to excited rhetoric; but the reader is held from the very preface by the power of expression which is neither the eloquence of Macaulay's New Zealander, nor the rhetoric of Ruskin, nor the jewelled fervor of Lothair; it is the calm, almost stately utterance of things which yet moves one strongly with a sense of color. Perhaps the difference is that the brilliancy of Macaulay, Ruskin, and Disraeli is a fictitious glow cast over common subjects; while that of the author of 'John Inglesant' is the splendor of a brilliant subject treated with very simple language." [Critic. **767**

JOSEPH NOIREL'S REVENGE. [by V: CHERBULIEZ: *Holt*, 1873.] "The action, which at the outset promised to be lit and amusing, with merely so much of tenderness and pathos as may belong to the hier comedy, becomes by degrees deeply tragical, and ends in a catastrofe which is saved from being horrible and revolting only by the shadows which forecast and the softening strains which attend it. In point of construction and skillful handling the story is as effective as french art alone could have made it. .. Marguerite Mirion is invested with all the fascination which beauty of face, simplicity of mind, purity of soul, sweetness of disposition and joyousness of spirit can impart. .. It is in simple obedience to the will of her parents that she marries Count Roger d'Ornis, and is carried from her happy home at Mon-Plaisir to a dilapidated castle in the Jura, where there are no smiling faces or loving hearts to make her welcome—where, on the contrary, she meets only hauty, spiteful or morose looks and a chilling and

gloomy atmosfere. It is Marguerite alone who, in the terrible struggle of fate, and of clashing interests and desires, rises to the hit of absolute self-abnegation; and this not throu any sudden development of qualities or intuitions forein to her previous modes of thôt, but by the simple application of these to the hard and complicated problems which have suddenly confronted her." [Lippincott's. **768**

JOURNAL OF A SUPERFLUOUS MAN. [with *MUMU*, by IVAN [S.] TURGENIEF: N. Y.,*Funk*,1884.] "These 2 stories are unquestionably to be ranked among the author's masterpieces. Their incomparable power has a spontaneity and impressiveness akin to that of nature herself." [Boston "Literary World".] "The 'Diary' is less interesting than most of Turgenief's work, but its theme is a good one. the sufferings of a class which exists in some form in all countries, aristocrats by birth or official station, to whom "noblesse oblige" means that they must not earn their living by such means as are used by the lower classes. while utterly unprovided for the position where they find themselves." [Critic. **769**

JUDGMENT OF GOD (A). ["Ein Gottesurteil") by "E. WERNER," i. e., E.. Bürstenbinder: *Munro*, 1889.] "Danira and her brother have been captured by the austrian commandant [in **Dalmatia**] as orfan children, and whilst the boy is retaken by his insurgent kinsfolk, the girl remains at the castle to share the education of the soldier's dauter Edith. Gerald, the betrothed of Edith, arrives, and Edith finds herself of less value than his soldierly ambition, whilst Gerald's arrival accelerates matters, and Danira escapes to rejoin her people. Against her tribe the aspiring young officer is sent. The two meet when he has been tempted into danger by the stratagem of the insurgent chief. Danira can save Gerald only by showing him the wild sanctuary of the rocks where no blood may be spilt: 'The Wilaquell endures nor blood nor vengeance.' The insurgent chief dares the protecting spirit of the

'Wilaquell," and—a "judgment of God"—his life is the penalty. The scenes in which love and pride of race on both sides struggle for mastery, are well given." Spectator. **770**

——, SAME ("Danira"), Chicago, *Rand,* 1888.

KATE KENNEDY [by—( ) NEWBY: *Newby,* 1865.] "The heroine is a beautiful orfan, whose father has left her an enormous fortune on condition that she marries a young nobleman, Lord Werter. If, however, she refuses the alliance, the money is to go to a charity. Such a will mit be supposed to place the young people in a great difficulty; but fortunately Kate has no heart (or rather thinks she has none), and frankly accepts Lord Werter by letter before she has ever seen him. Thus all seems to be comfortably arranged; but a certain young hero comes in the way, who, tho much despised at first (being only a young surgeon), obtains Kate's affection by degrees, and convinces her that it is better to be Mrs. Smith than to wear a coronet. Of course, Kate has to write to the Earl and explain the altered state of affairs. Instead of threatening her with an action at law, he behaves like a true gentleman, and is willing to release her; but he still cherishes a hope of being able to secure her, and entreats her to meet him in the midst of his noble relatives at Werter Hall on the 10th proximo, and then and there formally accept or reject him. The arrangement is not so inconvenient as mit be supposed, since she has promised to be married to Mr. Smith on that day, and it is agreed that they shall go up to the Hall together, settle the little affair with the earl, and then proceed with their more important business. The great day arrives, and Kate, blushing in her bridal robes, gives her hand to the earl, but only in frendship and gratitude, for it is about to be bestowed for life on another. The disappointed nobleman behaves with dignity and propriety, but implores her to look him once in the face before leaving him forever; and then, what is her surprise to see that the earl and Mr. Smith

are identical! The extreme improbability of this plot is compensated to a great extent by the care with which it is worked out, and the interest which we are made to take in Earl Smith's chivalrous experiment." [Athenæum. **771**

KATHERINE AND THE MOMENT OF FORTUNE. [by F: W: HACKLANDER: *Bentley,* 1856.] "Most of the personages who figure in the tale belong to the humbler ranks of life; the heroine herself, the cherry-lipped, black-eyed, black-haired, oval-faced, graceful Katherine is a flower-seller, and dauter of a washerwoman; but there is another beauty, Rosa by name, concerning whose relations to the 'moment of fortune' the reader soon learns to be curious. The latter part of the history introduces these persons into a court atmosfere with a regent as the centre-piece, and barons and ladies revolving about them in vicious, glittering circles. The episodes and groupings are skillfully contrived, and suggest the idea that the writer is copying from living models. We have found 'Katherine' an uncommon and interesting novel—quite a contrast, in its spirit and simplicity, to the vapid 3 volumes composed of half-sentences in false french and of hysterical english which are announced as 'now ready' for ever." [Leader. **772**

KING OF THE MOUNTAINS (The). [by EDMOND [FR. VALENTIN] ABOUT: Boston, *Tilton,* 1860.] "The story is supposed to be told by a young german botanist. He proceeds to Greece with the purpose of herbalizing in the mountains. Carried away by a scientific enthusiasm, he becomes the prisoner of a remarkable brigand, Hadgi-Stavros, the 'King of the Mountains.' He is not alone in his captivity. An english lady and her dauter—the former a striking portrait of a class of weak and consequential tourists, and the latter a thing to be admired and loved by any german, or any american, for that matter, under the circumstances supposed—are the hero's fellow-prisoners. The greater part of the book is taken with a description of the character, positions, re-

230

sources, habits and influences of the brigand chief; the temporary captivity of the party, who are made prisoners for the sake of a large ransom." [Knickerbocker.] "As 'Tolla' was the roman question dramatized, so is the 'King of the mountains,' the greek question dramatized. Neither of these semi-political novels seem to us so sweet, so far-reaching as Germaine; but the present one in wit, in humor, in admirable character-sketching, is unequalled by any other work of the author's, unless it be the novelette, 'Trente et Quarante'. If ever there was a mirror held up to english and american humanity it is that now wrôt of the mingled glass and quicksilver which enter so largely into this witty frenchman." [Dial. 773

KINGS IN EXILE. [by ALPHONSE DAUDET: tr. Clavequin, *Tinsley*, 1880.] "In this story is shown the degradation of a king, of Illyria, we are told, who having been driven from his throne by a revolution, takes refuge in Paris until such time as his people shall have grown tired of governing themselves. This King Christian II. is an easy-going pleasure-loving young fellow, without enthusiasm, caring only for enjoyment, who much prefers the easy joys he finds in Paris to the cares of ruling a remote kingdom. His wife is a very different person. She has the most earnest desire to see her husband, or their young son, on the throne of his ancestors. She believes fully in the divine rit of kings, and she chafes under exile. She is wholly indifferent to her husband, except as the possible filler of a throne, and her life is spent, not in forgiving, so much as in trying to hide and condone, his many villainies ... Without sermonizing, without contempt for the poor king, Daudet has written what is a serious defense of uprit conduct, simply by showing a weak, vicious man, and the consequences of his faults ... As to the way in which the characters are drawn, too much cannot be said in praise. They are all set vividly before us by their position, while the pathetic story is one that is every day repeated before our eyes in other circles of

society. But a king who is worthless seems more worthless than, say, a worthless coal-heaver, and a woman like this queen, who 'incedit regina,' adorned with every virtue, wins our sympathy at once from the contrast between her hi estate, even when in exile, and her heart-breaking sufferings. She endures everything with a proud patience which sets in a more shameful lit her paltry husband's misdceds, aad she suffers doubly, as an outraged wife 'and as a betrayed queen. It is this exalted setting which gives the book its really poetical flavor; what would have been touching under any circumstances is only the more touching on account of the magnitude of the interests involved, and the book is a real contemporary tragedy." [Atlantic.]—"Daudet describes the life of the Prince of Orange ("Axel") under a disguise so thin as to be none at all. At the same time he has worked with an idea; the idea was fresh; he has taken pains, and the result is a novel of much power, containing several character which may live as types." [Athenæum.] "The charm of the book, for it has charm, we need hardly say, as well as repulsiveness, lies in the tenderness with which royalty is treated throuoût. Even such a character as Christian II. hardly makes his painter cynical, and the pathetic beauty of heroism and devotion in Frédérique, in Élysie Méraut, in the old duke of Rosen, even in his unfortunate son Herbert—all sacrificing life, love, honor, fortune, to that crown of Illyria from which the king has had the precious stones pried out to pay his scandalous debts—makes a picture of fallen royalty hardly to be surpassed. The portrait of the little prince, too, is touched by genius; the child, the last of a worn-out race, yet the one hope of his mother and her friends; a little flame of life shooting up in him when his father has abdicated in his favor, as if in answer to his daily prayer that God would make him a good king; and then, throu a miserable accident from which his constitution has no strength to recover, the loss of sit, health, courage, hope, all but the love of the mother whose pride and ambition have till now been as strong as her love. Among the children of history and fiction we hardly know a more exquisitely painted figure than this little Leopold of Illyria." [Spectator.] The king and queen are the ex-king and queen of Naples; the duke of Palma is Don Carlos, the queen of Galicia is Isabella II.. Don Léonce is Alfonso XII., the king of Westphalia is Georg V. of Hannover. 774

——, SAME, Boston, *Lee*, 1880.

——. SAME, Chicago, *Rand*, 1890.

——, SAME, transl. by ENSOR, *Routledge*, 1890.

KING'S TALISMAN (The) or the young Lion of Mount Hòr. [by SYLVANUS COBB JR., BOSTON, *Elliot*, 1865.] "The mere sale of a book is deceptive. Before you decide upon its probable character or claims, ascertain who buys it. Fame is not conferred by the number of copies sold, nor by the multitude of readers, but by the quality of those who read. "The London Journal" sells 300,000 copies every week. But it never made a fame. Mr. PIERCE EGAN is its chief writer. He ôt to be a rich man, if he gets his share. But he is certainly not famous. His stories are probably read by 10 times as many people as Thackeray's or Dickens', but they are not a part of english literature. So with Mr. Reynolds. . . Perhaps you have commiserated the unhappy drudge who was compelled to scribble endless stories of nothing for a scanty living. . . Spare your sorrow, then. The income of the worthy REYNOLDS, whose name you will find in no Cyclopedia of Literature, is $70,000. Now the exact conditions of this success are incalculable. To call stories trashy does not explain it, for thêre are plenty of trashy stories which are not in the least popular. Thêre is an american writer who has a large english audience. Probably all the works of all american authors together are not so widely read as those of Mr. SYLVANUS COBB, who is not known exactly as 'an american author', altho we are all

familiar with his name. If Mr. Cobb's worldly fortune bear any proportion to the fortune of his writings in finding readers, and we hope they do, he is a very comfortable citizen. Now there are printed every week and every month stories which are apparently no better and no worse than his, whose difference from his it would be difficult to describe or to perceive, and yet they have no particular success, and the editor of the Ledger would not probably care to pay very large sums for them. Yet you may enumerate all the conditions of a fine novel. and perhaps not find Mr. Cobb's to conform in a single point. And you may lay down all the requirements of popular success, and still be unable to say why Mr. Corn does not succeed and Mr. Cobb does." [G: W: Curtis. 775

LADDER OF LIFE (The) [by AMELIA BLANDFORD EDWARDS: *Routledge*, 1857.] "is an uncommonly spasmodic production. Miss Edwards belongs to the startling school, which rises above sense and grammer. Her pages coruscate with fosforic figures of speech, miraculously brilliant eyes, litning glances, strange fire, blue-branching veins streaking pale brows under piles of rich glossy hair. Miss Edwards seems to have been infected with wide-wide-worldism." [Leader. 776

LADY AUDLEY'S SECRET [by M.. E .. (BRADDON) MAXWELL, 1858.] "The perversities of literary destiny are certainly strange. Miss Braddon is conducted by inscrutible fate to the novelist's desk, there to squander a forty-clerk power of persistent penmanship in turning romance into ridicule. She has little imagination, an indifferent taste, and no humor; yet she has written nearly 2 score of novels, which have been read by hundreds of thousands of readers, and the pages of which are unstained, as far as we are aware, by anything worse than sensationalism and vapidity." [Spectator. 777

LADY BELL [by "S.. TYTLER," i. e., Henrietta Keddie: *Strahan*, 1873.] "is a specimen of the semi-historical novel, and has a spice of freshness which will commend it to those who are weary of the uniformity of what passes among novelists for a picture of modern life. The pair of charming ladies whose history is sketched for our entertainment are cast in their early womanhood upon the times which witnessed the disruption of the american colonies, and just preceded the heroic era of the struggle with Bonaparte. . . Launched upon the world and on her own resources, she finds refuge first with the great actress, whom she worships with all the ardor of her simple but apprehensive nature; and next becomes companion to the most good-natured and stupid of educated country ladies, whose fatuous warm-heartedness is not the worst thing in the book. Her random reasoning about the inherent wickedness of uncles is uncommonly refreshing. Afterwards, when the wickedness of a different style of husband, the elegant roué of Chevely, drives Mrs. Sundon also forth upon the world, the two young exiles set up an elegant hermitage together, on the model of Lady Eleanor Butler and Miss Ponsonby, the once-famed ladies of Llangollen. This tranquil interval is but of short duration; and when the death of Trevor has freed the young widow of 18, she returns to the town, which was to her as to so many, the native heath on which alone real existence was attainable. In London she meets her fate, and Captain Fane is far from an ill-drawn portrait of an honest warrior. On the whole this is a graceful and readable story." [Athenæum. **778**

LADY RUSTIC, see *CAPTAIN'S DAUGHTER.*

LADY WITH THE RUBIES (The). [by "E. MARLITT," i. e., Eugenie John: *Lippincott*, 1885.] "A great rambling german house, with suites of disused apartments shut away from sunshine and air and haunted by vanished forms and silent voices, while its open rooms are tenanted by a nest of gentlefolk of all degrees of relation,—some united by love and others at swords' points,—offers a lively field for the romancer. 'Belief in the Powers of Darkness will never die so long as poor human hearts love, hope, and fear,' is the moral, so to speak, of the book; and the author has used with good effect this vein of superstition which 'makes the whole world kin.' Little Margarete's encounter with the family spectre, her flit from home, her lonely and terrifying nit, are touchingly described; and, in fact, the book is full of pretty child-pictures, which enhance the pleasantness and charm of the love-story." [Lippincott's. **779**

——, SAME, ("Lady with the Garnets") *Stock*, 1886.

LAJLA [by JENS ANDREAS FRIIS: *Putnam*, 1888.] "is an attractive tale of northern Norway and the Lapps. The human interest of the story is not without a primitive charm, but the raison d'être of the book is to be found in the descriptions of the nomadic life of the Lapps 100 years ago, their wanderings from mountain to coast and back again with the season's change, their meek acceptance of their position as a race inferior to the Norwegian, and their pathetic opposition, notwithstanding, to a merging of their language in that of the 'hauty Daro'. The reindeer plays a conspicuous part in the pages of Lajla, necessarily, since he is to the Lapp life, liberty, and currency; and one reads the tale with a bracing sense of driving the fleet animal over crisp snows litened by auroral flashes or by the midnit sun." [Nation. **780**

LAMPLIGHTER (The). [by MARIA SUSANNA CUMMINS: Boston, 1857.] "Whither are gone those stories which, a few years ago, could not be printed fast enuf,—'The Lamplighter', and the rest of that brood? They are hidden under the dust in the alcoves, or have been carted off to the pulp mills. Could mind of man have fancied an oblivion so swift for those favorites of the public? Could mortal tell have foretold its present fate for the 'Wide, Wide World'?—a story now quite dropped out of sit, but once the town's rage, and whose heroine I remember as a sort of inexhaustible human watering cart with the tear tap always turned on."

[Galaxy. 781
LAST ALDINI (The). [by G: SAND: *Churton*, 1847.] Here "principle is made to triumf over passion, but under circumstances which tempt the reader to regard it as Quixotism. Nello, the gondolier, loving and beloved, refuses to marry a beautiful woman of rank, lest he should injure the idol of his affections by lowering her position in society. This would be well if the idol were one to merit worship; but the first pages of the novel introduce us to the lady in question,— Biánca, as a person by no means careful of the world's opinion; and so weak, and frail and fickle, that when Nello breaks off the connexion, we commend his prudence rather than his virtue. The self-sacrifice intended to be portrayed assumes almost the form of self-interest." [Westminster.] "G: Sand has here recounted the adventures of a typical artist, an opera singer, who had the good fortune to win the affection of a countess, and also, 15 years afterward, to fascinate her daŭter, the last scion of a noble race; but who had the courage and wisdom to resist the advances of both ladies. On the other hand, the prosaic truth is sometimes told very plainly. The artist is occasionally represented as neither very fortunate nor very virtuous." [National Review.] "Take again that exquisite little story, 'La Dernière Aldini;' I do not know where one could find a finer illustration of the entire sacrifice of man's natural impulse, passion, interest, to what mit almost be called an abstract idea of honor and principle. I have never read this little story without wondering how many men one ever has known who, placed in the same situation as that of Nello, the hero, would have done the same thing, and yet so simply and naturally are the characters wrôt out the incidents described, that the idea of pompous, dramatic self-sacrifice never enters the mind of the reader, and it seems to him that Nello could not do otherwise than he is doing." [Justin McCarthy. 782
LAST OF THE MOHICANS (The),

see *LEATHER-STOCKING TALES.*
LAST ASSEMBLY BALL (The) [by M .. [ANNA] (HALLOCK) FOOTE: *Houghton*.) "is a close study in the inchoate society of Leadville, a typical mining city. Mrs. Foote looks deep into the apparent chaos, and shows the struggling forces which are at work to shape the social structure ... It is not a pleasant picture, it must be said, and the reader feeling its truth is the more thankful that the peculiar fäse it shows is a transient one; that altho this is a truly historical novel, it will, in a few years, be ancient history. The elements have been put into the flask and thŏroly shaken; soon they will adjust themselves, the chemical affinities will do their work and the laws of gravity fix the level of each individual. Then equilibrium, more or less stable, will be established, and the result of the process will be clear. But Mrs. Foote holds the flask before us just at the moment of mixing, while the chemical action is most fierce, the dregs stirred with the upper layers, and the whole compound indeterminate and cloudy. The social chemist may be able to gather some facts from observing the process, and so 'The Last Assembly Ball' will have its permanent value, even tho it is not a pleasant story." [Overland. 783
LE REVE. [by ÉMILE ZOLA: *Peterson*, 1889.] "Mr. Zola appears to have written 'The Dream' with the idea of showing his critics that he can write with perfect purity if he so desires. The result is one of the most exquisite romances in any language, told with a beauty of style which even a poor translator cannot conceal. The whole atmosfere of the book is sweet and true. Angélique, the saintly embroiderer for the cathedral of Beaumont, is a beautiful figure, and the romantic world in which she has her inmost being is opened to the reader with a master's hand. We should especially commend 'Le Rêve' to two classes of readers—those persons who take pleasure in Zola's usual filth and those who have been so far repelled by the report of it as not to read it

at all. We hope the first may learn how much finer an artist the author is when he regards purity as one law of life, and we know that the second will acknowledge the genius of Zola, which they may have doubted." [Boston "Literary World.] "In 'Le Rêve', Mr. Zola has attempted to show that his studies of the lowest forms of life have not unfitted him to treat a theme of mystical purity, but it is impossible to congratulate him on having achieved a complete success. There are passages of marvellous beauty in his picture of the girl bred in the shadow of an old cathedral, who developes a fervid imagination which, fed on the glories of the Church and the legends of the saints, absorbs her whole being, and culminates in an ecstasy of love for one almost as far above her us the angels." [Athenæum.**784**

LEATHER-STOCKING TALES (The). [by JA. FENIMORE COOPER: 1823-27.] "Were it not for one great creation, we should have to pronounce Cooper unsuccessful in the delineation of character. "Leather-Stocking" is, indeed, a most memorable and heroic yet pathetic figure, as living and impressive almost as any we know, and we should be sorry to believe that the world will ever willingly let die the delitful books which tell of his battles, his friendships, his unhappy love, his integrity and grand simplicity of character, his ungrudging sacrifices for others, his touching isolation, and his death on the lonely prairie. American fiction has no other such character." [Spectator.] "The order of the Leatherstocking Tales is (1) The Deerslayer, (2) The Last of the Mohicans, (3) The Pathfinder, (4) The Pioneers, (5) The Prairie. **785**

LEAVES FROM THE LIFE OF A GOOD-FOR-NOTHING, *Lippincott*, 1890.=*MEMOIRS OF A GOOD-FOR-NOTHING.*

LED HORSE CLAIM (The) [by M.. [ANNA] (HALLOCK) FOOTE: *Osgood*, 1883.] "has the striking merit of a very distinct purpose, so far as literary form goes, and of keeping very closely to that purpose. It may be only the unconscious

fidelity to experience which gives the story so purely and simply from the woman's point of view, but the merit is none the less true. Picturesque and graceful description is likely to be a woman's forte, but the fine balance which keeps Mrs. Foote's eye and hand true is a rare power. Not even the sharp contrasts, the swift tragedy of the wild mining-life tempt her to venture imagination, but so much the more powerful is her picture of the women waiting at home. It seems something more than a chance coincidence, that the return to the older life in the East appears now in more than one novel. Whereas once there was only the escape from it to the more brilliant possibility of the West, now more than one comes back in story to the old home, and finds a friendly lit in the sky, a content in the hills, a sense of refuge in what was once a hated narrowness. All the years from Plymouth Rock to the Golden Gate are embodied in the home of the "Led-Horse Gulch" and the home at "Little Rest" on the New England hillside. It is hard to say which picture is the better; but by way of minor figures, one must go far to seek even in a novel a more gracious pair than the 2 boys, half-brothers of the hero. They are most slitly sketched, but one-half the readers will flatter themselves that they were once such boys, and the other half will know that they have at some time loved and watched over their like." [Nation. **786**

LEFT-HANDED ELSA [by RO. E: FRANCILLON: *Loring*, 1879.] "is an honest little story. It has an odd mixture of reality and diablerie; but just that is attractive to some people, and homely honesty and truth at last win the day." [Nation. **787**

——, SAME, in *Tales from Blackwood*, N. S., 23.

LEFT OUT ON LONE STAR MOUNTAIN [in "On the Frontier," by BRET HARTE: *Houghton*. 1884.] "the justification of this book lies in the third of its 3 sketches. Here we have a composition which in all its details exhibits Mr. Harte's best manner. Here in the rugged mountain solitude is Lone Star cabin; here are the 5 picturesque partners of the played-out claim, whimsically known to each other as the Rit and Left Bowers (brothers), Union Mills (who had once patched·his trousers with the branded fragment of an old flour-sack), the Judge (a singularly inequitable Missourian), and the Old Man (whose downy lip proclaimed him still in his teens). For 5 years these 5 partners have been toiling at their claim, with nothing to show for it but debts, lost credit, and disgust. Four of them are plotting to 'vamose the ranch,' deserting the Old Man to sole inheritance of the claim, the debts, and the dangers. The shamefaced, shambling way in which they perfect their plot, and steal forth on the performance of it, is done to the very life. You can see the 4 men as they steal away from the cabin. And in the midst of it, the Old Man, all unsuspecting · their treachery, hopeful and true to his partners to the last, is out on the mountain side still prospecting. And Lo! the sudden avalanche discloses the auriferous seam, for which they have so long been searching, and he hurries back with the joyful news, and meets his skulking partners, and confronts their disheartened spirits and traitorous purposes with his discovery, and they are just in time to save themselves from the final step ... It is but a touch—those last words, but it illumines the whole scene with a flood of kindly feeling, and lifts the reader to a hi outlook. The picturesqueness in this story, the pathos of it, the life-likeness of the group of discouraged miners, their down-hearted desertion of their comrade, his lofty, unselfish devotion to the common interest, the swift turn in their affairs towards prosperity and brotherhood; these are the traits of one of Harte's better portraitures." [Boston "Literary World." **788**

LEONE [by L: MONTI: *Osgood*, 1882.] "There is a great deal to please in 'Leone'. It has to do with brigands, romantic captures, and surprises, but it is not sensational. The style is pure, graceful, refined;

the characters are outlined in successive strokes of self-revealing portraiture; there is variety of incident and a well constructed plot which baffles while it does not confuse. The heroine is a beautiful american girl who is neither a chatterbox nor a blue\stocking. There is a noble-minded captain of banditti without a trace of melo-drama about him. Two italian artists, a monk, and the father of the heroine form the principal dramatis personæ. The scene is entirely in **Italy**, where the author is so much at home as to be able to describe a sunrise with some degree of fidelity to nature. There is of course a love affair in which the fiery italian is placed in picturesque contrast with the sweet calmness of the less emotional dauter of the North, altho we hardly pardon Edith for giving up her Silvio so readily. The rapidity of the action, careful marshalling of scenes, and skillful dénoument show dramatic talent of a hi order." [Boston "Literary World." **789**

LES MISERABLES. [by V: HUGO: trans. Wilbour, N. Y., *Carleton*, 1862.] "From this bare abstract, the story does not seem to promise much pleasure to novel-readers, yet it is all alive with the fiery genius of Hugo, and the whole representation is so intense and vivid that, it is impossible to escape from the fascination it exercises over the mind. Few who take the book up will leave it until they have read it throu. It is morbid to a degree that no eminent english author, not even Byron, ever approached; but its morbid elements are so combined with sentiments abstractly christian that it is calculated to wield a more pernicious influence than Byron ever exerted." [Atlantic.] "It is a production of extraordinary power, in whatever lit regarded. The characters are original, marked and drawn with sharp distinctness; the scenes are described with minute fidelity, and yet without redundance of epithet; and the plot of the story, tho by no means complicated, is intensely interesting. It moves on more slowly than the course of most french novels, and there is no attempt to produce surprises or startling effects. There is a singular union of calmness and tragedy, and the last impression is at once pleasant and painful ... We shall not attempt to give an analysis of a story in which so much of the interest is in the details of description, and in the beauty of style. Each of the 5 books into which it is divided is complete in itself, and mit be given as a separate sketch. The bishop, and his household of 2 women quite unlike, make an admirable cabinet picture. The portrait of a perfect christian pastor has never been more beautifully drawn... Another striking character is the convict Jean Valjean, who is introduced first to show the consequences of unjust judicial sentence and harsh penal administration, and afterwards, in his changed and regenerate condition, as a mayor, to show what may be done by one man of energy and influence ... Fantine, the heroine of the story, does not appear until the third book. She is first shown in one of those characteristic Parisian groups,—students and their grisette companions taking a holiday. The inevitable issue comes in desertion, shame, poverty, struggle between womanly pride and maternal love. The beautiful, pure, and confiding girl becomes gradually, throu the succession of persecutions, mishaps, and miseries which follow her, a jealous, reckless, abandoned woman, held to virtue only by the love of her child. Incidentally, in connection with this child, we have glimpses of the brutal side of peasant life. Fantine dies at last in comparative peace; but her death is only the end of a victim to society. We can feel for this poor creature ónly pity." [Christian Examiner.] "Victor Hugo is not a moralist, for instance, because he does not paint human life. He is a rhapsodist in sentiment and a caricaturist in delineation. He is like Doré. His works are grotesque and powerful, but they are all unreal. They are not men and women in his pages more than the figures are truly human or the houses actually brick and stone in Doré's sketches. ... The reading world has been going

into factitious hysterics over 'Les Miserables' of Victor Hugo, and will say that Thackeray's 'Philip' is the same old story. No man is foolish enuf, let us hope, to remonstrate with public opinion; but, speaking of old stories, what is 'Les Miscrables' ? Its moral is that a bad man may have good traits. But the treatment is in such excessive chiaroscuro, it so blazes and darkens, that the figures glimmer and glower and reel off in fantastic diablerie. The man is so good that the influence is lost, and the story vanishes like a fairy tale."—[G : W : Curtis.]— "This much it is rit to say in condemnation of the work. But we think the world of today and of future generations will prefer to estimate the book in a manner which will allow a warmer recognition of its merits as a work of art and a romance. Thus criticized, it must be pronounced one of the masterpieces of the age which produced it. Faults, eccentricities, redundancies, extravagances, errors against good taste, it unquestionably has. Any critic who liked the task mit devote an essay to these. But when the most invidious criticism had done its worst, the immense power, the noble character of the book would remain uninjured. The foundation for half-a-dozen great reputations mit be discovered in its pages. Perhaps no hier praise could be given to the work than to say that, heralded as it was by months and months of the most vehement preliminary laudation, bily wrôt up as public expectation had purposely been, the world was not disappointed in the end. The presence of genius is felt by the reader in every chapter and page. A deep insit into human nature, a warm and almost passionate sympathy with human suffering, a pictorial power scarcely rivaled in our days, a dramatic force which strikes out new and thrilling effects in every new situation, an inexhaustible variety of character, incident, and illustration, and a vivid eloquence absolutely unequalled by any living author of the same class,—these are some, and only some, of the leading qualities." [Westminster

Review. 790
——, SAME, trans. Wraxall, London and N. Y., 1863.
——, SAME, trans. Hapgood, *Crowell*, 1887.
LICHTENSTEIN, by W: Hauff, *J. Blackwood*, 1860.
LINDA. [by C. L. (W.) HENTZ: 1850.] "The school-girl of the period will hail with delit the announcement of the Messrs. Peterson that they are about to publish a complete edition of the novels of the late Mrs. Hentz. Her books have always.been dear to the extremely juvenile mind. They introduce the reader to such delitful young men with classic brows and raven hair, and to such superbly beautiful and romantic dauters of the Sunny South, that it is impossible for the young heart not to be drawn towards such perfect creatures, and for the young intellect not to admire the author who created such sweet boons in the shape of lovers, and who described them with such wealth of flowery and poetic diction. Especially has 'Linda' been fortunate in its wonderful popularity. There has, probably, never been another book which has been hid under so many virgin pillows, and suffered from so much maidenly bread and butter, as has 'Linda'. It has been the solace of countless Sundays in young ladies' seminaries, and has rivaled its kindred, but lmore material milk and water, in the affections of parlor boarders. It is, therefore, fortunate, in vue of this remarkable popularity, that Mrs. Hentz' novels are entirely blameless. Except in the one respect of utter vacuity, there is no fault to be found with them. Their estimable author discovered that literary milk and water would meet with a large demand among the customers of the innocuous beverage which is known by that attractive name. She therefore set herself to provide for this demand, and for many years pursued the business with eminent success. To criticise severely such stories as 'Linda', and its numerous companions is quite impossible. The author intended to make them as weak and foolish as the school-girl heart could wish. She had an undoubted rit to pursue her|work, and deserves our gratitude for not writing vicious as well as foolish books. If her stories are worthless they are at least harmless, and he would be morose and cruel indeed who would deprive the girlish mind of the pleasure of reading them in stolen moments by the lit of surreptitious gas,. or behind the artfully raised lid of the school-room desk." [Citizen and Round Table. 791

LITTLE DORRIT. [by C: DICKENS: 1856.] "No sooner have you read a few pages than you seem to be in the midst of the world and daily life, with all its infinite varieties and currents. No novelists in english literature have this power of putting the reader, and interesting him in the characters as a part of the world, so much as Fielding, Thackeray, and Dickens. Their novels are not so much the story of the isolated fortunes of individuals, as vast panoramas of great masses of .the world. In this way they have a kind of cosmopolitan interest. It is not a thin thread of story which you pursue, so attenuated often that it is not strong enuf to sustain attention, but you move, lãf, and cry with a crowd. There is in 'Little Dorrit' plenty of that pungent satire with which Dickens always bears down upon great national abuses. Nothing in all his writings is better in its way than the *Circumlocution office*. It is broad satire, yet how cuttingly true, and how purely english! The stupid confusion of the impotent young official, who lives in precedents and an agonized and reverend chaos, when he drops his eyeglass—which is symbolical of the entire humbug of the system of which he is a cipher—is admirably drawn and severely dramatic . . . One thing must forcibly strike every american reader of this and other stories of Dickens. It is the intense englishism of the tale. There are certain conditions imperative upon a novel, which it seems almost impossible to attain in America, a kind of picturesque perspective, a romantic association of place and systems, which are entirely unknown to us. Thus the scene of 'Little Dorrit' is **London**, and all the local painting is, doubtless, strictly true. But how would it be possible to treat New-York, or any american city, in that way? We have no romantic setting for novels. What are you to do with Broadway, with the Park, with Avenue B. ? Of course there are plenty of characters, and life enuf, but there are no mellow distances, no grimed and venerable buildings and places. All these must be renounced in an american novel." [G: W: Curtis. **792**

LITTLE LORD FAUNTLEROY. [by F.. [ELIZA] (H.) BURNETT: *Scribner*, 1886.] "It is hard to find words hi enuf in which to commend this charming story. It is only a child's tale, but it is not the less genuine literature, and so worthy of any one's attention ... It is easy to call the story well-plotted and well written, but that does not explain why it sometimes clutches us at the throat and presses the moisture from our eyes before we are aware. In truth, it touches in the simplest and directest fashion the main chords of human feeling; it is dignified by an atmosfere of honest sentiment which a fine reserve rescues from the natural and almost inevitable fall into sentimentality. We suppose, if the truth must be told, his young lordship is too fine a fellow to have been a real boy, and we are inclined to hope that behind the scenes in which Mrs. Burnett has chosen to show us this manly, frank, sweet-tempered peer in embryo he indulges a small nautiness or two, if only that he may be a friend, on something like equal grounds, of the very recognisable human boys and girls who will make his acquaintance throu his biografer. We do not know any reason why he should not be as charmingly unselfish as he is, however, nor why he should not be brave and simple-minded, thinking no evil; and as these are the essentials of his character and make the point of the book, we need not question his other perfections, especially since Mrs. Burnett has the art of flattering us to belief in their reasonable-

ness while we read of them. His conquest of his surly and ill-favored grandfather, the Earl, by means of his innocent attribution to him of all the virtues, is admirably conceived, and carried out with touching truth; and it is not only his grandfather who is the better for the knowledge of Lord Fauntleroy's generous young heart. He carries love and sunshine with him, and every one who knows him is the happier for his living. By the subtlest and least didactic means, Mrs. Burnett implies this as the inmost meaning of her story; that this fruit of character is the chiefest good of life for every one of us. 'It was really a very simple thing, after all', she says—'it was only that he had lived near a kind and gentle heart, (that of his mother, who is scarcely less well done than little Lord Fauntleroy himself) 'and had been taut to think kind thôts always, and to care for others. It is a very little thing, perhaps, but it is the best thing of all. He knew nothing of earls or castles; he was quite ignorant of all grand and splendid things; but he was always lovable because he was simple and loving. To be so is like being born a king." [Church Review.] "It is full of spirit and originality, of brit surprise and captivating sweetness. It reminds one of some graceful allegretto or scherzo coming with gay relief and charm among slower and sadder strains—of life or art. The beautiful child-nature of the little hero is rendered with the utmost felicity. His small lordship is meant to be, and is irresistibly winning. Perhaps the best thing in the book is the clear showing of his innate nobility—a strength and sweetness of character quite independent of circumstances or condition, which conquers even the hardheartedness of the selfish old earl, his grandfather. This may not suit believers in total depravity, but to any other readers, old or young, we recommend the story as most fascinating; and tho as previously hinted, it is almost too charming for reality, there are not wanting touches of humor and pathos to make it lifelike." [Nation.] "It is already too well known and too much admired to need futher words of introduction ; but it is a pleasure to dwell with emfasis upon anything so perfect of its kind. It is piquant, amusing, instructive, beautiful, and not unnatural : and it has an excellent tho unobtrusive moral. While not written above the children's heads, its literary quality is something which the children can not wholly appreciate. There is, therefore no one whom 'Little Lord Fauntleroy' will not please. The child of 6 will listen with delit to the pretty story, and the man of 60 will not regret being called upon to read it aloud to the 6 year-old. It is full of touches which betray an insit into human nature like Hans Andersen's or the Autocrat's. Such is the capital way in which Mr. Hobbs' prejudice against earls is overcome as soon as he is able to associate with them in even the mildest way. These, of course, will not be wholly appreciated by the very youthful readers; but neither will they friten them away from the rest of the dainty story of a little fellow making his way in life by simple lovableness and lovingness." [Critic.] "The scene is nominally laid in New-York, and in England; it is really laid in that delitful and impossible country, a near nébor to fairy-land, which was first discovered by Dickens, where the good people are so very good, and beautiful in mind and manners and body as they are in character, where the funny people are too funny for anything, and the bad people are horrid, yet so little set in their wicked ways that the slitest thing, as a kind word or act, or the innocent trust of a little child, has been known to turn them from very bad people to very good ones. This story of the 7 year-old american boy who lives among all sorts of queer people in New-York, and is discovered to be the heir to an earldom, who goes to England, astonishes the aristocracy by his beauty and bravery and delitful bonhommie, wins the affections of the tenantry on his ancestral acres, softens the heart of the grim, cruel old earl his grandfather so that he turns into a sort of little Cheeryble, and rewards his old friends Mr. Hobbs the grocer and Dick the boot-black with a munificence that is unknown out of fairy-tales and Christmas-books,— this story is simply a stroke of genius." [Lippincott's. **793**

LITTLE MAID OF ACADIE (A) [by MARIAN COLHOUN LEGARÉ REEVES: *Appleton*, 1880.] "is a clever domestic story of the canadian border, having a pathetic interest and showing some skill in the arts of construction and expression. The 'little maid' seems rather a neglected good-for-nothing at the outset, but develops under experience and native force of character into a personage who challenges respect." [American. **794**

LITTLE MOORLAND PRINCESS (The) [by "E. MARLITT," i. e., Eugenie John : tr. by A. L. (F.) Wister: *Lippincott*, 1872.] "is a skillful blending of the fanciful with the real, the latter element being made subordinate without being absolutely deficient. In other words, the charm of these stories lies not so much in their fidelity to Nature as in the graceful and agreeable visions which they summon before the mind. . . The earlier scenes, in which the heroine, ignorant of her origin and unconscious of her attractions, runs wild upon the moor, have a peculiar attractiveness, and show to advantage that freshness of fancy which is the author's hiest gift, and which lends to her pictures something of the fascination with which the roseate tints of morning invest the commonest landscape." [Lippincott's.] "Neither Miss Marlitt nor her readers appear to tire of the pretty stories in which low-born virtue triumfs over aristocratic pride and prejudice, and in which german Lutheranism is always held up to open scorn. For our part, we confess to sharing in the pleasure which the rest of her public doubtless get from her performances, and to finding her last story, despite its similarity to its predecessors, as entertaining as the first one. There is an innocent freshness about them in despite, as it were, of their author, for she seems to have an ever-present sense of her responsibilities as a social reformer. She succeeds better as a story-teller, however, than as a preacher." [Nation.]—"There is a young girl brôt up in the country, a gentleman of middle-age who falls in love with her at first sit, an absent-minded father; various persons who draw the girl into difficulties, from which her elderly lover rescues her, and a faithful old servant, to whom she flies, in order to be brôt back by the said lover. But this particular heroine is so very wild and childish, that she evidently ôt to have been 7 instead of 17; and it passes even the most indulgent novel-reader's powers to believe that Mr. Claudius' 'large, blue, fiery eyes' could have seen anything attractive in her." [Spectator.　　795

——, SAME ("Little Princess of the Moor") transl. by Sprague, in *Ladies' Repository*, Jan.-Dec.. 1872.

——, SAME, ("Princess of the Moor") *Tauchnitz*, 1872.

——, SAME, *Ward & Lock*, 1882.

——, SAME, transl. by Slade, *Remington*, 1883.

LORD KILGOBBIN. [by C: LEVER: *Harper*, 1872.] "It is, unfortunately, very seldom that one finds a novelist whose work, extending over so many years, shows only steady improvement, but such is the case with the novels of the late Mr. Lever. His military novels, with the young dragoons ever ready for fiting, and for love or punch-making, were, and will be for a long time, the delit of youth, but in these novels of his later years there is the same britness, a much acuter study of character, and the evidence of a much wider experience. '*Sir Brooke Fosbrooke*' is one of this sort which can be recommended. '*That Boy of Norcott's*', altho of less merit, is very readable; but perhaps the best of all is his last, '*Lord Kilgobbin.*' The scene of this story is in **Ireland**, and the author has drawn an admirable picture of the gloom and dulness of its country life, and of the interruptions to this dulness which Fenianism and irish devotion to causeless brawling are capable of producing. The characters are numerous, and are sharply sketched; there are

many irish, a greek princess, young englishmen, officers, adventurers, a motley and entertaining crowd. One of the most amusing one of them all is one Atlee, who is simply a civilian sucessor to the soldierly heroes of the earlier novels. Instead of madly galloping in the charge, or jangling his spurs in the ball-room, he, while yet a young man in college, writes for all the best papers in Europe instructing statesmen in their craft, and taking all sides of every political question ... The two young women are well drawn; and, in a word, the interest we are made to feel in the characters, the skill shown in telling the story, the good nature and refinement of the author, make this a very readable novel." [Nation.　　796

LORENZ STARK, see *MARIA WUZ*.

LORENZO BENONI. [by GIOVANNI [D.] RUFFINI: *Chapman*, 1853.] The author "has narrated, in this charming book, his school-boy republicanism, his connexion with Mazzini (called Fantasio), and his part in the conspiracies and revolution of 1831. His elder brother was shot by the sardinian government, and he was able to escape to Paris only by a most romantic flit and swimming across the swollen Var before the sardinian police." [Athenæum.　　797

LORNA DOONE [by R: D. BLACKMORE: 1869.] "is one of the stories which gain and grow on you by repeated reading. It is a perfect handbook to some of the most picturesque districts of **Devonshire**, and a storehouse of Legendary and archæological information. Yet that is perhaps among its lesser merits. For no living novelist is more master of the art of introducing one to the innermost intimacy of his personages. Our liking for John Ridd changes, like that of Lorna, into affection and esteem, as we learn to appreciate the striking and straitforward qualities of that sturdy representative of the english yeomanry. Nor is Lorna herself less of a reality to us; while the casual references to such personages as the savage Chancellor bring out the man to the life in his coarseness and moral deformity..."

[Blackwood's. 798
LOST MANUSCRIPT (The). [by
GUSTAV FREYTAG: *Chapman*, 1865.]
"However, the professor's search brings
us into various scenes and strange company. It leads us first to Rossau, where
instead of finding the MS., the professor
takes himself a wife; it then brings us
back to the university, and shows us the
ways of professors and students; last of
all it carries us to a small court afflicted by
a prince who suffers under the same mal-
ady as the Cæsars. Details of country
life and farming, the visit of a learned
country lady, an adventure with gypsies,
a controversy between professors about
a forged leaf of Tacitus, a professors' ball,
a students' 'commerz,' a students' duel,
an inauguration of a rector, a long-stand-
ing quarrel between 2 nébors, court intrigues and scandal, the pranks of a mischievous young prince and the machinations of a mischievous old one, an attempt
on the life of the professor and the honor
of his wife, are some of the incidents
arbitrarily connected with the search for
the lost Tacitus . . . But the dénoument of
the whole story disappoints us, and has a
melodramatic look which is neither in
keeping with the outset, nor equal to the
parts we have specified." [Athenæum. 799
——, SAME, Chicago, *Open Court
Pub. Co.*, 1891.
LOST MOUNTAIN (The). [by [T:]
MAYNE REID.] "The real cause of the
popularity of Reid's novels, which, as regards 1 or 2 of them, may last long, is
that they gratify not the boyish, but the
human love for pure romance, for stories
in which there are practically fairies, tho
they are called mexican ladies, and genii,
tho they are dressed as american filibus-
ters, and devils, tho they appear as Don
Rafaels or Antonios; and probabilities are
set aside, and every thing happens as it is
convenient it should happen, and nobody
cares a dump whether there are any laws,
human or divine, or not. Adventures
are adventured, and the adventurers fall
into fritful dangers, and get out of them
again by wonderful means; and laws,

literary or other, are simply a burden . . .
It is to be rid of the coercing, compress-
ing, and therefore limiting chain of cause
and effect,—to set the imagination free,
and let it revel for a moment in an uncon-
ditional world. It does revel, and we all
like the momentary sensation even altho
we are all the while critical enuf to be
annoyed with our own pleasure . . . But
we can dispense with it, and find pleasure
even in Mayne Reid, and the marionnettes
which caper in the glowing air, furious
storms, and vast over scenery of the slopes
from the huge mexican plateau. We see
no harm in the enjoyment; it is only
'Jack, the Giant Killer' for the grown-ups;
and we firmly believe that some day Romance will again be a widely popular
form of fiction. Man grows gloomier and
gloomier, but the childlike element in
him is happily not dead yet." [Spec-
tator. 800
LOTHAIR. [by the EARL OF BEACONS-
FIELD: *Appleton*, 1870.] "A hero implies
a heroine; in this case we have three,
whose various form of relation to the hero
are happily enuf conceived . . . The
Church of Rome, in the person of Cardinal Grandison, having marked him for
her own, we are invited to see what part
the world shall play in contesting or confirming her influence. We have, in the
first place, Lady Corisande, the lovely
dauter of a mity duke, a charming
girl and a good Protestant; in the second,
we have Miss Arundel, equally lovely,
and a keen Papist; and lastly, we have
the "devine Theodora", an Italian patriot,
married, oddly enough, to a "gentleman
of the South" of our own country. Jewels, castles, horses, riches of every kind
are poured into the story without measure,
without mercy. But there is a certain
method, after all, in the writer's madness.
His purpose—his instinct, at least—has
been to portray with all possible completeness a purely aristocratic world." [At-
lantic.] *Key to Lothair:* The Oxford
Professor, Goldwin Smith; "Grandison,"
Cardinals Manning and Wiseman;
"Lothair", Marquis of Bute. "Catesby",

Monseigneur Capel. Duke and Duchess, Duke and Duchess of Abercorn. The Bishop, Bishop Wilberforce; "Corisande", either of the Ladies Hamilton. [Notes and Queries, 9 Jan. 1886. **801**

LOVE AFTER MARRIAGE see *COURTSHIP AND MARRIAGE.*

LOVE AND MIRAGE; or the Waiting on an Island. [by MATILDA B. ED-WARDS : *Hutchinson*, 1890.] " 'Love and Mirage' is a pretty and sentimental story delicately told. Arthur Venning and his younger brother Hervey go off to an island which is not geografically defined, tho it is described as "a veritable Eden under the northern star." Here they come across two lovely German sisters, and fall in love with them. Arthur's friend, however, refuses his offer, on the ground that a disgrace is attached to her family throu the conduct of an elder sister. The girls go away, but on the same island Arthur discovers a prince's castle and a mysterious lady; and here there is a second fase of love-making. The mysterious lady turns out to be the eldest of three sisters, the author's confidence must be preserved as to the fate of the two unfortunate ladies on whom Arthur Venning had successively bestowed his preference. This "out-of-door romance" is well worth reading for its own sake. It is painful in a sense, but extremely pathetic, and with a good deal of pastoral charm." [Athenæum. **802**

LOVE OR PRIDE? [Adapted from the Swedish, by ANNIE WOOD: *Bentley*.] "The book reminds us somewhat, in manner, of the liter style of baroness Knorring, and is a tolerably good example of the second-rate class of swedish romances, stronger in incident than plot, but always innocent and pretty. The plan of the story slitly recalls 'The Heir of Redclyffe.' A young man of immense fortune determines to become a tutor in a noble family, in order to accustom himself to self-restraint and obedience. Of course, there is a proud and lovely dauter, with whom he falls in love, and, equally of course, she declares a reciprocal pas-

sion a few hours before his rank and wealth are revealed. Her own family becomes ruined, and the ci-devant tutor buys the estate and presents it to her brother." [Athenæum. **803**

LOUISA [by K.. S. MACQUOID: *Harper*, 1885.] "is one of those stories which are really works of art in the skill with which what is thrilling is mingled with what is exquisite; so that every possible story-reader will find in it something to his taste. Nothing could be simpler than the material. Nothing happens in the book from beginning to end. There is an absolute dearth of incident; but the cunning of the writer keeps the reader perfectly absorbed in the development of character and the action and re-action upon each other of varying temperaments, until a fit of jealousy affects the reader like an incident, and the play of the passions seems the most exciting of dramas. 'Local color' of whatever nature, is always a great feature for a book; but if we could choose our local color, we should probably always say, 'Let it be of Italy'. The story of 'Louisa' is vivid with this rich italian coloring, sometimes of scenery, sometimes of character, as in the cleverly drawn servants and the admirable portrait of the count—for once a lovable Count. There have been times when we were ready to denounce any novel which rested its claim to interest on illegal love or jealousy; but altho this element is one of the pivots for 'Louisa', it is used in a way to disarm criticism and even win applause. The love of the countess for the serene englishman is not mad passion, but intellectual devotion. The calm, intellectual 'Louisa', the jealous but gentle count, the impulsive Francesca, the clever american widow, the interesting englishman, about whom, simple and unassuming as he is, all these inflammable characters revolve, make together a story which is at once as dramatic as a play, and as delicate as a dream." [Critic. **804**

LOYALTY GEORGE [by LOUISA (TAYLOR) PARR: *Holt*, 1888.] "is a story of **Devonshire** coast life during the days succeeding the french wars, when 'Bony' was the name which fritened nauty children into seemly behavior, when stories of the press gang were memories as well as romance, and smugglers had little trouble to ply their trade. Scores of novel writers have made the times and places familiar, notably Mrs. Gaskell, whose 'Sylvia's Lovers' will inevitably come to mind as one opens Mrs. Parr's book. But the times and places lent themselves to fiction so readily that one is only glad to meet them again, and 'Loyalty George' is in no sense an imitation. If we have with Mrs. Gaskell climbed these [these? not Yorkshire?] cliffs and looked upon this sea. hurried to the sands to see the fishing boats come in, hunted birds' nests in the rocky walls, pushing a way throu gorse and bramble, listened to the sea stories of soldiers and sailors, and passed the time of day with fishwives, it is with a guide of a humor more subtle than even Mrs. Gaskell's that we walk the streets of the twin villages, Ferrers and Fairstoke, and sit at the villagers' tea tables, or listen to Mrs. Coode's private interpretation of Providence. The heroine, with her disreputable surroundings, is so sweet and loyal a vagabond that it is a pity she fixed her affections on a man who knew how to love better than to trust, and that so she had to be sacrificed to the needs of a tragic consistency. Dunchy, the deaf boatman, with his malodorous past, and his wise affection for his little maiden friend, is a character to be put among the realities; so, too, the gentle Wesleyan minister; while Mrs. Coode is not unworthy of the hand that drew Sister Glegg and Sister Pullet."—[Nation   805

LUCK OF ROARING CAMP (The). [by [FR.] BRET HARTE: *Fields*, 1871.] "is but one very brief tale out of a dozen. It is a narrative of a short life—that of a baby—in one of those curious colonies of gold-diggers. It bears every evidence of being true to the life, as a picture studied from the life mit be expected to be. It is full of rude figures, without a pre-

tense at civilisation even—much less refinement—men without conscience or restraint, careless in body and in mind, and ruf as the rocks they work among; yet it is long since we have read anything so touching . . . Nothing is softened in the picture—there is no sentiment—nobody is reminded of the innocence of his own cradle in words, as so many moralist humorists would take pleasure in reminding him. The camp is not changed at once into a nursery Bethel. But nevertheless, the whole community, in which there is not a single woman left, gets gradually absorbed in the child, and with a shame-faced submission to the soft new yoke which is thus put upon its neck, it knows not how, grows a little cleaner, a little quieter, a little kinder, with a clumsy surprise at itself which is perfectly well rendered and thoroly natural. . ." [Blackwood's.   806

MACLEOD OF DARE [by W: BLACK: *Harper*, 1879.] "is much more like a great poem than a great novel. It begins like a modern tale, but it ends like an ancient ballad. We have noticed before that the halves of some of Mr. Black's best efforts do not entirely correspond. He seems to have a constitutional objection to ending on the common chord. In 'Macleod' his theme is extremely, poetically, simple. There are really only 2 characters: the untamed, and intrepid, yet gentle and chivalrous, Highland chief, with a chorus of wild retainers; and the fine London lady, the actress spoiled by flattery and feining, with her natural 'entourage' of relatives and friends. The lover is impassioned, generous, constant; the lady beautiful, of course, selfish throu timidity, fickle, and shallow . . . Macleod of Dare is a book of a thousand for its unity and fire. It is eloquent, tender and profoundly touching. It soars to a hit of simple passion seldom attained in those sofisticated days, but it topples over at the very last, and misses the crown of ultimate symmetry." [Atlantic.]—The "customary relation between the principal characters is exactly reversed, and it is a trusting, faithful, and noble-natured man whose life and happiness are wrecked upon the shoals of misplaced affection. Partly for this reason, and partly because of the overwhelmingly tragical catastrofe of its close, the story will probably be less popular than most of the author's previous ones; yet it contains some of his very best work, whether in the portrayal of character, the artistic adjustment of incident, or the poetical description of scenery ... In many cases the disenchantment follows so close upon the charm that no great harm is done; but when the comedy is played with an intense, passionate, fine-strung nature like Macleod's, the result is likely to be tragic, whether, as 'would commonly be the case, the victim summons resolution to brave his fate and silently endure the inevitable, or whether, as in the more soul-piercing catastrofe of Macleod of Dare, his dethroned and distempered reason prepares for both betrayer and victim an oblivion-luring draft of 'Death's black wine'." [Appleton's. **807**

MADAME DELPHINE. [by G: W. CABLE: *Scribner*, 1881.] "The characters move in the quaint, half oriental **New-Orleans** of other days. There is a group of singularly interesting persons,—an ideal pirate sanctified by a great and sudden love; a beautiful quadroon, sad with all the tragedy of her class; a wise, liberal, noble-hearted priest, and a few admirably sketched minor characters." [Amer. **808**

MADAME THERESE. [by ERCKMANN and CHATRIAN: *Scribner*, 1869.] "The story is told in the simplest manner by one who was a boy at the time of the scenes described, and lived in a little village in the midst of the **Vogesen** with his uncle, a filanthropic old doctor, a filosofer, and a lover of peace, but ready to be awakened by that great volcanic movement which began to upheave all Europe in 1792. Without any apparent purpose of making the novel historical, the authors, in their descriptions of the village discussions over the ominous rising of the french people, and of the military movements and spirited engagements which

sweep ruthlessly over the quiet village, give a glance into the strange, unsettled life of the time, which brings it before us with wonderful reality and distinctness. Madame Therese is a vivandière of rare elevation of character, who is left for dead in the streets of the village, after a fierce conflict in which her soldier comrades are engaged with the austrian troops, and rescued by the good Dr. from the inhumanity of the villagers and from the vengeance of the Austrians." [Galaxy. **809**

MADEMOISELLE [by F.. M.. PEARD: *Smith*, 1890.] "is a pretty little story telling of the days of the war of 1870, and the Commune. It is put into the mouth of a young country girl, who goes to **Paris** to visit a sister, and finds herself well-ni unprotected in all the horrors of the time. There is nothing original or remarkable about it; but it is simply and nicely told, and the personality of the narrator is well sustained. 'Mademoiselle' is a heroic figure, not exceeding real or moving, perhaps, but a fine conception of womanhood, and, as such, worthy of admiration." [Athenæum. **810**

M'LLE DE MALPEIRE [by HENRIETTE E. F. (A.) REYBAUD: in "The Albion", 3d to 31st. Jan.,1857.] "is an interesting story, told in a simple, unaffected manner. The plot is very slit, and the characters, tho distinctly marked, are by no means elaborated; they are mere sketches, outlines of persons who lived and suffered in the early days of the french revolution, and the incidents are narrated with such apparent truthfulness and candor as to leave the impression on the mind of the reader that experience rather than imagination had suggested them. The heroine, Marie, is the dauter of the baron of Malepeire, a staunch loyalist, whose wife, Madame la Baronne, is a fine lady of the 'old school', born and bred among the biest in the land, and imbued with all the ignorant prejudices that rendered the aristocracy so blind to the dangers which surrounded them. Marie is rather wearied by her mother's constant regrets and never ending complaints about the loneliness of their country life, their want of society, the distance of their château from her beloved Paris, and the life of exile to which she is condemned, and as her childhood has been passed among the mountains, altogether secluded from the great world, she has naturally imbibed many of the new opinions which were freely uttered by the discontented peasantry in the néborhood. The consequence is that when the marquis of Champeaubert arrives at Malepeire to claim the hand of the baron's beautiful dauter she takes refuge in the arms of a stalwart peasant, who is utterly incapable of appreciating the sacrifice which she makes in marrying him." [Round Table.] "Miss Shore has made a good translation of Mrs. Reybaud's well-known story, which has attracted more than one generation of novel-readers. Its cleverly contrived effects and the pathetic character of the of the setting relieve the sombreness of the central narrative, and that which chiefly takes the fancy is not the murder committed by the outraged wife, but the mystery surrounding the last of the Malepeires in her after life, which is dramatically sustained to the close. C: Reade's keen appreciation of the romantic elements of crime committed under certain exceptional circumstances led him to adopt Mrs. Reybaud's plot in his 'Story of a portrait' [?], which is rather a remodelling than a rendering of 'M'lle de Malepeire'. He undoubtedly deepened the dramatic interest; but there must be many readers who will be glad to have the original tale in a literal english version." [Athenæum.] "Now, this story, "The Picture", has either been borrowed by C: Reade from the owner of it, for the sake of its better "setting", or has been purchased by him from the owner, with an occult understanding that the credulous american public shall in the transaction be laudably cozened, whether bôt or borrowed, the plot, the essential fases of dialog, and the accessory descriptive padding, to the minutest detail, are abstracted from "The Portrait in My Uncle's Dining-room." [Corres. Nation.811

——, SAME ("Where shall he find her?"), *American News Co.*, 1867.
——, SAME, ("What the papers revealed") in *The St. James Magazine*, 1868.
——, SAME ("The Portrait in my uncle's dining-room"), [reprinted from "The Month"], *Littell & Co.*, 1870.
——, SAME ("The Old M'sieur's Secret"), *Carleton*, 1882.
——, SAME ("The Picture"), [free translation by C: Reade] *Harper*, 1884.
——, SAME ("A Daughter of the Malepeires"), *Remington*, 1885.

MADEMOISELLE MORI. [by MA. ROBERTS: Boston, *Ticknor*, 1860.] "This is a remarkable book, by a person familiar with **Rome** and with the Romans, who has thôt seriously and felt deeply in regard to their character and fortunes, who has studied with keen and sympathetic imagination the hearts of the people, and observed closely the outward aspect and common shows of the city. The story is well constructed, and has the essential merit of interest. Not only are the characters distinctly presented, but there is in them, what it is rare to find in the personages of our modern novelists, a rare and natural development, which is exhibited not so much by what is said about them as by their apparently unconscious words and acts .... The book, indeed, has a double character. It is not a mere novel; for it contains, in addition to its story, a sketch of the course of public affairs in Rome during the 3 memorable years from the accession of Pius IX. to the fall of the Republic.... The author has not the genius of Mr. Hawthorne, but the descriptions which the book contains of Roman scenes and places are full of truth, and render the common, everyday aspect of streets and squares, of gardens and churches, of popular customs and social habits, with equal spirit and fidelity. The interest of the story is sustained by the distinctness with which the localities in which it passes are depicted." [Atlantic. 812

MAID OF KILLEENA (The), and

other Stories. [by W: BLACK: *Macmillan*, 1874.] "The principal one, laid in those isles beloved of his Princess Sheila, will remind the reader of his most successful novel. It is a Highland love-story, dealing with the simple people and manners of the **Hebrides**. Ailasa Macdonald is a fit heroine for such an idyl. She has much of the grace and strength of character we were charmed by in the "Princess;" but being a simple peasant girl, is a less elaborated and less complex study. *Queen Tita's Wager* is humorous, and shows that the author has an eye for other scenes and people than those of Scotland. The desperation of Charlie's love is vividly displayed in his atrocious claim to the honor of vulpicide, when the fair Franziska Zahler desires a yellow fox-skin. *A Fight for a Wife* is farcical and funny, tho perfectly extravagant. *The True Story of a Billiard Club* contains some awful revelations of the advance made by 'woman' in the art of revolutionary combination, and the futility of man's attempts at resistance." [Athenæum. **813**

MAID OF SKER (The). [by R: D. BLACKMORE: *Harper*, 1872.] "The story opens in 1872, and closes soon after the battle of the Nile, in 1798, in which Davy was a prominent participant. Its pictures of life in a little welsh seacoast town, naturally developed in the progress of the narrative, are very effective, and the storm and the shipwreck, and the scenes which follow, are described with thrilling power. The author has evidently been a close student of welsh life and character, and sketches them with great skill of satire. From Newton-Nottage the exigencies of the story transfer Davy to Devonshire, where he has some very strange adventures and becomes acquainted with parson Chowne. This man,—a demon in human form—holds his parish under the sternest tyranny, scoffs at religion, and scorns all the restraints of civilization and society. His life is a long defiance of God and man, and his death by hydrofobia is a fitting end to it. We

are at a loss for words in which to convey an idea of this dreadful man, in whom there seems to have been nothing human but his form. Dramatic and fascinating as are his figure and the events which cluster about it, it is taxing the reader's credulity too far to ask him to believe that such a state of society existed in England within a century—a whole community crouching like dogs under the lash of the parish priest, who cared for public opinion only because he made it, committed the most heinous crimes unquestioned, and acknowledged responsibility to no power, human or divine. The introduction of a community of savages, too, brutish humans, who scorned habiliments, and fed on bugs and roaches, protegés of the fierce Parson, seems to us to be a rather bold stroke of the imagination. But it should not be understood that the general effect of the story is repulsive or extravagant. On the contrary, its leading characteristic is humor—a queer unaccountable humor—which pervades almost every sentence of the admirable Davy; and there are not a few passages full of tenderness and pathos." [Boston "Literary World." **814**

MALBONE, see No. 78.

MALCOLM, by G: MacDonald, see notice of sequel: *THE MARQUIS OF LOSSIE.*

MAN WITHOUT A COUNTRY, (The) [by E: E. HALE: *Ticknor*, 1864.] "When the war had passed it was found that a new classic had been added to american literature. It is impossible to conceive of a time, as long at least as the United States remains a nation, when the story of 'The Man Without a Country' shall not be able to stir the american heart. Its art is like most successful art, simple, quiet, and spontaneous. A hi moral purpose gives energy to the narrative, and the management of the details is singularly felicitous. No wonder that people apply to the author for a glimpse at Philip Nolan's scrap-books, or that government officials acknowledge the substantial truth of the tale [?]. It is one of those stories which are realistic in the best sense of the word. It has the elements of an enduring and unimpeachable veracity." [Boston "Literary World."] See, also, *IF, YES AND PERHAPS.* 815

MANON LESCAUT [by ANTOINE FR. PRÉVOST D' EXILES: trans. by A. W. GUNDRY: *Belford*, 1889.] "Mr. Gundry regards this book in a different lit from Mrs. Grundy: with him it is a classic, and so all but Mrs. Grundy agree; yet *Mrs.* Grundy mit he somewhat puzzled to say why she puts her fan up when the book is mentioned. To the reader who comes upon it by accident it seems dull and commonplace; no impropriety could be more decorously and blamelessly set forth; there is not a simper in the book. One has only to accept the intrigues as in the course of nature, and one has a mild narrative of personal adventure, told serenely and with proper grace." [Atlantic. 816

——, SAME, London, *J. Thomas*, 1841; Boston, *D. Ruggles*, 1845.

MARBLE FAUN (The) [by NATHANIEL HAWTHORNE: *Tieknor*, 1860.] "is a fascinating story. And yet, when we turn back to it, the material of plot and incident is meagre, compared with the array of circumstance, complication of events, and all the cunning machinery by which a novel generally moves on to an end carefully adjusted to the means employed. It is almost a story without an end, and we have heard much discontent that things were not made plainer in the last pages. Many good people are looking for a sequel which shall discover if Donatello's curls really hid the Faun's furry ears, and whether Miriam had Cenci blood in her, and what became of Hilda in those days when the Virgin's lamp went out, and the doves were unfed, and Kenyon wretched, and just who the queer union of spectre, model, and Capuchin was. But, as a story, and for the excitement of plot and issue, the book would seem to have little beside this mystery. For the characters are few, and the events, save the one fearful crime, not marked and

striking. Its fascination lies deeper than the romantic interest excited by deft handling of stirring adventures and strange destinies, and by the portentous followings of consequence, throu remarkable crises, to a nicely fitted close, where all get justice and the riddles are all solved." [Christian Examiner.] "Donatello is the opposite of Arthur Dimmesdale. One is the type of intense intellectuality; he is all mind, heart, conscience; and his body is comparatively weak. The other typifies the fysical in man; he is an animal, speaking and thinking; he is an Adam before the fall, his heart full of simple joy, his life empty of cares and sorrows, the trusted friend and playmate of nature. Remorse has now to act upon a stronger subject than Dimmesdale, and itself is weaker than before. The attendant circumstances, which in The Scarlet Letter tended to sharpen pain and to quicken its action, now act to soothe it. Hilda brings her purity; Kenyon, his friendly care; Miriam, her love. The Faun has changed indeed, but for the better. That supreme moment of self-denial, that release from the bondage of a purely selfish sorrow, that glimpse of something really worth while to live for, which came to Arthur Dimmesdale only in death, brot added life to Donatello. The test had put a new element into his being. R m rse had developed him. 'In the black depths, the Faun had found a soul.'" [G : P. Lathrop.] "It was sketched out", the author says, in the preface, "during a residence of considerable length in Italy, and was rewritten and prepared for the press in England." He proposed to himself "merely to write a fanciful story, evolving a thôtful moral, and *did not* propose attempting a portraiture of italian manners and customs." And yet, so faithful are the descriptions of objects and scenery in **Rome**, that it mit serve a visitor to that city as a guide-book. Those who see in the "fanciful story" a deeper meaning may regard the work as an allegory, illustrating the "war of sense with soul". Vued in this lit, it would be easy to imagine the animal instincts impersonated in Donatello; the moral sense, in Miriam; æsthetic taste, in Kenyon; and a severe type of probity, in Hilda. In the conduct of the story, the reciprocal influence of these qualities would produce the "transformation." [C: M. Barrows. **817**

MARGARET [by ÉLIE B. BERTHET: London, *Weir*, 1845.] "is an interesting tale. The scene is laid in a séquestered valley among the french Alps. The principal man of the valley, Martin Simon, styled by the inhabitants King of Peloux, without any ostensible source of wealth, has performed wonders in the valley, the whole of which is his property . . . The rumor was raised that Martin Simon had discovered a gold mine in some of the almost inaccessible mountains surrounding the valley . . . At the appointed hour all the parties meet at the rendezvous. Each, believing himself to be exclusively the favored party, is for getting rid of the others, and a regular fit almost ensues, which is stopped by Simon's proposing to conduct them to the gold mine, which is situated near the summit of a hi peak, accessible only by a rude sort of stair formed of piled blocks of granite, and that only on one side. After gratifying their curiosity, he reminds them that nit is coming on, and that they must immediately descend, which they reluctantly do. When all are safe in a cavern, Simon fires a train of gun-powder, which, exploding, undermines the only approach to the gold mine; the rocks roll down into the valley with horrible din, and the goldmine is forever cut off from human access." [Westminster Review. **818**

MARGARET MULLER. [by — ( ) BERSIER: *Seeley*, 1872.] "This unpretending tale deserves to be read by everybody to whom the example of kindness, self-denying generosity, and courage, will be an incitement 'to go and do likewise,'— not, perhaps, in a repetition of the actual facts, but in works of a like spirit, which in one shape or other lie ready to the hands of each one of us. The story itself

is delitful: it is almost worthy of Erckmann-Chatrian." [Athenæum. **819**

MARGERY. [by G: EBERS: *Gottsberger*, 1889.] "It is the first business of a novel, as of any other work of art, to 'enjoy' people, and they never attain their final end in any other way. 'Margery' eminently fulfils that purpose. Its readers must feel themselves indebted to the man who could so wholesomely and so fully entertain and recreate their minds. The time of the story is the first half of the 15th century, the place old **Nurnberg**, the actors all catholics, and the narrator, Margery Schopper, one of the 2 most charming young women lately introduced into fiction, the other being her dearest friend, Anna Spiesz. But the tale depends so little upon plot or motive, and so much upon style and character-sketching—the latter done with bold strokes and no niggling—that no attempt at condensation could do it any justice. It is full of incident, too, and what looks like excellent local color." [Catholic World. **820**

MARIA WUZ [by JEAN PAUL F: RICHTER] and LORENZ STARK [by J: JAKOB ENGEL: *Longman*, 1881.] "No task in prose translation could be much harder than to give an idiomatic and intelligible version of Jean Paul, with that abrupt and rapid fancy of his, for which no combination was too elaborate, no allusion too remote, no digression too sudden or too long. The first part of this dainty little volume is a bily successful attempt to defy these difficulties. *Maria Wuz*, 'the merry-hearted Dominie' of Auenthal, is among the earliest and simplest of Richter's romances: a charming little idyl, of less than 50 pages, which ôt to meet a warm welcome from english readers who appreciate 'Sartor', and who, if justly weary of the imitators of Carlyle, may still be able to relish his more genial and tender literary progenitor. The second tale, by ENGEL, is an interesting picture of middle-class life in the last century." [Spectator. **821**

MARIE, by PUSHKIN, = *The Captain's Daughter*.

MARIE DE BERNIERE [by W: GIL-MORE SIMMS: *Lippincott*, 1853.] "is a story of **New Orleans**, all about an old house and secret passages, and a ghost mystery, solved by the trapping of an artful father confessor with the wax mask of a dead man's face. The story is well told." [Westm uster. **822**

MARJORIE'S QUEST . [by JEANIE T. .. (GOULD) LINCOLN: *Osgood*, 1872.] "is a story for 'young people' who are not disposed to look too critically into a novel for a study of character, or an enunciation of social problems, but quite ready to be satisfied, as long as there are plenty of interesting incidents, and everything comes rit at last. The book before us fulfils these conditions admirably. Marjorie, the heroine, is twice lost herself, besides having to find her father; loses her memory; gets it back again; rides 18 miles into the Confederate camp (the story is written from a unionist point of vue), to have an intervue with General Early, in order to speak to the character of a prisoner, who, tho she does not know it, is her old playmate and future lover; saves him; finds her father; and at last marries, or is to marry the rit man who has been marked out for her, since as a boy of 16 he played with her, a child of 10. Of course there must be a little shade in this cheerful picture. So we have the nauty little girl and the ill-natured big boy, whom we have been familiar with from a very early age, and we have a wicked old woman who steals Marjorie, and a man who somehow knows all about her first disappearance, and comes at the rit time to tell her where to find her father, and gets killed directly afterwards; but these are, as all the world knows, necessary as examples of what happens to bad people, and do not spoil our pleasure at the satisfactory disposal of all persons. Well, a story of this kind is not hi art, but it is pleasant as serving to show that there is still some demand among young people in America for the same kind of simple amusement as has satisfied them in all ages, and that . love of children and

reverence for parents flourish no less in the New World than in the Old. As to the children, indeed, Miss Gould introduces us to some of the most delitful with whom we are acquainted." [Athenæum. **823**

MARMORNE [by PHILIP GILBERT HAMERTON: *Blackwood*, 1878.] "We seem to see the very spot in the wooded hits of Bourgogne whêre these strange events took place. Still more unusual, there is no character-painting in this strange book. We are not excited by analysis of motives or anatomy of passions. The book is a narrative throuôut, simple, straitforward, and reticent. The story enthrals the reader, and leaves an impression of power entirely controlled and under discipline, which of itself is a strengthen'd sensation. Not often do we meet with this sentiment of fresh cool strength, able to grasp its subject thôroly, to manage it calmly, and to resist all those currents of emotion and tradition which shape a novel into the mold of its kind, in most cases whether the author will or not ... The very atmosfere of the district, which is curiously unlike the lafing country which we realize under the name of Bourgogne, is in the book; and the old house of Boisvipère, morne, silent, shut in with its surrounding woods, is like a fotograf—while the happier dwelling of Marmorne itself gives one of the truest sketches of a thôroly french country-house which we remember to have met in english literature." [Blackwood's.] Time: the war of 1870. **824**

MAROUSSIA, A MAID OF U-KRAINE. [by "P. J. STAHL", i. e., P: Jules Hetzel: Paris, 1878,—*Dodd*, 1891.] "is a story of devotion and heroism such as flowers out of russian despotism.. The end is sorrowful enuf, but the sacrifice which it records is the fit end of a most beautiful and significant life. Such a story of patriotic matyrdom is like a trumpet call." [Atlantic. **825**

MARQUIS DE LÉTORIERE. [by EU-GENE SUE: Boston, *Nichols*, 1873.] "We think no more enjoyable story will issue from the press this year, than this dainty little volume. It exhibits the best qualities of french fiction,—grace, spritliness, epigrammatic vigor, and admirable deftness of characterization, and not one of its bad ones. It proves—what the reader of fiction mit reasonably doubt—that it is possible to make an intertaining novel with very little, or not any love-making. Love-scenes drawn by a skillful hand are pleasant to read; but we are sure no one will lament their absence in this book." [Boston "Literary World." **826**

MARQUIS JEANNE HYACINTHE, see *TEACHER OF THE VIOLIN*.

MARQUIS OF CARABAS (The) [by H. [E..] (P.) SPOFFORD: *Roberts*, 1882.] "is powerful, fascinating, and brilliant, romantic to a degree which is almost fantastic, and descriptive of entirely improbable people in utterly impossible situations. There is the usual elegance of surroundings; it is not enuf that a young man's name should be Gascoigne instead of Smith; he must spell it with a 'y' to suit the fastidious taste of the author, and it is never to be forgotten for a moment that her marquis could have been a marquis if he had chosen. Mrs. Spofford can do nothing without a great many ruby rings and superb gardens and heroes whose faces are an 'impersonation of impassioned splendor." [Critic. **827**

MARQUIS OF LOSSIE (The). [by G: MACDONALD: *Lippincott*, 1877.] "Malcolm, the hero, is a favorite groom of a Scotch nobleman and also his legitimate son, tho ignorant of his relation till informed by his father on his death-bed. His half-sister, Florimel, dauter by a second wife, succeeds to the title and estates of the Marquis. Malcolm is possessed of evidence that his mother, tho believed to be dead, was living when Florimel was born, so that his sister has neither title nor name. But throu affection for her he suppresses the facts, and serves as groom to the Marchioness of Lossie, not revealing the true state of the case till the close of the story, and then only in order to prevent his sister's marriage with a dis-

solute earl. While acting as her groom in London, he wins the heart of a lady of hi rank, and finally her hand, which is given while he is believed to be but a stable-boy. The principal characters are strongly drawn, and there is no lack of incident and romance. No one can read such a story without receiving good impulses. In both the plot and the minor incidents there is, however, a hi degree of improbability; and the delited reader can not forget that conversation like these between countesses and grooms never occur in life, least of all in english life." [Boston "Literary World." **828**

MARRIAGE OF MOIRA FERGUS [in Lady Silverdale's Sweetheart, by W: BLACK: *Low*, 1876.] "belongs in an episodical way to the most delitful of Mr. Black's novels—'The Princess of Thule.' They will not be sorry to hear a little more about the manners and customs of the inhabitants of "The Lewes," and to have a glimpse at Sheila Mackenzie (now Mrs. Lavender) in the settled life which has succeeded to the early troubles of her not over well-assorted marriage. Lavender himself has improved since the reader first made his acquaintance, but of his friend and mentor, Ingram, we have only a hint, tho, as before, he appears as the practical man who gives good advice in an emergency. This story ends happily enuf." [Athenæum. **829**

MARRIED IN HASTE, see *BERTHA'S ENGAGEMENT*.

MARRIED TOO EARLY. [by S.. B. WILLETTS: *Brentano*, 1885.] "The better type of southern fiction is represented by this unpretending story. The tone is dignified and restrained, the style quiet and clear, the quality pure and wholesome, and the interest decided. The time is that before the Civil War, tho the 'peculiar institution' is nowhere prominent. Plantation life in several fases affords the background. The beginning is at **Charleston**, the scene shifts to the sand-hills of Aiken, and then to the lower Mississippi Valley and **New Orleans**; later there are digressions to Europe and to the North, with a vue in particular of Nantucket and of its village of doll-houses (Siasconset) on the ocean side. There are 2 persons in the book who are 'married too early', Gertrude Moreland to Philip Rodney, and Fred Masterton to little Theresa, the german girl. There is a reasonably happy married life in both cases, with some alternation of clouds and sunshine, and with a measure of variety in incident amounting almost to plot. At last Philip dies, and Masterton and Gertrude, who had been early lovers, come together for the remainder of their years. The book wins respect." [Boston "Literary World." 830

MARTIN CHUZZLEWIT. [by C: DICKENS: 1844.] "I do acknowledge that Mrs. Gamp, Micawber, Pecksniff,— and others have become household words in every house, as tho they were human beings; but to my judgment they are not human beings, nor are any of the characters human which Dickens has portrayed. It has been the peculiarity and the marvel of this man's power that he has invested his puppets with a charm that has enabled him to dispense with human nature. There is a drollery about them (in my estimation, very much below the humor of Thackeray) which has reached the intellect of all; while Thackeray's humor has escaped the intellect of many. Nor is the pathos of Dickens human. It is, stagey and melodramatic. But it is so expressed that it touches every heart a little. There is no real life in Smike. His misery, his idiocy, his devotion for Nicholas, his love for Kate, are all overdone and incompatible with each other. But still the reader sheds a tear. Every reader can find a tear for Smike ... Tho they are not human beings, we all remember Mrs. Gamp and Pickwick. The Boffins and Veneerings do not, I think, dwell in the minds of so many. Of Dickens' style it is impossible to speak in praise. It is jerky, ungrammatical, and created by himself in defiance of rules—almost as completely as that created by Carlyle. To readers who have taut themselves to re-

gard language, it must, therefore, be un-pleasant. But the critic is driven to feel the weakness of his criticism, when he acknowledges to himself—as he is compelled in all honesty to do—that with the language, such as it is, the writer has satisfied the great mass of the readers of his country." [Anthony Trollope. 831

MARUJA [by [FR.] BRET HARTE: Houghton, 1885.] "is clever. The nervous, energetic style tells to advantage in a tale like this of the wilful and beautiful Maruja—with her odd mixture of puritan and spanish blood and her queer assortment of lovers—where surprises are constantly awaiting one, and the approach to a tragedy is just near enuf to keep one's interest pitched hi . . . With the tramp lover, the successful one, with the brit sayings of the civil engineer, and the amusing figure of the California Aladdin, one can forgive the occasional want of simplicity." [Nation. 832

MARY ANERLEY [by R: D. BLACK-MORE: Harper, 1880.] "is a Yorkshire tale of such proportions and variety that we can not attempt an epitome of its plot, and must be content with saying that its characters are very numerous, and divided into 4 or 5 sets, each of which illustrates a different tho convergent action; that it is partly a sea-story, the hero being first a daring smuggler and afterwards a junior lieutenant on the 'Victory' at Trafalgar; and, in fine, that it contains the elements of 2 or 3 ordinary novels, and elaborates them all with ease. The time is the beginning of the century, and the book is a picture of english life which has a real value as well as a romantic interest." [Nation. 833

MASTER OF BALLANTRAE (The). [by RO. L: STEVENSON: Cassel, 1889.] "A tale of more unmitigated gloom, with less admixture of any consolation human or divine, it has seldom been our lot to read ... From beginning to end the brothers of · Durrisdeer hate each other with boundless and unchangeable animosity. There is no relenting on either side,—even less perhaps on that of the virtuous and otherwise tender-hearted brother than on that of the reprobate. We are made to feel that his utter odiousness, falsehood and selfishness have been revealed with such pitiless distinctness that Henry hates in James the incarnation of every evil quality ... There are abundance of beautiful sketches of Durrisdeer and the surrounding country. But in the story itself the sun never shines, the air is lowering and ominous, a constant consciousness of calamity, of wrong and injustice, brooding over the house. In the midst of this gloom, however, the two prominent figures revealed to us are masterly ... The Master of Ballantrae is thus, even when he risks his life for it, without faith or principle, a mere interested adventurer. He is afterwards a vulgar traitor betraying his friends to the government, sucking the very life-blood of his family by a pretense of danger which no longer exists for him, —a pirate on the seas, by land a chevalier de l'industrie, living by his wits wherever he goes, betraying everybody who trusts him: he is full of taunt and intolerable mockery, a man with the gift of driving others almost mad with his tung, as well as of putting a remorseless knife into them with the greatest coolness if they happen to come in his way. This monster is, however, the most charming and delitful of men. He is gay and polished and debonair; he has every social gift, and, in addition to everything else, a perception of character and of goodness." [Blackwood's. 834

MATT [by RO. BUCHANAN: *Appleton*, 1885.] "is a very brit and amusing bit of narrative. It has none of the extravagant scenes and descriptions which are scattered throu Mr. Buchanan's longer stories. The pleasant personality of the young artist who goes gypsying in a caravan shines throu all his erratic behavior, and Matt, whenever she appears, manages to conduct herself with the cool independence which may naturally belong to a girl who 'wasn't born at all, but come ashore.' The events of the last chapter are hurried, and the reader has to give up

trying to reconcile the very unprincipled Mr. Monk's knowledge that Matt was true heir to all his acres with his ignorance of the existence of the fatal prayer-book and the marriage lines. The puzzle, however, is not so annoying as to detract from the pleasure of a story told directly and frankly for the story's sake." [Nation. 835

MAUPRAT [by "G: SAND:" transl. by Hays, *Churton*, 1847.] "opens with a grafic sketch of the state of France prior to the revolution, and the manners and influence of the nobility in provinces distant from the capital." [Westminster.]— "The plot, which turns on the moral education of a fierce, undisciplined boy, under the guidance of a refined, hi-spirited girl, enables the writer to avoid drawing the perfection of love by drawing the imperfection of an unformed character ... And certainly the picture of the 2 cousins, Edmée and Bernard is exquisitely drawn, and the gradual progress of the education conceived with great nicety of thôt and worked out with admirable skill. Edmée caut in the robbers' stronghold of Roche-Mauprat, purchases her delivery from disgraceful violence by a vow never to belong to anyone but Bernard, then a hot headed young savage ... The comprehension of this, the realization to himself of the fact that a woman would rather die than allow herself to be brutalized to his level, is the great awakening force which stimulates him to a new life. It is impossible to describe the beauty with which the action of Edmée's influence is conveyed. 'Mauprat' is not written according to an english model. The handling is broad. George Sand tries to imagine clearly, and she certainly expresses openly, what would be the real feelings of a hot-blooded boy. She neither shrinks from the subject of fysical sensations, nor vêils it in the obscurity of penny-a-lining eufemisms. But if she is so far truer to nature than would here be thôt decorous, she is also true to nature in a manner which is truly admirable. She is true to the power of purity, to the sustaining force of generous thôts, and to

253

the docility of a passion great enuf to be humble." [National Review. 836

——, SAME, transl. by Lord, *Roberts*, 1870.

——, SAME, transl. by Miller, *Laird*, 1891.

MEDUSA. [etc.] [by ADELAIDE (KEMBLE) SARTORIS: *Loring*, 1868.] "This volume of sketches is to be praised, like its predecessor, 'A Week in a French Country House' [No. 558], as giving in its fulness the pleasure which one gets from a perfectly easy, graceful, unaffected, and yet thoroly artistic style. We do not know of more delitful lit reading, and have found our enjoyment of them quite unimpaired by several re-perusals. The theme of nearly everyone of these sketches is music—the well-known love of their author for that art, and her successes in it, furnishing her with material which is wonderfully well adapted to her peculiar literary talent. The little romance which gives its name to the volume, and which most nearly resembles an ordinary story, having in it a curious love episode, and 2 shadowy appearances which bear an odd resemblance to a hero and heroine—is the least successful. Like the rest, it is of course full of charming writing; but the pleasure one gets from that is quite dissociated from any interest in the story. Mrs. Sartoris is neither a romancer nor a novelist; but we know no one who excels her in the use of artistic language—in the faculty of so sketching persons and places that her presentation leaves in the reader's mind a clear and definite impression which he feels to be precisely that which he was intended to receive. There is, we think, not one page of either of her books from which we mit not quote passages which would amply prove our case. We content ourselves, however, with advising everyone who can take delit in the manner, without making too serious demands upon the matter, of books to read them at once." [Nation.] See *PAST HOURS*. 837

MEMOIRS OF A GOOD-FOR-NOTHING. [by JO. VON EICHENDORFF: *Leypoldt*, 1866.] "The tale which Mr.

Leland translates so gracefully is an extravaganza, in marked contrast to all the other romances of Eichendorff, inasmuch it is purposely farcical, and they are serious; but we imagine it does not differ from them greatly in its leading qualities of fanciful incoherency and unbridled feebleness. An idle boy, who is driven from home by his father, the miller, and is found with his violin on the road to nowhere by 2 great ladies and carried to their castle near Vienna,—who falls in love with one of these lovely countesses, and runs away for love of her to Italy, and, after passing throu many confused adventures there, with no relation to anything which went before or comes after, returns to the castle, and finds that his lovely countess is not a countess, but a poor orfan adopted by the great folk,—and so happily marries her,—this is the Good-for-Nothing and his story. A young student of the german language, struggling throu the dusty paths of the dictionary to a comprehension of the tale, would perhaps think it a wonderful romance, when once he had achieved its meaning; but being translated into our pitiless english, its poverty of wit and feeling and imagination is apparent; and one is soon weary of its mere fantasticality." [Atlantic.]— It "is one of those artistic, bohemian, semi-mystical tales of love and music and wander-years of which 'Wilhelm Meister' is the head and front. The old castles are the old castles of Goethe; the orange-trees and pine-forests, the wandering minstrels, students and painters all have their prototypes in that universal romance. The characters, especially the women, with their mysterious disappearances, their bewitching songs and Lorelei-like advances to bewildered youths, are lineal descendants of the filosofic-æsthetic dames of the second part of 'Wilhelm Meister.' The Good-for-Nothing, or Taugenichts, is a youthful gardener's assistant, with a lively imagination, a disgust for honest toil, and a romantic habit of falling in love with nymf-like beauties on a hi plane, as he supposes, of society. His pursuit of a fair lady leads him over the mountains to the land where the oranges grow, and throu a variety of pleasing and fantastic adventures which bring him back at last to the old castle from which he started, where he is united in marriage with the lady of his love, and the mysteries of the plot are explained—after the manner, again, of 'Wilhelm Meister.'" [Critic.   ·   838

——, SAME ("Leaves from the Life of a Good-for-Nothing") *Lippincott,* 1889.

MEMORIES, = *GERMAN LOVE.*

MILLIONAIRE OF ROUGH AND READY (A) [by Fr. B. Harte: *Houghton,* 1887.] "Bret Harte, like Homer, sometimes nods in telling his tales of the Argonauts. But in 'A Millionaire of Rough and Ready' he is very wide awake. His crisp, firm, direct style is the best possible medium for the stories he has to tell. Here he effectively teaches the lesson that circumstances do not bring happiness, and above all, that riches may bring worse evils than poverty. The story is a work of art without the exaggeration which mars some of his other stories and without their false sentiment. A miner named Slim finds gold at last. But, having tasted by anticipation the joys of wealth, he is stricken with paralysis. Alvin Mulrady, instead of squatting on the land, went to the owner, Don Ramon Alvarado, and offered to manage a farm 'on shares'. Don Ramon and his son, Don Cæsar, are drawn truthfully and delicately. Their hi-breeding gives them even in poverty an incalculable superiority over their rich but vulgar nebors." [Cath. World.   .   839

MINISTER'S WOOING (The). [by H. (Beecher) Stowe: *Ticknor,—Low,* 1859.] " 'The Minister's Wooing' is a love tale, a religious novel, and a historic —or, rather, biografic—fiction, all in one. Regarded as the first, it deserves almost unqualified praise . . . The scheme of that part of the story on which the rest of the narrative is hung is simple and pretty enuf. The drama opens with a tea-party in the parlor of the Widow Scudder, who

is a lady blessed with a small farm and a gambrel-roofed cottage on the outskirts of **Newport**, a charming dauter (the heroine),—a sweet little maiden just emerging from childhood,—and a hi reputation for the possession of 'faculty' . . . The good man is a bachelor, something over 40 years of age, and besides officiating zealously amongst his congregation, ministering to his afflicted black brethren, and writing a profound system of divinity, finds time to act to the fair Mary Scudder (his landlady's dauter) the part that Abelard did to Héloise. He is her tutor in religious and secular studies, and she, in return, instructs him in the art of loving; but unlike Héloise of old, Mary conceives for him only that reverential affection which a young maiden naturally entertains for her pastor, who appears to her as the expression of all the goodness that is possible in humanity. The Widow Scudder would gladly see her dauter love the pastor dearly enuf to wish to be his wife; but the meek, gentle child, wilful in one thing only, bestows her heart on a wicked scapegrace of a cousin, James Marvyn, who having run away to sea, returns from forein countries to láf at the sanctimonious ways of the godly people of Newport, and to question the doctrine of election and predestination . . . Instead of being drowned, James Marvyn has returned rich. The rest of all this pretty romance can be imagined. Mary acknowledges to James that he has her heart; but she is, nevertheless, determined to keep her promise,—her solemn engagement to good Dr. H., and bids her lover not to hinder her from doing her duty. There is a pause of uncertainty and suspense. The awful day draws nearer; but ere it has arrived, a jolly little dressmaker, Miss Prissy, who acts the part of an amiable sprite all throu the play, informs the Doctor of the state of the case. The fine-hearted man takes all the sorrow of the position to himself, surrenders the timid child he loves so dearly to the man of her choice, and sets his face resolutely forward to do his duty in that unwedded

ROMANTIC NOVELS.

life which it seems Providence has designed for him ... If the book should
become popular, its success will be won,
not by its polemical qualities, but by the
winning graces of the heroine and her
little friend of the great world, Virginie."
[Athenæum. **840**

MIRAGE OF PROMISE (A) [by HAR-
RIETT PENNAWELL BELT: *Lippincott*,
1886.] "is a beautifully written story of
the early part of this century. It does
not claim to be an historical romance, but
much of actual history is interwoven in it,
and a vivid picture is given of the sufferings of abolitionists as well as slaves in
the conflict that waged for so many years
before the actual war. The scene in the
hero's rooms when the mob threaten him,
is a capital picture, and the entire story is
a novel of vivid and picturesque effects
illustrating the sternest truth, and certain
therefore to give pleasure to both 'romantic' and 'realistic' readers." [Critic. **841**

MISSION FLOWER (A). [by G: H :
PICARD: N.-Y., *White*, 1885.] "Those
who enjoyed Mr. Picard's 'A Matter of
Taste' will come to this new novel with
expectations of choice literary work, a
refined and delicate atmosfere, gentle
irony, dainty humor, and careful study of
character. All this they will find, and
more. This new story has fresh elements;
is placed in a section of the country not
yet made over-familiar to us by writers;
is planned and carried out with exquisite
skill; deals with the deepest emotions of
human hearts; is tender, is tragic; and
has the power of holding the reader's interest in a tense strain, tho it is not overwrôt or untrue to life in its portrayal of
the complexities which involved the 6
men and women who are the chief actors.
The period covered is short; the scene, a
valley in what the author designates as
'midland country' of America; the personages are Manuel Silva, of spanish and
english parentage; Dona Solace, his nominal ward; Roger Paradise, who has come
from England with his sister Nellie;
Madame Clement, who is the head of a
sisterhood from Port Royal; and Father

Caron, Superior of the great mission
called St. Xavier's-in-the-Valley ... After
a brief moment of rapture, she has the
truth from her lover's lips—he did kill her
father, but in self-defense. The crisis,
towards which everything has been moving, has this almost unlooked-for feature
of Dona's love, for her admission just referred to has left us mystified. She is a
new kind of heroine in american fiction,
as the finely-delineated Silva is a new
hero. The chapter which shuts them off
from each other is one of intense power
and painfulness. He has told her all ...
Silva, who has our sympathy (we have
had a suspicion of the crime from the
first), gives himself up, but the authorities
will not accept him; and after great prostration he is nursed back to partial health
by Nellie, and promises to follow her and
her brother to England, but the end
comes in a different way. Such are the
leading features of a story of such consummate skill, that as a purely artistic
piece of work it deserves to be placed beside 'Ramona.'" [Boston "Literary
World." **842**

MR. ISAACS [by FR. MARION
CRAWFORD: *Macmillan*, 1883.] "thoroly
deserved the reputation it made. As a romance of eastern life, open, by its very nature, to those encounters of the magical
which are foreign to our colder prose—
belonging still, notwithstanding modern
habits and western culture, to the period
of the 'Thousand and One Nits'—the attractions of mystery, wonder, passion and
romance, the latter all modern, the former
all antique, which united in this book,
were very great. The hero himself in
his complicated personality was so real,
altho so improbable, that there was nothing to be said against him." [Black-
wood's. **843**

—— SAME, [*parody*] "Mr. Jacobs, A
tale of the drummer, the reporter, and the
prestidigitateur," by ARLO BATES, Boston, *Clarke*, 1883.

MRS. KNOLLYS. [in The Sentimental
Calendar, by F: J. STIMSON: *Scribner*,
1887.] "Tho at times a too pronounced

256

literary manner is perceptible, a conscious effort for unconsciousness, there run throu the sketches strains of gentleness and tenderness, wtth flashes of worldly wit and fun, which help to make a very attractive style." [Nation. **844**

MISTRESS OF IBICHSTEIN (The) [by FRIEDERIKE ( ) HENKEL: *Holt*, 1884.] "is one of the good old-fashioned court stories, full of intrigue and plot, secret rooms and secret marriages; sensational, it is true, but sustaining the interest to the end. It is at least original in having for a heroine a young lady who is neither very good nor very bad, but cold and scornful, and doubtless somewhat startled herself when she learned from the will that she had been selected as heiress because 'in her I was charmed to find a person capable of acting with heartlessness, selfishness, and cold understanding.' The story is well worth reading." [Critic. **845**

MODERN MEPHISTOPHELES (A). [by LOUISA MAY ALCOTT: *Roberts,— Low*, 1877.] "At times the story is enigmatical, the parallel is not very closely maintained, and the author's diction, never mean, often becomes so sublime as to be unintelligible." [Athenæum. **846**

MODERN MIDAS (A). [Man of Gold) by MAURICE JOKAI: *Worthington*, 1885.] "Maurice Jokai reveals the complex and hily romantic fortunes of 'A Modern Midas' most skilfully. The selection of fields comparatively fresh to the English reader, and of character's nearer to nature than the ultra-civilized ladies and gentlemen whom most of our novelists struggle to mold into heroic form, gives him a great advantage for dramatic purposes. Very probably the fact that few of us are on terms of familiar intercourse with the dwellers by the lower Donau may add much to the charm of the story, for we are not called upon to determine what passions or emotions are natural or possible to a multitude of Greeks, Turks, and Hungarians. From the moment that Timar and Timea appear in the grainladen vessel on the Donau, the reader

must mentally let himself go. .Timar is the supercargo, and Timea the dauter of Ali Tschorbadschi, flying, with great treasure, it is whispered, from the wrath of the sultan. Tschorbadschi dies on the voyage, and Timar gets possession of his priceless jewels in a way which, not to put too fine a point on it, is far from honest. He thus lays the foundation of the fortune of Midas and of the great unhappiness of Timar. His practical restitution by marriage with Timea is vain, and vain, too, are his enormous public charities. The man is afflicted with a moral nature which, to quote the author, "longed for honesty, human respect, filanthropy, and self-sacrifice; but by a strange and sad destiny he had, throu temptations too great, for him to withstand, become a man whom others esteemed and honored, but who must despise himself." Only on "No Man's Land," cut off from the world by the waters of the Donau, can Timar find any peace for his soul. And even here there is always the sting that Namoi, the loving Eve of his Paradise, knows nothing of his true position, and nothing of his cold, faithful, wronged wife, Timea. The methods which the author adopts to free Timar from his burdens, insuring long life and happiness, are not at all in harmony with the english standard of morals, nor has he been trammelled by any prejudice in favor of the final reward of good and punishment of evil. He has, however, followed the prompting of a thoroly artistic nature, and brot his story to a logical and natural if unriteous conclusion." [Nation.] "Those to whom Jôkai Môr is a time-honored name will not be gratified to see him dubbed 'Herr,' and called 'the V : Hugo of the german tung.' That the translation is not direct from the magyar is self-evident, and that it is from the german is equally clear. In many respects 'Timar's Two Worlds' may not only be regarded as its author's masterpiece, but as a master-piece of european literature. Had 'Monte Cristo' never been written, Timar mit never have made his fortune; but there is an individuality about the Hungarian's personages the famous frenchman's do not possess. Altho the work possesses much of that oriental profusion of incident characteristic of hungarian fiction, and the changes of fortune and variety of adventures which beset the hero seem, to the occidental mind, to savor of the miraculous, the thread of the tale is never lost sit of, nor do the personages ever lose their respective individualities. To all classes of novel-readers the story should prove attractive." [Athenæum. 847

——, SAME ("Timar's Two Worlds") *Blackwood*, 1888.

MONSIEUR MOTTE [by G.. KING: N.-Y., *Armstrong*, 1888.] "is a collection of 4 stories illustrative of **Louisiana** life and character. Miss King's creole studies have a quality of fineness which is frequently lacking in Mr. Cable's work in this sort. The '*Marriage of Marie Modeste*' strikes us as the most charming of these stories, tho in this, as in the other tales, Miss King falls into an error that destroys the illusion. She makes her characters speak a mixture of french and english. Their dialog should be wholly in french or wholly in correct english translation." [Atlantic. 848

MOOR OF PETER THE GREAT, see *CAPTAIN'S DAUGHTER*.

MORE SAIL THAN BALLAST. [by C. A. MONTRESOR: *Allen*, 1889.] "Miss Montrésor has taken as the ground-work of her story a passage which will be familiar to readers of Carlyle, referring to certain domestic reforms introduced into the court of Carl Eugen, duke of Würtemberg. With the assistance of Körner and Vely she has treated the historical incidents with some degree of verisimilitude. The duke himself and his friend Franziska von Hohenheim appear in this narrative as their traditional repute mit have led us to expect, and we seem to get a fair idea of life and manners in the Ludwigsburg of 7 score years ago. The greater part of the volume, however, is occupied with the fortunes of Hans Ritter, a musician without much moral ballast, with his thoroly human wife, Olga, and with their friends,

as to most of whom history is silent. The story is romantic, and quite prettily told." [Athenæum. 849

MOSAIC WORKERS (The): and ORCO. [by G: SAND, i. e., A. L. A. (Dupin) Dudevant: London, *H. G. Clarke*. 1844.] "The mosaic 'masters' of Venice are the heroes of this tale; and we may remark that it does not contain a sentence to which the most fastidious reader could object." [Westminster Review.] "It cannot fail to delit the reader and inspire him with an interest in art and artists. The 2 master mosaists, or workers in mosaic, of which it treats are Francesco and Valerio Zuccato, who were commissioned by the Senate of Venice to execute some of the mosaics in Saint Mark's. In describing and illustrating their character and career the author is naturally led to touch upon events and persons of historic importance, so that her work presents a lively picture of venetian life at the period, while it is penetrated throuout with a lofty artistic enthusiasm." [Athenæum. 850

——, SAME, ("Mosaic Masters"), tr. by ASHURST, London, 1847 (177 pp.)

——, SAME, in "The Crayon", Jan.-Sept., 1856.

MOUMOU. [by IVAN TURGÉNIEF: In *Lippincott's Magazine*, Apr., 1871.] "Like everything of Turgénief's, it is deeply tragical: but there is a poetical element which relieves the somberness, and which brings it about that the effect which he produces is not, on the whole, depressing; unprosperous and sad tho his conclusions may be. Perhaps it is that he so surely in every case gives us, amid much which may be base, sordid, cruel, and unhappy, some aspect of human nature which is so lovely or so strong that we cannot but feel in the end elevated and strengthened. Even the cruel inscrutableness of fate, and man's subserviency to it —a thot very familiar to Turgénief's mind, is in a way very elevating and strengthening. And were it not, we should say that this writer has never presented it without, as we have said, giving us at the same time some vivid presentation of some beautiful or strong quality in the victim which causes us to rise unsaddened and even braced. This is to be truly tragical in the best sense. Compare, or rather contrast, with this the effect produced by the reading of another great master of the sombre and tragical, Hawthorne. Turgénief's very great merits as a poet, as a delineator of character, as a thinker, and as a story-teller it would be well if our reading public appreciated more fully than it does. This tale of "Mou-mou" is a simple little thing as regards its story, and will be best enjoyed by readers who have some training in the reading of poetry, and not so much enjoyed by those who care more for novels strictly so-called. It treats of some passages in the life of a russian serf, a gigantic deaf-mute. It is exquisitely pathetic and beautiful with true beauty, both in the few and slit details and in the main conception." [Nation.] "There are some half-dozen of Turgénief's short stories absolutely perfect, each in its way, but none perhaps quite so exquisitely as 'Moumou' shows the artist's power to transfigure to our eyes the tendernesses, passions, agonies, which lie beyond speech and almost beyond sign in the silent heart of a strong, simple man. Carlyle gives the tale mention in one of his letters, and awards it hi praise. The tragedy of the little story, is, like all Turgénief's tragedy, of the most hopeless kind. No vista of happiness opens out of the harsh, savage facts of every-day life. We can see no prospects for Moumou except that of dogged endurance: no good comes out of the evil he has endured and must continue to endure. There is no consciousness either for him or for us that his suffering is made important even by its relation to the general sense of human struggle and heroic example." [Lippincott's Magazine.] In Mumu the chord of pathos is sounded with an art so exquisite that it ceases to be art; it has the supreme reach of the whole gamut of human sympathy, and its appeal is irresistible. The materials are so simple that one wonders how such an effect is produced. It is only the story of a poor deaf and dumb serf, a mute Herakles, whose love for a little dog works as a transforming element in his life, and yet, as Turgénief unfolds it, the narrative becomes a profound revelation of character. It is full of human possibilities. We see that we, under like conditions, mit have felt and acted thus. The intense sympathy becomes at times painful. The expression of the elementary emotions is almost too realistic. How carefully each detail is worked into place; and nothing superfluous, nothing which does not have a vital part in the desired result! the minor personages, those that appear but once or twice in the course of the tale, are outlined as firmly and truly as if fotografed from life. Moumou will bear a great amount of study; it marks out a whole method in fiction." [Boston "Literary World". 851

——, SAME ("The Deaf-Mute") in *Ladies' Repository*, feb., 1878.

——, SAME, transl. by Gersoni, *Funk*, 1884.

MY HOME IN THE SHIRES. [by Rosa Mackenzie Kettle: *Weir*, 1876.] "This pleasantly written volume derives its interest from the description of italian country life, rather from any english experiences. The heroine, dauter of an englishman by an italian mother, is much perturbed in childhood by the circumstance that the tenure of her country home by her family depends on the pleasure of a distant and unknown relative. The fact that Guy L'Estrange is half austrian, as she is half italian, does not tend to make her more sympathetic with this ogre of the nursery. At length, Guy comes home, and, as Mr. Lester, he wins Margaret's affections, and so completely belies her ideal of him, as to prove a good fairy to her italian connexions, and even to give his only dauter in marriage to a fantastic patriot of that nation. Tho by no means exciting, this is a readable and pleasant tale." [Athenæum. 852

MY LITTLE LADY. [by Emma F. Poynter: *Holt*, 1872.] "It is to be doubted, if the author will ever create a character more charming and lovable than Madelon, the Little Lady. Madelon is the only child of Monsieur Linders, an adventurer, a professional gambler. From city to city, from watering-place to watering-place they roam; living in hotels, in lodgings, always gay, never alone, but having no true home, no real friends. At last the poor, reckless, unprincipled, but loving father dies suddenly in a Paris hotel, and the 10 year old Madelon would have been left to the mercy of the land-lady, but for the accidental presence of a young english surgeon, who has seen her 5 years before at a german spa and learned to pity and love the pale, elf-like child. The adoration which Madelon had felt for her father she transfers to Monsieur Horace, the young surgeon; and, tho he disappears from her life for years, the devotion never wavers. Madelon's life in the convent of which her Aunt was the Superior, her escape, her refuge with Jeanne Marie, a village inn-keeper, her going alone to the gaming tables at Spa, to win a fortune for Monsieur Horace, her strange rencontre with him there,—all these scenes are vividly told, and are by far the best in the book." [Scribner's.   853

MY LORD CONCEIT [by "RITA", i. e., Eliza M—J—(Gollow) Booth: *Maxwell*, 1884.] "opens well, but the interest flags when the heroine becomes engrossed in her babies. Rita is almost as fond of babies as 'Miss Mathers,' and writes quite as much pretty nonsense about them. It is a charming trait, and one for which the reader is very thankful, for he soon learns that all the baby talk may safely be skipped. It does not at all interfere with the story—it is, in fact, wholly irrelevant. In 'My Lord Conceit' the two babies are killed with a sudden ruthlessness which would have made even Dighton and For-rest shudder. Perhaps "Rita" was afraid of herself, and saw no end to her story if those babies were to go on talking. An-other attraction in the book is an italian villain who really is a quite first rate vil-lain—one who not only lives by his vil-lainy, but makes it the charm of his life.

It is his recreation as well as his profession, and one rather regrets that he makes such a mess of it in the end." [Athenæum. 854

MY UNCLE BENJAMIN [by CLAUDE TILLIER: Boston, *Tucker*, 1891.] "is a fascinating sketch of the manners and customs of the 18th century. By a few masterly strokes Tillier has endowed his chief character with flesh and blood and placed him in full life before the reader. It is a rare creation, one of those which by a blending of the real and the ideal become the common property of all times and places, and are handed down with-out ever becoming trite or tiresome. The style is simple, concise and direct; the narrative natural and without reserve, combining a genuine feeling for nature and mankind." [Critic.   855

MYSTERIES OF THE PEOPLE (The) or The Story of a Plebeian Family for 2000 Years. [by EUGÈNE SUE: 1849; N.-Y., *Clarke*, 1867.] "To afford the readers of fiction a new sensation—to awaken in their minds a powerful interest for a large portion of the human race whose history has rarely been invested with much of the romantic element—and, above all, to im-part, throu the medium of a story of un-paralleled length and infinite variety, an amount of instruction the acquirement of which would necessitate years of severe study, is a task which none but a man of the hiest order of genius, combined with warm sympathies for all humanity, could hope to accomplish." [Round Table. 856

MYSTERY OF THE LOCKS (The). [by EDGAR WATSON HOWE: *Osgood*. 1884.] "An old, failing town, by a sluggish Western river; a gloomy, uncanny man-sion, on lonely hill-top, with a tradition of ghostly footsteps coming and going over its stairs and corridors; a handsome, cultivated stranger, who hides his identity under an assumed name, and lives alone in the gloomy house; a girl, a dainty speci-men of sporadic beauty and genius; a vil-lain as ugly and captivating as ever ap-peared in the pages of fiction; an almost equally fascinating ne'er-do-well; a lurk-ing shadow of danger threatening the happiness and life of the stranger; a coterie of quaint gossips; an 'ancient maiden,' delitful in her sharp-spoken antiquity; a dreary background of decayed shops and warehouses, of mist and rain and mud, of sluggish waters roused to a fury of destruction; and a climax of grotesque, hi-wrôt tragedy—these are the elements going to make this strong, vivid, strikingly original, uncouth, impossible—possible novel. The impression left after a perusal of the book is anything but agreeable; it is like that which remains from the inspection of some terrible realistic painting like Rembrandt's 'Anatomical Lecture;' and yet one cannot deny the sombre genius employed in its production. It is indicative of Mr. Howe's essentially artistic power, that he occupies himself very little, if at all, with mere description. Before he has finished 2 chapters, the reader has in mind as clear and definite a picture of the decaying river-town of Davy's Bend as if he had spent a life-time within its borders, and yet with how few, firm, broad touches does the author convêy his meaning! And so of the men and women who figure in these pages—they are unlike, most of them, any of the men and women we have known; but we do not think for a moment of doubting their reality. They are flesh and blood; in speech and manners they are untrammeled by our limiting conventionalities; even the exquisite portrait of the heroine ('the only flower in a community of weeds') has a wild grace which differentiates her from all other pretty and accomplished women; and the love-making toward the close of the book is as fresh and artless as true passion and natural refinement can make it." [Boston "Literary World." 857

MYSTERIES OF UDOLPHO (The). [by A.. (WARD) RADCLIFFE: 1794.] "The opening chapters breathe the spirit of domestic peace and enjoyment. The peasants in the twilit shade dance on the banks of the Garonne, 'after the use of mild antiquity,' and in the distance we behold 'the long waving line of the Pyrenees' ... It is impossible to specify

all the beauties of this gorgeous romance. There are in it some fine descriptions of Venice, with its isles, palaces and towers, rising from the water and reflected on its calm surface; gondolas flit by, from which issue soft music and sweet voices, adding to the beauty of summer seas and moon-lit-nits ... The transition from the gayety and glittering splendor of Venice to the gloomy and savage grandeur of the Castle of Udolpho is described in Mrs. Radcliffe's happiest manner. The castle is filled with mysterious sounds, gloomy corridors, banditti, vaults, trap-doors, appliances and means which the lovely authoress knew how to use so well. Annette, the chattering, superstitious waiting maid, has her heart and mind occupied, and Emily comes in for her share of trouble, anxiety and heart-aches, but is at last amply rewarded both in wealth and love. Perhaps the scene and adventures at Chateau La Blanc possess the hiest interest. The disappearance of Ludovico, (from a haunted chamber,) after reading a fritful tale; the visit of Emily, at midnit, to the apartments of the marchioness, which had been closed for 20 years; their magnificence and gloom, the black pall on the bed, articles of dress scattered around the room; the strange resemblance of Emily to the marchioness, which likeness is hitened by her putting on her vêil, and touching the lute whose strings had been silent throu so many long years; the deep silence;—all these are described in a solemn and affecting manner." [American Review. 858

NANON [by "G: SAND": Roberts, 1890.] "is the prettiest of stories,—so pretty, so pure that it cannot be called french at all. It is a tale of peasants in eastern France just prior to the Revolution, and the story is so enveloped in green woods and pastoral ways, such tinkling waters and rural sweetness, that it becomes a poem before many pages are wrôt, and one follows its autobiografic revelations as quietly yet as intently as the lamb follows his mother ... Gradually, however, sounds more harmonious are heard.

261

Nanon and her, now, armless · lover go
back to the old home and the old ways,
and live beautiful lives of love and gratitude, and their union shows the complete
reconciliation of peasant and proprietary
class." [Critic. 859

NARKA. †by KATHLEEN O'MEARA:
Bentley, 1888.] "These are the raw
materials of a story rich in picturesquely,
conceived characters, in effective incidents,
and in pathetic situations. The story of,
Ivan Gorff is specially interesting as an
illustration of the manner in which the
condition of things in Russia may betray
a man naturally noble-minded into crime
of dastardly character; and yet, while the
author evidently feels keenly the force of
her impeachment, she does not lose her
head, and 'Narka' mit easily be regarded
either as an assault upon russian autocracy,
or upon the utterly unscrupulous revolutionary movements by which it is assailed. Apart, however, from all political
significance, the book is a thoroly interesting, well-constructed, and well-told story."
[Spectator. 860

NESTLENOOK. [by LEONARD KIP:
Putnam, 1880.] "There are some people
in the book whose love affairs serve to
lighten the somewhat serious tone of the
main plot. The story as an attempt at an
american romance has considerable merit.
The author has hit upon just the tone
which alone is capable of lending a romantic lit to the practical, prosaic outlines of
american life, but he is more successful
with his tone than with the execution of
the details of his picture. A romance of
this sort to be good needs to be perfect,
and Mr. Kip is not a master of romance.
The book is chiefly interesting as a suggestion of what mit be done in romantic
writing with the materials afforded by
ordinary modern life." [Nation. 861

NEW ANTIGONE (The). [by—BARRY:
Macmillan, 1887.] "There is a provoking
quality to 'The New Antigone.' It is so
good that we long to have it a little better.
There is great charm in the opening chapters. Their scene is the beautiful country
seat of an earl, their dramatis personæ

are ladies and gentlemen described by one
who knows the species; there is a flavor
of art and antiquity to redeem the commonplace of rank and prosperity, and a
beautiful entourage is well and picturesquely sketched. And the 'New Antigone' is
a delitful creature, in spite of the fact
that she is dauter to a well-born nihilist
and thoroly imbued with all his wildest
notions. It is in the carrying out of these
principles, in which she puts an innocent
credence, that she shipwrecks her life and
that of her lover. But the story is what
it terms itself, a romance rather than a
novel, and with all its flaws has a redeeming originality about it which lends it interest." [Boston "Literary World." 862

NEW PRIEST IN CONCEPTION BAY
(The) [by RO. T. S. LOWELL: Boston,
Phillips, 1858.] "brings us into perfectly
fresh and unhackneyed scenery and manners, in the island of Newfoundland;
certainly as unknown to most of us as if
it had never been found at all. Its great
charm lies in its descriptions of the life
and character of the primitive fishermen,
among whom the story is placed, and the
constant lovely bits of word-painting, sea,
sky, and shore, in that lonely region,
given with such lingering and constantly
recurring delit, that one sees well what
dear companions they were in the author's
island life." [Christian Examiner.] It is "a
book of power and beauty, combining
true pathos with irresistible humor, masterly in its delineation of character, hily poetic in its descriptions, betraying in the
strength and compactness of its language its
author's familiar acquaintance with the
masters of our tung, and giving in the
guise of a most attractive story well put
and telling arguments for the faith of England's Church. This book from the first
established its claim upon popular favor,
as striking out a new path in our literature, and giving us fresh and living creations attractive from their originality, and
brot before us with unusual skill."
[Church Monthly. 863

NEW RACE (A). [by "GOLO RAIMUND", i. e., Bertha (Heyn) Frederich,

1810-83: *Lippincott*, 1880.] "What purity so pure, what sweetness so sweet, as that of a really pure, sweet German story, such as the judicious [see No. 595] Mrs. Wister now gives us? It is short, graceful, and tender; full of the warm lit which glimmers over the Rhein, redolent of the virtues of charity and consecration. It opens, to be sure, with a dark chapter of family wrongs, but the worst comes first, and the end is peace. The old Zährenburg, the central scene of the story, stands before us like a picture; and the figure of Eva von Zähringen is one of angelic loveliness. There is a real freshness in the scheme by which she seeks to make restitution to young Waldemar for the injury which has been done him in her name; but when, in her disguise, she enters his mother's service, to minister to him in his blindness, it is easy enuf to foresee the conclusion. The restoration of his eye-sit by a stroke of litning is an uncommon piece of good fortune, but we do not know that it is incredible. The beauty of the story is in the quietness of its movement, the loftiness of its motive, and the simplicity of its style." [Boston "Literary World".]—" 'A New Race' is the rather misleading title of Mrs. Wister's latest translation, which has the qualities, albeit a good deal diluted, of its predecessors. The heroine, whose mother has been wrongfully deprived by her husband's family of her fortune, is reinstated by her grandfather, who accomplishes the task, however, by very sharp practice, which his desire for revenge justifies to him. After his death she attempts to redress the wrong her cousin has suffered at his hands, and her success is followed by their happy marriage, and 'the new race' which grows in the old castle promises to inherit only the virtues of its ancestors—a fulfilment which would certainly entitle it to a new label. The story, it will be seen, is sufficiently mild, tho it has romantic episodes." [Nation. 864

NICHOLAS NICKLEBY. [by C: DICKENS: 1839,] "As for the charities of Mr. Dickens, multiplied kindnesses which he has conferred upon us all; upon our children; upon people educated and uneducated; upon the myriads here and at home, who speak our common tung; have not you, have not I, have not all of us, reason to be thankful to this kind friend, who soothed and charmed so many hours, brot pleasure and sweet lafter to so many homes; made such multitudes of children happy, endowed us with such a sweet store of gracious thots, fair fancies, soft sympathies, hearty enjoyments? There are creations of Mr. Dickens' which seem to me to rank as personal benefits, figures so delitful, that one feels happier and better for knowing them as one does for being brot into the society of very good men and women. The atmosfere in which these people live is wholesome to breathe in; you feel that to be allowed to speak to them is a personal kindness. You come away better for your contact with them, your hands seem cleaner from having the privilege of shaking theirs. Was there ever a better charity sermon preached in the world . than Dickens' *Christmas Carol?* I believe it occasioned immense hospitality throughout England; was the means of liting up hundreds of kind fires at Christmas time; caused a wonderful out-pouring of Christmas good feeling; of Christmas punch-brewing; an awful slauter of Christmas turkeys, and roasting and basting of Christmas beef. As for this man's love of children, that amiable organ at the back of his honest head must be perfectly monstrous. All children ot to love him. I know two that do, and read his books ten times for once that they peruse the dismal preachments of their father. I know one, who, when she is happy, reads 'NICHOLAS NICKLEBY;' when she is unhappy, reads 'Nicholas Nickleby;' when she is tired, reads 'Nicholas Nickleby;' when she is in bed, reads 'Nicholas Nickleby;' when she has nothing to do, reads 'Nicholas Nickleby;' and when she has finished the book, reads 'Nicholas Nickleby' over again. This candid young critic, at ten years of age, said : 'I like Mr. Dickens' books much better than your books, papa,' and frequently expressed her desire that the latter author should write a book like one of Mr. Dickens' books. Who can? Every man must say his own thôts in his own voice, in his own way: lucky is he who has such a charming gift of nature as this, which brings all the children in the world trooping to him, and being fond of him." [W: M. Thackeray. 865

NIGEL FORTESCUE. [by W: Westall: *Ward*, 1889.] " 'Nigel Fortescue' fulfils very well the requirements of what are called in the trade "adventure books." Such books are not to be judged from a literary standpoint, being written to catch what one must call the taste of a class of readers who have no literary taste." [Athenæum. 866

NINETY-THREE. [by V: [M..]Hugo: 1874.] "Throu all his works, what a mixture of genius and grotesqueness, of majesty and absurdity! Take his 'Ninety-Three' ——a novel monstrously nonsensical and surprisingly splendid——a novel demonstrating that to pass from the ridiculous to the sublime, as well as the other way, needs but a step. With what magnetic power one of its first incidents, the rushing about of the loose gun on shipboard, is wrôt out! You begin by despising the frivolity of the scene, and momentarily wait to see the writer ludicrously break down in his preposterous attempt at imposing on your credulity. By degrees the situation is filled in till each successive objection of skepticism is somehow spirited away, and even the forein reader, sympathetically following the working of the french mind, is startled at his yielding. The episode of the roving cannon ranks with the devil-fish scene in the 'Toilers of the Sea,' where also the reader finds appreciated horror overcoming his first impulse of contemptuous incredulity." [Galaxy. 867

NO RELATIONS [Sans Famille], by Hector Malot: *Lippincott*, 1880.] "is the story of a foundling picked up in the streets of Paris, nurtured by a peasant woman, and finally, after divers adventures, discovering his ritful connexions. There is nothing original in this plot: what makes it so is the extremely skilful treatment it receives at the hands of its author. From first to last the fortunes of little Remi form a series of vivid and grafic pictures, true to life and thôroly pure and excellent in tone. Whether trudging at the heels of old Vitalis the showman, with Joli Cœur, Capi, and Zerbino, or floating in the Swan with Mrs. Millegan and Arthur, or exhibiting in company with little Mattia, his sworn comrade, or shut up for dark days of starvation in the Truyère mine, or earning the cow for Mother Barberin, or in the custody of the London thieves who personate his parents, he is everywhere the same truthful, affectionate, loyal child." [Boston "Literary World." 868

NOBLE SACRIFICE (A) [by Paul Féval: *Brentano*, 1888.] "is a fiction of the troublous times of the rebellion in Bretagne in the 17th century. It is a tale of noble lords and lovely ladies, with dungeons, escapes, and a grand wedding at the end. The romance is as satisfactory as a good fairy-story, and is so well-written that the pleasure is complete." [Critic. 869

NOBLESSE OBLIGE, see *ATELIER DU LYS*.

NORICA [by A: Hagen: *J. Chapman*, 1852.] "is a simple story, narrated in a quaint, pleasing manner. The rich Frankfurt merchant visits Nürnberg, with the vue of gratifying, in his simple way, his tastes for art and science. He arrives on the festal day of St. Sebaldus, the patron of the city; and in one of the processions he cast his eyes on a maiden whose modest beauty henceforth haunts his imagination. The heroine of the story, after many pretty mysteries and fluctuations between hope and disappointment, is wooed and won, finally accompanying the worthy Heller to Frankfurt. On this thread of romance the author skilfully strings several entertaining legendary episodes. But, while instructive, it never loses the unity and vivacity of a tale, and while unexciting in its incidents, it is hily romantic." [Westminster Review. **870**

NOTRE DAME DE PARIS [by V: [M..] Hugo: *Little & Brown*, 1887.] "was Hugo's coup d'essai in fiction, and it stands by itself, a work, so far as we know, without parallel—a piece of mediæval life and of universal tragedy, vivid, terrible, appalling. To think that Quentin Durward, fresh and simple, was just then walking into that lurid Paris, with its gloomy tumult and horror, to him a glorious daylit city, full of wonder and delit! The honest, open record may no doubt suffer in some points as compared with the other, in which the intensity of the effects suggest a constant flicker of torch-lit and all the fantastic shadows and illuminations of nit, rather than any shining of the sun. But Claude Frollo and Quasimodo, and even Esmeralda, are all spectres which vanish in the distance, wild semblances that breathe of fever and fancy; while the manly Scot and the solid figures about him stand fast as men and friends. Human nature with the one is ever cordial and honest and kind, which, all miseries notwithstanding, is its ordinary strain; but with the other it is dark, hapless, tragic,—a thing of misery struggling among blind and terrible forms, uncomprehended or unknown." [M. O. (W.) Oliphant.] "Esmeralda is a charming creation. She is a gypsy girl who gains her living by dancing in the public thorofares of the Paris of a former age ... She displays her visible beauties freely to the crowd; and yet she is chaste as assuredly no gypsy girl and dancer in the public streets ever was ... For this young creature, so graceful and so modest, we could have wished one of those lovers so common in romances—some young man of hi birth and great wealth—to extricate her from the grovelling impurities by which her outside only had been sullied, and elevate her to rank and fortune by making her his wife. But Mr. Hugo has disposed of her differently: he has made her enamored of a captain in the gendarmerie of Louis XI. The creature

who can love Esmeralda as she ôt to be loved is the poor bell-ringer, Quasimodo. ... deaf, hunch-backed, one-eyed—who lives sequestered in the farthest recesses of the cathedral, and has grown to manhood almost unvisited by the lit of day. Nothing can be more touching or more naif than the scenes between Esmeralda and Quasimodo on the platform of the tower. The unconquerable repugnance of the maiden, struggling with a gentle feeling of compassion for the poor bell-ringer— her efforts to reconcile herself to that countenance, so ungrateful and repulsive a mirror of a delicate and sensitive soul— the anxieties of Quasimodo, his devotedness, his intelligence—the sort of grace which love imparts to this monster—the conversations between these two beings, when Esmeralda softens towards the unfortunate bell-ringer, and permits him to remain a short time by her side; all this belongs, no doubt, to another world, but it is all interesting and touching; and if we may say with truth that it is overdrawn, it is an ingenious overdrawing of one of those all-but-impossible passions which we yet occasionally meet in life; between hideousness and beauty, old age and youth—between two beings, one of whom loves, but cannot be beloved; the other loves not, but is unable to hate. Mr. Hugo's writings appear in more favorable colors when remembered than when read. In that gentle and pleasing impression which a book leaves on the memory, the exaggerations disappear, the asperities are softened, the superfluities retrenched, the excesses of an ill-regulated imagination are blotted out, and the overdrawn figures (for they are all overdrawn, even when the original conception is in nature) are replaced by genuine and simple ones. Seen from a distance, Esmeralda and Quasimodo are beautiful creations of a romantic fancy." [Westminster Review. **871**

——, SAME ("The Hunchback") *Bentley*, 1856; N.-Y., *Dick*, 1862.

OBLIVION [by M .. Greenway Mc-Clelland: *Holt*, 1885.] "shows striking ability on the part of its author, and ability of a hi sort. Fresh and vigorous in handling, with a certain exaggerated force of feeling as well as expression, and real picturesque power, it stands head and shoulders above the rank and file of ordinary fiction. The scenery and people and dialect of the **North Carolina** mountains, among which the scene of the story is laid, are admirably rendered, with true pathos and humor. The plot turns on an accident. A lady, traveling alone with her child, is surprised by a freshet at a river-side inn. The house is swept away, most of its occupants lose their lives, the child is killed, but the lady is rescued with mind and memory utterly alienated by a blow on the head. For 3 years this hapless stranger lives among the ruf but kindly mountain folk, who adopt her into their lives, as it were, and give her the name of 'Lady.' Gradually her powers of speaking english return, and a certain interest in and ability for every-day matters, but all the past is still a blank to her up to the nit of the freshet. Dick Corbyn, a splendid young mountaineer, learns the road from pity to a passionate love, and she is on the eve of marrying him, when a second illness re-awakens the slumbering memory, saves her from innocent crime, and restores her to her old life and the husband who has long mourned her as dead." [Boston "Literary World." 872

ODDS AGAINST HER. [by MARGARET RUSSELL MACFARLAND: *Cassell*, 1888.] "Family life with us is so simple, and the descent of landed property so equitable, that it is hard to fully realize the intrigues incident to a state of society where exist primogeniture and entail. In 'Odds Against Her,' Margaret Russell Macfarland gives us a picture of the internal dissensions which divided a noble german family. A crusty, erratic old count; his headstrong sons and nefew; a beautiful, intriguing russian, beloved of 2 of them, herself determined to marry for his wealth the one she did not love; a little american girl, the dauter of the old Count's runaway eldest son and there-

fore [?] heiress to the family estates,—such are the characters of whom the story is woven. The story is well told, in a simple direct style, but is decidedly a development of plot rather than of character." [Critic. 873

OLD COUNTESS, See *BERTHA'S ENGAGEMENT*.

OLD CREOLE DAYS. [by G: WASHINGTON CABLE: *Scribner*, 1879.] "The fugitive sketches of G: Cable, collected under the attractive title of 'Old Creole Days,' are as fresh in matter, as vivacious in treatment, and as full of wit as were 'The Luck of Roaring Camp' and its audacious fellows when they came, while they are much more humane and delicate in feeling. The scene of all these 7 sketches is laid in **New Orleans**, and certainly no other city on this continent ever began to exhibit such bizarre conjunctions of race and lively clashings of race prejudice as did the gulf city during the earlier half of the present century,—for a generation or so after the cession of Louisiana ... Mr. Cable draws powerfully upon his reader's emotions also, touching rapidly and surely the stops of lâfter and of tears. Some of his plots are better made than others, and occasionally he is almost over-dramatic, relying solely upon the action of his puppets, and hardly pausing or condescending to explain sufficiently, in his own person, to make his motive intelligible. But again, in the smiling tale of Madame Délicieuse, the construction is perfect;—airy as gossamer, and yet firm as steel. '*The Belles Demoiselles Plantation*' is the most pathetic of the 7 legends. *Jean-ah Poquelin* is darker and grimmer in its tragedy but singularly impressive. '*Posson Jone*' is exquisitely droll. One and all have an ardor, a spontaneity, a grace of movement, a touch of fire, which are severally present as elements, and summoned in that rarest of endowments, an original and delitful style. Mr. Cable's dialogs are so concise and complete that quotation cannot illustrate them. Each one is a dramatic whole, which to break is to mutilate." -[Atlantic. 874

OLD FRENCH CHATEAU NEAR TOULOUSE (The) [by EDGAR W. DAVIES: Boston, *Loring*, 1879.] "is a nice, lively, bugaboo story, apparently of modern times; a suitable mixture of haunted castles, gypsies, grated vaults, smugglers, battles in the dark, and the inevitable english peer traveling with his family. Things seemed a little 'mixed' at the end; but this is natural, and in the course of the story there are various points from which the reader does not see his way out at all, which we take to be the object of a mysterious plot." [Nation. 875

OLD KENSINGTON [by A.. [ISABELLA] (THACKERAY) RITCHIE: *Harper*, 1873.] "needs no words of ours to commend it to a host of readers. It is a more ambitious story than any she has yet written; and if it is inferior to her *Story of Elizabeth* [No. 533], which reads like truth itself, it may yet be deserving of praise. The story is long and quiet; the plot is ingenious, tho perhaps a trifle artificial; but the characters are all well drawn, and the whole novel is marked by a repose which is never dulness. Miss Thackeray always draws young girls and children well, and here, with the honest, frank girl in contrast with her crafty friend, her usual skill does not desert her. Dorothea's earnest and affectionate nature is admirably described. Especially good is the way in which is told the gradual decay of her love for Robert Heſley, as she sees him grow, and she gets a clearer vue of his vanity and selfishness. The story abounds, too, in clever, but not too clever, remarks about the different characters, and of delicate descriptions of scenes and places." [Nation. 876

OLD MAM'SELLE'S SECRET (The) by "E. MARLITT," i. e., Eugenie John: *Lippincott*, 1867.] "A more charming story, or one which, having once commenced it, seemed more difficult to leave, we have not met for many a day. The abstruse and often incomprehensible theories with which german novels are so frequently burdened find no place in these pages, nor are they crowded with any

strange filosofical speculations. Nature, its outward form and beauty; life, its quiet enjoyments, its cruel injustices, its bitter dissensions; man, and the heart of man, the author has thoroly studied; and the strongly-marked characters—few in number, but all of importance to the narrative —stand out before us as complete human beings, their faults and their perfections skilfully laid bare, their motives and their actions clearly defined ... But the power and ability of the author are not fully called forth until a later period of the story. In the terrible conflicts between love and pride by which both man and woman are equally, tho from different causes, torn, the contrast between man's fierce struggles and the inner workings of the woman's spirit, strong by nature and strengthened by adversity, are drawn with nice discrimination, and display on the part of the writer a freshness and vigor of thôt sometimes uttered with fierceness, but never exaggerated or unreal." [Round Table.] "The mystery in 'The Old Maid's Secret,' when it comes to be revealed, is the record of a deed of dishonesty committed by the old maid's father, and concealed by her from motives of filial duty; but it has really very little to do with the story. The history of an orfan girl forced upon the reluctant charge of a bitter, harsh-tempered woman, who, without knowing all the pain and grief she causes, crushes down the child, depriving her of all education and even of common kindness—training her to domestic drudgery without the wages—despising her because her father was a conjurer: the child in spite of this upbringing, growing up a beautiful young woman, having been secretly taut and trained by the old maid, Aunt Cordula. The eldest son loves her, but he is too proud of his respectability to marry the dauter of a conjuror, and she is too proud to accept him; but they are reconciled in the end. He discovers that his 'house' has shared the ill-gotten wealth, and the girl forgives the past. After much storm and tempest and violent emotion, restitution is made, and all ends happily. The style is very hi-flown; the story is often obscure and enigmatical; but there is a substantial interest in it, which will carry the reader to the end." [Athenæum.   877

——, SAME ("Secret of the Old Mademoiselle), transl. by Sprague, in *Ladies' Repository*, May-Oct., 1868.

——, SAME ("Old Maid's Secret"), *Strahan*, 1871.

OLD MONSIEUR'S SECRET, *Carleton*, 1882, = *M'LLE DE MALEPEIRE*.

OLD MORTALITY. [by SIR WA. SCOTT: 1816.] "Scott is one of the poets (we may call poets all the great creators in prose or in verse) of whom one never wearies, just as one can listen to Beethoven or watch the sunset day by day with new delIt. I think I can read the *Antiquary*, or the *Bride of Lammermoor*, *Ivanhoe*, *Quentin Durward*, and OLD MORTALITY, at least once a year afresh. Now Scott is a perfect library in himself. A constant reader of romances would find that it needed months to go throu even the best pieces of the inexhaustible painter of 8 full centuries and every type of man; and he mit repeat the process of reading him 10 times in a lifetime without a sense of fatigue or sameness. The poetic beauty of Scott's creations is almost the least of his great qualities. It is the universality of his sympathy that is so truly great, the justice of his estimates, the insit into the spirit of each age, his intense absorption of self in the vast epic of human civilisation ... Such is Scott, who, we may say, has done for the various fases of modern history, what Shakspere has done for the manifold types of human character. And this glorious and most human and most historical of poets, without whom our very conception of human development would have ever been imperfect, this manliest, and truest, and wildest of romancers we neglect for some hothouse hybrid of psychological analysis, for the wretched imitators of Balzac, and the jackanapes frasemongering of some Osric of the day who assures us that Scott is an absolute philistine." [F: Harrison.   878

OLD TUNE (The). [by H. F. CRAVEN: *Tinsley*, 1876.] "The author has earned the credit of a happy thôt in selecting for his hero the nearly forgotten author of the tune of 'Rule Britannia'. His plot deals with the loves of the composer and Miss Cecilia Young, and the story is prettily told, from the first appearance of the young lady as a ballad-singer on a snowy Christmas nît, to the eventual triumf of Arne's affection over the wiles of a designing widow and her bullying brother. Captain Flabberly, like too many others in the story, is a purely farcical personage; but the bold scheming of these reprobates for the hand and fortune of the "poor simple fiddler" is, at any rate, less excruciating reading than the gloomy sentimentalism which pervades most modern novels. Cecilia's character is piquant, a pleasant mixture of modest simplicity and shrewdness, and the gentle good faith of the hero is picturesque and pleasant. 'The Old Tune,' tho by no means transcendental in its aims, is a readable and lively story, tho the plot is naively improbable, and the wit occasionally a little thin and overstrained." [Athenæum.   879

ON THE EDGE OF THE STORM. [by MA. ROBERTS: *Putnam*, 1869.] "Without any especial merits beyond its good taste and cleverness, which, however, are qualities rare enuf to be noteworthy whenever they are found, this story is still very pleasant reading. Its scene is laid in France, and the time is the beginning of the Revolution. What has pleased us most in it is the even-handedness with which the author deals with both parties in the contest, neither making the aristocrats all angels nor the republicans all fiends, but describing both with impartiality. The same evenness is found in other respects throuôut her work, her characters being all well and carefully drawn. Another pleasant thing about it is the care with which painful scenes and incidents are avoided, while, at the same time, one is made to see the possible ease with which the reader's feelings mit have been harrowed." [Nation.   880

ON THE HEIGHTS. [by BERTHOLD AUERBACH: *Leypoldt*, 1867.] "We do not wish to do this book the injustice of telling its story in a hasty and necessarily imperfect manner, and shall merely indicate its main current, in order to speak intelligibly of the thôt which underlies it, and honorably distinguishes it from the rank and file of recent novels. The story turns, then, as we have said, upon the requited love of the king for a maid of honor to the queen, a woman not only as young and beautiful as her rival, but even equally beloved by her husband. She is, however, a woman full of romantic feeling, and lives habitually on hits of sentiment and enthusiasm which the king finds slitly fatiguing. Irma, on the other hand, has a charming vivacity, a fine and untrammeled intellect, and an aversion from all laws but those of her nature, which make her attractive by contrast with the queen and doubly so by sympathy with the king. ... These letters throw a bomb-shell into the midst of the king's domestic arrangements. The queen had long been the only person at court who was unaware of the true state of things, and she has been kept from the knowledge only by her own purity and her confidence in that of others. Her anger and contempt for those who have violated her trust are doubly bitter for this reason. She upbraids the king for the deceit practised on her, and declaring that his guilt and Irma's death must always remain a barrier between them, lives thereafter in a state of virtual separation from him. Irma, however, is not dead. Almost at the moment when about to accomplish her design of suicide, she was saved by Walpurga, a peasant woman who had lived for a year in the palace as nurse. Walpurga is a charming character, full of naiveté and goodness, and some of the most delitful writing in the book concerns her and her household belongings. With her, Irma lives on a farm in the mountains for 4 years, occupying her time in carving on wood, and her thôts in speculating on the problem of her existence ... The theme of sin and expiation is one constantly recurring in fiction: but we remember no instance in which it is treated on grounds so lofty. We all know how Hawthorne used it—the positive form in which evil appeared to him, and the terrible immortality with which he endowed it. His books, therefore, notwithstanding their artistic power, are morbid and depressing. Like his Hester Prynne, we chafe, and grow rebellious under the too heavy yoke imposed upon us. Mr. Auerbach, on the contrary, does not outrage the individual, altho he rigidly circumscribes his individuality. His heroine, voluntarily shut out for years from all companionship with her equals and all intercourse with books; with the memory of her sin always before her, and saying to herself, 'I will quietly bear the consequences of my actions alone by myself, looking for no material or spiritual help from without', has the rare courage to contemplate things as they are, and arrives at last at a state which is neither resignation nor despair, but a calm serenity in which the outworn consequences of the past drop from her, and she has a rit to say: 'Whatever may have happened, it is atoned for. There is a renewal of life, a deliverance achieved out of ourselves." [Nation.] "In "On the Heights" there is at once a large and exacting plan, and a worthy execution of it. It is a wonderful double poem, running on in 2 currents of narrative, which now meet and blend, now separate widely. The simple life of the village on the mountains, and the elaborate and formal life of the court, and the same human nature in the actors and the spectators of both! Finely conceived also are the characters in both groups— Walpurgis and her husband and the village inn-keeper on the one side, and the king, the queen, and the Countess Ida on the other. Nowhere else in modern german fiction have we a book which comes so near to the novels of Goethe in their union of artistic simplicity with deep meaning." [Penn Monthly.   881

ONLY A FIDDLER. [by HANS CHRISTIAN ANDERSEN: N. Y., *Hurd*, 1870.]

"In their childhood, this little Naomi and Christian (the fiddler) meet, and he never ceases to love her throu all the changes of fortune which lift her so far above him, when the count takes her and rears her as his own dauter. She grows to be a brilliant, lovely, wicked girl, who attracts all which is bad from her surroundings. She has a strong brain and a strong will, and submits them both to a handsome, ignorant savage,—a gypsy circus rider, with whom she elopes and with whom she wanders about Europe in a man's dress. But finally she marries a french marquis, and is left in perfect prosperity and unhappiness; while poor Christian, the musician, having failed to win the fame on which he had set his heart, greatly for her sake, dies in poverty and loneliness. This is an outline of a work which is full of the most charming flts, the most melancholy shadows, the most pathetic blending of both." [Atlantic. **882**

ORCO, See *MOSAIC-WORKERS.*

ORTHODOX [by DOROTHEA GERARD: *Longman*, 1888.] "is a fresh, brit, and absorbing story, purporting to be written to an austrian officer, and telling in the first person how his comrade, Rudolph von Ortenegg, fell into the hands of the 'polish Jews; how he fell in love with the beautiful Salmoe, and all the complicated and disastrous results." [Boston "Literary World."] "In 'Orthodox' we have a strong and dramatic story, characters drawn with unflinching power, no scenery, no setting, except what is necessary; no softness, no beauty, and only the sad and stern side of what we call romance. Count Ortenegg's love story cannot be called attractive; it is, in fact, told with a certain reticence, not to say coldness, which makes it more like a man's work than a woman's. There is hardly one superfluous word in the book, and every slitest touch is in its rit place, leading to the catastrofe. This masterly directness is uncommon ... Ortenegg himself, with his persistent self-deception, his proud, unswerving faith in human nature, even in Jewish nature, generous and noble hero

as he is meant to be,' has the common weakness of heroes: he is a little unnatural ... It is the Orthodox Jews of a town in austrian Poland who give the story its name. They are the chorus of the drama. ... But of all the characters in the story, the cleverest and most original is Surchen, imp of darkness as she is, the lovely little incarnation of all the vices that have ever been ascribed to the jewish character ... In short, 'Orthodox' is an extremely clever story. It will be perceived that it is also a painful story, and many readers, no doubt, will feel themselves injured by the end of it. For our part, we admire the courage of a writer who dares to bring her story to its most likely and natural end." [Spectator. **883**

OTHMAR. [by "OUIDA," i. e., L.. de la Ramé: *Chatto*, 1886.] "This novel bears the name of a man, but its chief interest consists in the analysis of a woman's character. It is a continuation of Princess Napraxine; both books deserve perusal for their careful and artistic realisation of a very original conception of female character,—whether drawn from life or evolved out of the depths of the author's inner consciousness, we are puzzled to determine. Can Kirké exist without the faintest trace of sensualism, and can a woman breathe absolutely without the instincts of passion and of maternity? Princess Napraxine, afterwards Countess Othmar, is made to do so, and her personality is so vividly rendered in these pages, that notwithstanding her apparent incongruities and impossibilities, she lives and breathes and interests us far more than either of her rivals can do, lovely, innocent, and loving women tho they be. She is the spoiled child of fortune, the queen of society, beautiful as a flower, brilliant as a diamond, with a keen intellect and a powerful understanding, a woman's wit and a man's courage, chaste as an icicle, and proud as Lucifer. In spite of her coldness (or, perhaps, because of it) men are attracted to her, as moths to the candle; she rejoices in her power, and amuses herself with the adoration of her slaves, but feels no more pity for them than the senseless flame can do for the singed wings and shrivelled corpses of its victims. Partly cosmopolitan by birth, entirely so by education, she is equally devoid of patriotism and of religion. To her, all creeds, all countries, all prejudices, are alike sources of curiosity and objects of contempt; she neither loves, nor hates, nor believes, but coolly analyses every emotion and every passion which crosses her path. A careful but unloving mother, a cold tho faithful wife, tolerant of folly, indulgent of weakness, impatient only of sentiment, she yet possesses noble instincts, which occasionally flash throu all the selfishness, cruelty, and cynicism which distinguish her. She is a woman 'fashioned like a sword'—a most courtly rapier doubtless, cold, true, and cruel as steel—one who mit have played a great part in life, if fate had brôt her the occasion of heroism, but whose finer qualities have been left to rust in the lap of luxury until her life is full only of the weariness of satiety. She is a female Solomon, weary of all things, and wise in all things, more especially in the science of love, much as Solomon himself must have been. . . . The history of this ice-queen's awakening is told with some art, and the dénoument shows much dramatic power. When she finds reason to believe that her husband's neglected adoration has been transferred to another woman, the passions of ordinary female humanity suddenly awaken in her, much to her surprise and disgust." [Spectator. 884

OTTILIE [by "Vernon Lee" i. e., Violet Paget: Unwin, 1883.] "is a short and slit story, pleasantly and carefully written. The characters are german, the scene is laid in 2 small german towns, and the time chosen is the last quarter of the 18th century. The tale is one of sisterly affection. Called upon to choose between her young brother and her lover, the sister prefers her brother's happiness to her own. The brother, less self-denying, makes a foolish marriage, afterwards is separated from his wife, and ultimately

finds consolation in the unchanging affection of his sister. The author lets the reader have a glimpse of Germany in the "Sturm und Drang" period, and vividly, and without tediousness shows society changing from the old to the new ideas. The story is pathetic without being passionate, and is elaborated with sufficient care and restraint to deserve to be called an idyl." [Athenæum.] "Her story certainly vindicates the author's claim to the privilege of presenting "imaginary lives in a quiet imaginary german town ?' They are sad and solitary folk, leading shadowed lives, but the remoteness of that still calm life is a restful picture amidst the hurry of ours." [Nation. 885

OUT OF THE WORLD. [by M.. (Healy) Bigot: Low, 1875.] "Very much 'out of the world' is the scene of Miss Healy's story laid, even in a solitary little Pyrenean village, the old château of which, tenanted by the marquis of Varenne, a Legitimist nobleman, poor, but of ancient family, is one of the kind with which we have long been familiar . . . Miss Healy has managed, not unskilfully, to complicate this element in her story by making her heroine, tho french by birth, american by education: and consequently, when she arrives at the château of the Varenne family, and finds out that a plot is formed to marry her, whether she will or not, to 'count Paul', eldest son of the old marquis, it is not so much a sense of the injustice which a marriage de convenance may do to a possible lover 'waiting in the vale of years' as a spirit of republican independence, which makes her resolve to hate the proposed suitor . . . So far, Miss Healy has told her story pleasantly enuf: the characters are natural, the incidents probable, and both act and react in a consistent manner." [Athenæum. 886

OUTBREAK OF THE FRENCH REVOLUTION (The). [by Erckmann-Chatrian: Bentley, 1871.] "The story is told by an old soldier of the First Revolution, who was born to the hard and cruel lot of a peasant under the old régime. The scene lies in an **Elsass** village. ... Marguerite, his dauter, is also his friend and assistant: on her first introduction she is only a young girl, but she grows before the reader's eyes into a young woman;—it is no wonder that Michel falls in love with her. The picture of the misery and abasement of the peasants,—the little stream of life from the outside world which comes with Chauvel, and the gradual awakening amongst the younger men of a sense that it is only justice, that in addition to paying taxes, they should also know how they were spent,—the *gradual consciousness that they, too, are human beings,—and their loyal faith that if the king only knew of their misery and oppression he would give them help,—is all vividly set forth. It is a domestic drama going on in the midst of the great events which were to change the face of the world." [Athenæum. **887**

——, SAME("The States-General"), 1877

OWL'S NEST (The). [by "E. MAR-LITT", i. e., Eugenie John: *Lippincott*, 1888.] "This latest translation from Miss Marlitt's [*sic*: fancy speaking of "George Eliot", as "Miss Eliot"] legacy of novels, if not quite up to the mark of 'The Little Moorland Princess' [No. 795] and other of her earlier books, is yet a very good story. It gives a picture of the intrigues and jealousies of a small german court, where Claudine, the heroine, passes unscathed throu a fiery ordeal of criticism and slander. The situation becomes painful when the young duchess, stricken by a mortal disease, is at last enlitened as to the court gossip about the duke and Claudine. The struggle of the wife who believes herself wronged, at least in feeling, by her friend and confidant, is very delicately and naturally given. [Compare plot of 'On the Heights'.] The duchess has too little strength to bear such excitements. Her very life seems at stake when Claudine, rising to the hits of feeling which prompt heroic self-sacrifice, offers to give her blood to save the duchess. This operation of 'transfusion' is rather a favorite one with novelists, and is always effective,

altho it is perhaps more uniformly success-ful in fiction than in life. The story is best at its close, and comes out to the satisfaction of the reader." [American.]

"Mrs. Wister lifts the gift of translation into one almost of creation, for it is the spirit of the original which she seizes, and at times puts into better form than the author. 'The Owl's Nest,' her latest rendition from the german of E. Marlitt, has the many delitful characteristics which have so individualized that author. It is a story of court life, and one gets domestic pictures of german men and women, of their constrained social attitude towards one another, of their forein point of vue—pictures which satisfy an interest which amounts to curiosity in readers of a different type and nationality. Marlitt's women, his [sic] heroines especially, are always charming. The fine integrity with which she bore herself as friend to the invalid duchess, the tact with which she repelled the duke's protestations, the disregard which she showed to the criticisms of gossip, her delicate reasonableness in the strained and difficult relations which had sprung up between her lover and herself, display a character of sweetness and strength. As in all of Marlitt's court-stories, a mild current of intrigue flows along, without ever breaking into a stormy surface." [Critic. **888**

PARISIANS (The). [by BARON LYTTON: *Harper*, 1874.] "The time is the period immediately preceding the war of 1870 and ends with the siege of Paris. The underplot is managed with great skill. Until we have almost reached the conclusion, there is no clue to the mystery of Louise Duval, and when the secret is unfolded, it turns out by no means as the acutest novel reader would have expected. Paris society, with its salons and clubs and cafés, passes before us. There are 1 or 2 of the old noblesse, some chevaliers d'industrie, devotees of the Bourse, sharpers, bohemians and workmen. The canvas is crowded; but the characters do not jostle one another." [Canadian Monthly. **889**

PASCAREL. [by "OUIDA", i. e., L.. de la Ramé: *Chapman*, 1873.] "A work, not of rich nature, but of bily wrôt art, with art itself, and genius and Italy for its theme, 'Pascarèl' is far in advance of Ouida's earlier novels. Those who liked them will be disappointed in this book; those who shunned them as flippant or immoral, while they guessed at the hidden power of the author, will find in 'Pascarèl' the accomplishment of the promise of 10 years. The story is a simple one:— the heroine, a deserted girl of half-english, half-italian blood,—the hero, a strolling tuscan player of noble family. She loves him with the innocent love of an almost child. He loves her, too, as Wilhelm Meister loved Mignon, but has a mistress with him, passing as his sister. Jealousy causes the peasant-girl to reveal Pascarèl's deceit, and thus blast 2 lives. The heroine recovers the position of her father; Pascarèl becomes great and famous, and, after years of misery, the lovers meet and love again. A charming novel, tho somewhat overburdened with allusions not quite gracefully introduced." [Athenæum. **890**

PASSE ROSE [by ARTHUR SHERBURNE HARDY: *Houghton*, 1889.] "is altogether charming; neither in plan nor execution, neither in scenes, in characters, nor in style would we have it other than it is. And yet the time chosen is the time of Charles the Great, more than 1000 years back, therefore; and he who compasses a space so great, and so adjusts it to the vue that his reader, while conscious both of the strangeness and the charm, is neither repelled by awkward modernisms nor irritated by cheap and ill-chosen archaisms, cannot be less than a consummate artist. The story is not one to be talked about and discussed in parts, for, altho it has both well-contrived plot and incident in plenty, it yet remains in memory as a series of charming pictures, so delicately conceived and finished that they seem to rise spontaneously, like a mirage, and one's impulse is simply to enjoy, and to call others to enjoyment. Yet the workmanship is substantial and masterly, and the characters stand out clear cut and full of life. Who will ever forget Passe Rose again, her beauty, her vigor, her pure love and sane sweet womanliness, after once making her acquaintance?" [Catholic World.] It "is an exquisite piece of literature but it has no more hold upon the facts of life than a 'Märchen.' Fairyland, or, at least, the land of mediæval romance, is the home of the figures in this story. We can hardly look upon them as creatures of flesh and blood, or upon their emotions as those of prosaic mankind. This matter of standpoint clearly understood, the reader who is prepared to give himself up to the poetical imaginings of the writer may be prepared to enjoy himself rarely. Guy of Tours, the Prince Charming of the tale; Passe Rose, the warm blooded provençal maiden; the great king himself, and the men and women of his court, are all creations of a singularly vivid imagination, and all inhabit, with peculiar fitness, their realm of fable. Descriptions of the kind which it is fashionable to call 'word-pictures' abound in these pages, being very acceptable. And all together, scenes and figures and passions, have a very genuine tho subtle charm for minds weary of realism and glad to breathe for a while the liter and purer air of fancy." [Dial.] "The design seems to have been rather to take a time remote enuf to allow free play to the fancy, and a picture of people swayed by the simple passions and impulses of humanity, undisguised by modern conventions. These Franks and Saxons are barbarians, not because of the rudeness of their manners and style of living, for these are not made prominent in the narrative, being softened to an extent that will make the judicious antiquarian grieve, but because they act throu fear, or love, or hate, unmixed with policy, and unrestrained by inherited self-control. For this reason the bad are very bad, and the noble are as boundless, in their generosity and self-sacrifice,—the same person may indeed be either bad or good as the one side or the other of his nature is appealed to, but at the moment the ruling motive has free course. The king, for instance, has no curb for his passions, his cruelty roused by opposition is terrible, and yet appealed to by Passe Rose's artless tale, his magnanimity is equally bqundless. Rothilde, gentle maiden tho she is, marks her victim for death without a tremor, and even Passe Rose pauses not for an instant to learn the fate of her rival, whom she has thrown over the battlement. Brother Dominic, under the influence of a superstitious fear, is no more of a reasoning being than his ass; and lured by the voice of the temptress, his yielding is sudden and complete in in spite of his monkish frock. In short, these people are children. Their brains can hold but one idea and that idea is followed with absolute abandon. Dealing with his unmixed colors, Mr. Hardy has wrôt a fiction which is like a stained glass window, besides which some of the modern realistic work looks like a fotograf." [Overland. **891**

PAST HOURS. [by ADELAIDE (KEMBLE) SARTORIS: *Smith;* 1881.] "Tho Mrs. Sartoris' slit sketches and stories cannot possibly be called important, they are full of a characteristic grace and humor. As mit, perhaps, have been expected, they chiefly turn on some point connected with the life and history of a great musician. But, on the literary side, the two stories of *'Medusa'* and *'Judith'* are quite the most interesting and powerful. There is a peculiar weird vein running throu the former, which is rather french than english, and gives it a certain strangeness. 'Judith' is but a fragment. The wilful little heroine is excellently described. The finished story, as we gather from the preface, would have been sad enuf; that warm, petulant, impulsive heart would have dashed itself to pieces in a hard struggle with the restraints of society. Genius would have brôt fame, but would have been no security against trial and temptation." [Athenæum. **892**

PATHFINDER (The). [by JA. FENIMORE COOPER, 1840.] "I have just read

'The Pathfinder', and it has given me a still hier opinion thou ever both of Cooper's head and heart. It is an admirable production, full of noble pictures of exalted virtue in the humbler paths of life. The characters of 'The Pathfinder' and 'Mabel Dunham' are noble conceptions. The old salt-water captain, also, is a masterpiece, with his nautical wisdom, his contempt for fresh water, and his point-no-point logic." [Washington Irving. **893**

PAUL PATOFF. [by FR. M. CRAWFORD: *Houghton,* 1887.] "The opening scenes are so good that did but the rest of the story fulfil what they promise, there would remain little to be desired. Mr. Crawford,—always an effective scene painter,—launches the characters admirably, with a rich oriental background, brilliant without false color, and elaborate without improper detail, and sets in motion in their behalf a succession of novel and exciting incidents ... These are the two chief personages of the story: Paul Patoff, and his brother Alexander, who is paying him a visit. The brothers are far from being congenial in tastes or habits. Paul is discreet and sensible, and disciplined to perfect self-command; while Alexander—a spoiled child—insists on the gratification of his most aimless impulses in order to dispel his ennui. He overrides all his brother's warnings that he is in a strange country, among strange people, and lâfs at the turkish customs. He addresses a vêiled woman with an impertinent compliment. This breach of propriety enrages Paul, and the brothers quarrel. The quarrel is followed shortly by Alexander's mysterious disappearance while he is looking on at some religious rites in the mosque at St. Sophia. He vanishes, is nowhere to be found, and there is not even the faintest clue by which to follow him. It is an unlucky circumstance for Paul that he is known to have quarreled with his brother, for not a few believe that he has murdered Alexander. So far the situation is interesting. A mysterious disappearance is an effective beginning for a sensational story. But Mr. Crawford proceeds to spoil the effect he has created by introducing a variety of new characters, scenery and incidents, which eclipse each other. He brings to pass strange events, describes hallucinations, mysterious encounters. The scene shifts from **Constantinople** to the Black Forest, and thence to England. Mr. Crawford is used to traveling the earth as if he possessed the magic carpet of the arabian tale. A mad doctor and a patient whose sanity or insanity is one of the problems presented to the reader, become two of the leading characters, and the tangle of events is not a pleasant one, altho a love-story is finally resolved by a conclusion wilder than anything in the Thousand and One Nights." [Athenæum.   **894**

PEARL POWDER. [by ANNIE EDWARDS: *Bentley,* 1890.] " 'Pearl Powder' belies its name. There is nothing of the rouged and white-leaded sort in it but the face of old Lady Joan Carr, a relic of the mid 18th century. And even she is so naturally drawn, in a soft half-lit, that from amusement we pass to liking; and not even the morning toilet scene, where she moralizes on her shipwrecked beauty for the benefit of her young friend, excites any feeling of repulsion. The heroine is all the more charming because she is not perfect. She pledges her hand to Oliver Arden and gives her heart to Henri Germaine, alias Liston, but we cannot blame her much. The artist, Oliver, is the weakest character in the book, and is happily very little in it, being away most of the time. Liston, on the contrary, is a fine gentleman of the old school, with a mystery about him which, when dispelled, discloses some folly, but more generosity. Philippa, who is also generous, loses her lover to save him. Later, when she falls heiress to Lady Joan's wealth, her generosity prompts her to throw herself and her fortune at Arden's feet, who, having at this time grown sensible, accepts them. The scene is near **London**. The wars of the Consulate thunder in the distance.

Lady Joan, who brings to bear the experience and the knowledge of scandal gleaned in a long and not too virtuous life in behalf of the innocent Philippa and the reckless Germaine, gives card parties by tallow-candle lit at Carr's Folly, and dies in a blaze of wax-tapers over the card-table, 'fiddlers playing, lits ablaze, the house looking on.' " [Critic.   **895**

PEG WOFFINGTON. [by C: READE: 1852.] " 'Christie Johnstone' and 'Peg Woffington' had a great success. Their crisp, sparkling, compact sentences went off like the volleys of a well drilled regiment. There was a dramatic intensity of interest and rapidity of action which were inspiring after the slow evolution of elaborate plots. The very brevity of the books seemed to be brilliancy. The style had a happy audacity which was irresistible. It was fresh, too, and poetic; and there seemed to be a certain earnestness under the stinging persiflage. The books promoted Mr. Reade immediately to a place among the chief living english novelists; and it was pretty clear why he was so popular." [G: W: Curtis.   **896**

PENELOPE'S SUITORS [by E. LASSETTER BYNNER: *Ticknor,* 1887.] "is a charming little story. Mr. Bynner has been bold but not reckless. He has avoided tragedy, even intensity, and has simply told, in Mistress Penelope Pelham's words, why she threw over her young lover, Edward Buckley, and wedded the Governor, Richard Bellingham. In the writing of this short diary the author's cleverness is most evident, because the author is nowhere to be detected. Neither Mr. Bynner nor any other man appears in a line of it. Its innocence and unconscious cunning, its simplicity and skittishness, even its neat sarcasm, are all pure maidenly." [Nation. **897**

PERE ANTOINE'S DATE PALM. [by T: BAILEY ALDRICH: in "Margery Daw," *Ticknor,* 1873.] "Mr. Aldrich's first essay in fiction was strictly romantic. It was that little story, called 'Père Antoine's Date Palm', printed nearly 20 years ago. Hawthorne gave himself the pleasure of writing to the young poet in recognition of its charm. Its tragedy is of an airier sort than his own; it is rather allied to the pathos of Mr. Curtis in his 'Prue and I' [No. 348] sketches; but the master of romance felt its exquisite art with sympathetic satisfaction." [Atlantic. **898**

PHILOSOPHER'S STONE (The), by H. DE BALZAC, N.-Y., *Winchester*, 1834.

——, SAME ("Balthazar"), London, 1859.

——, SAME ("The Alchemist"), N. Y., 1861. *Which See.*

——, SAME ("The Alkahest"), Boston, 1887. •

PICTURE (The), "by C : READE," See *M'LLE DE MALEPEIRE.*

PILLONE [by WILHELM BERGSöE: *Lockwood*, 1878.] "is a charming story. The bandit of our childhood reappears in the most gorgeous costume, with underground passages leading in every direction, a purse full of unset jewels, and all proper apparatus. We had forgotten what a delitful creature he is; how he deceives and outwits the stupid police, whom we feel to be our natural enemies; by what feats of strength, if necessary, he transcends all their foolish combinations; how he blows up old castles in a thrice; and where luck goes against him, how naturally he takes refuge in the crater of Vesuvius and there bides his time. There is nobody like him, and when the story is threaded together with telegraf lines, railroad trains, and modern politics, the effect on our nerves is doubled." [Nation, **899**

PIONEERS (The), see *LEATHER-STOCKING TALES.*

PISTOL SHOT (The), see *CAPTAIN'S DAUGHTER.*

PLANTER'S DAUGHTER, see *ALL FOR LOVE.*

PLANTER'S NORTHERN BRIDE see *COURTSHIP AND MARRIAGE.*

PLÉBISCITE (The) = *STORY OF THE PLEBISCITE.*

PORTRAIT IN MY UNCLE'S DINING-ROOM = *M'LLE DE MALEPEIRE.*

PORTRAIT OF CONCITTA P., by "E. GERARD", see *HIDDEN PICTURE.*

PRAIRIE (The), see *LEATHER-STOCKING TALES.*

PRETTY SISTER OF JOSÉ (The) [by F.. [E.] (HODGSON) BURNETT: *Scribner*, 1889.] "is a short story of **Madrid** —a love-story full of the passionate vehemence of the South. Pepita had soft, langorous dark eyes, which lured men on to love her. But in her soul she had neither womanly compassion nor the tenderness that comes from loving. Scorn and a mocking merriment she felt even towards Sebastino, the brave young matador whom all the women adored when he stood so proud and courageous in the bull-fit. And she sent him away with little jibing taunts, and she lafed at his profecy that some time she would know what suffering was, and that some time she would catch at the device which she now trod under her feet and pray for the love of its owner. And he went his way, and Pepita's eyes grew grave; and in a year it all came true. She knew what it was to love and to suffer, and the device which she caut and hid in her breast was covered with blood from his torn shoulder. Dramatic, simple as nature is simple, with a charm of youth and fervor, the story has throu it the warm vivid coloring which comes to our cold northern clime only at the sunset hour, and which in Spain is the very day and nature and life itself." [Critic. **900**

PRINCE OTTO. [by RO. L: STEVENSON: *Roberts*, 1886.] "The romantic portion of it is delitfully romantic,—a tale of the emotions, never overwrôt or melodramatic. The scene is laid in the mountains of Germany and the feeling of the freedom and freshness of this region is admirably caut. The last chapters of the book, describing the reconciliation of Seraphina and the Prince, her husband, are simply idylic, and are full of the most exquisite touches of that literary art which effaces the signs of its own handi-work. Mr. Stevenson is certainly a genuine lover of nature, and his descriptions have the true feeling, altho not at all trumpeted, or apparently put in except as a matter of routine. But his petty german principality and its court, its scheming prime minister, gossipy atmosfere, intrigues, etc., are palpably stage properties." [American.] "They are pure romances, intended only to excite and entertain—and yet about Prince Otto a sort of moral clings, in the miseries of both Prince and Princess on their throne with discord, and their happiness, as commoners, with love. It is, take it all in all, a rather tender and romantic tale; and take it in detail, a spritly and entertainingly humorous one. Nothing could be more demurely amusing than situation after situation. The encounters between the english tourists and the Prince and Princess are especially good." [Overland. **901**

PRINCE RODERICK. [by JA. BRINSLEY RICHARDS: *Bentley*, 1879.] "Moralhunters will be disconcerted by 'Prince Roderick,' for while perfectly unobjectionable it is eminently non-moral; but pleasure seekers will find their reward in its pages, which are full of sparkle and life. There is abundance of satire in it, but it is of that tolerant kind which suggests a lurking sympathy for the object satirized. He tilts at everybody in a partial, but cheerful cynicism, from the prince who never could see any harm in what he did, down to his secretary's soldier servant addicted to the use of hair-dye. He is sincerely fond of his heroine, but he scruples not to describe her as reduced to a state of imbecility by her love for a weak and eccentric Hamlet of the 19th century. The author is no respecter of persons. All ranks and creeds and races are ridiculed alike. The canvas is perhaps overcrowded with figures, and few are drawn without a touch of caricature. The author's sole aim has probably been to amuse, and in this he has been signally successful, tho such success cannot be obtained without prejudice to the verisimilitude of the story. Life is not altogether made of the unforeseen, and the constant and kaleidoscopic mutability of the characters in 'Prince Roderick', coupled with the strongly farcical nature of several of the incidents

therein recorded, gives the whole book a fantastic and unreal coloring ... Altho the prevailing tone of the story is comic, or even farcical, the few serious incidents which occur are handled with sincerity and force ... Mr. Richards has the trick of investing his characters with a whimsical and airy caprice which renders them attractive in spite of their lack of all solid qualities and virtues. The book is full of good sayings ... The minor personages —Montenegrins, Bulgarians, german students, and opera-singers, court chaplains, and party politicians—are drawn with a vigor and skill possible only to one who has seen a good deal of Continental life and studied it in a sympathetic spirit." [Athenæum. **902**

PRINCESS AMELIE. [*Roberts*, 1883.] "It is a little romance of rare beauty; an idyllic picture of innocence and britness and love, set amidst historic scenes and characters which by contrast enhance its charm. Its new version of the theme of 'Noblesse Oblige' shows an ideal side even to the loveless and compulsory marriages which are among the most objectionable essentials of an aristocratic régime. The heroine of this story accepts the distasteful alliance to which her ambitious kinsman condems her, in a spirit of self-sacrifice and real devotion to her family and to what she deems the general weal, ennobling what is otherwise discordant and ignoble. Tho mismated with a sullen and rebellious boy, her fate is eventually a happy one. The manner in which this end is attained it would not be fair to indicate, as the half mystery which veils the sequel is maintained with some care by the author. It would be difficult to match elsewhere the delicate beauty of those later scenes of the story in which Princess Amélie fulfils a profecy and finds her fate under the cherry bows. The historic characters incidentally introduced are touched in litly but with grafic clearness." [American.] "While dealing with historical episodes and lords and ladies of hi degree, it is an almost perfect little book. There is much originality besides delicate skill, in the way the author has taken one of the royal marriages of the last century, where a grand duke of 11 marries a great heiress half a dozen years older, and woven into it a love-story of real charm. The book shows careful reading, but is never pedantically encumbered with what is non-essential, and contemporary personages and historical events drop into their places naturally and without destroying the vraisemblance." [Lippincott's. **903**

PRINCESS' CASAMASSIMA (The) [by H: JAMES: *Macmillan*, 1887.] "is a great novel; it is his greatest, and it is incomparably the greatest novel of the year in our language. It has to do with socialism and the question of richer and poorer, which grows ever more burning in our day. And the scene is contemporary London. Its people are the types which the vast range of London life affords, and they are drawn not only from the hiest and the lowest, but from the intermediate classes, who are so much more difficult to take alive. The Princess Casamassima is our old acquaintance, Miss Light, of Roderick Hudson [No. 525] fame, come with her beauty and splendor to forget her hated husband in semi-sincere sympathy with the London socialists, and semi-personal love-making with the two handsomest. The hero is the little, morbid, manly, æsthetic bookbinder Hyacinth Robinson, son of an english lord and a french girl, who kills her betrayer. For the climax, Robinson, remembering his mother, kills himself,—inevitably, not exemplarily—rather than shoot the political enemy whom the socialists have devoted to death at his hand." [W: D. Howells.] "It is the best thing he has done, if we leave out his short stories. The Princess has no principle, no constancy, no morality; but she is clever and interesting. Hyacinth Robinson is a type, perhaps somewhat too refined, of the state of mind to which unsuitable education and impossible aspirations, joined with a taste of luxury, bring a great class of young men. He is singular only in having skilled hands and in using them as a workingman in

love with his work. He is led by the princess into loving her ... The novel has no story; but the play of character on character is direct, and there is little tiresome analysis. The prince and Madame Crandoni, the honest german lady with the italian name, are genially painted, and are as true to their national natures as Thackeray's De Florac." [Catholic World. **904**

PRINCESS NAPRAXINE, see *OTH-MAR.*

PRINCESS OF THE MOOR, *Tauchnitz*, 1872, = *LITTLE MOORLAND PRINCESS.*

PRINCESS OF THULE (The) [by W: BLACK: *Harper*, 1874.] "is a novel full of romance and pathos. We recall few heroines of modern fiction more charming or more lovable than Sheila Mackenzie. She is a woman perfect in her nobleness, humble-minded, but full of Hiland pride, full of sympathy for the poor and suffering, and womanly enuf to show her sympathy in the most natural ways, despite her snobbish surroundings during her married life in London. This entire absence of affectation and snobbishness constitutes her chief charm. She is the central feature of the book, and the story tells of her sweet and gentle efforts to make a man of Mr. Lavender, who, when she marries him, is an attractive and talented snob, but whom she succeeds in the end in making a true man ... Mr. Black's style is admirable for its force and its purity. His wonderful descriptive powers have been already displayed in his earlier works. He seems to delit in describing the everchanging sea and richly-colored sky of Borva, and the primitive manners and the honest and simple lives of the fisher peasants over whom Sheila's father ruled by Hiland hereditary [?] rit." [Penn. Monthly.] "Its grand descriptions of rocky shores and broad waters would, of themselves, make this book worth reading. Its pictures of the Hebrides under the changeful skies of their short summer are full of breeze and color ... 'The girl was somehow the product of all the beautiful aspects of nature around her. It was the sea that was in her eyes, it was the fair sunlit that shone in her face, the breath of her life was the breath of the moorland winds.' Lavender, the careless, pleasure-loving artist, transplants this delicate northern flower to the hot-house air of London, where she pines and withers until his neglect drives her to escape into the freedom of her natural life, only to find its content and britness gone. Her loss startles Lavender back to the knowledge of his better nature, and after due penitence, and the discipline of hard work which wins him fame while making him worthier of her, they meet again in a reconciliation which is very pathetically and charmingly told." [Scribner's. 905

PROPHET OF THE GREAT SMOKY MOUNTAINS (The) [by "C: EGBERT CRADDOCK," i. e., M.. Noailles Murfree: *Houghton*, 1885.] "is a remarkable story. It has the charm of freshness in the type of life it delineates, of beauty in its descriptions of natural scenery, and of vigor and subtlety in the presentation of character ... The main interest of the tale, considered as a development of human experiences, concentrates about the love-story of Dorinda Cayce, and the spiritual struggles and destinies of Hiram Kelsey, the introspective, ignorant, noble, but half-crazed preacher and 'profet' of the Big Smoky Mountain district. Their 2 lives touch each other at many points. ... Dorinda is throuóût a distinctly conceived, beautiful and noble character. One wonders, indeed, how so much fysical loveliness as is hers could blossom out of such a family-stock as the brutal, whiskey-drinking tribe of the Cayces. It is like the gorgeous flower which bursts forth from the uncouth and savage cactushedge, but there is nothing impossible about it. And from the first moment of her apparition, holding the plow-handles on the June morning of the first page of the volume, to the last glimpse of her, brooding over the Profet's conjectured transit like Elijah to the skies, she is in every

way a creature of womanliness, purity, and lit ... One of the great charms of this author's writing is the beautiful and subtile delineation of the aspects of fysical nature amid the scenes of which her actors have their being. Nothing can surpass the frequent felicity of these descriptions and the delicacy of observation which they indicate." [Andover Review. 906

PROVENCE ROSE (A). [by "OUIDA," i. e., L.. De La Ramé: in "A Dog of Flanders' [etc.] *Lippincott*, 1871.] "People accustomed to lâf at 'Ouida' will temper their justice with mercy and their contempt with respect and liking after reading her 'Provence Rose',which is innocent, pretty, and touching. The Provence rose is a rose-tree in a poor girl's room." [Nation. 907

QUEEN OF SPADES (The) [by AL. PUSHKIN: in *Lippincott's Magazine*, Sept. 1876.] "has the genuine russian tinge of tragedy, and, while it does not suggest that eminence which Pushkin enjoys in another field of the imagination, it is not without both ingenuity and a certain kind of power." [Nation. 908

QUICKSANDS. [by ADOLF STRECKFUSS: *Lippincott*, 1884.] "In the selection of 'Quicksands' for translation, Mrs. Wister has shown her well-known discrimination [? See No. 595]. 'Quicksands' is a frank romance, making no shamefaced compromise with realism. The hero, Egon von Ernan, is superlatively daring and accomplished, and in the heroine, Elise von Osternan, the virtues strive for mastery. It is no blemish that most of the people talk by the page, making opportunities to express lofty moral sentiments. One does not think, "What bores! no human being ever talked in that strain"; but rather, "How truly beautiful and refreshing it would be to meet human beings who talked just in that way." The first situation is capital. The contrast between Egon von Ernan, meditating suicide to escape from a superabundance of this world's goods, and Golliet Pigglewitch, prompted to the same act throu lack of them, is very effective. We are not moved to tears by Egon's rhetorical cynicism, or by the life and sorrows of the wretched Pigglewitch. On the contrary, the sense of comedy, not tragedy, in the situation is uppermost, and the bargain struck between the two despairing mortals excites the liveliest curiosity about coming complications. Tho the story hardly fulfils its first promise, the intrigue is carried on very well, especially until the surprising candidate takes leave of Castle Osternan, and in Berlin resumes his identity as Egon von Ernan. Many of the subordinate characters are old in german fiction, but, being necessary to the development of the plot, and being kept in due subjection, they are not tiresome. We are so impressed by the romantic nature of everybody and everything, that we regard Bertha von Massenburg with all the disfavor properly accorded to the proud, unriteous sisters of Cinderella. Until the book is closed, it never occurs to us that her device for keeping Egon and Elise apart was a very trivial one for a clever woman of the world. It is only after reflexion that we see any improbability in the blasé Egon's swift and sure conversion to the paths of rectitude. And no amount of reflexion would convince us that Elise, as Frau von Ernan, could degenerate into a terrible curtain-lecturer, or that she and Egon could be less than happy ever after." [Nation.] "It is another example of the unerring instinct [? ☞ No. 595] with which Mrs. A. L. Wister detects the best german fiction of the day and rehabilitates it for american readers." [Boston "Literary World." **909**

RAMONA. [by H.. MARIA (FISKE) (HUNT) JACKSON: *Roberts*, 1885.] "There is a rare idyllic charm in the opening chapters, where she gives a picture of an old spanish rancho and its inmates: the household life, the pastoral occupations, the time-honored religious ceremonials, into which is carried a deep and simple fervor, are all described with the vivid and effective touches which mark the artist. In taking for her hero one of the

Mission Indians of Southern **California**, she must have been confronted with difficulties had she not thus carefully prepared the scene for him. As it is, Alessandro rouses sympathy and interest at once, and like all the rest of the characters, lives, moves, and pleads for himself and his race. There is no hasty or superficial work in the story, which is beautifully and pathetically told. There is no declamation and no argument, and the reader is impressed not so much by the author's vues and convictions, as by the vital and inexhaustible meaning of real action and suffering." [Lippincott's.]— "We find here "the mellowness of a long-continued pastoral form of civilization as witnessed in the remains of the mexican occupation of California. The contrast extends to the treatment, for Mrs. Jackson shows a ripeness of art and a richness of color which make one feel that he has come unexpectedly upon a Murillo in literature. The story is not a new one. A girl bred as a foster-sister to a boy whose mother is coldly just to the alien and passionately devoted to the child of the house, is secretly loved by the generous youth, but returns the love only as a sister. Then comes a stranger, who shows her what the power of love is. The alliance is held disgraceful by the mother, who obeys a sense of family pride when she has no obedience to give to family love. The lovers flee, are married, pass throu a terrible experience which ends in the violent death of the man, and the widow is rescued in dire extremity by the foster brother, who has gone in search of her after the mother's death, and now recovers her to ease and quiet, finally marrying her, or that part of her which has not died with her husband. It will tax the credulity of the reader to tell him that the story wrôt from such materials is one of the most artistic creations of american literature. Nevertheless, the most jaded novel-reader and indianfobist may be trusted to finish the book, if once induced to enter upon a reading. We will answer for it that as such a reader glides upon the smooth, gentle current of the earlier chapters he will forget his prejudices, and be borne quickly along by the hastening current." [Atlantic. **910**

RAPHAEL. [by A. DE LAMARTINE: *McClurg*, 1890.] "It is a painful fact that one lives to outgrow one's love for Lamartine, to re-read his once enthralling romances with an accompanying consciousness that there is a good deal of printed matter in the book,—to popo his moon-struck heroes, wandering about in the wake of other men's wives, sying by nit under the vault of heaven, and by day filling page after page of a journal with melodious lamentings about the cruelty of fate, and finally lying down to die in solitude, lamented only by village folk ignorant of their sad heart histories l 'Raphael', however, whose memoirs, newly translated, are told in the linked sweetness of Lamartine's beautiful prose, will hold his own as a classic of the great revival of romantic literature that made memorable the early days of this century." [Critic. **911**

RARAHU. [by "PIERRE LOTI," i. e., Jules Viaud: *McClurg*, 1890.] "The translation hardly gives us the indescribably sweet, melancholy sentiment of the original. The pretty polynesian idyl is sad, but the sadness is not in the fact, it is in the temperament throu which "Loti" looks at the world and which tinges everything he sees. It is a poetic temperament, contemplative and sensuous, receiving complete impressions instantaneously, and uttering them in a vivid, penetrating, fragmentary way. In a dozen disconnected passages he convêys perfectly the exotic charm which the islands of the Southern Pacific have for the wandering European. One can hear the ceaseless roar of the ocean breaking on encircling coral reefs, and the sob of the perfumed winds in primeval forests. In the same detached, forceful fashion, we are made to realize the enchanting grace of the tahitian girl, Rarahu ... The letters of Rarahu to Loti are like oriental love-songs, a naive declaration of profound passion

revealed in exquisite imagery." [Nation. **912**

RAYMOND'S ATONEMENT. ["Gebannt und Erlöst.) by "E. WERNER," i. e., E .. Bürstenbinder: *Bentley*, 1884.] "Werner is the one german novelist whose works appear to be popular in England. This is to a great extent due to the excellence of the english versions. 'Raymond's Atonement' is hardly equal in interest to 'Success; and How He Won It,' but it has plenty of incident and romance, and is free from the stiffness of expression which often mars a translation." [Athenæum.] see No. 600. **913**

——, SAME ("Banned and Blessed"), *Lippincott*, 1884.— *WHICH SEE*.

——, SAME ("Enthralled and Released") N. Y., *Knox*, 1886.

REATA. [by "E. D. GERARD", i. e., Dorothea Gerard and Emily (Gerard) Laszowska: *Blackwood*, 1880.] "It is long since we have read a story in which excellence of plot and excellence of character painting are so well combined. From the first page to the last the reader is thöroly interested in the story ... Such evenness of execution, such admirable balance between the interest of the story, the interest of the characters, and the mere interest of the local coloring, is very rare ... One great charm of the book is in the character of the heroine, Reata, who is half .of german, half of mexican blood. The wild fun of her first capricious practical joke, the romantic desire to be loved for herself alone, and not for any extraneous advantages she mit possess, which gradually induces her to continue for a time in earnest the deception which had begun in fun; the deep personal pride, and the contempt she feels for what she begins to discern doubtfully in her lover's character, which hardens this intention into a serious design, and the embarrassment she experiences when she has to confront seriously, in European society, the results of a mad freak conceived in the solitary freedom of a mexican forest, are all admirably painted, and so painted as to make what would otherwise seem an impossible plot perfectly natural ... All the scenes in Mexico are admirable." [Spectator. **914**

RECHA. [by DOROTHEA GERARD: *Blackwood*, 1890.] "has the same singular power as its companion story "Orthodox", but intensified; for its strength, simplicity, and directness are even greater, the characters are fewer and more thŏroly worked out, the descriptions are more vivid, the tragedy is darker and more hopeless. It is better art too, we think, that the story should be allowed to tell itself, instead of being told by a friend of the hero, as in Orthodox. Recha is another of those unflattering pictures of jewish and christian life in Austrian Poland, in painting which Miss Gerard shows such talent;—we mit say genius, for these stories give the reader a certain thrill which cannot be the work of any amount of mere cleverness. ... For the Jew, like Shylock, like so many Jews in fiction, was not all made of stone. It was with him, too, "My ducats and my dauter," and he was ready to lose 10,000 florins rather than let his dauter marry a christian. The beauty of Recha was used by her villainous father —who had however, a well-grounded faith in her power of taking care of herself—to draw foolish fish into his net. The young officers found it hard to refuse her anything; and it was by her persuasion that Theodor signed that terrible bond, at the same time falling desperately in love. Recha is a very powerful study.· Her pride, her courage, her strong sense, her aspirations, the secret religious doubts into which she is drawn by circumstances and by an irresistible sympathy to confide to Theodor; the intense sadness of a life which, for a soul like hers, is nothing but one long degradation; and yet the loyalty to her father which stands between her and every kind of happiness,—all these make a noble and touching character. It was not only Recha's beauty which roused such passionate devotion in Theodor. His long pleading, her long resistance, seem only to gain in strength from standing out against that unutterable dreary background of Horoweska, the

half-built, miserable, decaying galician town. And when at last Recha finds fate and love too strong for her, these lovers have a rendezvous so dismal, so tragic, that one cannot from the first believe in any happy end to the story." [Spectator. **915**

RECHERCHE DE L'ABSOLU, *translations of*, see *ALCHEMIST, ALKAHEST, BALTHAZAR, PHILOSOPHER'S STONE.*

RED CROSS (The). [*S*: *Tinsley*, 1880.] "The Red Cross is hily romantic and hily improbable.. It is, however, readable. The scene is laid in **France** at the time of the war of 1870. The hero is a member of the Red Cross fraternity, who is quartered in a french house and falls in love with the fotograf of a young french girl. Her brother, a prisoner of war, returns the compliment by falling in love with a german girl. After the usual complications all ends with marriage bells." [Athenæum. **916**

REJECTED WIFE, see *BERTHA'S ENGAGEMENT.*

REPROACH OF ANNESLEY (The) [by "MAXWELL GRAY", i. e., M. G. Tuttiet: 1889.] "has unusual merit. It abounds in passages of more or less poetic prose, descriptive of nature in her various moods. Many of these are fine in a way. The words are·well chosen and full of color, the sentences are musical ... There is more than one sufficient reason which mit prevail to·set asunder, with their free will, a man and woman between whom exists that unique and pure·passion which alone deserves the name of love, and which Maxwell Gray essayed to describe. For the most part she has imagined it very well. But, granting its existence, it·is not in nature that a man laboring unjustly under the suspicion of a foul crime, from which he can clear himself by incontestable evidence, should not do so to the woman he loves, when that ·is the only obstacle to possessing her; especially when, as is the case with Edward Annesley, the truth could not injure any living soul. With this serious exception, Max-

282

well Gray has managed the details of her story with much skill. Her manner of telling it is rather jerky and disconnected, the successive chapters being apt to come upon one with a certain shock of unpreparedness. The book is a clever one, nevertheless, and more than usually worth reading." [Catholic World.   **917**

RETURN OF THE NATIVE (The) [by T: HARDY: *Holt*, 1879.] "loses the rīt to be classed among the really great novels only by reason of being devoted too assiduously to the portrayal and dissection of a type of character which is repulsive in proportion to the vividness and fidelity with which it is painted. Eustacia Vye will remain a living reality in the mind of the reader long after the conventional men and women of other novels have receded into the shadow land of memory, and her tragic fate lends a certain mournful and pathetic dignity to her figure ... A certain instinctive modesty of the person is said to be the last of the purer sentiments lost by a woman as she sinks below the horizon of respectability; but Eustacia Vye never had such a sentiment to lose. She quite evidently and consciously looks upon her beauty, and her capacity for passionate ardor of feeling, as so many instruments for the procurement of those pleasures and excitements which she craved; and her quarrel with life was that the narrow conditions of her life did not allow these advantages to be availed of to the full. One feels a certain apprehensiveness in following the successive steps of such a character; and profoundly sorrowful as is that final castrofē, to most readers it will bring a sense of relief and a conviction that the impulse which carried Eustacia to Shadwater Weir was the happiest of her ,wayward and ūnpromising life." [Appleton's.   **918**

ROBERT HELMONT [by ALPHONSE DAUDET: *Routledge*, 1880.] "is a book which no lover of its author's exquisite art can afford to pass unnoticed. Less a story than a panorama of character, scenes, and events in the suburbs of **Paris** during the german occupation, it has the pulsating fervor of reality, and it portrays, with subtle perceptiveness, the not wholly imaginary experiences of a poetic mind confronted by the terror, the destitution, the tragic chances of war." [Boston "Literary World."   **919**

ROBINSON CRUSOE. [by DANIEL FOE, called DEFOE: 1719.] "It is not Robinson Crusoe we care about, but the account of his adventures, the solution of the problem of how to live under the circumstances. His name calls up the idea not of a man, but of a story. Say 'Lear', and you think of a man; you have the image of the white-haired king—the central point, about which the division of his kingdom, the disaffection of his dauters, the terrors of the tempest, the soft pity and sad death of Cordelia, group themselves in subordinate places: say 'Robinson Crusoe' and you see a desert island, with a man upon it ingeniously adapting his mode of life to his resources; the imagination of a solitary existence, reproduced in a special form with wonderful vividness, consistency and particularity,— there is the source of our interest. It would be to impugn the verdict of all mankind to say Robinson Crusoe was not a great work of genius. It is a work of genius—a most remarkable one—but of a low order of genius. The universal admiration it has obtained may be the admiration of men: but it is founded on the liking of boys. Few educated men or women would care to read it for the first time after the age of five-and-twenty. Even Lamb could say it 'holds its place only by tuf prescription.' But the boy revels.in it. It furnishes him with food for his imagination in the very direction in which, of all others, it loves to occupy itself. It is not that he cares for Robinson Crusoe,—that dull, ingenious, sea-faring creature, with his strong mixture of cowardice and boldness, his unleavened, coarsely sagacious, mechanic nature, his keen trade instincts, and his rude religious experiences; the boy becomes his own Robinson Crusoe—it is little Tom Smith himself curled up in a remote corner of the play-ground, who makes those troublesome voyages on the raft, and rejoices over the goods he saves from the wreck; who contrives his palisade and twisted cables to protect his cave; clothes himself so quaintly in goat skins; is terrified at the savages; and rejoices in his jurisdiction over the docile Friday, who, he thinks, would be better than a dog, and almost as good as a pony." [National Review. **920**

ROMAIN KALBRIS. [Les Adventures de R—C—, 1869.) by HECTOR MALOT: Phil'a, *Porter*, 1873.] "Mr. Malot has all the vivacity and delicate humor which are characteristic of the best french writers. The hero of this story is a most interesting and entertaining personage, and his inventor does not find it necessary to spice his adventures with the horrors which english authors seem to find indispensable. The story of how Roland and Mr. de Bihoret lose themselves in a fog on the sands, and how they are saved by the ready wit and presence of mind of the *boy*, is excellent." [Spectator. **921**

——, SAME ("Roland Kalbris"), London, *Hutchinson*, 1890.

ROMAN SINGER (A) [by FR. MARION CRAWFORD: *Houghton*, 1888.] "is a good, honest story, vigorously told . . . Here is the passionate, Romeo-like lover, the northern Juliet, the obdurate father, the hoary villain, the castle with the maiden immured in its tower, the rescue, the marriage, and the unreconciled father—all the "stock, well-worn, and acceptable properties of the novel—transmuted into a story of today, and presented with the well-restrained garrulousness of a professor who has a story of his own, which he won't tell. What more could one ask? The charm of it is that while it mît have been melodrama it is not; that the situations are not impossible, nor bily wrôt, yet are ingenious and follow in swift succession; that the romantic element, while fervent is not blatant; and above all, that the love which is the theme of the book is honest and straitforward . . . It may be said of this book—and it is a fine thing to

say of any novel—that it really does carry one away, and when one comes back one is none the worse for the adventure." [Atlantic.] "Mr. Crawford has brôt forward for his latest hero a handsome peasant youth with a tenor voice, who takes the stage at 20 with éclat and success, bewitches the ears of all Europe, gains wealth and eminence at once, wins the heart of a young and noble lady, and carries her off from her appointed suitor with the prowess of a young Lochinvar. We are inclined to say that the best point of the story is in the telling of it, for there is a naif garrulity and an artless self-complacency about the professor who plays the part of raconteur which go far to relieve the rest of the characters of their lack of reality . . . But the story, whether striking or trivial, flows on all the time with freedom and joyousness, like water from a fountain." [Lippincott's. **922**

ROMANCE OF A GERMAN COURT (The). [Le Roi de Thessalie) by "ARY ECILAW": *Remington*, 1886.] "The book is the story of the well-known scandal of the treatment by the grandduke of Hessen of the Princess Kalomine . . . The tale is a dramatic story, full of power and pathos, and admirably told. How far the details of the romance correspond with the details of the true story, only the king of Thessaly himself could say. Whether they be true or false, they are related with consummate art, and it is impossible for anyone to read the book without having his soul purged by the passion of pity and sympathy for the unfortunate heroine, and without being completely carried away by the grace and force of the teller of the tale." [Spectator. **923**

ROMANCE OF BEAUSEINCOURT, see *CARDINAL'S DAUGHTER*.

ROMANCE OF DOLLARD (The) [by M.. (H.) CATHERWOOD: *Century Co.*, — *Unwin*, 1886.] "is more than a romance in name. It is a bit of the real thing at last, and proves that Mrs. Cathwood is amongst the few who know how to animate the past and to recreate bygone deeds of heroism—is, in fact one of the chosen few in whom the lit of true romance is still burning. The tragic figure of Dollard, leading the handful of brave men who hurled themselves against the hordes of Iroquois, is historically familiar, but we find the episode now for the first time 'done into' fiction. This is matter for wonder, but not for regret, for tho it is an event, as one may say, to the manner born, it has but waited for the touch of the true magician. Of the many romances imbedded in history none is, perhaps, more inspiring than Dollard's. It has all the elements of real romance, and Mrs. Catherwood's treatment of the historical side, and her introduction of fresh material, make it quite an artistic and striking bit of work." [Athenæum. **924**

ROMANCE OF THE FOREST (The). [by A.. (WARD) RADCLIFFE: 1799.] "Mrs. Radcliffe's inspiration was a genuine sensibility to the beautiful, the wonderful, the adventurous. However little an elève of art, she was, in this regard, a child of nature, whose voice, however latent, she inly heard and emfatically interpreted; thus adding to the english novel, already rich in social pictures, the ineffable charm of imaginative, picturesque, and inspiring impressions, long since neglected for more finished and artistic creations, but still instinct with a native force and feeling that mark an era in english fiction." [H: Th. Tuckerman. **925**

ROMOLA. [by "G: Eliot," i. e., M.. A.. (EVANS) CROSS: *Smith*, 1873.] "The purely imaginative part of the story is far more powerful than the historical. The ideas of the time when the revival of learning took place had quite possessed themselves of "George Eliot's" mind, and had stirred her into a wonderful imaginative effort. But her conceptions of the purely imagined figures,—of Bardo, of Baldassare, and of Tito,—are far greater than her study of Savonarola ... In looking back on the story, Savonarola fades away from the scene. It is Bardo, the old enthusiast for the greek learning, or the fitfully vindictive gleam of Baldassare's ebbing intellect as flashes of his

old power return to him, or the supple Greek's crafty ambition which stands out in one's memory, while the devout and passionate Dominican is all but forgotten." [Spectator.] "There are few things requiring a more delicate touch than such stories as that of Tessa and her little ones; yet what an air of idyllic beauty is thrown over the episode by her ignorance and their innocence! "George Eliot" is always charming in the treatment of children; they have not yet become the theatre of those conflicts which she hates, and she loves them without distrust or remorse. How admirably this episode is made to show that a man may be a villain and yet have soft affections, and a noble woman be jealous of something hier than mere personal fidelity. In her treatment of Baldassare the author displays all the qualities on which we have remarked. His remorseless vindictiveness and thirst for blood seem to her so near an approach to lunacy, that she makes him mad whenever he has a chance of action. It mit be insinuated that this is done in order that the avenging sword may hang a little longer over Tito's head, and it is but an artifice to prolong the effect of the hovering Nemesis of his hate. But there are no artifices in "George Eliot's" art. The true reason is, that she does not sufficiently sympathize with such depths of passion to give them adequate expression; they are so repugnant to her that she hardly compassionates the wronged old man, and certainly does not sufficiently display those features of his character which caused him to be successively forsaken by the woman he loved and by the boy he had adopted and tenderly cared for. How was it that he who so longed to be loved was denied all answer to his yearnings where he had set his heart? It was only because his vindictive hate had so debased him, even in the mind that conceived his character, that no room was left for sympathy; and the savage animalism of his passions, lowering him to the brutes, made George Eliot less than humane to one who had put off what alone interests her as distinctively human. This concentration of self in the reckless pursuit of a personal gratification is the strongest expression of that tendency in our race which is uniformly decried throuout "Romola," whether it shows itself in the luxurious self-indulgence of Tito or in the noble Romola when she essays to throw off the trammels of a life which no longer answers to her ideal." [Westminster Review. **926**

ROSE OF DISENTIS (The). [by [J:] HEINRICH ZSCHOKKE: *Sheldon*, 1873.] "The scene is laid chiefly in the swiss mountains, toward the end of the last century, at the time when Austria and France were contending for the possession of that part of the country in which Disentis lies ... The background of the story is one of war and treachery, while in the foreground stands out the heroic character of the enthusiastic and patriotic Flavian, his pleasing sister, the countess of Schauenstein, and the charming Viennese whom he loves. He is an old fashioned hero, full of fire and love, and of contempt for the low and sordid ambitions of the mass of mankind, devoted to everything noble and good, and withal, and above all, a fiting man. His characters represents a type that has almost completely disappeared from modern literature ... Of course the novel ends happily." [Galaxy. **927**

ROSINE [by J: G: WHYTE MELVILLE: Toronto, *Lovell*, 1877.] "is a vivid story, in a rapid, lively style, of the terrible days immediately preceding the french revolution ... The style is vivid and lively, and the action well-sustained; and tho there are no profound studies of character, no psychological analysis, no introduction of the hier problems which did not then apparently much trouble men's thôts, we close the book with the feeling that it is a pleasantly told story, well conceived and executed, and with a good deal of historical vraisemblance." [Canadian Mo. **928**

SACRED VOWS [*Remington*, 1877, *Ward and Lock*, 1886.] = *AT THE ALTAR*.

ST. GEORGE AND ST. MICHAEL. [by G: MACDONALD.] "Even in 'St. George and St. Michael,' where the author sets himself to tell a pleasant tale of the english civil wars after the manner of Scott, the noticeable thing is his characteristic mode of treating the relations between his puritan hero and royalist heroine. Parted at first on account of their conflicting opinions, Dorothy and Richard join hands and hearts at last, not because of any conversion of vues, but because they have been led by the simple following of conscience to a hier conception of truth, and have learned to recognize each other's sincerity of soul and steadfastness of duty, and to value it infinitely beyond any mere coincidence of opinion. This romance is proof that Mr. MacDonald, however seldom he may choose to do it, has the power to make a story which is interesting for its own sake, and that it is from no lack of inventive ability in the author that his novels in general have so little of plot and incident. When he does deal in these, they are apt to be of a bold and striking kind." [Boston "Literary World." **929**

ST. RONAN'S WELL [by W: A. SCOTT.] describes "life at a wateringplace in Scotland in the author's time. A gloomy and painful story." [Boston "Lit. World." **930**

ST. TWEL'MO: or The Cuneiform Cyclopœdist of Chattanooga. [by C: H: WEBB: N. Y., *C. H. Webb*, 1867.] "How much 'St Elmo' deserves ridicule and how hard it must have been to make an effective travesty of it sufficiently appear from this, that Mr. Webb has been able to incorporate with St. Twel'mo whole pages of 'St. Elmo'. His premeditated absurdities are so exactly in keeping with Miss Evans' unconscious silliness that only one who remembers 'St Elmo' would ever suspect in 'St. Twel'mo diversity of authorship;—to use Mr. Webb's joke, 'a little Evans leaveneth the whole lump.' We have not critically compared Mr Webb's former burlesque which this one, but 'St. Twel'mo' appears to us almost as amusing as 'Liffith Lank'; not quite as

good, for to burlesque Miss Evans' book
properly there would be necessary a far
more protracted course of the jim-jims
than that described by Mr. Webb the
other day, and we can hardly require a
humorist to make delirium tremens a
habit, even for the sake of getting on a
level with Miss Evans. A good deal of
Mr. Webb's fun is aimless, as fun ōt to be,
but in his serious use of it he does a service to the cause of sense in literature—a
service which, if he likes, he can vastly
increase—which entitles him to thanks."
[Nation. 931
SALAMBO [by GUSTAVE FLAUBERT,
1821-80: transl. by Chartres, Vizetelly,
1886.] "is an archæological novel of the
hiest pretensions. Salambo is a Cartha-
genian princess ... It is not easy reading, nor is the book in the least agreeable;
but it displays in the biest degree what is
called the historical imagination. There
are passages in it in which the literary
expression of that refined, subtilized and
erudite sense of the picturesque which
recent years have brōt to so hī a development, seems to have reached it hiest
level." [H.: James. 932
——, SAME, tr. by Sheldon, London.
Saxon, 1885. Transl. bad.
SANT' ILARIO [by FR. M. CRAW-
FORD: Macmillan, 1889.] "is the continuation of 'Saracinesca'—the continuation
but not the conclusion of that much-
praised tale. On the contrary, for after
taking his amused and interested reader
throu nearly 450 pages of exciting incident, bloody battles, family feuds, forgery, blackmail, suicide, unwarranted
jealousy and renewed confidence between
his married lovers, Sant' Ilario and Corona, and such other solids, liquids, and
confectionery as he is continually spread-
ing before the public, Mr. Crawford
leaves Faustina and Mr. Gonache still unprovided with a suitable dénoument for
their remarkable adventures and their romantic love." [Catholic World. 933
SCARLET LETTER (The) [by NA-
THANIEL HAWTHORNE: Ticknor, 1850.]
"is a psychological romance. It is a tale

of remorse, a study of character, in which
the heart is anatomized, carefully, elaborately, and with strikingly poetic and dramatic power. A woman in the early days
of Boston becomes the subject of the
discipline of the court of those times, and
is condemned to stand in the pillory, and
wear henceforth the scarlet letter A attached to her bosom. She carries her
child with her to the pillory. The other
parent is unknown. At this opening
scene her husband, from whom she had
separated in Europe, preceding him by
ship across the Atlantic, re-appears from
the forest, whither he had been thrown by
shipwreck on his arrival. He was a man
of cold intellectual temperament, and
devotes his life thereafter to search for his
wife's partner and a fiendish revenge.
The young clergyman of the town, a man
of a devout sensibility and warmth of
heart, is the victim, as this Mephistophe-
lian old fysician fixes himself by his side
to watch over him and protect his health,
an object of great solicitude to his parish-
oners, and, in reality, to detect his suspected secret and gloat over his tortures.
This slow, cool, devilish purpose is perfected gradually and inevitably. The
wayward, elfish child, a concentration of
guilt and passion, binds the interests of
the parties, but throws little sunshine
over the scene. These are all the characters, with some casual introduction of the
grim personages and manners of the
period, unless we add the scarlet letter,
which in Hawthorne's hands, skilled to
these allegorical, typical semblances, becomes vitalized as the rest. It is the hero
of the volume. The dénoument is the
death of the clergyman on a day of public
festivity, after a public confession, in the
arms of the pilloried, branded woman."
[Knickerbocker.] "There is in his works
a mixture of puritan reserve and wild
imagination, of passion and description,
of the allegorical and the real, which some
will fail to understand, and which others
will positively reject,—but which, to ourselves, is fascinating, and which entitles
him to be placed on a level with Brockden

Brown [!] and the author of 'Rip Van Winkle'. 'The Scarlet Letter' will increase his reputation with all who do not shrink from the invention of the tale; but this is more than ordinarily painful. We recollect no tale dealing with crime so sad and revenge so subtly diabolical that is at the same time so clear of fever and of prurient excitement. The misery of the woman is as present in every page as the heading which in the title of the romance symbolizes her punishment. Her terror concerning her strange elfish child presents retribution in a form which is new and natural:—her slow and painful purification throu repentance is crowned by no perfect happiness, such as awaits the decline of those who have no dark and bitter past to remember. Then, the gradual corrosion of heart of Dimmesdale, the faithless priest, under the insidious care of the husband (whose relation to Hester is a secret known only to themselves,) is appalling; and his final confession and expiation are merely a relief, not a reconciliation.—We are by no means satisfied that passions and tragedies like these are the legitimate subjects for fiction: we are satisfied that novels such as 'Adam Blair' and plays such as 'The Stranger' may be justly charged with attracting more persons than they warn, by their excitement. But if Sin and Sorrow in their most fearful forms are to be presented in any work of art, they have rarely been treated with a loftier serenity, purity, and sympathy than in the 'Scarlet Letter.' The touch of the fantastic befitting a period of society in which ignorant and excitable human creatures conceived each other and themselves to be under the direct 'rule and governance' of the Wicked One, is most skilfully administered. The supernatural here never becomes grossly palpable:—the thrill is all the deeper for its action being infinite, and its source vague and distant." [Athenæum.] "It touches the lowest depths of tragic woe and passion—so deep, indeed, that the representation becomes at times almost ghastly. If Jonathan Edwards, turned romancer, had

dramatized his sermon on 'Sinners in the Hand of an Angry God,' he could not have written a more terrific story of guilt and retribution than The Scarlet Letter." [E: P. Whipple. **934**

SCOTTISH CHIEFS (The), by J.. PORTER, 1809.

SEAGULL ROCK. [by [LEONARD SYLVAIN] JULES SANDEAU: *Low*, 1872.] "A story more fascinating, more replete with the most rollicking fun, the most harrowing scenes of suspense, distress, and hairbreadth escapes from danger, was seldom before written, published, or read. It is all set in a framework of lovely family life and affection, which gives the finishing touch to the charm which envelops the book from the first page to the last. The story of 'Sea Gull Rock' is thŏroly french: the boys are all french boys, the fathers and mothers are french, and all the people in the little sea-board hamlet in **Bretagne** are french too." [Athenæum. **935**

SECOND WIFE (The). [by " E. MARLITT", i. e., Eugenie John: *Lippincott*, 1874.] "We rarely encounter a novel which we can read with so much pleasure and can commend so unreservedly. It is a striking psychological essay, a masterly study of character, and at the same time a vivid and fascinating picture of life. The theatre of the story is very narrow, the action being confined almost exclusively to one house, and its burden resting on the shoulders of 4 or 5 persons of both sexes. ... The incidents of the story are intensely, tho not sensationally dramatic, and the reader's interest increases from the arrival of the bride to the simple but sufficient and satisfactory *dénoument* ... The countess embodies in beautiful union the hiest ideal of womanhood and the most intelligent ideas as to feminine culture. In her it is demonstrated that a woman may cultivate her intellect without prejudice to her heart; that she may write and paint and study science without neglecting those softer duties which attach to her sex. The victory of the countess' intellect over her husband's honest but sturdy prejudices is not less signal and admirable than the triumf of her purity and devotion over the machinations of the priest and the 'Hoffmarschal'." [Boston "Literary World."] "The heroine, a poverty-stricken countess by birth, marries a baron, whose sole purpose in marrying is to affront a woman with whom he had formerly been in love, but who had married a loftier suitor; now this faithless one was a widow, and in love with .him, but his pride and vanity alone control him. The baroness is the second wife, and has a very hard time in her new home—what with her husband, a vicious old uncle of his, an odalisque living in a house in the garden, and a priest, who is continually coming and going, and watching everything with his black eyes, and making love to her. It would be hard to say which of the characters is the greatest caricature. The whole book is overdrawn, strained, and absurdly unnatural; still it is 'from the german', and will be read, as if the Germans were famous for writing novels, and only once in a while wrote a dull one by accident." [Nation.]—"The german novel and novelette are apt to be a terror to the reader and revuer. Badly written and composed, dull, full of 'drowsy placidity', and void of wit and humor, to get throu them often demands a combination of qualities rarely forthcoming, namely, dogged determination, a sense of duty, fixity and singleness of purpose. And even when reader or revuer is endowed with these virtues and peruses to the bitter end, he is likely to get nothing more profitable than the indigestion which, if Heine is to be believed, Father Rhein got from swallowing the verses of Nicholas Becker." [Spectator.

SECRET MISSION (A) [by EMILY (GERARD) LASZOWSKA: *Blackwood*, 1891.] "contains an apt contrast of character between 2 polish brothers, a lively delineation of the rustic life of a country not known to englishmen, a strong element of female love in 3 different aspects, and a narrative not marred by prolixity. Brotherly love is the cardinal feature of a 'Secret Mission,' and the almost fatherly care of Felicyan Starowolski —the patient agriculturist who, abiding on the remains of his ancestral acres, furnishes his young and brilliant brother with the means of a wider life of distinction in the german service—is more than matched by the self-sacrifice of Roman in his turn, who tears himself from ambition and from the imperial charms of Biruta Massalowska to redeem Felicyan from Siberia at the price of his life." [Athenæum. **937**

SHALONSKI FAMILY (The) [by "EUGENIA TUR," i. e., countess Salias: *Remington*, 1882.] "is a pleasant story, simple and fresh, and healthy in tone. In it a young girl describes the quiet life led by the family of which she formed a part previous to the french invasion of Russia, and the troubles which came upon the peaceful household when the enemy approached. The subject has been often treated by russian writers, and it has been turned to excellent account by Count Leo Tolstoi, whose 'War and Peace' is indebted to it for some of its most powerful chapters." [Athenæum. **938**

SHE. [by H: R. HAGGARD: *Harper*, 1887.] "It is said that 13 american issues of 'She' are in circulation. The fact must naturally be gratifying to the author, but it is not distinctly creditable to the literary taste and cultivation of Americans. Gross impossibilities without number, pages of platitudinous reflection, a smattering of learning, scenes which are indecent —all that is 'She' and that is all 'She' is. Nevertheless, thousands of people have read 'She' and probably thousands more are waiting for a chance. In the face of this spectacle, the only criticism of any value would have to take the shape of an essay on the advantages of not knowing how to read." [Nation. **939**

SHE'S ALL THE WORLD TO ME. [by T: HALL CAINE: *Harper*, 1885.] "The title is as misleading as it is unworthy. On the wild west coast of the **Isle of Man** the author has heard and idealized the "history of a love that was lost and a love that was won, of death that had no sting and the grave that had no victory." He has written a poem in strength and beauty of idea, in artistic unity and completeness, and in the harmony between the expression and the scenes, incidents, and thôts presented. It inculcates no more direct moral than may be derived from an extended and sympathetic contemplation of life. Every day, somewhere, an heroic deed is impelling a weak or erring multitude toward well-doing and hi-thinking; of the multitude, there are some to whom the nature of the heroism pleads so especially that the impulse becomes a controlling power. Christian Mylrea was weak, selfish, untrustworthy, measured by just such standards of human conduct, yet we may believe that the splendid devotion of Danny Fayle effected a moral revolution in the man, and that the memory of it would shine before him as a star lîting the way to better things than he had ever known. The author believes such a result to be possible, and his moral has a much wider significance than that of many works which discuss exclusively situations and sentiments of austere, conventional virtue. It is the moral inevitably taut by martyrdom even for a mistaken cause, and by that art which, representing only the sublime, the héroic, and the beautiful, is the híest." [Nation. **940**

SHOOTING THE RAPIDS. [by AL. INNES SHAND: *Smith*, 1872.] "Yet, these deductions made, a story of much interest remains, replete with the varied experiences of the man of the world and of action, accurately descriptive of many fâses of modern life, on a scale far wider than that of mere conventional society, keen and clear if not profound in delineation of character, original, so far as accurate powers of observation and reproduction can be called original, and everywhere rendered grafic and vivid by an eye for scenery, the gift of the soldier and the poet, priceless to the reader who would follow and assimilate a narrative. For the latter quality, the changing scene,—

laid sometimes at campanian villas, sometimes in roman piazzas, now among the hills and glens of the **Schwarzwald**, and again in the ruder moorlands of the northumbrian border,—has afforded ample scope. For the delineation of character the various actors in these scenes,—Martin Hardcastle, Garibaldian and queen's messenger, half knît-errant, half buccaneer,—Gaboche, the financier and wirepuller, low-bred, greedy, profligate, a noxious particle floated to the surface of seething parisian life,—stout old Von Heppenstall—Napoleonic De Rocheguyon, —diplomats, forein ministers (not distant likenesses to life),—healthy, steady, country gentlemen,—unwholesome, feverish votaries of the turf and the Stock Exchange; last of all, as a refreshing contrast, some true english ladies,—present a sufficient and suggestive field . . . There is not a spark of romance in it from first to last. As we have seen, it is far from tame: both the incidents and the characters command and rivet our attention." [Athenæum. **941**

SIBYL SPENCER [by JAMES KENT: *Putnam*, 1878.] "has a wholesome, old-fashioned atmosfere about it. It is well in these days to be reminded of the material and the influences which built up the country, and this book gives a sense of the steady resolves and severe sacrifices which were needed to win freedom. An imaginative outline of the hí-toned federalist gentleman, a very well drawn yankee private, and a deacon who is quite unlike Mrs. Stowe's deacons, furnish some of the material for the story, which is free from anachronisms (so far as we have observed), and of its kind good." [Nation. **942**

SICILIAN ROMANCE (The) [by A.. (WARD) RADCLIFFE: 1792.] "glows with all the splendid hues of a southern climate, and is well worthy of its title. From the first page, describing the ruins of the Castle of Mazzine, to the last, the interest is deep and absorbing—the characters are depicted with force and truth, and stand boldly from the canvas. After reading a few chapters the fair authoress lays her spell upon you,—a lit appears throu the broken window-shutters of an apartment belonging to a division of the castle which had for many years been shut—Vincent, an old and confidential servant of the marquis suddenly dies before he can make confession of some grievous sin wĕing on his heart; voices and groans are heard from deserted apartments, while more than echoes talk along the walls, and shadowy forms glide by in the obscurity. 'Sicilian Groves, or Vales of Arcady,' are painted in a style equal to Claude, and the savage grandeur of rude magnificence has all the force of Salvator. There is no lack of life in this work; there are plenty of hairbreadth escapes, faithful lovers, cruel fathers, stern abbots, banditti, ruinous castles; while the convent bell is heard in the twilit hour, or comes borne solemnly along on the midnit air. . . The most delicious portion of the Romance is the description of swiss scenery around the abode of La Luc, a pastor, whose character is one of the finest in the entire range of fiction; one whose life was passed 'in the deep Sabbath of meek self-content'." [American Review. **943**

SIGNOR MONALDINI'S NIECE. [by M.. AGNES TINCKER: *Roberts*, 1879.] "This is not so much a novel as a romance. The first thing which charms us in the book is that it removes us at once from daily life, american or english: and it not only carries us amid distant scenes and forein people, but out of the circle of those commonplace characters, circumstances, sentiments and emotions to delineate which faithfully appears to be the hiest aim of most modern story-tellers . . . A few lively pages bring several pictures of Roman life before us. There is in this description, and throuŏut the book, not good word-painting alone, but the impression of that which constitutes the power or charm of a face, a locality, an inanimate object, a time of the day or nit —that characteristic look, whether, habitual or fugitive, which every true artist endeavors to seize." [Lippincott's.]

"The literary grace and refinement of the book are exceptional . . . Yet the fine workmanship is the least of its attractions. The greatest and rarest is its fullness of feeling,—a sad, unfathomable flood, over whose hi surface, made smooth and tranquil by the very repression of the waters, the tenderest love-story since Doctor Antonio [No. 435] glides quietly, until it shocks us by its final plunge. The 2 principal characters seem almost ideal personages; the exquisite heroine, gentle, proud, and spotless, harassed and saddened, but never once moved from her serenity of soul by the suffocating espionage and insulting precautionary measures of her vulgar gardian; and the king of men who loves her from the hit of his throne with so glorious an ardor, tho, until the very last, may be, with such a magnanimous mindfulness of the barrier between them. These two and their love are thus hily romantic, they are linked with admirable skill to the commonplace beings around them; the latter are depicted with the lit and accurate touch almost of a french society novel, the intensest situations appear unforced, and we believe absolutely even where we readl with most emotion." [Atlantic. **944**

SIMON [by "G: SAND," i. e., A. L.. A. (Dupin) Dudevant: *Churton*, 1847.] "is presented with a play of cross purposes, very tantalizing and very aimless. Simon loves M'lle Fougères and M'lle Fougères loves Simon. Their rank in life is unequal; but as both despise aristocratic prejudices, and are, in other respects, persons of very independent character, why mademoiselle will not marry Simon till she has nearly turned his brain with the misery of hope deferred, appears an inexplicable enigma; and its solution in the last chapter, by the most improbable and painful reminiscences (not after all very clear or intelligible) does not amount to a reasonable justification of apparent caprice." [Westminster Review. **945**

SIMPLE STORY (A), and Nature and Art. [by E.. (SIMPSON) INCHBALD: 1791, *De La Rue*, 1880.] "A new generation of readers will find the 'Simple Story' what their grandmothers found it, a narrative of strong interest, excellently told. It is divided into 2 sections, which relate respectively the fortunes of a mother and a dauter of the aristocratic class, the husband of the first and father of the latter being a priest of very commanding character, who on succeeding to an english peerage is released from his vows. The incidents are forcible and often romantic, and not such as mit be expected from the title. The characters of the priest, Dorriforth, Lord Elmwood, is said to be studied from that of John Philip Kemble. 'Nature and Art' is a sliter and less distinguished performance, yet very readable, and with some strongly emotional situations." [Athenæum. 946

SIR PERCIVAL. [by J: H: SHORT-HOUSE: *Macmillan*, 1887.] "The author shows a sense of fitness in putting this story into a woman's mouth. He appears to recognize the truth ₜhaₜ men will hear of knitliness and devotion more readily from a woman, and will believe in it more cordially. The story itself is of a young englishman who seeks for the Holy Grail in 19th century fashion. The pictures of a refined society drawn in the early part of the book are exquisite. One can accept the grace, and let the painter's idealism refine the whole memory and knowledge." [Atlantic. 947

SLAVE KING (The) [Bug Jargal, 1826] by V: [M..] HUGO: London: *Library of Romance*, 1833, *Smith*, 1852.

——, SAME ("Bug Jargal") N.-Y., *Mowatt*, 1844.

——, SAME ("The Noble Rival, or Prince of Congo") London: *Pierce*, 1845.

——, SAME ("Jargal") N.-Y., *Carleton*, 1866.

SMOKE. [by IVAN [S.] TURGÉNIEF: transl. by Sprague, *Ladies' Repository*, Jan.-July, 1868.] "Turgénief thinks, feels, hates like a Russian, and writes like a frenchman. We mit add that it seems as if he must have loved like a madman, and reasoned like a filosofer, all his life. The charm of the strangely-mingled passion,

and analysis of passion, of history, and subtile satire on history, in his stories can hardly be described. One can not read them without an absorption so great as to be exhausting. It is as if, by some miracle of expanded or multiplied personality, one were to be actor, audience, and critic all at once, in a most exciting play ... 'Smoke' is one of the most powerful of novels. Its leading interest, like that of so many of his stories, centers in the short-lived but irresistible passion which a man feels for a woman whom he only partly trusts, respects less, and really does not love, yet for whose sake he breaks his betrothal vows, abandons all the purposes and hopes of his life, and except for her capricious and cowardly drawing back at the last moment would have plunged with her into utter disgrace and ruin ... His words are distinct yet reticent: intense as passion itself can be, yet forever decorous of sound; true and real, but neither naked nor drunken." [Scribner's. 948

——, SAME, *Holt*, 1872.

SNOW-BOUND AT EAGLE'S. [by FR. B. HARTE: *Houghton*, 1886.] "The story is too good to be told except by the book. The grotesqueness of life in the mountains in the stage-coach days is kept well under control, tho the temptation to overdo it must have been strong. Yet Harte does not neglect his opportunities, and the expressive slang of the colonels, captains, and judges, the nonchalance of the "old-timers" when a coach is robbed, as well as the wonderful scenery of the Sierras, all have their due wet in making the story pleasant and taking. The unconscious metamorfosis of John Hale from the precise, law-abiding Bostonian to the comical figure presented before his wife after a week's hunt for the hiwayman,— when Mrs. Hale objects to his hat, to his trousers being rolled up over his boots, and to the familiar bearing which had been assumed towards him by the colonels and captains—is delicious. As a rule, the slang is of the soil." [Nation. 949

SNOW MAN (The) [by "G: SAND,"

i. e., **A. L. A.** (Dupin) Dudevant: *Roberts*, 1870.] "is a novel of surpassing interest. It is a novel, pure and simple, unburdened with filosofy and unmarked by those idiosyncrasies of the author which, while beautifying some of her books to the eye of culture, have made them 'caviare to the general.' The action of the story moves with a grace which charms, and a rapidity which gives no respite to the reader's attention; the scenes are strange, the characters such as novel-readers rarely meet, the plot is vigorous, and worked out with pleasing effect. The scene of the story is **Sweden** a century ago; Baron Olaus, despotic ruler of half a province, is 'the Snow Man.' He gives a great entertainment at his castle, of several days' duration, and hundreds of guests are assembled. For their amusement he has hired Christian Waldo, a player of marionettes, who has made a sensation, not only by his performances, but by the mystery which surrounds him. This Waldo is the leading character in the book, and we know of none other in fiction which takes a stronger hold upon the reader's sympathies. He proves to be the lawful heir of the barony, and comes to his own at the end of a series of events which the reader follows with increasing interest. The pictures of swedish life and society, and the magnificent descriptions of winter scenery, sleing tournaments, and bear-hunts, fill most acceptably the interstices of the plot. We have never read a novel which we could more unreservedly commend as absorbingly interesting and unexceptionally wholesome." [Boston "Literary World." **950**

SNOW STORM (THE) by A. S. PUSH-KIN, see *CAPTAIN'S DAUGHTER.*

SOUCI. [by JULIA H. TWELLS: *Lippincott*, 1878.] "Souci, a wild little waif of the Paris streets, who grows to be prima donna, is the heroine of a tale of misplaced constancy. She idealizes the boy friend of her wandering days, and when she meets him again struggles to recover his allegiance, which he has long forgotten. In a sense she has outgrown him, tho her superiority to the brave, sincere soldier is not marked. Even in youth her impetuousness and passion rather repelled him, and he breaks no pledge when he abandons himself to a hopeless love for Viola. But the terrible disappointment of the hopes for which Souci has so faithfully waited is a blow sad enuf to win the sympathies of the most cynical, and the castastrofe by which poor Tonis is removed from a stage on which he has no place is powerfully and tragically described. Souci's true mettle shows itself among the horrors of that blood-stained glen, where she finds her soldier dead. She is quite of that french type of woman which both for good and evil has so much more grandeur than the men. Viola is a patient and pure-hearted german, as brave as Souci, and possessing an endurance which does not require hope to sustain it. The idyllic picture of life at Vogogna is not the least happy portion of the story. Tonis is as little successful there as poor Souci with him. When the englishman has destroyed his hopes, Tonis leaves the glen, and so misses the opportunity of supporting Viola in the darkest hour of her trouble. His subsequent generosity at Paris to the starving pair of maidens awakens all the gratitude he could wish, but no change of fealty, tho he certainly does more to deserve it than the easy-going Mr. Rawdon. The numerous characters have much distinctness and originality, and the common uational types are described with skill. With the moon-struck Heinrich Häblemann we have little sympathy. Whether the lapse of Souci after her misfortunes into a humble, loving woman, who is content to reward the long fidelity of her old patron, is altogether probable may be doubted; but at any rate, it is a restful conclusion of a series of storms and sorrows." [Athenæum. **951**

SPRING FLOODS. [by IVAN [S.] TUR-GÉNIEF: *Holt*, 1874.] "Those who know Turgénief only in an english dress have here what is perhaps the best of his novels.

Like many which he has written, it is a painful story; the tragedy it describes is of the most melancholy sort. Sanin, the hero, a young Russian of 21 or 22, happens to be detained in **Frankfurt** on his way back to Russia from Italy, and just as he is about to leave that city he goes by chance into a café, where he finds a family in great anxiety over a boy who is lying in a prolonged fainting-fit. He manages to bring the boy to his senses, and the others, who are italians, in their gratitude will not let him go. He spends the evening, and having missed the diligence, he very willingly consents to spend a few days in the city. The dauter of the house, Gemma by name, is engaged to another man; but Sanin, fearing no danger, goes about with her a great deal, and soon manages to fall in love with her, and she with him. A quarrel with some officers, ending in a duel, in which Sanin makes a much better appearance than her betrothed, gives her an excuse to throw the last named over and to accept Sanin. He, in order to get money enuf to settle in Frankfurt, goes reluctantly to Wiesbaden to sell his estates in Russia to an old school-friend of his who is there with his wife. It is with wonderful beauty that this first part of the story is told; nothing could exceed the delicacy with which Turgénief describes the young man's ardor and the modest pride and reserve of Gemma. He leaves her without dreaming of the possibility of any mischance, for merely a 3 day's absence; but in that time his friend's wife, a beautiful coquette, and worse, manages to make him interested in her and to win him as her lover. He despises her, but he cannot escape her snare. He is unable to return to Gemma. She, however, does not die of a broken heart; she marries someone else a few years later, while Sanin drags out a miserable, remorseful, broken existence. No analysis of this sort can give a fitting idea of the merits of the story. What we have said of it may read as if 'Spring Floods' were some ordinary french novel; but in point of fact this story is elevated above

such works by the great and touching beauty of the innocent part and the solemn impressiveness of the rest. No adjectives can do justice to its vividness. It is a chapter out of life. In that way the novel is both natural and moral." [Nation.] "We must express our feeling of its great power. Nowhere else do we believe the terribleness of a guilty passion has been so nakedly and unsparingly portrayed, and rarely can the beauty of the lawful love it ruins have been so sweetly touched. It is an awful tragedy, far beyond the power of any comment to impart; the reader must go to the book itself for a full sense of the fatal spell that binds the weak-willed but well-purposed hero, and the intolerable shame and despair to which it leaves his wasted life." [Atlantic. **952**

SPRINGHAVEN. [by R: D. BLACKMORE: *Harper*, 1887.] "Mr. Blackmore could never write another 'Lorna Doone', so let us take 'Springhaven,' and be thankful for Dolly Darling and Faith, for the rare bits of his characteristic description, for the glimpses he gives us of his love for dumb creatures, for the portraits of true heroes, and, most, for his fidelity to human nature in depicting the ruf but kindly fisher folk and gossips. Altho the author has taken so much pains to make Nelson and Bonaparte objects of interest, they are altogether overshadowed by the obscure Tugwell and Stubbard, capital characters out of real life, and the lovable old Admiral Darling, with his sweetness and fidelity, and the simplicity of his humor that he is never conscious of himself . . . It is a strong and fine novel, with breadth in its conception and careful finish in its details; vigorous in treatment, but with that underlying delicacy of sentiment which is a charm in Mr. Blackmore's books; and a genial feeling towards human kind." [Boston "Lit. World". **953**

STATES-GENERAL (THE) = *OUTBREAK OF THE FRENCH REVOLUTION.*

STATION-MASTER, see *CAPTAIN'S DAUGHTER.*

STEADFAST: the Story of a Saint and a Sinner [by ROSE (TERRY) COOKE: *Ticknor*, 1887; *Trübner*, 1890.] "is a fine story of New-England life in the later colony days—fine because it is just as faithful to the permanent and universal characteristics of humanity, as it is to the features of the time and place in which its incidents are set. Several people deserve the name of sinner in Mr. [sic] Cooke's narrative; at least 2 women and 1 man are saints, being free from conscious malice, and capable of any reasonable self-sacrifice. However, quite apart from the title and its inferences, 'Steadfast' is a thoroly good and life-like story, which anyone mit be glad to read." [Athenæum. 954

STELLA [by FANNY (LEWALD) STAHR: *Low*, 1884.] "without being in any wise great, is decidedly readable, and the translation is more than commonly easy. The scene is laid in and near Rome in 1845, and the election of Pio Nono is introduced. The author does not wander into long descriptions, but keeps in business-like fashion to her love story, which tells how 2 men loved a fair roman maiden, while she loved a third, who did not care for her. It is just a prose version of Heine's exquisite lyric of the old, old story which is ever new, and which breaks the hearts of those to whom it chances to befall." [Athenæum.❖ 955

STORY OF AN AFRICAN FARM (The) [by "Ralph Iron", i. e., OLIVE SCHREINER: *Chapman*, 1883.] "shows considerable power. Mr. Iron has followed no recognized model of romance, but contrives to tell his tale in a series of studies illustrating the wild life of an ostrich farm, and setting before the reader with striking vigor the problems which trouble a strong intelligence and an imaginative ambition remote from any possibility of culture. His descriptions are wonderfully grafic, and his pathos is forcible. The book is too melancholy to be altogether pleasant; but Mr. Iron obviously writes about what he knows with a successful result which is well de-

served." [Athenæum. 956

STORY OF A STRANGE MARRIAGE (The). [by H.. FALCONER: *Remington*, 1885.] "The central thread of its plot is the rescue of an earl's dauter from the grave by a german carpenter, which exploit introduces a love story as pretty and delicate as the reader could wish. Perilous as the theme may sound when thus barely stated, the author has known well how to handle it, and the result is a decidedly charming romance. Fritz Hübner, with his wife and their grown children, secures our sympathy at the outset of the story, and so prepares us for the unfolding of his pleasant life history. Miss Falconer's readers will be grateful to her for selecting scenes and characters so little hackneyed; for eschewing the conversational platitudes supposed to be appropriate to these; and for relying upon the unsofisticated interest of a genuine, homely, but altogether exceptional story of love and wedlock." [Athenæum. 957

STORY OF KENNETT (The) [by BAYARD TAYLOR: N.-Y., *Hurd*, 1866.] "is singularly straitforward, unpretentious, and impersonal in style. The tale is simply and not ineffectively told. It is pitched in a noticeably low key. But it leans toward the error of lack of incident (not, perhaps, of interest) and towards that monotony which usually follows the diffuse explication of unimportant truth in place of more entertaining, if less common, fiction. It is a record of a place rather than of persons; for Kennett is a township of Pennsylvania. The object of the book is obviously to depict the former country life of that region. The time is the end of the last century . . . Mr. Taylor here furnishes us with a picture of simple, unstrained, matter-of-fact, everyday life, placed among the beautiful hills and charming valleys around his home, with every feature of which he claims the familiarity of an old acquaintance. The traditions and habits of the people among whom the greater part of his life has been passed, the rustic dwellers and the legends of the country,—in themselves but homespun materials for a work of fiction,—in his hands have all the charm of novelty which Goldsmith invested the everyday life of the family of the Primroses, till, in their way, 'The Story of Kennett' and 'The Vicar of Wakefield' may be regarded as true pictures of the simple manners and customs of rural England and America at the date in which the action of either tale is placed." [Round Table. **958**

STORY OF NOEL (The) [by "OUIDA", i. e., L.. de la Ramé: in "A Dog of Flanders," *Tauchnitz*, 1871.] "has a bad ending, as both a good story-teller and a good story-reader would say; but, taking us into **Flanders** as it does, among the peasantry, and telling its tale of domestic affection and boyish aspiration in art and love, it pleases the reader by the goodness of feeling which pervades it, and by the comparative freshness of the scenery in some of the incidents." [Nation. **959**

STORY OF THE PLÉBISCITE (The). [by ERCKMANN-CHATRIAN: *Smith*, 1872.] " . . . Those two men of genius "rolled into one" have taken Christian Webber, miller and 'maire' of the village of Rothalp, in the valley of Netting, between Lorraine and Elsass, his wife Catherine, his dauter Gredel, and a son named Jacob, as the characters who represent the peasantry under the imperial régime." [Athenæum. **960**

——, SAME ("A Miller's Story of the War") N.-Y., 1872.

STORY OF THREE SISTERS (A) [by CECIL MAXWELL: *Holt*, 1876.] "is a charming novel, with a pensive strain in it which belongs especially to those novels that treat of the domestic misery caused by bullying or ill-tempered relatives, or by those wise people who interfere in love-affairs. The three sisters were reared amid all the dreariness which seems to sit like a cloud on english country-life. The proper heroine is the second one, Pamela, a most attractive girl, with a nature as surely bound to be miserable as sympathy and a sort of helpless innocence can make it. Her lovers are well described, and indeed the reader cannot

help noticing the large amount of observation and intelligent interest which the writer shows, and regretting that it should be given to so perishable a monument, for probably in 10 years the book will be as much forgotten as the daily newspapers of to-day. Meanwhile, however, it is decidedly pleasant to read. Its pathos is touching." [Nation.] Time: reign of George III. **961**

STORY OF VITEAU (The). [by FR. R: STOCKTON: *Scribner,—Low*, 1885.] "We have here a stirring tale of adventure, the scene of which is laid in **Bourgogne** in the 13th century. There are knits and ladies, squires and pages, monks of the Inquisition and robbers of the forest. Jasto, the worthy brigand who poses as a scholar, is a comical person." [Athenæum. **962**

STRANGE STORY (A). [by BARON LYTTON: *Low*, 1862.] "It is a mortifying reflexion that a very clever man, who has been Secretary of State, and a conspicuous member of Parliament, should write such intolerable rubbish as this, and should condescend to identify himself in ever so transient a manner with all the blue fire, hollow turnips with fiery eyes, magic lanterns, and fortune-telling, of which it is made. It is perhaps still more irritating that, instead of being content with telling his silly story to those who are foolish enuf to like it, and going about his business, he should put on throuout the airs of a christian filosofer. The preface, the notes, the reflexions, and calm rebukes of the venerable christian sage, are stuffed with matter of this kind, and are so many ways of saying, Know all men, that tho I am talking nonsense, and playing the fool, I am nevertheless a great scholar and profound filosofer. You will be pleased to observe that tho this is mere play, it is the play of a giant. I could if I chose overwhelm you with science in all its branches . . . No, doubt, he is not only a good but a very eminent novelist; but tho he struts as if he knew all mysteries and all knowledge, he has never written anything serious worth reading, except a few pamflets ... The Caxtons was a re-cast of Tristram Shandy, and the Strange Story is made up in about equal parts of 'Godwin's St. Leon' and 'Dumas' Mémoires d'un Médicin', the whole being crowned, in the famous scene of the 'Veiled Woman and the Giaut Foot', with an adaptation of the hobgoblin scene in the Freischütz." [London Review. **963**

STRANGE TRUE STORIES OF LOUISIANA. [by G: W. CABLE: Scribner, 1890.] "Everything in the collection is good, with agreeably varied time and place, and with naturally contrasting joy and woe. Some are so coherent, so full of opportune coincidence and unlooked-for compensations, that one needs to have had wide experience to know how easily they may be true. Few french comedy-writers, for instance, have arranged a neater knot and climax with more deliciously comic minor situations than those unfolded in an episode of the life of Attalie Brouillard. Retributive justice in hi tragedies never meted out more appropriate punishment than the death decreed to Mme. Lalaurie, the fiendish woman who, 60 years ago, kept splendid state in the "Haunted House of Royal Street." Decidedly, the more of such true stories that Mr. Cable can unearth, the better shall he be beloved of critical and uncritical readers." [Nation. **964**

STRANGE WATERS. [by Ro. E: FRANCILLON: Bentley, 1878.] "Andrew Gordon, the fanatic and self-torturer, who lives so entirely for music as an art as to crush his own affections, and do his best to reduce the gifted jewess his wife, and her patient but not musically gifted dauter, into machines of wood and wire for expounding his ideal, is interesting for his concentration of energy, and the intensity of the fire which, under a cold exterior, consumes his soul. When by a strange blow he is stricken with deafness before his work is concluded, his faith in its future carries him throu even the trial of having to stand aside without reaping the blest form of personal reward. The last scene of his earthly struggle, when the ears of the deaf are unstopped, and he reaps in a short hour the reward of hearing his opera,—successful, and made successful by the sudden repentance and assistance of the wife so long estranged from him, has a good deal of grandeur in it. One's mundane sympathies, however, are all with the ignorant italian woman, who cares only for the man, and nothing for that art in the name of which he so gracefully thanks her. The good, cultivated, restrained and oppressed Celia has a character of her own, too, in spite of all her father's efforts." [Athenæum. **965**

STRATHMORE. [by "OUIDA", i. e., L.. de la Ramé, 1866.] " 'Ecce iterum!' Here is the learned "Ouida" once more flinging about all the volumes of the biggest cyclopedias. Here she is again with her big talk and little sense. Here she is with her old blunders and her new follies. We have watched her from the day when she first broke forth in 'Strathmore' into her dog-Latin and Greek, and let loose her cheap scraps of Italian and indecent Spanish oaths; and have noted with interest her progress in blundering in 'Chandos', with its grouse in Devonshire, and its copper-colored beeches as old as the Druids. By this time we are thoroly acquainted with all the peculiarities of her delirious style. We could tell it in the dark. We could distinguish it by the flavor of her fine writing, and the peculiar air of her blunders. Hers mit, in short, be called the servants'-hall style. It bears the servants'-hall mark ... A repletion of ignorance peculiar to the lady's-maid marks each chapter. The characters, too, unmistakably breathe the lady's-maid's ideal ... For love, the lady's maid gives us the passion of animalism; for wit, the sparkling of putrescence. If there is anything good, it is sure to be borrowed. And, unlike the cock in the fable, the lady's maid does not find a jewel in the dung hill, but discovers a dung hill for the jewel. Finally, the lady's-maid's women are about as much like nature as milliners' blocks, and her men as hair-dressers' dummies." [London Review. **966**

STRING OF PEARLS (The). [by G: P. R. JAMES.] "This author has taut us how readily the novel-reading public acquiesces in a few simple conventions in the composition of the historical novel. Let there be a party of travelers journeying at eventide over a fertile plain in Auvergne; a conversation formed out of the permutations and combinations of such frases as, "I 'troth," "By'r Lady," "Grammercy," and "Gadso," or the substitution of "palfrey" for horse, and "housings" for horse-furniture; and the reader's imagination is forthwith adjusted to a tale of the middle age, anywhere between the First Crusade and the time of the League; and this understanding, once established between writer and readers, proceeds steadily and uninterruptedly throuout, altho they know, and he knows that they know, and they know that he knows that they know, that the ideas enunciated, the jargon in which they are expressed, the scenery, characters, incidents, and general accessories, never had any counterpart in any time or country on this earth." [London Review. **967**

SUN MAID, see No. 537.

SWIFTER THAN A WEAVER'S SHUTTLE [by JA. W. GAMBIER: Sonnenschein, 1887.] "is fresh and stirring, tho based on nothing newer than "original sin" in various guises. A really exciting novel such as this, depending for interest on plot and counterplot, is just now as welcome as rare. The action, which is quick and clear as well as complex, has a good deal of reality about it; and with all the mining and counter-mining there is no lack of character, miners and counterminers being every one of them individual, mostly exceeding wicked, or at the least self-seeking . . . Such a personality as Heræa, the gorgeous Greek, has often been attempted, but not so successfully as here; the perfection of her beauty and her extraordinary mental capacity are dazzling even in print. The

union in her nature of unscrupulousness and self-interest on a large scale with natural goodness and mercy is excellent, while the story of her treatment of the love-sick and despairing Rosalie is a pretty piece of writing. There is interest, too, tho the rendering is somewhat slit, in Rosalie, Nellie, and their companions, while the villain in chief is all, and more than all, one's fancy painted. There is about the book an unusual directness and plain speaking, with a surprising absence of anything like sentiment." [Athenæum. **968**

SYLVESTRES (The): or The Outcasts [by MATILDA [B.] B. EDWARDS: Lippincott, 1872.] "is the story of a young english lady, with property and a mind of her own, who gets interested in socialism, or more truly, perhaps, in some socialists, whom she has met abroad, and who come to her in England in abject poverty. She puts them on their feet, gives them a farm, and falls in love with one. We will not tell the story, but we recommend it to our readers. The leading socialist Père Sylvestre, is admirably drawn, with just that apparent exaggeration which in fact is only realism. There is not a word of ill-nature or of fanaticism in the author's treatment of this subject, and that in itself is singularly meritorious in a work which treats of socialism." [Nation. **969**

SYLVIA'S LOVERS. [by E.. CLEGHORN (STEVENSON) GASKELL: Smith, 1863.] "The story of 'Sylvia's Lovers' is laid in humble life, and is related chiefly in broad dialect, which, altho it gives the local color, is a drawback to the comfort of the reader. But for true artistic workmanship we think 'Sylvia's Lovers' superior to any of Mrs. Gaskell's former works. The scene of the story is laid at a fishing-town on the Yorkshire coast; the time, the close of the last century, when the war with France was rife, and press-gangs were in all their cruel authority." [Athenæum.] "Mrs. Gaskell has, we fear, mislaid the pen which wrote 'Cranford.' It is difficult to imagine that charming tale, with its wealth of quiet power and restrained and therefore infectious emotion, the work of the same hand as these 3: volumes of unreal or exaggerated sentiment. That was written as tho its author were relating a series of facts known to her from childhood; this is composed as tho every sentence involved an effort, and every scene depended for interest on a visibly manufactured agony. The plot is almost as old as fiction, but it has seldom been treated with more contempt for probability, or the nature of ordinary human beings. Sylvia herself is a character who never can have existed, and can only be accounted for by remembering that Mrs. Gaskell is a writer who, belonging to one breed of english society, passes her life in watching and describing another." [Spectator. **970**

SYRLIN [by "Ouida", i. e., L.. de la Ramé: *Lippincott*, 1890.] "has every conceivable fault except that of being dull. The hero and most of the other characters are sticks, there is no more movement than in a frog-pond, there is no story, and the long-drawn agony which takes its place is uninteresting as a chronic toothache. Syrlin is an actor, a man of genius, the natural son of a Bourbon prince. He is the most conventional specimen of the unconventional hero. which we know of. He is received in the hiest english society, which, as we know from Ouida's former novels, is completely eaten with ennui. He falls in love with a married woman, and excites her husband's jealousy. He spouts Coppée's poetry and speculates about socialism. He has his revenge on the needlessly jealous husband by writing him up in a play. The heroine of the play draws unwelcome attention to the lady in the case; the lady draws his attention to that little circumstance; and he goes off and shoots himself, leaving the reader as happy as a small boy at an accident. Still there is on almost every page some mark of talent; and 'Syrlin' will be read because, if its author had so chosen, it mit have been worth reading." [Critic. **971**

TALE OF TWO CITIES. [by C: Dickens: 1859.] "In epical unity, in power of imagination, in breathless and tragic interest, in masterly delineation of the inward and outward aspect of national life in an utterly gloomy period, [the revolution of 1780] and in the portraiture of the noblest self-sacrifice, rising into sublimity at last, it would not be easy to find a parallel to the, 'Tale of Two Cities.' The last 'Idyl' of Tennyson and the conclusion of the 'Tale of Two Cities' strike the hiest and sweetest note in modern literature, if not in all english literature. In the poem, King Arthur is depicted as a man fulfilling the requirements of the christian ideal of human character, without forfeiting perfect respect for his manliness; and in the novel, Sydney Carton offers his life, with the most utter self-renunciation, for the happiness of the woman he loves." [G: W: Curtis. **972**

TALES FROM BLACKWOOD. [*Blackwood*, 1860.] "This number contains several startling and effective stories, told in language at once powerful and vigorous, and the incidents of which are all wrôt to the very hiest pitch of excitement. "Antonio di Carara", the "Vision of Cagliostro," and "The Haunted and the Haunters" are severally perfect masterpieces of ingenious construction, and it would be impossible for any reader, having once plunged into the midst of one of these exciting narratives, to withdraw his eyes from the pages before arriving at its conclusion. *Antonio di Carara*," which is placed at the beginning of the present volume, is a tale of Padua, laid in the time of the Emperor Franz, in which the chief characteristics of the Italians, revenge, and the lengths to which they will go in order to gain their darling object, is subtly and vividly delineated. "*The Haunted and the Haunters*" is a tale of so intense, thrilling, and ghostly interest, that we will not anticipate the reader's enjoyment of it." [Leader. **973**

TARANTELLA. [by Mathilde Blind: *Roberts*, 1885.] "Throuôut the first book the fidelity of the delineation of

South German life does not compensate for its lack of vitality. Not till the second book does the author show the hits to which she can rise, and indicate the peaks beyond to which she may aspire. There is a genuine sense of the picturesque and dramatic in making the destiny of a poor violinist, Emanuel, turn on a chance visit to **Capri**, where he plays for a beautiful girl, Antonella, so that, as the superstition goes, she may dance out the venom of a tarantula's bite. In the virtuoso's narrative of his life his nature is admirably revealed ... Antonella comes on the scene first as the Countess Stargia; she occupies the 'belletage' in the house with 'frau professorin' Lichtenfeld; she piques the gossips of the coffee parties, and patronizes the little Minna. She is a tarantula of a kind most attractive to the woman novelist, and it would be interesting to know whether men avoid her as a model throu discretion or disbelief in her existence. In her cruelty and infamy she is a type of a large class of women, born, let us say charitably, as destitute of moral sense as a savage." [Nation. **974**

TEACHER OF THE VIOLIN (A). [by J: H: SHORTHOUSE: *Macmillan*, 1888.] "After so much crude nonsense there is a distinct relief in taking up this collection of Mr. Shorthouse's short stories where 'The splendor falls on castle walls and snowy summits old in story,' in which the author summons noble and familiar figures and permanent and beautiful ideals of thôt and imagination. There is always a quiet serious charm about Mr. Shorthouse' work, and if he errs a little on the side of intense sentiment, it is always the best and truest sentiment. His perception is deep and fine and true. We like his persistent note of aspiration, self-abnegation, fidelity, and wish that it could be made more audible in this generation which listens too little to such voices. 'A Teacher of the Violin' is a pleasant story of the career of a music-loving boy in **Germany**, and the description of the influences at work upon the lad's mind when he heard the winds sweeping throu

the woods is very delicate and full of charm. All the stories are good and we find something fine and chivalrous even in the names of 2 of them, 'The Marquis Jeanne Hyacinthe de St. Pelaye' and 'The Baroness Helena von Saarfeld.' We gain an impression of fine manners and noble character, and in each talc the expectation is fully answered. It is indeed an unusual pleasure to come upon so graceful and symmetrical work which brings up the old ideals and 'sets the wild echoes flying' from the old time world of poetry and romance." [American.] *The Marquis Jeanne Hyacinthe de St. Pelaye* seems to be the best. It is a 'little classic' in a hi sense of the term. These short stories, no less than the author's longer works, exhibit a literary art which is rare even among our careful writers; in them we find also the spiritual touch that marks 'John Inglesant' [No. 767] as one of the noblest of english novels." [Dial. **975**

TEMPLE HOUSE. [by E.. DREW (BARSTOW) STODDARD: *Carleton*, 1867.] "To tell the story is not to take the edge off the reader's appetite. The house which gives its name to the story is an ancestral mansion in a **New-England** seaport. In process of time it has been built about and walled in by the encroaching town, so that with its garden and few trees it has become isolated, but not more so than the persons who occupy it, who have withdrawn themselves almost wholly from the scrutiny of their townsmen ... Mathematicians have amused themselves with speculation as to the possibilities of life in a world where there is a fourth dimension of space. Mrs. Stoddard's art aims at quite as difficult a problem, the exemplification of life in one where there is only a single dimension: her world has thickness, but no length or breadth. The density of the atmosfere throu which the reader follows her characters is immeasurable. One feels now and then that the sun is shining, but no direct rays reach the landscape; only such lit as makes its way throu the circumjacent vapor. The singular thing about it is that the reader is convinced that if the cloud would only lift, he would see figures of remarkable force, beauty, and symmetry. There they all are, these men and women in this New-England seaport; they have names something like other human beings; they have 3 meals a day; they smoke; they read; they talk, occasionally. One catches glimpses of various human proceedings, and feels that the author meant her persons to be real, yet the show goes on behind a thick glass screen; if we could only get this screen out of the way, we think we mlt get a clear vue; every one is near enuf, but there is this dense medium throu which we see them and their actions. We are aware that by this confusion of terms we are not clearing the mystery of the book at all, but we are trying to convey to the reader something of the impression made on our mind by this intense, provoking, startling, and nltmareish book. The Philistine in us is constantly on the point of jeering; the poor little profet who occupies the hall bed-chamber of our mind is quite as often holding up his finger in warning." [Atlantic. **976**

TEVERINO [by "G: SAND", i. e., A. L. A. (Dupin) Dudevant; N.-Y., *Fetridge*, 1855.] "is one of her prettiest tales." [Nation. **977**

THADDEUS OF WARSAW. [by J.. PORTER, 1803.] "and 'the Scottish Chiefs' (1810) still hold their own. Thaddeus, a polish refugee teacher of languages, is described by Sophia Egerton 'as a soldier by his dress, a man of rank from his manners, an Apollo from his person, and a hero from his prowess.'" [Quarterly Review. **978**

THAT BOY OF NORCOTT'S. [by C: LEVER: *Smith*, 1869] "Novelists may be rufly divided into 2 classes; those who know nothing, and those who know something and have repeatedly told it. Mr. Lever belongs to the last class. But if he repeats himself, he does it with such new graces that we willingly forgive the offense. He is, perhaps, the only living novelist of whom it may be said that he is

never dull . . . Young Norcott accepts a clerkship in a Jew business house. Here he falls in love with the Jew's only dauter. Sara Oppovich sends him on a mission of importance into Hungary. At the house of a Hungarian noble he encounters Madame Cleremont, who is now his father's wife or mistress, as the courts may decide. His father is away on a hunting expedition, in which he receives a fatal wound. Madame Clermont hurries away from the scene as fast as her immense wardrobe will allow. And the curtain falls upon the marriage of young Sir Roger and Sara Oppovich. Such is the bare outline of the story. The interest is entirely in the characters." [Westminster Review. **979**

THEKLA. [by W: ARMSTRONG: *Lippincott*, 1887.] "Thekla is a peasant girl of Bavaria, with a marvelous voice. She is sent to Vienna to study by her miserly father, who hopes one day to win a fortune from her prospective career as an opera singer. From the time of her first appearance in public her success is great; she becomes the intimate friend of the Princess Weissenberg and is loved by Count Larisch, but refuses to forsake her career to become his wife, because she feels bound to make good her father's demands. At a critical moment, however, she inherits a large estate, the half of which she makes over to her father, after which she marries the count. The story is pleasantly written and has some humor in the portrayal of the minor characters. The descriptions of musical performances are admirably done and the wooing of Thekla is made a charming idyl." [Boston "Literary World." **980**

THREE MUSKETEERS (The). [claimed by ALEXANDER [DAVY] DUMAS: *Routledge*.] " 'Of your heroic heroes,' writes Thackeray, 'I think our friend Monseigneur Athos, Count de la Frère, is my favorite. I have read about him from sunrise to sunset with the utmost contentment of mind. He has passed throu how many volumes? 40 ? 50 ? I wish for my part there were a hundred more, and would never tire of him rescuing prisoners, punishing ruffians, and running scoundrels throu the midriff with his most graceful rapier. Ah! Athos, Porthos, and Aramis, you are a most magnificent trio. I think I like *D'Artagnan* in his own memoirs best. Dumas glorifies him, and makes a marshal of him if I remember ritly. The original D'Artagnan was a needy adventurer who died in exile very early in Louis XIV's reign. Did you ever read the *Chevalier d' Harmenthal?* Did yon ever read the *Tulipe Noire*—as modest as a story by Miss Edgeworth. I think of the prodigal banquets to which this Lucullus of a man has invited me with thanks and wonder. To what a series of splendid entertainments he has treated me! Where does he find the money for these prodigious feasts? They say that all the works bearing Dumas' name are not written by him. Well? does not the chief-cook have aides under him? Did not Rubens' pupils paint on his canvasses? Had not Lawrence assistants for his back-grounds? "—"The 'Three Musketeers', for example, of which Mr. Thackeray was so fond, was written entirely by AUGUSTE MAQUET, whose acknowledged works prove that the claim advanced on his behalf is not unfounded." [Fr. Hitchman in National Review. **981**

TIMARS TWO WORLDS = *A MODERN MIDAS.*

TO THE BITTER END [by M.. E.. (BRADDON) MAXWELL: *Maxwell*, 1872.] "is carefully written, and even re-written, and yet it is full of all the old ruf vigor and dash, the keen sense of the many pleasures and enjoyments of life, the love of green fields and blue skies, and pleasant gardens, and the quick impatience of all that is hollow and conventional ... As for the story itself, it is sufficiently simple, and here and there is told very prettily and naturally, and with evident feeling. ... Such is the 'situation'—an effective one, it must be admitted. And Miss Braddon takes much pains in working it up into an elaborate climax and catastrofe,

which, when all is said and done, has about it far less of the sensational element than mit have been expected." [Athenæum. **982**

TOILERS OF THE SEA, by V : HUGO : *Low*, 1867, see No. 867.

TOLLA [by EDMUND [F. V.] ABOUT : Edin., *Constable*, 1855.] "is a perfectly charming tale. The incidents of this little story are very simple, but they are made of absorbing interest by the artistic mastery with which the writer transports us beneath the skies of Italy, and shows us the life of the modern italian grandee, or the romantic barbarism still existing in the italian peasant; by the living, unexaggerated reality of the characters; and by the pure and tender spirit which breathes throu the whole narrative, and tempers the french point and vivacity of the style. Since George Sand's "André" we remember no picture of character at once amiable, infirm, and selfish, superior to this of Lello, and the delicacy of the touches which indicate the love of the peasant Menico for his hi-born mistress, is a kind of excellence which "Sand" has never attained." [Westminster Review.] "'Tolla was a social satire on the habits of the long-descended roman nobility. But the satire was softened by an engaging picture of the simple heroine, and by admirable sketches of the domestic life in the gloomy interior of one of the poverty-stricken roman palaces. It was relieved by brilliant fotografs of the Campagna and Sabine hills, with shepherds in their sheepskins, shaggy buffaloes, savage hounds, ruined aqueducts, huts of reeds, vineyards, oliveyards, gardens of wild-flowers, fountains overgrown with mosses and maidenhair, and all the rest of it." [Blackwood's.]—"We learn that Tolla is a real story, that the letters it contains are translations of the letters written by Vittoria Savorelli, and published in Rome, and that the invention of the author is confined to the manipulation of this story into a novel: thus he had to vary the monotony of the single situation which the story has, to surround the principal actors with minor actors, and to person-ify the public. The way in which he has done this shows that he possesses the true artistic capacity." [Leader. **983**

TOM CRINGLE'S LOG. [by MICHAEL SCOTT: *Blackwood*, 1862.] "This book is a reprint from Blackwood's Magazine of 1830, which gained from a hl authority the praise of being 'the most brilliant series of Magazine papers of the time.' We can say, from personal ex-perience, that they are not the sort of thing to put in a boy's way when he öt to learn his lessons .... Having read this book with all a boy's relish for illicit pleasure, we now find, after the lapse of more years than we like to reckon, that the task of revuing it is rendered easier when it comes in the shape of a new edition, to entice from their tasks, a new generation of school-boys. When we say that Tom Cringle was a midshipman, and that this book is the history of his adventures, it may perhaps be thôt that the reading public has had enuf of such books ... Tom's adventures among the smugglers, privateers, or pirates, who in those days haunted the West Indian seas, are various, and told with admirable spirit and grafie power. He gets kid-napped by some Americans, part of the crew of 'the tidy little 'Wave',' one of whom, he says, told him that 'if I was tired of my life, he calculated that I had better speak as loud again' ... We can only hope that all readers of this and other chapters of 'Tom Cringle's Log' will be as well pleased with them as we have been, on our last as well as on our first perusal." [Saturday Review. **984**

TRAGIC COMEDIANS (The). [by G: MEREDITH: *Chapman*, 1881.] "There is a process familiar to those who have studied latin composition by the name of oratio obliqua. Mr. Meredith's 'Tragic Comedians' is a study in oblique narra-tion; he has turned the 1st person of his original into the 3rd and added comments. It accordingly becomes somewhat difficult to see what there is in the book to criti-cize. The plot and much of the conver-sation are due to Mrs. von Racowitza, and the interest its characters arouse is as much owing to historical suggestion as to the art of the novelist. What remains as Mr. Meredith's is his style, and this, as everyone knows, is peculiarly his. Mr. Meredith has a habit of condensing epi-grams into adverbs and allegories into adjectives, which render his sentences stimulating, but at the same time some-what hard reading ... It is somewhat difficult to judge this novel 'on its merits.' If we had not read Mrs. von Racowitza's book we mit have placed 'The Tragic Comedians' very hl among the brilliant productions with which Mr. Meredith has enriched english fiction. And certainly readers who are ignorant of the original will do well to read Mr. Meredeth's adap-tion, which is as stimulating in style, and at least as lucid in arrangement, as any-thing else he has given to the world." [Athenæum. **985**

TRAIL OF THE SERPENT (The) [by M.. E.. (BRADDON) MAXWELL: *Ward & Lock*, 1861.] is "very spiritedly told. It begins with 2 murders and a suicide, diverges into an attempt at poi-soning, and has a dumb detective police officer, with a half-mad scapegrace un-justly convicted of murder, as its heroes. Those who like an english novel re-sembling in its incidents a french ro-mance, and repeating in its best-written passages many of the peculiarities of Dickens, will be greatly pleased with 'The Trail of the Serpent.'" [London Review. **986**

TRAJAN. [by H: F. KEENAN: *Cas-sell*, 1885.] "The title page of Mr. Keen-an's novel, Trajan, without being dis-tinctly apologetic, may not unreasonably be taken to disclose the author's conscious-ness of that characteristic of his work which will be most likely to invite criti-cism. If the reader becomes impatient, as he very likely will, at the frequent eddies which divert the stream of the narrative, he will please to remember that the author forewarned him, when he began his voyage, that the course was not clear. Mr. Keenan's hero is a young american artist, living in Paris at the bit of the Second Empire, and critical of the times throu his affiliation with men who afterward were active in the scenes which followed Sédan. The other principal characters are the members of a rich, cultivated american family, and of a french family which for 2 generations had been domiciled in America, but had returned to its more natural french circumstances. The time of the story is the year between May 1870, and May 1871, with necessary references to the history of the several characters. The place is chiefly **Paris** and its nêborhood, with occasional brief transfers of action to America. It will be easily seen how lurid a background was possible for the figures which are to engage the reader's attention." [At-lantic. **987**

TRANSFORMATION, see *MARBLE FAUN.*

TRANSFORMED, or Three Weeks in a Lifetime [by FLORENCE MONTGOMERY: *Lippincott*, 1886.] "is like all Miss Montgomery's books, written to inculcate moral and religious truth, and shows how the ministrations of a good little boy softened a hard worldly heart. John Ramsay has devoted his life to the acquirement of wealth for the sake of being able to buy back the lost family estate. By the time he has gained his coveted riches, he has, nevertheless, lost all capacity for pleasure. All the illusions which make life beautiful have flatly vanished; family ties are meaningless and old associations devoid of pleasure. Many of the scenes between the old man and the little boy are handled with a delicate sympathetic touch, and the book is well suited for those who like a story, but prefer that it should not invade the territory of man's actual existence." [American. **988**

TRASEADEN HALL [by W: G. HAMLEY: *Blackwood*, 1882.] "is certainly above the average of contemporary english novels. The plot develops too slowly, and the action perhaps extends over too long a period, but these defects

hardly strike the reader; he floats on, down a gentle stream of rational and agreeable reading which, tho never very exciting, is never either frivolous nor morbid. The scene is laid partly in a country town in England, and partly in **Spain** and Portugal. The time extends from the beginning of the Peninsular war to the peace so deadly won at Waterloo. The representation of the country town life is fotografic rather than pictorial, thereby sometimes recalling Miss Austen; but regimental life, whether at home or abroad, in peace or in war, is painted out of a fulness of knowledge which permits of idealization without any sacrifice of accuracy. We have perhaps said enuf to show that it is well worth reading." [Westminster Review. **989**

TRICOTRIN. [by "OUIDA", i. e., L.. De la Ramé.] "The passionate subtlety and vigor which distinguished the works of C.. Brontë are translated by 'Ouida' into sensuous animalism glossed over with words which rather indicate impurity than hide it. In the first there was something refreshing and healthful, despite the gloom in which the authoress constantly enveloped her pictures, a gloom like that in which Beethoven liked to compose; in the second, we get theatrical lits half down, a melodramatic strumming of fiddles, and a notion of something going on under the stage which is done in a few houses at Christmas under the mistletoe." [London Review. **990**

TRUMPET MAJOR (The) [by T: HARDY: *Smith*, 1880.] "is not Mr. Hardy's best, but it has much of his best work in it, and the subject is one calculated to show the author in his happiest lit. The heroine, Anne Garland, belongs to a class of women who are found only in Mr. Hardy's novels. Anne is personally lovely and attractive; she is, moreover, amiable, innocent, and generous and tender-hearted, and yet she makes woful havoc of the heart of a worthy man. She is selfish, as Mr. Hardy's heroines are selfish,—not wilfully or intellectually, but by dint of her inborn, involuntary, unconscious, emotional organism. She recognizes John Loveday's goodness, his self-abnegation, his lovableness; and she can no more justify herself in not loving him than she can in loving his scamp of a brother; nevertheless, and despite all obstacles of self-respect, gratitude, and expediency, she marries Bob, and sends John to die on a spanish battlefield. It is Mr. Hardy's delit to show his chosen women doing these things;. a hasty criticism mīt deem him cynical, but to us this judgment seems uncalled for. The truth is, such a character is not only picturesque in itself, but the cause of picturesqueness in others, and is, therefore, eminently suited for literary purposes. Compare a woman like Anne Garland with a woman like—to take an extreme case—David Copperfield's Agnes, or any of Scott's pattern heroines. When a woman is governed by reason, conforms to the canons of respectability, obeys the dictates of prudence and strict propriety, and sacrifices herself on the altar of what she is pleased to deem her womanhood, the less we hear of that woman [in fiction], the better we are content. What we wish, and what artistic beauty demands, is color, warmth, impulse, sweet perversity, pathetic error; an inability to submit the heart to the guidance of the head, a happiness under conditions against which a rational, judgment protests; and all this, and more, we get in Anne Garland and her kindred ... The story, from beginning to end, is conceived and put together with capital ingenuity." [Spectator. **991**

TWO CORONETS. [by M·· AGNES TINCKER: *Houghton,* 1889.] "Several of the characters are Americans; and in defiance of all dramatic unities, the scene constantly shifts from Italy to Maine, while the time covers the long period embraced between 1830 and 1874 ... 'Two Coronets' indicates the titles and estates of the heroine, Beatrice, born the rītful heiress of the Giorgini and Alinori, but who becomes the victim of a conspiracy by which her father is killed outrīt, and her mother so cruelly calumniated that

she dies of grief, while Beatrice herself is left to grow up nameless and penniless, a dependent in the very houses which rītfully belong to her. The real story is of Beatrice and her life-long effort to regain her name and property ... In contrast with Beatrice is Atalanta, the american girl, who comes to Italy and finds her fate involved in that of the Alinori and Giorgini. Atalanta is a charming creature, and her caressed and garded girlhood, surrounded by tenderness, worship, and exclusion, showing as it does all that Beatrice ōt to have had, but lost, must be accepted as a sort of vindication of the elder woman who has had to fīt for her own, and contest every inch of her way. The book is full of charm, touched everywhere by the felicities of a style which is the author's own, and as poetic and delicate as it is individual." [American. **992**

TWO DAUGHTERS OF ONE RACE. [Die Andere) by "W. HEIMBURG", i. e., Bertha Behrens: *Worthington,* 1889.] "That a novel which has no plot, hardly any incident, and very few characters, may be entertaining is proved by this one. Helena and Carlotta von Werthem are the 2 dauters in question. Helena tells the story; but it is her sister whose selfishness and caprice, pride, and recklessness make it. The 2 girls .with their grandmother, reduced to poverty,. are befriended by old-time acquaintances, the Von Rodens. Helena falls in love with Fritz von Roden and he with Carlotta; but Carlotta marries a princeling from whom she has to be divorced 'for court reasons;' Fritz goes to the war in France, comes home wounded, and recovers from his wound and his passion to conceive a new one for Helena. Carlotta also marries again, and that is all. But the pictures of the simple and refined home life of the Von Rodens; the glimpses of the ridiculous little court of Rotenburg, with its palace finished in the style of the first french empire; the pranks of the young. prince with his tīt-rope dancers, his elefant and his actors, leave not a dull page, and the reader soon begins to feel some regard for the stupidest and least respectable of the persons to whom he is introduced." [Critic. **993**

TWO LITTLE WOODEN SHOES. [by "OUIDA", i. e., L.. De la Ramé: *Chapman*, 1874.] "The earlier portion of Ouida's new story is, in spite of the writer's mannerisms, pleasing and interesting. Evidently, the author took at first a great deal of trouble with the character of Bébée, and with success. She also has bestowed much pains on the descriptions of Bruxelles and the néboring country in the first chapters ... But these are minor faults; and the tale is so graceful, and the writer's power so considerable, that readers will forgive even the more serious defects we have mentioned." [Athenæum. **994**

UNCLE TOM'S CABIN. [by H. [E..] (B.) STOWE: Boston, *Jewett*, 1852.] "It has always seemed to us that the anti-slavery element in the 2 former novels by Mrs. Stowe stood in the way of a full appreciation of her remarkable genius, at least in her own country. It was so easy to account for the unexampled popularity of 'Uncle Tom' by attributing it to a cheap sympathy with sentimental filanthropy! ... We had the advantage of reading that truly extraordinary book for the first time in Paris, long after the whirl of excitement produced by its publication had subsided, in the seclusion of distance, and with a judgment unbiassed by those political sympathies which it is impossible, perhaps unwise, to avoid at home. We felt then, and we believe now, that the secret of Mrs. Stowe's power lay in that same genius by which the great successes in creative literature have always been achieved,—the genius that instinctively goes rit to the organic elements of human nature, whether under a white skin or a black, and which disregards as trivial the conventional and factitious notions which make so large a part both of our thinking and feeling." [Ja. R. Lowell.]—"There are certainly some curious aspects of this comparison. Alarmists as to the undue influence of forein literature may well take note of the fact that of these 10 leading favorites all but 2 are of american origin. Curious is also the disappearance not only from this list, but from the wider detailed list, of some earlier favorites, as Miss Edgeworth. Most extraordinary of all is the prolonged supremacy of 'Uncle Tom's Cabin', which excels all competitors by nearly 2 to 1; and this among a race of children [of public schools in Cambridge, Mass.] born long since slavery was abolished! One eager little girl in the seventh grade, and therefore probably about twelve years old, writes at the head of her abstract of 'Uncle Tom's Cabin': "I think this book is lovely. I cried more over this book than any other." It is interesting to note, moreover, that this ardent young reader has a name unmistakably Irish." [T: W. Higginson. **995**

UNDER A CHARM, *Bentley*, 1877 = *VINETA*.

UNDER SLIEVE-BAN [by Ro. E: FRANCILLON: *Holt*, 1881.] "is a regular irish story of the Lever type, full of gayety and spirits, crowded with adventures and 'situations', interesting for its narrative rather than for the character painting, piquant, rapid, and humorous. In construction and execution it is a drama rather than a novel ... From beginning to end there is a sort of effervescence of wit and fun; and a collection of 'bulls' mit be made from its pages that would reflect credit upon Sir Boyle Roche himself." [Appleton's. **996**

UNDER THE STORK'S NEST [by ADOLF E. KATSCH: *Lippincott*, 1875.] "is a queer story. It is full of incidents,— a duel, a false marriage, murders, mysterious disappearances, etc., which make a really fascinating drama. Intrinsically objectionable and repulsive as these materials are, they are so treated by the author that their effect is not seriously unpleasant. The plot of the story is rather harum-scarum, and the style is eccentric; but pleasant humor and many odd situations make the book readable." [Boston "Literary World." **997**

UNDERTAKER (THE), see *CAP-TAIN'S DAUGHTER.*

VANITY FAIR. [1847.] "Few more fascinating novels were ever written. All THACKERAY is in it. All the acrid, remorseless sarcasm, all the rollicking fun, all the easy banter, all the wonderful flow of slang, of which no gentleman was ever perhaps a more thoro master. This was his first work; written while he had his reputation to make, and which at once made his reputation. There is no carelessness in it; every scene is elaborated to the last degree of minuteness; and the result is an effect of perfect ease, such as none but a master can hope to attain. And the strangest feature of the whole book is the keen relish which the writer evidently has for his work. Never was gathered such an odious company; never such a coil of swindling, hypocrisy, intrigue, and unmitigated folly unrelieved except by the tireless devotion of poor Dobbin to the flattest of Amelias: and yet Thackeray not only revels himself among this 'tas d'hommes perdus de dettes et de crimes', but makes us enjoy it, almost as much as he. What other writer could, out of such materials, make any but the most disagreeable of books? To us, no one mark of Thackeray's genius is more striking than this,—that, in "Vanity Fair" as in his other novels, but more in this than in the others, we read from end to end this most dismal of histories, surrounded by scamps of every description, by schemers, rakes, misers, cowards, and fools; annoyed, protesting, provoked, but fascinated. Only Dobbin's foolish fidelity redeems the wretched story, as Colonel Newcome's foolish fondness redeems another, hardly less wretched." [Christian Examiner.]—"Vanity Fair, tho not in my opinion the best, is the best known of Thackeray's works. Readers, tho they are delited, are not satisfied with it, because Amelia Sedley is silly, because Osborne is selfish, because Dobbin is ridiculous, and because Becky Sharp alone is clever and successful,—while at the same time she is as abominable as the genius of a satirist can make her. But let him or her who has read the book think of the lessons which have been left behind by it. Amelia is a true loving woman, who can love her husband even tho he be selfish—loving, as a woman should love, with enduring devotion. Whatever is charming in her attracts; what is silly repels. The character of Osborne is necessary to that of Dobbin, who is one of the finest heroes ever drawn. Unselfish, brave, modest, forgiving, affectionate, manly all over,—his is just the character to teach a lesson. Tell a young man that he ot to be modest, that he ot to think more of the heart of the girl he loves than of his own, that even in the pursuit of fame he should sacrifice himself to others, and he will ridicule your advice and you too. But if you can touch his sentiment, get at him in his closet,—or perhaps rather his smoking room,—without his knowing it, bring a tear to his eye and perhaps a throb to his throat, then he will have learned something of that which your less impressive lecture was incapable of teaching. As for Becky Sharp, it is not only that she was false, unfeminine, and heartless. Such attributes no doubt are in themselves unattractive. But there is not a turn in the telling of the story which, in spite of her success, does not show the reader how little is gained, how much is lost, by the exercise of that depraved ingenuity." [Anthony Trollope. **998**

VENETIA. [by LORD BEACONSFIELD: 1837.] "Better in some respects was 'Venetia' which quickly followed 'Henrietta Temple', and which has for its central thot the intense love of a dauter for her unknown father, separated from her as Byron was from Ada. In many other respects there is a close reproduction in 'Venetia' of incidents and exhibitions of temperament in Byron's career, and no less Shelley's. As the melancholy events in the lives of the 2 poets were of very recent occurrence when the novel was written, its use of them, especially its blending of them with fictitious events, was perhaps unwarrantable; but as a

ROMANTIC NOVELS.

study of cnaracter and conduct in certain
strange fäses, cunqingly wrôt out without
much plot, 'Venetia' is superior to most
of Disraeli's novels." [Athenæum. **999**
VESTIGIA. [by "G: FLEMING", i. é.,
Julia Constance Fletcher: *Roberts*, 1884.]
"Italy is again the scene, but in exchanging Rome for Livorno, and in choosing her
characters from humble folk, the author
has placed herself on new ground. Yet
to name the characters in 'Vestigia' is to
suggest familiar and oft-tried combina-.
tions—an old fisherman and his lovely
dauter, an ardent young patriot with his
foster brother, handsome, gallant, prevailing, and, in the background a secret
society striving to win liberty by the hardest of tyranny. But the reader who presupposes therefrom a commonplaçe novel
will find that he has never been so completely and agreeably surprised. Such a
story puts the revner to extreme disadvantage. To praise it as it deserves would
be treason to his readers as well as to the
author, for due comment upon the plot
would betray its secret. Not that the interest, the surpassing charm of the story
depends on mystery, or on involved intrigue. It is not the solving of a riddle,
but the development of 2 or 3 simple,
noble motives; and the conclusion, however tragic, throws over the whole previons story a clear white lit of truth and
purity ... Thêre is only so much of the
fair Italian sky and sea as to throw into
relief the figures; but so deft so sympathetic is the choice, the few pages give
the sense that all Italy is in the book.
It is like a returning sunshine to feel that
humble life need not be low life, that
laborious days need not be sordid and
base, that hope, filial love, and unselfish devotion illumine the poorest home."
[Nation.]—"The originality of the story,
the touching pathos of the plot, the minor
excellences compared with the vivid portrayal of character and the hi moral purpose which pervades and dominates all",
give it hi value. "The scene is laid in
Italy, but we are not detained by descriptions of its beauty nor charmed by the

subtle witchery of sky or land or sea.
The writer is too intent upon the tragedy
in which the characters are involved to
linger by the way, or revel in the soft
charm of the sunny land. 'Vestigia'
deals with the great questions of civil
liberty and the divine rît of kings ... In
accepting the mission, the struggle between love and duty is finely shown, and
the strength and weakness of the brilliant
youth are brôt out with genuine power.
In the passages between the lovers we
are refreshed by the pure and elevated
tone, the sweet sincerity and perfect
trust." [Manhattan. **1000**
VICAR OF WAKEFIELD (The) [by
OLIVER GOLDSMITH: 1786.] "is a prose
idyl, the first domestic novel. It is also
the first novel which contains no indecent expression. To critical eyes it appears full of absurdities, inconsistencies,
and improbabilities. The maxims seem
sententious, the villain a stage ruffian, the
incognito of Burchéll a theatrical mystery. Yet results only prove the truth of
Goldsmith's advertisement, that a book
'may be amusing with numerous errors.'
The 'Vicar of Wakefield' is better known
than many works of a more nearly perfeet character: few books have furnished
so many literary allusions. Full of practical wisdom, cheerful contentment, humorous observation, and without a touch
of malice, it has the added charm of the
unconscious ease of perfect simplicity.
Dr. Primrose is one of those characters
which posterity never allows to die ...
No greater praise can be bestowed upon a
book than Goethe's testimony, that it
exercised a soothing influence over his
mind at a crisis in his mental history, and
inspired him with a new ideal of life and
letters." [Quarterly Review.] "It has
been truly said of the Vicar that it contains more improbabilities than can be
found in any other work of the same
length, and yet it remains the most popular and delitful novel in our language."
[Spectator. **1001**
VILLETTE [by C.. (BRONTÉ)
NICHOLLS.] "There are 3 methods of

308

treating the human character, corresponding to the 3 principal classes into which the fraternity of novelists may be most appropriately divided. In the first of these classes are to be placed the favored few whom Nature has gifted with real conceptive genius. They paint not so much what they have seen, as what imaginative intuition enables them to shadow forth from the recesses of their minds. They form an ideal; and instinct, rather than experience, convinces mankind of its inherent truthfulness. Millions of people have felt Hamlet or Lear to be natural characters, not because they ever *saw* anybody like them, but because a hier sense than sit is appealed to, and something within bears witness to their reality and consistency throuóùt. Of this hier order of story-tellers, C .. Bronté may be accepted as the type. She goes to the very core of her characters and works gradually outward. Their closest secrets are those she knows the best, and interests us most about. Their outward demeanor, the events of their life, the evolution of the tale, concern us merely as evidencing the process which is going on within. We compare them with nothing but our consciousness, and unhesitatingly pronounce them to be true." [London Review. **1002**

VINETA. [by "E. WERNER", Boston, *Gill*, 1877.] "German novels have for a long time been popular among american readers, who have swallowed indiscriminately whatever publishers have seen fit to give them; but among the rather motley collection thus made, Werner's novels deserve good mention. Vineta deals mainly with life near the Polish frontier during the revolution of 1863; but it is by no means filled with matters not belonging to a novel. On the contrary, the usual subject of fiction has due prominence, and a new turn is given to the story of the young girl with 2 lovers, to which the picture of political intrigue and rebellion forms an impressive background. Often in german novels there is to be noticed a tendency to exaggerate the qualities of the different characters: the indolent man, for example, never lifts a finger; the ruf man is always ruf as truly as the genteel lady of the game is always genteel; but here there is no such working in plain tints without lits and shadows. The mental ripening of Waldemar, the frivolity of Leo, the frankness of Wanda, were clearly seen by the author and are clearly portrayed. The plot is an ingenious one, and the chance it gives the author to draw the various conflicting interests of the ambitious princess, for instance, who is intriguing for Poland, and of her son, who is averse to such doings, of the girl who is enthusiastic in behalf of her down-trodden country, etc., has not been neglected. There are very few recent german novels with more life in them than this. The reader does not have a sort of sympathetic pain with the subject, which is, as it were, dragged out to cover more space than it should properly do; on the contrary, there is decided repose and certainty in the author's treatment. The legend of Vineta, it may be said, by the way, has wonderfully little to do with the story, which is good, for all that." [Atlantic.] "It has the interest attaching to a fresh scene and unfamiliar types. It relates the gradual triumf of the spell of love over the national family prejudices which divide a polish countess and a german landowner in her native country. Both are ardent patriots, and both are influenced by family circumstances which place them in the strongest antagonism. But, in the end, the manly honesty and nobleness of Waldemar prevail over the hostility which Wanda tries to cherish against the enemy of her country and the supplanter of her race, and the victory is complete when she saves the german from a murderous attack of her own countrymen, and when Waldemar at the risk of his own life rescues her father from the russian vengeance for his share in unsuccessful insurrection. The characters of the main actors, and of Princess Baratowska, whose affection is as hard to be won by the son of her first marriage as is the hand of her equally patriotic niece; of the sensitive professor, whose devotion to his pupil first tames the harsher elements in Nordeck's nature; and, in a sliter way, of the merry Gretchen, and her unlucky admirer, the fussy officer of police, are exceedingly well drawn; while, more Germanico, there is a funny bit of mysticism in the story, which plays a vague part in uniting the discordant affections of the lovers." [Athenæum.]—"Novel readers owe a debt of gratitude to the translator of this fascinating story. The translation [Tyrrell] is so well done that one would never suspect the book to be other than of english origin, and the narrative is so absorbing that few who take up the book will lay it down without finishing it ... Nearly all the fascination of the book centres round the commanding figure of the hero, and the skill with which the reader is gradually drawn into feeling an intense personal interest in his sorrows, his bitter struggles, and his dangers and triumfs is of no mean order ... How the struggle between love and race ended we must not disclose. We have revealed enuf to make known the characters of this story, and can assure its readers that its interest is maintained to the last page." [Spectator. **1003**

——, SAME) ("Under a Charm"), *Bentley*, 1877.

VIOLETTA. [from the German of URSULA Z. VON MANTEUFFEL: *Lippincott*, 1886.] "The blasé reader of romances will sit up late over this one; and the most inveterate disciple of the new school will enjoy this spirited and tender story, which is by no means destitute of plot and incident, tho owing its interest equally to the perfection of its detail. The book is quite a novelty as a variation of the popular version of a prima-donna in private life, tho the new-version is by no means a goody-goody one; and every personality in it, tho there are more than the usual number of characters, is as clearly and carefully drawn as if each were the only one. The story is thus remarkable

for its even perfection; it has not a dull page, nor a superfluous paragraf, nor an uninteresting character in it, and it has the great merit of giving on the whole a noble view of life." [Critic. **1004**

VISCOUNT OF BRAGELONNE, see *COUNT OF MONTE CRISTO.*

VULTURE MAIDEN (The). [by WILHEMINE (BIRCH)' VON HILLERN: *Tauchnitz*, 1876.] "A brutal father, a wilful dauter, a swarm of lovers, all daring mountianeers, superstitious retainers, rivalries, fits, and images, furnish elements for a tragedy, the scene of which is the savagely romantic Oetzthal. Elsa, the dauter, is the pride of her father, the Head-peasant, because of her strength and fearlessness. Before her 14th year she, hanging by a rope over a precipice, captures a young vulture, kills the parent bird, and is known always afterwards as Vulture Elly. Two years later, she sees a handsome young fellow who has killed a bear—Bear-Joseph, and falls so entirely in love with him, that no other aspirant has the smallest chance of winning her. Sunshine fills her heart, but is soon driven out by a blow from her father's staff, which lays her senseless. That blow she never forgives: it changes her whole nature. A lover is forced on her: she knocks him down with an axe; is banished to the uppermost pasture among the glaciers, and in that dreary spot endures solitude and suffering while her heart grows harder. Does Bear-Joseph care for her? that is her one absorbing thôt. She had met him, in a furious storm, one day carrying a helpless maiden across a pass; and from that moment feared the worst. Her father dies. She goes down to her old home, becomes Head-peasantess, but Bear-Joseph holds aloof, and one day mocks her at a dance. In her rage, she promises to marry the man who shall lay him dead. Remorse seizes her on hearing rifle-shots, she rushes forth in the darkness, hears faint cries for help from the deep, misty gorge of the roaring Ache: insists on being let down by a rope, a fearful adventure;

but is at length hauled up, with Bear-Joseph in her arms, dead or dying. The wounded man recovers; the young girl, whose appearance had caused so much trouble, turns out to be a sister, not a sweet-heart, and, in the end, Vulture Elly and Bear-Joseph are married ... The book is worth reading; it presents "a powerful picture of the inner life of a tyrolean village." The story, however, notwithstanding the marriage, is essentially a tragedy." [Athenæum. 1005

——, SAME ("Geier-Wally"), *Appleton*, 1876.

——, ("Elsa and her Vulture") transl. by Wallace, *Longman*, 1876.

WANDA. [by "OUIDA", i. e., L.. De la Ramé: *Lippincott*, 1883.] "The scene is laid in the mountain fastnesses of Austria; and those who remember Ouida's descriptions of scenery will be glad to find themselves with her, no longer in rose-scented boudoirs, but under the clear shining skies of snow-covered hills, with keen breezes in the air, and stars glittering in the frosty heavens. The surroundings are still elegant ... But this time, it is a noble woman who wears the ivory velvet and pearls, living in her beautiful castle a life stately and austere; and Wanda will, we believe, take her place among the great heroines of fiction. It is a story of love, but it is the love of a husband and wife; the long courtship is full of dignity and sweet reserve, and the picture given of nine years of married happiness is one which we believe has never been excelled; while it is perhaps unnecessary to add that the children play a part in the drama unequalled for exquisite appreciation of children's natures. Husband and wife separate at last, not because they are tired of each other, or have been unfaithful; but because the wife has discovered that in one point her husband has deceived her, and she is a woman to believe that where there is one fraud there can be no truth. Sympathy is curiously enlisted for the husband; for he is no mere base-born impostor. In assuming the title to which he had no rit

tho he wore it so well, he wronged no ritful heir; and that he had inherited illegally his instincts of a gentleman and his desire for luxury only hitens one's appreciation of his temptation ... The story is brôt to an exquisite and artistic close, with forgiveness sealed by death." [Critic. 1006

WAR AND PEACE [by LYOF N. TOLSTOI: *Gottsberger*, 1887.] "is incomparably his greatest book. It has been called the russian epic, and in the vastness of its scope as in the completeness of its performance it is not unworthy the name. It is the story of the great conflict between Koutouzoff and Russia and Bonaparte and France; it begins some years before Austerlitz, and it ends when Borodino and Moscow are already ancient history. The canvas is immense; the crowd of figures and the world of incidents it is made to contain are almost bewildering ... But when all is said in blame which can be, so much remains to praise that one scarce knows where to begin. His pictures of warfare are incomparable. None has felt and reproduced as he has done what may be called the intimacy of battle—the feelings of the individual soldier, the passion and excitement, the terror and the fury, which, taken collectively, make up the influence which represents the advance or retreat of an army in combat. But, also, in a far greater degree none has dealt so wonderfully with the vaster incidents, the more tremendous issues." [Saturday Review. 1007

WARD OF THE GOLDEN GATE (A). [by FR. B. HARTE: *Chatto*, 1889.] "The ward herself is a delitful creature, and the mingling of courage, frankness, impulse, and refinement, real innocence, and arch, lovely girlishness, in her mother's story, and her own pathetic ignorance, are described with skill not to be surpassed. The dashing originality of the notion of the "trust" is captivating, and the group of men who furnish the action of a story composed of humorous and pathetic elements after the unique fashion of Mr. Harte, is perhaps his most

remarkable achievement in prose."
[Spectator. 1008
WATERS OF HERCULES (The). [by
"E. D. GERARD", i. e., DOROTHEA GE-
RARD and EMILY (GERARD) LASZOWS-
KA: *Blackwood*, 1885.] "With an unusual
play of fancy in the design, and considerable originality in the treatment, 'The
Waters of Hercules' must be pronounced
a most agreeable work of fiction. But its
chief merit lies in the local coloring, which
in itself, and quite apart from the story,
charms the reader. The scene is laid in
Lower **Hungary**, on the borders of Rou-
mania, and the people, scenery, and
superstitions of this wild region are vividly depicted. The whole story turns upon
the Gaura Dracului, a fathomless abyss
hidden in the heart of the densely wooded
mountains, whêre, according to an ancient
legend, a roman soldier, of the time of
Trajan, had slain his wife in a frenzy of
jealousy. A young german Professor
accidently discovers the spot, and is so
fascinated by it that he marks a tree close
by with the intention of revisiting it at
some future time and thôroly exploring
the chasm. Twenty years later, crippled
by an accident, he is ordered to the sulfur
springs of Hercules, situated in the adjacent valley of the Djernis, when the
chance finding of an old MS. in his desk
recalls to the Professor his youthful enthusiasm for Gaura Dracului, and at the
same time fires his dauter—the heroine of
the tale—with the determination to discover it. She encounters almost insur-
mountable difficulties, arising partly from
the arduous and perilous nature of
the ground, but still more from the superstitious secrecy of the natives. We will
not spoil the story by following the
search in detail; suffice it to say that the
dénoument is artistically brôt about and
some hîly dramatic incidents introduced."
[Westminster Review.] "The terrible
legend of 'Gaura Dracului' is admirably
told. The grim fatality with which the
awful rift in the solid earth is still invested,
the inexorable demand of the god for
human victims at fixed periods, with the

strange lingering belief in the legends of
the pagan times held by the bohemian
and roumanian peasantry, make the
desired impression upon the reader ...
The resumption of the legend, the
weaving of it with the modern story,
which it invests with a captivating mystery
and awe; the local traits of scenery and
manners, the incidental persons and
illustrative sketches; the haunting influence of the legend upon Gretchen's
mind; the fine scene in which the action
reaches its climax, and the grim fulfilment
of the fatal exaction of the god; all these,
and other features of the story, deserve
cordial recognition and praise. For us,
'The Waters of Hercules' possesses a
charm which surpasses that of its romantic interest and narrative power; it is the
author's love of Nature. To the beauty of
hills and valleys, woods and streams, her
heart and fancy are attuned; and her descriptions are at once pictorial and melodious. The finest pages of this charming
book are some in which the author discourses of the woods in spring, and of
the vast, lonely grandeur of the Donau."
[Spectator.] "It is a thôroly charming
story, made of so many pleasing elements
as to seem like a delitful jumbling of
several of the best stories we remember—
'The Initials [No 473] the 'Roi des Mon-
tagnes, [No. 773] and others of such goodly
company. It is long, but the interest,—
sustained first by a gentle curiosity as to
the fate of the earnest german doctor and
the firm little coquette (as mercenary as
Bella Wilfur and much more engaging),
and later by a forcible and clever mingling
of hî tragedy with graceful comedy—does
not lapse for a moment. The characters
are well drawn with a distinctness of individuality which makes them almost
equally entertaining. The mercenary
Gretchen, the frivolous little countess, the
stern, strong doctor, the lît, irrepressible
Tolnay, the pert boy, the flegmatíc Englishman, the tragic and indolent roumanian
princess who was 'fond of caves',—these
would make the story an admirable one,
even without so thrilling and mysterious a

plot." [Critic. **1009**

WELLFIELDS (The) [by JESSIE FOTHERGILL: *Bentley*, 1880.] "is in some respects the best story written by the author of 'The First Violin.' It is, of course, a love story, and the scene is laid partly in **Germany**, in that sort of artistic society which the author describes so well, and partly in England. Jerome Wellfield is a young man of extraordinary beauty and accomplishments, the heir of an old family once Catholic. There is also close by a Jesuit priest, who determines, after the manner of Jesuits, that the best thing for Jerome is that he should marry Nita and return to the fold, bringing the property under the control of the Church. For this purpose he schemes and intrigues. His plan works admirably. He contrives to establish a complete mastery over the weak character of Jerome, and to fill him with the idea that it is essential to him to break off his engagement with Sara Ford and marry Nita Bolton ... This outline gives a poor idea of the story. The description of the means by which Father Somerville establishes his hold upon Wellfield, and brings about his marriage, is admirably done, and the whole plot of the novel is managed with a firmer hand than the author has hitherto shown." [Nation. **1010**

WHAT THE SPRING BROUGHT. [Frühlingsboten) by "E. WERNER", i. e., E.. Bürstenbinder: N.-Y., *Munro*, 1880.] "A german novel in which the interest never flags, whose characters are natural and well drawn, and which is free alike from sentimentality and literary pretence, is a fenomenon rare enuf to be worth noting. All these virtues, and more, are offered to the reader of "E. Werner's" 'Frühlingsboten'. The plot is the old one of a contested inheritance, complicated by the fact that the possessor and the claimant have been bred as brothers, and are very fond of each other, and by the additional circumstance that both love the same woman. The heroes are as opposite in appearance and in character as they are in fortune: the one handsome,

lit-hearted, careless, and affectionate; the other distinguished-looking, industrious, firm-willed, imposing. How he discovered the flaw in his cousin's title to wealth and station need not be detailed here. The enforcement of his claim would involve the forfeiture not merely on the young count's part of his position, but the sacrifice, also, not of personal but of family honor. The ritful heir, therefore, resolves upon silence. But of course the young count discovers the secret, and, as the only way out of the difficulty, allows himself to be run away with and hurled over a precipice. The tale thus becomes a tragedy, but, given the circumstances, both the end and the steps which lead to it are natural. The dénoument is not suspected till one comes upon it in the last chapter, and one rises from the book without feeling any of the disgast often produced by the blue lits and other melodramatic devices by which the real pathos of such a story is too often obscured." [Nation. **1011**

——, SAME ("Fickle Fortune"), London, 1884.

WHERE SHALL HE FIND HER? *American News Co.*, 1867 = *M'LLE DE MALEPEIRE.*

WHERE THE BATTLE WAS FOUGHT. [by "C: Egbert Craddock," i. e., M.. NOAILLES MURFREE: *Osgood*, 1884.] "In spite of structural offenses, the book impresses one as the work of a man of strong, vivid imagination. His representation of character, where the character is, so to speak, in a state of nature, is uncommonly vigorous. We do not care much for the villain and his accomplices, but the moody Estwicke and the chivalric Vayne are capitally delineated. The women, too, are excellently discriminated, tho they play a very subordinate part in the story. Antoinette, tho not the heroine, is better drawn than Marcia. There are, besides, special scenes in the book which show a strong hand. Such is the gambling adventure, in an early chapter. It has very little to do with the development of the plot, but we suspect it will remain longest in the reader's mind; and it has a value, not understood when first read, as explaining the mind of Captain Estwicke. The pictures of ruf Tennessee life are also good, altho one is constantly afraid that the author is about to press the pathos too far. The temptation to exaggerate, not the actual feeling of ruf men and women, but the expression of that feeling in terms which belong to more analytic minds, is one which seems to be a sore one to this author." [Atlantic.] "We know of no author save Hawthorne, who could, like him, have invested the battle-field, the bridge, and the river with just such adjuncts of human passion, pathos, and mystery. The tramp of the advancing columns, the cries and moans of the wounded and dying, which belonged to that old, half-forgotten battle, are made a refrain to which the writer returns on almost every page with melancholy iteration. But such results appertain to poetry and romance, not to the domain of the novelists. The whole setting of the story abounds in picturesqueness, and the presentation of the various figures who go throu their parts is in almost every instance both brilliantly and effectively done ... Not one of the characters but enjoys a chance to do something striking and characteristic. There is also rare and delicate skill shown in the minor incidents, and they all reveal in logical sequence the traits and passions of the men and women behind them ... But, in spite of a certain woodenness in the plot and an over-subtile and complex set of characters, we find Mr. Craddock's book singularly impressive, fulfilling much in those hiest requirements where american novelists have generally disappointed us." [Lippincott's. 1012

WHITE LIES [by C: READE: Trübner, 1857.] "is written with Mr. Reade's usual dash. A rattling fire of italics and interjections, backed by a great artillery of capitals and short paragrafs, distinguish his style. He adopts french idioms freely, and defends his system in a pre-

face. In spite of his affectation and bumptious arrogance, he is really an artist. He has french characters, and he makes them thoroly french. They talk, think, and act french. The story is remarkable for its ingenious exposition of a few of the endless intricacies of female character. Mr. Reade would have us think that he knows women off-hand. He marshals Madame before us, and turns her in and out with a juggler's ease of legerdemain; and after it is over, has the air of posturing to an astonished people to ask them what they think of that for a show? Adam could not have done so much, 'tis certain. Mr. Reade is never bewildered by his Eve. He labors to expose the original woman, bare of all her shifts, for the benefit of noodles." [Westminster Review.]—"The narrative is of the last century, the chief locality is a château in Bretagne; the principal personages are Madame de Beaurepaire, her dauters Laure and Josephine, Jacintha a maid, St. Aubin a friend of the family, a hero or two of iron fabric, and lovers proper for each of the damsels. These gentry become involved in misfortunes, and a long history unwinds in order to make them all happy again. In the first volume many chapters pass without the slitest dramatic action; they are made almost wholly of description, ejaculation, and dialog; in the second the narrative moves with more spirit; in the third, altho interrupted by large digressive passages, it becomes comparatively interesting." [Leader. 1013

——, SAME ("The Double Marriage"), Chatto, 1882.

WHITE MONTH (The) [by F.. M.. PEARD: Smith, 1880.] "opens with an admirable description of the scenery in the more desolate part of Brétagne, and an equally admirable sketch of the chief characters in the book, the priest, and the heroine, then 'little Marjor'. The current of the story joins, in the end, the great stream of the german war, and assumes a more vivid interest. But from the beginning it attracts and pleases, not only by the skillful management of incident and character, but by the feeling which the reader has from the start, that he has before him a real work of art. There is no feeble or casual stroke in the picture; everything is done with a purpose, and produces its effect." [Spectator.] "The heroine is a Breton maiden charming enuf in her single self to make all her readers hope that she is real. Marguerite has many virtues and as many misfortunes; but the author is not hard-hearted nor unkindly, and she leads her heroine into difficulties only to have the pleasure of bringing her out of them, and of making her as happy as possible. All this she does, and does with a certain union of intelligence and charm, of insit and accomplishments, which makes her little book uncommonly pleasant reading ... Her landscapes and interiors, too, are very neatly and prettily done; they have the quality of being quiet and faithful in themselves and of producing a picturesque and vivid impression on their readers. Altogether, 'The White Month' is a book of exceptional freshness and force, and one that should certainly have as many admirers as readers." [Athenæum. 1014

WHITE WINGS. [by W: BLACK: *Harper,* 1880.] "A tender, graceful love-story, with feeling flecked by touches of gay humor and healthy pathos untinged by tragedy, set in a frame-work of winds and waves, cliffs, skies, and the alternate glow and gloom of Highland weather and Highland landscape as seen from a yacht, and told in Mr. William Black's clear and excellent English, could hardly fail to please. Such a story is *White Wings.*" [Literary World. 1015

WIFE TO ORDER (A) [by F: GERSTAECKER: *Routledge,* 1860.] "possesses much to interest and even to excite the reader, being full of strong dramatic situations, and exhibiting every now and then considerable skill in the delineation of character; the language is, moreover, easy and graceful and adapted both to illustrate and enliven the incidents of the novel ... In this slit analysis, we have made no

mention of a most skilful and interesting underplot, which is, perhaps, the most exciting portion of the book; but it is too complicated to admit of any mere outline of its leading characteristics." [Leader. 1016

WILHELM MEISTER. [by J: W. VON GOETHE: *Bohn,* 1852.] "Ask 19 out of 20 moderately educated persons what they think of Wilhelm Meister, and the answer will probably be—"I think it an immoral book; and besides, it is awfully dull: I was not able to read it." Whatever truth there may be in the first half of this judgment, the second half is a sufficient guarantee that the book is not likely to do any extreme injury in english society. Parents may let it lie on the drawing-room table without scruple, in the confidence that for youthful minds of the ordinary cast it will have no attractions, and that the exceptional youthful mind which is strongly arrested by it is of too powerful and peculiar a character to be trained according to educational dogmas. But *is* Wilhelm Meister an immoral book? We think not: on the contrary, we think that it appears immoral to some minds because its morality has a grander orbit than any which can be measured by the calculations of the pulpit and of ordinary literature. It is said that some of the scenes and incidents are such as the refined moral taste of these days will not admit to be proper subjects for art, that to depict irregular relations in all the charms they really have for human nature, and to associate lovely qualities with vices which society makes a brand of outlawry, implies a toleration which is at once a sign and a source of perverted moral sentiment. Wilhelm's relation to Marianna, and the charm which the reader is made to feel in the lawless Philina, many incidents which occur during Wilhelm's life with the players, and the stories of Lothario's in the present, preterite, and future, are shocking to the prevalent english taste. It is no answer to this to say—what is the fact—that Goethe's pictures are truthful, that the career of almost every young man brings him in contact with far more vitiating irregularities than any presented in the experience of Wilhelm Meister; for no one maintains that *all* fact is a fit subject for art .. Everywhere he brings us into the presence of living, generous humanity—mixed and erring, and self-deluding, but saved from utter corruption by the salt of some noble impulse, some disinterested effort, some beam of good nature, even tho grotesque or homely. And his mode of treatment seems to us precisely that which is really moral in its influence. It is without exaggeration; he is in no haste to alarm readers into virtue by melodramatic consequences; he quietly follows the stream of fact and of life; and waits patiently for the moral processes of nature as we all do for her material processes." [Leader. **1017**

WILL (The) [by ERNST ECKSTEIN: *Gottsberger*, 1885.] "is a decidedly clever and agreeable novel. The movement is founded on a promise made by a young man not to break the seales of a package handed to him on a death bed, unless he should have exhausted every earthly hope and should find himself in misery from which there was no possible escape. Bound by this solemn pledge, the youth sets out to conquer the world. He has the hardest kind of a time of it and is often inclined to think that the period for opening the mysterious document has arrived, but each time manfully sets to work again. At length he wins a secure place in the hurly-burly, when it also happens that the paper is opened, tho there is no need of it. Then it is found that the hero instead of being of obscure lineage is of noble race and vast inheritance. He has however made his name and fortune, which are of more value to him than the fruits of accident or chance." [American. **1018**

WILLY REILLY AND HIS DEAR COLLEEN BAWN: a Tale founded on Fact. [by W: CARLETON: London, *Hope*, 1855.] "This is a charming story, a kind of irish chivalry poem. Mr. Carle-

ton has the good luck never to leave irish ground, nor to go far from the irish peasantry, amongst whom his strength of delineation chiefly lies. There is a good deal of extravagance and exaggeration, no doubt; but the whole story is founded upon incidents so romantic that no fiction can exaggerate the actual truth. The character of old Squire Folliard is true to the irish human nature as developed in that class and in that day. As to the 'dear Colleen Bawn,' Mr. Carleton succeeds admirably in impressing upon the reader the reality of her beauty ... Willy Reilly himself is a darling, and there is an atmosfere of romance and nobleness about him which can scarcely fail to win all hearts." [Athenæum. **1019**

WOOING OF CATHERINE (The). [by EMMA F.. POYNTER: *Hurst & Blackett*, 1886.] "*In an Inn Garden'* is a very short piece,—a kind of literary instantaneous fotograf, so real, so vivid, that the scene will dwell in the reader's memory as tho he had himself assisted at the déjeuner à deux, where the grisette takes silent farewell of her nonchalant lover. She loves him, and he is tired of her; and she knows it, and will not betray her knowledge of his faithlessness ... The best tale in the series is called '*An Island Grave.*' It tells of the escape of a Jacobite gentleman after Culloden ... The tale is of the simplest, its whole interest centring in the devotion of the two hunted creatures to each other, and in the presence of mind and affection of the wife and mother, who sees her child sicken and die without any power of relieving its sufferings—a sacrifice to the safety of its father who, in the supreme moment of its death, secures his escape by her ready wit and courage. We have seldom read a more moving narrative, or one which appeals more forcibly to the noblest instincts of human nature. '*A Tragic Hero'* is amusing, even absurd, and gives us the impression of being a true story, as it certainly is not a very uncommon one. This cannot be said of the last piece: '*The Story of a God-dauter'* is an extraordinary flit of imagination, telling of a luckless passion which turns into a grim fate, pursuing the hapless heroine with unceasing and pitiless persistency. In vain does her sense of duty, of family honor, save her once from its fatal attraction; she succumbs to it at last, helpless as the moth in the candle." [Spectator. 1020

WORLD WENT VERY WELL THEN (The). [by WA. BESANT: *Harper*, 1888.] "Take it all in all, we have never read anything of Mr. Besant's which seems to us so agreeable as this. It is full of spirited action and delitful situations, notwithstanding that there are inconsistencies in the characters of his hero, with which we should be inclined to quarrel had we the time. The book is free from the strained moral and social speculations with which Mr. Besant is so prone to strew the pages of his novels of more modern life. The time of the story is the middle of the last century. The scene is Deptford town on the Thames, the very gates of London, and the decks of the ships that carry the hero in his expeditions to and fro. The business of life was simple enuf then; love, war, and adventure filled up the measure of man's conception. And if loyal Bess clung with meek and desperate devotion to an unworthy lover, it need not in the life of torpor of these modern days seem a violent price to pay for life—for to her poor primitive soul, love was life itself. Mr. Besant is never so much at his best as when he contents himself with the simple annals of the virtues and failings of human nature, the former of which he uses with so much charm and for the latter of which he has so much charity." [Critic. 1021

WUTHERING HEIGHTS. [by EMILY BRONTÉ: 1850.] "The accumulated horrors of the close, however possible in fact, are wanting in the one quality which justifies and ennobles all admissible horror in fiction: they hardly seem inevitable; they lack the impression of logical and moral certitude. All the realism in the

work will not suffice to convey this impression; and a work of art which wants it wants the one final and irreplaceable requisite of inner harmony. Now in 'Wuthering Heights' this one thing needful is as perfectly and triumfantly attained as in 'King Lear' or 'The Duchess of Malfi,' in 'The Bride of Lammermoor' [No. 617] or 'Notre-Dame de Paris' [No. 871]. From the first we breathe the fresh dark air of tragic passion and presage; and to the last the changing wind and flying sunlit are in keeping with the stormy promise of the dawn. There is no monotony, there is no repetition, but there is no discord. This is the first and last necessity, the foundation of all labor and the crown of all success, for a poem worthy of the name; and this it is that distinguishes the hand of Emily from the hand of Charlotte Brontë. All the works of the elder sister are rich in poetic spirit, poetic feeling, and poetic detail; but the younger sister's work, is essentially and definitely a poem in the fullest and most positive sense of the term." [Swinburne.]—"With "Wuthering Heights" we found it totally impossible to get along. It begins by introducing the reader to a perfect pandemonium of low and brutal creatures, who wrangle with each other in language too disgusting for the eye or the ear to tolerate, and unredeemed, so far as we could see, by one single particle either of wit or humor, or even psychological truth, for the characters are as false as they are loathsome." [North British Review. 1022

YELLOW MASK (The). [by [W:] W. COLLINS: N.-Y., *Dix*, 1855.] "For dramatic interest, and for artistic skill in the conception of its plot, as well as its development, we think it far superior to any novel of the day." [Crayon. 1023

YOUNG PHILISTINE; and other Tales. [by ALICE CORKRAN; *Burns and Oates*, 1887.] "We find here a delicacy of touch, a fine humor, and a pathos which give to these little stories something of the charm and finish of a miniature. The first tale, '*The English*

317

Teacher at the Convent,' takes hold of the reader by its fine portraiture, its quaint coloring, and its underglow of passion . ... Two of the other stories are based on a sad conception—that of the obscure, unknown artist, penetrated with intense love for his art, but ignorant, powerless to inform his ignorance, and producing only grotesques, which bring down on him lâfter and derision. '*Père Perrault's Legacy'* strikes altogether a new note; the strange little story is a thing apart. It is to be hoped that Miss Corkran may before long bring out another volume of such charming studies." [Athenæum.   **1024**

Novels are as a rule written for the young, and from their pages most young men and women get their first picture of life; they supply the gorgeous scenery, the heroic characters, and the thrilling events of those day-dreams on which the fancy of youth dwells, and so furnish unconsciously its ideals for future life. With regard to love and mariage, for instance, novels are the sources from which in early life, long before we can know anything about the matter from experience, we derive some of our most deeply-rooted pre-conceptions. Most people in mature life can look back upon some one or two novels which suggested to them new objects of existence, a clearer insit into the poetry of life. [Nation.

"Every year the influence of revues has less to do with the circulation or failure of a book. The public mind enlarges itself, and must be fed with printed matter of some kind. Readers are gluttons, not conaisseurs, and so the cannons of taste are set at naut, and the niceties of intellectual and imaginative work meet less and less appreciation." [Spectator.

"There are multitudes who habitually read a good deal, and much to their satisfaction, whose provision of books is almost entirely drawn from the middle and lower classes of literature. Very many of them, indeed, have read DICKENS, some few THACKERAY, wholly or partially; but for them, Miss AUSTEN wrote drivel, and SIR WALTER SCOTT prosy inanity. They would as soon attack John Locke as "GEORGE ELIOT"; and if they read a book of Mrs. OLIPHANT, they feel as if they had had a Sunday in the middle of the week. They like Mrs. CRAIK well enuf, because, tho didactic, she is sentimental. They take Miss BRADDON and "OUIDA" as the salt and spice of their reading; but what they live upon is the enormous mass of novels and stories which fill the pages of cheap periodicals and serve as ballast to the circulating libraries. It seems, then, that the laws of demand and supply account for the existence of thousands of novels, and since thousands of novels are required and manufactured, it is reasonable enuf to expect that they should lose the character of works of art, and be as commonplace as the daily bread to which we have already likened them." [Spectator.

PRICE: ONE COPY, $2.00; TWO COPIES, $3.50; THREE, $5.00; FIVE, $7.50; TEN, $10.00; TWENTY, $1.00 ₵.

A

DESCRIPTIVE LIST

OF

BRITISH NOVELS.

COMPILED BY

W: M. GRISWOLD

EDITOR OF "THE MONOGRAPH", A COLLECTION OF FIFTY-FOUR HISTORICAL AND
BIOGRAPHICAL ESSAYS; AND OF "TRAVEL", A SIMILAR SERIES
DEVOTED TO PLACES.

CAMBRIDGE, MASS.:
W: M. GRISWOLD, PUBLISHER,
1891.

It is a very pleasant thing to finish reading a book and feel that one has made a charming new acquaintance. Men and women who are entirely congenial and delítful are by no means common in this world, even if one lives in the midst of its best society; and some of our dear friends are people who live all the year round in the little three-walled houses made by book-covers. Yet *their* every-day life is as real to us as *ours*; their houses and their fortunes and misfortunes are well known to us, and we are sure of a thousand things about them that we never saw in print. The inner circle of our friends mít be a broken one if it were not rounded and completed with such companionships as these. But one thinks not so much of the luxury of having these friendships as of the necessity for them, and of the good it does everybody to know nice people, of the elevating power a novel may have if it carries its readers among people worth knowing. It is certainly a great force in raising the tone of society; it is a great help in the advance of civilization and refinement. A good story has a thousand readers where a biografy has ten. Who is not better for having associated with the ladies and gentlemen to whom certain novelists have presented us? One instinctively tries to behave his very best after meeting them, and admires their hospitality, their charity, their courage in adversity, their grace and good-breeding. How many tricks of speech and manner we have caut in such society! How often we have been moved to correct some carelessness or rudeness, of which we were unconscious until they taut us better! Trollope, Miss Thackeray, Mrs. Oliphant, a hundred others, have unwittingly done much more than entertain us with their stories: they have taut many people good manners; they have set copies for us to follow in little things and great. To have spent a Week in a French Country House—as I hope we have all been lucky enuf to do—will save us from seeming awkward on any repetition of that charming visit. If we have never been abroad at all we feel that when we are in France, by and by, and go into the country, it will not seem at all strange. It is a pity that so little is known of *our* pleasant people from the story-books. The best of our gentlemen and ladies have kept very much to themselves; at any rate, they have few representatives in fiction, and do not mix much with the familiar types of character in American novels. Do they have themselves privately printed, and are they rít to be so shy as they are, and to keep their fashion of doing things to themselves? Are the authors who write about american life afraid of seeming to copy forein stories if they say too much of the people who, from a social point of vue, are best worth knowing and reading about? The country lífe and local dialects and peculiarities, with their ridiculousness and pathos, the energy and restlessness and flashiness and unconventionality, the ostentation, of americans have been held up for us to look at again and again. There are many of our nêbors across the water who think the american girl of the period, with whom they have become acquainted, is the best type that can be found. It is too bad that there have been so few stories of agreeable, hí-bred american men and women, and that our best society has been so seldom represented in fiction. It is certainly not because it does not exist, and more books which show us such characters as these would do much good. [Atlantic.

BRITISH NOVELS.

The object of this list is to direct readers, such as would enjoy the kind of books here described, to a number of novels, easily obtainable, but which, in many cases, have been forgotten within a year or two after publication. That the existence of works of fiction is remembered so short a time is a pity, since, for every new book of merit, there are, in most libraries, a hundred as good or better, unknown to the majority of readers. It is hoped that the publication of this and similar lists will lessen, in some measure, the disposition to read an inferior NEW *book when superior* OLD *books, equally fresh to most readers, are at hand.*

This list will be followed by others describing EUROPEAN, ECCENTRIC, *and* FANCIFUL *novels and tales. The compiler would be pleased to have his attention called to any works deserving a place which have escaped his attention. It may be observed that the compiler has tried to include only such works as are well-written, interesting, and free from sensationalism, sentimentality, and pretence. But in a few cases, books have been noticed on account of the reputation of their authors, or their great popularity, rather than their merit. The selected " notices " here given are generally abridged.*

ACADEMICIAN (THE) [by H: ERROLL: *Bentley*, 1888.] "impresses one as being pleasant and lit, yet by no means shallo. The heroin, a charming person, improves as her story advances, for her 'niceness' is sufficiently qualified to preserve her from any suspicion of insipidity. The dialog is smart and neat, but is never fatiguingly over clever or over subtle..... The book's main interest is artistic." [Athenæum. **1025**

ACROSS THE GARDEN WALL [by — ( ) GREENE: *F. V. White*, 1886.] "is a little comedy which occupies the reader's attention very pleasantly. A novel which affords simple relaxation, and makes one forget to criticize, should meet with grateful recognition." [Athenæum. **1026**

ADAM AND EVE = No. 579

ADAM BEDE [by " G: ELIOT," i. e.,

M .. A .. (Evans) Cross: *Blackwood*, 1859.] "is remarkable, not less for the unaffected saxon style which upholds the graceful fabric of the narrativ, and for the naturalness of its scenes and characters, so that the reader at once feels happy and at home among them, than for the general perception of those universal springs of action which control all society, the patient unfolding of those traits of humanity with which commonplace writers get out of temper and rudely dispense. The place and the people and the language ar of the simplest; and what happens from day to day, and from year to year, in the period of the action, mit happen in any little village. We do not kno where to look, in the whole range of contemporary fictitious literature, for pictures in which the sober and the brilliant tones

320

of Nature blend with more exquisit harmony than in those which ar set in every chapter of 'Adam Bede.' Still life — the harvest-field, the polished kitchens, the dairies, with a concentrated cool smell of all that is nourishing and sweet, the green, the porches which hav vines about them and ar pleasant late in the afternoon, and deep woods thrilling with birds — all these wer never more vividly and yet tenderly depicted. The characters ar drawn with a free and impartial hand, and one of them is a creation for immortality. Mrs. Poyser is a woman with an incorrigible tung, set firmly in opposition to the mandates of a heart, the overfloes of whose sympathy and love keep the circle of her influence in a state of continual irrigation. Her epigrams ar aromatic, and she is strong in simile, but never ventures beyond her depth into that of her author." [Atlantic. **1027**

ADDIE'S HUSBAND [by — ( ) SMYTHIES: *Appleton*, 1885.] "is charmingly told, and so full of tender human feeling, with such an unmistakable moral, as to the absurdity of secrecy between husband and wife, and the wickedness of anybody cherishing malignity, that one closes the book feeling that one has gained a good deal more than even a pretty story." [Critic. **1028**

ADMIRAL'S WARD (THE). [by "MRS. ALEXANDER," i. e., Annie (French) Hector: *Holt*, 1883.] "There is a fineness about the whole life in this book which was sometimes missed in the author's previous novels. It is the old story of the gain and the loss of an inheritance, but imagined with motivs so unusual, and situations so unexpected, as to giv it positiv originality. The incidents ar simple, almost homely, but every-day life is transformed to something like poetry by the patience of the heroin in her humble duties, and by the beautiful, enduring affection of the 2 women of whom love and fate mit hav made enemies. The 'Admiral' and Mrs. Crewe, 'who does not take lodgers, but only consents to receive a gentleman or two, personally recommended' ar of the best of the whimsical oddities with whom Mrs. Alexander enlivens her tales — best, becaus drawn with more reserve. The plot develops so quietly that there is no suspicion of the catastrofe until the last moment. It startles, but it proves its fitness, for it makes the reader at once turn back to re-read the story in the lit of it. Too often the end of a novel is only like the solution of an enigma. The tangle untwisted, one cares no more, but, as in this case, real skill will lead to a result which impels us to turn back and judge of character by our knoledge of final deeds." [Nation. **1029**

ADRIAN BRIGHT [by — ( ) CADY: *Harper*, 1884.] "will giv the same sort of pleasure to the reader that he gets from some of his acquaintances — people whose goings-on seem to him altogether unwarrantable, who never accomplish much, nor say anything to be remembered, but who are brit, chatty people, who always hav a good time, and ar always ready to share it with their friends. The hero and heroin could not be of less account and maintain their positions. One takes but a mild interest in their fortunes as compared with the ways and deeds of a family of artist associations and occupations, as nearly bohemian as the respectability of Welbeck street will permit. It is rather a curious study, the pass to which bohemianism has come under the influence of the æsthetic craze, and the author has succeeded very well in rendering it with hearty appreciation and yet keeping all

the time her little smile of amusement."
[Nation. **1030**

ADRIAN VIDAL. [by W: E: Norris: *Harper*, 1885.] "Mr. Norris'
novels always bring before us living men
and women, and they ar always interesting. Adrian Vidal is, if anything, superior to the author's previous works.
It is a study of modern life, rather remarkable for its realism, and its analyses of character ar clever without being overwrôt, pitiless, but never cynical.
The tale folloes a portion of the career
of a young novelist, and the plot turns
on certain infelicities which arise soon
after his marriage. Having on one side
an easy-going nature, a keen susceptibility to flattery, and a fondness for society, and on the other a jealous disposition and a mind wholly domestic in its
tastes, one quickly recognizes the elements of an unhappy destiny which requires something more than mutual confidence, and this Adrian and his wife
attain only after bitter experience which
comes near to driving them apart forever..... Nor should we forget to mention the author's gift of humor which
bubbles unobtrusivly on every page.
Altogether a more thŏroly readable
novel than Adrian Vidal we hav not
met for many a day." [Boston "Literary
World." **1031**

ADVENTURES OF HARRY RICH-
MOND = No. 580.

ADVENTURES OF PHILIP (The),
Showing who Robbed him, who Helped
him, and who Passed him by. [by W:
Makepeace Thackeray: 1862.] "The
title tells what plan the author has pursued in writing it. He has carried out
that plan well. To say that the book is
interesting, original, full of singular
humor, containing passages which excite our wonder and amazement at the
author's penetration and almost unique

ability in exposing social shams and errors, would be superfluous. Mr. Thack-
cray's name on the title-page, and his
acute, sarcastic, almost bitter face for
the frontispiece, say all this to those who
hav read his former works. This one,
in neither interest, nor in the peculiarities
of the author in style, nor in the characters he portrays, falls behind them.
Philip, the hero, is made to struggle
throu his early life entirely at the mercy
of his Levites and Samaritans. Considering the disposition and proclivities ascribed to him by the author, the wonder
is excited why everyone did not pass
him by, and why so many dared to stay
their steps and offer him aid. He is a
ruf, loud, boisterous fello. Becaus his
father was a polished villain (having
early discovered this pleasing fact) he
immediately sets about being as different
as possible. Deeming polish insincerity,
and politeness treachery, he ostentatiously exhibits disdain for these pleasing social qualities. Being large in
frame, and strong, and red-haired, he
can sho to some purpose his aggressiv
and quarrelsom, yet not ungenerous
temper. He alienates those who try to
be his friends by his determination to
indulge his head-long independence of
speech or action. He insults people he
does not fancy, ignoring the bonds of
past obligations. In consequence of
these little singularities, he has several
enemies, and one is strongly inclined to
add to their number. Nevertheless, he
has a friend, the Little Sister, the most
like a woman of anything in the book,
who clings to him with a blind adoring
love which is neither useless nor fruitless. Again and again, this little woman,
poor, disgraced, to all appearance powerless, comes to the aid of this great
burly son of her adoption, and saves
him and his Charlotte, and his children

322

almost from starvation," [Church Monthly. **1032**

AGAINST TIME [by ALEX. INNES SHAND: *Smith*, 1870.] " is a really interesting novel, free from cant, verbiage, or undue sensation — the work of a man endowed with a clear and fertil fancy, who can describe the scenes and people of the present day without depressing the reader with the sense of their vulgarity. He is modern, but not mean, and imaginativ without being maudlin. Equally at home in the City and on the Highland hills, he givs a vivid and enthusiastic, yet truthful, description of both.....The characters ar all excellent, and many original." [Athen. **1033**

AGATHA'S HUSBAND [by DINA MARIA (MULOCK) CRAIK: *Chapman*, 1850.] " is, in its strong interest, a painful book; and for this reason it is more likely to be a favorit with the young, the hopeful, and the enthusiastic — who, after all, ar the great novel readers — than with those whose lives and thôts belong to the sober realities of life, and whose experience of sorro inclines them to shrink from the exposition of mimic woes. Agatha herself is drawn with such power and delicate skill that she livs in the memory with the individuality of a well-knôn personage. She is a true woman of the hi-toned class. Her 'husband,' tho apparently representing the author's ideal of a man, pleases us much less. The simile of the 'oak and the ivy' is all very pretty for poetry, and possibly for sylvan vegotable life. But the human ivy, we suspect, sometimes groes sadly tired of doing all the twining, and at any rate would like the oak to bend its branches and somewhat reciprocate the embrace. Nevertheless, we kno thêre is a large class of women who admire the 'style'; and while a tender-hearted, demonstra-

tiv man is often in life wedded to a shrew, or an automaton, we as usually find hi, generous-natured women lavishing thêir affection on some calm, stern, self-possessed ideal, like the Nathanael of the present volumes." [Ladies' Companion. **1034**

AGNES HOPETOUN'S SCHOOLS AND HOLIDAYS [by MA. OLIPHANT (WILSON) OLIPHANT: *Macmillan*, 1872.] " is a very pleasant story. The heroin is a rather bad-tempered and intractable little girl, who, throu painful disciplin, learns how to be good and useful." [Boston "Literary World." **1035**

AILEEN FERRERS. [by SUSAN MORLEY: *H: S. King*, 1874.] " Those who prefer quality to quantity of fiction will here not be disappointed. The young lady with the pretty irish name is an admirable heroin, whose sound sense, womanly heart, and fine discretion by no means detract from her character as the central figure of a neat little romance. Nor is Aileen alone in the possession of qualities which, however they may influence our common life, are generally deemed quite unworthy of fiction. Aileen's patrician aunt and plebeian grandmother vie with each other in the justness of their vues, and the tact with which they treat their young relativ." [Athenæum. **1036**

AIRY FAIRY LILIAN. [by MA. (AROLES) HUNGERFORD: *Lippincott*, 1879.] " We hav here a thôroly delitful novel, to be read with interest, lâfed over, and enjoyed from beginning to end by everybody who likes to look into english country life in its sunniest mood, to kno intimately a small party of pleasant people, to be a party to sparkling and witty conversation, to make the acquaintance of one of the most engaging young ladies whom recent fiction has presented, and to watch the course of 2 very pretty love affairs throu a tortuous and troubled grôth to a happy consummation. The book is as fresh, fragrant, brit, and exhilarating as a June morning. The only clouds in the sky ar made to be radiant; no disagreeable villains ar allowed; no taint debases the life recorded; Lady Chetwood is just a lovely old lady; and the ' airy fairy Lilian' is all which the epithets attached to her name suggest. The dainty social slang in which she and her irrepressible cousin Taffy indulge, givs special zest to the book." [Boston " Literary World." **1037**

ALDERSYDE [by ANNIE S. SWAN, N.Y., *Carter*, 1880.] is "a quaint, tender, pathetic story, illustrativ of a fáse of the social life of the Scottish border seventy years ago." **1038**

ALDYTH. [by JESSIE FOTIERGILL: *H. S. King*, 1877.] " There is some power in Miss Fothergill's domestic story. The sad trials throu which Aldyth passes (first in refusing, from a sense of duty to her younger sisters, to emigrate with the man to whom she is engaged, and lastly in being treacherously supplanted in his love by her younger sister, when 10 years of waiting have spoiled her looks) serve only to make her character hier and purer than before. The minor personages hav all their distinctiv traits. The style is simple and correct." [Athen. **1039**

ALEC FORBES of Howglen. [by G: MACDONALD: *Hurst*, 1865.] " It is something to rejoice the heart that even in these days a novel can be written full of strong human interest without any aid from melodramatic scene-painting, social mysteries, and the fysical force of incidents. ' Alec Forbes ' is merely the history of some of the inhabitants of an obscure village in the north of **Scotland.** A country lass, left an orfan,

and a boy, the son of a wido, a little better placed in the world, ar the main figures in the story; but innumerable threads of interest ar interwoven with them: the human hearts by which they all liv ar opened to the reader; and this is the real source of interest — an interest deeper and stronger than can be woven out of mere circumstances, however complicated or perilous.....The sketches of university life in Glasgow ar very good; the temptations and fall of Alec ar firmly handled, and the friendship of the whimsical and learned librarian is admirably introduced and worked out. But the reader must read for himself; no account of the story would giv any idea of the profound interest which pervades the work from the first page to the last. ' Alec Forbes ' is the work of a poet. The ballads and poems, which ar introduced here and thêre, ar all touched with grace and beauty." [Athenæum. **1040**

ALEXIA. [by ELEANOR C. PRICE: *Bentley*, 1887.] " It is not often that so much delicate art is displayed in the telling of so slit a story. Not only is the plot so skilfully interwoven with the finer passion of the tale that it is almost spun, as it wer, out of the very texture of that passion....but all the sketches of character ar complete to just the same extent and depth, so that we seem to be looking at a fine bas-relief whêre every figure is definitly, tho only superficially, chiselled out, and each is in keeping with the others. Miss Price tells us quite truly and simply at the conclusion of her tale : ' This is only a sketch of a few years in a girl's life, and there is no need to carry it on any further. Alexia and Charlie wer, of course, meant for each other from the beginning; they wer lovers always, and I shall be surprised if they do not continue lovers to the end. They wer neither of them faultless, and both made mistakes in their lives, which mit very easily hav severed them for ever.' But what interests us in this brief but delicate story is the beauty and simplicity of the workmanship, — the perfect ease with which not only the hero's and heroin's far from faultless characters ar drawn and made visible, but the secondary figures ar sketched in, so as to enhance the vividness of the principal interest....In a story so slit, we hav seldom seen so true an art displayed, so much finish and simplicity in delineating the relation between the characters, and so much skill in weaving a plot which shall really express, as human destinies very rarely seem to express, both what is truest and what is faultiest in the characters concerned, and that shall correspond so accurately, and yet so naturally, to the expectations and wishes of the reader." [Spectator. **1041**

ALFRED HAGART'S HOUSEHOLD [by ALEX. SMITH : *Strahan*, 1866.] " is a very charming tale.... Quiet, thoroly good, capitally told, with every here and thêre a sprinkle of really beautiful, poetic prose. Thêre is also a relish of mild Scottism, not only whêre the characters speak, but whêre the author himself speaks, which is of itself a charm in these days of clipped hedges and wire fences. The book mit almost hav for its second title ' Quarrels made up.' The chief figure in it next to its hero, is a rich old aunt, who has fallen out with her well-descended niece for marrying beneath her, but who does all kind things under her crabbed surface of pride: one great kind act above all others, buying a partnership for Alfred Hagart, of which, to the end, the recipient never knôs. Then we hav a lovers' quarrel, very well told, and nobly adjusted, by the working of a hint given by the same original old lady. Next to her character, the best drawn in the book is that of Alfred Hagart himself. The intermixture of the folly of the head with the wisdom of the heart; the combination of restlessness and yearning for change with safe anchorage in affection and respect for a good wife, ar capitally described." [Contemp. Review. **1042**

ALICE DUGDALE. [with " Why Frau Frohmann " by ANTIONY TROLLOPE : *Isbister*, 1882.] " Mr. Trollope fully succeeds in making Alice Dugdale really lovable and charming, in spite of the drudgery in which she is always engaged, the unromantic butteriness of her little brother's kisses, and the much pricked fore-finger which has gone throu so many trials in the mending of torn clothes. Nay, he makes, as, of course, he ôt to make, the buttery kisses and the pricked forefinger essential parts of the lovableness of the girl who carries her dignity so well throu all her trials, and wins her prize at last, by virtue, almost, of her resolv to thro it away." [Spectator. **1043**

ALICE GRAEME [*Chapman*, 1868.] " is a charming story. The personages ar well-drawn, and with the exception of the one incident (the father's acceptance of the proposal of a french nobleman to hav Alice taken abroad and educated for a public singer), all is quiet and life-like. The peaceful household and sunny garden of the scotch schoolmaster touch the reader like a pleasant home whêre he would like to dwell; the motherly Mrs. Graeme, the stern father, the old grandmother, ar like good dutch portraits. The sudden shame and grief which come to them throu thêir son, the sorro which overtakes the beautiful Alice ar well done. The mystery of affliction which is meted out to the whole household, is full of subtle teaching in the good that is worked out of trials which seem only dark and hard and cruel at the time. The picture of Alice when forsaken by her lover, her misery and her temptations ar well told. The author justifies the seeming cruelty of the trial by the beauty and delicacy with which the purifying influence of sorro is shön. Alice begins by being a lovely girl; she ends by becoming an angel." [Athenæum. **1044**

ALICIA TENNANT [by F.. M.. Peard: *Bentley*, 1886.] "is a story of good society, written in that pleasant and refined style to which readers of Miss Peard's books ar accustomed. Her characters ar well drawn, even the men, one of whom is particularly good, a precise, well-bred gentleman, studious and irreproachable, but a dreadful bore; and tho as a rule thêy ar a little wanting in incisiveness, thêre ar delicate touches about them which ar admirable.... but Miss Peard has been cruel in bringing her story to so sad an end." [Ath. **1045**

ALL IN THE DARK [by Joseph Sheridan Le Fanu: *Harper*, 1866.] "is a simple story excellently told, a reproduction of certain quaint fâses in life, which, while they display no lofty power, ar marked by much artistic excellence, and a series of pictures and incidental descriptions not extraordinarily brilliant, but evidently drawn and colored after nature. The mind of the reader is never unduly excited by overwrôt scenes of passion, and not even a sprinkling of crime disturbs the smooth current of the story, which floes so easily and is so charmingly related that each character seems to be the portraiture of an old friend whom we rejoice to meet, and from whom we ar unwilling to part even when assured of his ultimate felicity." [Round Table. **1046**

ALL SORTS AND CONDITIONS OF MEN. [by Wa. Besant and Ja. Rice: *Harper*, 1882.] "One of the most attractiv elements in the stories of Besant and Rice has been the genial belief in human nature, and we ar not surprised to find this becoming at last the dominant element in a story written with a purpose. 'All Sorts and Conditions of Men' is the record of a young lady who, having become an heiress by her father's immense operations in beer, decides to forego the privileges of her position, and liv among the people from whom she has sprung. She is convinced that she can do more good by her presence than by her money, but she very prudently takes the money too; establishes herself as a dressmaker, under an assumed name, in a co-operative association whêre the employées ar given opportunities to rest, to eat, and to play tennis; and finally builds 'A Palace of Delit' for the poor. She discards all knôn theories of political economy, and it is an excellent point in the story that she labors, not to foster a spirit of content in the humble, but to rouse discontent with misery and wretched surroundings which is knôn, when it appears in hi circles, by the name of aspiration. To the same boarding-house comes a young gentleman who, having learned that he was not entitled by birth to the social privileges he had enjoyed, decided to return to his people and become a cabinet-maker." [Critic.] — " Rice and Besant worked together with ease. One or both of them was gifted with a sort of french vivacity of description and narration which prevented their stories from ever being dull, and one or both of them had a considerable power of humorous caricature — enuf to make extravagant characters entertaining when most unreal..... Among other queer characters is an american heir, who has come to England to get his rits and be restored to his title. He and his wife, respectable citizens of Canaan City, N.H., ar knön among their friends as Lord and Lady Davenant, but their claim to the name has not received legal recognition, oing to a difficulty in making out the chain of descent. This difficulty is never overcome, but they, like everybody else in the book, ar taut a wholesom lesson, and kindly provided for out of the ample purse of the benevolent heroin." [Nation. **1047**

ALMA [by EMMA (   ) MARSHALL: *Sonnenschein*, 1888.] "is a simple offering to the now neglected shrine of poetic justice. Out of hackneyed materials is woven a graceful, tho improbable romance of the struggles and ultimate success of a girl reduced by poverty to teaching." [Ath. **1048**

AMERICAN SENATOR (THE) [by ANTONY TROLLOPE: *Chapman and Hall*, 1877.] "mit just as well have been called 'The Chronicle of a Winter at Dillsborough' ....This name will conjure to readers of Mr. Trollope's books a picture of pleasant recollections. Dillsborough is not, it is true, a cathedral city, nor even an assize town; but is buried in the depths of the country and apparently exists for no purpose whatever. This is Mr. Trollope's proper ground. He has made it familiar to his readers, but they see it again and again without weariness. Those who try to analyse the charm will fail to detect in what it consists. The detail is minute, often, as it seems, irrelevant, but thêre is an indefinable humor running throu it, and all helps to produce the general effect." [Athenæum. **1049**

AMONG STRANGERS [by "E. S. MAINE": *Smith*, 1870.] "is simple and unpretentious, but is told in so fresh and graceful a manner as to render it most acceptable. ....It will be seen that the story is of the simplest kind; but the book possesses a charm rarely to be met. Naturally and pleasingly written, it should find a place in many a home circle." [Athenæum. **1050**

AMOR VINCIT [by M.. E. MARTIN: *Ward & Downey*, 1887.] "is a pretty, unpretentious story of a girl who was kidnapped from her mother by her grandmother, and who does not seem to hav been in any sense the worse for it. She is brit and loving, the favorit of all whom she meets; and two or three eligible young men ar in due time captivated by her charms. To one of these, the humblest in worldly advantages, she is attracted; and tho her mother turns out to be a fine lady, and eventually recovers her lost child, the legend of the title-page is illustrated by the romantic fidelity of Lois Stanley. The central incident of the narrativ is painful, but it is not too obtrusiv, since the reader is interested from the beginning in the love story of Lois and Alan. The kidnapping grandmother, too, is not so repellent as mit be supposed." [Athenæum. **1051**

AMY WYNTER [by T: A. PINKERTON: *Tinsley*, 1880.] "is a pleasant story of simple life, warm with kindly feeling and redolent of natural charms. The prolog is a romance in itself, and serves, as a good prolog must, to secure the interest of the reader for the more detailed narrativ which folloes." [Athenæum. **1052**

ANGUS GRAY. [by "E. S. MAINE": *Smith*, 1878.] "The characters of Eveleigh and his dauter ar well imagined and successfully developed. The sudden fury which places the easy-going unprincipled virtuoso in such imminent danger, his wild despair and the

ALMOST A HEROINE [by E.. S..
SHEPPARD: *Hurst, Ticknor*, 1859.]
"may fairly take its plaçe amōng the many
which liv happily throu a season, and ar
then forgotten. Ernest Loftus, its hero.
is so unskilled in the ways of men as tŏ
be "almost a heroin" . . . The plan sucçeeds
admirably. Ernest sets ŏff with his £20,
leaving the old servant so disconsolate
that he wil eat nothing but bread and
cheese, and continues his menial work
during the whole epoch of his wealth.
Meanwhile the hero, when he has ōnly
sixpençe left, finds a friend in a philanthropic nobleman, whŏ has established a
mad-house, using, tŏ keep the patients in
order, a young ladv whŏ is possessed of a
marvelous magnetic influençe. With her
Ernest falls in lōve, but insanity runs in
her blood, and marriage is thĕrefore impossible. We need not follo him throu
the 3 years in which many lăfable, even
despicable, weaknesses ar mixed with
several strong qualities. The development of his character is an impossible
ōne, and the author in painting it, has
endeavored tŏ combine cōlors which can
not effectivly be blended. A much worthier creation is that of Loftus' friend,
Arnold Major, a man whŏ struggles
bravely against a crowd of troubles, and,
in the end, stands victoriously upon them.
His persistent lōve, marred as its working is by jealousy and pride, is powerfully described. He and the sparkling,
wayward, noble-hearted woman whŏ becōmes his wife ar the true hero and
heroin. The book has cleverness and
good purpos, which make it worth reading; but it also has many failings." [Ex-
aminer.]—"If ever the pulses of a woman's soul wer laid bare, thĕy ar so in this
book; and this is dōne quite as much by
what is written in the character of the
professed relator of the story whŏ is a
man, and in the description of the hero
and his life, as by the thôts and acts
which ar attributed tŏ her whŏm the
author styles "almost a heroin." This
"almost," by the way, is a bit of affectation which has ōnly its shado of reason in
the fact that "Horatia" is not a faultless
and (happily) impossible creature, but
ōnly ōne of the lōveliest, most lōvable,
and most lōving of women. The storv
can not be told in epitome; for its inçidents ar trifling, disconnected, every-day
occurençes. The interest of the book is
tŏ be found in its characters and in its
masterly portrayal of emotion, and its
exquisitly delicate anatomy of passion;—
not ōnly of the master passion, lōve, but
of all ōthers. Its hero and its heroin ar
London people of hi birth and culture:
he, poor, and a man of letters; she a rich
independent woman of fashion. Oddly
enuf thĕy dŏ not see each other til the
story is half told, altho it prōves in the
end that thĕy hav met before tŏ thĕir cost;
and no small part of the development of
the grand passion tŏ the workings of
which the hook is devoted is made throu a
description of thĕir behavior, while a
third person (the relator) is talking tŏ
each about the ōther. The stvle of the
book certainly can not be commended for
its purity, its clearness, or its eloquençe.
It is fragmentary, disjointed, elliptical,
affected, and contaminated with not a
little slang. The thôt, too, which this
style convĕys is feverish and hĭ-strung."
[Albion. **1048 f**

breaking down of all his prejudices under the reaction of unexpected relief ar forcibly dramatic. The true nobility which, overlaid with selfishness in the father, has unfettered sway in his innocent, unselfish child, and atones for the perversities of both, reflects credit on the writer. Angus is more commonplace, but in gentle manliness contributes as much as he gains from his educated friends." [Athenæum. **1053**

ANNE FURNESS. [by F.. ELEANOR (TERNAN) TROLLOPE: *Chapman*, 1871.] "It is impossible here to do justice to the rare merits of 'Anne Furness.' By adopting the autobiografic form the author has voluntarily encountered peculiar difficulties, with which a true artist alone can cope successfully. In saying that the author has succeeded, we mean that we recognize evidences of genius — marvellous imaginativ power, and great power of analyzing character. The subject of the memoir is a woman of a rare type, with all the instincts, tact, and sympathy, without the littleness of the feminin nature. Her lot is cast in the nêborhood of a town in Yorkshire. Much of her early life is spent in the house of her grandfather, with whose nature and household she feels herself more in sympathy than at home, and there she meets, while a mere child, a scotch lad, whom she worships from the first." [Ath. **1054**

ANNE WARWICK. [by GEORGIANA MARION (CRAIK) MAY: *Hurst*, 1876.] "The hero's one thôt is to secure the heroin from want. Hence he prevails upon her to marry him on what he supposes to be his death-bed. But she is not to kno what his real object is. She is to look upon it as the half-capricious request of a man doomed to die. The reader, of course, forsees that he recovers. How she is won to love him is the real sub-jcet of the story, which is told with much skill. The diplomacy of Mrs. Travers is especially clever. The reader will not find many novels more readable and pleasant than this." [Spectator. **1055**

ANNIS WARLEIGH'S FORTUNES. [by "HOLME LEE," i. e., Harriet Parr: *Smith*, 1864.] "From this point the interest of the story naturally increases, and is sustained without a check to the close. The character of the heroin, a wild and wilful little soul, who, tho in poverty and subjection, has all the instincts of her class, and all the family spirit in her disposition, is grafically drawn, and ably and consistently worked out, as is the retribution or the destiny due from the hands of ideal justice to all connected with her. Thêre is plenty of variety, both of scenery and incident, in these pages, and many agreeable pictures of quiet domestic life in rural rectories and sea-side cottages. That the whole ends happily for Annis Warleigh, and those who had cherished and benefited the little wildling in her days of peril and adversity, we need not say." [London Review. **1055a**

ANTHONY FAIRFAX [*Bentley*, 1885.] "is pleasant and full of promise. The author has not aimed hi, but the interest is maintained throuout and the characters ar consistent and true to nature. The secularist working man and his wife ar excellent portraits, and in Beatrice Clare we hav a charming picture of a healthy and rit-minded girl. Thêre ar abundant evidences in the pages of this novel of a close, but not unkindly study of human nature." [Athenæum. **1056**

APRIL DAY (AN) [by PHILIPPA PRITTIE JEPHSON: *F. V. White*, 1883.] "is well named. Thêre is the tearful britness of the spring about Kathleen

Desmond's love idyl. When the gallant hussar seems to love and ride away thêre is a sad contrast between the sombreness of her lonely days and the pleasant companionship in the glen which made her country life so endurable; and in proportion to the melancholy which, in spite of herself, has overshadoed her brave tho tender heart is the joy which dispels all sorro when her warrior returns. We ar bound to say that in life the earl who makes so praiseworthy and adventurous an effort to learn the character of the charmer who has bewitched his son would hav promptly married her himself; but both Lord Lowestoft and Mr. Desmond ar models of chivalry, and Kate's constancy is undisturbed by selfish machinations. There is enuf which is local in description to mark the scene of action sufficiently; but this graceful story is a lovetale, and not a book on the savage realities of life in **Ireland.**" [Athenæum. **1057**

ARMOREL OF LYONESSE. [by WALTER BESANT: *Harper*, 1890.] "Of all the novelists Mr. Besant is the most fertil, fluent, and uniformly agreeable. Dear to him is every kind of romance, and doubly dear the romance of love. He can tell a stirring tale of military adventure, a pathetic tale of the grievances of the poor, the sorroes of the oppressed; an amusing tale of transient fashionable follies — but he is most at home and most attractiv when he is leading young lovers throu deep waters of affliction to joy everlasting. The romance of 'Armorel of Lyonesse' is a very pretty one, packed full of romantic events and situations for which no apology is offered. .... The singleness of her devotion to her prince when, after several years, she finds him again, a pauper and bond slave to a cruel-hearted

villain, is quite beautiful to dwell upon; so ar the combined delicacy and pluck with which she forces him to strike for freedom and lay the villain lo. Laying him lo is no child's play, for his villainy is not vulgar and superficial; it is subtle, intellectual, with ramifications many and deep. He preys upon the brains of the needy, buying very cheaply thêir stories, thêir poems, thêir paintings, and, thus being enabled to pose as a universal genius, waxes fat, famous and fashionable at thêir expense. Thanks to the fidelity and courage of the girl from Scilly, his discomfiture is complete. Nobody can feel quite sure after reading 'Armorel of Lyonesse' that the most cunning sinner may not dig pits for his betrayal, or that riteousness never triumfs in a wicked world." [Nation. **1058**

ASPEN COURT. [by [C: W:] SHIRLEY BROOKS: *Bentley*, 1855.] "Mr. Brooks has written no book to compare with this in matter — so full of thôt, humor, and observation. To a style at all times lît, airy, brilliant, he has now added more serious graces. We hav the airy satire, the fresh expression, the humorous suggestion; but we hav these in a closer relation than was the wont of this lît and graceful writer, to the more sacred sympathies of human life." [Athenæum. **1059**

ASPHODEL [by M .. E .. (BRADDON) MAXWELL: *Maxwell*, 1881.] "is a story written in Miss Braddon's later manner. It does not depend upon intricacy of plot, upon crime or mystery; it is as simple a tale as could be contrived, with its interest centered upon one character. The style is wonderfully easy and fluent; the conversations ar brilliant, pointed, and vigorous; and the description, of which there is a great deal, is always vivid enuf not to be tedious. The tale is one of mutual love at first sit. The early scenes ar charming. There is a school girl sketching in the forest of Fontainebleau while her friend sits apart doing wool-work. A stranger looks over the artist's shoulder, amused at her energy, and makes a comment upon her work. Then comes an extemporized picnic, and next day a more or less accidental meeting at the château. The girl is perfectly frank and perfectly inquisitiv, and amongst other things finds out that the stranger is engaged to be married. Soon afterwards she goes home, and when her sister's fiancé appears, he turns out to be the stranger of Fontainebleau. Then the trouble begins. Both strive against their love, and it is not till near the end of the story that it bursts out on both sides. The power of the author is shōn not so much in her invention as in the ease with which she makes events suit her purpose and happen so naturally as to leave the impression that they could not hav been otherwise. Here and thêre a masterly touch is obvious. The love of the two sisters for each other shōes an imagination and delicacy which those who hav read only the author's earlier works would hardly expect from her. The book also shōes skill of a kind which is rather to be regretted. Having really but a short story to write, Miss Braddon fills it out by taking her people to **Switzerland,** when the book becomes in effect what used to be called a ' picturesque tour.' But in spite of all this the reader will find himself forced to admit that it is readable throuōut." [Athenæum. **1060**

AT ANY COST [by "E: GARRETT," i. e., I .. Fyfie Mayo : *Oliphant*, 1884.] " is the old story of the good boy and the bad boy, without the old ending. The heroes do not meet with

their traditional fate : outward prosperity comes to them both, but they bear it with a difference. Robert Sinclair and Tom Ollison are nativs of the Shetland Isles; it is among ' the crags and storms of the far, far North ' that we first make their acquaintance. They set forth to seek their fortune. Cold and selfish Robert Sinclair is bound for a Surrey village whêre his mother's old friend, the miller, is to take him in, while the brave and cheery Tom Ollison is to be assistant to an old London bookseller. On the road they came across Mr. Brander, a rich stockbroker, and his dauter. The handsom face and brit ways of Tom Ollison attract Mr. Brander, but the attraction is not mutual ; Tom draws back, and his more worldly-wise companion steps into the breach, and the journey becomes Robert's steppingstone to fortune. His sojourn in Surrey is short; he is taken into Mr. Brander's office. London life tries the lads, and brings out their strength and their weakness. The tale is admirably told, and we can strongly recommend it." [Athenæum.] — The book " is quietly, calmly written, and is the story of one who believes in having not love, or money, or power, ' at any cost,' but truth. Nor does it refer to religious truth, but simply the truth about ourselves and others, too often concealed from mistaken ideas of what is best. The plot, tho the hackneyed one of an illegitimate child deserted by his mother, is original in having the child knoing always who he is, and the mother ignorant that the man who has sheltered her is her son, while he knōes that he is her son." [Critic. **1061**

AT FAULT [by HAWLEY SMART : *Chapman*, 1883.] " is a tale which he who runs may read. No psychical analysis or subjectiv filosofy causes misgivings in the heart of the unspeculativ reader who likes his fiction lit and frothy. The gravest problem in the book is the dual identity of Fossdyke or Foxborough, the mysterious adventurer who is at once a 'topping' solicitor in rural Philistia and manager of a bohemian music-hall. [Compare the plot of 'The Hundredth Man,' — No. 275] As the hero has a wife to share either fáse of his fortunes, it may be supposed how complicated is the strain upon his energies and affections. His secret is not unravelled until the violent close of his life at the hands of an enemy, who, having endeavored to trade on his discovery of the truth, makes full use of the mystery to escape for some time the hands of justice. On the whole, the plot is well imagined and sustained. Marlinson, the old-fashioned inn-keeper, Sturton, the Radical, but fashionable tailor, and other minor characters ar very lifelike." [Athenæum. **1062**

AT HIS GATES. [by Ma. O. (Wilson) Oliphant: *Scribner*, 1873.] "Robert Drummond, a painter of fair repute, has a wife (Helen) and a dauter, whom he maintains in comfort by the practice of his profession. Reginald Burton, a cousin and rejected suitor of Helen, and now a rich merchant, becomes a frequent guest at Drummond's house, and infects him with the itch for rapid money-getting. Finally the artist is induced to become a director, with Burton, in a great banking-house. Not long after, Burton withdraws from the institution, pleading a press of other business.....At last the bank 'bursts,' and Robert finds that he has been a tool for working the ruin of many of his friends who had intrusted their funds to the bank. He writes a letter to his friend Dr. Maurice, announcing his intention to leave the world, and adds:

'Burton and Golden hav done it.' Secretly he disappears.....How time brôt about its revenges, how, in many years, fact after fact cropped out, throing a gleam on the mysterious tragedy; how, almost simultaneously, Burton fled, a hunted fugitiv, and Drummond, a white-haired, broken man, reappears on this earthly scene, — the telling of all this makes up the bulk of the story. But, long before this consummation, a new generation of personages come on the stage, — children of the original characters, — complicating the relations of these, and adding the disturbing element of love to the already tempestuous res gestæ. Mrs. Oliphant is not a mere fabricator of fiction; she is a thinker, a filosofer; and for the development of a plot which is in no respect remarkable, she has created sundry characters, original, individual, and finished, with a conscientious fidelity and power of handling which ar unmistakable marks of genius. The strength of the story is in its characterization." [Boston "Literary World." **1063**

AT SIXES AND SEVENS [by A. Weber: *Mozley & Smith*, 1877.] "defines the relations of an amiable party of youths and girls in a pleasant village in the valley of the Thames. The heroin is the self-sacrificing eldest dauter of an absent-minded student and his invalid wife, who occupy the village rectory. A very charming specimen of an enthusiastic yet sound-headed maiden is Grace.....Mrs. Wyatt, and the two excellent old maids, who ar alone in their thŏro understanding of their favorit, ar well drawn portraits. There is also an Oxford don, with an insit into character not common in the race, who is evidently described from some living model." [Athenæum. **1064**

ATHOL [by **M. R. H. POTT**: **N.-Y.**, *Young*, 1873.] "is the modest title of a singularly pure, modest, wel-written and interesting novel. The main point on which the narrativ turns is on which has always prŏved a favorit with women novelists, tŏ whŏm the sight of a young girl, gradually and unconsciously falling in lŏve with a grave, staid, strong, manly, middle-aged gardian seems tŏ hav had a grĕat, and tŏ sŏme minds, unaccountable attraction. But if the essence or most suggestiv element of the plot is not original, the fresh, naive, wholesŏme manner in which it is treated, and the distinct and strongly-marked individualities of the characters, giv the storv itself an indescribably fresh and healthy air, reminding ŏne of the odor of new-mōn hay . . . The characters ar drawn with grĕat distinctness and attention tŏ detail; the plot, tho stale, is nicely elaborated; the descriptiv passages ar vigorously drawn; and the whole tone of the book is pure and noble. Altŏgether we recommend it warmly tŏ every lŏver of healthy and legitimately exciting fiction." [Arcadian. **5 p**

ATHELINGS (THE) [by MA. OLIPIANT (WILSON) OLIPIANT : *Blackwood*, 1857.] " is written with simplicity and tenderness. The story is, in some respects, original ; and altho the main incident has an ancient tinge, the author never loses for a moment her power of making the situations and characters peculiarly hers. Without outlining the drama, we may mention that it turns upon three moral gifts, bestoed by nature upon 3 of the personages, and that this conception is cleverly kept in vue from first to last, without being strained into disagreeable prominence." [Leader.] — "Two sisters and one brother, a father, a mother, and baby twins, lived in Islington and comfort on £200 a year. The elder sister is an author ; the younger a beauty ; the brother is a boisterous boy who gets articled in a lawyer's office, and helps by his acumen and energy to save the family property and defeat the bad man of the book, Lord Winterbourne ; the twins remain subordinate and come in for the ladies' petting ; the father and mother ar also in the background.....The author is clever : she can describe society : Mr. Agar, the old epicurean exquisit, and Mrs. Edgerly, the vapid woman of fashion, ar well touched ; and thêre is a dainty naturalness in the sisters which makes it pleasant to remember them." [Westminster Review. **1065**

ATHERSTON PRIORY [by L. N. COMYN : *Estes*, 1874.] " is a story of english life, marked by refinement and healthful morality. Its heroin, Lisa, is a young girl of the harum-scarum order whose moral and intellectual reformation is effected gradually, but surely, by the influence of love. The masculin instrument in the case is a very grave, dignified, and, so far as personal charms ar concerned, an unattractiv man.

The book is filled with details of daily life in a large middle-class family, and is entertaining in a quiet way." [Boston " Literary World." **1066**

AUNT DIANA [by ROSA NOUCHETTE CAREY : *Lippincott*, 1883.] " is a pretty tho sentimental story about a girl named Alison Merle, who, under the inspiration of one of those delitful maiden aunts, unhappily more commonly found in fiction than in life — an earnest, influential, self-controlled maiden aunt, full of talent and benefactions, always appearing with help in her rit hand at the rit moment — does a hard bit of duty well, and helps and changes the moral attitude of her whole family. There is one rather exciting episode with an embezzling clerk, but otherwise the plot is simple, and enuf is to be learned from Alison's experience to make the book good reading for those who, like her, wish to do the rit thing tho at the cost of their temporary comfort and pleasure." [Boston " Literary World." **1067**

AUNT MARGARET'S TROUBLE [by F.. ELEANOR (TERNAN) TROLLOPE : *Chapman*, 1866,—*Peterson*, 1867.] "is a simple and touching little story which comes to delit us with its pure and refreshing influences.....It is a tale of unselfish love and devotion ; of cruel wrong and just retribution ; of noble thôts and aims in all which regards human life ; of womanly tenderness ; of christian resignation and forgivness. There is nothing startling in incident or style, nor is the plot remarkable for originality ; but there is a secret charm about Aunt Margaret which attracts us to her in her early childhood, and causes us to resent the injustice she is made to suffer — which enlists all our sympathies for the loving and confiding girl — and which, while sharing the sorro so cruelly brôt upon her young heart by another's treachery, causes us scarcely to regret the bitter trials throu which, in after life, her hier nature is developed..... The whole tone of the book is thôroly healthful, and tho, from the nature of the story, necessarily tinged with sadness, it is wholly free from any morbid tendency; on the contrary, Margaret, after the first gush of sorro, accepts her situation heroically — the lit and joyousness of life had gone; but thêre was serious work before her, and in its accomplishment she found consolation." [Round Table. **1068**

AUNT RACHAEL. [by D : CHRISTIE MURRAY: *Macmillan*, 1886.] "'A Rustic Sentimental Comedy' is a very modest sub-title for as dainty a bit of literary work, combining romance and humor, as we hav had for many a day. The book is, in its way, a gem — one of those richly humorous tales which ar all the more amusing becaus the actors in the drama hav not the least consciousness that they ar funny. The story moves with the greatest precision and dignified solemnity, while the audience is not convulsed with lâfter, but listens and looks on with a not less pleasing sense of being well entertained by persons who hav no intention of entertaining anybody. The story is nothing compared with the perfectness of each chapter in a series of little genre pictures as delicate in finish as they ar clever in conception." [Critic. **1069**

AUTOBIOGRAPHY OF M : RUTHERFORD, see "REVOLUTION IN TANNER'S LANE."

AUTOBIOGRAPHY OF A SLANDER (THE) [by "EDNA LYALL," i. e., Ada Ellen Bayly: *Appleton*, 1887.] "is a half-pathetic, half-humorous novelette exhibiting the clever powers of Miss Lyall in a new lit. 'The Autobiografy'

is quite unlike any thing else she has produced, and it will certainly enhance her reputation. It is a story of mischief wrôt by idle tale-bearing. The idea is worked out with much spirit and originality." [American. **1070**

AUTUMN MANŒUVRES. [by M. MOORE: *Bentley*, 1886.] "There is a lodg in a garden of cucumbers at Netherby whêre a jealous wido and her 3 charming dauters dwell in strict seclusion; and the reader will understand that in this situation thêre ar the makings of a pretty story. The wido seems to be a particularly silly specimen of her sex, for she has labored to keep her dauters out of the reach of possible suitors for no better reason than that her husband died of a sunstroke. But it is eventually proved to her satisfaction that sunstroke is not hereditary, and that the children of the sunstruck ar not specially in danger of being moonstruck. So the manœuvres ar fairly successful, from the day when the military besiege the wido's fastness by way of the garden wall, to the day when the last of their enemies surrenders at discretion." [Athenæum. **1071**

AYALA'S ANGEL. [By ANTIONY TROLLOPE: *Chapman*, 1881.] "Mr. Trollope has a knack of converting prevalent fâses of thôt into flesh and blood, so that in an individual may often be recognized the embodiment of some characteristic peculiarity of society, or some form of idea which is common to most of us; and evidence of this power is to be met in the book now under consideration. By dint of subtle appreciation of character and of these arts, which must surely result from an unusual quickness in feeling the social pulse, he accomplishes a feat which no less able writer could perform, and takes his readers pleasantly throu 3

AUNT ANNE [by Lucy (Lane) Clifford: *Bentley*, 1892.] " is őne of the most charming stories it has been őur good fortune tő meet in a very long while. It is as fresh and original as it is human. Few people hav gòne throu the world without knőing an ånt Anne ; most people hav a similar product in their ōn families, őthers hav met her amőng their friends. It was no easy task tő portray her faithfully and not disgust őne thőroly with her. As it is, őur patience is őften exhansted by her, őur interest and sympathy never. Her intense pride, her courtliness and dignity of manner, her kindheårtedness and generosity, her utter disregard of all indebtedness tő tradespeople, whőm she looks upon as inferiors whő must be content tő wait until it is the pleasure of their superiors tő remember their hils, and her perfect simpliçity of mind and character, which enables any designing person tő impose upon* her tő the last extent, prepare us fully for her inconsequent career, with its pitiful conelusion. As thére is nőthing more diverting than ånt Anne in her more prosperous days, so thére is nothing more touching than that same old lady in the midst of her shame and her disappointment. She is simply delightful." [Critic.]— "The old lady is 'digne' in every way, perfectly independent, perfectly irresponsible ... But we trust that every reader wil make the acquaintançe of ånt Anne for himself. We can assure him (or her) that he knoes nobody like her in fiction. Tő kno her in life might be perhaps a mingled pleasure, but in print she is at őnce the most original and most true creation which we hav met for a lőng time. The present writer has folloed the old lady throu the severe test of a magazine mőnth by mőnth, disappointed when the younger people filled the scene, and ånt Anne ceased tő be the first figure, but with unfailing interest in the old heroin, with all her big words and queer, irresponsible ways. Her lőve-story is ridiculous, but most touching and pathetic. and true. She herself is never for a moment ridiculous, even when she makes us låf ; and throu all those portions of the story in which she őt tő be most absurd, it is the tears which we find it difficult tő restrain, and the old, forlorn figure in her trouble wrings őur heårts. Mrs. Clifford has dőne nőthing before at all equal or tő be spoken of in the same breath with this delicate and most affecting picture. Tő reçeive it from hands accustomed tő portray "worldly women," is a surprise as wel as an extraordinary pleasure. The outside is almost worthy of Miss Austen ; the heårt much deeper than anything Miss Austen ever touched." [Spectator. **1066** v

AUSTIN ELLIOT. [by H : KINGSLEY [1830-76]: *Tirknor*, 1863.] "It warms the heârt tŏ read such a book. We can not say, indeed, that thĕre is anything profoundly original or affecting in the plot of the story; but thĕre is nature, life, character, genuin feeling in every page of it. A manly spirit, a tender heârt, a liberally cultivated mind, and a deliçiously humorous habit of seeing and of thinking, all these contribute tŏ make it ŏne of the few vital works in the literature of this scribbling century. It is a book tŏ be lŏved; and ŏne lŏves it—not because it denounçes duelling, not because it suggests that the organization of society is not altŏgether perfect, and that a little tinkering, now and then, has its uses— but because it deals so directly and honestly with men and women as thêy ar, inculcating lofty prinçiples and encouraging noble ideals. It has, in short, the combined fasçination of strength and sinçerity. Its writer had a story to tel, a story eloquent of lŏve, honor, fidelity, and . all the graçes of delicate culture—and he has told that story in the simplest and most direct style. We shal not undertake tŏ analyze his plot, nor tŏ point out excellences which the sympathetic reader wil readily diseŏver without guidance; but we wish tŏ record, in the strongest language, ŏhr approbation of the book, both as tŏ manner and matter. Like "Ravenshoe" [No. 1723], it is an earnest exponent of the dignity and beauty of manly virtue; and the weak friends of abstract goodness, whŏ write novels in præise of rectitude, and thĕreby—so far as in them lies—bring it intŏ contempt, may herein study with profit the example of a sturdy champion of the Right, whŏ hits from the shŏlder, and at whŏm it would not be safe tŏ lâf. Excepting Thackeray, we remember no modern novelist whŏ has exercised a better influençe over the age, than H : Kingsley." [Albion.] The time is that of the repeal of the cornlaws. **1069 k**

volumes, without the usual aids of plot and incident; the thread of the story in 'Ayala's Angel' is too slit to be called a plot, yet the book is amusing, in spite of that deficiency." [Spectator.]— " Ayala is a charming creation. Hating the dull life at her uncle's, she is yet true enuf to herself and her ideals to refuse 3 eligible offers. The story is written with great skill, and the reader succumbs to the attractions of the red-haired Jonathan long before Ayala does. Mr. Trollope has a genius for being generous to foibles. He hates the harshness of life and manner developed so often, alas! merely by the necessity for small economies;....yet he reminds us here that life at the 'bijou' had a charm and ease and affectionate hospitality apt to be lacking whêre minds ar too closely occupied with the payment of debts." [Critic.   **1072**

AZALEA [by CECIL CLAYTON: *Harper*, 1877.] "takes its name from the pretty, flower-like heroin, a young girl born in Lugano of a hebrew mother and an english father. She becomes an orfan when a child, and goes to England to liv with her grandfather.....The rest of the story floes on in a quiet limpid stream, neither quarrel nor misunderstanding interrupting the course of true love, and not a single murder, or sensational incident of any kind appearing to disturb the dreamy calm which gradually takes possession of the reader's senses." [Library Table.   **1073**

BABY'S GRANDMOTHER (The). [by LUCY BETHA (COLQUHOUN) WALFORD: *Holt*, 1884.] "No one is more successful than Mrs. Walford in gathering a dozen people and making them as interesting as our own friends. She has grouped this set about a beautiful woman, whose charm thêre can be no denying. It is her method to make

people talk, and thereby sho the development of character. This accounts for the length of the book in proportion to the number of incidents. How the author could work out of the situation anything like a happy issue was an anxious question while the story was running in 'Blackwood.' It may be said that the knot is cut, not untied. Still, it is as true to human experience that death should sometimes make a way out as that it should often stop the path. There will be two sides taken as to whether Lady Matilda should hav forgiven Challoner, yet that is only a proof of the reality of the creation, for life is seldom so convincing as to make all judgments agree. At least the author has shon great skill in enlisting the reader's sympathy. He, too, resents the assumptions of the Hanwells, and he feels that the punishment has been severe enuf for the almost unconscious sin of too easy compliance with the sister's ambitious schemes. Mrs. Walford's work needs no praise for anyone who knoes 'Mr. Smith.' To her new readers this book is a better token of her powers than anything since that first. She not only succeeds in making her heroin worthy a man's despair: she makes in Teddy a perfectly new figure in fiction; and by that one trait of hi-minded reticence which she hestoes on poor Mary Tufnell, she wins for her what would hav seemed impossible — respect and regret." [Nation.   **1074**

BACHELOR OF THE ALBANY (THE). [by MARMION W. SAVAGE: 1847.] "From first to last this story was told delitfully. It still remains in a great measure, altho among his minor works, the novelist's masterpiece. The name of the book was 'The Bachelor of the Albany,' the hero of it being Mr. Peter Barker, a thoroly humorous crea-

334

tion. This rollicking fun was surpassed by the drollery and the more caustic vivacity running throu the incident relating here to the oddly-contrasted households of the Spreads and the Narrowsmiths — the former so winning, the latter so repulsiv. Almost as good as the delineation of the Bachelor himself was that of Dean Bedford, the jovial pluralist, resident at Far Niente." [Athenæum. **1075**

BACHELOR'S BLUNDER (A). [by W : E : Norris: *Holt*, 1886.] "We hav endeavored, in noticing some previous books of this author, to express our hi appreciation of his grafic powers, and his rit to be reckoned one of the leading english novelists — one who has been compared to Thackeray in his delicate humor and his ready seizure of the foibles, as well as the virtues of mankind, and to Anthony Trollope in a certain minuteness of finish in the depicting of people and of scenes. This story of a natural and unsofisticated girl in the midst of the intense worldliness of modern english society, and of a marriage deliberately vued in advance and by both parties as one entirely of convénance, is not one of the author's best, but affords an excellent field for his characteristic modes of treatment. We observ in the style the same naturalness and frankness as in earlier writings; and to any readers not yet acquainted with Mr. Norris we commend his works as likely to afford much pleasant literary recreation." [Boston "Lit. World." **1076**

BAFFLED CONSPIRATORS (The). [by W : E : Norris: *S. Blackett*, 1890.] "Mr. Norris has never had a happier thôt for a novel, nor worked out his idea more felicitously, than in this brit story. The conspirators wer 4 spoiled children of society, who formed a mutual protection league against the wiles of the piscatory sex, agreeing with each other that if either of them ' saw that he was about to commit suicide' by swalloing a hook, he should consult his felloes, and be bound by their decision for the space of 6 months Evidently thére is room for any amount of spritly writing within the 4 corners of that agreement, and Mr. Norris is spritly on every page. His title is not so appropriate as it mît be, for the conspirators ar not baffled in the object which they set before themselves. The story has two heroins, and in the end thére ar only 2 bachelors left to lament, after greedily snatching at the bait, that they wer contemptuously thrön back into the water. The ' Baffled Conspirators ' is intentionally slit, but it is thöroly picturesque and sparkling." [Athenæum.] — " There is less body in this one-volume story than in any of Mr. Norris' previons works but, in its slit way, it is simply perfect. The masters of hi comedy ar much rarer than the masters of either lo comedy or melodrama; but Mr. Norris is one of them, and his present story never lapses from the true hi-comedy tone." [Spectator. **1077**

BANNING AND BLESSING [N. Y., — *Whittaker*.] "is a first-rate story of quiet life in a secluded nêborhood near the sea, with plenty of picturesque characters and incidents. It is written in good style by one who knoes how to interest and hold the attention of boys, girls, and all who ar young in spirit." [Critic. **1078**

BARBARA ALLAN, THE PROVOST'S DAUGHTER. [by Ro. Cleland: *Blackwood*, 1889.] "Thére is a great deal of charm about ' Barbara Allan '; it deals with extremely dull people, and contrives to make them interesting in spite of thére dulness. The portrait of the provost in his success and in his decadence shoes real ability, and the other characters, tho here and thêre improbable, form, as a whole, a pleasant and natural picture. The author seems well acquainted with scotch life, and manages his dialect well — it is genuine without being incomprehensible." [Athenæum. **1079**

BARBARA HEATHCOTE'S TRIALS [by ROSA NOUCHETTE CAREY : *Lippincott*, 1885.] "narrates the home life of an agreeable family, in which the author is chiefly concerned in differentiating the characters of 4 sisters. 'Barbara' herself seems built on the lines of Miss Alcott's 'Jo,' and her 'trials' ar chiefly the misunderstandings she suffers throu her bluntness and candor. The tale throuout is pleasing and brit." [American.] — "Given a family of girls well contrasted, utterly untrammeled, and each in possession of a will and a way of her ôn, materials for a romance ar not hard to find; and in telling the story of the Heathcotes Miss Carey seems to hav jotted down a series of events exactly as they fell out in life. Thêre is plenty of sentiment but its expression is dealt out with a sparing hand; thêre ar pretty sylvan scenes, and the woodpaths, the warm homesteads, the meadoes and fields all enter into the story and make a pleasant part of it." [Lippincott's. **1080**

BARBARA'S HISTORY. [by AMELIA BLANDFORD EDWARDS : *Hurst*, 1864.] "Just as Mrs. Radcliffe used to season her stories with the requisit amount of ghostly horrors, capable of explanation in the last chapter, so has Miss Edwards effected a compromise between her sense of rit and the depraved appetite of the public, giving zest to her romance by the introduction of a bigamist who, as the curtain falls, is proved to be a man of exemplary character." [Athenæum. **1081**

BARCHESTER TOWERS. [by ANTHONY TROLLOPE : *Longmans*, 1857.] "Thus [this novel being a continuation of the history begun in 'The Warden'], Mr. Trollope has not to contend against the difficulty of interesting us, at the outset, in his personages or in his narrativ; we ar by no means strangers in Barchester; but he has, perhaps, to meet a worse difficulty, — that of prolonging successfully the interest of a tale which seemed some time ago to hav been brôt to a natural conclusion. Yet we doubt whether 'Barchester Towers' is not a more satisfactory book than 'The Warden': it is certainly more dramatic in its construction; the characters ar more varied; an infusion of romance gives litness, and britness to the ecclesiastical picture." [Athenæum.] See *DOCTOR THORNE*. **1082**

BARREN TITLE (A) [by T. W. SPEIGIT : *Harper*, 1886.] "opens exceedingly well and is original throuout." [Critic. **1083**

BARRINGTON'S FATE. [Boston, 1883.] = *SELF-CONDEMNED*.

BASIL GODFREY'S CAPRICE [by "HOLME LEE," i. e., Harriet Parr : *Smith*, 1868], "is a g'raceful, healthy, and thôroly pleasant story of true love, enduring trials, trusting throu absence, giving no heed to false reports, but feeling them to be false by the talisman of its truth, and finally clearing away all obstacles by virtue of its royal nature. The difficulties and obstacles ar such as wer inevitable from the nature of things — not fantastic fancies, nor the cobwebs of conventionality. The difficulties ar genuin; they ar met in good faith, and yield to the true hearts which encounter them. Nothing is more remarkable throuout this story than the strong common sense which underlies the romance. Basil and Joan do not make miseries for themselves; they do not sin against the loyalty of each other by mistrust, nor do they torment each other by freaks of self-sacrifice which sin against justice as well as generosity." [Athenæum. **1084**

BASIL PLANT (A) [by ETIEL COXON: *Bentley*, 1881.] "enforces a moral against the unequal yoking of the artist with the philistine. A worldly Delilah shears away the strength of Roland Trench, a young man with the artistic temperament and full of hi purposes, but too susceptible, as is the manner of artists, to mere external beauty. Eve Goring understands him, if she somewhat idealizes him; and in sliting her affection for that of Gertrude Auley he makes the false step which it is too late to retrieve, when, after the tragic end of his first marriage, he is united to the woman whose influence mit hav enabled him to realize his biest ambition. The tale is simple, but strongly told." [Athenæum. **1085**

BASIL ST. JOHN. [*Edmonston & Douglas*, 1866.] "We breathe here a pleasant West Highland atmosfere which givs charm to a narrativ somewhat wanting in incident. The descriptions which it contains of the **Sutherland-shire** mountains and rivers ar as truthful as they ar picturesque, and the author shoes a thoro acquaintance both with the scenes he describes and the people who inhabit them. It is a pleasure to meet with a novel in which titled personages figure, without any solecisms betraying the author's ignorance of the world in which such persons move.... The hero goes to a shooting-box in the Highlands, and falls in love with a young lady who possesses every charm but that of wealth. His grandfather compels

him for a time to give up the object of his affections, but eventually yields on finding that a very eccentric old general is ready to settle a fortune on her. Meantime, Basil's chief friend, an excellent, but poor government clerk, named Charlie Hay, wins the hand of Miss Susan Mackenzie, an heiress of extensive possessions. . . . .The ladies ar charming. Evelyn Moncrieff and Susan Mackenzie ar two delitful studies, the trusting, kindly nature of the one, and the independent, noble spirit of the other being excellently described. Two so striking figures, set off by so picturesque a background, ar quite enuf to render the book attractiv." [London Review. **1086**

BATEMAN HOUSEHOLD (THE). [by JA. PAYN: *Hall, Virtue & Co.*, 1860.] "We can not speak in complimentary terms of this somewhat lengthy narrativ of complicated misfortunes, misdeeds, and misadventures, in which thêre is not a single point of interest for the reader. All the characters ar ill-conceived and ill-developed, without any individuality or purpose. The incidents ar generally commonplace, or, if otherwise, forced and exaggerated. The author evidently delits in rendering probable the improbable, and possible the impossible; he also deals too much in the revelation of horrors to allow him to develop his story in a natural or artistic manner. The book, however, betrays evidences of natural capabilities; and we hav no doubt that had Mr. Payn been more careful in his delineations and less indiscriminate in his choice of a subject, the result would hav devolved greater credit upon himself, and been decidedly more satisfactory to the reader." [Leader. **1087**

BEAUCHAMP'S CAREER. [by G: MEREDITI : *Chapman*, 1875.] "A prompt amount of compression which should bring ' Beauchamp's Career ' down to the proper limit and form of a work of art would make it a really admirable book. As it is, its cleverness and striking brilliancy ar lost in a sea of froth and foam. It is not interesting; it is not even coherent. The story does not develop; the characters act spasmodically, talk wildly, and the end is grievous. It is well knòn that a living british admiral was the prototype of Beauchamp, — but even that knoledg fails to giv the chronicle of his career an air of reality. In fact, to our thinking, the one novel in which Mr. Meredith has distinctly grasped his idea and realized it to his readers in a way worthy of his undoubted power, is ' Diana of the Crossways ' ; all the others furnish brilliant kaleidoscopic hints of what mit be beauty, but ar not worked out in a perfected novel." [American.] — " We hav not hitherto found Mr. Meredith easy to read, and in acknoledging the greatness of his power in this instance hav had to silence some prepossessions or some principles. Realistic the book certainly is not, unless we stretch that elastic term to cover a case in which the inner truth burns throu an outside of sufficiently conventional english-novel material; — squires, lords and ladies, country-house sojourning, parliamentary elections, dining, poaching, yachting, and all; with a gallic background of an unhappy marriage and love of the elderly french nêbor's wife. Out of this collection of antiquated properties a great, fresh, and noble ideal of conduct evolves itself in the character of Beauchamp, the valiant young aristocrat turned democrat." [W : D. Howells.] — " They say that he draws his men and women from the men and women he knoes; that Sir Austin Feverel, for instance, is himself; that the Redworth

of ' Diana of the Crossways ' is his idea of F : Greenwood; that the hero of ' Beauchamp's Career ' is a compound of admiral Maxie and Auberon Herbert; the Vernon Whitford of ' The Egoist ' is a portrait of Leslie Stephen; the Diana and the Dacier of his last book the Mrs. Norton and the Sidney Herbert of 40 or 50 years ago." [Critic. **1088**

BEAUTIFUL EDITH, The Child-woman. [Boston, *Loring*, 1877.] " It was in an evil moment that the author chose this name for her novel. It is a most unfortunate title, suggesting the most oppressiv silliness, while in fact the story is as entertaining and clever as any which has appeared for some time. It would be, perhaps, too much to say that it is as good as ' The Wooing O't,' but it is very like that favorit, while it is free from the somewhat snobbish aw of the aristocracy which marred ' Mrs. Alexander's ' novel. But the amount of cleverness, the knoledge of the world, of observation, of kindly humor which has produced this story is very unusual. Take any one of the characters, — Mrs. Lisle, for instance — and it will be hard to say in what respect the resemblance to life could be made greater." [Nation. **1089**

BEAUTIFUL WRETCH (THE) ETC. [by W : BLACK : *Macmillan*, 1881.] " Those qualities which hav made Mr. Black's writings so widely popular — his good sense, his geniality, and his delicate humor — go a long way towards making ' The Beautiful Wretch ' a successful tale..... The very young man who is brother to the beautiful wretch and several more pretty sisters is perhaps the best figure. He is drawn with wonderful fidelity, vivacity, and humor. It is equally impossible to help lâfing at and liking him. As for the heroin, her nickname is the one thing about her to which one must object." [Ath. **1090**

BEDE'S CHARITY [by "HESBA STRETTON," i. e., Hannah Smith: *Dodd*, 1872.] " is by no means an exciting tale. It does not deal with complications of the heart, but rather with the exercise of christian virtues. It is a religious story; but it has merits which we would gladly see in profane works — simplicity and naturalness. It lacks vulgarity, and that is, perhaps, even rarer praise for religious tales than those of other sorts." [Nation. **1091**

BELINDA [by MARIA EDGEWORTI.] " is superior to *Patronage* in construction and in liveliness of interest. Here, too, we hav to remember that whatever lack of freshness the characterization may hav for us is due to the multiplication of novels at the present time and the countless number of our fictitious acquaintance. The story of Belinda, the good angel of the fashionable worldling, Lady Delacour, is cleverly told, with a plenty of wit and of animated dialog, and the author cannot help it if her sinner is the most interesting person in the book." [Boston "Literary World." **1092**

BELL OF ST. PAUL'S (THE) [by WALTER BESANT: *Chatto*, 1890.] " mit hav for its second title 'The Belle of Bankside.' She is the dauter of a poet — a poet of whom no one has read..... These elements will be gratefully received by the old-fashioned reader, who likes his novels seasoned with plot and mystery; but Althea roing the australian to Chelsea, or taking him throu the Southwark slums to sho him whêre once stood the Globe Theatre, the Falcon Inn and Paris gardens; Althea in her turn being led, by the poet, past the tavern haunts of his old associates, while Fleet Street rings with applause of The Poet,

not the same but a prize fiter, and the two tâke the ovation to themselves; Althea again, in her boat, in a wonderful, Turneresque sunset — these ar pictures which will remain in the reader's fancy and to which he will turn again ere he takes up a fresh volume." [Critic.] — "The hero comes home as a prosperous australian youngster to search out, by his mother's behest, the decaying remains of her family..... With this good old 'revolution-and-discovery' plot ar interwound two minor plots : the story of a child bôt by a benevolent but eccentric doctor from the gypsies, and educated to the full of modern education in the fond belief that this will develop in him not only all the mits, but, as Mr. Carlyle mit hav said, all the ôts; and the story of a minor bard. That the man of pure science turns out a greedy, heartless young scoundrel, and the man of pure literature an amiable, chivalrous old dotard may be anticipated; but, still, tho these ar interesting studies ehuf, they ar not the main charm of the book." [Academy. **1093**

BELLES AND RINGERS [by HAWLEY SMART: *Chapman*, 1880.] "is a lively story of two pairs of lovers and the anxieties of a match-making mama. It is the slitest and frothiest of social sketches. ....When an author knoes his ground, and refrains from cynicism or exaggeration, it is not unwholesome that the better side of conventional life should sometimes be presented. The dramatis personæ, tho occasionally frivolous, ar strait-forward, honest specimens of english men and women of thêir class; and even Lady Mary and the intriguing old bachelor Pansey hav kind hearts beneath their worldly crust of small diplomacy. The heroins are well contrasted, and the dénoûment is as

happy as befits a merry tale." [Athenæum. **1094**
BELTON ESTATE (The) [by Antiony Trollope: *Harper*, 1866.] "is a very readable, if not a very exciting tale. Clara Amedroz draws our sympathy, if she does not win our love; Will Belton is a fine fello,— one of nature's noblemen; and Captain Aylmer, a fine gentleman in the world's very questionable acceptation of that ambiguous term. In these 3 characters, we hav the major premise, minor premise, and conclusion of the book. Clara is decidedly our major premise,— a very good, brave, and sensible girl of 26." [Church Monthly.] — "Mr. Trollope is intent on a life-like, external reality; he holds the mirror up, not to nature, but to the exterior of a hily artificial society; he strives that the people in his pages shall precisely correspond in language, thôt, taste, and behavior, to the millions of ordinary beings who form the population of Great Britain. He catches the last mode, and is never more than a month behind the Paris fashions. He is a great artist to sketch the lace shawls, and artistic bonnets, and undulating dresses, in which his performers go throu thêir parts. The resemblance to contemporaneous life is exact, and the slitest incongruity catches our eye and provokes criticism. We watch his young ladies and gentlemen with the same scrutinizing exactness which enables us, unhesitatingly, to define the social position of our fello-guests at a dinner party. We kno, for instance, that the young ladies by no means belong to the cream of society, and lapse occasionally into absolute vulgarisms; and we kno this by some one of a hundred tiny tests with which the author has provided us for the purpose of gauging them. Everything depends on re-

semblance, as the resemblance is one which everybody is able to test; the task of securing and maintaining it is one which few people like Mr. Trollope ar clever enuf to achieve successfully." [London Review. **1095**
BEN MILNER'S WOOING [by "Holme Lee," i. e., Harriet Parr: *Roberts*, 1877.] "is a pearl among novels, so fresh and pure. Pattie is the daintiest and most bewitching of heroins — a perfect brier-rose, like the Heidenröslein Goethe sings. And dear honest Ben is such a true matter-of-fact 19th-century lover!" [Boston "Lit. World." **1096**
BENEDICTUS [by Emily Marion Harris: *Chapman*, 1887.] "will prove attractiv to all readers in love with noble thôt and graceful fancy. Some acquaintance with 'Estelle' is taken for granted. . . . .People as good in thêir way as Estelle Hofer, the twins, and the eccentric M. Becquer ar worth knoing in any stage of development. Thêy ar of the kind who master the reader's attention till insensibly he interests himself in all their affairs, listens to their talk, and even takes to guessing their thôts. Seemingly unremarkable and seldom overstrained as thêy ar, they gradually become entertaining and sympathetic enuf to make parting a regret. 'Estelle' shôed that the writer possesses a thôro knoledg of **Judaism**, as it pursues its unchanged and solitary existence. . . . . Estelle in her union of feminin softness with mobility and strength of character is touching and excellent. The twins, in a different way, ar even better." [Athenæum. **1097**
BERTRAMS (The) [by Antiony Trollope: *Chapman*, 1859.] "has the same amount of acute and sarcastic perception of life and character as distinguishes his former productions. . . . . The two characters which stand out in

the strongest relief ar George Bertram and Caroline Waddington, his cousin. The first is a young man of plain exterior, but of cultivated and fastidious mind, of hi and ultra-romantic principles of honor and disinterestedness, and passionately attached to Caroline Waddingtou. The lady is beautiful, accomplished, hi-spirited and wayward, but with a touch, and but a touch, of worldliness. She, too, is secretly attached to George Bertram. The uncle, a money-getting millionaire, on whom his nefew and his grand-danter ar to a certain extent dependent, is desirous of seeing them married, in order that he may hav heirs to his vast wealth. A series of misunderstandings arise between the young people, and an estrangement ensues, which results in Caroline Waddington giving her hand, but not her heart, to Sir Henry Harcourt.....Thêre ar several episodes of no very inferior interest; one in particular — the loves of a young clergyman, Arthur Wilkinson, and Adela Gauntlet — which contrasts agreeably with the love passages in the life of the hero and heroin." [Leader. **1098**

BESSIE. [by JULIA KAVANAGI: *Hurst*, 1872.] " Of Bessie herself, it is superfluous to say that she is naive and charming, conscientious, affectionate, and unselfish. She is a born hero-worshipper, as most heroic natures ar. In spite of coldness and discouragement, and all the mysterious circumstances which surround the life of Elizabeth De Lusignan, Bessie remains stânch to her belief in the integrity and virtue of her friend; while her ōn love-story, the story of a real passion, which groes upon her unconsciously, until gratitude and early associations convince her reason that she is attached to her morose and exacting cousin, is one of the best bits of autobiografy. Miss

Kavanagh has produced.....The french life at **Fontainebleau** is well described." [Athenæum. **1099**

BESSIE LANG. [by ALICE CORKRAN: *J. Blackwood*, 1876.] " ' Bessie Lang' is a variation of a sad old story. A captivating stranger comes into a village, falls in love with a country girl, wins her love from the worthy country lover, carries her away, and finally deserts her. But, if the story is an old one, the writing is pure and graceful. Thêre ar brit glimpses of beautiful scenery, and good bits of human character. The description of the girl, dying and bequeathing her child by another father as her last and only gift to the lad she had forsaken, may seem unnatural, but it is touchingly pathetic." [Athen. **1100**

BETHESDA. [by " BARBARA ELBON," i. e., Lenora B. Halsted: *Macmillan*, 1884.] " The reader must not consider it as a novel, scarcely even as a romance, but rather look upon it as a psychological study. The characters delineated ar few, and the incidents related fewer. The whole force of the slôly moving narrativ is concentrated in the presentment of a man and a woman, alike gifted and strong, mutually attracted by powerful sympathies, yet held apart from closeness of union by the unloved and unloving wife of the man, who stands between them. For awhile Rêné persuades Bethesda that the conflicting elements of the situation can be reconciled by a close friendship under the guise of a literary co-partnership, but they soon discover that Platonic love is (as Cherbuliez says) ' not a house, but a tunnel'; and Bethesda, — a really strong and noble character, — awakes to the dangers of thêir situation, finding no ground safe under her feet but entire renunciation of her lover and utter separation of thêir lives and interests.

341

"Réné has not the same conscientious impulse to thêir separation, but loyally submits to what he deems the over-strained scruples of the woman, and they part with mutual love and sorro." [American. **1101**

BETWEEN THE HEATHER AND THE NORTHERN SEA [by M.. Lins-kill: *Harper*, 1884.] " is a careful and refined story. Thêre is a good deal of sentiment and a great deal of quotation; but a really admirable thing is the de-lineation of the artist-father whose life is made a picturesque and effectiv illustration of the pathos in the life of genuin workers whose work is never available." [Critic. **1102**

BETWEEN TWO LOVES [by Ame-lia Editı (Huddleston) Barr: *Dodd*, 1889.] " is a charming story of english provincial life. Jonathan Burley's love for his mill, his delit in the whirring music of the looms, his interest in the hands, his sturdy self-respect, his human-ity, and his broad vue of life, ar fases of human nature which we believe ar fast being starved out of existence.....No-thing, however, mars the insit, the deep knoledge of human strength and weak-ness of the other characters. One is swept on with the impulses of the life which stirred them. The abounding faith in human goodness, the simple naturalness of the village life, the beauty of the writing and the solidity of the work hav produced a charming story." [Critic. **1103**

BEYMINSTRE [by Ellen Wal-lace: N.Y., *Rudd*, 1856.] " is a book we can cordially recommend: — it is clever and interesting, the two cardinal virtues of a novel. The hero is drawn with spirit and individuality. His qual-ities ar not smoothed down to the per-fectness which is de rigueur for the heroes and heroins of fiction. He is

essentially a gentleman, tho he is full of defects; and, what is worse, behaves in the worst manner to the heroin. Regina, the heroin, is charming: she behaves well, but not too well to secure the reader's sympathies. All the other characters in the book partake of the nature of human beings; and the story itself, altho slit, is well and firmly woven." [Athenæuni. **1104**

BITS FROM BLINKBONNY [by J.: Strathesk: N.Y., *Carter*, 1882.] "is a story unpretending enuf, but with the inimitable scotch flavor. If heroin thêre be, it is a faithful servant-woman; but the chief incident is the leaving of manse and kirk by her master, the minister, at the ' Disruption ' of 40 years ago." [Nation. **1105**

BLACK ABBEY [by May Cromme-lin: *Low*, 1880.] " deserves a good word from all who can discriminate between careful workmanship and in-artistic looseness.....The characters ar an absentee landlord, who shôes him-self only about once in 6 months, staying just long enuf to make everybody miser-able; his 2 grandchildren, with a little ward, Nannie White; a presbyterian minister, his nefew, and his grand-child. The master of Black Abbey, Mr. de Burgo, is a repulsivly selfish and cruel old man, and the author describes somewhat too minutely the severity of the treatment which he ac-cords to the little girls. He is perhaps the least natural character in the book. The children gro together, and Hector manages to win the love of both Nannie and Bella, whilst Ailie captivates Luke Cosby. It is with the love story of the two first-mentioned girls that we hav principally to do; and this story is as pathetic as any one could wish it to be. The real heroin of the book, Nannie White, is charmingly drawn, and we ar

342

engrossed in her good and evil fortunes to the last page. Bella Hawthorn is a handsom Delilah, who successfully tries her wiles upon the simple giant Hector, to the great grief of the scrupulous old minister. She is less distinctly sketched than her rival, but still thêre ar signs that the author has devoted a good deal of labor to the portraiture of the two girls." [Athenæum. **1106**

BLACK SPIRITS AND WHITE [by F.. ELEANOR (TERNAN) TROLLOPE: *Appleton*, 1877.] " is a good novel both in plot and in treatment, in its conception of character, and in its delineation of the mental and moral changes brôt about by the working of circumstances. The gradual debasement of Sir Cosmo and Lady Lowry; the softening and refining effect upon Dr. Flagge of his hopeless affection, as far as Œnone is concerned, while all the rest ' of his offensiv personality is left as detestable as before; the moody and fitful unhappiness of the poor little artiste, as the conviction of her fate opens slõly before her ; all these ar wrôt with delicate and strong handling. But the chief attraction of the book lies in its vivid and lovely portraiture of Mary Lowry, in whom the author has drawn an ideal of womanly sweetness and strength, while at the same time she has made her deeply interesting." [Boston "Literary World." **1107**

BLANCHE SEYMOUR [*Lippincott*, 1873.] " is simply the story of the love of a young and charming girl for a man who was unworthy of her. It is not made a pretext for tragic denunciations of heartless men, nor of pathetic appeals for sympathy for neglected maidens; it is nothing more than a picture of a not uncommon life, which everywhêre is agreeably set before us. The author's great merit consists in the commendable

naturalness of all her characters. She is, too, very amusing with her side-remarks and the feminin cleverness which is to be seen on every page. In fact, except for the small tragic pang at the end of the book, which occurs at what is perhaps the only solution of the complication of the plot, we hardly know a more entertaining novel than this." [Nation. **1108**

BLUE BELL OF RED NEAP, SEE *JOHN THOMPSON.*

BLUE RIBBON (THE). [by ELIZA (TABOR) STEPIENSON: *Harper*, 1874.] " We kno few more delitful novels. It is a story of life in a cathedral town, tho ecclesiastical personages do not figure prominently in it. The hero is a young man who rises from obscurity to eminence in the world of science, and the heroin is a german girl, employed in the same factory. The latter is a musical genius, and this endowment, as often happens, brings her into trouble, from which she happily escapes. The tone of the book is singularly pure and quiet, and the sketches of society, especially the reports of the courteous contests between Mesdames Balmain and Ballinger, ar very skilfully done. The effect of the book is ennobling, and its interest never flags. We take pleasure in commending it as a thõroly good novel." [Boston " Lit. World." **1109**

BLUEBEARD'S KEYS, ETC. [by A.. I.. (THACKERAY) RITCIIE: *Smith*, 1874.] " No doubt the taste for these (we can hardly say, ' this kind of,' for they ar unique) daintily and delicately told little stories must be acquired, like that for dry wine, and like that too, we must not take them in too large a quantity, or our sense will become deadened to the aroma, and conscious only of the dryness; for, indeed, the stories ar of the simplest, and please far more by reason of the delicacy and accuracy of the drawing, and the just proportions of all the parts than by a vivid interest which the subjects ar likely to kindle in us. [Athenæum.] See *FIVE OLD FRIENDS.* **1110**

BLYTHE HOUSE [by R. F. H.: *Virtue*, 1864.] "is a very interesting story, pleasantly told. The moral is not set forth in words; but a sweet and gentle spirit pervades the whole, like a delicate fragrance, which imparts a pleasure to the reader independent of its literary merit. The story is simple, and thêre ar occasional observations, arising from the incidents, which sho a graceful goodness of heart. . . . . The reader will find pleasure in folloing the history of Ida Bernstein to her adoption into the family of the kind Dr. Blank and his pleasant sister Milly, and her happy marriage to her benefactor, all of which is charmingly narrated. The old-fashioned, quaint mansion in which they liv makes an agreeable framework to the 3 chief personages." [Ath. **1111**

BONNIE LESLEY [by — ( ) Martin: *Griffith & Farran*, 1878.] "is spirited, interesting, refined, and humorous, and deals, not obtrusivly, but amusingly, with the movement in favor of 'lady-helps.'. . . . And a charming story it is. . . . . But we can well forgiv a little bad english in our pleasure at the fascinating description of Bonnie Lesley, not only bonnie, but handsom, activ, lively, and humorous ; more praetical, perhaps, than imaginativ, but with that perfect health of mind and body which diffuses cheerfulness by its mere presence with a power almost magical. Her more sensitiv sister is also more conventional, and when the two ar left poor and orfans, is shocked with Lesley's boldness in accepting the offer of Lady Thornley." [Spectator. **1112**

BORN COQUETTE (A). [by Ma. (Argles) Hungerford : *S. Blackett*, 1890.] "Every reader who knoes what is what opens a novel by the author of *Molly Bawn* with a feeling of pleasant expectation . . . . The author has never drawn a more attractiv and life-like group than that formed by the members of the Delaney household, and thêre hav not been many heroins of fiction so wilful, so perverse, even so cruel, and yet so irresistibly fascinating, with that indescribable fascination which is peculiarly irish, as Nan Delaney, the 'born coquette.'" [Spectator. **1113**

BOUDOIR CABAL (The). [by Eustace Clare Grenville Murray: *Smith*, 1875.] "Mr. Paradyse ' is the educatee, not the educator of his disciples,' and 'intends to bring forward a motion (backed by agitation out of doors) to pledg the House of Commons to the program of the Home Rulers.' To meet this, Mr. Paramount moves a counter-set of resolutions, declaring ' that in the opinion of this House it is inexpedient to debate such a momentous question as the dismemberment of the empire until the voice of the whole people has been appealed to, and that in consequence this House is of opinion that the time has arrived for enfranchising those of her Majesty's subjects, of both sexes, who hav reached the age of 21 'years,' and so on, till we feel for a moment half inclined to believe we ar reading history. Upon this piece of tactics on the part of the Conservative leader, the story in a great measure turns; becaus the young Lord Mayrose, with whose affairs the book deals, sticks to his leader, and gets promotion, but deeply offends more than one of the 'ruling houses,' whose members ar not all prepared for universal suffrage, and hav, therefore, formed a 'cave,' and sit in it, furious against thêir former colleagues. Thêreupon, too, the ladies of these families sho themselves fiercely hostil to Mayrose, who has also committed the crime of marrying the dauter of a City knit, and the heiress to estates which had once belonged to his family. Out of this feud rise divers difficulties, which meet the unlucky hero in every walk of life, he all the while trying to act on the most uprit motivs.....The author has somewhat of Balzac's genius for inventing a society, and certainly, while we move in it, it seems strangely life-like. Take Lord Beaujolais, the great M. F. H., inventor of bits and harness, with his ' mity, determined face, adorned with a floing hay-colored beard, and piercing blue eyes,' who tries experiments in Grosvenor Square; or Lord Hornette, the prospectiv head of the great ducal family of Drone, (who bear ' an escutcheon of drones rampant, with the motto " Sans miel ni fiel,"' dry, ' cantankerous,' disagreeable, yet not without some humor and much queer chivalrous feeling; or several other prominent characters, not perhaps including the hero, who is too much the ideal young nobleman for his features to be quite distinguishable; but, for the rest, we see them all as plainly as possible. Of course, a good deal of the book is of the nature of a political squib, but it is not unamusing; and we may congratulate the author, since whatever we may think of his political vues he can put together an interesting story." [Athenæum. **1114**

BRAMLEIGHS OF BISHOP'S FOLLY (THE) [by C: LEVER: Smith, 1868.] "ar a family of wealthy parvenus, who, tho the head of the house, Col. Bramleigh, has married the dauter of an earl, hav never been able to take the position in society which many of them covet. They ar divided into 3 camps. Lady Augusta, who has avowedly married for money, livs in Rome, and keeps her life and her interests distinctly separated from those of any other member of the family; Col. Bramleigh is supported by his dauter Marion, and his second son, Temple, a budding diplomatist. The third camp is composed of the eldest son, Augustus; the youngest son, Jack, a sailor; and a dauter Nellie. These last ar honorable, straitforward people, whose only ends in life ar to 'liv and let liv,' and 'love and let love.' A claimant for the Bramleigh estate appears in the shape of a young Frenchman, who signs himself Count Pracontal de Bramleigh. His introduction, and the very respectable claim he is able to advance, serv to bring to lit the characters of the various members of the family — Marion, who has married an old diplomatist, Viscount Culduff, and Temple, treat him as an impostor. Colonel Bramleigh fits him resolutely, by fair means or foul, until excitement brings on death by apoplexy. Augustus, Jack, and Nellie, who compose what may be called the peace party, resign occupation of the estate, and depend upon their exertions for support until the question of proprietorship shall be settled. Lady Augusta arranges to retain her interest in the estate by marrying the Frenchman should his attempt prove successful. Accident reveals documents proving the claim to be unfounded. The claimant disappears, the whole family is restored to its rits, and the story ends.....In the reader's admiration of the wit of the dialog, and the power of the characterisation, inadequacy of plot and want of art in the conduct of the story ar almost forgotten." [Fortnightly Review. **1115**

BRANDRETHS (THE). [by A. J.

BERESFORD HOPE : *Hurst,* 1882.] "After the success of ' Strictly Tied Up,' the author had some justification for continuing in a second book the history of the principal characters of his former novel. ' The Brandreths' is a pleasant book to read, but it is not a good novel. It is an unusual treat to the reader of novels to find himself in the company of a man of the world who is also a man of wide knoledge and culture, and one who possesses the power of writing with ease and with point." [Athenæum. **1116**

BRAVE LADY (A) [by DINAH MARIA (MULOCK) CRAIK : *Hurst,* 1870.] " is the dauter of a french émigré, who is a viscount, and also a dancing-master. The lady marries an irish parson, the only son of a wealthy but vulgar merchant; and the history of the married life she leads with this parson constitutes the book. This life is most commonplace. The parson is rather an inferior man, who, without being exactly a brute, makes his clever wife experience a most trying time of it from his selfishness, want of ability, and lack of rectitude. The merchant becomes bankrupt and dies. The parson thereupon has to take a curacy in England; and, what with a large family and a small income, he finds his life anything but a rosy one, notwithstanding the companionship of his wife. Things gro worse and worse, and the parson, having embezzled funds entrusted to him for building purposes, is on the eve of being found out, when the rector dies, leaving the whole of his large fortune to the ' brave lady.' For a time thêre is a lull in thêir troubles; but the husband does not improve in conduct with the improvement in his monetary matters, and, by diverse acts of misconduct of a somewhat trivial but irritating nature, wearies his poor wife almost to death, until,

finally, partial misery becomes complete misery, and the children all die within a remarkably short time: the husband folloes; and the ' brave lady' is left all to herself for some years, then dies peacefully, and the novel ends. This is not a promising subject; but the author's style is so good that the work is readable, and no hier tribute could be paid to the power of this writer than in saying that a reader will be able to go throu the 3 volumes w.chout being bored." [Athenæum. **1117**

BRIARS [by A. M. MUNROE: *Griffith, Farran & Co.*, 1890.] "is a pleasant and genial tale of a snug estate, of its manly owner, of his companionable son, and of the more or less companionable and happy creatures brôt into contact with them. Thêre is a good character-plot in the story, exceptionally good and interesting; its men and women ar fair samples of the better class of refined gentlefolk, and most of them ar decidedly piquant." [Athenæum. **1118**

BRIDGET [by MATILDA BARBARA BETHAM EDWARDS: *Hurst,* 1878.] "is happy in its conception, and, in spite of some traces of haste, fairly successful in setting forth some interesting characters. Mr. Starffe, the hard-working, simpleminded curate, who is the better, as only a good man could be, for setting his affections on an ideal which is in all respects but that of moral wealth completely out of his range, is the most pleasing, and in spite of his awkwardness, the most dignified figure set before us..... Helwyse is all that is womanly and charming, and she does rit in preferring the aspiring workman Freeland, to the slitly conventional, and somewhat superfine artist, Kingsbury..... But the main merit of the tale is the delineation of its principal character Bridget, the impulsiv child, the motherly elder sister of a

young family, half French, half Irish, who thro themselves in thêir orfaned helplessness on the already overburdened resources of thêir uncle, a city clerk.... Acting with unhesitating confidence on that promise, she makes her appearance 2 years afterwards and quarters herself upon him, reminding him of his promise to assist her in studying for the stage. . . . . His horror and despair ar gradually allaved, till the selfish man about town is reclaimed and chastened into the adoring husband, and Bridget is developed from a thôtless girl into a loving woman." [Athen. **1119**
BROKEN TO HARNESS. [by EDMUND YATES : *Maxwell — Loring*, 1864.] "The hero is strong, manly and good at heart. A better work of fiction has not for many a week come under our notice. From beginning to end we hav read it with lively interest, and we lay it aside with an agreeable sense of refreshment and increased strength. Readers of every class will find in the story a liberal fund of amusement; and thêre ar those who will thank the author for certain wise lessons and many fine pictures. Taken as a whole, it is a man's novel, dealing far more with Bohemia, club-rooms and masculin absurdities, than with the refinements and graces of woman's life. But, tho it is a man's novel, women will relish it; for throuout its diverse scenes thêre is a chivalric and unobtrusiv recognition of feminin goodness. . . . . Apart from Barbara's troubles, the story contains much good matter. The sketches of the club-life of authors and artists ar capital. Enuf has been said of Mr. Yates' cleverness and power; but we have scarcely done justice to the unaffected amiability and manliness which ar amongst his most agreeable qualities." [Athenæum. **1120**
BROTHER GABRIEL. [by MATILDA

BARBARA BETHAM EDWARDS : *Hurst*, 1878.] "Three friends, an american archæologist, a young english governess, and an irish monk, become acquainted in a town of southern France. The intimacy between Delmar and his cousin soon ripens into love, while the effect of intercourse with both on Brother Gabriel is enlitening, delitful, and, finally, fraut with pain. For the ardent devotee of Romanism learns to chafe at the spiritual bondage of the monastery, and the vowed celibate to feel the thrills of a passion which startles and shocks him. When Delmar reveals too late that he has a wife beyond the seas, and Zoe is left alone with the feelings that she would but cannot eradicate, a strange chain of incidents leads her to taking up her abode with Gabriel, now an outcast from his convent, and alone and helpless in the world. They liv as brother and sister in a remote part of Finistère, till the falseness of their position is brôt home to them, partly by the censoriousness of their nêbors, partly by Gabriel's inability to maintain their romantic compact. To Zoe's distress, her simpleminded protégé discovers purely manly aspirations, and she is conscious, at the same time, that their fulfilment is impossible to her. When Delmar reappears, Gabriel acts with an unselfishness which lately would hav been impossible in the childish scholar of the cloister, and puts an end to Zoe's conscientious struggles by withdrawing from the field. There is a good deal of power in the way in which Gabriel's development is traced. . . . . Zoe is less interesting, but very womanly. Delmar presents little scope for observation. The minor french personages ar aptly described." [Ath. **1121**
BROWN AS A BERRY. [by G: DOUGLAS : *Tinsley Bros.*, 1874.] "The heroin is naïve and unselfish, passionate

yet pure, and just such a groth as mit hav been expected from a wholesom yet uncultivated soil. Briefly (for we cannot describe such minute and fleeting traits as giv charm to the undeveloped character of a girl of 17) she is, from the time we make her acquaintance, as she jumps from her school-room windo, a neglected girl in a french pension, to that in which we find her learning her capacities for love and suffering . . . . qualified to engross the interest of those who read her history. Our anxiety to learn whether Ferrier's love, which she has most innocently won in many a pretty scene of tender raillery, is to stand the strain of treacherous misconstruction; whether the inevitable explanation between two such frank spirits is to take place in time; finally, whether the estimable but inconvenient Dods is to be induced by fair means to resign the truculent part of a Minotaur, or as a last resource to break his respectable old neck, — is intense enuf to thro into the shade our critical appreciation of minor points in the story." [Ath. **1122**

BROWN PORTMANTEAU (The) [by Curtis Yorke: *Jarrold*, 1889.] "is one of several stories which ar not badly contrived, and ar told in a rapid and effectiv fashion without analysis or comment. There ar times when it is pleasantly soothing to the mind to run throu such stories of what mit happen to anybody any day." [Ath. **1123**

BROWNLOWS (The) [by Ma. Oliphant (Wilson) Oliphant: *Blackwood*, 1868.] "is perhaps the most artistic of Mrs. Oliphant's works. There is not a careless page, not a slovenly sentence in the whole. The materials ar slit, the characters ar few. The story, to be appreciated, must be read throu, and not dipped into for scenes. The progress may seem slo, and the steps by

which the drama moves ar very minute, and much in contrast with the ruf and ready slapdash which too many modern novelists affect. Mrs. Oliphant is not afraid of her trouble; and if the reader is impatient, so much the worse for him; he will get all the less good out of a subtle story. . . . The author knoes how to stay the storm she has raised, and to wind the skein she has tangled. The ending of the story is very skilfully managed. The reader will lay down the book with regret that the curtain has dropped, and that Jack, Sara, Pamela, Powys and Mr. Brownlow hav vanished, that he may hear no further about their after-fortunes, nor even kno what becomes of the malicious Nancy Christian, who did so much ill to everybody, — nor hear whether Mrs. Swayne and Betty at the Lodge lived contented under the new dynasty, — nor whether poor old cross Mrs. Fennel grew reconciled to the changed state of affairs; but such unsatisfied questionings ar only a tribute to the author's skill in telling the story." [Ath. **1124**

BURGLARY (A). [by E. A. Dillwyn: *Tinsley Bros.*, 1883.] " The plot is very fresh and clever, and by no means an impossible one. The two heroins ar sketched with a great deal of skill and truthfulness, and thêre is a buoyancy about the book, and especially about the out-of-doors life it contains, which is unhackneyed and very refreshing, after the ordinary drawing-room novel. Ethel's indolent sweetness, benevolence, and hi principle ar sketched with great delicacy; and Imogen's hi spirits, fresh enthusiasm, and awkward attempts to make herself useful in life present a true and pretty picture. . . . . Miss Dillwyn has a good deal of humor. The closing half-page in which Imogen accepts the young gentleman whom she has previously refused, closes a very ingenious and agreeable story with a touch of agreeable banter which pleasantly relieves the inevitable sentiment." [Spectator. **1125**

BURIED DIAMONDS [by " SARAH TYTLER " i. e., Henrietta Keddie : *Chatto*, 1886.] "is a domestic sort of story in which the principal events ar the experiment made by Bennet Gray in entering the family of her intended husband as a stranger and a governess, and the ruin which threatens that family from the dishonesty of one of its members. ....Jane Prior, her sister, and Bennet Gray ar good specimens of the modern learned lady ; — Jane a little too superior in her ōn esteem, but both of them very womanly. Mrs. Prior, a little undervalued by everyone but her son, is a pleasant portrait of a lady of the last generation, and beneath her gentle outlines decision and courage await oceasion for development." [Athen. **1126**

BY LOVE AND LAW [by LIZZIE ALLDRIDGE: *Smith*, 1878.] "is altogether pleasing, dealing chiefly with painters and painting....Of the heroin we shall only say that she is fascinating by her simplicity and directness of character, and that thêre is nothing ' heroic ' about her. Her father, who is at his wits' end to make the two ends meet and yet to keep up the position of the family, must also be drawn from life." [Athenæum. **1127**

BY MEAD AND STREAM [by C: GIBBON : *Chatto*, 1884.] " is a pleasant book, like its title. The love of singlehearted Madge Heathcote is of a stancher type than that of her friend Philip Hadleigh, but they ar an honest pair, and come in an edifying way throu the troubles caused by the eccentricities of thêir seniors, and the sudden overthro of Philip's mental balance by the pos-

session of wealth. The charm of the book lies in its rusticity.....But the reader in remembéring this story will recur to the meads and streams of Ringsford and its nêborhood and the peaceful contrast of the quiet country." [Athenæum. **1128**

BY THE WESTERN SEA : A SUMMER IDYL. [by JA. BAKER : *Longmans*, 1889.] The author "is fairly entitled to call his new story a summer idyl, tho it dōes, in a sense, turn on courtship and marriage. It is imbued with the simplicity of nature, it shōes the working of two human souls in harmony with the soul of nature, and it is a picture complete in itself. The leading characters ar a crippled artist and a lovely girl with poetic aspirations, and between these two thêre ar passages of great tenderness and truth. The hero has a well-tempered mind, reflected in a beautiful face, as frequently happens with the heroes of fiction who hav been crippled by aceident.....' By the Western Sea' is pleasant reading for a summer day." [Athenæum. **1129**

CAN YOU FORGIVE HER? [by ANTHONY TROLLOPE : *Chapman*, 1864.] "Alice Vavasor, whom we ar asked to forgiv, is not a captivating heroin; but a well-conceived and far from impossible young woman, who chafes under and breaks an engagement to an excellent, hi-minded gentleman, not, as she tells herself and her friends, becaus she has discovered that she is not good enuf for him, but becaus she has, half unconsciously, become deeply infected with the 19th century idea, that thêre was something important for her to do with her life — in other words, she was restless and craving for excitement, and her heart failed her when she thôt of long quiet evenings in the monotonous comfort of a country house. With his usual skill in depicting the working of half-acknoledged motivs, and the influence of slit causes in determining the most important actions, Mr. Trollope has placed his heroin in circumstances which ar admirably adapted to make her conduct appear natural, if not inevitable, and he succeeds in interesting us in a struggle which we feel has many counterparts in life." [Westminster Review. **1130**

CANON'S WARD (THE) [by JA. PAYN: *Harper*, 1884.] "is interesting, but it lacks harmony between the incidents and their surroundings. The characters fit well enuf in the placid atmosfere of scholarly life. Elderly men and women with soft faces and voices, and, about them, ingenuous youth, all, old and young, devoted to one opening rose, make another of those gracious pictures by which english life has become so pleasantly familiar. Such a setting should belong to a very different plot. Sorro comes surely even to such tranquil homes, but so strong is the feeling that it could come only gently, that it is a blo to meet a secret marriage at the beginning. The husband is at once drowned, and the secret is knön to but one man, who uses it to force the canon's ward to marry him. This leaves the story without a hero in the ordinary sense, for after such an outrage, the reader can only detest him. The canon is a suggestion of the dear old Warden, and he bears his reverses quite as patiently. But therein appears the superiority of the master hand. The Warden is left in his patience, but the canon's fortune is restored by one of the staple devices of the novel-writer." [Nation. **1131**

CAPEL GIRLS (THE). [by "E : GARRETT," i. e., I.. Fyfic Mayo: *Tinsley*

Bros., 1876.] "There is little sensationalism here, neither is thêre any morbid dissection of fashionable vices, yet the book is interesting as a picture of a family circle, such as we may see any day. The plot is evidently meant only as a peg for the characters, and the latter ar possessed of considerable individuality.....One of the best portraits is that of the eldest of the sisterhood, who is so charming a creation that many girls who read of her may be almost reconciled to the possibility of becoming some day old maids. All the dramatis personæ ar simply drawn, and we ar spared that straining after effect to which most modern novelists ar so much addicted. Neither ar there any painful endeavors to be clever and witty. In fact, the book is a homely chronicle of a homely family, and consequently will meet extensiv sympathy." [Athenæum. **1132**

CARITÀ. [by MA. OLIPHANT (WILSON) OLIPHANT: *Smith*, 1877.] "Agnes Burchell, to satisfy her desire for an ideal, leaves a very commonplace and ill-ordered home, full of discontent and petty wrangling, to become attached in a probationary state to a sort of anglican convent called 'The House.' Everything about this convent is admirably described. The place itself, the people, and thêir ways ar all treated with a kindly humor, the result of a comprehension of the motivs and aspirations which bring such things into existence. 'Comprendre c'est tout pardonner.' Agnes is soon discovered to hav no 'vocation,' and accident brings Oswald Meredith across her path. Mrs. Oliphant shöes a remarkable grasp over and insit into her character as her ideal shifts from the wide and rather impersonal vision of doing good to the poor, to the vain, and exceedingly worldly but charming, Oswald." [Athenæum.] — "Carità is an excellent story, so simple and in good measure uneventful that the plot of it hardly needs to be mentioned. To be sure, at the beginning of the book there is brôt in a woman who, to avoid the slo torture of inevitably painful death, takes poison. But apart from this everything moves as smoothly as only Mrs. Oliphant's skill can direct the course of novels." [Nation. **1133**

CASTE. [by EMILY JOLLY: *Hurst*, 1858.] "Thêre is much which is extremely good in this novel. The story is interesting, and it is well written. The heroin is the dauter of a tradesman who has educated her far above her nominal station. She being very proud and very ill regulated, chafes at the station of life in which she has been born. She first, out of pride, refuses a man above herself in rank whom she loves, and then, out of spite, marries another, also her superior in social position, whom she detests, and the result is what mit hav been expected. The tradespeople of the book ar refined and idealized . . . . Tho for the interest of the story that may be allowed, it does not add to its reality or probability." [Athenæum. **1134**

CASTLE BLAIR. [by FLORA L. SHAW: *Paul*, 1878.] "The scene is laid in **Ireland**, and the characters ar Adrienne, an orfan, niece of Mr. Blair, and 3 other young persons, the nieces and nefew of the same gentleman, who, indeed, as a bachelor, seems to hav been hardly dealt with by fortune in the matter of other people's children. The three ar wild and riotous; the cousin acts the part of healer and moderator. The narrativ is vigorous and lively, full of picturesque effect, and sometimes rising to a very considerable amount of interest." [Spectator. **1135**

CASTLE DALY [by ANNIE KEARY:

Phil'a, *Porter*, 1875.] " is a novel of more than ordinary merit. It deals mainly with life in **Ireland** in the years of the famin and the Smith O'Brien rising; and these elements, tragic and romantic, ar handled with remarkable power. The author's pictures of the country in the grasp of hunger, of the peasantry ground, as it wer, between pure fysical pain and the rage of fierce patriotism, ar far superior to the average portrayals of collectiv suffering. The pastoral life of the irish is depicted with sympathetic skill. Castle Daly was the home of a squire, who had married an english wife. They hav 3 children, — all approaching maturity, — 2 boys and a girl. The oldest son has been educated in England, and finds Ireland not much to his taste; the others ar irish in every thôt and act. We cannot trace the plot of the story; it is sufficient to say that, having passed throu strange and dramatic vicissitudes, the recital whêreof is extremely interesting, the oldest son marries an english girl, and Ellen, the dauter, marries an englishman. . . . . The author's mood is happy, adapting itself to all circumstances with good effect; and when she discourses seriously, she talks well." [Boston " Literary World." **1136**

CASTLE RACKRENT. [by MARIA EDGEWORTH: 1800.] "That Miss Edgeworth had the irish humor as well as the irish wit is manifest in *Castle Rackrent*, which she calls a piece of 'good-natured raillery' rather than a serious satire. It is Thackerayean in its rollicking extravagance, yet, in spite of the author's disclaimer, it has enuf resemblance to the reality of certain types of irish character to giv point to the caricature." [Boston " Lit. World." **1137**

CASTLE RICHMOND [by ANTHONY TROLLOPE: *Harper*, 1860.] " is a story of **Ireland,** told with a rich and racy humor, and ornamented with several of those mirth-provoking characters to be found only on irish soil. It differs materially from Lever's novels, is more refined in tone, and less given to exaggeration. The plot is well constructed, and skillfully developed. The interest of the story, too, is maintained unbroken to the end, and the reader puts the book aside, satisfied with the author, with the story, with the ending." [Crayon. **1138**

CHANNINGS (The). [by ELLEN (PRICE) WOOD: *Bentley*, 1862.] "To school-boys or to the families of school-boys, we can imagin nothing more charming than the first perusal of this book. It will probably be read again and again; and it is certain that it can never be read without profit both by parents and children. It is essentially a book for young people, yet it will interest the fathers and mothers of the rising generation. It is, in fact, merely the simple history of a certain eventful 6 months in the lives of 2 large families, the Channings and the Yorkes. In an old cathedral town, containing within its sacred precincts a collegiate school, liv these 2 families. The Yorkes are a harum-scarum race, badly bred by a foolish irish mother, of hi rank but small income. The Channings ar carefully educated, the wish to do their duty thŏroly being the chief object of their existence. The Channings and the Yorkes ar all much of an age..... The story is slit and unimportant. The merit of it lies in the detail, and the extreme truthfulness and simplicity in which it is related. We feel, while reading it, as if we had been living all our lives in the old town, and knew each college-boy by sit, and met the good-natured, jovial bishop and the stiff, dignified dean every time we went out.

Mr. Ketch, the great enemy of the school-boys and the victim of their choicest tricks, is a capital character; and Jo Jenkins, the clerk, so humble and faithful to his master, so terribly henpecked at home, and so beloved and respected abroad, wins all our sympathy and affection. It is impossible not to read every word with interest, and we feel real regret at parting with them." [Athenæum. **1139**

CHARLES DAYRELL, see "*LADY STELLA.*"

CHELSEA HOUSEHOLDER (A) [by EMILY LAWLESS: *Holt*, 1883.] "is Muriel Ellis, a girl of just that gentle independence of spirit which is so much more attractiv than positiv softness, or outrit strongmindedness. She is enuf of an heiress, too, to play very prettily at being an artist. The hero is a clergyman of Broad Church affinities, a puzzle to his kindred. While the book is not of great power, it has an individuality quite marked..... The descriptions of country landscape ar singularly happy." [Nation. **1140**

CHEQUERED LIFE (A) [by — ( ) DAY; *Hurst*, 1878.] "deals with life and its pleasures and pains, with love and marriage, and the blunders occasionally made in both, which ar so hard to remedy; but it is a genuin story, of well-sustained interest.....It is open to the objection that between 2 such amiable and perfectly well-intentioned persons as Lord Rewe and his innocent girl-wife, so ignorant of the world into which she had stepped out of her convent schoolroom, that she actually looked upon the pleasant vices of which she heard for the first time as deadly sins, silence and estrangement of so long duration would not, in life, hav been produced by anything said by a third party.....The sentiments and conduct of Valentina ar entirely consistent with her education and her character, with the shock of her introduction into a world in which men ar free to indulge in vice unblamed, and women ar supposed to kno all about it, but to be quite unaffected by that knoledge in their relations with thêir brothers, thêir lovers, and thêir husbands. — The truth is told in this novel; the woman's side of the matter is strongly, but delicately set forth.....It is well to hav a picture of the mind of a good, honest, sensitiv woman, loving, true, pure, full of the enthusiasm of love and respect which comes from lofty teaching concerning the meaning of duty and marriage, — of her acute shame and indignation, her horrified distrust and bewilderment when she finds herself established for life among people, who, holding hi places in the world, treat all which she abhors, without rendering count of it to herself, with the complacence of familiarity and indifference. The family party into which the young girl from her convent school is admitted is a perfectly respectable one, as the world measures respectability." [Spectator. **1141**

CHERRY RIPE [by HELEN (MATHERS) REEVES: *Bentley*, 1878.] "is a disgusting book. Not that it is coarse or delicately obscene. The diseased morality which Miss Mathers teaches is sicklied over with a nasty appearance of religious principle which makes it only 10 times more odious." [Ath. **1142**

CHILDREN OF GIBEON (THE) [by WALTER BESANT: *Harper*, 1886.] "is one of Walter Besant's most charming stories. The ease and grace, the delicate humor, the sweet humanity, which always distinguish his work, ar all thêre, while a deep problem underlies the whole, and the sympathetic suggestion of the trials of work-women make the

entertaining story also a thôtful one. The problem is whether we o our traits to birth or breeding, and the mother of the heroin thinks she has solved it in favor of breeding, when she brings up her own little girl and the little girl of a poor woman in ignorance as to which is which, with the result that both develop into gentle, interesting maidenhood. Such a plot is full of material and 'points,' around which Besant's delicate fancy plays britly and sweetly. The two girls ar introduced to the working man's son who is brother of one of them, and accept the situation, as they stand hand in hand, with the pretty little introduction, 'We ar your sister Polly.' The little touches which follo ar full of human nature, when the real heiress seeks to be the poor girl, while the poor girl feels it to be aristocratic instinct that she cannot bear the thôt of leaving fashionable comfort, and when the heiress inadvertently learns that she is the heiress, but keeps the secret patiently and nobly till the time comes when it must be revealed. Altogether the story is as pretty a one as we hav had for many a day, and it must be a hard heart which is not touched by it to finer issues." [Critic. **1143**

CHOICE OF CHANCE. [by W: DOBSON: *Unwin*, 1887.] "Something in the quiet style, the pathetic and humorous touches, perhaps the natural and simple autobiografical form and the wholesome and pleasant relations between a mother and dauter (who, by the way, ar not a mother and dauter, whereby hangs the tale), reminds one a little of ' My Trivial Life and Misfortunes.' — a book which had a kind of character of its ôn. The title is ill chosen. A sensational element, by no means of the best quality, pervades a story which, if rather fragmentary and disconnected, is pleasant reading. The heroin and narrator excites some interest and liking, and thêre ar a good many characters, amiable if somewhat slit, and altogether clean of hackneyed and conventional touches." [Athenæum. **1144**

CHRISTIAN'S MISTAKE. [by Dinah Maria (Mulock) Craik: *Hurst*, 1865.] "Christian is an orfan, the dauter of a gentleman of birth and education, and of great musical genius, but who lost his position from his habits of drunken profligacy. The sympathy of the reader is secured for Christian, and kept up to the end. Her father happily dead, Christian has been a governess in a respectable tradesman's family, and from their house she has just been married when the story begins. Dr. Grey, the husband, is described as a great scholar, a gentleman of most sweet and gentle nature, a man more like a father than a husband. His first marriage had not been happy, and he had been taut patience throu a weary course of domestic disciplin. His marriage with Christian had been one of real love, which is very delicately touched by the author — it is made both natural and interesting, and the reader's sympathy goes with it." [Athenæum. **1145**

CHRISTY CAREW [by May (Laffan) Hartley: *Holt*, 1880.] "is a quiet and simple irish story told with much nativ wit and a true keltic flavor; e. g., 'Thêre's elegant drowning at the end of the pier, Master Lanty, if you'll only consider it,' is the remark of an exasperated nurse to a veritable enfant terrible about to 'go fishing' thither. The characters ar well distinguished, and set forth with much ease, evidently from life in many cases, and tho the book is too long and the author neglects the elementary maxim that all episodes should conduce to the general action, and tho we must regard as premature the

judgment of an admiring critic who thinks her the successor of George Eliot, we can cordially commend the book as more interesting and decidedly abler than its class." [Nation. **1146**

CHRISTY JOHNSTONE = No. 639.

CHRONICLES OF CARLINGFORD (series), See "*THE DOCTOR'S FAMILY*," "*SALEM CHAPEL*," "*PERPETUAL CURATE*," "*MISS MAJORIBANKS*," "*PHŒBE JUNIOR*."

CHRONICLES OF GLENBUCKIE. [by H : Johnston : Edinburgh, *Douglas*, 1889.] The disruption of the scottish church "supplies the clever author with a convenient pivot on which the parochial politics of his Ayrshire village may revolv, and enables him to call into vivid life and action the ruf-hewn elders, the weavers and soutars of Glenbuckie. We hardly kno what minute piece of local portraiture to cite; whether the courting of the doctor and his housekeeper, Mrs. Forgie, whose gentle soul is so often confused by the wandering discursivness of that filosofic wooer, or the more practical union of the betheral and the 'oo-leddy, the piteous story of poor Maggie Winlestrae's ruin, or the loutish advances of Richie Necbikin to his Jean. ....Space fails to tell of Janet Pyat, the minister's maid, a much more energetic divine than that worthy man, — of Mysie the Spae-wife, or of Mrs. Haplands and her inferior half. Suffice it to say there ar no weak sketches in this gallery of originals, which lovers of Lowland Scotland will do well to study." [Athenæum. **1147**

CICELEY'S CHOICE [by — (   ) O'Reilly : *Bell & Sons*, 1875.] "is a pleasant story. Thêre is a good deal of humor in the way Ciceley's character is treated ; the picture of her as a young girl of 16, full of faults, but brit, brave, and honest, and with the promise of plenty of good sense to be developed hereafter. Her mistakes and her passionate, impulsiv temper, ar touched with a loving hand and ar true to the unformed but fascinating nature of a young girl. It is a book for girls, but grŏn people will also enjoy reading it." [Athenæum. **1148**

CINDERELLA. [*S: Tinsley*, 1876.] "We hav nothing but praise for this quiet little story, tho the title, we must say, rather fritened us. The vein of applied fairy tales, first so happily struck out by Miss Thackeray [see No. 1110] has, as Artemus Ward would hav said, been 'done too muchly.' There is certainly a want of sensation in this little book, and those who like thêir literature strong would better seek it elsewhere. But there ar others, we think, to whom this simply-told love-story will come quite refreshingly, after all the gushing immorality with which we ar surfeited. Some of the characters, particularly the family of the parvenu, ar cleverly sketched, and thêre ar one or two charming descriptions of scenery." [Spectator. **1149**

CITY GIRL (A). [by J : LAW: *Vizetelly*, 1887.] "Within the compass of 190 pages Mr. Law has given his readers a little romance of the East End which is wanting neither in pathos nor in force. The epithet 'realistic' is distinctly misleading as applied to 'A City Girl.' It is true that we move in squalid surroundings, but the author's method of treating his materials is wholly void of the Zolaistic taint. He is at heart somewhat of an optimist, and possesses the gift of a genial sympathy for those with whose vues he is not in accord. Daudet and Turgénief hav been his models rather than Zola, tho we doubt whether either of those great writers would hav contrived so happy an ending for what

threatened to be a tragedy." [Athenæum. **1150**

CLARISSA HARLOWE = No. 645.

CLAVERINGS (THE). [by ANTHONY TROLLOPE: *Smith*, 1867.] "The hero, Harry Clavering, is a young fello of good family and acquirements, but of small means, whose first love, Julia Brabazon, rejects him on account of his poverty, and marries a nobleman of great wealth. At the moment when his mind is bitterest towards the woman who, as he thinks, has betrayed him, and stands therefore in greatest need of affection which shall restore it to self-respect, Clavering meets Florence Burton. Tho fortune has denied Florence either money or family, in other respects it has not been ungenerous. Clavering accordingly ere long is betrothed to her. But the old love is not yet quite extinct. Julia Brabazon, now Lady Ongar, returns rich and a wido to offer herself to the man she has always loved. Clavering is sorely tried, and the story of the difficulties by which he is beset supplies the principal interest of the novel. He is a gentleman, however, and, in spite of some weakness of character, keeps the reader's respect throuout the story. He marries accordingly the girl to whom he is affianced, and Lady Ongar is left to muse disconsolately over the proverb, — 'She who will not when she may, when she will she shall hav nay.' Slit as is this story, it is deeply interesting." [Fortnightly Review. **1151**

CLEMENCY FRANKLYN [by ANNIE KEARY: *Macmillan*, 1866.] "is a charming story, well written and well told. It is a book to be read for the pleasure it will giv, and it is a book to be given to young girls for thêir profit. The reading will be an innocent pleasure, without any of the dulness that too often marks innocent pleasures for its ōn. Thêre is a zest in the story, — simple as it is, — a delicate discrimination of character, and a faculty for putting the various personages into action, which giv life and reality to the work. The tale is slit, and the skill of the author has been bestoed upon the delineation of character rather than upon the elaboration of incident. . . . . Out of all the cross purposes, disappointments, and mistakes, a better order of things arises than all the schemes and day-dreams which human self-will had purposed. The story is very satisfactory, and altho it may be a reversal of the usual order to make the heroin change her mind about her hero, Clemency makes the rit man happy at last, and the reader, if he be of our mind, will heartily sympathize with him." [Ath. **1152**

COLONEL CHESWICK'S CAMPAIGN. [by FLORA L. SHAW: *Longman*, 1886.] "A novel by the author of 'Hector' [No. 465] has been a pleasant anticipation, which is pleasantly realized. 'Colonel Cheswick's Campaign' is not a great book, but it is a charming story. The love of father and dauter forms the main theme, which is worked out throu all the manifold incidents of the attractiv life of an english country-house. A wider horizon bends round the whole, encircling with the english fens the egyptian sands. It would have been too much to expect, on the larger scale, the simple perfection of 'Hector.' Neither introspection nor analysis is part of Miss Shaw's method, and to fill her canvass she employs a number of minor figures which crowd each other, and which we could gladly hav spared. Not of these, however, is the beautiful old pair, in their death not divided. The main figures stand out very clear. It is no small power of characterization which, almost

without a comment, makes us understand the complex nature of the colonel and his wife. The latter, trivial, foolish, selfish, we can still see is lovable to the fond eyes of her loyal dauter. In the colonel is combined that reckless, happy-go-lucky spirit which justifies self-iudulgence which is even cruel to wife and children; and yet, in his place at the head of his regiment, he is the duteous, brave, ardent soldier. It was an early comment that the daughter, Ailsa, is only Zélie (from 'Hector') or Phyllis Browne (from the story of that name) grön. No one will admire or love her the less for that: it is very hi praise." [Nation. **1153**

COLONEL ENDERBY'S WIFE [by "LUCAS MALET," i. e., Rose G—— (Kingsley) Harrison : *Kegan Paul*, 1885.] "is an especially strong and thôtful novel. . . . The book tells the story of a heartless woman who wrecks the life of a trusting middle-aged husband — not by vulgar crime, but by mere heartlessness and selfishness. [Compare plot of "Marcia."] If the subject appears trite it is the baldness of this statement which makes it so. It is anything but trite, being strikingly original, passionate and impressiv." [American.] — "It is poignant, grievously pathetic, a fateful, disheartening book, but it is unquestionably clever, and when a work of art is clever, it is idle to quarrel with the artist becaus it is what he has made it, and not something else more agreeable to the taste of the reader. Our taste inclines towards art which does not seek to reproduce life, with its bitter cruelties, its inexorable hardness, but rather to waft us out of life into a golden age, to make us 'lie down in green. pastures' and to lead us ' beside the still waters.' " [Westminster Review. **1154**

COMEDY OF A COUNTRY HOUSE (A) [by JULIAN STURGIS : *Murray*,

1889.] " is something like what a comedy should be — brit and vivacious, rapid and amusing, yet with occasional touches and suggestions of deeper feeling. The cynicism is cheery rather than depressing, and thêre ar some typical men and women litly and knoingly sketched. The dialog is spritly and natural, and such things as pathos or tragedy ar but distantly hinted at. The tactics and sparrings of the ' smart' folk, the assembled guests of the rich and unappropriated young man of property, ar given with gaiety and humor." [Ath. **1155**

COMETH UP AS A FLOWER [by RHODA BROUGHTON: *Appleton*, 1868.] " is a simple narrativ of events occurring daily in social life, and is told in the form of an autobiografy, of which the heroin — the truly lovable, charming, warm-hearted Nelly Lestrange — is supposed to be the writer..... Early in life she acquires a painful knoledg of the bitter pangs, the heartburnings and humiliations of genteel poverty, which her brief experience teaches her is the heaviest load under which a man can groan..... Poor Nelly's troubles wer not occasioned by poverty alone, however— tho that may hav been one of the remote causes of her subsequent more serious griefs — but the absorbing passion of her life, her love for Richard McGregor, her hero,— this love, ' which was her doom,' was the source of all the happiness she knew, of all the misery which her gentle but passionate nature was called upon to endure. The picture of her life is a piece of pure womanly character-painting, in all respects consistent and natural, and her thôts and aspirations ar always in perfect harmony with her surroundings..... No word comes from McGregor — duns, bills, creditors, torment the poor father, his health fails, and the old story of Robin

Gray is enacted again, only Sir Hugh Lancaster is not an old man, but a good-hearted, not over-attractiv young one. This struggle between human love and filial duty forces our sympathies into a painful region of casuistry; Nelly's strength is tried to the utmost, and in the conflict her pure, steadfast love is sacrificed. She had withstood the doubts which McGregor's silence and Dolly's sneers forced upon her, but she could not see her father's honored head bowed to the dust, and, looking bravely and resolutely upon the blit which had fallen upon and withered all her life's spring and freshness, she determins to accept Sir Hugh and try to make him happy. The scenes ar full of painful interest, naturally drawn, beautiful in the tenderness which shôes itself toward the death-stricken father—sad in the hopeless love which still yearns toward the lost and absent one..... Throuout the book thêre ar passages of truly poetic thôt, and a vein of quiet humor which is really charming. The dialog is buoyant, sometimes witty, never vulgar; and the author possesses the happy faculty of shoing that earnestness and power ar perfectly consistent with purity of feeling and expression." [Round Table.] — " We hav here a little love story so fresh and unhackneyed in feeling that we hav read it with a great deal of pleasure. Its plot is one of the barest and simplest illustrations of the proverbial rufness of the course of true love, and the characters belong, with perhaps one exception, to types perfectly familiar in recent fiction; but the story is told with a directness, and the characters drawn with a freedom and grace, which quite giv the book the autobiografical air which it assumes. The exception to which we refer is to be found in the person of the heroin, who is also the narrator of the story. She smells neither of bread and butter nor of the stables, two almost equally odorous extremes between which the heroins of most english novels vibrate, and is at the widest remove from the metafysical and strong-minded nondescripts affected by our writers. She is merely a very genuin little girl, innocent, passionate, and with a genius for loving, the story of whose love and troubles is told with a simplicity and truth to nature which we think quite exceptional. Thère is in the book no attempt at any profundity of thôt or sentiment to which such a girl would not naturally be equal; the incidents ar not striking, and the conclusion is much too melancholy. Still we recommend it." [Nation. **1156**

COMIN' THRO' THE RYE. [by H.. BUCKINGHAM (MATHERS) REEVES: *Bentley*, 1875.] "In spite of a certain coarseness in its humor, and occasional solecisms in its diction, thère is a great deal of power in 'Comin' thro' the Rye.' The heroin groes before our eyes from the 'tom-boy' stage of girlhood to an excellent specimen of loving and truthful womanhood. Thère is originality in the tragic plot, and an unceasing current of rather rollicking fun, which saves the tragedy from becoming sombre. There is something lifelike and, at the same time, artistic in depicting George and Nelly when engaged in the most serious of discussions at the gravest crisis of Nelly's perilous love-story, as conducting thêir conversation in the close confinement of two nêboring piles of hay. George, whose sound sense and tender thôtfulness make him the safest of advisers and the most chivalrous of unselfish lovers, finds virtue, to a degree less common in novels than in life, its ōn reward." [Athenæum.] — "All the rowdiness of Miss Broughton's stories is

to be found here — if anything rather exaggerated — with a love-story different from hers in its strict preaching of exalted morality. The best part of the book is that which describes the heroin's childhood; the accounts of her 'governor's' domestic tyranny, his bad temper, and her pranks with her brothers and sisters, ar very amusing, and indeed they narroly escape being pathetic. When the love-story appears, the book falls off. Good taste is not this writer's strong point. Indeed, her vulgarity is amazing in quantity and quality, but yet she is brit, and her book is in its way entertaining. There is a great deal which is natural in the telling of the story, and a great deal of life in it. Slapping on the back, pillo-fits, and romps of every sort crowd the book; but the heroin, who never opens her lips except to talk the loudest slang and make irreverent remarks about her elders, is a well-drawn creature, and her two lovers, the good one whom she does not like, and the bad one whom she prefers, ar by no means sticks. The plot is not a very new one, but it is told so as to leave a lump in the throat of the unfastidious reader." [Nation. **1157**

COMMON SENSE. [by — (   ) NEWBY: London, *Newby*, 1866.] "We hav read this novel with pleasure. It is a healthy, sensible, and interesting story. The title is sober, and scarcely indicates the hi order of qualities which ar illustrated in the narrativ. But 'Common Sense' is a wide domain, touching genius upon one side, hi principle upon the other; it is an eminently practical virtue, and has the peculiar property of enabling its possessor to follo out his resolutions. The readers of the novel before us will see for themselves how interesting this matter-of-fact virtue can be made. .....
This is an old story, but it is told in a

fresh, unhackneyed manner. Martin Lorimer, the son, develops the heroism of common sense. The father and mother ar both crushed by thêir misfortune, unable to meet the emergency, or to act in any way. Martin, the boy, acts with an honest, clear-sited boy's wisdom; he does nothing which is superhuman, but he day by day acts up to the lit which is in him, developing his strong energy and unflinching will, groing in wisdom and in moral stature, and by the simple faculty of hard work and steady perseverance he works throu all difficulties, and restores the fortunes of the family. The mode in which he does it is interesting, and the reader's sympathy is thõroly engaged. Thêre ar no strokes of fortune, nor mysterious secrets, to change the face of affairs: the only talisman by which Martin Lorimer descends to the ranks, and, from being a workman in an ironfoundry, at a few shillings a week, rises to become a master and a man of wealth and influence, is energy and good sense, guided by religious principle. There is a touch of romance in the charming wife he wins, but the interest is concentrated on Martin and his father; the change which misfortune works in the poor man is pleasant to follo, and the setting free of his good qualities from thêir original alloy is cleverly done." [Athenæum. **1158**

CONINGSBY. [by LORD BEACONSFIELD, 1844.] " (whose hero must be identified as regards character and temperament, but hardly the incidents of his life, with the late Lord Lyttleton) — we see how a clever youth, intended by his grandfather the duke of Monmouth (who is a caricature of the late Marquis of Hertford), to be a model Tory of the old fashioned school, breaks loose from his training, and becomes a

leading member of the Young England party.....Conspicuous associates with Coningsby in this movement ar Oswald Milbank and Henry Sydney, who remind us only too strongly of Mr. Gladstone and Lord John Manners in thêir young days; and among two or three score of other well-knón persons, women as well as men, introduced into the book, by no means the least remarkable is baron Alfred Rothschild as the duke of Sidona." [Athenæum. **1159**

CODLINGSBY. [by W: M. THACKERAY.] " We marvel if Disraeli could ever again write one of his Oriental absurdities, after his trick had been so mercilessly exposed, his fustian so ludicrously reproduced, his style surpassed with such ease even in those parts upon which he most piques himself. It seems to us that if he had been laboring under the author's delusion up to that time, he could not continue in it. He may hav believed his melodious assemblage of words was eloquence, and that his descriptions had a gloing truth about them, until Thackeray shõed him how easy such eloquence is, how Holywell-street can be painted with an Oriental brush which shall make the Rose of Sharon gro in its gutters, and the splendors of Damascus glitter in its back-parlors." [Leader. **1160**

CONSTANTIA [by E. C. PRICE: Low, 1876.] "has a good deal of merit. .....Of 'Constantia,' a most refined, tho rustic lady, we can but say that she is the product of an old-fashioned education.....Mrs. Luttrell and Lady Heath, a trenchant old lady and inconsequent one, ar admirably contrasted, and all parties hav something to say." [Athenæum. **1161**

CONTRADICTIONS. [by F.. M.. PEARD: Bentley, 1883.] " Dorothy Leigh is a fresh creation, as pleasant as anything which can be found in the fiction of the year. Not that she is distinctly original or heroic, but she is a 'very woman' in the best sense of the term, shoing hi spirit in suffering as well as in triumf, and combining with infinit grace and tenderness a courage which disarms the spite of her enemies. She stands in contrast with a proud and more beautiful anti-heroin, who schemes unscrupulously to rob her of her lover, and contrives to mislead her in such a manner as to cause a good deal of misery.....On the whole the author has succeeded in producing a delitful narrativ in which the charms more than compensate for the short-comings." [Athenæum. **1162**

COQUETTE'S CONQUEST (A) [by "BASIL," i. e., R: Ashe King: *Harper*; 1885.] " is a well written and ingenious account of a young lady who married a hero so ideal that he mit have stepped out of, instead of into, a novel, and who thus attained the social position of her day dreams, only to find herself the most miserable woman in all England. Apart from this excellent moral, the detail of the story is entertaining." [Critic. **1163**

CORINNA. [by "RITA," i. e., Eliza M. J. (Gollow) Booth: *Maxwell*, 1885.] "The heroin is graceful and gracefully described. The lively little countess Nina, coquettish and worldly, whom we meet in her company at the outset of the story, is a good foil to the beautiful, single-hearted, and imaginativ author and poet who is her traveling companion." [Athenæum. **1164**

COUNSEL OF PERFECTION (A) [by "LUCAS MALET," i. e., Rose G. (Kingsley) Harrison: *Appleton*, 1887.] "is a refreshing novel of a merit quite above the average. There is a grace and delicacy in the style and in the air of the story which recalls that happy

hour when was made the acquaintance of 'The Story of Elizabeth' [No. 534]. The resemblance ends with these traits, for in the unwilling cynicism of the present volume ar touches which recall the elder rather than the younger Thackeray. The characters ar few, but of a distinctness which never hardens into exaggeration, and shōes the work of the artist no less than of the writer.....Dr. Casteen's dim study, the sparkling air of Switzerland, the mossy churchyard of Bishops-Marston, each lends itself in turn finely to the writer's deeper use. The wit which plays throu the book keeps the atmosfere free from miasma, and if it does pitilessly lit up some ugly troubles which beset humanity, it also brings into cheerful clearness the filosofy which can outliv and liv down worse woes than Lydia Casteen's." [Nation.] — ...."Love does not hav its whole beginning and end in the emotion of child-lovers, completely as young people may think it does. That fine arrogance of youth which will hav it that sweet-and-twenty is the heart boundary is a pretty spectacle enuf, but it shōes only the knoledg and experience which Twenty mit be expected to hav. The heroin of 'A Counsel of Perfection' has never loved until she is nearer 40 than 20, yet we dare affirm that a completer demonstration of the strength and elevation of that passion has seldom been made than in the case of Lydia Casteen. ....She has never knōn the buoyancy and hope of youth, and she had, when the story opens, definitly settled her life in line with the dust-covered existence of her father. At last, in a holiday most begrudgingly allowed her, she meets Anthony Hammond, a bachelor of uncertain age, worldly, cynical, a man entirely unworthy of her, as the author makes no secret of intimating.

This man Lydia loves, and the awakening is one of the most sadly-sweet pictures of abandon and faith we hav ever read. She loves this most imperfect hero, — but she does not marry him. Hammond is a trifler, and at first sets out to amuse himself with an unusual experience. He also pains Lydia by an appearance of wrong-doing which is worse for her than any neglect. But her penetrating beauty of character works at last its full sway on the sensibilities of her admirer; he is brôt to his knees, only to be told that the happiness of both is more certain in parting. This climax is the point of especial originality and strength of the book. Every sensitiv reader must rejoice that the woman for whom he has conceived so sincere an admiration has escaped the doubtful good of a marriage with such a man, while Lydia is left in the lasting possession of an imaginativ and emotional glo of feeling which we realize to be a far better thing for her than an illusion which, in the other event, would certainly be dispelled, leaving her indeed wretched. More than this we need only say that the book is excellent in construction and expression." [American. **1165**

COUNTERPARTS = No. 656.

COUNTESS KATE. [by C.. M.. Yonge: *Mozley*, 1876.] "It is hard to realize that the sickly Heir of Redclyffe, and the charmingly humorous Countess Kate come from the same hand." [G. R. Tomson. **1166**

COUNTRY COUSIN (The) [by F.. M.. Peard: *Harper*, 1889.] "is a very readable little story. It has rather an original situation for its raison d'être. The country cousin as knōn in fiction is commonly described as noble, pure-minded, and simple-hearted. She is usually brôt out in strong contrast against the shams of city life. She is almost invariably put in opposition to the cold-hearted, scheming city girl. But in this case the country cousin is at first extremely shy, and looks simple and ingenuous enuf to deceive the elect; but she soon loses her apparent naiveté and adapts herself most kindly to the ways of fashionable society. Within an incredibly short time she became the most worldly-wise girl in London. Her rival, the truly charming and unselfish Lady Millicent, who had been out many seasons, was not at heart nearly as frivolous as the country cousin. But the innocent face took the prize, and the empty-headed, vain little country girl succeeded in winning Lady Millicent's lover, and then made him a very bad wife. The story has a certain piquant flavor which makes it amusing reading." [Boston "Literary World." **1167**

COUNTRY GENTLEMAN (A) [by Ma. Oliphant (Wilson) Oliphant: *Harper*, 1886.] "and its sequel ar worthy of the only legitimate successor in English literature of Miss Austen. The first is the better. It is told with all Mrs. Oliphant's command of quiet humor, and that gentle sub-acid quality which is not satire or irony, but which answers the purpose of either. 'A Country Gentleman' introduces one of the most outrageous prigs in existence — a young man spoiled by his woman relativs. He marries a wido of an affectionate disposition, of perfect manners and knoledge of the world — a country gentlewoman with a touch of haute noblesse. Mrs. Oliphant is much at home in the delineation of persons who liv in those quiet, harmonious, luxurious interiors which she loves as backgrounds. She has no equal in her understanding of the 'social business' of life, and no superior in her manner of describing a well-bred woman. Her domestic comedies and tragedies ar not brôt about by the vulgar sensationalism of chance. Thĉy arise from the conflict or harmony of character, as they do in real life. *A House Divided against Itself* [See also No. 467.] is a sequel to 'A Country Gentleman.' The prig has lived a lonely life, apart from his wife, in the Riviera. His dauter Frances is with him; his dauter Constance, and his step-son, Lord Markham, the main cause of his separation from his wife, hav remained with thĉir mother in London. Frances is a simple and sweet young girl, bred by an italian nurse. Her amazement when she finds herself transported from the simplicity of italian life to the artificiality of London is great. She cannot understand the innuendoes of those around her, half-tolerant, half-condemnatory, of the immoral lives of the young men she meets and hears of. Her honesty and purity hav thĉir effects, one of which is the reconciliation of her father and mother, altho the reader who has followed them carefully cannot help wondering how long this will last." [Catholic World. **1168**

COUNTY VERSUS COUNTER [by TH. RUSSELL MONRO: *Chapman*, 1878.] "is rather an amusing story of county-town life, its social jealousies, feuds, and alliances. Both the Trevors and the Brooms ar well described, and Miss Penelope, the leader of fashion at Olton Priors, is a genuin lady..... With the exception of Conrad and his female confederates, thĉre is no utterly repulsiv portrait, tho the vulgarities of some of the Olton worthies ar amusingly set forth. Misfortune sometimes brings people out of the commonplace; and Mrs. Broom and her offensiv son sho themselvs in far better colors when real difficulties succeed their social struggles. The dénoument is the marriage of Diana

Trevor, the well-born heroin, with the hero, a timber merchant, of yeoman origin, but educated, and of fine moral proportions. The book is free from snobbishness, in spite of the delicacy of the subject, and tho unambitious, is not without its moral." [Athenæum. **1169**

COURTING OF MARY SMITH. [by F: W: ROBINSON: *Hurst*, 1886.] "To write an interesting love-story in which the heroin is a pretty and hi-minded girl of 19, and the hero a rugged, prosaic millionaire, an illiterate Lancashire cotton-spinner of 55 — to bring such a love-story to a satisfactory and even to a beautiful end mit well be pronounced impossible. Yet it is what Mr. Robinson has achieved. In truth, we should not go too far in saying that the attraction to a noble-minded girl like Mary Smith of a passion like that of Lovett — a passion deeper and purer and more self-abnegating than perhaps a younger man could feel for any woman — is one of the finest studies which any of our novelists has produced of late years. Mingled with the cotton-spinner's love of Mary Smith is a deep worship of ' the sweet glory of youth,' a reverence for the mystery and wonder of a beautiful girlhood, which could hav been rendered only by an english writer of the middle classes, among whom that which is lovely in the Puritanic idea may be said to flourish and liv. To read such a book as this is to strengthen the soul with a moral tonic." [Athenæum. **1170**

COUSIN HENRY. [by ANTHONY TROLLOPE: *Harper*, 1880.] "In ' Cousin Henry' we hav one of those curious chapters of english family history which Mr. Trollope is so skillful in reciting, and which in his hand become so nearly like leaves out of a veritable history. The disposition of a large estate is made to turn upon the mislaying and virtual concealment of a will, by which incident the wishes of the testator ar frustrated, and Cousin Henry is allowed to enjoy a good fortune instead of the nice and pretty Isabel for whom it was intended. But not 'enjoys,' for Cousin Henry's conscience givs him no peace while he guiltily possesses the secret of the will's hiding place, and not until its discovery do things rit themselvs, and all go well." [Boston "Lit. World." **1171**

COUSIN MARY [by Ma. Oliphant (Wilson) Oliphant: *Partridge & Co.*, 1888.] " introduces us to a country squire and his family..... Of course the curate marries Cousin Mary, and in spite of much mystery and conspiracy, including a madman who acts as a ghost, that well-kuon device of the novelist in difficulties, they liv more or less happily throu the remainder of the solitary volume." [Athenæum. **1172**

COUSINS. [by Lucy Bethia (Colquhoun) Walford: *Holt*, 1879.] " It is almost incredible that a rational man, in proposing for a young woman, should so muddle his meaning as to make his letter read like an offer for her older sister [compare plot of " My Neighbor Nelly," 1866] ; or that having committed such a bêtise, he should duly acquiesce in the consequences, and achieve explanation only when out of his mind with brain fever. Barring improbability, however, the plot is cleverly carried out, and the story thõroly well done and entertaining." [Boston " Literary World." **1173**

CRACK OF DOOM (The) [by W: Minto: *Harper*, 1886.] " has some originality and a good deal of britness; and had the author been able to cut away more completely from the conventionalities of the english society novel, he mit hav produced a really

noteworthy book. The story is ingenious, the thread on which it hangs — viz., the approach of a comet to the earth — original, and the intrigues with stock-market, love, and society, of an adventurer, personating an imaginary austrian count, ar raised to the dignity of a psychological study by the happy thôt of developing imposture into monomania. The conversations among scientific and literary people ar real and brit — such talk as does go on among them, instead of such as does duty for it in most novels; indeed the conversation is enuf above the level of the book to cause surprise." [Overland. **1174**

CRADOCK NOWELL = No. 661.

CRANFORD. [by E.. Cleghorn (Stevenson) Gaskell: *Chapman*, 1853.] "This collection of sketches should prove a permanent addition to english fiction. Possibly, it was not begun on a settled plan; but if this was the case, the author early became alive to the happy thôt pervading it; since she has wrôt it out just enuf and not too much — so as to produce a picture of manners, motivs and feelings which is perfect. Her theme, it is true, has not an iota of romance or poetry or heroism in it such as will attract lovers of excitement. There ar no wicked and hardened rich people — no eloquent and virtuous paupers in ' Cranford.' The scene is a small, drowsy town, the persons ar a few foolish and faded gentlewomen of limited incomes, moving round the young dauter of a deceased rector, as central figure, and thêir gentilities, thêir sociabilities, thêir topics, and thêir panics fill many pages. But the beauty of the book lies in this,— that our author has vindicated the ' soul of goodness ' living and breathing and working in an orbit so limited and among beings so inane and so frivolous as those whom she has displayed.

CRANFORD. "This is not a book tŏ be described or criticised ŏther than by a couple of words of adviçe—*Read it*. It is a book you should judge for yourself. If we told you it contained a story, that would be hardly true—yet read ŏnly a dozen pages, and you ar among real people, getting interested about them, affected by what affects them, and as curious tŏ kno what wil cŏme of it all as if it wer an affair of your ŏn. We should mislead you if we said that here is a book remarkable for the finish of its descriptions, the accuracy with which its characters ar drawn, the charm which it givs tŏ a variety of natural pictures of life—in short the etc., etc. which mark the good humor and hī satisfaction of the critic, quite as much as the particular merits of the writer. The real truth is that 'Cranford' contains hardly a bit of formal description from first tŏ last, that not a single person in it is thŏt worth a page of the regular drawing and cŏloring which is the novelist's stoc in trade, and that of variety it has ŏnly as much as a dul little town might at any time present you, with a parçel of not very wise old 'maids for its heroins, and, for its catastrophé, the failure of a county bank. But watch the people introduçed from chapter tŏ chapter—see them unconsciously describe themselvs as thêy reveal thêir foibles and vanities—observ, as you get tŏ kno them better, what unselfish and solid kindnesses underlie thêir silly, trivial ways —and confess that the writer of this unpretending little volume, with hardly the help of any artifiçe the novelist most relies upon, and shoing you but a group of the most ordinary people surrounded by the commonest occurrences of human life, has yet had the art tŏ interest you as by sŏmething of your ŏn experiençe, a reality you hav actually met and felt yourself the better for having knŏn ... Everybody whŏ has any business is of course ŏff tŏ the busy, commercial Drumble, distant ŏnly 20 miles, and Cranford is left tŏ a batch of faded old maids and widŏs, very poor but remarkably genteel, having a thŏro distaste for that sour-grapes— man, and tolerant ŏnly of Mr. Hoggins the surgeon and Mr. Hayter the rector as corporeal and spiritual neçessities. For a chapter or so, indeed, ŏne man dŏes sucçeed in planting himself at Cranford—and a thŏroly good man he is; but his voiçe is too large for the rooms, and his ways too brŏad and heârty for the plaçe, and, tho ŏne finds it difficult tŏ read what befalls him with unmoistened eyes, yet it is felt on the whole tŏ be better that he should disappear, no matter by what means. Miss Matilda, or Miss Matty as she is more frequently called, is quite the heroin of the book. Before it ends, we hav taken her entirely intŏ ŏur heârts—her and the whole of her little history ... It is all a pieçe of genuin truth—the reflection of a thousand such kind and blameless histories. Miss Matty is living by herself now, for sister Deborah is dead, and she has many old-fashioned prejudiçes, and silly little weaknesses and ways,—but thêre is such a riteous nature underneath them, such a true and tender heârt, such a noble regard for what is just tŏ ŏthers even at the cost of injustiçe tŏ herself—that the impression of all that human goodness, making itself felt in such simple, quiet, unromatic guise, has a thŏroly delightful effect."

[Examiner. **1175 +**

Touches of love and kindness, of simple self-sacrifice and of true womanly tenderness ar scattered throuout the record; and with no appeal and for no applause, but naturally and truthfully just as they ar found in the current of life. Then thêre is a rare humor in the airs and graces of would-be finery which the half-dozen heroins display, — in thêir total ignorance of the world, in their complacent credulity, in thêir irritable curiosity about all which touches matrimony. The main figure, Miss Matilda, is finished with an artist's hand. Her gentleness of heart and depth of affection, her conscientious and dignified sense of rit, her perpetual shelter under the precepts and counsels of beloved ones who hav gone before, — invest the character with an interest which is unique when her weakness of intellect and narrôness of training ar also considered. Thêre is not a single blemish of inconsistency to be pointed out; in short from first to last thêre is hardly a solitary incident which is not of every day occurrence. After its kind, this tale cannot be recommended too cordially." [Athenæum.] — "I first read the book when a girl in short dresses. I recently re-read the story, and am moved by the second reading to say a word in its favor. You see with stereoscopic clearness the prim little parlors, and really look in on the precise tea-parties, whêre the widoes and spinsters of the almost manless town meet so often for social enjoyment. Thêre is such a quietly eloquent plea in behalf of the "maiden ladies" underneath the little story. And our girls of to-day mit go to bible classes for many years and hear less beautiful illustrations of moral heroism than Miss Jessie Brown's sisterly devotion, and dear gentle Miss Mattie's unobtrusiv

and self-sacrificing life giv us. It would be hard to read of Miss Mattie's pathetic order to hav her caps 'somewhat in the style of the Hon. Mrs. Jameson's' without a quiver of the lips. And when the sister tells of poor Peter's life from his baby-days to his going to India, we see the boy as distinctly as he appeared to her simple, loving heart." [Corres. Boston "Lit. World." **1175** CREEDS = No. 662.

CRIPPS THE CARRIER [by R: Doddridge Blackmore: *Harper*, 1876.] "is a tale of life in a very rural town; most of its personages ar humble and rude; but the plot is unique, and the portraiture is very skilful. The hero — and the villain — is Luke Sharp, a lawyer, who devises a most startling plot to possess himself of a large estate, by abducting the dauter of Squire Ogland, with the intention of uniting her to his own son. So craftily did he lay his plans, and so propitiously did Fortune befriend him, that the missing girl was proved to be dead, and a slab erected over her remains. But some feeble forces wer at work counter to the lawyer's schemes, of which the chief instrument was Zachary Cripps, one of the most original and perfectly drawn characters we ever met in fiction. The development of the plot is gradual; but the reader's interest never flags, and the dénoument is at once hily tragical and poetically just." [Boston "Literary World." **1176** CROOKED PATH (A). [by "Mrs. Alexander," i. e., Annie (French) Hector: *Holt*, 1889.] "Mrs. Alexander's novels used to be excellent reading, but thêy ar groing poorer. 'A Crooked Path' is the story of a stolen will, and neither the plot nor the characters rise above the most commonplace sensational level. It is long drawn out, and much padded with irrelevant matter. It is one of those stories which hav no raison d'être, and leaves the impression of having bored the writer as well as the reader. A brilliant writer like Mrs. Alexander should not be forced to grind out a new novel every year. Her books ar losing their freshness, and very soon will hav few, if any, readers." [Boston "Literary World." **1177**

CROSS OF HONOR (The). [by ANNIE (THOMAS) CUDLIP: 1864.] "We congratulate Miss Thomas that she has turned aside from the path towards which in her former novels she so much inclined, and has in this one given us a charming story of domestic life, in which the interest is sustained throuout without the aid of vulgar sensation, horse-slang, or demi-mondeism; whêre the characters, with very slit exception, speak and move precisely as the same sort of people mit speak and move in every-day life, and whêre the plot, without being complex, is so well managed that, by apparently natural incidents, the several personages of the story ar brôt into close connexion, and the whole is invested with the air of a real history." [Round Table. **1178**

—. SAME ("MARRIED AT LAST"), *Peterson*, 1866.

CULMSHIRE FOLK. [*Macmillan*, 1873.] "The women's warfare, with its ingenious littleness, its unceasing activity, and its direful collateral effects upon the unoffending Doctor, is hily entertaining, especially when Mrs. Dimble, smarting under a repulse from Lady Culmshire, falls foul of Cecil Stanley's objectionable aunt, and her pet methodist minister....On the whole, the Culmshire folk seem to hav had a tolerably pleasant life, enlivened with considerably more funny people and good stories, than folk out of Culmshire hav to boast

of. They ar occasionally unhappy in the course of the 3 volumes, but they ar never bored, and they interest one about all their small affairs as small communities cannot interest, unless they be cleverly drawn." [Spectator. **1179**

CURATE IN CHARGE (The). [by MA. OLIPHANT (WILSON) OLIPHANT: *Macmillan*, 1876.] "Those who like novels of character will not be disappointed in this. Thêre is little incident in the story, the whole action of which is confined to a country parish, of which Mr. St. John, the gentlest and most unworldly of men, has been for 20 years curate in charge.....The absentee rector dies abroad, and the home of many years is threatened. The living is in the hands of a college, and naturally falls to the lot of the next clerical fello..... So agreeable and cultured a young parson mit hav been thôt to hav a soul above a country parish, but 'a man cannot liv for china,' and so it came about that Mr. Mildmay came down to Brentburn, and brôt upon him the indignation of Cicely St. John. How could she help but feel it? 'It is injustice, if it was the Queen herself who did it. But perhaps papa is rit; if he does not come some one else would come. And he has a heart. I do not hate him so much as I did last nit.' Herein is the gist of the story. Cicely finds he has a heart, and the process of that discovery is the staple of a charming tale." [Athenæum.] — " 'The Curate in Charge' is one of the simplest but most perfect of Mrs. Oliphant's shorter tales. Thêre is only the slitest scrap of narrativ; but how fresh, how tender, how true to nature it is — a village idyl, in which the simple english life and the simple english landscape ar touched with a softly pathetic lit. It is a distinct conception — absolutely graceful because absolutely simple — like a soap-bubble or a greek play or a Rafaelle. There is nothing by the way or out of the way; nothing which does not lend itself to the progressiv development of the history. If life could record itself as on a fotografer's glass we kno that this is the record which it would leave; thêre is the unambitious exactness, the homely sincerity, the inevitableness. And yet thêre is something more, — thêre is the imagination which realizes the immense pathos of human life, — of life, that is to say, into which no special adventure or misadventure enters, but which simply as *life* is so fundamentally sad, so intrinsically a tragedy." [Blackwood's. **1180**

DADDY DARWIN'S DOVECOTE. [by JULIANA HORATIA (GATTY) EWING: *Roberts*, 1885.] "From exaggerations and discords between intention and execution, it is like turning to the perfection of a flower to open Mrs. Ewing's last sketch. 'Daddy Darwin's Dovecote' is less than 'Jackanapes' only in that its simpler, homelier theme does not offer quite so full felicity of subject. How well done was 'the setting of a wild graft on an old standard' is told from the talk of two old gaffers gossiping on a sunny wall. Thêre is the same delitful, suggestiv commentary in homely proverb or tender household word as made her earlier story a poem." [Nation.] — "This slit but very pretty little story has about it a delitful breath of rural english life. Jack March is an Edgeworthian hero of probity, industry and thrift, and his progress to prosperity and happiness is quite what mit be deemed the legitimate result of such morality. Thêre is, moreover, a sweeter and purer strain of feeling in his story than is always found in such deductions from utilitarian filosofy." [Ameri. **1181**

DAISY AND THE EARL [by CONSTANCE HOWELL: *Tinsley*, 1877.] "is a pretty story, which leaves a distinct and pleasing impression. Daisy is a very fresh, unsofisticated country girl, of gentle birth; the Earl a somewhat blasé young man. She falls in love with him, and lets out her secret in the most artless way possible, never fancying for a moment but that he returns her affection. The scene of this disclosure, the Earl's surprise, concealed by him almost instantaneously under a well-assumed appearance of interest, but not quite enuf to deceive the girl, her shame and grief and courageous assertion of her dignity, — all this is very prettily told. We recommend the reader to follo the story to its close. He will not think the time misspent." [Spectator. **1182**

DAISY CHAIN (THE). [by C.. M.. YONGE: *J. W. Parker*, 1857.] "To young ladies generally, whose sunny ringlets confess to teens, perhaps even to those presumably young ladies who hav ceased to count birthdays, the 'Heir of Redclyffe' and other equally nice and pretty tho somewhat lengthy stories which hav been floing from the same facile and agreeable pen ar treasures of harmless intellectual recreation. We hav heard of a young lady who is in the habit of perusing that bepraised tale continuously and perennially, reading it over and over again as often as she arrives at the last sentence. 'The Daisy Chain' is more for the delit of that 'epidemic sect' of enthusiastic but severe young dévotes, who are addicted to the cultivation of pastoral theology, with the sister sciences of gothic architecture and mediæval upholstery." [Leader. **1183**

DAMOCLES [by MA. VELEY: *Smith*, 1882.] "is a story interesting, even fascinating, from first to last, — unique and picturesque in conception and execution, clever all throu, and often powerful; but difficult to criticise fairly, without greatly impairing the dramatic effect of the first-half of the book to those who ar reading it. They, however, must accept this warning, if they wish to enjoy it thōroly, and take our verdict as sufficient, without reading further, that it is a story which richly repays the trouble of the reader. The style is simple, forcible, and refined, and the english perfect..... However, the reader of this notice must not suppose that the story is all sad. The conversations ar lively and most amusing, the minor characters cheerful, and their little individualities lâfable; but the humorous passages depend too much on the context for quotation. The descriptions of scenery, and the few words here and thêre which giv reality to shades of color and to landscape, ar delicate. Altogether, 'Damocles' is a delitful book, and we may confidently affirm that not only did the sword never fall, but that the fear of it passed out of Rachel's busy life leaving only a shade of sadness behind." [Spectator. **1184**

DANIEL DERONDA [by "G: ELIOT" i. e., M.. A.. (Evans) Cross: *Blackwood*, 1876.] "is an æsthetically melancholy story. One groes sober over it. It has few stained windoes throu which strays the lit of humor and geniality. It has a gloomy interior, suggestiv of solemnity and gloom. It offers us no lâfter, few cakes and ale; and, in this deficiency, it fails as a picture of hi english life. In point of characterization, it is far beyond comparison. Deronda himself, if not quite true to nature, is absolutely unique. The influence of the suspieiou that he nurses hebrew blood in his veins, casts its sombre shado over his whole life. We see it in the habits of his

daily walk, in his taste and tendencies; and it has its most conspicuous manifestations in the memorable intervues with his mother. The sweet tenderness of his nature attracts us, while his sombre mien and manner repel. At his introduction, one likes him. His treatment of the wilful Gwendolen, on their first meeting, is simply admirable,—cool, gentlemanly, earnest, yet reserved. We pass on to Gwendolen's home life; to its hypocrisy, to its pretensions, its strivings between fashionable exigencies and stern necessity. We get a glimps of this rash young girl's nature in her flirtation with Reginald; and the idiosyncrasies of Mr. and Mrs. Gascoigne and thêir dauter stand out in clear relief in the complications which result from this callo affectional entanglement. The other members of Gwendolen's household appeal to us with no special force. She is queen among them, — nay, a tyrant; and, loving her mother with all the force of her strong nature, sets up her proud self, always icy and immovable, toward her. [Boston "Literary World."]
" What novels ôt to be,' she declared, 'is something you can turn to for pleasure and amusement — to forget one's troubles, and to relax one altogether. Something like dear Miss Austen's which one can read when one has a headache, and which make one lâf. I'm sure I love Miss Bates, and Mrs. Elton, and Mr. Collins, and all those dear, ridiculous people. It's a perfect delit to get among such old friends. But as for 'DANIEL DERONDA,' it's as dull as a sermon, and 50 times more difficult to understand. And I believe everyone agrees with me in thêir secret souls, only they dare not say so in this intense age. Call that a novel! I don't think myself stupid, but I declare I've read a whole

367

page without the words conveying a single glimmering of an idea..... Well, I don't quarrel with people writing filosofical, or metafysical, or any other sort of learned treatises; make them as deep as you like, and let learned people read them; but don't call them novels, and delude me into taking them up. Now her early ones, I grant you, ar novels — simple and full of human interest. I allow the genius in *Adam Bede*, and *Mill on the Floss*, and *Silas Marner*, but since she turned intense, I beg not to be forced to read any more of her books." [Character in novel by Mrs. H. Martin. **1185**

DARK COLLEEN (The) = No. 668.

DARK AND FAIR, See "One of Us."

DAUGHTER OF FIFE (A) [by Amelia Edith (Huddleston) Barr: 1886.] "is sweet and wholesom, and has a kind of virile energy and crispness which is very attractiv. The scene opens at the fishing hamlet of Pittenloch, the tiniest of towns, a place almost unapproachable except by the sea. These fisher-folk had characters which had been molded by their surroundings, and wer intensely religious, holding to the belief, ways, and modes of speech of their ancestors..... Not the least merit of this pure, uplifting, and charming story is the old fashioned love, the simple, honest wooing and winning, without the analysis and self-questioning of so many modern novels. Mrs. Barr's style is clear and strong; her literary workmanship that of an artist; her spirit, sentiment, teaching, sound and sweet; she has the real staying power, and knoes what to say and what to leave unsaid. Given all these qualities, and a unique scene with individuality of characters, we hav an uncommonly picturesque and

admirable novel." [Boston "Literary World." **1186**

DAUGHTER OF HETH (A). [by W: Black: 1860.] "Thêre ar two specialties in Mr. Black's writings for which we must always be grateful. The first is a strain of true chivalric feeling towards women and their relations with men, and the second is the great beauty of some of his descriptions of scenery. In his best works, such as the ' Daughter of Heth,' this tender feeling for women is very noticeable; and the account of the refining influence of Coquette, the heroin, upon the disorderly household and ruf children of the Scotch rector, is most cleverly and even pathetically painted. Indeed, this is by far the finest of Mr. Black's works, and the only one, in our opinion, which can be thōroly praised as a whole. [Spectator. **1187**

DAUGHTER OF THE GODS (A) [by J.. Stanley: *Hurst*, 1886.] "is very pretty. That is a description which specially suits the easy-floing, love-making story, in which the author is disposed on the whole to take cheerful vues of life, or at any rate to make nice people happy forever afterwards. The divinely tall and fair young lady is one Verena, who falls into the clutches of a villain at the age of 16, and subsequently meets an ideally perfect middle-aged man, whose love is proof against every strain, and whose confidence in Verena is finally rewarded. The dauter of the gods endures muêh sorro, and all throu the story thêre ar stern black-bearded kings, and one or two sharp-tunged queens, waiting tó see her die. Amongst other good points in the book there ar many clever little feminin touches which make the female characters stand out and liv. The heroin's spiteful friend Kate, who ensnares her future husband on the Underground Railway, is a capital sketch." [Athenæum. • **1188**

DAUGHTER OF THE PEOPLE (A) [by GEORGIANA MARION (CRAIK) MAY: *Harper*, 1887.] "is a pretty and healthful story, in which the dauter of the people nobly givs up the young artist who is nobly willing to marry her, while in the end another noble young lady comes into her kingdom. Not the least excellent point in the story is the evident fact that, fine as was the soul of the dauter of the people, it was a great deal better and wiser that the mésalliance did not take place. The climax of many stories on the plan of 'That Lass o' Lowrie's' is romantic and effectiv, but in life any mésalliance is to be regretted, and Mrs. May in her story has tried to be just to both sides of the question." [Critic. **1189**

DAVID ARMSTRONG. [*Blackwood*, 1880.] "The most striking character in the book is that of the hero. Whether he is a study from life or not, we do not pretend to say, but, at all events, he seems to be a study from human nature; tho he may never hav existed, yet thêre is no reason that he mit not hav done so. The genius in humble life has been frequently represented in fiction, but we think he has never been treated more satisfactorily than in the present instance. The hero is no ethereal being, with hectic cheeks and soul too big or brain too busy for the body which it wears out; he is, on the contrary, a giant in body as in mind, tall, handsom, and strong. Brave, tender-hearted, honest, clever, never appearing in the faintest degree conscious of his superiority to other men, he goes strait on his way, inventing and working at models in the intervals of his regular occupation, not out of vanity, or — until the last — out of

any very definit desire to benefit his fello men, but merely becaus, when an idea comes to him and takes hold of him, he can not help trying to carry it out..... But it is not only as an inventor that David Armstrong is portrayed. We ar shown his strong, earnest, simple, impressionable nature going throu various fases of life, and gradually molded by its trials and temptations.....All the scenes and characters ar taken from the poor, and giv us the impression of being drawn by one who is not only a genuin student of human nature, but also so sympathetic with humanity as to appreciate the good which is to be found everywhere in it. Consequently, we hav no picture of utterly repulsiv vice and villainy; and even the evil Peter Dobson has a redeeming touch of love for his idiot son. The characters ar • natural and well-drawn, especially the stern, yet loving, old mother, and the quiet, self-contained, unselfish Hannah Watson, with her gray life of hopeless love, and unceasing labor for others." [Spectator. **1190**

DAVID COPPERFIELD [by C: DICKENS: 1850.] "is the most finished and natural of his works; it is more than good. The boyhood of the hero; the scene in the church; the death of his mother; the story of Peggotty — poor Little Em'ly; that touching love, so true, so perfect, and so delicate and pure, which the ruf old fisherman has for his lost niece, cannot be surpassed. The mello strength and matured vigor of style, the modest ingenuousness of Copperfield's relation of his progress in literature, supposed truthfully to portray Dickens' career; the child-wife, her death, and David's final love for Agnes; all rush upon our memory, and put forward their claims to be admired. The original characters ar all good, and the

369

family of Micawber form a group as original as was ever drawn by Mr. Dickens. The dark and weird character of Rosa Dartle, and the revolting one of Uriah Heep, ar the only painful ones in the book. But they ar full of fine touches of nature, which also illumin the dark drawing of the Murdstone." [London Review. **1191**

DAVID ELGINBROD. [by G: MacDonald: *Hurst*, 1863, — Boston, *Loring*, 1869.] "D: Elginbrod is a Scotch peasant, such a one as Burns would hav gloried in, dignified, self-respectful, expressing himself always with force and vigor, and embodying a deep sentiment of piety in words which speak the simple needs and aspirations of his heart. The peculiarity of manner, and the veneration of good blood and ancient lineage inherent in the Scottish breast, ar made auxiliary to the development of this character, which is stamped, as it wer, with the impress of reality by the use of appropriate dialect. The old man's dauter is an exquisit sketch, inheriting the hier aspirations and deeper feelings which lay at the base of David's own nature, delicately reserved and self-abnegatory, but strong in her devotion to principle ; a ministering angel to her suffering friend, and worthy of the love which crowns her happiness at last." [Round Table. **1192**

DAYS OF MY LIFE. [by Ma. Oliphant (Wilson) Oliphant: *Hurst*, 1857.] "Hester Southcote is the dauter of a country gentleman; she is introduced walking home, when 2 strangers meet her. One of them is Edgar Southcote, her cousin, long supposed to be dead, who is coming to claim his patrimony and disinherit her. Expelled, with her father, from the Cottiswoode estate — on which he had long lived — she becomes the companion of his morose retirement. He is a reserved, harsh man, who has sapped every source of human felicity, and whose cynical pride is an hereditary taint in the character of Hester. After a laps of some years, proposals of marriage reach her from her cousin, and she rejects them, fancying they hav been offered in pity. Hester enters into society, and meets Harry Edgar, a gentleman after her kind, to whom her affections ar speedily surrendered, and who, ere long, is a suitor at her father's house. Of course, he is no other than the rejected cousin under an assumed name — but tho to the reader the artifice is, from the first, transparent, Hester is deceived, and the improbability is not, perhaps, too striking for a novel. The lady becomes Edgar's bride. Upon this event reposes the entire structure of the story. Hester, after a brief honeymoon, is bròt to her future home — the Hall of Cottiswoode — and discovers the deceit which has been practised upon her. Upbraidings follo. Hester, poisoned by her inherited pride, refuses to liv in a home to which she has been lured; but, after many wretched days, returns to her husband with an heir to Cottiswoode. Such is the story. The author writes with her usual fine capacity for the picturesque, her preference for simplicity, her knoledge of certain types of character, and her invariable good sense, good feeling, and good taste. No part of the narrativ is uninteresting, and the reader is not bewildered by boundless contiguities of digression." [Athenæum. **1193**

DEAD SECRET (The) = No. 671.

DEAN AND HIS DAUGHTER. [by A. C. Phillips: *Ward & Downey*, 1887.] "The heroin (who tells her story) is not without good points. Even for the reader she possesses a certain indefinable attraction ; while a round half dozen or so of 'gilded youth' of different types ar completely 'bōled over' by her. It is felt that she is beautiful, but thêre is not a syllable of description concerning her appearance. The poor creature has a singularly hard time of it on the whole; but the easy-going filosofy which carries her along is greatly in her favor. A friend and companion, one Ethel Fortescue, encourages her to a still closer walk with joy, and a calmer, if not more heavenly, frame. The said Ethel is a rather battered woman of the world and of a racy conversation and habit.... But she makes an excellent friend in an emergency, and sticks to Miriam bravely through good report and ill." [Athenæum. **1194**

DEAR LADY DISDAIN. [by JUSTIN MCCARTHY: *Grant & Co.*, 1875.] "The situation is cleverly devised, and we must confess that, having ourselves gone very near to falling in love with Lady Disdain, we may perhaps take a prejudiced vue of the way in which she acts towards her lover..... The book is never dull; the incidents ar well woven into the story; and, tho the plot is not intricate, the interest is excellently kept up, and the book is brit and healthful throuout." [Athenæum.] — "Mr. Justin McCarthy has not always succeeded in writing the best novels in the world, but his last one — 'Dear Lady Disdain'— is certainly deserving of commendation. The heroin, whose nickname givs the title to the book, is an attractiv creature, as honest as possible, with a sort of manly generosity and heartiness which distinguish her from most heroins, and bring her close to some real human beings. The name, Lady Disdain, does not suit her over well, for, so far from being disdainful, she has a very pleasing comradship with every one she meets. The men ar reasonably well drawn; the

successful lover is somewhat vague and misty, but the aspiring barber, Natty Cramp, and the lover of old china, Ronald Vidal, ar well set before the reader — the former especially. Throuout, Mr. McCarthy has shōn his earnest desire to improve, and his knoledge of the right method by holding his hand and not overdoing either the unattractiv or the ridiculous side of what he has undertaken to describe. In what he has written about this country this discretion is very noticeable, and he has avoided the easy temptation to make too much of its lack of fascination and rawness. Even Natty Cramp, whom many story-writers would hav blackened with obloquy, is treated with great fairness, and there is something very pleasing in the lack of exaggeration in describing the woman's-rits advocate — Miss Sibyl Jansen." [Nation. **1195**

DEEMSTER (THE) = No. 672.

DEERBROOK. "I hav recorded a list of the novels that I deem to hav been of use to me in the formation of character..... They ar 'Robinson Crusoe,' 'Helen,' 'DEERBROOK,' by Miss Martineau, 'Jane Eyre,' 'Coningsby,' 'The Heir of Redclyffe,' 'The Wide, Wide World,' 'Pride and Prejudice,' Dickens' 'Christmas Carol,' and 'Pendennis,' or any other of Thackeray you choose." [E : Everett Hale. **1196**

DELICATE GROUND [N.Y.], See "ORDEAL FOR WIVES."

DELICIA [by BEATRICE MAY BUTT: *Holt*, 1879.] "is charming; lo in tone and careful in construction, it describes a little corner of the world and a few people with uncommon freshness and originality. The dull London square whêre the action passes is a piece of reality, and the lives led thêre, with their blunders, retrievable and irretrievable, their weakness and strength, their hopes

371

HISTORY OF DAVID GRIEVE, (The) [by M.. A.. (ARNOLD) WARD: *Macmillan & Co.*, 1892.] "is an account of the life of a man from boyhood tŏ maturity. David is introduced tŏ us as a child in the north of England. The scene is afterward changed tŏ Manchester, whêre it remains, except during an expedition tŏ Paris, til the end ... 'David Grieve' is partly a religious book: it folloes David throu the changes in his belief, as wel as throu his temporal fortunes. Here it is that Mrs. Ward shōs her grêatest power; just as the religious thôt in 'Robert Elsmere' is what gave it its grêat interest. But David's thôts and aspirations wil not interest the reader as Robert Elsmere's did. Thêre is throuoŭt a sense that, tho you hav never read just this before, you hav read in ōther books sōmething very like it. It maintains the interest throuoŭt better than 'Robert Elsmere;' it is more natural; and its characters ar, perhaps, more real. But it dōes not appeal, as 'Robert Elsmere' did, tŏ everyōne whŏ has thôt over his religious belief, and doubted and believed and doubted again." [Commonwealth.]—"All whŏ hav read "David Grieve" with intelligent thôtfulness can not fail tŏ agree that the impression it leaves is ōne of depressing disappointment. While the workmanship and what might be called the spiritual texture of the book ar just as fine as in 'Robert Elsmere', the touch even more firm and sure, and certain portions of it far more brilliant than anything tŏ be found in the latter, we can hardly as a whole look upon it as much better than a failure. ... It is all interesting and fascinating from the first, and the author brings enthusiasm tŏ her task too, yet, tŏ quote her words, it sōmehow 'all dies intŏ space, like the flaming corona of the sun," and leaves no mark or lasting effect of any kind behind it. The most brilliant portion of the book is beyond question the **Paris** episode, and no ōne with even the spark of an artist in his or her composition can fail tŏ be delited with the general treatment of it all. The glimpses given here and thêre of Paris, of its light and cōlor and gayety and joyousness and general charm, ar admirable, and giv ōne a better picture of the grêat and wonderful city than pages of description. True, the general situation, the relation of David tŏ Elsie, is bad enuf, quite as much so as in the better French novels, but with what exquisit taste and delicaçy and refinement it is all handled! After this, however, the story seems tŏ flatten out. We dŏ not think it necessary that David should repent those few weeks in Paris in saccloth and ashes all the rest of his life. They wer tŏ be deplored of course, as every fall from perfect purity and rectitude is tŏ be deplored,—ōur hearts ar sōmehow full of sorro for him,—but we can not think that he committed an offense past all pardon. For on his part, at least, it was not a surrender tŏ a mere attraction of the senses; his heart was in it, he was not infringing on the rights of any ōne else, and moreover he was not only willing but anxious tŏ marry and devote his life tŏ the woman, if she had consented. But for his marriage with a woman so inferior as Lucy, whŏm moreover he did not lōve, (and surely a lōveless marriage is not the least immoral relation in the world) thêre seems no excuse and no reason whatever." ["Stuart Sterne." **1192 k**

and failures, ar genuin. Miss Butt is a keen but gentle observer of human nature, and the pauses and levels in her plot ar true to life. Betty Stevens is a very attractiv and very original creature, whose future rather wês on the reader, and Delicia, with her gentle weakness, rectitude, and ingrain refinement, is delitful." [Nation.] — It "is remarkable for its delicate truthfulness, its moderation and simplicity, its occasional wit, naif and irresistible, and thöroly refined, also for a certain quaint but hi-bred plainness of manner, a blending of perfect polish with utter absence of parade.....The characters ar very deftly balanced and discriminated, their destinies most naturally intertwined. There is not a melodramatic situation in the whole book, hardly, one would say, a dramatic one, until it is remembered how seldom the retiring author speaks in her ön person, how entirely and with what entire clearness the tale is told by the dramatis personæ." [Atlantic. **1197**

DENNIS DONNE [by ANNIE (THOMAS) CUDLIP: *Tinsley*, 1864.] "is a cheerful, entertaining story, dealing with more tangible matters than the distresses of extreme refinement. The writer has evidently a strong sense of humor, and enjoys unmasking the weakness of some of our conventional batteries, and exhibiting the mean compound of spite and petty jealousies, which is often their chief ammunition. The heroin, a beautiful, scheming adventuress, who fancies herself too poor to carry a conscience or a heart, contrives to entrap and marry a peer by a method as ingenious as it is novel. Her character is well drawn throuout; but even better is that of Mrs. Donne, her rival in beauty and coquetry, who outrages the moral sense of a cathedral town by

appearing with the new bishop in her train, and entirely subjugates, for the time, the bishop's chaplain, thèreby causing the rupture of his engagement to a harmless young lady, very respectable, but wholly uninteresting, and suffering sadly from comparison with the radiant lady who could giv appreciativ sympathy and words which fire ambitiou, instead of flat matter-of-fact congratulations. The real heroin is Stephanie Fordyce, as honest and truehearted a damsel as the others ar false and scheming, and who is given, with true poetical justice, to the chaplain aforesaid — the only man in the book who deservs her." [Westminster Review. **1198**

DERRICK VAUGHAN, NOVELIST [by "EDNA LYALL," i. e., Ada Ellen Bayly: *Appleton*, 1889.] "like so many heroes of women novelists, is too near perfection. However, Derrick's really noble traits and his renunciation of self and of the girl he loved, from a sense of duty to his disreputable old father, command both pity and admiration. Freda Merrifield, the girl, does not for a long time comprehend the position, and underrates him, but discovers her mistake before it is too late, and the brave, loyal, patient, long-suffering Derrick is rewarded in the end. Not the least interesting portions of the story ar those where the author reveals something of her personality in Derrick's aspirations and trials in writing his novels." [Boston "Literary World." **1199**

DESPERATE REMEDIES. [by T: HARDY: *Holt*, 1874.] "It is rit to say to such readers of ours as formed hopes of Mr. Hardy's work from 'A Pair of Blue Eyes,' that this is hardly worth their reading. The heroin has the charm of girlish naturalness which he contrives to impart to all his women, and thère ar strong impressions of character in other persons of the story. But they ar not mastered by his imagination; they feebly change into something else, at times; and the plot is a wearisom confusion of motivs and purposes, in which thêre is little color or definitness or probability." [Atlantic. **1200**

DIANA OF THE CROSSWAYS [by G : MEREDITH : *Harper*, 1885.] "easily takes the first place among Mr. Meredith's clever, subtle, and often baffling novels, from the fascination of its central figure and extraordinary vitality and movement of the whole story. The author has chosen a theme which stirs alike sympathy and cûriosity. His heroin is no graceful abstraction labeled with all feminin graces and virtues, but a real woman whose daily life, crying necessities, problems, loves, friendships, triumfs, and humiliations ar clearly revealed to us: not only by the skill of the romancer, but from our traditions of that dazzling, charming dauter of Sheridan's knön to all the world as Caroline Norton, and who is the prototype of Diana Warwick. The story shöes the career of a woman of unusual wit, beauty, and fascination married to an uncongenial husband, who, soon discovering that he commanded neither the affection nor respect of his wife, grew antagonistic, then jealous, and finding suspicious circumstances attending her intimacy with a man of hi rank and position sued for a divorce. He did not prove his case, and Diana Warwick remained legally a wife, altho separated from her husband. She supported herself by her pen, kept up a charming and costly little house, and drew about her a choice and brilliant coterie of friends. Diana is a character who exactly suits Mr. Meredith's powers. She is a true woman, exuberant, incoherent, unequal;

she perpetually utters epigrams, gets off witticisms which convulse her hearers, and altho her epigrams ar labored and her wit tortuous, we see the dimple about her charming lips and the lit in her irish eyes, and accept the sky-rockets as a rich illumination." [American.] — ...." Thêre ar many who so frankly regard Mr. Meredith's novels as ' told by an idiot, full of sound and fury, signifying nothing,' that total extinction of fiction would seem to them preferable to a reconstruction in harmony with his theories. On the other hand, thêre are some who love him, laud him as ' one of the breed of Shakspere and Molière ' and in whose breasts the brutal insensibility of the larger faction rouses the angriest passions. It is a case whêre the security of the middle way tempts one to brave its imputed ignominy. Dispassionate judgment suggests that few authors hav Mr. Meredith's store of wise, far-reaching ideas, and that for expressing them obscurely he is beyond compare. Then his work cannot be separated from an obtrusiv personality. By a wanton interpolation of venom in the narrativ, thêre is ever present a sour, malicious being who blits delicate fancy and poisons the tip of the shaft flying strait to the core of existence. A perpetual display of ill temper is not excused even by his honest, scathing contempt for sham virtue, sham decency, and for all the shuffling hypocrisies which the world heaps into a rampart of defense against the shock to self-love consequent on looking fairly at the facts of life and the mainsprings of action." [Nation.] — " It is full of mannerisms, ruf and unshaped in parts, tedious and even dull in others, but throu this outlying crust of superwordiness gleam here and thêre the facets of one of nature's jewels. Diana is truly a fascinating creature, whom we see in side-lits, as it wer, never full-face; and she is palpitating with life, overfloing with witty sayings, a centre of resplendent womanhood. " [Boston "Literary World." **1201**

DICK CHICHESTER. [by E. M. Roach: *Arrowsmith*, 1890.] The scene "is a type of that rural England of which Barsetshire is the most famous example, and out of its politics and society and love-making a very pleasant tho somewhat placid story has been evolved. The presence of but one villain would have lent animation to the plot, for as it stands the only obstacles in the way of the happiness of the principal characters ar put thêre by themselves." [Athenæum. **1202**

DICK NETHERBY [by Lucy Bethia (Colquhoun) Walford: *Holt*, 1882.] " is a plain story of temptation, the yielding, the punishment, and the final struggle into a new life of the hero, a humble country lad..... The side figures ar drawn with that same lit, accurate touch which gave us Lord Suffrenden in ' Mr. Smith '; and in ' Troublesome Daughters' Marjorie, the brîtest, truest portrait of a girl of the period which has ever been painted." [Nation. **1203**

DICK'S WANDERINGS. [by Julian Sturgis: *Houghton*, 1882.] "If this open-hearted young hero, Dick Hartland, is too typically british to be knön to us precisely as he is fotografed, — with his obsequious tenants, and his ambition to educate a constituency — he is true enuf after a particularly charming fashion, to world-wide human nature, to arouse much sympathy, and to waken an especial interest. The history of Dick's boyhood days is related at the outset, with sufficient minuteness to sho him then the father of the man. An affectionate, quick-witted, self-reliant young fello, he is generous to a fault, and pure-

minded as a woman. He groes, studies, and investigates unhurriedly, and finally falls in love with a pretty american girl. A series of small misunderstandings keep the lovers apart for many uncomfortable months; but fate is kind at last, and a roseate glo of happiness illumins the final pages of the book, to everybody's satisfaction." [Californian. **1204**

DINGY HOUSE AT KENSINGTON (The). [*Cassell*, 1881.] "The heroin is a comely, brit, affectionate, rather commonplace girl, whom the writer introduces with the remark that ' her name was Polly, and her nose turned up.' Her career is complicated between the attentions of two lovers, and the impracticable selfishness of a meagre and miserly father..... Robert is an admirable study of the honest, limited, commonplace, obtuse, warm-hearted youth, whose ambition never looks beyond a partnership in ' the firm,' and whose ideas of love and marriage ar of the strictly domestic, humdrum, and unromantic order. He is manifestly unfitted to do justice to Polly's requirements, and thêre is much good comedy in the description of their relations; and when it finally appears that the marriage is fated to take place, we ar distressed on his account scarcely less than on hers. The situation here is so sympathetically felt by the author that she makes the reader share her feeling; and all our respect for Robert's moral character, and our liking for his natural goodness do not prevent us from protesting with Polly against the inevitable woollen comforter which he persists in wearing round his neck, or from understanding how it was that ' his cheery voice always carried dismay to Polly's heart.' Richard Brandford, the other hero, tho well introduced and described, does not impress us nearly so much, in spite of his

374

aristocratic qualities. We ar told that he is reserved, clever, handsom, and imperturbable; but we ar nowhere told that he does anything worth a man's doing or a woman's loving. This, of course, does not prevent Polly's loving him; and we ar bound to say that the incident is probable enuf, and further, that we accept it with the better grace, inasmuch as it affords opportunity for the development of some very charming traits in Polly herself. Richard Brandford 'never said a word that her heart could find food in remembering; but in refusing to let her conquer him, he conquered her.'" [Spectator. **1205**

DISHONORED. [by " THEO. GIFT," i. e., Dora Henrietta (Havers) Boulger: *Hurst*, 1890.] " The subject — the mental agony suffered by a peculiarly noble-minded girl on discovering that thêre is a stain upon her birth — is fruitful of pathos, and if the writer shõed as much power in developing a story as in imagining individual scenes and in sketching characters, Theo. Gift's charming book mit hav secured a more than efemeral success. The portrait of the heroin is both winsom and vivid, and thêre ar some scenes — especially the one whêre she is compelled to listen to the pleadings of Mrs. Rice on behalf of her love-stricken son — which blend pathos with humor so ably that they mit pass for the work of a more ambitions novelist than we take Theo. Gift to be. The descriptions of Stoneham — the hïly self-respecting Stonehamites — and especially of the good Nonconformist folk who attend the chapel to admire, in an intensly critical spirit, the Rev. John Rice's sermons, would hav been more remarkable than they ar had they preceded and not folloed Mrs. Oliphant's marvelous descriptions of the Nonconformist world in ' Salem

Chapel'....Old Mr. Benison, the father of the heroin, who underneath his ruggedness of manner hides a natufe so loving that his life is wasted in the forlorn hope of the return of the wife who has betrayed him, is sketched in a few pages with that easy strength which only an entire sympathy with the character depicted can lend to any writer. It, indeed, lifts the story into literature." [Athenæum. **1206**

DISSOLVING VIEWS. [by LENORA BLANCHE (ALLEYNE) LANG: *Harper*, 1884.] " The author doubtless had herself in mind when she makes her heroin say, ' Any book I wrote would inevitably be for women. The moment a man took it up he would drop it. I kno a man drops a woman's book as if he had taken up a jelly-fish.' Still, the story is quite worth while as a lively picture of a London season. A good deal of the talk is evidently borroed, not made, and the diversions of the moment — greek plays, cricket, æsthetic teas, and all the rest, ar well set forth. The heroin is engaged to the wrong man, but marries the rit one." [Nation. **1207**

DISTURBING ELEMENT (THE). [by C.. M.. YONGE: *Appleton*,1879.] " A wonder among books; a tale from Miss Yonge in which saints' days ar hardly mentioned — daily service not at all; in which thêre is not even one of those noble beings, compounds of the loftiest birth and the finest sentiments, whose existences find their nutriment in the history of the peerage and ' the ritual year of England's Church '; in which no description of the exquisit anguish endured by those distant descendants of noble families who ar obliged to contaminate their lives by trade rends the soul of American readers. ' The Disturbing Element ' is a simple, natural story — telling of the home-work of two old ladies who help the lassies of a little seaside town, first to a sense of their ignorant inaccuracy, then to a little careful and thōro work, and to the various mental and moral rectifications which attend on work well done." [Nation. **1208**

DITA. [by Margaret Majendie : *Blackwood*, 1877.] " Dita, or Perdita, is the pet name of the heroin of a rather pretty story. A benevolent bookseller adopts the orfan heiress of a Highland family, disōned throu the treachery of an ambitious uncle. He persuades his mother, from whom he conceals the proof of the child's legitimacy, to countenance the wrong he does to the memory of his brother and the wife he secretly married. Lady Grisel is rather a pathetic character, but the author's tender-heartedness seems to hav prevented her working out her original conception, which, at the outset, appears to hav projected a sterner and more tragic figure. As it is, the lady's womanliness overpowers her pride, and what the story gains in pleasantness it loses in grandeur." [Athenæum. **1209**

DIVIDED [*Remington*, 1881.] " is a simple story of every day life, life in good society, amongst refined people in easy circumstances. The heroin is a charming, wayward girl, who loves whêre her mother thinks she ôt not, and weakly marries a richer man at her mother's bidding. The hero tries to follo a similar course, but fails on the eve of his wedding day, and in less than a year his first love is a wido. From this point a commonplace story would advance towards a commonplace ending, but ' Divided' is not a commonplace story. The heroin will not use her liberty as a well regulated heroin mit be expected to do. The girl's character is only begin-

ning to unfold, and, as it is worth the reader's while to study the process for himself, no more need be said about it here. Opinions may differ as to the poetical justice of the conclusion of this story, but it is, at any rate, sufficiently fresh and unhackneyed, and at the same time natural, to make it pleasant reading." [Athenæum. **1210**

DR. HERMIONE. [*Blackwood*, 1890.] " A clever story this, and eminently readable. If the author's intention was to sho that feminin aspirations after professional success ar apt to come o grief, ' Dr. Hermione ' is a decided success. Clever, enthusiastic, devoted to her work, and possessed of means which set her above the difficulties that encumber most women in her position, Hermione, it is easy to see, will be a failure as a fysician. She falls in love with a young man who can hardly be deemed good enuf for her. Is it worth while, the reader is disposed to ask, to take such a world of pains to attain an end which is, after all, so willingly abandoned? [Compare ' Dr. Breen's Practice ' (No. 25).] But whatever we may think of the construction or the meaning of the story, that it is ' readable from cover to cover' is beyond a doubt." [Spectator. **1211**

DOCTOR OF BEAUVOIR (The). [by W: Gilbert : *Tinsley*, 1869.] " Mr. Gilbert has the true secret of getting to the heart of things; it would be difficult to find a life containing fewer incidents than that of the Doctor of Beauvoir, who does not tell us even his name ; and yet he has contrived to make it thōroly interesting. This autobiografy is written exactly as a parish doctor mit be expected to write, only that the total absence of all pretence and effort and the skill with which the narrativ is knit together betray a practised artist. The

Doctor of Beauvoir is also a hero, and, apparently, without being in the least conscious of it. The manly,' uncomplaining spirit in which he bears his troubles, and the courage with which he makes his modest and useful way in the world, sho qualities of a fine nature, and of one which would hav done well in any walk of life. The background of family affection, and the different members of the home circle, who, altho only sketches, hav an individual interest for the reader, add to the pleasant elements in the book. The account of the 'poor patients' is charming, and has the appearance of being perfectly true. The interest of the story is real and substantial, and the closing chapter of the Doctor's life, when he is left quite alone in the world, is not only touching but cheering. The Doctor will, we think, exercise as good an influence on his readers as he did among his patients and nêbors of Beauvoir." [Athen. **1212**

DR. THORNE. [by ANTHONY TROLLOPE: *Chapman*, 1858.] " Mr. Trollope is strong and indefatigable, and we ar thankful for the robust, vigorous, and amusing novels he bestoes upon us. He has a real sense of fun, — a thing not common in these days. We can promise a hearty lâf to all who undertake ' Dr. Thorne,' a lâf which does good to the lâfter, not cynical and cruel, but hearty and sympathetic, and thêre ar so few books now-a-days which make us lâf. Thêre is genuin humor in ' Dr. Thorne,' not strained or ambitiously displayed, but arising from the natural play of the characters, who ar real creatures of human nature, flesh-and-blood, vigorously and broadly drawn — they would be likenesses if they wer not types..... Dr. Thorne is the good genius of everybody in the book, and is repaid by being indispensable — whether loved or hated,

nobody can do without him.'' [Athenæum. **1213**

DOCTOR WORTLE'S SCHOOL. [by ANTHONY TROLLOPE: *Chapman*, 1881.] " The mystery which shrouds the connexion between Mr. and Mrs. Peacocke, which so severely exercises the consciences of sundry spinsters, matrons, and clerical gossips, and drives the warm-hearted Dr. Wortle to the verge of lunacy, is revealed at the outset, and the remainder of the book is occupied in describing, with much skill and a good deal of quiet pathos and humor, the effect produced by the discovery, on a number of average, but by no means equal or identical, minds." [Athenæum.] " Mr. Trollope's tale is more than interesting, more than ingenious; it is bracing, which is much to say of a story dealing with delicate conjugal relations. Many novelists undertake the delineation of vice and its consequences with a sincere desire to make sin hideous; even Zola has at heart a terrible warning in his 'realism'; but he who would hav a garden must not only pull up weeds, but plant flowers. Mr. Trollope has planted flowers, not by depicting the troubles of a man who sins; but by drawing a man who sins and does not even repent, yet who accepts the consequences of his sins with a frankness, manliness, and patience which leaves us intensely impressed with the fact that honesty is — not the best policy — but best, whatever the policy." [Critic.**1214**

DOCTOR'S FAMILY (THE). [by MA. OLIPHANT (WILSON) OLIPHANT: *Blackwood*, 1863.] " A little, lithe Australian fairy, she has seen her silly sister ruined by her lout of a husband, — and the children groing up savages, and calmly takes them all on her shoulders, brings them to England, and plays in Carlingford earthly providence, — keeping

the husband in order, ruling the children,
doing all which the fretful wife is too
helpless to attempt, too silly to thank her
for accomplishing. Women hav done all
this often enuf in fiction as well as
reality, but it has been from love, or
pity, or religious emotion, or some feeling which rises in its intensity to the
hit of passion. But the speciality of
Nettie is that she does all this, not from
any of these motivs, but from the im-
puls of what seems to her common-
sense, and is common sense strengthened
and made activ, cool, and sensible, by
an idea of duty..... The merit of her
creation, in an artistic sense, is that she
has placed her heroin in such a position,
yet made her simply a girl, a natural,
warm-hearted, impulsiv being, always
alive with humor and incisiv good
sense, addicted to clever rapid chatter,
and as free from the self-consciousness
of virtue as she is from priggishness.
.... But Nettie is none of these, only
one of those girls whom most men hav
met once in life, who add a manlike
efficiency and decision to their feminin
acuteness of perception and capacity for
enduring love, and who, when once
understood, make those to whom that
fortunate comprehension is given listen to
arguments about woman's want of capacity with a smile which has in it some
tolerant scorn. Who has not seen such
a being, girl or woman, with a head as
clear as her heart is soft, whose instincts
ar as safe guides as other people's experience, whose perception never errs as
to character, or as to the road which
must willingly or unwillingly at last be
pursued, who cannot speak vaguely or
diffusely if she would, and who is called
by weak men satirical because she cannot help being pointed. It is impossible
to read the ' Doctor's Family ' with the
eager attention enforced by ' Salem

Chapel,' but very few readers will lay it
down without feeling themselves the
happier and the stronger for their intimate personal acquaintance with Nettie
Underwood." [Spectator. **1215**

DOLLY [by F.. [E..] (HODGSON)
BURNETT: Phila., *Porter*, 1877.] "is
a story of English domestic experience.
A group of motherless sisters ar the
leading characters, one of whom, Mollie,
is made just to escape the greatest disaster of a woman's life. The figure-
drawing is spirited, and the dialog salient
and good. Dolly's and Grif's misunderstandings are well portrayed for the
teaching of ardent young lovers that
they should not be jealous and fall out by
the way." [Boston " Literary World."]
— " 'The heroin is an attractiv girl who
is a capital combination of coquetry and
kindness; the troubles which beset her
and her brothers and sisters ar calculated to wring the heart, not excessivly,
but in discreet moderation, while a good
ending closes the book." [Nation.] —
" ' Dolly ' and " Theo ' ar not strikingly
new stories, with their accounts of the
happiness, after much suffering, of very
charming girls, who gro in out-of-the-way
places, breathing the air of genteel poverty, which they exchange very naturally
for the perfumes of the gilded drawing-
room. It is not the plots which ar noteworthy, but the animated, fascinating
style in which these threadbare incidents
ar recounted. Where so many novel-
writers ar pompous or affected, Mrs.
Burnett is as simple, as natural, and as
amusing as any one could wish. For
me, I find her hi spirits and her pathos
much better reading than the cold discussion of a ' problem ' in ' That Lass
o' Lowrie's ' and the willful accumulation
of distressing incidents in ' Surly Tim.' "
[Atlantic.] — " Upon the principle that it
is better to read a good book twice than an

indifferent one once, we welcome an old friend under a new title in ' *Vagabondia*.' Dolly as ' Dolly,' was altogether delitful. Revised by the author and veiled by the temptingly suggestive title we quote, she allures us as irresistibly as when we made her acquaintance. Jolly, deep-hearted, rattle-pated Dolly, is our darling as ever, but Toinette, Grif, Mollie, Annie, and the ubiquitous cherub Tod, to whom we ar introduced as he ' sits in the coal-box, eating Phil's fusees,' interest us with the freshness of new creation, draw upon our heart-strings, with the tender violence of old loves. We ar not sure that Mrs. Burnett did not giv us her best wine at the beginning of the feast of which we never tire." [Homemaker.] — " We ar not sorry to miss the storm and stress of her recent novels, and we think the drollery and overfloing good humor of ' Vagabondia,' a fair exchange for them. The male reader, at any rate, who does not fall in love with Dolly or Mollie, Aimée or Toinette, must be hard to please. But we ar sure that all will be delited to be admitted to that slipshod but otherwise charming household." [Critic. **1216**

DON JOHN. [by JEAN INGELOW : *Roberts*, 1885.] " The *motif* seems to be hackneyed; but it is not so, for here we hav the time-honored expedient of changing children at nurse treated in an entirely unprecedented, and yet perfectly plausible fashion. The irresponsible young wet-nurse whose imagination has been fired, and her lit head turned, by an immense consumption of the fiction furnished by a cheap circulating library, makes, in the first instance, in mere wantonness, the experiment of substituting her child for the one which had been confided — somewhat too unquestioningly — to her care, while a severe epidemic of scarlatina took its long course

throu the nursery of her employers. Again a chain of curious and very creditably-devised chances favor — almost necessitate — the maintenance of the deception; and at length it comes about, throu the sudden death, by accident, of her accomplice in the dangerous game she had been playing, that the nurse herself is not entirely certain whether it is the Johnstone baby or hers which the family reclaim, while she is herself prostrated by severe illness. The fritened woman keeps her guilty and yet rather absurd secret for a little while, but then the miserable confession will out, and the unhappy parents who hav been the victims of this enraging trick find that they can do no better than pack the unprincipled nurse off to Australia, adopt the other child, and bring up the twin boys exactly alike. The history of the groth of their characters, and the development of their fates, is a singular and affecting one. It is the best told of Miss Ingelow's tales, — the most direct and dramatic and symmetrical; and, in short, Don John is, to our mind, a beautiful little story; a finished and charming specimen of that minor english fiction which is often as good, from a literary point of vue, as the best produced elsewhere." [Atlantic. **1217**

DONALD GRANT. [by GEORGE MACDONALD ; *Paul*, 1884.] " .... However it must be confessed that in laying down ' Donald Grant' the most grateful of readers — and surely the author of ' Sir Gibbie ' and ' Within and Without ' has many grateful readers — is obliged to confess that Dr. MacDonald has been suffering from an attack of kleptomania, and does not supply us with such good material as when he came by it lawfully. Nothing need be said of his pilferings from Mrs. Radcliffe. He mit inform us that in helping himself to her ' properties' he is only folloing the example of Sir Walter Scott, whose 'Woodstock' was found on search to be stuffed with her paste jewels, and who, instead of shoing any penitence, gloried in the cleverness of the theft. But the counsel for the prosecution, after citing the sound tho startling critical maxim that literary robbery can be justified only when accompanied by murder, produces a witness who has survived being robbed by Dr. MacDonald — Mr. Sheridan Le Fanu to wit, the plot of whose 'Uncle Silas' has been bodily transferred to the pages of 'Donald Grant.' Ill-gotten gains never prosper. Dr. MacDonald finds his pillage as much in his way as Lady Cork did a hedgehog she once carried off from a garden for wánt of better prey, and his story pursues its mild path almost oblivious of the incident that the villain has tried to murder his heroin for the sake of her fortune." [Contemporary Review. **1218**

DONOVAN. [by "EDNA LYALL," i. e., Ada Ellen Bayly: *Appleton*, 1886.] "The author of 'Donovan' and what may be called its sequel, 'We Two' is a pretty fair preacher, but a better novelist. She carries a good story and a religious controversy side by side throu two thick volumes with indisputable success. She keeps both well in hand, guiding her people skilfully throu strange vicissitudes, and in argument always putting the rit thing in the rit mouth. The arguments ar far from original, so far that they seem to us profitless iteration, but they ar also so fair that it is at times possible to forget that the author is the soul of orthodoxy. She means to call in wanderers from the christian-fold, but she neither asserts dogmatically, nor threatens, nor scolds. She provides people of absolute faith, people of little faith, and people of no faith, and treats

all with impartiality. She displays serious thôt, some humor, a good deal of knoledg of life's by-ways, a joy in the good, with or without creed, and a wide charity for sinners. The prominence of her serious motiv presupposes some prolixity and dulness, but it is easy to get the whole of the story and the gist of the arguments without weariness." [Nation. **1219**

DORIE [in "A Maiden Fair," by C: GIBBON: *Maxwell*, 1886.] "is a pretty sketch of a lâfter-loving english maiden who at first does not kno her mind, but in the end makes up very satisfactorily to her harassed lover for the searchings of heart she has caused him." [Athenæum. **1220**

DOROTHY. [by MA. AGNES (COLVILLE) PAUL: Oxford, *Parker*, 1856.] "'Dorothy' is an excellent little story. Thêre ar no exciting incidents nor bilywrôt sentiments, but a great deal of excellent delineation of character. Dorothy herself is well drawn, and her progress from a self-willed, selfish, spoiled, domineering young woman to a well-regulated, self-controlled, rational being, is true to nature and extremely interesting. The sketch of her stepmother is happily hit off, and is a lifelike bit of portrait painting." [Athenæum. **1221**

DOROTHY FOX [by LOUISA (TAYLOR) PARR: *Strahan*, 1871.] "is a complete success from the first page to the last. There is not a character in whom we do not feel an interest. And the success is won by legitimate means — careful studies of life, and careful character drawings. Altho the story is in a great measure taken up with scenes from Quaker life, yet it is full of worldly knoledg. Here for instance is a bit of wisdom : — 'Love without money can not giv happiness; but money without love, tho it may not giv happiness, can giv many things which enable you to bear your life very contentedly.' And this wisdom of the market-place is excellently illustrated in the character of Lady Laura, who preferred her dismal, unhealthy house, to all other houses, however cheerful and healthy, if in a less aristocratic situation." [Westminster Review. **1222**

DOUBLE DUTCHMAN (THE) [by CATHERINE CHILDAR: *Hurst*, 1884.] " is above the average of novels of its kind. It deals britly and grammatically with scenes of quite modern social life. Mrs. Hazlewood and her 3 dauters ar eminently modern. Judith, the outspoken, dashing beauty, is the most interesting figure, so tender and strong a heart underlies her almost masculin manner. She is the good genius of her sister Blanche, the shy, gentle student of the 'sweet girl graduate' type.' [Athenæum. **1223**

DOUBLES AND QUITS. [by LAWRENCE W. M. LOCKHART: *Blackwood*, 1869.] " Two military gentlemen very much resemble each other, and ar always crossing each other's path. After this has gone on so far as to create some enmity, one of them, Captain Bruce, receives a billet at the opera from a young lady who mistakes him for Captain Burridge..... He visits at Mr. Badger's, her uncle's, and is at first received as Captain Burridge. The mistake is cleared up in time, but in the meanwhile Bruce has fallen 'in love' with her sister Rose, and is placed on 'calling' terms with the family. Mary, the young lady who had sent him the billet at the opera, is 'in love' with Burridge; but Burridge, tied to an odious, immoral woman, who is he knoes not whêre, is tung-tied and cannot propose. How these confusions ar cleared up, and

each of the gentlemen marries the girl of his choice at last, it would not be fair to tell." [Contemporary Review. **1224**

DOUBTING HEART (A). [by ANNIE KEARY: *Macmillan*, 1880.] "Thêre is a restful quality in Miss Keary's writings, which makes them always acceptable to one who is weary of the excitements offered by much of current fiction. In this story we hav the experiences attending a mother's efforts to marry and settle her dauters; with the result to them of some trial and disappointments, and the advantage to the reader of grafic portraitures of a peculiar aspect of english domestic life. Thêre ar many touching passages which must be read entire in their connexion to be enjoyed, and indeed the whole book is one not to be missed. It 'turns out' beautifully.' [Boston "Literary World."] — "A character who deserves mention is old Madame Florimel, the english wido of a french count, and Wynward Anstices' relativ. She livs at Roquette, and some of the scenes in the book — not the least important either — ar laid here. One, of almost idyllic beauty, called 'Madame's Fête,' givs a charming picture of a french village match-making. Madame de Florimel takes a strong fancy to the pure-hearted, honest, and impressionable Emmie West, and forms a plan for matching her to her kinsman, — a plan which comes at one time to a miserable shipwreck, causing Emmie much sorro. But 'all things find rest at their journey's end,' and, on the whole, we ar not disposed to quarrel at the fate to each assigned. One thing we may say in conclusion, and we deem it hi praise. There is no villain in the book, no character of extravagant wickedness. All ar human — the good and the bad — and tho some may be shadoy and distant, never impressing their individuality on the reader, none ar repellent. Even the Kirkmans ar tolerable, the worst of them, the old millionaire, being kept quite in the background. As for the old judge, Sir Francis Rivers, we get to like him much ere the story is over. Successful, easy-going, worldly, kindhearted and disappointed man as he is, the fine traits of his mind come out when bitterness and sorro overtake him." [Spectator. **1225**

DRAMA IN MUSLIN (A). [by G: Moore: *Vizetelly*, 1886.] "Mr. Moore can depict human beings in an original and consistent fashion; he can tell a story well, and he has an excellent eye for effect, so that his novel is picturesque, well constructed, and full of human interest..... It is as well to say that 'A Drama in Muslin' is not fit · for the drawing-room.....At the same time it is not too much to say that it is one of the ablest and most original novels of the year. It has been Mr. Moore's object to make a study of the life of a group of girls in good society. By laying the scene in Ireland he has secured the advantage of strong contrasts and good opportunities for his biting humor. His picture of **Dublin** in the season is exceedingly clever." [Athenæum. **1226**

DRAUGHT of LETHE (A) [by Roy Tellet: *Smith*, 1891.] "is an exceedingly clever book.....Of course, in a story of this kind, character-drawing is subordinated to plot-weaving; but the sketches of Vaux, the non-exhibiting painter, with his surface cynicism and his underlying kindness, and of Mr. Badgerly, the intervuer, whose being's end and aim is the procuring of piquant 'copy,' ar thŏroly life-like and entertaining. — The only serious artistic blot is the introduction of that horrible epi-

sode, the attempt of Dr. Falck to murder his rival by means of his new anaesthetic. It is quite unexpected, it stands out of all relation to the action, and has the look of being an afterthŏt which is quite out of place in a book that is otherwise so admirably planned." [Spectator. **1227**

DRIVER DALLAS. [by J: Strange Winter," i. ꞓ., Henrietta Eliza Vaughan (Palmer) Stannard: *Harper*, 1887.] "Captain John Dallas is a stalwart, honest, clear-eyed young fello; and when the bewitching Mabel Rivers, left motherless, comes to Drive to make her home thêre with his sister Betty and his great-aunt Miss Aurora, the result usual in such contingencies folloes. The course of love does not run at all smoothly, however. Mabel assumes for the time being the character of a coquette, when a handsom officer of the Lancers appears on the scene." [Boston " Literary World." **1228**

DUKE'S CHILDREN (The) [by Anthony Trollope: *Harper*, 1880.] "is, like all Trollope's novels, an extremely simple story. It belongs to the series, in which the Duke of Omnium and Phineas Finn and his wife appear, and narrates the fortunes of the duke's eldest son and dauter. Lord Silverbridge has two love-affairs, one with Mabel Grex, the fortune-hunting but attractiv dauter of a ruined earl, and the second with an american girl, Miss Boncassen, whom he finally marries..... Meanwhile he is disappointed in other things. His dauter, a charming girl, falls in love with Frank Tregear, who, tho a gentleman, has no rit to dream of such good fortune as marrying the dauter of the Duke of Omnium. This attachment the duke does his best to break up, of course without success. In the end Frank Tregear marries Lady Mary, just as Lord Silverbridge marries Miss Boncassen, and the duke consents. This is the sum and substance of the story, and thêre could scarcely be less." [Nation. **1229**

DUKE'S DAUGHTER (The) and THE FUGITIVES [by Ma. Oliphant (Wilson) Oliphant: *Blackwood*, 1890.] "is a story of very hi life indeed, since it tells of the Duke of Billingsgate, head of the house of Altamont, and of his dauter, Lady Jane, who falls in love with a man of inferior rank — wealthy, and a thôro gentleman, but not up to the mark of what the duke thinks fitting for his only dauter. Thêre is another duke in the story, and duchesses, and lords and ladies, and just a glimps of a royal personage. Mrs. Oliphant rejoices in the portrayal of these exalted people; and it is needless to say that they ar all instinct with life and verisimilitude, being as remote from the colorless fantasms of the professedly fashionable novelist as they ar from the crude monstrosities of the incompetent tyro in fiction. Since the death of Anthony Trollope we hav had no one who could so faithfully and appreciativly depict in words the pompous, overweening, intractable duke, who, subject to the common and vulgar lot of humanity, worships the fetish of his extravagant pride even at the moment when it is shattered and pulverized.....It is Lady Jane Altamont with whom tho story is mainly concerned, and the relations of father and dauter are drawn with a skilful hand. [Athenæum. **1230**

DUMBLETON COMMON [by Eleanor Eden: *Bentley*, 1867.] "is a charmingly pleasant book; it is full of genial kindheartedness, and thêre is a thôroly well-bred tone throu-out. The story itself is as slit as can hold together; but every individual in it has a distinctiv

character, and is made of flesh and blood, with a reasonable soul to match. The reader is effectually interested in the characters, all and sundry, from dear 'little Miss Patty,' the narrator of the annals of Dumbleton, to the Lady Venetia Verney, the siren and fine lady of the book.....Dumbleton Common is about 5 miles from London, and readers will giv it the exact locality they please; we hav our own idea of the particular spot indicated, but we do not wish to impose it on our readers. As for the story, we will not detail it, but recommend all who wish to have a lit, pleasant book, to get it for themselves." [Athenæum. **1231**

EARL OF EFFINGHAM (The) [by Lalla M'Dowell: *Tinsley*, 1877.] " is pleasantly told, and will repay the expenditure of time necessary to get throu it. It is an irish story, tho its scenes shift from Galway and Dublin to London. The distinctions between the several pictures of irish and english life ar well marked, in framework, background, coloring, and association; and whilst the former ar racy of the genuin character and tone of the Emerald Isle, the latter ar scarcely less grafic and legitimate imitations of good originals.....It is before all things a brit and interesting novel, with much to recommend it; and it deservs to be received with favor. The story is a pretty one, and the heroin is thôroly charming; the characters ar all well drawn, and the style, tho not perfect, is good." [Athenæum. **1232**

EAST LYNNE [by Ellen (Price) Wood: *Bentley*, 1861.] " is one of the best novels published for a season. The plot is interesting, intricate and well carried out ; the characters ar life-like, and the writing simple and natural. There is nothing forced, nothing disjointed or unfinished about

it; no discrepancies in the story."....
"East Lynne was a romance — a
love story of the most exciting and
complicated nature: it may hav been
a little exaggerated in parts — it may
hav had trifling discrepancies — portions of the story may hav been improbable; but no one can deny that
'East Lynne' was a work of absorbing
interest, this interest being concentrated
in the conjugal life of a lawyer in a
country town, and in the fate of his two
wives." [Athenæum. **1234**

EFFIE OGILVIE [by Ma. Oliphant (Wilson) Oliphant: *Macmillan*, 1886.] "is one of Mrs. Oliphant's
ever charming stories, in which, as
usual, even hackneyed plot and time-
honored situations ar turned to favor
and to prettiness. There is novelty in
the turn given to the crisis, keen insit in the study of a proud young girl's
heart, and ingenuity in the way things
ar brôt out rit, without the railway
accident or tyfoid fever, by which most
novelists rid themselves of one hero too
many." [Critic. **1235**

EFFIE'S GAME [by Cecil Clayton: *H. S. King*, 1873.] "is a simple, pretty love-story. Effie and her
sister Constance go to liv with a bachelor uncle, who has a general's command in Portsmouth. Constance's fortunes ar easily told. She finds a
match of a most prudent and respectable kind. Nor is thêre anything very
remarkable or heart-breaking about
Effie's. A young aide-de-camp, who
has nothing but his pay, falls in love
with her, proposes, is accepted, and
then cries off. Effie consoles herself
with a rapidity which speaks much for
her good sense. For a moment we ar
allowed to suppose that a respectable
post-captain, of the same stamp as the
respectable colonel who secured Con-

stance, will be the happy man; but a
brilliant writer in the Piccadilly, a
journal which we congratulate on possessing so eligible a person on its staf,
steps in before and carries off the prize.
In truth, the book is of very slit texture
but it is well written. The characters
ar not very profound studies, but they
move and act, and, above all, talk like
human beings, and we hav liked reading about them." [Spectator. **1236**

EGLANTINE [by Eliza (Tabor)
Stephenson: *Harper*, 1876.] "is one
of the pleasantest stories of the day.
More charming pictures of english
country life we hav never seen."
[Boston "Literary World."] — "The
narrativ is one which mit hav been
written for her ôn satisfaction by a
refined and cultivated woman, whose
life had been spent 'far from the madding crowd's ignoble strife,' whose
experience had scarcely transcended
the bounds of the domestic affections,
but who had passed beneath the chastening hand of sorro. Skilful as it is
in construction, however, the strength
of the book lies in its character
sketches." [Appleton's. **1238**

EGOIST (THE). [by G: Mere-
dith: *Paul*, 1879: *Roberts*, 1888.] "No
summary can do justice to the cleverness of Mr. Meredith's characters.
The Egoist livs for himself; but the
vues he takes of that self and the
duties of his position ar so lofty as to
be ideal. Called by Providence to be
the greatest magnate in his county, it
is not for him to frustrate the intentions
of fate by seeking the society of those
who ar his equals or possibly his superiors. A baronet, he mistrusts the
peerage. London he feels to be destructiv of all individuality, but at
Patterne Hall his talents hav room to do
themselves justice. Thêre he is in his

clement, worshipped by the country-side in general, and by Lætitia Dale, the dauter of a half-pay officer, in particular.....While Lætitia Dale's history exposes the cruel side of egoism, Clara Middleton brings to lit the ridiculousness of it. An admirable contrast to Lætitia, she makes a delitful heroin. With her sense of fun, and healthy instincts of liberty and enjoyment, she is more than a match for 20 egoists. The distress Sir Willoughby causes her is nothing to the agonies she makes him undergo. Mr. Meredith, tho he has created these two charming pictures of womanhood, does not allow himself to be diverted from his main object — the pursuit of egoism.....Mr. Meredith's style is a cross between Mr. Carlyle's and Mr. Browning's, if such a compound be imaginable. It is a nut confessedly hard to crack. He is so artificial as to seem to hav lost the power of using straitforward language. The simplest statement becomes an epigram; his epithets contain the pith of elaborate metafors; his metafors ar like the bursting of rockets, which sho new aspects of familiar scenes in a flash of fantastic lit. The objections to such a method of composition ar obvious. It is perhaps enuf to say that it is apt to be unintelligible." [New Quarterly Mag.] — "The Egoist is 'monstrous clever;' and to be that is a great deal, — but it is no more than that. ....That impression is never given by the Egoist, supremely clever as very much of it is. The insit of it is often so keen and penetrating, and its expression so clear-cut, that one strong tho not abiding result of it is a sense that in Sir Willoughby Patterne Mr. Meredith has created an illusion by reproducing a real man, vued from the coolly critical standpoint of his felloman. Here, one

feels inclined to say, is the self-seeking, vain, egoistic heart of 'that kind of man' laid bare, not as he appears to himself and wishes to appear to women, but as he looks under the lens of a singularly disinterested fraternal regard. And, to be just to Mr. Meredith, that seems to be precisely what he aimed at — not to paint one egoist, but to give 'a chosen sample, digestibly'; to condense into an acrid yet nose-tickling essence the mildly unpleasant odor of a whole garden full of dahlias and London-pride. And as he aimed at that result, and hit it, he must be acknoledged an artist, often supremely adroit in his manipulation, and irresistibly comic in his achievement." [Catholic World.] — "I should never forgiv myself if I forgot 'The Egoist.' It is art, if you like, but it belongs purely to didactic art, and from all the novels I hav read (and I hav read thousands) stands in a place by itself. Here is a Nathan for the modern David, here is a book to send the blood into men's faces. Satire, the angry picture of human faults, is not great art; we can all be angry with our nêbor; what we want is to be shōn not his defects, of which we ar too conscious, but his merits, to which we ar too blind. And 'The Egoist' is a satire; so much must be allowed; but it is a satire of a singular quality, which tells you nothing of that obvious mote which is engaged from first to last with that invisible beam. It is yourself that is hunted down, these ar your faults that ar dragged into the day and numbered, with lingering relish, with cruel cunning and precision. A young friend of Mr. Meredith's (as I have the story) came to him in agony. 'This is too bad of you' he cried, 'Willoughby is me!' [sic!] 'No, my dear fello,' said the author, 'he is all of us.'

I hav read 'The Egoist' 5 or 6 times, and I mean to read it again; for I am like the young friend of the anecdote — I think Willoughby an unmanly but a very serviceable exposure of myself." [Ro. L: Stevenson. **1239**

ELIOT THE YOUNGER [by BER- NARD BARKER: *Tinsley*, 1878.] "at least merits the praise of being lively and entertaining. It is smartly and some- times wittily written. The father of 'Eliot the Younger' is a figure drawn not without considerable skill, and talks in a way which we do not the less enjoy becaus it reminds us very strongly of Miss Austen. The intellectual man, placed in the midst of rural society, and married to the most liberal minded of women, and finding a certain satisfac- tion in a quiet sarcasm which no one about him understands, is a person whom we ar glad to hav met." [Spec- tator. **1240**

ELIZABETH MORLEY [by K .. S. MACQUOID: Bristol, *Arrowsmith*, 1889.] " .... is pleasant and not uninteresting. It is the story of a misunderstanding between husband and wife on their wedding tour, and if thêre is a little insufficiency in the reason of the dis- sension, Mrs. Macquoid may say that her story is therefore true to life." [Athenæum. **1241**

ELSIE [by A. C. M.: *Macmillan*, 1875.] "is a pretty rural tale at the outset.....There is little that is re- markable in the character of the selfish, but not wholly rascally male actor in Elsie's misfortune. The girl is a more substantial entity, tho she is unnaturally influenced by fear of a Calvinistic father. A true Lowland lass would hav shôn more spirit than our unhappy friend. But thêre is much pathos in the recon- ciliation between the poor girl and her parents, and the miller is a well drawn

sketch. The scene in which the hard, proud old man, blind and chastened by mortal illness, recognizes by her voice the child whom he has prayed his eyes may never more behold, is one which will linger in the reader's memory." [Athenæum. **1242**

ELSIE GREY [by CECIL CLARKE: *Griffith*, 1881.] "is an honestly-told, simple, and straitforward story, without veneer, and with no straining after grand effects. The heroin is the niece of a bricklayer whose wife is house- keeper in the city; where liv all the leading personages.....From Barbary Court the scene is shifted, about the middle of the tale, to a quiet Saxon town, and here again we hav some simple and truthful description, appar- ently based on personal acquaintance with the locality. Throuout the book thêre ar currents of genuin romance, with barely a fleck of crime or gust of passion to disturb the even flo." [Athe- næum. **1243**

EM. [By M. BRAMSTON: *Ward & Co.*, 1817.] "The feat of overleaping the conventionalities in his wooing speaks well for the strength of the hero's affec- tion. Fortunately his justification is very complete, for Emily Madock, the pretty grand-dauter of the old Devonshire farmer, is a pure rustic, with no half- bred gentility about her, and full of all the good impulses which lead her to take training well.....Indeed, it is the merit of the author that, without much resort to incidental subjects of interest, she manages to make all her characters distinct, if not ambitious in their pro- portions. The best of them is Em, a by no means faultless tho very winning heroin, who learns much in the period of suspicion and humbled pride which separates her for a time from happiness." [Athenæum. **1244**

EMILIA IN ENGLAND. [by G: MEREDITH : *Chapman*, 1864.] " Parts of it ar undeniably clever, and some of the scenes ar strong and natural, as for example whêre Emilia pleads with the father of her lover to obtain his consent to their marriage, tho she knoes, but will not apprehend the fact, that he is engaged to another woman; and also the intervue between Lady Charlotte and her unstable lover. The character of Emilia is the best sustained in the book. Perhaps this may be becaus we ar less sensitive to aberrations and extravagances in ' forein ' natures than in our ōn more familiar and more evenly balanced english contemporaries. Then too Mr. Meredith can draw better a character entirely unconventional and exceptional, than an ordinary figure in modern society dress. The Miss Poles ar overdṛawn to the point of caricature, and Mrs. Chump, tho sometimes amusing, is often disgusting, and has the tung of an irish Mrs. Gamp. Every now and then thêre is a glorification of ' english beef and beer ' that is almost Rabelaisian in its proportions, and with which the present generation cannot easily keep pace. Force and wit Mr. Meredith undoubtedly has, but he wants the faculty of lucid representation and the delicate perception necessary to make a novelist of the first rank." [American. **1245**

EMMA. [by J.. AUSTEN : 1816.] " So far as mere story goes Emma does not equal *Pride and Prejudice*. It is prolix, and the misapprehension under which the heroin acts throuout, and which furnishes the chief motif, is so patent to the reader that the story as such falls flat. The characterization, however, is as admirable as any in *Pride and Prejudice*. If not so notable for balance of mind as the agreeable Elizabeth, Emma is a more lovable heroin, and we find her all the more interesting for the little flits of her lively fancy and her impulsiv foolishness; while good sense never makes itself more attractiv than when combined with dignity, intelligence, and a genial temper as in the person of Mr. Knightly. Nothing of its kind could be better than the portrait of Mr. Woodward, the father of Emma ; . his kindness of heart and gentle fussiness, his amiable twaddle and benevolent bestoal of trivial advice, make him as delitful an old woman as Miss Bates herself, the humble friend and nêbor, whose cosy, gossipy presence was so welcom at the great house as a solace in the occasional absence of the beloved dauter. In all these tales the portraiture is less humorous than satiric, but it is a not unkindly satire : the author's wit has sharpness but no malice. It is the clever comment of a woman of observant and rational mind upon the folly and foibles of the human nature she has seen about her." [Boston " Literary World." **1246**

END OF A LIFE (THE). [by EDEN PHILLPOTTS : *Arrowsmith*, 1891.] " It must not be imagined, however, that the book is all villainy. The two sisters, Mary and Rose, ar delitfully natural studies of pure and truthful womanhood — truthful, that is, in all but the one deceit for which thêy and thêirs suffered so sorely, but which was justified, if deceit is justifiable.....In short, ' The End of a Life ' is well written, well considered, and well planned. The plot is original, the characters ar distinctly pictured and ably grouped, the dialog is excellent and thêre ar not a few true and striking sayings; and tho the central figures ar hateful, thêy ar meant so to be." [Athenæum. **1247**

ENTANGLED. [by E. FAIRFAX

BYRRNE: *Harper*, 1885.] "Written with a refinement of style and depth of sentiment which mit make it the kind of story which ladies delit in for a summer afternoon, it is also noticeable for a strength and intricacy of plot which will hold the reader most fastidious in requiring power in a story throu fascinated hours of close reading. Its situations ar all a little strained, if you analyse them closely, yet none of them affects one as absolutely unnatural; and thêre ar certainly many thrilling ones. But the grace of style is such that neither the most sensational of the incidents nor the well-sustained mystery of the plot appeal to one as earnestly as certain single scenes, like that when Colonel Woodworth hangs the portrait of his detested son-in-law among those of his ancestors." [Critic. **1248**

ENTHUSIAST. [by CAROLINE FOTH-ERGILL: *Ward & Downey*, 1887.] "Miss Caroline. Fothergill tells very well the story of an original and rather fascinating heroin, who has a secret which, even when revealed, leaves a mystery unexplained.....The hero discovers her secret — that she is married and separated from her husband, she admits the fact, and, while wishing that the secret shall be kept, refuses to answer several of the young man's questions. He is a most unamiable person, and makes it his object in life to discover all the rest, to hold the heroin in his power, and bide his time. The story then goes into a new channel, and the end of this episode is that the heroin marries a second time. The inner mystery is admirably kept up, and the ultimate explanation has the advantage of being simple." [Athenæum. **1249**

ESTELLE. [by EMILY MARION HARRIS: *Bell*, 1878.] "The sensitiv and

shrinking, but no less strong and patient nature of Estelle forms a fine contrast to the narroness of her strict but loving parents, and to the impetuous self-indulgent character of her lively younger sister. The hebrew household is planted in an old and picturesque setting, a quaint mansion in a cathedral town, in the sit and nêborhood of the gray pile which symbolizes an antagonistic creed. To such a fancy as Estelle's no root of bitterness springs up to mar the solace of such calm surroundings, tho to her orthodox father the position seems rather to intensify the isolation in which he glories. It is against his will, tho he is too proud and unsuspicious to feel concern about the matter, that a perilous intimacy grōes up between his young dauters and a christian family. Thêy are in fact 'taken up' by a pair of conventional young ladies, who having formed very esoteric notions of Judaism, ar at first charmed with the novelty of cultivated simplicity in an unexpected quarter. Estelle is a noble woman. Her days end as they begin, in the promotion, not the fruition of happiness of the hiest kind. She is an artist without living for art; sorro as much as joy continues her education to the end." [Athenæum.] — See "*BENE-DICTUS.*" **1250**

ESTHER [by ROSA NOUCHETTE CAREY: *Lippincott*, 1887.] "we can cordially recommend, both as pleasant reading, and as leaving behind it helpful and profitable impressions of life and character. It is an old story told anew, of the struggles of a widoed mother, who has to face poverty with a large family of children, and gain by dint of hard work and persistent efforts the daily maintenance which has hitherto come without thôt. The motivs which actuate the two eldest dauters of the family ar brôt into contrast, and a good moral is to be drawn from théir different careers. One is carried away by lofty enthusiasm, and wishes to do only what captivates her imagination and inspires her hiest energies. The other, Esther, is a girl of the rit sort, and putting poetry and picturesqueness out of sit, tries to perform the duty which lies nearest. She tells the story, and altho it is a difficult task to sho that one's self is invariably in the rit and the other in the wrong,—she continues to do it without injuring our impressions that she is a brave, sensible girl, who deservs the good fortune which comes to her like the reward of virtue in a fairy tale." [American. **1251**

ESTHER DUDLEY'S LOVERS. [by — (   ) Daniels: *Skeet*, 1874.] The "characters, bad and good, ar nicely balanced; by which we do not mean that they ar so moderated as to be mediocre, but that they ar tolerable approximations to concrete and composit humanity.....Esther, young and loving, and informed too late that the object of her affections has been always true, is on the verge of being false to her promis, or sacrificing her peace of mind and her husband's happiness. How the difficulty mit have been solved, we kno by sad experience of shattered hearts and broken vows, of elopements by moonlit, of death-beds, whêre consumptiv heroins perish as loquacious as the swan. Miss Dudley backs out of her engagement, and telling her story fully to an honorable man, meets his forgivness, and, in a sense, his gratitude. This natural conclusion, well told, exhibits more of what may fairly be called character, than could have been set forth in several volumes of a tragedy of errors. Mr. Carrington, pompous, narro-minded, and selfish in

his normal mood, comes out on an emergency in the character, unusual in fiction, of a hi-bred gentleman, while Esther, losing, by a first Nemesis, the dignity upon which she stood in her inexperience, shôes that true womanhood can be honest as well as sentimental. This moral of itself would stamp a tale less distinguished than the present by really careful work in its subordinate parts. The characters ar all good, Mrs. Hartleton admirable; and we can accord to the author the rare tribute of unqualified praise." [Athenæum. **1252**

EUSTACE DIAMONDS (The). [by Anthony Trollope: *Harper*, 1872.] "The more prominent characters ar quite fresh, and thêre is a background of old friends from 'Phineas Finn,' and 'Can You Forgive Her?' which serv to giv a home-like air. Mr. Trollope forestalls any possible accusation of want of originality in the conception of his principal character, by calling Lady Eustace, at the outset of the story, an 'opulent and aristocratic Becky Sharp,' but the very fact that her beauty, position and wealth giv her such immense advantages over her less fortunate prototype, lessens the resemblance. A better comment on the text of 'Honesty is the best policy' could hardly be made than the history of her career affords, and her unbounded capacity for lying makes it impossible to unravel the mystery of the diamonds, and thus brings about sudden turns in the story which both amaze and amuse the reader. Frank Greystock and Lucy Morris ar less uncommon and more agreeable characters. The former is not an unfair representation of a man of the world, with expensiv tastes, who has his way to make and is not very scrupulous as to the manner of making it, but poor little Lucy with her brave heart and generous temper, is surely worthy of a better fate than she is likely to meet in marrying such a man." [Penn Monthly. **1253**

EVAN HARRINGTON; OR HE WOULD BE A GENTLEMAN [by G: MEREDITH: 1861.] "is .a story of contemporary life, full of subtlety and spirit, depending for its impression upon the skill and detail with which its characters ar delineated. It is — curiously enuf, and perhaps unconsciously — a tale in which the women ar more variously and strongly pronounced than the men, and they ar the cleverest and most effectiv actors throuout. The ' argument' is the love of a tailor's son, whom Nature made a gentleman, for a baronet's dauter, whom Nature also made a lady. Thêre is no mawkish moralizing in it, but the simple and frequent experience of all society confirms the justice of the plot. The book is quiet, but most interesting, from the author's ability to state the shadoy, evanescent, and glimmering emotions that play throu every sensitiv mind brôt in contact with what it despises as prejudice, and yet cannot exactly escape. The Countess is a portrait of very great skill — so is Rose — so is Evan himself — so is his mother. The moral of the book is not that every tailor is as much a gentleman as every nobleman, but simply that gentlemanhood is determined by causes that cannot be calculated, and may appear in a tailor's son and not appear in an earl's. Its farther moral is the picture of the perfectly heathen spirit of modern christian society which stigmatizes one man becaus he is useful, and worships another becaus his great-grandfather was useful.....In Evan Harrington we hav one of the most fascinating heroes of the modern novel. Usually the fascinating people in novels do not fascinate. But Evan does. Rose's love is perfectly intelligible. Every girl who reads the book will fall in love with Evan, and that not becaus he is described with tinted ink as a pirate, or a statesman or a saint, or a hero; nor becaus he is invested with some obscure antecedents full of the possibility that he is a king's son after all. Thêre is nothing of this: nothing of the rose romance. The book is pure daylit throuout, dear young lady. Mr. Evan Harrington is a tailor's son; but he is somehow so essentially noble and lovely, that it is like the warmth of a June air, inevitable and universal..... And Rose, surely she is a true-hearted girl; and her mother, Lady Jocelyn, a most womanly woman. Every one must admire the cool, neutral tint of the story, while the passionate romance of love is touched with a power which few possess. Among the many novels it is remarkable for its masculin nerve — a tone which springs from knoledg. Too many of the clever novels, now a days, which ar written by women, lack a centre of gravity. They ar vague and unsatisfactory. Apparently they ar the product of intolerable ennui — with obscure aims and efforts, but without experience. A great novel is written by a man of great genius, whether he hav experience or not. Genius is vicarious. It interprets for us emotions it never itself experienced." [G: W: Curtis.]— "Evan is not a bad fello, manly and hi-minded enuf; but he has a weakness not uncommon in the ' heroic' character, which does not usually abound in common sense; he neglects the very obvious and immediate duty of an honorable man to explain his false position, and afterwards stoically performs monstrous works of supererogation and self-sacrifice for a principle, and this conduct in due time is of course rewarded by the heroin. The scheming countess with her little forein languors and affectations is an admirable figure, as is also 'Mrs. Mel,' the stern embodiment of duty, and the cheery little hen-peeked brewer. The book has the weakness of novels, that of opening with more strength than it closes; but, in spite of rather lengthy and dragging passages to fill out the relentless 3 volumes, there is a fresh, racy atmosfere throu the pages, a vigorous wit and strong human sympathy with all classes of men, which make very refreshing reading. [American.   **1254**

EVIL GENIUS (THE). [by [W:] WILKIE COLLINS: *Harper*, 1886.] " In these days of many, and pleasing, books, a book which enthralls the attention is almost as rare as in the days when the publication of any book was an event. Wilkie Collins' 'Evil Genius' is one of these absorbing stories, and it is all the more remarkable and enjoyable for not thrilling by the methods usually employed by its author. Wilkie Collins has been essentially one of the writers whom we regard as born to amuse us; and even his greatest admirers will be surprised at what they find to admire in this latest work — a depth, a tenderness, a wise and gracious insit, which has not relied on anything meretricious or startling in effect for the interest it inspires, and which has created a really noble, as well as entertaining, novel. The story is on the hackneyed subject of an unhappy marriage; but thére is nothing hackneyed in the treatment, tho the events ar all moral events in the development of character, utterly independent of striking incident. The precision of style, the concentration on the

subject in hand which never lets the author wander off into tiresome by-paths, the quickness of the movement, the exceeding ingenuity of telling situations constantly varied but never in the least improbable, the deep pathos, the delicious absurdities of the Evil Genius, who, by the way, is a mother-in-law, and the underlying, never conspicuous but always interfused, moral, lift this tale to a hit never reached by what is merely entertaining." [Critic.]—

" The opening of the story, after a prelude which is a minor tale in itself, is not altogether unusual — the young governess whose beauty and gratitude for kindness shōn to her prove dangerously seductiv to her employer, and the child who by close association of pupil with teacher becomes passionately attached to her. But the development is not commonplace, and its shifts and changes of evil and of good will enchain the reader's attention and interest..... We may especially recommend this story becaus of its pleasant ending and the absence of that concentration of horrors found near the close of some of this author's novels." [Boston "Literary World."   **1255**

EYE FOR AN EYE (AN). [by ANTHONY TROLLOPE: *Harper*, 1879.] " We hav here a tale shōing the evil consequences of weakness of character. This, at least, is the only moral we can extract from the story, which is not altogether a pleasant one, turning, as it does, on the base behavior of the son of an earl to a pretty young irish girl, her ruin, his desertion, his murder by her mother, and the consequent confinement of the latter in a private asylum. The story is a painful one; for the weakness of the young man in refusing to marry Miss O'Hara is not made tragic but simply weak, while the repulsivness of her

disreputable father is made so glaring that the reader is at times left in doubt whether a marriage is not as entirely out of the question as the young man feels it to be. It is needless to say that all the story is well told. Mr. Trollope has the art of narration to perfection." [Nation.]
—"Similarly tragic in its close, and even more painful in its course, is 'An Eye for an Eye,' which is a shorter novel than many he has written, but quite as interesting as any. It is the old story of a loving woman suffering from a selfish man the cruelest wrong which it is possible for him to do her, with the added element of a horrible revenge taken upon him by the infuriated mother of his victim. As in everything he writes, Mr. Trollope's purpose here is to sho the heartlessness of much of the english pride of family and name; and with this he associates some other lessons which giv the story a strong, tho not direct, moral bearing. [Boston " Literary World." **1257**

FAIR BARBARIAN (A) [by F.. E.. (HODGSON) BURNETT: Osgood, — Warne, 1881.] "is an excellent little story. Without the passion which Mrs. Burnett shōed she could powerfully portray in 'That Lass o' Lowries,' it shōes minuteness of observation combined with a freshness amounting to originality. Thêre is, too, a touch of humor of that delicate kind which Mrs. Gaskell possessed so richly — Indeed, the early part of Mrs. Burnett's story will probably remind every reader of ' Cranford ' [No. 1175]. The brilliancy of the contrast between the pretty, fashionable american girl and the staid society into which she is plunged at her aunt's in a small town in England is the essence of the happy invention upon which the book depends. The story is short enuf to prevent the effect from losing any of its britness, and

it is an artistic touch which brings the tale to an end so as to raise a smile and complete the general impression of litness and vivacity. Not content with the fair barbarian alone, Mrs. Burnett has given a picture of another charming girl of the opposit kind, an english home-staying young lady, timid, tender-hearted, and stânch. Both ar so admirably drawn and so fascinating that one hardly knoes which to prefer." [Athenæum. **1258**

FAIR TO SEE [by LAWRENCE W. M. LOCKHART: Blackwood, 1871.] "is precisely the book for those who wish to be amused, and not to be perplexed with any moral questions or doubts. The narrativ is rapid, the characters natural, the conversations humorous, and the author knoes thŏroly the ground he goes over. One especial recommendation we can give to the story — that tho it deals with military and sporting men, thêre is nothing whatever of the 'Guy Livingstone' tone about it. It is thŏroly healthy. The scenes abroad remind us of some of the best of Lever's tales. The plot, too, is good." [Westminster Review.]—"'Fair to See' is an exceedingly readable novel. The characters ar two officers, one an enamored youth, the other a friend; two scotch girls, one a flirt, the other sincerity itself. It is a very simple tale of a certain passion not wholly unfamiliar to the novelist, and it is very well told — in fact, it is just what a novel that is to be read once ôt to be. At times it is very amusing, and it is never dull." [Nation. **1259**

FAITH AND UNFAITH [by MA. (ARGLES) HUNGERFORD: Smith, 1882] " is well written, amusing, and decidedly readable. It is just one of the pleasant, dawdling narrativs of life in country-houses and town-houses which appear in such interminable succession, and whose

average ability is so remarkably hi."
[American. **1260**

FALLEN ANGEL (A). [*Tinsley*, 1878.] "The heroin's will is so pure, and her imagination is so hi-toned, that not the faintest stain of circumstance can affect her; while the woman who accidentally, one may say, becomes a lawful wife givs a sad example of the coarseness which must accompany a mercenary marriage. Laura's repulsivness is the greatest drawback to the pleasure of the book, but the description cannot be called untrue, any more than Harlowe's deterioration after his criminal desertion of Mildred is other than the usual result of selfish policy. The early scenes of love-making in the country ar spritly and idyllic; the farewell, when Harlowe first learns the nature he has gone so near to injure, is dignified and tender; and tho, in some parts, a little condensation mīt hav been effected, the book, on the whole is promising."
[Athenæum. **1261**

FALLEN FORTUNES. [by JAMES PAYN: *Appleton*, 1876.] "Those who remember the novels they read, and who now hav a distasteful impression of some of Mr. Payn's recent writings, will be able to do that author more justice and to think of him more kindly if they will look at his last story. Here, as elsewhere in his work, the main interest of the reader is the whereabouts of a fortune, which is always a fascinating subject. Mr. Dalton loses all his money, and his family at once finds how much pretence there is in all the assurances of affection they had hitherto received. It would be unfair to tell the plot of the story, which is so ingeniously constructed and well managed that even the reader who knoes how generous Mr. Payn is with his millions in the last chapter is kept in an unpleasing state of doubt as to whether, after all, the supply may not have given out, so that all the virtuous characters will be left sweeping crossings when the book ends. While the plot is good the drawing of the characters is much better. It is not too much to say that there is hardly an unlifelike person in the story— unlifelike, that is to say, so far (and it is not far) as the people ar described at all. Mr. Dalton, for instance, is not only said to be amusing, he is amusing; he makes good jokes and tells good stories and tells them well. His dauter Jenny also shōes herself as hi spirited as she is announced to be, so that the reader does not lack for entertainment. Another good character is Mrs. Campden. Her coldness and selfishness, and power of giving offense, ar so far beyond the invention of even the most suspicious soul that they bear the earmark of being observed and not imagined. How it has happened that Mr. Payn, after writing so much which was no more than the empty, lifeless shell of a good novel, should hav suddenly bloomed into such comparativ excellence, it would be hard to say."
[Nation. **1262**

FALSE AND TRUE. [by ELEANOR EDEN: *Booth*, 1859.] "'Easton and its Inhabitants' was a lively, sketchy, pleasantly improbable story. 'False and True' is an improvement on the first in many respects. It is written with more care and more unity of purpose— it is amusing and fictitious, — all the incidents fall out as in a comedy, and ar rounded off into a happy conclusion, such as the reality of things would hav scarcely brōt to pass. Vamela Dynely, with her honesty and brusquerie, has a pleasant ruf flavor. Vere, the curate, cousin and half hero of the book, is unfinished. Alba St. Maur, about whom a great deal of fuss is made by everybody, is a natural young lady, with a susceptible heart and fine voice. She, of course, prefers the Birmingham-gilt love of the dashing and fascinating Dudley Harcourt to the true, tho rather dull gold of Louis Delorme. But she gets better treated in the novel than she would by even-handed Justice. The true lover bides his time, — a coup de théâtre makes him a baronet, — Alba comes to her judgment and a sense of his merits, — her false love is banished in a way worthy of Theodore Hook, — Vamela marries the rit man — and all ends as happily as possible. The book is lit and brit and of the stuff of which farces ar made." [Athenæum. **1263**

FALSE HONOR [by T: Bentley: E: Walker, 1879.] " is a clever and amusing story, original in plot and in many of its incidents; so strongly tinged, however, with the dramatic element, that we never lose a sense of unreality in the characters introduced. The book purports to be a picture of some fâses of London society. We do not kno why it would not answer all requirements for the popular comedy, even to the last scene." [Boston "Literary World." **1264**

FAMILY AFFAIR (A). [by "Hugh Conway," i. e., F: J: Fargus : Holt, 1885.] It " is a pleasant thing for a popular author to leave behind him a novel worthy of lasting favor. ....It is less the story — the plot — tho that is strong, original, and im-pressiv, than the detail, which charms lastingly. The characters, the con-versations, the social incidents, ar fairly delitful, and the Talberts ar a creation as enjoyable as Dickens' famous brothers. The housekeeping idiosyn-crasies of the charming Horace and Herbert, making it possible for them to identify a doubtful little boy by the

fact that he wiped his shoes before daring to enter their house ar a constant fascination." [Critic. **1265**

FAMILY FEUD (The) = No. 689.

FAMILY FORTUNES [by " E: Gar-rett," i. e., I .. Fyfie Mayo : Dodd, 1882.] " is well worth reading, — a sim-ple, natural chronicle of a few lives, with little incident and less love-making, but with much shrewd observation of men and things. The real heroin is the family servant, whose acute remarks reconcile us even to the painful scotch dialect." [Critic. **1266**

FAR ABOVE RUBIES [by C .. Eliza Lawson (Cowan) Riddell: Lippincott, 1867.] " is an interest-ing and simple story, gracefully and fluently written, pure and healthful in tone, depicting scenes and characters for which it comes within the experience of nearly every reader to find a paral-lel; and, if it be wanting in that power and depth of thôt which hav hitherto marked the writings of this versatil and most industrious novelist, it is nevertheless surrounded by that pleas-ant quiet atmosfere which renders novels of country life particularly refresh-ing. The narrativ runs smoothly, undisturbed by any violent or stirring events, and is interspersed with many charming descriptions and sensible re-flexions which hav the merit of not being wearisom." [Round Table. **1267**

FAR FROM THE MADDING CROWD. [by T: Hardy: Smith, 1874.] " Sensationalism is here all in all. If we analyze the story we shall find that it is nothing but sensationalism, which, in the hands of a less skilful writer, would simply sink the story to the level of one of Miss Braddon's earlier performances. Take the career of Gabriel Oak, who is the least sensa-tional of the chief characters. He loses the whole of his property in a sensation scene of 200 or 300 sheep being driven by a dog over a precipice. He finds his mistress in a sensation scene of blazing ricks. He regains her estimation in another sensation scene of thunder and litning in the same rick-yard. So the story progresses in a succession of sensation scenes. But sensation scenes ar no more Mr. Hardy's strong point than they ar G: Eliot's. The scene in which Troy woos Bathsheba with his sword is a piece of mad extravagance, fit only for the boards of some transpontine theatre. The whole chapter is simply a burlesque upon the cavalier poet's lines, 'I'll make thee famous by my pen, and glorious by my sword.' Mr. Hardy has not done this, but only made the one step from the sublime to the ridiculous. Of course Mr. Hardy has had good reasons for dealing us such a dose of sensation. He knoes what true art is, but he prefers, in this story at least, to giv his readers a bastard substitute." [Westminster Review.] — "'Far from the Madding Crowd' depends for its interest not so much upon an exciting plot, as upon natural delineations of character, keen observation of nature, shrewd remarks, and quaint humor. The scene is laid among homely rustics and sheep-farmers, of whom it can truthfully be said, in the well-kuōn words of Gray, that : —

'Far from the madding crowd's ignoble strife, [stray.
Their sober wishes never learnt to Along the cool sequestered vale of life, They kept the noiseless tenor of their way.' [Canadian Monthly. **1268**

FELIX HOLT, THE RADICAL. [by "G: Eliot" i. e., M.. A.. (Evans) Cross : *Blackwood*, 1866.] "Beyond the plot thêre is in George Eliot's new novel a portrayal of character and of english country life whose exquisit fidelity can scarcely be realized except by those who hav gone throu those midland regions with which her story is connected. All who hav with charity and interest studied the characters of the best dissenting ministers, will feel with gratitude that the character of Mr. Lyon is a faithful picture of many a faithful man.....There is a notable change in the tone of G: Eliot since the appearance of 'Adam Bede' [No. 1027]. Her style is quieter, her spirit calmer, her social protestantism less bitter. In humor, certainly Mrs. Holt falls much behind Mrs. Poyser — than whom, by the way, no more original character has appeared in English fiction since Pickwick." [Round Table. **1269**

FELLOW-TOWNSMEN. [by T: Hardy: *Harper*, 1880.] "Anything from Mr. Hardy's pen, however slit, is worth reading; thêre is little of the dramatic in it, which is unusual, and the women ar rather shadoy, which is still more so ; but thêre is the same insistence upon the irony of fate, and the same intimation that if you let things take their course in this world they will turn out sadly and impotently, but in general bearably — or at least this happens oftener than other novelists ar apt to think." [Nation. **1270**

FERNYHURST COURT. [by F: Parthenope (Nightingale) Verney: *Strahan*, 1871.] "We ar indebted to the author of 'Stone Edge' for another excellent story. We cannot call to recollection a book in which women, as distinguished from feminin lay figures, have played so distinguished and diversified a part.....Our author should win the gratitude of her sex for a series of charming portraits of what hundreds of english ladies ar and may be. May Dimsdale stands out their queen by rit divine. The story of her love, fairly and naturally won, not lavished on the least worthy object, after the fashion of most heroins, reveals to us the character, nowhêre formally described, of a pure, hĩ-minded, warm-hearted, honest english maiden..... Other varieties,—the worldly mother, the Belgravian woman of fashion, the limp but loving girl, who leans for support upon a curate,— ar described with kindliness and skill; and the male actors, tho not one of them but the Squire is quite worthy of their gentler relativs, hav all their places and functions in the tale. Not a few sound and honest observations on society, instinct with Liberal thôt of the hier type, contribute to the value of a book which, on every ground, will well repay perusal." [Athenæum.   **1271**

FERNLEY MANOR [by — ( ) DANIELS: N. Y., *Brady*, 1866.] " is a pleasant picture of old-fashioned country life. The story is a simple one, fairly and unaffectedly told. Thêre is a carefulness and truth in the delineation of the characters not always observable in works which claim a hier place in modern fiction." [Round Table.   **1272**

FIVE CHIMNEY FARM = No. 699.

FIVE OLD FRIENDS AND A YOUNG PRINCE. [by A .. I .. (THACKERAY) RITCHIE: *Smith*, 1868.] The five tales ar not so much the 5 old tales of childhood rationalized and 'improved,' as the frãse is — that is, having all their poetry and beauty taken out of them — but transformed into a second and nobler meaning..... But whêre other writers hav so ignominiously broken down, Miss Thackeray has won her greatest success. Whêre they always prove dull and wooden, she is lit and graceful, — whêre they paint with heavy, coarse

strokes, she sketches with the most delicate touches.....Lastly, we must not forget the many touches of real poetry, pictures of the sea, and of the earth, of spring and of harvest, which ar scattered up and down these tales in such profusion. We have selected ' *Jack the Giant-killer*' for especial praise, but it perhaps contains less poetry of this kind than many of the others." [Westminster.] See "*BLUE BEARD.*"   **1273**

FLOWER AND THE SPIRIT (THE). [by FREDERIKA MACDONALD: *Blackwood*, 1887.] "The opening chapters ar excellent, hitting off the humors of the strange cosmopolitan society of a Bloomsbury boarding-house with much humor and point.....There is humor, too, in the sketch of Stephen Bloxam, the heroin's step-father, whose perpetual vacillation between self-reproach and self-compassion is cleverly illustrated. ....In contrast with such actualities we hav the heroin and her old danish friend, representatives of ascetic mysticism and romanticism respectivly. The latter is a thõroly sympathetic personage, charmingly drawn." [Athenæum. **1274**

FOOLS OF FORTUNE [by F: BOYLE: *Chapman*, 1876.] " must not be confounded with the average novel. It is rather bohemian, but full of life, movement, picturesque scenes, and brilliant talk. Literary men should certainly read it, as thêre is much in it which concerns them." [Westminster Review.   **1275**

FOR BETTER FOR WORSE. [Boston, *Burnham*, 1862.] "The author of this charming novel has had the hardihood to marry her heroin at the beginning of her story. We find much to praise in this well-told story and very little to dislike or blame." [Church Monthly.   **1276**

FOR CASH ONLY. [by JA. PAYN:

Chatto, 1882.] " Mr. Payn has long ago established a certain reputation as a romance writer. His strength lies in the narration of wild and more or less impossible adventures. But when, as in ' For Cash Only,' he comes before us as a painter of men and manners, he is far less successful. He wastes a good deal of virtuous indignation on a recent well-knōn novel, whose title he thinly veils under the pseudonym of ' Butterflies ' [' Moths '], but in so doing he loses sit of the old proverb about people who liv in glass houses, for the picture of morals with which he presents us is little, if at all, less revolting than that which he condemns, with the aggravating circumstance of being infinitly more vulgar." [Westminster Review. **1277**

FOR LILIAS [by Rosa Nouchette Carey: *Bentley*, 1885.] " is a thōroly wholesom and charming story, in which types of graceful womanhood predominate, tho the writer has given us one finished portrait in Capel Frere, whose whimsical fancies reconcile the reader to that absence of hearty humor noticeable in most books by women. The plot is effectiv in that it affords the writer full scope for the delineation of domestic life, in which she excels, and for the devolopment of the character of the heroin, who is no paragon, but nevertheless a striking and attractiv figure by reason of her very faults. Miss Carey's method is none the less successful becaus it is a little old-fashioned; the dialog is easy and natural, but singularly free from all approach to slang; and her latest work will maintain, if it does not advance, her reputation as a genial and refined writer." [Athenæum.] — " In ' For Lilias,' the author avails herself of all the agreeable traditions of english fiction; thêre ar warm and well-lited rooms, well-to-do people, regular meals, afternoon tea, plenty of bread and butter, and a gentle ripple of friendly, soft-voiced conversation. This may not be original or exciting, but ' ways of pleasantness and paths of peace,' ar refreshing to the critic, who believes that altho the novelist should not sacrifice his meaning to the requisitions of mere agreeableness, out of regard for art and the taste of his readers, he should still hav beauty in some degree or other as his chief end in vue." [Lippincott's. **1278**

FOR OLD LOVE'S SAKE [by Maria G. Fetherstonhaugh: *Bentley*, 1882.] " is avowedly a prose expansion of Mr. Gilbert's comedy ' Sweethearts,' and the theme has not suffered in the hands of the novelist. The story is slit enuf, but those who do not despise a mere love tale will not be disappointed in the troubled course run by the loves of Cornet Dundas and Lady Margaret. She is proud, tho honest enuf ; he hot-tempered ; and the two manage to be strangers to their better selvs for some five-and-twenty years, when the cornet, now a general, makes his peace with the woman he left in pique as a girl. Not an unparalleled situation ; but it is drawn with a lit hand, and yet not without pathos. The gravity of Dundas' embarrassment, when his pledge has to be exchanged with one kept faithfully for years, and the question arises, ' Whêre the devil did I put that rose?' makes a good foil to his almost too easy recovery of his place in Margaret's affections." [Athenæum. **1279**

FOR PERCIVAL. [by Margaret Veley: *Lippincott*, 1878.] " It is not often the critic's happy lot to be able to praise a book unreservedly, but we can truly say that For Percival is a most lovely story, one of the most charming works of fiction which hav appeared for the last ten years.....And this book is infinitly better, both for the pleasure it givs and for the influence which it may exert, than books remarkable only for the extraordinary talent and cleverness displayed by their authors. It shōes admirable drawing of character, especially in Lissy,— absorbed in her love, and sensitiv to every breath of coldness,— in the proud, frank, passionate Lottie Blake; and in Percival himself, an instance of that rare union of strength of mind, honesty of purpose, and gentleness of heart, which more than any other, probably, attracts the deepest affection of women. But thêre is something better than the most skilful description or the shrewdest observation: thêre is sympathy, and a great deal of it. In the author of this story we hav a person who answers The New Republic's definition of a woman of culture: one who ' as I speak of love or sorro, makes me feel that she herself has knōn them; as I speak of ambition, or ennui, or hope, or remorse, or loss of character, makes me feel that all these ar not mere names to her, but things.' Perhaps the best idea we can giv of the author is by saying that if we can imagin the George Eliot of Middlemarch, minus filosofy and Greek, and plus a certain all-pervading gentleness, we shall hav before us the writer of *For Percival*." [Boston " Literary World." **1280**

FOR RICHER, FOR POORER [by " HOLME LEE," i. e., Harriet Parr: *Smith*, 1870.] " is precisely the sort of book which mīt be expected from the author of ' Sylvan Holt's Daughter ' and ' Basil Godfrey's Caprice.' It is the story of a young clergyman of ability, but precarious health, who goes throu many struggles with an attached wife; but, at last, finds himself blessed by fortune, and may reasonably be expected to

' liv happily ever after.'....Equally true ar the descriptions of the little inland town, with its microscopic squabbles, jealousies, and cliques, whêre Mr. Lampleigh commences his career, and the miniature sea-coast community — a cross between a rural parish and a watering-place, whêre he begins life again as a curate. It is not a novel of thrilling interest; but most people will read it with pleasure, and those who delit in domestic scenes will accord to it still hier praise." [Athenæum.] — " Holme Lee's success does not end with her sketches of north country manners and scenery. We hav never before met so charming pictures of Brétagne. How the actors pass and repass from Cumberland to Brétagne, and how they liv at the Villa de l'Espérance, the reader must find out for himself· We hav dwelt so long upon the setting of the tale that we ar unable to do justice to the characters. But thêre ar few people who will not take an interest in the lives of Robert Rawstroun and Nan." [Westminster Review. **1281**

FORTUNE'S BUFFETS AND REWARDS [by E. D. PRIMROSE: *Unwin*, 1886.] " is a study, rather close than masterly, 'of some fāses of university life in **Edinburgh**. Its strength is of the conscious and conscientious kind, but thêre is plenty of keen observation, quick intelligence, and insit into character. The moral intention is nnmistakably hi, and the realism of one side of the picture, tho unpleasant, is. not coarse for coarseness' sake.....But the book, tho it is redeemed by more than one example of quiet courage and unobtrusiv heroism, is scarcely cheering. ....The process by which the students and their ways ar presented is fotografic. Their adventures, friendships, hoaxes, and foregatherings ar evidently as like the real thing as can be. Throu all this realism runs a vein of something akin to romance." [Athenæum. **1282**

FORTUNE'S MARRIAGE [by GEORGIANNA MARION (CRAIK) MAY: 1882.] "is a fine instance of what mit be termed the novel of conversation. It is almost a drama. The characters who ar for the most part before the reader ar only 3; the dialog, throu which the author works out her story, is handled in a masterly way; and the whole work has a certain natural charm, a grace and skill in portraiture, an impression of refined realism, that has no parallel in the productions of any contemporary novelist..... Briefly Ronald Glyn, the thriving barrister of 30, a well-meaning but cold and rather egotistical man, found few points of sympathy with Fortune Denbigh, the warm-hearted girl of 20, who had been petted all her life. It was Ursula, Ronald's maiden-sister, who acted as dea ex machina, and brôt about the union of these two, until, like Benedict and Beatrice, they succumbed to one another's charms. The incidents leading up to the marriage ar cleverly managed; and the subsequent estrangement, culminating on the one hand in wounded pride, and on the other in pathetic resignation, is no less admirably wrôt out. During a period of separation and sorro, Fortune learns the virtues of self-restraint, and Ronald at the same time begins to realize what he has lost. Nothing could surpass in delicacy the story of that second wooing, in which the man found himself repelled by the woman who had once been at his feet..... The situation is novel and piquant; and it is carried to obvious ending with exquisit delicacy and tact." [Boston "Lit. World." **1283**

FOUR CROTCHETS TO A BAR. [Smith, 1881.] "There is no elaborate character-drawing, and no elaborate plot-

making, but it is full of a lively knoledg of the world, and of rattle almost always amusing and now and then very clever. ....The story is cleverly contrived, and the conversation brit, with just enuf tendeney to flippancy to bring the reader into that state of mind half-way between amusement and superciliousness, which most conciliates his self-love. The author understands more classes than one: perhaps his best male sketch is that of an assistant in a dispensary, subsequently a professional fotografer, who is a very vulgar-minded young person; and his best female sketch is that of a vain and shōy young woman, — a chemist's dauter, — who becomes his wife, and whose beauty he describes as taking his breath away — 'She's just like peppermint and water.'" [Spectator. **1284**

FOUR MACNICOLS (THE) [by W: BLACK: Harper, 1882.] "is only a bit of a sketch which the reader will wish longer, of brave, hearty scotch fisher-lads. It has in it all the best traits of Mr. Black's work, and the peculiar charm with which he always depicts life upon the sea. It has, too, a special wisdom, in that the boys work their way up in a natural manner. No miraculous discovery, no prodigy of benevolence smooths the path for them; they make their modest fortune with only such help as diligence and perseverance may expect." [Nation. **1285**

—. SAME, with A BEAUTIFUL WRETCH. Macmillan, 1881.

FOUR SCHOOLFELLOWS. [Skeet, 1878.] "The 4 schoolfelloes in the french convent, tho not very attractiv, ar not uninteresting. Thêre is something rather grand about the proud beauty Adrienne de Coralae, who loses at one fell stroke her wealth, her beauty and her lover, and parts with the latter with a scorn which hides effectually the terrible wound she sustains. Old Lady Caroline is somewhat too fantastic in her cynicism to be quite real, but she, as well as the other matrons, is consistent in her oddities. Gertrude Calverly is both womanly and spirited, and is well rid of the selfish barrister who so nearly married her for her wealth. On the whole, thêre is character in the story, which involvs a large number of parts in general ably sustained." [Athenæum. **1286**

FOXGLOVE MANOR [by Ro. Buchanan: *Chatto*, 1884.] " is a powerful study. Mr. Buchanan has firmly grasped the character of a man of a sensuous and even refined imagination, but without any moral fibre. Tho the man is a clergyman the author disclaims the intention of making an attack upon the clergy generally, but he has made an opportunity for a great quantity of controversial matter by introducing as the chief contrast to the clergyman a professed agnostic. Mr. Buchanan has drawn the central figure with consummate skill, and told his story with great vigor, directness, and rapidity of narration. At the opening the clergyman is set clearly before the reader, fascinated by the charms of art and religion, and yet haunted by doubts as to his creed, keenly sensitiv to opinion, emotional, and vaguely ambitious. He is half attracted by the unconcealed adoration of a simple little girl when, in the midst of one of his impassioned sermons, he sees before him the face of the woman he had once loved. She is married, and has come to liv in his parish. Then begins the story of his moral failure, and Mr. Buchanan has revealed the workings of his mind and his spiritual degradation with complete success." [Athenæum. **1287**

FRAMLEY PARSONAGE. [by An-

thony Trollope: *Smith*, 1861.] " Too many hundreds hav read this beautiful novel for it to be necessary to giv any account of it as a story. Every one who reads novels at all is familiar with the little brown Lucy, and how she won the golden prize at last, and chiefly by seem· ing not to care for it; with Mark Roberts, soft, easy, pleasure-loving; and dear Fanny, all that a pretty young wife and mother should be; with Lady Lufton, despotic and benevolent, narro and generous, proud and Christian-hearted; with Mr. Sowerby, eaten by creditors and the great duke; with Griselda Grantly, that matchless marchioness, who gave to dress what others would giv to passion, or to pleasure, or to heaven.....Here is a man's book, written by a man in a thŏroly masculin spirit and with every adjunct and circumstance mâle, as the French say, to the back bone. We regard this work of Mr. Trollope as matchless in its way, being so perfectly pure and yet so manly, such fitting food for men, but with no odor and no savor which shall hurt the tenderest maiden." [London Review. **1288**

FREDA [by — (Smedley) Hart: *Bentley*, 1879.] " is a most entertaining book. ' Freda' happened to come in the revuer's way as a book to be read for pleasure, and not for business, and he can therefore say in the most unhesitating way that he found it a delitful story. To say that it is eccentric would not be an exaggeration. Such creatures as Freda, happily for the peace of male mankind, are not found wandering about the world; but they ar not the less attractiv to read about. Of course, she represents something in life; she is a type of a number of very inferior realities, but the writer has contrived, without making her in the least unnatural, so to glorify and idealize her, to make her so charming, so naïve, so amusing, that we recognize in her a creation of singular merit. To hav made so striking an addition to that gallery of imaginary portraits which a reader's mind possesses is no slit achievement in a novelist, and the author of Freda has attained it. As a tale, it is needless to criticise it. Of course, it is hily improbable, but the improbability is quite in keeping with the whole of the book. We ar better pleased with such delitful creations as these, than we hav often been with characters drawn on the strictest rules of art, and plots constructed with a most dutiful regard to probability. We feel that we hav not given our readers the least idea of what Freda is, and can only recommend them to find out for themselvs. Men will probably share our enthusiasm, but some women will think it silly." [Spectator. **1289**

FREDERICK RIVERS; INDEPENDENT PARSON. [by FLORENCE ( ) WILLIAMSON: *Williams & Norgate*, 1864.] "The author's object is to sho the vulgarity, narro-mindedness, intolerance and petty tyranny which prevail in Dissenting circles when a minister of more enlarged and liberal vues than the majority hold, dares to act in accordance with his conscience. . . . . Mrs. Williamson exhibits a good deal of ability in the development of her characters, and her book is clever and striking. Frederick Rivers, the hero, is a Dissenting minister who, while admiring the courageous protest of the old Puritans against tyranny in Church and State, heartily dislikes the gloomy and forbidding principles they hav transmitted to the nonconformists of the present day. He sees no harm in the theatre; he is fond of secular literature; and altogether he is a frank, open-hearted, genial, we mit even say jolly, young fello, with a

world of energy and serious thŏt in him, nevertheless. Necessarily, he is persecuted by the narro-natured tradesmen and their wives who 'sit under him;' and he has other trials as well. His sweet-souled, quiet, helpful wife dies in the course of the story, which ends in his second marriage to another equally-charming woman, Effie Holmes, who, her father having been ruined by the dishonesty of a clerk, has been getting her living as a shop-woman, and thereby mortally offending her rich and selfish uncle. The story is altogether slit, tho it includes an underplot in which this uncle is duly brŏt to shame and unhapiness. Too much of mere talking, description, and discussion is the great fault of the book, which, however, shōes also a great deal of humor, observation, and good sense." [London Review. **1290**

FRERES (THE) = No. 456.

FROM BIRTH TO BRIDAL [by — ( ) DAY: *Hurst*, 1873.] "is a wholesom and pleasant novel, with plenty of fresh air, free country life, and talk about children and dogs in it. The girl whose story it tells is an original character, but quite natural, and very charming. . . . . Then thêre is an admirable little episode, in which a quiet, sensible, unselfish, fair-minded man wins his wife's love, without letting her discover that he has suspected the lack of it. The story, very simple in the beginning, gradually groes into a complication involving a difficult situation, a father and son being respectivly in love with the same person. This position is so skilfully treated, with such nice delicacy and simple grace, that while all that is pathetic in the story is put forward with power and effect, no unpleasant impression is produced." [Spectator. **1291**

FROM MOOR ISLES [by JESSIE FOTHERGILL: *Bentley*, 1888.] "is pre-eminently a pretty story. It has delicate sentiment and picturesque scenes, and the language has at times a quality quite musical. The reader may make his choice of a hero, for our attention is divided between the devoted gardian of the young Inez, and the casual violinist who was the victim of a bluff at the destructiv game of poker which lost him his estate. One may choose, too, his heroin, whether it be Alice Ormerod, who spent her life in unreciprocated love for the fitful öner of Moor Isles, or Inez, who folloed the dictates of her heart in spite of external surroundings which seemed to impel her in other directions. Miss Fothergill, in all she does, shöes a literary instinct of the first order." [Critic.] —"Brian Holgate is a really fine presentation of the artistic temperament, a temperament which Miss Fothergill understands thöroly, both in its weakness and in .its strength. The early chapters, in which Brian is the prominent figure, ar the strongest in the book; and the noble portrait of Alice Ormerod makes them the most attractiv as well. Never, indeed, has Miss Fothergill given us a more graciously molded heroin than this Yorkshire dauter of the people who is Brian's good genius; and probably most novel-readers will be disappointed that her loving devotion does not receive what they will deem its natural reward; but we incline to think that this is one of the cases in which the old fairy-tale ending — 'They wer married, and lived happily ever afterward' — would have been a sacrifice of imaginativ veracity to superficial effectivness." [Spectator. **1292**

FROM THE HEATHER HILLS [by — (   ) PERKS: *Hurst*, 1887.] "is a graceful, interesting, and pleasant story. As may be inferred from the title, it is largely an out-of-doors book, and it is not one of those books in which nature smells of the lamp, but rather one which answers us by some intangible suggestion, that the writer has had long and loving familiarity with the springy moorland carpet and the keen moorland air. Even when Peggy Dalrymple is taken by Lady Erinwood from her Highland home into the whirl of a London season, we hardly lose the out-of-doors feeling, for

"'She brings the scent of heather with her,
To sho in what sweet glens she grew; —
Whene'er she trips in any weather,
She steps as if she trod on heather,
And leaves a sense like dropping dew.'"
[Spectator.   **1293**

GABRIELLE VAUGHAN [by M.. E. SHIPLEY: *Seeley*, 1876.] "has the merit of increasing in interest as the story proceeds. The scene and actors ar at first unattractiv. A struggling doctor's family in the outskirts of London does not promis to afford anything exciting in the way of incident, and a large household kept in submission to domestic disciplin does·not at first seem likely to present any extraordinary varieties of character. Yet, tho the circumstances of Miss Shipley's heroin ar sombre, and the episodes of her story tame, Gabrielle is so consistent in her adherence to duty, so steady in her unselfishness and submission to petty slits, so capable of self-sacrifice in the more important matter of her engagement to Gilbert Selwyn, that in the end she secures the reader's sympathy, and one takes more pleasure in her final happiness than at first seems possible. The drawback from one's complete enjoyment of her triumf arises from the vexatious and unnecessary nature of the trial to which she is exposed. Gabrielle is the artistic member of a commonplace family. It will be seen that the story has nothing of the sensational kind to recommend it;

that in spite of its neutral coloring, several situations and dialogs ar sketched with much force and truth to nature, and that the large party of youths and maidens ar drawn with much clear distinction of théir several characters, should be sufficient to recommend the book to those who ar content with an unpretending 'moral tale.'" [Athenæum. **1295**

GARDEN OF EDEN (The) [*Bentley*, 1882.] "is the work of a cultivated and observant mind, and possesses merits which raise it above the level of mediocrity. . . . . It is thōroly readable, unexceptionable in tone, and written in an intelligible and pleasant style. . . . . The hero, John Clifford, and the heroin Althea Biron, ar clearly, even powerfully drawn characters, and each possesses a distinct and marked individuality. They ar not puppets ticketed with some form of vice or virtue which they ar continually called upon to display, nor ar they dummies, introduced in the first chapter, with a minute description, to which the progress of the story adds not a single feature. They ar more life-like creations, whom the reader feels he comprehends better every moment while the plot is being developed." [Athenæum. **1296**

GARDEN OF MEMORIES (A) [etc.] [by Ma. VELEY: (†, 1887) *Macmillan*, 1887.] "contains three stories, all of them somewhat slender in texture, but all worked out with much delicacy and skill. We can imagin the old picturesque garden, a genuin 'rus in urbe,' which is the bone of contention between Mary Wynne and Thomas Brydon, — she wanting to keep it becaus it is associated with a sweet sentiment, he eager to buy it becaus he sees in it the only possible way of furnishing improved dwellings for a population in whose welfare he feels a keen interest. And the conflict between these two sentiments impresses us as being real, and one in which it is possible to feel a genuin interest. And thêre is skill, too, in the way in which the two ar ultimately reconciled. In 'Mrs. Austin,' a young man falls passionately in love with a woman older than himself; half out of compassion, half from affection which her lover's passion has called into being, she makes up her mind to accept him, and lo! he has changed. The third story is another variation on the familiar theme that first-loves ar often variable. The lover in 'Mrs. Austin' is a fine young fello, in spite of his fickleness; the other characters, both in this and the third story, fail to interest us." [Spectator. **1297**

GARSTANGS OF GARSTANG GRANGE (The). [by T: Adolphus Trollope: *Smith*, 1869.] . . . . "In their way we hav lately read nothing better than the sketches of the firm of Slowcomb and Sligo, solicitors in Silchester. The temptation to burlesque in the case of Mr. Sligo must hav been very great. A folloer of Mr. Dickens would most assuredly hav given us a gross caricature, whêre Mr. Trollope has finely shaded off the character. Mr. Slowcomb, altho we do not see so much of him, with his old-fashioned watch chain and seals, hanging like a kitchen clock's pendulum, and his anecdotes about the county families and their secrets, is equally well sketched. But the real power of the book is shōn in the skillful way in which the plot is gradually developed, and brōt to a climax only in the last chapter. Plot-interest is excessivly difficult to manage. The plot-interest of such writers as *Mr. Wilkie Collins* and *Miss Braddon* is not the plot-interest of true art, but of a kind akin to the morbid curiosity which is excited by an

Old Bailey trial. **Mr.** Trollope's plot is dependent upon the development and evolution of his characters." [Westminster Review. **1298**

GENTLE AND SIMPLE [by M<small>A</small>. A<small>GNES</small> (C<small>OLVILLE</small>) P<small>AUL</small>: *Paul*, 1878.] "is a good story, and of a kind that demands a hearty welcom, in these days of insolently-careless writing and lo motivs in the literature of fiction. It is admirably written, in a style which combines ease and carefulness, and it is as refined as it is clever. . . . . The scheming german girl is an admirable foil to the noble and uprit Millicent, but tho contrast is never drawn coarsely, nor ar the two brôt face to face in any broad rivalry." [Spectator.] — "'Gentle and Simple' is a pleasing novel of character. . . . . In spite, however, of her treatment at the hands of her purse-proud uncle and her plebeian aunt, in spite of the doubtful attentions of a worthless fortune-hunter, and the enthusiastic patronage of her cousin, Millicent is a marvel of delicacy and good feeling." [Athenæum. **1299**

GENTLEMAN VERSCHOYLE. [by L<small>AURA</small> M. L<small>ANE</small>: *Low*, 1875.] "The plot is simple, almost commonplace. The style, however, is free from blemish; some of the characters ar well drawn, and in their delineation the author displays considerable knoledge of human nature. The tone of the book is healthful throuoût, and the author, tho venturing to deal with questions not generally supposed to fall within a woman's province, treats them in a thôtful, temperate, and reasonable manner. What we most like is the tender, charitable, and sympathetic feeling evinced, and the care the author takes to avoid making the dramatis personæ unnaturally vicious or virtuous. . . . . The book is characterized by delicacy and refinement. [Athen. **1300**

GEOFFRY HAMLYN [by H: K<small>INGS</small>-<small>LEY</small>: *Macmillan*, 1857.] "is full of power of the most varied and different kinds, descriptiv, analytical, and humorous. We do not kno in fiction a complex character better described or more thôroly analysed than the heroin, who, as her father regretfully says, 'is not a lady,' but a passionate village girl, with a tropical nature, an unregulated brain, and all the instincts of an actress of the loer type. The portrait of this girl, with her fierce, yet not hateful egoism; her capacity of mixing real emotion and histrionic abandon; her rude, and, so to speak, animal, yet true affection for lover, husband, son and friends; her lawless wilfulness, and her latent capability alike of a goodness to which she never reaches, her nature being too vulgar, and a criminality to which she never falls, her training and circumstances being too favorable, is a work of the biest art, and shôed in H: Kingsley not only unusual powers of observation, but power of description of a severely restrained kind, such as is given only to the masters of fiction." [Spectator. **1301**

GEORGE GEITH OF FEN COURT [by "F. G. Trafford," i. e., C.. E<small>LIZA</small> L<small>AWSON</small> (C<small>OWAN</small>) R<small>IDDELL</small>: *Tinsley*, 1865.] "is an excellent novel, powerfully and carefully written. George, the runaway clergyman, tho plodding man of business, with the secret which has darkened his life, but also developed his energy and strength of purpos, is an excellent portrait. He has thrôn away his gown, changed his name and become a man of hard work, — giving himself no rest that he may earn money to retrieve the fatal error into which he has been led as a young man. The reader's interest in the man and his fortunes is thôroly aroused; he has been so deeply wronged, not only by his ōn act of which he is conscious, but by the wrong of another, which has changed the aspect of his fortune. Throuōut he is a deeply injured man, but he is so strong, so uprit, and, above all, so full of hard work, that the reader never deems him a victim; he is fiting a brave battle, and only for a foul blo, a treachery against which he could scarcely hav garded, he would hav won the victory. When he is struck down, he endures like a man. Few heroes of novels win the respect of the reader like George Geith. The other characters ar well drawn. Mr. Molozane, the. proud gentleman ruined by mining speculations, is excellent. Beryll, the young dauter, is a charming creature. The incidental sketches of character ar all good; as ar also the descriptions of the city, of the country, both in summer and winter. We abstain from telling the plot becaus we recommend our readers to get the book for themselves." [Athen. **1302**

GEORGY SANDON. [Boston, 1865.] = *A LOST LOVE.*

GERALD [by ELEANOR C. PRICE: *Chatto*, 1885.] "if only a story, is an original and interesting one. The last few chapters, on life in **Cape Colony**, ar written with a good deal of power, and the touch at the close is to be commended both from the artistic and the moral point of vue. It is a pleasing innovation for a heroin with two lovers, who marries the wrong one, not to be released by her husband's death from her unfortunate fetters, to marry at last the rit one. Theo is not released, but learns to love her chains." [Critic.] — 'Gerald' is a very pretty tale, with enuf of continuous interest, character, and lively dialog to keep the reader pleasantly engrossed. . . . . Theo is a hi-bred, disdainful young lady, whose features ar

constantly liting up with a fine scorn, and who likes to tell her friends in word and action, especially when she is going against their wishes, that she always does what she chooses. Fortunately, however, she nearly always chooses to do the rit thing at the rit moment, from happy instinct and pure goodness of heart, so that nothing very mischievous comes of her obstinacy." [Ath. **1303**

GERALDINE AND HER SUITORS. [by M. C. M. (S.) SIMPSON: *Hurst*, 1881.] "Thêre ar people whom even the unsocially disposed greet with alacrity whêrever they may come across them, and whose books the burdened revuer and the most rit-minded reader alike take with a smile of serene consciousness that they will find in them neither bad sense nor bad grammar, neither ill nature nor slang, and neither be introduced into the society of ruffians or profligates, nor yet into the blinding splendor of that company of Olympos to which Lord Beaconsfield is good enuf to act the part of Hermês. Among these universally-welcom people, Mrs. Simpson has for some years taken her place . . . . .. In turning out these smooth, brit, and well-written novels — 'Winnie's History,' [No. 560], and 'Geraldine' — she is always 'mistress of the situation,' dealing with her subject with perfect ease and tact, and the grace of a gentlewoman. Her heroin in this book is a young wido, a pleasant variation on the perpetual theme of clits of 18 endowed not only with all the solid sense of 28 but also with the savoir-faire and knoledg of the world to be acquired at 80. The story of this charming wido is prettily told, and placed in a part of South **Wales.** Everything in the book is perfectly natural, and the talk, of which there is abundance, is never tedious." [Spectator. **1304**

GIANT'S ROBE (The) [by F:
ANSTEY [GUTHRIE]: *Appleton*, 1884.]
"is a very clever book. It is satirical
but not cynical, amusing but not shallo;
without being in the least didactic, it
preaches a powerful sermon, and the
moral it draws is that dear to the heart
of Mrs. Opie: ' Nothing is safe but the
truth.' The hero is a young man with
many pleasing traits and much surface
brilliancy which make him attractiv to
all about him, but the truth is not in
him, and the literary imposition into
which he is allured appears to him a
venial error — so long as he is not found
out. It is not till the very last of the
peacock plumes is torn from the poor
shivering jackdaw that he sees himself
as he really is, and is brôt to the state
which the mystics call ' vastation,' in
which the planting of a new life becomes possible. Such a theme for a
story sounds grim and severe, but in
point of fact its treatment is not at all in
the tragic vein. The brilliancy of the
style is that of hi comedy, and thêre is a
kindly tolerance of tone which extends
even to the deeper-dyed villain of the
story. Ideal goodness is sustained in
the character of Mabel, who is as charming as hi spirit, intelligence, rectitude
and feminin softness combined can
make one." [American.] — "As it is
neither fantastic nor funny, extended
comparison between it and ' Vice Versa '
would be idle. It is a more solid and
thôtful work than Mr. Anstey's earlier
novel. The plot is an excellent one;
the characters ar well chosen, and the
expression, if not always free, is never
inadequate, often happy. The author
has already been accused of stealing his
central situation, but his preface ac-
knoledges a debt to the intrigue of a
Christmas story. Fortunately it makes
little difference whether the incident is

borroed or not, since the treatment is
strikingly original and vigorous. Mark
Ashburn's appropriation of his friend's
accepted manuscript is something more
than a common theft for money and notoriety; it is the extreme expression of
belief in his ōn literary talent; it is the
forlorn hope upon which hangs the fate of
his hitherto unappreciated ' Sweet Bells
Jangled.' In the drawing of the vain,
shallo, but not wholly worthless Ashburn, every stroke tells. While his
literary hallucination lasts, he does infamous things, and is comparativly
happy. Forced admission of his mistake about the quality of his genius
brings some dim perception of the extent and variety of his errors, and pangs
of remorse for the suffering and sorro
so uselessly heaped upon Holroyd.
Then his natural impulse to help other
people, chiefly that he may be comfortable, takes possession of him, and he
tells the truth." [Nation.] — " The story
of ' Tom Singleton ' [by W. F. SYNGE:
Chapman, 1879.] turns upon the difficulties which arose from a man's ap-
propriating to himself the glory and the
profits of a play, the manuscript of
which had been sent to him from India
by his friend the hero. The author's
invention is happily contrived." Compare, also, plot of No. 273. [Athe-
næum.] **1305**

GIDEON FLEYCE [by H: W.
LUCY: *Holt*, 1883.] " created, it is reported, a sensation in London becaus
of its life-like sketches of certain well
knōn public characters. This may well
be, but the book challenges admiration
on its merits as a story, and will be read
with pleasure by readers who kno nothing and care as little about London notabilities. It combines various kinds of
merit more or less rare by themselvs,
and rarer still in combination. Its style

is attractiv in its artful, or rather, artistic simplicity. Its plot is more intricate and more full of surprises than one is accustomed to look for now-a-days, and, tho hovering on the brink of melodrama, never actually loses its air of every day, newspaper reality." [Nation. **1306**

GILBERT RUGGE [by H : Jackson: *Harper*, 1866.] "is a very clever, gracefully written story. The hero is the well-born young gentleman who starts in life under the most favorable auspices, is lured away from his first love by a city beauty with whom his suit eventually prospers, only that she may jilt him heartlessly upon the discovery that he is the offspring of a mésalliance, hitherto successfully concealed by his family from himself and the world; poverty and other misfortunes accumulate about him that his character may be purified by adversity in the orthodox manner, which being happily accomplished, and having furthermore achieved success, as usual, in literature, he wooes for the third time his first love, is accepted, and married; while retributiv justice in various forms overtakes the evil-minded." [Round Table. **1307**

GIRL HE DID NOT MARRY (The). [by Iza Duffus Hardy: *White*, 1889.] "Thêre is much pathos in Miss Hardy's description of a wayward, hï-spirited, lâfing coquette gradually being reduced by several bitter experiences to a sad and solitary woman. It is a pitiful story, but it is redeemed by the really lifelike character of Hazel, who under her frivolity and heartlessness, as far as wooers ar concerned, bears a courageous and a tender spirit, and has that strong family affection which is the deepest feeling of many of the best of her sex. . . . . The book is britly written, and the author wins our sympathies for the luckless heroin." [Athenæum. **1308**

GIRL'S ROMANCE (A). [Edinburgh, *Edmonston*, 1867.] "The story is as natural as it is graceful, and it has the merit of being very touching and pathetic without leaving a painful impression. So many of the romances which we meet now-a-days ar either hopelessly vapid and unmeaning, incurably morbid, or repulsivly unnatural, that it is a real pleasure to lit unexpectedly upon one which is pure and fresh and healthy, which tells a charming love-story in a style deserving of hi praise, and which throuôut teaches an excellent lesson in an unobtrusiv manner. . . . . It is a very simple story, with little incident in it, its merit arising chiefly from the excellence of its delineation of one character. Janet Radway has been bred almost alone. Her mother is an invalid, her father a scholar, almost always absorbed in his studies. . . . . And so she groes up enthusiastic and romantic, eager to solv the mysteries of life, and little qualified to bear the sorroes which they involv. Chance throes her in the way of a wandering artist, who greatly admires her, and amuses himself by flirting with her. He means no harm, and he has no idea of intentionally deceiving her, for he is not entirely heartless. But he is sufficiently selfish to allow himself the pleasure of winning this young and confiding heart, and cold enuf to be able to withdraw and leave it to grieve for its loss without troubling himself about its sorroes. Thêre is great charm in the description of Janet's almost overwhelming joy when she finds out that he cares for her, and her belief that a happy time is at last beginning for her, and the pictures in which she figures by his side, while wandering throu the woods or by the riverside, ar full of life and color. . . . . Life gains by degrees a firmer hold over her; the possibility of happiness again enters into her meditations, and she learns to look calmly back on the past, and to estimate at its true worth the character of the man whom she used to adore. At the same time she learns the value of such a true affection as that which a very different man from the romantic but selfish artist who won her girlish heart has felt for her since the days of his boyhood. The conclusion of the story is well managed, there being a very dramatic scene just before its close. It is a book of very decided and unusual merit. We ar sure that we shall deserv the thanks of our readers, many of whom mit be led by the modesty of its appearance to overlook it, if we induce them to read this charming record of ' A Girl's Romance.' " [London Rev. **1309**

GIRTON GIRL (A). [by ANNIE ( ) EDWARDS: *Bentley*, 1886.] "The girl never goes to Girton; neither is she the chief personage of the story. Nevertheless, she is a charming and original girl. . . . . The true ' motiv ' of the story, apart from the love troubles of Geoffry and Marjorie, is very like that of 'Ought We to Visit Her?' The selfish, indolent, half-cynical worthlessness of the man in both novels and . . . . Dinah's character ar worked out perfectly; the little touches of unreasonableness, due to her entire ignorance of that kind of life in which Gaston is a blasé adept, ar supplied with great skill. The reader's sympathy with her is sometimes taxed a little, but it never quite givs way. And the britness and movement of the story, sarcastic and sardonic as it is, around the honest, frank, honorable, loving woman's figure in the centre, ar

very pleasant. The married flirt, of the confidential, 'incomprise' kind, with a facility for depreciating men's wives, with a deadly skill, tho she is charming to and concerning her husband in public, is always a success in the hands of Mrs. Edwards. She has never surpassed the typical flirt of this novel, Linda Thorne." [Spectator. **1310**

GLAMOUR. [by "WANDERER:" *Sonnenschein*, 1886.] "The hero of this pleasant and readable book is a young man who is somewhat of a paragon without being a prig, and is sorely perplexed as to whether or not he shall marry a charming, sensible, and in every way desirable girl, becaus he cannot be sure that he is in love with her. Tho his opinion inclines to the contrary, he is, nevertheless, quite open to conviction; and as, on recounting his symptoms to, and taking counsel with, various friends, he finds they ar all confident of his amatory condition being what it should be, he supposes they must be rit, and marries accordingly. Thanks partly to *his*, and partly to his wife's merits, they get on happily, except twice, when chance brings him in contact with a woman who has a fascination for him, and whom he no sooner sees, than he flirts with her in a manner most unbecoming to a married man. On both occasions, retribution followes swiftly." [Spectator. **1311**

GLENCOONOGE [by R: BRINSLEY SHERIDAN KNOWLES: *Blackwood*, 1891.] " is a well-written and litly-conceived story. . . . . At Glencoonoge the narrator stumbles upon a pretty romance, which begins in a sufficiently commonplace fashion, groes upon one as it develops, and gradually passes throu the fäses of mystery and dénoûment." [Athenæum. **1312**

GLENNAIR [by H.. HAZLETT:

Phila., *Claxton*, 1869.] "is a simple, but by no means uninteresting story, the scene of which is laid in the **High-lands** of Scotland. The diction is familiar; the incidents, tho somewhat commonplace, hav all the charm of probability, and thêre is a general tone of directness pervading the narrativ which suits well its subject. The characters of the chief personages ar nicely balanced; they ar neither marvels of goodness nor monsters of iniquity, but just such men and women as we meet every day, with the same proportional mixture of good and evil. The author does not present us with a series of incredible adventures; she passes quietly throu the shaded paths of private life, conversing with gentle natures and patient sufferings." [Round Table. **1313**

GOLDEN BAR (A). [by E. M. (TAYLOR) ARCHER: *Hurst*, 1883.] "Old Squire Haseltine is a county magnate, with a grand park and house, which bear the name of their lord. As death draws near, he meets for the first time pecuniary embarrassments. He cannot leave his property to his eldest son, who has died; nor to his younger son, with whom he has quarreled; and he cannot take it with him. . . . . Suddenly they come to understand each other, — but whether throu an increase of wisdom, — each of them having learned that pride is not a thing to be proud of, and that true love is not a thing to be spurned, — or throu some skilful device of the lawyers allowing each to be happy, in spite of the codicil, and without either of them condescending to humiliation, we shall not record. The tale is wholly free from the pretentious bad taste now so common. It is written with singular felicity of style, and uniform purity and refinement; it abounds in lively dialog and vivid description; and while it is free from all which is 'sensational,' it does not lack scenes of passion, in the hier sense of that often misused word." [Spectator.

GOLDEN BUTTERFLY (The). [by WA. BESANT & JA. RICE: N. Y., 1874?] "We hav here a rather clever educational idea joined to another marked quality of Mr. Besant's mind — his love for exaggeration; so that as a whole story it is simply an extravaganza. Every character, with the exception of Jack Dunquerque and Capt. Ladds, is overdrawn, altho faithful enuf to certain parallels of truth. Gilead P. Beck, the nervous, loquacious, egoistic, whole-souled american, who, thanks to the luck of the Golden Butterfly, 'struck ile,' is a type everyone knoes off the stage. Delitful, genuin Phillis Fleming, the charming illustration of the very suggestiv educational experiment, is alas! an impossible girl. The twins ar, we ar glad to say, more conceited imbecils than we find in life, broad as that latitude is. Yet the book is remarkably clever. Could anything be keener in its sarcasm against modern dilettanteism than the talk of the twins over their picture and their poem? Who does not enjoy the droll satire of that inimitable dinner of authors which Gilead Beck gave in hopes that the literary lions would sho their points, and the satire of the points which they did sho — appreciation of mulligatawny, clear, and an intimate knoledge of horseracing? Taken in connexion with the description of the vulgar display, the menu cards, the allegorical fountain, the Stars and Stripes, the rock-oil lamp, and the fact that the man of oil felt instinctivly that he was being guyed by the great moralists — a more spontaneous bit of humorous writing could scarcely be conceived." [Critic. **1315**

GOLDEN MILESTONE (The) [by SCOTT GRAHAM : *Wyman,* 1885.] "records some 'passages in the life of an ex-Confederate officer,' and the Virginian whose unexpected claim to represent the elder branch of the family of Stacpoole Court has so far-reaching an effect upon the fortunes of his english cousins, is a good specimen of an american gentleman. It is obvious to the practised novel-reader that the union between Radcliffe and his fair cousin is merely a matter of time, and that in this will be found the solution of the difficulty. Love at first sit is seldom entirely unappreciated by its object; and when Radcliffe imperils his life to save that of Dulcie's objectionable brother he wins entire forgivness for his imaginary offenses. .A good deal of the story is taken up with the struggles of Dulcie and her father in the provincial town to which the latter, after his ruin, has betaken himself as an organist; and the more or less vulgar society of Westlake, with its petty system of persecuting those it does not understand, is very fairly described. There is a tolerable and not exaggerated yankee, or naturalized yankee who acts the good fairy all round, and combines dollars with infinit good nature." [Athenæum. **1316**

GOLDEN SHAFT (The) [by C: GIBBON : *Chatto,* 1882.] "is a genuin work of art, fashioned out of materials which mit seem meagre but for the skill with which they ar manipulated. The actors ar few in number, and hav not the prestige of exalted rank, great wealth, or even exceptional personal attributes. The scene lies in the south-west of **Scotland,** in a small town and its néborhood. Tho thêre is no lack of incident, thére is little which verges on the sensational. Nevertheless, the story, even from the first chapter, fixes the attention and enlists the sympathy of the reader, and the interest never flags. Whêrein the charm consists it is not difficult to say. Entire naturalness in the march of events, and in the dialog, force and delicacy in the delineation of character, telling descriptions of scenery and atmosferic conditions, sound morality, and good, unaffected writing — such is the bill of fare here offered." [Westminster Review. **1317**

GOOD MATCH (A) [by AMELIA PERRIER : N. Y., *Ford,* 1873.] "is an amusing, hoydenish novel, told in the first person by a poverty-stricken young woman. She livs with grand but also poverty-stricken relativs, who ar trying in vain to marry her to a vulgar, but rich and aged widoer, who livs at Texton Hall, the seat of Lord Texworth. Lord Texworth himself has disappeared from human ken in order to make enuf money to buy back his estates, which, under stress of poverty, he had sold, with the rit of buying them back at the same price at the end of 25 years. The heroin falls in love with a young and handsome stranger, and the two ar married. Of course he turns out to be the missing ōner of Texton Hall, and, after some years of hard work, they liv in happiness and affluence. The plot is as transparent as it is artificial; but the story, altho it does not always preserv the elegant proprieties which should adorn the noble line of Texworth, is often funny enuf." [Nation. **1318**

GOSAU SMITHY (The). [by LOUISA (TAYLOR) PARR : *Daldy,* 1874.] "Mrs. Parr's tales ar not wanting in graceful passages. Some of them ar rather sad, as that of 'The Gosau Smithy,' a story of Swiss peasant life, in which a pair of faithful lovers ar ruthlessly drowned in a lake. 'La

Bonne Mère Nannette,' too, has a painful history, tho her self-sacrifice and fidelity bring their reward in the evening of her days. 'Little Nan' is the pathetic story of an orfan girl, whose early life among a set of kind-hearted tramps, and later trials under the severe disciplin of a 'respectable' school, produce a discord which mars her girlish days, tho in the end she finds happiness as the wife of a good man, who attempted to be her benefactor in childhood. The second volume consists of love-tales in a hier grade of society, mostly natural and pleasing, tho a little inclined to be 'goody.' Yet they smack of observation, and ar true enuf to that peaceful type of nature to which the author is wise in confining her attention." [Athenæum. **1319**

GRAPE FROM A THORN (A) [by JA. PAYN: *Harper*, 1881.] "is a hily amusing novel. The amusement consists in the delineation of a group of characters collected at a watering-place. The plan of the story is simple, and the author's effort is chiefly expended on portraiture and dialog. The result givs a new and enlarged sense of Mr. Payn's powers. He writes here with a delitful humor and even with occasional brilliancy, and nothing could be better in its way than some of the touches with which he takes off the follies and vanities of a set of fashionable people. [Boston "Literary World." **1320**

GREAT EXPECTATIONS. = No. 722.

GREAT GULF FIXED [by "GERALD GRANT," i. e., Gertrude Grant (†, 1883) *Tinsley*, 1877.] "is not a conventional novel. Neither is it more than reasonably sensational. The hero is not perfect; nor is the heroin divinely beautiful. The char-

acters ar neatly and naturally, rather than powerfully drawn. The women ar womanly without being insipid, and the leading lady is a charming creature. Mr. and Mrs. Lane, the little cosy, comfortable, good-hearted middle class couple, ar well described; and it is possible to feel that we hav knôn them somewhêre." [Athenæum. **1321**

GREATEST HEIRESS IN ENG-LAND (The) [by MA. OLIPHANT (WILSON) OLIPHANT: *Hurst*, 1880.] . . . . "is noticeably good among the great number of Mrs. Oliphant's good novels. The story runs along so pleasantly and maintains the reader's interest so completely throuout, that one hardly cares to pick it to pieces in order to sho how cleverly it is put together. The heiress and her friends ar depicted both before and after she comes into her fortune. The society is chiefly that of a provincial town. First one sees the people enuf to understand them and to form some opinion upon their characters; then the heiress becomes great, and begins to be petted and courted by the women, and made love to by the men, and thus an excellent opportunity is created for working out the diversities of ordinary people." [Athenæum.] — See *SIR TOM*. **1322**

GREEN HILLS BY THE SEA [by H. C. DAVIDSON: *Hurst*, 1887.] "is a story of the **Isle of Man.** With none of the fierceness which certain latter-day novelists affect, the book has enuf of personal atmosfere and grace of manner to compel the attention and to silence, for the time being, the noise of the world without. Nothing, perhaps, either in fiction or life, is so pleasant as to fall into the spirit of a tiny island, except to escape from it when the spell ceases to work. In 'The Green Hills by the Sea,' in spite of di-

411

gressions and unnecessary complications which somewhat mar its symmetry, this spell outlivs the reading, and even the revuer may feel regret in laying down the fatal ' last of three.' . . . . The author's forte consists in getting his readers well into a certain train of thôt and emotion, and thêre holding them in contentment with a skill which amounts to art. . . . . The appearance, the atmosfere, and the general ' sentiment ' (so to speak) of Manxland ar vividly felt and rendered; yet imaginativness of treatment and softness of outline ar preserved throuout." [Athenæum. **1323**

GREEN PASTURES AND PICCADILLY [by W: BLACK : *Macmillan*, 1877.] "begins very pleasantly. Has not Mr. Black a simple and peculiar grace of literary entrance ? On this occasion it seems charmingly proper that we should o to an old and much-admired acquaintance, Queen Tita of the Faeton, our introduction to a new heroin, and one of the loveliest and most clearly individualized of them all, Lady Sylvia Blythe. We like her scotch lover too, and entirely believe in him. Balfour, whose name is historic if he is in trade (so aristocratic do we all become in the charmed ' Liberties ' of english fiction!) — Hugh Balfour, of the hi mind, the hard head, the true heart; of enlitened and wary but ungrudging benevolence ; of strict but unsentimental sense of honor, scornful integrity, and hauty, quarrelsom temper." [Atlantic.] — " We hav not scrupled to tell a good deal of the story, becaus no one's stories suffer less than Mr. Black's from such treatment. We ar never tempted to look at the end ; for the secret of their success lies much more in the manner than the matter. IIis people ar real people, and pleasant,

too, as a rule; and they say and do pretty much what we hear said and see done when we ar among persons and in places whêre we like to be. IIis genius resembles very closely that of Mr. Trollope, but his taste is better : he is a purist when the elder writer is a naturalist [realist?]." [Athenæum. **1324**

GREEN PLEASURE AND GREY GRIEF [by MA. ( ) (AROLES) HUNGERFORD : *Smith*, 1885.] " is what many of its readers will be inclined to call a sweetly pretty story. Thêre is no question as to its sweetness and prettiness, for it is full of delitful love-making, and is told with dainty tenderness by one who understands both idyllic love and the art of romantic writing. ·The author is never tired of describing the happy intercourse of fresh young hearts, and folloes with evident zest the fortunes of 3 pairs of lovers throu the chequered course of their mutual passion. Perhaps her story would hav been better described by an inversion of the title, for the grey grief is not allowed to overwhelm the pleasure of any character who figures in its pages." [Ath. **1325**

GRISEL ROMNEY. [by M.. E. (FRASER-TYTLER) GREENE : *M. Ward*, 1881.] " The reader who asks, when he has finished ' Grisel Romney,' what has carried him throu the story without any feeling of tediousness, will not easily find an answer. That it is written with good-feeling and good-taste, in a style which never offends by incorrectness or extravagance, is the chief merit which he will be able to find in it. . . . . But these criticisms will probably not occur till the end of the story has been reached ; and that it should hav been reached not only without difficulty, but with pleasure, is no slit commendation." [Spec. **1326**

GUIDE, PHILOSOPHER, AND FRIEND [by — ( ) MARTIN : *Griffith*,

1884.] "is well worth reading. The guide, filosofer and friend is Phillis Carr, charming and distinguished, but penniless, who consents to act as bearleader to a rich mushroom family. The mushrooms ar good, honest folk; in spite of being homely and unfashionable they ar true gentlefolk, and they win upon us as we follo them in their timid siege of London. The son of the house, a handsom, silent, and true-hearted young giant, inevitably falls in love with Phillis, and the course of his love does not run smooth. The by-play is pretty, and the earnest, downrit Dick Harrison, the hard-working East-end curate, is very amusing." [Athenæum. **1327**

GUILD COURT. [by G: MAC-DONALD: *Hurst*, 1867.] " When we speak of ' Guild Court' as a very entertaining story, abounding with wholesom interest and wise counsel, it must be understood that our commendation of the book is addressed specially to a seléct class of readers, who ar capable of appreciating the author's method, and do not accuse a novel of unreadableness merely becaus it lacks the devices of sensational artifice, and to be enjoyed must be examined instead of ' skimmed.' . . . . Tom Worboise defeats the dishonest contrivance of his selfish father, and rehabilitates himself in the respect of his nébors and the heroin's love. Even those who only value prose fiction for the excitements which may be derived from it, will acknoledg that this latter part of ' Guild Court' is capital." [Athenæum. **1328**

HAGAR [by M., LINSKILL (†, 1891): *Clarke & Co.*, 1887.] is " a delicate and tasteful piece of work. The love of Christopher Fane for Hagar makes a beautiful little story, strongly tinged, indeed, with the melancholy throu which Miss Linskill seems to regard her world,

but very attractiv. In fact, this time she has put a certain constraint on herself, and not buried the happy lovers under the landslip which overwhelms poor Phil. She may take our word that the story is not the worse for it." [Spectator.] — " We can heartily recommend ' Hagar.' Even those who hav once read it will, we ar sure, read this picturesque story again with pleasure, so fresh and touching in its simplicity is it. Miss Linskill is in her element upon her **Yorkshire** coast, with its ruf but good-hearted country-folk, and its wild, fascinating beauty. Her Yorkshire dialect is capital, and Hagar, with her shy, girlish love for her idol — the poor village schoolmaster, — is a most charming character." [Spectator. **1329**

HALF A MILLION OF MONEY [by AMELIA BLANDFORD EDWARDS: *Tinsley*, 1866.] "in spite of some extravagances, is one of the pleasantest novels of the season. It is full of crisp writing and easy dialog. The writer has lived in a world of books, and has also made the world her book. The title alone ôt to render the work popular in a country whêre the 11th commandment, ' thou shalt not be poor,' if not always obeyed, is always feared. But the book givs far more than the title promises. The hero, who has been bred in the wildest part of Switzerland, inherits four millions, and a wicked cousin. The young savage, up to the time of his windfall, does not kno what a Bank of England note is. The barbarian is ignorant of I.O.U's. Civilization, however, acquaints him not only with the latter, but with forgeries. Good society shões him ingratitude, and other polite vices. The work is full of clever, incisiv sayings, and is marked by an absence of all vulgarity." [Westminster Review. **1330**

413

HAND OF ETHELBERTA (The). [by T : HARDY : *Holt*,,1867.] " In taking up Mr. Hardy's new story, one instantly re-discovers how great is the charm of a book in which the style everywhère givs token of a sensitiv personal touch from the author, where the words do not, as in average novels, shrivel and harden into their ordinary aspects, but continually freshen in the quiet dew of thòt which the author lets fall upon every detail. . . . In Ethelberta thère is certainly no lack of interest of a kind which must be acceptable to a wide variety of readers. The heroin is a butler's dauter who, from governessing, has passed into London society as the dauter-in-law of Lady Petherwin; and the strange predicament of her parentage, together with her personal attractions and the motiv of marrying in a way to profit her poor relativs, which greatly complicates her love-affairs, — these elements ar all of lively efficacy. The turns of the plot, at the close, ar extremely clever and absorbing." [Atlantic. **1331**

HANNAH. [by DINAH MARIA (MULOCK) CRAIK: (†, 1887) *Harper*, 1871.] " Hannah Thelluson is such a woman as Mrs. Craik delits to draw, and such as few writers can draw so well. She admires beauty of soul, and invests with it all her heroins. While we do not find Hannah herself to be really fascinating — becaus, probably, her charms ar too spiritualized to affect our earthly judgment — we yet admire her as the embodiment of the very hiest qualities of womanhood, sympathize with her throu her long trials, and rejoice in her final bliss. She is the only character in the story to which the thòtful reader can giv his unqualified approval. Bernard, tho drawn with great skill, and a character in some respects really novel,

sometimes merits a feeling a little milder than contempt; but he ' comes out strong' in the end. Of the other personages in the story little need be said; they ar all mere foils to set off the principals. The incidents ar few in number, and not striking; in fine, thère is little in the book to divert attention from the leading actors in a quiet, tho intense, drama. One of the most beautiful things in the story is Hannah's love for Rosie, in the setting forth of which thère ar frequent touches which probably no one but a mother [!] could hav effected, and which will bring tears to many maternal eyes. While, as we hav said, ' Hannah ' is a painful story, it is absorbingly interesting. No novels of the time, we think, ar so influential as this author's, in promoting a love for moral beauty, and developing those virtues which, in the language of Mr. Butler ' — Grace and gladden all our Saxon homes.' " [Boston " Literary World." **1332**

HAPPY WOOING (A) [by H. CLIFFE HALLIDAY : *Hurst*, 1889.] is " a capital bit of comedy. The earlier part of it is poor as regards literary effect, but as the plot develops one becomes thòroly interested. A young lady and her supposed gardian ânt arrive from Pelican Island, and as they ar reputed to be millionaires they create a great sensation. Their names ar Jennie and Minnie Money, and they ar wooed rit and left for their great wealth. Thère may be such nincompoops in the peerage as Viscount Daffodil and the Hon. Robin Redwood, but scarcely any, I should think, so absolutely devoid of sense and grammar. One makes love to Jennie and the other to Minnie, and each learns to his horror that all the money has been left to the girl wooed by his friend. In the end a fine young fello, Valentine Silver, carries off the ânt; and Adam Ash, an out-at-elboes scribbler, who makes a gigantic success with a novel, wins the other. Upon the wedding-day genuin surprise is evoked by the discovery that the two ladies ar sisters, with £250,000 each, besides real estate galore. They hav resolved to yield only to the feeling of love for themselvs alone; and the end justifies the means, tho it causes considerable scandal and remains a nine days' wonder." [Academy. **1333**

HARD CASH. [by C: READE: *Blackwood*, 1864.] "The book which re-introduces us to the pair we left [in 'Love me Little, Love me Long'] in the first glo of bridal happiness is entitled 'Hard Cash.' The Hard Cash of the work is David Dodd's cash, £14,000, which in those 20 years which hav passed since we saw him, he has amassed for his children. He is 20 years older, when we see him, every day of it. He is all mello experience, benignity, the softened, widened soul of natural charity which it requires years to develop. That is the only change which has come over him. [Blackwood's. **1334**

HARRY BLOUNT [by PHILIP GILBERT HAMERTON: *Roberts*, 1875.] "is a wholesom, brit, and interesting story. It gives pleasant and faithful pictures of english school-life, and grafic sketches of hunting and yachting adventures, and embodies some useful moral lessons together with considerable practical information." [Boston "Lit.World." **1335**

HARRY MUIR [by MA. OLIPHANT (WILSON) OLIPHANT: *Hurst*, 1853.] "tho sad 'is over true'—a real picture of the weakness of man's nature, and the depth of woman's tenderness—and in its sadness true to the country in which the scene is laid. From the introduction of Harry Muir, his case will be perceived to be hopeless; it is the manner in which out of its bitterness gracious influences and pure affections ar developed, which givs the charm to the tale. Some of Martha Muir's less amiable peculiarities ar exaggerated in an old relativ, Miss Jean Calder—who is one of those grim, parsimonious crones who figure often in domestic tales of the 'North Countree.' The narrativ has its relief of serene sunshine, amidst so much gloom, in the loves of Cuthbert and Rose—and, to repeat our praise, is not one to be entered on or parted from without our regard for its writer being increased." [Athenæum. **1336**

HARVEYS (The) [by H: KINGSLEY: *Tinsley*, 1871.] is a "slit but readable story;—instinct with the author's peculiarities of thôt and style. The conversations ar terse and animated and really like the speech of every-day life. The Harvey family do not fail to sho a great variety of individual peculiarities, and resemble one another only in the bohemianism and generous recklessness which thêy inherit from a puzzle-headed and simple-hearted father. Mr. Harvey, much exercised by theological scruples, yet too humble to regard his fine scent for mare's-nests as a feather in his intellectual head-gear, devoted to his family, yet as incapable of providing for them as a hen for her adopted ducklings, and struggling cheerily and patiently with a very sordid entanglement of pecuniary troubles, is a sketch which would be well worth more complete development, wer not the type unfortunately common. In the autobiografy of the young artist, his favorit son, we hav an amazing series of adventures compressed into a field of very limited compass. In the school-life so capitally described, in the struggle of his artistic novitiate, in his relation to the congeries of religious and theatrical fanatics which surround his disastrous but amusing experience of german dungeons and duelling, the buoyancy of young Harvey's character produces the very complications which set it forth to such advantage." [Athenæum. **1337**

HATHERCOURT [by M.. L.. (STEWART) MOLESWORTH: *Holt*, 1878.] " is a singularly pure, graceful, simple, and pleasing story, with an air of refinement and hi-breeding about it. . . . . She takes men, women, and things as she finds them, and all she attempts to sho is that the life and possible experiences of two young ladies in the quietest of country rectories ar adequate and attractiv materials for the novelist willing to make the best of them. . . . . The narrativ never becomes exciting, but the interest is steadily maintained throughout." [Appleton's. **1338**

HAWORTH'S [by F.. ELIZA (HODGSON) BURNETT: *Scribner*, 1879.] " is a strong story but not a good one. The people to whom it introduces us ar not in any sense good company; and thêre is very little in the book to inspire a generous sentiment or to quicken a worthy purpose. 'Life' enuf, of a certain sort, the book contains; but it is a kind of life of which most of us kno far too much already; the writer deservs no thanks who makes us 'liv it over again, and seeks to awaken in us a savage pleasure as its tragedy goes on before our face." [Good Company. **1339**

HE THAT WILL NOT WHEN HE MAY. [by MA. OLIPHANT (WILSON) OLIPHANT: *Macmillan*, 1880.] " This is a novel which no one can read without pleasure. In plot, in treatment, and

as regards most of the characters, it is almost devoid of faults. . . . . The plot of the story, if not novel in its essential features, is made interesting by the manner in which it is developed, and by numberless little incidental refinements and devices. It has a mystery in it, but not a harroing or portentous mystery — in fact, one foresees very early in the story what the general course of things is likely to be; but the charm of the tale is enhanced rather than diminished by this transparency, becaus we ar constantly called upon to admire the simplicity, naturalness, and dexterity whêrewith the successiv complications ar introduced and unravelled. The idea of introducing, out of a clear sky, a claimant to an estate the inheritance of which was supposed to be as settled as the succession of the seasons, is not unknôn to novelists, but to make the disinherited gentleman deserv his fate by the whimsical and empty perversity of his disposition is a delitful stratagem, and renders the good-humor of the reader imperturbable throu all vicissitudes. Again, the honesty, simplicity, and mingled gentleness and firmness of the 'little gentleman' who represents the disturbing element in the tale is a most happy variation upon the conventional treatment in such cases. And Mr. Paul's love affair is ingeniously contrived to sound an accompaniment to the prevailing sentiment of the story, and at the same time to humiliate the objectional persons, and to gratify the well-disposed ones." [Spectator. **1340**

HEALEY [by JESSIE FOTHERGILL: (†, 1891) *Harper*, 1875.] " is a rather unpleasant novel, but givs evidence of considerable originality and power; thêre is nothing humorous, or even cheerful in it, except the dénoument, whêre the lovers ar married. But they ar lovers of an odd sort, and their courtship by no means realizes the ideal felicities of that relation. The heroin is a remarkable character; thêre is a strong heroic element in her nature, and tho she does not fascinate the reader, she gains a strong hold upon his respect and interest. Thêre is nothing romantic about her; she is plain, and attractiv only to those who hav learned to love her. The scene of the story is laid in **Lancashire**, and the dialect of that region is often puzzling to the reader." [Boston "Literary World." **1341**

HEART SALVAGE. [by K.. (SAUNDERS) COOPER: *Chatto*, 1884.] "This collection goes to sho that the author of 'Gideon's Rock' has not lost her skill, and several of her tales ar marked by a good deal of pathos. The fiery, unhappy, warm-hearted, unsuccessful Tom Bailey is a figure one will remember, tho his secret trouble is only the fancied estrangement of a friend, and tho his more palpable sufferings ar the commonplace troubles of unromantic poverty in a suburban villa. Besides Tom, his good wife and gentle danter ar well described in '*By the Stone Ezel.*' *The Harpers of Min-y-don* ar more picturesque in their surroundings. The characters of the father and son—the former full of the weaknesses as well as the strength of genius, and shalloer than the son even in his art, tho for that reason more at his ease in its exercise and so far more successful—ar well contrasted. And the filial devotion of Lewis is touching. '*The Silver Line,*' the story of a feat of courageous humanity, and some smaller tales make up a sufficient issue of wholesom provender for summer idleness." [Athen. **1342**

HEARTH GHOSTS [by H: JACKSON: *Low*, 1871.] "would hav been more appropriately named, 'The Chron-

icles of Market Mudling,' but for the suggested comparison with the charming stories of Mrs. Oliphant. . . . . We recommend these narrativs as wholesom and agreeable reading." [Athenæum. **1343**

HEARTSEASE [by C.. M.. YONGE: Oxford, *Parker*, 1855.] "is the most *true* looking story we hav read for a long time. It is simple enuf. The honorable Capt. Martindale has fallen desperately in love and married in a great hurry, quite unknón to his father, the dauter of a country lawyer; Violet is little more than a child,— she is the 'Heartsease' of the book, and a charming creature. She is not endowed with any talent, nor any great strength of character,—with nothing but the simple idea that she must do her duty; and her gentle, straitforward simplicity works like a charm upon the whole family. Her amiability and gentleness mature gradually into hi principle and firmness,—without losing their unconscious gracefulness." [Athenæum.] —"'Heartsease' is a novel whose success would not speak well for our national literary taste, did we not kno that thêre is always a large and respectable reading public with no taste at all, but plenty of comfortable leisure which hangs terribly on their hands, when neither gossip nor tea is going forward. The book does not much exercise even the most ordinary impulse which leads to reading—curiosity; and can lay claim in no hi degree to any dramatic, narrativ or descriptiv excellence. . . . . Of insit into character, analysis of human passion and emotion—of intellectual strength, we find no trace." [Westminster Review.]—"The virtuous men and women of Miss Yonge ar so free from any touch of earthliness, and ar characterized by a purity so far removed from anything which is met among everyday persons that thêy ar sure to be enthusiastically admired by all lovers of morbid intellectual and spiritual fenomena. On the other hand, her bad people ar so wholly and preposterously bad that no one could dream of imitating them, and thêir acquaintance can not, therefore, contaminate her readers. The colorless creatures whom Miss Yonge mistakes for women, and the weak and feminin beings whom she presents as her ideals of manly perfection, hav no element of interest to the normally healthy mind. Still, thêre is a very large number of people who admire these novels, and regard Miss Yonge as an infinitly nicer writer than, say,— C : Reade." [Round Table.   **1344**

HEATHCOTE [by ELLA MACMAHON: *Ward & Downey*, 1889.] " is a pretty and lifelike, rather gushing story of a cathedral town. The heroin is the archdeacon's dauter, and the hero is sub-editor of a daily paper. The sub-editor's father was a music-master; but as his mother belonged to an old and proud family, which had proved its pride by rejecting the dauter who disgraced it, Heathcote Grant was admitted to be superior to his position, and his presumption in falling in love with the beautiful Violet Ward was not so overweening as it mit otherwise hav been. Thêre is some good drawing in this story; the characters ar decidedly like human beings, and its tone is hi and well sustained. . . . . The love story is admirably contrived, and wiلl giv pleasure to every one who reads it." [Ath. **1345**

HEIR OF REDCLYFFE. [by C.. M.. YONGE: 1850.] "Thêre is another class of novels — novels of the domestic class — which has also a great influence. I recollect hearing Mr. Guizot say, that the literature of France would match

(by which, of course, he meant would beat) all our literature, with one exception, and that was our domestic novels. He said : ' In science we match you; in poetry we match you (tho in that he is quite in error) ; in history we match you; but we hav not anything in our literature like " The Heir of Redclyffe" and your [other?] domestic novels. All books of that class ar peculiarly english. They ar books describing a virtuous domestic life. They do not go to the tragic or dramatic for interest, but thêy draw it from the simple springs of natural life. This we hav not in the literature of France.' Our previous want of acquaintance with this Pusey-novel arose from no barbarous indifference to the important literary events of our age and country. We abstained from reading it, solely from the dread of the effect which it mit hav in unfitting us for enjoying any other works of fiction afterwards. We wer well aware, from our knoledge of the disastrous influence in this respect, which the work had exercised over that large and discriminating portion of the reading public of England which is chiefly composed of curates and young ladies. Among other sad cases, in our circle of acquaintance, we met two which especially struck us. One instance was that of a curate (still living, and still, throu the scandalous neglect of his friends, unprovided with proper accommodations in an asylum for the insane), who, after reading ' The Heir of Redclyffe,' expressed himself critically in these terms : ' Thêre ar only Two Books in the world. The first is the " Bible," and the second is the " Heir of Redclyffe." ' The other instance is still more afflicting. A young and charming lady, previously an excellent customer at the circulating libraries, read this fatal domestic novel on its first appearance some years ago, and has read nothing else since. As soon as she gets to the end of the book, this uninteresting and unfortunate creature turns back to the first page and begins it again. Her family vainly endeavors to lure her to former favorits or to newer works; she raises her eyes from the too-enthralling page, shakes her head faintly, and resumes her fascinating occupation for the 1000th time, with unabated relish. Her course of proceeding, when she comes to the pathetic passages, has never yet varied. She reads for 5 minutes; and goes upstairs to fetch a dry pocket handkerchief, comes down again and reads for another 5 minutes; goes upstairs again, and fetches another dry pocket handkerchief. No later than last week it was observed by her family that she shed as many tears and fetched as many dry pocket-handkerchiefs as ever. Medical aid has been repeatedly called in; but her case baffles the doctors. The heart is all rit, the stomach is all rit, the lungs ar all rit, the extremities ar moderately warm. The skull alone is abnormal. [Compare No. 1344.] This is the ·story of the Pusey-novel which is the Wonderful Lamp not to be found in France. . . . . The characters by whose aid the story is worked out, ar simply impossible. They hav no types in nature, they never did hav types in nature, they never will hav types in nature. . . . . Throuout the book up to the scene of his last illness, Sir Guy is the same lifeless personification of the Pusey-stricken writer's fancies on religion and morals, literature and art. He is struck speechless with reverence when a rhapsodical description of one of Raphael's Madonnas is read to him. He occupies 3 summers in studying the Morte d'Arthur (not Mr. Tennyson's poem, but the old romance)

and, in spite of this romantic taste, when he gets to Italy he will not read the magnificent descriptions of scenery in 'Childe Harold' becaus Lord Byron was a profligate." [C: Dickens.] — "Here ar Sir Guy Morville and poor little Amy, both of them virtuons to a degree which would hav put Miss Edgeworth's most exemplary characters to the blush, yet Guy, after being bullied and badgered throu the greater part of his short life, dies of the fever which should hav carried off Philip; and Amy, besides being left widoed and heartbroken, givs birth to a dauter instead of a son, and so forfeits the inheritance of Redclyffe. On the other hand, Philip, the most intolerable of prigs and mischief-makers, whose cruel suspicions· play havoc with the happiness of everybody in the story, and whose obstinate folly brings about the final disaster, — Philip, who is little better than his cousin's murderer, succeeds to the estate, marries that very stilted and unpleasant young person Laura (who is after all a world too good for him), and is left in a blaze of glory, a wealthy, honored, and distinguished man. It is true that Miss Yonge, whose conscience must hav pricked her a little at bringing about this unwarranted and unjustifiable conclusion, would hav us believe that he was sorry for his misbehavior, and that his regret was sufficient to equalize the perfidious scales of justice." [Atlantic. **1346**

HEIR OF THE AGES (The) [by JA. PAYN: *Harper*, 1882?] "is one of the delitful stories which may not liv forever as literature, but ar as welcom as the flowers which bloom in the spring when they appear. Besides its humor and epigrammatic charm, the story has the merit of a dramatic and novel *dénoument*, which, instead of endless happiness after a long series of catastrofes, winds up with a catastrofe after the happiness." [Critic.] The motiv seems to hav been suggested by the literary career of George Eliot. **1347**

HEIR WITHOUT A HERITAGE [by E. Fairfax Byrne: *Bentley & Son*, 1887.] "is undeniably clever. . . . . Brit Judith Romilly is bred in a strait sect of Dissenters. To the narroness of her religious creed is added the narroness of the middle class before the poor gent'y has at all amalgamated with it. The description of life in Wesleyan circles at the beginning of the century is probably true enuf. Old Romilly and his wife ar kindly specimens of a race which had many virtues not seen conspicuously in their descendants, altho the mill-öner saw nothing but dishonesty in labor combinations and his charming old wife believed in the verbal inspiration of the Bible. An ardent spirit like Judith's naturally would revolt against her home; and when an enthusiast like Gervase Germayne made it his business to enliten her intellect, and inspire her with doubts of the truth of her creed, there was scarce the semblance of a struggle. . . . . Gervase is a fine character, apart from a little young-mannishness; he behaves like a gentleman at the fire, and in the matter of the sale of an estate ; while his forgivness of the picturesque ruffian Rick Blakedeane, and the method in which he returns good for evil, quite transcend the expectations we ar led to form of him at the outset." [Athenæum. **1348**

HELEN BLANTYRE [by A. E. A. Mair : *Smith*, 1875.] "herself is a pleasant specimen of a simple, freshhearted young girl, and the friends of her sex who surround her ar fairly described. Lady Jane Wynchester is a genial, worthy soul; Agatha Blantyre something more — a woman with hi principles, but soured and case-hardened by an early disappointment in life. . . . . On the whole, the characters engage our interest, and the story is a fairly interesting love-tale of the modern school." [Athenæum. **1349**

HENRIETTA TEMPLE. = No. 730.

HER DEAREST FOE. [by " Mrs. Alexander," i. e., Annie (French) Hector: *Holt*, 1876.] The author here "recovers, in part, her descent, but hardly reaches the grade of her first book. Her best characteristics, however, ar manifest in ' Her Dearest Foe,' which will be read with the quiet, reasonable enjoyment which results from natural pictures of life, marked sketches of character, and an unvarying spirit which sustains the reader's interest. The plot of the story is not complicated, and is quite possible. . . . . Mrs. Travers is very nearly a perfect woman, but the author has made her, in one or two cases, unnatural and untrue to herself. Lee has much *espièglerie*, and makes an admirable foil for grand Mrs. Temple. Tho not so satisfying a novel as ' The Wooing O't,' this should rank next in merit to that popular book. It is admirably pure in tone, and, tho not didactic, teaches useful lessons." [Boston " Literary World." **1350**

HER GREAT IDEA [by Lucy Bethia (Colquhoun) Walford: *Holt*, 1888.] "contains 7 stories. All ar of a humorous nature, and that Mrs. Walford possesses a fund of humor every reader of her novels knoes. In these tales she is seen at her best — the crisp, nervous style, the keen but never ill-natured satire, the ready command of interesting situations all going to the enhancement of the reader's enjoyment. Nothing could be better in their way than *Paul's Blunders, A Tumbler of Milk,* and *Ada.*" [Boston " Literary World." **1351**

HER MOTHER'S DARLING [by C.. ELIZA LAWSON (COWAN) RIDDELL: *Tinsley*, 1877.] "is as pleasant a character as Mrs. Riddell has ever introduced. Left fatherless and poor at an early age, and soon afterwards losing her invalid mother, she makes use of her talent as a singer to support herself, which she does very bravely and honorably, tho, öing to the unscrupulousness of some of her companions she does not escape slander. Her adventures in the strange world to which Miss Rodwell introduces her, the contrast between her hi-minded and womanly nature and the coarser clay of such as Archer and the Rodwell, her stay with some rich 'vulgarian' relativs, and the final happy resolution of all her difficulties, make up in their relation 'a very readable novel." [Athenæum. **1352**

HER SECOND LOVE. = *A LOST LOVE.*

HER TITLE OF HONOR. [by "HOLME LEE", i. e., Harriet Parr: *King*, 1871.] "The plot is slit and the story lacks proportion, but the author has displayed several good qualities which compensate for these defects. Pengarvon, on the Cornish coast, is the chief scene of the story; and Francis Gwynne, the son of a miner, is the hero, whose career without being vicissitudinous is described with such skill as to interest any novel-reader not hopelessly a slave to sensational literature. Some of the characters ar admirably sketched. . . . . Altho the characters lived at the end of the last century, their ways ar our ways and their lives ar our lives." [Athenæum. **1353**

HERIOTS (The) [by H: STUART CUNNINGHAM: *Macmillan*, 1890.] "is

a love story of the most modern kind, in which the passion is so unobtrusiv and reasonable that it is discovered only by those most interested when the circumstances ar all in its favor, and it could almost be done without. Olivia and Jack ar poor, but Olivia has rich relativs in whose house she meets a Mr. De Renzi, a brilliant man of the world, who amuses himself in Parliament and elsewhere with a whole-souled devotion to that employment, as the son of a great London financier should. He, however, falls in love with Olivia, and his father's consent is won by coupling the marriage with a splendid business opportunity. After her engagement, Olivia is introduced to the cream of the cream of english society, including vulgar Americans, manufacturers' wives from Manchester, insufferably rich Londoners, cynical Frenchmen, dull poets, and a duke or two. But tho the reader finds it enjoyable, Olivia does not like it. She and De Renzi quarrel, and it begins to dawn upon her that she loves Jack. He makes a similar discovery, and they ar married in the last chapter. There ar many more than usually clever passages in the book; it is thoroly readable, and almost too uniformly amusing." [Critic. **1354**

HERIOT'S CHOICE. [by ROSA NOUCHETTE CAREY: *Bentley*, 1880.] "The principal feature of the book, except a consistently polemical purpose in the High Church direction, is the great inferiority of the male to the female characters. Mildred is vividly described, and brings a fine nature before us; Olive, the poetess, is also an original conception, and mit be drawn from life, and the rest of the pleasant group of maidens hav their special attributes; but the imbecil clergyman and the brutal squire, — Richard, the opinionativ young 'priest,' who marries the heiress, and Polly's moonstruck lover, ar all sad specimens of the worst half of humanity." [Atheuæum. • **1355**

HERO (A) etc. [by Dinah Maria (Mulock) Craik : (†, 1887) *Harper*, 1853.] contains 3 stories. "The hero is a boy, but a true hero; and the story, related by a bachelor uncle to a group of nefews and nieces, is designed to sho that heroism is not a matter dependent on age or sex, hi or lo birth; that the hero is not, ex officio, girt with a sword; nor is it essential that he slanter others, or be slautered himself. '*Bread upon the Waters; a Governess's Life,*' is the title of the second story, and is sufficiently descriptiv to convey an idea of its spirit. '*Alice Learmont*' closes the volume. In this the scene is laid in scottish cottage life." [N. Y. "Literary World." **1356**

HERO CARTHEW. = *PRESCOTTS OF PAMPHILON.*

HESTER [by Ma. Oliphant (Wilson) Oliphant : *Macmillan*, 1884.] "should rather hav been called 'Catherine,' for the reader's interest is more warmly bestoed upon the proud, masterful, loving old lady, who receives so scant measure of gratitude from those she has befriended and adopted, than upon the equally proud and passionate young girl, who has youth on her side when the hardest trial of her life besets her. Tho at the opening of the story Catherine cannot endure the hi-spirited dauter of John Vernon, yet Hester is really her counterpart, and when a great blo falls upon them, when Hester loses her lover and Catherine the son of her old age, when disappointed affection and trust ar more grievous to bear than the repetition of financial trouble supposed to hav been vanquished long before, the two

noble souls draw together, and understand that their repulsion was meant only to unite them finally. All the story of Catherine's second struggle, the success of which cannot mend the broken heart which the discovery of Edward's heartlessness, not his dishonesty, has caused, is pathetic and impressiv." [Athenæum. **1357**

HESTER'S VENTURE [by Ma. Roberts : *Longmans*, 1886.] "'Hester's Venture' is long without being tedious, wholesom, but never mawkish, and marked throuóut by the kindly wit, refined protraiture, and acute perception which hav been observable in former works by the same hand. Thêre ar at least half a dozen finished studies of character and as many clever sketches. Of the former, Olivia Vane, the actress, 'a lovable, faulty creature, with a divine spark in her,' whose 'moral squint' brings such trouble on the heroin and herself; Mrs. Torrington, a charming picture of serene old age; her grandson John and his lo-born wife; and lastly, Hester herself, with her hi-bred scorn of all pettiness, her courage and conversational charm, ar perhaps the most successful." [Athenæum. **1358**

HIDE AND SEEK [by [W:] Wilkie Collins : *Bentley*, 1854.] "is a well-intentioned novel, exposing the dreariness of the existence of a religious family of the middle class, and the evil influences of a 'sound and serious' education on an impetuous and warm-hearted youth." [Westminster. **1359**

HIGHER LAW (The). [by E : Maitland : *Chapman*, 1870.] "The art with which these characters, altho all good, ar made to differ, and with which their several idiosyncracies ar brót out, is not slit. Sophia and James ar so constituted as to render a union between them, if it could take place, essentially a happy one, by reason of the affinity of their natures. Similarly, Margaret and Edmund wer 'made for one another.' By a great misfortune, James and Margaret ar thrön together before they meet their several affinities, and James falls in love with Margaret. She, on the other hand, altho experiencing a most friendly affection for him, is quite untouched by that divine fury and passion of love without which no wedded pair ar likely to be happy. James perceives her coldness, but trusts that time will change the friendly into a lover-like attachment, and persuades Margaret to marry him. Their married life is not a happy one. Margaret's coldness remains unchanged altho she esteems her husband, and tries in every way to please him. The husband's anger and misery at the want of reciprocity in his affection is vented on his wife and himself alike, and causes great unhappiness to both. While they ar living in this state Edmund Noel, a friend of the husband, but up to that time a stranger to the wife, comes to them. Instantaneously the capacity for passionate love, which had slumbered so long in Margaret's nature, is awakened at the sit of the being for whom by the 'hier law' of nature she has been intended, and with whom she ôt to hav been mated. The love is mutual, and soon acknoledged between the two; but altho they permit themselvs many endearments, their respect, and affection for James prevent them from yielding to temptation. The struggle of the affections and the lives of the unhappy trio ar given with great force; and simple as the tale may seem from this account of it, the reader will find much to interest and excite in the way it is told. The end is as happy as the circumstances will permit. James Maynard is killed. Margaret, after a decent interval, marries her lover." [Athenæum. **1360**

HIS COUSIN BETTY. [by F.. M.. PEARD: *Bentley*, 1888.] "Betty, the blunt, impetuous, half-boyish, but gently bred and lovable heroin, does not seem at all a likely person to be drawn to the quiet, prim, and at first sit rather priggish hero; and indeed the acquaintance of the cousins begins with a quite unreasonable amount of dislike, not to say hatred, on Betty's side. . . . . Very cunningly poor Betty is persuaded that John is in love with her, and still more cunningly— for this feat requires greater delicacy of treatment— John is persuaded not only that Betty loves him, but that she expects him to make her an offer of marriage. The stratagem succeeds; but before the wedding, John has discovered one half of the truth, and shortly afterwards Betty discovers the other. The situation is both interesting and pathetic, for the poor girl has given the love which she supposed to be spontaneously sôt, while the man's passion is only less absorbing and less certain of itself becaus it has been artificially forced into a hurried maturity. We will not tell more of the story, which from this point onward becomes less and less dependent upon mere incident; but it is difficult to praise too hily the deftness, the subtlety, the fine imaginativ insit which mark the book from the time when the hero and heroin ar drawn into the wretched labyrinth, to the happy day in which, having threaded all the devious mazes, they emerge upon the brit open land which lies beyond. 'His Cousin Betty,' whether regarded from the intellectual or the literary point of vue, is a singularly able and attractiv novel." [Spectator. **1361**

HIS HELPMATE. [by FRANK BARRETT: *Appleton*, 1887.] "This author

HIS GRACE. [by W: E: NORRIS: *Methuen*, 1892.] "Of all the imaginary dukes with whom we are acquainted, Mr. Norris' is the most delightfully human. His grace of Hurstbourne is a grown-up boy,—boyish in his tastes, in his recklessness, in his frank good-nature, most boyish of all in his determination to outshine, baffle, and in every way discomfit that very adult cousin, Paul Gascoigne, whose wealth and cleverness make the contest from first to last a very unequal affair. Of course, we know all along that the duke will be victorious; and there is real cleverness in the adoption of the expedient by which, in the final encounter, the duke's strong muscles rather than his wits extricate him from the very tight place in which he finds himself. The struggle on the floor of Gascoigne's chambers for the possession of the document with which the better-equipped combatant has threatened a 'coup-de-grâce,' may not be warfare of the legitimate kind, but it has a barbaric magnificence, and, dramatically, it is one of Mr. Norris' happiest effects." [Spectator.]—"In construction, as in writing, Mr. Norris has eminently 'le style coulant,' which is a very different thing from mere fluency. His novels hav the virtues of the oyster in an old, a vulgar, but an excellent apolog—they "go down so easily." There may not be very much in 'His Grace.' When Mr. Norris, in the first few pages, has introduced you to the self-depreciatory narrator, and to his Eton friend who comes into a dukedom and offers him a sort of agency just when he is very much down on his luc, and to the narrator's sister who, being penniless, has engaged herself to a harmless, but not charming, parson widoer, and to the duke's cousin, who has had the ready money left him, and is a detestable creature—you smile superior and say "I kno what is coming." You *do* kno what is coming; but you entirely mistake Mr. Norris' cleverness if you think that he is not perfectly aware of your knoledge, and resolved to take advantage—a quite good and craftsman-like advantage—of it. Pleased with yourself, you ar also pleased with Mr. Norris, and with the ornaments and surprises which prevent your satisfaction from being mere patronage. And then it goes down so easily! There ar no chees, no breaks, no puzzles, no false notes. It is like a very good dinner, whereof you hardly remember the details, but ar aware, after digestion, that all was and is peace. There is a touch of greatness in this." [Academy. **1361 q**

has been identified with sensational novels, but this one is mainly domestic. It has a spice of exciting incident, but the interest as a whole is subdued. It is a brit and wholesom little tale." [American. **1362**

HIS SISTERS. [by HERBERT P. EARL: *Low*, 1887.] "Mr. Earl has a pleasant story to tell of certain young men and maidens, of a quiet english type, set in a quiet background. Thêre ar several beroes and heroins, who receive impartial treatment at the author's hands, and who rouse impartial, if not quite indifferent interest in the mind of the reader; and thêre is at least one cold and calculating villain, of a sort not unusual in fiction, who makes a great deal of mischief before his time of reckoning comes. He is a lawyer, with an inordinate taste for other people's money; and he contrives to indulge his taste pretty freely. Of course thêre is a virtuous young man on his track, and in the end he gets his deserts. But Mr. Earl does not overdraw all his characters. Some of them are thöroly natural creatures, in whose joys and sorroes it is easy to sympathize; and if the narrativ is not very exciting, at any rate it deals with persons and things as they ar." [Athenæum. **1363**

HISTORY OF A WEEK (The) [by LUCY BETHIA (COLQUHOUN) WALFORD: *Blackwood*, 1886.] "is eminently a feminin work. It has a good deal of clever tho slit study of character. The 2 shallo and flirting, but essentially goodhearted sisters, the cousins of the heroin, ar a pleasant contrast to some of the equally shallo, but spiteful young women who seem to form the ideal of some novelists; and the heroin herself is identifiable." [Athenæum. **1364**

HOLLYWOOD. [by ANNIE L. WALKER: *S: Tinsley*, 1880.] "A

good book, simple in plot and unobjectionable in its manner of narration, is 'Hollywood.' It is a tale of true love and of the interruptions by which its course is impeded. . . . . Miss Walker is natural and simple throuöut. She weaves her plot quietly, without hurry or strain, and eschews the gaudy-colored threads by which a feebler worker or a novîce would hav been tempted. Iler characters, tho not commonplace, ar ordinary types of humanity; they do what we should expect of them at the rit moment, and possess our sympathies becaus they do not excite our ridicule or disgust. Thêre is no villain to speak of in the book, and no impossible hero; the interest excited is perfectly legitimate, and the inconsistencies fairly intelligible. 'Hollywood' is likely to please its readers without taking them by storm; it is a book which cannot offend and cannot leave a bad impression." [Ath. **1365**

HOME AGAIN [by G: MACDONALD: *Appleton*, 1888.] "is not in the author's old vein, being less elaborate, less didactic, and less solemnly thötful; but much tenderness and feeling underlie the britness and spirit of the new story; and perhaps the tenderness has all the more chance of making itself felt whêre the lesson is needed, for being concealed a little more than usual under the cleverness. Thêre is a too painfully appropriate moral worked out unrealistically at the close, when the thötless and almost cruel hero suddenly melts into all the most desirable fäses of unexpected manliness, common sense, filial devotion, and affectionate respect for the rit woman; but his nanty ways ar worth reading about, even if his conversion is felt to be purely a literary one; and the first part of the volume is really very entertaining. The ins and outs of both fashionable and literary snobbery ar well worked, and the reader will delit in much intellectual by-play of spirited thôt and talk." [Critic.] — " The hero goes home to the father he has looked down upon becaus a farmer could not be a gentleman, and in the loving, wise companiofisbip of a true-hearted man, under the tonic influence of his sturdy, sensible cousin Molly, and with honest work to do, he groes into worthy manhood. Such a story, earnest, thôtful, far-reaching in its purpose, is good to read and to think about." [Boston " Literary World." **1366**

HOME SWEET HOME [by C.. ELIZA LAWSON (COWAN) RIDDELL: *Tinsley*, 1873.] "consists of the autobiografy of a girl, who, òn the death of an affectionate and somewhat puritanic grandmother, with whom her early years hav been spent, is transplanted from her nativ soil, a stratum of small dissenting trades-people in a provincial nêborhood, to the somewhat different region of musical and theatrical Bohemia. Anne, who has been early left an orfan, inherits from her father a strongly artistic bias, possessing likewise the endowment of a glorious voice. The conflict of feeling is decided mainly by the insidious influence of a german musician who is acquainted with some friends of hers in the country, and has had the sagacity to foresee in Anne's voice a possible source of emolument to himself. The character of this wily Herr Droigel, with his effusiv demonstrativness and sentiment, his calculating regard for the main chance, and dogged tho not ungentle tenacity of purpose, his flo of talk, his amazing candor, his unchivalrous diplomacy, is the best part of the book. The adventures of Anne under his roof, her zest for her art, her distaste for its profession when her eyes ar opened to the knoledge of certain hard facts of

the life she has to lead, constitute the substance of the three fairly readable volumes." [Athenæum. **1367**

HONOR BLAKE. [by — ( ) KEATINGE: *King*, 1872.] " The heroin is one of the most genuin characters whom we hav for a long time met in fiction. The scenes abroad ar sketched with great spirit. The chapter ' Bayonne' in the first volume is alone worth scores of ordinary novels. Mrs. Keatinge can describe the wild coast scenery and the fir woods with the same skill with which she can paint Honor's first ball. The episode about the Simmonds family, and the story of the forged check ar also told, the first with some humor, and the second with some dramatic power." [Westminster. **1368**

HONOURABLE ELLA (The) [by the EARL OF DESART: *Hurst*, 1879.] " is a lively book. The author's caustic humor, his vivacity, his witty and unexpected comparisons, make his pages sparkle, and giv the reader many a pleasant lâf. . . . . The conversation, for instance, between the vulgar millionaire and Lady Lorton, is as much over done as if it had been written for a farce to be played before a very undiscriminating audience. . . . . Lord Desart certainly succeeds in keeping his readers in a good humor. He is never dull, and if he has a taste for moralizing at times, and is delited to gird at the follies of society, he does it shortly and sharply, and lets one see that his own estimate of human nature is not that of the worn-out cynic." [Athenæum. **1369**

HONOURABLE MISS (The) [by " L. T. MEADE : ", *Methuen & Co.*, 1891.] " is a brit and lively story, with a fine heroin, whom it really does one good to read about. The vulgar people of the country town whêre the little drama is played ar sometimes a little tiresom.

Perhaps it mit be said that the comedy sometimes verges upon farce. But the novel is worth reading." [Spec. **1370**

HONORABLE MISS FERRARD. [by MAY (LAFFAN) HARTLEY: *Bentley*, 1877.] " Since we read Miss Edgeworth's Castle Rackrent [No. 1137] we remember no such grafic pictures of life among the spendthrift class of irish gentry as is here afforded. It is a singularly original story, told with a pre-Rafaellite fidelity to detail, a steady sacrifice of romantic effect to truth, which make it read like a real history. Helena Ferrard, its heroin, a beautiful, tameless, utterly untrained creature, is dauter of Lord Darraghmore. The ancestral home has long since passed from his hands, and he and his family ar, to all intents and purposes, vagrants, living here and thêre, banqueting with ruf profusion when the quarterly stipend is paid in, and starving for the rest of the year. . . . The interest of the tale centers in the fortunes of the wayward and beautiful Helena. At one time she is sent to some maiden ânts in Bath; but alas! the process of civilization is too bitter for her, and after a fortnit of regular and decorous living, she escapes to her wild brood in Ireland. Continually in hope, we ar continually disappointed; and when, at last, she turns from the fairer fortune which mit hav been hers, and to which the deeper instinct of her heart invites her, and follooes her peasant lover to America, it is with a constriction of grief and regret that we see her vanish. Did she really come? It is hard to accept the story as a mere story, and to say this is to offer hi praise to the story-teller." [Boston " Literary World."] — " It is rustic Ireland that is now described, and the central figure is a wild irish girl, the dauter of a ruined peer. Helena Ferrard groes up unedu-

cated and uncared-for, folloing the sordid vicissitudes of her father's shiftless life, and without companions except her ruf poaching brothers. . . . . Accordingly, we think none the less of her for preferring the love of the honest young farmer, with whom she seeks a wider and more tolerant world in Canada, to the equal devotion of the educated Englishman, whose kindness has been so constantly directed to her; her first allegiance is untarnished, and the wrong she does to Satterthwaite never dawns upon her. It is of a piece with her rejection of her ânt's kind overtures, and yet in neither case is thêre mere ingratitude." [Ath. **1371**

HORRID GIRL (A). [*Bentley*, 1876.] " " The lady who is unjustly characterized as a ' Horrid Girl ' is one Mary St. Felix, who, in her old age, tells some incidents of her life to her nieces, or rather allows them to read some old letters which relate them. Mary's worst fault is having been rather hoyden, having caut some wild habits, including that of swearing, from the sailors and other ruf characters in whose company the motherless girl spent a portion of her childhood. On the death of her grandfather she goes to a school which is kept by a pair of very evangelical ladies, kind souls enuf, but naturally apt to be scandalized at their fiery pupil. She is much relieved by the diversion of going to spend some time at a large country house whêre under the easy rule of a good-hearted but vulgar dowager, young men and maidens do much as they list, in the way of amusement and intrigue. . ... . Mary groes out of her reckless girlishness into a very lovable young woman. Her conduct is good and true to nature, at least to the nature of a thôroly honest and affectionate girl, gifted with good spirits and healthy nerves." [Athenæum. **1372**

HOSTAGES TO FORTUNE. [by M.. E.. (BRADDON) MAXWELL: *Harper*, 1875.] "It would be hard to find a more unequal writer in her field than Miss Braddon. . . . . Her 'Hostages to Fortune' is one of her successes. It tells the story of an easy-going self-indulgent London littérateur who, tired by his work and his social duties, flies for rest to a distant spot in **Wales,** whére he falls in love with a very charming country girl. Altho he has already decided the question of marriage in the abstract unfavorably, he was led to break his resolution, and he married her and bröt her to London. Thére he fitted a house for her extravagantly and wasted his hard-earned substance in little dinners, old china, etc., until bankruptcy stared him in the face. The wicked people ar a Mrs. Brandreth, an actress, who had formerly been engaged to him, but had thrön him over to make a better match, and who, being now a wido, is anxious to marry him, but who becomes a fury on account of her second love, and the other is a wealthy pursuer of pleasure who falls in love with his wife. These two come to bad ends, while the man of letters resumes domestic life in Wales, well out of the way of danger." [Nation. **1373**

HOUSE ON THE MOOR (The). = No. 744.

HOUSE PARTY (A). [by "OUIDA," i. e., L.. De la Rame: *Lippincott*, 1886.] "The last story in the little volume, entitled 'A Rainy June' is all that saves the production from absolute worthlessness. This little tale is told with striking cleverness in a series of letters, and in its least effects, Ouida's artistic skill comes out in clear relief. It is cynical, but the cynicism is often delitfully

amusing and compels a lâf." [American. **1374**

HOUSEFUL OF GIRLS (A). [by "SARAH TYTLER," i. e., Henrietta Keddie: *Smith & Innes*, 1889.] "The author has considerable knoledge of girl nature, and she has found a congenial theme in her present story. The four sisters, Annie, Dora, Rose, and May Millar, ar charming in their different ways. Their characters ar developed by the bracing necessity of taking their ön paths in life when the county bank fails, and the good old doctor, their father, loses his savings." [Athenæum.] — Compare plot of "Not like other Girls." **1375**

HOW IT ALL HAPPENED, etc., [by LOUISA (TAYLOR) PARR: *Strahan*, 1871.] contains "not one good story, but a whole collection of good stories. Each is excellent in its way. 'How it all Happened' is a tale of two marriages, which happen in the most improbable way, but to which Mrs. Parr, by her happy humor, which wards off all criticism, contrives to give the air of probability. . . . . Mrs. Parr is as happy in describing forein characters and forein scenery, as those of her nativ land. We most heartily recommend her volumes to all those who can appreciate true humor and true pathos." [Westminster Review.] — "The author has solved the problem of being domestic without being tame. This is partly the result of her undoubted power of description, and her insit into character, and partly of the kind of life which she describes — life mostly of the quiet rustic sort lurking in old country towns and odd seaside villages, which hav not yet been crushed into uniformity by the march of 'progress.'" [Athen. **1376**

HUGH MOORE. [by EVELYN STONE: *Blackwood*, 1885.] "A yacht in the

Ionian seas, a golden evening in Corfu, the english öner of the yacht and his companion, younger son of an irish lord, a wily consul and his pretty dauter, with the intriguing spirit of her Levantine mother strongly developed — such is the opening scene and such ar the leading characters of this acceptable story. The impressionable young irishman is the hero whose adventures ar related in terse english, studded with natural incidents and dialogs. Thêre is nothing out of the ordinary beat in Hugh Moor's experiences, and when the reader knoes that thêre ar more heroins than one he may make a tolerably confident surmise as to the development of the plot which dates its origin from that autumn trip in the Mediterranean." [Athen. **1377**

HURST AND HANGER [*Paul*, 1886.] "is an attractiv picture of a group of families in hier middle-class life, and concerns itself with loves and affections of the younger members, coming to an end only when the entire company hav been settled off in well-assorted couples, after many chances and changes, and without the slitest reason for anxiety as to their future lot in life. Apart from the usual lottery of love thêre is not much in the way of incident. . . . . It is not a rare thing to meet a story which rests its claims on nothing more exciting than the vicissitudes of domestic affection and conventional courtship, but it is rare to find one in which the feeling is so true and the descriptions so delicate as in 'Hurst and Hanger.'" [Athenæum. **1378**

IDA CRAVEN [by JESSIE ( ) CA- DELL: *Holt*, 1876.] "is a very good novel. Its subject is the married life of a young woman, who, after a scrappy education in different parts of Europe, when still very young, marries an east indian official 20 years her senior. She takes this

step without loving him, as much from a careless curiosity about her fate as from any other motiv, while at the same time she loves him as much as she does any one. When in India she tries to be a good wife, but her romantic dreams ar far from satisfied, and when she has much idle and lonely time on her hands the appearance of an attractiv but slitly scampish former lover arouses her from her apathy and threatens to cause considerable confusion. . . . But she has eyes to see her duty, and does it; she turns off her filandering lover and tells her husband, who swalloes the pill as well as he can; and in time the curtain falls on a reunited and happy couple. These few lines do but scant justice to the clever way in which the author has drawn the heroin's character and has folloed its gröth from the stony-hearted indifference of youth to its maturity throu experience." [Nation. **1379**

IDEALA [*E. W. Allen*, 1888.] "is a strange but intensely interesting volume. It is not a novel, but a portrait of a single character ' by suffering made strong,' a character full of inconsistencies and warring impulses, lofty aspirations and sensuous promptings — the character, in fine, of a woman who, to quote the author's words, 'had gone down to the verge of dishonor, but whose goodness had raised her again above the best.' Ideala is certainly one of the most original figures to be encountered in the whole range of contemporary fiction, but she is at the same time one of the most unmistakably true to life. The author is in love with his creation, and he certainly succeeds in rendering the brilliant and wayward personality of his heroin singularly attractiv to the reader. The descriptiv passages ar picturesque, and the dialog dashed with humor." [Athenæum. **1379A**

ILL-REGULATED MIND (An) [by K.. WYLDE: *Holt*, 1886.] "is a curious and somewhat strained little story, but full of vividness and pathetic interest. None of the people would probably behave in life as they do in the book, but that does not necessarily lessen the pathos and prettiness of the story in these days of almost too much realism. The characters stand out with singular clearness, and the story is one to linger in the mind." [Critic. **1379B**

ILLUSIONS [by H. MUSGRAVE: *Bentley*, 1887.] "mit well hav been called ' Disillusions.' The sweet women characters, drawn with much care, ar all more or less rudely awakened from the dreams of human perfection in which their visionary training had allowed them to indulge, and scarcely one of them is happy enuf to keep her illusions to the end. It is true that they come across unfavorable specimens of the illuding sex. . . . . Her sisters ar only less delitful than herself." [Athenæum. **1380**

IN A CATHEDRAL CITY [by BERTHA THOMAS: *Bentley*, 1882.] "is a slit but pretty story. The most prominent character is a young man of humble birth, endowed with a fine voice, who, after having been looked upon as a black sheep and a ne'er-do-well in his nativ place, becomes a member of the choir of ' St. Martin's Minster.' There ar some love passages between him and Elsie Ford, a pretty little dressmaker, who has fled from a worthless husband. Leonard tempts her to cast off her fetters, but she resists in spite of her liking for him; and when he is bròt out in London, and makes a sensation, he soon displays the worst side of his nature. Elsie's husband comes to a tragic end, and a modest lay clerk is eventually rewarded for a love much more genuin and faithful than that of

the inconstant young tenor. There is some very charming work in Miss Thomas' volumes." [Athenæum. **1381**

IN DURANCE VILE. [by MA. ( ) (AROLES) HUNGERFORD: *Lippincott*, 1885.] "The work of ' The Duchess ' is noted for its unevenness; but in this collection of short stories she is at her best. The best is *A Week in Killarney*, which is a most entertaining, and at the same time most natural, description of the woes of a young couple who had undertaken to chaperon on a trip throu Ireland a young lady with 2 lovers. We ar not at all sure that we hav not enjoyed it as much as the similar adventures of the famous ' Phaeton.' " [Critic. **1382**

IN FAR LOCHABER. [by W: BLACK: *Harper*, 1888.] The author's "delineation of the ' dour Scotch,' the stiff-necked, Free-Church Scotch, who swear by the Covenant and hate the Establishment, who ar incomparable killjoys, is an illustration of justice without mercy. He givs credit for many recognized virtues to the minister and even to his elders and their wives. He refrains, too, from suggesting that almost every one of them may be possessed of a cruel and vindictiv spirit of fanaticism. But he doesn't like the ' unco guid ' nor wish any body else to like them; he is glad to get off to the moor and heather, and sing the hospitality, the prodigality, the impulsiv, warm-hearted shiftlessness of the keltic Highlanders. Arriving at ' Far Lochaber ' he is delitedly at home, and infects the reader with his sense of pleasure." [Nation. **1383**

IN GLENORAN [by M. B. FIFE: Edinburgh, *Oliphant*, 1888.] "is a pretty tale of scottish village life. The good genius of the story is Kate Cameron, the minister's dauter. She, while suffering from a cruel disappointment in her lover, tries to comfort her poorer friends and to act as peace-maker. Too much sympathy is demanded for Allan Campbell, a ne'er-do-well, spoiled by his devoted sister. Nevertheless one folloes his fortunes and those of Miss Kate with interest." [Athenæum. **1384**

IN LONDON TOWN. [by K.. LEE : *Bentley*, 1884.] " The stammering young assistant at the British Museum, with his wonderful shyness and his solid worth; the girl who has been bewildered by lectures and ' hier education,' and who is rescued from the terrors of Girton by the aforesaid assistant; the old museum-haunter, who vainly tries to establish his claim to a title and property, and ends by starving himself, and worse ; the dauter of this man, by an Italian mother, who shares her father's garret and nurses a Socialistic hatred of the rich in her tempestuous heart — all these ar well imagined and designed, and they ar by no means arbitrary creatures wherewith to people the flöors of a London lodging-house. Much depends upon the telling; and in describing these personages, with that of the Perseus who delivers the little Andromeda out of her garret, Mrs. Lee has been for the most part bily successful. No doubt she puts occasional temptations in the path of a hypercritical reader, who mit find something to lâf at here and thêre, and something on which to base a serious homily. But ' In London Town ' is an unusually interesting story, and it treats sundry topics of the day in a well-informed and rational manner." [Athenæum. **1385**

IN LOW RELIEF [by MORLEY ROBERTS : *Appleton*, 1890.] " is clever enuf to hav a very distinct success. It is an intense love-story, but its every incident goes to illustrate the prevalent ideas, habits and characteristics of half a dozen men who occupy a group of studios in London. All the men ar ' bohemians,' and the heroin is a ' model.' Thêre is no effort made to sho off any of the characters under hi lits, — quite the reverse, — but no one can help feeling that the story helps rather than hinders our faith in the real greatness of humanity. The hero is a literary man; he haunts his friends' studios, and is something of an art critic. He wastes a good deal of time, as they all do, and we see the gropings of genius in pursuit of its true work; — its patient waiting with an instinct that if one waits long enuf, something must drift up from the unknōn. . . . . Success has not sapped the integrity of any of this little coterie, and they nurse thêir illusions and follo thêir ideals with the most disinterested disregard of consequences. . . . . This is a shiftless, unthrifty way of living, but it is at any rate enuf of a contrast to the rich, sordid, materialistic world we hear most about, to enable us to believe that thêre may exist a possible medium if the balance be ritly struck. The story lies entirely outside the world of society. Its climax concerns only 3 people, each of whom has gone throu an arduous struggle. Thêre ar 2 touching intervues between Armour and Torrington, who ar in love with the same woman, which sho the power of the author, and ar indeed the triumf of the book. The effect produced by the heroin is also something to be remarked. She can hardly be described, for she creates her atmosfere, moves in it, and carries it with her from studio to studio. But to discern how modest, pure, and charming a woman may be, even without the ordinary conventions and safegards which society imposes, the reader must go to the book." [American. **1386**

IN ONE TOWN [by EDMUND

DOWNEY: *Ward & Downey*, 1886.] "tho a little pragmatical and matter of fact, is not uninteresting. It has no hits and depths, but confines itself entirely to the commonplace joys and mishaps of every-day men and women, including an old sea-captain, a friendly ship-broker, a sailor-lad, a giddy clerk or two, a nice young woman, and so forth. The various dealings of these characters with each other ar described without much spirit or excitement, and the story is eked out with some of the usual business of narrativ fiction. There is the 'Auld Robin Gray' business, and the stolen will business, and a shipwreck, and a few other familiar incidents; but, all put together, the action of 'In one Town' does not amount to anything like a sensational romance. The author has written for quiet and mildly disposed readers, and for them he has written successfully. It is a great thing in these days to conceive and write an unobjectionable story." [Athenæum.] — "The scene is an old seaport in the south of **Ireland**, and several chapters ar devoted to the talk of the shippers — each man of them a character. The story is that of a girl, who pledged herself on the eve of his sailing on a long voyage, but was forced by her mother into a marriage with Captain McCormick. While the latter is absent the old lover returns, and then begins her struggle between love and duty, made desperate by the rumor that her husband's vessel has gone down, but when further word comes that it is not true, she thanks God that she can meet him with the consciousness that she has 'sinned only in thôt.' However, the worthy captain is really lost at sea, and in the end the lovers ar married. Many threads of other lives ar made to cross the chief

story, and the every-day events in the old seaport ar made to go rit along as they would outside of a book." [Boston "Literary World." **1387**

IN SILK ATTIRE. [by W: BLACK: *Tinsley*, 1869.] "Allowing for the improbability which lies at the root of this novel, and which leads to some minor faults of the same kind, we say at once that it is thôroly pleasant and readable, marked by much and varied cleverness. Mr. Black's plot is not in itself a new one. The unavoidable rivalry between 2 girls who ar in love with, and almost equally loved by, the same man, has often been treated. But in the present instance, the contrast is not so strongly felt as usual. Both girls ar worthy, both ar unselfish, and each seems to wish the other to win." [Athenæum. **1388**

IN THAT STATE OF LIFE [by HAMILTON AIDÉ: *Smith*, 1871.] "is a very charming story. The character of Sir Andrew Harrieson, whose family was so intolerably proud, yet not too proud to add to its wealth by marriages with plebeian heiresses is a sketch in which the author excels. . . . . We shall not spoil the reader's pleasure by telling him the way in which Mr. Aïdé undoes the knot which he has so skilfully tied. We shall simply say that the last chapters in the book ar by far the most interesting." [Westminster Review. **1389**

IN THE FLOWER OF HER YOUTH. [by MABEL COLLINS: *White*, 1883.] "She is the dauter of a burly man of letters, large-hearted, extravagant, careless of opinion, but with a genuin love for the dauter who has been his comrad since her infancy and her mother's death. Alone with her father in the country she groes to be a charming girl of 17, with all the imagi-

431

nativ side of her nature strengthened by a purely literary and poetic education. . .. So Lil becomes Mrs. Newman, and few pictures ar prettier than that of love in a suburb which maintains its charms for some 5 years of domestic life. Then, when offiee-work and domesticity ar beginning to pall upon 'Charlie,' comes a change of fortune; the Newmans, now rich people, visit Rome, and the blo falls which darkens Lil Newman's life. Very striking is the description of what occurs in the ilex grove in the Ludovisi gardens. . . . . Adelaide can talk of art with her eyes full of unshed tears, and presents a delicious problem to the art-loving husband, who thinks he knōs all about his wife's resources in that line." [Athen. **1390**

IN TRUST. [by Ma. Oliphant (Wilson) Oliphant: *Longmans*, 1882.] " Its interest turns on the contrast between the noble simplicity of Anne, who is as royal as her name, and the 'comparativness' of Mr. Cosmo Douglas, the rising man of business and conventional clubbist. Mr. Douglas is quite presentable both in manners and morals, and thêre is nothing more lifelike in the book than the struggle between his horror of making an impecunious marriage, which from his point of vue will be disastrous to both parties, and his feeling that a young man on his promotion cannot afford ' to behave bad'y ' to a lady." [Athenæum. **1391**

IN WHITE & GOLD. [by Mrs. F. H. Williamson : *Hurst*, 1888.] " With all its inconsistencies and improbabilities is a pretty story, wanting neither in strong situations nor in graceful narrativ. . . . . However, if they had been rational mortals the story mit hav been told in 1 volume instead of 3, and we should hav lost a good deal of agreeable flirtation, alternating with the more

serious portions of the story. The whole plot hinges on womanly devotion, on a love for a sinner which proves stronger than loathing for his sin. Happily, the object of the heroin's mingled feelings turns out to be wholly innocent of this imaginary offense, and the curtain descends amid showers of kisses." [Athenæum. **1392**

INCHBRACKEN [by Ro. Cleland : Glasgow, *Wilson*, 1883.] " itself was an estate lying near Kibundle, a little scotch village so far away from the world that they knew the time only from the watch of the mail-coach gard. The lady of Inchbracken, the Laird of Auchlippie, and the minister of the Free Church, ar all people who mit hav stepped out of one of Mrs. Oliphant's novels. The story is quite of her kind, vivid in its delineations of the hardheaded, opinionated Scotchman. The reader is likely to turn a second time to some of the chapters." [Nation. **1393**

INCHFAWN. (N. Y., 1887.) = *THE O'DONNELLS OF INCHFAWN.*

IS HE POPENJOY? [by Anthony Trollope: *Harper*, 1878.] " The interest of this novel gathers under 3 heads : the problematic legitimacy of an italian-born heir to an english title, the problematic birth of another heir to the same, the italian claimant having died in infancy ; and the problematic issue of a double-and-twisted flirtation between several married people and others. These various problems ar closely and curiously interlaced, and their solution cleverly postponed until all is ready for a happy consummation. Mr. Trollope uses his old colors, familiar by reason of many past combinations, but he mixes them with undiminished skill, and lays them on with an almost perfect touch. His people, as usual, ar of all sorts, strongly marked and violently contrasting; Lady Mary is a very spirited and lovely figure, and the Dean, her father, we like in spite of his obvious faults." [Boston " Literary World." **1394**

IT MIGHT HAVE BEEN [*Chapman*, 1877.] "will be appreciated more on its cheerful side, as a well written and amusing picture of irish life. Thêre is nothing exaggerated in its humor, but it is the britest and pleasantest story of its kind which we hav seen for some time, and tho thêre ar sufficient unconscious hibernianisms, 'up a declivity' for instance, to sho its nationality, the style is fairly correct. The family at Drury Castle ar most life-like and natural, not the least so pretty Marney. Thêre is plenty of comedy in the pertinacious love-making of Mr. Peter Dakins." [Athenæum. **1395**

IT WAS A LOVER AND HIS LASS. [by Ma. OLIPHANT (WILSON) OLIPHANT: *Harper*, 1883.] "From fine frãses and strained self-questionings it is delitful to turn to the gentle simplicity of Mrs. Oliphant's people. True story teller that she is, the coming of a new book of hers givs the same assurance of sweet, fresh pleasure as the tidings that the June roses ar in bloom. She takes us this time to **Scotland,** whêre we first knew 'Katie Stewart,' a life time ago for some of us. Thêre is old Sir Patrick, who lived twice as long as was expected, and his son, who was as old as himself. Thêre is the manse, full of gay voices, whither, for the sake of the bonnie Kate, come 'the langleggit laddies'; and the dim old manorhouse whêre sit the ladies of Murkley, Margaret queening it bravely — queen-regent only, tho she be — and Jean, that sweetest of all women, 'an old maid who is still a young one.' Above the village rises their father's folly, a great palace uninhabited and unfinished;

white and splendid, but all naked, vacant, and silent. The hero is a preux chevalier, and the heroin, tho with a very distinct self of her õn, is another of the tender, impulsiv, hi-hearted girls whom Mrs. Oliphant has so long loved to draw." [Nation. **1396**

JACK THE GIANT-KILLER. See *FIVE OLD FRIENDS.*

JACKANAPES [by JULIANA HORATIA (GATTY) EWING: *Roberts*, 1884.] "is a most beautiful little story. Its literary art is as perfect as its moral lesson is ennobling. The skill and taste which framed for its humor and pathos so appropriate a setting will rarely be surpassed." [Nation.] — " These, Jackanapes, Daddy Darwin, A Short Life ar beautiful little tales, simple, even to the simplicity that is generally dedicated to children, yet only one of them could properly be called a child's story. Two of them ar pitiful, and a sensitiv child would cry hard over them, yet they ar not in the least morbid, but hav in a hi degree that sentiment of even romantic courage, knitliness, and love of duty which comes out with an unexpected charm from under the prosaic english character." [Overland. **1397**

JAMES HEPBURN [by SOPHIE F. F. VEITCH: 1888.] "is a story of significant power, filled with unusual and even tragic incidents, and yet far removed from the sensational order of fiction. Rarely indeed, in fiction or out of it, does one encounter so strong and noble a character as the Rev. James Hepburn, but he is none the less thõroly human from his ruf and almost uncouth exterior to his honest, uprit, courageous, loving heart. The tale involvs the fate of many personages, all well and carefully individualized, and the benign and wholesom influence of the good minister on the little scottish

IRON COUSIN (The) or Mutual Influence, [by M .. V .. (NOVELLO) CLARKE: *Appleton*, 1854.] "The two principal characters ar a young girl of genius, character and independençe, invested with extraoṛdinary personal attractions, but, from a defectiv education, self-willed, blunt, hauty and domineering; and her cousin, a young man, clear-sited, wel disçiplined, self-controled, calm, profoundly affectionate, severely just, of unbending wil. The theme, of course is the mutual attraction and repulsion, the curious play of affinities between them, by which each modifies and impròves the character of the ōther, until both melt into ōne." [National Era.]—"The chief interest is attached tŏ the fortunes of the heroin, the child of an unfortunate marriage, and the orphan nīece of a kind-hearted, uncultivated, squire. Kate as a child is od, clever, beautiful, and affectionate; but self-willed, obstinate, and provoking, full of lāve for an old nurse and her uncle, both of whŏm indulge her in everything, but not disposed tŏ sho respect for any ōne else until she meets her "Iron Cousin," whŏ exercises a strông and benefiçial influençe over her career. As Kate groes intŏ girlhood and womanhood her mind becōmes developed under the operation of a fitful and aççidental proçess of education, her influence upon the squire is strongly felt, sōme of the finer chords of his character ar touched, and from being a mere country gentleman, hunting and drinking, he becōmes a very lōveable person, and enlists ôur sympathies tŏ no small extent. This portion of the story is told with grêat skil, and evinçes an accurate knoledge of character such as few writers possess. Fermor Worthington groes from boyhood tŏ manhood with a character in which the sense of duty and self-control ar predominant elements; but he is rather tiresome in his perpetual goodness, and while ôur author is very happy in shoing his influence upon Kate, hers upon him is imperfectly exhibited. Many of the minor characters ar admirably sketched, such as the old nurse Matty, the fashionable Miss White, with an unexçeptionably polished surfaçe but neither depth nor heart, and the quiet, gentle monitress Ruth." [Atlas. **1393** r

hamlet is depicted in a very impressiv way. The theme, of course, is not new, but it is treated in a new way, with a quiet, irresistible air of reality. Miss Veitch has a distinct and eloquent style and the purely literary charm of the book is something to be thankful for. Her method is that of George Eliot, and she does not suffer by the comparison, becaus it is never imitativ; it is rather the spontaneous expression of her mind." [Boston "Lit. World." **1398**

JAN OF THE WINDMILL. [by JULIANA HORATIA (GATTY) EWING: *Roberts*, 1876.] "A more perfect book than this we think we never read. It passes all the tests of successful authorship without a failure. Its plot is original, its action lively; and that its characters seize upon our sympathies, the reading of it will fully demonstrate. Into the family of Robert Lake, the wind-miller, a child was brot and left to be cared for. He at once took an equal place in the family with the other children; the mother seemed to love him even more than her ōn. The child was called Jan, and was strongly precocious. He manifested unmistakable marks of genius, having a strong fondness for drawing. . . . . We cannot weave into the meagre outline of the story the warm and life-like portrayal of country life, which is really the sweetest charm of the book. Temptations to quote assail us on every page — all kinds of matter, descriptions of nature, pathos, violence, sentiment of the finest. . . . . Strength, knoledge of human nature, great discriminating power, concise and effectiv narrativ, a gentle humor, argument, and description, characterize this book, which we do not hesitate to pronounce the best of its class." [Boston "Literary World." **1399**

JANE EYRE = No. 762.

JANET. [by MA. OLIPHANT (WILSON) OLIPHANT: *Hurst*, 1891.] "The few who can appreciate fine workmanship employed upon any not unworthy theme, will find in this novel much pleasant reading. At first it bids fair to be one of the quietest of quiet books; for when Janet, after the death of her ånt, begins her career as a governess in the house of the gentle old wido, Mrs. Harwood, her lines seem to be cast in a place which is certainly pleasant enuf, but is as certainly decidedly humdrum. . . . It is the discovery by Janet of the well-concealed skeleton in the Harwood family cupboard, and her something more than indiscreet action in revealing it to Meredith, which really bring about the catastrofe; and the situations in the third volume, which hav freshness of invention as well as vigor of presentation, ar of a kind to appeal to the lover of exciting narrativ as well as to an admirer of good workmanship. It is clear that Mrs. Oliphant's hand has lost none of its cunning, and while 'Janet' does not rank with her most noteworthy performances, it is certain to be enjoyed." [Spectator. **1400**

JANET'S HOME. [by ANNIE KEARY: *Macmillan*, 1863.] "To write a novel which contains no startling incidents — indeed, scarcely any incidents at all — no elaborate plot, no characters out of the common range of human experience, and no grand flits of passion or pathos, and yet to make it interesting and impressiv, is undoubtedly evidence of great ability. This is what we find accomplished in 'Janet's Home.' The story records the everyday life of a middle-class family with some rather hi connexions, and dōes so with a simple, realistic power which enlists our sympathies at once. It is the air of actual experience which givs the tale its charm. We find it difficult to believe that we ar not reading some veritable autobiografy, or to forbear fancying that we hav, at some time, met the characters described, and shared in the emotions they ar made to suffer." [London Review.]—" The home is a type of many english firesides; the father bravely earning the daily bread as head-master of a school, and giving professional lectures besides; the mother, fond, careworn, and a little tiresome, living only in and for her children. She can never forget that she was well-born, the ritful heiress to a large property when she gave her hand to Mr. Scott, a poor tutor, and has taut her children to think of their mother's early history as a dream of fairy land. The characters of the 4 children of which the family consists ar well drawn, and that of Janet, the narrator, is made to unfold itself gradually and naturally amidst the cares, distractions, and sorroes of her home. A great calamity, the failing sit and ultimate blindness of her father, calls forth the latent strength of her dreamy imaginativ nature, which excites a deeper interest than that of her softer and beautiful sister. The character of Lady Helen Carr, the disappointed, false-hearted woman of the world, is well drawn, and also that of her clever son, who, while yet in his early youth, has discovered that ' naut is every thing, and everything is naut' and has written a poem which is intelligible only to readers under 20." [West. **1401**

JANET'S REPENTANCE in ' Scenes of Clerical Life ' [by " G: Eliot:" 1866.] " is the last and longest of the 3 clerical stories. The subject of this tale mit almost be qualified as ',scabreux.' It will be difficult for realism to go further than in the adoption of a heroin stained with the vice of intemperance. The theme is un-

pleasing; the author chose it at her peril. It must be added, however, that Janet Dempster has many provocations. Married to a brutal drunkard, she takes refuge in drink against his ill usage ; and the story deals less with her lapse into disgrace than with her redemption, throu the kind offices of the Reveren.l Edgar Tryan." [H: James. **1402**

JEAN. [by — ( ) Newman: *Harper*, 1875.] " The name of Mrs. Newman is strange to us, but if she writes any more novels as good as ' Jean,' it is likely to become familiar and beloved. ' Jean ' is one of the very best novels of the year, — satisfactory in almost every respect,—fresh, brit, novel in plot, shrewd in characterization, an.l singularly felicitous and forcible in the development of points. The heroin spends her childhood in a boarding-school, friendless and contemned. When she is 16, her father recognizes her, and givs orders that she shall make her home in the family of his sister, a wido with 2 grön children. He makes ample pecuniary provision for her, and her ânt's family make her welcom. She is lâfed at for her unworldliness; but the strength and brilliancy of her nature soon assert themselvs. Her cousin Maud has long expected to marry Nugent Orme, a rich nêbor. He is at first contemptuous of Jean, but soon learns to admire and presently to love her. He inspires a like passion in her, and an accident makes thêir attachment kuôn. Maud is transformed from an elegant, well-bred girl to a fiend. News comes of Jean's father's death. He seems to hav died without making a new will, and his property goes to his sister. Jean flees, unable to endure Maud's persecutions. She goes to London, seeking the position of governess, and has an experieuce of positivly fascinating interest.

The episode of the Drakes — two old ladies, sisters, who had not spoken to one another for 30 years — is one of the most original and well-executed 'tours' we hav ever seen; and few can read, without tears, the story of Jean's relations with Lady Roughton, who, as the reader will at once suspect, is her mother. We cannot name a tittle of the excellencies of the book, which is refined, very entertaining, and full of truth and good lessons. Thêre ar few novels that we can commend so heartily." [Boston " Literary World." **1403**

JESSIE CAMERON. [by RACHEL BUTLER : *Blackwood*, 1857.] " A simple story simply told is a boon to literature, and ' Jessie Cameron ' wês more than a pile of fashionable novels in the critical scale. The narrativ is quiet and vigorous. The ' Scotch ' is excellent — natural, and never intrusiv. The central figure is a leal lassie, and how she loves, and proves her worth, we recommend our readers to find out for themselves. Thêre is nothing to criticize, for thêre is nothing to condemn." [Westminster. **1404**

JEWEL OF A GIRL (A) [by MAY CROMMELIN : *Hurst*, 1877.] " is well written and pleasing throuôut. From the first we ar charmed with the gentle Miss Ina and with her strong-willed niece. But thêre is one part which has a quite unusual freshness and force. Bridget Colbert, looking back with pride to her old huguenot ancestry, and at the same time feeling the .cruel pinch of need, made all the worse by the nêborhood of the place whêre her family had once been wealthy and prosperous, devises a plan such as is often imagined but very seldom executed. The religious troubles which had exiled her family to Ulster had sent another branch of it to Holland. To the head of this branch she writes. She details her circumstances. Will he look out for employment for her? Then the scene of the story is transferred to **Holland.** Here thêre is no mistaking the touch of familiar acquaintance. The dutch family and its belongings ar charmingly described, and the relations of Bridget with her wayward pupil and her lovers form a picture full of interest." [Spec. **1405**

JOAN. [by RHODA BROUGHTON : *Appleton*, 1877.] " Given a hi-bred, noble-looking girl, with ripely, dewily red lips, a milk-white throat, and a willoy form, and an amorous gardsman, 5 feet 11 in his shooting boots, with wicked gray eyes. . . . . Joan herself is altogether charming — quite the most hi-minded and lovable girl in the gallery of Miss Broughton's heroins. . . . Joan who has been reared in all the comfort, refinement, and luxury which wealth can command, at the outset of the story suffers a reverse of fortune throu the sudden death of the relativ upon whom she has been dependent, and is plunged at once into poverty. She goes to liv with an ânt and two cousins — girls — all warm-hearted, but horribly vulgar. Her journey to her new home, at which she arrives in a butcher's cart, is told with much humor; and her new life, and the constant jar which the tawdriness and coarseness of her surroundings produce in her, ar described with truth and power." [Canadian Monthly. **1406**

JOHN. [by MA. OLIPHANT (WILSON) OLIPHANT : *Blackwood*, 1870.] " John is simply insufferable. Pious, stupid and bilious, it is simply incredible that any girl in full possession of her faculties could fall in love with him. He dôes not hav a single point in his favor, unless we except the one shining quality — that he says little. As to the young lady, she is a trifle better, but not much.

She giggles, and is one of those 'giddy, vain things' whom we ar always hearing of, altho she is supposed to improve towards the end of the tale. The only sensible person in the book is the cruel father, who is much to be pitied in being surrounded by such trying people as the dauter, John and John's parents. Had this been the work of a novice, we should not, perhaps, have spoken out so plainly; but we ar justly entitled to be indignant when Mrs. Oliphant wastes her powers so thŏroly as she does in this 'love story.'" [Athenæum. **1407**

JOHN-A-DREAMS. [by JULIAN STURGIS : *Appleton*, 1878.] "It is a relief to turn from a french novel, however clever, to an easy, natural, healthful, but withal interesting story like this. . . . . The hero is a near kinsman, but not a dependent, of a wealthy baronet; he loves, and is loved by, his kinsfolk; he cherishes a close affection for an excellent young lady connected with the family, of which, however, he is himself not thŏroly aware. Then he travels in Italy, whêre he is fascinated by the lovely voice and not unlovely character, of the dauter of a somewhat 'shady' countryman. But he breaks away in time from the charmer, and returns to his true love, whose hand, after some trials, a natural result of the break in his allegiance, he at length secures. The style of the earlier chapters, describing the hero's boyhood, is delitful, and the conversations ar natural, spirited, and often bily amusing." [Boston "Literary World." **1408**

JOHN BOWERBANK'S WIFE, See *TWO MARRIAGES*.

JOHN CALDIGATE. [by ANTHONY TROLLOPE : *Harper*, 1879.] "The hero makes a fortune in Australia, and after his return, woos and wins the dauter of an old banker at Folking, near Cam-

bridge. After the marriage has taken place, and a son has been born, the sin of John's Australian life crops out in the form of the woman aforesaid, with whom it appears that Caldigate had a liaison, and who claims to be his wife, to the exclusion of the very lovely lady now enjoying that position. . . . . The report of the trial is extremely interesting, and we ar kept in a state of tension till the end, when the verdict of 'guilty' is pronounced, and John Caldigate is sentenced to be imprisoned for 2 years. How he gets out again, how Euphemia Smith is proved to hav perjured herself, and never to hav been his wife, and how the story ends happily, we forbear to explain. As a study of character alone the novel is well worth reading." [Boston "Literary World." **1409**

JOHN HALIFAX. [by DINAH MARIA (MULOCK) CRAIK : *Hurst*, 1856.] "The hero has risen from the loest dregs of society to fortune and position by the force of innate integrity of character and determined energy of will. He is often placed in somewhat improbable situations, but his conduct never fails to be marked by courage, mother-wit, and a triumfant sense of honor and propriety. The brave affectionateness of Ursula, her sweet conjugal devotion, and her unfailing womanly dignity in every change of scene, admirably blend with the robust virtues of John Halifax, and create a perpetual interest in thêir fortunes. Few passages in recent fiction ar more touching than the closing chapter of this novel, which completes a domestic history, marked throuδut by simple pathos." [Harper's.] — "A boy who begins by being a farm-servant until he is 14, and who then is employed in a tan-yard to fetch the skins from market, mit possess all the fine characteristics bestoed on John Halifax, — his self-reliance, his energy, his integrity, his passion for self-improvement, — but he would not — he could not — attain the bearing and manners of a gentleman; he could not by mere effort of self-culture attain the tone of good society. . . . . The story is, however, interesting; the attachment between John Halifax and his wife is beautifully painted, as ar the pictures of their domestic life and the grōth of the children. The strife between the brothers when they discover they ar each attached to the same object is vigorously drawn, and the conclusion of the book is beautiful and touching." [Ath. **1410**

JOHN JEROME [by JEAN INGELOW : *Roberts*, 1886.] " is a work so full of wit, humor, wisdom, and charm, that we not only recommend it to every reader, but should like to insist that it should be read. For it is full of a delicious quality which only the reader can feel. It seems quotable from beginning to end, and yet to quote is to lose the setting, which is an essential part of the dainty and exquisit little pictures. It is not a story, and yet it indicates a delitful story." [American. **1411**

JOHN MAIDMENT [by JULIAN STURGIS : *Appleton*, 1886.] " is a wholesom novel, well-written, manly, and having a purpose. John Maidment is a handsom, strong-brained, well-educated young englishman. He starts in life encumbered by only one thing — a debt of gratitude. He sacrifices his convictions and principles to success. He gains all that he wishes, and yet, tho no outward calamity overtakes him, tho he has married an earl's dauter who adores him, tho he seems on his way to the cabinet, he feels that he has not gained the truest success. Mr. Sturgis manages his story with consummate skill." [Catholic World. **1412**

JOHN NEWBOLD'S ORDEAL.

[by T: A. PINKERTON : *Sonnenschein*, 1889.] " The hero is the son of an archdeacon, a young man healthy in body and in mind, who can do nothing but what is straitforward, and who consequently runs his head against all kinds of obstacles. The moral stone walls which giv John Newbold most trouble ar fortunes and nice young women ; he could hav a wife and a fortune more than once if he would take them both together; but he is the sort of man who is always seeing difficulties. Without much plot, the story is interesting and pleasantly written, with many a natural and artistic touch." [Athenæum. **1413**

JOHN SMITH. [by — ( ) CRADOCK : *Chapman*, 1878.] " Of course it turns out that the real name is not Smith, but something more aristocratic ; so that Mary's friends ar spared the humiliation which threaten them. Apart from this blemish, Mrs. Cradock has written a pleasant enuf story, containing nothing repulsiv, and very little that is unnatural. Nearly all the many characters ar such as we should be delited to reckon amongst our acquaintance ; and indeed the narrativ is, on this account, almost monotonous for want of relief. ' John Smith ' is a story on which every reader is likely to pass favorable judgment." [Ath. **1414**

JOHN THOMPSON, BLOCKHEAD. [by LOUISA (TAYLOR) PARR : *Lippincott*, 1871.] " Many of our readers will remember that very pretty story, ' Dorothy Fox,' and will be glad to see more work by the same author. The volume contains 10 tales from her pen, some of which ar very good. But if thêy ar not all equally good, they hav in common certain merits which ar rarer in stories than is pleasant for either writer or reader. Love, and occasionally jealousy, is the burden of them. There is no complex plot to baffle us, no great wit to fascinate us, nothing but a pretty tale, told with considerable humor, and with such gracious enthusiasm that one is interested even in the flimsiest of the sketches. *The Blue Bell of Red Neap* is rather longer than the rest, and may be taken as a very good example of the author's merits, which ar simplicity, naturalness, and delicacy." [Nation. **1415**

JOHNNY LUDLOW. [by ELLEN (PRICE) WOOD: (†, 1887) *Bentley*, 1874–80.] "Shrewd observation, a certain vigorous realism, and a power of pathos, used, for the most part, quietly and with good taste, hav characterised these stories all along. Mrs. Wood distinctly increases her reputation by being able to claim the authorship. To be quite candid, we did not think that she could hav dŏne so well. It is the restraint, the moderation in the use of her power, which especially strikes us as something that the author's longer tales would not hav led us to expect. Take, for instance, 'East Lynne,' with its extravagant incidents, its more than tragical, — its melodramatic situations; or such a book as 'The Shadow of Ashlydyat,' with its dismal scenes, to which the word 'pathos' seems quite inappropriate, and we hav something which differs, toto cœlo, from Johnny Ludlow, with its subdued tones and carefully moderated style. Mrs. Wood shŏes that she dŏes not need to walk us over a battlefield or throu a hospital to move our hearts, but can bring all the effect she wants out of a plain, simple story of life as it is, and persons who may be conceived as possible. To prolong such criticism as this, however, would be ungracious. Let us say at once that having had the pleasure of speaking very hily of

the first series of these papers, we hav found in these volumes a successor scarcely equal, indeed, but not unworthy. Johnny Ludlow is the ward of a Worcestershire squire; and he relates in these stories his experiences and observations. A slit thread of connexion runs throu them, but they may be read separately with quite sufficient understanding. Johnny acts as a sort of chorus; sometimes he plays a minor part. In every case he tells the story, and the admirable way in which Mrs. Wood preservs throu-out the genuinly boyish tone is not the least of the merits of her book." [Spectator.] — "Johnny is an observant school-boy, with a gift of reading characters by fysiognomy, whose healthy country life affords him opportunities of exercising his faculty upon a number of oddities in different walks of life, and his descriptiv powers upon not a few domestic tragedies. The stories, altho essentially distinct, ar threaded by the presence in each of them of the narrator and his immediate connexions. Both lads ar pleasant portraits, and go far to relieve the sombreness which from the choice of subjects, pervades many of the stories. On the whole the author shŏes vigor in description, and a certain strong grasp of such traits of humanity as strike her, but fails somewhat in delicacy of handling, makes her dialog too ruf and vernacular to be altogether suitable to the supposed narrators." [Athenæum. **1416**

JONATHAN [by CHRISTINA C. FRASER (TYTLER) LIDDELL: *Holt*, 1875.] "is a drama of the common people: it has no glitter, no pomp; but a deep pathos pervades it, to which the inevitable tribute is of tears. Readers of 'Mistress Judith' need not be told with what fidelity the author paints the fāses of rural society, and the features of rural character; the same ar characterized in this story, whose tints, however, ar far more sober. The most notable and beautiful character in the book is Jonathan, who sacrifices even his love — such a love as only a pure, strong man can feel — to the obligations of friendship. His mental struggle over the temptation to betray Falk's guilt, and thus prevent him from marrying the woman he (Jonathan) loves, is delineated with great power, and the estrangement between him and Andrew is indicated with remarkable delicacy. Andrew is less individual; but his steadfast trust in his old friend, givs him a dignity which it is impossible not to admire. The character of Falk is made effectiv by its very simplicity. He stands out a man of good intentions, of good repute and good life; his one error is unexplained, and he drops out of the story with singular naturalness. Miss Linn is an admirable figure; one can almost see the britness of her gray eyes, and feel the sunny emanations from her presence. That she would marry Falk, tho not loving him, was a venial fault; for her blind mother urged her on, and the toil of teaching was hard, and the Falk gardens wer lovely." [Boston "Literary World." **1417**

JOSHUA HAGGARD'S DAUGHTER. [by M.. E.. (BRANDON) MAXWELL: *Maxwell*, 1876.] "The plot depends for its development upon analysis of character, rather than complication of incident. A minister of the most stern and uncompromising type marries a pretty, flaxen-haired child — a waif, from a company of strolling players, — whom he has picked up by the roadside. For the rest, it is almost that of 'The Winter's Tale,' but very few readers of Miss Braddon would giv her credit for the skill with which she has worked her idea out.

Thêre is a local color and a 'humor of the soil' about 'Joshua Haggard's Daughter,' which givs evidence not so much of careful study as of an ability to produce good and lasting work." [Athenæum. **1418**

JOYCE. [by MA. OLIPHANT (WILSON) OLIPHANT: *Macmillan*, 1888.] "The young lady whose portrait is the last addition to Mrs. Oliphant's gallery will prove no discredit to the collection. A decidedly gracious figure is that of Joyce, gentle-born and peasant-bred, cultured in virtue of her innate attraction to what is noble, sympathetic as she would not hav been by a more artificial training. Her constancy to duty reminds one, at a distance, of 'Jeanie Deans,' whose words she uses touchingly when she is recovered by her father and introduced to the soft charms of the Thames at Richmond. . . . Scotch, above all, is pragmatical Andrew Halliday, with his self-sufficiency, which he takes for 'proper pride,' and his information, which he takes for culture. Thêre is pathos in the ignorance of dour, stiff, tender Peter Matheson; nothing but provocation and vulgarity in the educated school-master. . . . . Another good portrait is sharp-witted Mrs. Hayward, the colonel's commanding officer, and step-mother to the heroin, whom she tries not to like. On the whole, thêre is much good reading in 'Joyce.'" [Athenæum. **1419**

JUNIA. [by M.. A. OLNEY: *Blackwood*, 1878.] "The heroin is all which is noble, pure and unselfish; her patient sweetness wins upon us even when we ar almost moved to contempt by the unresisting feebleness of the poor 'trembling slave,' as one of her friends describes her. She is crushed and broken by what she endures, but not soured or hardened; and in this, as in many other respects, the narrativ of her sufferings is made to seem thŏroly consistent and natural. The majority of the characters ar clear and life-like, and the reader who once makes acquaintance with them is not likely to leave the book unfinished, in spite of its monotonous melancholy. The scenes borroed from italian history ar treated with vigor and success. The death bed of the old marchese, the champion of republicanism and 'humanity,' yet accepting the kingdom as a compromise, and insisting upon the ministrations of a priest, in order to leave what he considers a wholesom lesson of conciliation behind him is well done." [Ath. **1420**

JUST A LOVE-STORY. [by " L. T. MEADE:" i. e., — Smith: *Blackett*, 1890.] " Nothing of the kind could be sweeter, simpler, or more innocent. This is a story of an author's troubles, and of one girl's love and of another's magnanimity. The contrast between Patty Beaufort and Elizabeth Cunningham is admirably brŏt out. Mr. Beaufort is almost too good a specimen of the genus irritabile; but Louis Stanhope is not represented as much of a hero. He is, indeed, nothing better than a straitforward young englishman." [Spectator. **1421**

JUST A WOMAN. [by E.. ( ) EILOART: *Bentley*, 1871.] " Christine Ruddfield is a noble type of womanhood. Gifted with beauty and genius, all those powers which we venture to think render really great characters quite superior to that distinctness of position which women ar now rebelling against as an injustice to thêir sex, and endowed with the tenacity of attachment and susceptibility to disinterested love which is one of the biest attributes of woman, — she leads throu long years of secret sorro a life of self-denial for the sake of an injured sister; sacrifices her early hopes for the benefit of the object which inspired them; withstands with rare constancy the shafts of misrepresentation, and never suffers the intensity of her particular affections to' narro the range of her activ and large-hearted benevolence. It argues some kindred spirit to conceive such a character; it is a proof of genius to bring it home to others; to invest it with life and attractivness; to giv it voice and action. When we say that in this leading character the author has thŏroly succeeded, we mit fairly add that this portrait alone would render the book worth reading. But it abounds also in other pictures drawn with no small degree of skill. Country-town life is grafically treated." [Ath. **1422**

JUST IMPEDIMENT [by R: PRYCE: *Ward & Downey*, 1891.] " is a rare example of the way in which a novel should be wrôt. Mr. Pryce's work recalls the style of Feuillet by its clearness, conciseness, its literary reserv, and brilliancy of touch. . . . . Mr. Pryce is realistic in the true sense. He handles fearlessly the uglier side of life as well as its pleasing and conventional surface, when it is necessary to his purpose. But when he deals with repulsiv matters he does so with a rare art, and with a clear and sure discretion. . . . . Nevertheless the path which leads to the final crisis is full of pleasantness. Mr. Pryce has steeped himself in the subtle charm of London, which he reproduces rather than describes. The main actors in the drama ar filled with the breath of life. The hero and heroin ar both delitful, so is Lady Heron. The conversations ar excellent and full of point. Every reader would be prepared to kill his fatted calf for Billy, most warm-hearted and dreadful of prodigals. It is impossible not to share in his anxiety lèst his ânt should ' get lecturin'' when he forsakes his very evil ways and returns to the domestic hearth. The Fate which suddenly appears with a bared sword in the path of the happy lovers is as remorseless as in a greek tragedy, and wholly free from melodrama." [Athenæum. **1423**

KATHARINE REGINA. [by WA. BESANT: *Arrowsmith*, 1887.] " Then the little volume may be read either quickly or sloly. One can dash throu it with one's interest sustained in every page, or take time to note the artistic method of its arrangement, the happy irony of circumstances, and the vein of buoyant earnestness which runs throu it all without cropping up too obviously. It is a model of what a short story should be." [Athenæum. **1424**

KATHLEEN [by I.. HARWOOD: *Hurst*, 1868.] " The author of ' Raymond's Heroine ' is entitled to our thanks on two grounds. Besides the gratitude which critics feel to the writer who givs them a work which deservs a second perusal, we ar obliged to her for the excellencies of a book which more than justifies the hi opinion which we expressed of her capabilities when passing judgment on her previous story. Litly and closely written, and remarkable for the ingenuity of a very unusual plot, ' Kathleen ' is the strongest and most exciting narrativ which we hav read for many a day. . . . . From a desire to say nothing which mit lessen the reader's interest, we hav spoken vaguely of the details of its plot; but we hope we hav said enuf to satisfy all lovers of a good novel that they will find diversion in the pages of ' Kathleen.' " [Athenæum. **1425**

KATIE STEWART [by MA. OLIPHANT (WILSON) OLIPHANT : 1850.] " in delicate pathos and grace, reached a point which the writer at her best has never ex-

ceeded — which indeed it would be very difficult for any writer to do." [Blackwood's. **1426**

KENELM CHILLINGLY. [by Baron LYTTON: *Harper*, 1873.] " We trust thêre ar still readers who may be persuaded to take up this interesting novel; for, with all its faults, it is interesting, and it is not an unworthy curiosity which makes one anxious to read what is so nearly the last word of a man who, for nearly 50 years, has been steadily writing. The novel is full of capital things; wit, knoledg of the world, and generous sympathy with goodness, ar to be found on almost every page. Admirable ar the letters of both Kenelm and his father; Cecilia is well drawn; thêre is plenty of caricature in the descriptions of the ' Wandering Minstrel,' Mivers the critic, and others, but generally thêre is a very fair vue of men, and the exaggeration in these cases is at times very slit. On the whole, we hav good cause to be grateful for a story which shôes so much sympathy for the young, such constant belief in all which adorns and softens life. We may look leniently on the faults, in consideration of the undimmed kindliness of heart which is so conspicuous in the novel, and also in consideration of the fact that the author is now a much less seductiv example of all sorts of literary faults than he was 20 or 20 years ago [See Nos. 674, 685, 963]. . . . . It is a melancholy fact, tho we may easily allow ourselvs to be too melancholy over it, that the most artificial writer of the last 2 generations — or almost the most artificial, for we must recollect Disraeli — should hav been at the same time one of the most popular. . . . . No one could deny his talent; and thêre was a humbug about him that imposed upon and pleased the undiscerning. This is by no means unusual. We suppose, for instance, that Dickens' excruciating pathos and fearful Tiny Tims and Little Pauls got him 10 readers for one who appreciated his distinctiv and good gifts. So of Bulwer; the Aspiration and the Ideal which made him justly the lâfing-stock of his best admirers wer to himself and his worse admirers the bread of life." [Nation. **1427**

KEPT IN THE DARK. [by ANTHONY TROLLOPE: *Chatto*, 1882.] "The plot is simple. The story turns on the concealment, by a woman from her future husband, of the fact that she has already been engaged to another man. The husband, of course, learns it in the end from the man, and is made furious by the discovery, imagins in his jealous rage all sorts of additions to the story, refuses to liv with his wife, leaves her, but after an interval of separation is again completely reconciled. Thêre is a naturalness about the tale which makes it pleasant reading, tho no one can help feeling that the wife is punished rather too severely for a concealment which is not oing to any desire to deceive, but to a combination of perfectly innocent motivs. The husband's misinterpretation of the facts when they come to his knoledge, is what mit hav been expected." [Nation.] — "Mr. Trollope excels in describing girls, thêir little vanities, thêir ways, thêir thôts; he is especially happy in his portraiture of nice, thôroly english girls, who ar decidedly a type by themselves, and well worth knoing, whether in fiction or in life. Cecilia is no exception; one learns to kno her, understand her and love her, and one can almost go along with her in the difficulty she made for herself by putting off speaking, as she did from day to day, for what seemed at the time good and warrantable reasons, till it was too late, and her life and her fate wer

taken out of her keeping. . . . . The mixture of tenderness and humor with which the girl's love troubles ar treated is a happy specimen of Mr. Trollope's insit and observation, and is a very good bit of character-painting. . . . . Mr. Trollope has no love for women who go in for rits and advanced vues, and he evidently thinks that ridicule is the best weapon with which to assail them, — and exceedingly ridiculous poor Miss Altifiorla manages to make herself. It is a very pleasant little book, altogether; we feel intimately acquainted with all the characters, we sympathise throuôut with the heroin, and ar spitefully delited when Miss Altifiorla meets her match." [Spêctator. **1428**

KILCORRAN [by MARIA G. FETHERSTONHAUGH: *Bentley*, 1877.] "has nothing exciting about it, nothing even original. The 2 principal characters ar each engaged when they meet. One gets his engagement broken off; the other marries, and her husband has to be killed to make way for the obvious end. . . . It is not the story which givs 'Kilcorran' its interest, but the characters. The heroin is charming. She is a brit, fearless, honorable little girl of the best type. It is quite rit that she should be the central figure in the story." [Athenæum.] — "It is a bit of an irish story, adorned with the gushing sub-title of 'Fair, fair, with golden hair.' A very good story. Fresh, clear, pleasing. The theme is a hopeless attachment springing up between a young man and a young woman who ar 'otherwise engaged.'" [Boston "Literary World." **1429**

KILMENY. [by W: BLACK: *Low*, 1870.] "Here is a simple story, which is pure in its style, and wholesom in its moral, without any want of vigor in delineation of character or power to sustain a simple but original story from beginning to the end. We will not betray any portion of this story, since that would interfere with the reader's pleasure, but we may tell him — if his appetite has not had its edg destroyed by sensational romances — that it is a story which will please, perplex and interest him from the first chapter to the last, and yet thêre is no glamor in it. '. . . . This sort of gray sky alternates with sunshine and positiv storm about 3 cleverly-traced characters — Hester Burnham, Bonny Lesley (who is not the Kilmeny of the book) and Polly Whistler. Thêy come before the reader, alone or in groups, as soft, clear and natural as figures by Meissonier. The passages in which they appear rest upon the mind like memories of pictures done by a master-hand. Even the subordinate characters ar marked by touches which keep them fresh in the memory." [Athenæum. **1430**

KING ARTHUR [by DINAH MARIA (MULOCK) CRAIK: (†, 1887) *Harper*, 1884.] "is a return to the strong and beautiful stories with which its author first charmed us. It is much the best thing she has written lately, and besides its interest as a touching story, full of clever points as well as pathos, it is original in taking for a heroin, not the typically 'sweet' woman, but the strong woman, with a will and insit and a determination not to be imposed upon." [Critic. **1431**

KING'S BAYNARD [by M.. A.. DANET (NORBURY) GIFFORD: *Hurst*, 1866.] "is pleasant and readable. It is interesting without being over-exciting; its tone is satisfactory, and it is told in an easy style. It is a story of society written by one to whom good society is familiar, and whose pictures of gentlemen and gentlewomen may be accepted as genuin portraits. The hero is a little too good,

and the villains ar somewhat hard in outline and crude in coloring; but the heroins ar very pleasant. One little sketch, that of Miss Town-Eden, is especially charming. Altogether, the book may be cordially recommended." [London Review. **1432**

KINGSDENE. [by MARIA G. FETHERSTONHAUGH: *Bentley*, 1878.] "We wish to speak litly of the shortcomings of 'Kingsdene,' becaus it possesses certain excellent qualities. It is fresh and lively, and yet thêre is not a trace of that sort of impropriety with which, one is almost ashamed to say, women generally delit to flavor thêir novels. It is written with far more correctness than usual; and if the story is wanting in originality, it is told directly. The heroin's character has evidently pleased the author. On the whole 'Kingsdene' is a brit, pleasant, readable book." [Athenæum. **1433**

KIRSTEEN. [by MA. OLIPHANT (WILSON) OLIPHANT: *Macmillan*, 1890.] "The merit of Mrs. Oliphant's latest story lies not in any strange path of ineident or change of groove. To many thêre will be almost a sameness in the accessories. An old scotch country-house, the inevitable old servant, the maiden ânt, the ponderous minister, the ailing wife, the 'long-leggit' laddies, the buxom girls — we hav seen them or thêir like before. But the true human nature, in its infinit variety, which custom cannot stale, has seldom been more freshly treated;" [Athenæum. **1434**

KIT AND KITTY. [by R: DONDRIDGE BLACKMORE: *Harper*, 1890.] "The story is a very charming piece of work — so charming that it forces one to consider whether the common belief that Lorna Doone [No. 798] must for ever stand alone and unapproachable, as well by its author as by other novelists of the period, is, after all, more than a fond superstition. Not that the present fiction takes the hier imagination by anything like so powerful a hold as its great predecessor. Kitty Fairthorn, sweet as she is, stands as remote from Lorna's unique and lofty charm as the ideal dairy-maid from the ideal duchess, and Downy Bulwrag, tho a remorseless ruffian, is by no means so convincing in his villainy as Carver Doone. But Kit himself, the loving and soft-hearted and forgiving, who stands compassionate above his deadly enemy and says truly: 'I have been throu 10 times worse than death, and the lesson I hav learned is mercy,' is, on the whole, as pleasant a figure as one shall meet in the entire collection of contemporary fiction. True he is only a market-gardener, earning 5s. a week and his board from 'Corny the topper,' his close-fisted, wider-hearted uncle, and having no ambition beyond that of dwelling in peace with Kitty while he diligently brings his fruits and vegetables to thêir hiest perfection. . . . . It is delitfully old-fashioned in its whole scheme and lay-out, and altho the secret of Kitty's mysterious absence is sufficiently well kept to baffle the most penetrating novel-reader, yet when it is divulged it turns out to be of a piece with the narro simplicity of all the rest. . . . Still no reader of the latter novel is likely to care much for it unless he is still capable of being interested in very primitiv english rural life and can be charmed by the most innocent, pure, and honest sort of love." [Catholic World. **1435**

KITH AND KIN [by JESSIE FOTHERGILL: (†, 1891) *Bentley*, 1881.] "deservs to rank, in grace of touch ánd sustained interest, with the author's earlier stories. Its hero is a certain Bernard Aglionby, only child to the dis-

inherited son of a North Country squire. He is earning a living as clerk in a warehouse. Accident brings him into contact with his grandfather, and the meeting unmasks a deception practised on the old man years before by which he was made to believe that his grandson was adopted and provided for by rich friends of his mother, who rejecte.l all aid from himself." [Boston " Literary World."] — "Thêre is in it enuf genius — that is, enuf imaginativ insit, vital realisation of character, and dramatic presentation of situation — to place it almost in the first rank of english fiction. . . . . The situations ar strongly conceived and splendidly handled. . . . . All the scenes between Bernard and Judith testify, both in conception and execution, the hand of a master; and one scene in particular . . . . has that grasp, vividness and directness of treatment which impress us as we ar seldom impressed by any thing in contemporary fiction. Equally fine, —tho fine in beauty and pathos rather than in simple power — ar the scenes in Delphine's Studio, whêre Rhoda Conisbrough delitedly exhibits her sister's sketches to Randulf, and the touching intervue between Delphine and Sir Gabriel Danesdale, when the old man comes to plead his son's cause, and has to retire sorroful anl disappointed, but more than ever convinced that his boy has made a noble choice." [Spectator. **1436**

KITTY. [by MATILDA [BARBARA] BETHAM EDWARDS: *Hurst*, 1869.] " The fascination which holds all the male characters in this novel spell bound at the feet of the heroin, is, to some extent, communicated to its readers. None of the men can exactly explain the cause of their devotion; the reader cannot quite account for his interest. Like the heroin, indeed, the story is lively and clever, but it is also disappointing . . . The artistic Bohemia which the author sketches with such ability, is of an impossible vulgarity. We lâf at Polly Cornford a little too heartily, especially when she breaks out in proverbs, as she does in a marked way with the beginning of the second volume. Perry Neeve, too, is given to trespassing on the indulgence of society rather more than is customary with the wildest artists, and the abnormal development of his eccentricities at the supper given after his marriage is far from reconciling us to the large share they hav had in the conduct of the story. Still, these scenes of artist life ar amusing; thêre is a certain dash in every description; the dialog is brit and sparkling, and Miss Edwards' farce has the more refined air of comedy." [Athenæum. **1437**

LADY ANNA. [by ANTHONY TROLLOPE: *Harper*, 1874.] "We hav here a young woman of hi birth, who has been kept out of her ôn by the misdeeds of her father, coming finally into possession of an enormous property. She has already engaged herself in the time of her obscurity to a young tailor [compare No. 1254.] and the book is made up of the attempts of a doll-like earl, her cousin, to marry her and so get money enuf to maintain his title. All of Lady Anna's friends and relativs urge his claims; but she keeps to her word, marries the tailor, and makes over a large share of her money to her cousin — for Mr. Trollope always has a large unclaimed fortune for the consolation of young heroes crossed in love." [Nation. **1438**

LADIES LINDORES (The) [by MA. OLIPHANT (WILSON) OLIPHANT: *Blackwood*, 1883.] "— the dauters of

a gentleman who has been living a needy life abroad, but succeeds to a scotch peerage just as his girls gro up, and is thêreby changed from a somewhat useless dilettante to a stern, scheming man-of-the-world, — ar to the lasting sorro of the elder and the scorn and dismay of the younger made the pawns in the game of social ambition their father is engaged in. 'Poor Lady Car,' the gentle and refined, but not beautiful elder sister has just been handed over to the coarse grasp of brutal Pat Torrance, a newly wealthy laird, who treats this last trofy of his importance according to his nature; and Edith is the subject of much anxiety to Lord Lindores, and of more to 'Rintoul,' when J: Erskine, who has been educated in England, comes as a young man to his modest inheritance near Lindores, and gradually becomes acquainted with the strange world of which his house of Dalrulzian is to him the centre. He has knôn the ladies in their happier and poorer days, and is by no means conscious of the damage his presence is doing to the elaborate plans which surround him. True love triumfs, and Edith takes the sober young laird in preference to the excellent, but rather comic marquis whose hand is pressed upon her." [Athenæum.] — "The little nêborhood has in it a less attractiv group of people than those we ar used to expect from Mrs. Oliphant, but she could not tell a dull story. [? See notice of John.] It is a tale of suffering scarcely compensated by a late-come happiness, 'a wistful pale sky, clear shining after rain.' The tragic part of the story is well contrived. The reader feels that moral justice is dône, tho legal acumen is entirely at fault. The 2 or 3 delitful old servants ar worth knoing." [Nation.] — See *LADY CAR*. **1439**

LADY BABY [by DOROTHEA [GERARD) LONGARD : *Blackwood*, 1890.] "is an entertaining novel dealing with the oppressiv treatment by the scarce mature heroin of the hearts of her hereditary enemy, Sir Peter Wyndhurst, and of a thŏroly blasé man of the world, Mr. Carbury. The scene is on the scotch border, whêre Lord Kippendale, Lady Baby's father, has a fine estate, maintained by the revenues of an english copper-mine. The mine is drowned by the sea in consequence of reckless blasting, and, the family being reduced to comparativ poverty, Lady Baby breaks her engagement with Sir Peter, unwittingly encourages Mr. Carbury, and innocently plunges her unhappy family into embarrassments of all sorts. The 'Dea ex machina' who delivers them is a Miss Maud Epperton, a female fortune-hunter of a new type, who, having fairly netted Sir Peter, instead of marrying him, brings about a reconciliation; and whose interest in Lady Baby's brother leads her to the discovery of a new copper-mine on the Kippendale property. She finally spoils what Sir Peter calls her 'artistic possibilities, by marrying a ,retired tallo merchant." [Critic. **1440**

LADY BEAUTY [by ALAN MUIR: *Low*, 1882.] "is the youngest, and after the rule of fairy tales, the best of 3 sisters. Of the other 2, one is a beauty and the other a blue-stocking. 'Lady Beauty' is simply a good and charming woman who seeks to do her duty in life, and does not forget that one important part of that duty in a woman is to please. The moral of the story, if so formidable a word is to be used of a thŏroly simple and unaffected book, is how much blessing and happiness may come from carrying out such a theory of life. The heroin, of course, has a love-story, and it is as prettily told as anything of the kind which we hav seen for some time. Sophia — that is this delitful young woman's name — is quite perfect in this particular character, as indeed she is in most parts of life. It is no small proof of Mr. Muir's that he makes her as interesting after her happiness is secured as before." [Spec. **1441**

LADY CAR. [by MA. OLIPHANT (WILSON) OLIPHANT : *Longmans*, 1889.] "Those who hav read that tragic book 'The Ladies Lindores' will regret to find that Lady Car, the gentle creature who was handed over to the rude grasp of ruf Pat Torrence, fails in 'the sequel' to find any compensation for her youthful sufferings . . . The ideal hero she made of her old lover E : Beaumont, to whom she is married after her rude master, the navvy's son, leaves her a wido with two black-browed children, was to be a knit errant of the pen and platform, a man who by inspired verbosity was to redress social 'evils, and hasten the apotheosis of the simple citizen. But Beau has become elderly and lazy. [Compare plot of No. 1448.] . . . Tom Torrance, that carnal youth, who has assimilated all the newflŏn insolence and innate brutality of the moneyed loer orders, is in his frankly antagonistic way nearly as sad a disappointment as his gentlemanly step-sire. Nor is the dauter much more satisfactory. With twice Tom's brains and sympathy, she is quick to recognize and resent on his behalf her mother's disapproval. Yet Janet has her merits. She has some of her mother's apprehension and a little of her tenderness." [Athenæum. **1442**

LADY DENZIL, See *NEIGHBORS ON THE GREEN.*

LADY HETTY. [*Daldy*, 1875.] "Humor and some wit ar here blended with

447

shrewd observation. The story is also suggestiv of serious thôt. Lady Hetty, with her tangled and incomplete, tho not unhappy love-story, the minister with his proud humility and struggles with a feeling which he thinks must lead to a compromise with duty,—all hav the quintessence of their several natures envoked by the Socratic irony of a subtle questioner . . . With these we will take leave of one of the most genial stories we hav lately met, tho its plot is not untinged with sadness." [Athenæum. **1443**

LADY ISABELLA, See *NEIGH-BORS ON THE GREEN.*

LADY JANE [by MA. OLIPHANT (WILSON) OLIPHANT: *Harper,* 1888.] " has the inexplicable charm of all novels which succeed in being delitful in long paragrafs. It is not too much to say of it that it is an exquisit love-study, told with an airy and delicate grace. Its chief charm is in the gracious refinement of its tone and in the picture it givs of maidenly simplicity mingled with womanly dignity; thêre is much britness in it." [Critic. **1444**

LADY LEE'S WIDOWHOOD. [by E: BRUCE HAMLEY: *Blackwood,* 1854.] " This is a pleasant book. The characters ar not very complex specimens of human nature, but they ar britly colored, and drawn with spirit. The character of Col. Lee is of a hier class, and well worked out. The contrast between him and his swindling associate is delicately marked, and thêre is a certain pathos in the ruin which overtakes him. The incidents ar not such as to excite any anxious interest; but it is a brit, healthful book, with a dash of hearty humor in it." [Athenæum. **1445**

LADY OF LAUNAY (The) [by ANTHONY TROLLOPE: 1878.] "is a very clever and pretty story, having, you may say, but 2 scenes and 3 figures. The

' Lady of Launay' is a conscientious, family-proud woman, whose lo-born but lovely adopted dauter becomes betrothed to her manly and well-beloved son Philip. A very attractiv pair thêy ar, but the Lady of Launay does not ' see it.' Poor Bessy is sent off in semi-disgrace to a protectress in Normandie. But Philip has his way, after all, his mother finally relenting. This is the whole of it, but how the heart is made to warm toward the deserving and persecuted lovers, and yet what respect one conceives for the stern parent. Her conversion in the end makes quite a saint of her." [Boston " Literary World." **1446**

LADY RESIDENT (The) [by HAMILTON PAGE: *Macmillan,* 1880.] " has practically no plot, and can scarcely be styled a novel, but the entirely imaginary picture of life as it mit be in a university town of which a ladies' college was a leading feature affords the author scope for delineations of character and a great deal of amusing dialog. Bertie Ravenshaw is a hi-spirited and warm-hearted girl with intellectual aspirations, and the desire of whose young life is the freedom and opportunities of cultivation afforded by college life. She is supported by her father, a shrewd but kindly observer of his favorit dauter's character, and thwarted by an acute but commonplace mother . . So discursiv a book is somewhat hard to estimate, but, in spite of inequalities in construction, it has the merit of being eminently readable. The author has a keen eye for modern varieties of crotcheteers, and is as sympathetic with the simplicity of children." [Ath. **1447**

LADY SILVERDALE'S SWEET, HEART (etc.) [by W: BLACK: *Low-* 1876.] "is a sad little sketch of the gradual discovery on the part of a man who, at the age of 40, has married his old love of many years ago, that youthful ideas do not bear translating into the prose of middle life [compare plot of No. 1442]; and illustrates the great truth, which, however, is seldom admitted, that far more often than not, man is the sentimental, woman the practical animal. We certainly do not blame Lady Silverdale, with two dauters nearly gron up, for preferring her house, in Belgrave Square, to a villa at Ouchy; and yet we cannot but sympathize with Frank Chestnut's disappointment at seeing the romance of his life vanish irrevocably just as he seemed to hav found it at last." [Ath. **1448**

LADY STELLA. [by H: SOLLY: *Ward & Downey*, 1888.] "'Charles Dayrell' had many admirers; thêre was no contesting the hi aim of that fresh and adventurous story of human effort and development. The hero's friends will be able to follo his fortunes in 'Lady Stella and her lover'— for Charles Dayrell is the Lady Stella's lover. A good part of this new story is poetry, filosofy, quotations, agnosticism, and love, well mixed and delitful. The protracted struggle between the hero and heroin, two strong-minded yet transcendental natures, is finely described, and when the reader groes accustomed to the atmosfere in which they breathe and talk, he will probably be very much taken by the author's account of them. In fact, Mr. Solly's romance is of a distinctly superior character, without any straining of a word which has been soiled by much ignoble use. Stella and her lover pass under a yoke of severe disciplin, and they beat their music out at the cost of a great deal of fysical suffering. Their reward, if it is not without an element of chastening sorro, is at any rate enjoyed in common." [Athenæum. **1449**

LAIRD OF NORLAW (The). [by MA. OLIPHANT (WILSON) OLIPHANT: *Hurst*, 1858.] "Scottish character and scottish manners ar the topics of her theme, with a racy blending of scottish feeling in its old and its modern forms. Mrs. Elphinstone of Norlaw is the mother of an extremely reduced house of 3 sons. She combines in herself the feudal family pride of an ancient chief, with the religious faith of a covenanter, and the rusticity of a straitened scotch farmer's wife; while a national sagacity and resolution dominate over all. Her eldest son, Huntley, has at the bottom some of his mother's pride of family and of landed substance. But that social atmosfere, which reaches almost as far as the air itself, has shön him the necessity of burying his feelings in his breast, so as not to interfere with the worldly struggle he sees before him. Patrick, the second son, is intuitivly a 'practical man.' Altho scarcely knoing anything by experience beyond his nativ district, the newspapers he has seen and their reports of steamboats, of the railway experiment just begun, and of the other wonders connected with the mity changes steam was even then working, hav given him lit. He has a conviction that the family dreams ar of the past, and must be thrön aside by a man who has his bread to win and his way to make. The yungest and favorit son, Cosmo, is a loftier likeness of his father. A poetical spirit elevàtes and refines the good-natured but weak and somewhat selfish character of the sire — selfish, that is, in no coarse and vulgar way . . . The story of the novel is of course the career of these 3 sons. Huntley emigrates to Australia, determined to acquire means to discharge the encumbrances on the land of Norlaw. Patrick, thröing aside the notions of scotch gentility, resolvs to become an engineer, and begins by studying the mechanical part as a workman. Cosmo devotes himself to discovering a first love of his father's, whose memory tho she jilted him was green to the last, and her name uttered in his dying moments. This devotion dões not altogether originate in romance — tho there is a romance connected with it, and which shaded his mother's life. The validity of a will and the succession to an estate depended upon discovering 'Mary of Melmar' or proving her death. With the separation of the family consequent upon these resolvs the interest of the story will probably begin for the library reader. In a critical sense, the introductory narrativ and scenery possess the most quiet attraction. They hav not indeed the movement, variety of persons and incidents, or the surprises of the latter and larger section. But these things rather partake of the character of the general novel in their conception, tho possessing freshness from the style of the author. Her original observation and minute lifelike painting mingled with reflexions appear more distinctly in the scenes at Norlaw." [Spectator. **1450**

LANCELOT WARD [by G: TEMPLE: *Harper*, 1884.] " is delitful; the plot being simple and unpretending, without resort to complications unnecessarily hideous, and the style possessing that unconscious finish of tone dear to the critic's heart. The cõnversations ar admirable, and the individuality of the characters perfectly distinct, while every character is deserving of its portraiture. It is a story to be read, not for the sake of the ending, but for its continued unwearying level of excellence. The gentlemen ar not too gentlemanly, the heroin is not too heroic,

the simple country girl is not too simple; but, dealing with average human nature, there is a pleasant intimation that on the whole human nature is a good thing — as we all kno it is." [Critic. **1451**

LAND AT LAST [by EDMUND [HODGSON] YATES: *Chapman*, 1866.] "is a love story, enlivened with sketches of bohemian character and life. It introduces a few people whom we should like to kno at their firesides, and as many persons whom we should not like to meet anywhêre. The Bohemia thus bròt under notice is that of painters and picture-dealers; and in describing the tone and ways of pipe-smoking artists, the writer exhibits the same litness of humor which made the popularity of his sketches of literary and dramatic Bohemia." [No. 1120. [Athenæum. **1452**

LAODICEAN (A) [by T: HARDY: *Holt*, 1881.] " is a pleasing story, with some brit character drawing, and some agreeable incident . . . The heroin, a dauter of the people, succeeds by purchase to the possession of the castle and estate of an old and ruined family, and the complications of feeling and incident groing out of this juxtaposition of the old and the new giv the author fit opportunities, — more, in fact, than he has availed himself of. The story goes on to elaborate the conflict in this young woman's breast between folloing her natural bent in loving a person of her ōn class, and an attempted reconstruction of the old family throu marriage with one of its poor and disreputable offshoots." [American.] — "Mr. Hardy is an ingenious novelist, and he has managed to convey to the mind of the reader a subtle doubt with regard to her character which pervades the book almost to the end. Somerset falls in love with her, and in the end marries her, but the obstacles thrŏn in the way of this terminątion ar numerous . . . Miss Power's feeling for Somerset has now reached a point far removed from the Laodicean mean of lukewarmness, and she determins to rit the wrong she has done by hunting him up and confessing her error. Her pursuit of him is attended with some difficulties, but the reconciliation is in the end complete. At the last moment, the old castle, which has been the scene of so much of the story, and has seemed to exist as a sort of gloomy fate overhanging the lovers, is burned by the incendiary hand of Dare, leaving Somerset and his wife to begin their new life freed from the moldy associations of the past." [Nation. **1453**

LASSES OF LEVERHOUSE (The) [by JESSIE FOTHERGILL: (†, 1891) *Hurst*, 1888.] "is a 'story revived,' having made its first appearance when as yet 'The First Violin' was not. It is a sketch of a healthy, poverty-stricken Lancashire family, done in something of a Broughtonesque vein, but with less smartness and flippancy in the dialog, and an undercurrent of stronger feeling. Thêre ar pretty touches of humor and pathos in the picture of child life, and thêre is some character as well; but the general effect is not of strength nor certainty, and the blindness inflicted upon one of the 'lasses' is both unnecessary and unkind." [Athenæum. **1454**

LAST CHRONICLE OF BARSET (The) [by ANTHONY TROLLOPE: *Harper*, 1867.] "has all the good qualities of his other works — the exceeding naturalness of the dialog, the homely fidelity to english character of the men and women, the absence of all coarse appeals to sympathy, the entire freedom from all straining after effect. But its superiority to his other stories

arises from his selection of a situation as deep in its pain as any that could be brôt within the range of ordinary english experience. We hav a country curate miserably poor — that is common enuf. He is placed in a parish mainly inhabited by a population less stolid perhaps than a purely agricultural peasantry, but whose better wages induce only greater surliness and a somewhat coarse independency. Then this curate is a man of fiercely intense piety and strong character, a ripe scholar, full of antique learning, but almost mad from the pressure of the daily, hourly, biting ills which come from household want. As a clergyman he is brôt into a kind of contact with the hiest personages of the nêborhood, and thus the peculiarities of his character become the public property of village gossips of all ranks. He is accused of having stolen a cheque; the facts tell against him; even his best friends fear that, driven wild by debts and duns, he may hav committed the crime; and his wife, heroically patient and loving, half thinks that he must be mad when he cannot tell even her how he got it. This in itself is a striking situation. The depth of the man's anguish as he tries to realize that he — with his hi conscientiousness, his ever-rigid preaching of duty, and his stern vues of the holiness of a moral life — is held to be a thief; the awful dread of the wife that this crowning calamity, her husband's public disgrace as a felon, is coming on, and that he is perhaps insane, present a combination of as keen an agony as is possible in ordinary englishlife. To these elements is added another which hitens and yet relieves the whole. The curate's dauter, a graceful girl — drawn in slender outlines, but with suggestiv touches, — is loved by a gentleman of the county, who, before

451

the cloud had come on the poor man's home, had almost declared himself. He hesitates for a moment, but is drawn on by circumstances and his love to act a chivalrous part, and his constancy — not heroically unflinching, but still natural and true, — keeps, as it wer, a bit of blue sky in the upper distance, even in the darkest part of the story; while the comparativly petty vexation of his father at the impending mésalliance is good foil, most artistically designed, to the gaunt and deep agony in the other parsonage home. We do not remember any situation in any modern novel in which the pure tragedy of the circumstances is so deep; for it must be borne in mind that the sufferers ar people made sensitiv by early refinement and educated thôt; that they cannot hav even the solace of suffering in solitude, for the pain is a public event; and that becaus thêy ar of the educated classes their sufferings come clearly home to our conception and consciousness." [J. H. Stack.] — . . . "The dramatis personæ — church dignitaries, church drudges, church hangers-on, pleasant people, vulgar people, designing people — old acquaintances and new, ar alike admirable . . The decline and death of dear old Mr. Harding, who, as the Warden of Hiram's Hospital, was our carliest friend in Barsetshire, is exquisitly pathetic. With all these people Mr. Trollope's descriptions — his bits of mental anatomy, his analysis of actuating motivs, his exposure of meannesses and pettinesses — ar fine. His observation has taut him not only what a man will do and what he will feel in given circumstances, but what the man will do and feel whom he has under consideration." [Round Table. **1455**

LAST OF HER LINE (The). [by ELIZA (TABOR) STEPHENSON: *Hurst*,

1879.] "It must be said that the picture of these two old ladies, if overworked, is at least a real picture, recalling something of the manner of Mrs. Gaskell, without her humor, and too diffuse. The reader cannot fail to hav a kindly feeling towards the author, for her writing shôes refinement, and, if it is not impertinent to say so, a very estimable character." [Athenæum. **1456**

LAST OF THE HADDONS (The) [by — ( ) NEWMAN: *Tinsley*, 1878.] "is far from being a sensational novel, yet is extremely interesting. The chief merit of the author consists in the harmony and logical sequence of her plot, and the consistency of the dramatis personæ. The heroin rises to a hi standard of unselfishness, yet somehow her self-denial never seems unnatural. All the other characters ar well-drawn, and the distinction between conventional and true vulgarity is skilfully illustrated. Thére is also some originality in several of the characters, yet, tho none of them is hackneyed, we cannot but feel that we hav come across them, or mit any day meet with them in life. Humor is not usually a characteristic of female novelists, but in 'The Last of the Haddons' thére ar one or two touches which in a quiet way are very humorous. The book is throuôut pure, refined, and amusing." [Athenæum. **1457**

LAST OF THE MORTIMERS (The) [by MA. OLIPHANT (WILSON) OLIPHANT: *Hurst*, 1861.] "is a charming book — simple, quaint and fresh. As in 'A Life for a Life,' the story is carried on by two different people — not by lovers, as in that case, but by two women — one, a quiet, inoffensiv maiden lady of fortune, timid, nervous, and unsofisticated; the other, a young officer's wife, a frank, lively, affectionate girl, devoted to 'Harry' and the baby, and thinking herself only too hily favored in being able to add to Lieut. Langham's happiness. Very poor, the young couple ar after a runaway match, but very gay an l happy . . . With the help of some old books and pictures, and a few coincidences, it transpires that Milly Langham [born Mortimer] is the next heir to the old ladies at the Park, and she is joyfully acknoledged, and taken out of her poor lodgings and made a pet of, while Harry is away fiting. The mystery of the italian Count must be unravelled from the book, as it would be unkind to spoil the pleasure of its future readers by detailing the whole of the very ingenious plot." [Athenæum. **1458**

LATE LAURELS. [by H: STUART CUNNINGHAM: *Longmans*, 1864.] "To those who remember 'Late Laurels' when it first appeared, its republication will giv an opportunity of appreciating its merits more fully, and the favorable anticipation which 'Wheat and Tares' may hav raised in others, will not be disappointed. Indeed thêre is a decided advance both in the design and the execution of the latter work, tho the canvas is small and the characters few. To paint the contrast between the simple force of a noble nature, and the artificial, factitious brilliancy of a character altogether molded by the influences of modern society, is the object attempted in 'Late Laurels,' and it has been ably achieved. The style is always pure, and often brilliant, and the dialog displays considerable mastery of that peculiar lit repartie which would promise the author success in comedy. If the people in ordinary society seldom talk with such point and wit as flo naturally from Florence Vivian and her friends, and if they never display

their well-bred cynicism so ostentatiously, it must still be granted that the atmosfere of half-real, half-affected despair, moral and intellectual, which pervades modern drawing-rooms, has rarely been better indicated, or its modes of expression more accurately reproduced." [Westminster. **1459**

LAUREL BUSH (The). [by DINAH MARIA (MULOCK) CRAIK: *Harper*, 1876.] "One gets a world of counsel an l comfort from Miss Mulock's novels. She seems to put her heart in them, and from the vicissitudes of every-day life draws lessons which linger and impress. 'The Laurel Bush' is a simple little story, with common-place scenery, and few characters." [Boston ."Literary World." **1460**

LAW AND THE LADY (The). [by [W:] WILKIE COLLINS: 1874.] "In spite of the utter poverty of language, the entire absence of humor, the lack of any one character in whom any interest is felt beyond curiosity, and the painful suspense into which the reader is plunged in the very first page, and kept to the close, 'The Law and the Lady' must be read throu by those who venture upon the opening chapter. It is not fair to state what the plot is, so as to giv any key to it, but we may indicate generally the materials used in its construction. With an audacity almost amounting to wickedness, the novel opens with the marriage of the hero-and heroin, a gentleman and lady of good fortune and family. The match is all but forbidden by the relativs of both; why offensiv to the husband's mother is the grand secret which torments the reader until the book is finished. The wife, Valeria, discovers in the first week of wedlock that she has been married under an assumed name; she resents the indignity, yet passionately loving her deceitful mate suffers it not to cool her love, tho it excites her curiosity until it masters her devotion to him, and one step she takes to discover why this was done leads to a separation, as it reveals to her a terrible episode in the life of her husband, which has necessitated his assumption of a false name — he has been tried for a crime, and the verdict was ' Not Proven.' Confident that this verdict should hav been ' Not Guilty,' she devotes herself to searching enquiry into the facts, and is rewarded for all her anguish, her toils, her unshaken faith in her husband's innocence, by the discovery of evidence which fully clears him from all taint of guilt. The unravelment of the plot is accomplished in Mr. Collins's unrivalled style ; the reader is led off on false scents to rit and left by the most ingeniously puzzling suggestions, until all is ripe for a startling revelation of facts, which justify the husband in his great deceit, explain the mother's severe condemnation of his marriage, clear the mystery of both to his wife, and rewarding her for her fidelity by restoring a husband who oes the proof of his innocence to the wife he has loved and wronged. That is a dish to satisfy to repletion the lovers of — a good story." [Canadian Monthly. **1461**

LEADEN CASKET (The) [by MA. (RAINE) HUNT: *Chatto*, 1880.] "is a novel of various excellencies, and the story is of sufficient interest to giv continuity to the several episodes which form its main merit. The dramatis personæ ar, for the most part, a collection of character sketches, and the incidents ar studies of different society crazes, from the vagaries of the ' æsthetes ' to the extravagance of the ' professional beauties.' These somewhat disjointed fragments ar deftly woven into the semblance of a whole along the thread

of a needlessly improbable plot, principally by the skill of the author in keeping her pictures in a lo tone. The heroin, the dauter of an east-indian englishman, is reared in the family of her uncle, who, finding that she has been left to her ön devices throu the neglect of a novel-writing änt, and is better acquainted with sensational novels than with studies suitable to her age, despatches her to his sister in the country . . . Recalled to London she develops into a sensible young woman. Her änt introduces her into society, but only the literary and ' æsthetic ' portion of it, and when her mother suddenly appears from India she finds her dauter wearing the costume of her great-grandmother. All this is quickly changed, however, and Lady Brooke mortgages to a fashionable dressmaker her dauter's chances of a wealthy marriage for the necessary wardrobe for court circles, precipitates the young woman a last time into the æsthetic whirlpool, in order to carry off the only eligible man, a rich young lord, and then länches her dauter as a professional beauty. The latter proves refractory, and finally, after the melodrama alluded to chooses the ' leaden casket ' and is appropriately happy. The ' nincompoopiana ' is admirably done for lit satire." [Nation. **1462**

LESLIE TYRREL [by GEORGIANA MARION (CRAIK) MAY: *Loring*, 1867.] " is a very agreeable story. The personages ar few, and the incidents simple, yet the interest never flags : a large part of the dialog consists of love-making, yet it is neither affected, silly, sentimental, nor dull. The characters ar all pleasing, and the book is one of the few novels which we hav found too short." [Southern Review.] — " It is one of those charming little sketches — it can scarcely be called a novel — which at once rivets the attention and commands the sympathy of the reader, rendering him incapable of closing the book until he has completed its perusal. The situations ar neither new nor unusual, but the character of Leslie is drawn with great skill and discernment, and evinces a just perception of all which is good and noble in woman's nature. At the outset we ar not prepared to succumb to the controlling influence of this self-reliant and determined young woman; but by degrees she wins upon us by the purity and sincerity of her truly affectionate nature, and Frank Arnold rises in our estimation as he gradually learns to appreciate her real value, and to love her with the earnest devotion which such a woman unquestionably deservs. A strong-minded woman Leslie undoubtedly is, according to the best and most correct acceptance of the term, and if all who aim to be so regarded would emulate her nobleness of character, and become in reality what they desire to be thôt, the term would no longer be used as one of opprobrium, but as a distinctiv mark of respect and admiration. The quiet, unobtrusiv way of Leslie's life, her tender and judicious care of children, her gentle ministering to the sick, and the hi moral purpose by which she is guided under all circumstances, ar described with such simplicity and apparent truthfulness, that we ar led to believe in the absolute existence of such a woman, and to indulge the hope that the writer has drawn her sketch less from imagination than from experience. In presenting such a portraiture to the world the author not only confers a pleasure upon her readers, but renders a service to her sex." [Round Table. **1463**

LESS BLACK THAN WE'RE PAINTED. [by JA. PAYN: *Chatto*, 1878.] "Mr. Payn's eloquent portrayal of the character of a hi-minded actress should win him the thanks of that profession . . . When circumstances again draw them together, Lucy declines to be managed, and the 2 ardent spirits start in wedded life without the approbation of their friends. How Lucy comforts herself with her spendthrift husband, and after grievous trials makes a man of him, and secures her ôn happiness, is the gist of the story — a story as well told as it is wholesom. The different actors in the piece ar well placed upon the stage. Thêre is much humanity about Dick and the rector, the gamekeeper, and Squire Pole. The women, too, ar well imagined, which is noteworthy in a masculin author." [Athenæum. **1464**

LETTICE LISLE [by F. PARTHENOPE (NIGHTINGALE) VERNEY: *Smith*, 1870.] "deservs her pretty name. Her lot is cast among an old-fashioned society of farmers and fishermen. It is refreshing in the days of hi pressure and sensation to come across a novel which it is a pure relaxation to read, and the charm of which consists in good dialog, grafic but not needless description, and characters drawn from nature, creatures of common daylit, not 'creations' of a dyspeptic fancy. Lettice is what Americans mīt call an 'all-day' heroin, who makes up for want of sublimity by the 'staying' power of a strong but gentle nature. In childhood she endures the yoke of an ignorant and puritanic grandmother with exemplary fortitude, and returns the love of the poor gentleman, her yeoman uncle, with a dauter's piety. In early womanhood she is embarrassed by the attentions of the 2 lovers, and being a girl of that period, is honest to both. We hear little of her later days. Her story is a simple one, but well told, and deserving of gratitude, in that it describes a character which englishmen still admire, and which is not yet extinct among us. The subordinate characters, tho inferior in interest, ar good types of the better side of an age which is passing away, and in their speech is a ring of the forest and the sea." [Athenæum. **1465**

LIEUTENANT (The) [by EMILY MARION HARRIS: *Bell*, 1882.] "is a peaceful story, its main theme being the romantic friendship between little Monica Carr and a young officer on duty in the Tower. Monica is a delitful, quaint, imaginativ child, and her conversations with her friend ar excellent. A still more refined conception is the character of her sister Louie, who rewards in a different way the pains spent upon her by a somewhat puritanic, but gentle and hi-minded mother." [Ath. **1466**

LIFE FOR A LIFE (A) [by DINAH MARIA (MULOCK) CRAIK: *Harper*, 1859.] "is a bold, instructiv, and even fascinating book. Thĉre is the same clear insīt into human nature, the same clever dissecting of its most eccentric elements, the same graceful and pure style, which distinguish all we get from the pen of this gifted lady." [Crayon. **1467**

LIFE'S AFTERMATH [by EMMA ( ) MARSHALL : N.Y., *Dutton*, 1876.] "is one of the best stories we hav recently read, — fresh in matter, refined and elevating in manner, and peopled by some personages whom it is a blessing to kno. Most of these ar Quakers, and very charming ar the glimpses of their placid life. The atmosfere of the book is delitful, — unalloyed purity . . . In Winifred, we find one of the few successful efforts to portray an absolutely ingenuous, con-

science-dominated maiden, whose love is as pure and perennial as a mountain spring. A few more sunbeams in these pages would hiten their charm; but thĉre ar several passages of exquisit pathos, which truly illustrate the 'luxury of grief.'" [Bostón "Literary World." **1468**

LIFE'S LONG BATTLE WON [by "E: GARRETT," i. e., I.. Fyfie Mayo · *Dodd*, 1889.] "is in every sense good reading. With quite sufficient plot, ineident, and story to keep up interest, its strength lies chiefly in its characters. Not the least attractiv of these is that one which, standing behind the scenes, and busy only in bringing the personages of the little drama before the audience, has been unable to prevent its shado from looming behind them all. Lifelike and interesting as thĉy ar, the gossiping Gibson woman, gentle Lesley Baird, common-sense, shrewd, practical, and yet unworldly Clementina Kerr, the 2 old Scotchwomen, Alison Brown, and Jean Haldane, patient and loving-hearted Mrs. Crawford, and the womanly, aspiring Mary Olrig, — the personality of 'Edward Garrett' is, on the whole, the predominant attraction of the book. A woman, one would say, who has kuón how to love and how to suffer, and who has been won to wisdom throu both experiences. Shrewd, too, and observant, with as quick an eye for a foible or a fault as for a natural virtue or a grace." [Catholic World. **1469**

LIFE'S MISTAKE (A) [by — ( ) CAMERON : *Ward & Downey*, 1886.] "returns to the old, yet ever new story of 'Auld Robin Gray,' and her version of the 'life's mistake' is pretty and pathetic. Here, as in the ballad, the girl who is faithless to an absent lover at the bidding of her father tells the tale of her weakness, and does not spare herself; but the sympathy of the reader, as is meet and rit, remains with the old man rather than with the young one. At any rate, this is so before the story ends, and it must be confessed that the young lover is well able to take care of himself. The plot is brit and cheerful on the whole, both hero and heroin eventually proving the truth of the motto, according to which, if hearts cannot be torn away ' by sudden wrench,' yet love may sink by slo decay. As 2 new loves rise to replace the love which sinks, the reader is amply consoled for his sympathetic sorro, and he puts down the book with a feeling of satisfaction. Thêre ar 4 to sympathize with instead of 2, and at least twice 4 in whom it is impossible not to be interested." [Athenæum. **1470**

LIFE'S SECRET (A). [by ELLEN (PRICE) WOOD.] Mrs. Wood "is securely enthroned in the affections of her readers, in virtue of an unsullied career. Her worst enemies can never accuse her of an attempt to soar for a subject above the beneficent institutions of her nativ land. The modest coroner's inquest, the homely justice-room, the unassuming smuggler's cave, ar full of inspiration for her; and she is thŏroly consistent. She resorts to no garnishes for her plain english fare, but servs up murders and mutton, suicides and rice-pudding, stolen cheques and thick bread and butter; and as she never fails to say an emfatic grace over each heavy meal, she satisfies alike the appetite, the taste, and the conscience of her readers." [Spectator. **1471**

LIGHT THAT FAILED (The). [by RUDYARD KIPLING: *Ward & Lock*, 1890.] "Fresh from its perusal, we willingly ōn to having read it with great pleasure, and we think no one can put down ' The Light that Failed' without giving it the hearty word of praise it deserves. We find

ourselves carried away by its dash, its humor, its pathos; and our first idea is that here is a bit of life fotografed for us by an experienced hand. The outline of the story is simple in the extreme; indeed, it can hardly be said to possess a plot at all. Dick Heldar, the hero, falls in love with a little girl, who has, as well as himself, the misfortune to be under the care of a female virago calling herself a gentlewoman. After a long separation, the 2 meet again by chance. Dick is now a ' special artist' and war-correspondent, and Maisie is giving herself up to art. The point of the book lies in the question whether she loves Dick well enuf to marry him, or whether she prefers the pursuit of art, for which she has no real talent." [Spectator. **1472**

LIL. [*Lippincott*, 1878.] = *KIL-CORRAN.*

LIL [*Roberts*, 1889.] "has its scene in a quiet english village. Its attractiv characters ar Dr. Murray, his 5 boys, and his dauter Lil who is laid up with a spinal complaint, Ken Wyat, the heir to the manor, and his cousin Sylvia who comes from far Australia to dispossess him. The plot is simple, and the character-drawing lit but firm in touch. The charm of this writer is in her wholesom faithfulness to the quiet life she describes, and the unaffected teaching she gathers from experience." [Boston " Literary World." **1473**

LILLIESLEAF: Concluding Series of some Passages in the Life of Mrs. Margaret Maitland of Sunnyside, [by MA. OLIPHANT (WILSON) OLIPHANT: *Hurst*, 1855.] "is in our thinking superior to the beginning, and this we take to be about the most satisfactory compliment we can pay the author. Thêre is a vein of good simple sense running throu, for which no reader can fail to be the better." [Athenæum. **1474**

LIFE FOR A LIFE (A.) [by DINAH MARIA (MULOCK) CRAIK (†, 1887) : 1859.] "Its readers will be many; but those whŏ strictly sympathise with its vues of life must be comparativly few. The thread of its narrativ is the birth, grŏth, and consummation of the lŏve of twŏ singular characters, under singular çircumstances. Theodora Johnson is the second dauter of a clergyman. Her elder sister has personal attractions, but a narro soul, tho an earnest ŏne; her younger sister is a beauty, sballo in feeling and in thôt, but with that ever smiling good-nature which in the every-day life of woman so wel compensates for the absençe of unusual intelligence. Theodora has a broad, deep, placid-seeming, but really impetuous nature, and a keen, wel cultivated mind ; but tŏ these she joins a person, not ugly or even disagreeable, but simply insignificant, and not distinguished for graçe or breeding. She is neglected, and eaten with envy; when she acçidentally meets a Dr. Urquhart, whŏ is her masculin counterpart. They gradually, but with the sureness and certainty of fate, approach each other, and finally ar united by the bonds of a lŏve, which, they being what they ar, makes them inseparable, in soul at least, for life. But there is a slight difficulty in thêir way. Dr. Urquhart has a gloom hanging over him from the first; and it prŏveş that in his boyhood he, in a soli-

tary fit of drunkenness, unintentionally killed the elder brŏther of Theodora, whŏ was a bad fello, and had led him intŏ the very exçess which terminated so fatally tŏ his tempter. The tale is told in a sŏmewhat singular style. We look over the sholders of Theodora and her lŏver as thêy write thêir diaries. This form of narration has the advantage of directness in its relation of the inner experiençe of the principal characters, which in this case could not be so wel protrayed, perhaps, in any other manner. It belŏngs tŏ the class of psychological novels which is now so notably on the increase, and the interest of which depends not in the variations of the fortune of the characters, but in their emotional and intellectual experiençe under circumstançes which ar established at the outset of the narrativ, or soon after it . . . It is ŏne of the gloomiest, and, in spite of the final marriage of its hero and heroin, ŏne of the most hopeless and depressing books we ever read. It contains, however, many fine studies of character; prominent amŏng them being that of the heroin. Her sisters, too, ar sketched intŏ the picture with boldness, spirit and knoledge; and her father is a fine type of the man whŏ allows his religious faith, almost, but not quite, tŏ crush his affectionate and charitable nature." [Albion.

LITTLE CHATELAINE (The). [by the EARL OF DESART: *Sonnenschein*, 1889.] "Charlie Garland — the weak man who cannot see, except at times, that his ruin and that of the pet dauters whom he fondles, and who repay him with the whole love of their childish hearts, is attributable to his personal selfishness — is a common character, but he tells his story uncommonly well before he dies. 'Captain Carr,' the truer friend of poor Geraldine and Ethel, is a gentleman in the finest details. Major Dobbin may hav suggested him, but the suggestion is faint. Fortunately for him, Gerry is not an Amelia. Lord Desart supplies plenty of animated description, and genial Lord Liscannor and his 3 irish dauters in their nativ land form an excellent sketch. John Joxam, the book-maker, and the amusing butler and his better half will not be forgotten by the reader of 'The Little Chatelaine.'" [Athenæum. **1475**

LITTLE WORLD (A) [by G: MANVILLE FENN: *King*, 1877.] "is a story of humble life, not badly sketched. Jared Pellet, the organist, is one who, with much natural refinement, has not the counter-balancing element of hardness which enables a man to be successful in the world. Accordingly, in middle life he finds himself glad to accept the management of the organ at St. Runwald's, which enables him just to maintain his large family in decent poverty. From this post he is near being expelled, an undeserved slur upon his honesty having alienated his friends, the kind-hearted vicar and church warden; and it is on his conduct under this trial that one thread of the narration depends . . . The author takes, for the most part, a kindly vue of human nature, and his book will be read with interest." [Athenæum. **1476**

LOB LIE [by JULIANA HORATIA (GATTY) EWING: *Bell*, 1873.] "is a story which neither young nor old will read throu without having their feelings strongly moved. It is the history of a child whose natural or unnatural parents hav left him exposed under a bush of broom. The infant is found and adopted by 2 of the dearest and most primitiv of old ladies; they call him John Brown, and try their best to rear him in a god-fearing manner, and to make him a useful member of society; but the child inherits gypsy blood and gypsy ways. He is the most fascinating of nanty children, idle to the back-bone, and with that restless adventurous nature to which comfort and a quiet life ar irksom, whilst all restraint or coercion is simply intolerable. The boy runs away and finds hardships to his heart's content. Home-sickness and the recollection of his kind benefactress come over him on the other side of the world. He makes his way back, a cabin boy, as he went out; and then ashamed to go back, he lingers about the barracks in a town, running errands for the soldiers and forming a boy's friendship, full of worship and admiration, for a magnificent Highlander. The pathos and beauty of this little episode will go to the heart of every reader. The boy returns to his old friends, but too ashamed to sho himself til he has made some amends, he hides in a stable and does the work secretly, and the nêborhood declare it is the old family brownie come back to bring luck to the house. Of course he is discovered and welcomed by the old ladies and all the nêborhood. The real love and gratitude which hav been roused keep him tolerably industrious, and he does not run away again, tho the tramp's nature never quite dies out in him. The story is delitful." [Athenæum. **1477**

LOGIE TOWN. [by "SARAH TYT-LER," i. e., Henrietta Keddie: *Ward & Downey*, 1887.] "Miss Tytler's new volumes ar likely to be read with appreciation by those who feel old associations stirred by a clever and truthful description of life in an old-fashioned scotch town. That the dialect is good goes without saying, and the dramatis personæ ar numerous and fairly original. Mrs. Mally, of course, suggests Meg Dods at once, but it is by way of contrast, tho probably the aristocratic old dame of the Crown oes her literary existence to her ruder prototype. The contrasted 'beaux' of Logie Town — Adam Lauder, with his strong health and gay spirits, and the sentimental, rather supercilious Steenie Oliphant — ar less complete portraits than ar the female figures, yet hav much individuality. Those who can be touched by scotch humor and scotch pathos will find plenty of both in 'Logie Town.'" [Athenæum. **1478**

LONG SUMMER'S DAY (A) [by M. C. M. SIMPSON: *Smith*, 1873.] "is unpretentious, aiming at nothing more remarkable than the description of a country girl's experience of a London season. [compare No. 1168.] It is written in a cheerful spirit, the crumpled rose-leaves being few and far between . . . Mrs. Hamilton is a good-humored woman-of-the-world, with better principles than ar sometimes supposed to appertain to that character; Lily is a pleasant child; Mrs. Barlow is a well-drawn sketch of a selfish invalid. Of the men, a lively old vicar, of a school less common than it was, strikes us as the best. The tale goes off trippingly." [Athenæum. **1479**

LOOK BEFORE YOU LEAP. [by "MRS. ALEXANDER," i. e., Annie (French) Hector: *Bentley*, 1865, (*Holt*, 1882.)] "Mrs. Alexander sel-dom writes a dull novel and she has the art of making use of the improbable in such a way as to make it seem natural, and yet not lose its interest. Her tenderness of heart will not permit her to bring her characters to bad ends, and 'Look Before You Leap' is far from being a tragedy. Yet thêre is suffering enuf in it to bring a tear to the eye of a sympathetic reader; in fact, the description of poor Marie Delvigne's distress and misery when, on her wedding day, her husband falsely accuses her of imposing upon him and leaves her, is heartrending. The women ar good throuóut, and the men ar far from bad, tho as a woman 'Mrs. Alexander' understands, and is able to describe, better the operations of the feminin than the masculin mind and heart. But the ingenuity with which the improbable incidents of the tale ar worked together is really its most remarkable feature. That Marie should be able to hide herself away in London, notwithstanding the activ search which is going on for her, is probable enuf, but what shall we say of her falling in with, and being protected and shéltered by, her husband's half-brother, without either discovering who the other is? And yet, óing to the quarrel between Neville and Watson, all this seems natural enuf in reading it." [Nation.] — "The hero of the story, Capt. Neville, elopes with a pretty governess whom he takes to be an heiress. In the first transports of his disappointment he treats her with an unwarrantable cruelty, whêreon she quits him, and for a year he is made to pay the penalty of his fit of ill-temper by separation from the woman he loves and by complete ignorance as to her fate. In the end all is happily arranged, the impecunious and reunited pair ar furnished with an incom, and the true

LITTLE MINISTER (The) [by Ja. Matthew Barrie: *Cassell,* 1891.] "There could hardly be better evidençe of the reality of the author's powers than the charm exerçised by this story, in spite of the absurdity of its plot. It may be from some defect in the Southern imagination, but tŏ us the heroin whŏ is the pivot round whŏm the story all revolvs, is even vexatiously impossible. A girl whŏ is at ōnce a lady and a gypsy of the fields, whŏ is ōne minute the fiancée of a peer, and the next a barefooted Egyptian, dançing with a tamborine in the streets of a Scotish fishing-village, whŏ is all goodness and forever lying, whŏ is at home with all classes and an object of suspicion tŏ all, whŏ is full of wild blood and mad capriçe, and falls in lōve with a bit of an "Auld-Licht" minister solely because of his virtues, is an incredible and even preposterous figure. We can never forget her, or avoid the reflection that, for all the author may say, she could never hav been there, or hav dōne that, or hav said, either as lady or as Egyptian, what she did say. The lōve of the Little Minister for her is like the lōve of a mortal for a kelpie, so unnatural and improbable that the account of it givs an impression like that which would be produçed by a book half written in prose, and half in wild snatches of lyric poĕtry. It jars throuŏut with the realism of the rest of the book, which is Mr. Barrie's true element. For he is realist first of all, in the healthiest and truest sĕnse of the word. It has becōme a fashion tŏ call him a humorist and master of pathos; whōse insight is so deep and his heârt so broad, that he perçeives alike the pathos and the humor—tho more perhaps the pathos than the humor—which lie hidden in common events and common folk, espeçially when both ar Scotch." [Spectator]—"The story is told by that dominie whōse acquaintance is made in 'A Window in Thrums' [No. 1820 p.] It is a poetical, passionate story, with a plot so romantic as tŏ appear quite old-fashioned. An Auld-Licht minister is, after all, but a man, espeçially when at the age of twenty-one. When Gavin got the "call" tŏ Thrums, and was able tŏ establish his devoted mōther in the manse, the troubles of life seemed tŏ lie behind and the future shon fair, provided his physical vigor should prŏve equal tŏ the demands of Thrums for loud-voiced denunçiation of all things natural and agreeable tŏ weak humanity. Poor Gavin had not counted on an "Egyptian limmer" cōming dançing out of limbo, strait intŏ his cut-and-dried life, dictating heaven or hel for him by the ring of her voice and the light of her eyes. But when, at last, he understands the wōnderful, terrible forçe which sweeps away all his wel-knōn self, except his stanch integrity, then let Thrums rise and with imprecation stone him from its limits. Babbie is his and the joy thĕreof passes understanding. Mr. Barrie leaves us in doubt about the action taken by Thrums when the news of the marriage over the tōngs was confirmed, but the inferençe from the behavior of "lang Thammas" is that thĕy accepted what couldn't be helped, and proçeeded tŏ vindicate outraged riteousness by prŏving tŏ Babbie how far from a bed of roses is the lot of a minister's wife." [Nation **1475 m**

heiress with a truer admirer." [Boston "Literary World." **1480** LOST BATTLE (A) [by ELEANOR C. PRICE: Edinburgh, *Douglas*, 1878.] "leaves us satisfied, and ready to do justice to the excellence of the author's drawing of her characters . . . Thêre ar no monsters of vice or paragons of virtue, but people such as one may often meet, with their several characteristics just sufficiently accentuated to save them from being commonplace. Perhaps the best is the foreman of the quarry, in whom the educated artisan is depicted to a nicety, sober, honest, cleanly, but allowing self-respect to verge closely on selfishness, and tho not neglecting duties, thinking still more of rits. But it is invidious to select whêre all ar good." [Athenæum. **1481**

LOST IDENTITIES [by M. L. TYTLER: *Sonnenschein*, 1888.] "is a story which may giv reasonable satisfaction. Its language is hi flön and not always correct; its incidents ar often sensational and sometimes melodramatic; but thêre is no doubt about the buoyant and pathetic freshness which characterizes the narrativ from beginning to end. It is based upon the old foundation of a pair of changeling babies. The heroin is supposed to be the child of nobody in particular, and as she takes this very much to heart, and refuses to ally herself to the man she loves, some years of wretchedness hav to be endured before things ar finally put rit. With such a threadbare theme 'Lost Identities' mit hav been a terribly commonplace story; yet it is nothing of the kind. The author has a sympathetic heart, and she makes her reader sympathize with her characters — a score of children, the heroin and a dozen or so of her unsuccessful lovers, several old men and women, and a fairly worthy hero. Most of these people ar

pleasant, some of them positivly charming; and the interest of the story, bily colored as it is, compensates for a number of little shortcomings in its manner and method." [Athenæum. **1482**

LOST INHERITANCE (The) [1852.] "is a gentle, agreeable story, — so free from folly, exaggeration and bombast as to be more than ordinarily grateful. This said, however, the revuer has little to add: since the author's effects ar made by continuous narration and description — and not by violent surprises, brilliant aforisms, or hily-wrôt dialog. The heart-story of Marion Harcourt, and the slo cure (not without its relapses) wrôt on the suspicious, cynical man by the truthful, sensible, and not insensible, girl could not hav been shön in shorter compass." [Athenæum. **1483**

LOST LOVE (A) [by "ASHFORD OWEN," i. e., Annie Ogle: *Smith*, 1855, — *Loring*, 1876.] "is a little story full of grace and genius. The incidents ar slit and common, such as mit be picked up either in the streets of London, or in the most stagnant town. Thêre is little or nothing bily colored, either in character or emotion. The story resembles a delicately finished outline rather than a fully colored picture. — It is the heart which magnifies this life, making a truth and beauty of its ön. — The opening of the life which lies at the root of the dull, cheerless, uneventful career of the heroin has a deep and touching interest which would be too painful wer it not for the skill with which the conclusion is so managed as to leave the reader indifferent to what is called 'a happy ending.' After folloing poor Georgy throu the deep love which made her life, we feel that it was 'well with her' at the last; and we leave her without unavailing pity. We recommend our readers to get the book. No outline of the story would give them any idea of its beauty." [Athenæum, 1855.] — " It is but an hour's reading, but the hour is one of rare and memorable pleasure." [Leader, 1858.] — It " is a very pleasant love-story, peopled by some very nice persons. Georgy, the heroin, is betrothed to Stephen Anstruther, who goes away soon after their engagement for 3 years' absence. Georgy, living with unpleasant relativs, repents her rashness, and refuses to marry Anstruther. She leaves her home and goes to London to Mrs. Erskine, the mother of the man she had learned to love. He loves her, too, and they ar betrothed. But Cornelia Everett, his old love, is in the same house, and Georgy suspects that his heart has returned to her. She tells him this, and breaks their engagement. He marries Cornelia, and Georgy marries Anstruther, and presently dies." [Boston " Literary World."] — " In reprinting ' A Lost Love,' the publisher has done something more like a personal favor to certain people than he probably knoes. I am not going to revue it, — and I wished to speak of it only becaus of the curiously enthusiastic folloing — worship, cult—which it has among certain refined american women. I do not kno anything about the fact, but I should doubt, on general principles, whether it has equally a cult with english women. My observation is that it was expressly written for some 10 or a dozen ladies of my acquaintance, who read it 15 or 20 years ago, and who hav since gone about proselyting people to it . . . It is not at all an exciting story, I should say : the scene is largely that everlasting english country house, which is in itself almost enuf to render any action and person loathsom; but the manner

in which the skeptical reader is convicted of his former hardness of heart and darkness of mind, as the story progresses, must be hily gratifying to the early Lost Lovers, — as I may call them. What should be so wonderful about a young girl's not getting the man whom she loves, and who loves her as much as, if not more than, he loves the brilliant woman who does get him? That is the author's secret, and you ar made to kno that it is a very great matter, — a matter of life and death. The book is truth and life, treated with consummate, unfailing, uninsistent art." [Atlantic, 1876. **1484**

LOST REPUTATION (A) [*Stock*, 1887.] " is an affecting story, not original in plot or general construction, but treated in such a manner as to make it fresh and attractiv. Graham Murray, the hero, is the only son of a scotch laird, and he loses his reputation by associating with an unscrupulous swindler whom he knoes to be detested by his father . . . But from this point onward all is natural and engrossing and pathetic. Language and reflexions, incidents and conversations, ar alike simple and in good taste. The reader will follo Graham's later fortunes with interest to the end, and will be rewarded by a conclusion which, if not altogether free from shado, is purely artistic and true to life." [Athenæum. **1485**

LOST SIR MASSINGBERD [by JA. PAYN: *Low*, 1864.] " is a story, which, having professedly more of the characteristics of romance than the ordinary works of fiction, is calculated rather to amuse the young than to entertain the reader of matured and cultivated taste. If any one be desirous of reopening his mind to early impressions, or should wish to realize his idea of what his childish predelictions probably wer, he may hav recourse to this truly extraordinary narrativ. The preternatural gloom with which the annals of the Heath family ar overshadoed; the unexceptional and increasing iniquity with which each successive generation is credited; the glaring and acknoledged depravity which renders every scion of the family tree an outcast almost from civilized society while living, and insures him, at his end, a reception in unconsecrated ground, — remind one, with a pleasant thrill, of the imperfectly-kuòn antecedents of Bluebeard and of certain passages in the memoirs of the Life and Times of Dr. Faustus. To this, altho the modern agencies of Bow St. runners and one-pound notes ar introduced, the wonderful and woful end of the hero, which, in its horrible retributiv justice, has a touch of the grotesque, not a little, indeed, contributes." [London Review. **1486**

LOVE ME LITTLE, LOVE ME LONG [by C: READE: *Harper*, 1859.] "is exquisitly simple in conception, and the narration is mostly full of ease and grace, altho the unfolding of the plot is less direct than mit hav been expected from an author who professes so deep a regard for the dramatic order of development . . . The whole work is as spritly and agreeable a love-story as any english writer has produced, — always amusing, often flashing with genuin wit, sometimes inspiring in its eloquent energy." [Atlantic.] — "David Dodd, beautiful, tender, simple, rit-minded soul, chivalrous as Don Quixote, guileless as a child, fine seaman, impassioned lover. One's heart warms to the man so broadly, simply, forcibly drawn, who is no fool and no piece of perfection, but one of the finest human creatures who has ever set foot in a book, and that is saying a good deal.

The fun in him, the unconscious poetry, the benign mildness and charity, the simple, unaffected courage and strength, ar not to be surpassed — unless it is by the utter unconsciousness of the man that thère is anything in him which is admirable or unusual. Mr. Reade makes him gro into the maturity of middle age before our eyes, melloing the young seaman into the experienced commander with a skill which commands our biest plaudits . . It is not a book which it is usual to distinguish as Mr. Reade's masterpiece; but of all the little library before us, it is the one to which *we* turn with the warmest partiality. Thère is so little in it which we can wish out of it — so little redundancy, so much originality, — such truth and naturalness, such charming ease and undemonstrativ power. It is not a great work like the 'Cloister and the Hearth' [No. 646.]. It is a little idyl, a homely poem. Only one of the 2 most deeply concerned is even impassioned; thère ar few sensational events, — none, indeed, except the voyage, but yet the story attracts is like music. Lucy is like the 'melody that's sweetly played in tune.' She is not brilliant, splendid, commanding, like Mr. Reade's first favorit. The grand charm about her is that she is a perfect lady — courtesy is almost her passion . . She is sweet to everybody, taking every one's feelings into consideration, smoothing matters everywhère, sparing no pains, excusing, petting, putting pretty glosses upon all the doubtful proceedings of her relativs. Thus she glides about the story in maiden meditation fancy free, softly eluding a lover at every corner, very happy in her freedom and her youth, and the affection of her friends. She is so sweetly in tune among all the jars of the surrounding figures, that she soothes the reader and the writer, as well as the other personages in her little drama. Thêre is something in the idea of this soft, tender, passionless feminin creature which has always had a wonderful power. Passion is grander, but it is, in its way, always a descent from that pedestal on which chivalry has placed the abstract woman — a creature above passion, spotless as sno, almost insensible, affectionate, serene, and sweet, with none of the thrills and throbs of feeling which belong to the senses rather than to the heart." [Blackwood's. **1487**

LOVE, OR MARRIAGE? [By W: BLACK: 3 vols., *Tinsley*, 1868.] "is rather an original novel, and by no means a dull or uninteresting one. The tale is simple enuf, but well told, and in .that lies its chief charm. Thêre ar 2 heroins, Fanny Glencairn and Marie Kirschenfeld, and 2 heroes to correspond, C: Bennett and Mr. Helstone. The latter is an atheist, and a bitter opponent of the custom of marriage. With the exception of these blemishes, he has no particular faults. Charles and Mr. Helstone contend for the love of Fanny Glencairn, who is a pretty but bily independent young lady. Charles has the best of the rivalry at first, but the lady's independence of character induces her to listen to Mr. Helstone's theories of religion and marriage, and she becomes captivated by his brilliant ability, and ultimately coincides with his opinions and theories. As a sequel, she becomes Helstone's mistress, with the tacit consent of her mother, who has been also convinced by Mr. Helstone, and leaves her father broken-hearted. Charles nursed by Marie . . . soon forgets his misery, falls in love with his kind nurse, Marie, and marries her, and

the pair ar perfectly happy. Whether the other couple ar equally blest, or whether any or what punishment ultimately descends upon them, we ar not told by Mr. Black. This certainly sounds a very strange kind of a story to found a novel on, and one which in most hands would make the book unreadable. We must, however, in fairness state that all coarseness of expression is avoided, and tho the facts we hav mentioned ar not obscurely told, they ar not forced upon the reader's notice." [Athenæum. **1488**

LOVE STRONG AS DEATH. [by ROSE BURROWES: *Remington*, 1878.] "The plot, tho simple is interesting, the characters ar original, and the story is full of tenderness and refinement. The author, however, has too daringly ventured on the improbable, in making 2 brothers so much alike that the woman who loves one of them is for a series of weeks deceived by the resemblance. The title is well justified by the contents of the book, and a very pretty little tale of wooing and winning is told. The account given of the gradual refining, taming and awakening to love of a young hoyden is decidedly attraetiv. As a contrast, the villain of the story is a little too atrocious for this civilized and conventional age and country. Usually women hav little sense of humor, but this writer is an exception, and if the reader is here and thêre moved to melancholy, he is many times excited to lâfter." [Athenæum. **1489**

LOVEL THE WIDOWER. [by W: M. THACKERAY.] "It seems as if much mit be said, and without any unseemly strain, of such stories as 'Vanity Fair' [No. 998] and 'Lovel the Widower.' They ar certainly lamentable pictures of human nature. If Life wer only that, it would be hardly worth living. **Ex-**

actly, and there the satirist begins. 'See what it may be; what it often is. Be warned; be simple, honest, pure.' That is the moral of such books and of such pictures. They do indirectly, inversely, what others do directly and positivly. But certainly the artist may choose whether he will warn you or win you. For a long time it seemed to be thot essential that the hero of every novel should be brave and handsom, rich and strong, and picturesque; and that the heroin should be beautiful and graceful. That fashion has gone by. Major Dobbin is very tall and very gawky; but what a man he is compared with *Pelham*, or *Vivian Grey*, or *Ivanhoe!* — who ar not men at all, but school-girls' puppets. The point of departure of Thackeray, and all the realists in Art, is dependence upon nature." [G: W: Curtis. 1862. **1490**

LOVER OR FRIEND? [by ROSA NOUCHETTE CAREY: *Bentley*, 1890.] "concerns a noble fello broken in health by wounds received in the struggle which won for him the Victoria Cross, who hides a love which mit hav been returned, until such time as he can undertake the responsibilities of marriage, only to discover, when he is in a position to make his declaration, that he has been forestalled by a younger and more impetuous rival. There is also a substory, the central figure in which is a fascinating but vaguely unsatisfactory wido introduced to us as Mrs. Blake, who turns out to be in reality the wife of a living husband named O'Brien, who for the crime of forgery has been sentenced to a long imprisonment, and whose involuntary intrusion upon the woman who has made herself dead to him comes, of course, at the most inopportune moment. [Compare plot of 'Tale of a Lonely Parish.'] The two

stories ar, however, so skilfully wedded that they ar practically one, for Mrs. Blake, or O'Brien, is the mother of the handsom, loyal-hearted Cyril, who, by winning the love of Audrey Ross, has unwittingly robbed the strong and tender Michael Burnett of a hope which, faint as it is, has been for years his most cherished possession." [Spectator. **1491**

LOVERS' CREED (The). [by F., S., (J.) HOEY: *Chatto*, 1884.] "Here there is no lack of incident cunningly fitted, all captious objections being foreseen and provided against . . Mavis Wynn is a heroin with just enuf strength of character, and the Bassets, father and son, ar attractiv, mauly figures. Add to these merits the pleasant bits of french domestic life, and a style which is familiar without vulgarity." [Nation.] — The cause, duration, and ending of this estrangement must not here be told; the reader will find it well worth his while to take the whole story, as its author chooses to tell it, with its fluctuating interest, its rather humdrum style, its bits of Latin, and its quiet simplicity and tenderness. Capt. John's betrothed is a charming character." [Athenæum. **1492**

LOVING AND SERVING [by "HOLME LEE," i. e., Harriet Parr: *Smith*, 1884.] "is a pleasant story in which the heroin meets just enuf unhappiness to hiten the happiness with which she is ultimately rewarded. There is a succession of pictures of comfortable home-life passed in an atmosfere of goodness; the incidents ar not exciting, but they ar always pleasing." [Athenæum. **1493**

LOYS, LORD BERESFORD (etc.). [by MA. ( ) ARGLES HUNGERFORD: *Smith*, 1883.] ("These) 17 short tales ar harmless, spirited little love-stories; some pretty, and even a little touching;

some absurdly farcical, — witness ' *The Dilemma*,' and the one in which Snooks, at the suggestion of a friend, proposes to 4 sisters at the same ball, to help him out of the scrape in which his first thótless proposal has involved him; but all deal with exceedingly pretty girls, and handsome felloes with handles to their names; and everything happens in beautiful summer, and all comes delitfully rit in the end, tho not always with sufficiently poetical justice . . . The slitness of the tales will be indicated, when we say that ' *Lydia*,' for example, is a brief account of how Lord Fenton begs Lydia not to cultivate the acquaintance of a certain gentleman; how Lydia indignantly refuses to grant his request, and does so in offensiv language; and how, after a few days of misery, they fall into each other's arms. ' *Krin*,' again, merely narrates how Corinna Crofton got locked in a ruin with Lord Rowden, [compare plot of ' Quits'] and came home as the future Lady Rowden, which appeased mamma's displeasure for the frit her prolonged absence had given her." [Spectator. **1494**

LUCKY YOUNG WOMAN (A). [by F. C. PHILIPS: *Ward & Downey*, 1886.] "We can besto unstinted praise on the unflagging spirit and genuin humor with which Mr. Philips tells his story. Sir Hugo Conyers, a sort of aristocratic Pecksniff, is an exceedingly clever sketch, while Marcia, the ' lucky young woman,' is an excellent specimen of a hi-spirited and straitforward girl, whose indiscretions ar the result of her confidence. The tone, while remarkably unreserved, is never unwholesom. The author's filosofy, if earthy, is distinctly optimist." [Athenæum. **1495**

LUCY CARTER. [by T: C. JUNIOR: *Sonnenschein*, 1887.] "No one who considers what ar the essentials of a

pleasant work of fiction will be disposed to take Mr. Junior to task for his minor defects of style, or for a certain want of finish in the working out of his ideas. The narrativ itself is natural and straitforward, tho one of the incidents with which it concludes mit well hav been dispensed with . . . The simplicity, directness, and quiet good taste of the story ar conspicuous. The heroin is admirably drawn, and her actions ar inspired by delicacy and good feeling throuout." [Athenæum. **1496**

LUCY CROFTON [by MARGARET OLIPHANT (WILSON) OLIPHANT: *Hurst*, 1859.] "is a sequel to a former onevolume story by the same author; but it stands intact and intelligible in itself. It is a piece of home-painting, very nicely touched. The interest is quiet, but it is sustained, and made up of the simplest material. A happy marriage overshadoed to the wife by the one great sorro of her life, the loss of her only child in its first infancy, — the husband, kind, loving, indolent, a rich country gentleman, whose very ' ease ' chokes up his talents, rendering them unfruitful — an orfan relativ whom théy adopt, and whose self-possessed reticence and perfect ability to take care of her interests, ar the chief personages of the book. Lucy Crofton's serene deportment, and skilful manœuvring to obtain her ends, and always to be in the rit to give no shado of handle against herself, is cleverly dône. The faint struggle betwixt herself and her ânt, who, whilst vaguely feeling that all is not rit in her extremely sensible and well-deported young companion, is also conscious that she is no match for her, the aggravating obtuseness of the husband, and his perverse commendation of Lucy on all occasions as ' an excellent girl,' — is all shôn with a quiet humor which prevents the story from seeming slo; and when, at the very last, Lucy throes off the mask, amply justifying her ânt's dislike of her, the reader feels pleased, tho even the stickler for poetic justice will, we fear, hav been so far biased by Lucy's cleverness and prudent management of her affairs, that even he will be rather glad that she carries her point at last, and wins everything she had set her heart on attaining. The secret of this very slit and simple story giving pleasure is, that the persons ar painted not in black and white, but in flesh color, as human nature should be. Thêre is no affected or exaggerated sentiment in the story, — it all rings true; the inner hidden life of the wife, and the sorro of her bereaved motherhood, into which her husband, kind and good as he is, cannot enter, is touched with a skill and delicacy which attests its truth, whilst it keeps clear of becoming wearisom or morbid." [Athenæum.] — " It is another of Mrs. Oliphant's clever little stories, always satisfactory, always interesting, always completely different from anything she has written before." [In the ease of " L. C." this is not strange, as the book was pub. in 1859. — W: M. G.] [Critic. **1497**

LUNA. [by M. C. HELMORE: *Smith,* 1873.] "Miss Helmore's little story is slit enuf, but it attains the modest aim proposed. It is the tale of some personages in fashionable life, redeemed from insipidity, or worse, by the influence of pure and passionate affection. Diane or 'Luna' is a charming heroin, tho capable of silly freaks, and devoid of any sound training which mit hav prevented the dilemma in which she finds herself placed. Lancelot, a lazy dandy, more harmless than most of his kind, is elevated by being surprised into a genuin passion . . . For the homelife we hav nothing but praise, and

Minnie and her irish cousin ar admirably suited to their friend. The soldiers, too, ar good in their excellent tho heavy way, and deserv their success with a dainty group of damsels." [Athenæum. **1498**

MABEL'S PROGRESS. [by F., ELEANOR (TERNAN) TROLLOPE: *Chapman,* 1867.] " In order that the hero and heroin may come to an understanding before the end, the fair Mabel, the triumfant young actress, who has refused Clement Charlewood's proffered love when he was rich and she was poor, is compelled to make something very little short of a point-blank offer to him when their positions ar reversed . . . Thêre is not much plot, but the narrativ is interesting and eventful, and the characters ar well designed and carefully finished, and the tone and language ar pure and good throuóut. 'Aunt Margaret's Trouble,' tho well written and full of character, was somewhat deficient in life and movement. Thêre is no such deficiency here. The difference between the former and the present work may be in some part likened to that which exists between a secluded village and a busy metropolis, or between a solitary and plodding student and an accomplished man of letters. The humor of the dialog, and the epigrammatic remarks occasionally thrôn in by the author, form an agreeable seasoning, and the groundwork of the story is natural and sensible, while at the same time it deals too much with the ups and downs of life to be open to the charge of tameness. Among the most amusing scenes ar the occasional tilts between Miss Fluke — a strong-minded and ultra-evangelical young lady, — and Penelope Charlewood, equally strong-minded, but not addicted to the distribution of tracts. Some of Penelope's retorts ar excellent; but her humorous sallies ar scarcely more provocativ of lâfter than her stolid antagonists' utter inability to understand them." [Athenæum. **1499**

MACDERMOTS OF BALLYCLO-RAN (The) [by ANTHONY TROLLOPE: 1847.] "was in some respects a better book than some of its successors. Treating of irish life and character with plenty of humor and vivacity, but in a more earnest spirit than Lever's works, then at the hit of thêir popularity, it set forth very cleverly the social and political evils which the author wished to guide english opinion in helping to cure . . . But apart from its preachings, 'The Macdermots' was cleverly constructed and britly written." [Athenæum. **1500**

MADAME [by MA. OLIPHANT (WILSON) OLIPHANT: *Harper*, 1885.] "is slīter than we hav had of late from Mrs. Oliphant, but it is a beautiful treatment of a subject by no means common, — the devotion of a dauter to the father's second wife, who has been grossly wronged by him in a momentary fit of impatience." [Nation. **1501**

MADAME FONTENOY [by MA. ROBERTS: *J. & C. Mozley*, 1865.] "is a quiet, and pleasing story of domestic life . . . Madame Fontenoy — strict, stately and sedate, of simple habits and austere manners — is sketched with some skill; while Helena, her granddauter and adopted heiress, reared under the shado of her ancient relativ — a shado as real and distinct on her mind as that of the cathedral on the house in which she lived — and who finds, at the death of her protectress, that she is completely isolated in the world, and has not a single recollection, aspiration, or thôt in unison with the rest of her family, — is so drawn as effectivly to interest the reader. Other characters — Helena's mildly sarcastic papa; Annette, her

busy unimaginativ sister; Roger, the young vicar, whose mind is totally absorbed in the manifold and apparently almost incongruous duties of a country parson; and Robert Leicester, who is the first to understand and appreciate the stranger in the family — ar agreeably and truthfully outlined, if not very grafically defined. The solution of the story, by which reconciliation is effected, confidence restored, and all difficulties cleared away, is at once ingenious, simple, and satisfactory." [London Review. **1502**

MADAME LEROUX [by F.. ELEANOR (TERNAN) TROLLOPE: 1890.] "is clever and well-written. The conception and presentation of the numerous characters ar throuôut admirable, and the ōnly structural defect of the story is what in a picture we should call want of composition. Thêre is no sufficiently striking centre of narrativ interest, for tho Madame Leroux is the strongest, most original, and most interesting of the author's characters, her place in the narrativ is subordinate to that occupied by her dauter Lucy, who is the real heroin . . . The opening chapters, which deal with life at Enderby Court and in the village of Westfield, ar especially attractiv; and not less so ar those devoted to the bohemian circle of Mr. Hawkins, and to the relations existing between Mr. Tudway Didear, the dentist and the 'young ladies' whom he employs as secretaries." [Spectator. **1503**

MADAME SILVA'S SECRET [by E.. EILOART: *Hurst*, 1869.] "is a very pleasant, readable novel, with a gentle interest which will neither fatigue nor unpleasantly excite the reader . . . Madame Silva herself is the charm of the book. How a poor, broken-down, timid and foolish woman can be made to enlist so much sympathy as we feel for Madame Silva testifies to the skill and delicacy with which the character is drawn. Madame Silva is a gentlewoman, and that fact is kept in vue throu all her weakness and poverty, and if the truth must be told, all her tiresome foolishness; but the refinement of her nature is so inherent and true to the life that the reader feels as much affection for her as 'Mrs. Captain' or the terrible Mrs. Hitchcock, who both make themselves her gardian angels. The glimps given of Madame Silva's life in the old days is touching." [Athenæum. **1504**

MADCAP VIOLET [by W: BLACK: *Harper*, 1877.] "is certainly a readable novel, and indeed it deservs much more than this faint praise, for it is in many ways one of the best, if not the very best, of this writer's stories. It oes its great merit, for the most part, to the capital way in which the heroin is not described, but brôt before the reader with all her fascination and those qualities which in combination with unfortunate circumstances bring the book to a gloomy end. We see her first at school, the leader in every kind of mischief, and Mr. Black takes considerable pains to impress upon his readers, by the prominence he givs to her escapades, what a curious compound the girl is of wilfulness, impulsivness, and affection, while at the same time it is made clear that her education has done nothing in the way of remedying her faults. She is ill-treated at home by her step-mother, and spoiled by her father; at school she knoes no authority, and is very conscious of her freedom from responsibility; and the other influences of her life, her relations to George Miller and to the Drummond family, ar not of a sort certainly to repair the harm that has been done. In writing at this date about

the novel, it may be fairly taken for granted that every one has read it, and there is no need of referring vaguely to the complications of the plot from dread of disclosing it to those who do not yet kno the story. Assuming this, it is fair to say that all those things which wer intended in part to prepare us for an inevitable mörnful end hav more certainly the effect of making us fond of the heroin." [Atlantic. **1505**

MADE OR MARRED [by JESSIE FOTHERGILL: (†, 1891) *Bentley*, 1882.] "is a pleasant, quiet tale, containing nothing exciting or striking, very slit and unpretentious, not aiming at depth of plot, close study of character, or great effect in any way, but carefully finished, and good as far as it goes. The title is explained by the story turning upon a disappointment in love, whéreby the hero imagined his happiness to hav been marred, but by which it eventually proved to hav been made.'' [Spectator.] See No. 1646. **1506**

MADELON LEMOINE [by ALICIA A. (ADAMS) LAFFAN: *Lippincott*, 1879.] "Not since 'Margaret Chetwynd' [No. 1523] and 'Through a Needle's Eye' [No. 1849] hav we read so thöroly good and enjoyable a novel of its kind as this. Madelon is a lovely woman, with an unknön history, who settles in a town on the west coast of England, and becomes by turns a source of blessing, a mark for gossip, an object of love, and a victim of trial, until in the end she wins the reward of her goodness and sweetness. Around her stand the representativ figures in an english picture, conventional it is true, but drawn with much power and lifelikeness . . . Seldom is it that a novel which covers so much ground as this introduces so little which is disagreeable in person or incident. Yet the moral contrasts ar strong, and the finest lessons of self-abnegation, of heroism, of repentance, of patient continuance in well-doing, of maidenly purity and manly courage, in a word, of *duty*, ar taut in impressiv forms . . . and at other points the author has command of a pathos to which *we* hav been compelled to surrender." [Boston "Literary World." **1507**

MADONNA MARY. [by MA. OLIPHANT (WILSON) OLIPHANT: *Hurst*, 1866.] "The principal charms of the work ar the subtle humor, fineness of touch, and seeming ease with which Mrs. Oliphant delineates and contrasts her numerous characters . . . Nor is the author less successful in her picture of the domestic circle to which Madonna Mary returns on the death of her husband, bringing with her the 3 boys, whose education becomes henceforth the chief care. Nothing but true poetic insit could hav enabled Mrs. Oliphant to bring her readers. face to face with the unselfishness and womanly purity of ånt Agatha, in whose heart, deeper than the strong love which she bears to all her kith and kin, thêre burns, inextinguishable for years, almost unrecognized by herself, a sacred lamp of maidenly affection for one whose wife she mit hav been had he been as simple, brave and strong as she. Very pathetic — all the more so becaus the circumstances of the case ar not wanting in something which borders closely on the ludicrous — is the joy of this old spinster on learning after her lover's death that throuoūt his long career of selfish dilettantism he had cherished a sentimental tenderness for the woman to whose devotion he had responded with neglect." [Athenæum. **1508**

MAID ELLICE. [by "THEO. GIFT," i. e., Dora Henrietta (Havers) Boulger: *Holt*, 1878.] "The heroin is a

charming creation, and one mit go far without finding a pleasanter and more real picture of english country life. The quiet home, the eccentric and strong-hearted squire, the manly Oxford lad, the morbid discontent of the sister combine into a perfectly natural group, and the story is told with great power. It portrays simple and strong characters which may be enjoyed apart from the dark plot which finally involvs it, and out of whose shado it at length emerges more admirable." [Nation. **1509**

MAIDEN ALL FORLORN (etc.). [by MA. ( ) (ARGLES) HUNGERFORD: *Ward*, 1885.] "Tho 'A Maiden All Forlorn' is only the first of a number of stories, it contains as much romance and incident as many novels of the full regulation length. It mit claim to be considered as a novel condensed, and the same remark would apply to at least one other story in the present collection. All of them ar lit and brit. Thêy ar, at the same time, harmless enuf, full of comical situations, and frant with comfort and encouragement for pretty young women not yet engaged to wealthy young men. The ease with which the forlorn maiden, for instance, slips into a great fortune which has a very endurable encumbrance attached to it is a little more than remarkable. But it is safe to say that the reader who once begins to take an interest in Ronny and Cecil Rivers will not care much whether the story of their good fortune is probable or not. They descrv to be happy; and very improbable things ar wont to take place for such as deserv happiness." [Athenæum. **1510**

MAIDEN FAIR (A) etc. [by C: GIBBON: *Maxwell*, 1886.] "The principal story is laid in Scotland, and it need not be said that the fair maid of Newhaven and her sailor lover ar admirably protrayed. The character of Bell Cargill — strange mixture of rufness and tenderness — and the pathetic end to which disappointment in the 'sumpish' son she has toiled for directly leads, ar the most original bits of the story, tho all the characters ar natural and locally true." [Athenæum. **1511**

MAJOR AND MINOR. [by W: E: NORRIS: *Bentley*, 1888.] "The history of Brian Seagrave's love for Beatrice Huntley is certainly not new in its main features. One can hardly think of a novelist who has not tried his hand at least once on a similar situation; but it always remains pleasing to read of a young fello, who is in every way worthy and hi-minded, loving hopelessly above his station, and finally being loved in return, and perhaps suitably rewarded. There is a sense of consolation for the young men readers in such a tale. And the young ladies, who, we ar told, now form the chief audience for novelists, will always, one fancies, be partial to such a history; especially if it turns out as charming as Brian's affair." [Nation.] — "The action is divided between Brian's struggles and Gilbert's Nemesis. Miss Huntley, the beautiful heiress who constitutes herself the instrument of his punishment, is a wonderfully clever creation, perhaps one of Mr. Norris' greatest triumfs in brilliant and subtle portraiture . . . But apart from this, our enjoyment is unalloyed, for 'Major and Minor' is a thoroly brit story, rich in lifelike character and pleasant humor." [Spectator. **1512**

MAJOR LAWRENCE [by EMILY LAWLESS: *Holt*, 1887.] "is a novel of the kind one lays down with the praise, 'a very pretty story.' There is nothing new in it, the plot being the old one of a staid bachelor falling in love at last with the girl he had knon as a child, and marrying her in her widohood after her first luckless marriage with a youth of her ön age. All of this we hav had many times before; but there is a good deal of grace and spirit in the telling of it this time, and the book is extremely readable." [Critic.] — "It shöes the hand of an expert in novel-writing. Its well-defined form, its clear and ingenious characterizations, its expressiv and elastic language, make it hily readable. It will find many pleased readers in its flo-ing style, its brit epigram, its agreeable incident and charming conversation." [Nation. **1513**

MALCOLM. [by GEORGE MACDONALD: *Lippincott*, 1874.] "To say that a story is written by George MacDonald implies that it is inspired by the power of a peculiarly rich and delicate imagination, a true and beautiful idealism, a pure and noble filosofy of life, and, last but not least, a deep, far-reaching spiritual insit . . . The story has more of a plot than some of the author's works, but its interest depends much less upon that than upon the portrayal and development of character, the exquisit and poetical descriptions, and the beautiful thöts with which it is profusely enriched. The little town of Portlossie, with its Seaton or sea-town; the old castle and church, with the few thatched cottages clustering about them; the sandy beach, with its rocky cliffs and grass-covered downs; ar so vividly painted, as to become to us real places which we have seen and knön." [Canadian Monthly. *See notice of sequel*, No. 828. **1514**

MANSFIELD PARK. [by J.. AUSTEN: 1818.] "Miss Austen is so good at her best that we the more regret the inferiority of Mansfield Park, Sense and Sensibility, Northanger Abbey, and Persuasion. It is only justice, however, to

470

estimate an author by his strength rather than by his weakness, and to value him or her according to the worth of the best which is given us. Miss Austen's imagination was neither rich nor wide-ranging; her mind was practical rather than poetic, her intelligence shrewd and activ rather than fine or subtle. Her personal experience of men and manners was narro, and she wisely contented herself with portraying the characteristics of the quiet middle-class she moved in." [Boston "Literary World."] — "It is none the less an exceptional case to find a lady under 40 who has read Mansfield Park or The Absentee; and with those who hav, it has been more a matter of duty than inclination — a tribute of respect to the taste and judgment of elderly friends, or a sort of compromise with their conscience, by the reflexion that they are perusing works of sterling merit instead of what they ungratefully call the 'trash' of circulating libraries." [Lippincott's.   **1515**

MARCH IN THE RANKS (A) [by JESSIE FOTHERGILL: (†, 1891) *Holt*, 1889.] "is such a healthy novel that it is a pleasure to read it. It deals with the struggles and successes of a family of clever young people who hav to make their way — a situation which always enlists one's sympathy. Godfrey Noble is a strong character. In his decided individuality, which is far from eccentricity, and by his bearing in the various trying situations in which he is placed, he givs an impression of positiv manliness. In the midst of the morbid sensationalism of to-day, it is pleasant to encounter a courageous, simple nature like this. In the character of Hilla, the author strikes a subtle blo at Woman's Rits. She shoes how an intellectual woman can rise by her exertions to a hi and responsible posi-

tion, and yet that these very exertions so undermine her strength that she becomes unfitted for her work and is almost forced to accept the more protected and dependent position of a wife. It may be said that it is not Hilda's work alone which weakens her, but every woman has a soul history, and even our intellectual sisters would not wish to be exempt. On finishing the book one does not cast it aside as one does most novels, but keeps it to lend or re-read." [Critic.   **1516**

MARCHCROFT MANOR [by C. A. ROBERTS: *Remington*, 1882.] "is a pretty love story, in which a double thread of interest is well sustained, and the heart's history of 4 exceptionally nice and fortunate young people is told with freshness and simplicity. Olive and Ella Maloney ar the dauters of an eminent fysician, who allows them to spend a good deal of their time with their ant, the wife of a country rector. Here they ar seen by the young squire and his friend Osborne. The girls ar a delitful pair, fine in nature and character; and whilst their lovers ar in every way worthy of them, the course of their love is interrupted by more than one misunderstanding, caused by somewhat exaggerated scruples and points of honor. In the end, however, all comes rit, and the reader is allowed to put down the book in good humor with everybody." [Athenæum.   **1517**

MARCIA. [by W: E: NORRIS: *Murray*, 1891.] "When a young lady meets a man whose fortune and social standing ar such as to command the approval of her family, whose character is good, whose personal appearance is not unpleasing, and who seems to be as much attached to her as it is within the range of masculin capacity to be attached to anybody, parents and gardians in general ar of opinion that she would be extremely unwise to refuse him . . . Marcia givs a description, from girlhood to middle age, of the career of a woman who acts on the above mentioned principle, with the discouraging results that incompatibility of taste and character leads speedily to estrangement between her and her husband . . . Eustace is conscientious, sincere, and capable of true love in his stern, cold fashion, but is unsympathetic, rigid, formal, and outwardly unemotional; Marcia is vain, frivolous, pleasure-loving, and too purely egostistical to be really fond of any one but herself . . . Of the two, he is unquestionably the least to blame, but in fiction, as in life, a person so devoid of sympathy as he is does not easily excite it in others, and thèrefore, whilst pitying him sincerely, and indignant at his wife's abominable behavior to him, one cannot help thinking that perhaps, after all, her conduct was not altogether to be wondered at. The book strikes us as one of the cleverest which Mr. Norris has produced, tho, until tōards the end, hardly the most agreeable. The study of everyday people which it contains is so good as to be rendered painful during the first volumes by its very excellence; for the men and women ar so like life that they bring home to one the pettinesses and unworthinesses of human nature with disagreeable force . . . Fortunately, however, the third volume makes amends, and enables us to leave off with a pleasant taste in the mouth, by introducing a sort of fresh hero in the shape of Marcia's son, a charming young fello who, with his sweetheart, Lady Evelyn, servs to reconcile us once more to our common humanity, and whose love-making by land and sea, at golf and yachting, is told delitfully, and

rouses a keen interest and sympathy." [Spectator. **1518**

MARGARET AND HER BRIDESMAIDS. [by A.. (CALDWELL) MARSHCALDWELL: *Hurst*, 1856.] "We may save ourselvs the trouble of giving any lengthened revue of this work, for we recommend all who ar in search of a fascinating novel to read it. They will find it well worth their while. Thére is a freshness and an originality about it quite charming, and thére is a certain nobleness in the treatment both of sentiment and incident which is not often found. The morality is not enforced by sententious preaching, but by the skilful management and careful working out of the story. We imagin that few could read it without deriving some comfort or profit from the quiet good sense and unobtrusiv words of counsel with which it abounds. The story is very interesting; it is the history of 4 schoolfellōs. Margaret, the heroin, is, of course, a woman in the biest state of perfection, and so falls rather too smoothly, and with too little individuality, to lay much hold on our sympathy; but Lotte — the little· wilful, wild, brave, fascinating Lotte — is the gem of the book, and, as far as our experience goes, she is an original character, — a creation, and a very charming one." [Athenæum.] — "It is a novel of domestic life, in which the plot, apparently simple, is yet artistic and skilfully managed. The thread of life of the bridesmaids is held with that of the bride, the development of character, distinctly marked in each, progresses throu a series of natural events. . . The book is charming. Its moral is unexceptionable, its characters well drawn, its plot and incidents simple and natural, and its interest sustained from beginning to end." [Continental Monthly. **1519**

MARGARET CHETWYND [by SUSAN MORLEY: *Lippincott*, 1878.] "as a source of pure, wholesom, and unalloyed enjoyment, surpasses any of the others. It is a story of large proportions and careful workmanship, marred by no extravagances of style, nor monstrosities of character, nor improbabilities of incident, nor vulgarities of wickedness; but full of agreeable people, and engrossed with an interesting family history, which takes the reader into the very intellectual, social, and spiritual interior of the mother country, presenting at almost every point a picture which it is a pleasure to look upon. There is an indescribable air of good breeding about the book, which sets it apart by itself from the great mass of its kind, and tho there may be places in it which ar weak as compared with the general fabric, it is as a whole singularly well designed, woven and colored; a work in which any cultivated taste must find great satisfaction." [Boston "Literary World." **1520**

MARGARET JERMINE [by "FAYR MADOC": *Macmillan*, 1886.] "is the work of one who knoes more of women and children than of men. A peculiar father is responsible for the peculiar infancy, education, and subsequent fortunes of Fayr Madoc's heroin. In despair at the loss of his wife, he rushes from the worship of love to an opposit extreme, in which he discovers, declares, and would fain propagate a filosofy which should exclude love, and therewith suffering, from the human race. He is mad enuf to try the experiment in sober earnest on his only child. Her desolate, wayward childhood is pathetic, and pretty, too, in a way [Compare plot of No. 366]. Mrs. Minimy and her dauter ar charming. The mother is a genial 'prattler among men,' a rather worldly,

but amiable and naïve old lady." [Athenæum. **1521**

MARGARET MAITLAND. See *MERKLAND*.

MARGARET MALIPHANT. [by ALICE (   ) CARR: 1889.] "The subject of this story is how an anxious sister schemed and labored to make two beautiful young people think they wer in love with each other, out of the purest and most generous motivs in the world — a motif not unlike that in 'Emma,' but managed, we need scarcely say, in a very different way: tho it is hard upon Miss Margaret, after her innocent but silly scheming, to hav her lover carried away by the beautiful sister, whose happiness she was so anxious to secure, tho not in that way. . This sister, however, in her beauty and reasonableness, is charmingly drawn, and so is the mother, and the ways of the homely but refined yeoman's house." [Blackwood's. **1522**

MARGERY TRAVERS. [by A. E. N. BEWICKE: *Hurst*, 1878.] "The heroin is perhaps a little too reckless to be so successful a schemer, and the pretty italian girl, who is the most injured of many victims in the novel, is a little too much idealised. We cordially like the american heiress, Lottie Spluck, and ar grateful to Miss Bewicke for letting her recover from the threatened consumption, which, for so fritfully overworked an expedient in fiction, is admirably used, and with novel effect; and we ar glad that the virtuous hero, after having been cruelly jilted by Margery, marries the kindly, sweet-natured, original little yankee girl. The vicious hero is good enuf for Margery, and tho he is penitent, and also married, at the end of the third volume, we hav no doubt that they plague each other a good deal, in that untraveled country to

473

which people in novels retire after the honeymoon." [Spectator. **1523**

MARION FAY. [by ANTHONY TROLLOPE: *Harper*, 1882.] "Mr. Trollope has here written a long story, and used for it materials which hardly hav the recommendation of novelty. Thêre is a marquis of Kingsbury, who has much trouble with his family, and especially with his second wife; thêre is his son, Lord Hampstead, who falls hopelessly in love with Marion Fay, a poor quaker girl; and his dauter, Lady Frances, who engages herself to a post-office clerk, Mr. G: Roden. The quaker girl dies, leaving Lord Hampstead inconsolable, while George Roden turns out to be an italian nobleman, and Lady Frances makes him happy . . . Thêre is some lo comedy introduced throu the medium of the adventures of a vulgar young woman named Clara Demijohn and a pair of rivals for her hand. Thêre is a great deal of love, but very little incident . . . The best drawn character is that of Mr. Sam Crocker, whose vulgar vanity, self-assertion, curiosity, good humor, and untruthfulness make altogether quite a perfect modern cad." [Nation. **1524**

MARJORIE BRUCE'S LOVERS. See *MR. LESLIE*.

MARJORY [by "Milly Deane," i. e., — ( ) ERSKINE: *Macmillan*, 1872.] "is a most unambitious tale of the sufferings of a charming young girl, who falls in love with a young man, and who then is tortured by the familiar passion — jealousy. More serious troubles, too, befall her, an l the result is that we hav a very good story. It is told with the utmost simplicity, and we hardly kno any novel that we should so soon recommend as a model . . . But any one who reads this story will see for himself its apparent simplicity

(it really contains a great deal of art) and will feel the direct singleness of impression which it makes upon him. The supernatural part is admirably managed; the quiet tone of all the rest makes this seem possible and very impressiv. Thêre is in some books a way of making even ghosts almost as awkward and unnatural as the shadoy heroes and heroins of the story. The girl's feelings ar well told, quietly and decorously, as she suffered; it reads as would a true story tol l by a good narrator, who was wise enuf to kno what to leave out. Thêre is no rule for the writing of good stories, tho thêre ar certain conditions which the author must bear in min l if he wishes to do satisfactory work. But in such matters example is better than precept, and once more we recommen l 'Marjory' to writers as well as to readers who would like a pretty tale." [Nation. **1526**

——, SAME [by F.. E.. GEORGINA (BAYNES) BROCK: *Longman*, 1880. "The author has tried to present studies of life in an english cathedral town, mainly among the middle class. The method is descriptiv rather than analytical, and the characters ar at times vague and shadoy. But the author has considerable skill in sketching natural scenery, as may be seen from the description of a hot day with which the story opens. The heroin is an old-fashioned girl." [Boston "Lit. World." **1527**

MARK RUTHERFORD'S DE-LIVERANCE. [by W. HALE SMITH: *Trübner*, 1885.] "No reader of the 'Autobiografy of Mark Rutherford' can hav forgotten the last words of the editor: 'I can only hope that it may be my good fortune to find the materials which will present him in a somewhat different lit to that in which he appears now.' So strong is the abiding sense that the life was an actual one that we

· 474

open the sequel, 'Mark Rutherford's Deliverance,' with the involuntary exclamation — 'The hope has been realized!' But we ar no better able than before to settle the question whether the book is a purely imaginativ creation, or a fearlessly candid and exact self-portraiture. The writer has not lost one bit of his skill. whether it comes from an elaborate training or is a gift of inspiration. The brief story is resumed at the point whêre Mark finds a slender occupation as correspondent for a country paper. The one fortunate chance of his life throes in his way again the lady to whom he was early engaged, and from his marriage to her come the few happy hours of his life. 'If a man wants to know what the potency of love is, he must be a menial; he must be despised . . I cannot write poetry, but if I could, no theme would tempt me like that of love .to such a person as I was — not love, as I say again, to the hero, but love to the Helot.' He had called himself commonplace, truly enuf, so far as education, opportunities, circumstances go; but the impulse of honesty, the clear-sitedness, and the fidelity to awakened conscience which nervd him to close against himself the one narro opening offered him to the world's comforts, ar above commonplace. Call it motiv, fibre of nature, or grace from above — whatever one may — the same superiority of nature which carried him out of the darkness of his early Dissenting surroundings, survived in the hard, joyless round in which the remainder of his life was spent. It manifested itself in the effort of which not one in a thousand of his class among working people would hav been capable, to do good to the suffering souls about him. His personal problem was no longer how to escape from a false position, from insincerity, but how to keep for his soul some vision of the invisible, while toiling to utter weariness for bare existence. Mark Rutherford kept it by trying to bring some knoledge of it to his fello-men. For this reason the later part of the life will appeal to the sympathy of a wider circle of readers than the first. However much the opinions of some of our sects may resemble those of the english Dissenters of 40 years ago, thêir homes and thêir ways ar very remote from us. On the other hand, the poor — not the starving, but the poor who hav only the narroest bit of the day for living thêir ôn lives when work is done — these offer the most urgent problem of the moment. Thêir hearts Mark Rutherford knew, for he was one of them. The history of his efforts to reach and comfort those worse off than himself ôt to be closely and humbly studied by all those who ar now thinking about help for the working classes." [Nation. **1528**

MARRIAGE. [by M.. FERRIER: 1818.] "Miss Ferrier was not a Miss Austen — she more closely resembles Miss Edgeworth; but her amusing and wholesom stories well deserv to be read and remembered, and it is to be hoped that this revival of them may meet with the success it merits. The later editions hav been poor in type and the text was mutilated, so that Mr. *Bentley* should receive the thanks of all lovers of fiction for the favor he has conferred upon them." [Athenæum. **1529**

MARRIED AT LAST. [N. Y., 1864.] = *CROSS OF HONOR.*

MARRIED BENEATH HIM [by JA. PAYN: *Macmillan*, 1865.] "is a thôroly lively and diverting book, and sufficiently interesting to induce the reader who begins it to go to the end; but thêre is not a character in it for which anyone can care in the least, and it contains nothing calculated to dwell in the memory, beyond some tolerably humorous scenes and a variety of jokes, good, bad and indifferent. As for moral, it has none, unless it be that a housemaid may not prove a good wife for a literary man . . . Its plot defies criticism by its absurdity, and most of the characters ar carelessly and feebly drawn. But thére ar a few which appear to hav been sketched from life, and their merits make up, to a certain extent, for the defects of their companions . . . The best characters ar those of Mr. Jonathan Johnson, editor of the Paternoster Porcupine, and his colleague, Mr. Percival Potts, a journalist greatly given to classical quotations. These 2 literary gentlemen ar very amusing companions, and we can conscientiously state that their acquaintance is well worth making." [London Review. **1530**

MARVEL. [by MA. (   ) (ARGLES) HUNGERFORD: *Ward & Downey*, 1888.] "The ingenious author of 'Molly Bawn' is as readable and ridiculous as ever. She has discarded the present tense, but remains constant to her quotations and 'ingrammaticisms' . . The final cause of life as conceived by the writer is flirtation; we never remember to hav encountered a male character in any of her books who seemed to hav any serious occupation. The nearest approach to it in the present story is the manufacture of bustles for dolls by Mr. Kitts." [Athenæum. **1531**

MARY BARTON [by E.. CLEGHORN (STEVENSON) GASKELL: *Chapman*, 1849.] "is a most striking book. It is an appropriate and valuable contribution to the literature of the age. It embodies the dominant feeling of our times — a feeling that the ignorance, destitution and vice which pervade and corrupt society, must be got rid of. The ability to point out how they ar to be got rid of is not the characteristic of this age. That will be the characteristic of the age which is coming. Compare Mary Barton with the Evelinas, Cecilias and Belindas [No. 1092] which superseded the Romances of the Forest [No. 925], the Children of the Abbey, and the Haunted Towers of the age which preceded theirs! Mary Barton is no heiress, nursed in the lap of luxury, without knoing how it comes to her — refined, generous, capricious, indolent — dying first of ennui, then of love, and lastly falling a prêy to a fortune-hunter, or a military swindler. Mary Barton is heiress of the struggles, vicissitudes and sufferings consequent upon the ignorance and prejudices of the society into which she is born." [Westminster Review. **1532**

MARY MARSTON. [by G: MAC DONALD: *Low*, 1881.] "William Marston, the father of the heroin, is a hi-principled, religious, and honorable man, who keeps a shop in partnership with a man who is just the reverse, but whose roguery he never finds out. Tho Marston is a Baptist deacon, we ar not troubled with his peculiar ideas, as what is made prominent about the man is his intensely conscientious and sincere practice of that morality and religion which ar — or ôt to be — common to all denominations. We do not see much of him, as he dies before the end of the first volume; but the impress of his life remains permanently stamped upon his dauter, who, tho never hier in the social scale than a shop woman, and becoming at one time a lady's-maid, is yet ever a lady in heart and feeling, because ever simple, true to herself, unselfish, and free from any shade of mauvaise honte, in whatever circumstances she may be placed . . . The book contains many carefully drawn characters. Thêre is Hesper, the well-born young lady, who is sold by her parents to the rich, elderly, vicious Mr. Redmain. Hesper loathes the bargain from the bottom of her heart, but has not stamina enuf to resist the pressure put upon her; and thêre is a striking and pathetic chapter describing, first, the intervue with her mother, when the latter informs her of the hateful marriage which she is expected to make, and subsequently Hesper's turning in despair to her cousin Sepia, as the only human being who may, she thinks, love her. Sepia, however, is one of those altogether evil and heartless women who may justify the common belief that when a woman is bad she is worse than any man ever is; and so it is, of course, worse than useless to look for counsel or help from her . . . Another very interesting character is that of Letty, the ignorant, impulsiv, well-meaning, affectionate girl, living with a hard, unloving, old ânt, and a grave, kindly, very superior cousin Godfrey, who wishes to educate her to his ôn level. Letty believes in and looks up to him with her whole soul, but aw and reverence alone do not satisfy the girl's nature; she wearies almost unconsciously of the seriousness and sternness of her surroundings, and yearns instinctivly after something liter, briter, more demonstrativ and playful. This she finds in the homage of the ardent, gay, superficially clever Tom Helmer, whom she marries, and whose affections stray sadly far from his poor wife." [Spectator. **1533**

MARY ST. JOHN [by Rosa Nouchette Carey: *Bentley*, 1882.] "is a simple little story told with unprovoking simplicity. Miss Carey shôes a pleasing power of delineating the liter

traits of character, and refrains from trying to depict any very strong passion. Her most able study is that of a beautiful woman, with a natural taste for refinement and luxury, married to a poor curate in the East-end, always revolting against her life, and yet sustained in it by her deep love for her husband. The heroin, if not a commonplace character, is, at all events, one well knôn to every novel-reader; and the young men ar equally drawn after a recognized model." [Athen. **1533a**

MASTER OF HIS FATE. [by Amelia Edith (Huddleston) Barr: *Dodd*, 1888.] "Again Mrs. Barr has a Yorkshire story; its few characters a rich, shrewd mill-ôner, his handsom son, his sister-in-law, Edith Bradley, and Perkins the lawyer. These 5 ar absolutely all who hav much part in the tale except old Samuel Yorke, but thêy fill the foreground in fine, strong portraiture, and ar vital beings. Amos has elected that his only son shall be a mill ôner; the son prefers to be a lawyer; neither will yield after having said the word, and Jo leaves his home forever in consequence; the ânt also departs; Jo tries in vain to earn money by his profession, falls in love with Edith, the heiress of Luke Bradley, who was a deadly fo to Amos, and marries her. The position of husband to Mrs. Braithwaite becomes galling, made especially bitter becaus she still leavs the management of the estate in the hands of Perkins, instead of transferring it to her husband. Jo comes to a manly resolution, apprentices himself for two years to Samuel Yorke, his father's old friend in Manchester, and learns cotton spinning, confident that at the expiration of that time he will hav gained his self-respect and that of his wife. Jo and Edith, Amos and Aunt Martha, all being made of sterling stuff, with practical sense, hearts warm at the core, and principle, the result is easily foretold. It is a sound, sweet book, so captivating that the reader will not lay it down till the last page is reached; full of humor, delitfully set forth in the person of Amos, who is a most original being; and full of sunshine from the genial and lovable Jo." [Boston "Lit. World." **1534**

MATRIMONY [by W: E: Norris: *Smith*, 1881.] "has almost all the qualities which make a good novel — that is, a good man's novel · · · We congratulate Mr. Norris on the constant variety and vivacity of his scenes and events, and on the truth and humor of his drawings of character. The book is wonderfully rich in types. Even the young heroes hav an individuality which is rare. The first hero is Claud Gervis, a young fello of excellent parts, who has been reared in the course of w wandering youth by a father who rarely says a kind thing, and never does an ungenerous act. He has the sense to appreciate and like this bitter old diplomatist, who is a fine gentleman first, and in the second place, a human being who has been soured by a misfortune which would hav injured any temper." [Saturday Review.] — ' The story is interesting, tho not thrilling; but the charm of the book lies in its bits of talk and of characterization. It has been called cynical; but thêre ar two kinds of cynicism; that which tries to make things not actually ridiculous appear so, and that which simply enjoys the ridiculousness of things which ar ridiculous." [Critic. **1535**

MATTER-OF-FACT GIRL [by "Theo. Gift," i. e., Dora Henrietta (Havers) Boulger: *Tinsley*, 1881.] 'is an honest-hearted little maid, tied by force of circumstances to a tyranni-

cal old ånt and a coarse and not too devoted sweetheart in her father's rank of life, that of u peasant farmer. "Berrie's' loyalty to her home, and especially to her father, keeps her true for a long time to this unequal engagement, in spite of the half-acknoledged influence of an admirer of a different calibre, who has unwittingly opened her eyes to the existence of a contrast she had not hitherto suspected." [Athen. **1536**

MAY [by Ma. Oliphant (Wilson) Oliphant: *Hurst*, 1873.] "is õne of the best novels of the year." [Ath.] — "May herself is essentially feminin and natural, loveable and tender, but planned on a nobler scale than is usually assigned to the marriageable young ladies of novels. . . Here we have a woman still young and beautiful and fresh, but with a fine matured dignity and common sense which enrich the story with possibilities of action denied to callo innocence." [Saturday Review. **1537**

MAYOR OF CASTERBRIDGE (The) [by T: Hardy: *Holt*, 1886.] "will be welcomed becaus of its introduction to a fresh company of those english rustics who, if not real, ar as good as real, in Mr. Hardy's stories. It is, besides, a strong, vivid story, which makes one ask if thêre is any english novelist who combines in better measure the qualities of a great story-teller than Mr. Hardy." [Atlantic. **1538**

MEADOWLEIGH [by M.. A.. Manning: *Bentley*, 1864.] "is a tale with a mild, pleasant interest, refined and gentle, as refreshing as a breath of country air . . The materials of the tale ar slit enuf; Miss Clairvaux, a benevolent elderly gentlewoman, whose originality borders on eccentricity, takes, from motivs of kindness, a young girl to be her companion, — the dauter of an artist, who has died, and left his family in reduced circumstances. Miss Clairvaux is a charming person, drawn with a delicate and firm touch; with all her peculiarities of temper and manner, she is a genuin english lady, about whom it is pleasant to read. Eleanor Graydon, her protégée, is a very nice young woman, who enjoys living with Miss Clairvaux; and well she may, for their life at Three Parks is a tempting picture of elegant thrift and rural comfort. 'Meadowleigh' is a good picture of a retired, quiet, and rather dull english village, and the style of society is well described." [Athenæum.   **1539**

MEADOWSWEET COMEDY (The) [by T: A. PINKERTON: *Vizetelly*, 1886.] "is a short and hily readable novel, smart without being flippant, and trenchant without being cynical. Mr. Pinkerton has a good eye for portraiture and a fair insit into character. He seems to hav a considerable knoledge of the world and of books, and can use it without affectation   The description of comfortable upper middle-class society with which the story deals is excellent." [Athenæum.   **1540**

MERE CHILD (A) [by LUCY BETHIA (COLQUHOUN) WALFORD: *Blackett*, 1888.] "is a capital specimen of its author's agreeable style. It is refreshing to read a story in which there is no bad character and no pretension to any other aim than those of pleasing the reader. The characters ar sketched with artistic decision, and the setting of the story, both in the Highlands and in London, is excellent." [Athenæum.— "There ar few writers more successful than Mrs. Walford. If her limits ar natural, she is an instance of the advantage of restriction; had her experience or her imagination been wider, she mit hav done different work: she could not hav done what she has done, better,

nor so well. *A Mere Child* is one of the pleasantest of her stories. It does not come near 'The Baby's Grandmother,' [No. 1074] for either originality of conception or nicety of finish; but wild little Jerry of Inchmarew, with her boy's love of out-door life, and her great lady's sense of the grandeur of her position, makes an amusing, life-like, and very pretty picture. Nor could anything be truer than the figure of Mrs. Campbell; we must hav knon Jerry, and this was precisely the grandmother she had. We ar sorry to admit that Bellenden, too, was fact. Why so charming a girl should be wasted on so selfish, commonplace, and wholly inferior a man, is a melancholy mystery. It is a mystery which confronts us in all Mrs. Walford's books. She draws us very winning portraits of women: her men — or at least her young men — are uniformly of a lo type in character and manners." [Church Review.   **1541**

MERKLAND. [by MA. OLIPHANT (WILSON) OLIPHANT: *Colburn*, 1851.] "The Athenæum was one of the first to recognize in *Mistress Margaret Maitland* an old-world quaintness and gentle pathos truly welcom in days like these. It should seem as if in her second venture the author of that story had tried to add to those gifts the excitements of wonder and strong interest, — and in some measure she has succeeded. The efforts of Anne Ross to clear the fame of her brother cannot be watched without as much trust as curiosity; — the trust naturally engendered by her steadfast determination, — the curiosity adroitly kept alive by the far-scattered traces which serv as her clue and taper throu the maze and throu the 'mirk midnīt.'" [Athenæum.   **1542**

META'S FAITH [by E.. (TABOR) STEPHENSON: *Hurst*, 1869.] "tho a sober and tranquil tale, deficient in action and notably devoid of stirring incidents, creates strong interest by the naturalness and force of several of its delineations of character, and by the cleverness with which it inculcates certain wholesom lessons respecting the affections and moral life of men and women in the middle and later terms of existence . . On these and other kindred points the lads and lasses differ from the author of ' Meta's Faith,' who insists that a middle-aged widoer, or an outwardly austere old maid, is as capable of romantic affection as any boy and girl now for the first time plunging into love's sweet madness. In a manner which will win the approval, and in some cases the gratitude of mature novel-readers, this doctrin is very delicately and cogently urged by the scribe who displays her sex in such passages as the one in which she remarks : ' Life at Percy Cottage, as is generally the case whêre a household consists of a very moderately gifted woman, was a rather worretting process. A family without the masculin element is something like an egg without salt, or a dish of trifle without the concealed ring which imparts such wonderful flavor and piquancy to the rest of the compound. Women wer never intended to cluster in close bōros, paying their taxes, looking after their rīts, slipping along throu the world without that wholeṣom, disciplinary friction which the presence of the sterner sex is so well calculated to produce. Even if a man can do nothing else in a house, he seldom fails to giv the women about him abundant opportunities for self-denial, and so brings out the noblest part of thêir nature.' In the same vên of humor the author observs — ' But a man does more in a general way than keep the women about him from having

time to think too much of themselvs. Tho undeniably productiv of an untold amount of trouble in the shape of hot dinners and carefully prepared sauces, and various other little gastronomical dainties for which he has a natural appetency ; and tho when, having seen him safely off to his office or warehouse after a good breakfast, his wife is conscious of a bounding sense of independence until such time as he comes home again to dine ; still a man, if he is worthy the name, and not just a mere machine for bread-gathering and rent-paying, dōes bring with him a clear, invigorating, health-promoting air into the house. He supplies the needful oxygen without which the līt of home-life is apt to burn dim, and the atmosfere to become stifling.' " [Athenæum. **1543**

MIDDLEMARCH [by " GEORGE ELIOT," i. e., M.. A.. (Evans) Cross : *Blackwood*, 1872.] is " the one novel which alone will make its mark on the age, the one book which will outliv all its fellōs, the book from which future generations will learn not only our outward lives, our daily doings, but our inmost thóts and aspirations. As to its supreme literary merits, thére can be but one opinion. Upon this point critics ar unanimous. Style has never reached such perfection of art. Humor of so rare a quality has not been given to the world since the days of Shakespeare.' [Westminster Review.] — " This discrepancy between fact and comment excepted, the figure of Dorothea is nobly conceived and exquisitly finished. She commands the reader's admiration in spite of her illusions, altho it can hardly be said that she wins his love. Her victory over the shalloer nature of Rosamond is complete in every respect — and is altogether the most powerful passage in the work. Dorothea's second marriage is also dwelt upon as the unfortunate result of 'the meanness of opportunity.' Having first married a cold-blooded pedant, ' old enuf to be her father, in a little more than a 12-month after his death she gave up her estate to marry his cousin — young enuf to be his son, with no property, and not well-born.' Will Ladislaw was a somewhat rash, capricious, and petulant young reformer, but this second marriage was one of mutual affection. ' They wer bound to each other by a love stronger than any impulses which could have marred it.' Still the author thinks that a love-match, happy as this one admittedly was, was another mistake. Dorothea's life was necessarily a life of emotion, and her affections wer satisfied. But her great ideal was to remain forever unfulfilled ; her personality had been lost in her husband's, and not remained for her but the activities of domestic life." [Canadian. **1544**

MIGNON. [by " MRS. FORRESTER,' i. e., — ( ) Bridges : *Hurst*, 1877.] The author " has had the courage to follo the maxim that the chief interest of a woman's life is probably to be found after her marriage. And she does it, too (and this is a still greater difficulty), without going too far into dangerous ground. Mignon is a beautiful girl, with whom a man of middle-age falls frantically in love, and whom he marries, knoing well that she cares nothing for him. The story of their after-life is well told, and Mignon is well contrasted with another fascinating creature, Kitty by name, who begins with very mercenary professions indeed, but ends by being much better than she professes. The Nemesis which overtakes at last the heartless Mignon is finely described, and the justice which brings a deservd punishment on Raymond l'Estrange is not the wild imagination of

that name which has the epithet ' poetical' attached to it, but a genuin reality. Genuin realities, too, ar the men, whom Mrs. Forrester draws with quite unusual force. This is a good story well told." [Spectator. **1545**

MILDRED [by GEORGIANA MARION (CRAIK) MAY : *Harper*, 1868.] " is a thoroly well-conceived, well-sustained, and artistically developed story. The characters hav meaning, consistency, and genuin resemblance to possible human beings throuout ; and the author has shŏn not only fertility of invention, but admirable self-restraint in the touching incident which forms the climax and catastrofé." [Round Table.] — " It is very pleasantly and unaffectedly written, has a well-conceived heroin, and a hero who, tho he may possibly hav prototypes in nature, certainly has none in recent fiction." [Nation. **1546**

MILL ON THE FLOSS (The) [by " G: ELIOT," i. e., M.. A.. (Evans) Cross : *Harper*, 1860.] " is emfatically a story of destiny. From first to last thére is a fate pursuing the heroin which she cannot escape, and which casts its baneful shado over every incident of her life. With a warm and yearning heart, an overfloing affection, a passionate desire to love and to be loved, she is tormented even in childhood by the constant feeling of her shortcomings, and a too sensitiv conscience poisons every spring of happiness in her nature. Struggling as she advances to maturity with the great mystery and burden of existence, groping blindly in her ignorance, searching for the path of duty, but always in doubt, and distress, and anxiety, suddenly the lĭt flashes upon her . . . She develops into a superb and beautiful womanhood, the clouds of domestic misfortune and poverty which hav so long hung over her seem to break away, and if not a briter, a more tranquil and cheerful future opens before her. But her evil angel is still thêre, to inflict a new form of suffering—the most poignant which a woman can kno—that of a deep, absorbing, hopeless passion—a passion which is returned, but which she cannot indulge without ruin to the happiness of those who ar nearest and dearest to her heart, without requiting by the basest ingratitude a more than sisterly affection. Every reader must hav observed how in the last part of this novel the two leading characters appear to be urged forward in their disastrous course by a power which is beyond thêir control, and against which the most strenuous resolutions, the most fearful self-conflicts, the most bitter tears — all the struggles of pride, of friendship, of honorable feeling, of womanly delicacy, and manly shame — ar of no avail. Thêre is nothing finer in the whole range of fiction, but the fatalism which underlies all the author's writings is nowhêre so strikingly manifested. The world may blame them, but we cannot; and the unutterably mȯrnful effect of the close is not marred by a single misgiving with regard to her who lies in Dorlcote churchyard, lost in the final triumf of love and self-sacrificing devotion, and by whose grave we can stand and weep, as that of one whom we had ourselvs knȯn and loved with the intensity of years." [Lippincott's.] — "This very elaboration, tardy and idle tho it may seem, was necessary to the completion of the author's plan, and — in our eyes—instead of being a blemish upon a fair story, is one of its principal charms. On this account, the book will be less popular, and fewer persons will admire it wholly; but, as thȯtful readers draw near to the end of the

narrativ, and anxiously hasten on past trial, temptation, and conflict, to the dreaded and yet inevitable downfall, muse mȯrnfully over the agony and remorse which follo, and sloly close the volume upon tender forgivness and final joy, they will be thankful for the far-seeing genius which, by this gradual process of education, enable them to understand clearly the fateful scroll at last unfolded to them, and which, if they hav read in the true spirit, has made them wiser and better." [Atlantic. **1547**

MINE IS THINE [by LAWRENCE W. M. LOCKHART: *Blackwood*, 1878.] "is a tale of the most amusing and agreeable order, full of picturesque situations and piquant events, brisk in conversation, sustained in interest, abounding in humor." [Atlantic.] — "As far as the plot and characters go, we hav nothing but praise to giv it. It is really delítful to read a story of lȯve-making between a gentleman and lady in the good old fashion." [Athenæum.] — "Who Cosmo Glencairn really is, and how he eventually marries Esme Douglas, we leav the reader the pleasing task of finding out for himself, tho we think the actual catastrofe is somewhat hurried, and not very artistically brȯt about. One merit Col. Lockhart possesses to a remarkable degree . . . He excels them all in the way in which he presents to his readers, in every position and under all circumstances, that rare plant of home grȯth, so difficult to describe, so impossible to analyse, but so easy to recognise, — an english gentleman." [Spectator. **1548**

MIRIAM'S MARRIAGE. [by K.. S. MACQUOID: *Smith*, 1872.] "We may congratulate the writer on having constructed, out of very ordinary materials, an interesting narrativ, which evinces insít into the various conflicting elements which go to make character . . . Our sympathies ar so strongly enlisted on her side as the story proceeds'that we tremble when her happiness is imperilled by the appearance of a formidable rival, and we feel that we could never forgiv the author if, at the end of all her troubles, none of which result from any fault of hers, Nancy should not be rewarded by the full fruition of the love which, passionate as it is, is yet dwarfed by hers. We may assure intending readers that poetical justice is meted out to every personage in whose future any possible interest is likely to be felt." [Athenæum. **1549**

MIRK ABBEY [by JA. PAYN: 1867.] " is at once extravagant and feeble, improbable and commonplace; the characters ar vaguely conceived, and the plot unskilfully carried out." [London Review. **1550**

MISADVENTURE. [by W: E: NORRIS: *Blackett*, 1890.] " Mr. Norris has a manner of treatment peculiarly his, so that it makes little difference to his admirers what subject he takes in hand, old or new, conventional or original. Like a painter who clings to the quiet and sober style which happens to suit him best, and disdains to vie with the vivid colorists whose pictures draw the uninstructed crowd, he is best appreciated by those whose taste he has cultivated. In ' Misadventure' we hav nothing fresher than a country girl with a train of lovers — the despised sailor, whose race for a wife is sŏmething like the race of the tortoise against the hare; the free handed young man who is involved in a fatal ' misadventure' with her brother, and who comes to a violent end; and the traveled ŏner of a nêboring estate, who is mixed up with a russian lady of a decidedly intrïguing bent, and who also comes to a violent

end. These ar familiar types, and their haps and mishaps ar equally familiar; but Mr. Norris plods on with his story in an easy, unbroken, mildly cynical fashion, and makes himself interesting without visible effort." [Athen. **1551**

MISS BRETHERTON [by M.. A.. (ARNOLD) WARD: *Macmillan*, 1884.] "was sure of a kind of early popularity based on the personal element, so to speak, which the public would read into it, whether the author intended it or no. Miss Bretherton is' said to be Miss So-and-so. The american man of letters is such an one; the hero, another veritable personage. The world of fashion will thus be content; but this first wave of success will meanwhile hav carried the book within reach of eyes which will see the inadequacy of this surface comment, and will appreciate its depth and its fineness. Tho the heroin is an actress, it is not in the least a story of the stage. The motif underlying the plot and action is the insufficiency of natural gifts, and the mistake of the world's easy acceptance of them. True of all the arts, it is most true, most evident, in that of the stage; above all, if the actor be a woman. In a few incidents so briefly told as sŏmetimes to be broken, we hav a concrete presentation of the problem, How shall an exceptional natural endowment of fysical perfection, with no inheritance of cultivation from the past, no accumulation of personal thŏt and experience, reach the hīts of artistic excellence? Will Undine find a soul? . . . We hav to trace the steps of Miss Bretherton's development. Sometimes thêy ar given rather by hints or in flashes than in full detail, but the story affords manifold suggestions as to training in art, not for the stage only, but in any perfected skill. The lŏve of Eustace Kendal for Isabel makes no part of her artist life, tho he is most vitally connected with it. To her, till the very last, he is only a judge, an authority, an embodied standard. In the relation between them Mrs. Ward has attempted, and, it seems to us, worked out with rare and delicate insīt, a situation of great difficulty. Blankly put, it is, How can a man, with only himself and a moderate fortune to offer, address a woman on the hīts of fame? Over and over, again novelists hav evaded the question by bringing the man to help or to rescue at the moment of failure. In that guise cōmes Kendal's first vision of his bitherto unsuspected love — a dying fame, u forsaken and discrowned beauty, finding in his affection a fresh glory and an all-sufficient consolation. Her triumf leaves him no hope. He watches her on the nit of her reappearance, conscious that the moment is so vital, so desperate, that life on the other side will bear the mark of it forever. When it is over, he knoes that in the halo of her great success she stands afar off from him, divided by an impassable gulf from the lōve which cries to her, unheard and hopeless, across the darkness. Yet by chances of life so simple, so inevitable, as to seem ōnly daily human experience, these two, so wide apart, ar brŏt to the common ground where neither wealth nor fame can separate, where only the heart's need and the heart's lōve can ask and giv." [Nation.] — " The main interest lies in the fact that it is all about Miss Mary Anderson. Whether the picture is true to life or mostly fanciful is a question of no moment. In either case it will satisfy those readers who like prying into the private life of an actress, while those who look for some touch of art in fiction will be disappointed. Tho the book is well written and is obviously the work of a woman of much ability

and knoledge, it is not in any true sense a novel; it is merely a talk about Miss Anderson and her friends." [Athenæum. **1552**

MISS DEFARGE. [by F.. [Eliza] (Hodgson) Burnett : *Lippincott*, 1887.] " The influence of character in very unpromising surroundings forms its theme . . . Miss Defarge sets things rīt by single-minded intrepidity. She cōmes as a governess in a house of which the master is a wicked baronet, a drunken, gambling scoundrel, tho fortunately for the most part an absentee, the mistress cowed and helpless, the eldest son a boor, the children savages, and the servants thievs. The governess conquers .them all, except the wicked baronet, who is conveniently shot at a gaming table at Homburg. She givs her eldest charge a very severe whipping, she infuses some spirit into the mother, makes the hĕir take the management of the estate, and even dares to dismiss the ' wicked, slippery, good-looking housekeeper.' However difficult these achievements seem, Mrs. Burnett is well able to carry her reader along with her, and the journey is all the more pleasant for the company of a charming goddess in shabby white merino, unconscious of her beauty, inconsequent, and idle, but unselfish and kind-hearted almost to the point of nobleness." [Athenæum. **1553**

—— SAME. [" A Woman's Will"], *Warne*, 1887.

MISS FORRESTER. [by " Annie Edwards:" *Tinsley*, 1865.] " The tale of ' Miss Forrester ' is unhealthy; it has not the excuse of being a study of morbid anatomy of human nature, for the characters ar utterly unreal. Mrs. Edwards is not true to herself nor to the talents intrusted to her : in writing such novels as ' Miss Forrester ' she is employing them to do mischief to the utmost of her power." [Athenæum. **1554**

MISS GASCOIGNE [by C.. Eliza Cowan Riddell: *Appleton*, 1884.?] "is a beautifully told little story, artistic in plot and in detail. The author accomplishes what really requires very great skill: she puts her heroin in a ridiculous position, and yet never lets her appear ridiculous. This in itself is no mean triumf; and the whole story deals with picturesque situations, never improbable, set in a frame work of delītful humor and thŏroly keen insīt into human nature. Miss Gascoigne is past the youthful age supposed to be essential to a heroin; but she is not without adorers. So neatly is it all managed, that your imagination is constantly exercised as to who will eventually carry the day — the boy lover, the aristocratic suitor, or the impertinent curate, who for sōme reason or other you suspect may turn out to be less impertinent than appears on the surface; or whether, indeed, Miss Gascoigne may not decide to braid St. Catherine's tresses. And even then the one who triumfs is not the one you expected. [Critic. **1555**

MISS MACKENZIE. [by Anthony Trollope: *Harper*, 1865.] "Miss Mackenzie is a worthy gentlewoman, who, coming at the age of 36 into a comfortable little fortune, retires to enjoy it at a quiet watering-place, whêre in course of time, she is beset by a brace of mercenary suitors. After the laps of a year she discovers that she holds her property by a wrongful title,' and is compelled to transfer it to her cousin, a widoed baronet, with several children, who, however, gallantly repairs the injury thus judicially inflicted, by making her bis wife." [Nation. **1556**

MISS MARJORIBANKS [by Ma. Oliphant (Wilson) Oliphant: *Black-*

wood, 1866.] "is perhaps the cleverest of all of the extremely clever chronicles of Carlingford, and is indeed a great triumf . . . Thêre is more both of satire and of sympathy in the admirable figure of Miss Marjoribanks than in any other which we remember by this author, unless it be that of Mr. Tozer, the butterman. Thêre is something in the conception of Lucilla Marjoribanks which reminds us, — completely different as the external world in which she moves is, — of 'Emma' [No. 1246.] . . . The picture of Lucilla and her father, and the sort of society at Carlingford of which she is the centre, is one of the hiest skill. Indeed it is seldom enuf that one reads throu 3 volumes about mere social manœuvres with such sustained interest and continual food for the sense of humor." [Spectator.] — "Miss Marjoribanks is the dauter of the dry, unromantic, hard-headed doctor of Carlingford, who is left, early in the story, a not inconsolable widoer. Mrs. Marjoribanks having been for years a somewhat tiresom invalid, her departure from the scene is almost a relief to the doctor; but Miss Marjoribanks, who is sent home on the occasion from the boarding-school at which she is being educated, takes a very different vue of her father's feelings. The first chapter contains a most amusing account of her return, her attempt to play the part of the devoted dauter over which she has so often wept as described in novels of sentiment, and the utter frustration of her plans due to the callousness of the doctor, whose heart is not in the least broken and whose feelings refuse to be soothed by his dauter's entirely unlooked for attempts at consolation. Lucilla is obliged to postpone for a time the realization of her dreams, and to gò back to school for 3 years more;

but at the end of that time she returns to Carlingford full of ideas which ar truly great, and bent on filling a really grand position. Having made up her mind that her father must be dull and lonely in his solitary house, and that it is impossible his life can be a pleasant one as long as he has no one to take care of him, she resolvs to devote her energies, which she feels ar great, to the task of being ' a comfort to her dear papa.' Nor is this all. Besides taking care of his interests, other occupations await her. The state of society in Carlingford appears to her entirely unsatisfactory, and she determins to reform it. There is no one to take the lead in social matters — no master mind to sway less competent intellects, to guide them into new directions of thôt, and to teach them to form correct conclusions on subjects to which they hav hitherto paid little attention. All this she determins to do herself, and the story shōes how thōroly she succeeds in all she undertakes ᣟ. . . The doctor, who has a keen sense of humor, is greatly tickled by the grand air with which his dauter occupies her new position, and acquiesces with an inward chuckle in her gravely announced determination to be a comfort to him." [London Review. **1557**

MISS MISANTHROPE [by Justin McCarthy: *Chatto*, 1877.] is " a charming portrait of a girl whose story brings her into an amusing and lively company. Minola herself with her premature and innocent cynicism, which breaks down at the first touch of true affection, is consistent and well sustained throuôut; and the men she cômes in contact with ar fairly real specimens . . . Very good fun is made of the heroin's third admirer, Mr. Blauchet, the poet . . . A fourth lover, Mr. Sheppard, is a smug Philistine,· who

is totally antipathetic to her, but whose prosaic persistency has its respectable side. In the end the happiness of Minola and Heron is secured by pretty, trivial Lucy Money making a sacrifice which all three ar generously emulous of making. The dénoûment is perfectly natural·and artistic, and a hopeful moral is conveyed without preaching." [Athenæum. **1558**

MISS MOLLY [by Beatrice May Butt: *Blackwood*, 1876.] " is a charming little tale, of a slit kind, but without a flaw. We do not say that it proves genius, or even very great talent in the author. Thêre is no great breadth of character-painting in it, for ' Miss Molly ' is about the only person in it whom, when the tale is dõne, we really kno; but then, thêre is no particular reason why we should kno more. It is in her that the whole charm of the story centres, and one does not much expect or desire to understand the other figures, except so far as thêir relation to her is concerned, and that is easily understood without understanding the details of their individual natures. Unfortunately, we cannot, without spoiling this fascinating little story, giv our readers any adequate insit into the charms of Miss Molly. If we gave them a picture of her before her troubles begin, they would think too little of her; and if afterwards they would miss the real beauty of the sketch, the mingled contrast and harmony between her gaiety and the depth of her devotion." [Spectator. **1559**

MISS MONTEZAMBART [by M., A. (Hoppus) Marks: 1885.] " for readers who ar sensitiv to the delicate, sleepy charm of village life, will be one of the most successful of this autumn. The old Gloucestershire village, with its simple pleasures of nature and scandal, the quaint interior of the parson's house, the parson himself, the general effect of life being a more or less tranced survival of energies which rusted long ago." [Boston "Lit. World." **1560**

MISS OONA McQUARRIE, sequel to *ALFRED HAGART, which see.*

MISS SHAFTO. [by W: E: NORRIS: *Bentley*, 1889.] "Thêre is no novelist of our time whose work exhibits a greater equality of excellence than Mr. Norris . . . We kno that in his books we ar certain to find the results of keen observation, shrewd reflection, and brit, fresh humor, embodied in a story made attractiv by thõroly capable literary craftsmanship. Mr. Norris' work is good all round, but it is as a humorist that he shões himself at his best, and in 'Miss Shafto' this special gift is displayed very pleasantly. The love-story of the heroin and the aristocratic sculptor, Lord Walter Sinclair, tho pleasantly told, is not of absorbing interest: we enjoy it mainly becaus it is the means of introducing us to the entertaining circle which is composed of the horsey, hard-headed, but loyal-hearted young nobleman, Lord Loddondale, the ineffably conceited æsthetic poet, Mr. Basil Morely, who servs as a butt for the caustic humor of that terrible but charming old maid, Miss Nell Travers, and Mrs. Lämmergeier . . . The good things of the two ladies would in themselves suffice to make 'Miss Shafto' a very brit book; but thêre can be little doubt that Lord Loddondale is Mr. Norris's crowning success." [Spectator.] — "Mr. Norris writes of good society with refinement and good taste, in a pleasing style, and with a careful and yet easy avoidance of any touch of what mit offend the most sensitiv reader. But whatever he does is done gracefully." [Athenæum. **1561**

MISS TOMMY [by DINAH MARIA (MULOCK) CRAIK: *Macmillan*, 1884.] "is a very simple, sweet, and tender story of a queer old lady, whose full name was Thomasina." [Boston "Literary World."] — "The tale is an exceedingly simple one; its unaffected narrativ is undisturbed by any exciting passages, and quietly unfolds a story within a story — of two young lives whose prosperous love is interrupted by some transient adversities, and of two other and older lives which had drifted asunder when life was young, and had come together again when it was old, but was still rich in the capacity of tranquil happiness." [Harper's.] — "The story concerns itself mainly with the quiet loves and sorroes and joys of two middle-aged, indeed, rather elderly people, rather than with the stormier youthful passions which form the stock-in-trade of the ordinary writer of fiction. So far, indeed, from being a romance, 'Miss Tommy' is hardly even a novel; it is little more than an exquisitly sympathetic study of a single situation — the revelation of a lõve which for years has been a sacred secret, at a time when the day of lõve's warm delit has been left behind, and õnly its tranquil joys remain." [Spectator. **1562**

MISS WILLIAMSON'S DIVAGATIONS [by A.. I.. (THACKERAY) RITCHIE: *Smith*, 1881.] "in spite of its unpleasing title, is a very interesting volume of stories. The peculiar grace which belongs to all Miss Thackeray's writings is never better displayed than in short stories. These ar slit enuf — mere threads of fiction on which to string the pretty pearls of Miss Thackeray's sweet ideas and tender thõts, and graceful turns of frase, but they answer their purpõs well enuf. Thêre is a story of love. playing at cross purposes which ends happily enuf in a box at a theatre where 'Romeo and Juliet' is being performed, affording a pretty contrast between the fortunate love on the one side of the footlits, and the unhappy passion presented on the other. Then thêre is a ghost story which, as far as its supernatural element is concerned, must be pronounced but poor enuf, and thêre is of course a story about an old French town, and a tale in which Miss Williamson herself figures as heroin. No one of the stories leaves much to be carried away by the memory, nothing, that is to say, beyond a pleasant recollection of agreeable ideas and delicate language." [Westminster Review. **1563**

MR. BUTLER'S WARD. [by F.. MABEL ROBINSON: Vizetelly, 1885.] "After the heroin, the dauter of a murdered bailif, having received her education in a french convent, has half forgotten her tragic childhood, and married an artist, she livs almost constantly in England, and her life is that of the typical happy matron, merging her nationality and youthful prejudices in complete devotion to her husband. This marriage occurs very early in the book, and Deirdre goes throu her most moving experiences after she has become a wife. Between the death of her father and the birth of her baby the feelings which possess her mind ar not very intense, or at any rate thêy ar not described with much intensity. But her story is, perhaps, all the more natural on that account; and Miss Robinson has so far succeeded in her aim as to produce a conspicuously natural romance. A quite unusual fidelity in reproducing the interior life of young married people is the distinguishing mark of the story, which, without being a masterpîece, is both artistic and simple . . . It may be recommended as a charming book, poetically

conceived, and worked out with tenderness and iasit." [Athenæum. **1564**

MR. HARRISON'S CONFESSIONS [with "Lizzie Leigh," by E.. C. S. GASKELL: Chapman, 1855.] "is a genuin bit of comedy, from the same mint as gave out 'Cranford.' The steadiness with which the gay and clever young fysician was beleaguered by the old maids and widoes of the country town in which he had pitched his tent, is a thing to giv young bachelors in like circumstances a shudder; — since few amŏng them may really be able to extricate themselvs so felicitously as our young man is made to do." [Ath. **1565**

MR. LESLIE OF UNDERWOOD. [by M.. PATRICK: Smith, 1879.] "The author of 'Marjorie Bruce's Lovers' is well enuf knŏn to the novel-reading public to dispense with any introduction beyond her name on the title-page, which is a guarantee of a prettily conceived, well-arranged, femininly written romance. This is a story with 2 heroins and a hero.' [Athenæum. **1566**

MR. SMITH. [by LUCY BETHIA (COLQUHOUN) WALFORD: Holt, 1875.] "A short, stout, gray man, middle-aged, a bachelor and rich, comes as a stranger to settle near the village of Eastwold. The vulgar genteel families of the place ar distracted between the professional advantages and social disadvantages of calling upon him, till they discover, late in the day, that 'the county' knŏes him. The beauty among a set of flirting motherless sisters had given such heart as she had to giv to a snob of a soldier, who kisses her at home and denies her in the better houses of the nêborhood; but for marriage she schemes to catch the rich, middle-aged man, honored with the friendship of eligible acquaintance. Mr. Smith, thinking no guile, and equally grateful to kind friends of all sorts and conditions, falls in love with the beautiful girl, but can hardly bring himself to believe that the prize is for him. He thinks no scandal nor will listen to it. And then, suddenly, on the eve of his marriage, he died. His life and his death left the book, as they lifted Eastwold, out of what had otherwise been a dead level of unendurable vulgarity. The soldier and girl marry; but with eyes opened to see their unworthiness and with a 'quickened sense of the compass of human feeling' from having once knōn a simple noble christian gentleman, Mr. Smith." [Macmillans'.] —" Mr. Smith had a flavor and a humor entirely his ōn. The artless vulgarities of the Hunt family could hardly hav been more carefully studied or more faithfully represented by the creator of the immortal Mrs. Bennett; but in the conception of her hero, — the plain, modest, pious, instinctivly chivalrous, and inevitably honorable english gentleman, — with the simplicity of his love, and the perfectly unconscious disinterestedness of his motivs, Mrs. Walford givs proof of hier sympathies and deeper estimates of human nature than wer often betrayed — whatever may hav been felt — by her accomplished model. Lord Sauffrenden is another delitful type, not in the least romantic, or ideal, except in the fine touch, at once lit and firm, with which he is drawn; and his wife is another; while the story of the vain, yet not ignoble heroin, and of her moral awakening and virtual regeneration by the brief, humble, wistful passage throu her life of one thōroly good man, is as well told as possible. Indeed, excellent as is the faculty of characterization shōn in Mr. Smith, and racy the humor, the most remarkable thing about the little book is a certain sober unity and masterly simplicity of method, — a resolute subordination of all details to the general design." [H. W. Preston. **1567** MR. WYNYARD'S WARD [by " Holme Lee," i. e., Harriet Parr: *Smith*, 1867.] " is a story which, if not very deep or strong, at all events is very attractiv and touching. Thêre is not much plot in the book, nor is that which exists over-probable. But the heroin's character is charming, very true and life-like, and marked by a number of those agreeable little peculiarities which giv a pleasing individuality to a fictitious personage. Pennie Croft is left by her father under the gardianship of Mr. Wynyard, a well-meaning but weak-minded country gentleman, who not only contrives to run throu *his* property, but is led by an unprincipled attorney into unconsciously performing the same feat with respect to the money of his wealthy ward. But as this performance of his is not discovered for some time, she is long deemed a great heiress. The scenes ar very good in which she is depicted while visiting among her relativs, who ar of an inferior class to that in which she has been reared, her father having made his money by lucky speculations. The contrast which her unenlitened cousins offer to the members of the cultivated family circle in which she has moved is well expressed, and so is the effect which the commonplace life they lead has upon the spirits and feelings of one whose tastes have been educated and refined, and in whom aspirations hav been ventured for something hier than the ordinary aims of an unreflecting middle-class family. She makes the acquaintance of a nêboring land-ōner who possesses 'the charm of a great sorro' and gradually she loses her heart to him. He, who has been crushed by adverse fate, and has given up all hopes of happiness, suddenly finds a change wröt by her in all the current of his being, and a flood of unfamiliar sunlit pours in upon his path whenever she appears. The story of their courtship is charmingly told, and thêre is something so frank, and brave, and straitforward in all she says and dões, that it is impossible not to feel a strong personal liking for her. Such a good, trusty, probable little heroin is worth any number of the unreal adventuresses, the impossible criminals, with whom sõme novelists delĩt to shock us. We ar the better for having been in Pennie Croft's presence; her healthy talk and honest thóts ar to one who has been condemned to much reading of sensational romance, wbat a fresh seabreeze is to the weary denizen of an inland city." [London Review.] — " Foremost amongst the qualities which make the goodness of this clever and charming tale ar a freshness of style and a peculiar newness of arrangement and manipulation in the presence of much which shões Holme Lee's readiness to profit by the example of other artists . . No purer, brĩter, or more delĩtful tale has for many a day come under our notice." [Athenæum. **1568**

MRS. ARTHUR [by MA. OLIPHANT (WILSON) OLIPHANT: *Hurst*, 1877.] "tells of the only son of a baronet, who falls in love with the handsom, but vulgar and ignorant dauter of a taxcollector in a London suburb. His family oppose the match as best they can; his most intimate friend remonstrates with him with the usual success, and the bad-tempered Nancy soon attains the position she had so longed for. The husband, Arthur Curtis, finds the awakening from his dreams anything but pleasant. His wife shocks him by

her taste in dress; he takes her to Paris, but the pictures, the theatres hav no charm for her, and she sis for her congenial home. They return to England and lead an utterly miserable life together, until, in an access of unusu-ally violent rage, she runs away from her husband and returns to her family. Arthur leaves the country to take a diplomatic position at Vienna, but in time Nancy sees her follies and devotes her energies to self-improvement. Gradually, by some unexplained process, she becomes like other people; she manages to charm Arthur's father and mother before they kno who she is, and the book ends well. Nothing could be better than the description of the poor young fello's infatuation and his impatience of opposition. But nothing could be saintlier than his behavior after his marriage, when his wife gave frequent exhibition of her ungovernable temper. Mrs. Oliphant draws the unhappiness of the poor hero with a clever pen, and too much cannot be said in praise of her description of Nancy's family. Alongside of the main love-story runs an account of the love the remonstrating friend bears for Arthur's sister, which is a very different piece of business from the romance of Arthur's life. It is in just such subjects of social complications in english life that Mrs. Oliphant is at her best. The mantle which Miss Austen first wore and Mrs. Gaskell inherited now covers her shölders; but it is made over to suit the present fashion, and it is a most useful as well as becoming garment." [Nation.] — " The good youth who makes the mistake of marrying Nancy Bates does not do much to excite the reader's sympathy; tho his affliction at finding he has married the tax-collector and his wife, as well as sisters Matilda and Sarah Jane, both admirable in their way, is sufficiently well founded. In describing these really good specimens of a certain class the author by no means makes the mistake of allowing no moral virtu to those who ar totally without refinement, tho how nearly parallel gentleness and virtu run is a lesson the little back parlor at Mr. Bates' mit hav taut any one but a lover. Of two different types of sisterly affection, honest Matilda Bates and Lucy Curtis ar excellent specimens; while the sketch of Hubert's gentlemanly selfishness is an outline for an excellent picture." [Athenæum.　　　　　**1569**

MRS. FENTON. [by W: E: Norris: *Holt*, 1889.] "Mr. Norris is never less than entertaining, even in his liter efforts. The heroin is a clever australian adventuress who swoops down upon a fortune not ritfully hers, captures it, and with it the good graces of half of London, and all but succeeds in winning a noble prize, the heart of the man she loves. Withal, she is so generous and so merry and charming in her way, that she captivates the reader as well, and we ar half sorry when she is exposed and disappears from the scene, leaving her lover to wed the somewhat colorless girl, and be happy after a dull and regular fashion." [Boston "Literary World."　　　　　**1571**

MRS. GEOFFREY. [by Ma.( ) (Argles) Hungerford: *Smith*, 1881.] "The irish maiden who enchants and marries Mr. Geoffrey Rodney is a very charming heroin, and as a love story the tale of her adventures is worthy of the author of 'Phyllis.' The talk between this honest-hearted pair is especially lively, and tho amorous enuf it is neither gushing nor silly. To be able thus naturally to reproduce the dialog of lovers without immediately becoming

intolerable to the general reader is a remarkable gift, tho we trust the author will be wisely sparing in its exercise. For the characters, Geoffrey is a manly fello, a trifle slangy, perhaps, but a gentleman; while his thöroly worldly mother and the conventional and rather cool-tempered Violet Manser form a good contrast to the impulsiv Mona. The process of Mona's reconciliation to these outraged relativs, who ar by no means prepared to welcom her entrance into the family circle, is well told." [Athenæum.　　　　　**1572**

MRS. HALLIBURTON'S TROUBLES. [by Ellen (Price) Wood: *Bentley*, 1862.] "The scene is laid in the same old cathedral town in which dwelt the Channings [No. 1139.] . . . The great merit of the book is the true and simple manner in which every scene and character ar depicted. They may be all living human beings for aut we kno. The bad ar perhaps a little too bad; they ar seen always on the worst side, and the good, again, ar drawn like Queen Elizabeth, with no shadoes. But still they ar real, and we kno them and .believ in them, and take an interest in them; and tho the story is long and not always lively, we ar compelled to read on to the end, and to see the last of the Halliburtons. The. moral and religious principles inculcated are unexceptionable." [Athenæum.　　　　　**1573**

MRS. HORACE [by Alex. Kepler: *Remington*, 1887.] "does much to set off the directness and simple pathos of his study of two lives, for which he fully secures the interest of his readers. Rosa Horace is a woman of an easily recognized type, who never ceases to be a girl, forever young in heart, with a girl's exulting sense of liberty and power, rarely conscious of an earnest soul within, yet capable of a deep and abiding fidelity to the man who first awakened her from her moral sleep. The sketch is well executed, and the touches take the shape of incidents rather than of reflexions. Reflexions thêre ar in plenty — many of them inspired by Mr. Kepler's appetite for good food and moral conundrums. But he has drawn his heroin with a loving hand, and in virtue of this the reader will freely forgiv him." [Athenæum. **1574**

MISTRESS JUDITH. [by Christina C. Fraser (Tytler) Liddell: *Low*, 1874.] "Those who hav read that most delicious of modern stories, 'Under the Greenwood Tree,' will understand what we mean when we describe this book as an idyl of rural life. Tho less worldly and humorous than that book, it cannot fail to recall pleasant memories of it, and in respect to the almost exclusiv rusticity of its scenery and personnel deservs to be classed with it. Not only does 'Mistress Judith' lack humor, but it is really painful; yet despite this sombreness, which will, perhaps, repel the average novel-reader, it is a charming and wholesom story. Its personages liv within the narro limits of an obscure hamlet, whêrein the several acts of a homely little drama ar enacted under quiet skies and with the simplest imaginable surroundings." [Boston "Literary World."] —"We do not ever remember to hav read a story more perfect of its kind thar 'Mistress Judith'; and since 'Sylvia's Lovers' [No. 970], we hav not read a sadder one. Indeed we can hardly imagin the frame of mind in which a person could compose, and still more, write such a story, ending in sorro hopeless and irreparable to those who ar left alive at the end of it. Of course, as in all perfectly sad stories, misunderstanding is the cause of the sorro,

aggravated in the present instance by treachery. We question how far an author less great than the greatest has a rit to employ such a motiv: there seems to be a kind of profanity in thus handling a grief almost too great for human nature to bear, especially when it is told with all the vividness given by commonplace surroundings." [Athen. **1575**

MRS. KEITH'S CRIME [by Lucy (Lane) Clifford: *Bentley*, 1885.] "is marked by a total absence of plot and incident, and of the kind of interest which has been usually thôt necessary to novels; and ovs its interest to the fact that it is a picture of a state of mind which has met these problems with a negativ answer, and finds the world empty of all but human love. Human love under such an aspect seems to gain a strange new intensity. It finds a vast legacy, as it wer, suddenly put at its disposal. That craving for the infinit which no belief or unbelief can repress, losing, as far as consciousness goes, its eternal object, stimulates imagination to create one within the limits of mortality. The mother who believes her love for her child to be but a drop from the ocean which surrounds her can but acquiesce in all the appointments of supreme care; the mother who regards her love as an ultimate and original reality, finds it a law to itself. Mrs. Clifford's heroin learns that the disease which is preying on both her and her child is to make her its first victim; she feels that in the universe is no parental care greater than hers. We cannot see any harm in the overdose which givs the child a painless death, from Mrs. Clifford's point of vue; and we presume that she intends her title to indicate the different moral ideal belonging to her creed and that which it is to supersede. Mrs. Keith ends her child's life as the god in whom she has ceased to believe takes it: she givs it the best she has to giv. It is a decision of unselfishness as absolute as that of the divine appointment. She deprives herself of the sweet solace of those offers of service which ar her heaven, lest they should be missed when she is not thére to giv them." [Contemporary Review. **1576**

MRS. LANCASTER'S RIVAL. [by ELEANOR C. PRICE : *Low*, 1880.] "The heroin eclipses Mrs. Lancaster in the eyes of two men, — in the heart of one, and the calculating judgment of the other; and we follo the complications which ar the results of this rivalry, if it is to be so called, with unwearied interest. The characters of the men ar particularly well drawn. The sailor lover, the bluff old captain, and the chivalrous rector ar 3 excellent portraits, such as should alone make the fortune of a novel." [Spectator.] — "It is neatly written, well imagined, and carefully done, and may be read with not a little pleasure. The third volume is completed by a novelette called ' Miss Monckton's Marriage,' which is ingeniously turned and forms acceptable reading." [Athenæum. **1577**

MRS. LORIMER [by "LUCAS MALET," i. c., Rose G. (Kingsley) Harrison : *D. Appleton*, 1880.] "is called a ' sketch in black and white' from the fact that the heroin at the opening of the story appears in morning for her young husband, and at the close ' in a gown of soft, ivory-white cashmere, plentifully trimmed with rich old lace;' the white, however, being symbolical not of second love and marriage, but of the shroud in which she is too soon enfolded . . . In the remaining pages the Vicar seeks her only to be repulsed; she meets her first love, who proves to be less interesting than she had supposed,

and on the verge of marrying some one else, and she refuses to marry her Platonic friend for no reason perceptible to the reader, and returns to her ânt's, whére she dies. This is all, and it is certainly very little, but the padding is a series of short, pleasant essays on the events of every-day life which ar certainly interesting and well-written. It is a book to be read quietly, not with any impatience to kno the end; and such as like digesting a chapter thóroly will find much food for reflexion, and tranquil enjoyment of good things, in the keen analysis of character and motiv, and the shrewd comments upon men and things." [Critic. **1578**

MRS. MAINWARING'S JOURNAL [by EMMA ( ) MARSHALL: *Seeley*, 1873.] "is the tale of a quiet married woman's life, from the day when she arrives, a girlish bride, at the quaint house in a cathedral town whére her husband livs and has his business, to the time at which she celebrates her golden wedding, with her children and grandchildren around her. If it is not very stimulating food for the intellect, its appeals to the heart ar often forcible, and its literary skill, tho of no unusual order, is sufficient to prevent resentment on the part of those who detect under the guise of a novel the very sufficient modicum of sermon which is artfully submitted for théir digestion . . . This is the acme of good story-telling; and accordingly, altho the subject-matter is tame, and altho the religious element in the book will deter a large number of readers from its perusal, its method should attract the notice of more pretentious writers." [Athenæum. **1579**

MRS. MERRIDEW'S FORTUNE. See *NEIGHBORS ON THE GREEN*.

MISUNDERSTOOD. [by FLORENCE MONTGOMERY: N. Y., *Randolph*, 1877.]

" This little and unpretending story is *about* children rather than *for* them, being written evidently with the intent of warning parents against the danger of partiality, and of illustrating the painful sense of isolation which may cōme upon a tender-hearted child, who feels that upon another is lavished the whole affection in which he would only too gladly hav a share, but for which he is too proud to ask. The story is well written, and has sōme very touching passages. It is, neither long nor elaborate." [Boston " Literary World."]—" It is the story of two little motherless boys, whose father honestly tries to do his duty by both, altho his affection for the delicate little ' Miles' is greater than for his more robust and reckless brother. The writer's sympathy with the joys and sorrōs of childhood, and keen appreciation of their natures, ar evidenced in every page ; and their naturally dramatic thōts and actions lose nothing throu her representations . . . Thēre ar pleasant little bits of poetical descriptions of nature, and it is quite easy to see how the brīt skies, beautiful fields, and waving trees tempted the restless ' Humphrey,' and how his activ imagination delīted to linger over the fatal and forbidden pond, whēre the old tree stretched a limb over the water, so exactly like the one described by ' Uncle Charlie,' in a story of wild adventure. It is not surprising, either, that a father should believe that a child so full of life and health, so careless and happy under every circumstance, would be quite indifferent to an extra caress or word of affection for his more delicate brother ; and it is almost as much of a shock at the last, as it was to the father, to find out how simply the boy had accepted his share of affection as a part of an inexorable system of things, which he

mīt comprehend when he grew to be a man, but now could only receive unquestioningly. The pathos of the closing chapters is characterized by the same quiet good-taste which pervades the humorous parts." [Overland. **1580**

MITCHELHURST PLACE [by MARGARET VELEY: (†, 1887) *Macmillan*, 1884.] " is admirable in style, and this terse, vivid, and nervous style is not wasted on platitudes. Miss Veley's pages ar brīt with flashes of insīt, and abound in touches of sympathetic tenderness . . . The story rivets the attention from the first page to the last, and the writer's management of the plot is perfect. Reynold Harding, the purposeless and ill-tempered son of a dauter of the ruined house of Rothwell, visits the home of his mother's ancestry (his father's father had been a pork-butcher) and thēre meets his fate in Barbara Strange. She had already met hers in Adrian Scarlett, a brīt, good-humored artist and poet, and a previous visitor to Mitchelhurst Place. But she thōt her love was not returned, and is brōt, without loving him, into such relations with Reynold, that she would hav married him if he had asked her. It is impossible to speak too bily of the skill and delicacy with which this portion is worked out. Reynold is moved by his love for Barbara to write a letter which will put him on the road to wealth, and secure him, as he has reason to hope, the hand of the woman who has transfigured him. How that hope was baffled the reader must discover for himself; and we can only assure him that the discovery is well worth making." [Spectator. **1581**

MODEL FATHER (A). [by D: CHRISTIE MURRAY: *Harper*, 1882.] " The model father is Montgomery Bassett, a tall, portly person, with a pale magenta nose, and a rich bass voice in which the öner takes prodigious pride. Mr. Bassett enjoys a certain fame as an interpreter of Shaksperian parts on the London stage, and is knön as a star in the provinces. When his pretty dauter Mary falls in löve with the handsom Jack Cameron, the impecunious but promising artist, Mr. Bassett, having an eye to his future, naturally objects, and tries to force her into a marriage with young Weatherly, a good-natured weakling . . . The course of true love runs smooth at the last, and in the final chapter thére is an affecting reconciliation. The strength of the story is in the portrayal of Bassett's personality and character, which is of singular life-likeness, altho with here and thére a touch of exaggeration." [Boston "Literary World." **1582**

MODERN GREEK HEROINE (A) [*Hurst*, 1880.] "The heroin's experiences ar gained amongst english and french people, clergymen and artists, and the narrativ clings to England all throu . . . But the romance is strong enuf to stand on its merits, without any assistance from its title . . . Miss Valettas is carefully drawn after an ideal which has several distinctly greek characteristics. She is subtle, ingenious, full of resource, large-hearted in adversity; she is insincere, untruthful, a schemer, and an actress — yet frank and candid at intervals, and especially with those whom she likes. Whether sincere or insincere, her creator molds her in such form that the reader löves her throuöut, and admires her even more than he löves. The author may be congratulated on a pretty and clever story." [Athenæum. **1583**

MODERN LOVER (A). [by G: MOORE: *Tinsley*, 1883, Chicago, *Laird*, 1890.] "What Tito Melema was in the grand life of Romola, 'A Modern Lover' is in the several lives of three women who löve him, trust him, and sacrifice themselves to him, each in a different way, and according to the opportunities afforded them by his various needs at the time. Of the refined and poetical tone and atmosfere of the book which gave us an unrivalled picture of moral good-for-nothingness in old florentine days, thére is no trace in this essentially modern story; they ar replaced by plain prose, and realism which, while it is not coarse, and, unlike the tone of the 'naturalistic' writers, döes not offend, takes the gilt off the gingerbread of sentiment, and ignores romance in a more thörobred style than we ar accustomed to, except in the utterances of professed cynics. This author is not a cynic; he not only recognises, but he respects goodness, purity and disinterestedness, and altho the story he tells is all about the woful waste of those feelings upon a person absolutely unworthy of them, he is quite alive to the pity of it, and givs his readers the notion that he would hav liked to make Lewis Seymour a better fello, if he could. He cannot, however, for 'A Modern Lover' is not a bit of a built-up story; it has a very uncommon note of spontaneity; it tells itself, and its faults ar the defects of its qualities of moderation and sincerity. The book has more power than the story; the characters hav more interest than the incidents; the first volume is the best as a conception and a composition, but the third is superior to it as a picture of society: it givs a clearer evolution of character without exaggeration, and a vue of modern life, which, while it is tinged with pessimism, is not scornful or bitter, but on the whole tolerant and good-humored . . . It would be difficult to praise too hīly the strength, truth, delicacy, and pathos of the incident of Gwynnie Lloyd, and the admirable treatment of the great sacrifice she makes when, in his utter destitution, and under the influence of his threat to commit suicide, she consents to sit to Lewis Seymour for the nude figure of Venus. The incident is depicted with skill and beauty. The author dōes not again reach that point; his later materials are more commonplace . . . Mr. Moore's, then, is not an ideal novel; it is a study from life, and lifelike, — more's the pity! It is faulty, but always interesting; it has both pathos and humor, and it is pervaded by a frank, revealing spirit which tells of observation of men and things, intelligent, not malicious, and commonsensical. The world and its ways neither take in this writer, nor do they disgust him; he sees the poetry of things, but he knoes that it is the prose of them which lasts." [Spectator. **1584**

MOLLY BAWN. [by Ma. ( ) (Argles) Hungerford: *Lippincott*, 1878.] "Anyone who delits in repartee, or in the exquisit charm which sōmetimes half extenuates the cruelty of flirtation, should read 'Molly Bawn.' Altho the story is well constructed, and the simple plot affords strong characterization and many interesting situations in the development of the relations between Mr. Amherst and his 8 grandchildren, each of whom is the only child of a detested marriage and receives from him open maltreatment and frequent insult; and altho the minor characters ar well marked and amusing, the central interest is in the captivating power of Molly and her readiness to use it. She has a talent for flirting, and in her it is a graceful sin. The fault in moral quality which injures

the story is the skill which has made her actions seem so much the product of nature as to be irresponsible, so that the anger which they continually excite is like that felt at the barbarities of children. She pulls a man's happiness to pieces as a 3-year-old demolishes a costly toy, and treads on her lover's feelings as if they wer of no more consequence than a cat's tail. This goes on until she is sobered by an unexpected misfortune, and opportunity is offered for the development of noble qualities. Still, with all her charms, her gifts of youth and beauty and song and wit, and all the prettiness of her 'petulant, quick replies,' we confess to a gladness that such explosiv bonbons ar not the daily fare of men. It would indeed be but a sorry world if she and her peer, Lady Strafford, wer representativs of many women. The other great charm of the book is its conversation, which is plentiful, brit, amusing, and never flags." [Nation.] — " In the case of 'Molly Bawn' we ar for a time propitiated by the saucy graces of the irish heroin and the genuin ardor of feeling which she appears to kindle in her numerous admirers. And since, if man, woman, or book cannot be useful, it is doubly incumbent upon them to be agreeable, it may be worth while to inquire a little more carefully what it is which makes this frivolous 'Molly Bawn' so uncommonly 'fetching.' It is partly, perhaps, the entire and audacious naturalness of most of the conversation . . And the insignificant portion of the book which is not slang is in very nice, plain, few-syllabled english. Thêre is also a good and quite fresh situation among the minor characters, whêre the parties to a marriage of the coolest convenience knōn in the biest circles, who had agreed to separate directly after the wedding ceremony, meet accidentally, and fall honestly in love with each other." [Atlantic. **1585**

MONA'S CHOICE [by "Mrs. Alexander," i. e., Annie (French) Hector: *F. V. White*, 1887.] "is a very good specimen of Mrs. Alexander's familiar workmanship. The 'choice' is, we need hardly say, a choice of lovers. Mona, who is an orfan, is introduced into society by a wealthy ânt, and frequently meets a certain Captain Lisle, a singularly attractiv man, to whom, believing that he loves her, she givs her heart. Lisle, on his side, has not been untouched; but when Mona is left destitute, the Captain is too self-regardful to risk marriage with a penniless girl, and instead of proposing to her himself, suggests that she should accept the addresses of his rich but very clumsy and shy friend, Waring. Out of consideration for her ânt, Mona accepts Waring's offer, tho she frankly tells him that she has no love to giv; but when, just before the marriage, her ânt dies, she feels that she cannot go on with the sacrifice, and breaks off the engagement. She sees nothing of either Lisle or Waring for some years, which ar spent partly with an old friend, whom she assists in giving music lessons, and partly with an eccentric scotch uncle, who takes her with him to his northern home. At this place the two men reappear, and Lisle now claims her love; but Mona, having discovered the difference between gold and pinchbeck, rejects his suit, and givs herself, this time finally and unreservedly, to the faithful, loyal, Waring. The story is pleasantly told, and some of the subsidiary characters ar specially good. Mr. Craig, Mona's uncle, is, indeed, a triumf of truthful and humorous delineation; and we think that on the whole, 'Mona's Choice' must be deemed Mrs. Alexander's best novel." [Spectator. **1586**

MONKS OF THELEMA (The). [by Wa. Besant & Ja. Rice: *Chatto*, 1879.] "Mr. Besant's love for caricature finds here an open field and no favor. No English nobleman was ever so simpleminded as to carry his theories of the elevation of the tenantry to the point of marrying ône of his dairy maids out of pure altruism. The motiv of the book, the order of Thelema, is directly traceable to Besant's studies in old French literature. It is the transformation and modernization of a religious order into a very delitful community of clever people whose motto is 'Fay ce que vouldras,' and whose patron saint is Rabelais. Here also is occasion for one of those barbed shafts of irony. It is personified in the person of Rondelet, fello of Lothian, and directed against certain tendencies in exclusiv literary coteries to believe that within their holy circle they alone contain the profet of the new Messiah of the hier culture. But on the whole, one is baffled a bit that Besant should permit a matter so closely connected with his favorit idea about the elevation of the working classes to be conceived in seriousness and executed only in levity." [Critic.] — "But perhaps still better handled is Mr. Paul Rondelet [Wa. Pater?], the profet of that mysterious School of Thinkers who 'keep the Renaissance bottled for themselvs,' circulate little poems, liv well, sī over the ignorance of their elders, and talk of the 'hier thôt, the nobler aim, the truer method.' Nothing is more characteristic of Rondelet than his wooing of Miranda, the abbess and the heroin. He is driven to this step by the awful thôt that his felloship is about to expire, and that he will hav literally no means on which to liv the hier life, except by taking orders. He, thêrefore, offers to share that life with the richest and most beautiful woman of his acquaintance. He is good enuf to say that, in woman the hier receptivity alone is required." [Athenæum.] — "In this picture of life thŏroly pleasant and perfectly luxurious, untroubled by any responsibilities, never invaded by satiety, undisturbed by jealousy, and safe from the selfish passions which will intrude into the best defended paradise, the aspirations of a worldling's better nature find their ideal; while that which is worse finds a satisfaction which is not too grossly cynical in the kindly satire directed against those who ar not content with acknoledging social wrongs, but madly try to set them rīt." [Spectator. **1587**

MONKSFORD [S: Tinsley, 1879.] "is a pleasant story of life in a provincial town, not the domestic life of a family or two, but the life of the town itself, of the gentry and professional men, of the mayor and corporation, of the officers and the inhabitants in general . . . Other incidents, which mīt hav been stale and commonplace enuf in the hands of a clumsy storyteller. But thêre ar matters treated in these annals of Monksford which stir finer chords and wake other music than questions of municipal government." [Athenæum. **1588**

MOOR COTTAGE (The) [by MAY BEVERLEY: Macmillan, 1861.] "is a good little innocent story, the interest not very exciting, but the spîrit in which it is written kind and genial. The good people who set an example and the middling people who ar intended to profit by it, ar all pleasant in thêir way; thêre is no false pathos nor affected sentiment to disturb the reader's good-nature. Thêre is a gentle humane influence perceptible throu the book; and when the course of true love runs strait, the reader feels pleased, and sympathizes, mildly it may

be, but quite sincerely, with the fortunes of the characters." [Athenæum. **1589**

MOORLAND COTTAGE (The) [by E.. CLEGHORN (STEVENSON) GASKEL: Chapman, 1850.] "like 'Mary Barton,' is a tale of passion and feeling, developed among what may be called every-day people : — but, unlike 'Mary Barton,' it is not a tale of class-sufferings and class-interests. It is merely a story intended to soften the heart and sweeten the charities at christmas time by the agency of pity and sympathy. The idea is simple, but the execution is of no common order. The characters ar nicely marked. Mr. Buxton, the great man of the town, — his saint-like invalid wife — Mrs. Brown, with her jealous hardness towards her dauter and her credulous indulgence of her son — ar as well made out as they ar artfully, because artlessly, contrasted . . . Rarely has woman drawn a fairer study of self-sacrifice in woman than our author in Maggie Brown; and if we refrain from quoting some of the scenes in which this is developed, it is simply becaus we will not take the edg off the reader's curiosity with regard to a story of so deep interest and wholesom moral : — for wholesom beyond the usual fashion of novelists is the form of Maggie's self-sacrifice, and her standing for those rīts which in life count for so much while in fiction they are disregarded as it wer by receipt." [Athenæum.] — "So healthy and powerful and pathetic a story of woman's love, woman's endurance, and woman's generosity, claims honor, not merely for its ōn sake, but as illustrating a taste among english authors and readers, for work in which fancy and feeling graciou\-ly consort with, and ar harmonized by, virtue and reason." [Ladies' Companion. **1590**

MORALS OF MAY FAIR (The). [by ANNIE EDWARDS: 1857. N.-Y., *Sheldon*, 1873.] "Another of Mrs. Edwards' novels has been exhumed by her enterprising publisher, and we presume that many who hav been entertained by her later stories will be inveigled into buying this her first ōne. We can assure them, however, that thĕy will be disappointed. Occasionally, it is true, we find a frase which givs promis of the cleverness she has since shōn, but such exceptions ar rare; and we ar put off with a very sensational story of a disagreeable kind — of the lōve, namely, between one married man and another's wife, all of which is told with a certain amount of force, but with a greater amount of crudeness." [Nation.] — Mudie refused to circulate ōne of "Mrs. Edwards'" earlier novels; we suppose this is the ōne. **1591**

—— SAME ("Philip Earnscliffe") [*American News Co.*, 1866.]

MORNING GREY [by G. M.: *Ward*, 1885.] "is made most entertaining and readable by a crisp and lively style, a playful humor, and an occasional spice of real wit. But, altho amusing episodes ar in the majority, the chief interest centres in the fortunes of the heroin, a sympathetic character of considerable charm. Her relations with a little boy friend ar touchingly told, the interchange of līt and shade being skilfully managed. Thĕre ar plenty of quaint and incisiv sayings in these pages, but they hav the merit of being justified by the context, and do not suggest any conscious effort on the author's part. 'G. M.' is particularly felicitous in hitting off the foibles of provincial society." [Athen. **1592**

MOTHER'S IDOL (A) [by LYDIA HOPE: *Tinsley*, 1882.] "is a Capt. Davenel, who falls in love with the governess of his nĭece, very much to his mother's annoyance. Mrs. Davenel, the wife of a worthy magistrate, keeps her house, and all it contains, in exemplary order; she is, in fact, a commander-in-chief of the sternest type, whom no one can thwart or disobey, unless it be the object of her maternal adoration. The heroin says of her, quaintly enuf, that ōne always had a sort of apologetic, guilty feeling in Mrs. Davenel's presence, as if one wer an uncompleted effort. It is certainly much to the credit of the little governess that she is able to conquer the whole house of Davenel. How her engagement to the idol prospered, and what end she made to her chequered career, may be learnt from the pages in which Miss Hope has related her experiences. The relation is simple and pleasant, tho thĕre is no attempt to soar much abōve the level of straitforward narrativ." [Athenæum. **1593**

MY BRIDES [by EMILY G. NESBITT: *Newby*, 1869.] "is a very readable and pleasant tale . . Truthful, frank of speech, and overfloing with strong natural affections, Dorothy finds out that to secure the happiness of her father and cousin, and other persons who ar dear to her, she must amend her manners, get the better of her unruly hair, conquer her hoydenish propensities, and acquire the tender touch and delicate tone which do not cōme of thĕir ōn accord to damsels of her sort, and having made this discovery by the līt of affection, the same illuminator shōes her how to remove her faults and assume the gracious qualities with which Nature omitted to endow her. From a clumsy, boisterous girl she becōmes the unselfish and considerate woman, to whom every one cōmes for sympathy in joy and comfort in trouble. Of course she is everybody's bridesmaid, and in the autobiografic fragment to which we ar indebted for the pleasure of her acquaintance, she lets us into the secrets of her friends' lõves and joys and sorroes . . . The story which ends thus agreeably is by no means an important or perfect achievement; but whilst under perusal it has so strong and wholesom an effect, that it would be sheer ingratitude to qualify praise of its goodness with needless talk about its shortcomings." [Athenæum. **1594**

MY DUCATS AND MY DAUGHTER [by Hay Hunter & Wa. Whyte: C. K. Paul, 1884.] "does not lack variety of character and incident. Tho the plot and situations ar far from novel or ingenious, their development is not uninteresting. The story begins with a filanthropic capitalist's disastrous attempt to improve the condition of the working man and found 'the factory of the future.' It turns with marked deliberation upon the benefit accruing to the son from õne of the misguided father's acts of kindness. It folloes this son throu failure at college, failure in journalism, failure in lõve, and makes sudden prosperity the crucial-test of character. It is rather a bold protest against the traditional efficacy of adversity, and in the hero the author depicts successfully a nature which is commoner than moralists choose to believe." [Nation.] — "Not only is it extremely well written, but it treats several widely diverse fãses of life with a sureness of delineation and fulness of detail to be acquired õnly from experience. Many of the characters are finished studies, and all ar thõroly human and life-like. Two of them ar so finely drawn as to call for more especial notice; õne is a rigid scotch Puritan, narro, bigoted, austere, yet underneath this repulsiv crust the real nature of the man is lovable and estimable; he is just, faithful, affectionate and grateful. Under extreme stress of af-

fliction, his unyielding armor of self-rîteousness falls from him shattered, and leaves him humbled and perplexed. It is an unusually keen and delicate psychological study. The other is editor of a London daily paper, and author of a book called 'Martyred Humanity,' a man of consummate ability, not a charlatan. Too often in novels we hav to take the author's word for the cleverness and learning with which certain of his personages ar accredited, but such is not the case here; the reputation of the editor of *The Forum* is fully borne out by his conversation, which is really brilliant." [Westminster Review. **1595**

MY ENEMY'S DAUGHTER. [by Justin McCarthy: Harper, 1870.] "The enemy in question is a very rich, proud and insolent M.P.; and his dauter, if not very new or strange, is very tender, sweet, and true. She is lõved by the hero, a mediocre singer, who has first lõved and lost a german girl, — later a great prima-donna and wife of an italian patriot. Of course Emanuel Banks marries Lilla Lyndon, and the irreclaimable M.P. is duly carried off by the avenging gout of his class. This is the outline, not very surprising or promising, of a singularly good novel, — good enuf in plot, and thõroly good in tone and conduct of character . . . The hero, in whose mouth the story is put, is also pleasant, a manly, generous fello, whom you like. Italian conspirators we do not get on well with, nor with opera-singers of any nation; but we ar bound to say that Mr. McCarthy has managed these contrary people with great skill. No part of the book is dull. A hî level is kept, and the story abounds in neat and truthful touches, capital sketches and studies of persons and places." [Atlantic.] — The leading character is drawn from G: H: Lewes. **1596**

MY FRIEND JIM [by W: E: Nor-ris: *Macmillan*, 1886.] "is certainly one of the author's best stories. Its charm is difficult to analyze, as it lies chiefly in the shrewd yet genial interpretation of human nature. It is realistic in making use önly of the average incidents in life of the kind depicted; and it strains nothing for the sake of romance, allowing the good sömetimes to die young and undeservedly, and the wicked often to triumf so far as this world's goods are concerned. One can hardly tell what the story is, thêre seems to be so little of it when one would sum it up; yet the reader will find nothing more entertaining for a summer afternoon or a winter evening. The style is precisely that of the perfectly unpretentious, straitforward, keen-sīted, yet by no means remarkable young man, who is supposed to tell the story." [Critic.] — "Mr. Norris' brīt and lively story is perhaps the best he has written. It is very unambitious, containing no very striking type of character, and not depending either on any ingenuity of plot or on exciting incidents. But it is a finished _pi_ece of work, both as a novel of ·character and as a narrativ. The simplicity of style and the gentle humor lead one to guess that Mr. Norris has taken Goldsmith as his model, and if that be so it should be added that he has avoided the dangers of imitation. At all events, he has written gracefully and in good taste, and if at times one wishes for a little more vigor, criticism is disarmed by the author's modesty. The principal character is a heartless and entirely selfish woman of the world, but Mr. Norris refuses to be so harsh as to bring even her to a bad end. Here he is doubtless rīt, for the picture would hardly hav been complete if she had not been perfectly successful." [Athen. **1597**

MY FRIENDS AND I [by Julian Sturgis: *Holt*, 1884.] "is a fresh, original and charming contribution to literature. It contains 3 short stories. In the first, — one of those tales of hero-worship always enjoyable and in this case especially so, — the delicious, unconscious egotism of the old fello supposed to be telling the stories is wonderfully well sustained. Thêre is little plot to any of the stories: but the breezy style, and the gentle, genial tone which the real author manages to giv while quoting the narro one of the supposed author, make the book a wonderfully attractiv one." [Critic. **1598**

MY GUARDIAN. [*Appleton*, 1879.] "We hav found not a little pure and wholesom enjoyment in this story of a little orfan girl. It is simply and sweetly told, and pre-eminently a book for mothers and dauters." [Boston "Literary World." **1599**

MY INSECT QUEEN [*Bentley*, 1869.] "is a fanciful name for a very lit, brīt, readable novel. The story purports to be told by a country doctor, of sufficiently good birth and fortune to make him öne of the gentry. He is a worthy, good-hearted fello, a bachelor, who has the amusing peculiarity of believing that he can marry any, if not every, pretty girl he sees, and he makes filandering löve to all in the nêborhood, in a half-gallant, half-fatherly fashion . . . He is, however, a good fello in spite of being an old coxcomb; and he is 'a gentleman, after all,' as sömebody says of him. He falls into the toils of a little coquette, Miss Monica Greysbrooke, who is very destructiv to the hearts of all the men who come near her, and she herself at last becömes entangled amongst her own snares. She is the 'Insect Queen' regnant over the heart of the doctor at the period of the story. Thêre is an innocent mystery running throu the book, which is cleverly handled; and thêre ar sharp sketches of character and of country society. The story is altogether a clever, pleasant novel." [Athen. **1600**

MY LADY CLARE [by E.. EIL-OART: *F. V. White*, 1882.] " is an extremely readable novel. As the plot is apparent at a glance, thêre is no unfairness in saying that it is based upon the inequitable possession of Hailsham Hall, the property of the Crewe family. Mr. Robert Crewe had run away with his wife to Scotland, whêre the form of marriage thêre valid was duly gone throu. After the birth of Anthony Crewe, the document shoing his legitimacy was lost, and a second ceremony was performed, by the english chaplain of a Continental watering place. Accident reveals this to the younger brother, Charles, who claims the estate, which Anthony, to avoid disgracing his parents, at once surrenders. Later, as the eldest son of Robert Crewe, he succeeds to the fortune of Mr. Vane, his father's old friend. How Dollie Crewe becomes the mistress of Hailsham, how she learns the crime of her mother, Mrs. Charles Crewe, how she loves her cousin Randall, and how all ends satisfactorily, must be gathered from the book. Dollie herself is fresh, natural, and charming." [Spectator. **1601**

MY LADY LUDLOW [by E.. CLEGHORN (STEVENSON) GASKELL. N.-Y., 1882.] " is in sôme respects similar to 'Cranford' [No. 1175]. In the latter the humorous portraits of the circle of quaint old gentlewomen ar doubtless taken largely from life; 'My Lady Ludlow' is probably an imaginativ conception, and to our mind a very charming one; while the humor of the little book, if not so unfailing as that of *Cranford*, is, perhaps for that reason, the more delītful." [Boston "Literary World." **1602**

—— SAME, in *ROUND THE SOFA.*

MY LITTLE GIRL [by WA. BESANT & JA. RICE: *Tinsley*, 1873.] " is as disagreeable a book as one often finds. It is a story reeking in its most innocent passages with brandy-and-soda, and with accounts of black mistresses, mock marriages, illegitimacy, gambling, horse-racing, and every form of evil-doing, which cannot fail to hav a bad effect upon readers who may mistake its vulgarity for profound knoledge of the world, and its offensiv description of human degradation for a valuable picture of human nature and civilized society. It is, in fact, a shocking book, and it is not rendered more tolerable by the mock jocosencss and artificial sentiment with which it is filled." [Nation.] — " Let it be understood at once, that with all its faults, and everything to the contrary notwithstanding, we unhesitatingly recommend this charming little book. It is by turns fantastic, improbable, sentimental, occasionally insipid, too often even disagreeable, and yet it is undeniably interesting. But that is not its only, nor nearly, its greatest charm; it abounds in quaint humor, in beautiful little tender passages, and in exquisit bits of description." [Spectator. **1603**

MY MARRIAGE. [*Roberts*, 1881.] " The story is quickly told: a girl who has married a rich, admirable young man after a short acquaintance, not becaus she loves him, but becaus she believes the arrangement will be of general service to her burdened family, she being ône of a number of dauters in a vicarage, spends her time for several months in acquiring the love which should hav been precedent to the marriage, the only obstacle to the acquisition being her obstinacy and her passionate affection for one of her sisters. Her husband, a model of patience and stupidity, loves her in the grave manner which is becoming in such cases, and after a series of misunderstandings and petty accidents, subdues her somewhat obtuse heart. What renders the reader impatient of this couple is that they are both so unnecessarily blind and incapable." [Atlantic. **1604**

MY MOTHER AND I [by Dinah Maria (Mulock) Craik: Isbister, 1874.] " is sure to hav a greater number of admirers than any other novel this season. We cannot reckon ourselvs amongst them. We hav but little sympathy with the heroin. We regard one-half of the fine-spun sentiment as namby-pamby nonsense, and the other half as mere morbidness. We ar quite aware that in saying this we differ from the rest of the world." [Westminster Review. **1605**

MY NEIGHBOR NELLY. See *NEIGHBORS ON THE GREEN.*

MY OWN CHILD [by Florence (Marryat) (Church) Lean: Appleton, 1876.] " is refined, ladylike, and fully interesting. An orfan girl, left in charge of an utterly unsympathetic maiden ânt, falls in löve with a nêboring student, and a promise of marriage passes between them. The ânt exhausts the resources of tyranny in the effort to subdue the little rebel; but the latter effects her escape, and is married. The happy pâir go to Paris, whêre Hugh dies. The wido goes to her grandfather's, in Ireland, and thêre givs birth to a babe, of whose education the grandmother at once assumes control. When May is grön, she goes with her mother to Bruxelles, whêre they encounter Lord

Annersly. He offers himself to the wido, who loves but rejects him; then to the dauter, who becömes his wife, and soon dies. In Sir John Power and his wife, and Mrs. Delancy, we find some fair character-drawing; and the story throuöut is pervaded by a sad but strong interest." [Boston "Lit. World." **1606**

MY QUEEN [Appleton, 1879.] " is an heiress, and the tale runs on her löve for a poor cousin, Max, — and her money, the barriêr that disturbs its course till she takes a fever in nursing his wretched tenants. Then his pride givs way, the troubles ar cleared away, and the very pretty and well told story comes to its happy end. One may ask why should it hav been written: *Cui bono?* We giv it a welcom, knoing how much our vigor, moral and mental, depends on association with others whose interests and pursuits ar not ours, and that to many this rubbing of minds must cöme largely from books like this, which givs a half-hour's chat with charming people." [Penn Monthly. **1607**

MY TRIVIAL LIFE AND MISFORTUNE [Blackwood, 1883.] " is a work of great ability, by one who observs keenly and sees deeply into character. She has the power of presenting real people. Description and analysis hav not made them mere bundles of qualities and defects — the lay figures which often stand for human nature in the work of even the better sort of novelists. The Trivial Life is passed chiefly at a dull country house. So dull is the house, and so lively is the author's picture of it, that the reader feels oppressed by it himself, and is thêrefore ready to giv to the heroin that warm sympathy which a skilful writer must always try to get. Tho she endures the life shado, as no man could hav endured it, she suffers terribly from its crushing monotony, its aimless punctuality, the repetition of the same useless occupations, the ever-recurring remarks about the weather, and the daily wonder as to whether what happens every day will happen again. Worst of all, however, is the evangelical piety of the ånt who, subject to the absolute authority of her maid, is mistress of the house." [Athenæum. **1608**

MYSTERY OF MRS. BLENCARROW (The). [by Ma. Oliphant (Wilson) Oliphant: *Blackett*, 1890.] " A sketch thröu off by a practised hand should hav had a little more *motif* than we can find in the rather sordid mystery of Mrs. Blencarrow. The misery of a sensible and withal sensuous woman who has contracted a secret marriage with a handsom dullard cannot be and is not overdrawn in the story of this unhappy lady. Kitty Bircham is lifelike, as far as she goes, but she is rather a slît Miss Hoyden. Thêre is no moral in the story, which is so far well; but it is somewhat sad, and not so suggestiv as usual." [Athenæum. **1609**

NAME AND FAME. [by A. S. Ewing Lester and Adeline Sergeant: *Bentley*, 1890.] " The authors hav endeavored, with more success than mît hav been expected, to justify a bold step across conventional boundaries. Lettice Campion avows to Alan Walcott, a married man, that she will cõme to his arms whether or not he obtains the divorce he is justified in seeking. Alan, a poet and a man of hî refinement, has been put for years to the most terrible torture by an unfaithful and malignant wife; he has suffered unjustly at the hands of the law as the result of her violence and deliberate falsehood; in Lettice he has found his equal in mind and his superior in generosity anl candor; Lettice

has believed in him when his life was shadoed by disgrace, and has braved hostil opinion by receiving him when released from prison, and when he had not another friend in the world; and to these circumstances of inducement may be added the all-important fact' that Lettice is in lõve." [Athenæum.] — The original of the hero (as in " My Enemy's Daughter," and " Heir of the Ages ") seems to be G: H: Lewes. **1610**

NANCY [by Rhoda Broughton: *Bentley*, 1873.] " pleased the author's established admirers less than any of its predecessors, but had previously undiscovered attraction for readers who had not cared about her former works. Thêre was more heart in ' Nancy,' more true womanhood, and much less suggestion of a mental attitude which mît be described as having its fysical counterpart in slang, hands-in-pocket, cigar-in-mouth, devil-may-careishness. The quick observation, and the odd, piquante way of putting things, which made the author's preceding stories attractiv, wer as fresh as ever in ' Nancy,' and tho the ideal of the story was not a very lofty one, it was hier than its forerunners." [Spectator.] — " Thêre ar plenty of smart things and plenty of amusing things in ' Nancy,' and very few indeed which ar thõroly coarse. Nancy, like all Miss Broughton's heroins, is a girl with a mind above her life, and the history of her young experiences is admirably told, and is full of delineations of every-day adventures of a large family. This part of the book mît be described as the ' autobiografy of a tom-boy.' In the second volume she is wedded, and we hav an equally clever treatment of married life between two persons, both good and true, who hardly suit each other." [Athenæum. **1611**

NEIGHBOURS [by M.. L.. (Stew-

ART) MOLESWORTH: *Hatchards*, 1889.]
" is a graceful study of life in a country
town. Pretty, shy Susie Thicknesse is
ŏne of a motherless family ruled over
by an admirable, but stern elder sister,
anxious abŏve all to keep her flock from
the world and the wickedness thĕreof.
To the quiet place cŏme a family out
of the great world — not wicked, not
even frivolous, but branded in the stern
Lavinia's eyes as titled and traveled.
Susie and her sisters ar drawn towards
the new-cŏmers, and then begins a struggle between the old ways and the new —
silent, but nŏne the less deadly. How
the fĭt is fŏt, and how true worth wins
in the end, Mrs. Molesworth tells in her
charming way." [Athenæum. **1612**
NEIGHBOURS ON THE GREEN.
[by MA. OLIPHANT (WILSON) OLI-
PHANT: *Macmillan*, 1889.] " Several
of these 9 stories ar among the best
things she has written. Tho published
anonymously, the authorship of ' *My
Neighbour Nelly* ' and its successors was
an open secret to any reader with a feeling for style; and the publication of
that exquisit novel ' A Rose in June '
[No. 1743], rendered it obvious to the
outside world, as several characters wer
common to the novel and the short
stories. A general idea of the nature
of the rare treat here provided may
perhaps best be given by saying that in
its pages Mrs. Oliphant dŏes for a quiet,
refined, almost aristocratic rural community, just what Mrs. Gaskell did for
an equally quiet, almost equally refined,
but decidedly less aristocratic urban
community in the pages of ' Cranford.'
[No. 1175; compare also, No. 1231.]
Dinglefield Green is a village ' far from
the noise and smoke of town,' inhabited
by a little colony of well-bred, well-
mannered people who hav somehow
drifted towards the quiet, lŏvely spot,

and, one by one, hav pitched thĕir tents
thĕre. Sŏme of the tents ar more
imposing than others, for tho Sir T;
Denzil at the lodge, and Mrs. Spencer
and Lady Isabella, who liv together
not far away, ar decidedly rich, Mrs.
Stokes and the Merridews ar certainly
poor; while Mrs. Mulgrave, the kindly,
middle-aged chronicler of her nĕbors'
lives, is troubled by neither poverty nor
wealth . . . This story of ' *The Stockbroker at Dinglewood*,' with its opening
of brĭt refined comedy, and its sad,
almost tragic close, has a wider range
than sŏme of its companions, and is, we
think, among the finest, tho it seems
ungracious to make comparisons when
all ar so charming. The tale which
occupies the place of honor is a delĭtful
record of the beginning and end of a
blunder, which, strange as it seems, —
has been made more than once in life,
whĕre it has not always been rectified
so happily as it is rectified here; but
even ' *My Neighbour Nelly*,' graceful
as it is, must yield the palm to the
story of ' *Lady Denzil*,' the dignified, sweet, sympathetic queen of Dinglewood, whose sad secret, kept for
so many years, is so suddenly and
sŏ startlingly revealed. The close of
' *The Scientific Gentleman* ' is powerful, and such stories as ' *Lady Isabella* '
and ' *Mrs. Merridew's Fortune* ' could
not well be better than thĕy ar; but
it is in ' Lady Denzil ' that Mrs. Oliphant's genius touches its hĭ-water
mark." [Spectator. **1613**
NELLY'S MEMORIES. [by ROSA
NOUCHETTE CAREY: London, 1868;
Lippincott, 1880.] " Nelly is an english
girl who is left by her mother's death in
charge of a family of children; and
her experiences relate to the duties,
responsibilities, and trials which she
encountered in that position. Her story

is sweetly told, and has that indefinable but perfectly distinct charm which attaches to so much english fiction of the less ambitious sort." [Boston "Literary World." **1614**
NEW ANTIGONE = No. 862.
NEW GODIVA (A) [by STANLEY HOPE: *Lippincott*, 1880.] "is a novel of full proportions, and of more than ordinary ability and interest, written with a good deal of power and self-command, introducing many pretty little touches of landscape, but characterized chiefly by its strong portraiture of the leading personages, and, in particular, a wife whose devotion to an invalid and unfortunate husband nervs her to a sacrifice in his behalf which few true women would offer. The nature of the offering we will leav the reader to find out for himself; simply saying that the title furnishes a suggestion of it, and that the point of the story is revealed with the greatest delicacy, and in a way to avoid offense to the most refined and sensitiv taste. The steps by which the wife advances to her supreme resolution, and the thotless and selfish ignorance with which her husband drives her on, ar depicted with great skill and strength. There is something almost pitiless in the fate which crowds them both, but there is a happy ending, and the sorroes of poverty ar forgotten." [Boston " Literary World." **1615**
NEW REPUBLIC (The). [by W: HURRELL MALLOCK: *Spottiswoode*, 1878.] " If cleverness wer the one thing needful in a book, ' The New Republic' would leav little to be desired. Only a man of wit, and of much confidence in his wit, would hav dared plan such a work; but tho the author's interest in his performance flags a little after his brilliant outset, his epigrams ar not exhausted before the close . . .

A young man of fortune and distinction assembles at his sea-side villa a party comprising the chief leaders of english thot, — some typical representativ of each of the contending schools. The disguises ar so thin that even the american reader is in no danger of mistaking the characters. Matthew Arnold comes under the name of Mr. Luke, Ruskin as Mr. Herbert, Professor Jowett as Dr. Jenkinson, Huxley and Tyndall as Mr. Storks and Professor Stockton, and a certain Mrs. Singleton, who has published rather nauty and enormously silly poems, figures as Mrs. Sinclair. Then there ar Mr. Rose, a præ-Raffaelite poet and critic, presumably Mr. Pater; Mr. Saunders, a particularly tuf and unscrupulous young materialist, identified with Professor Clifford; Lord Allen, a modest and boyish peer, of immense wealth and benevolent purposes; a rather hazy and sentimental Scotchman who has seceded from the kirk to join the ranks of free thot, and suggests G: MacDonald; a charming Miss Merton, who is a devout Romanist; Lady Ambrose, a thoro woman of the world, with manners so delitful that they impart a certain fascination to a positivly defectiv intelligence; Mr. Leslie, the intimate friend of the host, who givs us some of the keenest ' mots ' with which the book is adorned, but who is heart-sick over the death of the woman whom he had loved in secret, and so cannot openly morn; and finally the host himself, Otto Laurence, who also fancies himself in a state of deep disenchantment with ' life, love,' literature, and ' all things,' yet who is swayed by romantic and re-actionary impulses toward Mr. Herbert and Miss Merton. The fact that the author of the volume appears to divide his on languid and fluctuating opinions about equally between these two friends tends rather to confuse the personalities of Leslie and Laurence, but a little care will keep them distinct, and the portrait of Laurence, the host, in the first chapter is one of the most caustic bits in the book." [Atlantic. **1616**

NEWCOMES (The). [by W: MAKE-PEACE THACKERAY: *Smith*, 1855.] "Let us say a word about 'The Newcomes.' The story lingers and loses itself willingly in those bypaths of humor and sentiment which ar worth all the beaten tracks of all the most exciting novels in the world. To enjoy Thackeray demands the palate of a dégustateur, not the gross appetite of a novel-reader, ravenous for plot and incident. To drain a number of the Newcomes at a dråft is to drink Lafitte or Clos-Vougeot in pewter, and to insult your host by swalloing what you ar expected to sip, and pouring down your mouth what you should first taste with the breath of your nostrils. Thackeray's stories, we say, ar to be sipped like the finest and rarest wine; and it is neither to his praise nor to his shame, but simply to his liking, to invite nōne but the epicures of life's various feasts of joys and sorroes to his select table. Only those who hav shed their illusions and passed throu a premature cynicism into a larger and more complete filosofy of life — less bitter and more compassionate, less trustful and more sympathetic, saddened rather than sad, and smiling genially throu unshed tears at human weakness and human vanity — only those can feel the subtle charm of a humorist like Thackeray." [Leader.] — "In 'The Newcomes' whose fortunes it is so pleasant to follo from month to month, as thêy thus acquire a reality, and becōme, as it wer, a part of the actual circumstance of life, Thackeray will undoubtedly con-

vert to his side the many of the gentle sex who hav hitherto refused allegiance to him upon the ground that all his women wer either fools or knaves, while the heroic gentlemen who did not believe that, like Dobbin, all heroes must hav clumsy hands and feet, and be great gawky louts, will find that Thackeray is of their opinion. For, to the ladies, Ethel, if we mistake not, will be lōvely without the weakness which is so deprecated in Amelia, and brave and noble without the subtle knavery of Mrs. Rebecca Crawley. And, to the gentlemen, the father of Clive Newcome will prove to be just such a father as every son would be glad and proud to remember, — such a father as he could never recall, after all the long years of life, and when he saw his ōn grandchildren around him, without an affectionate melancholy quite beyond tears . . . We thêrefore heartily advise all the friends about our chair to enrich their lives with the monthly perusal of this tender and touching, as well as severe and amusing, story. It is a great mistake that it is dull to read stories in numbers. You hav to take life in numbers. You ar compelled to wait patiently until every day is regularly issued. How long ar the dénoûments in coming! How eagerly and delîtedly, or how anxiously and sorrofully, you await the crisis! It is sure to cōme. It cōmes sometimes rather more quickly than you hoped. The story ends suddenly. Two lovers ar married, and go into endless festivity; perhaps you may be one! Or thêre is a bell tolling — perhaps for you! Besides, we hurry on so rapidly that if you wait until the convenient monthly number has swelled into the volumes of a complete work, you ar likely never to find the moment for attending to it. Thêre ar many adherents of this chair

507

who complain bitterly that they hav not read Copperfield, for instance, or Bleak House, becaus they did not read it in numbers when they mīt hav taken it just before dinner, or in the cars, or just before going to bed — in fact, at a hundred times when they would ₄ not think of beginning a book. And lo! after a dozen or score of such spicy hours scattered throu a year, not felt by their loss, but önly by their pleasant gain, the book would hav been read, and read with enjoyment. For it must be remarked, too, that it is quite a peculiar enjoyment. You speculate about the fate of Ethel Newcome — you hope, you ẏear, you doubt, as you do about your cousin Jane, or your nïece, the gentle Annie. You digest the whole matter. You taste the tale drop by drop. You forecast probabilities, you balance chances. The book becõmes a graceful àrabesque around the actualities of life.'' [G: W: Curtis. **1617**

NINE DAYS' WONDER (A) [by HAMILTON AIDÉ: *Osgood*, 1875.] ''is a short and simple story, which presents sõme novel complications, the unfolding of which is very interesting. A rich widoer is living in a village, happy in the possession of a lõvely dauter. During the latter's absence a lady cõmes to him, in whom he recognizes her whom he had lõved in youth. She is still beautiful and fascinating, and the widoer's thõts turn to marriage. Kate, the dauter, cõmes home, and tells her father about a yung officer whom she lõves. Presently this officer arrives, tells Mr. Vavasour his sad history, — how his father was a villain, and how his mother had deserted her husband, fleeing with another man. Mrs. Fitzroy recognizes in him her son; he resolvs, for her sake, and in vue of her probable marriage with Mr. Vavasour to

abandon his suit. But the mother, stained tho she was, would not permit this sacrifice, and with the vows of Mr. Vavasour thrilling in her ears, departs to return no more. So the yung officer and Kate wer married. Thêre is a good deal of pathos in this story, and its pictures of a gossiping nêborhood ar lively." [Boston '' Lit. Worll." **1618**

NO NAME. [by [W:] WILKIE COLLINS: *Low*, 1862.] ''The third class of readers finds its undoubted chief in Mr. Wilkie Collins; here thêre is neither insīt into character, as in the first instance, nor careful imitation of external, as in the second. On the contrary the characters ar moral monstrosities; not shocking önly becaus they ar too monstrous to suggest the idea of their possibility, while the resemblance to life is the very faintest possible, and önly just sufficient to enable author and reader to forget the fictitiousness of the whole . . . We ar forever on the verge of a crash; a look, a word, a pïece of ribbon, a stray envelope, a late train, a talkativ maid, or a careless postman — may at any moment tumble the whole fabric to the ground. We hold our breath til the author has safely landed us in the next secure position, and allows us a few moments' rest before another entanglement, another crisis, another stroke of luck, another fortunate escape . . All this is, we think, a little overdõne in ' No Name :' the reader really gets too flurried, and his attention is too hard-worked, to be compatible with artistic enjoyment. We arrive at the close almost as exhausted as at the end of a difficult cross-road railway journey ; thêre hav been half-a-dozen different trains, any mistake in any õne of which would hav marred our traveling for the day; the carriage which took us to the station was within a second of being too late; we hav been within a few yards of a collision; in each train we hav unexpectedly met an old acquaintance; we hav several times lost our luggage, and recovered it by miracle. All is over now; but ōne's nerves ar shaken, the mind still continues to hope, calculate, prepare for disaster, or devise expedients for success; our host mercifully dismisses us to bed, and our troubles haunt us in our dreams. The thousands who hav devoured ‘No Name’ as it appeared, hav probably experienced the same sort of fluttering spirits, nervous anxiety, and weary restlessness." [London Review. **1619**

NO NEW THING. [by W: E: NORRIS: *Holt*, 1883.] "The story revolvs about the career and fortunes of an anglo-italian boy, who is adopted by the kind-hearted heroin, and the analysis of his pleasure-loving, superficial character is very good. It is his fate, and leads him a strange dance, throu failures and misfortunes and mistakes, and a good many lies, to a queer end. The contrast of his selfish, facile disposition with the stronger and simpler english characters with whom he is thrön in contact is well drawn, as is also the contrast between his subtle half italian intellect and thêir coarser mental fibre. The story is very natural." [Nation. **1620**

NO SAINT. [by ADELINE SERGEANT: *Macmillan*, 1886.] "So true a picture of middle-class life and its religious aspirations is most welcom. The writer has chosen for her central figure a man on an entirely different intellectual platform from hers, and has succeeded in rendering him both interesting and admirable. Added to a fine feminin perception she has a dispassionateness and a sense of humor, tho the latter quality is greatly restrained by the sombre character of the story . . . It is

a fine feature in the writer that she is always ready to recognize the existence of noble qualities under unprepossessing exteriors. Mrs. Crockett, an eccentric and angular little woman, vegetarian, homœopath, teetotaler, and anti-vaccinationist, nevertheless by her acts of unselfishness and delicate reticence fairly proves her kinship with the heroic souls of the earth. The attitude of aristocratic orthodoxy towards bourgeois dissent and vice versâ is pointedly set forth, but with perfect impartiality; and thêre ar sōme admirable chapters describing the false position of a girl belonging to the latter class, who marries into the ranks of the former, but ōing to her husband's death has ‘to accomplish her elevation’ without his help. In short, ‘No Saint’ is a story of remarkable merit." [Athenæum. **1621**

NOBLE BLOOD. [by JULIAN HAWTHORNE: *Appleton*, 1884.] "Nothing is more certain than that Mr. Hawthorne can do very pleasant work, except the fact that for some unconscionable reason he chooses to do a good deal which is very unpleasant. It is a pleasure to record that ‘Noble Blood’ shōes him at his best; not becaus it exhibits weird imagination about things which never wer or ōt to be, but becaus it is human, possible and pretty. This may seem slīt praise to those who would like Mr. Hawthorne to be always Hawthornesque; but in being enjoyable, ‘Noble Blood’ will appeal to a much wider class of readers. The mise-en-scene of the opening chapters is delicious; the genial, breezy, lovely bit of description is follōed by a tale which, if little more than a story, is nevertheless an entertaining story, full of irish humor, and leaving one with an impression that life after all is worth living, and human nature worth lōving." [Critic. **1622**

——, SAME ("Miss Cadogna"). *Chatto*, 1884.

NOBLE LIFE (A). [by DINAH MARIA (MULOCK) CRAIK: *Harper*, 1866.] "The story of a man born cruelly deformed and infirm, with a body dwarfish, but large enuf to hold a large heart and clear brain, — and of such a man's living many years of pain, happy in the blessings which his great wealth and hi rank, and, abŏve all, his noble nature, enable him to confer on every one approaching him, — could hardly hav been told more simply and pathetically than it is in this book, but it mĭt certainly hav been told more briefly. The ŏne slĭt incident of the fiction — the marriage of the earl's protégée and protectress and dearest friend to his worthless cousin, who, having learned that the heirless earl will leav her his fortune, wins her heart by deceit, and then dŏes his worst to break it — occurs when the book is half completed, and scarcely suffices to interest, since it is so obvious what the end must be; while the remaining pages, devoted to study of the earl's character, do not develop much which is new in literature or humanity. Still, the story has its charm: it is healthful, unaffected, and hopeful; and most people will read it throu and be better for having done so." [Atlantic.] — It is "intensely moral in its character, but not healthily moral becaus the goodness of the chief character borders on ' namby pamby.' " [London Review. **1623**

NOR LOVE, NOR LANDS [by CECIL GRIFFITH: *Tinsley*, 1873.] "is a picturesque tale of rustic life. The plot is slĭt, and the characters few; but thĕre is a grafic power in the description of scenes and people which will leav more than one mental fotograf on the reader's memory. The action proceeds

alternately in a decayed mansion, fallen upon evil days and the uses of a farmer's homestead, and a town in the nêborhood. The latter is described principally in its social aspects, which we vue in the hi-polite society of retired tradesmen; the former is more tenderly dwelt upon, being the home of an ancient race, who hav declined to the rank of yeomen, but retain in their adversity sŏmething of the strong character and traditional pride which raised them in old times to prosperity." [Athenæum. **1624**

NORA'S LOVE TEST. [by M.. CECIL HAY: *Harper*, 1877.] " Mrs. Hay differs from a good many writers of fiction in this, that she takes the trouble to invent a complicated plot, whêreas many of her craft seem to regard that part of their occupation as an obsolete and superfluous bit of trouble. She by no means stops thêre, however, for the dry bones of the plot ar hidden beneath a good deal of talk and action. ' Nora's Love Test' concerns itself in a thŏroly new fashion with the persecuted country-girl, ignorant of the world and its ways, as penniless as ŏnly pretty-faced heroins can be, and tells how she is snubbed by envious yung women who notice that Mark always gets her into a corner and talks to her in a lo, earnest voice when they ar singing, but how, not otherwise than as a perfect lady, she manages to say the last word, which is of a sort to confound and abash the would-be snubbers and drive them to shoing before Mark (who draws his ŏn conclusions) how bad tempered the sweet-looking, hily educated Victoria and Genevieve can be. Of course this yung person at the proper time cŏmes into the possession of a large fortune by a series of incidents which do credit to Mrs. Hay's head, and, it may be added, to her heart, for Nora deservs a generous reward for the unflinching way in which she performs the intricate duties of the leading lady of the story. This is not a novel which will be very well knōn a few years hence, unless the supply of novels should miraculously cōme to a sudden end; but for a season it will deserv to be read, and any ōne who does not find it better than 3 novels out of 5 has made a very good selection." [Nation. **1625**

NORTHAM CLOISTERS [*Smith*, 1882.] "is a quiet study of a little provincial university, and the loves and misunderstandings of 8 gentlemen and 3 ladies, who settle down as comfortably at last as the lōvers of the sweet Midsummer Nīt, when the Puck of real life has opened their eyes to their blunders . . . Her style is quiet and meditativ even, as becomes the subject-matter with which it deals, and confirms the promise of 'Alcestis' [No. 582] in that respect. Moreover, it co-exists with a distinct power of working out and analysing still-life, even commonplace character, in a progressiv way which ōne can watch with interest . . . The life in 'Northam Cloisters' is made up of quiet characters and quiet deaths, homely flirtations and misunderstandings; small pólitics, collegiate and ecclesiastic; and a great deal of music . . . The 6 lovers, with another yung lady of a loer class of life interfering at one period, who looks at first as if she mīt be nauty, but soon dispels any such dangerous suspicions, ar all in their ways well drawn, particularly the heroin, Althea, who leaves a sweet and womanly impression." [Spectator. **1626**

NORTHANGER ABBEY. [by J.. AUSTEN: 1816.] "Mr. Payn holds up to admiration the courage of Miss Bronté's remark about J.. Austen's novels: — 'I kno it's very wrong, but the fact is I can't read them. They hav

not story enuf in them to engage my attention. I don't want my blood curdled, but I like it stirred. She strikes me as milk-and-watery, and to my taste, as dull' . . But this imperious craving for a story, this desire to hav the blood 'stirred,' if not curdled, by fiction, betrays a certain puerility of literary feeling, and when it goes so far as to render any clever person insensible to the extraordinary humor and literary piquancy of such a writer as Miss Austen, it really dōes limit their horizon to a very unfortunate extent. Such limits may well be expected of what Miss Austen somewhēre calls 'strong, natural, sterling insignificance;' but they disappoint ōne in Miss Bronté and in Mr. Payn. One passes over it in people remarkable, to use another of Miss Austen's admirable expressions, 'for want of sense, either natural or improved,' but it always shocks one when a man or woman of real imagination confesses to feeling no delīt in those most wonderful and perfeet of all miniature pictures." [Spectator. **1627**

NORTHERN LILY (A). [by JOANNA HARRISON: *Macmillan*, 1886.] "The story of Elsie Ross is ōne of the most touching things we hav lately read, and like all writers who hav the gift of true pathos, Miss Harrison has the keenest appreciation of humor. A 'Lily among Thorns' is the second and more appropriate title of the book, for first in her northern home with her intensely 'dour' and proud but loving father, and afterwards in England among worldly and other-worldly matrons, maids, and men, Elsie's ingenuous purity contrasts with all who surround her. Not that thêre is an unmitigated bad character in the book, nor, if we except some hoidenish girls, is thêre a really vulgar ōne, which is another blessing . . . Her men and women talk exactly as people do talk, and in their talk reveal the great variety of their characters." [Athenæum. **1628**

NOT LIKE OTHER GIRLS. [by ROSA NOUCHETTE CAREY: *Lippincott*, 1884.] " It is a refreshment of soul to turn to anything so brit and sweet as ' Not Like Other Girls ' . . . The story ranks with the best of its kind ; and the kind is a very good one, which leaves would-be filosofy and pretentious theories quite out of sit, and givs us the home life of gentle, hi-hearted maidens. A dauter's devotion, and the old-fashioned fidelity of lōver to lady, still offer worthy opportunities to the novel-writer. Thêre is sōmething curious in the difference in a story of this calibre, by an english hand and an american ōne. The latter is more ambitious, puts more ideas into it, intends to mean more; but the former rounds out and finishes by adding a host of details which make the picture more interesting as well as more beautiful. Sōme people may say the difference is in the life itself, but it is not yet proved that it is not for want of some special faculty, call it perhaps literary patience, which will gather a full store, and then spare no pains to use it all to the utmost advantage." [Nation.] — " The 3 yung women characterized by the title of ' Not Like Other Girls ' ar not, it may be hoped, so very unlike the rest of their sex, after all, since they ar 3 brave, activ, sensible girls with so wholesom a taste for work that while in affluence they make their dresses, and when reduced to poverty turn their talents to account in making dresses for other women, instead of trying to gain a foothold in the overcrowded tho possibly more ' genteel' occupations of governesses or companions . . . How they achieve social suc-

cess, also, in spite of their industrial pursuits, and ar asked in marriage by the cream of the nêboring bachelors, and ar finally restored to affluence by a rich relativ from India, ar mere matters of detail, not essential to the point of the story, but adding to its agreeableness." [American.] — " The story of the Misses Challoner, who ar ' not like other girls,' shōes their unlikeness to their compeers to be merely superior adaptability and cleverness, charm and energy. It is an engaging history of a family, consisting of a mother and 3 dauters, who ar suddenly reduced from easy circumstances to poverty. Thêre is no vagueness in the recital: the girls ar clear headed enuf to see all the difficulties and dangers of their position, and canvass them at ōnce. Altho pretty, refined and clever enuf to hold their place in society, they hav no special accomplishment or talent which mīt enable them to be governesses : so they resolv to turn to account their skill in dress-making ; and this is effectivly done in a little, dull, sea-side town whêre their enterprise makes a nine-days' wonder. There is a cheerful naturalness and good sense about the heroins, and an attractivness besides, which win the reader's liking, and it is inevitable, we suppose, that such pretty damsels should enlist the sympathies of all sorts of gallant knīts who rush to their rescue." [Lippincott's. **1629**

NOT WISELY, BUT TOO WELL [by RHODA BROUGHTON: *Tinsley*, 1867.] " is, comparativly, free from the faults which provoked so much hostil criticism in the author's first novel [No. 1156] . . . The theme of both stories is an unwise and disappointed affection, and in each the leading character is a girl whom lōve has the power of sending into almost mad raptures, and who under its influence, is capable of performing the wildest and most unreasonable of actions. In each story, also, the greatest stress is laid upon the strength and stature, the thews and sinews, of the hero, and a great deal more is said than is at all necessary about his 'vine-tendril hair,' the 'stately column of his throat,' 'the knotted muscles' of his arm, his deep chest, and his broad sholders. Kate Chester, the lady who lŏves too well, is a beauty of the irregular kind, her nose being slītly turned up, and her hair inclining in hue to red. But she is so brīt and animated, and her figure is so charmingly proportioned and so provokingly plump that she wins all hearts, and almost reduces her commonplace sister, Margaret, to despair by carrying off from her all her admirers. Unfortunately for her peace of mind, she gains the affection of a Col. Stamer, and in return she givs him her whole heart. The chief merit of the book — and it is great — lies in the description of her lŏve, of the joy with which at first it fills her being, of the fierce restlessness which it brings upon her afterwards when disappointment begins to overshado it, and lastly of the blank despair to which it surrenders her when all hope of its being rewarded has passed away." [London Review. **1630**

NUGENTS OF CARICONNA (The) [by Tighe Hopkins: *Ward & Downey*, 1890.] "ar all which can be desired by those who enjoy līt character studies divorced from too much plot and incident. The opening chapter is quite delītful, nor is the rest disappointing. It has lately been our fate to read more than ŏne so-called irish novel with no irish flavor about it. But this is distinctly **irish** in feeling from first to last with a whimsical yet not exagger-

ated air which is Erin in essence. The effect is produced by artistic and quite simple means. Thêre is no description in the ordinary sense — the whole thing is conveyed to the reader in the surest and happiest manner. Humor, truth, kindliness of feeling, and good taste ar the principal ingredients. Miss Barbara, who keeps house for her brother Anthony, and Anthony himself, ar an excellent pair. In a certain quality, which we call quaintness, only for want of a less hackneyed word, these two ar not alone. Most of the people in the story ar human, natural, and individual to an uncommon degree, and their talk is like them." [Athenæum. **1631**

OCCUPATIONS OF A RETIRED LIFE (The) [by "E: Garrett," i. e., I.. Fyfie Mayo: *Routledge*, 1868.] "is a very pleasant story, written in an easy, graceful style, abounding in good sayings, in charity, and in common-sense. Thêre is nothing in it which can properly be called a plot, and very little incident, but a good deal of character-drawing very well done, and a good deal of sound reflexion on manners and life. The story is the autobiografy of an old bachelor who has lived in London long enuf to becŏme rich, and then retired into the country and gŏne to house-keeping with his maiden sister, who is *the* character of the book, a somewhat shrewish person in appearance, but in appearance only, her outward sharpness masking a world of inward tenderness . . . Some of the minor characters of the book ar very pleasant, and one of them, at least, Ewen McCallum, the proper hero of the book, and a real hero, is made by a few stray touches to stand out vividly." [Nation. **1632**

ODD COUPLE (An) [by Ma. Oliphant (Wilson) Oliphant: Phil'a,

Porter, 1876.] " portrays a milder and more frequent form of marital unhappiness, which leads to the separation of the husband and wife. The father retains the dauter and the mother takes the son, and both suffer from Mrs. Oliphant's gentle satire, who always writes as if she had observd countless households and was never weary of describing the amusing scenes which took place before her. Her field is a narro ōne; she seldom goes outside of the parlor in her simple but charming stories, but on her ground she is without a rival. She is a worthy successor to Jane Austen." [Nation.   **1633**

O'DONNELLS OF INCHFAWN (The). [by " L. T. MEADE," i. e., E.. Thomasina (Meade) Smith: *Harper*, 1887.] "The plot is conventional, but the characters ar interesting, and fit naturally into the scenes in which they play a part. The author, tho very kind to their virtues, is not blind to those peculiarities which do not exactly endear the **irish** to other nations. The O'Donnell tenantry ar impulsiv, turbulent, absolutely ignorant, and hopelessly lazy. If they could, by honest work, extract subsistence from the land, they would wither in despair. Thêre would be no excuse for begging and picturesque starving, for mysterious conspiracies, and for incredible noise about wrongs. But noise and notoriety hav becŏme essential to them, and with plenty of these, their bliss is completely expressed in such a vision as that inspired by the thŏt that the evicted O'Donnells wer coming to their ŏn again." [Nation.   **1634**

OLD HOUSE IN THE SQUARE (The). [by ALICE WEBER: *Routledge*, 1883.] "Thêre ar sŏme stories which hav the quiet homely merit of a dutch picture, and Miss Weber's is of that order. No involved plot wearies us in its unraveling, no very brilliant sallies dazzle us as we read, but we enter with a certain satisfaction into the life of the Bertrams, and thêre is a gentle charm in the family chronicle. We kno all the children who liv in the old house— giant Roger, fiery Fergus, and dreamy little Jane, on her beloved Peg, or Pegasus, the wooden horse who livs in the attic. We feel that thêy ar all real and we like them." [Athenæum.   **1635**

OLD INIQUITY [by PHŒBE ALLEN: *Sonnenschein*, 1886.] "is a simple and pleasant tale, without pretensions to be anything else. The nauty old man who furnishes it with a name is comical enuf, however malicious; but it is the story of Elizabeth Laurence and her lovers which Miss Allen sets herself to tell. The reader will like Elizabeth, and will tolerate Ivo Carmichael as her favorit and for her sake. He will lâf at the discomfiture of old Richard Smith, and still more at the disappointment which he inflicted on the too sympathetic Mrs. Grey. And he will not be ungrateful for his hour of mild and modest entertainment." [Athenæum.   **1636**

OLD MAN'S LOVE (An). [by ANTHONY TROLLOPE: *Harper*, 1884.] "The 'old man' fell in lŏve with his orfan ward, and she, out of gratitude, promised to marry him, when all the while she had a true lŏver far away, she knew not whêre. Three years before the lŏver had left her, without a word of lŏve spoken between them, and had promised to come back to her, but in all this time she had heard no word from him, and for aut she knew she mît never see him again. Besides, was it certain after all that he loved her? Under these circumstances she promised to marry good Mr. Whittlestaff, old enuf to be her father. The very day she made this promise, who should cõme in to claim her, but the long lost lover. He had been at the diamond fields to make his fortune, and had made it." [Boston "Literary World." **1637**

OLD ORDER CHANGES (The) [by W: HURRELL MALLOCK: *Putnam*, 1887.] "is a novel of considerable ability. The social problem discussed is that of poverty and of the revolt against aristocracy . . . For the rest, the book is decidedly readable; many a point is put with brilliant precision and memorable shrewdness . . . As a story it has sõme merit: its characters ar picturesque, and talk well, and with distinctly preservd individuality; and thêre ar many bits of good observation, as when Miss Consuelo accomplishes sõmething with 'that tact which rarely deserts a woman until she is so much in love that her happiness hangs upon its exercise.' His hero, upon whose words the whole story hinges, is, however, a weak and fickle person." [Overland. **1638**

OLIVE BLAKE'S GOOD WORK [by J: CORDY JEAFFRESON: *Chapman*, 1862.] "is extremely interesting. The plan dões not reveal itself to the guesses of the sagacious reader until he comes face to face with the solution at the author's appointed time . . . With all faults found and objections made, the reader will not fail to read the book from first to last for the sake of the story, and he will return to its pages for the sake of many noble and excellent sentiments which in the interest of folloing the story he may not read with the attention they merit." [Ath. **1638a**

OLIVER'S BRIDE. [by MA. OLIPHANT (WILSON) OLIPHANT: *Ward & Downey*, 1886.] "The incident on which this novel is founded is sad and sordid enuf, the only relief to its sombre character being found in Grace's noble simplicity. Oliver Wentworth, on the

eve of his marriage with Grace, a woman worthy of all devotion, is summoned to the dying bed of an unhappy and unworthy creature, with whom he has had such relations as, now that his conscience is awakened by contact with a hier nature, he dares not ignore. So he goes and marries Alice on her deathbed, with a miserable hope that the sacrifice need not cost him much in time, or in the pain of revelation to the woman who respects as well as lõves him. Alice dões soon release him, but the gratification of her last wish so far revives her for a time that Oliver has to make the confession he shrinks from so unutterably. Grace, in the best manner of womanhood, not õnly forgivs, but approves what she thinks to hav been his duty. [Compare plot of No. 1897.] It is a slît tale, but the picture of a good woman is noble, and should give male readers much food for reflexion." [Athenæum. **1639**

OLIVIA RALEIGH [by W: FOLLET SYNGE: (†, 1891) *Lippincott*, 1877.] "is a pleasing and innocent tale. It is lît and can be read throu in half an hour, but it cannot fail to leave an agreeable impression. This is but little to say about a book, but it is more than nine-tenths of the novels published deserv, and applies with justice to this story, which is neither remarkably clever nor by any means thrilling." [Nation. **1640**

OMBRA. [by MA. OLIPHANT (WILSON) OLIPHANT: *Hurst*, 1872.] "Tho the sorroes and perversities of Ombra occupy an almost undue share, our interest is from first to last concentrated in her charming cousin, an original portrait of a brît yung englishman with a character and a temper of themselvs good enuf to raise a worse book to popularity." [Athenæum. **1641**

ON TRUST [by T: COBB: *Hurst*, 1891.] "is eminently english without being dull, for Mr. Cobb has managed to keep up a good deal of interest in the fortunes of his characters till the end. One may feel that it is just a little too 'kept up,' as it wer, and that certain things which occur to delay the dénoûment ar forced rather than inevitable; yet thêre is cause for gratitude all the same. The leading situation is not a bad one for a novel of the kind, and is not so overworn by constant use and misuse, that the mere introduction of it sets the reader yawning. On the contrary, he gets interested in the drama and this in spite of some improbabilities in its working and a little not unnatural confusion at the close. The heroin is a nice creature, and thêre ar others who interest becaus they ar natural and well drawn. Mrs. Swanley is rather humorously dõne, tho occasionally too farcical. On the whole, 'On Trust' is anything but dull." [Athenæum. **1642**

ONCE! TWICE! THRICE! AND AWAY! [by MAY PROBYN: Remington, 1878.] "is a pretty little lõve-story. It is that and nothing more, for thêre is no plot, no character-drawing, and no incidents except those which mark the course of a romantic courtship and a runaway match. A yung artist cõmes to a nobleman's country-seat to paint the portraits of his lordship's dauter and nefew, who ar engaged to be married. He saves the heiress' life, falls in lõve with her, talks over her mother with great ease, and wins her affection; and, in the most ingenuous manner, the two lovers take matters into thêir õn hands, cut the knot which has fettered many more skilful folks than they, and marry. All this will sho clearly enuf that Miss Probyn is a novice at the art of fiction; but thêre ar sûfficient grace and tenderness in the romance of Dudley Wyld and Diamond FitzOswald to make one pass litly over

the improbabilities and incompleteness 'of the rest of the story.'" [Ath. **1643**

ONE ANOTHER'S BURDENS [by M.. E. MANN: Bentley, 1890.] "is a pretty and carefully written story. Libbie Strong is a healthy and natural yung creature, who tells her sister the most refreshing home truths. Mr. Elgard is a fair success in the matter of villains. Miss Mann fortunately relents so far as to end with the happy and long-deferred marriage of two of the martyrs, tho with incorrigible obstinacy her last word is a morbid question as to its advisability, most inappropriately placed in the mouth of our courageous and cheerful yung friend." [Athenæum. **1644**

ONE OF OUR CONQUERORS. [by G: MEREDITH: Chapman, 1891.] "Mr. Meredith has great merits, as we all kno, and it has long been the pride of his admirers — we mĩt call them his enthusiasts — to aver that while his writings ar caviare to the general, they ar nutritious to the superior mind. Nutriment, however, both for mind and body, may be so conveyed as to ɓe almost impossible to swallo, and Mr. Meredith's tales, and very notably this one, is written, it must sadly be confessed, in such a florid, inflated, execrable style that it would take a very much better story than the present õne to atone for it. Story, indeed, would seem to be the very last thing the author aims at, the book being simply a theme on which may be hung variations of fraseology." [L. B. (C) Walford.]—" 'One of our Conquerors,' by G: Meredith, will be liked by a certain class of readers only; the class which likes G: Meredith's novels. To others the hard cracking of the nut will not be paid for by the quantity of the meat within, however superior its quality. These novels may be taken as the intellectual tonic their devoted admirêrs claim them to be; but few people take tonics for pleasure, and none savor them with satisfaction. Meredith givs us character, and he givs us emotion, but all so piled hi with verbiage, actual verbiage, even tho intellectual, that ' character' is pressed flat and proportionless, and emotion squeezed dry of all effect. The present story has all the Meredith mannerisms. The wise people chop logic after the manner of sausage machines; the foolish ones never escape the presence of their pet foolishness, whatever it may be." [C. Tribune.] — " The initiated may be left to analyse the elements of greatness in this book. To the reader bred on intelligible literature, the game seems hardly worth the candle. He finds characters enigmatically named whose story, simple in its main lines, is so swathed in envelopes of fräses which constantly suggest occult meaning as to make him wonder if he is not at work upon the inversion of a parable. The book is apparently loaded to the muzzle with meaning, and the result is likely to be nearly fatal to the innocent reader who touches it off." [Atlantic. **1645**

ONE OF THREE [by JESSIE FOTHERGILL: (†, 1891) *Holt*, 1881.] " consists of two stories, of which the first is decidedly the best. The plot is the not unusual ōne of a lōvely heiress disguised as the governess of a sickly and exacting boy; but the story is treated with originality, and possesses at least one very unusual feature in the fact that the hero is not the best man of the book. Moreover, the marriage is neither the ideally blissful one of old-fashioned romances, nor the miserable one of more modern fiction; the hero is simply the man whom the heroin lōves. The second story is *Made or Marred* [No. 1506.]" [Critic. **1646**

ŌNE OF US. [by EDMUND RAN-

DOLPH: *Low*, 1882.] "'The talk is excellent all throu. We cannot recall anything quite like it, with the same mingling of good breeding, 'irresponsible chatter,' and wit so deftly placed that it seems frankly accidental, except the talk in a novel by the late Count Jarnac, called ' *Dark and Fair*,' probably quite unknōn to the present generation, but which is an extremely entertaining book. We could not exactly describe why it is that Mr. Lessenden reminds us of Sir Charles Rockingham, and the banter of ' One of Us ' of the wide-ranging, witty absurdities of Cammy, Vinny, and the incorrigible but irresistible Lord Walter of that novel; we ōnly kno that we hav never enjoyed any book since ' Dark and Fair' in precisely the same way that we hav enjoyed ' One of Us.' Of course, the tone of Mr. Randolph's story is more large and liberal, and its dramatis personæ ar more various and representativ. Sir Charles Rockingham would never hav thōt of admitting a Yankee tourist to his learned and leisurely retreat, and no Yankee tourist would hav knōn what to do, had he found himself thêre. Mr. Randolph introduces a delītful Yankee at Haversham, likewise an Irishman, of whom we deeply regret to see so little; and a certain Skipwith, who has not been approached since Major Pendennis' time. Not that he is like Mr. Thackeray's masterpiece, but that he is as good in his way, and for so much, or so little, as we see of him. And then thêre ar the ladies, — Mrs. Indigo Smythe, who is a charmingly natural, frank, clever creature, much oppressed by her gorgeous, golden-calf-like condition, but with a fine talent for organization and ' mise en scène ;' the two scheming women who do the mystery and mischief of the story . . . Mrs. Golightly is a gem. She is not absolutely novel; she

517

has been sketched before, but rarely with such fidelity, impartiality, and moderation . . . Thus happily introduced, Mrs. Golightly is, as may be supposed, a delītful element in the story, which is at once more and less than a story, being a singularly fascinating book." [Spectator.   **1647**

ONLY THE GOVERNESS. [by Rosa Nouchette Carey: *Bentley*, 1888.] " Miss Carey's novels may be compared to a tranquil backwater out of the main current of the turbid stream of modern fiction. The graces and charities of domestic life ar treated by her with never-failing sympathy and refinement. It is not that she closes her eyes to the existence of evil or suffering, for in the pages of her new novel the general placidity of the story is varied by occasional passages in the minor key, so to speak. ' Only the Governess ' has no dwelling on the sordid or repulsiv actualities of life. The female characters largely predominate; indeed, Miss Carey has given us a whole gallery of portraits of womanhood in its most gentle and attractiv fāses. The hero and good genius of the story has hardly a redeeming vice. The style is that of a cultivated writer throuŏut." [Athenæum.   **1648**

ORANGE LILY [by May Crommelin: *Hurst*, 1879.] " is really a charming story, ŏne which, without any surprise in its plot, by simple power of description and vivid presentment of character, arrests and holds fast the attention. The writer has a quite uncommon skill in using both humor and pathos; thêre will be but few readers who will not find both tears and lâfter at hand while they read . . . The interest of the heroin's life centres in a love, which groes with her grŏth, for a cottager's son who has to struggle with the

difficulty of social inferiority, and who manfully overcomes it. Nothing could be better drawn in its way than the ' Lily's ' sweet and gentle steadfastness; and Tom is a specimen of the best type of northern irishmen. The minor characters, the gentle ladies of the Hall, the noisy, kindly stepmother, and ' big John,' the ruf, honest lover, who seeks, but in no dishonorable way, to fill the place of the absent Tom, ar all excellently sketched. This is a book far abŏve the average." [Spectator.   **1649**

ORDEAL FOR WIVES (The) [by Annie Edwards: *Hurst*, 1864; N. Y., *Sheldon*, 1878.] " is far inferior to Mrs. Edwards' later stories, and bears much stronger resemblance to the sensational novels of Rhoda Broughton than to any better models. But thêre is besides much of the humor, of the keen observation, which make her later writings so very readable." [Nation.   **1650**

ORDEAL OF RICHARD FEVEREL (The) [by G: Meredith: London, 1859.] " givs us the history' of a motherless boy who is reared by his father, according to an exact ' system' founded on carefully framed theories. Sir Austin is a man of formula; every fāse of human expression is summed up in epigrams and antitheses. His hobbies ar many, but as a parent he proceeds to train Richard on the principle that a boy should be kept ignorant and thêrefore innocent; he should enjoy entire freedom within certain bounds, so as to giv his powers and ambitions free play, but must be watched and garded by a neverceasing espionage, in order that he shall imbibe no idea concerning the mysteries of a man's existence. When he approaches the age of 18, every effort is made to prevent his finding any suggestions of lŏve and love-making in his surroundings, or any temptation to meet anything youthful and pleasing of the feminin kind. Nature abhors a vácuum, however, and this void is filled. At the very moment Sir Austin intends to lay the top brick on his ' system ' Richard falls in lŏve, and in spite of every obstacle marries against his father's will. The remainder of the story is unnatural in situation, complex in treatment, and the end is grievous. The novel may enforce a strong moral, but it pushes to extremes the desire to pluck good out of evil." [American.] — " It is a story with a most comic beginning, and a most tragic end. Thêre ar many characters which ar almost perfectly drawn, if we allow for the medium used and peculiar treatment which the artist adopts. Among them, the reader cannot miss those of Adrian Harley, the old nurse, Berry, and the yung scapegrace, Ripton. The book is certainly not what Mr. Meredith calls elsewhêre of the ' rosepink' order. It occasionally treats of or alludes to subjects which ar very important, but ar as rarely met in novels as they ar frequently met in life. Yet it is not realistic, tho it mĭt in sŏme quarters be deemed morbid." [Spectator.] — It is " a book which, we cannot forbear to say, ŏt never to fall into the hands of a boy or girl, or of any ŏne in sickness or depression of mind. The result will inevitably be bad." [Boston " Literary World." **1651**

ORLANDO. [by CLEMENTINA BLACK : *Smith*, 1880.] The heroin " has reveled in the woman's triumf of being coveted by coveted men; and then at last she herself begins to covet too late. Yet throuŏŭt she dŏes not cease to claim our respect, whilst her story touches us more deeply than that of any of the men and women with whom she is brŏt in contact. She remains pure and lovable to the end, even when, with

a supreme effort, she puts aside the cup of consolation which Orlando holds to her lips. For a moment, by the last deceit which lŏve has power to practise on her heart, she dreams that she may be happy . . . Thêre is a pathetic charm in Miss Black's stories which must compel the sympathy of her readers. ' Orlando' has beauties, and even blemishes, which wer not clearly manifested in the earlier work, but it is distinctly a clever, wholesom, and affecting romance." [Athenæum. **1652**

ORLEY FARM [by ANTHONY TROLLOPE : *Chapman*, 1861.] " is, we think, the most interesting, as it is certainly the most powerful and the most carefully finished of Mr. Trollope's novels. In spite of a good deal which is tedious, and more that is commonplace, the story is well conceived, and its details worked out with marvellous industry. Readers of all classes will delĭt in Sir Peregrine and his grandson, Judge Stavely and his dauter, the tragi-comedy of Mr. and Mrs. Furnival's ' querelle de ménage,' and the broad fun of the Christmas festivities in Great St. Helens. But it is on the character of Lady Mason that the author has expended the most study, and which is worked out with his best dramatic efforts. Opinions will differ as to his success, and still more as to the possibility of developing such a character in the midst of such surroundings. For us, we cannot think it altogether successful. Lady Mason cŏmes before the reader as a woman oppressed for 20 years by the secret consciousness of a crime; we ar told of her extraordinary strength of character and of her devoted lŏve for the son for whose sake her crime was committed, and we ar made to feel that her beauty of person and a certain irresistible attractivness win for her a place in the dry heart of Mr.

Furnival, her counsel, the romantic love of poor old chivalrous Sir Peregrine, and the beautiful affection of Mrs. Orme. It may be that, as the reader suspects her guilt from the first, he is intended to feel the contrast between the outward woman, whom all love and respect, and the inner blīt upon the soul, which makes him dislike while he pities. At any rate, this is the result; we see only a poor wretch, whose power over the hearts of the good and' pure we believe, but do not understand . . . How far it is consistent with the true principles of art to associate a crime [forgery] and its frītful and inevitable fruits with careful fac-similes of the decorous and prosaic characters which Mr. Trollope knoes so well how to draw, we hav no space to discuss. But whatever may be its faults, thêre ar scenes and passages in 'Orley Farm' which abundantly sho that the author can touch the finer and more plaintiv chords of the heart with a true and delicate hand, as well as exhibit to an unpoetical generation its lineaments in unadorned and unmitigated simplicity." [Westminster Review. **1653**

OUGHT WE TO VISIT HER? [by ANNIE EDWARDS: *Sheldon*, 1872.] " is ōne of the best novels which has appeared in a long time. The heroin is Jane Theobald, who before her marriage was a dancer, or about to become one,—at any rate of origin and associations altogether bohemian. The people who will not visit her ar the relativs of Mr. Theobald, and all the respectable people in Chalkshire, among whom he takes her to liv after a free, happy, hap-hazard life on the Continent. [Compare plot of No. 1634.] It would be a pity to tell the story, further than to say that the pretty, good-hearted, witty, charming victim, shunned for no reason by these good people, and deserted by her

worthless husband, who takes up an old flirtation with an old reprobate finc lady to beguile the dulness of Chalkshire, cōmcs near being driven into wickedness, but is saved on the way to elopement by one of those sudden fevers which lie in wait in novels, and is reconciled to her husband, and joyfully leaves Chalkshire with him and goes back to thêir free life on the Continent. Dull respectability and convention ar too much for them, and they must fly or be crushed; yet she has done no wrong. The merit of the story is in the clearness with which Jane's character is portrayed as of that strength and simple goodness and fidelity which perhaps as often go with a fair face as with a plain one; and in the evident reality of the pictures of society. Since Thackeray we do not kno better studies of social meanness and feebleness; and all is done with temperance and self-restraint wonderful in woman." [Atlantic. **1654**

OUR LITTLE ANN [*Roberts*, 1886.] " is a pleasant little story by an author who has an eye for the kindlier attributes of the race and could not make a villain if she tried, much less introduce one into her households of gentle mothers, brotherly brothers, and the friendliest of people who rescue such estrays as the simple Ann. Thêre is a vein of sentiment running throu her, of which she seems half shy and half ashamed, making a pretty mockery of it, but blending it in most fittingly with the lovers of Will and Ann, and with the idyllic life of Ann at Filbert Farm, her fondness for the boy Hal, his fealty to her and the tenderness of the old man who livs his lost youth over again in this little irish governess. Thêre is a sweet and pure atmosfere about the book; pictures of a genuin home, tho a humble one, in London, and also of rustic living amidst the delīts of country ways and scenes; and the influence leads to more confidence in human nature and a feeling that the world is not so bad as has been represented." [Boston "Literary World." **1655**

OUR MUTUAL FRIEND. [by C: DICKENS: 1805.] "The 'Boffin, Wegg, and Venus business' is no doubt full of farce, but of farce so excellent, so genuinly lâfable, that it would take us back almost as far as Martin Chuzzlewit to eõme upon anything of Dickens' production more admirable after its kind. On the other hand, Mr. Ward is not half severe enuf when he says, 'What sfere or section of society would feel itself especially caricatured in the Veneerings or in thêir associates, — the odious Lady Tippins, the impossibly brutal Podsnap, Fascination Fledgley, and the Lammles, a couple which suggests nothing but antimony and the Chamber of Horrors? Caricature such as this, representing no society which has ever, in any part of the world, pretended to be good, corresponds to the wild rhetoric of the superfluous Betty Higden episode against 'the gospel according to Podsnapery;' but it is in truth satire from which both the wit and humor hav gone out. An angry, often spasmodic, mannerism has to supply thêir place.' This is true enuf, but it dões not express half adequately the sense of disgust which this ostentatiously self-rīteous bit of vulgar and flaunting moral satire produces on the mind. It is not merely that it is so bad, but that the author is so pleased with himself, almost in such rapture with himself, for every dull or heavy stroke of his brush. He givs himself all the airs of a noble evangelist, while he shões the vulgarity of this sleekly-bad society in a travesty at least as purblind and dreary as the conventional selfishness and hard-heartedness which he was seeking to expose. Thêre is something in Dickens, when he abandons his part of humorist to play that of a spiritual purifier, which is to our mind beyond measure repellant. More than self-confident, at once shõy and shabby in his moral make-up, at once proud of his spiritual functions, and without éven an incidental flash of that self-suspicion and self-distrust which alone could hav enabled him to fulfil them." [Spec. **1656**

OUR VILLAGE. [by M.. RUSSELL MITFORD: Low, 1840.] "We hav often wondered that this, one of the most charming books of country life which has ever been written, has been so long suffered to remain inaccessible, — not forgotten, indeed, by the older generation, who must remember its brīt, loving descriptions of rural life, whether animate or inanimate, but unknõn to the yunger . . . The cheery, cultured lady, with her inseparable comrade, the greyhound May, is a delītful companion." [Spectator. **1657**

OVERMATCHED. [*F. W. J. Baker*, 1877.] "This is a clever, well-written story. An elder son is disinherited and robbed of the property which the late repentance of his father would hav given to him, by the wickedness of the yunger brother's wife. The tale of how things ar brôt rīt, how the promis is kept which the injured man has exacted from his son that he will never consent to enjoy the ancestral estate, except in his rīt — for it has cõme into the hands of an heiress, the yunger brother's dauter, — all this is told with excellent effect." [Spectator. **1658**

OWEN GWYNNE'S GREAT WORK. [by AUGUSTA NOEL: *Macmillan*, 1875.] "Owen Gwynne is a painful scholar, smitten late in life with the 'cacöethes scribendi' and urged to exertions beyond his power by an ambitious wife. Both ar pathetic portraits, tho their selfishness is combined with much not ungenerous self-deception, and the woman, at any rate, is buoyed up by hope and a pride which is not selfish. To enable the bodily machine to stand the strain of authorship, this anxious couple call their artist son from Rome, and make him exchange for humble bread-winning as a banker's clerk, the career which is dearer to him than anything but duty. Lance is a fine character, tho the touch of dourness inherited from his mother mars the grace of his self-sacrifice, and in the crisis of his life makes him unforgiving to a woman whose fault arose from loving much. Readers will be moved to sorro by Mary's death, and as infinitly relieved as was Owen when the too precious 'History of the Fifteenth Century' is lost in a shipwreck, and all hearts gladdened except poor Mrs. Gwynne's by the removal of the family." [Athenæum.] — "A novel like this, in the modern tumult of hï-colored fiction, is like a bit of blue in a thunderous sky. It is a novel of a thousand, and fame is the just reward of its writer. Very quiet it is, and in its later pages, very sad; but a refined grace pervades it, whose charm never relaxes. It is full of gentle wisdom, set forth with a singular eloquence of laconism; thêre is hardly a superfluous word in its pages, and not a fräse or figure which will not bear the test of criticism. In artistic and literary respects, it is a nearly perfect book." [Boston "Literary World." **1659**

PAIR OF BLUE EYES (A). [by T: HARDY: *Holt*, 1873.] "No just novel-reader can complain that he has not full measure of most delicious love-making, in this very pretty story. In fact, thêre is no stint of that mental sweet (if it *is* mental), and the quality is so delicate that it dões not cloy. But the author had need to lavish it with a generous hand, for he brings his romance to but a sad close at last, of which we feel it our duty to forewarn all tender-hearted readers, who do not want character, or life, or subtile analysis, but marriage, and marriage and again marriage, in a novel. To be sure thêre is marriage in A Pair of Blue Eyes; but it is not the marriage of the two people who ôt to marry; the author effects a compromise; the heroin marries the wrong person — and dies. We try to carry it off lïtly, but we will privately õn that poor, pretty Elfrida's fate has been an affliction to us, and that we would willingly hav had her innocent guile, her simple duplicity, bring her to a happier if less probable end than they do. Her character is nearly all thêre is of the book, tho neither of her lovers is drawn with a touch wanting in distinctness . . . She has no pride, she has only love; she has no arts save in love . . . We cannot giv any just idea of how gracefully and modestly all this pure analysis of character is managed . . . The charm, the sweetness, the tenderness of the story ar not excelled by its truth; and for a good, solid, intolerable bit of tragedy, we commend its close as sõmething which may almost stand beside the close of Liza." [Atlantic. **1660**

PARIAH (The). [by F: ANSTEY [GUTHRIE]: *Smith*, 1889.] "The character who givs the title to the book is the yung man, Allen Chadwick, the underbred, neglected son of a vulgar father, who, finding himself in middle-age a man of wealth, determins to take his boy out of the sordid surroundings in which his early years hav been spent, and giv him a position to which, as he imagins, his ōn money entitles him. Chadwick père is, however, compelled to realize the force of the homely proverb about the silk purse and the sow's ear. He makes the acquaintance of a well-bred, worldly, impecunious wido with her eldest dauter Margot, and the father and mother, inspired by motivs superficially different but essentially identical, conspire to bring together the loutish lad and the beautiful, proud, wilful girl, whose charms eclips her faults, save in those moments when her faults blind us to her charms. The scheme is a failure, and as an alternativ method of establishing himself and son in good society, Mr. Chadwick marries the wido, and Allen finds himself ōne of a family by every member of which he is more or less openly detested and despised. The situation is a pathetic one for the poor lad, uncivilised cub as he is, raised from the region of contempt into the region of sympathy by an obvious doglike devotion, and a latent capacity for heroism, and even for real refinement of chivalry. The combination described thus briefly may seem somewhat unreal, but the portrait as drawn at full length by Mr. Anstey is a triumf of harmonious art . . . The picture is powerful, but it is too painful; we ar harroed all throu, and imaginativ compensation is ruthlessly denied us." [Spectator. **1661**

PARISH OF HILBY (The) [by—( ) Mann: *Stock*, 1883.] " is a sensible, characteristic, and thōroly entertaining ' story of a quiet place.' It is refreshingly straitforward. The picture of still life in the heart of an english county may not be particularly attractiv for the lovers of intensity in tone and color, but it is very careful painting nevertheless. She givs some glimpses

of the ' merry England' of our day which will charm the majority of her readers. Few more genuin or delītful romances hav recently made their appearance.'' [Athenæum. **1662**

PARLEY MAGNA. [by E: Whitaker: *Smith*, 1876.] " We really think thêre ar few readers, however blasés, who could easily put down this book without finishing it. It contains plenty of tokens of original thôt and careful writing, and, moreover, is instinct throuōut with an honest and commendable purpos. Altho the amusing denizens of the gossiping village furnish matter for thôt apart from the main interest of the story, it is in the history of Arthur's character, as developed by the refining fires of passion resisted and temptations overcōme, the simple but not unheroic triumf of a pure and generous nature over the stumbling-blocks which warm imagination and soft-heartedness cast in its path, that the best part of that interest will be found." [Athen. **1663**

PARSON GARLAND'S DAUGHTER. See *TWO MARRIAGES.*

PASSION IN TATTERS (A) [by Annie (Thomas) Cudlip: *Chapman*, 1872.] " is certainly a book which cannot fail to be entertaining. The author has a happy knack of introducing a variety of totally distinct characters. We hav the fast yung lady of the bohemian type, — the vacillating but enthusiastic artist, distraut by loving in the wrong place, — the traveled yung gentleman of ' god-like beauty ' — the stately old lady, full of kindly impulses, — the crafty governess, — and the professedly religious but uncharitable wife of a country vicar; and all ar admirably depicted . . . The plot is well carried out and you ar brôt only to the brink of the precipice. The authoress does not admit a breach of the 7th com-

PASSAGES FROM THE LIFE OF MRS. MARGARET MAITLAND [by Mr. OLIPHANT (WILSON) OLIPHANT: 1849.] is "a book which charmed and soothed us when we wer young, and which we can read over stil on summer days and winter nights with undiminished satisfaction. Mrs Margaret Maitland is no echo and no wraith, but a real living woman, set in the midst of the loving, hoping, fearing, stirring little world of a Scotch rural parish. The plaçe in ôur regard that dear old lady of Sunnyside originally achieved she keeps, and we think of her always as a person whŏm we hav knŏn. Her story is very simple, but her way of telling it is delightful; and when, after the lapse of a few years, she takes up the thread of it again, and in *Lilliesleaf* [No. 1474] relates the married trials of the dear bairns whŏse early days ar the britest passages in her ŏn life, we take it up with her, and listen tŏ the story as if it conçerned personal friends. It is a grêat merit in a writer when she can thus compel us tŏ realize her characters, and it is a power which Mrs. Oliphant possesses in a very hĭ degree. Mrs. Maitland has had her griefs, and very bitter they ar, but the main story is that of her brŏther's children, Claud and Mary, at the manse of Pasture-Lands, and of Grace, a little lassie whŏm she rears in simple, pious ways, quite unwitting that her charge is an hêiress. In her sweet bright maidenhood Grace is reclaimed by her selfish father, and put under the care of his fashionable sister, tŏ be mysteriously suppressed, and, if possible, bullied out of her inheritançe which is derived from her il-used mother. Grace, however, bêars a hĭ spirit, and having discŏvered the truth she calmly resists her persecutors. We ar very indifferent tŏ this part of her adventures. She is much more at home at Sunnyside than in Edinburgh; and her heârt being given tŏ Claud Maitland before she is carried away, she returns eventually in triumph, having defeated wicked father, bad ânt, and foolish suitor, with her gardian's commands not tŏ quit Sunnyside again at anyŏne's bidding but his; and whŏ should this gardian (a sarcastic old bachelor) be, but the lost lŏve of Mrs. Margaret Maitland! Between Claud and Grace thêre ar no difficulties but such as true lŏve makes light of, and soon overcŏmes; but between Mary and Allan Elphinstone thêre ar wêighty obstructions, fears, and sorrŏs of his ŏn causing, and which we kno wil hav thêir sequel when the twŏ ar married, and the first series of the Sunnyside Chronicle ends. During the interval which elapses before Mrs. Margaret Maitland again takes up her pen the clouds hav begun tŏ gather about the house of Lilliesleaf; and that she has a prescience of them is clear, from the saddened strain in which she resumes her narrativ . . . At sight of the young generation of 'Miss Mary's four darlings', 'Miss Marget' catches sŏme of her old servant's cheerful and wise philosophy. Was thêre ever a sweeter picture than this, tho you see the shado of an invisible trouble in the bacground of it? . . . Thêre is heartache in the story of 'Lilliesleaf,' but not heartbrêak, for lŏve abides stil between the ŏne whŏ strays away and those whŏ stand fast by duty." [British Quarterly. **1663 v**

mandment; neither is thêre anything coarse. She delineates the working of the female mind with an artistic touch, and we congratulate her on having produced a novel which is fit to be read." [Athenæum. **1664**

PASSION'S SLAVE. [by R: ASHE KING: *Appleton*, 1890.] "Thêre ar sõme novels — not too many — in which the good characters ar good, but the bad ar merely indifferent. Such is 'Passion's Slave,' its hero, the 'slave' in question, being a very respectable yung land-õner; the Vicar, his nefew, and the Vicar's nîece Kate, amiable and mildly interesting; but the yung landlord's wife and her lover as dull as vicious folk generally ar in life. But in Biddy Devine the author has touched a point abõve what yung ladies, to whom novels ar a necessity of life, mît be supposed to be content with. Biddy is a gem of the purest water, who shines amid the troubles of the Carew family like a diamond set in bog-oak. Her simplicity in dealings with the butcher and the grocer, her broad vues on money matters, her lack of conscience — what should she, or an angel, do with a conscience? — her superstitious terrors and ingenious speculations about the powers and immunities of irish banshees on english soil, mît redeem a dull book wer it conceivable that the writer of such a book could hav created her. The author dões not overtax her capacity in making her do double duty, accounting for the success of his heroin's novel, and warming and illuminating his õn." [Critic. **1665**

PATRICIA KEMBALL [by ELIZA (LYNN) LINTON: *Chatto*, 1874.] "has the first merit of a romance: it is interesting, and it improves as it goes on . . . We advise our readers to send for it." [Athenæum. **1666**

PATTY [by K.. S. MACQUOID: *Harper*, 1871.] "is a novel of more than ordinary merit. It is the story of a yung girl in humble life, who suddenly becõmes rich. Just before this stroke of good fortune she had met an artist, who, fascinated by her remarkable beauty, asked her to be his wife. She lõved him or thõt she did, and they wer betrothed. Becoming a rich woman, she repelled him, and, going abroad, gained a passable education, and soon married a wealthy gentleman. By chance the artist, who was married to a lõvely girl, is employed to paint her portrait. She endeavors to reassert her dominion over him, and sõme serious complications ensue, which ar described entertainingly. The characters of Patty and Nuna ar drawn with much skill, and the closing pages of the story ar intensely interesting." [Boston "Literary World." **1667**

PAUL FABER [by G: MACDONALD: *Lippincott*, 1879.] "is an activ, able atheist, whose hiest life is his profession, and the book describes his gradual conversion by means of the severe experiences of his life, applied and explained by the clergyman of the parish. He is called to see a beautiful stranger whom he finds at his second visit almost dead from loss of blood. He transfuses blood from his arm and saves her life. He falls in lõve with her, and, knoing nothing of her antecedents, marries her. After a time she is wrõt up to confess to him that she has been another man's mistress. He rushes away and when he returns finds her gône. He endeavors to put a good face on the matter, and to go about his work as usual, but falls into a severe illness and suffers in every way, discovering, by the by, that a little girl whom he has seen groing in the village is an illegitimate child of his õn.

Mrs. Faber is all the while hidden in the nĕborhood with a friend, and her husband being called in to her, again performs the operation of transfusion, without recognizing his patient. We see in sõme of the english papers enthusiastic praise of this book, and we do not profess to hav said all that may be said in its favor, but we doubt if it is by books like this that men ar convinced or sins abated." [Nation. **1668**

PAUL FOSTER'S DAUGHTER. [by DUTTON COOK: *Low*, 1865.] "It was the brilliant success of his excellent novel ' Paul Foster's Daughter ' in which he drew with a masterly hand so many portraits from the life, studies for the most part in the Bohemia of art, which finally determined him to make literature his profession. This, perhaps the most varied, fresh, and original, if not the most hĭly finished of his stories, was always prized by him." [Athen. **1669**

PAUL'S COURTSHIP [by "HESBA STRETTON," i. e., Hannah Smith: *C: W. Wood*, 1867.] "is deserving of much praise. It is a work ably planned and cleverly executed. Tho it relates almost wholly to lõve, the 'old, old story' is retold with a grace which renders it not ŏnly very readable but even impressiv . . . Paul is a medical man of independent means, who, together with his brother Rufus, and his sister, Mrs. Margraf, reside at a place called Monkmoor. In the same town dwells an elderly lady, Mrs. Aspen, who, conceiving herself to be a poetess, collects a number of her poems for publication. This character is very cleverly drawn. Thêre is much good humored irony in the description, and the dreams of the poetess at the prospect of seeing herself in print ar related with real humor. To assist her in this ambitious design, she advertises for an amanuensis. A yung

girl, named Doris Arnold, responds to the advertisement, and after a short time takes up her abode with Mrs. Aspen. Between these two thêre presently arises a very warm friendship. In Doris Arnold we hav the nucleus of the book; the centre from which the whole of the interest radiates. Three men fall in lõve with her, of whom õne is Paul Lockley, Rufus another, and a deformed painter named Atcherly another . . . The sacrifices which this triple lõve necessarily entails awakens no doubt as to their probability. They ar exactly as they would hav occurred in real life: and they ar narrated with a simplicity which captivates the ear, whilst it lends additional beauty to the pathetic portions of the story." [London Review. **1670**

PAULINE. [by LUCY BETHIA (COLQUHOUN) WALFORD: *Holt*, 1885.] "Much is made and skilfully, in the first and last parts of the story, of the local color of the Hebrides. Thêre was an almost passionate intensity in certain portions of ' Pauline,' suggesting another, and perhaps hĭer order of power than any which the earlier book had revealed, — õne touching upon the veritably tragic. This book certainly had a moral. A good woman is not to marry a bad man with the vain hope of making him better. Such devotion is not useless, merely, but sinful. On this austere text, the author, in the person of her saint-like yet perfectly simple and natural heroin, not so much preaches a homily as makes a plea, — a tearful, regretful, yet inflexible plea. We recall few passages in modern fiction more seriously beautiful than the last scene vouchsafed to us of her pensiv story, in which she receives the tidings — told carelessly and incidentally — of the violent end of the man she loved." [Atlantic. **1671**

PELHAM. [by Baron LYTTON (1805-73): London, 1827.] 'Pelham," "Devereaux" and "Paul Clifford' ar works of which the tendency is to bring into repute folly and viçe, and even crime—works from the perusal of which we arise with much the same feeling as if we had escaped from lo, disreputable, and impure company, into which we had unwillingly been brot by accidental çircumstances,—with a sense of contamination, a feeling as if our mind had been soiled by the contact of the grossness and viçe around us" [Amer. Monthly Review.]—"We pronounçe any man a perniçious humbug who professes to inculcate useful and ennobling lessons of duty, and does the very reverse; who dresses sophistry and viçe in the garb of wisdom and virtue, and thus deludes the thotless into worship of the monsters, whose hideous mien, if undisguised, would fil them with hatred. And does not Mr. Bulwer do this? Ar not all his works saturated with voluptiousness, replete with false and meretriçious vues of life? And does he not at the same time assert that he is applying fiction to the most salutary. the most elevated purposes? We make 3 distinct charges against the author of the Pelham, or rather of the Falkland series,— for the republication of that precious mass of filth, after the çelebrity of the writer was established, indicates a desire to hav it regarded as entitled to the honors of the first born darling. We assert that his characters ar for the most part full of affectation and exaggeration; that his philosophy is in the main but sounding brass and tinkling cymbal, and that he is wholy defiçient in that hi moral sense, that perception of the beauty and sublimity of religion, without which a novelist can never succeed in giving a true picture of life, in unfolding the mysteries of existence, and in impröving his fello-men. He is the most artifiçial writer, we hav no hesitation in saying, of the day; more addicted to frigid ecstaçies and studied enthusiasm than any of his fellos. We never seem to see the inçidents he relates or hear the dialog he puts into the mouths of his characters; but always to hear him repeating the latter and describing the former." [Amer. Monthly Mag. **896 m**

PEARL [by EMILY JOLLY: *Hurst*, 1868.] " is a refined and charming story; the incidents and characters ar managed with delicate subtlety; and thêre is a careful finish about each character which raises the story into a work of art . . . Mrs. Doynton is a dear old lady. The other characters ar more sharply designed and less finished; they serv to thro out the delicate coloring of Pearl and Mrs. Doynton." [Athenæum. **1672**

PEN [*Roberts*, 1888.] " is a sweet little story, well written and well conceived. Both the sisters, Pen and little Tre, ar charming, and Sandy and his löve-affair enlist from the first a sympathy which his red hair and yello-green eyes hav no power to do away with. The book is entirely wholesom and to be commended." [Catholic World.] — " Penelope and Theresa Brand, to whose fortunes the tale relates, ar the children of a shiftless and not very meßitorious artist, who has married, against the wishes of her family, a rich man's danter. The marriage is never forgiven, and the children gro in poverty, but so long as thêir sweet mother livs her influence keeps her husband tolerably strait. When she dies he goes to the bad rapidly, takes to drink and opium, and little Pen, just 15, with all her mother's capacity for self-devotion and all the honorable instincts of a lady, has to face debt, disgrace, and penury, with but one friend to turn to for aid. This friend is Sandy MacClaren, a man yunger and better off than Louis Brand, but still from sõme old attraction his warm friend and the devoted servant of his wife and children . . . How Pen redeems her promise 10 years later we must leav to be found out from the book, which will be found full of the delicate charm which characterizes

the older stories of its author." [Boston " Literary World."] — " It is a tale of early trials, ending happily throu the girl's strength of character and nativ virtue. The author shões the possession of real feeling and of good taste, and she has an effectiv style. The pathos of the book is unforced and touches a true and responsiv note. The moral tone is hi, and better recreation and instruction than it offers could hardly be asked." [American. **1673**

PENANCE OF JOHN LOGAN (The). [by W: BLACK: *Low*, 1889.] " Of the 3 stories 2 ar good enuf to lead one into the temptation of overpraising the unexpected. It is at all events a pleasure to read 'The Penance of John Logan,' and '*Romeo and Juliet*,' and one cannot help saying that they seem better than Mr. Black's recent novels. The third story, '*A Snow Idyl*,' is a story of love and salmon-fishing, in regard to which one must be thankful that thêre is no yachting in it. 'The Penance of John Logan' is so well contrived, so brïtly told, and so lifelike that its simple pathos is irresistible." [Athenæum. **1674**

PENDENNIS. [by W: MAKEPEACE THACKERAY: (†, 1863) 1850.] " Pendennis is an unsteady, ambitious, clever but idle yung man, with excellent aspirations and purposes, but hardly trustworthy. He is by no means such a õne as an anxious father would wish to put before his son as an example. But he is lifelike. Clever yung men, ambitious but idle and vacillating, ar met every day, whereas the gift of persistency in a yung man is uncommon. The Pendennis fäse of life is one into which clever yung men ar apt to run. The character if alluring would be dangerous. If reckless, idle conceit had carried everything before it in the story, — if Pendennis had been made to be noble in the midst of his foibles, — the lesson taut would hav been bad. But the picture which becōmes gradually visible to the eyes of the reader is the reverse of this. Tho Pendennis is, as it wer, saved at last by the enduring affection of two women, the idleness and the conceit and the vanity, the littleness of the soi-disant great yung man, ar treated with so much disdain as to make the idlest and vainest of male readers altogether for the time out of lōve with idleness and vanity. And as for Laura, the yunger of the two women by whom he is saved, she who becōmes his wife, — surely no female character ever drawn was better adapted than hers to teach that mixture of self-negation, modesty and affection which is needed for the composition of the ideal woman whom we love to contemplate." [Anthony Trollope.] — "Here we hav 2 characters totally distinct, as different in thêir daily life and habits as it is possible to conceive, and yet each marking the author's self-consciousness, each in thêir degree a prototype of the man. We refer, of course, to Pendennis and Warrington. Some hav thôt that in the latter he drew himself, and at first sīt it seems natural to couple the thôtful, grand, slītly cynical, becaus hard-tried man, smoking his lonely pipe in his chambers, and wearing his tattered clean shirt, with the sarcastic, vigorous writer; this may seem more natural than to couple the latter with the prig Pendennis, — selfish, dandified, preferring claret to beer, conceited, vain, and spoilt, and yet with Thackeray's ōn honest heart, which eschewed vice, and tried hard and successfully against the power of the Evil Nature to withstand temptation." [Westminster Review.] — "My father

scarcely ever put real people into his books, tho he of course found suggestions among the people with whom he was thrōn. I hav always thôt that thêre was sōmething of himself in Warrington. Perhaps the serious part of his nature was vaguely drawn in that character. Thêre was also a little likeness to his friend E: Fitzgerald, who always lived a very solitary life." [A.. I.. (T.) Ritchie.] — "Yet as to Warrington, we must quote Thackeray against his dauter. When Pendennis was published, he sent a copy to ōne of his intimate friends, G: Moreland Crawford, Paris correspondent of the 'News,' who had nursed the novelist throu the long and dangerous illness which nearly put an end to Pendennis. The copy was accompanied by the folloing letter: 'You will find much to remind you of old talks and faces, — of W: J: O'Connell, Jack Sheenan, and Archie Archdecne. Thêre is sōmething of you in Warrington, but he is not fit to hold a candle to you, for taking you all round, you ar the most genuin fello that ever strayed from a better world to this. You don't smoke, and he is a consumer of tobacco. Bordeaux and port wer your favorits at the Deanery and the Garrick, and War. is always guzzling beer. But he has your honesty, and, like you, could not posture if he tried.' Warrington, thêrefore, seems to hav oed his being to the novelist's acquaintance with Crawford, altho thêre is undoubtedly [and possibly unconsciously] much of Thackeray himself in it, — more, perhaps, than in the character of Pendennis." [Lippincott's. **1675**

PENRUDDOCK [by HAMILTON AÏDÉ: *Osgood*, 1873.] "is a good novel. It is written as an autobiografy, and sets before us the youth and early manhood of a man who leaves his home and

527

makes the best way he can in the great world. He is an honest, simple-hearted yung fello, a favorit with all except his relativs; but his enthusiasm and over-confidence in others as well as in himself ar continually getting him into hot water. All his deeds, the most innocent as well as those which ar rather dubious, ar harshly judged, the ears of the girl he lōves ar filled with calumnies about him, and his life is by no means an easy one. A german lady, who is 10 years older than he, is a kind friend and counselor to him, but this fact is not ignored by a censorious world . . The author has written a very readable novel, which we trust givs an exaggerated representation of the improprieties of London society." [Nation. **1676**

PERIL [by JESSIE FOTHERGILL: (†, 1891) *Holt*, 1886.] "dōes not disappoint readers who remember ' The First Violin ' [No. 698] and ' Kith and Kin ' [No. 1436]. It is long, elaborate, and sŏmewhat involved ; but it is not tedious, and at times is startlingly vivid and intense. It is the story of a yung lady with a ' temper,' who rarely dōes anything but what is dangerous, and who wrecks *her* peace and the fortunes of the man she lōves by the caprice of a vengeful moment. But thére is food for reflexion in the very evident fact that the girl's ' temper ' is due to circumstance as well as temperament, — to the people who did not lōve or understand or disciplin her, as well as to her ōn recklessness; while sŏme of the scenes ar powerful enuf to make it that really ingenious and rare thing, a novel which suggests thŏt while dealing with what is sensational." [Critic. **1677**

PERPETUAL CURATE (The) [by Mᴀ. OLIPHANT (WILSON) OLIPHANT: *Blackwood*, 1864.] "tho perhaps it contains no single sketch quite so fresh and full of humor as Tozer, the dairyman and principal chapel-warden of the Independent congregation at Carlingford, is a more perfect work than ' Salem Chapel ' [No. 1756] mainly becaus it has no vein of melodramatic alloy like that otherwise inimitable story . . The workmanship is not ŏnly good but singularly uniform; thére ar skilful intellectual touches in every page, and even when the last thread of the story is displayed, we read with quite as much interest as before, to the very last page, confident that the minute strokes of insît and humor with which every character is shaded will not cease till the end. In ' Salem Chapel ' the rubbishy element connected with Susan's romance sounded so striking a discord in the tale, that we had to reassure ourselves repeatedly that we wer under no delusion as to the realistic power of the more striking features. Here thére is nearly perfect keeping in the whole . . For the rest, the critic has little to do but to point out the many slît but admirable sketches, lîted by a delicate humor which seldom exaggerates even by ᴀ hair's-breadth, which the tale contains . . . The dismay with which the rector's wife sees her husband, of whom up to her marriage she had hoped to make a hero, indulging in what she thinks almost malignant feelings against his rival, and eagerly catching the iʒle gossip unfavorable to him, the despair with which she tells herself that these petty feelings would not hav gained any hold on him had they not waited so patiently for their marriage during those 10 years for his promotion, the feminin sagacity with which she half controls her regrets and half vents their bitterness on the unlucky curate who fans her husband's clerical animosity, ar blended most delicately with the over-nicety of a woman still half a spinster in habits and tastes. The glaring pattern of a drawing-room carpet with which the previous rector had provided the rectory, and which it was thòt too expensiv to replace, is an especial theme of constant irritation to poor Mrs. Morgan, — not that humorous irritation which a woman would feel to whom such matters had assumed their rĭt subordination in life, — but the grave irritation which they would cause to one who had long looked forward to marriage as the beginning of a full true life, and yet found it setting in motion a variety of petty annoyances, and cares, and trials of temper which had never before beset her . . . The great artistic merit of the story is the *evenness* of the literary workmanship. Almost every page is saturated with delicate and earnest observation of life and character." [Spectator.] — See *MISS MARJORIBANKS.* **1678**

PERSUASION. [by J.. AUSTEN: 1810.] "Whatever draws attention to Miss Austen is a boon to mankind and a benefit to literature, and it would not be easy to find anything about her and her novels which would not be pleasant to read, if the treatment be only appreciativ and the style good. It is only too lazily delîtful to wander in spirit about the lanes of Highbury with Emma Woodhouse, [No. 1246] or linger in the glades of Mansfield Park, [No. 1500] with Fannie Price, or look out on the sea from the Cobb of Lyme Regis with Anne Elliot, or accompany Elizabeth Bennett [No. 1697] to her pitched battles at Rosing's or her triumf at Pemberly. We could read Miss Austen's novels almost for ever, and anything concerning them has, of course, its borròed charm." [Spectator. **1679**

PETRONEL. [by FLORENCE (MAR-

RYAT) (CHURCH) LEAN: Bentley, 1870.] "Petronel is a yung lady of somewhat explosiv and fiery temperament, but very charming and lovable, — whose story is pleasantly told. She is the dauter of a 'bohemian' artist, who, having eloped with a lady of rank, deserts and leaves her dependent for the last offices of friendship, and her danter for parental care on the kindness of their cousin . . At length, when an unusually sharp passage of arms between her cousin Marcia and her charge has compelled the Doctor's interference, he selects a school for her at Antwerp, whêre is laid the second scene of Petronel's history . . . A happy reconciliation of the family party forms an appropriate end to a slĭt but ably-written story." [Athen. **1680**

PHANTOM FUTURE (The) [by H. S. MERRIMAN: Bentley, 1889.] "is readable for several reasons. It introduces the bar-room life of struggling literary men, actors, medical students and others who turn nĭt into day; it describes a David and Jonathan sort of friendship; and it contains a pretty lŏve story . . The friendship between Crozier and Valliant is delicately handled — between the strong, steadfast sailor and singer, and the brilliant artist, who conceals beneath a careless, rather dissipated mask the consciousness that his days are numbered, and that he is in the grip of mortal disease." [Athen. **1681**

PHARISEES. [by — ( ) EDWARDS: Maxwell, 1884.] "The Pharisees ar the county folk who welcom, after 9 or 10 years of australian exile, yung Squire Oldcastle with his wife Star, formerly an actress, on whose account principally he had gône into banishment [Compare plot of No. 1634] . . . He is gradually made to feel ashamed of his wife, to think that she stands in his way, and to act with

529

cruelty toward her, even when he fancies that he is playing an unselfish part. The situation is complicated by his yunger brother Errol, who falls madly in love with Star, and by his friend Major Peveril, tho both these men in their different ways ar guided by honorable motivs, and by a desire to befriend the unfortunate wife. Guy and Errol ar worked at by the author with much care, and with sõme success, but it is Star who holds our attention fixed throuõut. She is prouder in her soul than all the Oldcastles, and better, and more worthy to be loved. Her pride leads her throu great sufferings, and subjects her to much insult and humiliation. The author dões not shrink from painting scenes of tragic intensity, and her novel is painful in the hīest degree. But its power is unquestionable, and the reader becōmes engrossed in watching the martyrdom of a wayward, over-sensitiv, and yet noble woman. The story is far above the average." [Athenæum. **1682**

PHILIP EARNSCLIFFE. [*Amer. News. Co.*, 1866.] = *MORALS OF MAY FAIR.*

PHILISTIA [by " Cecil Power," i. e., [C :] GRANT [BLAIRFINDEL] ALLEN: *Chatto*, 1884.] " is an unusually clever novel. It has a very apparent political and social bias. The most prominent characters ar Socialists, and all the intellectual and cultivated men in the book are represented as thõroly convinced of the absolute truth and rīteousness of the Socialist doctrin, even tho self-interest may restrain them from personally obeying its dictates . . . It is the spirited and pithy dialog which givs to ' Philistia ' its undoubted superiority to the ordinary run of novels ; for it must be confessed, the incidents ar farcical, and not a few of the personages either exaggerated or

unnatural; and thêre is, too, a jumble of classes which is quite bewildering. For instance, ' Little Miss Butterfly,' the dauter of a small grocer in a petty town, is depicted as the very akmē of elegance, cultivation, and refinement; yet with her surroundings, how could she escape being what G: Eliot called ' spotted with commonness ' ? And this is no solitary example : few indeed of the characters ar the legitimate outcom of thêir antecedents. But the gravest drawback to Mr. Power's work is its marked Socialistic teaching. It is mischievous to disseminate error in an attractiv form, and no error could be more signal than that which attributes to a social scheme of human devising, the power to suspend or materially modify a great natural law like that of the struggle for existence." [Westminster Review.] — " Thêre is a quiet, pleasant tone about ' Philistia' which recommends it to one's liking in spite of an occasional straining of the socialistic note. If Ernest le Breton is somewhat tiresome at first, in the pertinacity with which he obtrudes his socialism on all with whom he cōmes in contact, we forgiv him afterward for the troubles his conscientiousness and his principles bring him into, for his quiet resignation and gentleness under their wêt. The main thread of the story runs very simply. Le Breton is driven by his opinions from his tutorship of Lord Exmoor's son, and then from his schoolmastership, on the strength of which he had married, into journalism. Here, but for the help of friends, he would hav starved, again on account of his opinions, until the success of his pamflet on the poor of London brõt him prosperity and the editorship of a socialist paper. The tale is told mīldly, yet with vivid incidents. and with minor threads ingeniously woven in, which make it full of interest. Thêre is no study of a social fâse, as in '*Alton Locke*,' no sensational use of socialistic organizations, as in ' Sunrise'; but merely the recognition that thêre is a new faith groing up which is already strong enuf to be the guiding motiv in the lives of some men of culture and breadth, as well as men of narro and intense ideas." [Nation. **1683**

PHINEAS FINN. [by ANTHONY TROLLOPE : 1868.] " In writing ' Phineas Finn' I had constantly before me the necessity of progression of character — of marking the changes in men and women which would naturally be produced by the laps of years . . So much of my inner life was passed in their company, that I was continually asking myself how this woman would act when this or that event had passed over her head, or how that man would carry himself when his youth had becôme manhood, or his manhood declined to old age. It was in regard to the old duke of Omnium, of his nefew and heir, and of his heir's wife, Lady Glencora, that I was anxious to carry oût this idea ; but others added themselvs to mind as I went on, and I got round me a circle of persons as to whom I knew not only their present characters, but how those characters wer to be affected by years and circumstances. The happy, motherly life of Violet Effingham, which was due to the girl's honest, but long-restrained love ; the tragic misery of Lady Laura, which was equally due to the sale she made of herself in her wretched marriage ; and the long suffering but final success of the hero, of which he had deserved the first by his vanity, and the last by his constant honesty, had been foreshadoed to me from the first . . . Lady Laura

Standish is the best character in ' Phineas Finn' and its sequel ' Phineas Redux ' — of which I will speak here together. They ar, in fact, but one novel, tho they wer brôt out at a considerable interval of time . . . But I found that the sequel enjoyed the same popularity as the former part, and among the same class of readers. Phineas, and Lady Laura, and Lady Chiltern — as Violet has becôme — and the old duke — whom I killed gracefully, and the new duke, and the yung duchess, either kept their old friends or made new friends for themselvs." [Author's Autobiografy. **1684**

PHINEAS REDUX. [by ANTHONY TROLLOPE : *Harper*, 1874.] '' Many novel-readers will recall with pleasure Mr. Trollope's Phineas Finn, which in some ways is among the best of his stories, and they will welcom a continuation of the adventures of the yung irishman who made a great many friends in his struggle with life, as depicted in the earlier volume, and by his disappointed hopes of success as he approached middle age. We left him then returning to Ireland to marry the simple girl whom he had first loved, and in Phineas Redux we hav him returning to London, a widoer, after 2 years' absence, and once more taking part in politics." [Atlantic.] — See *EUSTACE DIAMONDS, PRIME MIN., etc.* **1685**

PHŒBE, JUNIOR [by MA. OLIPHANT (WILSON) OLIPHANT : *Hurst*, 1876.] " purports to be a last chronicle of Carlingford, and the reader will not regret the renewal of his acquaintance with that typical old-fashioned town. The present chronicle deals with the fortunes of the minister's dauter whose father and mother, finding the jealousies of their nêbors too much for them at the outset of their married life, emigrate to the North, and finally to London, raising themselvs in the social scale of dissent by these changes, and dropping in the process much of the belligerent nonconformity which was natural in their former position. The filosofy of hereditary dissent, as opposed to the mental attitude of the original separatist, is amusingly analyzed, tho no fair-minded person will accuse her of an unfriendly spirit; and types of character differing as widely as Copperhead the contractor and Sir Robert Dorset and Mrs. Tom Tozer ar effectivly sketched in the author's happiest manner. Phœbe is capital. The self-possession with which she guides herself throu the difficulties of her position as a thoroly educated girl, who has quite left her relativs behind in a social point of vue, but whose polish has gone sufficiently deep to make her act toards them without the slitest indication of meanness, or false shame, is excellent. Her honesty (which was an effort to the fair bourgeoise) in this case proves the best policy as also does the frankness with which she accepts both the task of civilizing and cherishing the loutish Clarence Copperhead, and the gage of battle promptly thrōn down by her future father-in-law. Every one will sympathize with her clever defeat of that gross specimen of the monied proletariat . . . Of course a perfect lady would hardly hav góne in for the prize, with or without the expectation of such a struggle to retain it; but Phœbe is not perfect, nor quite a lady, and obtains in her Clarence the opening she desires for further social success." [Athenæum.] — "When Mrs. Oliphant writes about yung girls she is sure to be entertaining, and generally she shōs herself in her best novels a worthy follower of Miss Austen, while thêre is hardly ōne, even

of those most hastily written, into which she dōes not put some few pages of such simplicity and apparent artlessness that the reader wonders why all domestic tales ar not like hers. 'Phœbe, Junior' shōs both her excellences and her faults. Thêre is a great deal which is clever in it. Phœbe is well drawn, and all of the family life of Ursula and her yung sister is well described. The difference between the two yung men, one of whom is a nonconformist while the other is a churchman, is set before us in a most lifelike way. But what is disappointing is the upshot of the whole story. Why should Phœbe, after all, marry the man she does? That termination is a disappointing ōne, and, if it was intended for satire, it is too suddenly thrust upon the reader to make him sure of the intention. We becōme too fond of Phœbe not to pity her fate, and, with all her faults, she seems too sensible a girl to choose such a fate. Still, Mrs. Oliphant knoes her public better than we do." [Nation. **1686**

PHYLLIS [by MAY (LAFFAN) HARTLEY: _Smith_, 1877.] "is a lōve story of the post-nuptial period, which has a great deal of merit and interest, tho it is not strikingly original, and has the ōne recommendation which tells most strongly for a book intended to be amusing, — it amuses . . . In 'Phyllis' we find a very fresh and pleasant atmosfere . . . The author writes perfectly good English, and she possesses both refinement and humor . . . The story of the girl-wife, whose husband has ignorantly dōne her a great wrong, and who is content with the liking which an unawakened heart givs him, until he shall be able to win a warmer and more satisfying sentiment, would hav been more true and pleasing without the incident of Sir Mark Gore, a commonplace and over-dōne specimen of the false friend and unprincipled man of society. It is much to the honor of the lady who has written this clever and interesting novel, that she fails in all the scenes of dangerous flirtation, while she succeeds perfectly whêre the sentiments and the difficulties with which she deals are entirely honest and natural." [Spec. **1687**

PHYLLIS BROWNE, See No. 1153.

PIQUE. [by S.. (STICKNEY) ELLIS: *Smith*, 1850; Boston, *Loring*, 1863.] "The manner of narration is so easy, earnest, and pleasant as to hav enticed us on from chapter to chapter, with a charm which is by no means of every week's experience." [Athenæum.] — "It is probably destined to become as popular as the novel of which it frequently reminds us — 'The Initials' [No. 473]. The characters develop throu spirited conversations, always natural and without exaggeration. The pages are never dull, the story being varied and full of interest. It is a tale of the affections, of the home circle, of jealousies, misconceptions, perversions, feelings, the incidents groing naturally out of the defects and excellences of the individuals depicted. We commend 'Pique' to all lōvers of refined, spirited, and detailed home novels." [Continental. **1688**

PLAYWRIGHT'S DAUGHTER (A) [by ANNIE EDWARDS: *Bentley*, 1884?] "is an admirably told story. It is not the story, but the telling of it, which is striking, for we hav had much the same material before, but seldom do we hav such spirit in the rendering of a more than twice-told tale." [Critic. **1689**

POINT OF HONOR (A). [by ANNIE EDWARDS: London, also *Har-*

per, 1863.] "The heroin remains at Chesterford, leading her solitary life and loving him. Meantime the vicar, a man of strong nature, much tenderness, and great tact, whose character is admirably drawn, lōves Jane, and bides his time. After 10 years, however, Mohun returns, walks into Jane's parlor, and asks her to be friends with him. She, loving him no less than ever, assents gladly . . . But, altho she forgivs, she will not receive him again on the old footing, and he drives off with his handsome adventuress wife, and Jane lōves and is married to Mr. Follett. The story is told with great yet with very simple skill, and the characters of the few personages ar revealed rather than portrayed." [Galaxy. **1690**

POLLY [*Tinsley*, 1867.] "is essentially a village portrait. The author pays a flying visit to a garrison town whêre sōme amateur theatricals ar going on, and occasionally peeps into the palace of a bishop; but with these exceptions the incidents ar transacted in a village, the changes of scene not extending beyond the vicarage, the mansion house, and the inn. Polly Churchill, the heroin, is ōne of those charming characters far less frequently met in the fiction of modern days than we could wish . . . She is merely a simple, true-hearted little girl, the dauter of a parson; she looks after a crowd of little brothers and sisters, and is a devoted believer in ōne of the most worthless parents who ever existed." [London Review. **1691**

POOR GENTLEMAN (A). [by MA. OLIPHANT (WILSON) OLIPHANT: *Hurst*, 1889.] "The contrast between the boisterous family life of Penton Hook and the solemn grandeur of Penton Hall, whêre old Sir Walter rēgns childless but for an ōnly danter and her elderly husband, is not all in favor of the latter. Mrs. Oliphant has not lost the art of delicate contrasts in female character. Ally and Anne ar a charming pair of sisters, and their gentle mother is admirably described. Of the men there is less to be said. Mr. Russell Penton, the prince-consort of the queen regnant at the Hall, has the most individuality. His gentle disapproval of his wife's attitude to the heirs of entail, and his generally loyal and tactful submission to the necessities of a position which bores him to an extent none of his family circle quite appreciates, ar excellently set forth. For a lazy, acquiescent sort of a man he manages to hav a great influence in the rit direction over his wife, who, in spite of her prejudices and force of character, is sensitiv to his inarticulate judgments on her vues and ways . . . Rochford, the smart yung lawyer, is only a sketch. The filosofic old roadman is another. ' One like me, as sits here hours on end, with nant afore him but the clouds flying and the wind bloing, learns a many things.' One would hav liked to hear more of them." [Athen. **1692**

POOR SQUIRE (A). [by " HOLME LEE," i. e., Harriet Parr : *Smith*, 1882.] " It is always a pleasure to read one of ' Holme Lee's ' novels, a pleasure not a little increased when we turn to them from the tedious frivolities or dismal moods of passion and crime with which sõme writers would amuse or instruct. The ' Poor Squire ' is a lõve-story, pure and simple. When we ar introduced to the hero, he has had his disappointment. His father, offended by the too evident ennui which the girl to whom he is engaged shõs in her first visit to the family home, leaves away from him the greater part of his wealth. He is now a poor man, and her friends break off

the match. Some years afterwards, their influence makes her contract a new engagement, a grand match, for the new lover is a duke, only old enuf to be her grandfather. But tha Squire is stirred to rebellion, and she, too, when she finds that he is faithful to his old passion, asserts herself. Thêre ar no grand emotions, no harroing scenes, or startling surprises. The tale has just the quiet charm which surrounds the Squire's home, ' a land of ancient peace.' But we follo it with unfailing interest, so natural is everything, so graceful the touch with which the author brings her men and women before us." [Spectator. **1693**

PORTIA. [by MA. ( ) (ARGLES) HUNGERFORD : *Lippincott*, 1882.] "There is an exceeding amount of excessiv playfulness in the pages of 'Portia,' for a novel with so formidable a secondary title as ' By Passions Rocked.' A serene and slender mystery dões, indeed, try to meander gracefully among the puns and frolics of the heroes and heroins, and a great deal of agony is piled suddenly on the last page; but on the whole the book is amusing rather than tragic." [Critic.] — " It is a rather painful story, told in this author's sprĩtly manner — always in the present tense — of a man's lõve for a woman, which she rejected becaus thêre was an ugly story afloat of his being a forger. She believed it. By-and-by the besotted old clerk who had really committed the forgery confesses his crime, and Portia turns to her old lover, but it is too late." [Boston "Literary World." **1694**

PREMIER AND THE PAINTER (The). [by J. FREEMAN BELL : *S. Blackett*, 1888.] " The theme is politics and politicians, and the treatment, while for the most part satirical and prosaic, is often touched with sentiment, and sŏmetimes even with a fantastic kind of poetry. The several episodes of the story ar wildly fanciful and ar clumsily connected; but the streak of humorous cynicism which shōs throu all of them is both curious and pleasing. Again, it has to be claimed for the author that — as is shŏn to admiration by his presentation of the excellent Mrs. Dawe and her cookshop — he is capable of insīt and observation of a hī order, and thêrewith of a masterly sobriety of tone." [Athenæum. **1695**

PRETTY MISS BELLEW. [by "Theo. Gift," i. e., Dora Henrietta (Havers) Boulger : *Bentley*, 1876.] "To readers lookiñg for a fresh, pretty, and wholesom story, with a good deal of honest sentiment, sŏme pathos, and in places a considerable strength of passion, we commend Mr. Gift's latest book . . . The realness of his people is so firm, and the charm of his yung heroin so abiding, that he is able to take the most curious liberties in talking about them." [Atlantic.] — "The author has told very cleverly a story of home life, with a heroin modern, independent, thŏroly natural and without a tinge of fastness. It is a capital study of character, and if it convinces any would-be heroins that everything natural in character is certain to be interesting, it will add sŏme tone to the great army of men who are searching for home life of the rīt kind. The readers aimed at would probably observ that the hero is quite a useful example of how not to do it for men. He is the stereotyped englishman, delīts in his rufness, asks the girl he loves to marry him as he would his 'tiger' to bring him his boots. It is needless to repeat our conviction that the hero, when introduced into the sfere of home life, will adorn it as all english husbands do." [Penn. **1696**

PRIDE AND PREJUDICE. [by J.. Austen : 1816.] ·"An often quoted passage from the diary in Lockhart's 'Life' contains the fullest recognition of this. 'Read again, and for the third time at least, Miss Austen's finely written novel "Pride and Prejudice." That yung lady had a talent for describing the involvments and feelings and characters of ordinary life which is to me the most wonderful I ever met with. The big bow-wow strain I can do myself like any now going; but the exquisit touch which renders ordinary, commonplace things and characters interesting from the truth of the description and the sentiment is denied to me. What a pity such a gifted creature died so early!" But much more, of course, than "truth of sentiment and description" goes to the creation of Jane Austen's power and charm. A profound insīt into the workings of the calmer and commoner human feelings and motivs — this and a marvellously subtle humor wer the two gifts which she was the first to bring in anything like profusion to the "novel of manners." And the purest novels of manners, in the sense in which I hav endeavored to define the frase, her stories ar. They giv, and they confine themselvs strictly to giving, a picture of life as it presents itself under the most rigid rules of social convention, with only such actions described, such characters and feelings depicted, as these rules permit of being displayed.'" [A. Trollope.] — "Pride and Prejudice must be deemed, on the whole, her best book. The heroin, Elizabeth Bennett, is, in the frāse of Miss Austen's day, a fine yung woman, clever and agreeable, good-looking and good-tempered, tho with a hī spirit which enables her to hold her ōn in all situations; and she is well matched with Darcy, who, in spite of his aristocratic prejudice and stiff manner, is a thōro gentleman. All the figures in this novel ar well drawn, particularly those of the pompously stupid Collins, and of Mr. Bennett with his cynic filosofy, under which he hides his disappointment at his matrimonial mistake, and the satiric humor with which he revenges himself upon his wife and yunger dauters for their exasperating silliness." [Boston "Lit.World." **1697**

PRIME MINISTER (The). [by ANTHONY TROLLOPE: *Harper*, 1876.] "Formerly, whenever Mr. Trollope had written a new novel, it was customary for critics to giv full descriptions of his style, and to say that it was much more like such a representation as is given by a fotograf than like one of Turner's paintings, for instance; but now every one knōẹs ōnly too well how Trollope writes, and pretty nearly what measure of sentiment and romance he is to furnish us in the story which he unwinds like so much tape. 'The Prime Minister' stands true to the author's old traditions, and why it is not as good, or as bad, or as indifferent as sōme 20 others of his less successful novels, it would be hard to say. Thêre is the dose of political life, as the title of the novel suggests, whêrein we read of our old friends, the Duke of Omnium and Lady Glencora his wife, and then for the body of the novel we hav the story of the unhappy married life of the english woman who took the bit between her teeth and married, against everybody's advice, the disreputable Jew. There is about it all a calmness which is not classic, nor yet by any means romantic, and which is as monotonous as the bricks in the walls of city houses which belong to no school of architecture." [Nation. **1698**

PRIMROSE PATH. [by MA. OLI-PHANT (WILSON) OLIPHANT: *Hurst*, 1878.] "A prettier or more idiomatic scotch story it would be hard to find, and tho its subtler touches will be lost on the general reader, the refinement of its humor and the picturesqueness of its descriptiv setting cannot fail to be to sōme extent appreciated. The picture of the gray, turreted manor-house, the home shared by Margaret with the stately old father, and John and Bell, faithfullest of ancient serving-folk; the contrasted beauty of the english grange, with 'its mass of flowers and leafage and blooming old walls,' in which she leads the more conventional existence preferred by her anglicised sisters, ar both excellent in their kind; while thêre is not a character without individuality." [Athenæum. **1699**

PRINCE FORTUNATUS. [by W: BLACK: *Harper*, 1890.] "Mr. Black's singing hero lōves abōve his station, ōnly to hav his affection blīted by a 'no,' sweeter, however, than another's 'Yes.' After a proper season of self-abnegation and desperate follies, winding up in brain-fever, he consoles himself with the faithful adoration of a young italian person no better than himself socially, and rather worse artistically. No genius is needed to extend these simple sorrocs into a very dull romance; the wonder here is, that, interwoven with equally simple joys, they make a very readable story, which gently stimulates curiosity to the end, and then modestly effaces itself from memory." [Nation. **1700**

PRINCESS OF THULE, = 905.

PRINCESS SUNSHINE [by C.. ELIZA LAWSON (COWAN) RIDDELL: *Ward & Downey*, 1889.] "is a pretty, domestic, 'middle-class' tale. But the best part of it, perhaps, is the description of the old fashioned house, in the suburbs of London 25 years ago, in which

Gregory Gifford, author and pressman, labors to support the ungrateful gentility of his commonplace sisters, and the airs and graces of his would-be fashionable yung brother. For nooks and corners of the London which is disappearing Mrs. Riddell has the sympathy which is essential to good description. Of the characters, Gregory is a marvellons example of unobtrusiv sacrifice of self for family loyalty and ties of honor, such as is uncommon, but fortunately not unknōn in daily life. Sunshine, as becōmes her, rewards her patient hero at last, in spite of the faded 'ladies' who oppose her." [Athenæum. **1701**

PRIVATE SECRETARY (The). [by G: TOMPKYNS CHESNEY: *Blackwood*, 1881.] " Apparently, the whole work has been produced for the sake of the ōne figure to which reference has been made, and no competent reader will fail to perceive that Robert Clifford's private secretary, Hilda Reid, is a remarkably interesting and indeed masterly creation . . . She is represented as beautiful, but her beauty dōes not seem to hav been of that type which especially appealed to her lover; and apart from fysical charm, thêre is nothing to excite, but everything to repel passion in a purely business relation with a yung lady who, so far as can be seen by him, is distinguished mainly by good business habits, unfailing reserv, a suspicion of satire, and a noteworthy ability to take care of herself. To depict such a woman with unflinching veracity and with no softening of the angles of character, and at the same time to represent her as inspiring a lōve which is made to seem natural and even inevitable, is a task of amazing difficulty, but it is performed here with the ease of effortless strength, and it is ōnly

on reflection that we perceive how great a triumf of subtle and delicate art has really been achieved. We ar reminded of 'Jane Eyre' [No. 762] not only by the central character, but by the central situation. Clifford, the employer and lover of Hilda, is represented as in sōmewhat peculiar circumstances. He is the possessor of a temporary incōme of £5,000, but this incōme is forfeited, in the event of his marrying anyone but his cousin . . . He confides to Hilda his lōve and his embarrassment, and pleads for her consent to a permanent union consecrated only by mutual lōve and fidelity. At first, Hilda is firm in her refusal. She has had no religious training, and holds no religious belief, and is free from conventionality of thôt; but she feels that wer she to consent she would be degraded in her eyes, and ultimately in the eyes of her lover. She has, however, miscalculated her strength and the strength of the forces brôt to bear against her. She is 'proof against her lover's pleadings, and even against his reproaches; but when she has sent him from her side, she goes to see her little brother at the school whêre Clifford's money has placed him, and thêre a plea is made which she cannot resist. Tho a silent plea, it is more effectual than the spoken ōne. The agonized look on the face of the little boy — too yung to understand more than that sōmething is wrong — when she hints at a return to his old life, is too much for her; it is something that her imagination has not grasped, and she can hold out no longer . . . Apart from considerations which could appeal only to a religious mind, the argument for her lover's plea was logically unanswerable; for the circumstances wer such that by giving way to him she could injure none but herself, while she could giv unspeakable joy to those dearest to her, and help and comfort to many more . . We will not spoil the pleasure of intending readers by folloing the process by which the tangled web in which Clifford and Hilda hav enmeshed themselvs is at last partially disentangled. Enuf has been said to sho that thêre is in 'The Private Secretary' a sufficiently strong element of human interest to make it well worth reading." [Spectator. **1702**

PROBATION [by JESSIE FOTHERGILL: (†, 1891) *Bentley*, 1880.] "is to be cheerfully and unreservedly commended. It is a well told, thõroly healthful novel, abounding in effectiv and sympathetic touches, such as only an amiable and intelligent student of one's kind can command. The scene of this pleasant tale is laid in a Lancashire cotton-manufacturing district during the cotton famin of 1863. The distress and suffering of that melancholy period form a darker background to the homely and romantic experience of the several artistically individualized characters which figure in the interesting drama here unfolded." [Penn.] — "Altogether, 'Probation' is the most interesting novel we hav read for sõme time, and we can giv no better proof of this than the paucity of otr critical notes, conspicuous by their absence; for criticism is forgotten when the interest is real and sustained, and when the style and sentiments do not interrupt, by arousing a spirit of antagonism. We closed the book with very real regret, and a feeling of the truest admiration for the power which directed and the spirit which inspired the writer; and with determination, moreover, to make the acquaintance of her other stories . . . She is equally appreciativ of the eager, wealthy girl,

who, in impatience of the useless idleness of her class, becõmes a hot defender of woman's ríts, as of the clever and cultivated man who gets her to work, instead of raving; and finally modifies her opinions and subdues her antagonism, by the power of his lõve." [Spectator. **1703**

PROFESSOR'S DAUGHTER (The). [by A. EUBULE EVANS: 1882.] "Thêre is much sprïtliness in the sketch of the foibles of the rich old ânt and the feats of the little german professor. The shade of G: Eliot falls upon the pages; — the earnest yung doctor is surely a descendent of Lydgate." [Athenæum. **1704**

PRUDENCE. [by LUCY CECILIA (WHITE) (LILLIE) HARTE: *Harper*, — *Low*, 1882.] "This novelette will serv as a pretty sketch of æsthetic life. It is not powerful, but it is attractiv in its graceful pictures, and will not fail to appeal to the feminin mind, throu its delicate little details of dress and situation. Throuõut the story runs a thread of stronger fibre, which is worked out in the charactêrs of Helena Armory and Jonas Fielding, and the book is wholly free from vulgarity, — no small praise to the taste of the author, when a story deals with 'Æsthetic London.' It is amusing to see the evident admiration, not to say reverential aw, with which the author speaks of this enchanted ground; but, after all, if pretty colors and picturesque attitudes may not be admired, it would go hard with those who kindly do their best to contribute to the pleasure side of social existence. The story is but a sketch, but it is a sketch suggesting sõme reserv power." [Spectator. **1705**

PUT YOURSELF IN HIS PLACE. [by C: READE: *Sheldon*, 1870.] "Successfully to resist the machinations of the Trades, and to overcōme the shy, aristocratic instincts of the yung gentle-woman, who has nothing in common with the hero but youth and a taste for carving, is the problem which Mr. Reade has to solv. As it is throu the artistic and inimitable manner in which this is dōne that the story becōmes a work of genius, a mere outline of the incidents would neither do the author justice, nor satisfy the reader . . . Considered, then, as a work of art, quite free from that quality of genius which defies analysis, it is an extraordinary pro-duction. If it lacks the exuberance of genius, it has at least no wasted power. Every incident tells. Even the poetry, which Mr. Reade uses but sparingly, bears upon the plot; the mysteriously līted windoes of the old church, the legend of the Gabriel hounds, the 'bad music' of the flawed grindstone, all prove to hav a purpose beyond their intrinsic interest, and giv us that double pleasure of which we hav spoken. It is ōnly when the book is finished, that the reader really begins to appreciate the completeness of that skill which has held him often breathless over its pages." [Overland. **1706**

QUAKER COUSINS [by AGNES MACDONNELL: *Harper*, 1879.] " is a pleasant, readable story, which givs the history of an orfan boy and girl left by their devout quaker mother to the care of almost unknōn cousins. The pros-perity, the ill-doing, and the downfall of these cousins, and the steady rectitude and disinterested fidelity of the cheated wards, make the story . . . Mrs. Burton, we think, is rather a favorit of the author, who describes with much care her muffled worldliness, her shallo content, and eternal striving for her ōn ends. Our favorit is rather Mr. Forbes-Stokes, who, cheated into marrying an

unloving beauty, gradually and pain-fully rectifies his lot by sheer nobility of nature. The opening of the story, which describes the life and household and the death of Susan Marsland, is very good indeed." [Nation. **1707**

QUATREFOIL. [by M.. DEANE: *Chapman*, 1883.] " M.. Deane's geese ar all swans; and most of her ganders may be included in the same category. If the 4 delītful sisters who ar hinted at in the title of this delītful story had been described as the pretty and natural geese that they ar, and not as the superb birds which it was almost impossible for them to be, the record of their fortunes would hav been no less attractiv, whilst it mīt hav been even more simple and pleasing. They ar welsh girls, living on a retired part of the southern coast, neglected orfans, and bound by a bond of exquisite lōve and confidence. A wandering artist discovers the four-leaved shamrock, and the usual conse-quences follo . . . The welsh scenes hav a glamor; but the account of the house-keeping in London is singularly pathetic and amusing." [Athenæum. **1708**

QUEEN MAB. [by JULIA KAVANAGH: *Hurst*, 1863.] " Mr. Ford's character is very tenderly drawn, and the reader's sympathy with him never fails . . . The rest ōf the book is taken up with the efforts of Mr. Ford to make sōme atonement to Mabel — the name of the child left at his door — by earning money for her. The £500 found with her had set him on his legs and given him a fresh start in life, and with varying fortune he never fell back into beggary. The mutual attachment between him and Mabel is touching. Queen Mab, as she is called, is charming; the story of her life in the family is extremely well dōne; the gentle, scrupulous maiden ānt, who after the mother's death keeps the house, is a good element, and Mab is well trained by her . . . The book is well worth reading, it is well and solidly written, and the interest is sustained to the last page. It illustrates Miss Kavanagh's leading article of faith, which pervades all her novels — the idea of a love existing throu all trials, which nothing can change or weaken, and upon which time and absence take no effect. This is very beautiful and a true ideal, but considering how short human life is, and how soon youth passes and old age comes on, we could wish that Miss Kavanagh would be more merciful to her characters." [Athenæum. **1709**

QUEEN OF CONNAUGHT (The) [by HARRIET (JAY) BUCHANAN: *Bentley*, 1875.] '' one would suppose to be written by an irishman : — the handling of long words is sōmetimes more bold than accurate. But the picture of **irish** life would be deemed libellous if penned by an englishman. The queen is one Kathleen O'Mara, a yung irish lady of hĭ descent and romantic patriotism, who endeavors to preserv in thĕir primitiv vigor all the customs of feudal, or rather clannish, hospitality, — and, as far as possible, to revive the glories of the nativ princes from whom she is descended. As these projects require wealth, and the O'Maras hav long been groing poor, she overcomes her prejudices so far as to marry a rich englishman, to whom she eventually becōmes sincerely attached. Her husband, a generous and honorable man, is, on hĭs part, devoted to her, and willingly supports her in projects which move rather his curiosity than his admiration. The two natures, however, ar on all points of feeling divided by the national characteristics of each, and misunderstanding soon arises, which is fostered, for their ōn purposes,

by every member of Kathleen's numerous family, from the priest to the poorest ' coshera' in the hall. Only at last, when her passionate heart is broken by the treachery of all around her, which culminates in an attempt to murder the open-handed stranger to whom most of them o thĕir bread, dōes she recognize the full worth of the brave man whom she has been taut to undervalue as cold and ungenerous. Thĕre is much merit in the contrast between 2 fine natures of different national types, and great varieties of the peasant species ar fully described, whose traits, however, do not seem to be deemed as repulsiv as thĕy certainly ar." [Athenæum. **1710**

QUEEN OF THE COUNTY (The) [by A.. (CALDWELL) MARSH-CALDWELL: (†, 1874) *Hurst*, 1864.] '' is the record of a good woman's life, and much of it has the air of being the genuin recollections of life and manners as they existed in an age gŏne by, tho not so long passed away as to be without a charm for the present generation. The story of the heroin's early years, the nursery life of a large family, the sketches of Newcastle-upon-Tyne and Gateshead 80 years ago ar charming . . The first volume is occupied with the history of the youth and maidenhood of the heroin and her sister; it is a pleasant picture of 2 good, happy girls in the secluded house in Devonshire ; the old-fashioned mode of education, and the 3,000 punctualities insisted on, ar told with freshness and spirit; the friendship of the 2 sisters, their innocent confidences, their rambles throu the deep lanes, will be read with pleasure even in these days of sensational novels, becaus they ar true to a pure type of girlish life. The return of Dulce to her home, full of yunger sisters, and the gradual ripening of her girlhood into womanhood, under the warm and gentle influence of her mother ar charmingly given. The eventful dinner-party, at which Dulce meets Peter Maladean, is told with a pleasant simplicity which secures the reader's sympathy." [Athenæum. **1711**

QUEEN'S HOUSE (The) [by LIZZIE ALLDRIDGE: *Bentley*, 1886.] " is exceedingly pleasant reading — so pleasant, indeed, that such an expression seems scarcely adequate. Its great charm consists in the descriptions of the Tower and its surrroundings. In these she displays a delicacy of touch and powers of observation and imagination beyond the common order . . . All the same, thêre is much directness and honesty of purpos in the execution of some of her characters, and she makes no secret of her regard for õne or two. In Alison, the heroin, she takes peculiar delĩt, and her readers will be likely to agree with her; for Alison is such a creature of health, sweetness, and (as it wer) a certain subtle unripeness, held in combination by a strong dash of individual reality, as is not usual in modern fiction." [Athenæum. **1712**

QUEENIE. [by MAY CROMMELIN: *Hurst*, 1874.] " 'Queenie' Demeric is õne of an orfan family of 5, who liv under the gardianship of a thin, hard ànt, and stout, choleric uncle, at the family mansion of 'Ballymore, in the north of Ireland . . . We need not detail the whole story. By and by, of course, all goes merry as a marriage bell, and Queenie gets what many women never get, — the rĩt man at last, in spite of an intriguing wido — and a lost fortune, for her uncle consents to the match with the poverty-struck Wyverne out of pure contradiction to his wife. The story is, it will be seen, almost purely personal and devoid of plot, but it is

not without interest, and it is here and thêre clever." [Spectator. **1713**

QUEENIE'S WHIM [by ROSA NOUCHETTE CAREY: *Lippincott*, 1881.] " relates the adventures of 2 orfan sisters, the elder of whom supports the yunger by teaching. They find a friend in one of the boarders at the school whêre thêy ar oppressed, who invites them to visit her in her country home. Thêre the opportunity of taking the village school at a comfortable salary is accepted, when 'Queenie' falls heir to an immense fortune, which it is her 'whim' to conceal for a year, and still to appear among her friends as the village school-mistress. Of course her reason is the dislike of her friend's brother for heiresses, and of course she dões not acknoledg it. It is needless to state that this brother's affairs become involved soon after, and 'Queenie' induces the rector to lend the gentleman £2,000 of her money in his name. The rector's sister inadvertently discloses the true source of the loan, and the beneficiary, who has by this time fallen in lõve with 'Queenie,' decides that he must discharge his debt before he breathes his devotion. This a legacy enables him to do with but little delay." [Nation. **1714**

QUESTION OF HONOUR. [by W. COSMO MONKHOUSE *Chapman*, 1869.] " Side by side with the story of Jermyn, the literary man, runs that of Stuart Orme, a gentleman who has married, after the scotch fashion, a hĩ-spirited girl, who, believing afterwards that the marriage is not genuin, and that she is a clog to her husband, runs away from him and hides herself. After she has been absent a good many years, Stuart falls in lõve with another girl (who is very happily drawn), and the knot has to be cut in one way or another. How it is cut we hope a gopd many persons will fin.l out by going to the book. Thêre is not an unreal or slŏvenly figure or character in it. Many of the persons strike us as being drawn from life." [Contemporary. **1715**

QUIET LIFE (A) [by F.. (Hodoson) Burnett: *Peterson*, 1879.] includes "2 short stories. In the first we hav a rector's dauter dying of a broken heart throu unrequited lŏve — a pathetic and saddening picture; the other, *The Tide on the Moaning Bar*, tells the old story of man's inhumanity to woman, and of her consequent despair and death. Neither is in any sense powerful, tho neither is unworthy of the author." [Boston "Literary World." **1716**

QUIXSTAR. [by E.. Taylor: Edinburgh, *Edmonston*, 1873.] "The commonplace life of commonplace people in a small scotch town dŏes not, at first sĭt, promis to be interesting, and thêre is neither diversity of incident nor any great intricacy of plot to make up for the tameness of the subject; yet, so marked ar the natures of the homely folk described, so fully do thêy liv and move before us, that we hav not seen many novels this season which we should be inclined to rank abŏve it." [Athenæum.] — [*Putnam*.] "It is a novel which contains a great deal of cleverness rather than a clever novel. It givs an account of many of the inhabitants of a scotch village, describing every one with intelligence and humor. The writer is a very sharp-eyed person, who manages to see into the secret hearts of many characters, and who puts them before us very clearly. The story is very simple, even, it mĭt seem disproportionately so to the thŏroness with which the people ar described, and thêre is sŏmething cloying in the continual flo of epigram, and sŏmething disappointing in the way in which what would, in more skilful hands, be the

material of many novels, is lost sĭt of by the author." [Nation. **1717**

RACHEL GRAY [by Julia Kavanagh: *Hurst*, 1856.] "is a charming and touching story, wrŏt from the humblest and simplest of materials; but the interest is genuin, and the story is narrated with grace and skill. A yung seamstress, neither beautiful nor clever, is the heroin. Thêre is neither lŏve nor the shado of a lŏver in the whole book, — the heroin begins and ends unmarried, — yet the interest is sustained, and the reader's sympathy never fails. The sombre, homely details amongst which Rachel's life is passed ar made beautiful and almost saintlike, by the gentle, single-minded obedience with which they ar fulfilled. No ŏne can read the story and not feel a good influence from it. The characters ar vigorously sketched, and hav a life-like reality." [Athenæum. **1718**

RACHEL RAY [by Anthony Trollope: *Chapman*, 1863.] "is richer than any other of Mr. Trollope's many works in two of the qualities which hav made him an eminently popular novelist. Like the name of its heroin, the tale is homely, with a cheery lĭt pervading its homeliness; but by the delicacy of its delineations of feminin character, and by the pleasant humor animating its sketches of ordinary domestic experiences, it is far removed from the merely readable and entertaining stories of practised writers. Its incidents ar but the events which every inhabitant of a country town can match from the occurrences of his daily life, or from the treasures of local gossip . Even the charming lŏve-passages of the hero and heroin, — his dashing confidence and her simplicity at the outset, their subsequent misunderstandings and final reconciliation, — derive their interest in no degree

from uncertainty as to the fate in store
for them. At every stage of the story,
after Rachel has incurred her grim sister's disapproval by 'walking with a
yung man,' it is clear that the truthful,
pure, hi-spirited girl will, in the end,
marry 'the yung man,' and that the
yung man will make her an excellent
husband, notwithstanding his imperious
airs and firm conviction that Devonshire ot to giv up drinking cider, and
the entire universe concede to the will
of the masterful Mr. Luke Rowan."
[Athenæum.   **1719**

RALPH WILTON'S WEIRD [by
"Mrs. Alexander," i.e., Annie (French)
Hector: *Bentley*, 1875.] "describes
prettily how an honest soldier defied
fortune in the person of a wealthy and
patrician uncle, and married for lŏve a
bohemian sort of yung woman. The
lady turns out well; we find at last that
she is really her husband's long-lost
cousin and the rĭtful heir to the fortune he magnanimously throes away.
In spite of the plot being so far commonplace, the story runs well in the
artistic hands of the author; the characters ar definit, the heroin charming,
and the result agreeable to the reader."
[Athenæum.   **1720**

RANALD BANNERMAN'S BOY-
HOOD. [by G: MacDonald: London, 1871.] "Ranald is a man writing
the life of his boyhood; and that boyhood is gilded with 'the lĭt of the setting
sun.' It has a look of romance and
mystery seen in the dim distance, and
yet it is the real ordinary and sŏmewhat
hard life of 3 motherless boys, in a
scottish village. The incidents ar trivial and common; the glamor of dear
'long ago' hangs over them, and they
ar touched in the spirit of tender reverence, with which every good man
regards his father, and the home of his

youth. It may be that even these elements would not hav made of it the
charming book it is, if it had not also
been written by a poet, who can so
penetrate common things with the spirit
of lŏve and tenderness and beauty that
(for the moment at least) the reader's
ŏn life shines with the lĭt reflected from
its pages, and his heart gioes under the
influence of the lessons of 'plain living
and hard [*sic*] thinking,' which ar here
set forth." [Athenæum.   **1721**

RARE, PALE MARGARET [*Low*,
1878.] "deals with a bevy of boys and
girls, all well bred and well disposed,
amongst whom the heroin exercises a
strong, salutary influence. As they gro
up she is, of course, lŏved by more than
ŏne of her companions; and quite enuf
is made of the rival passions to relieve
any sense of excessiv juvenility in the
plot. Indeed, sŏme of the latter scenes
ar thŏroly effectiv." [Athenæum.] —
"Thêre is nothing especially 'rare' or
'pale' about the Margaret who is the
heroin of this story. She is a hi-spirited
girl, who lŏves both open-air life and
books, and who would scarcely be distinguishable from her felloes but for the
accident of a divided and doubtful lŏve.
Circumstances hav created a peculiar
relation between her and a yung nêbor,
a man of culture and even genius, and
of commanding moral qualities, but
suffering under the affliction of being
a deaf-mute. On the other hand her
heart is solicited by a less romantic but
not less sterling affection on the part of
the Vicar's son, a gallant yung sailor.
This lŏve-history, entangled as it is
with that of a village beauty, is told
with much vivacity. We follo it with
interest, while we recognise in its
personages genuin types of character.
Of these personages, perhaps sŏme of
the less important ar the most skilfully

drawn. Nothing in the book is better than Margaret's shallo, clever mother, with her art of sympathetic talk." [Spectator. **1722**

RAVENSHOE. [by H**:** KINGSLEY: Boston, *Ticknor*, 1862.] "The whole tone and spirit of the book ar thŏroly english. It represents the best aspect of english life, character and manners. Whatever is most generous, heroic, tender, and true, is here to be seen, and not drawn in colors any more flattering than it is the rit of fiction to use. We think the author carries us too much into the stable and the kennel; but this, we need not say, is also english. But we hav yet to mention what we deem the hiest charm of this charming book, and that is the combination which we find in it of healthfulness of tone and earnestness of purpos. A healthier book we hav never read. Earnestness of purpose is apt to be attended with something of excess or extravagance; but in 'Ravenshoe' thêre is nothing morbid, nothing cynical, nothing quernlous, nothing ascetic. The doctrin of the book is a reasonable enjoyment of all which is good, with a firm purpos of improving the world in all possible ways. It is ŏne of the many books which hav appeared of late years which sho the influence of the life and the labors of the late Dr. Arnold. It is as inspiring in its influence as a gallop over ŏne of the breezy downs of Mr. Kingsley's Devonshire. It is, in short, a delîtful book, in which all defects of structure and form ar atoned for by a wonderful amount of energy, geniality, freshness, poetical feeling, and moral elevation." [Atlantic. **1723**

RAYMOND'S HEROINE [by I.. HARWOOD: *Hurst*, 1867.] "is told in simple, solid, and dainty english; such english as Daniel and Taylor wrote, we

should say, for it floes and rolls in unforced, limpid sweep . . . Its tale is written by ŏne who has a master's eye for scenery, and that in the double sense; an eye for a landscape, — for the peculiarities of moorland, sward, wood, water, village — and also for the moral significance of these visible marks, for what may be called the sentiment of external nature The pretty fineries, and the weird and yet monotonous misery of the busy town and port, ar only less strongly marked by character than the surroundings of Black Moor Farm. Then, again, we hav real conversation in this book, not the stilted and mechanical frȧseology nowhêre to be heard except in bad novels and bad plays." [Athen. **1724**

READY MONEY MORTIBOY [by WA. BESANT & JA. RICE: *Tinsley*, 1872.] "is not a book which we should recommend yung people of either sex to read; and yet it is a clever book, not without grave faults both of style and of tone, it is true, but ŏne which no man who has experience of life can read without being the better for it." [Athenæum.] — "Nothing could be more healthful in tone than this story. Its incidents ar original, its treatment dramatic, and its atmosfere that of the broadest humanity. Thêre is no playing with souls, no hot-bed forcing of emotions, no straining after psychical effects — nor on the other hand is thêre any reflexion. The story is a straitforward, vigorous, and withal humorous narrativ of events. It has, besides, a sound moral. Retributiv justice of a Lear-like order arrives without waiting for the life-to-cŭme." [Critic. **1725**

REBEL ROSE (The). [*Harper*, 1888.] "The scene is London, whêre the Honorable Mary Stuart Beaton, a legitimate descendant of the Stuarts, and a very striking reproduction in face and figure of queen Mary, has come to press her claims to sŏme estates bequeathed to ŏne of her ancestors but confiscated . . . She is a most charming yung girl, who presently leads into captivity, wholly without intent to do so, and with no effort save that unconsciously exercised by her beauty and pure womanly charm, the two men most able to advance her cause in the House of Commons — Sir Victor Champion, the Liberal leader, and Rolfe ·Bellarmin . . It is not a great novel; it allows itself to be laid down without difficulty, altho it must be taken up again with pleasure. But it shŏes an easy and sympathetic mastery in nearly all its touches, and a keen insīt in human nature in both its noble and its meaner aspects. It is written, too, in singularly even and well-bred english, which is always quite equal to the stress laid upon it by the exigencies of the business, the sentiment, or the passion of the moment. And as all of these, tho natural and real, ar yet lifted out of the rut of the ordinary tale of contemporary life and manners, chiefly, perhaps, by the skill with which Mary Beaton herself and her would-be Bothwell ar invested with imaginativ charm, the book fairly deservs the title of a romance rather than a novel." [Catholic World. **1726**

RECTOR'S WIFE. = *VALLEY OF A HUNDRED FIRES.*

RED AS A ROSE IS SHE. [by RHODA BROUGHTON: *Appleton*, 1870.] "Throuʊut this romance thĕre is a great and explicit loathing of all persons in sickness, poverty, old age, or calamity of any kind except unhappy lŏve, and most of the virtues ar put whĕre they belong, amongst the humbugs. You may say that the characters ar vulgar in their lives and words, but it

is all nothing to the vulgarity which appears when the authoress speaks of herself in a parenthetical passage. Thĕre is no denying that she has dash; but you can not call it anything better. Her wit would not save a well-meaning book, but a very little wit goes a great way in a reckless or evil book." [Atlantic. **1727**

RED HOUSE BY THE RIVER (The). [by G: DOUGLAS: *Tinsley*, 1876.] "The author of 'Brown as a Berry' [No. 1122] has produced a readable little story. Thĕre is a good deal of pathos in the lŏve of E.lna Heron for her cousin Robert, who is a fine specimen of an ambitious, self-respecting man, shrewd on all points of worldly knoledge, and an able judge of character, except whĕre the most important domestic event of his life is to depend upon his choice. Of course, such a man wastes the tenderness of his first passion upon the most flīty and fickle of all his feminin acquaintance, who is all the time to jilt him, and dŏes so when a gentleman seems inclined to take the carpenter's place in his absence, exeludes every one else from Robert's attention and finds easy room for repentance when her fashionable swain has deserted her. Thĕre ar many touches which sho appreciation of character; and the local peculiarities of the scene (the east coast of Scotland) ar well preservd." [Athenæum. **1728**

RED TOWERS (The). [by ELEANOR C. PRICE: *Bentley*, 1889.] "The author of 'Alexia' [No. 1041] has charm, ease, and lītness of manner, and her latest novel is more than well planned, well told, and well sustained; it has also a way of its ŏn — a way which seems more simple and natural, and less the resʊlt of art, than it is. The truth is that, of its kind, 'The Red

Towers' could not easily hav been better. The author has a knack of compelling the reader to take an interest in her puppets. Without seeming to go far belo the surface, she has an almost unerring instinct as to the manner in which people speak, think, and generally comport themselvs. Her creatures never surprise by exploding into new and incredible developments; they gro logically, according to circumstances and the unalterable law of their being. The dialog, too — which is appropriate, and nearly always apt — is a pleasure in itself; while thêre ar at least 2 or 3 people to be fond of, and 2 or 3 more to be watched with the interest of a pleased uncertainty." [Athenæum. **1729**

REGENT ROSALIND. [*Tinsley*, 1878.] "It is pleasant to meet a book of so 'old-fashioned' a type, — old-fashioned in the sense of being cool, quiet, sedate, and unpretending, like the lavender silk gowns and the black silk modes of our grandmothers. It is to be hoped that thêre exist even now a certain number of yung persons whose taste is sufficiently unvitiated to permit them to read this simple story — written in unusually good english, and which deals with nothing out of the way of the homely life of thousands of english homes — with appreciation and interest. The 'situation' is not a novel one; we hav made the acquaintance of a great many yung ladies on thêir leaving school 'for good,' and taking their position as mistress of a widoed relativ's household, and we hav generally been interested in them, even when they hav not been such imposing personages as Mrs. Oliphant's Miss Marjoribanks [No. 1557], or Mr. Trollope's Mary Thorne [No. 1213]. Miss Yonge's responsible yung people ar indeed too vir-

tuous, too self-conscious, and too full of a technical kind of scrupulosity, to interest us; but even for them we feel concerned when the 'Daisy Chain' [No. 1183] seems quite endless, and the 'Pillars of the House' ar 13. The author of 'Regent Rosalind' has drawn a brīt, honest, lōvable, pleasant girl's portrait for us, and the accessories ar all natural and well-developed." [Spectator. **1730**

REPENTANCE OF PAUL WENTWORTH (The). [*Bentley*, 1889.] "Thêre is much variety of character and much literary excellence . . In Muriel Ferrars the author has drawn a decidedly charming portrait, and it is consistent with her true and loving nature that, in spite of the sad knoledge she acquires of the stains and flaws in her ideal, her affection for the man remains. But thêre is infinit sadness in the shock which awakes her to the fact that this man has deceived her in the vital point of his marriage at the moment he won her lōve. Harder still is the fate of this girl who learns so cruel a lesson at 19, when she takes the advice of an austere young cleric, and puts, as she thinks, a barrier, in the shape of a lōveless marriage, between herself and the treacherous suggestions of her heart. Utterly contrasted with the course of Muriel and Wentworth's affection is that of her sister's attachment to the clerical hero aforesaid. Philip Irvine is vowed to missionary work in East London, and has resolved to assume no domestic ties which can hinder him in his work. The descriptiv portions of the book, the swiss and italian scenes especially, ar generally well written, and the minor characters distinct, tho the lovers engross most of the interest." [Athenæum. **1731**

RETURN OF THE NATIVE

(The). [by T: HARDY: *Smith*, 1879.] "On this heath Mr. Hardy places a retired sea-captain with his granddauter, a handsom, dissipated civil engineer, who has failed in his business, and now keeps the lone inn; the wido of a farmer, herself the dauter of a gentleman; her niece; and her son, the Nativ who returns. He cōmes from Paris and an uncongenial occupation, with culture and a burning desire to help his fello men; he cōmes into the midst of crass superstition, whêre witches abound, and fried adder's fat is a specific against an adder's bite; and, a half-unconscious positivist, (for at one time he thinks of taking orders) he resolvs to devote himself to teaching and raising the Egdon folk. Can Eustacia Vye help him in this — the sea-captain's granddauter, a glorious woman as he thinks, one of larger culture and hīer aims than those about her, and on that very ground considered as a witch by the simple heath folk? Surely not, for she loathes the heath, to which she is not 'nativ.' Weymouth is to her the world, and Paris almost a dream of heaven, the band on the parade sweeter music than the wind on the desolate upland, the flagged pavement suits her feet better than do the white quartz paths of the hill side. The bitter disillusioning of this eager, passionate girl, to whom ōne man's love seems to offer a means of escape, whose sensuous nature is attracted, on the other hand, by a flashy, handsom scamp; the patient acquiescence of Clym Yeobright, the Nativ, in what he cannot control; his no less persistent struggle with what can still be bent to his ends, ar two of the elements in a tragedy of no common power and sadness. Thêre is also the pathetic severance between a noble mother and a noble son, throu a misun-

derstanding; thêre ar failed purposes, and death, which, when it comes untimely, is an insult and an impertinence to life. The sombre heath is the background to all, the weird sounds of this heath ar the constant orchestral music." [New Quarterly Magazine. **1732**

REVOLUTION IN TANNER'S LANE (The). [by W. HALE SMITH: *Putnam*, 1887.] "Appreciativ readers of that remarkable book, *The Autobiography of Mark Rutherford*, which appeared a couple of years ago, will need but the mention of this new novel by the same writer to induce them to purchase it. Neither Mark Rutherford nor his friend Mr. Shapcott appears here, but the story is of the same grim, uncompromising sort . . . With a powerful touch, not free from cynicism, the author sets before us the contracted life of the people of Cowfold, with their narro horizons, intellectual, social, and religious. In this part of the story, too, thêre is a central unhappy marriage of a thôtful tradesman to the silly dauter of the minister. The revolution is a church revolution which results in the overthro of the gross ministerial hypocrit. This is no romance of lōve and wedded bliss in the last chapter, but a moving tale of 'martyrs without a cause,' of visitation upon the good and true for the sins of others, — a record drawn from 'a world of incompleteness, a sorro swift, and consolation laggard,' which the līt-minded will shun, the cheerful dismiss with a sī, and which others will read with the same mingled feelings with which they face the spectacle of life itself, in which romance plays so small a part, and whêre the best solution reaches us as it reached Maggie Tulliver [No. 1547]." [Boston "Literary World." **1733**

RHODA FLEMMING [by G: MEREDITH: London, 1865.] "is as superior to ' Emilia in England' [No. 1245] as if it wer the work of another man. The labored, almost uncouth style, and the distorted, exaggerated character-drawing hav well-ni disappeared. Thére is a touch of Browning now and then in the speech, and in the dramatic presentation of ône or two of the scenes; but the book is full of warmth and life and action; the story, with a slit pause in the middle, interesting throuôut, and is not spun out to undue length. Some of the characters ar vividly distinct, and almost all hav life and individuality, if one or two ar sômewhat incomplete. The first part of the story is idyllic and charming, with the picture of the old farm in the midst of the blooming kentish landscape; the thrifty mistress, the gloing flower garden, and the two handsom dauters who 'carried erect sholders, like creatures not ashamed of shoing a merely animal pride, which is never quite apart from the pride of developed beauty.' But a shado soon cômes over this sunny landscape, when Dahlia, the beautiful elder sister, goes to London, and lôves and trusts her lover too well, and brings shame to her father, and locks the heart of Rhoda, the yunger, in iron bands which seem to hold her whole nature rigid till she has found, and as she thinks rited, her beloved sister. Mr. Meredith is impatient of the tame and commonplace in incidents and characters. He cannot subdue his voice to the regulated, well-bred monotone of conventional speech; or, to borro an illustration from decorativ art, his hand is too ruf and quick and bold for the skilful lo-relief which Mr Norris and Mr. H: James employ so cleverly. Rhoda is the best drawn figure. Her strong and restrained nature has becôme over-concentrated in her isolated life. Her pride has grôn fierce, her tenderness hard, and her vi-

sion narro. Her obstinacy at last shatters her poor sister's returning gleam of long deferred happiness. The knoledge that she too had been mistaken and had sômething to repent of is the solvent which at length melts the proud nature; and we hav a glimpse of her tamed and softened, in the keeping of the lover who had deserved her so well." [Amer. **1734**

RIGHT AT LAST, ETC. [by E., CLEGHORN (STEVENSON) GASKELL: *Harper*, 1860.] " Mrs. Gaskell has been singularly successful in domestic stories. These ar here collected, and will prove a welcom offering to the numerous readers who hav learned to prize the exquisit felicity of delineation, the sagacions judgment of character, and the hi moral tone which distinguish the productions of the author." [Harper's. **1735**

ROBERT ELSMERE [by M., A., (ARNOLD) WARD: *Macmillan*, 1887.] " is a great novel. It will attract the lôver of the best literature becaus of its literary power and charm, and it will gain the absorbed attention of all men and women who see that religion, ' the most overwhelming of human interests,' as Mrs. Ward calls it, is undergoing a transformation . . . The author has made so much use of actual personages for her leading characters, she has drawn Thomas Hill Green, the Oxford professor of moral filosofy, so frankly, for instance, as the Henry Grey of this book, and the whole temper of her story is so realistic, that one reads Robert Elsmere much as if it wer an actual biografy. Probably Arnold Toynbee has furnished more than ône feature for the portrait of Elsmere." [Boston " Literary World."]—" Of ' Robert Elsmere,' after what Mr. Gladstone has said, who will dare to deny that it is a great work? Yet Mr. Gladstone's enthusiasm is itself evidence that the merit of it is not as a novel. Mr. Gladstone is many-sided, but he has never proved himself to be a lover, student, or critic of lit literature. Had 'Robert Elsmere' been 'lit,' he could not hav admired it. The librarians class it among novels and romances; but it provides the parsons with subjects for pulpit discourses, and is, really, an overgrōn theological tract. It marks, too, more than any other work of our time, the overweening self-consciousness which has attacked our fiction and is sucking away its vitality. What an exhibition of feeble sentimentality! Everywhêre 'trembling lips,' 'blanched faces,' ' deadly paleness,' men and women dropping into chairs, wringing their hands, flinging themselves into each other's arms, sobbing, bursting into bitter tears . Thackeray spoke of novels as ' sweets loved by all people with healthy literary appetites.' The popularity of such books as ' Robert Elsmere ' points rather to the morbid craving which indicates dyspepsia." [Wa. Lewin.] — " But when all is said by way of criticism, how much remains to admire! No ōne who had not steeped himself in the atmosfere of Oxford and its changing currents could write so feelingly and unerringly of its outer and inner life. No ōne who had not been born to generations of culture, sprung from a race british and bookish to its core, could picture so intimately its intellectual fâses. No ōne who knew not the hills and dales of Westmoreland and the downs of Surrey as well as the electrical, throbbing heart of London could hav rounded this story as its author has dōne. Profounder minds than Mrs. Ward's may pick flaws in reasoning and errors in judgment, but as an expression of the intellectual life of to-day, especially of that side of it which touches on science in its bearings on theology, it is a remarkable book.

Ponder this history of ' a soul on fire; ' note the development of the austere, puritanical Catherine into perfect womanhood, the portrayal of the hard, selfish, stunted nature of Langham, the creation of the wilful, human yet aerial-like Rose Leyburn, the delineation of the hunted Newcome, the cynical Wendover, the hearty, happy Flaxman and the passionate Mme. de Netteville, — surely a woman who can thus create, develop and delineate so varied elements as these — pit against each other almost every knōn type in the great whirling, complex world about her, — not only possesses a marvellous power but is mistress of it. Unforgettable pictures rise to the mind as ōne revues his reading — the scene on the crags whêre Elsmere woos Catherine in the nit-winds; that other ōne, whêre he tears open his heart to her while hers is breaking; the chapter whêre they humble themselvs before each other and life begins anew for them; the last tense chapter, with the death-bed scene in Algeria. And in thinking over that terrible nit when Langham questions the little soul and conscience left to him, we ar perhaps forgetful of the tender fireside duet, whêrein the impulsiv child, Rose Leyburn, opens her life to him as a flower unfolds to the sun . . With the death of its founder, we see no more of the ' New Brotherhood.' The needs, the conditions, the promises of the present age ar thêrein typified. To perfect and fulfil them will take ages yet. We ar shōn the Promised Land; then the pen is silent: its attainment is not even profesied. Hope is held out, but no pledge offered. Such forbearance as this deservs the name of art." [Saturday Review. **1736**

ROBERT FALCONER. [by G: MacDonald: *Hurst*, 1868.] " Robert is a scotch laddie brót up by his grandmother, who is a fine religious character; a strong Calvinist, and deeply religious, with no conception of any religion apart from her creed, but with a heart full of loving kindness, and a sense of justice which is stronger even than her love. She has ōne heart-grief — her ōnly son, the father of Robert, has gone to the bad, and after a career of drunkenness and debauchery in which he wasted his fortune and broke his wife's heart, he has utterly disappeared in a slōu of degradation . . . When he is free to go out into the world, — after a long and difficult training, in which all hope or desire for any personal happiness has been taken from him, — he givs himself up to the search for his father, . and in the course of that quest he goes about doing good in the dens of London misery, working out the author's ideas of the principles and method upon which such things should be dōne. Whilst Robert is undergoing the training of education and circumstances the reader is in sympathy with him; but when he becomes the author's idea of a perfect filanthropist, he has acquired a touch of self-consciousness, which mars the effect." [Athenæum. **1737**

ROBERT ORD'S ATONEMENT, by ROSA NOUCHETTE CAREY: *Tinsley*, 1873.

ROGER NORTH. [by — ( ) BRADSHAW: *Sonnenschein*, 1885.] "The author has succeeded in investing an every-day romance with considerable charm, the result of keen and sympathetic observation of country society . . . This is in no way a remarkable book, . . but it is thōroly agreeable reading." [Athenæum. **1738**

ROGUE (The) [by W: E: NORRIS: *Holt*, 1889.] "is in the delītful vêin of the author's best books . . . The humor, the knoledge of men and affairs, the

glossy style, the easy progress of the tale, the faint satire, the clever way of talking about anything and everything charmingly — these are here in friendly naturalness . . A. man of easy-going disposition, who has been a skalawag all his early life, finally cōmes home to his family and palms himself off for the decent fello that he afterward becōmes, tho everyōne, without being able to prove it, feels sure that he is a rogue. There is a clever, shrewd old society woman, and thère ar yung people who fall in lōve and marry." [Critic. **1739**

ROMANCE OF A GARRET (The) [by SYDNEY WHITING: *Chapman*, 1867.] "is lit and readable, and contains a very pleasant story. Thère is not much plot in it, and what thère is servs chiefly as a series of props on which to hang the author's experiences as a journalist; but its tone is so pure, and at the same time so genial, that no one can fail to be delīted with it. It is chiefly the record of the discouraging, but ultimately successful, struggles of a needy man of letters, who is obliged to take up his quarters in an attic . . . The lōve-story is as charming an idyl as has ever been made to grace the somewhat prosaic records of London life." [London Review.] — " But tho Mr. Whiting's scenes of London literary life ar truthfully drawn, they do not convey the whole truth. The shadoes, tho deep, ar not deep enuf. The līt is too brīt. Not all of us, who ar literary men, hav, like the hero of Mr. Whiting's tale, noble relativs and friends who ōn shooting-boxes. Our luck does not cōme so easily as his, tho we drink the full cup of all his troubles. This is the great fault of all tales of London literary life, even of Thackeray's 'Pendennis.' The world hears ōnly of the successful writers. The great charm, however, of the book is the O'Aisey. He is, so far as we ar aware, unique in english literature. And yet every literary man knoes some O'Aisey, with his unblushing, good-natured impudence, and utter want of all principle and morality." [Westminster Review. **1740**

ROMANCE OF A SHOP (The). [by AMY LEVY: *Cupples*, 1889.] " The story is of 4 sisters, left orfans, who attempt to support themselvs in London by fotografy. The different characters of the sisters and the various ways in which their new life affected their dispositions ar admirably described. The strong-minded Gertrude, the conventional Fanny, the industrious Lucy, and the beautiful Phyllis win places in our affections, and ar real persons to us before we close the book. The writer does not content us by merely picturing the outer lives, but she lets us see the hopes and fears, the temptations and sorroes, which came to each sister in livilually while they lived together. Besides these character sketches the writer givs us a delitful picture of bohemian London and the artist life. She takes us to picture exhibitions and studio receptions, and with an artist's löve of contrast presents us often to a representativ of conventional middle-class life in the shape of the sisters' rich but disapproving ânt Caroline. Bohemian London with all its fascinations is of course full of perils for yung, unchaperoned girls. In the sad story of poor little Phyllis' life and death we ar shön the dangerous side of what otherwise would be the most charming society in the world." [Boston " Lit. World." **1741**

ROSAMOND FERRARS [by M. BRAMSTON: *S. P. C. K.*, 1878.] "is a well-written, healthful and most interesting story, which we can cordially recommend; grön people will read it

with as much pleasure as yung önes." [Athenæum. **1742**

ROSE IN JUNE (A). [by MA. OLIPHANT (WILSON) OLIPHANT: *Hurst*, 1874.] "Mrs. Oliphant has written nothing more delicate than ' A Rose in June ' . . . She paints still life with a lïtness of touch which is unsurpassed. This is at önce her weakness and her strength. The hand which lifted the vêil from the homesteads of Carlingford and disclosed a turmoil of passion still sweeps the finer chords of the human instrument with rare skill . . . Her latest novel is the story of a summer shower . . . The wife is a woman nobly planned, yet by no means perfect. On her, when the rector dies penniless, falls the burden of maintaining the family. But she is no longer passiv. Rose has a poor lover at sea, and a rich lover at hand, and Rose's heart is at sea. Her mother determins that the girl shall learn the meaning of self-sacrifice, shall sell herself for the benefit of her brothers and sisters, and she is already engaged to the rich suitor, when her family becömes prosperous again. Rose, bound by her engagement, throes herself on the mercy of her affianced husband, and he releases her, not without reproaching the mother. It is an idyllic story. Thêre is pathos in it, but not the depth of pathos which was fathomed in Nettie Underwood [No. 1215]; thêre is humor, but not the breadth of humor that played upon Pigeon and Tozer [No. 1756]" [Academy. **1743**

ROSE TURQUAND [by ELLICE HOPKINS: *Macmillan*, 1876.] " possesses the charm of style, culture, and breadth of thôt. So far as art is concerned, it is nearly perfect. We may or may not agree with the writer's vues, and we may or may not answer the great problem of life as Rose Turquand does, but this has nothing to do with art. It would be hard in contemporary fiction to match the early scenes in which the life of this poor desolate orfan is painted — her attachment to the good-hearted but somewhat narro-souled pedant of a tutor — the agony of her parting with him, and the conflict of emotions which is ever going on in her mind . . No õne, in short, can possibly read 'Rose Turquand' without feeling his hier nature awakened, his sympathies widened. It is a book to be read and re-read." [Westminster Review.] — " Most readers will be a little repelled by the opening chapters, so vulgar ar the rising generation of Adairs and so hard and unnatural their mother, a lady with projecting eyes, who indeed becõmes still more outràgeous as the story proceeds. But they will do well if they hav courage and persevere; the little weakly waif of a heroin really turns out to be a character worth knoing; and tho her adventures ar of a homely character, they ar sufficiently stirring to prove the true metal of a noble and self-sacrificing nature. In small matters and in great she shõs herself womanly and admirable." [Athenæum. **1744**

ROSSMOYNE [by MA. ( ) (ARGLES) HUNGERFORD : *Smith*, 1884.] "is a pretty story, in which all the ladies ar charming and almost all of them in lõve, and most of the men nice and all of them in lõve. That, at any rate, is the impression left upon the reader, and it is accurate if one or two minor characters ar not taken into account. As to them thére is uncertainty only for want of more minute information. Probably the coachman and the cook and the tenants had their love affairs as well as the ladies and gentlemen. But the story

is not at all ridiculous. It is very pleasantly told, with plenty of spirit, and a great deal of archness and womanly fun." [Athenæum.] — [*Lippincott*.] "It is a pretty and amusing little lõve story. The scene is laid in Irelind, and thére is much of the always enjoyable irish humor. The yung, very yung lõvers, ar very entertaining, but best of all ar the delîtful maiden ânts, never better than when trying to reconcile lõve and disciplin." [Critic. **1745**

ROUGH HEWN [by — ( ) DAY: *Hurst*, 1874.] "exhibits vivilly the grõth of a strong nature, which is improved and refined by conflict with the trials of life. Edmund Barton, like many energetic people in uncongenial circumstances, shões symptoms of turning his activity into wrong directions. Confined to the life of a clerk in a small town, he is beginning to get involved in petty dissipations, and more seriously in a lõve affair with a girl who is no match for him in education or character. At this crisis, he conceives a real attachment for another yung woman, who is abõve him in both respects. The impression awakens him to a more worthy vue of life, and he wrenches himself from his unpromising surroundings, and seeks a better field for his energies in the ruf life of Australia. Rose Lester, who thus proves his good genius, is a pleasant specimen of womanhood (as indeed ar all the female characters), and the interlude of her attachment to Ashley, and its effects in ripening her to receive the mature affection of Barton when he returns a wiser man to the haunts of his boyhood, ar very well told." [Athenæum. **1746**

ROUND THE SOFA. [by E.. CLEGHORN (STEVENSON) GASKELL: *Low*, 1859.] "On this account we always look forward with pleasure to any work by the author of ' Mary Barton' [No. 1532]. Here we hav no fear of slip-shod sentences — of fantastic torturings of speech, of turbid and confused imagery. The language is always clear, and pure, and sparkling, like the water of a mountain rill. There is no fine writing in 'Round the Sofa.' The very excellence of the style is proved by the fact that we ar at a loss to pick out pieces for quotation. We cannot, however, refrain from quoting a passage from the charming tale of 'Lady Ludlow,' in which that most delitful of grand old ladies is speaking about flowers . . . It is a relief to come upon writing like this, after reading such works as ' Queechy ' [No. 260] and ' Amy Herbert,' and the whole of that race of which the ' Heir of Redclyffe ' [No. 1346] is the crown and glory. It is like a draft of good clear ale to a stomach surfeited with ginger-beer and lemonade. There is one other specialty of all the writings of this author, to which we cannot help alluding. We hav in them none of that mixture of religion and romance which is the bane of our modern literature. There is no attempt to enforce the doctrine of justification by faith, throu a dialog between the angelic heroin and her earnest löver . . . Poor Clare, a weird north-country story, and The Half-Brothers seem to be new. Even if we wished it, it would be scarcely possible to tell in a few words the thread of any of these stories. To all our readers we can most sincerely recommend these volumes as worth reading for the stories alone, and almost, if not better, worth reading for the sake of the writing." [Leader. **1747**

RUSTIC MAID (A) [by A. PRICE: Low, 1885.] "is a very pathetic story,

more or less melancholy in every chapter, and yet sufficiently graceful and tender to sustain the interest. The heroin loses her mother in early childhood, and her father is separated from her by a cruel wrong. He is restored only to blit her happiness, and to destroy the proud belief in him which she had cherished. This is the chief motiv of the story, and around it clusters an abundance of pure and pleasant incident, with some admirable characterization and not a little entertaining by-play . . . Those who like a quiet novel with a true touch of pathos in it will take kindly to ' A Rustic Maid.'" [Athenæum. **1748**

RUTH. [by MRS. E.. CLEGHORN (STEVENSON) GASKELL: Chapman, 1853.] "The heroin is a dress-maker's apprentice, an orfan, alone in the world, a creature full of graces, — and, therefore, marked out for temptation. The misery of her apprenticeship is well described, becaus it is not exaggerated with a vue of exciting false sympathy. Her employer is no ogress, — she is merely a self-interested woman, pinched and præoccupied by her struggle with narro fortunes. Nor ar the chances which fling Ruth into error superfluously romantic. While attending on the ladies at a public ball, she is seen by the partner of a spoiled beauty, — she is subsequently thron in his way by chance, and the sad but strange consequences ensue which it is needless to specify . . . Mr. Bellingham is just beginning to weary for another world than that of her smiles, when he is seized with a fever at the little inn in Wales . . . Now begins the important part of the story, — the lesson of Faith, Hope and Charity to inculcate which the tale in hand has been undertaken. — The ill-starred outcast is not deserted in her anguish. — Ruth has, by chance, fallen in with a Dissenting clergyman, by whom the nature and the circumstances of her error hav been early discerned. He is present at the crisis of despair which threatens her death, — is touched with compassion, — and resolvs, almost instinctivly, to succor and to save her. Summoning to his aid a maiden sister, they nurse the desolate outcast throuout her illness, and take her home with them. — She is to be domesticated with them from thenceforth." [Athenæum.] —" Mrs. Gaskell's clear insīt and genuin christianity ar shōn in the novel, which deals with another deep social question; viz., how a society which calls itself christian should treat a fallen woman. Tho it may be said that Ruth is an exceptional person, and that it is the rule rather than the exception which society must regard, the book is a stirring and noble appeal and protest against the merely worldly judgment which condemns without discrimination and without mercy. The book is remarkable for its perfect good taste, for its lack of exaggeration and of that sentimentality which is the counterfeit of real sentiment." [Boston " Lit. World." **1749**

SAD FORTUNES OF THE REV. AMOS BARTON (The). [In Scenes from Clerical Life.] " Of the 3 tales, I think the first is much the best. It is short, broadly descriptiv, humorous, and exceedingly pathetic. The Sad Fortunes of the Reverend Amos Barton ar fortunes which clever story-tellers with a turn of pathos, from Goldsmith downward, hav found of very good account, — the fortunes of a hapless clergyman in daily contention with the problem how upon £80 a year to support a wife and 6 children in ecclesiastical gentility." [H: James.] — " We hav the image of the poor clergyman — not brilliant —

not a favorit with his parishioners — unable to cope with his turbulent vestry — shabbily dressed — thinking all the while of the little mouths at home which he finds it hard to fill; then of his invalid wife, wasting away before the bloom of youth is passed, but every moment sweeter in his eyes as the final, hopeless, irrevocable parting draws nearer and nearer; then his silent, speechless misery by the death-bed, and a simple intimation of a visit, years afterward, to the grave whêre all his happiness lies buried: this is the whole story; but, alas! no less lifelike than true." [Lippincott's.] — " The very first of these, produced without any previous indication of power, in the maturity of her years, affected the world at ōnee to enthusiasm, and she never struck a stronger or deeper note than in the simple story of Amos, or rather of Millie Barton, the poor curate's mild and lōvely wife, the mother of many children, the smiling domestic martyr, whose little tragedy has taken a place among our most cherished recollections as completely as if we had been members of the little rural parliament which discussed her simple story. The power and the pathos of the most remarkable beginning, and its heart-breaking catastrofꝫ, dōes not prevent it from being at the same time full of all the humors of a fresh and unexplored country, delītful in indications of rustic character, and in those wise sayings of village sages which afterwards rose in Mrs. Poyser to the climax of proverbial wisdom." [Blackwood's. **1750**

SAGE OF SIXTEEN. [by Lucy Bethia (Colquhoun) Walford: Blacket & Hallam, 1889.] " Mrs. Walford has written of all sorts and conditions of girls, but so far she has not discovered so sweet and likable a heroin as Elma, 'a sage of 16.' She endears herself to everybody in the story — and out of it — by her glad-hearted, winning ways and her simple little kindnesses. She is welcom whêrever she goes; amongst the 'best people' or amongst the 'half-and-halfs,' with whom she is particularly in sympathy. The nicest thing about Elma is that she is utterly ignorant that she has adopted a mission of any kind. She is one 'whom nature leadeth,' and it is into pleasant ways and places that she and those about her ar conducted. If thêre is a fault to find it is that Elma is perhaps a shade too irresistible in her influence, too invincible, and too entirely unspoiled by circumstances, and that those who seek to emulate her may find their task less easy than it looks. But her story is decidedly pleasant and healthful, and it is a relief to find thêre is sŏmething besides 'slumming' to be done by unselfish people." [Athenæum. **1751**

ST. AGNES' BAY. [*Low,* 1864.] "The main idea is very original, and the narrativ is fresh and lively . . . Still the conception of the various personages is good, and the old doctor, especially, with his alternate fits of angry madness and vigorous friendship, has in him the making of a very telling character. The whole story is supposed to be included in the short space of a few days, during which a yung Cambridge graduate is dwelling, from some curious whim, in a ruined tower perched upon a sea-washed rock . . . How all is explained at last, and the hero finds himself possessed of a father, a wife, and everything which he can possibly wish; all these things ar clearly brôt about in 200 pages without omission or overcrowding in the development of the narrativ. An 'Old Cantab' finds more life in a tiny bay than some

novelists in a crowded city, and puts as much incident in a week as many writers can sto away in a year." [Athen. **1752**

ST. MARTIN'S SUMMER [by SHIRLEY SMITH: London, 1880.] "is not an ill told story. Thêre is freshness and variety in it, and sŏme of its characters ar very prettily conceived . . Thêre is ease of manner and expression both in the descriptions and in the conversations, which enable the reader to go trippingly throu without any great stumbling or cause of offense. We ar introduced to at least 4 very pleasant yung ladies, and at least 4 worthy men, whose fortunes ar told in a natural and lively vein, with much spirit and abundance of lit and frivolous detail. The whole story is, in fact, narrated as a man or woman of the world would be likely to tell it to a group of friends." [Athenæum. **1753**

ST. MUNGO'S CITY [by "SARAH TYTLER," i. e., Henrietta Keddie: *Chatto,* 1884.] "will interest a wider circle than the 'Glasgow bodies,' of whom the author givs such an appreciativ account. The local coloring is rich and vivid . . . but the sterling sense and honor of the ruf, self-raised man of business, Auld Tam, hav a deeper interest, and we cannot but think he will be appreciated by students of character . . . Not less lifelike ar the characters of the 3 Misses Mackinnon — very natural their fencing with the kindly anxiety of Tam Drysdale when he indeavors to find a pretext to save them from what is literally starvation, and with stern politeness they do their best to make his purpos ineffectual. The mess in which they involv themselves by burning the will which has unequally distributed the long expected inheritance from Strathdivie is more comic, but hardly less pathetic. A pleasant contrast to these too austere gentlewomen of the olden time is sweet Eppie Drysdale, a perfectly idyllic heroin." [Ath. **1754**

ST. OLAVE'S. [by ELIZA (TABOR) STEPHENSON: *Hurst*, 1863.] "This charming novel is the work of ōne who possesses a great talent for writing, as well as sōme experience and knoledge of the world." It is distinguished by "discrimination of character, depth of thôt and felicity of expression. It is the work of an artist . . . The scene is laid in an ancient cathedral city. The heroin is a brĭt, sunshiny little creature, full of youth and hope, with 'a fitful maiden-like freedom in her ways and an unschooled gracefulness in her simple speech.' Living with a very old and infirm ânt, Alice Gray amuses herself in the best way she can, and her favorite pastime, after the Bruces come to St. Olave's, is to hear David playing long overtures and symfonies of his ōn composing. Janet likes to watch the gay little figure flitting about the quiet old house; and David is pleased to keep Alice enraptured at his side . . . David says nothing, but the thôt of Alice is never absent from his mind; and henceforth the quiet, gray organist has but one aim in life — to distinguish himself, to make money, to become worthy of Alice Gray, to be able to meet her on terms of equality." [Athenæum. **1755**

SALEM CHAPEL [by MA. OLIPHANT (WILSON) OLIPHANT: *Blackwood*, 1863.] "will take a permanent place in english literature. Thêre is scarcely any other tale of the present day which, for truth and humor and living effect, could take its place beside G: Eliot's 'Scenes of Clerical Life,' without being hurt by the comparison; but this, — that portion of it at least which relates to 'Salem Chapel,' and its organization, — mĭt fairly do so

. . . The Mildmay melodrama is what almost any novelist could do as well or better than the author of ' Salem Chapel,' and we could wish that in some new edition the Mildmay film mĭt be skilfully removed from the book, and the simple squabbles of the Salem Independents left in all thêir purity, — not that we would on any account object to the yung Independent minister's passion for Lady Western; — that is an essential and most artistic element of the story, — the azure background, without which the life of the Salem dissenters would lose half its vivid humor and many of its distinct features. But while this touch is true to art, the story of kidnapping and all but murder which groes out like a fungus on the Lady Western side of the story, is scarcely true artifice even. Having relieved our minds with this protest, we may pass to those features of the tale which we could scarcely praise too hily if we would. Mr. Vincent is the ambitious son of a minister of the Independent ' connexion,' and has just taken charge of Salem Chapel, Carlingford. He is a yung man of taste and refinement much abōve the level of Homerton College, but still penetrated with the maxims of the Independent school, and full of that youthful belief in eloquence, and argument and religious sentiment, which fancies that it can vanquish the world . . . All this is really wonderfully drawn, — with a delicacy and skill of which we can giv but very imperfect proofs in the limits of a single article. The two most perfect pictures in the story ar Tozer, the butterman and principal deacon of Salem Chapel, and Mrs. Vincent, the yung minister's mother. The latter is an etching of marvellous delicacy and art, with every line and shado separately touched in — the

former, a vigorous cartoon of massiv·
effcct and vigorous outline, representing a man who attaches us so much personally that it seems a real privation
not to hav been able to join the ''Omer-
ton students' in that testimonial presented to him for his great ungrammatical
speech in Salem Chapel on behalf of the
liberty of the ministry and against the
tyranny of the 'connexion.' To˷er, the
butterman, is such a character as we
should hav thôt scarcely any one but
G: Eliot could hav drawn. Throu all
the vulgarity of its surface thêre is so
much genial strength and breadth, so
much vulgar manliness, so much intelligence in the shopocratic shrewdness, so
much true mettle behind the stratum of
butter and bacon, such ̭ liberal feeling
within the limit which Salem ideas and
the narro personal vues of his womankind impose, that Tozer, who in the
opening of the story servs to represent
the vulgar pettiness of ignorant congregational aims, seems before its close ʈo
be a figure of more true dignity, tho,
perhaps less intellectual significance,
than even the yung minister." [Specta-
tor. **1756**

SANDRA BELLONI. = *EMILIA
IN ENGLAND.*

SARA [by JULIA BOSVILLE (DAVID-
SON) CHETWYND: *F. V. White*, 1887.] " is
a tale of misunderstanding between husband and wife, told with rather happy
contrivance as to the little accidents
which in novels nearly always, and in
life sōmetimes, hav important consequences . . . The heroin is well drawn
and makes rather an amusing figure. As
the story groes to be more concerned
with her its interest increases. Thêre
ar sōme good bits of character in the
minor people." [Athenæum. **1757**

SARA CREWE [by F.. [ELIZA]
(HODGSON) BURNETT: *Scribner*, 1888.]

" is a very pretty, interesting, and well-
written story . . . Sara livs in a London
boarding-school, whêre she is petted and
made much of until the death of her
only parent leavs her in poverty. Then
she is kept on as a drudge . . . She
becōmes an ill-used, neglected little ōne,
with no friend but her doll, and no
solace but a lōve for reading and a wonderful capacity for 'supposing things.'
. . . Of course it all cōmes rīt in the
end. Sara livs for ̭ while in what
seems a fairy tale made real, finding her
cold, ugly attic transformed in some
magical way into a nest of elegant comfort, new clothes supplied by unknōn·
hands, dainty suppers lying ready for her
when she climbs the garret stairs tired
out at nīt. Then her real, flesh-and-
blood benefactor cōmes to līt, and Sara
leavs Miss Minchin's for kindness and
luxury in a home of her ōn." [Catholic
World. **1758**

SARAH DE BERENGER. [by JEAN
INGELOW: *Roberts*, 1885.] "A poor
woman, of extraordinary character, the
wife of a convict just transported, unexpectedly falls heir to a competence; and
in order to secure it, for the benefit of
her two baby girls, from the possible
future claims of their worthless father,
she assumes a different name, takes the
position of their servant, and rears them
as orfan gentlefolk, of whose incōme,
slender for their false position, altho
amounting to wealth for their true ōne,
she passes for the scrupulously honest
trustee. A great deal of skill is shōn in
the contrivance of slīt chances, whêreby
the self-devoted author of this pious
fraud is continually enabled to escape
detection; and it was clever to conceive
of her as aided, however unwittingly, by
the inveterate folly and freakishness, the
long pampered eccentricities, of the
wealthy and addle-pated spinster who

finally leavs her money to the convict's children. The drawback is that the thing was, after all, so outrageous a fraud that our gratification at its success is felt to be uncomfortably immoral. Moreover the bizarre central figure of Sarah de Berenger, tho happily enuf imagined, is not well developed. She just fails of being an entirely credible, and thêrefor legitimately amusing character. The latter part of the story, from the time when the mother is forced finally to sever herself from her children and go back to her rehabilitated convict, is painful, but powerful also; especially in the way in which we ar forced to share both the poor wife's dispassionate conviction of the reality of her husband's repentance, and her invincible repugnance for his person." [Atlantic. **1759**

SCARBOROUGH FAMILY (The) [by ANTHONY TROLLOPE: *Harper*, 1883.] "is a picture of english life taken in his usual fotografic way; it opens well, drags throu the middle, and gets better again at the close. It concerns the fortunes of a county family, but has a dash of lo life for comedy, sõme fox hunting, a lõve affair in which the lady's family raise fruitless objections, and so on . . . The central figure of the book, however, is not the hero, but old Mr. Scarborough, who is a terrible rascal, judged by ordinary standards, but who, notwithstanding his defiance and violation of all law, human and divine, gains the reader's regard, partly becaus in Mr. Trollope's commonplace world, he is a very uncommonplace man . . All this Mr. Trollope has great difficulty in making seem probable, but interesting it certainly is. In reading this last of his long series of successful novels, in the lît of the admitted fact that they represent English life more clearly than the works of any novelist of our day, we

hav been reminded of õne striking feature of english life as he describes it, in which the criticisms brót out by his death was not dwelt on as much as it deservs to be. We refer to the extraordinarily strong, coarse flavor of money which pervades them. In most american novels, as in american life of our day, money is generally avoided or looked at and spoken of askance, as if thêre wer sõmething belittling about appearing to think too much of it. In Trollope's novels, the action of the book generally revolvs in sõme way about a question of £., s., d., whether a man may marry the woman he lõves, whether a yungster shall go into a profession or emigrate, whether a son shall honor or despise his father, — all questions, practical or sentimental, becõme a simple matter of money, until in the end the reader gets an impression of english society as a country pervaded not merely by a commercial, but by a positivly sordid tone. How much of this is due to England and how much to Mr. Trollope, we must leav others to determin; but as to the fact we think we can hardly be mistaken, for we never lay down one of his novels without regretting that in so rich a country as England it should always seem as if thêre wer rather too little money to ' go round' comfortably, and easily, and expansivly." [Nation. **1760**

SCENES OF CLERICAL LIFE. [by "G: Eliot": *Blackwood*, 1857.] = *SAD FORTUNES, MR. GILFIL'S LOVE-STORY, JANET'S REPENTANCE.*

SCIENTIFIC GENTLEMEN (The). See *NEIGHBORS ON THE GREEN.*

SCOTCH FIRS. [by "S.. TYTLER," i. e., Henrietta Keddie: *Smith*, 1878.] The first "is a well told tale, and the principal and his wife, Marget, and the wily Highlander, ar all racy of the soil. The second narrativ, that of a minister's visit to London, and the change of his vues on the subject of the stage, is equally well imagined, and enforces a generous moral." [Athenæum. **1761**

SCOTCH WOOING (A) [by J. C. AYRTON: *King*, 1875.] " has a good deal of merit. Arundel Fielding has a character which groes upon us as the tale proceeds. At first we see her under the unfavorable influence of a sudden change from english country life, gentle in its traditions, easy-going, uncommercial, to life in a scotch industrial town, among scotch bourgeoisie, whêre she finds sweetness and līt lying at a considerable distance from the surface, and everything except the hospitality of the nativs jarring dissonant from the impression and axioms of her childhood. ' Touch not the cat, but the glove ' is the motto which at first sīt seems appropriate for the guidance of all intercourse at Lairy. Not till sõme stirring experiences hav touched her does she learn to value the strong feeling which underlies the exterior angularity of such ruf-hewn specimens as her uncle Carmichael, and the disputatious earnestness of her uncompromising but devoted lover. When she dões recognize the honesty of thêir attachment her hi and truthful nature finds the discovery very satisfactory. In the revulsion of feeling which folloes, it is natural to her womanly ardor to condone even grave faults such as the frantic and unpardonable jealousy of Stewart, which so nearly wrecks their mutual happiness. This is essentially a novel of character." [Athenæum. **1762**

SCUDAMORES (The). [by F. C. PHILIPS & C. J. WILLS : *Gardner & Co.*, 1890.] " Thêre is movement enuf in ' The Scudamores' for 2 or 3 novels, if not for a play. It is full of down-

rīt characters, english and american, polished and unpolished, serious and comic; and thêrę is not a villain amongst them. The situations ar well conceived, and as thêre ar to 4 or 5 yung people, and two old widoers do the matchmaking and the matchmarring, the authors contrive to escape from the trite and commonplace into an atmosfere of wholesom freshness, they put no strain upon their readers, and consequently secure their attention without effort or difficulty. The cleverness of their story is all on the surface. It is a ' narrativ of incidents and humors, and it eschews analysis as completely as it avoids reflexions and morals." [Athenæum. **1763**

SEABURY CASTLE [by CECIL HOPE: *Lippincott*, 1869.] " is an exceedingly pretty and simple story. The principal personage is a man of hī moral character and great dignity. Sensitiv to a fault, he allows a disappointment in early life to cast a gloom over all his after years, which, tho it is never wholly dispelled, is in sõme measure relieved by the society of 2 very charming girls, his orfan nieces, whose grõth and culture he watches over with parental care. In due time these yung ladies, of course, fall in lõve; but, as they choose wisely, altho they do not escape suffering, and in one case a terrible catastrofē takes place, still their path is not strewn with the thorns which spring up in the way of modern heroins. The story is rather sketchy, but not encumbered with underplot nor surcharged with incidents, nor yet so destitute of them as to be without a considerable portion of life interest." [Round Table. **1764**

SEAMY SIDE (The) [by WA. BESANT & JA. RICE: *Appleton*, 1880.] " is a very readable tale. Its novelty in the way of character is an Albino boy, and a very original character he is. The story deals with a mystery of birth, a worthless scamp of a brother, a voluntary and sacrificial disappearance, and the bare rescue from undeserving hands of a large property. Anthony Hamblin, who is one of its central figures, is a fine man to meet even in a novel." [Boston "Lit. World." **1765**

SEARCH FOR BASIL LYND- HURST (The). [by ROSA NOUCHETTE CAREY: *Lovell*, 1889.] "The scene is a country nêborhood, with its quiet, conservativ society, its great place, its squire's family, and its rectory. The squire's family consists of two dauters, ŏne of them a wido; and the 'search' is for her son, abandoned when an infant by his mother in a paroxysm of half delirium, caused by cruel treatment from the husband with whom she has made a runaway match. Out of these materials is made an entertaining novel, brit, well-bred, and gracefully told." [Boston "Literary World." **1766**

SECOND SON (The) [by MA. OLIPHANT (WILSON) OLIPHANT: *Macmillan*, 1888.] "is far from being the best of its author's stories, but thêre ar good points and situations in it, and thêre is that fidelity to truth in minor details which none but artists possess, and oing to which the reader is impressed with a sense of harmony which allows him to appreciate the plot and narrativ. Very admirable and consistent is the butler in her book, himself not a prominent person, but in his solemnity, and his appreciation of the tragedies and comedies around him, over which he rises in a sense superior, how good a modern substitute for a garrulous greek chorus! How just the sentiments of Pouncefort, the family lawyer; how clever thc glimps of the scotch gardener,

who thôt to add Lily Ford to his floral collection, and of the London fysician and the country apothecary! The plot is not complicated, but every way suffcient to produce a domestic tragedy, and the irony of fate is the 'ower-word,' or refrain, to which one listens." [Athenæum.] — "It is a strong story, clearly planned, allowing for much interplay of character, involving several striking episodes, and its conclusion, easily foreseen, is not at all commonplace. The description of the old manor house is an attractiv bit of realism. Thêre livs squire Mitford, a choleric, self-willed old widoer with his 3 sons — Roger, an accomplished man of the world devoted to the 'busy i·lleness of country life;' Edmund, at the outset of the book a rather motivless dreamer; Stephen, a noisy, imperious young fello with no manner or morals to speak of — and here, too, dwells Nina, an interesting specimen of the english girl transferred from the school-room to the drawing-room, and, for want of other resources, passing her time in eavesdropping and the exchange of scandal with the servants. In the keeper's lodge ar the Fords, with their beautiful, slender, golden-haired dauter, Lily. In the fine new mansion on the hill, not far away, is the sensible yung heiress, Elizabeth Travers. These, with Pax, the rector's elderly dauter, ar the chief characters, and readers of Mrs. Oliphant's novels do not need to be told that they play their parts well." [Boston "Literary World."] — "As a study of character, with deep feeling associated with perfectly simple and realistic incidents, it is ŏne of the best novels of the year. The grouping of the 3 brothers around the one woman is admirably managed; and Lily is a new creation . . . The choleric old

Squire is a strong feature; and his indignation when he learns, not that Stephen has tricked Lily, but that having meant to trick her, he had found the yung woman too 'smart' for him, is wonderfully natural and amusing." [Critic. **1767**

SECOND THOUGHTS. [by RHODA BROUGHTON: *Appleton*, 1880.] "Yes, second thôts ar best; and Miss Broughton's present way of illustrating and enforcing that maxim is entertaining. It is a very clever process of psychological art by which she brings round Dr. Burnet and Gillian, who at the outset ar back to back, so to speak, until they ar face to face. Little by little you see them turn — she from her antipathy and scorn, he from his indifference and neglect. Only, the end is foreseen from the beginning, and thêre is little in the book to pique the reader's curiosity. Sõme of the best things in it ar the contemporary portraits, as we will call them: Gillian's bedridden old father, a very perfect character-sketch; the meek and docile squire Marlowe and his majestic and commanding dauter Jane, who furnish between them much amusement; the stiff Miss Burnet, the doctor's spinster sister, well framed in her stately London drawing-room; and last, but not least, the sentimental and poetical Challoner, beneath whom lies, we must think, an intended caricature of the whole Swinburne-Rossetti school." [Boston "Literary World."] — "Miss Broughton has here dropped her sensational and somewhat hoydenish tone, and] has given us as pretty and proper a lõve-story as õne would care to read. The old process of the taming of a shrew has seldom been more neatly and effectivly depicted; and, aside from its sparkle and vivacity, the story possesses qualities which make it really valuable as a picture." [Appleton's. **1768**

SELF-CONDEMNED. [by MA. (RAINE) HUNT: *Chatto*, 1883.] "Barrington is a writer, and he and Miss Carey fall desperately in lõve, she under mental protest, he with selfish, or at least, thôtless, disregard of Roger Hackbloch's prior claims . . . Some use is made of the cooking school at Kensington, thêre ar touches of the literary and histrionic elements in the course of the story, in which Wentworth Wilbraham, a scapegrace son and Kitty's persecutor, is the unhappy victim. The strength of the book lies in the portrayal of eccentric characters, and their contrasts, and in the naturalness, to the extreme point of simplicity, of the delineation of feeling, motiv, and conduct. Thêre ar many lâfable things in the book — lâfable like the absurd actions of absurd people which we see going on before our eyes every day." [Boston "Literary World."

——, SAME ["Barrington's Fate."] *Roberts*, 1883.

SELF OR BEARER [by WA. BESANT: *Chatto*, 1889.] " is full of fun. It is, in brief, the story of a poor doctor who became a viscount and was extremely uncomfortable, and then lost his title and became happy. This is not the gist of the plot, but the fun of it depends upon this incidental contrivance of circumstances. It is not often that so much good reading is found in õne volume." [Athenæum. **1769**

——, SAME, with *TO CALL HER MINE*.

SEMI-ATTACHED COUPLE (The). [by EMILY EDEN: *Bentley*, 1860.] "It has really dõne our heart good to read this lĩt, slĩt, pleasant novel. It is clever, very clever, — tho we hav read dozens of novels with more talent in them; but we hav read very few which ar so pleasant as this 'Semi-Attached Couple,'

SEMI-DETACHED HOUSE (The). [by EMILY EDEN (1797-69): *Bentley*, 1859.] "There is freshness of humor and good-humor in this little story. It is full of a frank, sociable feeling, of the liter sort of talk which is one of the charms of good society, and of the sound instinct which exists where true human courtesies ar honestly exchanged, and kindly or affectionate relations can spring out of them. Character-painting so entirely unpretending in its manner, and so perfect of its sort, as that which givs to this novel its value as a work of art, is not often to be found among the novelists who do not stand in the front rank. The author has not attempted mity things but, after its pleasant way, the 'Semi-Detached House' is in many respects perfect. The heroin is a very young and happy bride, whose husband is for a few months withdrawn from her by a diplomatic appointment after the first half-year of marriage. She is a good girl, weak in health, and strong in imagination, lively, fastidious, and a little spoilt. Blanche can not, during her husband's absence, stay with her father-in-law, because he thinks it a good joke to call her Blanket; nor with her brother-in-law, because he would count the cost of her keep; nor with her ânt, because the doctor who would attend her there wears creaking boots. *Her* doctor has determind that she shal liv out of town, and her husband accordingly has rented for her a furnished villa on the Thames, to which there happens to be another and a smaller house attached, inhabited, as she learns from her sensible ânt Sarah, by Hopkinsons . . . As to the fastidiousness, the story tels that altho both the Hopkinson and the Chester households set out with strong prejudices founded upon fancy, altho Lady Blanche was connected only with the aristocracy, and Mrs. Hopkinson, the wife of a sturdy sea-captain, was really fat and unlettered, and wore mittens,—a good heart was the life of each of the two homes, the young bride and the motherly old lady each knew and did her duty to her nebor, and throu the little offiçes of human kindness simply rendered, became large debtors to each other. Neborly feeling is, in fact, the topic of the story, the superfiçial differençes of rank, person, and manner ar lost sight of in the unaffected interchange of kindly words and deeds . . . The spirit of the book we hav described, but its story we do not mean to disclose. Let it be cheerful reading to the idler, and welcome relaxation to the worker." [Exam. **1770 a**

oing to the spirit of kindness, charity, and good-breeding which pervades every page, we may say every line. Thêre ar brĭt little touches of humor which prevent the goodness becoming oppressive, giving a sparkle and briskness to the whole. Thêre ar no set descriptions, and the story reads more like the scenes of a genteel comedy than a novel." [Athenæum. **1770**

SENIOR PARTNER (The) [by C. ELIZA LAWSON (COWAN) RIDDELL : Harper, 1881.] " is a novel which will last — no small recommendation to people of busy brains, who turn to a novel for refreshment on the same principle that they go to see a good comedy. It is so solidly, carefully dõne, that thêre is no temptation either to skip it or skim it. It is in this respect more like Trollope's work than we should hav supposed a woman's could be. Much of it has that same fotografic fidelity. Robert McCullagh — ' plain auld Rab ' — is the head of a commercial house in London, but õne whêre everything is scotch — ' deeply, darkly, beautifully scotch.' His õne virtue is his unswerving honesty, as, cold of heart and hard of head, he makes his lõveless way to fortune. Such a man must needs be harsh to his children, and the plot deals mainly with his injustice to his son Robert and the heaping of coals upon his head by Robert's noble wife. But the interest is less in that side of the story than in the contrast between McCullagh and Pousnett, who is the veritable ' Senior Partner.' The contrast is never obtruded, but left to impress itself on the reader's mind in the development of events : Rab, always crabbed, repellant, grasping, but always with the fine fibre of strict honor in his nature : Pousnett, winning, suave, plausible — speaking never a falsehood, but, equally, speaking never the truth." [Nation. **1771**

SENIOR SONGMAN (The). [by ELIZA (TABOR) STEPHENSON : Harper, 1883.] " Whoever has kuõn the brooding sunshine, the creeping shadõs, the delicious quiet which make the charm of a cathedral close, will recognize the scenes of this story of ' The Senior Songman.' The romance is a double, if not a treble, õne, the first interweaving with the placid monotony of the close and a drowsy town the passionate hopes which waken under an italian sky. The second blooms and fades, or reopens to glad fruition in the very home of the songman as he goes in and out, ever graver and sadder with the pain of memory and the keen disappointment of present loss. Thêre ar two heroins. No two could be more different in their nature or their fate, but to each of them came the truest peace which either could hav asked, ' the peace of living up to the best they knew.' The chords ar minor chords, but patience, endurance, forgivness and faith make the music a tender harmony. The Senior Songman will be remembered as a gentle and modest companion in the little group of which the Warden of Hiram's Hospital is first." [Nation. **1772**

SENSITIVE PLANT (A) [by E. & D. GERARD, i. e., Emily (Gerard) Laszowska & Dorothea Gerard : Paul, 1891.] " is in many ways an able and pleasant book. The irascible Sir Alec, who makes a point of complaining of everything and disagreeing with everybody, is as entertaining in fiction as he would be terrible in life, and as a specimen of the perfectly amiable and perfectly tactless woman, Miss Penny, who is never daunted by ill-luck in ' breaking things' to her ' dear brother,' is simply a masterpiece. Mr. d'Osbon, the epicure, whose slõly but steadily groing passion for Janet is rooted in his belief that she was the compounder of a certain wonderful lobster soufflé, is drawn with rather coarse strokes; but he is amusing—at any rate, for a time." [Spectator.] — "A pale, frïtened child, whose natural timidity has been suffered to gro unchecked and unheeded until it has developed intb a sort of savage shyness, something absolutely painful to herself as well as to the beholder, is the heroin. . . . The scene is changed to Venice, the child becomes a woman and struggles alone with the self-asserting world; but the change from the hard, cold northern country in which she was born to the soft southern beauty of Italy has a happy effect upon her, and she livs and blooms in the sunshine which has cōme into her life at last." [Critic.] — "The entire motif of the story is the analysis of the painful shyness of an ingenuous girl, whose childhood has been shadoed by many circumstances tending to make her shrink into herself. The authors hav dōne their part with a good deal of success, not the least being the fact that they manage to make Janet's nervous misery, which is at first only not contemptible, becōme gradually subordinated to that unselfishness which is really a deeper-seated attribute of her character, and which eventually entitles her to the reader's consideration. Honest and loving as she is, we do not, any more than her lōver, feel a particle of respect for her until she rushes, as she supposes, into moral danger to save him from death, after the fashion of a valiant hen partridge or most magnanimous mouse. The local setting of 'the Mimosa,' the old house and policies left stranded in a grimy district of scottish coal fields, the sundial under the copper beech, the glen in which Janet first meets her lover, ar all real and suitable." [Athenæum. **1773**

SEVENTY TIMES SEVEN [by

ADELINE SERGEANT: Edinburgh, *Oliphant*, 1888.] "is a very beautiful, powerful, and pathetic story, the general effect of which we can best describe by saying that the book has reminded us very frequently of ōne or two of the best novels of Jessie Fothergill. We do not mean that the new story is at all imitativ, or that we can lay our finger here and thêre upon special parallelisms or reminders; but that the general handling, especially the conception and grouping of character, dōes undoubtedly recall the total impression left by such books as Probation [No. 1703] and Kith and Kin [No. 1436], tho in intensity of passionate imagination, Seventy Times Seven must certainly take rank belo the last named story, —ōne of the most impressiv novels which has been written since the days of C̈.. and Emily Brontê." [Spectator. **1774**

SHADOW OF ASHLYDYAT. [by ELLEN (PRICE) WOON: *Bentley*, 1864.] "It is in the working out of the main fact, and in the variety of incidents involved, that the strength and charm of the story lie. We think that Mrs. Wood has dealt too leniently with the gay and gallant G: Godolphin, whose sins bring so much wo upon innocent persons; but even the female reader will be constrained to forgiv Miss Charlotte Pain, unprincipled as she is, for the sake of her thōro good-nature. T: Godolphin is a noble character. The episode of Ethel Grame, the girl to whom he ıs engaged, is skilfully managed. Maria, the wife of G: Godolphin, is sure of the reader's sympathy; she is a sweet and perfect wife—too perfect, for if she had expressed her ōn good sense with more emfasis, it would hav been better, tho not so pleasant, for the erring Mr. George. In all the details of the personal and private troubles which follo

SENSE AND SENSIBILITY. [by J..
AUSTEN: *Bentley*, 1833.] "As the novels of Miss Austen never weary, thêir
interest is never lost; for, as in the prints
of Hogarth, we find fresh matter for
admiration upon every renewal of ôûr
acquaintançe. Her fables ar of the simplest construction; her inçidents in the
common course of things; and her characters ar extraordinary ōnly in the truth
of thêir delineation. The story she tels
in all her works is the story of human
nature in its most familiar phases. Thêre
ar no exaggerations, and no defiçiençies,
and it is by the completeness of the vue
of character that the fulness of the effect
is produçed. The persons described ar
such as we meet every day, but we hav
never seen thêir peculiarities in connexion
with thêir causes of action. The scene is
before us with all the reality of the world,
and, free from the engrossment of acting
a part in it, we discôver points of interest
which a divided attention had overlooked.
The commonplaçe characters of the town
and the village ar the characters which
Miss Austen makes of interest by making
them thōroly understood. In the story
before us what an example of the worthless is Mr. J: Dashwood—not worthless
as implying viçe, but the negativ of
worth, of which common character Miss
Austen has evinçed a perfect comprehension, and presented various illustrations.
Mr. Dashwood is incapable of a generous
sentiment or a benevolent action, but he is
a rigid observer of all the laws of the
world, and we kno full wel that so really
despicable a man would pass as a pattern
of propriety. He has a wife all selfishness and worldliness, tõ whõm he looks
with veneration, consecrating all her
foibles, and admiringly magnifying her
littleness ... Mrs. Ferrars is anōther excellently drawn character; ōne of those
creatures cankered with wealth, the
tyrants of the mōney-box, the capriçious
despots of the last wil and testament, whõ
make those about them slaves of expectation, tormenting them with fears of disappointment, and causing the interested
hopes of thêir death tõ be frant with
miseries and abasements during thêir
lives. Her merit considered, her perfection in ōne style, Miss Austen is the worst
appreçiated novelist of her time. She
labored under the disadvantage of having
the inferior stamp of circulating library
popularity put up n her works, before
the superior judges had becōme acquainted with them, and recognized thêir hī
degree of excellençe. The Quarterly Review was the first critical authority which
did justiçe tõ her merits, and that after
the grave had closed over her modest
genius." [Examiner, 1833. 1772 v

the great catastrofē of the Bank, Mrs. Wood has shōn skill; but it must not be supposed that ' The Shadow of Ashlydyat' is an oppressiv book — the reader's interest is never sacrificed, and it is a book which he may return to with pleasure." [Athenæum. **1775**

SHADRACH [*Bell*, 1879.] " is a very charming story. The modesty, the good taste and withal the vigorous performance of these delītful volumes (which ar ' dedicated with tender and reverent gratitude to the memory of Annie Keary '), warrant the reader in believing that a worthy recruit has been enlisted in the service of a public. If these impressions ar just, more than the mantle of Miss Keary has fallen on the sholders of the writer to whom we ar indebted for the romance of ' Shadrach.' It is not that the narrativ is at all times sustained on the bīest levels, that the workmanship is always of the finest and subtlest, that the conception is thōroly original, the plot faultlessly proportioned, or the style without blemish. ' Shadrach' has its faults. It is, perhaps, too ambitious; its characters and incidents ar here and thêre a little vague and overdrawn; its motivs, always lofty and pure, occasionally defy the efforts of the artist and elude her grasp. Admitting all this, this story is ōne which may charm even the exacting and fastidious." [Athenæum. **1776**

SHANDON BELLS. [by W: BLACK: *Harper*, 1883.] " In ' Shandon Bells ' we welcom a book which charms at the outset, and, if it dōes not maintain its fascination till the end, puts a sting of regret into our memory of it almost better than complete satisfaction. Mr. Black has indeed a supreme gift of endowing his women with charm, — a charm so ethereal and elusiv that it is, happily, to be felt and not described.

And Miss Kitty Romayne, besides making both the hero and the reader fall in lōve with her, writes lōve-letters which ar the treasure of the book, written with an overflo of fancy and feeling which the author has rarely surpassed. That the pretty, faithless, mercenary Kitty wins our heart, while to Miss Chetwynd's excellences and perfections we remain obstinately indifferent, may be true to every-day experience, but is, we think, one of the faults of the book. Master Willie Fitzgerald, the hero, is a very pretty hero indeed, — modest, lovable, clever, endowed with a warm heart and a capacity for intense sentiment which puts him wholly out of the category of modern heroes. The story of his entrance into London literary life is capitally given; and, ideal and fanciful as Mr. Black's imaginativ flīts may be, his realism is always the simplest." [Lippincott's. **1777**

SHE WAS YOUNG AND HE WAS OLD. [by M.. L.. (STEWART) MOLESWORTH: *Tinsley*, 1872.] " We ar introduced to the heroin at a pensionnat, in Switzerland, whêre an english lady is living with her two dauters, under the care of Mr. Montluc, a worthy little ' pasteur,' whose chiêf claim to recognition lies in his being the husband of Mrs. Montluc. — Mrs. Urquhart is hopelessly ill, and Eleanor, that her mother may die happy, consents to marry her gardian, Mr. Marshall, a prosaic, pompous, but unaffectedly honest and simple-minded country lawyer . . . Once established as the wife of a middle-aged, humdrum attorney, immersed in business, Eleanor begins to feel, tho she was slo to realize, ' the galling yoke of an uncongenial, unsympathetic marriage,' and would hav found her isolated life intolerable but for the little sister on whom all her passionate tho undemonstrativ affection was lavished . . . We cannot do more than allude to the admirable touches which the writer has hit off many of the weak points of provincial life. This is a book which we can honestly recommend." [Athen. **1778**

SHEBA. [by "RITA," i. e., Eliza M. J. (Gollow) Booth: *White & Co.*, 1889.] "The author retains her power of original portraiture of women, and Sheba, intellectual, imaginativ, and passionate, will hold a conspicuous place in her gallery. The tragic history of the wild australian girl, after her easy-going, but loving father's death, and when she has escaped from the thraldom of petty people with snobbish social aims, but no aspirations like hers, turns upon the terrible moral problem: given a lŏveless and sin-dishonored marriage, and an irregular connexion begun in ignorance, but riveted by sympathy and passion, which is the true marriage, which the outrage upon nature? It is not quite certain how far the author is in sympathy with Franz Müller, the old german violinist, who shakes Sheba's faith in the orthodox creed." [Athenæum. **1778a**

SHEPHERDS ALL AND MAIDENS FAIR. [by WA. BESANT & JA. RICE: *Chatto*, 1879.] "A wholesom contrast is here drawn between the vigorous honesty and purity of the yung canadian farmer, the suspicious isolation of his long estranged father in England, the crushed affections and acquired timidity of his father's ward Lettice Langton (a heroin as pretty as her name), and the precocious development of vulgar vice in the foolish yung clerk, her brother. The localities ar drawn with a descriptiv power which enhances the contrast of characters, and makes a picturesque setting to the story." [Athenæum. **1779**

SILAS MARNER. [by "G: ELIOT": *Blackwood*, 1861.] "A poor, dull-witted, disappointed Methodist cloth-weaver; a little golden-haired foundling chīld; a well-meaning, irresolute country squire, and his patient, childless wife; — these, with a chorus of simple, beer-loving villagers, make up the dramatis personæ. More than any of her other works, 'Silas Marner,' I think, leavs upon the mind a deep impression of the grossly material life of agricultural England in the last days of the old régime, — the days of full-orbed Toryism, of Trafalgar and of Waterloo, when the invasiv spirit of french domination threw England back upon a sense of its insular solidity, and made it for the time doubly, brutally, morbidly english. Perhaps the best pages in the work ar those telling the story of poor Marner's disappointments in friendship and in lŏve, his unmerited disgrace, and his long, lonely, twilīt life at Raveloe, with the sole companionship of his loom." [H: James.] — "It has less variety, its pathos is more quiet, the dialogs ar sometimes tedious instead of amusing, and the humor seems more an accident than an element of the book. The tale begins tragically and ends quietly . . . But Silas Marner is a masterly creation. It is evident that the author, with even more than her usual singleness of purpos, has coneentrated all her power on the artistic development of this, her leading character, and her efforts hav met signal success. The successiv changes sloly wrŏt in this man's soul by the vicissitudes of his life ar portrayed with marvellous effect. The insīt which enables G: Eliot to lay bare so thŏroly the heart, is equalled only by the rare skill shŏn in delineating these hidden springs of thŏt and action, which being so subtile and undefined, ar more difficult to embody than to conceive. In depicting the solitary life of the outcast weaver, the author has also clearly solvd the problem of how the love of gold for its ōn sake alone can becōme, in a nature generous as well as intense, not ōnly an absorbing passion, but an all-satisfying enjoyment. No one, after reading Silas Marner's nĭtly revels over his shining hoard, can wonder at such an infatuation, even while forced to deplore it. The loss of this gold, and the dawning of a new life upon the enfeebled intellect and heart of the weaver throu the gentle influence of a child, which not only brŏt him nearer to God but to the world, is most tenderly and charmingly told. And the gradual way in which the transformation is effected commends itself particularly for its naturalness." [Christ. Examiner. **1780**

SIMPLE STORY (A). [by E.. (SIMPSON) INCHBALD, 1791.] "Open to criticism on many points, bŏth literary and artistic, as it is, its appeal to what is tender and true in human nature is so genuin that the cool analyst is disarmed, and lured to recognition of the faith and feeling, the fondness and despair, in two eager, exacting, devoted, but perverse hearts. The magnetism of the story is its pathos, whêrein few works of fiction excel this of Mrs. Inchbald's, who gave to this quality a new charm, and a hitherto unappreciated value as a means and method of imparting vital human interest to fiction. *Nature and Art*, tho similar in tone, is less complete and impressiv in this regard. The 'Simple Story' marks a transition period in novel-writing, when the mutual interaction of character, softened and inspired by sentiment, creates a new world of emotional experience." [H: Th. Tuckerman. **1781**

SIMPLICITY AND FASCINATION. [by A.. BEALE: *Bentley*, 1855.] "The ōnly foolish thing in this novel is its title, which is certainly enuf to deter any but an adventurous reader from its pages. Those who begin will, however, find their virtue rewarded by as pleasant a novel as they would wish to read on a winter's day. It is a well-drawn picture of domestic life; the characters ar well contrasted, and the situations and incidents ar interesting. Aunt Betsey and Uncle Timothy ar our favorits; Jessiê, the mother-sister to her family, is charming, — which is saying no little for a model heroin. The book ends happily, and even a misanthrope must hav hopes of a world whêre so many happy marriages can take root and flourish. Thêre ar as many couples as in a country dance; and altho the figure is a little complicated, yet the rĭt partners find each other at last, and everybody marries precisely the rĭt person. If the candid reader had been consulted ever so much he could not hav arranged matters more to the contentment of everybody concerned." [Athenæum.] — [*Lee.*] "Simplicity and Fascination is unique in its pleasant old-fashioned directness, plainness, leisurely detail, and its great propriety, sincerity, and kindliness of spirit." [Overland. **1782**

SIR AUBYN'S HOUSEHOLD [by SIGMA: *Tinsley*, 1878.] "is the lōve-story of two sisters, one of whom is a beauty, the other, at least by comparison, plain. The writer has had the courage to contravene the common tradition in such a case; he makes the beauty the finer and the more interesting character of the two. How she gĭvs her heart away, and what cōmes of it; throu what rapids and ruf places the current of her lōve has to run, and how it finds itself at last in peace, is very

attractivly told. The characters ar
natural, if not striking; they talk like
possible creatures, they never cease to
interest us. The story is, indeed,
scarcely the ' plain unvarnished tale'
which the author is pleased to call it.
The lover is found to be sōmething like
a prince in disguise; the heroin passes
throu adventures which ar doubtless
possible, which may even be probable,
but which ar certainly romantic, and
scarcely enter into the calculable contingencies of life in the 19th century.
But we do not kno that the book is the
worse for the introduction of this more
novel and exciting element." [Specta-
tor.   **1783**

SIR BROOK FOSBROOKE. [by C:
LEVER: _Blackwood_, 1866.] "Several
years hav passed since Mr. Lever gave
us so good a novel as ' Sir Brook Fosbrooke,' in which we encounter much of
the pungent humor and mad frolic of his
earlier tales, combined with certain
hier qualities which ar looked for in
vain in his most popular stories. The
drama opens in the mess-room of a regiment quartered at Dublin, with a scene
which introduces us to a party of military men, who ar chatting about the
dissipations and scandals of the irish
capital with that caustic sprītliness which,
according to novelists, characterizes the
ordinary conversation of officers; and
from this lively introduction, written in
the author's happiest style, readers glide
without effort into the body of the vivacions and vigorous narrativ." [Athe-
næum.   **1784**

SIR FELIX FOY [by DUTTON COOK:
Low, 1865.] "is a story of every day
life, with nothing sensational or extravagant about it — a story which deals
with persons who for the most part mīt
appear, at first sīt, commonplace, and
even uninteresting. Sir Felix occupies

the most prominent position, or perhaps
shares it with Lydia Finch, the lady who
ultimately becōmes his wife; but the
pains which Mr. Cook has bestovd
upon his principal performers hav not
rendered him careless about the minor
personages of the drama. Mr. Foy, the
baronet's brother, an amiable, eccentric,
untidy clergyman, with a constant smile
and ' a habit of nodding his head in a
kindly approving way, no matter what
sort of observation mīt be addressed to
him,' is so pleasant a character that we
ar sorry not to hav more of his company. Especially charming is the story
of his quiet, unspoken lōve for Alice
Pratt — a yung lady in his parish, with
very attractiv eyes, and a chin ' charmingly fashioned, nibbed, as it wer, with
a dimple.' Then thêre is Lady Casey,
the baronet's ānt, a spirited old lady, of
a vagrant disposition, with a great belief
in sherry as a specific for all sorts of
ailments, both mental and bodily, who
spends her life in roaming about, able
to hold her ōn with all she meets, and
indulging in utterances of an original
and spicy nature." [London Rev. **1785**

SIR JAMES APPLEBY [by K.. S.
MACQUOID: _Harper_, 1887.] "is an original and entertaining story, in which a
yung man who givs up law for literature
exerts a decided influence on the fortunes of the characters by working a
true story into a romance. The romance
is read by people who follo the advice
in ' Dombey and Son ' to make an application on't,' with important results to
all concerned." [Critic.   **1786**

SIR JOHN [by CHRISTIANA J..
DOUGLÁSS: _Hurst_, 1879.] "is a good,
old-fashioned scottish tale, — a calm,
domestic narrativ. It has abundant
interest, without any straining after the
sensational . . . Jenny Setocun's lōvers
ar drawn with much appreciativ taste,

and the contrast between them is finely and firmly brôt out. Jenny's friend, too, has a pretty lōve story, which finally ripens into an arrangement such as men's sisters perhaps more fre- quently intrigue for than accomplish." [Athenæum. **1787**

SIR PERCIVAL [by J : H : SHORT- HOUSE : *Macmillan*, 1887.] "is perfect, and tho unpretentious it is beautiful in its simplicity. Sir Percival is a very modern lad, and the story is that of two girls who lōved him; both hī-bred and noble-hearted, tho' ōne was an ascetic and ōne a religious and social radical. The story is beautifully told, and tho the situation is a little strained, and both girls ar a little morbid, thêre is a charm in the fascination of the style which makes the book a grateful oasis in the desert of realism. It is a very little book, and one longs for more of its cool purity and gracious, aristocratic charm." [Critic.] — " It leaves an impression of being elevated and made better, and its moral beauty, spirituality, and nobility of motiv make most recent novels seem leaden, earthly and commonplace in comparison." [Spectator. **1788**

SIR TOM. [by MA. OLIPHANT (WIL- SON) OLIPHANT : *Macmillan*, 1884.] "Thêre is no indication in 'Sir Tom' of any failure of Mrs. Oliphant's well- knōn incisivness and ease, but the story will not be remembered as ōne of her happiest efforts. Perhaps that is partly the result of the uninteresting and common-place figure of Sir Tom him- self. Having spent a rather purposless and not very innocent life, principally abroad, he marries, in his forties, a yung heiress of unusual innocence, who enables him throu her fortune to take a leading part in his county for which he becōmes M. P. He is good natured and sincerely fond of his wife and infant

son; but his tenderness dōes not carry him the length of consenting to her deal- ing with her money according to the tenor of her father's will, nor his rever- ence to that of refraining from inviting into his house a certain Contessa di Forno-Populo and her *protégée* Bice, the former lady an acquaintance of his bo- hemian days, and the latter of entirely unknōn parentage and history. The principal part of the story deals with the endurance by poor Lady Randolph of her husband's neglect under the infin- ence of his fascinating friend — endur- ance which culminates in the sharp pain of discovering, on what seems good au- thority, that Bice, the brīt yung italian, with the morals of a savage and the im- pulses of an affectionate child, the ōnly one of the party who feels an honest friendship for her, is her husband's dauter. One of the best parts of the book is the contrast between the open- hearted Bice, who looks upon her pat- rouess's efforts to trade her away in matrimony as the most natural thing in the world, and the almost equally simple Lucy Randolph, who employs all the means in her power to prevent what she deems a revolting act of human sacri- fice. Bice's relations, too, with the ex- cellent Jack Trevor, a fine specimen of the mingled priggishness and callōness which blend with better qualities in the 'sixth-form' boy, and with that superior person M'Tutor, Jack's guide, filosofer, and friend, ar very amusing." [Athe- næum. **1789**

SISTER [*Smith*, 1888.] "is a domestic story of a superior kind, and deservs an appreciativ welcom. The language is pure, and this is the more satisfactory becaus the narrativ is not stiff and awkward, but has the freedom too often secured at the sacrifice of grace, if not correctness. That on which the author may specially congratulate himself is that he can produce the natural manner, expressions, acts, and expedients of ordinary men and women without suggesting anything like slavish imitation. The 'Sister' who is the central figure of the story is the eldest of a family of 4 girls, who lose first thêir mother and then thêir father, but ar kept fairly safe against the buffets of fortune by their good sense, thêir staunch friends, and, abōve all, by the more than motherly care of 'the hen,' as Jane Anderson is lovingly called by her yunger sisters. Two of the four ar made thōroly happy in the orthodox sense of marrying well; and the other two ar left, at the close of the story, possibly just as happy in another way, tho their path to happiness is thorny. Thêre is really not much more in the book than the lōve stories of the sisters, but these stories ar treated in such a way that the reader will not be likely to crave for more excitement." [Athenæum. **1790**

SISTERS OF OMBERSLEIGH (The) [by ROSA MACKENZIE KETTLE: *Unwin*, 1888.] "reminds us of Miss Austen. It is a placid bit of gentle life, in which, however, the characters ar distinct enuf. Agnes, the shy, undemonstrativ wife of a brilliant husband, who has married in haste to repent at leisure, is an excellent study, while her far more attractiv sister Isabella is in her way as pathetic a figure. The style is classical, with an old-fashioned ring about it. Altogether, slīt in texture as it is, the little story has more individuality than most modern novels." [Athenæum. **1791**

SIX TO SIXTEEN. [by JULIANA HORATIA (GATTY) EWING: (†, 1886) *Bell*, 1875.] "The author shōes a fine insīt into character in her portraits of infantine humanity, and the grōth of Margery and her friends into brīt and lovable girlhood is traced with rare simplicity and corresponding skill. Mrs. Ewing's story for girls is a pretty little volume suggestiv of many moral deductions, but never wêted with the least taunt of 'preachiness'—in which a small family party of boys and girls tell thêir stories and reveal thêir characteristics in a picturesque and unobtrusiv fashion. Girls, who reason partly with their hearts, should hav more leisure than men for this complete development. This brīt and suggestiv writer is responsible for apparent deviation from the grooves of the revuer's duty. To return to them, we may say that we hav rarely met, on such a modest scale, characters so ably and simply drawn." [Athenæum. **1792**

SKIRMISHING [by HENRIETTA CAMILLA (JACKSON) JENKINS: (†, 1885) N. Y., *Leypoldt*, 1866.] "is a simple and touching story, delicately conceived, and breathing throuōut a spirit of kindliness and christian charity, and a sympathetic lōve and appreciation of all which is beautiful in nature and elevating in thōt. The characters ar mere sketches, but marked by so distinct individuality as to render elaboration unnecessary. The scene is laid in the pleasant village of Eden, far from any hī-road . . The greatest interest centres in her child, whose sad and touching story awakens a feeling of deep sympathy akin to that which one experiences for 'Mignon.'" [Round Table.]—"Altho of a līter character than 'Who Breaks,' and shorter, we think it more complete. The racy dialog is racier. The plot unfolds with the dash and rapidity of a french comedy. The plot is a gem of a plot. Thêre is a spicy little mystery whose catastrofē is positivly a surprise even in these days;

569

and yet not a bit of a forgery or a particle of the Braddon machinery is employed. It is the kind of a story which suggests dramatization, ōnly that by making a play of it the clever descriptions, and the scraps of filosofy scattered throuoūt, would be lost. We read of all sorts of old ladies in books, sharp, or senile, or benevolent, or pious, but rarely ōne of that kind which is rare enuf, but still to be found in life — an old woman who adds experience to ability without extinguishing the warmth and spontaneity of youthful feeling; who joins to that fine result a quick wit, a keen sense of the ridiculous, a touch of defiance of public opinion, the utmost benevolence, and a mind well stored with the reading and events of the day. Mrs. Lescrimière remembers her part, too, in the revolution. She tells an apt story well. Her good-humored antagonisms to british prejudices is delītful. Her ruling principle is expressed in the motto quoted from her on the title-page : ' Never repent a good action, however it turns out for yourself.' Such a person in ōne's house would be a perfect specific for all sorts of selfishness and moroseness; we ar not sure that it is not a partial cure just to read of her." [Nation. **1793**

SMALL HOUSE AT ALLINGTON (The) [by ANTHONY TROLLOPE : *Smith*, 1864.] " is a capital sketch of country life, with its quiet pleasures and quiet sorrōs, — its ineffable sameness and appalling dulness. To this ar added pictures of London boarding-house life, and several scenes in hī life . . . The character of Mr. Crosbie is also well drawn, — his struggle between love of rank, position, property, — and innocence and simplicity, is given with a minuteness and truth that can be rarely equalled. The misery he entails upon

himself, not so much by his wrong-doing as from the inherent nobleness of his nature, is run into its minute moral results. We cannot help sympathizing with him in the manly way in which he accepts the results of his villainy, and resolvs to liv the hīest life in his power with his wife, whom he dōes not lōve. The two female characters ar masterpieces. Fresh, natural, simple, full of life and feeling and foibles, they move before us as living characters." [Christian Examiner.]— " Dōes any body wish to kno where to find the best and nicest girls in all England — the kindest, the purest, the pleasantest young ladies we hav ever met — at least in a book? They used to live in the ' Small House at Allington.' For aut we kno Miss Lily Dale livs with her mother still. And if thêre ar no better and nobler men in the world than such as Mr. Trollope has yet introduced to her acquaintance, we would hav this most lōvable of women abide still in her maiden home. Crosbie, Adolphus Crosbie of Sebright's Club, is a selfish, heartless coward, a slave to the vain pursuit of social ambition; Johnny Eames, with all his frankness and good feeling, is deficient in strength of mind. Neither of these could be worthy of Lily Dale. We like the custom which Mr. Trollope has adopted, — that of bringing into a later story, among its background figures, a few of the most interesting characters of a former tale. [See Nos. 1082, 1213, 1288, & 1999.] Thêre is the dear old warden [compare No. 1131, end], that pattern of christian meekness and fidelity, whom Crosbie meets at the cathedral door of Barchester; thêre is the pushing and prosperous archdeacon, with his dauter, Lady Dumbello, a mere monument of fashionable elegance, a superb and stately belgravian doll. In the same manner, if Mr. Trollope pleases, we shall again see Lily Dale. She will make the most agreeable and estimable of old maids. It will be such a comfort to her mother, the wido, that Lily should remain at the Small House — it will be such a blessing to the children of Dr. and Mrs. Crofts at Guestwick, — that for Mrs. Dale's sake and for Bell's sake, whom we care to see happy as well as Lily, we would rather not hav her married and carried away." [London Review. **1794**

SNAPT GOLD RING (A) [by F: WEDMORE: *Smith*, 1871.] "is, if we may venture to say so, a bohemian novel, but not unpleasantly bohemian. Ringley and Warner ar unmistakable Bohemians, of a hier class, however, than we generally meet. It is the old story, which will go on repeating itself as long as thêre ar artists and poets in this world, and pretty faces to enchant them. Our Shelleys will, to the end of time, fall in lõve with simple girls who cannot understand them. And so ensues the tragedy of life, ending only in death. Mr. Wedmore's book is full of life and spirit; thêre is not a dull page. It abounds with sparkling criticism on books, pictures, and men. It is, in short, the very reverse of the ordinary circulating novel." [Westminster Review. **1795**

SOAP [by CONSTANCE MACEWEN: *Simpkin*, 1886.] "is a sparkling little romance and is so much the reverse of shallo, that õne not accustomed to such style and diction mît look for an even deeper significance than really underlies the surface . . . Thêre is the rich and fantastic Gautier, who determines to be loved for himself, not for the sake of the 'soap' which 'made' him, and is still the source of his fortune. To this end he accomplishes his metamorfosis into a poor but portly german professor, of a vaguely speculativ turn, an l proceeds

(successfully) to induct the mystic Miss Ben-Israel into the deeper mysteries of intellectual affinities and others . . .. Besides her power of expression and fancy and her understanding of many fâses of human nature, Miss Macewen has a whimsical humor, often bordering on extravagance, which is really a very pleasing feature of her writing, much more so than a certain unprofitable mistiness which occasionally overtakes her. A keen, not to say trenchant vue of society is always present, with the excellent resûlt of spurring the dulled mind to fresh interest in and observation of its surroundings." [Athen. **1795a**

SOME DAY OR OTHER [by J.. M. KIPPEN: *Tinsley*, 1879.] "is pretty, moderately exciting, happy in its issue, and consolatory to the hearts of all true and faithful lõvers. Thêre is no great fault to be found with its matter or its manner." [Athenæum. **1796**

SOME OF OUR GIRLS. [by E.. ( ) EILOART: *S: Tinsley*, 1875.] "The dramatis personæ ar 4 inmates of õne household — a yung heiress, who, at the outset of the story, is under medical care for an indisposition which has deeper than fysical causes; Polly Brooke, a tradesman's dauter and governess in the doctor's family; Susan, a cockney servant of the modern school; and Madge, a work-house waif, sullen and debased by her pauperism, and despised for it by her fello-servant. The interest of the tale depends on the progress by which these four, isolated from each other as they ar at first by their several accidents and by a vast amount of natural antagonism of character, ar drawn together by circumstances into relations more consistent with nature and morality." [Athenæum. **1797**

SON OF HIS FATHER (The) [by MA. OLIPHANT (WILSON) OLIPHANT:

1837.] "is õne of Mrs. Oliphant's strong
and fine stories which captivate the interest and at the same time educate the
soul. The story is that of a yung fello
whose mother fears he has inherited the
unfortunate traits of his scapegrace of a
father; and altho the mother is a little
overdrawn in her capacity for cold, stern
judgment, she is nevertheless a type,
and the story is told with intensity and
fascination." [Critic.   .   **1798**

SON OF THE SOIL (A) [by Ma.
Oliphant (Wilson) Oliphant: 1865.]
"Colin Campbell is a scotch lad, who
makes his way from the shores of his
nativ Loch Lomond to õne of the pulpits
of his national kirk, gathering on the
road the best honors of Glasgow and
Oxford scholarship. This would contain
but little romance in itself, but the poor
farmer's son rather oddly saves twice
from drowning the youthful heir of an
english aristocrat. This complication
with the family of a wealthy baronet involvs the son of the soil in a fruitless
flirtation, first with the baronet's niece,
on whom the handsom, manly, brilliant
yung Scot made considerably less impression than she did on him; while the
second rescue threw yung Campbell
into a dying sickness which sent him to
Italy for health, whêre he found another
affair of the heart, which eventually,
and after much not over-smooth running,
grew from pity into affection, and from
this into wedlock." [Nation.   **1799**

SONS AND DAUGHTERS. [by Ma.
Oliphant (Wilson) Oliphant: *Blackwood*, 1890.] "The best thing in it is the
discovery by Gervase — the sensitiv, ul-
tra-refined, hypercritical moralist, who
nearly loses a healthy-minded girl who
lõves him rather than accept a sum of
money from an unknõn hand — of his
father, who has taken bankruptcy so
easily, living obscurely with a yung

wife and family. Old Mr. Burton's uneasy shamefacedness when he meets his
son under these novel conditions, and the
mutual relief with which they part, ar
in Mrs. Oliphant's best manner. But on
the whole the book is very slit, tho we
hav never yet been able to call the author
dull." [Athenæum.   .   **1800**

SOPHY CARMINE. [by "J:
Strange Winter," i. e., Henrietta Eliza
Vaughan (Palmer) Stannard: *Lovell*,
1889.] "Dões anybody ever tire of J:
Strange Winter and her delitful army
people? Here in Sophy Carmine ar
many of our old acquaintances — Bootles
and his wife, and their inimitable little
maids, Lil and Mignon, and comrads,
and the demure Sophy, for whom the
match-making Mrs. Bootles means to
secure a husband during the Christmas
visit at Ferrers Court — succeeding twofold better than she had dared to hope.
It is deliciously told, arch, and dainty,
and captivating; and the *dénoûment* is
all one could wish." [Boston "Literary
World."   .   **1801**

SPRIG OF HEATHER (A) [by
Geraldine Butt: *Ward*, 1878.] "is
picturesque in its tragedy, and domestic
in its happier fâses. It deals with pleasant people who crumple thêir rose leavs
for lack of serious trials. Marjory Gil-
mour, waiting for her lõver, falls in lõve
with another in his absence. The discarded suitor, being a gentleman, withdraws from the field." [Athen. **1802**

SQUIRE ARDEN. [by Ma. Oliphant (Wilson) Oliphant: *Hurst*,
1871.] "The interest which attaches to
the principal character arises from the
strange freak of destiny which places an
open-hearted youth, emancipated by a
forein education from the conventional
trammels of english society, in the position of an innocent usurper of the
possessions and honors of an old family.

The Ardens, with their cherished exclusivness and vindictiv traditions — the Thornleighs with their almost naive self-surrender upon the altar of fashion — the commercial Pimpernels, with their unblushing and out-spoken vulgarity — the cynicism of the doctor, — the worldly shrewdness of the family lawyer, — the æsthetic radicalism of Lord Newmarch, most priggish of patrician doctrinaires, ar all equally strange and perplexing to our honest and long suffering hero. Yet the dignity of an uprit and pure conscience sustains him worthily, alike in the lesser troubles of his uneasy eminence and in the more tragic downfall of his fortunes. We ar never indeed less inclined to despise him, gentle and tender-hearted as he is, than when the real value of his manhood is tried by the cruellest of tests, the collapse of all the ties which his affectionate nature had assimilated to himself in his prosperity. When he finds himself a stranger in the domain he has been taut to regard as an ancestral home — when the maiden of his choice resigns him as a sacrifice to the claims of society, — when his sense of justice compels him to enrich a bitter and insidious enemy, — and when ŏne whom he has learned to lŏve as a sister forsakes him to unite herself to his rival, he parts from all with resignation, even with a sad satisfaction in the thŏt that his out-spokenness has enabled him to reinstate the matronly good fame of the wife of his most fatal enemy. Yet thêre is nothing overdrawn or unnatural in his mental attitude." [Athenæum. **1803**

SQUIRE LISLE'S BEQUEST. [by A., BEALE: *Hurst*, 1883.] "The character of Aveline is uncommonly pleasing. A sweeter picture of a girl we hav seldom seen. The french retired teacher, too, is excellently drawn . . . Praise, too, must be given to the drawing of the characters of the 4 sisters. Their resemblances and their differences ar marked with a skill which is nothing less than subtle. We much admire the tact with which Miss Beale has worked out the development, which a nature substantially the same in these 4 women, a nature petty and narro, but not radically evil, receives under the various circumstances under which they ar placed." [Spectator. **1804**

SQUIRE OF SANDAL-SIDE (The) [by AMELIA EDITH (HUDDLESTON) BARR: *Clarke*, 1887.] "is a quiet, unsensational, but by no means uninteresting story of family life, and is thŏroly well written and healthful in tone. Iere and thêre may be found a touch of sentimentalism; but thêre is no mawkiness and thêre is no preachiness, for which we cannot be too thankful, as these ar the besetting sins of books written with an eye to the líter requirements of the religious public. The scene is the Lake District, and Mrs. Barr's descriptions could hav been written only by a loving observer of nature. She has also a keen eye for character; her conversations ar natural; and her incidents happily chosen." [Spectator. **1805**

SQUIRE'S LEGACY (The). [by M., CECIL HAY: (†, 1886) *Hurst*, 1875.] "Thêre is sufficient mystery in the story to sustain the interest evenly and without effort; the people ar nearly all pleasant and natural. We fancy that the sympathies of most readers will be with the yung squire rather than with the romantic and somewhat feminin yung lawyer who, by virtue of his being the heroin's accepted lover, is, we suppose, the rítful hero of the tale; we do not wonder that tho Doris never wavers in allegiance to Kenneth, she occasionally yields to the charm of Scot Monkton's chivalrous affection. Iow everybody who deserves to be happy is made so, including the readers of the story, who will be sure to see very early in the story whom Doris ôt, in the eternal fitness of things, to marry, we hav no intention of disclosing. The old lawyer is, we should say, a sketch from life, and the 2 ânts, Michal and Joan, ar charming." [Spectator. **1806**

STAND FAST, CRAIG-ROYSTON! [by W: BLACK: *Low*, 1891.] "Never has the author been more true to the national characteristics than here, but for that very reason we think the figure which is pathetic to us may be repugnant to the mass of readers, who hav little tolerance for rodomontade, and less for genteel poverty. Yet, granted a hī-strung, poetic temperament, saturated with all the ballads and lyrics which hav rung throu the North, given a lifelong hope, dear to patriotic pride, blīted to the extent of confusing a reason never very sane ; add privation and penury and the struggle of a hauty spirit to ignore the pressure of lo circumstances, and such a character as the hero of this book merits pity and not contempt . . . And Mr. Black knoes how to relïeve the monotony of Bethune's rather sordid surroundings. To say nothing of the lilts of song which diversify his mono-logs, his dauter Maisrie, as tender as her name, whose honesty is as intuitiv as the moral confusion of her grandsire; her excellent english lover, a typically straitforward gentleman ; and the more conventional, but not less vivid minor portraits, afford an excellent foil to the central figure. Lord Musselburgh and his wife, tho slītly sketched, suffice to contrast the modern actualities of so-ciety with the imaginary world in which the enthusiast has his being." [Athe-næum. **1807**

STARLING (The). [by NORMAN

MACLEOD: N.-Y., *Dodd*, 1875.] "One sees here how much it is in a novelist's favor to hav settled social custom to rest upon, for we fancy it is largely from that source that the little story draws its wholesom quietness and solidity. To this is added a fair measure of literary skill, however, which is by no means so unimportant a factor of success as many of our indigenous geniuses would seem to consider it. Thus it happens that a careful, educated writer, not confused by the notion that with him alone rests the duty of revealing to the world the real nature of an entire na-tional life, is able to make a credible and sufficiently entertaining story out of the lōve of an old soldier and his wife for a bird which excited sōme scotch children to noisy merriment on the Sabbath, and which the parish minister held should be put to death. The dis-grace and anxiety which for a time overshadoed them, and the circumstances which brôt all rīt again, ar detailed with a good deal of obviousness of edification and sōme padding, it is true, yet with the ease and completeness which come of a good school. In respect of construc-tion and simplicity of key ' The Star-ling ' is commendable." [Nation. **1808**

STEPHEN THE SCHOOLMASTER [by M.. E. GELLIE: *Griffith*, 1879.] " is called by its author a story without a plot, but it has as much plot as the majority of lōve-stories. It folloes the chequered fortunes of its hero from in-digent boyhood to comfortable maturity, and it traces the disturbed current of a true and romantic affection into smooth waters and a happy haven. Without lacking the savor of a good novel, the book is simple and pleasing; nothing which could possibly be obnoxious is forced down the reader's throat, and thêre ar no bad people to ruffle our serenity. In fact, the story mīt serv for an easy introduction to the mystery of lōve, which no parent or gardian need be afraid of placing in the hands of an unsofisticated girl." [Ath. **1809** STIFF-NECKED GENERATION (A). [by Lucy Bethia (Colquhoun) Walford: *Blackwood*, 1889.] " An uncommonly brīt and captivating girl is the Rosamund who is the heroin of this very readable story. It is her mother who stands for a stiff-necked generation, and who, insisting upon her dignity as 'Lady Caroline,' wife of plain Mr. Liscard, so restrains her brilliant dauter that she breaks loose in an unexpected way and becōmes engaged to the nucultivated Major Gilbert, instead of falling in with the maternal plan and fixing her affections on her cousin, Lord Hartland. Thêre is a most delītful match-making ânt Julia, whose character is drawn with sōme touches which remind one of Miss Austen. Thêre ar the loud sisters of the major and the 2 or 3 family groups, all very life-like. Lady Caroline's sudden death, just after the engagement, is made ōne means of opening the eyes of Rosamund to her mistake, and thenceforth all the circumstances move strait towards the dénoûment, which cōmes as ânt Julia would hav it, in spite of the poor girl's determination to do her duty by her betrothed. In the sudden development of manly traits in the major the author has shōn much skill, and she invests the close of his career with such a pathos that he becōmes the true hero. Thêre is a good deal of human nature in the father and the irrepressible Catherine; the glimpses of home life ar excellent, and the story has throuɡ̄ut an atmosfere of reality. ' [Boston " Literary World."] — " Rosamund is sufficiently like other girls to be quite willing to idealise a clever, kindly

yung man, and then to fall in lōve with her ideal, but she likes to do her idealisation for herself; and Lady Caroline, with the shortsītedness not unusual in her tribe, is so persistent in her panegyrics on Lord Hartland, that in his direction thêre is no vacant space in which Rosamund's imagination can exploit itself. What more natural than that she should turn from the solid but repelling perfections of the yung peer to the more shōy and superficial attraetions of the dashing soldier, Major Gilbert? We feel that it is not, only nạtural but almost inevitable; and it is certainly inevitable that in the case of a girl like Rosamund, the illusion should not be permanent . . . Mrs. Walford's most complex, and also most successful creation, is undoubtedly Major Gilbert. He is a thōroly vulgar person, utterly devoid of the tact which comes from the quick feelings of a gentleman, and he is placed before us in a series of situations in which we see him to the very worst advantage; but behind his vulgarity thêre is character; — thêre is even a certain nobleness, and we ar made to realise the latter as fully as we realise the former. Subtlety of handling which results in simplicity of effect is always fine art, and the portrait of Major Gilbert seems to us very fine art indeed." [Spectator. **1810**

STOCKBROKER AT DINGLE-WOOD, See *NEIGHBORS ON THE GREEN.*

STOKESLEY SECRET (The) [by C.. M.. Yonge: *Mozley*, 1861.] " is ōne of Miss Yonge's family histories, containing as many little boys and girls as ' The Daisy Chain.' It is rather confusing and difficult at first to distinguish ōne of the 9 yung Merrifields from the others, but they gro upon us by degrees, and their various characteristics stand out clear and distinct tōards the end. Thêre is sŏmething natural and true in the picture of school-room life : the little nautinesses, the petty teasings, the small vexations, will be familiar to every member of a large family. Miss Fosbrooke, the yung governess, is a delītful personage." [Athenæum. **1811**

STORY OF A SHORT LIFE (A) [by JULIANA HORATIA (GATTY) EWING (†, 1886) N. Y., *Young.*] " surpasses every thing the author had dōne, and is a little master-piece. We hav spoken of it as pathetic, but its pathos is not that of weak sentimentality ; on the contrary, the tale is as strong as it is touching, as natural as it is tender. The story of the handsom, brilliant, spoiled boy, instructed in the nobleness of the family motto ' Lactus sorte mea,' and remembering to shout it appreciativly as he rides away to what he feels to be the greatest joy of his yung life, ōnly to find that it leads him to his greatest sorro, is most beautifully told ; and the account of his suffering and death is all the better for not being that of a morbid ' little Paul,' but that of a headstrong, activ youth, whose patience under trial cōmes only with an effort." [Critic. **1812**

STORY OF VALENTINE AND HIS BROTHER. [by MA. OLIPHANT (WILSON) OLIPHANT: *Harper*, 1875.] " The plot is quite original, and is ingeniously wrŏt out. Lord Esskside's son marries a gypsy girl, who, having given birth to twin boys, unable to endure the restraints of civilization, disappears. Several years later, she secretly leavs ōne of the boys at his grandfather's house, whêre he is recognized and adopted. How, finally, all the members of the family ar reunited is told in a pleasant narrativ, in which a charming little lōve-drama is fittingly enacted." [Boston " Lit. World." **1813**

STRAIGHTFORWARD. [by "HOLME LEE," i. e., Harriet Parr : *Smith*, 1878.] " Thêre is always a peculiar pleasure in coming back, after other experiences in the field of literature, to ōne of ' Holme Lee's ' novels. They ar always carefully executed, for tho she writes much, she dōes not so over-task her pen as to be obliged to hurry its work. And they hav always a clear, wholesom purpos. ' Straightforward ' is one of the best. The hero is a foundling, and the story tells us how he wins his way in the world in the matters both of fortune and of love. The author has not, indeed, the courage to make him absolutely independent of all antecedents, and givs him, by a sort of afterthŏt, a respectable parentage. But when he fīts his battle with the world, and wins the lōve on which his heart was set, he is practically ' filius nullius.' And a very fine, manly fello he is, quite true to the word which is the motto of his story. A better picture of a real man, quite free from all affectations and meannesses, we do not kno in the range of fiction ; and we take it to be no small proof of genius that it cōmes from a woman's hand. The hero's boyhood makes a pleasant picture ; pleasant, too, the description of the golden hours which he spends at the italian lakes with the darling of his childhood, now grōn to womanhood. Of a more sombre color ar the scenes in his nativ town, whêre he has to liv down the suspicions in which the eccentric behavior of a friend has involved him. The minor characters, too, hav a genuin and natural hue, the most cleverly and subtly drawn being, perhaps, Mr. Douce, the vicar, ōne of those men, personally blameless and even aiming at good, who can do so much harm by narro-mindedness and want of courage, lending thêir prestige to abuses which they really hate, becaus thèy ar too timid to welcom the necessary movements of reform. This is an excellent novel, which we can recommend without reserv." [Spectator.　**1814** STRANGE ADVENTURES OF A HOUSE-BOAT (The). [by W: BLACK: *Harper*, 1888.] "The responsible heads ar the two who figure in the 'Phaeton,' in 'White Wings,' and other romances. But the central figure is an american girl, Miss Peggy Rosslyn, whose saucy wit and delītful freshness of character make her ōne of Mr. Black's most charming heroins. The descriptions ar not so felicitous as those of the earlier book, a canal tying the course of the voyage too closely. The plot is far too much of a repetition, if so slīt a story can be said to hav any. But after all is said, Mr. Black is surpassed by nobody in the genuinness and the freshness of his heroins, and Americans may welcom Peggy as best the attempt to depict an american girl which any british author has yet made. [American.　**1815** STRANGE ADVENTURES OF A PHAETON (The) [by W: BLACK: *Macmillan*, 1872.] " is a charming book, full of beautiful scenery, and just such a brīt and pleasant thread of story as beguiles the reader on . . . The journey made by the faeton is from London to Edinburgh, throu many villages and towns which hav fallen out of knoledg of travelers; and from the silvery reaches of the Thames to the moors and burns of the Border, thère occur landscapes enuf to make a picture-gallery well worth having to refresh ōne's mind with in stormy days. The party thus traveling carries with it, too, a romance — a delītful yung lady with a guitar, and an equally delītful yung lōver, who is characteristically, but not fatiguingly, german. How this romance

floes on along the pleasant road, throu all the summer sīts and sounds, with comments upon everything which cōmes across the traveler's path, and all manner of amusing discussions and disquisitions, the reader must find in the book. Thère is even room for complications, for an unhappy rival, and a considerable amount of that uncertainty which is so dear to the novelist, and everything cōmes to a delītful conclusion." [Blackwood's.] — "The yung people fall in lōve, as in duty bound, and the elderly couple look on approvingly. 'In this wise they went throu the sweetly-smelling country, with its lines of wood and hedge, and its breadths of field and meado' . . . We follo them under a spell of enchantment, woven of soft and rich colors, sweet and spicy scents, and tender melodies. Thère is a glamor over every scene, over the great parks, the open downs, the green woods, the stretches of heath, the picturesque villages, the breezy hills, the silver lakes, the splendid road-ways lined with hedge-rōs, the old-fashioned inns, the quaint towns, and the broad sweeps of meadōs, sōmetimes glimmering in the sunlīt, and sōmetimes shining in the white rays of the moon. Even the rain dōes not interfere with our enjoyment. It only givs an opportunity for varying the pictures, of bringing in the soft grays, and hanging līt mists about the woods." [Scribner's.] See also Nos. 813, 1015, 1324, 1815.　**1816** STRATHROWAN [*Chapman*, 1878.] "is a lōve story pure and simple; or, if it is complicated at all, the complication is due to the existence of ōne or two tributary streams of lōve floing into the main current. The simple tale which thus appeals to the reader is acceptable by its thōro ingenuousness, which characterizes both the manner of the narrativ and the majority of the personages who play their part in it. It is long since we hav found, in the production of an unknōn writer, the picture of a family so engaging, so unsofisticated, and, as a rule, so natural, as that of General Clifford, in which the delītful character of the heroin sparkles like a good stone well set. The author has been happy in the delineation of Helen Clifford, and has traced the course of her lōve with constant pathos, delicacy, and even subtlety. Her story and the story of her suitors ar told freshly, pleasantly, in a vêin of unpretentious art. One feels that the book is good to read, not becaus its writer has thōt it out deliberately or labored over it painfully, but becaus he has conceived a noble and lōvely character, and has delineated it with a tender solicitude." [Athenæum. **1817**

STRICTLY TIED UP [by A. J. BERESFORD HOPE : *Hurst*, 1880.] "is entertaining. It is irish in subject, irish in spirit, and written in the easy, dashing, humorous style which has characterized sōme of the best english fiction having its origin on the other side of the channel. The scheme of the story is well proportioned, and worked out in all its complications with much care and skill. The author evidently knoes his ground, and rarely convêys to the mind of his reader so much as a suspicion that he is overdrawing his characters for the sake of effect, or painting his scenery with brīter colors than ar warranted. If the plot confines the reader chiefly to Ireland and amongst **irish** people, this is by no means exclusivly the case. He finds himself at different times in the midst of a London season, in Lincolnshire, at Bath . . . 'Strictly Tied Up' is thōroly a novel conceived in a līt and happy vein, and

scarcely even demanding a serious thôt." [Athenæum.] See *THE BRANDRETHS*. **1818**

STRUGGLE FOR FAME (A). [by C.. ELIZA LAWSON (COWAN) RIDDELL :. *Harper*, 1883.] " One story has a hero, the other a heroin, the corresponding figures in either case being of minor concern. Both struggle for fame in the world of literature, 'that land which has no itinerary — no finger-posts — no guides — it is a lone, hapless country' . . . The story offers more than the usual number of entertaining figures. In contrast to the heroin is a lady of quality, who publishes at her ōn expense. 'She can't write a bit — but she sells.' And in contrast to each other ar the publishers, Vassett of the old school, cautious, honest to the last fibre ; and Felton, the ' Cheap Jack,' without a scruple." [Nation. **1819**

SUCH A GOOD MAN. [by WA. BESANT & JA. RICE : with 'Twas in Trafalgar Bay : *Chatto*, 1879.] " The satire upon sōme of our social, especially our mercantile idols, is here more pronounced. The great Sir Jacob Escomb, ironmaster and financier, is hardly a caricature of sōme very ill-favored fetishes which hav had thêir day. A farcical adventurer, genuinly in lōve with the astute wido who has twice disappointed him, makes an absurd, tho ununlikely contrast to the ponderous filanthropist." [Athenæum. **1820**

SUCH IS LIFE. [by MAY KENDALL : *Longman*, 1889.] " A little group of yung people of hī aspirations, and a serious way of taking life, ar the persons to whom we ar introduced in a lōvely rural home. By hap of ill fortune they all cōme to London, whêre the stuff they ar made of is put to the test; and it bears the strain. The pure and loyal artist Lionel, and brave Nan, — who spends herself for others, — find the deep peace thêre may be in self-surrender and acceptance of the inevitable. The rarely sincere Jim falls into line with the great, uncounted army of those whose ideals hav proved false, and whose lŏves hav been misplaced, but who can go on with thêir lives, loyal to truth and to themselvs. Readers of Miss Kendall's *From a Garret* will hav seen in these tender and touching studies and stories the qualities of this book — the same sympathy, and clear insĭt, probing to the deeps of the heart — the same delicacy, refinement, dignity, subtle analysis, and charm of expression." [Boston "Lit. World." **1821**

SUNSHINE AND SHADOW [*Newby*, 1856.] "is a well written story. It has a wholesom moral; and we can recommend it to those in search of a book to read aloud." [Ath. **1822**

SURRENDER. [by LESLIE KEITH [JOHNSTON]: *Low*, 1881.] The characters ar drawn with skill, and thêir individuality is sustained throuŏut. The story is carefully constructed . . . The book is well written, but in looking on the dreamy world which surrounds Joyce Daring we seem sŏmehow to remember Miss Thackeray . . . The by-play in the book is charming. Thêre is Miss Felicia, the little old maid, who has secretly adored Colonel Loveday for years, but is brave and meek enuf to giv place to her yung nîece. Thêre is Tina, Joyce's sister, a heartless, self-indulgent little flirt, who poses always as an innocent child and gracefully shirks all responsibility. And thêre ar two sisters, Barbara and Freda Dewhurst, with thêir bachelor establishment. On the whole, 'Surrender' may be safely recommended to all who care for a pleasant tale pleasantly told." [Athenæum. **1823**

SUSAN FIELDING. [by ANNIE EDWARDS: *Sheldon*, 1869.] "Portia Ffrench, however, is a very creditable study. She is intended to be the type of the ambitious woman of the world, and thus to work as a foil to the virtues of Susan Fielding. In point of fact she is much more intelligent, agreeable, and in every way more attractiv, than the immaculate Susan, and every reader will at once prefer her, selfish as she is, to her perfect, tiresom little country friend. Portia is an exceedingly careful and truthful study from life. In her we see the modern fashionable yung lady of english and american society. She is handsom, accomplished, and possessed of more than the usual feminin share of strong good-sense. She prefers the ease and luxury of wealth to any other earthly blessing; and, as for matters beyond the earth, she never givs them a thŏt. She would be kind and gracious to every well-bred person wer it in her power, and would be a true and affectionate wife to a man who could support her in the style which to her is synonymous with comfort. Without money herself, it is necessary for her to seek it in marriage, and hence it is quite impossible for her to lose time in an impracticable passion for a lover who possesses less than half a million. Nevertheless she is not heartless or selfish save in matters which concern her object in life — a rich marriage. Neither is she without noble possibilities, could she be freed from the necessity of fortune-hunting. No one has comprehended the real nature of the fashionable girl of the period more fully than Mrs. Edwards, and her embodiment of this conception in Portia is exceedingly creditable to her powers of mental and moral analysis, and her capacity for accurate and forcible portrait painting." [Round Table. **1824**

SUSSEX IDYL (A) [by CLEMEN-TINA BLACK: *Tinsley*, 1877.] " is in every way what its title implies, for the story has much freshness and grace, and its pictures hav a distinct local coloring and a fidelity to nature . . . But at the same time its reproductions of country life ar unquestionably clever and conscientious, its pathos is genuin, its style is natural." [Athenæum. **1825**

SWEET SEVENTEEN. [by ARTHUR LOCKER: *Chapman*, 1866.] " Those writers of fiction who season thêir pages with mysterious crime and repulsiv vice, should study the modes by which Mr. Locker captivates the imagination of his readers with scenes alike humorous and innocent. Instead of making them endure his characters by rousing a morbid curiosity as to the sequel and result of a startling commencement, he leads them to enjoy his story by inspiring them with personal interest in its characters. From first to last the book is fresh with nature, and unconstrained pleasantry. The actors ar neither tame nor commonplace; the incidents bear no resemblance to the conventional arrangement of story tellers; and yet the drama so impresses us with a sense of its fidelity to human nature and society that we seem to encounter old friends and familiar faces in every scene. Nor is this success the less noteworthy becaus much of it is due to the writer's prudence in confining his delineations to the kinds of life with which he is thōroly acquainted. The world described is that of professional men and merchants, clerks, and petty tradesmen; and with such never-flagging humor dōes Mr. Locker set forth the ways and tempers of the various persons who ar made to illustrate this comparativly humble life, that no idle reader will feel aggrieved by

the one fault of a tale which runs to more than twice the length of an ordinary novel." [Athenæum. **1826**

SYLVAN HOLT'S DAUGHTER [by "HOLME LEE," i.e., Harriet Parr: *Smith*, 1858.] " is a fascinating yung woman, with whom we recommend our readers to make acquaintance. The work is the best proportioned and best sustained story the author has written . . . Throuōut thêre is evidence of great care and painstaking. It is well and solidly written. Thêre is nothing slīt or superficial. The author has evidently wished to do her best, and she has succeeded in writing a novel which is well worth reading, and which possesses the cardinal virtue of being extremely interesting." [Athenæum. **1827**

SYLVAN QUEEN (A) [*Hurst*, 1880.] " is a picturesque and very pleasing story. Rural scenes, more or less unsofisticated characters, a quaint and almost affectedly old-fashioned style of narration, combine to make it read lītly and smoothly enuf . . The principal merit consists in its brīt little pictures of country life and character." [Athenæum.] — " In the village, nothing can be more happy than the sketches of the jolly landlady; the gossipy, plausible pedler; the nervous, plaintiv housekeeper; and the taciturn, but civil and trustworthy gamekeeper. The Sylvan Queen is his dauter, and her beauty, her ambition, her coquetry, her thōro, clever, household womanliness, her genuin and passionate devotion to her father, ar sketched with great ability." [Spectator. **1828**

SYLVIA'S LOVERS = No. 970.

TALE OF A LONELY PARISH (A). [by FR. MARION CRAWFORD: *Macmillan*, 1886.] " Mr. Crawford here excels all his former work, and in his pleasant, floing fashion has given us an interesting story, consistent, relieved by touches of humor, and made various by the well studied characteristics of a quiet group in a country place, consisting of 2 women, 3 men, a child, and a dog." [American. **1829**

TERRIBLE TEMPTATION (A) [by C : READE : *Chatto*, 1872.] " is intensely interesting. Its plot is singularly original, the action is exciting, and the characters ar drawn with great vigor . . . It is no worse than the majority of modern novels. These hint at, half conceal, and gloss over vice. Mr. Reade speaks of it in plain terms, as a positiv element in human life and society which will not be winked out of sît. Looking at the story with exclusiv reference to its power of entertainment, we must pronounce it very successful : the reader's interest increases from page to page ; the cardinal event of the plot is skilfully vêiled, and not until the closing pages ar reached dões the author explain just what the ' Terrible Temptation ' was." [Boston " Literary World."] — " Mr. Reade denies, in an explanatory preface to this novel, that he ever intended to make the '.temptation' õne to commit adultery, for the sake of securing an hêir ; but in so saying, he confesses failure. Everybody who read the book thôt that this was its motif. [Spec. **1829**

THAT CHILD. [by MA. ROBERTS : *Whittaker*, 1887.] " This is a well written story of yung people which older readers will find of interest. A little girl is the survivor of a railway accident and is taken as ward by Philippa Beaumont, who brings her up without much training. She is a wild creature altho noble-hearted, and when Miss Philippa dies and is succeeded by Miss Priscilla, the two do not get on very well. Avice forms a friendship with the old antiquary, Simon Ashbury, who teaches her

music. He givs his time to the writing of a history of his nativ town, and proposes to use his fortune in publishing the work; but just before his death he burns the precious manuscript and leavs his money to Avice. The characters, as one mît expect from the authorship, ar all skilfully drawn, and the account of a child's emotions and experiences is very faithful and very true." [Boston " Literary World." **1830**

THAT LASS O' LOWRIE'S [by F.. [ELIZA] (HODGSON) BURNETT : *Scribner*, 1877.] " has a somewhat fantastic plot, whose narration shões plenty of humor and pathos and a good deal of power. The story is briefly this : Joan Lowrie works at the mouth of a mine. Her father, a savage miner, conceives a great hatred for a pleasant yung civil engineer who has occasion to correct him for opening his safety-lantern in the mine against the rules. He has, moreover, a habit of beating his dauter when he is drunk. She is touched by the kindness of the engineer to her when she is suffering from a blo given by her father, and in return she saves him from her father, helps rescue him half dead from the mine after a terrible accident, and finally consents to marry him, seeing that he had long been in lõve with her . . . Now it is one thing to be told in a poem, whêre defects of dress and education ar not forced upon the reader's attention, that King Cophetua married a beggar maid, but it is another and very different thing to hav a similar story told in prose with all sorts of realistic details. In the one case we see lõve a rule for itself, and it is easy to imagin that in the fairy land whêre the scene is laid thêre is not much difference between kings and beggar maids, but when the romantic story is told of our contemporaries, and we hav abundant proof of Jean Lowrie's absolute ignorance, and see how ungrammatically she spoke, and that she was, in fact, totally unfitted, so far as education goes, to be the companion of a child 8 years old, it is impossible to avoid thinking with sõme concern of the future married life of Mr. and Mrs. Derrick. Indeed, everyone will but too surely feel that she will never be fitted to be the yung engineer's wife. Reading, writing, and cifering ar only a small part of what is needed before this girl could be turned into a civilized being [compare No. 1410] and it is a mistake for an author to giv such a conelusion to so clever a novel as this is in many respects." [Nation.   **1831**

THAT OTHER PERSON [by MA. (RAINE) HUNT: *Lippincott*, 1887.] " is of the hier grade, with a lesson of charity for an unfortunate girl which is unmistakable. Unusual treatment at the hands of the novelist a forsaken mistress — 'that other person' — receives [compare No. 1261], and it is this girl, Hester, who is the true heroin, and not ' Zeph,' the beautiful yung wife who drives her husband away by her insane jealousy. The characters of the antiquary and his wife ar delicately drawn, and so ar those of John Simonds and the noble-hearted old Doctor; no õne is perfect, and no õne is altogether bad; the different persons introduced act much like human beings, so that naturally it becõmes a pleasure to follo them from day to day, and see what is to be the outcõme. The action takes us into a pleasant region, and the descriptions of scenery, of both out-of-door and in-door life, add to the attractions of a book which is well worth reading." [Boston " Literary World."   **1832**

THAT UNFORTUNATE MARRIAGE. [by F.. ELEANOR (TERNAN)

TROLLOPE : *Bentley*, 1889.] " Those of us who hav learned the art of contentment ar satisfied to forego originality — in the sense of novelty — if we can now and then find a book which recalls the delīts of the old times, when a novel sõmetimes justified its name. Such a book as ' That Unfortunate Marriage,' which reminds us often 'of the work of Miss Austen and still oftener of Mrs. Gaskell; indeed, sõme of the sketches of life in Oldchester mīt hav come strait out of the pages of ' Cranford ' [No. 1175]. The strong-minded and large-minded Mrs. Dobbs and her faithful admirer and ally, Jo Weatherhead, who belīevs, not without reason, that she is a pearl among women, ar a delītful pair, but the most perfectly Gaskellian characters ar the Piper sisters . . Pleasant company is also to be found in the society of the good-natured organist, Sebastian Bach Simpson, whose mere name would hav crushed the vitality out of a less līt-hearted musician; but with all her musical people, professionals and amateurs, Mrs. Trollope is evidently at home; and the chapters devoted to them ar the liveliest and brītest portions of a book which is of lītness and brītness all compact . . . Really good līt comedy can be enjoyed in any mood, and becaus it is provided here, ' That Unfortunate Marriage ' is a book for every reader and for every season." [Spectator.   **1833**

THEREBY [by "FAYR MADOC:" *Blackwood*, 1885.] " is distinguished by a happy audacity of method, a crisp style, and a dialog which is always lively and occasionally witty. ' Fayr Madoc ' introduces us to a circle whêre servants and filanthropists, politicians and men and women of fashion, meet on common ground, and the discussion of social and religious problems which arise out of these meetings is conducted with considerable spirit and versatility. Thêre is also no lack of sensational incident, and the lõvemaking is carried on in a fashion that is at õnce original and entertaining. The plot is decidedly fantastic, and sõme of the details ar clumsily contrived. But such defects ar readily condoned when the general result is so exhilarating. The characters âr all well drawn, tho the author shũes to most advantage in the delineation of women . . . The whimsical vĉin, perhaps, suits ' Fayr Madoc ' best, but thêre is a good deal of serious thôt incisivly expressed in the pages of ' Thereby.' The author has a decided turn for epigram, and the conversation is enlivened by many felicitous sayings which hav the additional merit of spontaneity. In fine, thêre is food for reflexion as well as for mirth in ' Thereby,' and we shall welcom with pleasure any future work from the pen of a brĩt and amusing writer." [Athen. **1834**

THIRD MISS ST. QUENTIN (The) [by M.. L.. (STEWART) MOLESWORTH : *Hatchard*, 1888.] " is a contemporary version of Cinderella. Sõme years ago we had a similar adaption, on a smaller scale, from the delĩtful pen of Miss Thackeray [compare Nos. 1149 and 1273] . . . Mrs. Molesworth's adherence to the main structural lines of her classic original is characterized by as much fidelity as the prosaic conditions of real life will allow. Of course, the godmother has lost her supernatural powers, and the pumpkin coach, its rat horses, and mice footmen, ar exchanged for more familiar modern representativs, while the Prince is only a very charming yung english baronet; but so long as we hav the elder sisters, and the ball, and the 12 o'clock departure, and the loss of the slipper and the finding of the slipper, and the happy marriage of the Prince and Cinderella, what more do

we want? . . . At last, however, Ella's eyes ar opened; she wins at õnce her sister and her prince, and a very pretty story eõmes to an appropriately happy ending." [Spectator. **1835**

THIRLBY HALL. [by W: E: NORRIS : *Harper*, 1884.] " The lõve-making in ' Thirlby Hall ' is, like all Norris' lõve-making, consummately well dõne, and the hero's infatuation for a certain Lady Constance Milner is managed with cleverness and dexterity : the reader understands the worth of it, and, while he belĩeves in its present reality, feels sure that Charley Maxwell will finally be led out of the temptation and delivered from the evil of forgetfulness of his early lõve. Loosely twisted altho the threads of the novel seem, they ar nevertheless held by a strong and careful hand, and a hundred causes working together bring an excellent *dénoûment*. The date of the story is 30 years ago; but we trust that the retrospectiv tone which pervades it is merely a part of the novelist's stock-in-trade, and that Mr. Norris is a yung man [born 1847] with half a century before instead of behind him, which he may devote to the writing of books like ' Matrimony' [No. 1799] an.l ' Thirlby Hall.'" [Lippincott's. **1836**

THIS INDENTURE WITNESSETH. [by MA. (RAINE) HUNT : *Low*, 1875.] " Audrey, with many prejudices and infirmities of temper, is still a noble specimen of an english maiden. It is well for her in the end that she learns to lõve her honest cousin, the shopkeeper, whose manly faithfulness earns its reward in due time." [Athenæum. **1837**

THIS WORK-A-DAY WORLD. [by " HOLME LEE," i. e., Harriet Parr : *Smith*, 1875.] " This yung person, Winifred Hesketh, is, we must admit, as charming a heroin as we hav met for many a day. The dauter of the elder son of a London merchant, who has married a successful milliner in a small town, she is left fatherless at an early age . . . Whether as a 'half-boarder' in a yung ladies' school, or as a governess in aristocratic families, or when her one lŏve-passage has ended in regret, or in the alternate successes and disappointments of authorship, she is a pleasant picture of an unselfish, unselfconscious, thŏroly self-reliant woman." [Athenæum. **1838**

THOMAS [by Lucy (Lane) Clifford: in "Tales from Blackwood," N. S., I.] " — a story of an errand-boy who develops into an accomplished doctor and marries the dauter of the house in which he cleaned knives and boots, is declared to be that of a real personage, which, of course, disarms any criticism of the probability of his good fortune." [Athenæum.] — The tale is interesting and charmingly told. **1839**

THOMASINA [by Ma. Agnes (Colville) Paul: *King*, 1872.] " herself, is at first a delĩtful child and afterwards a charming girl, until she marries, and then the story cŏmes to an end: if we had not been acquainted with her from her birth we should, perhaps, hav been no more interested in her than in any heroin of a pleasant and well-written story, who falls in lŏve with the wrong man and flies in the face of her family traditions; but, having watched her course from the time when her mother was inclined to offer objections to the hereditary christian name of the ladies of the Bertram family, and throu childhood to womanhood and marriage, we regard her with different feelings. The merits of the book depend so much more on character than on incident that it would be absurd to giv any sketch of the story; and the style being rather 'plain in its neatness' than sparkling or epi-

grammatic, extracts would not giv a fair idea of it. So we will ŏnly assure our readers, that if they read 'Thomasina,' and do not agree with us when they hav read it, their moral tone must stand in great need of elevation, or else the cultivation of their taste must hav been sadly neglected." [Athenæum. **1840**

THORNEY HALL. [by "Holme Lee," i. e., Harriet Parr: *Smith*, 1855.] "Miss Grisel's example has a living influence; and tho she did not herself see the hope of her life realized, it still bears its fruit in the next generation. One of the grandsons of her yunger brother determins to restore the family to its ancient consequence; it is ŏne of those determinations which is the incarnation of a strong will, seldom failing to work out its fulfilment. He is attended by his sister, — named Grisel, after their great-ânt, — who, wĩhout an idea of being anything more than a plain, conscientious yung woman, anxious to do her duty day by day as it arises, stands beside her brother, strengthening him, watching over him, devoting herself to him so long as he needs her, — then leading her life as a wife and mother, — seeming to take up the tangled and troubled web of her ânt's life, and work it out to a true and worthy result. The story of the fortunes of the brother and sister is extremely interesting. The character of Hugh Randal is well drawn and sustained: his success in the grand object of his life — the restoration of the family to its former state — and the mortal sorro which dims all the beauty of the hope almost as soon as realized, giving him days of darkness instead of joy, giv an interest to the book, which is only kept from being tragic by the skill with which it is softened into 'the milder grief of pity.'" [Athenæum. **1841**

THORNICROFT'S MODEL. [by

"Averil Beaumont," i. e., MA. (RAINE) HUNT: *Chapman*, 1873.] " Thornicroft is an artist sufficiently eminent to draw a school round him, and to attract a certain amount of aristocratic patronage. Both these facts exercise over his rather morbid and self-conscious nature an influence which is specially unfavorable to anything like abandonment of his egotism in favor of idyllic lŏve. Yet he is effectually attracted by the complete womanliness of a gentle girl whom he picks up by chance, ŏne of the jewels which, according to novelists, ar to be found amidst the most sordid of surrounding circumstances. Thére is something pathetic in the way in which the connexion which Thornicroft's profession at first establishes between the fair model and himself leads to the connubial relation; on ŏne side such a complete sacrifice; on the other, such a mistaken estimate of the strength of a transient sentiment. Very sad is the misunderstanding which groes out of the inequality of true passion between this ill-matched pair; too facile expression of all that amounts to sentiment on one side, too unpractised an articulation of real devotion on the other." [Athenæum. **1842**

THORPE REGIS. [by F.. M.. PEARD: *Smith*, 1874.] "The plot is simple, the interest turning upon the effect of an unfounded suspicion of his honor on the mind of an ambitious and hĭ-spirited yung man. Anthony Miles is a pleasant type of academical youth at 24, ᴀ little of a prig, and very much of a despot — full of ineffable yearnings to sweep and garnish this old world — animated by a cheerful tho unconscious feeling of merit, — more dependent than he would at all allow on the néborly sympathy in all quarters which he takes for granted. Whére pathos is to be

found humor is seldom lacking; and, accordingly, we hav an undercurrent of irony which involvs and defines nearly every actor in the tale. We would gladly draw attention to the Mannerings and others of the minor personages; but as the book is a good book, we trust our readers will make their acquaintance for themselvs." [Athenæum.] — " It is entitled to the praise which is due to naturalness, purity of sentiment, and grace of style. The scene is laid in a sleepy village, of whose aspect and external characteristics a charming picture is sketched in the opening pages." [Boston " Lit. World." **1843**

THREE BROTHERS (The) [by MA. OLIPHANT (WILSON) OLIPHANT: *Appleton*, 1870.] " is ŏne of Mrs. Oliphant's quiet, interesting, natural, and every way healthful stories, in which thére ar no abnormal characters, no harroing prolongation of plot and counterplot, and no improbable transitions. A father's will puts his sons on ᴀ 7 years' probation before théy ar allowed to kno the disposal of the property, and théir behavior, adventures, and attachments form the plot of an excellent story." [Scribner's. **1844**

THREE CLERKS (The) [by ANTHONY TROLLOPE: (†, 1882) *Bentley*, 1857.] " whose histories ar narrated, belong to two government offices, and in a quiet family at Hampton Court they find their counterparts — 3 graceful girls, of whom ŏne is proud in her passion, another capricious, another wild. Perhaps the differences of their natures ar more strongly marked than Mr. Trollope intended. However, he now presents himself with a romance of modern lŏve, and subtly and delicately has he developed it, but without hanging before his groups a ganz of theatrical unreality pallidly glimmering with moonshine. The spirit of the book is healthy, natural, and vigorous . . . Without disclosing too much of the plot, we will add that the conclusion of the story is adroit and satisfactory, ' the everlasting fitness of things' being held in vue, without the introduction of any repulsiv catastrofe. Yet by many readers the principal charm of these volumes will be attributed to their rapid and sparkling flo of ironical portraiture — toned down, as the finest irony invariably is, by interludes of wise and wholesom seriousness." [Leader.] — " Two of his characters he confesses ar drawn from real persons. Sir Gregory Hardlines was intended for, and recognized to be, Sir C: Trevelyan, then 'the Great Apostle of the [by Trollope] much loathed scheme of competitiv examination,' and thèrefore a special object of his dislike." [Westminster. **1845**

THREE FEATHERS [by W: BLACK: *Harper*, 1875.] "deservs many admiring readers. It is not so flawlessly delitful as 'A Princess of Thule' [No. 905], becaus, probably, it deals with a life less strange and romantic; but it amply illustrates the author's peculiar skill in the delineation of character, and the description of scenery, and his pervading grace of rhetoric. Wenna Rosewarne, the heroin, is a very original and charming personage, and her affectional complications, in which she bears herself with admirable dignity and conscientiousness, invest her with an indescribable interest. She betroths herself to an old and by no means attractiv bachelor, and presently becomes aware that her heart is given to another. This other, Harry Trelyon, is a rich aristocrat, possessed of a terrible temper, and thoroly selfish. The reforming influence of Wenna upon him is indicated with singular skill. Mr.

Roscorla, the bachelor, is also a very original person and we kno little better worth in fiction than the account of his feelings and conduct during his engagement. This story seems to combine in just proportions all the elements of entertainment, — humor, pathos, skilful analysis of character, and graceful composition. [Boston "Lit. World." **1846**

THREE GEOFFREYS (The) [*Allen & Co.*, 1889.] " is likable just becaus it is simply, quietly, and not unskilfully told. It is of the domestic type, and tho ône or two rather surprising things do occur, they ar not presented in too thrilling a way; neither ar the majority of the people who figure in it too brit or good for every-day use. The villain, too, is not so deeply dyed as to be quite out of harmony with his surroundings. The heroin in particular has nothing remarkable about her, being ônly natural and quietly attractiv; but that is much. The eldest of the 3 has a pretty hard time of it, but he meets his round of misfortunes wisely and well, and even generously." [Athenæum. **1847**

THROSTLETHWAITE. [by SUSAN MORLEY: *King*, 1875.] " The scene is laid in the Lake district. It is of the quiet and domestic order, but dôes not lack the interest arising from an apt contrast of characters. The shiftless selfishness of Leonard Barrington, which culminates in positiv dishonor, is keenly brôt into relief by the frank simplicity and courage of the girl whose lôve is the best achievement of his life. Very slôly and painfully dôes she learn to rate her attractiv suitor at his proper value, and as gradually dôes she recognize the worth of the manlier lover who finally supplants him." [Athenæum.] — " ' Throstlethwaite ' is another readable story, the main interest of which lies in a yung girl's troubles with ône lôver who is unworthy of her, and her final freedom from him, and her attainment of greater happiness with another man much more deserving of her. She is well drawn, and in good contrast with her stands her fashionable married sister. The two yung men, too, ar natural and lifelike, and altho the villains of novels ar apt to carry with them a strong, unmistakable odor of brimstone, in this case the evil heart is hidden beneath a calm, but not too calm, exterior, and the good young man is no shadōy supporter of all the virtues, but is a very good copy of a human being." [Nation. **1848**

THROUGH A NEEDLE'S EYE [by " HESBA STRETTON," i. e., Hannah Smith: *Dodd*, 1878.] " is a description of a few lives livd almost entirely in a seaside village. It tells how lōve and wrongdoing, temptation and repentance, worked together to shape and to alter the quiet ways of the Squire and his family, and those committed to thêir charge. A picture, not exactly vivid but careful and finally effectiv, is drawn of the old house and its inherited acres, which was as a weapon in the father's hands, a stumbling-block and a snare to his successors, and which had so·strong a hold on the affection of all three. Justin, the hero of the story, is tempted to belie his true self in order to possess and manage the land he has loved all his life; and his wrongdoing and his repentance and its consequences make the story (with due accessories), and it is told with truth and delicacy. It is true to the laws of life that tho Justin can clear his ōn soul and restore twofold, his dauter, who is the lĭt of his eyes, should suffer from her knoledge of his frailty, suffer from its consequences falling on herself, and, unable to construct a new life out of the ruins of the old, should fade and die. Thêre is a true and kindly perception throuōut the book, and thêre is a marked absence of melodrama and of snobbishness." [Nation.] — " Hesba Stretton's fame is little, but her work is admirable, and her latest story, so compact and complete, that even to ōne who does not much mind its earnest moral purpos it must be very restful and satisfactory reading . . . The tale is always free from cant, but it becōmes deeply serious in tone. The author dōes not scruple to enforce the text which she has taken for a title, and sho the narro and perilous entrance of the man whom ambition has misled into the kingdom of peace and spiritual honor. His expiation is a sore one . . . Thêre is a depth, a verity, about the completed story which no brief outline can properly represent. The minor characters ar all clearly conceived : Richard, the half-unwilling reprobate ; Leah, the village girl, who lōved him so coarsely yet so truly in his prime, and servd him joyfully in his helplessness ; the Methodist preacher at the lithouse ; while the mother of Justin and Richard, and Mrs. Cunliffe, the worldly wife of the unworldly curate, ar delineated with abundant humor. The action of the tale is natural, smooth, and steady ; the style unstudied, but without blemish ; the impression which it leavs wholesom, grave, and sweet. Once more our thôts recur to G : Eliot. That 'Hesba Stretton' is less than she, goes without saying, but she is not immeasurably less. Her very limitations may serv her as a sort of artistic defense. She has studied in the same nobly realistic school as the greatest of recent novelists, and excess of power will never betray hemdinto a disregard of proportion." [Atlantic. **1849**

THROUGH THE LONG NIGHTS. [by ELIZA (LYNN) LINTON : *Harper*, 1884?] " She plans a good story, works it out neatly and makes it long. But she does not possess the faculty of exciting sympathy with her characters, without which, tho he speak with the tung of men and of angels, the novelist is fatally lacking. Thêre is about her descriptions a smoothness as of ice which chills one, and all about her writing an air of self-sufficiency which holds you aloof from close contact even with so much of emotion as it contains. 'Through the Long Nights' is the story of a yung girl, who to repair the family fortunes, was deceived into marrying a rich man whom she did not löve. A year after her marriage, the lover who was represented to her as dead cömes back, and she goes off with him. She has, however, but a short time of happiness, as he soon dies of consumption, and she of grief." [Critic. **1850**

THROWN TOGETHER. [by FLOR-ENCE MONTGOMERY: *Lippincott*, 1872.] "We would defy the coldest cynic, the most experienced novel-reader, to read 'Thrown Together' throu with tranquility. Many will remember 'Misunderstood' [No. 1580] by the same author, a work which was by no means a screaming farce, and this tale is quite as tearful as that öne. The book simply narrates the struggles of a yung girl of a sensitiv disposition, who is snubbed by her cold-hearted mother and unappreciated by her careless father; she has a cousin, a boy, who is petted by a doting widoed mother; and these two children, being thrön together, work upon one another's characters and giv the plot of the story, as well as the name. Nina's reserv and sensitiv pride ar melted by the boy's frankness and simplicity; a series of domestic tragedies softens the flinty hearts of the parents and we see two peaceful households without any traces of flirtation. The agonies,

temptations, and bewilderments of these yung people ar told with really remarkable power, and when öne remembers the widespread delusion of parents, that children hav no characters, but ar to be manufactured into the semblance of söme favorit model, — which delusion is probably necessary to persuade parents to be unceasing in their care of their children, — it is easy to see that a book of this sort may be of great service. The sufferings of children ar often, to our thinking, much greater than those of grön people, their reasons for grieving ar so capricious, their reticence so singular, and, moreover, their wo is so total, so absolute, they hav not the power of abstracting anything from their suffering which shall console them, and so their feelings ar keener then then at any time of their life. That parents forget this and fail to understand their children, is well knön, and to point out this truth is the design of the story. We hope it may be kept on a hï shelf away from the children, who ar ready enuf of themselves to take morbid vues of life, and that it may not turn out to be a sort of 'Uncle Tom's Cabin,' to be used in the nursery for the propagation of a society for the abolition of parents." [Atlantic.] — "The girl was a sensitiv, proud little thing, and was by no means appreciated by her parents; the boy was his mother's joy; gradually the children became friends, obdurate parents ar tamed by the example of the children and by domestic affliction, so that the book ends happily. It would be well, we think, if all parents wer to read this book; to söme it may seem exaggerated, yet we fancy that thêre is nothing in it but what mït be true, and indeed is true, of the lives of many children. One is so inclined to forget his childhood, or to clothe it with a purely

imaginativ interest, and thêreby to lack sympathy with his children, that they often really hav good ground for their belief that their father and mother never wer yung." [Nation.   **1851**
THYME AND RUE [by MA. B. CROSS: *Hurst*, 1890.] "is a pretty and an entertaining story, told with sufficient cleverness on the basis of a fairly novel plot. A man whom his friend describes as having been 'the brilliant prizeman and the most distinguished scholar of his year,' audacious, eloquent, a 'gourmet,' but a dealer in freaks and fads, suddenly flees from civilization with his motherless danter Juliet, and sets up the ideal of the Simple Life, to which he intends as far as possible to convert the world. A nêboring wido with one son adds herself to the communion; and what more natural than that the yung people should be destined for ône another by their ambitious parents. The girl is an hêiress, tho she dôes not kno it; and a sensible lawyer, discovering the eccentric arrangements of the filosofer's household, contrives to get her away, and place her with sôme good people who teach her the ways of the world. The story of her adventures will afford the sympathetic reader a great deal of pleasure and amusement; and perhaps it may be interesting to kno beforehand that the yung man who was left behind in the community of the Simple Life also cômes to kno the ways of the world, and that after a decent interval he meets Juliet again. The story is complex, and holds more than a single romance; for 'thyme and rue gro both in ône garden.'" [Athenæum.   **1852**
TO CALL HER MINE (etc.). [by WA. BESANT: *Chatto*, 1889.] "Mr. Besant must hav been working hard when he wrote the stories now pub-

lished. The pressure put upon a successful novelist is most severe, and in sôme cases it has a disastrous effect. Mr. Besant's work shôs signs of the stress under which it has been produced; but he is so well equipped that he can always fill his pages with interesting matter. With a little more leisure, perhaps, his imagination would be more varied and free, and his best is so good that ône wishes he could never be compelled to do anything less than his best. The volume contains 3 stories. One of them, *Katherine Regina*, has already been revued. [No. 1424]. 'To Call Her Mine' and *Self or Bearer* [No. 1769] ar the other two. Both ar good stories, full of incident and contrivance, and Mr. Besant, as he is wont, forges the chain of destiny with hearty blôs, so that the evil which overtakes the wicked and the happiness which is attained by the good seem thôroly satisfactory. But much of the interest of Mr. Besant's books lies in what in other books would be called the padding. For one reader who skipped pages in 'All Sorts and Conditions of Men' [No. 1047] for the sake of the plot, hundreds must have put up with the plot for the sake of the padding; and really in 'To Call Her Mine' the descriptions of Dartmoor ar the most enjoyable part of it." [Athen.   **1853**
TOM BROWN'S SCHOOLDAYS. [by T: HUGHES: Boston, *Ticknor*, 1857.] "In a sprîtly tone, a schoolboy's adventures at Rugby under Arnold ar dashed off, — with rather too much dash perhaps, and a little too much criticism of all the rest of mankind, — but still in a vivid, humane, and truly religious spirit. One gets somehow an impression, that bird's-nesting, wrestling, racing, quarter-staff, football, and the logical 'clenched fist,' (varied, may

589

be, by courses of the rhetorical 'open hand,') ar the grand apparatus of an english education. The brutality of the fagging system, and the odd compound of riotous lawlessness and an almost military disciplin in a great school, ar left just the painful problems thêy wer when Dr. Arnold took such a school for his liveliest type of hell. Yet, in a way ōne hardly understands, this is the soil in which the hardy Brown stock thrives; and along with its ruf vigor gets initiated by degrees in all gentle and generous, as well as manly ways." [Christian Examiner. **1854**

TOM BROWN AT OXFORD. [by T: Hughes: Boston, *Ticknor*, 1861.] "The author dōes not, on a superficial examination, seem to descrv the wide reputation he has obtained. We hunt his books in vain for any of those obvions peculiarities of style, thôt, and character which commonly distinguish a man from his fellōs. He does not possess striking wit, or humor, or imagination, or power of expression. In every quality, good or bad, calculated to create ' a sensation,' he is remarkably deficient. Yet everybody reads him with interest, and experiences for him a feeling of personal affection and esteem. An unobtrusiv, yet evident nobility of character, a sound, large, ' round-about' common-sense, a warm sympathy with english and human kind, a practical grasp of human life as it is lived by ordinary people, and an unmistakable sincerity and earnestness of purpos animate everything he writes. His ' School Days at Rugby' delīted men as well as boys by the freshness, geniality, and truthfulness with which it represented boyish experiences; and the Tom Brown who, in that book, gained so many friends whêrever the english tung is spoken, parts with nōne

of his power to interest and charm in this record of his collegiate life. Mr. Hughes has the true, wholesom english lōve of home, the english delīt in rude fysical sports, the english hatred of hypocrisy and cant, the english fidelity to facts, the english disbelief in all piety and morality which ar not grounded in manliness." [Atlantic. **1855**

TOM SINGLETON. [by W. Follett Synge: (†, 1891) *Chapman*, 1879.] "Tom is a fine fello, and modest. He is, however, nobody's ideal knīt, but a real, living, actual person, who takes the ups and downs of his life with quiet, unboastful courage, — is a good son, a true lover, a faithful friend, and a very clever man. The reader likes him cordially, and perhaps likes his father still better . . . Thêre is evidently a great deal of drawing from life in this story, but from life survêyed in a cheerful spirit by kindly eyes. The incidental sketches ar very happy, and the author is especially to be congratu- lated on Miss Vavasour. Thêre has not been a more amusing spinster in fiction since the immortal Miss Pratt, of Miss Ferrier's second best novel, ' The Inheritance,' and she is so genuinly good with all her oddities, that she dōes not contradict or clash with the bonhomie which pervades the book . . The story ends happily, after it has wound throu sōme troublous ways. It leavs an impression of a cheerful, manly, reverent mind, and a bīly cultivated intellect; thêre is not a jarring note in it; it is, as we hav said, a book which becōmes a friend." [Spectator. **1856**

TOO SOON [by K.. S. Macquoid: *Harper*, 1873.] "is a simple story of a yung girl's disciplin, — the painful processes by which her nature was purified of selfishness. It is quite unpretentions in plan, quiet in action, and in nowise remarkable save for its subtle and instructiv analysis of the heroin's mental operations; but we unhesitatingly commend it as an exceptionally profitable novel. We like it especially for its recognition of the old-fashioned sentiment of lōve, which is coming to be tabooed in modern fiction, and which the author shōes to be quite consistent with hi intellectual endowments and fine culture." [Boston " Lit. World." **1857**

TOWER GARDENS (The). [by LIZZIE ALLDRIDGE : *White*, 1883.] " The narrativ is of the domestic kind, but thêre is a picturesqueness in the setting [compare No. 1466], in the description of the bachelor uncle's dwelling, etc. For the rest, it deals with the lōves of Uncle Harbuckle's nîeces, and the constancy of their widoed mother, a natural flirt, to the remembrance of her dead and ruined husband. The triumf of her first lōve over a considerable temptation in the shape of a comrad of the late captain's, and a sharer of many common memories, is ōne of the best told things." ,[Athenæum. **1858**

TRAGIC MUSE (The) [by H: JAMES : *Houghton*, 1890.] " is the story of a yung lady of dubious extraction and vulgar surroundings, who yet possesses the artistic temperament so strongly that she pursues the rocky way to professional eminence. She is aided much in this by a yung diplomat, who struggles long between his lōve for her and his ambitions. The artistic moral of the story is further enforced by the introduction of an ambitious yung politician, who resigns a seat in parliament in spite of the pressure exerted on him by his political sweetheart, to pursue the divinely inspired calling of a portrait painter . . . All these characters discourse much and admirably on art, — dramatic, pictorial, and general, and an

interest in these subjects is necessary for full delīt in the book. Possibly it is this artistic tone, of which James is surely a master, which makes The Tragic Muse of special interest." [Overland. **1859**

TRAP TO CATCH A SUNBEAM (A). [by — (PLANCHÉ) MACKARNESS (†, 1881) : 1850.] " Few writers since Miss Edgeworth's time hav been so successful as Mrs. Mackarness in pointing out the value of domestic virtues. It is from the wholesom character of its teaching that ' A Trap to Catch a Sunbeam ' will liv in the hearts of its many readers for years to cōme." [Athenæum. **1860**

TRANSPLANTED. [by M.. E.. FRASER (TYTLER) GREENE : *Bentley*, 1883.] " The story is graceful and touching. The orfan girl, half english, half italian, with her simple faith in Mr. Frank, the hero of her childhood, and Mr. John, the kind old rector, who would gladly hav been something nearer to her had not his gentle self-restraint forbidden, is a pretty picture. The book closes, as most readers will desire, with a glimps of hope for her early lover." [Athenæum. **1861**

TRUE MARRIAGE (A) [by EMILY SPENDER : *Hurst*, 1878.] " is a thōroly pleasant and satisfactory book, without being too bily pitched, either in desiga or in execution. It is a genuin story of human concerns and interests, such as ar met in the world of every day experience. Mrs. Spender writes as one who knoes life from the fact of having lived, and of having watched with clear perception the life of her friends and acquaintance ; and this givs the charm which mere imitators never possess." [Athenæum. **1862**

TRUE OF HEART [by " KAY SPEN ": *Virtue & Co.*, 1868.] " is an unpretending but very charming story,

TOM JONES [by H: Fielding (1707-54): 1749.] "is the great prose epic of English literature ... In it, Fielding has comprehended a larger variety of incidents and characters under a stricter unity of story than in Joseph Andrews; but he has given to the whole a tone of worldliness which does not mar the delightful simplicity of the latter. As an expression of the power and breadth of his mind, however, it is altogether his greatest work, and in the union of distinct pictorial representation with profound knoledge of practical life, is unequaled by any novel in the language ... It would almost seem to argue an unreasonable skepticism to doubt the existence of such a veritable personage as Square, lover of Plato and Molly Seagrim, with his brain full of transcendental morality, and his heart full of descendental appetites; of Thwackum, malignant orator of grace, and most graceless of boisterous malignants: of Ensign Northerton, the very pink of rakes, braggarts, and upstarts, with his profane disrespect for "Homo," his contempt of all learning associated in his mind with pedagogic flagellations, and his exultation at deceiving his father out of his intention of making him a parson, of Blifil, the most sublime of didactic coxcombs, with his deep and solemn shamming of virtue, so completely a hypocrit that he almost conceals himself, and seems more an appearance than a being; of Allworthy, in whose delineation the author's whole beneficence of heart overflows; and of Tom himself, with his unguided heart gloing with all the impulses, disinterested and sensual, and allowing each to act of its own wil,—sincere, generous, affectionate, and unprincipled. But, above all, what shal we say of Squire Western, next

to Falstaff the most universally popular of comic creations, and as geniun a lump of clay and passion as ever started into being under the magical touch of a humorist? His shrewdness, his avarice, his coarse kindness, his sense-defying Jacobitism, his irresistible unreasonableness ... All these go to make a character so natural and yet so eccentric, as to disturb our faith in the dogma that reason is the separating line between man and beast ... We ar, in fact, made acquainted throu this book with England as it was in the middle of the 18th century. Every personage, from lord to chamber-maid,—every incident,—every description of costume, or amusement, or fashion of dress,—every form of colloquial speech, vulgar or delicate,—every allusion to political parties—is a mine of information: and the whole givs the lie direct to half the impressions we derive from history, and enables us to grasp the reality and substance of the national life." [E. P. Whipple, 1849]—"Fielding entered fully into passion, and is the only writer who has undertaken to trace it throu the double action of the heart and the senses the whole theory of which he lays down with his customary mixture of philosophy and wit. Undoubtedly the humanity of love was never so wonderfully anatomized as in that most wonderful of all stories. That Fielding was master of all the springs of the passion can not be doubted by any reader of 'Tom Jones,' or of another novel less widely knon, but not less remarkable for its power, in which he has portrayed it with consummate success in its biest and purest form, relieved of all sensual accessories, and existing only in the sweetness of its trust, its fortitude, and patience." [Albion. **1855 k**

descriptiv of a fåse of human life which is within the experience, and carries with it the sympathy, of a large class of persons. The heroin dōes not travel beyond the circle of domestic life, and with her individual biografy she givs us glimpses of refiñed, not fashionable society, and portraitures of quiet scenes of english country life, which ar very charming. In Ellen we find the picture of a true woman; not a remarkable ōne, nor ōne of that exaggerated class whose moral strength teaches them to despise happiness, but a sensible, refined, and practical woman, who, not born to work, yet, when her mother is suddenly reduced from affluence to comparativ poverty, resolvs to becōme the breadfinder for the family, takes a situation as governess, and, instead of presenting the usual picture of patient martyrdom and ill-requited labor, applies herself cheerfully to her duties, and finds in her vocation a sfere for the exercise of useful talents and a source of infinit gratitude. The characters ar natural, the men, women, and children ar such as we find them in real life, and the scenes throu which they pass ar neither inconsistent nor improbable." [Round Table. **1863**

TRUE STORY OF A BILLIARD CLUB = No. 813.

TRUE TO LIFE [*Macmillan*, 1874.] " is one of those rare stories which one feels happier for having read. It is not funny or jubilant; thêre is no conventional optimism or manufactured gladness in it; on the contrary, the sole touch of adventure turns upon a family migration in anticipation of a death, which afterwards takes place; but it is full of the cheerfulness of duty, piety without the least suspicion of cant, and a reasonable, well-disciplined vue of life and estimate of its responsibilities.

We kno no finer picture in modern fiction than that of Mr. Eversley and his dauters, nor a prettier simple love-story than that of Alice Eversley and Alice Sherborne. We cannot too hily commend yung people who talk good sense in good english." [Spectator. **1864**

TRUST (The). [by JEAN LE PEUR: *Tinsley*, 1877.] " Tho in outward characteristics the Friends to whom we ar introduced hav a general resemblance to each other, each of them has a strongly marked nature of his or her ōn, and the gradations from John Cave, the ' mïty stif, disagreeable Friend,' to loquacious Becky Wilson, who represents the extremest unreserv of which her sect is capable, ar both numerous and fine. The heroin whose autobiografy we read is happy in the possession of a most amiable pair of grandparents, whose sedate goodness has nothing repulsiv about it, and thêre is grandeur as well as kindliness in Joseph and Sarah Ellis which will make a pleasant and lasting impression on the reader. Even in dealing with the darker characters in the tale, the hypocritical Jilks, and unprincipled worldling Bob Graham, thêre is a deal of redeeming humor which lïtens the shadōs. Bob's boyish wickedness, tho sadly profetic of the selfishness of his maturity, ar lâfable enuf, the escapades at the fair and on the river being such as grōn people can pardon for the sake of thêir audacity. Thêre is, of course, a tender lōve tale running throu the story." [Ath. **1865**

TWO KISSES [by HAWLEY SMART: *Loring*, 1877.] " will be found to be very entertaining. It is what is called a society novel, describing the career of a yung wido, who, having buried a worthless husband, marries again. The plot is an ingenious and, what is more, a probable ōne, if we make allowances for a little straining here and thére; and the people ar clever and cleverly drawn. Thére is a great variety of character introduced to the reader: a sómewhat disreputable freebooter, whose position between respectability and swindling is not very certain, a sleek villain, a sensible husband of a coquettish wife, a very charming yung .girl, a would-be novelist, etc., and every ōne of these persons givs the reader a very agreeable impression of the author's humor and habit of observation." [Nation. **1866**

TWO LOVES. [by — ( ) Martin: *Tinsley*, 1878.] " Mr. W: Black's Uhlan Baron [in No. 1999] is one of the finest fellōs in or out of romance, and in this novel we hav another hero who is half german, and that is the best half. Max Wray is a good, true, brave man, and if he is u little too sentimental for the time, he makes up for it when he is in the midst of ' the slings and arrōs of outrageous fortune.' One of Dora Lee's two lōves is a worthy object, and thére is sōmething quietly and genuinly pathetic in the way in which he takes his punishment in the first instance, administered, as it is, under the influence of a mistaken notion of the rīt and honorable thing for her to do, by Dora Lee. Of course, in life (in which a family secret of the kind that makes all the mischief and misery in the story mīt ōnly too easily exist) Dora would simply tell Max ' all about it.' " [Spec. **1867**

TWO MARRIAGES [by Dinah Maria (Mulock) Craik: (†, 1887) *Harper*, 1867.] " contains two stories, each illustrativ of sad experiences in life, and each descriptiv of home scenes under different aspects, delicately, simply, and thótfully depicted. Tho lacking in power, the whole work is pervaded by a spirit of hī principle, of morality, u genuin love of nature, and

tender sympathy for the sorrōs and sufferings which flesh is heir to . . This paragon of commercial integrity becomes the bridegroom of a beautiful girl, more than 30 years yunger than himself, who marries him in disobedience to her father's will and who ʼleads a life of hopeless resignation, endeavoring to fulfil her duties as a wife, until consumption relieves her of the heavy burden. Not that Sir John Bowerbank was an unkind husband — far from it; but poor Emily had long before her marriage given her heart to another, and while she honored the old man and appreciated his goodness, yet to lōve him was out of the question. And so she died of what sentimental people call a broken heart, but in other words, from the havoc made by an unresting and oppressed spirit upon a frame too fragile to resist its influences. In the second story there is an old clergyman whose whole life and character ar more complete, more artistically drawn than anything of the kind we hav met for many a day." [Round Table. **1868**

TWO RIVAL LOVES [by Annie L. Walker: *White*, 1882.] " is a story more remarkable for the interest attaching to 2 or 3 of the characters than for originality of plot, tho the arrangement by which the hero is enabled to keep an estate, which neither he nor the reader believes to be his rītful property, is not without ingenuity; and the hearty earnestness with which the hero strives to make a beggar of himself is a novel feature also, and would be stranger still wer it not prompted by his lōve for a yung and beautiful wido. Virginie is delītful, and Marston would hav been strangely constituted if he had not felt her charms . . . We seem to be already acquainted with ' Miss Lydia,' but if that kindly fussy little woman has her prototype in former novels, Lucilla, tho slïtly drawn, strikes us as fresh in conception. She is a girl to be liked and lōved, and one feels sorry, on reaching the end of the story, to find her still unmarried . .. Enuf to say, that the man must be a hardened novel-reader who will read 'Two Rival Loves' without emotion and pleasure." [Spectator. **1869**

UNCLE ANGUS [by M.. S. G. Nichols: *Saunders, Otley, & Co.*, 1865.] "deals with what may be called the behind-scenes of journalism; in its dramatis personæ figure an editor, his wife and dauter, a literary speculator, and a poetical contributor, and with the fortunes of a magazine, entitled the Polyanthus, ar closely woven the fortunes of all the more prominent characters in the story [compare plot of Nos. 263 and 1777] . . . The exposure of this would-be contributor's device for detecting editorial 'laches' ōt to fall like vitriol on the consciences of the conductors of the 'magazines and weeklies:' the leavs of the manuscripts which they returned to him, marked 'not suited,' had been ingeniously gummed by their author before he sent them, and they went back to him gummed no less compactly." [London Review. **1870**

UNCLE BOB'S NIECE. [by Leslie Keith [Johnston]: *Ward*, 1888.]"Uncle Bob is a ruf and simple scotchman who has made his pile in the new world, and cōmes back to spend it on his niece in the old. The author paints her characters remarkably well. The heroin is as charming as her uncle, and a good deal more refined, whilst the best yung man, tho his goodness is of a somewhat vapid sort, is human in every way. A financial villain plays his part throuōut the narrativ, and is very nearly too much for the millionaire." [Ath. **1871**

UNCLE JACK (etc.). [by Wa. Besant: *Harper*, 1885.] "Whatever else a book by Mr. Besant may be, ōne may safely conclude that it will be readable and amusing; that it will take sound vues of life; that it will not humor fads or crotchety theorists; that it will 'sho up' the mean and selfish and scoundrelly people without mercy; and that all the good and pretty and well-behaved people will get what they wish and be happy. The very existence of such books in these times when stupid and foolish and morbid novels unduly abound is a mental solace akin to the knoledge of sōme refreshing retreat by sea or mountain when the dog star is in the ascendant. These stories ar in Mr. Besant's best vêin, and thêrefore to be read with delït. Every ōne will be interested in the fate of Uncle Jack's charming nïeces, who ar for a time the victims of an unjust will; and in the just fate dealt out to Miss Antoinette Baker and the other conspirators who try to get the property from the rïtful hêirs, and dedicate it to the 'cause.' '*Sir Jocelyn's Cap*' is a clever travesty. As for '*A Glorious Fortune*,' it is delïtful. Perhaps the Ambler family is made too much of, but 'Johnny' is an original, and the villain is disposed of in a wholly new way — he becomes a mere county respectability!" [Boston "Literary World." **1872**

UNDER A CLOUD [by Ma. Roberts: *Hatchards*, 1888.]. "contains much to attract and to please, but more by the way than in the main track of the story, more in the manner than in the matter. It is impossible to take much interest in the vagaries of so obstinate and wrôngheaded a person as Magdalen Rideolph, but it is pleasing to see how the yung lōvers and the crusty, friendly squire lead her back to sense and reason." [Athenæum.] — After the crash, when the hero has fled from the country, ruined and disgraced — for he had embezzled trust money — she sees her fault, and is stricken with the keenest remorse. She refuses to liv with her uncle, an old country squire — a most charming character — but retires with her only dauter to a farm house on his estate, whêre she livs a life of the utmost seclusion. It is at this point that the story begins. The old squire, who is a most ardent admirer of landscape painting, is struck by the picture of a struggling yung artist, who on inquiry turns out to be the chief sufferer by Mr. Rideolph's failure. He buys his picture, and invites him to his house. Thêre, while at work, the yung painter makes the acquaintance of the heroin, who has, he discovers, a wonderful talent for drawing. In the end, poetic justice is dône, and Walter Kennedy receives what he counts of far more value than his lost fortune . . . Altogether, the book is worthy of the hiest praise." [Spectator. **1873**

UNDER ONE ROOF. [by Ja. Payn: *Chatto*, 1879.] "Mr. Payn is a master in the art of making bricks without straw. It would be unjust if the critic did not stop to admire the skill which misses no opportunity for digressions, and even make opportunities for them almost without seeming to do so. Thêre ar probably few commonplaces in the english language and hardly any stock newspaper metafors, similes, and allusions which ar not to be found collected here, as the title happily suggests, under one roof. Mr. Payn has in his time written a great many stories, sôme of which, no doubt, plenty of readers will remember to hav read with pleasure. It would be impertinence to make any suggestions to so practised an author; it

must ônly be regretted that he knoes his business so well. His kindliness and good humor, which ar apparent throuôut this book, giv a pleasant complexion to his writing, but thêy ar only àn alleviation to the ennui caused by reading a very commonplace story." [Ath. **1874**

UNDER THE GREENWOOD TREE. [by T: Hardy: *Holt*, 1872.] "Thêre ar few pleasanter stories than 'Under the Greenwood Tree.' It 'is an idyl of english peasant life, so fresh and sweet and real, that in reading it one seems to be looking at a fine painting. It is a lôve-story in which the hero is a carter, and the heroin a school-teacher, — he simple and sincere, she a beauty, and a large bit of a flirt. Their wooing is not specially romantic; but its circumstances ar wholly fresh, and the sketches of life and manners in the hamlet whêre the scene is laid, which illustrate its progress, ar positivly unique. The atmosfere of the book is sweet with the odors of a fair english landscape; the hum of bees; and the lo of kine; the rustle of leaves animate its pages; and a peaceful summer-sky, with short-lived little rain-clouds dotting' it here and thêre, broods over the whole delîtful drama. So simple and pure and wholesom a story we hav rarely seen." [Boston "Literary World."] — "Fancy Day, the new school-teacher, is the heroin of the story, and she has no fewer than 3 lôvers . . . The story ends with a pretty marriage scene. The secret of her attractiv duplicity remains locked in the breast of the clergyman and in her ôn. The character of Fancy is admirably drawn. The author certainly manages to convêy the impression that he is a believer in the natural fickleness of the maiden heart, but his belief does not lead him into denunciation; on the contrary, he makes this fickleness not merely not repulsiv, but agreeable. The descriptions of village life, and of the village choir singing, and choir serenading, and choir festivities, ar very good. On the whole, we do not kno when we hav read a more interesting and pleasing book." [Galaxy. **1875**

UNDER THE LIMES. [by E. M. (TAYLOR) ARCHER: *Macmillan*, 1874.] "This is ône of those quiet, simple, stories that most modern novel-readers cast aside with disdain as not sufficiently exciting for thêir tastes, but which find in a few thôtful persons of well-balanced minds a hearty and appreciativ welcom. It is admirable by reason of its refinement and purity, its freedom from vicious personages and repulsiv or even rude incidents . . . To delineate the operations of 4 natures under the influence of the passion of lôve was the main task of the author, and she has succeeded marvellously. The sweet, womanly reticence of Rose is most lovable; but the equally womanly indecision of Etta is most artistic. The conduct of her relativs with Sebastian, the clear analysis of her feelings towards him, and the processes by which she passes from what she thôt was fond affection to the state of calculating his claims and deciding against him, represent the most delicate work which falls upon the novelist. Due praise should be awarded to the character of Sir Lawrence, which, tho slīt, is very effectiv. Thêre ar few other personages in the story than those named; but ône of these, a ritualistic clergyman, is a fine creation. What we especially like in this novel is its serenity and natural sweetness. The author has no hobbies, no friends to belaud, no enemies to punish; no reader will find his prejudices shocked in her pages, or be led into troublesom speculations. The book is

an expression of warm humanity, and its refinement and tender beauty ar beyond praise." [Boston "Literary World." **1876**

UNEXPECTED FARE. (An) [by "MAXWELL GREY," i. e., M. G. Tuttiet: in Tales from Blackwood, 3d series.] "is a brīt little tale. It tells what results may flo from earls' sons chafing under conventionalism and driving hansom cabs as a relíef to thêir feelings, and barons' dauters, whose 'english blood boils at the thôt of restraint,' setting up as independent workers to avoid pressure on the subject of matrimony. Mark Forrester's equivocal description of the pursuits of his rīt honorable parent and family, and Olive de Wynter's shortlived fury at the trick he plays on her, ar happily imagined." [Athenæum. **1877**

UNFORESEEN (The) [by ALICE O'HANLON: *Harper*, 1886.] "is a very clever and artistic story of the olden sort, full of intrigue, plot, and surprises. It relates how a Lady Macbeth of humble antecedents worked her way to quite unprecedented successes in the aristocratic world, ônly to find herself defeated at the moment of culminating pride. The story is exciting and entertaining; but the execution is sômething more than that. The style is unusually good for a novel of the kind, and the story is far abôve the average for its quality of construction and expression." [Critic. **1878**

UNLESSONED GIRL (An) [by M.. EMMA (LE BRETON) MARTIN: *Marcus Ward*, 1881.] "is short, pleasing, well-written, and has a natural plot and wholesom characters, several of whom ar drawn with sômething of that talent which distinguishes Mrs. Gaskell's delicions 'Cranford' [No. 1175] so far as regards observing and reproducing minute touches of every day domestic life, which at first sĭt may appear insignificant, but yet go far to giv an accurate idea of peoples' dispositions. Mrs. Martin has two heroins, who act most effectually as foils to each other. One is the pretty Gladys Byrne, who has spent all her life in a wild Irish home, and is consequently totally ' unlessoned' in the great school of the world; whilst the other one, Janet Ellison, has never been settled long anywhêre, but has always been knocking about with her mother from place to place, and habitually pinched for money, so that worldly wisdom has becôme a second nature to her . . . She is deceitful and full of faults, but is excellently drawn, and we must confess to having folloed her adventures with even greater interest than those of the legitimate heroin. Thêre is sŏmething pathetic in Janet's acute consciousness of her outward defects, her ceaseless struggles to rise superior to them, the way in which she makes the best of whatever happens, her stoicism, her rare fits of self-pity, and her passionate desire to be first in the affections of sŏme man or other . . . The scene whêre she proposes to Russel is very good, and mĭt almost be studied as a model of tact and delicacy by any plain woman resolvd upon securing, at all hazards, an unwilling lover; the proceeding is made to appear so nearly rĭt and natural, that we almost lose sĭt of the unwomanliness and unworthiness of Janet's despairing endeavor . . . In Janet, mind evidently predominates over heart, but in her cousin Gladys we hav a complete contrast to this. Gladys is almost the slave of her feelings, — constant, devoted, truthful, chivalrously anxious to help the weak and oppressed, ever ready to attribute to people whatever good qualities thêy chose to assume,

unsuspicious of evil, and unselfish." [Spectator. **1879**

UNTIL THE DAY BREAKS [by EMILY SPENDER: *Bentley*, 1886.] " is a delĭtful story. Cecilia Tremayne is very well drawn, and is in every way a fine character, lofty, courageous, and self-sacrificing. Thêre is more earnestness about the book as a whole than is found in the great majority of novels, but it is not earnestness of the sort which bores and repels a reader in quest of entertainment." [Athenæum. **1880**

UNSPOTTED FROM THE WORLD [by — ( ) GODFREY: *Bentley*, 1883.] " is a very touching story. The unselfishness of the tender elder sister and the naiveté of the ardent yunger one, whose first lŏve is exposed to so cruel a rebuff at the hands of the cautious man of the world on whom she has lavished the freshness of a sincere, if not very courageous nature, ar charmingly contrasted. It is hard on Dolly that the man she lŏves and the sister she lŏves hardly less should be driven by circumstances to turn to her to make their union complete; but in her self-renunciation she finally attains something more than the domestic happiness without which Psyche, the butterfly, must hav pined to death." [Ath. **1881**

URSULA. [by E.. M. SEWELL: *Longman*, 1858.] " Here we hav a sweetly written story of domestic life, — a book to warm the family affections. Sŏme of the family scenes ar exquisit in their warm simplicity, and it is hĭ praise to say that, with a distinctly religious purport, *Ursula* is neither didactĭc nŏr wearisomly serious. The author, tho capable of real pathos, writes often with a gay heart which gladdens the reader." [Leader. **1882**

URSULA'S LOVE STORY [by GERTRUDE (HEXT) PARSONS: *Hurst*, 1869.]

"has a picture of contemporary manners, of more than ordinary merit. Its tale is fresh, interesting, and in the main well told; its language is simple and correct, and its characterization is not wanting in power. Evidences of culture ar frequent in its pages over which hangs a pleasant aroma of refinement and good taste . . . So much of the strength and beauty of the story lies in dialog and in grace of narration and description, that a mere outline givs no just idea of the work. Ursula is admirably depicted. Her first intervue with Mrs. Daynham wins for her the reader's entire sympathy, and her subsequent behavior is womanly and rīt-minded. Irrational as is her attempted self-sacrifice, it has a moral grandeur which redeems its absurdity. Edgar Ravenel, Mrs. Daynham, and all the characters, even to the most subordinate, ar life-like. Their gossip and actions, loves, betrothals, and marriages ar well described, and constitute with the main interest a very pleasant novel." [Athenæum. **1883**

VAGABONDIA. [*Scribner*, 1889.] = *DOLLY.*

VALENTINA [by ELEANOR C. PRICE: *Chatto*, 1882.] " is a graceful, cheerful, fairly clever sketch of character. The heroin is a wayward girl, not happily situated in the way of gardianship or early training, who is guilty of many indiscretions, and who is constantly proving the truth of the adage that evil is wrôt by want of thôt far more than want of heart. She plays rather fast and loose with the hearts of her friends, not having much herself. As her brother-in-law says of her, she is a mad-cap who has never been trained. 'Everybody wants breaking in — sōme more, — sōme less — she decidedly more.' However, she falls into pretty

good hands, and they break her in; not cruelly, for that would hav broken her altogether, but naturally and gradually, and by allowing her better self to develop. One indeed — her second husband — tries to manage her in the other fashion, sōmewhat as he would hav tried to tame a horse or a dog, but he fails egregiously. The latter stage of the story is told with noteworthy skill, and nothing could be better or more delicate than the passage between the unhappy Valentina and the mother of the man who has lōved her purely and unrequited from the beginning. As for the conclusion of Valentina's history, the author tells it with more than ordinary taste and feeling." [Athen. **1884**

VALLEY OF A HUNDRED FIRES (The) [by JULIA C. STRETTON: London, 1867.] " is a most pleasing story of domestic life, in the delineation of which the author evidently excels. The scene is laid in Wales, in the midst of sōme of its lōveliest scenery, and the characters ar drawn with so much simplicity and evident truthfulness that we at ōnce recognize them as beings in whose presence we delīt, whose pleasures and interests we ar glad to share, whose trials and sorrōs ar reflected in our hearts. The excellent pastor, with his honest zeal, his passionate lōve of nature, his tender and genuine appreciation of all which is good and worthy in mankind, and his beautiful and helpful wife, make conquest of our affections when they arrive with their baby, and throuôut a long and not particularly eventful life, we ar content to bear them company, and part from them regretfully at the close. Thêre is no pretense of a plot, but the record of lives worthily spent, and of sorrōs borne with fortitude, can never fail to interest the reader, if the author be careful to avoid the unpardonable sin of being wearisom, and in the present instance thêre is so much variety thrôn round the several scenes and descriptions that, without being brilliant, they ar agreeable and often impressiv." [Round Table. **1885** —— SAME ("The Rector's Wife"). [*Peterson*, 1867.]

VANITY FAIR = No. 998.

VENUS' DOVES [by IDA ASHWORTH TAYLOR: *Harper*, 1884?] "tho belonging to the līter class of novels meant merely to entertain, dões more than entertain, and is at ônce original, amusing and graceful. Sôme reliance is placed on the time-honored foolish misunderstanding, and thêre ar signs of unhappy marriages and marriages for money; but every situation is delicately treated, and the signs never amount to more than signs, while the conversations ar brīt, the people interesting, and the moral, without being obtrusiv, healthful and unmistakable. The heroin has faults, and the way in which she nearly wrecks all her happiness by demanding happiness as a rīt instead of taking it as a gift, is a lesson, as well as a pretty story." [Critic. **1886**

VERY YOUNG COUPLE (A) [by — (SMEDLEY) HART: *M. Ward*, 1876.] "is a very pleasant and lively little tale, vivid in its interest, and the harroing part of it not too prolonge1 for endurance, not too artfully shaded to leav a loop hole for the entrance of a beam of hope. The very yung couple ar spirited as well as yung; they marry on £175 a year without any conception at all how small expenses add up . . . Moreover, the lively rattle of the story is not better painted for us than the tension of its deeper interest and the happy exultation of its close." [Spectator. **1887**

VICAR OF BULLHAMPTON (The). [by ANTHONY TROLLOPE: *Bradbury, Evans & Co.*, 1870.] "As the author has shunned the history of Carrie Brattle's fall, it is difficult to estimate the amount of merit in her subsequent reformation. That she is pretty and affectionate is nearly all we kno of her: we see that she is harshly regarded by many selfish relativs, but whether the hardness of her father or the tenderness of Frank Fenwick, the clergyman, has more true lōve in it, it is hard to say, or whether the justice of the ōne is less admirable than the mercy of the other . . . Thêre ar many Trollopean lawyers and clergymen, ōne thōro old gentleman, and the miller's wife, ōne of Nature's ladies, Lord St. George, a 19th-century improvement of his father the marquis, a dissenting preacher, of a type which is, we hope, uncommon, and a gallant captain, who rescues Mary Lowther from a marriage with the vicar's importunate friend, and so givs the story an orthodox conclusion. On the whole Mr. Trollope deservs our gratitude both for his story and his moral, tho we must protest against any confusion between the selfish fears of those who ar harsh to thêir unfortunate relativs, and an honest pride of race." [Athenæum. **1888**

VICAR'S DAUGHTER (The). [by G: MACDONALD: *Roberts*, 1872.] "The present is a genuin, pleasing home-story, which floes along, brook-like in its naturalness, its banks dotted here and thêre with rare and fragrant flowers of fancy. Ethelwyn Percival is permitted to tell her story in *her* way — a sensible, practical, live woman, innocent of all dreamy sentimentalities, or morbidly religious tendencies — a refreshing, healthy specimen of well-organized womanhood." [Overland.] — "Dr. Geo. MacDonald is hardly to be congratulated upon his success in his last novel, unless, indeed, an artful concealment, or rather attempted concealment of his personality, and his masquerading in petticoats, with a perpetual harping upon the joys of maternity, and the discomforts of pregnancy and the terrors of confinement alleviated by chloroform, can be deemed an admirable intellectual feat . . . He is at home in the nursery, in fact, he shōs a proficiency in the care of yung children that must make mothers, tormented by careless and ignorant nurses, sī with envy . . . If almost any other writer wer to draw such a character for a heroin, as if under the opinion that women wer nothing but producers and caressers of babies, and semi-hysterical housekeepers for their husbands, we feel confident that the women would be the first to raise an outcry against the narro-minded cynicism of such a vêin. They would naturally demand that sōme credit should be given to hier feminin virtues, to their grace, their dignity, their purity, to the real loftiness of their minds." [Nation. **1889**

VICAR'S PEOPLE (The) [by G: MANVILLE FENN: *Putnam*, 1882.] "ar the inhabitants of a Cornish village, half mining, half fishing. Thither cōmes a yung engineer, brīt, steady, and sturdy. How he won friends and enemies, suffered doubts of the most cruel kind, but finally triumfed over everything — even the powers of nature, — makes a very interesting story. The novelty in its settíng is the great ruins of the deserted mine down which fortune after fortune has gone. ' Wheal Carnac' seems as real a monster, devouring men, bodies and souls, as any dragon of mediæval legend." [Nation. **1890**

VICISSITUDES OF BESSIE FAIR-FAX (The). [by "HOLME LEE," i. e., Harriet Parr: *Smith*, 1874.] " ' The Vicissi-

tudes of Bessie Fairfax' is an agreeable novel of the utmost simplicity, recounting in a natural way a probable story. The heroin's vicissitudes ar not startling; she has both a step-father and step-mother, to be sure, and sōme of her relativs ar of hī birth, and sōme of her associates ar of humbler parentage; she has various lovers, and they hav life-like misunderstandings, and at last she marries the man of her choice, and all ends well without the introduction of any unnecessary horrors." [Nation. **1890a**

VIDA [by AMY DUNSMUIR: *Macmillan*, 1880.] " is a pleasant piece of writing, the various characteristics of the minor figures enhancing the commonsense and simplicity of the rustic heroin. Vida is the dauter of a minister on the coast of Arran — a man not so much originally cold-natured as numbed into selfishness by a humdrum life. The loss of her mother, which crushed the affection of Vida's father for his child, left the maid to gro up under the superintendence of an old scotch nurse of the ancient and faithful pattern. It was Nannie's care which sent her forth by herself on that adventurous errand of a morning call which led to the attachment of her life, and Nannie's anxiety for the future which secured the advantages of school education for the yung plodder in greek and latin in her father's study. Next to Nannie's faithfulness the' disinterested love of Mr. Jeffrey is the best thing which befalls Vida's childhood. When, in after years, that chivalrous lover makes the mistake of revealing the attachment to his yung pupil, and Vida mistakes for a season the impulse of gratitude for lōve, the rectitude and unselfishness of both convert what mīt hav been an unpleasant incident into one of the best parts of the story." [Athenæum. **1891**

VILLETTE [by C.. (BRONTÉ) NICHOLLS: *Smith*, 1853.] "is a work of astonishing power and passion. From its pages thêre issues an influence of truth as healthful as a mountain breeze. Contempt of conventions in all things, in style, in thôt, even in the art of story-telling, here visibly springs from the independent originality of a strong mind nurtured in solitude. As a novel, in the ordinary sense of the word, 'Villette' has few claims; as a *book*, it is one which, having read, you will not easily forget. It is true that the episode of Miss Marchmont, early in the first volume, is unneçessary, having no obvious connexion with the plot or the characters; but with what wonderful imagination is it painted! Whêre shall we find such writing as in that description of her last nît, whêrein the memories of bygône years côme trooping in upon her with a vividness partaking of the last energy of life? It is true also that the visit to London is unnecessary, and has many unreal details. Much of the book seems to be brôt in merely that the writer may express sômething which is in her mind; but at any rate she *has* something in her mind, and expresses it as no other can." [Westminster. **1892**

VIOLIN PLAYER (The) [by BERTHA THOMAS: *Bentley*, 1880.] "has a satisfactory theme and is a well-constructed story . . . In studies of character the book is unusually rich. The author understands the artistic temperament throuôut, and has traced it in a musician and in a sculptor, in a woman and in a man, with great skill. No less able is her delineation of the character of a fascinating woman of the world, a person with artistic taste but not an artist." [Athenæum. **1893**

VITTORIA [Sequel to "Emilia,"

by G: MEREDITH: London, 1866.] "has perhaps been one of the least popular of Mr. Meredith's novels, becaus of the repelling nature of the theme and the huge proportions of the book. But in its filosofy, its knoledge of human nature, its superb diction, its epigrammatic vividness, it will be found, if the rît point of vue is gained, not inferior in valpe as a social study to any of its stately companions." [American. **1894**

VIVIAN GREY [by Lord BEACONSFIELD: 1826.] "took the literary, social, and political worlds by storm . . . Notwithstanding the many flashes of genius in it, the novel wquld find few readers now wer it the production of an unknôn writer, but it was in complete harmony with the scandalous and scandal-loving tastes of the society to which it was offered, and throu its preposterous burlesque of the things and thôts around him was always expressed the daring indjviduality of the author. Neither Lord Lyndhurst nor Lord Clanricarde may hav been intentionally caricatured as the Marquis of Carabas; Foaming Fudge may not hav been purposly designed as a burlesque of Lord Brougham, nor Charlatan Gas of Canning, nor Fitzborn of Sir Robert Peel, nor even Stanislaus Hoax of Theodore Hook; but nône the less wer all these and nearly all the other persons in the book exaggerated reproductions, sôme clever, and some clumsy, of the characters and temperaments of actual persons conspicuous when the tale was written." [Athenæum. **1895**

VOICE IN THE WILDERNESS (A). [by CAROLINE FOTHERGILL: *Ward & Downey*, 1888.] "The man with a mad wife who falls in lôve with a more attractiv maiden is not exactly a novelty in fiction [compare No. 762], but unexacting readers may find quite as much of sentiment and entertainment as thêy care for in Miss Fothergill's new version. The style is very good. Thêre is no fault to find with it, and the dialog is managed as gracefully and easily as the description. Welsh scenery and town life ar painted with equal facility." [Athenæum. **1896**

WAGES OF SIN. [by "Lucas Malet," i. e., Rose G. (Kingsley) Harrison : *U.S. Book Co.*, 1891.] "James Colthurst was an artist, a man of great talent, who had forced a recognition from his countrymen, and placed himself at the top of the ladder of fame in the artistic world of London. In his early youth, while a student in Paris, he became entangled with a woman by whom he had a child, and to whom he always felt himself in a measure bound becaus she had supported him, by questionable and unquestionable means, when he was ill and starving. He became the head of ōne of the artschools in London, and thêre fell deeply in lōve with a rarely gifted woman who was his pupil. At first, knoing that his past life had rendered him unworthy of her, he made up his mind that he would never ask her to be his wife. Finding that she returned his lōve, however, his resolution weakened and thêy became engaged. His mistress, hearing that he was to be married, sōt his fiancée and told her the whole story of his life with her. On the spur of the moment, his sweetheart gave him up, but was soon convinced she had been too hard upon him, and was determined to recall him. In the meantime, the woman who had made the mischief was dying of consumption, and had sent for James Colthurst's intended wife to cōme to see her. Once arrived Mary sent instantly for James to come and make his peace

with the dying woman [compare plot of No. 1639]. It is just here that the extreme improbability of the 'The Wages of Sin' cōmes in. Mary renounced her lover forever, not in anger or in scorn, but becaus she deemed it rīt that he should belong to a woman whose hours wer numbered, tho she knew that his life would be ruined by her decision. It was not surprising that he threw himself from a cliff and was dashed to pieces." [Critic. **1897**

WARDEN (The). [by Anthony Trollope : 1855.] See Nos. 1082, 1455.

WATERDALE NEIGHBOURS (The) [by Justin McCarthy : *Tinsley*, 1867.] " is a good novel — well-written in good nervous english, — brīt and emfatic, without any appearance of striving. The story is interesting, the characters speak as people in life talk when they hav anything to say ; and all talk well. Each ōne has his or her individuality, and thêy speak for themselves. The interest lies in the frank reality of the characters, who follo thêir fortunes regardless of author or reader. This givs a freshness to the book which is as grateful as a drāft of sparkling water from a wayside rock to a thirsty traveler. The story turns on the power of a true and genuin nature to overcōme strokes of adverse fate, sorro, disappointment, and even grave mistakes in life and practice ; making all work together to a mature and perfect grōth of character." [Athenæum.] — " It is a book which no one can read without pleasure, nor close without regret ; it is interesting but never sensational, picturesque but not exaggerated, unaffected and natural without becoming wearisom or insipid. The story opens in a retired portion of Switzerland, whêre an English clergyman and his wife ar sojourning, and accidentally be-

come acquainted with Ralph Lennon, the hero." [Round Table. **1898**
WAY OF THE WORLD (The). [by D : Christie Murray : *Harper*, 1884.] "The history of. Mr. William Amelia and his paper, ' The Way of the World,' may be taken as a satire on the society journal and the methods of its editor. The man and vocation fit each other, and worldly prosperity ensues. Mr. Amelia is diligently and delītfully snubbed, but that is small comfort, since inability to recognize a snub is part of his fortunate nature. The characterization is a clever and amusing piece of work — so clever and amusing that it almost excuses the author for whipping up choice items from the daily papers before the ink dries, and presenting them to us as fiction. At the same time it shōes him scourging with the left hand what he imitates with the rīt. He holds Mr. Amelia up for detestation as an unscrnpulous gossip, knoing that the spice in the dish is, for a great many readers, the inferential identification of Mr. Amelia [E. Yates?] with very interesting current gossip." [Nation. **1899**
WAY WE LIVE NOW (The). [by Anthony Trollope : *Harper*, 1875.] "The good american will find in this novel not ōnly an entertaining story of modern life, but also a justification for his lōve of country. Whatever hard things hav been said in times past of America by english travelers, english newspapers, and english writers, no description of ordinary american life at thêir hands was ever made blacker than this picture of english civilization by Mr. Trollope . . . The novel contains descriptions of several kinds of life — the great world ; the yunger club life ; genteel country life and humble country life ; and we ar allowed to get a glimps or two of the journalistic world and of commercial life, and of

course learn a good deal of the condition of the matrimonial market . . . Mr. Trollope's picture of literary life is entertaining. We hav heard sōmething before now of that dishonest tribe, the critics, and it hardly needed the amusing correspondence of Lady Carbury, the doting mother of Sir Felix, with the 3 editors of the Bee-hive, the Morning Breakfast-Table, and the Evening Pulpit, on the subject of her venture, ' Criminal Queens,' to sho the real relation between authors and the conductors of the press. How Lady Carbury cajoles ōne editor and throes herself on the mercy of a second, and allows a third, without too much reproof, to kiss her in a moment of frenzied admiration, need not be told, nor how little her manœuvres help the sale of ' Criminal Queens.' Poor Lady Carbury, whose severe literary labors ar only varied by the performance of the maternal duty of letting her son in at day-break, when he is in a condition which renders the use of his latch-key difficult, has u hard life, and it would hav seemed ōnly fair for the author to hav disposed of Sir Felix in sōme way. But tho he is terribly mauled on ōne occasion by honest John Crumb, who suspects him, not without reason, of dishonorable designs with regard to the yung woman John desires to marry, he makes no sort of resistance, but allows himself to be beaten like a cur, and so preservs his valuable existence, to the inevitable future misery of his mother. Paul Montague, the honest yung man of the book, is so extraordinarily weak that we cannot help wondering that he cōmes out as well as he dōes. He is always getting into sōme mess, either being engaged to ōne woman when he is rapidly becoming interested in another, or gambling, or getting his property involved, or entangling himself in sōme other way.

He is well drawn, as all the characters in the book ar, but, ōne asks, why should so feeble a creature be thȯt worth drawing at all? He is in lōve with Hetta Carbury, and has been engaged to Mrs. Hurtle, an american wido, who has killed her man and been divorced from her husband, but with all her eccentricities is perhaps the nicest person in the book; and with Hetta her cousin Roger Carbury is also in lōve. Roger is an honest country gentleman, who is almost removed from the main current of the story, and who evidently thinks that ' the way we liv now ' is not at all a good way to liv." [Nation. **1900**

WE TWO [by " EDNA LYALL," i. e., Ada Ellen Bayly : *Appleton*, 1886] " is beautifully written, so that the style sustains ōne throu the length, and certain striking and dramatic situations at times relieve the monotony with startling vividness. It is chiefly remarkable as a book written in the interests of what is knōn as revealed religion, which yet has an atheist for a hero — and really a hero ; while the heroin, altho a converted atheist, is nōne the less a clear-sīted, liberal thinker. Besides being radicals, the father and dauter ar journalists, and the book is full of clever transcripts of the vicissitudes in the life of these ' two.' Incidentally, of course, thêre is a love-story." [Critic.] — " It givs the history of a father and dauter whose tender and intimate relation is defined by the title . . . She clings to her father, who is misunderstood, hated and denounced, and feels with all the warmth of her woman's heart the worth of the tie which binds them. Thêre is much which is truthful and winning in the book, and the character of both father and dauter rouse our interest and sympathy." [American. **1901**

WEARING OF THE GREEN (The).

[by "Basil," i. e., R: ASHE KING : *Chatto*, 1885.] " When hav we read a more delītful story than ' The Wearing of the Green '? It opens as the typical **irish** story, with the charming irish girl; and it holds us from the first page to the last with the genuin fascination of the wit and humor, the drollery and pathos, the winning warm-heartedness and contagious līt-heartedness, of that pathetic and interesting people." [Critic.] — " He who lōves a rosy cheek, and the nativ grace of irish womanhood, painted on a background of uncompromising green, shall here find as pretty a story as he wishes. The mingled simplicity and guile, the humor and geniality, the brogue and the politics of Erin, do not possess an equal charm for everybody, and thêre ar people with sufficient prejudice to decline beforehand the reading of a tale in which these things make up the whole plot and narrativ. Thêy will do themselves an injustice, however, if thêy refuse to read ' The Wearing of the Green,' for it is a brīt and pathetic novel, with good characters and a lively style." [Athenæum. **1902**

WEE WIFIE. [by ROSA N. CAREY: *Tinsley*, 1869.] " May every bachelor we kno be as well-mated as more than ōne husband in this pleasant story, albeit Fay has her humors, — and so with sōme other charming women enshrined in this book. It is a joy to be among them." [Athenæum. **1903**

WELLFIELDS (The) = No. 1010.

WENDERHOLME [by PHILIP GILBERT HAMERTON : *Roberts*, 1877.] " professes to be a study of Yorkshire life and character, but the representativ nativs who talk dialect and the middle-class mill ōuers who develop into millionaires ar not half as well depicted as the people of gentler breeding, the poverty-stricken Prigleys at the parsonage, with their patrician sympathies and their cruelly outraged tastes, and Colonel Stanburne, the commander of the militia, and his hī-born wife, Lady Helena. These last ar admirable. Colonel Stanburne is that very rare personage in fiction, a living gentleman — manly, kind-hearted, unintellectual, thōro-bred, lavish, — lapsing into pecuniary ruin more throu courtesy to others than indulgence to himself. His wife is a hī-spirited creature, a great deal more clever, conscious, and cautious than he, wiser, but not so sweet-natured, an exceedingly real woman, both in her pitiless anger at the discovery of her husband's folly and in her sudden and deep repentance for her severity." [Atlantic. **1904**

WHAT SHE CAME THROUGH [by " S.. TYTLER," i. e., Henrietta Keddie: *Dadly Isbister & Co.*, 1877.] " is a pleasant book. Pleasant in style, which neither aims at flippant brilliancy nor descends to important declamation or gush, but is that of a cultivated lady, — natural and pleasant in the persons and places with which the story deals, as well as in the happy end to which it is brôt. At the same time other characters besides the heroin hav to cōme throu thêir share of troubles enuf 'to make the story resemble life; and while the happy conclusion is sufficiently probable it is also sufficiently unexpected for fiction, and givs the reader genuin satisfaction. The heroin is a girl of gentle birth on her father's side, at whose death she and her sister wer left almost without money and with only two relativs." [Athenæum. **1905**

WHAT THE WORLD WOULD SAY? [by C: GIBBON: *Bentley*, 1875.] " The Major falls genuinly in love with Bess, and, when she finds she is thwarted by the indifference of Austin, and her

father fails in a rich marriage he projects for her, in a moment of pique she elopes with the soldier. Then cōmes the narrativ of thêir poverty and struggles, and our author, by very natural degrees, converts the tolerance with which she first regards her husband to duty and affection. The dramatic interest in the story is confined to there. But incidently we ar introduced to many characters worth knoing. Killiwar is an amusing and worthy Highlander; Miss Janet's oddities ar pathetically humorous; the gate-keeper is a fine specimen of the reckless Scotchman." [Athenæum. **1906**

WHAT YOU WILL [*J. W. Parker*, 1858.] " is full of cleverness and character. The incidents ar not numerous, and ōne, constituting a sort of turning point, is nothing more than a commonplace; but the writing is natural and pointed, the illustrations of human nature ar vivid, and thêre ar sōme charming sketches of home life. The clergyman of Acton Bars is an admirable portrait, sōmewhat in Mr. Trollope's style; but the best part of the narrativ is described as ' The winding-up of the thread; ' it is most tenderly conceived and most touchingly developed." [Leader. **1907**

WHAT'S IN A NAME? [by S.. DOUDNEY: *Hodder*, 1883.] "is a very romantic story. One H: Jervaux marries secretly a girl belo him in social positiou, and thêreby offends his family. He dies, leaving ōne child; and, we ar led to believ, that his wife dōes not long survive him. The child is adopted by his grandparents. Thên a wido lady, who undertakes her education, appears upon the scene. Who this lady is, how she is avenged upon one who had wronged her in former times, we may leav for the readers to find out. The

tale is written with considerable power."
[Spectator. **1908**
WHEAT AND TARES [by H:
STUART CUNNINGHAM: *Harper*, 1860.]
"is a capital story. Fresh, sparkling,
and cheerful as a summer's morning,
it has also the hier elements of a first-
class novel, in its striking delineations
of character, in its fidelity to life, and
in the essential nobleness of its sentiment and its filosofy. With sŏme free
and easy conversations, which may
scandalize those who would treat the
church and all its adjuncts as especially
sacred, it has a good sense in its vue of
things sacred, as well as things worldly,
which is very refreshing after the cant
of so-called religious novels. [See No.
1346.] It may not increase reverence
for bishops, deans, archdeacons, or popular preachers, but it will foster respect
for manliness, generosity, frankness,
and all christian virtues. Its vivacity
never degenerates into slang, nor dŏes
it overstate the graces or faults of any
of its personages. It is, we hav no
doubt, a very faithful picture of the
life in an english sea-side town." [Chris-
tian Examiner.] — "This is a *natural*
work. It will please all readers, whose
tastes and human feelings hav not been
utterly obliterated by the blood-and-
thunder 'sensation' romances of the
time . . . Altho thêre is nothing very
novel either in its incidents or situations,
the reader is agreeably interested to the
close. Like most other modern stories,
it is chîefly concerned with what may
be described as the superficial aspects of
'the course of true love;' but, unlike
most stories, so charmingly ar all these
adjusted and exposed, that the entire
work becŏmes an exquisit picture of
life. Trifles hav no undue importance.
We ar not requested either to wail over
exaggerated grief, or to prance with

spasmodic joy. Thêre is neither the
sickly whine of sentiment nor the lugu-
brious plaint of morality. The characters ar natural, and vividly portrayed.
The bits of description occur gracefully,
and sŏmetimes with excellent dramatic
effect. The conversations ar skilfully
managed. We seem to be hearing the
unaffected talk of clever people, who
ar always sprîtly and often brilliant.
And throuŏŭt, the story is pervaded with
a spirit of genuin humor, refinement,
good sense, and feeling, which makes it
altogether delîtful." [Knickerbocker.]
— "The man of whom all men speak
good becaus he dŏes well to himself;
who makes cleverness take the place of
hard work, and taste that of conscience;
and to whom 'the world appears merely
an " I writ large"' has no doubt always
been a recognized character, tho it has
been left to comparativly recent writers
to formulate him. Probably the ruffer
manner of a more plainspoken time kept
him in his place; it may be dŏubted,
indeed, whether even Tito Melema [No.
926], the type for all time of this character, could really hav risen to influence
in the Florence of his day, and whether
he is not a modern man projected on an
ancient state of society. However this
may be, he flourishes now, and several
writers of our time besides G: Eliot
hav studied him with precision. He is
an old acquaintance of Mr. Justice
Cunningham. Middle-aged people
remember as ŏne of the cleverest short
novels which thêy ever read a book
called 'Wheat and Tares,' in which is
sketched a brilliant yung man of this
sort." [Athenæum. **1909**
WHEN I WAS ᴬ LITTLE GIRL.
[by ELIZA (TABOR) STEPHENSON: *Macmillan*, 1871.] "The stories read
very like the genuin recollections of the
real girlhood of a charming woman, for

such a childhood could not help developing into a graceful and excellent womanhood. The stories ar generally cheerful; but thêre is ône which will bring tears into the eyes of all who read it. For simplicity and pathos we hav seldom read anything more touching than the death of little Callie; but the book ends cheerfully and it will be pleasant reading for grōn people as well as for children." [Athenæum. **1910**

WHEN WE TWO PARTED. [by S.. DOUDNEY: *Maxwell*, 1885.] " Thêre is much to praise and little to find fault with in this homely romance. The nonconformist minister and his surroundings, his puritan dauter and her lively maid, and the humors of his congregation ar drawn with a thōroly sympathetic hand. Shrewd sayings in a sententious form ar scattered thickly throuȯūt these pages, and prove the author to be a close but kindly student of humanity. She possesses, moreover, a vêin of quiet humor which emerges pleasantly at times, as well as an artistic restraint which spares the reader unnecessary details." [Athenæum. **1911**

WHERE TEMPESTS BLOW. [by M. W. PAXTON: *Ward & Downey*, 1885.] " So unpretentious is the opening af this novel, that not until the middle of the first volume is reached dōes the reader realize the welcom truth that he has lit upon an uncommonly clever and engrossing novel . . . Thêre is a great deal of local coloring, but the freshness and humor of these pictures of scotch provincial life can not fail to enlist the sympathy of the reader by their truth and unconventionality . . . Out of simple materials the author has wrôt a singularly effectiv story, steadily advancing in interest, and concluding by a simple and artistic dénoûment. We hav read ' Whêre

Tempests Blow' with genuin pleasure. The style is vigorous and unaffected, and in keeping with the bracing moral atmosfere which pervades the whole story." [Athenæum. **1912**

WHICH SHALL IT BE? [by " MRS. ALEXANDER," i. e., Annie (French) Hector: *Bentley*, 1866; *Holt*, 1874.] " If we call this a remarkable novel, it is less for what it performs than for what it promises. In itself it is rather a series of studies than a finished work, and the reader will find it a curious study rather than an interesting novel . . . Madame de Fontarce, born Blake de Ballyshanahan, is not ōnly a new character, but is drawn with consummate art. Her outward appearance and her ménage ar not new to us; but her religious principles, her cheap charity, her way of living on others and dying for them, ar sketched to perfection." [Athenæum. **1913**

WHITE HEATHER. [by W: BLACK: *Macmillan*, 1885.] " Mr. Black here displays more than ône attractiv quality of his art as a writer of fiction, and it is fortunate both for his readers and for himself that sōme of these qualities ar much fresher, at any rate in thêir manifestations, than others. Mr. Hudson and his dauter, for instance, who ar follooed in their holiday pilgrimage throu the scottish heather, ar american studies of the best kind, and will win their way at ōnce to the heart as well as to the critical approval of the reader. Still more directly will his heart be reached by the gentle Meenie, a veritable scottish lassie, drawn in Mr. Black's tenderest, if not his strongest style. Ronald Strang, the keeper, is the true hero . . . The verses constitute another element of freshness." [Athenæum. **1914**

WHITE HOUSE BY THE SEA

(The) [by MATILDA [BARBARA] BETHAM EDWARDS: *Smith*, 1857.] "is a novel of a class now uncommon, being made of lŏve, pure and simple, and in the form of an autobiografy. The heroin has two passions . . . The tender-hearted reader, however, must not despair; thêre is balm in Gilead, for the yung girl quaffs a sweet nepenthe of second lŏve, and livs with her husband in a place of pleasantness whêre all her paths ar peace. Then returns the false ŏne, base and haggard, and begs to be forgiven, which being dŏne, he disappears throu the shrubbery and embarks for the East. It is a tale told, apparently, by a youthful writer, and may be commended to readers old enuf to sympathize with its ecstacies of joy and grief, and not too old to believe in heart-blĭts and breathing passion-flowers." [Leader. **1915**

WHO IS SYLVIA? [by A. PRICE: *Harper*, 1883.] "Thêre is a 'bar sinister' in 'Who is Sylvia?' and so much misery descends upon her lŏvely head that it would be well to ·read the last chapter first, and then with a free mind to enjoy the always charming country life from which the book is made. Sisterhoods affŏrd new ground for the novelist, and the scenes in St. Mary's Refuge sho them at thêir best and worst." [Nation. **1916**

WILD HYACINTH [by — ( ) RANDOLPH: *Lippincott*, 1875.] "is a very good novel, rich in good sense, pleasant pictures of english life, and instructiv sketches of character. Its tone is exceptionally refined, and its moral, tho not emfatic, is excellent . . . The author is very severe on ritualism and woman's rĭts; but these subjects ar not prominent features of the story. The characters ar drawn with great skill." [Boston "Literary World." **1917**

WILFRED CUMBERMEDE [by G: MACDONALD: *Hurst*, 1871] "is extremely original, clever and interesting. But the fact that it satisfies these conditions will not make it popular in the face of ŏne defect: we mean the want of continuity in the narrativ, in which ar many lacunæ which one would like to see filled — perplexities which remain unsolvd, motivs which ar left unexplained, actions which ar never accounted for . . . The good-hearted, unworldly uncle to whose singular wisdom in dealing with children the boy oed whatever happiness of his boyhood he knew; the worldly lawyer, — his antitype — in whose fysiognomy the unerring instinct of the child read the base nature his conduct revealed, Charley Osborne, his school and còllege friend, ruined by his father (an evangelical) from whom he inherited an abnormal sensibility, and who hated his son for not having inherited also the dogmas of his school; Clara Coningham, a woman capable of infinit good and infinit baseness, if the motiv wer thêre; and abŏve all Mary Osborne, the 'Athanasia' of his dream who concealed, behind the vêil of a commonplace, expressionless countenance, a nature more divine than human, — in all these the reader will find tokens that Mr. MacDonald's hand has not lost its cunning. But besides the faculty of drawing character, Mr. MacDonald has a wonderful gift of word-painting, which is shŏn especially in his descriptions of alpine scenery, but còmes out whenever he has an occasion to make language supply the lack of pictorial illustrations." [Athenæum. **1918**

WILFRED'S WIDOW [by — (SMEDLEY) HART: *Bentley*, 1883.] "is a thŏroly amusing book, the interest of which carries the reader on throu every

608

page of a sufficiently brief story. We must say, however, that we hav seldom read a story so lively which is open to the old criticism that the bad character of the novel is more interesting than any of the good characters with which she is brôt into unfavorable comparison. It shôs a good deal of that quiet humor in which women, when they hav any humor at all, so often excel. The story opens with a picture of the deepest grief. News of Wilfred's death has just reached his family, who belong to the stiffest county society. Then folloes the announcement that he had been married in Australia, and that his wido is coming. She arrives, and every one is captivated by her surpassing beauty. But she shôes a strange forgetfulness or ignorance of all sorts of details with which Wilfred's wido ôt to hav been familiar [compare plot of ' Mrs. Fenton '] . . The pictures of refined country life ar excellent; and the yung wido's astonishment, her vulgarity and cleverness, and the absurd influence of her beauty sho a keen power of observation and a sort of genial shrewdness which charm the reader and interest him in the story, altho he cannot fail to see what the conclusion is to be. The author's warm sympathy prevents her insît into character leading her to becôme cynical. She succeeds in the cleverest way in raising a kind of pity for the ' wido ' at the very moment when her wicked imposture is unmasked. The style is brît and simple throuôut, without any affectation of cleverness, and the characters appear to unfold themselves in whole chapters of self-analysis." [Athenæum. **1919**

WILL DENBIGH. [*Roberts*, 1877.] " Herter Kenrick, its heroin, is a fresh, lovable bit of drawing. Her pretty rages and jealousies, her warmth, her impulsiv speeches, and loyalty to old friends and fixed ideas, ar well depicted, and very like the girls we kno in life. Of Will Denbigh, the ' nobleman,' we cannot say as much. He is a little too deep and earnest and self-abnegating, a little too unlike mankind out of novels, to excite our full sympathies. No such fault, however, is to be found with Miss Kenrick's other lôver, Frank Halliday, who is admirably natural; spoilt, attraetiv, versatil, uncertain." [Boston " Literary World." **1920**

WINNA [*Charing Cross Pub. Co.*, 1878.] " is interesting. The people ar ' nice,' and altho thêy hav their ' little weaknesses ' they never scare us by getting into any serious scrapes, or into doubtful company. The scene of the first half of the story is laid in Italy, at the house of a baronet. To him enter his nefew and his nîece Winna, who hav agreed to meet thêir widoed mother on her way from India to Florence. The society of Florence seems to be cleverly sketched, without any attempt at word-painting or picturesque writing . . . The scene changes to the Devonshire village . . . She continues to entertain us by brît passages of shrewd observation and characterisation . . . Each character has an individuality . . . The story is readable and thôroly pleasant throuôut." [Spectator. **1921**

WINTER STORY (A) [by F.. M.. PEARD: *Roberts*, 1877.] " is of rare excellence from every point of vue. Thêre is about it an air of good breeding — an artistic completeness, symmetry and finish — which sets it quite apart by itself . . . The landscape of the south of England is pictured with a loving and faithful hand. The atmosfere is fresh, pure, invigorating. The child life of Ronald and Jess, the earlier remorse and later peace of Philip, the gentle and

WINDOW IN THRUMS (A). [by JAMES M. BARRIE: Cassell, 1891.] "To the pleasure given by the records of life in the hamlet of Thrums, it is difficult to say whether humor or pathos contributes most. The grinding poverty, all the more severe because decent and self-respecting, the stern and unyielding religious creed practiçed by these poor weavers, the patiençe and dignity with which both poverty and "the decrees of God" ar borne, touch the heart with pity, while the pictures of their vivid curiosity as to their nebors, and the pains they take to satisfy it, and the conduct of their love affairs, ar replete with a quiet humor that is very taking. The author, tho principally occupied with the history of one family, givs glimpses of T'nowhead, Tammas Haggart, the minister—not Mr. Dishart [See No. 1475 m], his wife, and others of the village. The glimpses of Hendry's life open with the pleasing excitement attendant upon the minister leaving for a Sunday, and the conjectures as to the personality of the supply, and, more interesting yet, the probable lodging of the supply. Jess, Hendry's wife, and the dauter, Leeby, ar fairly beside themselvs with curiosity, and finally triumphant over certainty of knoledge. This description is full of dry humor and naturalness. Stil more amusing is the call which Hendry, Leeby and the dominie make upon the minister, during which Leeby assumes a downcast aspect and dumb manner, which deçeives even the minister's wife into a belief in her dulness, but the dominie listens as Leeby on her return home tels her mother the exact particulars as to the furnishings of the manse, of the darned spot in the carpet under the table, the worn plaçe in the chair cover and the chamber fire-irons which don't match. The interest of these sketches lies in the reçital of the homely pleasures, the pitifully small ambitions of the family (the struggles to attain a headed cloak ar of a gravity suffiçient for the conduct of a state), the sweetness of their affection, their pride in Jamie the son, and the bitterness of his neglect and final desertion which ar told by the sympathetic onlooker, who deeply pities tho he can not help. In this book perhaps more than in any other, Barrie evinçes his appreçiation of the Scottish character. Many sentençes contain whole volumes of evidençe as to the mingled narroness and ambitions of the people." [Springfield Republican.]—"These reminiscences of a very old man ar grouped about a lame woman who, for 20 years or more, sat at a windo looking down the brae toards the town with the dismal name of Thrums. The daily life of the deçent poor is pretty much the same the world over, always commonplace, frequently dismal. It is no more interesting in fiction than in reality, unless the people who ar obliged to put up with it hav some inborn strength, or grace, or purity which can't be destroyed by hard conditions. Such people Mr. Barrie has chosen to tel about very simply and plainly, as befits his subject. To appreciate the story fully, one must hav some acquaintance with English as it is spoken from Maidenkirk to John o'Groat's House, tho enuf is told in the uncorrupted tung to giv an idea of the fine spirit inhabiting Jess Hendry's poor body, and of the great love with which she inspired family and nebors." [Nation. **1920 p**

true Hester, quaint farmer Ben and his strong-minded wife, and the ins and outs of the Pollard Farm, make up an 'ensemble' of uncommon attractivness. The author writes with a reservd power, pleasantly mingles the humorous with the pathetic, and with great skill brings a spring-time of life and joy to succeed the 'winter' of grief, loneliness and despair with which her opening pages ar chilled." [Boston "Literary World." **1922**

WITH HARP AND CROWN. [by WA. BESANT & JA. RICE: *Tinsley*, 1875.] "The heroin has the advantage of most heroins, in that she has sõme value as an ideal. She is patient, loving and womanly; an energetic worker in the world without the cant of strong-mindedness; and faithful to a deep attachment without hysterics or selfishness. Her story is not an uncommon õne; sho simply finds that the lõve of men dões not bear the test of separation like that of women; her struggle with the world leaves external wounds, which impair instead of enhancing the only beauty for which her hero loved her; and she has to resign the happiest of her hopes in favor of one who has not earned them . . . Owen, the schoolmaster, is good and genial; the impetuous heartiness of his plans for regenerating society is excellent. Another figure at the zero point of moral excellence, is the sublime Lillingworth, the hermit of Lowland street, who deliberately contemplated the purchase of immortality by the production of clap-trap and sensation memoirs." [Athenæum. **1923**

WITHIN SOUND OF THE SEA [by C.. L.. (HAWKINS) DEMPSTER: *Paul*, 1878.] "is a novel of a kind which is not at all too common; short, natural, picturesque, never tedious, and thõroly healthful." [Contemporary Re-

view.] — "The author of 'Blue Roses' writes delītfully. In her present tale the scotch scenes ar particularly well-dõne. Only those who kno Scotland well will be able thõroly to appreciate their truthfulness. The description of the literary and scientific society at Edinburgh, when 'yung Robert' is at the university, is particularly good, and is not overdõne by fine writing. We can most thõroly recommend the story to all persons seeking a sound, wholesom novel." [Westminster Review. **1924**

WITHIN THE PRECINCTS. [by MA. OLIPHANT (WILSON) OLIPHANT: *Smith*, 1879.] "The heroin is Lottie Despard, the dauter of Captain Despard, a gentleman of irish descent and fallen fortunes, who has recently been elected one of the chevaliers . . . We feel greatly for these two yung people, whose troubles cõme home to us vividly; and we cannot repress a throb of sincere sympathy when their jaunty, pretentious father, in his shabby coat with the flower in the buttonhole, brings matters to a climax by providing them with a stepmother in the person of an atrociously vulgar and flippant yung dressmaker, who is a mésalliance even for him, and turns the already miserable home literally upside down . . . How Lottie wins a lõver, considerably abõve her in society, and how she is innocently and unconsciously brõt to the brink of ruin, is touchingly told; our sympathies go entirely with Lottie throuõut the story, and she wins our affection involuntarily. Within the Precincts is a pleasant, cheerful bit of life, with its touch of romance and sentiment, its clever but harmless irony, and its fidelity to human nature." [Boston "Lit. World." **1925**

WIVES AND DAUGHTERS. [by E.. CLEGHORN (STEVENSON) GASKELL: *Harper*, 1865.] "In 'Wives and

Daughters' Mrs. Gaskell added, we think, to the number of those works of fiction — of which we cannot perhaps count more than a score as having been produced in our time — which will outlast the duration of their novelty and continue to be read and relished for a hier order of merit. Besides being the best of the author's tales — putting aside 'Cranford' [No. 1175], that is, (which as a work of quite other pretensions ôt not to be wêd against it, and which seems to us manifestly destined in its modest way to becôme a classic) — it iṣ also ône of the very best novels of its kind. So delicately, so elaborately, so artistically, so truthfully, and heartily is the story wrôt out, that the hours given to its perusal seem like hours actually spent, in the flesh as well as the spirit, among the scenes and people described, in the atmosfere of their motivs, feelings, traditions, associations. The gentle skill with which the reader is sloly involved in the tissue of the story; the delicacy of the handiwork which has perfected every mesh of the net in which he finds himself ultimately entangled; the lîtness of touch which, while he stands all unsuspicious of literary artifice, has stopped every issue into the real world . . . these marvellous results, we say, ar such as to compel the reader's warmest admiration, and make him feel, in his gratitude for this seeming accession of social and moral knoledge, as if he made but a poor return to the author in testifying, no matter how ŝtrongly, to the fact of her genius." [Nation.   **1926**

WIZARD'S SON (The) [by Ma. Oliphant (Wilson) Oliphant : *Harper*, 1884.] "is in the author's less pleasing manner, the plot being of the mysterious and exciting kind; but she manages her old castle and her en-

chanter or her ghost better than any body else now writing can. The reader's approval of the tale will vary in proportion to his willingness to put up with unexplained mysteries, but all will agree in the charm of the yung girls. 'Hester' is as delîtful as any whom Mrs. Oliphant has drawn, while so different from the others as to strengthen the opinion long prevailing in circles whêre her books ar enjoyed, that she must take each one carefully from life, for how could ône imagination supply so many?" [Nation.] — "It is a book which cômes so near to positiv greatness that the sudden and amazing falling-off in the final chapters moves ône to a species of exasperation. A very commonplace yung man falling hêir to an ancient and ghost-encumbered inheritance in Scotland afforded a matchless opportunity for the calm and candid consideration of the relations between the canny and the uncanny, between the comforts of modern civilization and the venerable fenomena of second-sît. The story is accordingly conceived in a quaint spirit of equal hospitality to the two sets of influences; and it is most skillfully sustained to the last, being made to move smoothly and, so to speak, naturally along the narro line between the possible and the impossible. The human characṭers ar as distinct as need be, — altogether such as ourselvs, and visited only from time to time by the 'blank misgivings of a creature moving about in worlds not realized;' the 'revenant' is entirely '*comme il faut*.' All goes weirdly and well up to the moment of the final catastrofē, which it would hav been so easy, one would think, to manage with the same fine and faultless ambiguity. If only the haunted tower had been made to crumble without warning of its inevitable decay, putting forever beyond the reach of investigation the mysteries which had pervaded it, the conclusion would hav been perfectly consistent and credible, and the reaction in the reader's mind would probably hav been toward wonder and faith. The lovers mīt still hav been buried beneath the ruin, and then exhumed alive, if their merciful author absolutely would. But the antiquated and tawdry machinery of the secret chamber, the mystic lamp, the winking portrait, and the alchemist ' properties ' generally test our credulity too severely, and make us more than half ashamed of the sincerity of our interest. Loch Houran tower is reduced to the rank of the Castle of Udolpho [No. 858]." [Atlantic. **1927**

WOMAN OF MIND (A) [by — (JERROLD) SMITH: *Low*, 1879.] "is a pleasant tale told in a pleasant and unaffected manner. The style is fresh and brīt, the characters simple and straitforward, without a touch of that obnoxious fastness with which too many novelists think fit to pander to a corrupt taste. Her heroin, if a woman of mind, is nōne the less a woman of heart." [Athenæum. **1928**

WOMAN'S KINGDOM (The) [by DINAH MARIA (MULOCK) CRAIK: *Harper*, 1868.] " as a lōve story is a success. It is not easy to conjure so much out of so little; and the author deservs credit for having made so readable a book with only ' speaking parts' in it . . . But Letty, the bad angel of the book, is truly amusing; her airy selfishness, meant to be very wicked, is piquant and excessivly diverting. Her author called her into being to teach yung people how wicked it is to flirt and break yung men's hearts, by pretending to lōve them. But the yung persons will see that a fatal error had been made in

Letty's anatomy, by leaving out a heart; consequently, they will be diverted by her old speeches, and may possibly sī that thĕy ar not so beautiful as this heartless yung woman is represented as being. And, after all, is thêre not a certain flavor of wildness in the human heart that revolts at the prospect of such a dead level of humdrum goodness as that which we ar morally certain must be the lot of the married Doctor and Edna?" [Overland. **1929**

WOMAN'S VICTORY (A) [by AGNES C. MAITLAND: *Tinsley*, 1876.] " is a thōtfully written story . . . Wynward, a thōtful and noble sort of man, has married a cold-blooded lady of fashion, who is attracted to him by his fortune, and soon ceases to care the indifference she feels for his aspirations. [Compare plot of ' Marcia.'] The falling of the unequal yoke is described with painful fidelity. After the pair hav long lived separate cōmes the acquaintance between Acton and Miss Colquhoun. Sōme scenes of terrible trial which the latter pass throu together awake in the man the conciousness of his true feelings for the woman. In a moment of pain and weakness he reveals his secret. They part in an agony of lōve and shame, never to meet again. Helen, who is most wêd down by what she thinks her guilt, is enabled, by a strange turn of fortune, to save the life of the woman to whom she oes an act of reparation, and perishes in doing so. Such is the outline of the tale, and its powerful conception is equalled by the skill of its gradual development. The victory of poor Helen over her rebellious heart involvs a desperate conflict, but she cōmes out from it in the full possession of those faculties which throuōut her short life hav been devoted to the good of others. The incidents of life in a manufacturing town, which include the memorable famin during the american war [compare ' Probation '], ar told with a vividness which denotes either actual experience or large powers of observant sympathy." [Athen. **1930**

WOMAN'S WILL. [by F.. [E..] (H.) BURNETT, *Warne*, 1887.] = *MISS DEFARGE.*

WOODLANDERS (The) [by T: HARDY: *Harper*, 1887.] " is a story of the present epoch, yet it seems better to describe Shakespeare's England than the England of our ōn time; the England of May-poles, midsummer-eve wanderings in haunted woods, all sorts of rustic customs and old time observances. It is indeed the magic of the triumf of Mr. Hardy's art that he has thus wrôt imperishably into the mosaic of his novels the vanishing poetry and traditions of old England. The story before us is too hily and subtly colored by the author's genius to be fairly told except as he has told it. It is in a hī degree fascinating, but it is also one of the dreariest and most hopeless of books." [American.] — " The Woodlanders is a disagreeable novel; thêre is no disguising this melancholy conclusion. It arouses the keenest sympathies on the part of the reader, may, indeed, if he be of sensitiv fiber, wring him with anguish, and leav him at the last, baffled, stupified, cast down. The quality of inevitableness is thêre, and givs the book hī rank as a work of art, but the inevitableness is too irresistible, too implacable. Edgar Fitzspiers is a monster of selfishness — a man who, while engaged in a shameful intrigue with a village wench, is pursuing the courtship of the sweet girl who soon becōmes his wife, and whom within a few months he forsakes for the companionship of an adventuress. And when ōne nīt it is

thôt that Fitzspiers has been killed by a fall from his horse, these 3 women meet and shed thêir tears together; while the wife, altho in lōve with another — poor Giles Winterbourne, the most pathetic of all these victims of circumstances — the wife, wooed again by the returned husband, succumbs to his blandishments and consents to a reunion before the grass has grōn upon the grave of the guileless, chivalric lōver who gave up his life to save her from open shame. By the side of Giles Wenterbourne Mr. Hardy places another figure whose consistency of purpose and unyielding fidelity, ar equally pathetic and devoid of fruition. Mary South is a supremely successful embodiment of homely, faithful lōve, one who, made to play a thankless and even absurd part, at the last touches sublimity." [Boston " Literary World." **1931**

WOODLEIGH [by F: W: ROBINSON: *Hurst*, 1859.] " is a good novel, and one which will be read with interest not merely for the story — the interest of which is kept to the last — but for the knoledge of human nature and life-like characters it contains, with the sound common sense which is so deficient in most novels, but which is one of the especial attractions of the author of ' The Wild-flower.' There is no hī flōn description of beautiful heroes and heroins; the characters ar all poor earthly mortals, as plain as ōne meets in every day life, and painted with all their imperfections on their heads, as a warning to others with the same faults — as novel characters should be . . . Woodleigh is not a novel to be read and thrōu aside; it will be found quite as interesting in the second perusal. The author possesses two excellent qualities requisit for the novelist, namely, — a great knoledge of character and the art of telling a story." [Leader. **1932**

WOOED AND MARRIED [by Rosa Nouchette Carey: *Lippincott*, 1876.] " bears in its title a rather frank avowal of those subjects which writers of fiction hav seldom found it to their interest to eschew. Here we hav our old friend, the poor governess, apparently insignificant and girlish; but, altho she has a way of yielding to her quick temper, she has the good fortune to interest a number of people in her, and in time, after much delay, she marries the squire ' with the quizzical eyes.' Thêre is in all this a good deal of ' gushing'; but thêre is less of it when the author fairly buckles down to business, and it is her digressions which ar the most tiresome things in the book. Thêre is besides this a more serious fault — the wholesale slanter and maiming of so many of the characters. Rheumatic fever, dislocated ankles, blindness, heart disease, hunting accidents, and sudden death make the story almost as alarming reading as a report of sewage commissioners; but then thêy supply incidents enuf to interest the most callous." [Nation. **1933**

WOOING O'T (The). [by " Mrs. Alexander," i.e., Annie (French) Hector: *Holt*, 1873.] " Mrs. Berry is a good type, and so is the polished and scoundrelly M. de Bragance, who after he has married the wido and got hold of her property, begins his travels not ōnly with her but with another lady no better than she should be, not troubling himself afterward much about the former, who finds a refuge in England · · · Maggie Grey, the heroin, with her familiar eyes of changing blue, pensiv, sensitiv,—shy mouth, indescribable nose, frank, open forehead, delicately turned neck, and pretty figure, belōved by

Lord Torchester, her cousin John Grey, and by the hero, Geoffrey Trafford, always modest, always natural, always charming, has not infrequently been met by novel-readers; while Trafford himself, the aristocratic, sarcastic, witty, traveled man of the world, who at 32 has exhausted its pleasures, and who, tho ' steady,' would ' stick at nothing which he wanted very much,' who is always a perfect gentleman, however, with infinit depths of possible passion in his dark eyes, which makes all women say instinctivly to themselvs, ' How he could lōve!' who deeply lōves Maggie and is deeply lōved not ōnly by her but by a legion of other women — Geoffrey Trafford, too, has been playing his part for a long time." [Galaxy. **1934**

WORLD WE LIVE IN (The) [by Oswald Crawfurd: *Chapman*, 1884.] " is a capital novel. It is lively and sparkling throuōut, and ōne can ōnly regret that it is so short. The story is excellently contrived, and told not merely in an easy and racy style, but with admirable skill. The action all takes place in the course of a few days at a country house. The house party furnish the characters, and an excellent party they make. They ar drawn with a firm hand, and stand out distinct and intelligible. ' The World We Live In' will be popular with men as well as with women. It is the sort of novel which men like. Not much burdened with analysis, and free from disquisition, and description, it is full of good spirits, and lōve, and bits of good criticism. It is a pleasure to find a writer who takes a cheerful vue of life and is ready to believe well of human nature, and who yet writes like a man of the world, and, if it is not impertinent to say so, like an educated gentleman too." [Athenæum. **1935**

WORLD'S VERDICT. [by " Annie

EDWARDS : " *Hurst*, 1861.] " We could not giv a sketch of the story without greatly diminishing the reader's pleasure when he gets the book, for it contains a story, an l a very good õne, worked out with all the art which is necessary for concealing art. The only questionable point in the mere execution, is whether the first chapters, in which the hero, saddened by his wretched fate, is introduced to the reader at Brighton, should hav been the first chapters, or not. But the best beginning of a tragic tale is sõmetimes difficult to find; and poor G: Rutherford mĩt not hav excited the reader's attention, if he had not been introduced on his first starting in life as an artist. The character of Laura Bellayne is powerful in its truth; thêre is no word too much or too little about that woman. Vain, weak, coquettish, false, heartless, cold and sensual, yet beautiful outwardly, with brain and histrionic talent enuf to act any part they choose for thêir selfish ends, such women hav the power to lure the lõve of the best men, if those men ar too yung and unworldly to be aware of their dodges. Laura is a fine specimen of a bad woman — very different from Becky Sharp; but as clever a sketch as the latter is a finished picture. Laura, with her large, soft, hazel eyes, her small, white hands, and her graceful figure, is as clear to the mind's eye as the wonderful, piquante, plain, white-shõldered Becky." [Spectator.   **1936**

WYNCOTE [by — (   ) ERSKINE : *Holt*, 1875.] " is a very quiet story, remarkable for its pleasant pictures of village society, and its delineation of a noble family reduced almost to indigence, and restored by marriage into a rich plebeian family. Three of the feminin characters ar very lõvely, — Phœbe, the heroin, Rose Cooper, and

the brave, strong, yet tender-hearted Camilla." [Boston " Literary World."] — " Mrs. Erskine's heroin is a yung girl who has been brõt from Rome, whêre she was the much-tried dauter of a blind and starving artist, to officiate as companion to an ancient lady, under the eye of the latter's danter, a strenuous old maid of charitable pursuits and a romantic history. Miss Camilla, the old maid, is extremely good, and the author has happily commingled in her composition the disagreeable and the sympathetic. Thêre ar various other persons, especially a certaiń Lydia Ashton, a yung lady who ' goes in' for the hĩest æsthetic culture. She is very well dõne, her companions ar lĩtly but happily touched, and the story, albeit rather tame, is agreeable and naturally unfolded. It has a compactness and symmetry which denote an artistic instinct, and it is, in a good sense of the term, a ladylike book." [Nation.   **1937**

YOUNG MISTLEY. [*Bentley*, 1888.] " Except in a few scenes in which some melodramatic forein conspirator's play an eminently futil part, the characters of ' Young Mistley ' ar well drawn and in effectiv contrast . . . It is a graceful and pleasing story, with an attractiv heroin and a gallant hero, equally successful in diplomacy and private theatricals. The author has a wholesom regard for chivalrous adventurers, and metes out hard words to the disciples of asceticism, who ar described as ' damsels who mistake, in themselves, bodily weakness for mental wo, dressing in sombre misshapen garments in order to pass on the belief to others.' Nor is the pathetic side of life unrepresented in these pages. Laurence Lowe is an interesting figure, a taciturn, steadfast man who had ' stood by ' all his life." [Athenæum.   **1938**

YOUNG MRS. JARDINE. [by DI-
NAH MARIA (MULOCK) CRAIK: *Hurst*,
1879.] "It requires courage to write a
book, nowadays, in which the sentiment
is healthful and the characters healthy.
This book takes us back to a few such
simple ideas as lŏve, truth, honor, and
embodies them in strong personifications.
Thêre is a refreshing optimism which
abounds on every page, altho now and
then degenerating into 'gush.' Thêre
is no striking originality in the story or
the people it tells of. Roderick Jardine
fell in love with a young girl whom he
saw by the lake side at Neuchatel,
and afterward discovered to be Silence
Jardine, the dauter of the kinsman, who
had died . . . The poverty was the
graceful, self-respecting poverty of the
swiss protestant community, and the
picture of Silence is drawn with affectionate eagerness, as presenting a not
unknŏn type of puritan loveliness.
Roderick was enchanted with the village
refinement of life into which he was
suddenly thrust . . . The book is chiefly
an account of the love, life, and struggles of this yung couple. Roderick is
unused to poverty, is ashamed to work
at first, and learns the lesson with sŏme
bitterness of heart, coming out nobly,
however, at the last. 'Young Mrs.
Jardine,' who is, perhaps a trifle overdrawn, is an unselfish and devoted
character. We hav no hesitation in
pronouncing the book worthy of the hī
reputation of its author." [Californian
and Atlantic. **1939**

YOUNG MUSGRAVE. [by MA. OLI-
PHANT (WILSON) OLIPHANT : *Macmillan*,
1878.] "Pity that a thŏroly successful
writer should be stirred by the natural
but rather childish ambition to sho that
his or her power is not limited by ŏne
style, or ŏne tone of feeling, or to the
description of ŏne class of people and

manner of life. Mrs. Oliphant is so
thŏroly admirable — so unrivalled in
her peculiar department (country-town
life, and the strife between Church and
Dissent at the vicarage, the chapel
house, the squire's and the grocer's) —
that it is to be regretted that she should
try her hand at what approaches romance, — the castle, the lake, the fells,
the gypsies, the madman, and the murderer [compare Nos. 744 and 1927].
And yet this story had nearly been a
success. We read the first volume with
great pleasure and some genuin delīt.
The decaying grandeur of the castle,
the bleak fells, and the gleamy lake,
bordered by its storm-beaten pines, ar
described with a striking picturesqueness; and in keeping with them ar the
wiry old squire, who has been a hard
man in his day, tho venerable and respectable now, — for, as Mrs. Oliphant
rather cynically observes, 'age has a
way of counterfeiting virtue, which is
generally very successful;' and Mary,
his dauter, a timid, gentle, loving old-
maid, still blushing at the recollection
of her admirers, who devotes herself to
her old father and a little nīece and
nefew; and the said nīece and nefew —
motherless children — the former a most
attractiv picture of the motherly instinct
in little girls, which is capable of nerv-
ing them to unwonted courage, but which
givs way quickly to the timidity of the
child and the dependence of the woman."
[Spectator.] — "It contains many elements of a first rate novel. Had Mrs. Oliphant only been content to tell a simple
story instead of straining her inventiv
faculties to the utmost in order to construct a far-fetched, intricate plot, intended to keep on the tipto of expectation
to the end of the third volume, her present
book would be a truly charming work . . .
The interest of the story depends on the

author's nice discrimination of character, sympathetic insīt into child life, true sentiment, and fine descriptiv power. She has what Carlyle calls the faculty of ' seeing.' In a few words, sŏmetimes, she not only renders the outer aspect of nature, but its inmost expression. Sŏme of her descriptions rise to the hīt of poetry." [Athenæum. **1940**

ZAIDEE. [by Ma. Oliphant (Wilson) Oliphant: *Blackwood*, 1856.] " A charming family at a country house in Cheshire ar about to celebrate the coming of age of the hêir; the father has long been dead. A few days before the grand event, Zaidee, the orfan child of a yunger brother, finds inside an old book in a deserted garret, a lost will, — by which the estate is bequeathed to her

father, and consequently **she** is the rītful hêiress to the Grange. Dreadfully shocked at this discovery, she mopes about the house, not daring to destroy the document, and yet made miserable by keeping it, — her sorro betrays her and her secret is surprised; the fatal document is read by the family, who all acknoledge it as genuin, — and cousin Zaidee, driven to despair because her cousin will not accept the estate as a gift, obtains a very apocryfal letter of introduction to a family in London who ar in want of a nursery governess . . . All these impossibilities ar, however, so well and pleasantly narrated that the reader is carried along, step by step, until it pleases the author to unravel the tangle of affairs." [Athenæum. **1941**

"Who read english books? American young people read them—to their own undoing. Much has been said of the evil results of the reading of cheap sensational novels upon boys and girls. They are advised not to read these bad books, but to take good books. Thousands of our young people never see the dime-novel type of book because they have plenty of good novels, well written, refined, interesting, moral in tone, and apparently without any harmful tendency. Now the larger part of these (in a literary sense) excellent books are written in England by english authors, and are read by american young people to their lasting injury, and to the injury of our time and country. These english writers intend no harm; thêir books are strictly moral and convey many good and noble lessons; and yet the books do lasting harm, and to their influence can be traced much of the false pride, incompetency, idleness and vice to be found in our cities. These harmful lessons in so many english novels are writ between the lines — unread, yet clearly understood and believed . . . It is impossible to say what is the exact influence of these books on our young people. It is clearly not for good. Do they not explain in part much of the idleness, the false pride, the secret worship of rank that fills their minds? At any rate, they are un-american and we do not want them." [Maurice Thompson in Critic.

PRICE: ONE COPY, $1.00; TWO COPIES, $1.50; THREE, $2.25; FOUR, $3.00; FIVE, $3.25; SIX, $4.00; TEN, $6.00.

A

DESCRIPTIVE LIST

OF

NOVELS AND TALES

DEALING WITH

LIFE IN FRANCE.

COMPILED BY

W : M. GRISWOLD, A. B.

CAMBRIDGE, MASS:
W : M. GRISWOLD, PUBLISHER,
1892.

FRENCH NOVELS.

The object of this list is to direct readers, such as would enjoy the kind of books here described, to a number of novels, easily accessible, but which, in many cases, have been forgotten within a year or two after publication. That the existence of works of fiction is remembered so short a time is a pity, since, for every new book of merit, there are, in most libraries, a hundred as good or better, unknown to the majority of readers. It is hoped that the publication of this and similar lists will lessen, in some measure, the disposition to read an inferior NEW book when superior OLD books, equally fresh to most readers, are at hand. It may be observed that the compiler has tried to include only such works as are well-written, interesting, and are free from sensationalism, sentimentality, and pretense. But in a few cases, books have been noticed on account of the reputation of their authors, or their great popularity, rather than their merit.

The selected "notices" are generally abridged.

This list will be followed by others describing GERMAN, ECCENTRIC, and FANCIFUL novels and tales.

ABBÉ CONSTANTIN, by L. HAL-EVY, = No. 401.

ABBÉ'S TEMPTATION (THE). [Faute de l' Abbé Mouret.) by ÉMILE ZOLA: Peterson, 1879.] "The Abbé is pastor of a village church. He falls il. The means resorted tŏ for his cure bring him intŏ the companionship of a wildly fascinating yung girl, under circumstances which favor the grŏth of an absorbing passion between the twŏ. The prîest lŏses not ŏnly his heart but his head. The pair. exalted intŏ an unnatural state, ar left tŏ themselvs, like another Adam and Eve in Paradise. The conflicts which the soul may undergo hav seldom been depicted with greater intensity and exuberance—sŏme would say extravagance—of imagination than in the scenes in the lonely glades of Paradon. But the awakening cŏmes. He returns tŏ his altar, under the retribution of remorse; she makes expiation by death. Throu the whole romance runs the deep undertone of the most fervent type of roman-catholic faith and piety; and around the ill-fated lŏvers pass and repass the forms of a few ecclesiastics and villagers, whŏ variously contribute tŏ the līter or graver elements in the tragedy. The power in this original and striking tale is not tŏ be denied, but it is far from being of a wholesŏm kind." [Boston "Literary World." **1943**

——, SAME ("The Abbé Mouret's Transgression"), London, 1880.

ADÈLE, by J. KAVANAGH, = No. 403.

ABBÉ TIGRANE (The). [by FER-
DINAND FABRE: N.-Y., Ford, 1875.]
"Thére is something positivly startling in
the cleverness and novelty of this book.
Comparing it with óther stories of ecclesiastical life, from Le Maudit [No. 2297]
tŏ Barchester Towers [No. 1082] it
resembles nóne except perhaps ŏne or twŏ
of Droz' sketches, which ar faint and
slight beside it. Thére is no sketchiness
in the 'Abbé Tigrane': it is a full and finished picture in a masterly manner. It
would be diffićult tŏ say whether the outer
or the inner life, the words or the deeds
of the personages, ar most strikingly and
truthfully portrayed. The scene is laid in
a little town bidden amŏng the hils, of
which äny ŏne whŏ has been in the south
of France has seen the like, with narro,
crooked streets, a small but exçitable
torrent spanned by a stone bridge, and a
grand cathedral—an old quarter of respectability and religious houses, a new
quarter of factories and poverty. The
lay element plays but a subordinate part,
tho as ably handled as the rest. The magnates of the town ar ecclesiastics, and théy
ar mäny masters, oing tŏ the afflux of
religious orders and dignitaries tŏ this
favored spot. Of course the bishop is
híest in position, but the Abbé Capdepont,
vicar-general, etc., nicknamed the Abbe,
Tigrane, almost counterbalançes him by
personal wéight." [Lippincott's Magazine.   1942 s

AFTER-DINNER STORIES, by BALZAC, N.-Y., 1889] contains *The Red Inn*, *M'me Firmiani*, *The Grande Bretèche*, *M'me de Beauséant*. **1944**

ALAIN FAMILY (THE). [by ALPHONSE KARR: († 1890) London, *Cook & Co.*, 1853.] "Mr. Karr seems to kno and to lōve the district whêre he has laid the scene of the story. The christening of a new boat, with which the novel opens,—the simple orisons and fearful suspense of those left at home when their lōved ōnes ar out at sea in stormy weather,—with numberless like scenes and traits, endear the tale tŏ us, and giv it a close hold on the heârt.—Thêre is character in Pulchérie's experiences of parisian seminary life: thêre is humor in the miserable attempts of the Malins tŏ act the patronizing grandeur of country aristocrats, the humor shading naturally intŏ pathos when the 'seigneur' becŏmes impoverished." [Athenæum. **1945**

ALBERT SAVARUS, by BALZAC, in *Comédie Humaine*. **1946**

ALCHEMIST (The), by BALZAC . = No. 583.

ALIETTE ["La Morte"] by OCTAVE FEUILLET: *Warne*, 1886. **1947**

ALKAHEST, by BALZAC, = No. 583.

ALL FOR GREED. [by [M.. PAULINE] ROSE (STEWART) BLAZE, called "baroness" and "de Bury":* *Littell*, 1868.] "Those ōnly whŏ hav lived for a long period in France, and hav becŏme familiar with life in the provinces, can appreciate the faithful description which the author givs of the habits and customs, the ignorance and prejudice, and the marked peculiar-

* "Why? Blaze is Blaze,—son of Blaze the musician."—*P. Chasles* in Athenæum, 28 Dec. 1872.

ities of persons mŏving in very narro circles and dwelling in districts remote from the capital. Thêre is, of course, a noble vicomte, proud of his ancestry, an unsullied representativ of his "order", and "true tŏ his name" throu all the vicissitudes of fortune, living in the ancestral château in a condition of discomfort tŏ which no well-tŏ-dŏ tradesman would submit. . . The only expedient for enlivening the dulness of daily life among these quiet people seems tŏ consist of a murder, and as ōne is sure tŏ occur when the community arrives at the last stage of stagnation, its introduction is not only appropriate but looked for; and this incident, with its consequences, its mystery, the trial of those who ar wrongfully accused, the devotion of the yung girl whŏ saves her lōver at the risk of her reputation, and the final discovery of the culprit, form the ground work of this very interesting narrativ." [Round Table. **1948**

ALMOST A DUCHESS, by OLGA (GRANT) DE LONGUEIUL, = Nos. 407 & 586. **1949**

AMERICAN (The) [**Paris**] = No. 410.

ANDRÉ, by "G : SAND" (Paris, 1835) London,. *Churton*, 1847. **1950**

ANDRÉ CORNÉLIS, by · PAUL BOURGET: *S. Blackett*, 1889. **1951**

ANDREW THE SAVOYARD, [by [C:] PAUL DE KOCK: (†,1871)London, *Simms*, 1847.] "Humor is not the ōnly characteristic of de Kock; he has another virtue,—the truth of his pictures of life and society. In the representations of humorous scenes he may be charged with exaggeration. but when he cōmes tŏ the quiet development of character, by means of social and familiar scenes taken from common life. he is tŏ be equaled by ōnly ōne

writer of ŏūr coŭntry. The resemblance between the novels of Paul de Kock and those of JANE AUSTEN is as strong as can exist between the productions of a Parisian author and those of an English lady. The humorous scenes of the foreiner undoubtedly turn upon incidents, and ar supported with an extravagance. unknōn to ŏūr countrywoman; but when thêy cōme tŏ the nice distinctions of character, tŏ the play of domestic life, tŏ the detection of the small springs on which society hangs, and tŏ the accurate representation of nature, whether it be the nature of a bac-shop or of a drawingroom, of a village or of a city, they ar alike and unrivaled . . . *Andrew the Savoyard* is perhaps the most truly pleasing of all these romances; it is the least dramatic, and the least lively. but it is full of truth, and breathes an air of purity and innocence . . . Andrew and his brother,—mere children,—set off to seek their fortunes in Paris, and the novel is the history of their respectiv adventures, for their fortunes ar different." [Foreign Quarterly Review, 1830.] "Paul de Kock est consolant: jamais il ne présente l'humanité sous le point de vue qui attriste. Avec lui on rit et on espère." [Chateaubriand. **1952**
——, SAME (abridged) in *Johnstone's Magazine* [*Museum*, Feb.-Mar.. 1838.]

ANGÈLE'S FORTUNE [by ANDRE THEURIET: *Peterson*. 1880.] "A clerk in a lawyer's office in a provincial town of France has a pretty dauter, whŏ chafes under the restraint of her life and cherishes a secret ambition to go on the stage. One of the yunger clerks, René des Armoises, a litheaded and selfish aspirant for poetic

fame, has becōme her ideal, and when he goes tŏ Paris tŏ seek his reputation her heart goes with him. Meanwhile, her father brings home as a lodger another clerk. Joseph Toussaint, a country youth whŏ is the Virtue of the little Morality. He is captivated by the girl, but overpowerĕd with his modesty . . . The girl has already fallen in with René, and her lover, the moral Joseph, presently appears. The relations begun in Bay continue in the new scene. René receives Angèle's affection as a tribute tŏ his poetic sensibilities. and honest Joseph is the true friend whŏ dŏes all the good deeds for which René gets credit. The attempt tŏ go on the stage is a failure, the promised fortune vanishes in smoke, and the selfish poet. after having gŏne as far as he cared tŏ in pleasure, offers tŏ make the gigantic sacrifice of poverty and discomfort in witness of his noble character. The girl abruptly leaves him and her other friends. in order tŏ giv him liberty, and finally cōmes bac in wretchedness tŏ Paris, at the opening of the siege. René has meanwhile made a prudent and uncomfortable marriage, and has taken himself out of the country for safety. Joseph is the noble volunteer. and after the war marries Angèle and adopts her child as his." [Atlantic.]—"The tale is full of the truest and deepest lessons, as indeed is everything which this writer givs us. His pictures. if they introduce wrong-dŏing and its fruits. always leave a final impression for virtue and truth." [Boston "Literary World." **1953**
ANNETTE; or The Lady of the Pearls. [by ALEX. DUMAS: N.-Y., *F: A. Brady*. 1863.] "The plot is complicated. and the translation flo-

ing and spirited . . . No sense of rĭt or wrong ever seems tŏ dawn upon the heroes or heroins of this school. The events gro entirely out of human incidents, passions, and interests—conscience has no part tŏ play in the involved drama. After passing throu seas of naive intrigue and innocent vice, we ar quite astonished at the close to be landed upon a short Moral." [Continental.   1954

ANTOINETTE [by G: OHNET: *Lippincott*, 1889.] "is a translation of ·La Grande Marnière.' . . . In a general way we may say with entire fairness that Ohnet's writings ar not writings which it is worth anyŏne's while tŏ concern himself about. He is forever concerned with mysteries of crime, expressed in a voice of sicly sentimentality, which tŏ discriminating readers must be extremely disagreeable." [American.   1955

ANTONIA. [by "G : SAND," i. e.; Amantine Lucile Aurore (Dupin) Dudevant: († 1876.) *Roberts*, 1870.] "None of G : Sand's novels ar more perfectly artistic and finished than this lŏve idyl; which seems to exhale the fragrance of the rare exotic lily after which it is named. It is perfectly pure in tone and romantic, the style is masterly in its transparent simplicity, the characters ar true, beautiful and noble. The discussion of filosofical or social topics which characterize so many of her novels ar not tŏ be found in this book, but, as a romance, it has a distinct beauty and perfection in which it stands unrivaled." [Galaxy.   1956

APOSTATE (The), by ERNEST DAUDET: *Appleton*, 1889.   1957

ARCHIE LOVELL by "ANNIE EDWARDS," [Boulogne] = No. 412.

AROUND A SPRING [by [AN-

TOINE] GUSTAVE DROZ: *Holt*, 1870.] "deservs tŏ be read. It givs with a keen, incisiv toŭch the characteristics of society in France. The story is slĭt so far as incident goes; but it is suggestiv. The idea which underlies it and which it illustrates, is the position in which the men of old families with a long line of ancestors at their bac, but whŏse possessions ar dissipated and whŏ hav nothing left but the expensiv habits which represent past magnificence, find themselvs before men whŏ hav risen from nothing, whŏ hav achieved all the power which the possession of money can giv, combined with the genius for organizing vast and lucrativ schemes of material imprŏvement." [Athenæum.   1958

ARTIST'S HONOR (An), by OCTAVE FEUILLET: *Cassell*, 1891.

ASSOMMOIR (L') [by ÉMILE ZOLA: *Peterson*, 1879.] is "both poorer and less bad than we had supposed. It is neither so good as a literary product, nor is it so bad as a moral quantity. The story takes its name from a groggery, around which its incidents may be said tŏ revolv; and when we get down tŏ its "raw materials" they ar found tŏ be drunkenness, illicit lŏve, quarreling and brutality. At the same time, the handling is not needlessly coarse, tho we suspect the translator may hav deodorized the original tŏ sŏme extent. In the present form the work hardly shŏs the exceptional realistic power which has been claimed for it, and can be read without great pain or disgust by anybody whŏ may wish tŏ kno what it is. We cannot call it agreeable reading, but its lessons for the vicious and abandoned ar not tŏ be mistaken." [Boston "Literary World."   1959

ATÉLIER DU LYS (The) [1789]
= No. 596.

ATHEIST'S MASS (The), by BAL-
ZAC, in *Fame & Sorrow.*

—— SAME ("The Freethinker") in
We are All, by S : PHILLIPS, *Routledge*, 1854.   **1961**

ATTIC PHILOSOPHER (The).
[by ÉMILE SOUVESTRE: [†, 1854.)
Appleton, 1857.] "The happy man whŏ
publishes his journal is a virtuous, beneficent hermit, whŏ prefers exemption
from care, excitement and responsibility—a life of modest fortunes and
little kindlinesses—tŏ a strife in the
more bustling arena of enterprise
whêre the vicissitudes ar more exhausting, and the prizes more brilliant. He scarcely ever goes intŏ the
streets without dŏing or planning
sŏme little filanthropic surprise or
witnessing sŏme good action. Pressed
tŏ exchange his clerkship, with its
humble salary, for a position of greater risk and promis he declines; apos-
trofizing Poverty as his gardian-angel,
—his music as his incentiv and his
reward. Struc down with a fever,—
on recovering, he finds that he has
been tended more affectionately and
sedulously by the humble persons
whŏm he has befriended than by the
rich among his kinsfolk. Sŏme of the
incidents of the year embraced within
the compass of his journal ar gracefully touched:—let us instance the
pleasure-party tŏ Sèvres of the twŏ
old maids." [Athenæum   **1962**

AULNAY TOWER [1870-71] =
No. 597.

BAGPIPERS (THE). ["Les
Maitres Sonneurs") [by "G: SAND,"
i. e., Amantine Lucile Aurore (Dupin)
Dudevant : *Roberts*, 1890.] "The
charm of this crisp woodland romance
lies largely in the harmony of its soft
gray colors, its simple passions, the
poetry of its upland scenery, and the
sweetness of the author's style . . . Its
theme is deliciously rural, full of the
tinkle of silvery brooks. the twitter
of birds, the chatter of Bourbonnais
peasants, the music of 'musettes,' the
sits and smels of pastoral romance . . .
In "G : Sand" the country is the country : genuin, unmistakable, in sît,
smel, sound ; her country folk ar the
ancient peasantry. Thêre is no artificiality or sofistication about her tales
of the provinces : thêy ar as locally
distinct in thêir large horizons, thêir
murmuring woods, thêir mîty waters
as Auvergne, Berry, Bourbonnais can
be from the asfalt of the boulevards
or the emasculated landscape of the
Bois. In the 'The Bagpipers' thêre
is all the ineffaceable charm of grêat
landscape-painting set with simple
human passions which play and coun-
ter-play, contend and sport with each
other in a fashion altŏgether human.
. . . The characters tel the story
among them in a truly fascinating
way. It is of provincial laborers whŏ
lŏve the bagpipers and their old-fashioned music, the ways and wanderings of muleteers, the lŏves and hates
of simple people whŏ til the soil and
hav their rivalries : about all of which
flo the coronation-robes of G : Sand's
noble style in a way which lifts these
rustic existences tŏ a plane with
works of the hiest artistic excellence,
and makes ŏne read tŏ the last line of
the charming work." [Critic. **1963**

BALL AT SCEAUX (The), by
BALZAC, in *The Cat;* also in *The
Vendetta;* also ("Emily") in *Cham-
bers' Pocket Miscellany*, vol. X. **1964**

BALTHAZAR, by BALZAC. = No.
583.

BARBER OF PARIS (The), by DE

BABOLAIN [by GUSTAVE DROZ: *Holt*, 1873.] "is a tragica' little romançe which draws the reader along with it by every line in every page . . . Scientific and stupid, Professor Babolain enters the world of Paris armed with his innoçençe, his uncle's legacy, his deep learning and his utter ignorançe. A couple of adventuresses, mŭther and dauter, swoop down upon him as lawful prêy, and he is quicly a doting husband and a terrified sŏn-in-law . . . His wife never melts, exçept when he givs her diamonds, and, after finding a leisure moment tŏ giv birth tŏ a baby, rushes ŏff tŏ Italy with Count Vaugirau, folloed promptly by a certain Timoleón. This Timoleon, whŏ lŏves her unsucçessfully, is the benetiçiary of poor Babolain, borroing his mŏney at the same time that he tries tŏ borro his wifé, and returning with outrageous reproaches tŏ the hero impoverished and desolate . . . As the abused victim, starving and ragged, treads the road of sacrifiçe tŏ death, ŏur sympathy is checked by the consciousness of his unmitigated and needless pliancy, until we withhold the tribute of sorro due tŏ a Lear or a Père Goriot [No. 2206.] The novel however, tho sketched out extravagantly between hyperbole and parable, fairly scintillates with brilliancies and good things: we could hardly indicate anŏther imported novel of the length containing so much . . . The translator reveals his quality by calling pantaloons 'pants'." [Lippincott's Magazine. 1962 p

BARBER OF PARIS (The). [by
[C:] PAUL DE KOCK († 1871): Phil'a,
Carey, 1839.] "De Kock occasionally
reçeives a good share of abuse from various English critics of the newly-raised
school of elegançe and aristocraçy—whŏ
delight tŏ see mankind in embroidered
coats and satin smalls, and vote every
man a 'mauvais sujet' whŏ dōes not figure
in silk stockings. A novel, tŏ be good in
thêir estimation, must be devoted tŏ the
sayings and dŏings of the fashionable
world—a close portrayal of human nature
is of small avail, unless the characteristics of hi life form the text—in ōther
words, the sterling value of the metal is
not of so much importançe as the fashion
of the make . . . Paul de Kock is a painter
of life as it is—his pages teem with excellençe, but his readers require the possession of a certain worldly experiençe before
thêy can perçeive the full value of the
scenes presented tŏ thêir notiçe. Notwithstanding the volatility of the class of
people from which he selects his subjects,
thêre is less of 'outrance' or caricature in
his delineations than in the pages of
Marryat, altho, in ōther points, thêre is
much similarity between the twŏ. De
Kock's works wil exist when many of tlfe
popular writers of the day ar forgotten.
"The Barber of Paris" is the most powerful in its effects of all the author's
works. Lively narrativ, startling but
natural inçident, and grêat diversity of
wel-sustained character, combine tŏ make
it the most agreeable reprint of the season." [Phil'a 'Gentleman's Mag.' **1964 p**

KOCK, London. 1839, ☞ No. 1952.
BEATRICE. by JULIA KAVANAGH,
[Provence] = No. 419.
BELLAH [Vendee, 1793] = No.
606.
BELLS (THE) [Le Juif Polonais],
by ERCKMANN-CHATRIAN: Tinsley,
1872. 1966
——. SAME, "The Polish Jew."
BERTHA'S BABY = Papa, Mama & Baby. 1967
BESSIE. [by JULIA KAVANAGH:
Hurst, 1872.] "Of Bessie herself, it is
superfluous tŏ say that she is naive and
charming, conscientious, affectionate
and unselfish. She is a born hero-
worshiper; in spite of coldness and
discouragement, and all the mysterious circumstances which surround the
life of Elizabeth de Lusignan, Bessie
remains stânch in her belief in the
integrity and virtue of her friend;
while her ŏn lŏve-story, the story of
a real passion, which groes upon her
unconsciously, until gratitude and
early associations convince her reason
that she is attached tŏ her morose and
exacting cousin, is ŏne of the best bits
of autobiografy Miss Kavanagh has
produced. How far such minute
analysis of maiden meditation is desirable, how far it wil be possible for
Bessie's yung-lady admirers ever to be
Bessies themselvs, is anŏther question. Of the minor personages, the
women ar the best. Miss Russell,
infirm in body, and positiv and petulant in mind,—smooth-spŏken, treacherous Miss Dunn,—Mademoiselle, a
tender type of old-maidenhood,—ar all
touched with a skilful hand . . .
Life at Fontainebleau is well described." [Athenæum. 1968
BIGARREAU, by ANDRE THEU-
RIET, in Modern Age. June-July, 1884.
BLACK PEARL (THE). by V.

SARDOU, in Lippincott's Mag., Sept.,
1872. 1970
BONNE MARIE [by "HENRI
GREVILLE": i. e., Alice M .. Céleste
(Fleury) Durand, Peterson, 1878.]
"is a very attractiv and original story,
folloing an unusual line but fresh and
coherent." [Nation. 1971
BOURBON LILIES [Paris] =
No. 424.
BRETON JOINER (A), by É. SOU-
VESTRE, in Museum, 1836. 1972
——. SAME ("A Peasant Prometheus"), in Living Age, 13 Jan.. 1877.
BRETON MAIDEN (A), [1793]
= No. 616.
BRIDE PICOTÉE (A). [by MA.
ROBERTS: Bemrose, 1882.] "This is
a charming little story, the point of
which consists in the self-denial of a
little worker in lace, whŏ, tho she has
re-discovered for herself the particular
stitch which constitutes the secret of
the lace Point d'Argentan, yet conceals her discovery, in order not tŏ
disappoint the ŏne remaining lace-
maker whŏ has inherited the secret
and whŏ, after a long struggle, has
made up her mind tŏ reveal it tŏ the
crippled girl with such a ᵥgenius for
lace-making. This is a kind of self-
denial which is probably even rarer in
the world than martyrdom itself, and
very delicately has the accomplished
authoress of Mademoiselle Mori [No.
812] worked out the character and the
story of La Brisarde, and of Lise, the
heroin of this delītful tale. We hav
nŏt read for many years a tale of
greater beauty and simplicity."
[Spectator. 1973
BRIGADIER FREDERIC [1870-
71] = No. 619.
BRITTANY & LA'VENDÉE, [by
ÉMILE SOUVESTRE: Ed., Constable,
1855: N.-Y.. Dix, Edwards & Co.,

1857, 301 pp.] contains, besides the Brétagne tales of the original, *The Bargeman of the Loire* (from "Sous les Filets") and *The Lazaretto-Keeper* from "En Quarantaine." The tales translated from original ed. ar: *The Kourigan, The White Boat, The Treasure Seeker, The Groach and the Kakous, The Chouans, The Virgin's Godchild.* **1974**

BROTHER GABRIEL = No. 1121.

BROTHERS RANTZAU (The). [Les Deux Frères) by ÉMILE ERCKMANN & P: ALEX. CHATRIAN († 1890) *Low*, 1873.] "The scene is the village of Chaumes, in the Vogesen, and the story is told by the old schoolmaster. The "twŏ brothers" hav quarreled over their inheritance, and bring—the ŏne his sŏn, and the ŏther his dauter, tŏ hate each ŏther fiercely. The children fall in lŏve, and the book ends with the birth of a child whŏ wil reunite the divided properties of his grandfathers. The story is slīt almost tŏ a fault, but as a study of village life nothing could be more full of interest tŏ readers of a hī tone of mind. Those whŏ require plot or passion, must turn elsewhêre." [Athenæum.] "The story of this terrible passion, this 'idée fixe' common tŏ twŏ beings perverted by the lŏve of "proputty" in every shape, is sŏmetimes deeply tragical, sŏmetimes perversely ludicrous. always told with the simple directness which givs tŏ the Erckmann-Chatrian creations thĕir irresistible 'vraisemblance'. Along-side of it runs the simple story of the schoolmaster's life, with an admirably convêyed unconscious contrast in its contented poverty, its intellectual industry,its tranquil. homely affections and joys. The timid. time-serving.

cautious wife, whŏ is perpetually driving Florence tŏ risky outspokenness by her warnings against his siding with either Jean or Jacques, is a charming comic element in the drama." [Spectator. **1975**

BUREAUCRACY. [Les Employés) by HONORE "DE" * BALZAC: *Roberts*. 1889.] "Monsieur Rabourdin, head of a bureau, and next in succession tŏ the position of chief of division, is a statesman [*We* should say business-man—*G.*] rather than a politician, and conceives a comprehensiv scheme for reform. Rabourdin's scheme called for a large reduction in the number of officials. with a corresponding doubling and trebling of salaries. Tŏ commend this tŏ his minister he makes a list of all the clerks in his division. and annotates it as a guide when the time for dismissals cŏmes. The list is seen, and a stolen copy made by an underling, a cause of disaster tŏ Rabourdin. The chief of the division is il with a mortal illness, and the story of the book is made of the successful efforts of the incapables tŏ get ŏne of their number appointed over Rabourdin's head. In this they ar almost foiled by the counter stratagems of Rabourdin's wife, whŏ, faithful tŏ him and his interests, and a noble character, is yet enuf of a frenchwoman tŏ make the most of her personal attractions tŏ aid his cause. The scene being Paris. and the story a tale of intrigue, all readers of Balzac wil expect tŏ find a disheartening picture of life. and a gloomy end-

---

* "It was not til he became famous that he began to use the aristocratic prefix; in his earlier years he was plain M. Balzac. I believe it is more than suspected that the pedigree represented by this DE was as fabulous (and quite as ingenious) as any that he invented for his heroes."—*H: James.*

ing." [Overland. **1976**

BUT YET A WOMAN. [by AR-
THUR SHERBURNE HARDY : *Houghton,*
1883.] "Not so with the gracious
creatures tŏ either of whŏm the title
of 'But yet a Woman' mĭt be applied
—Renée. the delicate maiden, with
all the fearless ease of innocence;
Stephanie, the woman of the world,
'of a strange confidence and naturalness, blended with a dignity which
was almost imperious.' The other
characters ar not unfamiliar, the elderly Frenchmen, with their nĭtly
game of piquet, the prĭest, the polished
journalist, the yung doctor; but it is
only in the choicest and finest french
work—the best of Cherbuliez, for instance—that they ar presented with
anything like the delicacy tŏ be found
here. The story is strong and original withal. The reader wil find all
his conjectures as tŏ plot,—not disappointed. but contradicted and surpassed. Thêre is no smiling Kirkë tŏ
deplore, but a woman, noble, tho
sorely tempted. whŏ could strike the
death-blo tŏ her happiness rather than
win it at the price of shame and
treachery. The spanish episode, the
hapless fate of Felisa, is a model of
its kind, telling a tale ŏf guilty passion not for the sake of excitement,
but for the Nemesis. It wer a pity to
forestall the story. but without dŏing
so it is not easy tŏ giv it the praise it
deservs. The style is exquisit in its
limpid clearness; and, while we admire the beauty of description and the
power of characterization which givs
us living human beings, not critical
analyses, we ar inclined tŏ put foremost the conversations. Tŏ make
people talk as they dŏ in the *salon* of
M. Michel is a rare success." [Nation.]—"It is long since we hav seen

the finer qualities of womanhood so
generously and so subtly displayed as
in these figures. The minor characters also ar delicately touched. especially Father le Blanc, and the
flavor of the story given by the reflection and comment is always fine and
gracious. It is a positiv pleasure tŏ
take up a book so penetrated as this is
by pure and noble thŏt, and marked
by so hi a respect of the author for
his work." [Atlantic. **1977**

CADET DE COLOBRIÈRES (The)
[by HENRIETTE ETIENNETTE FANNY
(ARNAUD) REYBAUD : Phil'a, *Carey
& Hart,* 1847.] "is a very sprĭtly and
interesting tale, in which the difficulties of the old 'noblesse' ar very humorously contrasted with thêir indomitable pride. One is reminded, in the
struggles of thêir decayed fortunes, of
the domestic diplomacy of the Vicar
of Wakefield." [Democratic Rev. **1978**

CAMILLE = *LADY OF THE CA-
MELIAS.*

CAMILLE [by VALERIE (BOIS-
SIER) DE GASPARIN : Edinburgh.
Edmonston, 1867.) "is a regular story
with a lŏver, a heroin and a charming soldier brŏther, whŏ belongs tŏ
the army of Africa, and whŏ is as
dashing and impetuous as if he came
out of ŏne of the Dumas' novels, but
good and gentle and affectionate as
the heârt of any maid or mother could
desire. The lŏver is fascinating, full
of genius, and already a distinguished
man. with ŏne of the grandest of human natures; but he declines tŏ believe in revealed religion. Camille is
a christian, and tho she lŏves him as
passionately as even he can desire,
she refuses tŏ becŏme his wife, and
allows him tŏ go alone: and tho
her heârt is nearly broken, she holds
fast tŏ what she feels tŏ be her first

duty. The struggle is extremely wel drawn. The temptation, the sorroful victory over herself which leaves her nearly dead. is told with human sympathy and genuin feeling. There is truth tŏ human nature throuŏut, especially in the reaction after all is over and it is too late. But Camille dŏes not end miserably; she goes throu her trial bravely, but not too bravely; she is charming throuŏut." [Athenæum.

——, SAME, in *Hours at Home*, mar. 1868, *seq*. **1979**

CANON'S DAUGHTER (The), by E. ABOUT, in *Canadian Monthly*, apr. 1872; also in *Ladies' Repository*, Nov.-Dec., 1873. **Strassburg. 1980**

CAPTAIN FRACASSE, by GAUTIER, [**1498-1515**] = No. 624.

CARLINO [**Riviera**] = No. 428.

CASTLE IN THE WILDERNESS (Le Château des Désertes, Paris. 1847) by "G : SAND," in *Dwight's Journal*, 1857. **1981**

——, SAME ("The Castle of Pictordu") Edinburgh, *Gremmell*, 1884.

CAT AND BATTLEDORE (THE). ["Maison du chat qui pelote") by HONORE "DE" BALZAC : *Low*, 1879.] "The tales ar all of good quality, but they ar scarcely of Balzac's best, nor ar they of his most characteristic brand . . . Only perhaps, in *A Double Family* is sŏmething like a glimpse of the Balzacian cosmos, with its singular fysical and moral conditions. vouchsafed . . . *The Ball at Sceaux*, with the pleasant little story of *The Purse* and the more characteristic ŏne of *Madame Firmiani*, is probably most suited tŏ a purely english taste." [Athenæum. **1982**

CATHERINE, by SANDEAU, = No. 631.

CATHERINE'S COQUETRIES, a tale of country life, by CAMILLE DE-BANS, *Worthington*, 1890, 174 pp. **1983**

CENTULLE : a Tale of Pau [by DENYS SHAYNE LAWLOR : *Longman*. 1874.] "This is a pleasant, refined, and ingenious book. It personally conducts the reader throu the **Pyrenees** and the Basque provinces, in company with an imaginary pair of friends. whŏ meet interesting people and undergo curious adventures. The story cŏmes tŏ a melancholy ending, except in the case of ŏne pair of happy lŏvers, whŏ ar all they should be ; but as the general award is in strict accordance with morality and political justice, we must not complain. The idea of interweaving this charming volume of description with a story was a happy ŏne; the writer has opportunities for legitimate indulgence in enthusiasm, which would hav been out of place in the merely grave and more conventional book of travel. In the latter capacity it is valuable and minute. One closes it feeling that ŏne knoes the country. with all its present faculties and attractions. and all its past historic reminiscences and personages." [Spectator. **1984**

CÉSAR BIROTTEAU, see *HIST-ORY. ETC.*

CÉSETTE [by ÉMILE POUVILLON. *Putnam*, 1882.] "is a story which cŏmes from a clear artistic impulse. apparently as spontaneous as nature. and as simple in its methods; not a line seems forced, and not a cŏlor exaggerated. It is a picture of peasant life, homely and realistic in its details, yet suffused with idyllic grace and charm. . . . Each page suggests a Millet-like picture,—peasants setting forth tŏ their morning toil, the soing, the threshing, the winnoing. the shepherdess returning with her floc;

yet thêre ar few words wasted on mere description. Césette's artless lõve, and Jordi's more complex emotions, being called õne way by his passion for the little shepherdess and the other by the promis of decisiv advantage from Rouzil's mõney, makes a pleasant little comedy, which ends in the rĭt way. . . . The book is a very dainty translation of a charming and finished little work, which we hope may be read and appreciated." [Lippincotts'. **1985**

CHATEAU LESCURE [Vendee, **1793.**] = No. 635.

CHOISY [Paris], = No. 429.

CHOUANS (THE). by BALZAC, [Bretagne, **1798-9.**] N.-Y., *Street*, 1891: Chicago, *Rand* (423 pp), *Laird & Lee*, 1891. **1986**

CHRIS [Riviera] = No. 430.

CINQ-MARS, by A. DE VIGNY [**1640-2.**] London, *Bogue*, also *Routledge*. **1987**

CLARA MILITCH, by TURGENIEF, [Paris, **1865-70**] = No. 446.

CLAUDE BLOUET [Les Souffrances de C.-B., in "Nouvelles Intimes", Paris, 1870.] by ANDRE THEURIET, in *Old & New*, Feb., 1870. **1988**

CLÉMENCEAU CASE (THE) by ALEX. DUMAS: Chicago, *Laird*, 1891. **1989**

CLORINDA ["Son Excellence Eugène Rougon") by ÉMILE ZOLA: *Peterson*, 1880.] "is outwardly decent. The author is stil wading in the gutter but it is a gutter which runs around a palace. and the sewage of a court is, tŏ say the least, scented. Clorinda is the gilt (not golden) ornament of the' court of Napoléon III; and Eugène Rougon [Rouher], whŏ divides the interest of the story with her, has becõme a minister, and rises or falls according tŏ the whim of his

master. The hĭest circles during the flush days of the empire ar constantly before the reader, and sõme personages already notorious—the duke of Morny, for example—mŏve amidst them in thin disguise. Clorinda is a lobbyist among courtiers; whŏ pays costly prices for political favors for her friends, and, finally, tŏ cap the climax of her career, she returns õne day from Fontainebleau wêaring the glistening badge of an imperial alliance. The vêil thrŏn around her character and course is as thin as the gauze with which alone she sõmetimes protects her person in the presence of her guests; but we wil say this for Zola, that in this book he has managed tŏ be as little offensiv as it would be possible tŏ be in dealing with such a subject. The book shŏs the corruption, political and social. of the Napoleonic régime with a masterly hand. The descriptions of the baptism of the Prince Imperial, of the fêtes at Compiègne, and of the charitable "sale" at the Tuileries, sho a wonderful combination of simplicity and power." [Boston "Literary World."]—"The book contains sõme of Zola's best work; the study of each incident is exhaustiv, and at times subtle enuf tŏ sho a different fãse tŏ, and awaken a different judgment in, different minds —an effect justly tŏ be called artistic, and thŏroly antagonistic tŏ his most impressiv 'naturalism'."[Nation.**1990**

CLOUD & SUNSHINE by G: OHNET, *Vizetelly*, 1887, ☞ No. 1955.

COLOMBA, [Corsica] = No. 648

COL. CHABERT, by BALZAC. ☞ *Fame and Sorrow.*

——, SAME ("The Countess with Two Husbands") in *New Mirror*, 27 july tŏ 9 sept., 1837. **1991**

CLÉMENCEAU CASE (The) [by AL-
EXANDRE DUMAS: Paris, 1866; Phil'a,
Crawford, 1892.] "is an imaginary
cause célébre. The hero of the novel, or
tŏ speak in strict keeping with the form
of the work, the defendant in this "extraordinary case" is the illegitimate sŏn of a
poor young needlewoman, whŏ, after
having committed the ŏne grĕat fault
leads a respectable and industrious life.
She sends Pierre, when he is 10 years old,
tŏ a first-rate boarding school; but before
dŏing so, she reveals tŏ him the melancholy secret of his birth, telling him that,
in consequençe of this degradation, he wil
be exposed tŏ humiliating vexations and
insults. The foreshadoed sufferings of
Pierre ar ŏnly too soon and painfully realized . . . Clémenceau becŏmes a suc-
çessful sculptor, gaining fame and fortune
at a much earlier period than usually falls
tŏ the lot of artists; he enjoys also universal esteem on account of his hĭ qualities,
amŏng which the preservation of his
moral purity, in spite of the manifold
temptations by which artists ar surrounded, is emphatically commemorated. His
happiness seems tŏ hav reached its culminating point when he makes the
acquaintançe of a young countess of
dazzling beauty . . . Clémenceau's passionate lŏve is returned by Iza; but her
mŏther scorns the idea of throing away
her beautiful danter on an artist, however
çelebrated and wealthy. She has in vue
a Russian prince. The princely marriage
however, fails, and Iza throes herself in
Clémenceau's arms 'sans gêne et sans
façon.' The "énigme éternelle" makes

him a declaration of lŏve in so "emancipated" a manner that it ŏt tŏ deter him
from a matrimonial alliance with her.
Besides, he has also received several anonymous hints reflecting severely on her
character; but he sees ŏnly the incarnation of beauty before him, and can not
free himself from the fatal infatuation . . .
Clémenceau's happiness is beyond description, but, alas! the hŏneymoon is not
over cre the infatuated lover detects sŏme
ugly traits in his wife's character, and
after sŏme time, he is plunged intŏ the
deepest misery by the discŏvery not of
ŏne lŏver, but of a whole nest of lŏvers
favored by the danter of the Polish adventurer. His mŏther dies of grief at
seeing the disgraçe of her sŏn's wife, and
Clémenceau, repudiating the idea of killing his bride, repairs tŏ Italy tŏ solaçe his
broken spirit by an assiduous devotion tŏ
art. But life has no longer any charms
for him, and even art cannot heal his
smarting wounds. He might hav linger-
ed on and consumed his life in quiet
grief, but, hearing that he is an object of
pity and derision tŏ his friends, he starts
in a fit of rage for Paris. He finds his
wife leading a life of roval luxury, a fact
not tŏ be wondered at, she being the 'femme entretenue' of a prince. Once more he
is overpowered by her fatal beauty, and by
his ŏn stil more fatal sensuous feelings.
He sees her in her boudoir amidst the mute
witnesses of her shame, and "condones"
her guilt. Once more he asks her—"M'
aimes-tu?" Half-asleep, she answers,
"Oui," and he quietly plunges a knife intŏ
her heart." [Albion.   **1989**

COLONEL'S DAUGHTER (The), [Renée Mauperin, Paris, 1864.] by E. & J. DE GONCOURT; London, 1883. [It purports to be by "W. S. Hayward."] 1992

COMÉDIE HUMAINE (The) [by HONORE "DE" BALZAC: (†, 1850.) Chatto, 1879.) "consists of an introduction and 3 of the author's shorter tales,—'La Bourse,' "Gaudissart II.," and 'Albert Savarus'. "The first is much better dõne than was the version contained in No. 1982." [Athe. 1993

COMPANION OF THE TOUR OF FRANCE (The). [by "G: SAND," i. e., Amantine Lucile Aurore (Dupin) Dudevant (†, 1876): [Paris, 1840] London, Churton, 1848.] "A 'Companion' is a member of a trades' union; the "Tour of France," refers tõ the wandering of artizans from town tõ town, after the custom described in Wilhelm Meister's Apprenticeship [No. 1017.] The hero is the son of a carpenter, and the design of the author appears tõ hav been tõ paint the ideal of a man of the people, aiming at hïer objects than wealth or station, and devoting himself tõ the solution of the social problems most intimately connected with the welfare of his class." [Westminster Review.

——. SAME ("The Journeyman Joiner"), N.-Y., Graham, 1847. 1994

CONFESSOR (THE), ☞ UNDER THE BAN. 1995

CONQUEST OF PLASSANS (The). [by ÉMILE ZOLA: Peterson, 1879.] "Here we hav a stern, self-controlling prîest, indomitably resisting the seductiv worship of an infatuated woman. He cõmes off conqueror, and she. baffled and defeated, perishes. This is the true "conquest of Plassans." The author's motiv is executed with firmness. directness.

and clearness. But the whole atmosfere of the piece is somber and forbidding; thêre is nothing pleasant in its situations; the dénoument is direfully tragic and we cannot think that the specific utility of the book is an offset to its general unwholesõmness." [Boston "Lit. World." 1996

CONSCRIPT [The], by A. [D.] DUMAS: New-York. 1855. 1997

——, SAME, by ERCKMANN-CHATRIAN [Alsace, 1812-14] = No. 649.

CONSUELO, = No. 650.

COQUETTE'S LOVE (A), [Nôtre Coeur] by G. DE MAUPASSANT, N.-Y. Belford, 1890. 1998

——, SAME ("Notre Coeur") Chicago, Laird, 1890, 307 pp.

CORINNE, by A.. L.. G. (NECKER), baroness STAEL-HOLSTEIN, Carey, '36; Warne, '84' ☞ No. 2004.

COSETTE. [by K.. S. MACQUOID: Ward & Downey, 1890.] "Cosette chooses õne lõve for herself whilst her friends choose another for her; and thêre ar the usual complications, which ar told with good taste and feeling. The story has very little incident. but much play of character, so that the men and women whõ act their parts in the comedy appear almost real. The experiences of Cosette ar decidedly touching, and her fate is well contrived to support a french rather than an english vue of the theory and practice of courtship." [Athenæum. 2001

COUNT DE PERBUCK (The), by F: SOULIE, London, Newby, 1859. 2002

COUNT KOSTIA, = No. 653.

COUNT OF MONTE-CRISTO = No. 654.

COUNT XAVIER. [by "HENRY GREVILLE". i. e., Alice M.. Céleste (Fleury) Durand: Ticknor, 1887.]

CONFESSIONS OF A CHILD OF THE CENTURY (The) [by ALFRED DE MUSSET (1810-57) : Chicago, *Sergel*, 1893.] "Men ar always lâfing at what thêy call "women's men," as portrayed in the feminin novel; but "men's men" as ôften astound women, until thêy ar ready tŏ go tŏ thêir male relativs and ask: "Ar you really like this? Did you ever dŏ such things as that? Dŏ you suppose my husband and my sŏns ar at all like the men in this book? Such a character is "Octave" in these 'Confessions.' This very hysterical young person of 19, whŏ has run the gamut of all the viçe acçesible tŏ him in Paris, is the victim of a moral maladv which renders him unable tŏ believe in either sinçerity, generosity, or virtue. His passions of doubt, remorse and ŏther emotions têar him tŏ tatters, and he is forever being consumed by grief or convulsed with tears. Now and then, he opens his heârt tŏ joy and tranquil happiness: ōne of the most notable of these occasions being when he was about tŏ stab a most admirable young woman in her sleep, [compare No. 1989] but was prevented by the sight of a little blac cross upon her heârt. After having beheld this, he is at ōnce "converted," and, tŏ use with respect an old phrase, he "enjoys religion." He is in fact, so changed that he at ōnce passes the young woman, whŏ has out of pure philanthropy ruined herself— hoping tŏ regenerate him — tŏ the man whŏm she really lōves, and whŏ, tho poor and named Smith, is bily respectable. As the book is written by Alfred de Musset, it goes without saying that thêre ar sŏme fine things in it: the opening chapters, which describe the moral condition of the people after a war of invasion and defeat, being espe. cially remarkable." [L.. Stockton, 1893.] "It is tŏ Alfred de Musset that many of G : Sand's exquisit 'Lettres d'un Voyageur' ar addressed. She ôften repeats in them how truly she had lōved him, even at the very moment when she betrayed him... 'The Confessions' wer written while he was writhing under the anguish caused by his mistress' faithlessness, and the whole tenor of its contents is thêrefore strōngly imbued with the violençe of personal feeling. Altho these çelebrated 'Confessions' assume the form of a novel, they ar evidently, a narrativ of the author's life. The treachery of a heroin is the pivot upon which revolv all the events of the story. She is shōn tŏ the reader in every form which the mind of the writer, mad with passion, could depict: now, under the appearançe of the light, heârtless woman of the world — now, with all the tranquil homish charm of virtue—and then, again, under the bright dazzling cōlors of the courtezan. No details, however cynical, ar omitted. The author seems tŏ hav traçed his thôts as thêy presented themselvs in rapid sucçession tŏ his mind, with all thêir nativ singularity of contrast, hight of colōring, and crudity of expression. Thêre is, doubtless, much tŏ be admired in the work; but thêre is sōmething too nearly akin tŏ indelicacy in exposing tŏ the public gaze the private feelings and thôts which recur constantly during the course of the narrativ, tŏ award it unqualified praise." [Albion. **1994** w

"The story is very slīt, and the plot so simple as tŏ be almost hackneyed; but the freshness of treatment, and the grace and humor of the style, make it a most delītful little book. The old count's funeral, the devotion of the old servant and the obsequiousness of the new ŏne, the momentary temptation of the hero, the accidents which enable him tŏ triumf over temptation, and finally the young scapegoat's stratagem of the dynamite plot tŏ get himself recalled tŏ the lŏve from which he has been banished, ar all told with inimitable humor and vividness." [Critic. **2003**

CORINNE. [by A·· L·· GERMAINE (NECKER) baroness STAEL-HOLSTEIN: Boston, 1808, 2 v., 12°; London, 1856, 8°.] "One faculty the author possessed in an extraordinary degree,—the faculty of delineating character. She had the power of exhibiting it both by a few brīt touches of epigrammatic force, and by a long and unobtrusiv cŏurse of minute and delicate delineation ... Never was thêre a more successful example of true and delicate delineation than her character of 'Comte d' Erfeuil' in *Corinne*; and it possesses the rare merit of being not only a vivid and consistent portrait of an imaginary individual, but of ŏne in whŏm ar embodied all the most amiable peculiarities of the cŏuntry tŏ which he belongs. No ŏne can follo this personage throu the tale without being better acquainted ·with the French character." [Foreign Quarterly Review. **2004**

COUNTESS EVE (The) = No. 657.

COUNTESS SARAH, by G: OHNET: *Vizetelly*. 1885; N.-Y., *Waverly Co.*, 1890, ☞ No. 1955.

COUNTRY DOCTOR (The) [by HONORÉ "DE" BALZAC (†, 1850): *Roberts*, 1888.] "has for its theme the good work wrŏt by a man whŏ relinquishes his ŏn career, settles in a primitiv region and applies all his powers tŏ raising and benefiting the ignorant aňd debased peasantry whŏ hav hithertŏ maintained only a precarious existence from the results of their soing and reaping in a wretched soil, with neither health, hope, nor heârt tŏ rouse them out of a dul, almost imbeçil stagnation. Balzac, whŏ paints town and city life in so sombre cŏlors, têaring the vêil from their secret sins and mysteries, appalls us with the conviction that thêre is no cure for the terrible disease which is sapping the health of all modern society, takes quite a different tone in recounting tŏ us the simple details of Dr. Benassis' enterprise, and describes a veritable Arcadia. The doctor has found the peasantry sic, both in body and mind, tending tŏards crétinism, living in hovels, il-fed, il-kept, heârtless and wicked. Intŏ the little community he has infused health, good sense, good living, which hav brŏt about freedom from vice and crime. Dr. Benassis' early motiv in devoting himself tŏ the regeneration of this people had been tŏ overcŏme personal agony and revolt at his failure in life. He is ŏne of Balzac's typical personages; a truly grêat soul, simple, affectionate, without vanity or pedantry, wise, equitable and patient. Thêre is benefit and stimulus tŏ be gained from reading the quiet chronicle, and we ar glad tŏ see that hopefulness and belief can be breathed even from Balzac's pages." [American. **2005**

COURTIER OF MISFORTUNE

(The) [by EUSTACE CLAIRE GREN-
VILLE MURRAY : († , 1881) in "French
Sketches" *Smith*, 1878.] "is a fervent
and devotedly loyal Bonapartist, and
he risks his life, when all is over with
the emperor and his army, tŏ carry a
letter from her husband tŏ the Em-
press ... In time tŏ cŏme, when the
imperial tragedy shal hav faded intŏ
the distance, and shal be invested
with romance, 'la révérence de l'im-
pératrice' may take its place among the
historic pictures which illustrate the
troubled story of France, and the
lives of those whŏ in that fantastic
and fierce country hav been born tŏ
greatness, hav achieved it, or hav had
it thrust upon them." [Spectator.2006
COUSIN BETTE. [by HONORÉ
"DE" BALZAC († , 1850.) *Roberts*,
1888.] "Balzac aspired to paint
french life, especially parisian life, in
all its aspects,—'the great modern
monster with its every face,' tŏ use
his ŏn words; and in no ŏne of his
novels is his insīt keener, his cŏloring
bolder, or his disclosures of the cor-
ruptions of city life more painfully
realistic than in 'Cousin Bette.' Lisbeth Fischer, i. e., Cousin Bette, is a
peasant woman, and in spite of 25
years of parisian life, a peasant she
remains ... But tigerish as ar sŏme
of Bette's instincts, she is stil a woman within our keb,—we can understand and feel for her. It is tŏ
Crevel, tŏ the baron, tŏ the infamous
Marniffes that we go for types of a
corruption which sickens us of our
commŏn humanity. It is a picture
before which we shade our eyes and
turn away. Stil thêre ar contrasts
and varieties of character, throu
which as throu a rift iñ the blac
clouds cŏmes a hint of brītness. For
example, thêre is supreme delicacy of
touch in the portrait of Adeline Hulot
and of her dauter Hortense, in whŏm
nature and art have united tŏ make a
çharming character. So far as it is
an exposition of the passions, the
lust, the greed, the hatred and jeal-
onsy of mankind working out events
under the vêil of social fenomena, it
is a very grêat book, but it is a terrible ŏne. Not ŏne of the series shŏs
more breadth, skil, and sympathy
with every characteristic of the grêat
french author than dŏes this." [Amer-
ican. 2007
COUSIN PONS [by HONORÉ "DE"
BALZAC († , 1850.) : *Roberts*, 1886;
London, *Warne*, 1889 ; N.-Y., *Munro*,
1888 ; *Bonner*, 1891.] "continues the
series grimly entitled 'La Comédie
Humaine,' and shŏs like the rest the
vanity, the heârtlessness, the greed of
parisian life,—all those sordid vices of
civilization, which here thro intŏ relief the inexhaustible tenderness and
worth of a friendship between
twŏ men. Both ar musicians. Pons
began his career by winning a prize
as a composer, then dropped tŏ the
dead level of mediocrity, and makes
a living by giving lessons and conducting the orchestra of a theatre.
Schmucke, a German, is a pianist tŏ
an adapter of scores for Pons' orchestra. Poor and lonely, the twŏ men
liv tŏgether, and giv each other not
ŏnly companionship, but entire sympathy. Schmucke, whŏ is a senti-
mentalist, is entirely happy in this
life, but Pons, over and abŏve his
friendship for the German, has twŏ
passions ; he is both a gourmand and
a virtuoso. For years he has been able
tŏ gratify his lŏve of good dinners by
dropping in daily at the tables of his
rich relativs ; and by knŏing all the
curiosity-shops and being always on

the alert tŏ secure whatever is valuable and rare, he has made a collection fit tŏ rouse the envy of all the connaisseurs ... How he destroys himself, how he is momentarilv reinstated as a welcōme and honored guest ōnly to be turned out as a pariah; how his collection is appraised and how the beasts of prêy gather about the heârt-broken man; all this the reader will discover. It is a sombre and terrible picture,—the friendship of the twŏ men (which lasts tŏ the grave and beyond the grave) helping ōnly tŏ render the cruelty and greed of every other character in the book more hopeless and more intolerable." [American. 2008
——, SAME ("Poor Relations"), London, *Simpkin*. 1880.

CRIME OF SYLVESTRE BONNARD (The) [by ANATOLE FRANCE: *Harper*, 1890.] "is a charming story ... Sylvestre, the old booklōver, is a most lōvable creation: his very crime is endearing. His kidnapping of Jeanne seems the most natural thing in the world, and so dōes his fatherly jealousy of the young student whŏ is in lōve with her. The book is full of quaint scenes." [Critic. 2009

CRIQUETTE. [by LUDOVIC HALÉVY: Chicago, *Rand*, 1891.] "Halévy has a talent for writing very sweet, attractiv stȯries ... Criquette is a most charming character. We begin with her as a little girl selling flowers and barley-sugar tŏ the passers-by in the streets of a suburb of Paris. We follo her throu her first efforts in a juvenile part on a provincial stage, and thence tŏ her first grêat theatrical success at the Porte St. Martin. Her mother dies while she is thêre, and she is adopted by an actress ōnly tŏ be turned over later tŏ a hard, cold wonian, whŏ raises [*sic !*] her properly but without a particle of affection. The girl's lōving nature starvs in this atmosfere, and she runs away and takes refuge with a young friend whŏ has always been kind tŏ her and whŏm she genuinely belīeves she lōves. She is grêatly his superior, however, and awakens at last tŏ a realization of the fact that she has outgrōn him. She remains perfectly loyal, tho, even after he deserts her, and refuses tŏ accept the happiness which another offers her. She feels that she belongs tŏ her first lōve, but she givs her life for her second, dying of fever contracted while nursing him in the hospital at the close of the german war. The charm of the story lies in the beauty of Criquette's character, and in the tender interest with which she inspires us." [Critic. 2010

DADDY GORIOT = *PERE GORIOT*.

DEAD MARQUISE (The) [1789] = No. 670.

DELPHINE. [by A .. L .. GERMAINE (NECKER), baroness STAEL-HOLSTEIN: Phil'a, *Carey*, 1835.] "Our sympathies ar so strongly enlisted on her side, and she is exhibited in so interesting a lit. that whatever ŏūr judgments may decide, ŏūr heârts at least ar made tŏ tel us that if she and society ar at variance, it is rather society which ŏt tŏ be remodeled, than that Delphine should be turned aside from the wel intentioned cŏurse of her enthusiastic errors." [Foreign Quarterly Review. 1834. 2011

DENISE. [by MA. ROBERTS: London, *Bell*, 1863; N.-Y., *Gregory*, 1864.] "The promise of goodness if not excellence given in "Mademoiselle

Mori" (No. 812.) is more than fulfilled in this charming tale, which
endeavors tŏ portray a side of french
life which has not been sufficiently
regarded. The author's aim is tŏ
paint existence in a quiet, sunny, self-
absorbed town of Southern France, a
town chattering busily about its local
affairs, the feast of its patron saint,
the conduct of its mayor, the dŏings
of its gentry, but altŏgether careless
of the intrigues, ambitions and splendors of the Tuileries. The subject
indeed is regarded from an english
point of vue; the cōloring is english:
but notwithstanding its insular treatment, the picture is a veritable representation of french manners, and wil
please those whŏm it describes scarcely less than those for whŏm it is especially written." [Athenæum.]—
"Thêre is a strange charm about this
book. The story is common enuf,
the characters have nothing original
in their conception, and yet we ar fascinated by the detailed truth of the
portraiture . . . Mademoiselle Le Mar-
chand, an odd old maid, with a genius
for painting, is really the character
of the book. Denise, the heroin, is
quietly and faithfully drawn. Various picturesque fāses of the cathŏlic
faith ar artistically managed, while
the faith itself is not treated with
much courtesy." [Continental. **2012**
DEVIL'S POOL (The) [by "G:
SAND," i. e.. Amantine Lucile Aurore
(Dupin) Dudevant (†, 1876): N.-Y.,
W. H. Graham, 1847.] is "the most
perfectly idyllic composition of modern times. The characters ar as real as
the scenery. Everything is in keeping, and it is because the harmony is
so perfect, while the theme is so
simple, that we call the tale idyllic;
but if it had been less wel and artisti-

cally written, it would stil hav been a
pleasing story of rural life. It is not
the fruit of any theory about humanity." [Saturday Review.]—"The
books whŏse scenes ar chiefly laid in
the country wil, we believe, be G:
Sand's surest title tŏ immortality.
In these you fil your lungs with the
fresh air from the 'landes' and the
mountains. You hear the rush of the
mountain torrents, the murmur of the
gently-flōing brooks, the rustle of the
leaves in the summer breeze, or the
sying of the autumn breeze throu the
branches. The simplest and most
perfect of all is 'La Mare au Diable.'
. . . In point of genius, and perhaps
of interest, we must giv the palm, as
we hav said, tŏ 'La Mare au Diable.'
The triumf of its art is in its extreme
simplicity. The story is woven out
of a single adventure—the best part
of it is in the incidents of a single nīt;
the personages ar a laborer in homespun, a little peasant girl, and a child.
It would seem incredible that the
author of the passionate 'Indiana'
could hav made so much of such slīt
and simple materials. For ŏnce she
has discarded all her socialist fancies;
she dispenses with her analysis of
artificial passion, and is working after
nature pure and unadorned." [Black-
wood's. **2013**
——, SAME ("Enchanted Lake"),
London, *Slater*, 1849.
——, SAME ("Haunted Marsh")
with "Old Convents," London,
Simms, 1851.
——, SAME ("Haunted Pool"),
N.-Y., *Dodd*, 1890.
——, SAME ("Lovers' Pool"), N.-
Y., *Redfield*, 1871.
DIANE. [by K.. S. MACQUOID:
Chatto, 1875.] "The story is the old
ōne: lōve at first sīt on the man's part,

and not long after on the woman's, —misunderstanding. jealousy, separation, reconciliation, marriage. But the events succeed each other naturally and thêre is just enuf doubt as tŏ the parts which the various characters ar going tŏ play tŏ keep ŏur interest alive. Madame Poulain, Diane's intrîguing rival, is perhaps a little too wicked tŏ be in harmony with the general key of the story and the young baron whŏm we expected tŏ turn out a second Arthur Donnithorne (No. 1027.) is almost too good for human nature; but french people, whether good or bad, ar less conventionalized than english people."
[Athenæum. **2014**

DIANE CORYAL [by KATHLEEN O'MEARA: *Roberts*, 1884.] "is so wel written, and givs so graceful and faithful a picture of provincial life. that it takes its place in the pleasant list which comprises such novels as 'Denise' and 'The Rose Garden.' Acquaintance with the french provinces seems tŏ suggest books like these, whêre everything picturesque in the pretty towns, with thêir quaint houses with gables and shining pinnacles, the dresses, the household customs and belongings. is carefully sketched, each dainty detail indicated, even if ŏnly half cŏlored with human likeness and passion. This fresh and delicate little story is peculiarly felicitous in its treatment of french ideas and manners, and no ŏne can fail to enjoy the picture given of life at the abbaye ... The plot of the novel is Auld Robin Gray, but freshly and spontaneously enuf told tŏ please the reader. Diane, whŏ is a fine character, wins sympathy and affection from the outset, and holds it until the end." [Lippincott's.]—"A young french

girl, brŏt up among artists,'lŏses her mother, gets engaged tŏ ŏne of her painter-friends against his father's wish, goes tŏ liv with sŏme elderly cousins in Picardie, hears a false report of her lŏver's marriage tŏ anŏther woman, and in her despair and loneliness marries ŏne of her cousins. When she is the wife of Robin Gray young Jamie turns up again. Meanwhile the situation is sufficiently tragic tŏ giv interest tŏ the story, even tho the experienced reader knoes that in a novel of this kind things ar pretty sure tŏ cŏme rĭt at last. The ŏnly fault is that, as so often happens, the husband is a far more inter esting figure than the lŏver tŏ whŏse welfare he has tŏ be sacrificed. But in novels. at least, youth wil be served; and we can ŏnly be grateful when the author carries this maxim intŏ effect in the english rather than in the french method." [Athenæum.

——, SAME ("The Old House in Picardy"), *Bentley*, 1887. **2015**

DR. ANTONIO [**Riviera**] = No. 435.

DR. RAMEAU, by G: OHNET: *Lippincott, Lovell, Rand, Waverly Co.*, 1889. ☞ No. 1955. **2016**

DOCTOR'S FAMILY (The) [by [M.. ALFRED] JULES GIRARDIN: *Routledge*, 1876.] "is delĭtful. It is a tale of domestic life in a country town. The lĭt, pleasant zest of the original style is wel preserved. It exhibits a side of french life healthful and admirable, shoing that the usual "french novel" dŏes not represent the life of the mass of people in France."* [Athe. **2017**

DON JUAN, by BALZAC. London, *Scott.* 1890. **2018**

* Thêre is a proverb that one swallo does not make a summer. Compare Andrew Lang on French Novels in *The North Amer. Review*, Jai., 1892.—*W: M. G.*

DORA [Rouen], by JULIA
KAVANAGH, = No. 438.

DOUBLE FAMILY (A), by BAL-
ZAC, in *THE CAT AND BATTLE-
DORE.* 2019

DREAM OF LOVE (A) by ZOLA,
Chicago, *Laird*, 1891, = No. 784.

DUCHESSE ANNETTE (The),
Chicago, *Laird*, 1891, = No. 1954.

DUCHESSE DE LANGEAIS
(The) [by HONORE "DE" BALZAC:
Roberts, 1886.] "is a tedious tale as
if told after dinner by a guest whŏ
for the most part drowses but occasionally rouses himself tŏ startling
power. Few things of Balzac illustrate better how his narrativ faculty
gets the better of him. It runs on
and on. It is with him as H: Taylor
said of Macaulay, "his memory
swamps his mind." The story is in
reality all told in the prelude of the
convent scene . . . . It is as if the novelist played with his characters—
doomed and plainly declared tŏ be
doomed—as a cat plays with a half-
dead mouse." [Overland. 2020

DUKE'S MARRIAGE (The).
[*Bentley*, 1886.] The author "has
made the french character the
subject of study under the various as-
peets of Breton,—peasant and noble,
bureaucrat, imperialist, and demagog;
and if he is a bitter opponent of republicanism, it must be admitted that
he is at least as vigorous in exposing
the rottenness of the Second Empire.
The Duke himself is a fine and generous fello, but we can hardly resent
the endless embarrassments which
sever him so long from his bride when
they afford the writer scope for admirable delineation of country life, gentle
and simple. Jerôme Juva, the priest,
is a touching figure, and ŏne of the
strongest situations in the book is

that which arises out of the sudden
shattering of his belief in miraculous
apparitions. On the ŏther hand, thêre
is no little humor in the account of
the imprisonment in Paris of Little-
point, a .respectable english solicitor.
and the compromising circumstances
of his release along with a batch of
socialists on the downfall of the Empire. 'The Duke's Marriage' may be
read, both by those who ar fond of
France, like the author, and by all
whŏ appreciate a clever and original
story told with plenty of life and
spirit and an abundance of epigram."
[Athenæum. 2021

EDMÉE (Les Dames de Croix-
Mort) by G: OHNET: *Warne*, 1886,
☞ No. 1955.

ÉLIANE = No. 440.

EMBARRASSING WIFE (An)—
[18½ pages], by G. DROZ, in *Modern
Age*, Apr. 1883. 2022

ERSILIA [Pyrenees] = No. 686.

ESTELLE RUSSELL [Toul-
ouse] = No. 444.

EUGÉNIE [by BEATRICE MAY
BUTT: *Holt*, 1877.] "is a simple,
quiet story of home-life, having throuŏut a certain delicacy of touch which
is very pleasing. The characters ar
few, but clearly drawn; and while as
a story it is disappointing and unsatisfactory, we ar constantly charmed
by the fresh, natural way in which it
is told." [Boston "Lit. World." 2023

EUGÉNIE GRANDET [by Ho-
NORÉ "DE" BALZAC (†, 1850): N.-Y.,
Winchester, 1843; *Rudd*, 1860; *Bonner*.
1891; London, *Routledge*, 1859; Boston, *Roberts*, 1886.] "has amongst
Balzac's countless tales, the almost
singular merit. that it may be read by
a man without indignation, and by a
woman without a blush. It is, as it
wer. a dutch picture of an interior—of

the family and society of a penurious merchant of a country town. The details ar painted with vivid accuracy, and the characters ar worked-up with equal originality and truth. The character of Eugénie Grandet herself, combining the gentleness of her submissiv mother with sŏmething of the shrewdness and firmness of her avaricious father is ably conceived and happily executed." [Quarterly Review, 1836.]—Eugénie "shines out from Balzac's gallery of women with a beauty and charm beyond all others, and her reality givs worth to the grêat novelist's conceptions of different female characters. That he should hav knŏn how tŏ draw a Eugénie makes the dauters of Père Goriot, and the Duchess of Langeais more credible. The character of Eugénie is that of a perfect woman; it is portrayed within close limits, it is true, but limits wide enuf tŏ include sweetness, fortitude, faith, constancy, nobility and passion,—everything, indeed, which endears and sanctifies woman tŏ the imagination. She is at the beginning of the story a weed shaken by the wind at any thŏts of displeasing her father, the old miser, whŏ domineered his household, forbidding, depressing, thwarting every generous impulse which he could govern. It is impossible for reality or imagination tŏ surpass the picture of sordid gloom, apathy and dulness which Balzac paints with a wonderful minuteness and completion of detail as a bacground for the human lives whŏse secret he is tŏ disclose. You feel here the grimness, the bareness, the hideousness of the Grandet ménage: you shiver with Madame Grandet and Eugénie as they cower over the foot-warmer in the chilly autumn days before the fire is līted: you experience ennui at the scanty meals, the silence, the gloom, the intolerable wêt of a perpetual and crushing tyranny. This girlhood had been the long preparation for Eugénie's womanhood. which begins with the advent of her coŭsin from Paris. The little lŏve idyl which ensues, the occasional talks in the garden, the ŏne long deep kiss in the passage, is a momentary brêak of sunlīt in a long life of gloom. But Eugénie belīevs for a time that she possesses a secret of happiness which no ŏne can rob her of. Her cousin goes away, but he is tŏ return! A vain hope, but a long sweet hope; if a falsehood, a blessed falsehood which transmutes a gray, monotonous, isolated existence intŏ ŏne linked tŏ all which makes the worth of human experience. Her cousin, like everyŏne else in the book except Eugénie, her mother, and Nanon the servant, is sordid, faithless, willing tŏ sel his soul for gain. Eugénie redeems his honorable name,—promotes his ambitious marriage in Paris, and she goes on her ŏn lŏveless and joyless way. It is ŏne of the most sombre of sombre pictures. One mīt ask if Eugénie's faith and lŏve and religion and goodness wer not a līt unseen,—a fountain wholly wasted,—poured out in a desert which refreshed no thirsty soul. But it is not so. She has ŏne consolation which enriches her life; she has given her gift, and everything is made endurable by the faithfulness of her ŏn heârt." [American. **2024**

EVANGELIST (The). [by AL-PHONSE DAUDET: *Peterson*, 1883.] "We hav seldom read a more painful book. It is unrelīevd. gloom. This writer has been called 'the french

Dickens.' but it is certain that 'Boz' would never hav becŏme so popular as he was if he had given himself tŏ the morbid studies in which Daudet delīts. L' Évangéliste tels a story of religious zeal and intolerance so unnatural, depressing, and subversiv of common human feeling, that the reader's patience is put tŏ the test on every page, and he must hav a strong mental stomach whŏ can digest it at all. It develops a picture of french Protestantism which, if true at all, must certainly be exceptional, and not characteristic. It has been stated that Daudet, on being taken tŏ task for this book, declared that it was founded on facts connected with the experience of his family. It may, thêrefore, be necessary tŏ concede that such an episode, as that of 'L'Évangéliste' has occurred in the history of the extremest side of the religious mŏvement in France, outside the catholic church, and that the author is to that extent justified in making it the basis of a book, but the circumstances certainly cannot be accepted as more than an episode, historically, while, as a literary work, the story inflicts a painful labor upon the reader." [American.]—"We ar inclined tŏ call 'L' Evangéliste' his finest work, and the ŏne which most nearly approaches artistic perfection.—It is a story of direct and pitiless power. It is like a greek tragedy in its simplicity, and in the suggestion of an overriding and irrevocable fate against which all strife is vain. The Evangelist is a cold, proud, imperious, bigoted woman, controlling enormous wealth in the propagandisɔ of a hard and narro form of religion; going strait before her, tho her husband kils himself because of her frigidity, and tho a

mother goes mad because her dauter is taken from her by a pseudo-religious 'camp-meeting-revival' ecstasy. This figure of Jeanne is drawn with extraordinary vigor and sobriety, and is worthy to stand side by side with the 'Religieuse' of Diderot; indeed, as excess of ŏne kind is as bad as excess of anŏther, 'L'Évangéliste' is nearly as horrible as 'La Religieuse.' —The subject is of special interest here, whêre the same bigotry is much more ·frequent, altho perhaps less pernicious than in France, as all readers of Eggleston's excellent stories [Nos. 15. 30, 40, 52, 92, 131,] wil remember." [Nation. **2025**

——, SAME, ("Port Salvation"), *Chatto*, 1883.

EXTRACTS FROM THE MS. OF DR. BERNAGIUS ["Les Clientes du docteur Bernagius," Paris, 1873] by LUCIEN BIART: in *Time.* Aug.-Dec., 1880. **2026**

FACINO CANE, by BALZAC, in *LOUIS LAMBERT* **2027**

——, SAME ("Gold"), in *SHORTER STORIES*.

FADETTE = *LITTLE FADETTE*.

FAME AND SORROW. [by HONORÉ "DE" BALZAC: (†, 1850.) *Roberts*, 1890.] "The 6 tales ar 6 chalices brimful of unction, quivering with a play of beauty and sorro which captivates at the start. All ar sad. One, *Col. Chabert* [No. 1991], shŏs the sublimity of resignation tŏ a fate undeserved. In anŏther an artist winged with fire and caprice mates himself with a Parisienne whŏm he lŏves passionately for—a month, and then dismisses down the dismal lane of disillusioned women. The story of Chabert has a greek severity of outline, a keenness of logic, and a pathos in its climax shŏing the hīest art. In

'*The Purse*,' gentler elements meet and harmonize in an end beautiful and tranquil as a midsummer evening." [Critic. **2028**

FANNY. [by ERNEST FEYDEAU (†, 1873) : Paris, 1858 ; N.-Y., *Long*, 1860.] "Edward, whŏ is a mere boy, is in lŏve with Fanny. This is natural enuf. Fanny, whŏ is decidedly an old girl, whŏ has been married for 15 years, and has three children, is not less desperately in lŏve with Edward, whŏm she regards with a most charming sentiment, in which the timid passion of the maiden blends gracefully with the maturer regard of an ânt or a grandmother. This is not quite so natural. Certainly, it can hardly be that she is fascinated with Edward, whŏ is the most disgustingly silly young monkey tŏ be found in the whole range of french novels. But the mystery is at ŏnce disclosed when we read the description of Fanny's husband. He is 'a species of bull with a human face.' 'His smile was not unpleasing. and his look without any malicious expression, but clear as crystal.' We begin to comprehend his inferiority tŏ Edward,—tŏ sympathise with the youth's horror at the sīt of this obnoxious husband, 'whŏ seems tŏ him,' as Mr. Janin says in his preface, 'A hero—what dŏ I say? —a giant!—tŏ the lŏving, timid, fragil child? 'In fine, a certain air of calm rectitude pervaded his person.' Execrable wretch! could anything be more repulsiv tŏ true and delicate sentiment? 'I should say his age was about 40.' Our wrath at this atrocity can hardly be controlled. It seems as if Mr. Feydeau, by collecting in ŏne individual all the qualities which most excite his abhorrence and contempt, had succeeded in giving us, in Fanny's husband, a very tolerable specimen of a gentleman. We pardon all tŏ the sŏmewhat middle-aged lady, whose 'feelings ar too many for her'; and we only regret that Mr. Feydeau did not see the eminent propriety of increasing the lady's admiration by having this brutal husband pull Edward's divine nose or kic the adored person of the 'pauvre enfant' down stairs." [Atlantic. **2029**

FATAL PASSION (A). ["Gerfaut") by C: BERNARD [DU-GRAIL DE LA VILLETTE] (†, 1850.) : Paris, 1838 ; New-York, *Carleton*, 1874.] "Among minor novels, nŏne has been more read and esteemed than 'Gerfaut.' It is entirely free from those venturesŏme details whêrein french writers ar prone tŏ offend alike taste and propriety, it is in every way a refined book, thêre is a delicacy of shading about the lŏve-scenes, an imaginativ sensuousness, which is rare and has a legitimate fascination of its ŏn. The plot is not a complicated ŏne : it is a story of the seduction of a married woman, but thêre ar nŏne of those fatalities of circumstance which often play so considerable a part in such stories ; the precipices ar not inevitable ; the road tŏ them is taken by choice. not accident. But it is the character of the hero tŏ which we feel ŏur attention drawn, for tŏ ŏur mind he is the most singular hero ever depicted by a writer of imagination. Gerfaut is never, even for a moment, deluded intŏ the most passing fãse of that exaltation which we all connect inseparably with strong passion. and in which many of us see its partial apology. He seems throuŏut tŏ be aware that temporary personal gratification—the same in kind tho not in degree as that tŏ be derived

from an exceptionally good dinner,—
is the object of his pursuit; and his
nearest approach tŏ being swept away
by what he is pleased tŏ term his lõve
is when the idea occurs tŏ him that
the woman he is pursuing is playing
with him, and the emotion of wounded vanity swels the current of his
desires tŏ sŏmething resembling a cataract. His selfishness is näif in its
openness, his heârt never obtrudes
upon the scene tŏ complicate the action: he is of noble descent and proud
of his lineage, a poet of repute and
ambitious of fame. yet in his treatment of the woman he professes tŏ
lõve he never exhibits a spark of honorable feeling or romantic enthusiasm." [Lippincott's.   **2030**
——, SAME ("Lover and Hus-
band"). London, 1841.   **2031**
FIRST AND TRUE LOVE = *SIN
OF M. ANTOINE.*

FISHERMAN OF AUGE (The) [by
K.. S. MACQUOID: *Appleton*, 1879.]
"is a pretty story of village life, of its
lõve-makings, disappointments, and
marriages. The strong home-feeling
of the peasant, the reverence for parents and the parental interest, not
õnly for the welfare, but for the happiness of their children, the graceful
chattering of the old women. ar all
wel drawn. In õur ruder social life
we lac õne of the grêatest charms of
french society, the 'vieille femme,'
but in the hier civilization cõming tŏ
us. year by year, we may hope for an
old age in õur women, whŏm household drudgery and petty cares wil not
hav so far deadened tŏ the beauties
and graces of life as tŏ deserv banishment from thêir rītful place as the
authority of the Salon." [Penn
Monthly.   **2032**
  FLIRT.   by PAUL HERVIEU:

Worthington, 1890, 273 pp.   **2033**
  FLOWER GARDEN (The) by
É. SOUVESTRE: Baltimore, *Murphy*,
1864.   **2034**
  FOREIGN MATCH (A) [by M..
(HEALEY) BIGOT: *McClurg*, 1890.]
"with no wealth on the õne side and
no title on the other is, if õne is tŏ
judge from contemporary fiction,
sŏmething of an anomaly. But. no
doubt, marriages between penniless
american girls and impecunious french
artists sõmetimes occur, and dŏ not
always turn out bad. In Mrs.
Bigot's wel-told tale. however, the
lõve and romance ar. from the beginning, all on õne side—that of the
artist. He is called in tŏ teach drawing tŏ the dauter and niece of an
american millionaire, and goes on tŏ
fall in lõve with the latter, who is engaged tŏ be married tŏ a titled Italian.
But the Sanford's fortune is lost, and
Prince Cavalmonte, with tears in his
fine eyes, demonstrates tŏ Miriam that
it is impossible for him tŏ marry a
poor girl. She wil not quite giv him
up, tho. She wil stay in Paris, becõme a grêat actress and make a
colossal fortune ... Her hopes all
vanished, the remnant of her fortune
nearly eaten, Miriam marries Raoul
Bertrand. and goes tŏ liv in his shabby
studio with him and his invalid sister
Miette. Raoul is happy. Miriam dul
until the return of her cousin Mattie,
whŏ has married in America a half-
rich man, Mr. Silas Blizzard. Led
õnce more intŏ the old life of pleasure
and lavish expense, she drags her husband with her, intrîgues with picture
dealers. and, on the strength of fictitious orders, makes him set up a
fashionable studio. She again meets
the Prince, and falls a victim tŏ his
wiles; and the story ends tragically.

FOLLE-FARINE. [by "OUIDA," i. e., L.. De la Ramé: *Chapman*, 1871.] "Folle-Farine is the child of a miller's dauter, whŏ, in her quiet Norman home, had passed for a saint, until the miller's cruelty, and the gloom of her life in a dul atmosphere of superstition, had driven her tŏ run away with a handsŏme gypsy whŏ had visited the neborhood. That she had so run away was knŏn tŏ nŏne, and her disappearançe was currently attributed tŏ sŏme miracle by which she was taken tŏ heaven, and her saintship consummated, until six years afterwards, when her child was brŏt tŏ the miller's house by a kind-hearted gypsy of the tribe tŏ which the seduçer of the now dead maiden belŏnged. 'She was a saint,' the old miller exclaimed, conçerning his dauter; 'she was a saint, and the devil begot in her *that*.' The girl was thus looked upon from the first as a child of the devil, and the dark beauty and the stubborn strength that she inherited from her father, encouraged the ignorant villagers in the belief that she was a witch. That belief was further encouraged by the persistent cruelty of her grandfather, whŏ turned her intŏ an abject slave, and whŏ allowed her tŏ liv in his house ŏnly because she was cheaper than any beast of burden, and because in his brutish way he felt that he was dŏing a duty, as wel as gratifying himself, by thus scourging

the offspring of the devil and the disgraçe of his family. Of course, even in superstitious Normandy, it would be hard tŏ find people so degraded by bigotry, and rendered so inhuman by superstition, as ar this old miller and his nebors. But Ouida dŏes not here attempt tŏ paint life-like characters. Her characters ar embodiments, for the most part, of prejudiçes and passions which stil defaçe the beauty of the world, and render miserable that which might be happy. If the miller is inhuman in his cruelty, so ar the twŏ ŏther men whŏ ar the most prominent in the story. One of them is a rich old sensualist, whŏ lays cunning snares for the ruin of the heroin, hunts her from plaçe tŏ plaçe, and tries her with bribe after bribe, until, tho his ends ar gained, he ŏnly succeeds in making of her a martyr and saint indeed. The ŏther is a selfish devotee of art, so wedded tŏ his craft that, while he açcepts sŏme of Folle-Farine's slavish homage, he spurns the lŏve which she offers him, and thinking that he oes her nŏthing, is twiçe an ignorant debtor tŏ her for his life, and for the fame which he values more than life. [Compare No. 725.] The miller, the sensualist, and the painter differ in kind, but alike illustrate the cruelty of selfishness, the vileness of human greed, the worthlessness of that lust of power which finds favor with men." [Exam. **2034 m**

It is very wel written, with quiet force, and a tact which is beyond praise. The various făses of Paris life introduced ar faithfully enuf but not too realistically painted. Perhaps the most attractiv characters ar the invalid embroiderer, Miette, and the artist's stone-cutter friend, Pierre. But nŏne of the ŏthers is wholly bad, and even the hardened Miriam is allowed the grace of a death-bed repentance." [Critic. **2035**

FOREST HOUSE (The) & CATHERINE'S LOVERS [by ÉMILE ERCKMANN & P: ALEX. CHATRIAN (†, 1890.) : N.-Y., 1870.] "opens like a regular story of rustic lŏve, in, say, the second manner of G : Sand. You ar just looking out for the good old traditional dénoûment, when lo! you find yourself plunged intŏ a thrilling mediæval legend of crime and retribution, skilfully linked tŏ the present day by a slender thread of the supernatural . . . On the ŏther hand, in sŏme of the smaller sketches, the description predominates, or rather thêy ar all description: thêre is no plot worth the name. *Catherine's Lovers*, for example, so far as the story is concerned, mīt hav been written by Arthur or Titcomb. Thêre is a village hêiress and a poor schoolmaster. He is ashamed tŏ profess his lŏve, and she forces him tŏ confess it; and his rich rivals, whŏ hoped tŏ mortify and ruin him, ar awfully sold. Voila tout! The whole attraction of the sketch is in the delineations of village life and scenery." [C: A. Bristed. **2036**

FORESTERS (The) by ALEX. [DAVY] DUMAS : *Appleton*, 1854. **2037**

FORGET-ME-NOTS [by JULIA KAVANAGH : *Bentley*, 1878.] "contains a number of short sketches of life in a norman village, and ar connected solely by community of place. The great bulk relate tŏ the fortunes of various inhabitants of "Manneville," and all ar gracefully told." [Athenæum. **2038**

FORTUNES OF THE ROUGONS, by É. ZOLA : Chicago, *Laird*, 1891. **2039**

FOUR GOLDPIECES (The), by —— GOURAUD : *Low*, 1875. **2040**

FRENCH COUNTRY FAMILY (A). [by HENRIETTE (GUIZOT) DE WITT : *Harper*, 1868.] "Apart from the pleasure which old and young must derive from this story, it is useful in correcting sŏme erroneous impressions concerning french family life which many persons may hav imbibed from reading novels; and altho no absolute teaching is aimed at, few persons wil peruse this little book without receiving from it instruction as wel as delīt. The atmosfere of La Vacherie is wholesŏme, the life thêre picturesque; the children ar affectionate, dutiful, intelligent, but never priggish; filial lŏve and parental devotion contribute tŏ form a family picture." [Round Table. **2041**

FRENCH EGGS IN AN ENGLISH BASKET by É. SOUVESTRE, London, 1871. **2042**

FRENCH HEIRESS IN HER OWN CHATEAU (A) [by ELEANOR C PRICE : *Low*, 1878.] "takes us tŏ the pleasant towns and châteaux of Anjou, and among a society which, tho its bugbear is the Red Republic, has no notion of looking tŏ a pinchbeck Cæsar for its salvation. Indeed, these courteous and kindly marquises and marchionesses seem. on the whole, very wel content with the existing state of things. and when they marry ar not abŏve being escorted tŏ

FORESTERS (The). [by ALEX. DU-
MAS (1803-70) : *Appleton*, 1854.] "Turning his bac upon camps and courts, the
scene of his former triumphs, the author
here givs us u charming reminisçençe of
Villers Coterêts, his nativ village, und
relates a simple tale founded upon occur-
rençes which ônce happened in the nĉbor-
hood. The thread of the story is slight,
but it is wel managed and full of interest.
The sketches of character introduçed, and
the descriptions of woodland scenery, ar
lifelike, and evidently copied from nature.
Unlike sõme of his more pretentious
works, "The Foresters" seems the product of an unhacnied pen. Altõgether it
is a delightful episode of country life,
pure and healthful in its teachings, and
reminding us rather of that beautiful
pastoral, *Fadette* [No. 2108] and sõme of
the tales of Èmile Souvestre, than of any
previous production of this inexhaustible
writer." [Albion. **2037**

FRANCIS THE WAIF [by "GEORGE SAND," i. e., Amantine Lucile Aurore (Dupin) Dudevant (†, 1876) · *Routledge*, 1889, 304 p.] "is a story of peasant life. ... A 'champi' is a child abandoned in the fields ... The author introduçes the hero, at the tender age of 6, boarded by the parish with an old woman whŏ dwels in a hovel. The pretty young wife of the miller takes compassion on the child, and finds means tŏ supply him, unknŏn tŏ her brutal husband, with food and raiment. He groes intŏ a cŏmely lad, gentle, intelligent, and right-heârted, and devotedly attached tŏ Madeleine. He enters the serviçe of the miller given up tŏ the fasçinations of a wido, whŏ trieś tŏ seduçe the handsŏme Champi, and, failing of sucçess, instils jealousy intŏ the ear of the miller, whŏ drives François from his house. The young man finds occupation in a distant village, and returns tŏ the mil of Cornouer ŏnly when its master is dead and Madeleine il, tŏ rescue his benefactress from grasping creditors, by means of a sum of mŏney his unknŏn father has sent tŏ him. George Sand makes every woman fall in lŏve with the Champi; but he repulses all save ŏne, and that ŏne never dreams of lŏving him ŏtherwise than as a mŏther. At last ŏne of the fair ŏnes whŏ would fain hav gained his heârt, generously reveals tŏ him, what he himself has difficulty in believing, that he is in lŏve with Madeleine, and, further, compassionating his timidity, undertakes tŏ brêak the içe tŏ the pretty wido. It requires a talent like that of George Sand tŏ giv an air of probability tŏ all this. Thêre ar at most but a dozen years' difference between Madeleine and the Champi, but the reader has been so much accustomed tŏ look upón them in the light of mŏther and sŏn, that he is sŏmewhat startled on finding the boy of 19 enamored of the woman of 30. The lŏve-passages, however, ar managed with the author's usual skil. As a picture of peasant life, the book yields internal evidence of fidelity." [Blackwood's Magazine. **2040 k** their homes by the local National Gard. Nay, more; thêy ar willing tŏ admit that thêir recent ancestors wer not wholly free from blame in thêir relations with thêir inferiors, even tho the penalty thêy paid may hav been sŏmewhat too severe. As the chief personages in the story ar twŏ young Englishmen, it is needless tŏ say that it turns mainly on the "peculiar institution" of french society in regard tŏ marriage arrangements. Of course the twŏ english brothers, of whŏm ŏne is charming but selfish, the other less attractiv, but more genuin, fall in lŏve with french girls, and, of course, each succeeds as he deservs." [Athenæum. **2043**

FRENCH PICTURES IN ENGLISH CHALK. [by EUSTACE CLARE GRENVILLE MURRAY: *Smith*, 1876.] "Many of ôur readers wil remember these brilliant sketches as thêy appeared in the Cornhill Magazine. Martin Boulet, 'Our ruf, red Candidate,' whŏ so admirably out-manœuvres archbishop, prefect, and the rest of the authorities, is quite deserving of a permanent place among portraits of french personages. So is the young democrat, Camille Lange, and his father, Demosthenes Lange. Of course, our author is a little cynical, witness the end of 'Our Secret Society,' whêre fôur conspirators, whŏ ar bent on revolutionising France, not tŏ say the world, appear in a way which shŏs them tŏ be very fair 'friends of order.' 'L'Ambulance Tricochet,' however, is a capital story, free from this characteristic. Altŏgether, 'French Pictures' is a book worth reading, or even reading again." [Spectator. **2044**

FRIEND (A). ["L'Aimée") by "HENRI GRÉVILLE": i. e., Alice M ..

Céleste (Fleury) Durand: *Peterson*, 1878.] "The locale and the personages ar french, and all the conditions of french life amongst rising professors, sober old 'rentiers,' and aspiring officials ar very wel described by a person whŏ knŏs all about them." [Nation. **2045**

FRIEND FRITZ. [by ÉMILE ERCKMANN & P: ALEX. CHATRIAN (†, 1890) : *Scribner*, 1889.] "Thêre is sŏmething delītfully human, drŏll, and kindly in it, from the first page tŏ the last. Kobus' predestind but unconscious laps from the determind bachelorhood of a bon-vivant, easy-going and sweet-tempered, fond of good eating, good drinking, and shuffling about in old clothes, proud of his unhampered liberty and serene in the untempted security on which it rests, could hardly hav been described with greater simplicity and charm. True, thêre is nothing which can be called elevating about the story. But granting that the authors look at life like thŏro Sadducees, stil they not only hav no quarrel with the moralities, grêat or small, but they ar plumply and unmistakably enlisted on the side of the natural virtues and social decencies. And surely they have seldom been surpassed as delineators of those common, humble, and kindly aspects of elsatian village life with which they had a natural sympathy." [Catholic World. **2046**

FROMONT THE YOUNGER AND RISLER THE ELDER. [by ALPHONSE DAUDET: *Vizettelly*, 1880.] "Sidonie is the personification of cold, calculating worldliness; Désirée is the poor, patient, working-girl; Claire, the sweetest wife and mother in the world.—and both Désirée and Claire ar embodiments of self-devotion. Between the two stands Sidonie, working mischief to both and death to one. Sidonie in childhood livs under the same roof with Désirée; in her married life she is thrön constantly with Claire. From Désirée she steals her löver; from Claire, her husband. She is faithless in turn to both men, as she has been from the first to her husband; and cruel as she is to the women whö ar nearest to her, the men whö löve her suffer even more at her hands. The scene is laid in the middle-class life of Paris. Thêre is not a titled personage in the book; and thêre is a straitforward simplicity, and an absence of pretence and glamor, about the way in which the story is told, which is very striking." [Boston "Literary World." **2047**

——. SAME, ("Partners").

——. SAME, ("Sidonie"), *Estes*, 1877.

FUGITIVES (THE) [with "The Duke's Daughter" by MA. OLIPHANT (WILSON) OLIPHANT: London, 1890.] "is popular because it treats of and appeals to familiar emotions. The midnīt flīt of the dishonest financier from his luxurious english home with his two dauters—the young woman and the little child, neither of whöm can even guess at the meaning of the mysterious journey—provides a striking opening for a story the continuation and close of which amply fulfil the promise of these early pages. The life of the little french village of Latour, which the fugitivs make their final resting place, and in which poor Mr. Goulbourn finds not only his grave but the opportunity for the öne kind deed which makes that grave sacred to Blanchette and her husband, is portrayed with intimate knoledge and fine sympathy; and tho Mrs.

Oliphant has done more ambitious work than this story of the ordeal of Helen Goulborn, she has never excelled its quiet, tender pathos." [Spectator. **2048**

GABRIELLE ["La Maison de Maurège") by "HENRI GRÉVILLE", i. e., A. M. (F.) Durand: *Peterson*. 1878.] "is refined and charming." [Atlantic. **2049**

GALLANT LORDS OF BOIS DORÉ, by "G: SAND," = No. 711.

GAMBARA, by BALZAC, in *Louis Lambert*. **2050**

GAUDISSART II., = *ILLUSTRIOUS GAUDISSART*.

GÉRARD'S MARRIAGE [by ANDRÉ THEURIET: *Appleton*, 1877.] "is öne of those stories to which the term idyl may be wel applied. It is provincial in its locality, and its every page is pervaded by the sweetest of rural influences. Its heroin lifts her lövely head like a beautiful flower, and seems to bear about her the charm and the perfume of a rose just not fully blön. Gerard, whö is the son of an old chevalier of the 'petite noblesse,' is destined by his father to marry the not unattractiv dauter of a similar family; but he having seen Helen, falls straitway in löve with her ... All the personages in this most charming story ar full of character and vitality ... They all ar drawn with a pencil which seems to carry life and līt in its very touch. Not less remarkable is the use of the rural scenery among which the incidents of the story take place. Descriptions of scenery ar generally very tedious, and fail entirely to produce the picture which the writer designs. But in these not only dões the scene cöme vividly before the mind's eye, but the moral and fysical incidents blend with and illustrate each other, so that the result is a charming whole. We hav used the word charming more than ŏnce in this notice; wc let it stand; it is only by such tautology that the effect of 'Gérard's Marriage' can be expressed." [Galaxy.]— " 'Le Mariage de Gérard' is a charming tale, charmingly told, with a touch of quiet, gentlemanly humor, and possessing a pathos that has nothing sentimental about it." [Athenæum. **2051**

——, SAME ("Marriage of Gerard"), Chicago, *Laird*, 1891. **2052**

GERFAUT, ☞ (A) *FATAL PASSION*.

GERMAINE [by EDMOND [FR. VALENTIN] ABOUT: Boston, *Tilton*, 1859.] contains "fair delineations of character and faithful descriptions, and the usual number of dramatic situations. The heroin is a young girl of a noble but impoverished family, whŏ is sloly wasting away with consumption, her disease being aggravated by poverty. She becŏmes the wife of a rich spanish nobleman, throu an intrigue of a mistress [herself married], by whŏm he had a child, which child the father sŏt tŏ legitimise. This is ŏne of the conditions of the marriage, that the child should be accepted too. The mistress trusts tŏ the death of Germaine tŏ recover her lŏver, and, in the event of the death of her husband, for an opportunity tŏ marry him. Germaine, however, is restored tŏ health, and the plotting mistress is foiled." [Crayon. **2053**

——, SAME. *Munro*, 1882.

——, SAME, ("A Round of Wrong"), London, 1861.

GERMINIE LACERTEUX. by E. & J. (†. 1870.) DE GONCOURT: [Paris, 1865.] *Vizetelly*, 1887; Chicago, *Laird*.

1891, 222 pp.; N.-Y., *Street*, 1891. **2054**

GEROLSTEIN (sequel to "Mysteries of Paris") by EUGENE SUE: *Harper*, 1843. **2055**

GIRL WITH THREE PETTICOATS. by [C:] PAUL DE KOCK, London, 1839, ☞ No. 1952.

GODSON OF A MARQUIS (The). [by ANDRÉ THEURIET: *Appleton*, 1878.] "No novel in this series yet has pleased us more than 'Gérard's Marriage' [No. 2051] and in exquisit style and in all qualities of interest this is the equal of that. The godson was the marquis' illegitimate son, whŏse ignoble birth stood in the way of his marriage tŏ a lŏvely girl. Over this hindrance the unfortunate godson almost stumbled intŏ an intrigue with a married woman, but happily was saved from it; the repentant marriage of his father and mother finally bringing his lŏve troubles tŏ an acceptable solution. This, as will be seen, is a frenchy plot, but the wondrous delicacy and refinement of Theuriet relieve it of all coarseness. Thêre ar passages in it of grêat beauty, and the characterization is masterful and yet easy." [Boston "Lit. World." **2056**

GOLDEN MEDIOCRITY, by E. (G.) HAMERTON, = No. 461.

GOLDSMITH'S WIFE (The), by REYBAUD, = No. 718.

GOOD FELLOW (A). [by [C:] PAUL DE KOCK: Phil'a, *Carey*, 1838.] Kock "never soars intŏ the regions of fashion tŏ dazzle and regale his readers with descriptiv luxury, or the follies and eccentricities of the world on stilts. He seems quite unconscious of the existence of conventional personages, or that any degree of interest can be attached tŏ any other class, but that which he has specially selected tŏ furnish subjects for his pencil. Paul walks along the crowded thorofares of life, jostling and jostled, gleaning materials in every fresh contact with his fello-men for his amusing combinations—treasuring the nice traits and evanescent distinctions which individualize character, and transferring them tŏ paper with a fidelity which leaves nothing tŏ be desired, and a rapidity of execution which is truly surprising. His last work "Un bon Enfant," is the history of what is called among us. *A Good Fellow.* Charles Darville, the personification of this character, is the sŏn of a wholesale silk mercer, whŏ died, leaving his wido and son in excellent circumstances. Charles is a most dutiful and sober youth up tŏ the period when ôur history begins; when, with the best disposition in the world. he is led intŏ the commission of innumerable follies and absurdities, whioh reduce him tŏ distress." [Albion. **2057**

GRANDE BRETÈCHE (THE) *Eccentric Novels.*

GUENN, by HOWARD, = No. 725.

HAND AND GLOVE [by AMELIA BLANDFORD EDWARDS: London, Brown, 1858.] "is a slĭt, but very readable and interesting story—not sensible, indeed, but romantic and easy tŏ read. Thêre has been no great expenditure of talent or industry upon it, but thêre ar sŏme pleasant, life-like descriptions of french country-life." [Athenæum. **2058**

HANDSOME LAWRENCE, by "G: SAND." Boston, 1871, is sequel to *A ROLLING STONE.* **2059**

HAPPY FIND (A) [by — ( ) GAGNEBIN: *Crowell,* 1889.] "is a simple domestic tale, pure and wholesŏme, and full of unaffected kindliness. The 'happy find' is a foundling

whŏ grŏs intŏ a creature of so sweet and helpful a kind that she becŏmes a blessing tŏ all about her. Of course, in the end, she 'cŏmes tŏ her ŏn'." [American. **2060**

HAUNTED MARSH, 1851, Haunted Pool. 1890.. = *DEVIL'S POOL.*

HEADSMEN OF FRANCE (The) = *THE SURGEON'S STORY.*

HECTOR. [by FLORA L. SHAW: *Roberts,* 1881.] "It is a rare pleasure tŏ find such a book as 'Hector,' a little tale of country life. It tels of the lŏve and the sorro of grŏn people, but from the child's point of vue, and with such exquisit skil as tŏ make it ŏne of the most beautiful of children's books. It is a pure idyl, sweet and fresh as the songs of the birds which carol throu its pages." [Nation.]— , also. No. 465. **2061**

HÉLÈNE by HENRIETTE E. F. (A.) REYBAUD, London, 1849. **2062**

HENRIETTE, or a Corsican Mother, by FR. COPPÉE: *Worthington,* 1890. **2063**

HEPTAMERON (THE) = No. 703.

HESTER [by BEATRICE MAY BUTT: *Appleton,* 1880.] "is ŏne of the happiest little sketches of the french war, in the chronicle of a faithful lŏve crossed and a burden patiently borne. The style has vivacity and charm." [Penn Monthly. **2064**

HIDDEN MASTERPIECE (The), by BALZAC, in *The Duchess* [No. 2020.

HISTORY OF THE GREATNESS AND DECLINE OF CÉSAR BIROTTEAU. [by HONORÉ "DE" BALZAC: transl. by Wight & Goodrich. N.-Y., *Rudd,* 1860.] "We ar very glad tŏ see this beginning of a translation of Balzac. or de Balzac, as he chose tŏ christen himself. Without intending an exact parallel, he mĭt be called the Fielding of french literature,—intensely masculin, an artist whŏ works outward from an informing idea. ą satirist whŏse humor wil not let him despise human nature even while he exposes its weaknesses. The story of César Birotteau is wel-chosen as an usher tŏ the rest, for it is eminently characteristic, tho it dōes not sho the hīer imaginativ qualities of the author. It is ōne of the severest tests of genius tŏ draw an ordinary character so humanly that we learn tŏ lōve and respect it in spite of a thōro familiarity with its faults and absurdities. In this respect Balzac's 'Birotteau' is a masterpîece. The translation seems a very easy, spirited, and knōing ōne. The translators hav overcōme the difficulties of slang with grêat skil, rendering by equivalent vulgarisms which giv the spirit whêre the letter would be unintelligible." [Atlantic.]—"This narrativ of a bourgeois perfumer whŏ adhered tŏ the royalist cause, 60 years ago, gathered sōme money, was decorated, began tŏ speculate, grew extravagant, went up like the wel-knōn rocket and came down like its stie,—this is a partienlarly clean story and study of life. The family of Birotteau is a charming group. His faithful, sensible wife, and gentle, pure-minded dauter ar so different from the female characters in 'Père Goriot' that we can hardly understand why, since thêy must hav inhabited Paris at nearly the same time with the characters in "Père Goriot" we got in that work not a single glimpse of them, and wer forced tŏ conclude thêre wer no such species. But poor Birotteau himself is the best figure, because he ends honorably and cleanly. His death, after his recovery from insolvency and his reinstatement in credit, is a pathetic but true stroke of the novelist's art. And what is notable about it is that Balzac, in relating it, shōs his appreciation of the moral dignity of Birotteau's recovery and exit; he dōes not handle these incidents coarsely or cynically, but as sympathetically as ōne could ask. So, too, he sketches the characters of Popinot and Pillerault with a firm but gentle hand, and makes them both win ōur esteem. On the whole it is a pleasing study, and is made the more attractiv by its dashes of cheerful humor." [American.]—"It is a tale of domestic life in Paris, not a tale beginning with an intrigue, filled with passion, and ending in tragedy, as many suppose all Parisian life tŏ be; but ōne of homely virtues, of every-day suffering and sorro, of happiness and lōve, with sōmething of the social vice and treachery which belongs tŏ all sŏciety ... It is on this land speculation that the story turns. Of cōurse it failed; failed not because the calculation was not a good ōne, but because the guileless César was cheated by twŏ of his associates, ōne of whŏm ran away with all the ready mōney, while an ex-clerk of the perfumer whŏm he had dismissed for theft compelled the payment of the notes when thêre wer no funds. All this, however, is evolved in due season. In the meantime the grand ball is given, for Mrs. Birotteau, finding contention useless, resigns herself tŏ the inevitable. The cōurse of events is full of interest and incident. Ruin cōmes, but salvation cōmes also, ruin throu weakness and knavery, and salvation throu strength and self-denial. The close, perhaps, is a little too dramatic, as in life the happiness of success is seldom fatal." [Albion.] **2065**

——, SAME (transl. by J: H. Simpson), London, 1860.

——, SAME (César Birotteau), Boston, *Roberts*, 1886; N.-Y., *Bonner*, 1891.

HOPE DEFERRED. [by ELIZA F.. POLLARD: *Hurst*, 1872.] "The patient attitude of a lŏving woman, whŏ waits during long years for an affection which awakes too late, and is doomed tŏ find that when hope seems no longer possible, the passion which she has stifled so bravely is at length reciprocated, is a subject which, in any hands, must be difficult tŏ treat without profanation. That Miss Pollard, in her character of Jeanne, should hav succeeded so wel—placing before us a type of ardent affection without grossness,—trusting simplicity without weakness or insipidity,— shŏs that she possesses appreciativ insît and womanly delicacy of touch. We hav read few stories which hav left so pleasing an impression . . . The scene is laid in France, and the author writes with knoledge." [Athenæum. **2066**

HOTEL DU PETIT ST.-JEAN (The) [by C.. L.. HAWKINS DEMPSTER: *Smith*, 1869.] "is far superior. Even if we leave its main feature out of sît, we find in it much which throes lît on provincial society. A criminal trial, the election of a deputy, a sermon pregnant with the dramatic expression of french preachers, and ŏther scenes of equal force, giv a zest tŏ the story, and keep us from brooding altŏgether on the self-sacrifice of the heroin and the meanness of the man whŏm she had first chosen . . . We commend 'The Hôtel du Petit St.-Jean' as a careful study of manners, with a central figure of even grêater interest." [Athenæum. **2067**

HOUSE DIVIDED AGAINST ITSELF [Riviera] = No. 467.

HOUSE OF PENARVAN, by SANDEAU. = No. 742.

HOUSE OF THE TWO BARBELS (The) [by ANDRÉ THEURIET: *Appleton*, 1879.] "is full of touches revealing domestic life in a southern town. Twŏ bachelors of middle age liv with thêir ânt, an old maid, simple-minded, unsofisticated, eccentric creatures all; and ar in consternation when thêy learn that thêir privacy is tŏ be intruded upon, and thêir quiet disturbed, by 2 relativs from Paris, a lady and her dauter. If the 3 domestic recluses ar perplexed and in dismay at the advent of the 2 ladies of glittering plumage from the capital, the Parisiennes ar equally disturbed by thêir provincial surroundings . . . The current fiction of France bêars unmistakable testimony tŏ the place home holds in the affection of the french people. Sŏme of the most delîtful of domestic pictures hav in times past been furnished by french writers; but recent fiction seems tŏ us tŏ paint these scênes with more grace and artistic skil, tŏ delineate domestic life more distinctly on its artistic rather than on its moral side. Sŏme of the writers of the day ar admirable 'genre' painters: thêy delît in giving tŏ the most homely and simple incidents exquisit effects of cŏlor and contrast, in turning tŏ dramatic account groupings and details which writers of the past disdained tŏ heed. . . . Theuriet's stories ar full of these delîtful pictures, these domestic bits of cŏlor." [Appleton's Journal. **2068**

HUNTING THE ROMANTIC, or the Adventures of a Novel-Reader. [by [LEONARD SYLVAIN] JULES SANDEAU: N.-Y., *Stringer*, 1852.]

Here "unbridled youth is gently and adroitly led in the path of virtue by guides as delītful as thêy ar irreproachable." [Saturday Rev. **2069** ICELAND FISHERMAN (An). [by "PIERRE LOTI," i. e. Julian Viaud: N.-Y., *Gottsberger.* 1888; Chicago, *McClurg.* 1890.] "The scene is not laid in Iceland but in Brétagne, and his 'Pécheur d'Island' is ōne of those whŏ bear that name because they ar engaged in the cod-fishery off the coast of Iceland, and rarely see France in summer time. The story is a sorroful and yet not a glóomy ōne. It is lit by so much true and natural affection, and so full of natural beauty, that the tragic death of the twŏ young fishermen,—ōne sacrificed tŏ french ambition, the ōther never returning from the fishing expedition on which he starts six days after his wedding,— dōes not bring tŏ the rèader a sense of unrelîeved sadness. The central interest of the story is the lōve of the proud and sensitiv Yann for a girl his superior in wealth and social position. For twŏ years after thêir discōvery of thêir mutual affection, he is kept from avowing it by his feeling that he is not the man tŏ marry a fine lady. But her father's death as a bankrupt remōves the obstacle, and the story of thêir brief courtship, merry wedding, and early and final separation is wel told. Even tho the book dōes not comply with the requirement which Mr. Darwin would hav enacted by Act of Parliament, that all novels should end pleasantly, yet it may be read with pleasure by those who sympathize with his wish." [American.]— "The second translation of Loti's 'Iceland Fisherman,' the finished flower of his literary work, is better than the first. The translator has reproduced the marked onomatopoetic quality of Loti's language with singular fidelity and skil." [Nation. **2070**

IDLE TIME TALES, by Fᴀ· COPPÉE: Chicago, *Rand.* 1891. **2071**

ILLUSTRIOUS GAUDISSART (The), by BALZAC, in Nos. 1993 and 2020. **2072**

IMMORTAL (The). [by ALPHONSE DAUDET: Chicago, *Rand*, N.-Y., *Alden,* 1888.] "What is stil more remarkable than the correct and sparkling rendition of the original, is the fact that the illustrations really illustrate the text. It is a skit at the 'Académie' and the characters ar lītly disguised portraits from life. It is a powerful book, but, like most of Daudet's, it is not cheerful reading. Even 'Le Petit Chose' was not that, delītfully amusing as it is in parts. Daudet dōes not gloat over vice; we hav more than a suspicion that he cordially detests it. Nevertheless, the atmosfere of his books, even of this ōne, which is comparativly free, is, if not steeped in corruption, at least redly suffused with it. What a master of pathos he is! With what līt, unerring strokes he paints the dreadful scene in which Astier-Réhu's wife unvêils herself tŏ him after the cold intimacy of 35 years, strips of the last shreds of vanity and self-respect, and drives him tŏ suicide, that inevitable refuge for Daudet's disappointed heroes!" [Catholic World. **2073**

——, SAME ("One of the Forty"). *Sonnenschein.* 1889.

IN THE CAMARGUE [by EMILY BOWLES: London. 1873, *Loring,* 1875.] is "a story of Southern France. As a picture of a strange and sōmewhat fascinating·life it is quite remarkable, its dramatic interest being inferior tŏ the charms of its brīt and realistic sketches of character and society." [Boston "Literary World." **2074**

IN THE SPRING OF MY LIFE [by OLGA (CANTACOUZENE) ALTIERI: *Tinsley*, 1878.] "is a charming little romance which even an indifferent translation has not been able tŏ spoil. It is, indeed, only a variation on a wel-worn theme—"the course of true lŏve never did run smooth,"—but it is treated so delicately and simply, and is so free from vulgarity and bold commonplace, that it interests the reader from beginning tŏ end. No doubt thêre ar improbabilities in the story, and exaggerations of sentiment and manner; but these blemishes ar not of a sicly kind." [Athen. **2075**

INDIANA. by "G: SAND," = No. 753.

INTERIOR OF A DILIGENCE (The), by É. SOUVESTRE, in *Southern Lit. Messenger*, Nov., 1854. **2076**

IRENE'S DOWER, by C: DESLEYS, *Remington*, 1878. **2077**

IRONMASTER (The). [by G: OHNET: *Vizetelly*, 1884; *Rand*, 1888.] "Tŏ what is the success of 'The Ironmaster' tŏ be attributed? In the first place, tŏ the fact that Mr. Ohnet is manifestly a consummate playwrīt. The convent-school jealousy between Claire de Beaulieu and Athénais Moulinet, seems but a poor basis for a good story. Yet Mr. Ohnet's superstructure is undoubtedly ingenious and compact, and you never quite forget this early girlish rivalry in the duel between the wife of the ironmaster and the wife of the heârtless lŏver whŏ has deserted her, tŏ the all but tragic close of which the plot leads. The author skilfully transforms Claire and Athénais intŏ impersonations of moral lŏveliness and unlŏveliness in

woman . . . Philippe Derblay, the ironmaster, is a character of a kind seldom met in french fiction, a character of the teutonic rather than the gallic type. He is courageous, sagacious, disinterested, merciful, a worshipper of duty . . . He declines tŏ forgiv Claire long after he must hav seen that her old indifference tŏ him had been transformed intŏ an overmastering passion . . . The reader wil be grateful, not only for the story, but for sŏme of the characters. In particular, the mŏther and brŏther of Claire, a sprītly baroness and her good-natured scientific husband, and a notary of the old school, ar so good, that we can only hope that they ar not too good tŏ be out of place in a representation of French life at the present time." [Spectator. **2078**

——, SAME ("Claire"), N.-Y., N. L. *Munro*, 1884; *Lovell*, 1888.

——, SAME ("Lady Claire"); *G: Munro*, 1884.

ISHMAEL, by BRADDON, [1851-70] No. 755.

ISLE OF THE DEAD = *LAZARETTO-KEEPER*.

JACK [by ALPHONSE DAUDET: *Estes*, 1877, *Routledge*, 1889.] "is a bad book in its materials and atmosfere and a good book in its purpos and method. In its literary execution it is exceedingly fine . . . The characters here set before us ar, for the most part, a loose set. Jack, poor child, and the lŏvely Cécile, alone stand in the līt. In the Moronval Academy we hav a palpable reproduction of Dŏtheboys' Hall. The style throuŏut is bīly artistic, the posturings ar dramatic and absorbing, and the entire work that of a master, but the end is sad, painfully so." [Boston "Lit. World." **2079**

JACQUES. [by "G: SAND," i. e., Amantine Lucile Aurore (Dupin) Dudevant: *Harper*, 1847, 2 v.] "The story is told in the shape of correspondence; and thus, as incidents develop themselvs, we hav a running commentary supplied in the most piquant and artistic manner . . . The long and short of it is, that because Fernande cannot fathom her husband. she laments herself as a 'femme incomprise'; so she, too, goes on the search for sympathy. The slope she treads is so gentle at first as tŏ be almost imperceptible. She concerns herself about the sorrŏs of an unhappy lŏver, and offers herself as intermediary with the object of his affections. The perilous intimacy, sweetened by her tears and smiles, seduces him 'intŏ transferring his lŏve; and that power of sympathy which exercises an irresistible sway over its predestind subjects betrays her intŏ reciprocating his passion. Yet she never lŏses her regard for her husband—a regard which is scarcely tŏ be distinguished from her early lŏve. Jacques, who is preternaturally shrewd and clear-sīted, anticipates the cŏurse of her unlawful passion; and his fancies pass intŏ firm beliefs a full stage or so in advance of the reality. Finally, he dŏes what was possibly the best thing in the peculiar circumstances, and remŏves himself out of the way by a suicide which he adroitly disguises as an accident. The charitable consideration that has gŏverned his conduct is "No human being can command lŏve, and no ŏne is tŏ be blamed either for feeling it or for lŏsing it. What degrades a woman is falsehood.' " [Blackwood's. 2080

JAMBE D'ARGENT & M. JACQUES. by É. SOUVESTRE, in *Southern*

Lit. Messenger, aug.-sept.. 1855. 2081

JEAN TETEROL'S IDEA [by V: CHERBULIEZ: *Appleton*, 1879.] "is written with that precision, polish, grace and vivacity which hav always characterised Cherbuliez' work; and it has the additional advantages of a story interesting in itself and of sharply contrasted and piquant characters. Jean Têterol is an illiterate laborer whŏ has raised himself tŏ the position of a millionaire, and whŏ exhibits the egotism of a self-made man in its most vulgar and aggressiv form." [Appleton's.]—"Jean goes off, and finally cŏmes tŏ the folioing decision: he wil go away, and becŏme rich,— richer than this Baron de Saligneux, whŏ permits himself the pleasure of kicking. Then he wil cŏme bac tŏ the village, and hav his revenge. And —people wil see! That is the whole book. He dŏes it, and people dŏ see! He amasses a large fortune, and returns tŏ his nativ hamlet. Unfortunately the old baron is dead, but he buys all the land sold by his sŏn, the prodigal young baron, builds a grêat white house which cuts off his vue, and finally manages tŏ get possession of all the claims against him, and present them in a lump. The baron, a spendthrift man of the world, is at his wits' end; having tried all his methods of procuring mŏney in vain, he goes tŏ see the ex-gardener in his new mansion, preserving, however, throuŏut the intervue his air of the ancien régime. The ex-gardener meets him with an ultimatum: your dauter, aristocrat tŏ the tips of her fingers, shal marry my son. *Voila!* The twŏ fathers at last arrange it. Lionel, meanwhile. has had an excellent education, and has been bred among gentlemen. He falls in lŏve with Claire honestly; but when he discōvers that she is, as it wer, being sold tŏ pay her father's debts, he têars the paper which binds the baron before his father's astonished eyes, and, barely escaping being strangled by him, flees tŏ Paris, whêre he begins tŏ earn his living as a writer (how easily thêy dŏ that in books). Of course, the moment Claire (whŏ has been very scornful all along) finds him really gône, she turns around and now begins tŏ lōve him. An uncle fortunately dies and leaves her his estate, so that the throttling money obligation is ended. And then the twŏ young people come tŏgether again, and the idea is carried out." [Atlantic. **2082**

——, SAME ("The Wish of his Life") London, 1879.

JEANNE LARAGUAY [by EUGÉNIE (GINDRIEZ) HAMERTON: *Chapman*, 1864.] "exhibits so much feminin prettiness and piquancy that we ar constrained tŏ deal tenderly with it, notwithstanding a want of orignality which in ône place almost lays the author open tŏ a charge of plagiarism. Jeanne is the only child of a Parisian banker, whŏ in early life was guilty of forgery. In spite of the unwhōlesome influences surrounding her frivolous life, Jeanne is as good and clever as she is beautiful and belōved. She has been taken from her convent and introduced intŏ a brilliant, wéalthy, pleasure-seeking set . . . Ere he has declared his devotion, Jeanne has fallen deeply in lōve with her tutor. Thus the case stands when Sir Henry Luton appears on the scene. Sir Henry is already married tŏ a woman of whōse existence society is ignorant; but he is the ône person whŏ possesses the proofs of Mr. Lara-

quay's early error. He insists on making Jeanne his wife; and Jeanne, whŏ has learnt the awful secret of her house, consents tŏ marry the man whŏm she hates, and discard the man whŏm she lōves, in order that she may shîeld her father from ignominious punishment. The wedding is on the point of celebration, when the artist prŏves Sir Henry tŏ be a bigamist in intention, and compels him tŏ relinquish his claim tŏ Jeanne's hand, and also tŏ deliver the documentary evidence of Laraquay's forgery. Thus the villain is defeated; the virtuous forger is freed from dread of exposure; and the lōvers begin the world as man and wife.' [Ath. **2083**

JET [Riviera] = No. 475.

JOAN WENTWORTH [by K., S. MACQUOID: *Harper*, 1886.] "is a pleasant story of school-life and Breton manners." [Catholic World. **2084**

JOSEPH NOIREL'S REVENGE. [by V: CHERBULIEZ: N.-Y., *Holt*, 1873.] "Nowhêre has Cherbuliez drawn a character so fascinating as 'Marguerite." The way in which she is represented, first as a young girl at home, as charming and lōvely as possible, then married and in trouble, but grōing in fascination as in character with every affliction, retaining in spite of all her suffering her wōnderful innocence and purity, warrents us in declaring that Cherbuliez has shōn here a power which, previously, it was in ōne's power only tŏ predict. Tŏ draw a charming woman is no lît task; Cherbuliez has dōne it not only with the cleverness with which he gave us Didier's self-analysis and Ladislas Bolski's fiery passion—a quality in which, by the way, he stands almost alone—but with a pathos and sympathy far superior tŏ any such

cheap gift as cleverness. While Marguerite stands first in merit, Joseph is
not tŏ be forgotten; indeed, thêre is
no weakness shōn in the treatment of
any of the characters. The plot is
ōne of the sort in which Cherbuliez
delīts, it being complex and not too
easily unriddled, but yet ōne not too
heavy for its author—he is never wêd
down by its demands, it seems tŏ
trouble him as little as the utterance
of ōne of his numerous witticisms.
Sŏme of the descriptions, as, for example, that of the old castle, and the
meeting between Joseph and Marguerite in the sno, ar models of beauty.
One of the peculiarities of Cherbuliez'
novels is evident in this, thêir joyousness in spite of a tragic end. This
quality seems tŏ us ōne of the grêatest
an author can hav: tŏ give us sadness
but yet, without cheap consolation,
tŏ leave in ôur minds the impression
that thêre is sŏmething which no sadness can touch—a state of mind which
is neither hope nor indifference, but
the certainty of the grandeur of the
world outside of ôur petty misery.
This Cherbuliez has dŏne. If this
praise seems fulsŏme, we hope that
the fault-finders wil read the novel."
[Nation.] Compare No. 768.   **2085**
. JOSEPHINE, or The Beggar of the
Pont*des Arts, by W: HAUFF: Lon-
don, *Clarke*, 1844.   **2086**
——, SAME ("The True Lover's
Fortune"), Boston, *Munroe*, 1843, 91 p;
Shorey, 1869 (in "Emerald," 57 p.)
JOURNEY ROUND MY ROOM
(A) by XAVIER DE MAISTRE: *Long-
man*, 1871; *Chatto*, 1883.   **2087**
JOURNEYMAN JOINER (The) =
No. 1994.
JOYS OF LIFE. by É. ZOLA,
N.-Y., *Tousey*, 1880; Chicago, *Laird*,
1891.   **2088**

JUPITER'S DAUGHTERS. [by
HENRIETTA CAMILLA (JACKSON) JEN-
KIN: *Holt*. 1874.] "Mrs. Jenkin's
pretty stories hav all a charm . . .
Thêy ar written in agreeable english,
which, tŏ hazard a guess, has been
just enuf affected by an intimate acquaintance with french tŏ increase the
delicacy of style without rendering it
affected. 'Jupiter's Daughters' is the
story of a french girl whŏ, tŏ please
her parents, marries a Mr. de Subar,
when she is in lŏve with sŏme ōne
else, and regrets it for the remainder
of her life. Of course after her marriage, she falls in with Mr. Vilpont,
but this dŏes not make her any happier. She is a good wife, and nothing
is left for her, after her adventures
during the sîege of Paris. but a life of
duty . . . The descriptions of life in
St. Gloi, a little provincial town, ar
often very attractiv." [Nation. **2089**
KING APÉPI. [by V: CHERBU-
LIEZ: N.-Y., *J: Delay*, 1889.] "Entertainment, pure and simple, is what
Cherbuliez here provides for his readers, and tho it is ōnly a novelette,
and of very slīt pretensions, it is nevertheless thŏroly characteristic. It
may be briefly described as the
Fŏtheringay episode in 'Pendennis'
dŏne intŏ french. It is, of cōurse,
admirable in point of workmanship,
and reads itself from cover tŏ cover.
Thêre is no writer of fiction whŏm we
now recall from whŏm ōne can cōme
so near obtaining that ideal of the
novel-reader, the maximum of amusement with the minimum of effort, as
from Cherbuliez. Every detail of his
work is refined and polished tŏ the
last degree, distinctly tŏ that end;
and surplusage being rigorously rejected, the positiv seductivness whŏse
secret that genial cynicism knŏn as

Gallic wit alone possesses, is with him unusually potent. You dŏ not care tŏ read ōne of his books more than ōnce, but you wish tŏ read it aloud. In this sketch, as usual, thêre is no grêat amount or grêat subtlety of character portrayal; the personages ar types often enuf used by french romantic writers; but, after the romantic writer's privilege, thêy ar generalizations which afford all sorts of possibilities forbidden tŏ students of 'the human documents,' and which, in the hands of so vivacious and inventiv a romancer as Cherbuliez, ar very agreeably managed." [Nation.] —'"The 'affaire du coeur' in which the clever old diplomat finds himself pitted against an intriguing young wido and her mōther, is amusing throuout, while the character of the hero, an ardent Egyptologist, is wel conceived." [Penn. **2090**

——, SAME ("A Stroke of Diplomacy"), *Appleton*, 1880.

KINGS IN EXILE, by A. DAUDET, = No. 774.

LA BELLE MADAME DONIS, by H. MALOT: *Tinsley*, 1885. **2091**

LA BELLE NIVERNAISE. [by ALPHONSE DAUDET: *Routledge*, 1887.] "Daudet here sounds the vibrant, penetrating notes of pity and lōve. It is a charming idyl of the Seine. Good-heârted François Louveau, the bargeman, with his equally benevolent tho shrewish-tunged wife, ar portrayed with a subtle sympathy which brings them out clear against the bacground of poverty and toil. Victor is a poor little waif picked up by Louveau in the streets of Paris and cared for til he cōmes tŏ be the chîef prop and cōmfort of the worthy pair. The whole picture is before us; the trips up and down the river, the cheer-

ful, useful childhood of Victor and his foster-sister, the discōvery of Victor's father, the boy's departure for school, his pitiful longing for a return tŏ his previous life, his ilness, the family reunion—all is told with a grace and charm which we may wel call incomparable, and which lend tŏ the simplest incidents the glo and cōlor of romance." [Boston "Literary World." **2092**

LA TERRE. [by ÉMILE ZOLA: *Peterson*, 1888.] "If the peasants of France ar without exception jackals, wŏlves, and swine, tŏ the degree Zola depicts them, it is hard tŏ perceive how any ōther country could equal the abominable shōing. The title of the book is understood tŏ suggest not merely the occupation of the people as tillers of the soil, but also their excessiv greed for land ōnership, and upon this Mr. Howells dwels as the essential feature in their character, as shōn by this alleged 'study.' But the book dōes not indicate this: it shōs every form of sordid avarice, silencing every form of human feeling, developing hate and jealousy, and employing cruelty and crime without remorse; and while in the midst of this the greed for land appears prominent, it is but ōne detail in the evil catalog." [American. **2093**

LADIES' PARADISE (The) [by ÉMILE ZOLA: *Tinsley*, 1884.] "is prosaic, painful, full of a strange pathos which english novels wonderfully lac; and profoundly moral, if rītly understood. It is the story of a grêat Parisian monster shop, and the exhibition of the spirit of hard, brutal worldliness expressed in its colossal success, ruining all little shops in its nêborhood, and casting off scores of workpeople tŏ starv at a moment's

notice; of the demoralizing influence of the vast 'culte' of luxury, and the magnetic power—sensuous and deadening at ōnce—which it exercises over all whŏ hav tŏ take part in it. Thêre is sŏmething in the picture of a pure hard-working girl sitting up at nīt tŏ supply the necessities of a brŏther of 17, whŏ invents fresh tales of profligacy tŏ bêar out his demands upon her. and boasts of the advantage his youth givs him with his mistresses, which opens an instructiv vista intŏ the true meaning of the worship of luxury, and the tendency of a sensuous materialism." [Contemporary Review.   **2094**
LADY WITH THE CAMELIAS, by A. DUMAS: (Paris, 1848.) N.-Y., *Belford*, 1890; 251 pp.   **2095**
——. SAME ("Camille") *Peterson*. 1860, *Laird*. 1891.
LAKE SHORE (The) [by ÉMILE SOUVESTRE, Boston: *Crosby, Nicholls & Co.*, 1855; 12°, 239 pp.] contains 3 tales,—*The Slave, The Serf*, THE APPRENTICE.   **2096**
LAKEVILLE = No. 287.
LAST LOVE. [by G: OHNET: *Chatto, Ivers, Lippincott, Munro*. 1890.] "The characteristics of Mr. Ohnet's 'Dernier Amour' wer so much like the characteristics of most of his work as tŏ confirm a theory held by sŏme critics that thêre is no author so popular as the author whŏ givs the public exactly what it expects. A certain facility of construction, dialog slipshod but fluent, a knac of describing all classes of society with indifferent incorrectness, and, finally, a kind of bluntness of moral toŭch which tickles morbid senses without shocking them —these ar Ohnet's qualifications, and thêy appear in the history of the contest of Mrs. de Fontenay and Lucie

Andremont for the not particularly valuable affection of the former's husband as wel or as il as in most of his ōther work." [Athenæum.   **2097**
LATIN QUARTER COURTSHIP = No. 483.
LAWYER'S NOSE, ☞ *ECCENTRIC NOVELS*.
LAZARETTO-KEEPER   (The) ☞ No. 1974.
LE BLEUET [by "GUSTAVE HALLER," i. e., W.. J. (Simonin) Fould: *Brentano*, 1889.] is "a pretty story of alsatian life, full of tender feeling, of rural charm, and gentle manners. Thêre is a note of introduction by G: Sand which givs it hī praise for the delicacy of its character drawing. Possibly. the story in its english dress would not hav attracted such praise unaided, but few wil be inclined tŏ quarrel with 'G: Sand's' estimate. The picture given of the relations between the landed peasantry and the nobility is astonishing in the simplicity and freedom it indicates. A very pleasant half hour may be spent in the Alsace of this book." [Overland.]—"It is a charming, innocent little tale. of a kind not too common in french or indeed in any other language ... It would be unfair tŏ go further in recounting the story, which is full of delicate sentiment and chastened, unostentatious observation. That forêin readers wil admire it so warmly as dŏ the french can hardly be averred. for we ar accustomed tŏ stories in which innocence and poetry combine, and thêre is a faint trace of exaggeration in thêir union here; but yet the story is very pretty and the book is wel worth reading." [Atlantic.   **2098**
——, SAME ("Renée and Franz"), *Appleton*. 1878.

LE REVE, by Zola, = No. 784.

LEAH [Paris] = No. 485.

LEAVES FROM A FAMILY JOURNAL ["Mémoires d'un Famille") by Émile Souvestre: London, *Groombridge*, 1854; N.-Y., *Appleton*, 1855.] "is an autobiografic sketch of domestic life in a provincial town, written in a quiet, unpretending manner, but replete with the lessons of practical wisdom. The characters ar wel drawn, and the simplicity of the style, the purity of the moral tone, and the homely truths which the book inculcates, recommend it. Opening with the marriage of the hero and heroin, the diarist unfolds the family history throu many years, until the children, having reached maturity, prepare tŏ leav the family circle for new homes." [Christian Examiner. **2099**

LED ASTRAY, = *LITTLE COUNTESS.*

LES MISERABLES = No. 790.

LETTERS FROM MY MILL. [by Alphonse Daudet: *Trubner*, 1880.] "Few modern volumes hav the subtle charm of this. They sparkle with airy brĭtness. They depict an Areadia so delītful that we ar fain tŏ believe it real. Thêy please ŏur fancy without strain or fatīgue, as nothing but good french work can dŏ. Thêy dŏ not stir ŏur deeper feelings as german or english stories mīt. The author makes no appeal tŏ ŏur egotism by suggesting that we ar in any way concerned in his puppets, except tŏ note how gracefully thêy play thêir part; and his book is full of diffused lit, so that even the men and women in it cast less gloomy shadōs than those of real life. His Provence is like the sea which plays along its shores, now passionate, now serene, but never of the dul leaden hue which the northern atmosfere can giv tŏ Nature." [Spectator.]—"The grace and charm of Daudet's manner hav never been more apparent than here. Subtle as thêy ar, keen as is the touch with which his simplest sketch illustrates some depth or hīt or surface folly of human nature, the first and abiding impression of these little tales is thêir delītful delicacy. Thêre is not ōne of them but is full of point, either of wit or humor or pathos, and thêy ar as original as thêy ar simple. That anything so strongly intellectual should be so delicate is as wonderful as that anything so keen should be so sympathetic." [Critic.]—Thêy "ar only in part stories, for 7 out of the 17 ar descriptiv or meditativ essays, pure and simple. The stories ar delītful, with a peculiar tenderness and delicacy, a playful brītness, and a satire quite without bitterness of spirit, even when the subject matter is bitter, with ōne exception. The exception is upon the subject of making a living by literature. In addition tŏ his sympathetic expression of human experience, thêre is no less sympathetic expression of out-door nature of Provence. The delicate dramatic sense very rarely permits a touch of melodrama; and tho the perceptions of the artistic value of sorrōs and joys of the Provençals is far from naive, neither would it be fair tŏ call it self-conscious." [Overland.]—"Thêy ar unrivaled in grace, humor and pathos, while now and then a līt, swift gleam of satire crosses the page ... The english (Harper) version is far abōve the average." [Nation. **2100**

——, SAME ("Stories from Provence") *Harper*, 1886.

LIFE IN A FRENCH VILLAGE.

[by LISBETH GOOCH (SÉGUIN) STRA-
HAN: *Strahan*, 1879.] "The stories
contained in this little work ar all
very gracefully told. The reader is
taken tŏ a quaint seaside village called
St. Brie—a ro of stone, weather-beat-
en, wooden-shuttered cottages, strag-
gling along the edge of the clif.—and
thêre introduced tŏ various of its inhabitants, and tŏ sŏme of the grêat
folk living hard by. Each tale is
distinct, and yet a unity is preservd,
by reference in ŏne tale tŏ characters
figuring in ŏthers . . . Throuŏūt thêre
runs a subtle local flavor, a delicate
presentment of the quaint side of
french life, which is very attractiv.
'The Two Sisters' and the 'Curé's
Crime' ar very good samples of this
kind of presentment. We feel at
home with the people sŏmehow, and
understand thêir circumstances and
modes of thôt. Even the slit sketch
of the semi-idiot boy, 'poor Michel,' is
full of delicate touches, which stamp
it as work of a true artist. Altŏgether, we can heártily recommend
this little volume." [Spectator. 2101
LIFE'S DECEIT by E. DE GON-
COURT: *Chicago*, Laird, 1891. 2102
LIGHTNING ROD (The), by C:
DE BERNARD, 35 p., in *The Sapphire*.
Boston, *Shorey*, 1869. 2103
LILY OF THE VALLEY (The).
[by HONORÉ "DE" BALZAC: (Paris,
1835) *Roberts*, 1891.] "Balzac has
written no book which is regarded as
a better representativ of his genius
than this, and it is specially remarkable as being a novel in which the
heroin preservs her purity intact, preferring steadfastly her duty tŏ her
happiness, and sacrificing her life tŏ
her ideal standard of rīt. We follo
Madame de Montsauf throu all the
painful pitiful struggles of her daily

life; we see her turn aside from pleasure, nay, from happiness, and embrace her cross day by day; we contemplate her patience, her fidelity,
her noble self-renunciation; we see
her hŏūrly victories over self. and we
say tŏ ŏūrselvs, After all, thêre is
ŏne french writer whŏ comprehends
the saying that 'it is more blessed tŏ
lŏse ŏne's life than tŏ find it.' The
agonies, the sublimities of self-sacrifice ar not ignored or scoffed at by all
french novelists. Balzac has given us
ŏne woman whŏm we need not excuse
and pity, but can admire and adore."
[Lippincott's. 2104
LION'S SKIN AND LOVER
HUNT, ("La Chasse aux Amants")
by C: "DE" BERNARD [Dugrail de la
Villette], N.-Y., *Stringer*, 1853. 2105
LISE FLEURON. [by GEORGES
OHNET: *Remington*, 1885.] "No english writer could bring himself tŏ
depict a girl of Lise Fleuron's innate
delicacy and refinement, and then
represent her becŏming her lŏver's
mistress under no special pressure of
temptation, without making us feel
that she had, tŏ sŏme extent at least,
becŏme degraded in her ŏn eyes; but
here this is dŏne in such a matter of
course manner that it seems for the
moment a normal evolution . . . It is
impossible not tŏ pay a tribute of
admiration tŏ the skil and freedom
with which the artist works . . . All
the characters liv in a world in which
the impulses of emotion ar the only
law; and yet between the mistress of
the grêat financier, and Lise Fleuron,
the mistress of his parasite, we ar
made tŏ see a grêat gulf . . . Accepting the picture as it stands. thêre can be
no doubt of the pictorial and intellectual effectivness of the contrasted figures. In ŏne character, that of the

LION'S SKIN (The) and The LOVER
HUNT [by CHAS. DE BERNARD: N.-Y.,
Redfield, 1853.] ar "a pair of lively,
piquant stories. The first cleverly illustrates the distinctions between bravado,
courage, and temerity. The second shŏs
the Parisian consequençes of a marriage
between a studious, thôtful man, and a
young, beautiful, and frivolouş woman
[compare 1962 p]; and shŏs, also, how
such consequençes may be circumvented;
provided the parties possess as much
heârt, wit, and good sense, as ŏŭr hero
and heroin." [National Era.]—"Seldom
hav we read any more charming tales
than these. In the class of literature tŏ
which thêy belông, French writers
particularly excel; and amŏngst them C:
de Bernard is entitled tŏ a hĭ plaçe. He
is neat, terse, and clear in his style, has
withal an indefinable air of elegançe and
finish, and weaves a plot so skilfully, contrasts his characters so markedly, and
makes the action of each so complete, that
he really may be set down as a master.—
The plot of *The Lion's Skin* is rather too
intricate tŏ be unraveled in a paragraph;
but its moral is that ōne man may be thôt
a coward and yet be brave, whilst anŏther
may be thôt brave, and yet be a coward.—
The Lover Hunt teaches that a husband
is the best and the ōnly proper gardian of
the wife's honor.—If both these tales be
french, thêy ar so in the better and most
unexceptionable sense, in piquancy, in
wit, in tenderness—not in the fondness
for intrigue, and the proneness tŏ dally
with forbidden subjects. It is rare in
French pages tŏ meet with so much purity
which is neither sentimental nor insipid."
[Albion.   **2105**

play-writ, thêre is really sŏmething of moral elevation; at any rate, thêre is true poetic beauty in his selfless devotion tŏ the woman whŏ as a little girl had been his playmate; but De Barre is held in reserve until he can be used as a foil tŏ the poor, shallo creature whŏ leaves him tŏ be Lise's support in her hŏur of need; and the book, as a whole, is impoverished tŏ enrich the concluding chapters, which ar certainly full of very simple and genuin pathos . . . It is as bad a translation as we hav ever seen." [Spectator. **2106**

LITTLE COUNTESS (The). [by OCTAVE FEUILLET (†, 1890.) : *Peterson*, 1880.] "Nevertheless thêre is sŏmething very attractiv about Feuillet's work which makes 'The Little Countess' a refreshing contrast tŏ the writings of sŏme of his harshest critics. Altho it is not among the latest, it is in certain respects the best thing he has dŏne, which is probably due tŏ its slītness. Feuillet inclines tŏ melodrama, and in his more elaborate and ambitious efforts, such as 'M. de Camors'—a kind of 'Tom Jones' of the Second Empire—it involvs him in intricacies of ideas and feelings whêre it is quite impossible tŏ follo him without protest against his artificiality. But 'The Little Countess' is distinctly a minor work; it is simple and genuin, and its scheme permits the writer tŏ display all his cleverness, which is grêat; his tact, which is considerable, and his workmanship, which is perfect. It is not a large enuf thing tŏ tempt his imagination tŏ part with experience and observation, which is usually his main error; ŏne may even suspect that the little Countess is a portrait, so sympathetically and distinctly is she de-

picted. Thêre must hav been not a few such products of the artificial and yet haphazard society of the Empire; the merit of the book is that it dŏes not paint the manners of the period as illustrated in the conduct of a fiction of Feuillet's sŏmewhat sentimental imagination, but the effect of such manners upon a real and passionate nature. The dénoûment is very pathetic, and tho, as always, the hopelessness of the tragedy seems partly due tŏ the author's wilfullness, thêre is no slo music tŏ detract from its impressivness." [Nation. **2107**

——, SAME ("Led Astray"), N.-Y., *Carleton*, 1875.

LITTLE FADETTE [by "G: SAND," i. e., Amantine Lucile Aurore (Dupin) Dudevant (†, 1876.): London, *Slater*, 1849.] "is a tale of quiet, exquisite beauty, and rendered intŏ graceful, idiomatic english. [Harper's.]—"We hav not for a long time read so sweet a story. It is pure, natural and wholesŏme; thŏroly french—but not the french of Dumas or of Sue, the exaggerated and prurient abominations of the present day. It resembles the romances of Florian and St.-Pierre, but, while the purity and beauty of thêir morals ar preservd, the tone of the picture is reduced, by exchanging the pastoral and sentimental cŏloring, for the sober hues of country life." [Southern Lit. Messenger. **2108**

——, SAME ("Fanchon"), N.-Y., *Follett*, 1863, 230 pp; Phil'a, *Leypoldt*, 1863.

LITTLE FELLOW AT THE CORNER (The) [by [C:] PAUL DE KOCK: Paris, 1874, pp. 110.] "Of M. Dupont, the flourishing Paris grocer, whŏ givs his name tŏ ŏne of Kock's novels, we never think without associating the idea of Liston. His good nature, his simplicity, his vanity, his timidity, his ridiculous taste in dress, his awkward activity, and, tŏ crown all, his utter unconsciousness of not being as fine a fello, and as loveable an object as any in Paris, would all meet an admirable representativ in our inimitable comedian. What enjoyment the people would hav in his dancing at Romainville, with his sounding seals and watch chain, and his pockets full of crown-pieces, making tŏgether a little tambourine accompaniment. and his coat of skyblue," [Foreign Quarterly Review, 1834. **2109**

LITTLE GOOD-FOR-NOTHING ["Le Petit Chose") by ALPHONSE DAUDET: Boston, *Estes*, 1878.] " 'No Account' would hav been a better and a more taking equivalent for the original title than the ōne chosen, which givs the impression that the story is ōne for children. It is, on the contrary, by no means the least of the author's serious efforts, whether as regards carefully discriminated study of character, delicacy of touch, or sustained interest. The character of the hero, Daniel Eyssette, is a creation, or, rather, a transcription. We hav all seen him in life, if not in a novel. Of diminutiv stature and boyish manners, the first remark that rude people make on seeing him, and the first thôt of people whŏ say nothing, is always, substantially. "He is of no account." His character is a compound of childish weaknesses and masculin wil. When his father's business is ruined and the family is scattered, Daniel supports himself as a teacher in a grêat barrac of a place among the mountains, two days journey from Paris. Thêre he makes a

brave fît with his unmanageable classes, a race of Anakim, each pupil at least twice as big as himself, and thêre he devotes himself tŏ the task of restoring the fortunes of his family. Lŏsing his place, however, throu the treachery of a companion, he goes tŏ Paris, whêre his brother Jacques receivs and protects him. houses him on a fifth floor in the Latin Quarter, encourages him tŏ commence as a poet, and raises the money tŏ publish his first volume, which, being unsalable is also his last. Then the temptations of the city prŏve too much for Daniel. He succumbs tŏ them, and is rescued with difficulty by the devotion of Jacques. This part of the story is touching, and it describes traits of the french character of which we kno perhaps too little. It depicts their strong family attachments, the almost passionate lŏve of the country-people for home, and the same joyous sacredness of domestic affection as that which givs the imperishable charm tŏ the earlier chapters of Marmontel's memoirs. As in those memoirs, too, the escapades, the dissipations of the student-life in the capital form but an interlude. Thêy ar ripples, not interruptions, in the current of family affection. Sŏme of the incidents of the story ar enuf like sŏme which ar recorded of Daudet's ōn life tŏ lend a sub-autobiografic interest to the adventures of his hero. If the original is free from mannerisms, the translator has added nŏne. The version retains much of Daudet's abundant humor. That the story should be entertaining was tŏ be expected from its authorship. That it may serv tŏ illustrate the french character tŏ persons whŏ find in the word 'frivolous' a sufficient critical account of that

character is, perhaps, rather tŏ be hoped than expected." [Nation. 2110
——, SAME ("My Brother Jack"), . Low, 1877.

LITTLE HEAD OF THE FAMILY (The) [by ZÉNAIDE M. A. FLEU-RIOT: Ward, 1877.] "is an excellent story, wel translated. The heroin is a boy, whŏ, impoverished by the death of his father, endeavors bravely tŏ take the father's place tŏards his twŏ sisters. We hav a description of the characters of the 3 children, their life with their aged grandfather, the trials and temptations of the village schools." [Athenæum.   2111

LITTLE ORATOR (The)   by É. SOUVESTRE, Balt., Murphy, 1869. 2112

LITTLE PETER [by "LUCAS MALET," i. e., Mary (Kingsley) Harrison: Paul, 1887.] "is 'A Christmas Morality for children of any age.' It is a beautiful and pathetic story. 'Little Peter' is ŏnly ŏne of a fascinating group of characters, each of which is unique and piquant. The impatient old father absorbed in ancient history, the patient wife and mother, the older brother, the cat of the household, the charcoal-burner of the forest, Eliza the servant-maid, with her entertaining flirtations, and Gustavus the cowherd, all play thêir parts, and play them wel. The story is a touching ŏne, and yet escapes being entirely mŏrnful, even tho the terrible walk throu the sno-storm results in the death of Little Peter. The local cŏlor is wonderfully clear and strong, the descriptions of life in the pine forest vivid and impressiv, while the little tale leaves a sense of simplicity and pleasantness which wil not allow ŏne tŏ remember too painfully its mŏrnful elements." [Critic.]—"Not often dŏes a christmas book appear of

such charm as this. It is a scene from country life—an idyl with a half-sad, half-joyous ending. Tŏ giv a sketch of the beautiful, pathetic story would be dŏing it scant justice; but all whŏ can ŏt tŏ possess themselvs of this "christmas morality" for it is rare christmas reading." [Athenæ.   2113

LOST BATTLE (A) [Ed., Douglas, 1878.] "is a charming story, of a sort which has cŏme tŏ be so old-fashioned that it is very hard tŏ find, in these days . . . The author has perfect taste, considerable invention, and extreme delicacy of touch in description. The portion of the story which takes place in France is the best, and the author paints certain fāses of parisian life with grêat fidelity, spirit, and neatness. Best of all the qualities of the book is the true lŏve of honor and goodness in both men and women which shines throu it, and has inspired the writer with courage tŏ depend on those virtues for the interest of a story which is pure and lofty from beginning tŏ end, and has not a dul page." [Spectator.   2114

LOST ROSE AND OTHER STORIES. [by K .. S. MACQUOID: Chatto, 1876.] " 'Lost Rose,' 'A Wild Night,' 'A Sailor's Story,' 'Outside the Porte des Capucins,' 'Neptune's Tower.' 'Fifine,' 'My Daughter Molly,' 'The Courtyard of the Ours d' Or,' ar so many illustrations of the sad troubles which befall men and women, when thêy allow themselvs tŏ lŏve and tŏ be lŏved. The author excels in her flemish stories. She is at home in the quaint, old-fashioned towns of Flanders, and strongly imbued with a sense of thêir picturesqueness. 'Fifine' a 'Story of Malines,' may be taken as a fair sample of the author in her happiest mood. The

LOST ILLUSIONS. [by HONORÉ "DE" BALZAC (†, 1850): *Roberts*, 1893.] "Turning tŏ the idylic and pathetic pages of "Lost Illusions" is like turning from a grinning tragic mask tŏ the beautiful loered head of a stooping caryatid. Wŏnderful feliçity dŏes Balzac possess in describing rural landscape traversed by brimming rivers, jeweled and starred here and thĕro by antique towns, set thicly with even more antique people, and full of the poetry of provincialism. Here, in Angoulême, "Lost Illusions" unfolds its vivid pages, in the time of the good year 1822, when the Bourbon Restoration was wel under way and royalty seemed re-established forever. From this quaint surrŏunding Balzac placs a drama of graphic situations, tender lŏves and sublime hates, trimming it with all that extraordinary rococo embroidery of which he possessed whole museums. Finer characters than the David and Eve of this book he has never conçeived; a character more ficly brilliant, more Frencby, more 'insouciant' in its airv criminality than Lucien's it would be difficult even in Balzac's vast picture-galleries tŏ find. That plague-spot of the French social system, the married flirt, is thĕre in all her flŏunçes, and her correlativ the 'cavalière servente' is thĕre too as her complement. Surrŏunding these is an interesting assembly of provinçial nobility, mamas with marriageable dauters, pettifoggers, intriguers, misers, ecclesiastics, "newly-rich" and immemorially poor: a tableau living, crowded, mŏving, breathing, all more or less entangled in the meshes of an ingenious plot." [Critic.]—"This volume contains *The Two Poets* and *Eve and David*,—the first and third of a series. Thĕre is a connecting story, "A Great man of the Provinces in Paris." The book presents twŏ strikingly contrasted types of character: the young poet, brilliant, volatil, with the artistic temperament, but lacking genuin ability, and entirely devoid of firmness of character; and, in contrast, his sister Eve and her husband David, twŏ noble-minded, strenuous, and self-sacrifiçing souls. These characters ar all drawn with the wŏnderful power which Balzac puts intŏ his characterization. The stories ar also representativ because thĕy include ŏne of those very careful and elaborate studies of a form of practical activity which Balzac was so fond of making. He goes intŏ the details of paper-making, printing, and the legal proçesses attending commercial disaster with that grasp of detail and that exactness so characteristic of his wŏnderful mental vigor. The book is also representativ because it givs us a whole section of provinçial soçiety; not a group of names, but a group of people differentiated with the utmost particularity and realized tŏ the imagination by every possible detail. We feel as if we wer reading history and meeting people whŏse pedigrees wer tŏ be found in the books, and the story of whŏse ançestral lives could be gained by word of mouth in the little community in which thĕy liv." [Commonwealth. **2114 m** red-faced, good-natured, but outspoken laundress, Madame Popot, bustling about tŏ arrange a good match for her niece Fifine, the pretty, innocent girl in lŏve with a poor fisherman, and caring little, of course, for the old, rich, selfish bachelor, whŏm Providence, in the shape of her ânt, has destind for her; her girlish troubles and unexpected happiness in finding herself united at last tŏ the beloved Michel van Vorst, promoted in the meanwhile tŏ the post of railway-porter, make a charming story, all the more charming because every one knoes that the Flemish, taken as a whole, ar probably the dullest and most prosaic race in Europe. The other stories ar less attractiv. 'A Diligence Adventure.' tels the story of a poor Frenchwoman whŏ meets a terrible punishment, on account of a long and loud tung. This way of silencing women is, we trust, as obsolete as the expedient tŏ which the author resorts in the ghastly story entitled 'My Worst Christmas Eve,' Mrs. Macquoid dŏes not kno how tŏ manage a plot, but she has the knac of writing a pretty story." [Athenæum. **2115**

LOST WILL (The) or DOWERLESS, by H. É. F. (A.) REYBAUD. Phil'a, *Peterson*, 1847. **2116**

LOVE CRIME (A). [by PAUL BOURGET: *Vizetelly*, 1888.] "The husband is a good, honest, hard-working, innocent, and unsuspecting engineer; the wife is a romantic and dissatisfied person whŏ has made a marriage "de raison." She falls in lŏve with a friend of her husband, a man of the world, idle, clever, for whŏm lŏve is an occupation more than a passion. The woman dŏes not understand him; she lŏves in him the

man of her dreams; she is blind and becŏmes guilty. She sacrifices tŏ a dream, tŏ a chimera, her duty, her honor, her peace of mind;—and her sacrifice is vain. The twŏ criminals ar punished in a different way; the woman, by the gradual discŏvery of her lŏver's true character. She finds out in the end that her sacrifice has not been even understood. Her lŏver dŏes not believe that he is her first lŏver ... He sees a mere episode, a mere adventure, in what seems tŏ Hélène the object and foundation of her whole existence. The more she believes in him the less he believes in her. Her passion has a sort of repellant effect; thĕy dŏ not understand each other. She has given everything tŏ him, and he dŏes not kno it or comprehend it. He has been always looking, during the idle years of his youth and of his manhood, for real lŏve— for an absolute, boundless, unselfish existence; he has it, and dŏes kno it. His perverse egotism makes him blind and poisons everything for him." [Nation. **2117**

LOVE EPISODE (A) ["Une page d'Amour"] by É. ZOLA, Chicago, *Laird*, 1891. **2118**

——, SAME ("A Woman's Heart"), N.-Y., *Tousey*, 1880.

LOVE MATCH (A). [by LUDOVIC HALÉVY: N.-Y., *Delay*, 1889.] "The ambitious young lady, bent upon making a good match, is not new in fiction; but the girl, whŏ is an amusing, brīt, and nice little girl, and whŏ yet sets herself with all her mīt, and by every means in her power, tŏ secure the sort of husband she apprŏves —which is primarily a prince, and afterwards what Heaven may send— is really a delītfully new revelation. Such a picture could be only Parisian,

LOVE'S CRUEL ENIGMA [by Paul Bourget: N.-Y., *Waverly Co.*, 1893.] "describes the placid life of two ladies, poor and hily genteel, whŏ wer educating a young man, thêir sŏn and nephew, with the most delicate and tender care. The beginning of the book is charming; the description of this quiet home, this Eden of virtue, of respectability, of peaçe, in the midst of Paris, had real merit. Tŏ be sure, it reminded ŏne of many passages in Balzac's 'Scènes de la vie de province,' for ŏ̂ur grêat Balzac was admirable in these descriptions of humble and domestic lives; he knew how tŏ plaçe his pure figures in thêir 'cadre,' and how tŏ giv a sort of life tŏ this 'cadre.' But it is not everybody whŏ can make you think of Balzac, and I conçeived at ŏnce a hi opinion of the talent of Mr. Bourget. I saw also at ŏnce how the drama would develop itself; how this tender, delicate, refined, but too feminin education of the hero would il prepare him for the temptations of life. I was not deçeived; the young man falls under the influençe of a married woman, and you can imagin the rest—the struggle between the pure affections and the impure lŏve, the hesitations, the victories, the defeats of the human wil subjected tŏ the action of conflicting forçes. It is the old story of Hêraklês plaçed between virtue and viçe; it is, alas! the old story of the final and irreparable fall. This "cruel enigma" is no enigma at all: it is the common story. The work of lŏng years of education, the teachings of ançestors, even the clearest possible vision of right and wrŏng, the consciousness of a grêat fault and of a grêat folly— all is vain. Man must meet his fate, and the punishment cŏmes at ŏnce, in the diminution of the wil, in the impotençe of liberty, in the degradation of all the faculties which represent the divine in man. This book is not a bad 'analysis of the struggle which too ŏften ends in the subjugation of a fine nature tŏ a coarse, common, and bad nature. It is artistic in so far as it is analytic; it is inartistic in so far as the mind is never kept in suspense, and that you can see at ŏnce how it wil end. The young man whŏ represents Hêraklês between virtue and viçe, is not enuf of a Hêraklês; he is too weak, you can expect nŏthing of him. He is not very interesting; you can not help despising him almost as soon as you kno him." [A : Langel in Nation. **2119 m**

LOVER HUNT (The), with No. 2105.

or rather Parisienne. This young lady has the misfortune tŏ be Catherine Duval, the dauter of a rich papermaker—respectable, and bourgeois tŏ the last degree. Thêre is a very pretty little sketch of the serious, homely house, of the delĭtfuļ mother, modest, a little timid, a little 'dévote' —the best housekeeper, the best wife and mother imaginable, without a thŏt beyond her mild interior, or a preoccupation except that of finding for her dauter a secure and wel-established 'ménage' like her ŏn. The scene opens with a conversation between mŏther and dauter returning from a ball, in celebration of a marriage in that respectable bourgeoisie which M'lle Catherine déspises with all her soul, the mother asking anxiously, "How did you find him?" the dauter pretending not tŏ understand, tho she is very wel aware that the person in question is a young engineer of grêat promise, the most respectable and the most bourgeois that can be conceived. Catherine has already refused seven or êt, "all from the École Centrale or the École Polytechnique," and she is in despair. Nothing, however, can be prettier than the home scene. The marriage of the father and mother has been a lŏve-match—'absolument comme dans les romans anglais'; and thêy hav livd happy ever after, wer it not for a son whŏ lŏves pleasure too much and a dauter whŏ lŏves engineers too little, —whŏ dŏ thêir best tŏ spoil thêir parents' peace." [Blackwood's. **2119**

——, SAME ("Marriage of Love"), London, *Simpkin*, 1886.

——, SAME ("Marriage for Love"), Chicago, *Rand*, 1891, 106 pp.

LOVER AND HUSBAND = (A) *FATAL PASSION.*

LOVERS' POOL (The) = No. 2013.

LUCIE, by H. E. F. (A.) REYBAUD, in *Brother Jonathan*, 6-27 aug., 1842. **2120**

LUCK AND LEATHER, by BALZAC. ☞ *ECCENTRIC NOVELS.*

MABEL STANHOPE [**Paris**] = No. 448.

MADAME ALPHONSE by MAURICE TALMEYR: N.-Y.. *Tousey*, 1882. **2121**

MADAME BOVARY [by GUSTAVE FLAUBERT (†. 1880, Paris, 1857): *Peterson*, 1881; Chicago, *Laird*, 1891, 407 pp.] "is noted for having been the subject of prosecution as an immoral work. That it has a serious lesson thêre is no doubt, if ŏne wil drink tŏ the bottom of the cup. But the hŏney of sensuous description is spread so deeply over the surface of the goblet that a large proportion of its readers never think of its holding anything else. All the fãses of unhall0ed passion ar described in full detail. That is what the book is bŏt and read for, by the grêat majority of its purchasers, as all but simpletons very wel kno. That is what makes it sel. This book is famous for its realism; in fact, it is recognised as ŏne of the earliest and most brilliant examples of that modern style of novel, which, beginning whêre Balzac left, attempted tŏ dŏ for literature what the fotograf has dŏne for art. For those whŏ take the trouble tŏ drink out of the cup belo the rim of hŏney, thêre is a scene whêre realism is carried tŏ its extreme.—surpassed in horror by no writer, unless it be the ŏne whŏse name must be looked for at the bottom of the alphabet, as if its natural place wer as lo in ⁄the dregs of realism as it could find itself. This is the death-bed scene, whêre Madame

Bovary expires in convulsions." [O. W. Holmes in Atlantic.]—"In "Madame Bovary" the husband is a fool tŏ his wife. Tŏ the reader he is a simple apothecary, a weak, everyday sort of character, whŏ lŏves his offspring and adores the wretched woman whŏ deceives him. She is about equal tŏ him in station: his superior in intellect. Living in a provincial town. and sying for the unknŏn delits of Paris and splendor, her whole nature cries out tŏ be seduced. Of course she dŏes not go tŏ her grave without being satisfied. As the German poet writes—

"Ein Thor ist immer willig.
Wenn eine Thorin will."

The old blandishing graces of Dumas, Sand, and Balzac ar quite excluded from this story. All is severe matter of fact elaborated. We flung the book tŏ the four corners of the room; but we took it again, and finished it. The author is uncompromising: he givs Madame Bovary successiv lŏvers. She has not even the excuse of lŏve and its poor consolation when the end cŏmes. She endeavors tŏ persuade both lŏvers tŏ elope with her; she begs mŏney of both. She plunders her husband; ruins him; finally the discovery of her treason kils him . . . No harm can cŏme from reading Madame Bovary; but it is fysic for adults, as the doctors say. The author has no more lŏve for her than an anatomist for his subject. He dŏes not preach. He allows her patiently tŏ make her wickedness manifest. and leaves us tŏ contemplate the picture at ŏur leisure. He is a singularly powerful writer." [Westminster. **2122**

M'ME DE BEAUPRÉ. [by HENRIETTA CAMILLA (JACKSON) JENKIN (†, 1885): *Smith*, 1868.] "The ŏther

marriage" is much gayer. It is lively and pleasant, and ends most agreeably. The sketches of provincial society remind us of sŏme parts of 'Eugénie Grandet' [No. 2024.] The Vicomtesse de Beaupré, after being married when almost a child tŏ a horrid old man, and after bêaring her noble husband's tyrannical temper with a patience which must hav touched the heârt of her gardian angel, is left a widŏ. and then she enjoys her liberty, and is a most fascinating flue lady. til her time cŏmes when she falls in lŏve in so charming a manner that no man wil be able tŏ read of it without envy. Thêre ar grêat difficulties; but the man she lŏves is so worthy of her in every respect, so suited tŏ her in character,—tho his social position is belŏ hers,—that the reader's interest and sympathy ar secured. The wilful and bewitching little viscountess surmounts all obstacles but ŏne, and that is Raymŏnd Savoisy's duty tŏ his parents. His father is a protestant pastor, with a disapproval of popery which makes him feel he would rather his son should die than marry a catholic. The mother is even more sternly opposed. Deeply as Raymond is attached tŏ the viscountess, and she tŏ him. neither of them entertains an idea of opposing the parental wil. This deep sense of the obligation of duty, tŏ be obeyed at all sacrifice. makes a striking point in the story. and givs it a strong interest quite independent of the lŏve affair. However, at last all is happily ended by the impetuous little viscountess declaring her adhesion tŏ the pastor's religion! The protestant reader wil rejoice in so charming a convert, and even a catholic reader wil forgiv her under the extenuating circumstances."

[Athenæum. 2123

MADAME DE BEAUSÉANT, by BALZAC, in *AFTER DINNER STORIES.* 2124

MADAME DE MAUVES [Paris] = No. 489.

MADAME D' ORGEVAUT'S HUS-BAND [by H: RABUSSON: N.-Y., *Dodd*, 1891.] "treats a very serious problem in a most striking and interesting manner—the problem as tŏ whether a woman can be married tŏ a man and continue tŏ lōve him and be happy with him when she has ceased tŏ respect him. Mme. d'Orgevaut's second husband tels her, a few hŏurs after thêir marriage, that he has been a dishonest man and has used his employer's mŏney, but that he was successful in his gambling, has replaced the mŏney, and has lived an honest life ever since. She lōves him, and for the moment, overcŏme by her feeling for him, she forgivs him and permits him tŏ remain with her. Thêre is a certain charm at first in the sacrifice she imposes upon herself for his sake, but this dŏes not last. It is not forgetfulness; it is slo familiarization with a new kind of happiness, a progressiv initiation intŏ the art of being happy throu the benumbing of the faculties which can make ŏne suffer. It is the voluntary torpor of a woman whŏ dŏes not wish tŏ kno whether it was wrong tŏ lōve first and condone afterwards. She dŏes not blind herself; she goes tŏ sleep. Thêre ar, unfortunately, awakenings and sleeplessness. Madame first knoes the latter by short attacs, of which she hopes tŏ be cured; but it is not long before she also knoes the other, of which ŏne is never cured—the grêat awakening. Her husband's error—which is inevitable and fatally com-mon tŏ all those whŏ accept a rehabilitation—is tŏ becŏme used too quicly tŏ the climate of indulgent silence and forced abnegation which surrounds him. The situation becŏmes intolerable. The wife tels him that the guilty person whŏ is really worthy of being rehabilitated comprehends that thêre is no rehabilitation possible, save in a solitude courageously and voluntarily borne; he understands that thêre wil always be in his conscience and in the memory of others, in that of the being he lŏves, sŏmething which would protest against this pardon. She can stand the life in close companionship with him no longer, and thêy separate. The story thus draws tŏ a perfectly logical conclusion in its treatment of a moral question which men and women ar being called upon tŏ face every day." [Critic. 2125

MADAME FIRMIANI, by BALZAC, in *After-dinner Stories;* also in *The Cat and the Battledore;* also in *The Vendetta;* also in *The N. Y. Mirror,* 14 & 21 jan. 1837. 2126

MADAME JEANETTE'S PA-PERS, by ERCKMANN-CHATRIAN, in *Ladies Repository*, Sept. 1873. 2127

MADAME LUCAS [*Osgood*, 1882.] "is a charming little story, the gentle vêil of sadness tŏards the close scarcely interfering with the reader's delicate pleasure. Thêre ar many touches, indeed, of the positiv amusement ŏne anticipates from the headings of the chapters. Madame Lucas herself is a vivid little creation, illustrating pleasantly that when a french-woman is good, she is very, very good. She is eminently french ... She gathers about her a small circle of friends knŏn as the 'Lotos-eaters,' comprising many people of many

minds, from the brilliant critic tŏ the absorbed irish gentleman who did not kno a Fra Angelico from a Fra Diavolo. The plot is extremely slit and not in the least original; but the whole is a very charming bit of work from an author evidently of much cultivation." [Critic. **2128**
MADAME THERÈSE, by ERCKMANN-CHATRIAN, = No. 809.
MADAME'S GRANDDAUGHTER. [by F .. M .. PEARD (b. 1835) : *Hatchard*, 1887.] "Everyŏne acquainted with Miss Peard's charming novels wil welcŏme this, and not be disappointed. She takes her readers again tŏ the sunny South, whêre she herself, it is very apparent, lŏves tŏ be; and carries them to the spots she describes so wel. This time it is tŏ Grasse, on the Riviera; and thêre we liv for the time amongst the olivgroves, the gardens of exquisitly scented flowers for which Grasse is remarkable, the hils and valleys, and the vues on all sides of the bluest of blue seas, and wander over the dilapidated castle in Castelbianco, with its gray walls and interesting associations, and with the quaint and lifelike group of characters which she describes with so vivid power. Thêre is a spirit, humor, beauty, and pathos in Miss Peard's descriptions which seem tŏ us tŏ increase with each effort of her genius, and we thank her for adding so much pleasure tŏ the reading hŏūrs of ŏūr lives. Few of ŏūr present-day lady-novelists can vie with Miss Peard in unfailing interest of subject, delicacy of characterdelineation, purity of style, and a hī and refined tone of feeling." [Spectator. **2129**
MADELAINE'S FAULT [*Remington*. 1883.] "is pathetic enuf. and

short. The "fault" of Madelaine, tho french in character, wil not be deemed a very hêinous ŏne." [Spectator. **2130**
MADELEINE [by JULIA KAVANAGH : *Appleton*. 1852.] deals with "the simple-hêarted peasantry in ŏne of the wildest districts of Auvergne." [Norton's Lit. Gazette. **2131**
MADELEINE [by [LEONARD SYLVAIN] JULES SANDEAU (†, 1883) London, *Slate*r, 1849.] tho "a wel knŏn book, and ŏne deservedly honored with a crown, is perhaps a little utopian in its picture of a young roué, reformed by his cousin, and by the agency of honest labor in which she ingeniously engages him; but it is a charming sketch." [Saintsbury.]—
"It is as innocently charming s 'Madame Bovary' is the reverse. is the difference between the atmosfere of the dissecting-room and of primrose banks in the spring. Mr. Sandeau shŏs no lac of knŏledge of the world; but he passes lītly by the shadŏs on its shady side. resting by preference on simplicity and virtue. Young Maurice de Valtravers, tŏ use a vulgar but expressiv frase, is hurrying post-haste tŏ the devil. Wearied of the dulness of the paternal château he has longed tŏ wing a wider flīt. He soon succeeds in singeing his pinions, and has cŏme crippled tŏ the ground. Thêre seems no hope for him : he is the victim of remorse, with neither courage nor energy left tŏ redeem the past in the future; and he has found at last a miserable consolation in the deliberate resolution tŏ commit suicide, when his cousin Madẹleine, whŏ has lŏved him in girlhood, cŏmes tŏ his salvation as a sister and an angel of mercy; with the rare sensibility of a lŏving woman, she understands the appeals which ar

most likely tŏ serv her. She cŏmes as a suppliant, and prevails on him at least tŏ put off self-destruction til her future is assured. It prŏves in the end. that. by a pious fraud, she has presented herself as a beggar when she was really rich. That she resigns herself tŏ a life of privation, supporting herself by the labor of her hands, is the least part of her sacrifice. She has stooped tŏ appear selfish in the excess of her generosity. Maurice swêars, grumbles, and victimises himself. But the weeds which hav been flourishing in the vitiated soil, die ŏne by ŏne in that heavenly atmosfere. Madeleine's sacrifices hav thêir reward in this world as in the ŏther: and she wins the hand of her cousin, whŏm she has lŏved in her inmost hêart. as the prize of her prayers and devotion." [Blackwood's. **2132**

MADEMOISELLE, by F.. M.. PEARD, = No. 810.

M'LLE BISMARCK [by [V :]] I : [DE] ROCHEFORT [LUCAY]: *Putnam*, 1881.] ''is in form and construction an excellent novel, and in these respects mĭt hav been written by an academician, so far as it is possible tŏ judge from a translation. It is, besides. entertaining from cŏver tŏ cŏver, and contains at least ŏne portrait which is a character-study of a good deal of acumen. This is the heroin, whŏse tact in social diplomacy gave her the title of the book. her name being Antoinette Alibert. Miss Alibert's father is a professor and has but a small salary. Her mother is dead. She develops astuteness early. Realising, "at the age when little girls ar cutting dresses for thêir dols," that she never wil be pretty, she begins tŏ endow herself with ŏther attractions. She devotes herself tŏ

study. not because she desires tŏ read Goethe. Byron, or Tasso. but because she wished it tŏ be said of her when she entered a drawing-room : 'You see that young lady? Would you belíeve it? She knŏs 3 languages'." The next end tŏ compass is the entrée of sŏme drawing-room. After she has accomplished that, her effort is tŏ engage the affections of sŏme important personage, and she succeeds finally in entrapping no less distinguished game than the President of the Chamber. Tŏ dŏ this, however, she has been obliged tŏ forge lŏve-letters from a member of the noblesse, whŏ finds her out, and having her in his power, makes a very base use of it, compelling her tŏ sacrifice either herself or her hopes of Talazac. She chooses the former, and the viscount falls in lŏve with her. As she wil not recognize him and returns his letters unopened he falls il, and his cousin, whŏ is in lŏve with him and is his nurse, finds the letters and sends them tŏ Talazac. —This is too bad, for Antoinette's character is. in the main admirably sketched, and in point of art she deservs tŏ be ranked with more celebrated portraits of the same type, which is a favorit ŏne with french novelists." [Nation. **2133**

MADEMOISELLE DE MALE-PEIRE, by REYBAUD, = No. 811.

MADEMOISELLE DE MAUPIN. [by THÉOPHILE GAUTIER († 1872): (Paris, 1835) Chicago, *Laird, Sergel*, 1890, 423 pp.] ''It is not these things which the admirers of 'Mademoiselle de Maupin' admire. It is the wŏnderful and final expression, repeated, but subtly shaded and differenced, in the 3 characters of D'Albert, Rosette, and Madeleine herself, of the aspiration which, as I hav said, cŏlors

Gautier's whole work. If he, as has been justly remarked, was the priest of beauty, 'Mademoiselle de Maupin' is certainly õne of the sacred books of the cult. The apostle tŏ whŏm it was revealed was young, and perhaps he has mingled words of clay with words of gold. The creed may be an impossible creed, or an irreligious, or an immoral: that is for filosofers and priests and moralists tŏ decide. We may certainly agree with Sainte-Beuve when he says that he dōes not advise any of his female readers tŏ send for Mademoiselle de Maupin, tho we may doubt whether he seizes its spirit when he describes it as a book of medicin and pathology—õne which every fysician of the soul ŏt tŏ hav on sōme bac-shelf in his library. It would be difficult tŏ find a Bowdler for õur Madeleine, and impossible tŏ adapt her tŏ the use of families. But for those whŏ understand as thêy read, and can reject the evil and hold fast the good, whŏ desire sōmetimes tŏ retire from the meditation of the weary ways of ordinary life tŏ the land of clear cōlors and stories, whêre thêre is nõne of this weariness, whŏ ar not tŏ be scared by the poets' puppets or tempted by his baits, thêy at least wil take her as she is and be thankful." [Saintsbury. **2134**

M'LLE DE MERSAC [Algérie] = No. 491.

MADEMOISELLE DE SEIG-LIÈRE, by SANDEAU, in *American Rev.*, July, 1849 tŏ Feb. 1850. **2135**

MADEMOISELLE DESROCHES [by ANDRÉ THEURIET: N.-Y., Bonner, 1891.] "is the story of a fysician's dauter reared by a peasant family, whŏse good sense and delicacy of feeling ar strengthened by a

simple country life. Her subsequent history is full of interest, and shōs how closely character and truth and romance ar related." [Publisher's Weekly. **2136**

MADEMOISELLE GIRAUD [by ADOLPHE BELOT: Chicago, *Laird*, 1891.] "has reached us in a cleverly executed translation. The book had tremendous vogue in France. The public believed that it had here found food for its ünwholesōme curiosity, and continued tŏ devour what it united in decrying. It rests on delicate ground, but it is delicately and seriously handled. It is an indictment for a crime; it is a session of the court, during which the depravity of society is exposed with the utmost severity. Its author has the clear, cold tone of a judge whŏ probes human monstrosities and applies the eternal law of chastisement as an honest man. His offense is simply tŏ hav troubled the quietude of people whŏ preferred tŏ relate the story in question behind closed doors tŏ seeing it freely circulated with all its avenging consequences." [Critic. **2137**

MADEMOISELLE MERQUEM. [by "G: SAND," i. e., Amantine Lucile Aurore (Dupin) Dudevant (†, 1876): N.-Y., *Carleton*, 1868.] The reader's first "impression .is of the extraordinary facility in composition begotten by the author's incessant practice. Never has a genius obtained a more complete and immediate mastery of its faculties . . . These things it is which besto an incomparable distinction on this àctual "Mademoiselle Merquem" far more than any felicity of selection in the way of events and characters. The style, as a style. strikes us as so far superior tŏ that of ōther novelists,

MADEMOISELLE MERQUEM. [by G : SAND : N.-Y., *Carleton*, 1868.] "It is tŏ be regretted, we think, that English-speaking peoples ar so much attached tŏ the novels of thêir respectiv countries as tŏ care little for the masterpieces of forêin fiction, espeçially those of France. The critics of both countries feel, or affect tŏ feel, a horror of French novels, but, as the French would say, thêre ar novels and novels. We can understand and sympa-shize with the feeling which leads them tŏ censure such works as the 'Lady with the Camelias,' 'Indiana' [No. 753], and sŏme of the stories of Balzac, whŏ, after Thackeray, is the grêatest modern novelist. No French writer has suffered more from the prejudiçes and the ignorance of her English critics than George Sand. The works of hers which hav been translated ar few, and thêy hav never been popular. We can recall but 4 or 5 American versions of her novels and novelettes, as 'Consuelo' [No. 650] and the 'Countess of Rudolstadt,' 'Teverino' [No. 2606], and 'Little Fadette' [No. 2108] . . . For it is ŏne of the special qualities of George Sand that she is always and thŏroly an artist. The story of Mademoiselle Merquem is very simple, as the story of most grêat works is—thêre is hardly enuf of it tŏ make a chapter in ŏne of Miss Braddon's romançes—but as handled by George Sand, how charming it is, and how interesting, too, tŏ those whŏ prefer character tŏ plot, and art tŏ mere "sensation" writing! We shal not undertake tŏ tel it here, further than tŏ say that it shŏs that the coldest, most statuesque, and apparently least lŏving of women can be wŏn by the right man, and so wŏn is the sweetest, tenderest, and most womanly of women. The character of Mademoiselle Merquem is ŏne of the most beautiful in the whole range of fiction, and tŏ hav drawn it so that it produçes this effect is a triumph of genius . . . The portrait of Mademoiselle Merquem is as lŏvely in recollection as that of Miranda or Imogen. The hero, Armand, whŏ tels the story, draws himself very skilfully, and stil more skilfully the person and individuality of his rival, Montroger, a weak, vaçillating man, whŏ with the best intentions in the world, is a monster of selfishness. The scene of the story is a village on the coast, the life of which, hi as wel as lo, is painted with the idyllic freshness which is ŏne of the grêatest charms in the writings of this author. The adventures of Armand amŏng the sailors ar grafically portrayed, and wil linger in the memory when scores of clever novels ar forgotten." [The Albion. **2138** that while the impression of it is fresh in your memory, you must make up your mind tŏ accept her competitors wholly on the ground of thêir merits of substance, and remit for the time the obligation of writing properly . .. The romance before us is conceived and executed with a heârtiness, a good faith, a spontaneity, which assuredly justify our use of the word "immortal"." [Nation. **2138**

MADEMOISELLE SOLANGE. ["Terre de France") by FRANCOIS DE JULLIOT: Chicago, *Rand*, 1889.] "This is a dainty, graceful and thŏroly agreeable novel. It is a picture of provincial society of which the tranquil surface is rippled by the arrival of a young parisian lady, full of caprices, sensitiv, proud, and capable of entire devotion. The story is charming; ŏne may even be permitted tŏ say that it is a refreshment tŏ find a new novel which is not the apostle of sŏme theory, but a lŏve story pure and simple. Perfectly refined in quality, unexceptionable in incident, it is a romance suitable for young girls as wel as for their elders." [Boston "Literary World. **2139**

MAGIC SKIN (The), by BALZAC. ☞ *ECCENTRIC NOVELS*.

MAKING AN OMELETTE [by GUSTAVE DROZ: in *Lippincott's Magazine*, Oct. 1871.] "is charming and pure." [Nation. **2140**

MAN AND MONEY [by ÉMILE SOUVESTRE (†, 1854): Liverpool. *Howell*, 1854.] "is an interesting but painful story,—shoing how a rich, hard-heârted man of capital may crush a rival and hunt him tŏ poverty without in the least transgressing the laws. It is written on the text of "Competition," and shŏs how the battle of mŏney may be as fatal as

the battle of armies; and the moral is that brŏtherly lŏve ŏt not tŏ be entirely excluded from business." [Athenæum. **2141**
——, SAME ("Two Rivals"), N.-Y., *T. R. Dawley*, 1865.

MAN OF THE PEOPLE (A) [by ÉMILE ERCKMANN and P: ALEX. CHATRIAN (†, 1890.): London, *Bentley*, 1871.] "is an account of the revolution of 1848, from the point of vue of ŏne whŏ took no small part in it. Jean Pierre Clavel, the hero, is a cabinet-maker. He has cŏme tŏ the capital from Saverne, whêre his youth was spent; and the workshop in which he finds employment, is ŏne of those places in which the revolutionary spirit was nurtured by hot discussion and made ripe for an outbrêak. ... The quiet scenes of Saverne life ar more interesting than the tumult of the revolution. When Jean-Pierre is first taken up by Madame Balais after his kinsfolk hav abandoned him, —when he climbs the long flïts of stairs in the old-fashioned house which is tŏ be his home,—when he masters his alfabet by grêat efforts, and is led the keener in his enjoyment of ŏne day's holiday in the week,— when he puts his whole energies intŏ the work he is learning under the quaint old cabinet-maker,—a series of delïtful pictures is unroled. No wŏnder that Jean-Pierre himself looked bac with regret upon that life from the narro streets of Paris, remembering his runs throu the long grass and his swims in the clear stream under the leaves." [Athenæum. **2142**

MAN WITH THE BROKEN EAR, by ABOUT, ☞ *ECCENTRIC NOVELS*.

MANON LESCAUT = No. 816.

MARBLE BUST (The), by ABOUT,

in *Russell's Magazine*, 1859, 36 pp. **2143**

MARGARET, by BERTHET, = No. 818. •

MARGARET MULLER, by BER-SIER, = No. 819.

MARGERY MERTON'S GIRL-HOOD [by ALICE CORKRAN : *Blackie*, 1887.] "is a careful and quietly humorous study of the life of an orfan whŏ is placed by her father under the care of a maiden ånt in Paris. The ånt, tho elderly and wizened, is a good soul and sensible withal, and manages tŏ let her nïece be reared very much in the way that the girl herself likes best. Margery and her fello-students, the excellent Mrs. Réville, the not less excellent painter, Mr. Delteil, and. abŏve all, poor Rose Lifebore, ar delītfully sketched. Then thêre is a conspiracy tŏ prevent Margery from obtaining a prize tŏ which she is entitled, and thêre is anŏther conspiracy tŏ defeat that conspïracy ; and thêre ar rural adventures resulting in the arrival on the scene of a Prince-Charming in the person of Arthur Wilton, a young englishman, whŏ would doubtless hav married Margery in the final chapter, had marriages been permissible in stories for school-girls. The french simplicity which, whêre it really exists, is exquisit, and which is altŏgether the opposit of that abomination knōn as chic, pervades this story like a perfume. An amount of skil and subtlety has been expended—we dŏ not say wasted—on 'Margery Merton's Girlhood' which would hav made the fortune of more than ōne good novel." [Spectator. **2144**

MARGUERITE, or Two Loves, by DELPHINE (GAY) GIRARDIN : *Appleton*, 1862. **2145**

MARIE DERVILLE [by HOR-TENSE (GUIZOT) DE WITT : *Lippincott*, 1873.] "is a brīt and pleasant story of country life. The heroin is a dauter of a captain whŏ departs on a 3 years' cruise. In his absence pecuniary troubles overtake the family, and his wife and mother set up a boarding-school, life in which constitutes the principal material of the story." [Boston "Literary World." **2146**

MARINER OF THE LOIRE (The) by É. SOUVESTRE, in *Southern Lit. Messenger*. Dec. 1855. **2147**

MARKETS OF PARIS (THE) ["Ventre de Paris") by ÉMILE ZOLA : *Peterson*, 1879.] "is the most successful and the subtlest study the author has made of ōne of those cŏlorless characters which offer few or no salient points tŏ most students of life, but whŏse delineation always tasks the hīest powers of the novelist of the first class. The heroin, Lisa. belongs tŏ the Macquart family—with differ-. ent members of which all of Mr. Zola's books ar concerned—and unites her father's selfishness and her mŏther's industry ; she may be called, in fact, the embodiment of the reasons which led tŏ her parents' marriage. Her 'enlītened self-interest' assures her that it is in the orderly path of life that cŏmfort dwels, and it is ōnly by the unwisdom of disorder, weakness, poverty, and sin by which so poignant a passion as anger is aroused in her. Her husband's brŏther, an escaped exile, suddenly reappears. Lisa is at ōnce ready tŏ divide with him the inheritance which her husband received from his uncle, and is displeased at the arrangement between the brŏthers which leaves it all in her hands and givs Florent a home with them. Her dislike of her brŏther-in-law begins with her aversion tŏ anyōne whŏ has suffered such hardships; that he has suffered unjustly, and that his character is noble, ŏnly emfasizes her general sense of a hopeless muddle whêre everything should be so clear. His willingness tŏ liv without work, altho he dŏes not spend a tithe of what belongs tŏ him, increases this aversion by offending her sense of the necessity of work in any wel-ordered life, and in ŏne way and anŏther she forces him tŏ accept a position under the government which he hates as his persecutor. He is drawn intŏ a revolutionary society, which she discŏvers, and. frītened for the safety of her family, she denounces him tŏ the police, whŏ ar already in possession of her story throu anonymous letters from the nêbors. Florent is transported, and Lisa quiets her conscience by reflecting that her course was open, and that her brŏther-in-law had already been denounced, and abŏve all by the return tŏ the quiet and orderly life which had been interrupted. Thêre is nothing contemptible in Lisa, it is tŏ be remarked. She is ŏne of the elements of society, and a product of civilization; tho an incarnation of selfishness, from sheer force of selfish wisdom she escapes the patent failings of characters superficially similar; she has, indeed, the garnered worldly wisdom of ages, and mīt be offered tŏ Mr. Mallock as an example of the passion with which 'honesty is the best policy' may be worshipped, or tŏ sŏme of his critics as an example of the tragedy such a character develops when brŏt intŏ contact with a life ordered by ideas which, however completely thêy may pre-figure the wisdom of the future, nevertheless threaten the comfort secured by the wisdom of past. Like

the rest of his books, 'The Markets of Paris' shŏs M. Zola committed tŏ a theory of novel-writing, but, unlike sŏme of them, it shŏs his ability, when he is at his best, tŏ sink his theorizing in an acute and dispassionate study of life and character. The details of the story, aside from the development of its principal character, ar even slīter than is usual with him." [Nation. **2148**

MARMORNE, = No. 824.

MARQUIS DE LÉTORIÈRE by SUE, [in Omnibus, vol. 2., N.-Y., *Mowatt.* 1844.] = No. 826.

MARQUIS DE VILLEMER, by "G: SAND," Boston, *Osgood*, 1871. **2149**

MARRIAGE (All About) by "GYP," i. e., countess Martel de Joinville: N.-Y., *Tousey*, 1880. **2150**

MARRIAGE IN HIGH LIFE (A). [by OCTAVE FEUILLET (†, 1890): Phil'a, *Porter*, 1875.] "The hero is handsŏme, rich, and accomplished; but at the age of 30 is stil a bachelor. He desires tŏ marry; but the wives he sees in society dŏ not suggest tŏ him the idea of domestic bliss. At last, he is introduced by his match-making godmother tŏ Marie Fitz-Gerald, and the twŏ ar presently betrothed. The characters of the twŏ, and the circumstances of thêir marriage, ar unqualifiedly auspicious; and thêy begin thêir new life assured of a blissful future. Thêir delītful dream is soon interrupted. Mrs. de Rias, intoxicated by the excitement of parisian society, yields herself tŏ it without reserv, and her husband, thus robbed of the home happiness he had anticipated, withdraws from his wife. Under the influence of certain gay ladies with whŏm she is intimate, Marie accepts the easy filosofy of thêir set, and draws near the precipice of ruin. At the most dangerous crisis she is

saved." [Boston "Lit. World." **2151**
MARRIAGE OF GABRIELLE
(The) [by DANIEL LESUEUR : Chicago, *Rand*, 1890.] "is pleasantly told,
the tone of the lŏve-tale is good and
pure, and all ends happily." [Writer. **2152**
MARRIAGE OF LOVE (A), by
HALÉVY. = *LOVE MATCH.*
MARRYING AND GIVING IN
MARRIAGE = No. 494.
MARRYING OFF A DAUGHTER
["MARIER SA FILLE") by "HENRI
GRÉVILLE," i. e., Alice M.. Céleste
(Fleury) Durand : *Peterson*, 1878.] "is
an entertaining story. The heroin and
the hero stand out in bold relief
against the setting of thêir disreputable surroundings, and thêre is a
grêat deal of humor in the talk of all
the people. In short, the writer's
cleverness cannot be questioned, and
thêre wil be but few, it is fair tŏ say,
whŏ wil object tŏ the good-natured
way in which the good people ar rewarded for thêir virtue by a cŏmfortable incŏme." [Atlantic. **2153**
MATILDA. [by EUGENE SUE:
N.-Y., *Winchester*, 1844, 8°, 414 pp.]
"The 'young woman' whŏse memoirs
ar laid before us has hardly contracted a marriage with ŏne of the most
charming. fashionable and devoted of
men, before she discŏvers that her
husband is bound hand and foot in
the thrall of a Mephistopheles, whŏ
wil not be content unless she also is
made tŏ minister tŏ his satisfaction.
This demon has riches by the bank
full,—of cŏurse. agents by the hundred ; and the strong interest of the
book is excited by the perpetual
terror he maintains in the mind of the
heroin. whŏse reputation he destroys,
whŏse person he menaces, whŏse husband, finally. he bribes and degrades

until he becŏmes a partner in his designs." [Athenæum. **2154**
MAUGARS, JR., = *YOUNG MAUGARS.*
MAUPRAT, = No. 836.
MAURICE, by F: BÉCHARD,
Carleton, 1871. **2155**
MEMBER FOR PARIS (THE).
[by EUSTACE CLAIRE GRENVILLE
MURRAY (†, 1881) : *Smith*. 1871.]
The hero "mixes in the 'grande
monde,' makes acquaintance with
literary and ŏther celebrities, amŏng
whŏm we recognize Arsène Hŏussaye,
Jules Favre, Blanqui and Worth.
Thêre is a vacancy for the Corps Législatif and Macrobe urges Horace tŏ
stand for it, and so intrîgues that he
is triumfantly returned. The pictures
of Parisian society which the book
contains ar thŏroly life-like, and such
as only an intimate knoledge of it
would enable any writer tŏ depict"
[Athenæum. **2156**
MERE CAPRICE (A). [by M..
(HEALY) BIGOT : *Jansen*, 1882.]
"The writer has the power of reproducing thŏt and scenes from the
french point of vue which almost
amounts tŏ genius. The 'caprice' is
the whimsical fancy of a rich, heârtless. and idle woman for an orfan
girl. Her best motiv is revenge upon
her husband's relativs, so that it is
ŏnly natural that upon the discŏvery
that the girl has by her beauty unconsciously won the lŏve of the artist
whŏ is the object of her ŏn ardent
passion, she ruthlessly turns her out
of doors. The moral of the book is
hî and pure in intention : it is the artist whŏ dreams of 'an ideal of tender
lŏve. unlike mere fevered passion—
lŏve which dares sho itself tŏ all; a
healthy, honest lŏve, which would not
fear the blessed monotony of every-

day life, with its work, and rest, and lo talks by the common heârth, and the patter of little feet for its home music'; but it is taut ōnly by negativs, and the story groes more pitiful as each struggle of the poor girl is more hopeless. The plot is new enuf and exciting enuf tŏ compel the reader tŏ follo it tŏ the end, but the book wil never be opened the second time; for, wel written as it is, thêre is nothing beyond the plot tŏ counterbalance the painful impression of the catastrofē." [Nation. **2157**

META HOLDENIS. [by V: CHERBULIEZ: *Appleton*, 1873.] "The story is told in letters by a young man, a painter, tŏ a lady, a friend living on the Rhein, whŏ has written tŏ him that she has chosen for him the maiden he is tŏ marry. The latter is a charming girl, sentimental as wel as practical, and her eyes ar of a heavenly blue; but about those heavenly blue eyes he has his opinion, and the novel is the account of the manner in which his present opinion of them was formed ... Naturally, at an early opportunity, Tony and Meta seek an explanation, which has the usual result of explanations in complicating matters more than ever, bringing him again under the power of her fascination ... The intrîgues of the girl ar discŏvered, and she leaves the house. Afterwards she becōmes a protestant sister, and denounces the immorality of the French, taking an account of the conduct of Tony and M. de Manserre for her text. It is, as may be seen, the story of an intrîguer, and, in ōur opinion, it makes a very interesting novel." [Na. **2158**

MICHELINE [**Normandie**] = No. 495.

MILDRED VERNON [by HAMIL-TON MURRAY: *Colburn*, 1848.] "is a novel of more than ordinary excellence. It is unusually wel written; the characters ar wel sustained; the conversations natural and lively; the plot ōne of grêat interest and skilfully developed; and altho much of the society intŏ which we ar introduced is, both socially and politically, as bad as need be,—the scene being laid amōng the hier ranks in Paris tōards the close of Louis-Philippe's rêign,—yet the tone and feeling of the book ar good throuōut, and the morality, while neither narro nor severe, is on the whole pure, correct, and even hī-minded." [National Review. **2159**

MILLER OF ANGIBAULT (The). [by "G: SAND," i. e., Amantine Lucile Aurore (Dupin) Dudevant (†, 1876): London, *Churton*, 1847, *Simms*, 1853, *Weldon*, 1878.] "The author introduces us tŏ a fāse of french life, unfamiliar tŏ the ordinary reader; and, while working out a plot of extraordinary interest, givs us pictures of affairs such as could hav been drawn ōnly by the hand of a master, and which, of themselvs, unaided by the fascination of the story, entitle this novel tŏ rank amōng the author's best." [Boston "Literary World."]— It "is divided intŏ 5 parts, embracing a narrativ of 5 successiv days; and with the exception of the prolog, the scene passes entirely within the narro limits of a country parish. The blemish in the book is that the author pushes tŏ extravagance her dreams of an ideal equality of ranks. Marcelle, the beautiful baroness, has formed a platonic friendship during her husband's life with Henri Lémor, a working engineer. When her husband dies, it is her delīt tŏ believe that she can besto herself on the friend whŏ has avowed his attachment tŏ her. But Lémor is proud, and an enthusiast in the principles which hav won him her admiration, and the idea of Marcelle's riches revolts him. He decides tŏ fly from her, for a year at least; but, like the moth flickering round the flame of the candle, he cannot help cōming after her tŏ Blanchemont. He experiences a moment of transport in hearing that her late husband has ruined her. Then, again, thêre is a relapse tŏ despondency when he finds that enuf has been saved from the wrec tŏ giv the object of his adoration a tolerable fortune. Finally, a fire, which burns a bundle of bank-notes with the farm buildings of Blanchemont, reduces her means tŏ such a very modest independence, that he succeeds in shaking himself free from his scruples. Thêy marry, and look forward tŏ a life of unruffled lŏve in a cŏttage. Such is the outline of the romance; and so far it sounds, and it is, absurd enuf. Yet such is the inimitable skil of the narrator that the book dŏes not strike us as ridiculous in the reading; and we see in Marcelle a hī-minded and fascinating woman, by no means excessivly eccentric. Refined as she is, born and reared as she has been, it is barely conceivable that she could find a congenial spirit in Lémor, whŏ must appear tŏ a man of the world tŏ be a prig and an embodiment of crochets. But thêre is an easy and effortless abnegation of the habits and prejudices of her birth and breeding in the way ĭn which she associates with the boors of Blanchemont, altho it savors unquestionably of poetical license." [Blackwood's. **2160**

MIMI. [by ESMÉ STUART: London, 1880.] "But ŏūr readers must not suppose that this little novelette deals ōnly with a child's fancies, or with word-pictures of Normandy scenery and the homely prettiness of a farm. We hav a tale of really thrilling interest, told with the simplicity and vividness which ar ōnly natural in recalling sŏme exciting and startling incident of childhood; and exceedingly wel told." [Speeta. **2161**

MIMI PINSON, ☞ Musset.

MISERABLES (Les) = No. 790.

MISERIES OF PARIS, by EUGENE SUE: N.-Y., W: II. Davis, 1891. **2162**

MRS. DYMOND [Paris] = No. 500.

MODERN CYMON (The) ["Jean"] by [C:] PAUL DE KOCK: London. rep. Phil'a, Carey, 1833.] "is an interesting novel, by a writer of much celebrity. The story, which is the same with the "Cymon" of Dryden, is truly delītful, and has ever been fascinating, tho it be found in every language. A youth of wild passions and bêarish, uncultivated manners, which entirely conceal his naturally good heârt, is arrested at the beginning of his evil courses, by the sīt of a lŏvely woman whŏm he rescues from an attack of sŏme robbers in a lonely street in Paris. Being gradually impressed with a sense of his deficiencies by comparing himself with ōthers, he resolvs tŏ reform, and devotes a year tŏ intense and solitary study in an 'entresol' opposit the house of his mistress, whence he catches a glimpse of her daily as she walks out and returns. The dénoument is stil more interesting. His manners becōme polished, his address easy, rufness and forwardness giv plăce tŏ modesty and diffidence, and the lŏvely cause of this wondrous change becōmes his." [N.-Y. Mirror.]—"If we wer requîred tŏ mention anyŏne of Kock's numerous productions as a specimen and proof of his talent, we should select *Jean;* not becâuse it contains the most brilliant of his humorous sketches, but because it is the most regular and best conducted of his novels, the most complete, varied, and natural; and while it certainly would not disgust—as sŏme of his romances mît disgust a fastidious english reader—would prŏve the capability of the writer, and demonstrate the nature and character of his style . . . The skil of the author is not shŏn in the original conception of the subject, but in his admirable style of carrying it throu; first, in the naturalness of the character of Jean under the circumstances of his education, the amusing manner in which these circumstances are exhibited, and next, for the knoledge of human nature, which has enabled him tŏ trace all the changes affected by the operation of new motivs and new ideas of pleasure." [Foreign Quart. Rev. **2163**

MODERN FRENCH LIFE (translations. edited) by C. G.. F.. ( ) GORE: London, 1842. **2164**

MODESTE MIGNON. [by HONORÉ "DE" BALZAC: *Roberts,* 1888.] "Few of Balzac's novels appeal tŏ the taste and sensibilities of english readers so fully as 'Modeste Mignon.' The heroin is a charming young girl whŏ sets about falling in lŏve in a very original and striking way, and chooses her husband with a mixture of audacity and good sense, which provoke interest and sympathy. Stil, full of brilliancy and charm altho the story is, the essential unreality of the chief character is always before the reader's mind. Modeste is ardent, naive, innocent. but

she is not, after all, an actual girl, but a mere projection of Balzac himself. Behind her spontaneity is the author's intention—the intention of a deeply sofisticated mind, full of whim, resource, and experience. But Balzac, being always Balzac, is never less than grêat, and 'Modeste Mignon' is ŏne of the most delītful of his works." [American.]—"Inthis work Balzac deals with the līter and sunnier side of the Comédie Humaine, often more of a tragedy in his hands. It tels of the lŏve affair of a pretty dauter of a Havre merchant with the friend of a parisian poet, carried on in a correspondence in which the friend masquerades as the poet himself. The most amusing situation in the book is whêre Dumay, the watch-dog of the maiden, goes tŏ Paris tŏ pull the nose of the impudent scribbler whŏ has dared from his garret tŏ address the girl, and is amazed and confounded by the splendor of the Canalis mansion. Thêre ar tedious places in the book, connecting the various episodes, but the reader would as soon quarrel with life for its stupid hŏurs, as with Balzac, for it is impossible in reading him tŏ avoid the feeling that Balzac is life." [Overland. **2165**

MONEY. [by "JULES A. TARDIEU," i. e., J. D. de St. Germaine (?): London, *Allen,* 1879.] Here "we hav a quiet comedy, clean, fragrant. and wel written, rather crowded with characters, which, however, ar drawn with good effect, and flavored with a mild humor." [Boston "Literary World." **2166**

MONEY. [by ÉMILE ZOLA: Boston. *Tucker,* 1891, 435 pp.] "is, as its name implies, a record of the effect produced upon the human race by its greed for gold. Certain capitalists, men whŏ hav spent thêir lives in speculativ ventures on the Bourse, start a Universal Bank, in connection with which thêre is tŏ be a steamship company. At first the scheme succeeds brilliantly, then cōmes the inevitable crash, and with it the crush of the small, the trampling crowd which folloes large armies, passion descending from the parlor tŏ the kitchen, from the bourgeois tŏ the workman and the peasant, and which hurled intŏ this mad gallop of millions subscribers having but twŏ or three shares, the whole emaciated and hungry mass of tiny capitalists which a catastrofē such as this sweeps away like an epidemic and lays at rest in the pauper's grave. The originators of the scheme, those whŏ hav been the cause of all this, ar pursued by the endless wail arising from the frītful anguish produced by this tragedy of mōney. In its study of the subject, which it is the purpos of this novel tŏ treat, it is truly grêat. The descriptions of the scenes at the exchange, the development of the character of the man whŏ is the mainspring of this mad speculation, the horde of parasites whŏ cling tŏ him in thêir overpowering greed until he goes down and then desert him, ar certainly marvellous in thêir realism. It is a masterly work, unnecessarily revolting at times in sōme of its details, nevertheless a book in which a difficult subject is handled with the utmost skil and which sustains the most unflagging interest tŏ its last page." [Critic.]—"In his latest novel, L'Argent, thêre is a fairer balance than in his ōther books; thêre ar decent people, kindly folk, men and women of honest heârts and willing hands. We hav a pleasant glimpse

of the home life of Mazaud, the stocbroker whŏ commits suicide when he fails. The Jordans, husband and wife, ar perhaps the pleasantest pair tŏ be found in all Zola's novels. With the novelist's increasing fame, apparently, he is taking brīter vues of humanity. And Madame Caroline, despite her lapse, mīt almost be called an honest woman, if this is not a paradox, she is a strong, wholesōme, broad-minded creature, admirably realized. Thêre is no disputing also that Zola is a novelist of most extraordinary fecundity and force." [Brander Matthews. **2167**

MONEYBAGS AND TITLES. ["Sacs et Parchemens") by [LEONARD SYLVAIN] JULES SANDEAU (†, 1883): *Lippincott*, 1851.] "A certain epigrammatic vivacity of style and expression, occasionally amounting tŏ wit, and an ingenious plot, fully sustain the reader's attention. The types presented of certain important classes of frenchmen ar certainly not flattered but neither must thêy be looked upon as mere caricatures ... The pivot of the tale is the misplaced ambition of a wealthy parisian citizen, whŏse heavy purse and huge vanity render him the target of a host of inguers, and especially of a dowager marchioness, more proud of her pedigree than scrupulous in her manœuvres ... Its tone and tendency ar alike unobjectionable; and we ar quite sure that it wil be a general favorite with english readers." [Blackwood's. **2168**

MONKEY ISLAND, or The Adventures of Polydore Marasquin, by LÉON GOZLAN: *Warne*, 1888. **2169**

MONSIEUR ANTOINE = *SIN OF M. ANTOINE.*

MONSIEUR DE CAMORS, by

MONSIEUR DE CAMORS. [by Oc-
TAVE FEUILLET (†, 1890): N.-Y., Blelock, 1860, Phil'a, Peterson, 1870.] "Sŏme
persons hav taken 'M. de Camors' for M. de
Morny, ŏthers for the Duke of Gramont;
but the personage is ŏne of pure imagination, and is meant tŏ represent a class . . .
Camors, the elder, thŏt nŏthiug of religion, little of honor, a good deal of politics and fençing, and he concluded his
adviçe tŏ his sŏn by counselling him not
tŏ get angry, tŏ lâf seldom, and never tŏ
weep. Whilst he was penning these instructions, his sŏn was seduçing the wife
of an innoçent architect with whŏm he
had been at school . . . The acquaintançe
with Lescandre was renewed by an
aççidental meeting. Camors endeavored
n'ot tŏ fall in lŏve; but ŏne fatal opportunity got the better of his resolution. A dinner-party, the husband called away on business, an ânt obliged tŏ retire by a headache,
a young wife left 'tête-a-tête' with a handsŏme man of fashion, a few minutes spent
in the twilight, hands that met: 'Sir, I beg
you tŏ leave me;' a few seconds more,
and Mrs. Lescandre awoke from a trançe.
. . . Camors goes tŏ parliament, and becŏmes a working member. He was looked upon as a probable minister, and made
himself useful in committees. His father
had recommended him 'honor;' and a lot
of men about town thŏt the prinçiple a
good ŏne. Thêy formed a Patent Safety-
Club; no member of the club was tŏ trifle
with the wife or dauter of anŏther member. This rule was not applicable tŏ
people whŏ wer blac-balled, and so the
margin given tŏ the leading prinçiple was
large. Tho not muried, Camors joined it

and General de Campvallon did likewise,
and an extra barrier was thrŏn between
the rising Deputy and Mrs. de Campvallon. Wild resolutions, vows, reflections
on the regulations of the Patent Safety
Club wer all made in vain in presençe
of the suberb beauty and elegant woman
whŏ ruled the world of fashion, and whŏ
had never ceased tŏ lŏve. Thêre wer
moments of remorse; and Camors was
was very near confessing his crime at
the club. The poor general suspected
nothing til an anonymous letter half-
opened his eyes. From behind a curtain
whêre his wife plaçes him he is witness of
an intervue between the couple. Camors
arrives, is coldly reçeivd by Madame, and
immediately smels a rat behind the arras.
Charlotte persuades him tŏ marry, and in
the hearing of the general, he promises tŏ
espouse Mrs. de Técle's dauter. Camors
keeps his word, and an element of jeal-
onsy is introduçed: the mistress is jealous
of the neglected wife, whŏ ŏne day is
put in possession of a letter from Mrs. de
Campvallon tŏ her husband, which leaves
no doubt of the intimaçy existing between
them. The countess finds that she has
been married merely tŏ favor the intrigues of ŏthers. Mrs. de Técle had tŏ cŏme
from the country; thêre was no scandal;
but the young wife was carried home
broken-heârted. Camors did try tŏ becŏme better, but could not; he wrestled in
vain with his fatal attachment . . . Curious trials crop up now and then, and
Feuillet might select half-a-dozen tŏ sho
that his picture of French life is not overdrawn." [Examiner   **2170**

OCTAVE FEUILLET: N.-Y., *Blelock*, 1868; Phil'a, *Peterson*, 1870. **2170**
MONSIEUR D'HAUTERIVE = *ROMANCE OF A POOR YOUNG MAN.*
MONSIEUR FRANCOIS by IVAN TURGÉNIEF: in *Appleton's Journal*, May, 1880. **2171**
MONSIEUR SYLVESTRE. [by "G: SAND," i. e., Amantine Lucile Aurore (Dupin) Dudevant (†, 1876): *Roberts*, 1870.] "The hero is a young man whŏ has abandoned the house of his uncle, and his probable hêirship, because that relativ would force him intŏ a distasteful marriage ... In his retirement Pierre presently becŏmes conscious of twŏ nêbors—an old man and a young girl. In due time he becŏmes acquainted with both, finding ŏne tŏ be M. Sylvestre, and the ŏther tŏ be the lady whŏm his uncle desired him tŏ marry. The progress of the acquaintance of these three,—poor, proud, hī-souled creatures, each possessing a secret sorro,—is touchingly sketched. The reader falls instantly in lŏve with M. Sylvestre, and becŏmes penetrated with the keenest curiosity about him. In the development of the story twŏ ŏther ladies—tŏ each of whŏm, at different times, his uncle had wished tŏ marry Pierre—ar introduced, both of strong and striking individuality ; ŏne married, the ŏther single. Anŏther male character cŏmes in, M. Gédéon, a Jew of grêat wealth, powerful intellect and marked personal fascinations. Among all these personages, thrŏn tŏgether in the country, sundry lŏve affairs spring up, and the history of these make the volume." [Boston 'Literar y World." **2172**
MOTHER (A). by H. MALOT, N.-Y., *Belford*, 1890, 284 pp. **2173**

MOTHER AND DAUGHTER, by BALZAC, in vol. 5, of *Romancists' Library*, ed. Hazlitt. London, 1841. **2174**
MOTHER OF A MARCHIONESS (The) by ABOUT, in *The Great Republic*, N.-Y., aug.-sept., 1859. **2175**
MOTHERLESS = *A PARISIAN FAMILY.*
MOUSTACHE, or Three Students of Paris [by [C :] PAUL DE KOCK: in *The Novelist*, London, 1839.] "Paul de Kock is that in the literary world, which Michel Angelo was in the realms of sculpture—a perfect master, whŏ with a single touch can reproduce nature in all its truest and most various shapes. He is as much at home in the pathetic as in the humorous, and can extract tears from the eyes as readily as he can draw smiles tŏ the lips. His sensibility is natural and true; that of Dickens is insipid and mawkish. That half-school-boy—half idiot, Nicholas Nickleby, with his maudlin ideas of honor which scarcely repress the spirit of the adventurer, finds no parallel in the category of heroes whŏ figure in the novels of Paul de Kock. We cannot dŏ ŏtherwise than pronounce Nicholas Nickleby tŏ be a most unfortunate tale, written without palpable plot or design, interrupted by frequent astounding starts and leaps. and so forced in its 'dénoument', that the reader almost wŏnders what reference the last number bêars tŏ the preceeding ŏnes . . . Giving the full award of his grêat merits tŏ Mr. Dickens. we cannot admit that he is tŏ be named even in the same breath with Paul de Kock. The French author is a man of education,—Dickens dŏes not pretend tŏ possess this advantage: the former is as familiar with the pathetic style of writing, as

with the humorous; the pathos of the latter is bombast or bathos. Paul de Kock's writings contain a degree of interest which renders it impossible for the reader tŏ lay down the book until he has arrived at the end; his descriptions ar very brîef, but invariably contain a volume in a few words; and his scenes of life amongst the middling or loer orders of the Parisians ar indisputably the most faithful and natural pictures of the same subjects upon record." [Monthly Review, 1840. **2176**

MUSSET, [L: C.] ALFRED DE, SELECTIONS from his *PROSE AND POETRY* [N.-Y., *Hurd & Honghton*, 1870] contains *White Blackbirds*, and *Mimi Pinson*. **2177**

MY BROTHER JACK = *LITTLE GOOD-FOR-NOTHING.*

MY BROTHER YVES, by "P: LOTI": *Vizetelly*, 1887. **2178**

MY COUSIN, MISS CINDER-ELLA. [by LÉON DE TINSEAU; *Appleton*, 1888.] "It is a slight but agreeable performance, and the picture given in it of an old aristocratic french family has a striking air of reality." [American. **2179**

MY SISTER JEANNIE. [by "G: SAND," i. e., Amantine Lucile Aurore (Dupin) Dudevant (†. 1876): *Roberts*, 1874.] "The incidental contrast of the vehement lŏve-making of Laurent and Manuela with the timid, childlike, yet fervent drawing tŏgether of Laurent and Jeannie, is ŏne of the many wêighty lessons of the book. It might seem absurd tŏ commend ·G: Sand' as a moral teacher; but we venure tŏ say that no ŏne can read this book carefully and searchingly without feeling conscious of a refining and ennobling influence. It is unlike any of the author's earlier novels with

which we ar familiar, being simple in thôt and style, and pervaded by a certain gentleness of spirit which is very pleasant." [Boston "Literary World." **2180**

MY STORY [by K.. S. MACQUOID: *Appleton*, 1874.] "is a novel in autobiografical form, and is written with quiet power. It is singularly refined, and is ŏne of the most delicate and beautiful histories of the transformation of woman's nature under the influence of lŏve which we ever met. The plot is simple, and the action is so circumscribed that many novel-readers wil find no entertainment in the book. But it is ŏne of those stories whŏse charms ar subtile, not external and palpable ... The personages of the story ar strongly individual and drawn with sharpness and delicacy, the many french characters being especially winning, and the pictures of french country life, tho very quiet, ar not less delightful. The novel is a good, almost grêat, ŏne of its kind, and its tone is as pure as the ripple of a brook." [Boston "Literary World." **2181**

MY UNCLE BARBASSON [by MARIO UCHARD: *Vizetelly*, 1888.] "among the author's more or less fantastical novels ... has enjoyed exceptional popularity ... Thŏroly french in the character of the adventures it describes, but unlike much modern french fiction, it aims at being amusing rather than psychological." [Athenæum. **2182**

MY UNCLE BENJAMIN, by TILLIER, = No. 855.

MYSTERIES OF PARIS. [by [M.. JOSEPH] "EUGENE" SUE: N.-Y., *Winchester*, 1843.] "A sovran prince is the hero—his dauter, whŏm he has disŏned, the heroin; and the tale begins by his fīting a man on the street, and taking a fancy tŏ his unknŏn child. whŏ livs in ōne of the loest dens in Paris! The ŏther 'dramatis personæ' ar convicts, receivers of stolen goods, murderers, intrîguers of all ranks—the aforesaid prince, in the disguise sŏmetimes of a workman, sŏmetimes of a picpocket, acting the part of a providence among them, rewarding the good and punishing the guilty. The english personages ar the Countess M' Gregor—the wife of the Prince—her brŏther Tom, and Sir Walter Murph, Esquire. These ar all jostled, and crowded, and pushed, and flurried—first in flash dens, whêre the language is slang; then on farms, and then in halls and palaces—and so intermixed and confused that the clearest head gets puzzled with the entanglements of the story; and confusion gets worse confounded as the farrago proceeds." [Blackwood's.]—"The morality of 'Les Mystères' strikes us as worse, because of the hīer professions made in it by the author, and recognized by the throngs of his eager admirers. In this tale as we hav said. we encounter power in the cause of benevolence. The passion of the Grand-Duke of Gerolstein is tŏ bring mischief tŏ light, tŏ succor misery, and tŏ punish evil; he stalks throu all the moral filth of Paris, redressing crime by crime, detecting chicanery for artifice.—here, putting out the eyes of ōne sinner, tŏ giv him time and motiv for repentance,—thêre, awakening the vilest passions of anŏther, without satisfying them, that they may sting thêir possessor; telling falsehood after falsehood, employing tric after tric, tŏ recommend truth, and purity, and disinterestedness—and tŏ set right the

distortion in the relations between the small and the grêat, the wêarers of rags and of cloth of gold." [Athenæum.]—"We freely avow, that in the whole range of fiction-writing, we hav never met anything so thrilling and powerful as 'The Mysteries of Paris.' The works of Mr. Dickens, while thêy dŏ not surpass the "Mysteries" in bold and effectiv delineation of character and freedom and truthfulness of dialog, fall far belo them in interest of plot and general scope and purpos. Thêre is sŏmething of that indefinit vastness about the design and execution of the "Mysteries"—that shifting and far-stretching horizon which seems as if just subsiding from the infinity of chaos—that speaks of sublimity, and startles the sōul with a class of sensations seldom aroused by literary stimulants. Tŏ enter intŏ anything like an analysis of the plot of this wŏnderful book would be totally impossible—as nothing short of copying the whole would giv the reader an efficient idea of the power, pathos and poetry here strewn over the loest and most disgusting details of lo life as wel as the hypocritical and seductiv vices of the nobility and the cŏurt. Sŏme of ōur readers may hav met random assertions that the "Mysteries" contain much that is improper and impure, in thŏt and expression. This is not so. We profess tŏ despise and loathe the licentiousness of the press as heârtily and wholly as anyŏne; nor could any consideration tempt us tŏ gloss over a work which we thŏt had an improper tendency. Such, however, is not the "Mysteries of Paris." True, much which is evil, gross, disgusting, horrible. is thêre described. and with so vivid power and effect, that it is as if a broad glare of lightning had suddenly illuminated the dens of a vast metropolis and laid bare thêir secrets. Thêre is no maudlin attempt, as in Paul Clifford, tŏ sugar over crime, and sho ŏnly its fairer side. The picture is *truth;* and all truth is wholesŏme. The translator, Mr. Town, has performed his difficult and thankless duties with a neatness, a delicacy of finish, a clearness of perception, and an acuteness of comprehension, which dŏ him honor." [Ladies' Companion. 1843.

——, SAME (abridged), *Harper,* 1843. **2183**

MYSTERIES OF THE HEATH-ER, by F. Soulié: N.-Y., *Langley,* 1844. **2184**

MYSTERIES OF THE PEOPLE. by Sue. = No. 856.

NABOB (The). [by Alphonse Daudet: *Estes, Smith,* 1878.] "is a picture of Parisian life in the garish heyday of the Second Empire; and the evident intention is tŏ sho how essentially tawdry, hollo, contemptible, intellectually little and morally base, that superficially brilliant régime really was." [Appleton's.]—"The hero is a man from the south of France, whŏ has risen from grêat poverty tŏ the possession of enormous wealth by mysterious practices in Tunis. Of course his main desire, now that he has made a fortune, is tŏ spend it in Paris . . . One of the most prominent figures in the motley crowd is the Duke de Mora. This worthy nobleman is distinctly drawn, and so ar sŏme of the less aristocratic characters; but the nabob himself rises far abŏve them all. The story of his crude, boyish ambitions, of his sincere delight in his success, of his humility in defeat, of his affection for those he lŏved, and of his kindliness for every ŏne, is good reading, altho the narrativ is too profusely enriched with all sorts of scandalous titbits which forever tickle the reader's appetite." [Atlantic.]—"An irish doctor is ŏne of the leading personages in the story. His celebrity in Paris about 1860, his intimate friendship with de Morny, the description of his person, and even the decorations which he wêars, suggest Sir Joseph Olliffe. Mr. Daudet wished when he wrote the book that his readers should say tŏ ŏne anŏther, "Jenkins, you kno, is Olliffe." Yet he makes the Duke's fysician liv publicly with a lady whŏ turns out not tŏ hav been his wife, and, not tŏ speak of his minor crimes, he makes him murder his friend and patient, the duke. Sir Joseph Olliffe's wido and children ar living. Portraits, far from flattering, of Mr. Mocquard and of sŏme whŏ, like Mr. Jules de Lesseps, ar alive, ar also introduced." [Athenæum. **2185**

NANON, by G: Sand, = No. 859.

NATHALIE. [by Julia Kavanagh: *Colburn,* 1859.] "A sentiment, a tenderness, an old world, french grace ar commanded by Miss Kavanagh which ar as individual as thêy ar elegant. Nathalie is the long lŏvestory of a wayward heârt,—the narrativ of a contest perseveringly maintained between girlish wilfulness and fascination and middle-aged reserv and suspicion,—thêre being no lac of bystanders tŏ foment every misconstruction for thêir tortuous purposes, yet the tale never languishes intŏ sicliness—never becŏmes dragging and wearisŏm. By the side of the petulant, sprightly Nathalie the episodical character of her pale and saintly sister Rose, thus charmingly introduced, acquires a double beauty. Most especially, too, after her kind, dŏ we like ânt Radegonde, the old canoness. —But we should not soon cŏme tŏ an end wer we tŏ specify all the delicate touches and attractiv pictures which places Nathalie hĭ amŏng books of its class." [Athenæum. **2186**

NEAR TO HAPPINESS [*Appleton*, 1889.] "is a society novel. Like nearly all french stories it is readable and clever, but it is chiefly devoted to describing the lŏve affairs of married women." [Boston "Lit. World." **2187**

NEW LEASE OF LIFE (A) or Saving a Daughter's Dowry, by E. [FR. V.] ABOUT: *Vizetelly*, 1880. **2188**

NINETTE [by C.. LOUISE HAWKINS DEMPSTER: *Appleton*, 1888.] "is an attractiv story of peasant life in Provence. Possessing always a strong originality, the nature of the french peasant is replete with the germs of romance and song. "Ninette" is a very simple story, merely that of a bankrupt peasant-proprietor whŏse pretty little dauter was pursued by the roué of the village, and whŏse honor and happiness wer defended by her young soldier lŏver. But tho simple, the story has decided personality, tŏgether with a cŏlor and freshness which ar quite distinctiv. It has the delicate piquancy of french landscape art, with its simplicity of scenery and handling. Perhaps no ŏne knew the french peasant better than 'George Sand,' and we hav in this book, tho in an inferior degree, the same intimate knoledge of thêir nature. The carnival earthquake of 1887 at Nice servs for the timely taking off of those persons whŏ stood in the way of little Ninette's happiness, and typifies that retributiv justice with which a happy fiction fortunate-

ly beguiles us." [Critic. **2189**

NINETY-THREE, by HUGO, = No. 867.

NO RELATIONS, by MALOT, = No. 868.

NOBLE SACRIFICE, by FÉVAL, = No. 869.

NOSE OF A NOTARY, by ABOUT, ☞ *ECCENTRIC NOVELS.*

NOTARY'S DAUTER ["Un Mariage en Provence") by LÉONIE ( ) AULNEY: *Bentley*, 1878.] "The pictures of french manners and habits in the comparativly unconventional life of 'the provinces, both in 'The Notary's Daughter,' and in 'The House of Penarvan,'—ar lightly and grafically presented." [Athenæum.] —"A match is arranged for motivs of convenience, amŏng which certain political arrangements ar the most important, between Rose, dauter of the notary of La Ciotat, and the second son of Baron de Croixfonds. The notary looks for aristocratic connections and wealth; the baron looks for political influence. It happens that the second son is ŏne in whŏm he had been grîevously disappointed, grêat hopes of intellectual ability having ended in what seemed not far from imbecility. The marriage, however, takes place; but Rose betrays her disgust at the husband whŏ has been provided for her, and the twŏ seem alienated for life. How she finds out her mistake (for the young man is a genius, not an imbeçil),'and how all things cŏme right in the end, is very gracefully told in these pages. The characters of the story ar vivid and picturesque, and the interest is wel sustained." [Spectator. **2190**

NOTRE COEUR = *COQUETTE'S LOVE.*

NOTRE DAME = No. 871.

NUMA ROUMESTAN. [by AL-
PHONSE DAUDET: (Paris, 1881.),
Vizetelly, 1884; Chicago, *Rand*, 1890.
(337 pp.)] "Daudet here tels us how
the handsŏme young Provençal goes
tŏ Paris at the age of 24; frequents
a café in the Latin Quarter, the favorit haunt of a crowd of boisterous
countrymen, amŏng whŏm, because of
his strong lungs, originality, and lŏve
for music, he is at ŏnce installed as a
favorit; goes twŏ or three times a
week tŏ the opera or the play, and by
successful lying, for which he has a
positiv genius, gets a reputation as an
artist; is installed as fourth secretary
of a celebrated advocate throu a pretended enthusiasm for Mozart; by
audacity wins a beautiful wife with a
fortune; and, tŏ complete the story, is
at 30, Minister of Fine Arts. This
career Mr. Daudet depicts with almost cruel fidelity, and the public has
not been slo tŏ recognize the portrait.
It is probable, however, that not ŏne
person, but mäny, hav supplied the
details of a picture whŏse outlines wer
unmistakably drawn from the life of
the grêat Opportunist—Gambetta.
Thêre is an undercurrent of domestic
sorro running throu the ştory, a tale
of a beautiful and trustful wife, whŏ
finally learns of her husband's unfaithfulness but is tied tŏ him by the
convenances." [Boston "Literary
World."]—"Mr. Henry James and
Mr. Zola ar at ŏne in giving the first
place in Mr. Alphonse Daudet's remarkable series of fictions tŏ 'Numa
Roumestan,' of which we here hav a
translation which, altho free and flŏ-
ing, is nearly everything which could
be desired. Mr. James says:—"Daudet's ŏther works hav thêir inequalities, thêir anomalies, certain places
whêre, if vou tapped them, thêy

would sound hollo. The beauty of
'Numa Roumestan' is that it has no
hollo places; the logic and the image
melt everywhêre intŏ ŏne." ... It is
its bright realism,—bright even in its
satire,—and its equality of style
which constitute the charm of 'Numa
Roumestan' and mark it as Mr. Daudet's masterpiece, regarded merely as
a work of art. It is full of its author's **Provence**, of the mistral, of
the farandole, of "the song and sunburnt mirth," which cŏme, however,
from the soil and the climate, rather
than from the heârt or the conscience,
and which, while thêy express "joy
abroad," also conceal "grîef at home."
M. Daudet's light-heârted Provençals
whŏ, under a blazing sun, jostle and
lâf, and chatter in the amfitheatre,
and bepraise the Bourbon nose and
imposing appearance of thêir hero,
the Legitimist Deputy Numa Roumestan, ar quite as true tŏ life as the
Sicilian peasants of Theokritos, and
very nearly as entertaining. In fact,
Mr. Daudet's grêat triumf consists in
making his readers not ŏnly pity and
forgiv, but almost lŏve Numa, whŏ is
weak, shallo, vainglorious, self-indulgent, all things tŏ all men, and restrained ŏnly by cowardice from
being all things tŏ all women, not because he is a worthy man at bottom,
but because he is a typical Provençal,
and has in him, thêrefore, not even
the germs of those virtues of which
self-control is the first. One is almost
tempted tŏ be wroth with his wife
Rosalie,—cold, proud, a true child of
the North,—for not more readily forgiving him his weak mendacities, his
weaker "liaisons"; for being induced tŏ
return tŏ him ŏnly when her mŏther
tels her that "men ar deceivers ever,"
and prŏves what she says by telling of

678

the weakness of her ŏn father, whŏm she has hithertŏ regarded as immaculate. Is she not a bit of a prig as wel as of a prude? ... Even his political fibre is of the poorest; altho the enthusiastic champion of Legitimism, he is saved from taking office under the Empire ŏnly by the superior and restraining moral sense of his wife. But simply because he is amiable, impulsiv, tender, because, in his superficial fashion, he lŏves Rosalie better than ăny ŏther woman, ŏne is sorely pressed tŏ pardon him, or, at least, tŏ blame Provence, and not him, for his weaknesses." [Spectator. **2191**

ODD NUMBER (THE). [by GUY DE MAUPASSANT: *Harper*, 1889.] "The first of these tales is a picture of rural life which has its parallel in the paintings of François Millet. The atmosfere of the norman village, the simple and careful manners of the peasants, the grim fate which can depend from so slight a thing as a chance pîece of twine saved from the mud of the road, all ar rendered with depth and suggestivness of sentiment, and with absolute command of effects." [Boston "Lit. World." **2192**

OLD HOUSE IN PICARDY = Diane Coryal.

ON THE EDGE OF THE STŎRM = No. 880.

ON THE SCENT = No. 512.

ONCE AND AGAIN [by HENRIETTA CAMILLA (JACKSON) JENKIN: *Smith*, 1865.] is "a fitting title, for it is ŏne of those few novels, which, when ŏnce read, ar worthy of being taken up again. Its story is interesting, tho it deals with few startling incidents; it is touching and pathetic, and yet it dŏes not leave a dismal impression; it teaches a useful lesson, but it is thŏroly free from anything

like sermonizing. We can cordially recommend it as a book which we hav read with grêat pleasure, and which we belîeve wil meet with general approbation. The heroin is a very attractiv being, and her character is admirably sustained throuŏut the record of her childhood and girlhood, and the earlier years of her married life. Thêre is a grêat charm in the picture of her home in Paris; the house intŏ which she, as a child, brings happiness by her presence, and in which everyŏne adores her, from the marquis on the first floor tŏ the family of the dissolute professor in the attic. Equally pleasant is the account of the swiss paradise, in which, as a girl of 15, she inspires a passionate and il-omened lŏve in the breast of her former playfello in Paris." [London Review. **2193**

ONE OF THE FORTY = *THE IMMORTAL.*

ONESTA, by OCTAVE FEUILLET, N.-Y., *E. D. Long & Co.*, 1860. **2194**

ONLY A GIRL: A Tale of Brittany. [London, *Wells*, 1883.] "is a pathetic story of the Breton maiden, Françoise Dano. We find her an orfan in the first chapter, and leave her in the last solitary, with her hopes of happiness disappointed, yet not unhappy, because her heârt is wholly given tŏ caring for ŏthers." [Spectator. **2195**

ONLY SISTER (AN), by PAULINE (GUIZOT) DE WITT: *Low*, 1872. **2196**

OPERA-BOX (The), or Judith, by EUGENE SCRIBE, in *The Emerald*, Boston, 1869. **2197**

OUT OF THE WORLD, by M.. (H.) BIGOT, = No. 886.

OUTBREAK OF THE REVOLUTION, by ERCKMANN-CHATRIAN, = No. 887.

PAPA, MAMMA, & BABY. ["Monsieur, Madame, Bébé,") by [ANTOINE] GUSTAVE DROZ: *Vizetelly*, 1887.] "Nŏthing could be more realistic than this idyl of parentage and domesticity—a little too realistic perhaps at points for american taste, but stil always decent and tender, albeit it admits the reader tŏ scenes from which all strangers but the doctor ar generally excluded [compare No. 1889.] and takes him intŏ almost the inmost confidences of husband and wife, father and mother. But everything is as delicate and fine as the baby's wardrobe, and thêre ar uses in seeing how thêy manage these things in France." [Boston "Lit. World." **2198**

——. SAME, "Bertha's Baby," *Peterson*, 1881.

PARISIAN FAMILY (A). [by HENRIETTE (GUIZOT) DE WITT: *Low*, 1871.] "Mdlle. Louise becŏmes, by the death of her mŏther, mistress of her father's house, and in the receipt of 1.500 francs a year for the dress of herself and her twŏ sisters; she is ŏnly 16, and thinks it delītful tŏ order dinner, and be the mistress, and abŏve all, tŏ buy her dresses. All her follies and sorrŏs and errors ar very pleasantly told; and, of course, everybody, if not perfect, is at least in the way of being so, before the story ends. The work is beautifully translated." [Athenæum. **2199**

——, SAME ("Motherless"), *Harper*, 1871; *Munro*, 1879.

PARISIANS (The), = No. 889.

PARTNERS = *FROMONT.*

PASSAGES FROM THE LIFE OF A HAPPY MAN, by K: SPINDLER (†, 1855) in *Southern Lit. Messenger*, Dec. 1841. **2200**

PASSION IN THE DESERT (A).

by BALZAC, in *The Duchess* [No. 2020.] **2201**

PAST FORGIVENESS [by MARGARET E.. (LINDSAY) MAJENDIE: *Bentley*, 1889.] "has the author's old faculty of making french people real tŏ us; indeed Madame Brise, Mlle. Manchon, and the notary's wife in thêir first conversation would be enuf tŏ stamp the book in this respect. But besides the vividness of the dialog thêre is so much power and pathos in the central situation (the passionate lŏver turned priest, and afterwards discŏvering that the wife he mŏrns is living and lŏving him as old) as tŏ raise this portion of the story tŏ a hī moral level. The idea is ŏne which forms a feature in ŏne of Charles Reade's novels, but the treatment of it here is different." [Athenæum. **2202**

PASTELS OF MEN [by PAUL BOURGET: *Roberts*, 1892.] "first and second series, containing in the first the three titles *A Saint, Monsieur Legrimaudet*, and *Two Little Boys*. The skil of line, the touch of delicacy, the simplicity and yet subtlety of motiv, make these portraits not ŏnly charming in themselvs, but admirable studies in literature. If ŏne could but learn this deft art!" [Atlantic. **2203**

PASTORALS OF FRANCE. [by F: WEDMORE: *Bentley*, 1877.] "In thêir tenderness, thêir simplicity, thêir truthfulness tŏ the slo and remote life which thêy picture, in the quaint accuracy of thêir slight touches, in the atmosfere of them, these 'Pastorals' ar almost perfect ... . '*The Four Bells of Chartres*' is a very hīly finished study, so dŏne as tŏ preserv an appearance of simplicity ... '*A Last Love at Pormic*' includes sŏme admirable touches of french charac-

ter, as true as thêy ar carefully slight.
... Here is the slightest thread, upon
which it would be impossible tŏ hang
a story;—Mr. Wedmore has hung a
string of pearls upon it ... ' *Yvonne
of Croisic*' is a beautiful little story,
as sad as the 'lonely country, leading
nowhither,' whêrein Yvonne dwelt;
the country tŏ which inland France is
'abroad,' and Piriac, 'beyond the farthest point, five hours' sail,' so far
that the dwellers thêre ar foreiners,
and a girl of Croisic may not marry a
man of Piriac, because she cannot
leave her ŏn people and her father's
house. Mr. Wedmore draws a
strangely beautiful picture of the
place and the people, the lonely country which made lonely lives for those
whŏ dwelt in it ... 'Pastorals of
France' is a book tŏ be read with
grêat, and tŏ be re-read with increased,
pleasure." [Spectator. **2204**

PAVILIONS OF THE LAKE
(The), by THÉOPHILE GAUTIER, in
Aldine, Jan., 1872. **2205**

PEASANT PROMETHEUS (A) =
A BRETON JOINER.

PÈRE GORIOT [by HONORÉ "DE"
BALZAC: (†, 1850) *Roberts*, 1885;
Munro, 1886; *Rand*, 1886, *Routledge*,
1887.] "is a good name for a fine
book; yet I am not sure that 'La Maison Vauquer' would not fit the book
even better. True, the tragedy is the
tragedy of a father sacrificed tŏ his
dauter's lust and avariçe. But the
'pension' is the scene and very symbol
of his martyrdom, and the house, like
the book, has dark secrets not directly
connected with Goriot's story. In his
treatment of the Maison Vauquer,
Balzac reaches romanticism throu
realistic methods. This ŏne sinister
house stands out from the houses
about it with a lurid light upon it.

Picked out in this light, the mean
lodging-house reveals itself as a centre and heârt of suffering, scheming,
struggling, criminal Paris. Tŏ make
the work of the builder's hands cŏlor
and overshado the lives of men, tŏ giv
it a fysiognomy and a soul which
haunt the imagination as of a thing
alive and purposful,—this is a note of
romanticism. It is a function of romance tŏ read its appropriate legend
intŏ a tower, a ruin, a stream, a glen,
—the legend which expresses and
completes it by seizing and making
permanent its lurking and evanescent
suggestivness." [Macmillan's.]—
"What no ŏne wil dény tŏ Balzac is
grafic, realistic, all-enforcing use of
language. This is his, absolutely.
Perhaps he descends at times tŏ details too trivial, but his picture is vigorous beyond reasonable criticism.
In this novel the description of the
old, decayed, greasy pension, saturated with sordid circumstances, reeking with all that is ignoble and unpleasing, is ŏnly too complete. But
so, indeed, is the work throuŏut.
Miserable old Goriot, his shameful
progeny, all the despicable group of
figures which cluster around them,—
this is a chapter out of Dante, a new
fäse of Inferno. It requires, indeed,
not ŏnly a rare form of ingenuity, but
a mental nature which we must hope
is rare likewise, tŏ conceive so evil a
company. In all the chronicle, no
hope appears. Old Goriot, it may
hav been intended, should light the
horrid blaeness of the scene, but while
pity pŏurs its tears upon his wretched
clay, what more could be than that?
His dotage is grêater than his self-
sacrifice; his betrayal of his dauters
thrusts aside his affection for them.
If the author imagined himself tŏ be

681

drawing a portrait of an old man which should extort sympathy, his mental attitude is all the more curious." [American. **2206**

——, SAME ("Father Goriot"), N.-Y., *Winchester*, 1845.

——, SAME ("Daddy Goriot"), London, 1860.

——, SAME ("Unrequited Affection"), *Ward & Lock*, 1875.

PETER'S SOUL. [by GEORGE OHNET: Chicago, *Laird*, 1891.] "Tŏ see a good fundamental idea inadequately treated is as irritating as tŏ behold a valuable fabric fashioned by a clumsy tailor. Ohnet has never been a favorit of ōūrs, despite the '20 or 30 mille' which so glibly adorn the covers of his numerous works; but on taking stoc of his latest novel, we wer forced tŏ acknoledge that the author had for ōnce contrived tŏ stumble upon a really original motiv, which, treated by a Cherbuliez, Feuillet, or Bourget, would assuredly hav resulted in a powerful and thôtful study . . . When the doctor returns tŏ France nearly a year after Pierre's supposed suicide, he finds Juliette apparently dying, and Jacques utterly degraded by his infatuation for Clémence Villa. Judging it tŏ be hī time tŏ interfere and put an end tŏ this metempsychological farce, he recalls Pierre by telegram, and unites him tŏ Juliette, whŏ instantly recōvers her health and spirits. On Jacques, however, the re-apparition of his friend has a directly opposit effect, and having now discōvered that he has ōnly his original soul tŏ count upon, he promptly falls intŏ a decline and dies. Such is the substance of this fantastical story, which, if rightly treated, might hav afforded scope for so much delicate play of charac-

ter, but which in Ohnet's hands never rises abōve the commonplace. He fails tŏ interest us in any of his numerous characters, and fully half the book is taken up with descriptions of masked balls, 'petits soupers', and all the usual parafernalia of 'demi-monde' life, which seems tŏ present so irresistible and incomprehensible attraetions tŏ a large proportion of french readers." [Blackwood's. **2207**

——, SAME, Chicago, *Sergel*, 1890.

——, SAME ("The Soul of Pierre"), *Cassell*, 1891.

——, SAME ("What Pierre did with his Soul") N.-Y., *Belford*, 1890.

——, SAME ("A Weird Gift"), *Chatto*, 1890; [*Munro*, 1891.]

PETTY ANNOYANCES OF MARRIED LIFE (The). [by HONORÉ "DE" BALZAC, N.-Y., *Rudd*, 1860.] "When a man cōmes intŏ the world endowed with vigorous perception, a retentiv memory, and that species of imagination which is ōnly a potpourri of memories, made grotesque and fantastic by thêir incongruous intermixture, it is a matter of the merest accident what he wil write; or whether he wil write on paper, or on canvas . . . When a powerfully endowed man, such as Balzac certainly was with all his limitations, dōes chance tŏ spend a lifetime in writing fiction, and moreover, without the accident of any immediate popularity of ōne volume or anōther tŏ determine the particular form or quality of his work, so that he continues tŏ pōur out a flōōd of all manner of fiction—gōōd, bad, and indifferent, clean and unclean. romantic and realistic, it is like characterizing the surface of the globe tŏ characteriᴢ his productions. His mind was a grêat mirror—not without its cracs and blurs—and it imaged the whole fantasmagoria of superficially seen objects and events." [Overland. **2208**

PHILOMÈNE'S MARRIAGES. [by "HENRI GRÉVILLE," i. e., Alice M.. (Fleury) Durand: *Peterson.* 1879.] "Philomène is a country-woman of the middle class, honest and reputable, but a trifle vulgar; and the story of her "marriages" is the story of her anxious but lucless schemes tŏ secure a husband. The scene is a village which Hamerton would lŏve, and the atmosfere is as fresh and pure as that of a June morning. The comedy—for it is without a hint of tragedy—is quiet and unexciting, but amusing throuŏut, and at points very lâfable." [Boston "Lit. World." **2209**

PHILOSOPHER'S STONE (The), by BALZAC: N.-Y., *Winchester*, 1843, = 'The Alchemist' (No. 583.)

PHYSICIAN'S SECRET (The), by É. SOUVESTRE: in *Ladies' Repository*, mar., 1863. **2210**

PICTURES ACROSS THE CHANNEL. [by K .. S. MACQUOID: *Bentley*, 1873.] "We rise from the perusal of these tales with a dreamy feeling of not altŏgether unregretful surprise tŏ find ŏurselvs in England ... Our authoress vues of human nature ar sŏmewhat cynical, but find amusing expression in Captain Gragnac's opinions. Nevertheless, she is fully alive tŏ its beauty, tho she may deem it fitful, and has given us many sketches here of its more lŏvely characteristics. In the wife and sŏn of *The Fisherman of Auge*, [No. 2032] and in ŏthers, we hav pictures of unselfish lŏve and religious resignation; and, abŏve all, she has described with a most beautiful tenderness and insight the loneliness of a warm-heârted, imaginativ

child, always misunderstood, checked, and punished by a conscientious, but cold and shallo-natured mŏther." [Spectator. **2211**

PIERRE AND JEAN [by GUY DE MAUPASSANT: Chicago, *Laird*, 1890, 336 p.] "is tragic and full of sombre passion, scarcely relîeved by any slighter margin of incident, altho thêre is neither murder nor violence in it any more than lîght-heârtedness of any kind. The book is ŏne of those complete and careful studies of life in which certainly the hîer masters of the french school ar singularly successful, when thêy leave thêir ŏne favorit subject behind and address themselvs tŏ the consideration of those mute tragedies which may be carried on sŏmetimes within the closest enclosure of a family circle. The story in this book is of the slightest. We open úpon the apparent tranquility of a 'bourgeois' family of the most moderate means and pretensions ... Thêre ar twŏ sŏns: trained, the ŏne as a fysician, but without practice, the ŏther as an 'avocat' in the same condition, both at home and depending on thêir parents ... All the good things ar for Jean. The pretty wido prefers him; he is the happiest in temper and life, and the trust of his parents; and now this inheritance tŏ crown everything ... We cannot follo the tragical succession of thŏts, of questions, the pîecing tŏgether of small incidents and stray recollections, and a hundred things half forgotten, which lead the unhappy young man from ŏne step tŏ anŏther tŏ the dreadful conclusion that Jean is not his father's sŏn, but the sŏn of a man whŏ has left him this fortune. Pierre has adored his mŏther with the traditional fervor of a french sŏn, and the horror of finding out shame and sin in the life of the gentle and tender woman whŏ has made all the happiness of home for him makes him wretched, but dŏes not make him relinquish the terrible, keenly pursued, inquiry intŏ all the evidences of her guilt. The struggle of his thôts against this all-invading, all-absorbing passion ; the mingling of the pitiful jealousy for which he despises himself with this devouring horror; the tragic certainty which he acquires that she devines his suspicions, and awaits, helpless, the moment of discŏvery, with an anguish which he shares—ar all set before us with the finest skil and power. Thêre ar few sensational scenes—the ordinary incidents of life ar enuf tŏ create and bĭten the effect of the silent struggle in which the woman can dŏ nothing, paralyzed by her guilt and humiliation, and the man seems under the dominion of sŏme sombre demon, and cannot arrest himself in the awful investigation intŏ which he has been swept. Nothing can be more painful than the secret, infallible progress from ŏne certainty tŏ anŏther of the avenger, nor more terrible than the position of the mŏther, conscious almost from the first of the process going on against her . . . All this tremendous theme is wrŏt out upon the narro peaceable bacground of the matter-of-fact 'bourgeois' life with a reality and truth which givs it double force." [Blackwood's. **2212**

——, SAME ("The Two Brothers"), *Lovell Co..* 1890, 333 p.

PIGEON PRIZE (The), or Variations of a Paradox, by ALEX. DUMAS [Second] in *Southern Lit. Messenger*, Dec. 1860. **2213**

PLEASURES OF OLD AGE (The)

by É. SOUVESTRE : London,1868. **2214**

POET AND THE PEASANT (The), by É. SOUVESTRE, in *Southern Lit. Messenger*, Sept., 1854; also in *Cottage Hearth.* March, 1881. **2215**

PONT-DES-ARTS (BEGGAR GIRL OF THE), by W: HAUFF : in *The N.-Y. Mirror,* 31 Oct. to 5 Dec., 1840; also in *The Mirror Library*, No. 15.. 1844; also in *The Century,* 10 Sept. to 29 Oct., 1859; also in *The Sapphire*, Boston, 1869, 57 pp.

——, SAME ("True Lovers' Fortune"), Boston, *Munro,* 1843, 91 p., 8°.

——, SAME ("Josephine"), London, *Clarke*, 1844. **2216**

POOR RELATIONS, by BALZAC, = *COUSIN PONS.*

POPULAR TALES, by E .. C .. P.. (DE MEULAN) GUIZOT : Boston, *Crosby,* 1859. **2217**

PORT SALVATION, by DAUDET, = *EVANGELIST.*

PRANKSOME PAIR (A). [UN PETIT MÉNAGE) by —— GINISTY : *Belford*, 1890.] "recounts the fooleries of a young couple, not satisfied with a humdrum married life and determined on varying it by make-believ quarrels, adventures and reconciliations. Thêy at last venture on a moc divorce which the wife decides tŏ make real, at least for a season. The translator's 'preface' suggests the presence of improprieties of a sort not tŏ be found in the book." [Critic. **2218**

PRINCESS AMÉLIE (The) = No. 903.

PROSPER RANDOCE [by V: CHERBULIEZ : *Holt*, 1874.] "tels the story of a modern poet, an artificial nature, forever posing, more theatrical than most actors on the stage, extravagant in manner, assuming grêat warmth, but with a heârt of stone. The ŏther hero, Didier, is the

PRIVATE LIFE OF AN EMINENT POLITICIAN (The) [by E: Rod: London, *Allen*, 1893.] "is the story of a middle-aged statesman, prosperous and respected, beloved by his wife and children, the leader of a large minority in the Chamber. He poses a moral regenerator, his trump card being the revival of social purity and the abolition of divorçe, and his influençe is largely founded on the supposed fact that he is a good husband, and so forth: 'instead of which' he falls violently in löve with an unmarried girl whŏ is a kind of ward of his. Teissier's löve is not the passing fançy of an impressionable sensualist: but it is a complete absorption, and so is the girl's for him. Both ar moral and would be Platonic; but his wife discövers all, and preçipitates matters. Thêre is a scene between her and Teissier, which is curiously modern: 'We ar friends,' he says, 'partners if you wil, whŏ ar threatened by a common danger. We must combine tŏ resist it.' Beautifully reasonable, and so entirely ignorant of women's ways is Teissier. He stils feels affection for his wife, and the changing of that intŏ hatred as she opposes his desire is skillfully described. Ultimately, after a futil attempt tŏ save appearances, Teissier is divorçed, resigns his seat in the Chamber (very absurdly), and marries the girl. But the divorçe and the publiçity and the comments of the newspapers hav vulgarised their löve, and you ar left with the intimation that they wil probably be wretched. The questions of the relation of private morality tŏ public position and of the working of divorce in France ar, however interesting, merely questions of transient convention. Thêre ar deeper questions of sex and physical history which, intentionally or not, the book wil raise in many readers and leave unanswered. But it is cleverly döne, and, of course, is suggestív reading. By far the best thing in it is the character of Mrs. Teissier; she seems absolutely true. Teissier himself is possible, but dubious, and the girl is unconvinçing. An old school friend is as tedious as the most of his tribe. The English is rather ponderous but fairly good." [National Observer. **2218 m** very oppo'sit; he is kind, amiable, a skeptic tŏ the heârt's core, and born tŏ be the victim of delusions, altho confident of his ability tŏ see throu them. The contrast between these twŏ is strikingly given, with no more caricature than is needful tŏ make them life-like. The 'verve' with which the story is told makes it ōne of the most entertaining of modern novels. Every page bêars witness tŏ the qualities a novelist most needs, exhibited in wise profusion. The characters ar most vivid; Prosper is wel enuf drawn tŏ stand as the representativ not ōnly of the school of writers Cherbuliez had in his mind, but of that larger class of human beings whŏse characteristics ar the dramatic fire which imitates enthusiasm, and real, deepseated coldness." [Atlantic. **2219**

PROVENCE ROSE (A), by OUIDA, = No. 907.

PSYCHE OF TO-DAY (A) [by HENRIETTA CAMILLA (JACKSON) JENKIN: *Leypoldt,* 1868.] "is Regina Nolopoeus, [compare real names and incidents of *A Sister's Story* by Mrs. Craven] the dauter of a musical and constitutionally impecunious Hungarian and a noble French girl with whŏm he eloped. Regina, orfaned and disōned by her maternal relativs, is introduced tŏ the reader at the age of ten, a shy but dignified young person, whŏ keeps her sorrōs tŏ herself, and announces that she can cook, speaks Latin, and never tels lies. She is adopted and reared by a Parisian lady whŏ knew her mŏther. Madame Saincère is ōne of those women whŏm Mrs. Jenkin lŏves tŏ paint, and she dōes it so wel that we ar always glad tŏ see her. An old lady, full of the best kind of worldly wisdom, warmheârted and sensible, Madame Sain-

cère differs from her predecessors in being childless, and thêrefore with less experience of the ways of young heârts. She is a patroness of letters and art. With her dwels her nefew, whŏ is a painter and a genius. Latour's aristocratic mŏther in the provincial town of Juvigny had destined him for a gōvernment office, and would hav chosen him a proper wife. but he shocked her by refusing both. yîelding tŏ her influence ōnly so far as tŏ brêak his engagement with a young lady whŏm he lŏved and of whŏm she disapprōved. This young lady soon becōmes Madame Autry, without, however, lŏsing her affection for Latour . . . Thêre is nothing in the whole book so delightful tŏ ôur mind as the description of the society in this old town. It consists of a few Legitimist families and the respectable and wel-tŏ-dŏ people with whŏm thêy condescend tŏ mix; the former poor, despising trade.—thêir manners and thôts of the past, hopeless, ennuyed, yet indefinably elegant and attractiv, the latter, more modern in thêir ideas, upright, narro, provincial." [Nation. **2220**

PUNCHINELLO, by OCTAVE FEUILLET: *Appleton,* 1858. **2221**

——, SAME (in "Picture Storybooks"), *Appleton,* 1852.

PUPIL OF THE LEGION OF HONOR, (THE) [by LOUIS ÉNAULT: Phil'a, *Porter,* 1871.] "is the story of a young girl. whŏ was left an orfan and destitute, and whŏ, passing throu many and grievous trials, emerged intŏ the valley of wedded happiness and general good fortune. Her experiences ar interesting, and she is an admirable and fascinating character. The book givs striking pictures of hî society." [Boston "Lit. World." **2222**

——, SAME ("Woman of Honor"), *Peterson*, 1875.

PURSE (THE), by BALZAC, in *The Cat and Battledore*; also in *Comedie Humaine*; also in *Fame and Sorrow*; also in *The Vendetta.* **2223**

QUEEN OF THE WOODS, by A. THEURIET, = *A WOODLAND QUEEN.*

RANZAUS (The) ["Les Deux Frères"). N.-Y., *Tousey*, 1886. **2224**

RAPHAEL, by LAMARTINE, = No. 911.

RAYMONDE. [by ANDRÉ THEURIET: *Appleton*, 1879.] "With the simplest of plots and the tamest of incidents, the writer has made a very pretty story. One is pleased and interested, never in any way thrilled, even at the climax of ōne scene whēre the heroine, Raymonde, a girl of 18, is slapped by her mōther, which brings intŏ her eyes 'an expression fearful tŏ behold.' The power of french parents over thêir children is the hinge on which the story turns, and the ōnly situation at all dramatic is that in which it is made use of tŏ defeat the effort of Raymonde's mōther tŏ marry her tŏ a man she dōes not lōve, and enable her tŏ follo her inclinations. But it is the people in the story whŏ ar interesting, not what thêy dŏ or say. Mr. Nöll is a woman-hater; Raymonde's mōther simply a bad, selfish woman; her father, a nonentity; the rejected suitor, a good-natured lout. We make an exception as tŏ Raymonde herself, whŏ is thŏroly and vividly drawn—gracefully and delicately as wel." [Penn Monthly. **2225**

RED CROSS (Thē) = No. 916.

RED INN (The), by BALZAC, in *AFTER DINNER STORIES.* **2226**

RENÉE & FRANZ =*LEBLEU-*

ET.

RESIGNATION, by ARBOUVILLE, in *THREE TALES*, also in *Living Age*, 13 Oct., 1849. **2227**

REVERBERATOR (THE) [Paris] = No. 522.

RITA [by HAMILTON AIDÉ: London, *Mayhew*, 1860.] "is the story of an english girl born in Paris, the dauter of a scamp of an officer, a man whŏse principles ar as lo as his social position is hī, and whŏ is obliged tŏ seek refuge, not ōnly against the duns and bailiffs, but against the frowns and the contempt of the better part of the society intŏ which he was born. Intŏ the less scrutinising circles of the french capital he is freely receivd; and also intŏ that english set made up of men and women in a grêater or less degree like himself. In this society Rita makes her acquaintance of the world; and, her mōther being an invalid, she is brŏt out under the chaperonage of a lady in whŏse finely delineated character it is impossible not tŏ recognise the chief mental, moral, and fysical traits of the celebrated Countess of Blessington. "Rita" is thŏrŏly good, kind-hêarted, simple, and pure-minded, as wel as beautiful; and the motley crowd intŏ which she is thrōn, young and inexperienced as she is, soon disgusts her. All, however, is not distasteful; for now-a-days, as of old, thêre is always "a certain man" making his appearance, whŏ prevents the world from seeming a mere blank. Rita is not ōnly good and a beauty, but she has a grêat talent for painting, which amounts almost tŏ genius; and this she uses tŏ relîeve her father of the disgrace and the burden of sōme of his debts. After selling a sketch or twŏ at a paint shop, and finding that she dŏes not receive half thêir value, she bethinks herself of a certain Israelite whŏ made her acquaintance in the cŏurse of a business visit tŏ her father, and whŏ spoke kindly tŏ her and offered tŏ purchase her drawings. In this good sŏn of Abraham, the author has given us ŏne of the best of a series of portraits which constitute perhaps the chief attraction of the book." [Albion. **2228**

RIVAL RACES (The), by EUGENE SUE: *Trubner*, 1863. **2229**

ROBERT HELMONT, by DAUDET = No. 919.

ROLLING STONE (A). [by "G: SAND," i. e., Amantine Lucile Aurore (Dupin) Dudevant (†, 1876): Boston, *Osgood*, 1871.] "The tendency of this novel. whŏse central figure is the handsŏm Laurence, is the rehabilitation of the strŏling comedian. The theme is handled in a manner which strongly reminds us of 'Wilhelm Meister' [No. 1017] ŏnly that George Sand's characters ar more virtuous. The hero of the story, the sŏn of a peasant, is a sort of rural Antinous. His Marianne is a poor maiden of noble birth, whŏ has gŏne on the stage tŏ support an aged parent. Laurence, whŏse father desires that he shall make a figure in the world because he happens tŏ be the hêir-expectant of an uncle whŏ is a baron, is sent tŏ study law at Paris. At the Odéon he meets the heroin, whŏ appears on the boards in classic parts under the name of "Imperia." He at once falls in lŏve with her, and joins the cŏmpany in order tŏ be constantly near her. But his idol is as cold tŏ him as she is tŏ an admiring public, and even declares tŏ his face that she lŏves anŏther ... On the way tŏ Constantinople and Corfu the vessel in

which the actors hav taken passage is wrecked, and thêy ar cast on a barren roc, whêre thêy would hav perished by hunger and exposure but for the interference of the factotum of the troupe, a sort of cross between Hêrakles and Caliban. Rescued from death, thêy meet anŏther adventure in the castle of a semi-barbarous prince. ... At this conjuncture the wealthy uncle dies without a wil, and leaves him, if not a baron, at least the possessor of a barony—an event which kils the father with joy. Laurence meets the rich wido again and marries her. Imperia, for whŏm he now experiences no warmer feeling than friendship, marries Bellamare, long lŏved by her in secret, and everybody is left cŏmfortable and happy when the curtain drops." [Lippincott's.] See also the Sequel "*HANDSOME LAURENCE.*" **2230**

ROMAIN KALBRIS, by MALOT, = No. 921.

ROMANCE OF A CHILD (The). [by "PIERRE LOTI," i. e., [L: M..] Julien Viaud: Chicago, *Rand*, 1891, 179 pp.] " 'Pierre Loti' is too delicate and refined a writer tŏ be generally appreciated: he excels rather in suggesting the fleeting, intangible feelings common tŏ us all, than in depicting the violent emotions or passions by which a few individuals ar swayed. He brings home tŏ us as few authors hav succeeded in dŏing the subtle poetry of commonplace events, the cruel pathos of inanimate objects, when looked at in the light of after-years. More effectivly than ăny ŏther author we kno, he seems tŏ hav gaged the bitter contrast existing between ŏur unstable nature and thŏts and the terrible immutability of ŏur surroundings ... This book is not a

story in the strict sense of the word—
or rather it is the story of every ōne
of us, the record of the gradual development of the thôts, feelings, opinions, and aspirations of a child, whŏ,
having unconsciously invested his
surroundings with sōmething of his
individuality, experiences the disappointment common tŏ us all when,
being hereafter confrōnted with these
reflectors of oūr early years, we make
the discōvery that we ar no longer
oūrselvs." [Blackwood's. **2231**

ROMANCE OF A POOR YOUNG
MAN [by OCTAVE FEUILLET : N.-Y.,
Rudd, 1859, *Miller*, 1875, *Gottsberger*.
1887.] is "ōne of the best french
novels which has been translated. It
is deeply interesting, thōroly pure in
sentiment, and characterized by a certain nobility and loftiness of spirit
which is very admirable. The hero
is a fine creation, whŏse merit is
strikingly set ôff by his associates and
the circumstances of his life. Marguerite is unique, and the lōvely old
Mlle. Poerhoët-Gael is an exquisit
character. The general tenor of the
story is placid,—its tumults being
those of feeling ōnly ; but twŏ or three
dramatic scenes ar wŏnderful 'tours'
of descriptiv power. It is a charming
novel, which stimulates and elevates."
[Boston "Lit. World," 1875.]—
"Feuillet's most popular romance has
maintained its hold upon the affection
of at least twŏ generations of readers,
and seems tŏ be in a fair way tŏ retain its freshness of interest for sōme
time tŏ cōme. The simplicity of its
motiv, the charm of its style, the refinement of its passion, the purity of
its sentiment, all appeal tŏ tender
and thôtful minds, and awaken responsiv echoes from ardent temperaments which cannot escape such influ-

ences any more than a flower can
escape the solicitation of sunshine and
the dew. The author, tŏ be sure,
displays tŏ a certain extent in this
book the defects of his virtues. Max-
ime is perhaps a little too perfect;
ōne would hav more patience with
him if he occasionally lost his temper
—but he is a type far remŏved from
the prig, and his manly qualities of
head and heârt win frank admiration.
In Marguerite we hav the prototype
of mãny figures which hav appeared
again and again in modern fiction,
nōne of the conscious or unconscious
imitations having the reality of the
original. She is a distinct creation,
and ōne which bêars the test of analysis. And then the triumfant conclusion of the narrativ ; the hero cōming
victorious from all his trials, and
finding himself rewarded with a fortune and the hand of the woman he
lōves! It is like a fary tale, and in
spite of the realists, good wŏmen and
chivalric men hav not lost thêir appetites for the fairy-tale order of fiction." [Same, 1887.]—"No ōne can
fail tŏ be interested in the story of the
young Marquis, whŏ, on finding that
his inheritance had been dissipated,
resolutely settled down tŏ earn a
living for himself and his little
sister. Throu the influence of an
old friend, the family lawyer, he obtains the post of bailiff on the estate
of a rich wido whŏ has ōne beautiful
dauter. Unknōn tŏ the young man,
the lawyer purposly sends him tŏ this
place, in hopes that he may marry the
hêiress, and thus retrîev his fortunes.
The marquis drops his title, enters on
his work, and, as the old man had
hoped, the young people fall in lōve
with each ōther ; but thêre ar difficulties in the way. He is proud, and

she, always afraid of being married for mŏney, is prejudiced against him by the spiteful insinuations of her gŏverness. These materials the author works intŏ an exceedingly pretty story. The characters ar lifelike, and the style vivid and picturesque. Altŏgether, thêre is a freshness and grace about it, which is very charming." [Spectator.]—" 'Le Roman d' un Jeune Homme Pauvre,' for instance. with its stoc of wel-worn incidents, that air of lofty morality which is tŏ be found in frencʰ ŏnly in a novel which sets out tŏ be virtuous, and in english in the writings of Mr. T. S. Arthur,—this story doubtless oes its long life tŏ the fact, that it can be read in girls' schools." [Atlantic.

——, SAME ("Monsieur d'Hauterive") London, 1860.   **2232**

ROMANCE OF A SPAHI, by "P: LOTI": Chicago, *Rand*, 1890.   **2233**

ROMANCE OF AN HONEST WOMAN (The) [by V: CHERBULIEZ: Boston. *Gill*, 1875.] "is ŏne of the best french novels of the day. The author's style is charming. and its characteristics hav been wel preservd by the translator. A young girl, reared in seclusion by her father, a devoted arçhæologist, is brŏt intŏ contact with a Marquis Lestang, a man of various accomplishments, and in every way a desirable 'parti.' Thêy ar married and go tŏ the Marquis' château. He behaves very wel for à time, but his old associations ar too strong foɽ his sense of marital duty, and he resumes his attentions tŏ a certain pretty wido. The wife, aware of his infidelity, yet stil lŏving him fondly, maintains her womanly dignity amid many temptations, but suddenly and unaccountably finds herself in correspondence with a half-

demented youth whŏ intends tŏ becŏme a Trappist. While this intimacy is in progress, the marquis is learning tŏ lŏve his wife; he is aware of her relations with Dolfin, but is bound not tŏ abridge her freedom of action. In a maze, ŏne day, Isabel sets forth tŏ join her lŏver, but accident detains her; she meets her husband, and conjugal harmony is re-established. The plot, tho simple, is interesting; but it is of small account compared with the skil of the author in his portraiture of character." [Boston "Lit. World."]
—"The scene is laid in an artificial world, much jauntier than the familiar vale of tears. and the twŏ leading characters, whŏ ar about equally equippd with pride, self-possession, attractivness, and readiness of wit, play thêir amusing game of tit-for-tat. The reader's sympathy is secured beforehand for the abused wife, whŏ manages by dexterous strokes of wit and ingenuity tŏ turn the tables on her polite but overbêaring husband. ... One folloes the downfall of the husband from the hīghts of his foolish presumption with the satisfaction ŏne always has in seeing the right conquer. In this case, tŏ be sure, it is less the glo at the victory of rīghteousness over sin which ŏne is conscious of, than a sŏmewhat spiteful rejoicing at seeing a polished domestic tyrant beaten at his ŏn game: but the feeling, if a trifle malicious. is nŏne the less sincere. In spite of the triteness of the subject, thêre is so much freshness and originality in the treatment that it reads like a new revelation." [Atlantic.   **2234**

ROSA; OR, THE PARISIAN GIRL. [by E.. (DEHAULT) DE PRESSENSÉ: *Harper*, 1860.] "Its purpos is tŏ giv a correct idea of domes-

tic life amŏng families which retain
simplicity of purpos, and hav not cast
aside moral and religious principle as
an antiquated humbug. The little
volume abounds in charming pictures,
skilfully drawn." [Harper's **2235**
ROSE AND NINETTE. [by AL-
PHONSE DAUDET: *Cassell,* 1892.]
"With the evident motiv of shŏing
divorce as a failure in that it at most
givs temporal relief, sŏmetimes, in the
first moments of release, mistaken
for happiness, and that it dŏes not
effectually dissolv marriage, the author creates his characters. Regis de
Fagan, dramatist, recognizes that his
wife and self ar incompatible. Thêy
agree upon a plan by which they can
obtain divorce. In the consequences
of this act, "Rose and Ninette," a
Wagnerian devotee and the ex-wife
hav prominent parts. The hero's
characteristics ar in sŏme respects
those of "Père Goriot"." [Publish-
er's Weekly. **2236**
ROSE GARDEN (The) [by F..
M.. PEARD: *Roberts,* 1872.] "is not
english:—but the humor, the transparent refinement of the story, the
cool, moderate tints with which it is
drawn, ar unmistakably so, as wel as a
certain quiet pathos here and thêre,
which differs as widely from the thing
recognised as "sentiment" on the un-
english side of the channel as daylight from gas. It is the picture of a
french landscape from a british paint-
brush, and cleverly and justly given.
... The charm of the story lies in the
simple yet subtle methods by which
the characters ar made tŏ unfold
themselvs without visible interference
from the author, in the delicate sentiment which pervades like perfume,
and the picturesque setting of the
whole." [Scribner's. **2237**

ROSINE, by MELVILLE, = No. 928.
ROUGE ET NOIR ["Trente et
Quarante."] by EDMOND [FR. VAL-
ENTIN] ABOUT (†, 1885): Phil'a.
Claxton, 1873.] "A french writer is
generally seen at his best in his shorter stories. The plot is so carefully
worked out, the characters ar so vivid, and the language is so crisp and
sparkling that a book like this is tŏ a
story of the same size by Dickens or
Wilkie Collins as a diamond tŏ a lump
of quartz ... Wit, verve, and brightness, with just a dash of pathos, the
quic play of feeling and an exquisit
sense of the ludicrous—these wil redeem even a flimsy plot and conventional characters ... His story begins
with a family of three living in a
Paris flat; Captain Bitterlin, his dauter Emma, and his servant Agatha ...
He shuts up his dauter from all society and amusement, and is especially
on the watch against lŏvers. Nevertheless, a young Italian, Bartolomeo
Narni, whŏ has lost his home and
fortune, sees her at church, and the
pair instantaneously fall in lŏve.
Agatha is brŏt intŏ the plot; and after
sŏme weeks of hidden meetings Emma
tels her father boldly that she wishes
tŏ be married. He falls intŏ a paroxysm of rage, boxes her ears, sends off
poor Agatha, and locs Emma intŏ her
room. The confinement soon makes
her sic, and the captain, at his wits'
end, adopts his doctor's advice, and
takes his dauter tŏ Switzerland and
Baden. Meo goes in the same carriage, and by a lucky manœuver devised by a wiser head than his ŏn puts
the captain under an immense obligation, excites his impulse tŏ contradiction, so that he insists on dŏing just
what Meo secretly wishes, and finally
marries Emma with her father's full

approbation. How the result is achieved we wil leave the reader tŏ discŏver, but the critical moment is at the gaming tables of Baden." [l'enn Monthly.]—It "is ōne of the most enjoyable of About's novels, and is remarkable for the force and consistency with which Captain Bitterlin is drawn. Much of the story is occupied by records of travel, which ar very amusing. The book is bright, witty, and interesting, from the first page tŏ the last." [Boston "Literary World." **2238**

ROUND OF WRONG, by ABOUT, = *GERMAINE.*

SABINE'S DECEPTION [by OL-GA (CANTACUZÉNE) ALTIERI : *Harper*, 1888.] "is a good story of provincial life, wretchedly translated. Its atmosfere is pure and clear, and the people hav a moral excellence which would repay the study of Parisian journalists and play wrīghts. Sabine's whole life had been so open tŏ the sunlīght that the little deception practised tŏ insure her sister's happiness seemed tŏ her a deed of darkness, and doubtless caused her more anguish than did the relinquishment of her lŏver, so faithful in letter and faithless in spirit. Sabine is carefully drawn from nature. The author perceivs, as it almost seems that ōnly french novelists can perceiv, that truth has many sides. Sabine is positiv, prejudiced, rigid, but she is also courageous, loyal, and full of passionate tenderness for those dependent on her. No sort of perfection is ascribed tŏ Sabine, but a natural proportion is observd between her defects and her good qualities. Of course, the sacrifice which marks the victory of her strength over her weakness, is made for people whŏ can never remotely

appreciate its fineness. In fiction such a sacrifice is rewarded by the reader's sympathy. The Sabine of romance gets enthusiastic admiration; the Sabine of reality goes on tŏ the end, managing the farm, studying the causes of potato rot, and spoken of behind her bac as a hard, cross-grained old maid, whŏ has no soul above a sixpence, and never had." [Nation. **2239**

——, SAME ("Sabine's Falsehood") *Peterson*, 1881.

ST. MICHAEL'S NIGHT [by AG-NES HARRISON : in *Atlantic Monthly*, six numbers, 1868.] "is tŏ be praised as having much of local truth in its pictures of norman scenes and the character of norman peasants and fisherman; and certainly it is very honest and wel-finished writing, which mīght wel be given as a lesson tŏ 9 out of 10 of ōūr women whŏ write. Even better than that—we speak of the reader's pleasure, and not of the nature of the writer, as revealed by her style—the author shōs that she has an eye for character, and quic, true sympathies. Read, for example, her account of the touching conversation between Jeanne and Épiphanie as thêy walked tŏ Dieppe . . . It is a very fresh and agreeable little story, with plenty of old-fashioned lōve in it, and plenty besides . . . It groes upon us as we read, and turns out a story tŏ be heârtily praised; it is not saying too much tŏ call it beautiful." [Nation. **2240**

SAINTS AND SINNERS ["Noirs et Rouges") V : CHERBULIEZ : *Appleton*, 1882.] "is, abōve all things, amusing in the best sense—a sense which implies a first-rate romancer doing his best, and bringing tŏ his work qualities which many novelists

SAINT (A) AND OTHERS. [by
PAUL BOURGET: London, *Osgood*, 1893.]
"Of the 4 "portraits" (3 taken from his
'Nouveaux Pastels') the ōne entitled "*A
Saint*" is the lôngest and most lifelike.
In all of them we see ōne or twŏ points
ŏnly of Mr. Bourget's many-sided genius,
he is as profoundly analytical as ever,
idyllic, dramatic, tragic; but we hav nōne
of the subtle delineations of the mata-
physics of passion, no studies—except,
perhaps, faintly foretold in the youthful
heroins of "*Childhood Perfidy*"—of the
fin-de-siècle "mondaine," her luxurious
surroundings, her correctly attired lōvers
or the analysis of her emotions, tŏ which
we hav becōme accustomd. "*Marcel*,"
the first portrait in the book, is a remiu-
iscence of a boyish friendship, "the ŏnly
interest of which—if, indeed, it has ōne—
consists in the study, so rarely attempted,
of an aspect of a child's sensitivness." In
'A Story of a Child,' [No. 145 p] reçently
written by an American authoress, we
hav been strŏngly reminded of the child's
secret, tho futil flight, and of the heârt-
awakening which folloes. "*Monsieur

Viple's Brother" is the record of a bygône tragedy. The vail of an apparently
uneventful life, lifted for a moment, discōvers a hidden scar; the old man speaks
of a brŏther, lông dead, whŏ in his boyhood avenged an insult by shooting an
Austrian offiçer. But this brŏther was a
fiction; it was Optale Viple himself "whŏ
has avenged his outraged father, he, the
sōmetime assoçiate of the University,
whŏ, since that time, perhaps, had never
touched a weapon. What strange mys-
terv sōmetimes lies behind the most peaçe-
ful and humble career!" A *Gambler* and
"Childhood Perfidy" ar sliter sketches,
tho "study" is, perhaps, a more appropriate word for the dissection of human
nature that is a special characteristic of
Bourget. He turns his microscopic eye
even on the friendships of boys and girls,
thêir childish lōves and quarrels, and lavs
bare the intricaçies of hopes and fears,
the miseries which seem gigantic in proportion tŏ the size of the sufferers, the
action that for good or for evil may determin the future course of thêir lives."
[Spectator. **2239 t**

deem of too much public importance tŏ be employed merely in entertaining a frivolous public. But Cherbuliez has also, besides the felicity of manner which cōmes from presupposing his readers tŏ kno as much as himself about things in general, a grêat deal of a quality not usually tŏ be found in the imaginativ writings of his countrymen—the quality of humor, namely: Usually ōne is perfectly safe in looking for the best sort of humor in an english work, and the best sort of wit in a french ōne; but this writer is an eminent exception, and the flavor of his books is a compound which it would be puzzling tŏ analyze, but which is certainly as clearly humorous as it is witty. The title givs the key tŏ the substance of the book, which deals with jesuit intrigues on the ōne hand, and chronicles thè happenings in a radical interior on the ōther. Jetta Malaubret, the heroin, is left an orfan by the suicide of her father and the death of her mōther, whŏ had run away with an italian count. Tŏ expiate these sins she enters the hospital whêre her ânt, a nun, is a nurse, and declines the offer of a home with her grêat-uncle, whŏ is a radical Republican, and the next thing tŏ an atheist. Mr. Antonin Cautarel is an atheist outrīght, but a very different man from his brōther, being, amōng ōther things, a man of intelligence and a gentleman. He is a surgeon at Jetta's hospital, and the twŏ becōme fast friends just before his death, after which his wil is found tŏ leav her a large fortune on condition of her living twŏ years in Mr. Louis Cantarel's family. She is about tŏ decline this stipulation when Mère Amélie, her ânt, shōs her the folly of it, and the action of the book concerns

the efforts of the 'blac army' tŏ keep alive her intention tŏ take vows at the end of her probation in the world, and the efforts of various ōther people tŏ marry her. Her uncle Louis endeavors tŏ giv her tŏ the vulgar sŏn of a marquis whŏse favors he hopes thus tŏ win, and the executor of her Uncle Antonin dŏes his best tŏ bring aboṇt hẹr union with a young friend of thẹ latter's, in accordance with his dying wish. She hẹrself falls in lōve with this young gentleman, but deems it her duty tŏ becōme a nun, and her conflict with herself becōmes ōne between her and a fanciful vision of her benefactor, whŏ appears tŏ her from times tŏ time. It is in this sort of thing that Cherbuliez discloses a vêin of poetry now and then and it is very prettily managed here. As skilful as this is pretty is the social diplomacy which conducts the external conflict, in which also the author is an adept. The result is satisfactory, of cōurse, it being a pet theory with Cherbuliez that thêre is altŏgether too much tragedy in novels tŏ need any augmentation at his hand." [Nation.

——, SAME ("The Trials of Jetta Malaubret"), *Vizetelly*, 1886. **2241**

SAMUEL BROHL & CO. [by V: CHERBULIEZ: *Appleton*, 1878.] "In this story, a german Jew named Brohl has assumed the name and personality of a polish count whōm he has knōn, whŏ has died in grêat poverty, and under this disguise the Jew has wōn the lōve of a very charming french girl. All of ōur author's heroins ar attractiv and life-like; this ōne is no exception, but thêre is sōmething odious in the way in which Cherbuliez maltreats them. In this story the young woman givs her heârt tŏ this fascinating reptil, and the novel describes the net-work of intrîgue spun by him and by those whŏ suspect him of being the adventurer he is. It is enuf tŏ say that Cherbuliez has written this tŏ make it perfectly plain that the book holds the reader's attention fast, and that he is a bold man whŏ can say at any given chapter that he knoes what is cŏming next; all he can be sure of is that it wil be sŏmething very clever. But all the cleverness in the world wil not make up for the tone of the book, which is undeniably depressing. The hero is a most odious villain, the girl's feelings ar dangled before the public in a painful way, and ŏne cannot help a sort of shame at reading a story which, if true, ŏt tŏ be kept from the public out of respect for the victims. But yet it is entertaining." [Atlantic. **2242**

SAPPHO. [by ALPHONSE DAUDET: N.-Y., *Tousey*, 1885; London, *Vizetelly*, (abridged); *Maxwell*, 1886; Chicago, *Nile*, 1891.] "Daudet holds a peculiar place in ŏur romantic literature. He dŏes not belong tŏ the old-fashioned, sŏmewhat artificial school, which may be said tŏ be represented by Feuillet; he dŏes not belong any more tŏ the true naturalist school, which has Zola for its master. He is realistic without being systematically vulgar; he dŏes not prefer odious, hideous, loathsŏme subjects and characters; he is not a pessimist, and thêre is in him an irrepressible touch of the gay, cheerful, and optimistic South. Tho he has ridiculed the South in his *Tartarin*, in *Numa Roumestan* [No. 2191.] and quite recently in 'Tartarin sur les Alpes,' Daudet is a child of the South; thêre is no real sadness, no true melancholy in him. Thêre is a vêin of true sentiment, sŏmetimes an ŏutburst of real pathos in sŏme of

his works: in *Fromont* [No. 2047], in *Jack* [No. 2079]; but on the whole the balance always falls on the side of humor, gayety, and hope. What is very remarkable and even admirable in all Daudet's productions is what I can not call ŏther than life. Thêre is an extraordinary vitality and mŏvement throu all his work—no system, no elaborate style, no perception of effort; his descriptions ar fotografs, but thêy ar not dry: "il y a de l'air," as the painters say of a landscape. His characters also hav "de l'air": thêy ar all more or less volatil, thêy hav nothing statuesque, thêy ar carried away on the current of life —a current which is sŏmetimes so rapid that you can hardly follo ît. In this respect also Daudet belongs truly tŏ the South; he is not a dreamer, he is essentially an actor. Thêre dŏes not seem tŏ be much system in his choice of subjects. He dŏes not pretend. like Zola, tŏ giv us a new "Comédie Humaine." His receptiv mind takes in tŏ-day ŏne thing, tŏ-morro anŏther; he is a mirror. You can always recognize sŏme living character in his novels; every Parisian knoes whŏ the *Nabob* [No. 2185] was, and can giv the real names tŏ all the characters of that novel as wel as tŏ those of *Numa Roumestan*. The poet of 'Jack' is stil living: the verses which ar cited by Daudet in the novel were written by this poet "without a heârt." I dŏ not kno whŏm Daudet had in vue when he wrote his last novel, 'Sappho', for this takes us intŏ a world which is not familiar tŏ me— the world of the studios. This world is, in many respects, quite apart. It is very different from the real world, tho I hasten tŏ say that the artists of very grêat eminence ar a part of this real world; but the rising artists, the beginners, those whŏ ar ŏnly knōn in a small circle, form a sort of society which has a freedom unknōn in the regular society. In dress, in manners, in almost all the details of life, this artistic world affects a license and has an originality which make it worthy of study. It is not the "demi-monde," but it has its liaisons, which sōmetimes assume the seriousness of marriages. The women whŏ ar met amōng the painters, the artists, the literary men whŏ liv in thêir company, ar not venal, and in this respect thêy ar much superior tŏ the women of the "demi-monde." Thêy ar more intellectual, more imaginativ; thêy ar living in a hīer stage. Thêy ar tŏ be seen on varnishing day, with thêir friends, as anxious as these can be, as curious, as uneasy. Thêre is sōmething of the old "Bohemia" left in this world of painters, but it is no longer the Bohême of Henri Mürger, [No. 2244] composed ŏnly of very young men and women; it is a Bohemia whêre you meet men with gray beards, and old models whŏ hav becōme semi-respectable matrons." [A. Laugel in Nation. **2243**

SCENES FROM THE LIFE OF BOHEMIA. [by H: MURGER (†, 1861.): N.-Y., *Gould*, 1891.] "The *Vie de Bohême* stands apart from all preceeding works. In it the author explored unknōn solitudes, discōvered a fresh world, full of gaiety and tears, of ringing lâfter and the starkest poverty, of hopes unutterably eager, and of miseries which ar indicated rather than described ... Each chapter in the strange volume is a work complete in itself. yet the chapters lead ōne intŏ the ōther, til the whole, with its quips, its jests. its

delicate shades of humor and its fine strokes of wit, forms ōne of the gayest, naîvest books of even this century of fantasies ... But the charm of the Vie de Bohême, after its neverfailing gaiety, lies in the tenderness and the beauty of its lōve-scenes. In connexion with the student we naturally hav the grisette—now, alas! no more—devoted in her lōve, façil in her conquests, industrious and happy in her labors and privations. Tŏ Mimi and Musette we ō all the pathos of the volume. We may, after a cōlorless fashion, compress the gayer episodes—Rodolphe writing Mimi a gown, and. at her solicitation, adding, with so many more columns of matter, so many more flounces and furbelōs; but it is impossible tŏ deal in this meagre manner with the pathetic chapters. Mimi was Rodolphe's mistress, and her lōve, affected ōnly by too long a bout of starvation, for she was fond of dress and pleasure, is merely a reproduction from life. "The scene at the hospital," says Banville, "so poignant with misery, is completely true. Poor Mimi had livd too long amōng the poets, til she naturally came tŏ die at the hospital as a poet might." [Westminster.

——, SAME ("The Gypsies of Art"), transl. by C: G. LELAND, in *Knickerbocker*, Oct. 1853—Jan., 1854. **2245**

SCYLLA & CHARYBDIS, a Lesson for Husbands, by OCTAVE FEUILLET, in vol. 4 of *Cosmopolitan*. **2246**

SEAGULL ROCK. by SANDEAU, = No. 935.

SEASHORE GLEANER (The), by É. SOUVESTRE: Bristol. 1855. **2247**

SECRET OF HAPPINESS (THE), ["La Comtesse de Chalis.") by ERNEST FEYDEAU (†, 1873.): Edinburgh,

Edmonston, 1867.] "The author of 'Fanny' [No. 2029] has discõvered that the secret of happiness lies in dõing good. We hav hĕard sõmething like that before; but cõming from a gentleman whõ has been õnce or twice held up as the terrible example of modern french literature, the defini-tion acquires a startling novelty. We would not recall the author's past crimes, wer it not tõ point out the singular sort of nature in which french writers whõ endeavor tõ escape from the artificial and conventional gener-ally seek refuge. Nature tõ them is synonomous with ignorance; and the people whõm thĕy represent as dwell-in a state of nature ar merely over-grõn babies with a taste for aimless sentiment. 'The Secret of Happiness' is an effort in the 'Paul and Virginia' direction, Mr. Feydeau having appar-ently been stung by criticism intõ prõving that he was sõmething better than a worshipper of poetic adultery. The really valuable part of the book consists of the vivid description of scenery in **Algeria** and arab manners, with which the work abounds. The author tels us that he traveled leisure-ly throu this region, noting the most minute facts which came before him; and we ar not without a suspicion that the colonists whõ figure in these pages, and whõ discõver 'the secret of happiness' ar mere sketches from lay figures thrõn in tõ complete a picture. the chief merit of which lies in the faithful painting of the bacground. At the same time it must be said that the story is readable and interesting, and that it occasionally becõmes pow-fully dramatic." [London Rev. **2248**

SEMPSTRESS'S STORY (THE) [by [ANTOINE] GUSTAVE] DROZ: *West, Johnston & Co.*, 1877.] "is a

simple but touching little tale of a child in Paris whõ lay at the point of death with. croup, and was saved by the kind serviçe of a big-heãrted sur-geon. It is a fresh, bright, warmly cõlored picture of an ordinary 'inte-rior' and a not uncommon experi-ence." [Boston "Lit. World." **2249**

SERAPHITA, by BALZAC. ☞ *ECCENTRIC NOVELS.*

SEVEN YEARS. [by JULIA KAV-ANAGH (†, 1877): *Peterson*, 1860.] "The name is due tõ the period dur-ing which the hero, an honest-heãrted Flemish upholsterer, is obliged tõ work and wait for his capricious mis-tress. a quic-witted and not, perhaps, utterly heãrtless Parisian sewing girl. The tale is an interesting õne, and very wel told, and the soul-experience of the lõvers as thĕy go throu the trials consequent, chiefly. upon the waywardness of the girl—is described with a very clear perception of the modes of mental dõing, being. and suffering." [Albion. **2250**

SERGE PANIN. by G: OHNET, Manchester, *Tubbs*, 1883. **2251** —, SAME ("Prince Serge Pa-nine"), *Munro*, 1890.

SERGEANT'S LEGACY (The), by E. [B.] BERTHET; London, *Nimmo*, 1880. **2252**

SHORTER STORIES. by BALZAC. London, *L. W. Scott*, 1890. **2253**

SIBYLLE'S STORY = *STORY OF SIBYLLE.*

SIDONIE = *FROMONT THE YOUNGER.*

SIEGE OF BERLIN (The), by A. DAUDET, in *Swinton's Story-Teller*, Oct., 1883; also in vol. 4 of *Tales from Many Sources*, N.-Y.. 1884; also in *Cosmopolitan*, Aug., 1886. **2254**

SILVIA [Provence] by JULIA KAVANAGH = No. 530.

SIMON [London, *Churton*, 1847.] "But.'George Sand' has written several [novels] which ar fit for the perusal of the most spotless. These ar 'André' [No. 1950], 'Simon,' 'Les Maitres Mosaistes' [No. 850], 'Pauline,' 'Le Secrétaire Intime,' 'Les Sept Cordes,' and the 'Mélanges'." [Foreign Quarterly, 1844.] See also No. 945. **2255**

SIN OF M. ANTOINE (The). [by "G : SAND", i. e., Amantine Lucile Aurore (Dupin) Dudevant († 1876): N.-Y., *H. Long*, 1850.] "The husband in this novel behaves better, or rather the circumstances of the plot permit him tŏ take the step which G : Sand would hav society make open tŏ every husband. The offspring of the adultery is the heroin of the story, and she brings about a happy reconciliation between her father and the husband of her mŏther. An unfilosofical irritation has kept them asunder for years; but Gilberte, the heroin, when driven by a storm tŏ seek shelter, happens tŏ see a portrait of her mŏther in the house of what, speaking conventionally, we may call the injured husband, and she is struc by its likeness tŏ a miniature which she has often seen in the hands of her father, whŏ contrary tŏ the usual practis, has reared her. 'Her modest imagination refusing tŏ comprehend the possibility of an adultery,' she is naturally puzzled; but she takes advantage of the occasion tŏ make friends with the first possessor of the original, and at length gets him tŏ pardon the second possessor. Friendship survives the conflict and consequences of youthful passion, and thêy ar all happy at the'end of the book." [National Review.

——, SAME ("First and True Love"), *Peterson*, 1852. **2256**

SISTER ANNE [by [C:] PAUL DE KOCK († 1871.): London, *Henderson*, 1840; 396 p., 8°; N.-Y., *Wilson*, 1843.] is by "an author whŏ enjoys more celebrity than any living writer; that is tŏ say, if the extent of a man's reputation be judged by the number of his readers. From the hiest lady tŏ the poorest 'grisette', from the statesman tŏ the copying-clerk—all classes hav pored over those pages which teem with gaiety and mirth, relieved by the finest touches of pathos and feeling—all hav felt the magic charm of this grêat enchanter. A new novel by Paul de Kock creates a more powerful sensation than the speech of the king. His popularity extends tŏ the meanest and most distant cottage; thêre exists not a laborer, whŏ has not heard of Paul de Kock, and lâfed at sŏme village pedant's recital of the best episode in his last work." [Foreign Quarterly.]—"An Englishman whŏ turns tŏ Paul de Kock's numerous works tŏ form a judgment of thêir merits and defects, will be astonished tŏ find that, amidst an exuberance of familiar humor, which often passes the limit of good taste, thêre ar vêins of the most beautiful and elevating sentiment, and passages of tremendous, yet never exaggerated power." [Edinburgh Review.]—"This is ône of those novels in which we find the most exquisit humor and most beautiful pathos. It is a novel which abounds in strong contrasts. The wit and the pathos—the passionate lŏve of Sister Anne, and the calm but deeply-rooted affection of Constance—the sincere and honorable character of the elder de Montreville, and the levity and inexperience of his sŏn—the half swindler, half filosofer

Dubourg, and the upright, but easily duped Ménard—the tries practised by Dubourg, and the deeply interesting adventures of Sister Anne, form the basis of ŏne of the most amusing novels in the French language . . . "Sister Anne" is the narrativ of a beautiful young girl, whŏ, in her infancy, lŏses the faculty of speech throu a sudden fright, and recŏvers it eventually by a similar revulsion in nature. The fortunes of this orfan girl form the ground-work of the tale. She is seduced by a young count, whŏ is subsequently compelled by his father tŏ abandon her; and she sets out in search of the faithless swain. After experiencing all those dangers and difficulties which must necessarily hav attended an individual in her forlorn condition, she arrives at the very house whêre dwels her seducer's wife. The dumb stranger is kindly received by the unsuspecting wife. The husband's return however explains all; and the tale is wound up by the death of Sister Anne, whŏ recŏvers the faculty of speech ŏnly a few monents before she surrenders her spirit." [Monthly Review. **2257**

SISTER PHILOMÈNE [by ED-MOND & JULES DE GONCOURT (†, 1870): Paris. 1861, *Routledge*, 1890.] "is a sad and painful study of a wŏman's heârt which the cold and monotonous life of a convent in vain attempted tŏ subdue; a cry for human lŏve and sympathy which is hushed ŏnly with life itself. Marie Gaucher is a little french girl whŏ groes up as a dependent in a grêat french house. She is admitted tŏ unusual familiarity with the young hêir, and assumes airs far abŏve her true position in the social world. Tŏ recall her tŏ her proper sfere, her ânt sends her tŏ a

convent tŏ be educated. Without any real unkindness being shŏn, her health and spirits ar most successfully broken by the unnatural, repressed life she is forced tŏ lead. The steps ar then easily taken by which she becŏmes 'Sister Philomène.' As a nun she finds little happiness until her duties transfer her tŏ the hospital. Here, in the care of the sic, she finds her vocation, and becŏmes almost reconciled tŏ life. A grêat deal of space is devoted tŏ an account of life in a hospital ward, the talk of the medical students. and tŏ the feelings aroused in the innocent nun's heârt by the varied experiences she passes throu. She cŏmes constantly in contact with a young hospital surgeon, whŏ inspires her with what she believes tŏ be a strong sisterly interest. The gradual awakening tŏ the consciousness of her lŏve is described by a master hand." [Literary News. **2258**

SO FAIR YET FALSE ["Pourquoi"] by EUGENE VACHETTE, called "CHAVETTE": N.-Y., *Carleton*, 1874. **2259**

SOUCI = No. 951.

SONS OF THE SOIL. [by HO-NORÉ "DE" BALZAC: *Roberts*, 1890.] "The proprietor of a country place in Bourgogne endeavors tŏ imprŏve it tŏ the best of his knoledge and ability. In cultivating and imprŏving his estate, he wounds the sensibilities and tramples on the traditions (often without knŏing it) of the surrounding villagers. Instantly a legion of malign activities spring intŏ life: his trees ar 'ringed,' his vintage is lessened, his steward is murdered, and he. a general of the Empire. is threatened with murder. In the end the beautiful château and its lands ar laid waste, the general is driven tŏ ignominious sale and flight, and the peasants possess themselvs of his acres. One or twŏ bright spots relîev this diabolic gloom, across which Balzac shoots his sinister profecies of the results of peasant proprietorship. He has conjured not so much 'sons of the soil' in his Jeremiad as the gnomes and goblins which dwel beneath it, creatures of his dreams, monsters of his dyspepsia, a proletariat peopling hell, not the gay, gracious country-folk of Sunny France." [Critic. **2260**

SOUL OF PIERRE, by G: OHNET, = *PETER'S SOUL.*

SPECULATOR IN PETTICOATS (A), by H. MALOT: *Peterson,* 1887. **2261**

SPIRIDION, by "G: SAND," ☞ *ECCENTRIC NOVLES.*

STAR OF EMPIRE (The), N.-Y., *Tousey,* 1885, = *CLORINDA.*

STARTLING EXPLOITS OF DR. QUIÈS (THE). [by PAUL CELIERES: . *Harper,* 1887.] "As tŏ the involuntary journeyings of Dr. Quiès, thêy ʼar brŏt about in such a forced way, thêre is such a sameness in his discomforts on being disturbed from his quietude, that a little adaptation and arrangement wonld hav imprŏved the original work. Stil, pictures and all, the book presents a very pleasant vue of provincial life." [Nation. **2262**

STONE-MASON OF ST.-POINT (The), by ALPHONSE DE LAMARTINE: (†, 1869.) *Routledge,—Harper.* 1851.] "We dŏ not admire all which Lamartine writes, but of this, his last production, we can speak with almost unqualified praise. It is all it professes tŏ be, a simple village tale. The record of a very humble life, it breathes the spirit of lŏve and Christian meekness, exalted by the noblest sentiments." [National Era. **2263**

STORIES OF AN OLD MAID,ʼ by D. (G.) GIRARDIN: London, *Addey.* 1856. **2264**

STORIES OF PROVENCE = *LETTERS FROM MY MILL.*

STORM-DRIVEN [Paris] = No. 533.

STORY OF A DEMOISELLE (THE) [by E. C. PRICE: *Ward,* 1880.] is an "excellent story. Its grêat charm is the pronounced nationality of every word and thŏt of the members of the family groups which surround Clotilde de Mornay. The strong-minded marquis, the pleasure-lŏving and unscrupulous Madame de Belleville, the "good Jourdain" with her girth, her gruffness, her tender heârt, her skin-deep severity, ar all life-like. It is the story of a french marriage of arrangement. The author is too wise tŏ drag her heroin throu the mud, and the reader learns a lesson, sŏt tŏ be impressed on him, not throu the failure but the success of a sweet nature in coping with trials which would hav embittered and spoiled an ordinary character. The men ar as good, nearly, as the women, and the gallant old Legitimist obtains no more than his due when, after saving the life of his rival, he secures the affections of his bride." [Athenæum.]—"The characters ar sketched with force, and the french life is very delicately and vividly painted. A pleasanter tale, on the whole, it would not be easy tŏ find." [Spectator. **2265**

STORY OF AN HONEST MAN [by EDMOND [FR. VALENTIN] ABOUT (†, 1885): *Low, Appleton,* 1880.] is "the story of the plain life of a bourgeois lad, whŏ rose by virtue of his character and exertions tŏ be the head of a grêat business, a millionaire, and the father of a lŏvely and interesting family. The manner is realistic enuf tŏ giv the work the aspect of a veritable autobiografy; but it has all the true shape and cŏlor of fiction, gloes with the warmth of life, and appeals in the strongest way tŏ the tenderest feelings. The subjcet is full of interest, the style is masterly, the tone lofty and morally exhilarating; and while the fortunes of Pierre Dumont present little tŏ gratify a lŏve of the sensational, thêy wil be folloed with keenly sympathetic pleasure by every reader of refined taste." [Boston "Lit. World." **2266**

STORY OF COLETTE (The) *Appleton*, 1888.] "is a harmless and amusing tale, put intŏ very pleasant english. It opens on the first day of March with the little prayer Colette inscribes at the beginning of the journal she keeps tŏ relieve the weariness of life spent in a dismal château under the gardianship of a maidenânt whŏ dŏes not lŏve her, and ōne old servant . . . Colette is an ingénue of a rather sparkling type. With the exception of twŏ happy years in a convent—whêre her ânt placed her in order at ōnce tŏ keep and tŏ evade the promis made tŏ Colette's dying mŏther, by which she was obliged tŏ giv her nîece at least twŏ years in Paris, and thus a chance tŏ settle herself"—she has spent all her days in this gloomy mansion, and at 18 she is grōing very tired of being "full of ideas with no earthly being tŏ tel them tŏ; tŏ be gay alone, tŏ be sad alone, tŏ be angry alone—it is unsupportable." She has begun tŏ look for her "adventure." She is sure it wil cŏme . . . But when the 20th of March also cōmes and goes and brings nobody, Colette flies intŏ a passion,

seizes the statue and flings it throu her windo intŏ the road—whêre, of cōurse, it hits the "adventure" in the head as it is climbing the garden wall tŏ see what lies beyond, knocs it down, fractures its knee. makes a hole in its forehead, and throes it thus upon repentant Colette's good offices as nurse. The story is old enuf, as the reader sees, but it is charmingly told." [Catholic World. **2267**

STORY OF ELIZABETH (The), [**Normandie**] = No. 534.

STORY OF REINE (The). [by JEAN DE LA BRETE: *Roberts*, 1891.] "The opening chapters dŏ not appeal especially tŏ the reader, but the interest increases as the story is developed. 'Reine' is a young girl, whŏ, altho of aristocratic birth and rich by inheritance, is reared in a lonely country house by an ânt, whŏ is not ōnly ignorant, but lo-bred. The ânt has a most incorrigible temper, which she visits upon her young and pretty charge. The curé whŏm she lŏves, the ânt whŏm she hates. and the servants ar the ōnly companions Reine has during the formation period of her life. Endowed by nature with an impulsiv disposition, a lŏve of freedom, and an inclination tŏ ride rufshod over those whŏ hav her education in charge. Reine finds herself at 16 in open warfare with her surroundings, a condition the reader cannot but sympathize with. for the child possesses a warm heârt, and instincts which require ōnly judicicus training for thêir ultimate proper development . . . She promptly falls in lŏve with the first young man she meets, and from that moment life has unknōn charms for her. On the death of her ânt, she goes tŏ liv with an uncle, in the midst of a cultivated society. The scheme of the story is original ... The dialog, true tŏ its french origin, is sparkling and effectiv, the ready wit of Reine, and her delicate raillery at the exactions of social propriety, which she regards as a bugbear, being at ŏnce charming and infectious. ·Purely as a character study, 'The Story of Reine' is wŏrth reading." ·[Writer. **2268**

STORY OF SYBILLE (*sic* for Sibylle) [by OCTAVE FEUILLET (†, 1890.) Boston, *Osgood*, 1872.] "is a novel in which almost everybody is moral, the heroin an ultramontane catholic with sŏme of the instincts of a saint, and the hero a free-thinker, converted throu lŏve, is a curious thing tŏ get from a man whŏ afterwards wrote "Camors" [Nos. 2107 & 2170.] It is an interesting story, nevertheless, skilfully told, and put intŏ readable english. Sybille is a unique creation—not because she is either lifelike or possible, for we imagin her tŏ be neither, but because Mr. Feuillet seems tŏ hav tried his hand at making in her an incipient saint. Tŏ be a saint he has understood ·that ŏne lŏves God exclusivly ; and in his effort tŏ combine an exclusiv lŏve for God with an absorbing passion for a man, he has produced a character which has no consistency nor possibility. On its face it is a very simple, pretty, religious little tale, but it has a taint of insincerity throuŏut which would be as perceptible wer the novel an anonymous ŏne as it is when it bears its author's name." [Nation.]—"It is not likely tŏ win new laurels for its author. It is thŏroly french in its extravagant use of adjectivs, and equally so in the extremes of pietism and skepticism exhibited in its principal characters. Sibylle is ŏne of those

rare combinations of beauty, grace, intellect, and piety which abound in second-rate religious novels—a creature all too bright and good for human nature's daily food—and the reader is hardly surprised when she takes tŏ herself wings. The grandfather and grandmŏther Férias ar a fine old couple; but the majority of the characters ar very indifferent people, and the plot is poorly managed." [Hearth & Home.] G : Sand's "M'lle de Quintinie" is an answer tŏ this novel. **2269**

——, SAME, in *Hearth and Home*, 17 July, 1869, seq.

STORY OF THE PLÉBISCITE = No. 960.

STRAIGHT ON. [by author of "Colette." *Appleton*, 1891.] "Captain Bailleut's dying injunction tŏ his little· boy was keep "Straight on" throu life, and when· he was too weak tŏ convêy the message by words he wrote them. The child adopts this as his motto, and the result is a pretty, pathetic story of a lad's mastery of all sorts of difficulties. A military school is the scene." [Publisher's Weekly. **2270**

STROKE OF DIPLOMACY (A) = *KING APEPI*.

STRUGGLE (A), [**Normandie**] = No. 535.

SUCH IS LIFE [by ALBERT DELPIT], Chicago, *Laird*, 1891. **2271**

SURGEON'S STORY (The) ["Les Parents de Bernard"] by ABOUT, in *Appleton's Journal*, 18 nov. 1871. **2272**

SYBIL'S SECOND LOVE = No. 538.

SYDONIE'S DOWRY [by MA. ROBERTS : London, *Bell*, 1865.] "is a healthy little story, pathetic in sŏme parts, humorous in ŏthers and characteristic throuŏut. The scene is laid in a remote valley of Languedoc hemmed in by the hïghts of Cévennes; and the characters ar probably such as mïght be met in that Arcadian retreat, tho it is possible that thêy may be a little idealized. Sydonie, at least, appears tŏ be a little abŏve the peasant standard; but we must make sŏme allowances on account of her having been patronized and petted by the hĩ-born Thérèse de Parthenan. This young lady is the ŏnly dauter of a nobleman of the old régime whŏ has lost his parents by the guillotine and his lands by confiscation, but has succeeded in buying bac a fragment of the family estate which he cultivates as a farmer. Hence we hav occasional reminiscences of the bonnetrouge, the Carmagnole, and ŏther features of the Revolution, which is supposed tŏ be not so far bac but that elderly people can recollect its horrors. The local customs and superstitions ar lïghtly and pleasantly touched, and the character of the reputed witch is welded in with care and effect. Sydonie, of cŏurse, is the main figure and is a lŏvable tho wayward little heroin." [Athen. **2273**

SYLVIE [by GÉRARD DE NERVAL: *Routledge*, 1888.] "has the elegance, the purity, the translucency of a porcelain vase. When the Frenchman is charming, how charming!" [Boston "Lit. World." **2274**

SYLVIE'S BETROTHED. [by 'HENRY GRÉVILLE", i. e., Alice M.. Céleste (Fleury) Durand: *Peterson*, 1882.] The author here "manages a delicate situation with exquisit tact, and makes what mïght easily hav been, in the hands of the naturalist, a grossly offensiv story intŏ a charming romance of innocent lŏve and heroic self-devotion. A beautiful, wilful creature, she fascinates from the first with her delïghtful candor and dainty obstinacy. It is not strange that Sylvie, left an orfan at an early age, should gro tŏ lŏve her godfather, Pierre Clermont, with sŏmething more than the affection due from ward tŏ gardian. Nor is it surprising, perhaps, that he should find the education of this fascinating girl an agreeable task. But thêy ar on dangerous ground, as Sylvie is the first tŏ discŏver when Jacques Debrancy asks for her hand. The scene in which Clermont tries tŏ persuade his ward tŏ accept the young suitor is admirably written. The former is mŏved, he knoes not why; the latter cherishes her dream, loath tŏ see it shattered. She yields at last, ŏnly tŏ find that her innocent passion can not be overcŏme, and in despair she sends her young lŏver away. Meanwhile Mrs. Clermont, seeing herself isolated from her husband's lŏve, is obliged tŏ meet Jacques with sympathy and consolation. Thêir mutual pain brings them tŏgether, and neither is proof against the ŏther's pity. Only the noble sense of duty in the woman holds bravely out. Amélie is also forced tŏ confess that the dream is fair; but she bids him farewel without a murmur at her fate. "You must learn tŏ liv for ŏthers," she says. "We may not liv for ŏurselvs alone." We shal not undertake tŏ follo the characters throu the remainder of the story, or foreshado the end which is made so inevitable. It is easy tŏ complain of the monotony of the types chosen by Mrs. Gréville tŏ exemplify her art; but no ŏne can question the grace and freshness of her method, the purity of her motivs or the piquancy of her style, which even a nebulous translation cannot wholly obscure. Thêre is evidence of a firmer touch in Sylvie's Betrothed than in perhaps any ôther of the author's novels, and the absence of dramatic incident is largely compensated by a breadth of portraiture almost masculin in its grasp of contrasting personal traits." [Boston "Lit. World." **2275**

TALE OF TWO CITIES = No. 972.

TALES OF TO-DAY AND OTHER DAYS, by A. DE MUSSET, COPPÉE, BOURGET, MAUPASSANT, MÉRIMÉE, and GAUTIER: *Cassell*, 1891. **2276**

TEMPTATION (The) by [M.. JOSEPH] "EUGENE" SUE: N.-Y., *Winchester*, 1845. **2277**

THOROUGH BOHEMIENNE (A). [by HENRIETTE ÉTIENNETTE FANNY (ARNAUD) REYBAUD: *Appleton*, 1879.] "Sketches of life in an old breton manor-house, framed in pure and simple language, and a few characters wel defined and consistently sustained, combine tŏ make this a story of unusual merit. It wil be read with interest and remembered with pleasure, whilst in refinement of touch and delicacy of execution it excels most current novels." [Penn Monthly. **2278**

THREE RENCONTRES (The), by É. SOUVESTRE. in *Southern Lit. Messenger*, July, 1855. **2279**

THREE STRONG MEN, by ALEX. DUMAS [Second], N.-Y., *Dewitt*, 1850. **2280**

THREE TALES. [by SOPHIE (DE BAZANCOURT) D'ARBOUVILLE. *Harper*, 1853.] "These stories ar of such exceeding beauty and peculiar merit, that we should be inclined tŏ adopt the extravagant estimate of thêir value taken by the translator. if by so dŏing we could arrest the attention of ôur readers and provoke them tŏ a perusal

of the volume. Thêy ar simple, clear, sweet, truthful, free from all the vices of style, sentiment and principle which most beset the modern school of french romance. Thêir leading characteristics ar vividness of conception, depth of pathos, and closeness and clearness of pictorial representation." [Graham's.]—"Thêy exhibit an inimitable portraiture of refined and beautiful passion, in a style of singular sweetness, simplicity, and power." [Harper's.] See *VILLAGE DOCTOR*. **2281**

TOUR AROUND MY GARDEN by ALPHONSE KARR: *Routledge*, 1854. See Athenæum, No. 1214. **2282**

TOWER OF PERCEMONT (THE) [by "G: SAND", i. e., Amantine Lucile Aurore (Dupin) Dudevant (†, 1876.): *Appleton*, 1877.] "The elder dauter has been placed in a convent, and thêre her stepmŏther wishes tŏ keep her and compel her tŏ take the vail. A nefew of M. Chautabel named Jacques, a handsŏme, good-heârted fello, sees M'lle de Nives, while she is a noviçe, falls in lŏve with her and succeeds in contriving her escape. she, however, not yet being in lŏve with him . . . This sister Miette is lŏved by and lŏves Henri Chautabel, but a coolness has grŏn between them. The motiv of the story is tŏ bring this pair of lŏvers tŏgether, tŏ counteract the plans of Countess de Nives, and tŏ save the dauter of the latter from her mŏther's evil influence. The story is almost altŏgether ône of character." [Galaxy. **2283**

——, SAME [and "Marianne"] London, 1881, 240 p.

TRAJAN = No. 987.

TREASURE (The), by SOUVESTRE. in *Arthur's Magazine*, Nov., 1880. **2284**

TRIALS OF JETTA MALAU-
BRET. = *SAINTS AND SINNERS*.
TRUE AS STEEL [by —— ( )
COLOMB: *Routledge*, 1879.] "is a
spirited translation of a good story of
the War of 1870. The hero is a quiet,
retiring gŏvernment clerk, whŏ, thinking nŏthing of himself and everything
of his duty tŏards God and man, is
as "true as steel," and conceals the
heârt and conduct of a true hero
under a quaint, not tŏ say rather
absurd exterior. The character of
uncle Plaçide is beautifully drawn;
it reminds ŏne of "Cousin Pons" [No.
2008] in sŏme of its touches. The
ending is too sorroful and .the author mĭght, we think, hav turned the
faint "hope for the best." with which
she consoles her readers, intŏ a reality
without any sacrifice of truth."
[Athenæum. **2285**
TRUE LOVERS' FORTUNE
(The), by W: HAUFF: Boston, *Munroe*, 1843, 91 pp, 8°. **2286**
——, SAME ("JOSEPHINE, or
The Beggar of the Pont des Arts"),
London, *Clarke*, 1844.
TURKO (The), by ABOUT, in *Six-
penny Magazine*, 1886 [*Every Saturday*,
1st tŏ 15th Sept., 1866.] **2287**
TWINS OF THE HOTEL COR-
NEILLE (The) by ABOUT, in *Rus-
sell's Magazine*, vol. 6. Nos. 4-6. **2288**
TWO BROTHERS [by HONORÉ
"DE" BALZAC: *Roberts*, 1887.) "is
not entirely a story of Provincial
life, for the scene is partly Paris, and
the brŏthers ar Parisians born and
bred, tho thêir mŏther is a provincial.
Each novel of Balzac unfolds tŏ the
reader a little more of the marvelous
range of the artist's vision, the universality and fidelity of his insĭght.
Saint and sinner alike ar comprehen-
sible tŏ him; lŏve such as has given

human heârts the material for thêir
saintliest dreams of the relations of
Heaven, no less than lŏve in its coars-
est satyr shape. Material lŏve is the
theme of "The Two Brŏthers"—but it
is presented here less noble than the
typical material lŏve, because the
mŏther is herself a weak, dul woman.
Strong and unselfish as is her material passion, sweet and uprĭght and
loyal as is her character, Agathe is
not an impressiv enuf figure tŏ suffice
for the story, and it is largely ocen-
pied with the drama of Philippe's
contest with an interloper for the inheritance of his uncle's property."
[Overland.]— The elder brŏther is a
monster; he has fysical courage, but
absolutely nŏthing else good,—he is
sensual, dishonest, selfish, cruel, and
base. On the ŏther hand, his brŏther
is patient, unselfish, clean, honest,
and noble. The contrast is almost
too grêat a strain on belief. Associated with them ar ŏther figures which
may be classified almost as distinctly
as the brŏthers . . . It is not a book tŏ
be left in the way of all sorts of readers; but it is undoubtedly a powerful
study of life, and like the ŏthers of
its kind in the Balzac list, leavs no
doubt in the reader's mind as tŏ the
rĭght and wrong of living." [American. **2289**
TWO BROTHERS, by MAUPAS-
SANT, = *PIERRE & JEAN*.
TWO DUCHESSES (THE), by É.
ZOLA, N.-Y., *Tousey*, 1885.
TWO FRENCH MARRIAGES
[London, 1868] = *MADAME DE
BEAUPRE* [No. 2123.], and *A
PSYCHE OF TO-DAY* [No. 2220.]
TWO LILIES [**Normandie**] =
No. 548.
TWO MOTTOES (The), by SOU-
VESTRE, in *Southern Lit. Messenger*,

Jan., 1855; also in *The Sapphire.* Boston, *Shorey*, 1867. **2290**

TWO OLD CATS [**Riviera**] = No. 549.

TWO PUPILS OF ST. MARY OF GRENOBLE, by E.. C.. P.. (DE MEULÀN) GUIZOT, in *Southern Lit. Messenger.* June, 1854. **2291**

TWO RIVALS (THE) = *MAN & MONEY*.

ULLI. [by EMMA BILLER: *Trubner*, 1889.] "Ulrika de Watteville is the dauter of a ruined nobleman, and at an early age is thrōn upon the world without education, and with the most meagre equipment of common sense. Her adventures ar comical enuf, and she struggles most pluckily with her misfortunes. In twŏ or three years she becōmes formidably "educated." But the story need not be absolutely tabooed on that account." [Athenæum. **2292**

UNAWARES. [by F.. M.. PEARD: *Smith*, 1870.] "Written with all the sentiment and delicacy which distinguish The Rose Garden [No. 2237.] the story is even more charming. It dŏes not turn on the inconsistencies of a little wilful heârt like Renée's, but portrays the gradual grōth and development of a true wŏmanly nature ... We ar strue afresh in reading this story by the same odd inconsistency between spiritual and material atmosfere which was so remarkable in 'The Rose Garden.' The entourage is as distinctivly forein as the actors ar not. It is an english mind thinking in french, a french landscape whŏse figures ar full of the health, simplicity, and underlying reserv of english character. The point and delicacy, the finish of frase and picturable quality of the book cannot be too hīly praised. It

abounds in tender thôts and happy touches." [Scribner's.]—"We hav so often had tŏ condemn stories of french life, that it is both a pleasure and a surprise tŏ find ōne which we can unreservedly praise, both from its tone and its adherence tŏ truth. The picture of the old doctor is in every way excellent. The character, too, of Thérèse is stil more delicately drawn. It is in her female characters that the writers' strength is shōn. The descriptions, too, ar full of poetry." [Westminster. **2293**

UNCLE & NEPHEW, by ABOUT, *Graham's Mag.*, Jan., 1858; also in *The Independent*, Jan. 12, 1882; also *Cassell*, 1892. **2294**

UNCLE BERNARD'S SHELL, by ERCKMANN-CHATRIAN, in *Englishwoman's Magazine*, July, 1872. **2295**

UNCLE CÉSAR [by HENRIETTE ÉTIENNETTE FANNY (ARNAUD) REYBAUD: *Appleton*, 1879.] "is the story of a rich, aristocratic, pompous bachelor and his nefew, told in a vêin of light comedy. The action takes place in a provincial town. The nefew lōves and is belōved; untōard circumstances obstruct his marriage; the uncle finds the nefew tŏ be his rival and disinherits him; the nefew in turn lōses his avaricious lady, and marries a better and worthier girl whŏ had all the while adored him in secret. The story is pure and proper, without having, however, either the strength or beauty inherent in such a work as Theuriet's Young Mangars." [Boston "Lit. World."]—"The story is sōmewhat painful, but thêre is good character-drawing, and a certain persistent fidelity in treating the slo, disintegrating processes which affect human characters and action, which is anything but commonplace. The buoyant and successful selfishness which at first makes Mr. Fauberton the delĩght of his fello-townsmen is the same sentiment which shapes his subsequent cruel life, and the prudence which seems altŏgether admirable in Camille's youth slõly dries the sources of feelings which seemed sincere and mĩght hav been controling." [Nation. **2296**

UNDER THE BAN ["Le Maudit" by the ABBÉ * * *, i. e., —— Deléon: *Smith*, 1864.] is "a book of sŏme power tŏ which the controversies of the time impart adventitious interest. A second part, 'La Religieuse', folloes the rule, in being less powerful and more tedious than the first portion . . . It is not, however, chargeable with the acrimony and the open prejudiçe which too frequently disfigure novels of its quality." [Athenæum.]—"The individual sufferings of the La Clavières' (brŏther and sister, as supposed, and the hero and heroin of the narrativ)—sufferings attributable tŏ the machinations of the brŏtherhood of Loyola, and ŏther malevolent influences which bring the young and ardent reformer of his religious contemporaries 'Under the Ban'—ar delineated with a painful fidelity and verisimilitude which hav rarely been surpassed. The dulness of provincial, the vivacity of Parisian, society, and the charms and perils of Pyrenean solitudes, ar forcibly and appropriately depicted. The events related succeed each ŏther with rapidity, and the alternations of fortune frequently produce striking and sŏmetimes romantic effects. The work is ŏne of much talent and interest." [London Review.] See, also, continuation of abŏve in *THE CONFESSOR*, N.-Y.. *Brady*, 1868. **2297**

UNDER THE TRICOLOR [**Paris**] = No. 551.

UNDINE, by ANDRÉ THEURIET [Paris, 1872] in *Canadian Monthly*, June 1873 tŏ Feb. 1874. **2298**

UNFROCKED. by ERNEST DAUDET, N.-Y., *Tousey*, 1885, = *THE APOSTATE*.

UNREQUITED AFFECTION = *PERE GORIOT*.

URSULA. [by HONORÉ "DE" BALZAC: *Roberts*, 1891.] "Ursule Mirouët. in the series of "Scenes of provincial life," was published in 1841. "Ursula" is a most charming creation, a pure, lõvely young girl, reared by three old men, whŏ all succumb tŏ her tender influence. Her godfather, Dr. Minoret, is surrounded by a number of rapacious relativs, whŏ ar watching for his last breath, that thêy may pounce upon his wealth. Thêir meanness and viciousness ar vividly reproduced. The scene is **Nemours**, tbe life of a provincial town being carefully studied. The postmaster of Nemours, whŏ is the Doctor's cousin, forms, with his wife and sŏn, a remarkable character group." [Publisher's Weekly.]—"It seems as if for ŏnce in his life the grêat romancer had said tŏ himself, 'I wil be a poet and you—my poem !' Leaving Paris and its storms and dramas, the subject of 'Ursule' nestles amŏng the hils of the provinces, whêre a silver stream and a town of ancient houses make lõve-eyes at each ŏther and coquet in the piquant way knŏn ŏnly tŏ old french houses and swift french streams. Glimpses of Fontainebleau bring us near Paris; but the scene, the plot, the people. the drama ar entirely provincial. The study of provincial manners has always been a fascinating theme, for thêre is so much of individuality about the old town and château life, untainted with the glaze and polish of the capital, unspoiled in its naive nakedness, simple and good in its rural strength and 'bonhomie.' Here if anywhêre the true heârt of France is found, a pious, godly, often passionate life unsuspected by the hurrying tourist, which Balzac has caut in his vast net and made tŏ illustrate ŏne corner of his grêat comedy—the fireside corner, with all its precious and tender associations . . . In 'Ursule Mirouët' quite the contrary refreshes us, after a long 'spel' of barbaric and rococo Balzac. The lŏveliest Bermuda lily on its tall and tapering stem could not be lŏvelier than this sweet young girl or the circle of venerable old men tŏ whŏm she oes her education. The ŏne weak spot in the book is its use of the supernatural tŏ bring about the catastrofē. Balzac, like Dumas, had a 'penchant' for mesmerism and Swedenborg and has nearly spoiled several powerful books by introducing it. 'Ursule Mirouët' imperils the reader's interest by exciting his derision. and produces a feeling of incredulity that is unfortunate for the whole book. A new fāse of covetousness is analyzed with all the master's terrible knoledge of this passion, and new and beautiful lŏve-scenes gro ŏut of the complications in the old doctor's house, tŏ counterbalance it. The moral of the tale is good, and ŏne is thankful that Balzac wrote ŏne [ŏnly ŏne? See No. 2024.] book that, like Zola's 'Rêve,' [No. 784.] can be put intŏ the hands of a girl." [Critic. **2299**

——, SAME, in *The Dial*, Cin'ti, 1860.

VENDETTA (THE). [by HONORÉ "DE" BALZAC (†, 1850): Bos-

ton, *Redpath*, 1864, 85 p; also (transl. by F.. A.. Kemble) in *The Democratic Review*, sept.-nov., 1845; also in *Canadian Monthly*, mar.-apr., 1873.] "The first of the *Scènes de la Vie Privée* is entitled *La Vendetta*. The ŏnly dauter of ŏne of Buonaparte's Corsican folloers, whŏm he has raised tŏ rank and wealth, is, nevertheless a pupil in a common painting school, whêre she makes acquaintance with a proscribed officer 'de la vieille armée.' whŏm she persists in marrying. in spite of the advice. entreaties. and commands of her affectionate parents, whŏ had the deepest and best founded objections tŏ the match—namely, an old family feud, exasperated by recent bloody injuries. She at first supports herself and her husband by her grêat talents as a painter—but gradually she goes ŏut of fashion, and poverty cŏmes. Her parents ar inexorable; and then perish, of actual starvation—first her baby—for the sources of maternity ar dry—and then she and her husband. The parents repent when too late—the mŏther dies of remorse, and the father is left alone in the world—soon, also, tŏ die of a broken heârt, the punishment of his cruelty." [Quarterly Review. **2300**

——. SAME ("The Family Feud"), in *Chamber's Pocket Miscellany*, Vol. 15.

VILLAGE DOCTOR, (The) [by SOPHIE (DE BAZANCOURT) D'ARBOUVILLE: Chapman, 1853.] "is a tale of pure and pathetic feeling set in a bright and distinct framework of description. The arrival at a deserted country-house in Brétagne, of a gay party from Paris, opens the story; and the reminiscences of the village practitioner as tŏ what happened in a certain white cottage, which the lady of the manor thôtlessly talks of having pulled down, furnishes the matter. The Doctor tels the old tale of a secret marriage, follōed by the young husband's sudden death and the neglect of the wido by his proud relativs—simply and môrnfully—without that affected garrulity which writers ar apt tŏ introduce intŏ such narrativs when thêy wish tŏ be natural.'' [Athenæum. 2301

——, SAME, in "Three Tales" [No. 2281.] and in *Graham's Magazine*, Oct.-Nov., 1847.

VIOLETS OF MONTMARTRE (The) [by —— ( ) BERSIER: London, *Seeley*, 1874.] "is a collection of interesting stories. excellently translated. It is good and profitable for english girls tŏ vary thêir interests in reading, and these french stories wil sho them incidents in the lives of girls under ōther environments than thêir ōn." [Athenæum. 2302

VICTIMS [**Bretagne**] = No. 554.

WAS IT LOVE? ["Un Coeur de Femme") by PAUL BOURGET: Worthington Co.. 1891.] "Bourget ranks with the grêatest of modern novelists, and this marvellous effort places him on a plane which few if äny of his contemporaries wil ever reach. It was a natural supposition on the part of those whŏ knew him that the development of the 'Comédie Humaine' would cease with Balzac. that no ōther hand, however cunning, would possess the genius tŏ push the work tŏ further if not grêater successes. And yet this is what Bourget has dŏne, and in dŏing so has prŏved himself a worthy successor of that grêat master of the modern art of fiction. He has taken a theme upon which Balzac wrote at length, and has developed it in a most fascinating manner. It is the theory of the duality in feminin nature—a theory which forms the basic idea in Balzac's 'Seraphita.' With Balzac it was the development of a filosoficⁿl theory solely. Bourget has made a practical application of that theory, and has produced ōne of the most interesting psychological studies as wel as ōne of the most charming novels which we hav been treated tŏ in modern times. This is an expurgated edition, and in making what he deemed necessary excisions the translator has left ōut the point of the study. Either these books should be translated literally or thêy should be left alone: it is too grêat a wrong tŏ the author tŏ mutilate his work in this fashion. In an ordinary narrativ of blood-curdling events ōne or twŏ more or less tŏ the page would make no difference, but in a grêat psychological study such as this, whêre every link in the chain of thôt fits intŏ its proper place and cannot be dispensed with. it is vandalism and affectation tŏ introduce him tŏ a thinking public in an expurgated form." [Critic. 2303

WEDDED IN DEATH. by É. ZOLA, N.-Y.. *Tousey*, 1885, = *FORTUNES OF THE ROUGONS.*—Compare No. 1890.

WEEK IN A FRENCH COUNTRY HOUSE (A). [by ADELAIDE (KEMBLE) SARTORIS: *Loring*, 1868.] "The style of this little novel was singularly brĭght and accomplished, the humor original, and ·the characters sharply drawn. The fact that certain persons very wel knŏn in the world of art wer understood tŏ hav sat unconsciously tŏ Mrs. Sartoris for thêir portraits gave a further popularity tŏ an exceedingly clever and genial book." [Athenæum.] **See, also.** No. 558. 2304

WEIRD GIFT, = *PETER'S SOUL*.
WHITE BLACKBIRDS, ☞ Mus-
SET.
WHITE LIES, by C: READE. =
No. 1013.
WHITE MONTH (The). by F..
M.. PEARD. = No. 1014.
WILL (The). by G: OHNET. *Vizetelly*, N.-Y., *Brentano, Ivers*, 1888. 2305
WINGS OF COURAGE (THE)
[by "G: SAND." i. e., Amantine Lucile Aurore (Dupin) Dudevant (†,
1876) : *Putnam*, 1877.] "contains 3
rather long stories. But why "adapted?" and why is not George Sand acknoledged as the author? Thêre ôt tŏ
be an authentic translation of Madame Sand's fairy-tales, which ar so
full of fancy, earnestness, and charm.
These stories appeal tŏ a more imaginativ and cultured audience of boys
and girls than that tŏ which the realistic tales of american writers ar addressed. The beauty and simplicity
of the antique, wil, we fear, appear
dul when compared with the adventures of hoydens and newsboys, and
Young America is not partial tŏ the
young naturalist unless he justifies
the singularity of his pursuit by an
abundance of slauter." [Lippincott's.
—— SAME, [London, *Blackie*,
1883.]
"Thêre ar twŏ stories in this volume.
the first and most important being a
tale of Bretagne. in which the grêat
novelist has mingled fact and fancy
in a vêry happy fashion. We feel
sure that the lad whŏ makes his home
amõng the wild birds on the breton
cliff is a real person; but he is skilfully idealised, and his story made intŏ a genuin romance." [Specta. 2306
WINNIE'S HISTORY = No. 560.
WISH OF HIS LIFE = *JEAN TE-
TEROL*.

WITHIN AN ACE = No. 561.
WITHOUT DOWRY, by E.
ABOUT: in The Emerald, Boston,
Shorey, 1866. 2307
WOMAN OF HONOR = *PUPIL
OF THE LEGION*.
WOMAN'S HEART (A) = No.
2118.
WOMAN'S JOURNAL (A). [by
OCTAVE FEUILLET (†, 1890.) : *Munro*,
1878.] "Trivial as the story is, it has
the merit of being entertaining. All
of the woman ar cleverly drawn, thêir
talk is as natural as possible, while
the men ar mere vague creations . . .
Feuillet holds a hi place amõng contemporary french novelists, which he
has won by studying fashionable society, and by flattering the largest
class of his readers by putting them,
with thêir little ways, intŏ his stories;
thus he makes them interested. and
he wins those also whŏ hav grêat curiosity about the ways of the grêat
world. He dões his work cleverly,
but it is a poor pîece of business, and
õne which can hav õnly brief success.
His admission intŏ the Academy is
very much like the choice of a fotografer for a vacant seat in the Royal
Academy." [Atlantic.]—"In such a
book, tho it touches on delicate
ground, thêre is in the style a refinement and in the story an appreciation of the finer things in life which
speaks of an atmosfere of chivalry
and honor which is becõming less and
less common in France. The characters in the story ar few in number;
the interest turns upon the fate and
character of the woman whŏ tels it.—
It wil be seen that thêre is very little
incident in it. It is almost altõgether
a novel of sentiment; but, told with
that amazing cleverness of which
Feuillet is a master, the play of pas-

sion and feeling furnishes as much or more interest than the most exciting plot." [Nation. **2308**
——, SAME ("Diary of a Woman") *Appleton*, 1879.
WOMAN'S REVENGE (A), or the Count of Morion, by F: SOULIÉ: *Peterson*, 1847. **2309**
WOMAN'S TRIALS (A). [by "GRACE RAMSAY," i. e., Kathleen O'Meara (†, 1888) : *Hurst*, 1868.] "In this plain, every-day story, in which thêre ar no hïly wrôt sensation scenes, we hav a minute and vivid picture of an English girl's school life in Paris. Mr. Sala, in *Quite Alone*, givs sōme glimpse intô these establishments, whêre English girls ar, in more than ōne sense, finished, but his sketch is not for a moment tô be compared with that of Grace Ramsay. The place, the pupils, the teachers, ar singularly exact. It is a lifelike picture, with which imagination has nothing tô dô, and the picture is calculated tô make English parents pause before thêy suffer thêir girls tô experience its reality. Of course all the superintendents of these schools ar not harsh, sordid, and unscrupulous; of côurse thêy dô not all freeze and starv thêir pupils; of course Madame St. Simon is no more the exact likeness of all French schoolmistresses than was Mr. Squeers that of all English schoolmasters. But thêy both represent with a terrible distinctness a certain fâse of school life." [Englishwoman's Domestic Magazine. **2310**
——, SAME ["Mabel Stanhope"], Boston, *Roberts*, 1886 [No. 488.]
WOMAN'S WHIMS (A), by JO. XAVIER BONIFACE, called SAINTINE, N.-Y., 1850. **2311**
WONDERFUL EYE-GLASS [Le Lorgnon] by DELPHINE (GAY)

GIRARDIN (†, 1855) : in *Englishwoman's Domestic Magazine*, aug. 1871 tô jan. 1872. **2312**
WOODLAND QUEEN (A). [by ANDRÉ THEURIET : Chicago, *Sergel*, 1891.] "The 'Queen' is a sweet sensible girl whô has been educated abōve her rustic station, but leaves all her opportunities tô devote herself tô a paralytic old man, whôm she has always deemed her father. Her country home, with its many duties, changing seasons, and the rare beauty of the woods of Southern [?] France. is artistically drawn. Her lōve-story is rudely shattered by hearing from her confessor that she and the man she proposes tô marry ar children of the same father. She goes bac tô her devotion tô the half-witted old paralytic, and in the end wins the lōve of a truly noble man." [Pub. Weekly. **2313**
——. SAME (abridged) "The Queen of the Woods,' Chicago, *Laird*, 1891.
WORKMAN'S CONFESSIONS (A). [by ÉMILE SOUVESTRE (†. 1854) : *Longman*, 1851; N.-Y., *Hunt & Eaton*, 1891.] "Souvestre excelled in delicate description of the minutiæ of daily life. The workman here tels of the trials and pleasures of his life, his lōve, marriage. fatherhood and plan of making his children useful and happy. The details of home-life amōng the working classes ar very touching; and the picture he draws of himself and his wife in old age surrounded by thêir children is inspiring and helpful." [Publishers' Weekly. **2314**
WORLD'S VERDICT (THE). [**Riviera**] = No. 564.
YELLOW ROSE (The), by "C: DE BERNARD": in *The New Mirror*, Oct-. 1843. **2315**
YOUNG GIRL'S CONFESSIONS

(A). [by "G: SAND," i. e., Amantine Lucile Aurore (Dupin) Dudevant: N.-Y., *Brady*, 1865.] "The author endeavors tŏ sho that an impassioned character may be in the dark about its sentiments and wants in consequence of contradictions which may hav occurred in its educational progress, and of the various influences which hav by turns acted upon it. In order tŏ prŏve her argument, G: Sand introduces tŏ her readers several characters whŏ hav thêir peculiar notions about lŏve. Frumence, a stoical disciple of the ancient filosofers, and Jenny, an activ and devoted woman, deem lŏve an instinct which should be suppressed and even sacrificed in certain contingencies, and which, under all circumstances, must giv way tŏ duty. The vulgar Galanthée holds lŏve tŏ be nothing more than a 'grossier besoin des sens;' and for the selfish Marius it is simply a means tŏ repair the wrongs of fortune by a rich match. Lucienne, whŏ is the principal character of this subtly conceived story, has natural, womanly feelings. She marries ŏne MacAllan, whŏ, like her, was deceived in his first aspirations. The devoted Jenny wil marry the stoic Frumence; and the cŏvetous Marius must content himself with the sensuous Galanthée. The plot in this tale is rather slīght, but the delineation of the characters, and the psychological analysis, tŏgether with the descriptions of picturesque scenery, ar executed in a masterly manner." [London Review. **2316**

YOUNG MAUGARS. [by ANDRÉ THEURIET: *Appleton*, 1879.] "Those of ŏur readers whŏ remember Theuriet's exquisit story, 'Gérard's Marriage' [No. 2051.] wil learn with pleasure that in his latest work, he has produced very nearly, if not quite, its equal. All the charms of beautiful description, clear analysis, delicate workmanship, hī ideals, refined motiv, and elevating purpos, ar here found in full strength and equable proportion. The author's design is the hīest and best. It is tŏ bring out the strong contrast between the sordid and the unselfish life, tŏ trace the struggle in a human sŏul between the lŏer and the loftier nature, and tŏ prepossess the heârt in favor of that choice which secures virtue, and peace, and simplicity and the delights of home, even at sŏme sacrifice of things which the world commonly holds dear. All this is accomplished without a suggestion of cant on the ŏne hand, and without resort tŏ vulgar devices on the ŏther, so that the reader is guided along a flowery and fragrant path, even tho àt times under the shado of clouds, tŏ his happy destination ... Mlle. Marcelle's seductiv approaches and Étienne's sturdy resistance and final escape; the latter's present discŏvery of Thérèse in her retreat at La Joubardière and the fanning of the old flame which had already fired thêir pure and truthful heârts, the pleasant picture of the simple life which went on at the farm, while the bond that knitted the lŏvers grew stronger and stronger; the ruin which then burst upon Mr. Maugars, senior, and the unkind fate that ŏnce more threatened the uprīght-minded sŏn; these and ŏther passages which conduct the story tŏ its conclusion we forbêar tŏ enter upon in detail ... The extracts which we hav given wil convêy tŏ the reader a good idea of the soft and glŏing beauty of the pastoral scenes amidst which this story is laid, the tender delicacy of such of the dialog, and the sharp outlines of the figures which pass before the eye. We kno no european writer, unless it be Turgénieff, whŏ equals Mr. Theuriet in his power of setting a real landscape visibly before you and making his personages tŏ stand or mŏve with the vividness of life. Certainly the beauties of rural France hav been seldom if ever placed upon the printed page with more exquisit effect than in this story and in Gérard's Marriage. And yet the scene never obtrudes itself in the way of the drama; the development of character, the play of motiv, the succession of circumstances and incident, and the slo but steady and natural evolution of the result occupy thêir full share of the attention." . [Boston "Lit. World."]—"Mr. Theuriet is rather an optimist; his vue of life suggests gay ribbons and holiday jollity in the main, and tho it has its shadŏs thêy ar not very sombre. But he is very much of a poet, and in an idyllic story like "Young Mangars" is at his best. The lŏve-making is very charming and dŏne with grêat delicacy. It

quite atones for the author's naiveté in painting a villain of a deliberate and frank execrability with which Zola, whŏ knoes villains tŏ thêir fin-ger-tips, would never think of enduring his worst character.—The book is excellent for its contrast between the virtues of the peasants and the vices of the bourgeoisie in a small town, and for its mãny pleasant pictures of ŏut-of-doors. These, tho thêy giv a sŏmewhat episodical character tŏ the story, ar in a subdued key, and thêy ar admirable in technique." [Nation. **2317**

——, SAME ("Maugars, Jr.") *Vizetelly*, 1880.

YOUNG MAN OF THE PERIOD, by A. Theuriet, Chicago, *Laird*, 1892. **2318**

YOUNG STUDENT (The) by E.. C.. P.. (de Meulan) Guizot: *Appleton*, 1844. **2319**

ZADIG, by Voltaire: in *Brother Jonathan*, 12 Nov. 1842. **2320**

ZEMGANNO BROTHERS (The) by E. de Goncourt: [Paris, 1879.] *Maxwell*, 1886. **2321**

ZYTE, by H. Malot: *Warne*, 1888. **2322**

"I like the novel because it tels the eternal story of lŏve. And I like it abŏve all because, while I read, I liv a life different from that of every day: the novel carries me for sŏme hŏurs beyond this petty every-day life; it makes me for the moment realize my dream. In order tŏ charm and tŏ attract me it should be sentimental, impassioned, graceful, elegant, full of illusions, and not the simple fotograf of my ordinary existence which wêighs me down on account of its vulgarity and commonplace, which folloes me everywhêre,—which I kno too wel, and which I should like tŏ forget." [Quoted in Pall Mall Budget.

PRICE, ONE COPY, $1 00; TWO COPIES; $1.50; THREE, $2.25; FOUR, $3.00; FIVE, $3.25; SIX, $4.00; TEN, $5.00.

A

DESCRIPTIVE LIST

OF

NOVELS AND TALES

DEALING WITH

LIFE IN GERMANY.

COMPILED BY

W: M. GRISWOLD.

CAMBRIDGE, MASS.:
W: M. GRISWOLD, PUBLISHER.
1892.

[*From the "School Bulletin," Aug.*, 1892.]

We hope teachers will not fail tŏ recognize the work W. M. Griswold is dŏing in his classified bibliography. He sends us a Descriptive List of Novels and Tales dealing with Life in France (Cambridge, Mass., 1892, 8vo, pp. 94, $1.00), which is of immediate practical use tŏ the teacher of French history as well as of French literature.

[*From the "Central Christian Advocate."*]

Mr. Griswold has dŏne an excellent work, which will be appreciated by all librarians, and by many people of cultivated taste whŏ wish tŏ get on the track of the best French fiction, or at least tŏ secure sŏme guidance and information in regard tŏ its qualities and characteristics. His former "lists" have dealt with American City and Country Life, with Life in England, etc . . . Life in city and country, peasant life and soldier life, the reckless and adventurous career of the free and easy student in Paris, and the rude rustic amŏng the mountains,—all these phases of French life pass in review in the books which Mr. Griswold has here catalogued. A guide like this would be invaluable tŏ a student of French literature, telling as well what tŏ avoid, as what tŏ secure and read.

[*From the "Boston Commonwealth," 13 Aug.*, 1892.]

If all libraries wer generously equipped with these Lists, the long-suffering curator of books would find more pleasure in life. The compilation and selection ar made with rare skill. The poor book drops into deservd oblivion, while the worthy but neglected and forgotten good book is restored tŏ the eye of the world.

Sŏme not too busy people make note of the name of a novel recommended by a trustworthy critic, but when the time for use cŏmes the note seldom is at hand, and, if ready, generally givs the mere title and no idea of the contents. But here is a series of brochures that contain excerpts from the fairest critical notices, often from several sources, and ŏne is enabled tŏ form a sort of judgment of choice without actually glancing at the book itself. Of course, those dealing with foreign lands must for the grĕater part be translations, since with few exceptions the most truthful and vivid characterizations cŏme from the compatriot whŏ has summered and wintered his fellows. Few people realize the patience, skill, and labor involvd in such an undertaking as the publica-tion of these successiv lists, but those whŏ dŏ should urge upon ŏthers the use of so valuable a means of education and pleasure. As a series of 'condensed novels' they ar interesting, too.

GERMAN NOVELS.

———————◆———————

The object of this list is to direct readers, such as would enjoy the kind of books here described, to a number of novels, easily accessible, but which, in many cases, hav been forgotten within a year or two after publication. That the existence of works of fiction is remembered so short a time is a pity, since, for every new book of merit, there ar, in most libraries, a hundred as good or better, unknown to the majority of readers. It is hoped that the publication of this and similar lists will lessen, in some measure, the disposition to read an inferior NEW *book when superior* OLD *books, equally fresh to most readers, ar at hand. It may be observed that the compiler has tried to include only such works as ar well-written, interesting, and free from sensationalism, sentimentality, and pretense.* BUT *in a few cases, books hav been noticed on account of the reputation of their authors, or their great popularity, rather than their merit.*

The selécted " notices" ar generally abridged.

This list will be followed by others describing RUSSIAN, NORWEGIAN, SPANISH, — HUMOROUS, ECCENTRIC and FANCIFUL *novels and tales.*

———————◆———————

AARON'S ROD, or the Jewess, in *Southern Lit. Messenger*, Sept. 1846. **2323**

ADÉ [by ESMÉ STUART: London, The S. P. C. K., 1882.] "is the tale of an unlŏved husband and a forsaken lŏver, of duty faithfully discharged and of virtue rewarded in the end." [Athenæum. **2324**

AERONAUT, by A. STIFTER, in *Illus. Mag. of Art*, Feb., 1853. **2325**

AFTERGLOW [**Dresden**] = No. 405.

AGAINST THE STREAM, by E. ECKSTEIN, in *Masterpieces of German Fiction*. **2326**

ALL IN VAIN, by R. LINDAU, in *Masterpieces of German Fiction*. **2327**

ALOYS, by B. AUERBACH: *Holt*, 1877. **2328**

ALPINE FAY (The). [by " E. WERNER," i. e., E.. Bürstenbinder: *Lippincott*, 1889.] " Twŏ pretty mŏtherless girls, cousins, divide the interest. The father of ŏne is a wealthy man and the president of a grĕat railway; that of the ŏther a baron, and · possessor of an ancestral mansion amŏng the mountains, which the railroad president is trying to get for his railway. The struggle tŏ retain his home kils the old baron, and he dies cursing the originator of the road. Added to this curse is a legend of the ' Alpine Fay ' connected with a peak which is verified in the story just as the baron's curse seems tŏ carry out its evil work. The theft of an invention, the final punishment of the thief, several lŏve affairs, and many charming scenes from domestic life make up the story."

[Pub. Weekly.] It "is agreeable. . . Readers whŏ dŏ not relish the ultra emotionalism of the German novel may yet find in the strong and effectiv local cŏloring of this book a good excuse for giving it their attention." [American.

—, SAME (" A Heavy Reckoning.")
—, SAME (" The Fairy of the Alps.")
See No. 729. **2329**

AMAZON (The) [by FRANZ DINGELSTEDT (†, 1881) : *Putnam*, 1868.] "deals cleverly with artistic and theatrical life under the glare of the footlights." [Nation. **2330**

ANNA HAMMER [by HUBERTUS TEMME : *Harper*, 1852] "givs a vivid picture of the interior of german life, and is filled with passages of exciting interest." [Harper's. **2331**

ARISTOCRATIC WORLD (The) by FANNY (LEWALD) STAHR : in *Masterpieces of German Fiction*. **2332**

ASBEIN, by "OSSIP SCHUBIN, *Worthington*, 1890. See No. 2345.

AT A HIGH PRICE [by " E. WERNER," i. e., E.. Bürstenbinder : *Estes*, 1879] "A lŏve affair between twŏ young people as strongly affected by a feud of long standing between twŏ elderly men, whŏ stand in near relation and friendship to the lŏvers. One of the men is a physician of renown, the ŏther is the governor of the Province. The cause of the bitter feud is political. Gabrielle, the heroin, is the ward of the governor, whŏm she learns tŏ lŏve, and hence is ready tŏ sacrifice her early lŏver. The situation is elucidated by a tragedy." [Pub. Weekly.

—, SAME (" No Surrender ") *Remington*, 1879, *Munro*, 1883.

—, SAME, (" The Price He Paid ") N. Y., *Street*, 1891. **2333**

AT ODDS, = No. 593.

AT QUARANTINE, by FANNY

(LEWALD) STAHR : in *The Radical*, Nov., 1871. **2334**

AT THE ALTAR, by WERNER, = No. 594.

AT THE COUNCILLOR'S [by " E. MARLITT," i. e., Eugenie John (†, 1887) : *Lippincott* [*Bentley*] 1876] is " a story which compares wel with the best the author has written, while it is far better than her worst. She always runs the risk of overdŏing whatever she takes in hand, of exaggerating the goodness of her heroes and heroins, and the villainy of the wicked ones ; but if we overlook this fault, we find her capable of interesting the reader and of giving a fair picture of german life. On this occasion she has drawn upon her experience of the turmoil which has arisen in her country since the late war, and has shŏn the disturbance caused by the sudden gain and sudden loss of wealth. The councillor dŏes not belong tŏ ŏne of the fine old families, but he accumulates a large fortune and illustrates admirably the fate of those of his class whŏ ar put on horsebac, by riding rapidly in the familiar direction, expediting his journey by the awful explosion of dynamite. The main interest of the book lies not in him but in the heroin, Kitty, who is young, rich, handsŏme, fascinating — in fact, faultless ; and in the silent, uncomplaining, but able Dr. Bruck. Flora, whŏ was for a long time engaged tŏ Bruck, was a very mischievous young person, and is the object of the utmost virulence on the part of the author. She is aggressivly wicked ; and this exaggeration is the more tŏ be regretted because she is a wel-imagind character." [Nation.] — " We cannot say that any of the personages of the story ar very pleasing. The doctor, whŏ is the hero, is a good example of the half-scientific, half-military prig,

BEACON FIRES ["Flammenzeich-nen") by "E. WERNER," i. e., E.. Bürsten-binder: *Bentley*, 1891.] "is a German novel by a German, but it is written in good plain English. It is romantic, of course, and rather sentimental, but decidedly inter-esting. The struggle between father and son, which is the pith of the story, is wel conceived, and both hold the reader's sym-pathy. Von Falkenried, with his stern sense of disciplin, moral as wel as military, and with a kind nature hardened by a miserable marriage, is determined tŏ make his son go as strait as he and his ancestors hav always gône. Hartmut, however, has his Roumanian mŏther's blood, and it is not of the quality which goes strait. At 17 he is induced by the divorced wife, his mŏther, whŏm he believed to be dead, tŏ desert the military college where he is being trained, and tŏ which is attached a sort of parole of honor not so binding as the oath of service, but distinctly under-stood, and also tŏ brêak his promise tŏ his father. These ar deep offenses, and thêy ar folloed by ten dubious years of adventu-rous life, in which Hartmut's poetic gen-ius is developed at the cost of his morals and faith. How the gifted and unhappy son redeems the blited reputation by splendid service in the war with France, and reconçiles his iron father, may be read, alông with much more or less relev-vant matter, in the pages of the book it-self. Hartmut is a distinct individuality, and his story has interest. Thêre is, of course, plenty of lŏve-making of various sorts, and a grêat many weddings at the end, as German novels usually hav, and the ŏnly trouble is, that the fine fello Prince Egon has tŏ be shot, because he also was in lŏve with Adelheid, and she could'nt marry both him and Hartmut. [Saturday Review]— As a picture of various phases of life amông the "classes" in Germany, the book can be heârtily and unreservedly praised; and the humorous sub-story, which deals with the lŏve-affairs of the easy-going young giant, Willibald von Eschenhagen, is really a good deal more enjoyable than the greater part of the rather melodramatic romance in which the Byronic hero, Hartmut Falkenried, is the leading figure. There is, however, a point in the story at which Hartmut ceases tŏ be merely histrionic and be-cŏmes human; and from this point onward is, what the writer has meant him tŏ be all along, the true centre of interest. His midnight interview with the stern father whŏ has disŏned him, and whŏ refuses tŏ condone the dishonor of the stainless name of Falkenried, is a really strông piece of work,— a tragic situation quite unspoiled by anything in the way of sentimental un-reality; and hardly less impressiv is the pathetic and picturesque reçital of the succéssful issue of the deed of daring by which the sŏn saves the father's life." [Spectator.

——, SAME ("His Word of Honor"), N.-Y., *Street & Smith*, 1890 (284 p.)

——, SAME ("Northern Lights"), N.-Y., *Bonner*, 1890.   **2339 q**

ᴜ clasʂ wel knŏn in the Fatherland. The lady with whŏm he plays the game of fast and loose is 29 yearʂ old, writes, and speaks of herself as a ' rich perfumed plant;' while her grandmŏther and the other members of her family ar all disagreeable after their ways. Her half-sister, for whŏm her lŏver finally givʂ her up, an innocent and not wholy unpleasant young girl, tinctured, however, rather too deeply with Dresden culture, and the Doctor's ânt, an elderly lady of the ' goody' type, whŏ makes pancakes and talks piously, ar the ŏnly twŏ people in the book whŏm we dŏ not feel we should hate if we met them in the flesh. The descriptions ar good; tho, as is usual with descriptions of german life and scenery, they produce ᴜ sŏmewhat de-pressing effect, like the stove-warmed rooms." [Athenæum.] — " This is ŏne of the author's best stories, — a graphic picture of hi life; a vivid lŏve-drama; ᴜ gallery of striking portraits, with a moral echo infinitly impressiv. The contrast of Kitty, the heiress — a pure, innocent, sincere young girl, and the vain, arrogant, selfish Flora, her half-sister, is ŏne of the finest effects in fiction; and the characters of the councillor and the physician ar not less effectivly opposed. The history of the betrothal of Flora and Bruck is a tragical drama, forcibly illustrating the woman's perfidy and the steadfast justiçe of the man. Kitty is a lŏvely character, whŏ passes throu mãny trib-ulations tŏ her due reward." [Boston " Literary World." **2335**

BACHELOR OF GÖTTINGEN (The) in *The Symbol*, Jan., 1846. **2336**

BAILIFF'S MAID (The) [by " E. Marlitt," i. e., Eugenie John (†, 1887) : *Lippincott*, 1881.] is " a piece of fiction as faithful tŏ life as tŏ seem no fiction; a summer lŏve-idyl, invested with name-less charm and quaintness of old-world existence; a plot of the simplest and most transparent character, yet with mysteries and surprises skilfully handled, and a technique fresh and rich . . . The scene is ᴜ beautiful secluded manor in the Thüringian forest — just the place for the new hêir of the estate, a wealthy young manu-facturer from Berlin, tŏ fall in lŏve on occasion of his first visit; and fall in lŏve he dŏes, most hopelessly, and much tŏ his dismay, with the queenly and mysterious maid of the farm steward." [American. **2337**

BALDINE = No. 598.

BANNED AND BLESSED = No. 600.

BAREFOOTED MAIDEN = *LIT-TLE BAREFOOT*.

BARON LEO VON OBERG, Boston, *Loring*, 1868. **2338**

BARONESS BLANK, by A. Nie-mann : *Bonner*, 1891. **2339**

BEATRICE, by Heyse, = No. 669.

BEGINNING AND END, by Heyse, = No. 669 : also in *Every Saturday*, 23–30 jan., 1869. **2340**

BELINDA [Dresden] = No. 420.

BETROTHAL OF MR. QUINT, by H: Zschokke, in *Graham's Mag.*, Feb.–Apr., 1844. **2341**

BLACK FOREST VILLAGE STORIES. [by Berthold Auer-bach (†, 1882.) : Phil'a., *F. W. Thomas*, 1858; N. Y., *Leypoldt*, 1869.] " ar Præ-Raphaelite pictures of peasant life — pictures so simple and so vivid that with ᴜ little stretch of fancy we can see the figures mŏving in the fields or in the roads, the smoke curling from the rustic cottages, and almost hear the soft gutturals transforming themselvs intŏ the sharp aspirates of ŏur english speech. In each story we meet the same fresh-faced peasants, — the same homely, simple life. This is all delitful tŏ read about, because it is so fresh and new. The perfectly unaffected manner in which these tales ar told is anŏther of thêir charms, and the book wil hav a wholesŏm attraction for ăny reader whŏse taste has not been vitiated by the hily-spiced pictures current in the literature of tŏ-day." [Round Table.] — "All of them hav a wŏnderful air of truthfulness and naturalness and tenderness, tŏ which undoubtedly, their popularity is due. That this should be as grêat as it is, even in forêin parts, and with readers whŏse experience is so unlike that of the german peasants and villagers, is good testimony to the author's excellence. In ŏūr opinion, it is in these village stories, and in his shorter, less ambitious novels, that Auerbach is at his best; he is certainly infinitly more natural, and he cŏmes much nearer life, than he dŏes in the long novels in which he discusses vague theories of social philosophy." [Atlantic]. — "The sŏmewhat realistic english mind is rather repelled than attracted by Auerbach's peasants, whŏ ar anything but genuin boors. They ar german philosophers, folloers of Spinoza, tricked out for the nonce in peasant attire. Yet, for all these defects, the stories hav real merits, ar prettily told, and, save for the fault we hav named, ar true tŏ nature." [Athenæum.]

The tales in this collection ar: *The Gawk* [a story continued in *Aloys* (No. 2328), *The Pipe of War*, *Manor-House-Farmer's Vefela*, *Nip-cheeked Tony*, *Good Government*, *The Hostile Brothers*, *Ivo*, *Florian and Crescenz*, *The Lauterbacher*. "How shal we dismiss the other stories, *Brosie and Moni*, for example. Ar we not tŏ dwel even on the proud device of Brosie, ' I hav no equal,' which was quite true? Not a word about *Ivo*, whŏ was tŏ hav been a parish priest, and never became ŏne ; or his gentle mother, Christin, or *Lorle*, the village maiden whŏm the painter wedded, or his democratic and satirical friend, the *Kohlebrater ;* or the shy schoolmaster from *Lauterbach ;* or the story of *Seb and Zilge* and their house which was founded on sand? And *Hops and Barley*, and the sad disappearance of *Vefele*, and the adventures of *Joseph in the Snow*, with his witch friend, Lugard, Hecate's first cousin, and the wild *Roemannin* and *Aivle* and *Matthias* whŏ stole the May, ar these tŏ be lumped in a bare catalog when they would furnish a winter's reading? But the rehersal of such names wil tel us why Auerbach is a household word among his countrymen ; and why his death brŏt grief intŏ German homes." [Dublin Review. *See, also, GERMAN STORIES.*

—, SAME (" Village Tales of the Black Forest,") *Bogue*, 1846–7, 2 v.

—, SAME ("Ivo "), London, 1847.

—, SAME ("Florian and Crescenz "), London, 1853.

—, SAME (" Professor's Lady "), *Harper*, 1850.

—, SAME ("Lorley and Reinhart ") *Holt ;* 1877. **2342**

BLOODSTONE (The) = No. 612.

BLUE WONDER (The), by H: Zschokke, in *The Albion*, 8 july 1837. **2343**

BOARDING SCHOOL GIRLS, by E. Eckstein, in *Masterpieces of German Fiction.* **2344**

BORIS LENSKY [by "Ossip Schubin," i. e., Lola Kirschner: N.-Y., *Worthington*, 1891.] is "a continuation of ' Asbein.' The hero, whŏ appears as a violinist, is said tŏ be intended for Rubinstein. His selfishness and vanity ar further illustrated, and the last days of a grêat genius, whŏse powers ar waning, are depicted with a pitiful realism." [Pub. Weekly. **2345** BRAVE WOMAN (A), by "Mar- litt," = No. 936.

BREACH OF CUSTOM ("Geheim- niss des Geigers") by Reinhold Ort- mann, N.-Y., *Bonner*, 1891. **2346** BREAKING OF THE DIKES, by Th. Mügge : [**Schleswig**] in *Gra- ham's Mag.*, Apr., 1856. **2346 g** BREAKING OF THE STORM (The) [by F : Spielhagen : *Bentley*, 1877.] is " a powerful and vivid picture of social life in **Berlin** during the late financial crisis." [Athenæum. **2346 k** BRIGADIER FREDERIC, by "Erck- mann Chatrian,"=No. 619. [**Elsass.**] BRIGITTA [by Berthold Auer- bach : *Holt*, 1880.] "deals with simple peasant life and character. The heroin is the dauter of a peasant, ŏnce the ŏner of a farm and much forest-land, whŏ is defrauded, ruined, and finally brŏt tŏ a premature grave by the machinations of a swindler. The burning sense of wrŏng which fires the old man's blood passes at his death intŏ the nature of his dauter. She fights it with all the powers of wil and resolv, but when, years after, her enemy cŏmes for treat- ment tŏ the oculist in whŏse hospital she is serving as assistant, and she hears him boast of his crimes and their suc- cess, an uncontrollable fury seizes her; she tears the bandage from his eyes, tels her true name, and bids him go blind thenceforward as a judgment on his villainy. The terrible revulsion of remorse, her agony of relief when she learns that the operation was unsuccess- ful and in no case could her victim hav recovered his sight, the expiation she sets herself of tending her enemy and nurs- ing him tŏ the end of his days, her beautiful and peaceful life afterward as

landlady of the Golden Lamb, ar all powerfully depicted, and make a har- monious and flawless picture, full of fresh and vigorous feeling." [Boston " Lit. World."] — " Brigitta is a story which may be warmly commended. It is in Auerbach's best style, and dŏes not contain the discussions of the true in- wardness of everything which sŏme- times overburden his long novels. It is ·a short story, very much like the Vil- lage Tales [No. 2342], by which we ar safe in presuming that this author wil be remembered by future genera- tions. Indeed, it is tŏ be borne in mind that Auerbach deservs credit, not merely for his delightful stories, but also with inspiring other writers with a desire tŏ copy him. G :· Sand, for instance, was led by reading these village tales tŏ write ' La Mare au Diable ' [No. 2013] and her ŏther stories of simple peasant life. It is not given tŏ every man tŏ open a new path in literature, and that Auer- bach has dŏne this is sŏmething which should not be forgotten. Of late years, after abandoning the tale, he has tried more ambitious flights, which hav been less successful." [Atlantic. **2347** BROKEN CHAINS [by " E. Wer- ner," i. e., E.. Bürstenbinder : *Osgood*, 1875.] " The bonds riven ar those of matrimony. A young German, in a gushing mood, deserts his counting- house and his too domestic wife for the life of a musical composer and the society of a passionate Italian. Rein- hold is wel described, tho most english readers wil be rather repelled by his enthusiasm, and indignant at his artistic hypocrisy. Certainly, he is a selfish scamp, and the signora has more tŏ dŏ with his errors than the needs of his mental idiosyncrasy. His lamentations and rhapsodies ar wel contrasted with the plain sense of his brŏther, a merchant skipper, whŏ cŏmes home after a long absence just when Reinhold is on the point of escaping. His feelings ar not demonstrativ, but he is genuinly touched by his sister-in-law's distress, and makes a discŏvery about the color of her eyes which causes him, being a manly fello, tŏ go throu much repressiv self disciplin. The character of Ella, whŏse principal fault was being too youthful, is brôt out as wel as hardened by adversity. She gains a complete mastery over the truant Reinhold, tŏ whom she is reconciled by force of circumstances, which need not be revealed." [Athenæum.

—, SAME ("Riven Bonds"), *Remington*, 1877. **2348**

BUCHHOLZ FAMILY (The) [by JULIUS STINDE: London, *Bell*, 1886–7, 2 v.] "This series of letters from a middle-class, typical 'Hausfrau,' whŏ is utterly devoid of sentiment, poetry, of any feeling save jealousy, of any instinct save the maternal ŏne, has passed intŏ its 50th edition. . .
The truth is, that the grêat success of these briêf sketches of middle-class people and their ways, drawn by ŏne of themselvs, is due to the fact that they hav been recognized as perfect likenesses by the people whŏ unconsciously sat for them. . . . More than this, Dr. Stinde has made his Wilhelmine Buchholz so vitally feminin in her pretty traits that she wil appeal tŏ the hêart of mãny a woman in ŏther ranks of society, whŏ would, nevertheless, consider this german woman 'common.' Common she certainly is; but the way, for instance, in which she brêaks off and renews her connection with the hated Bergfeldt family, is not unknŏn in ŏther lands and circles. The ŏther actors possess the same vital quality, tho they ar limited tŏ casual exhibitions

of it, in subordination to Wilhelmine. As a whole, they present a perfectly real but depressing class of the community, which is wholy wrapped up in its petty interests, which has no ambition tŏ elevate itself in ãny way — which indeed, seems unconscious that there is anything hier than itself and its unintelligent ways except when sŏme member of the circle, like Emil Bergfeldt, chances tŏ recall the fact by marrying a little more mŏney than it is accustomed tŏ. Frau Bergfeldt has not an idea beyond snubbing or conciliating her dearest female friends, whŏ ar also her natural enemies, and getting her dauters married; yet her nativ mŏther wit enables her tŏ say things which ar clever and droll enuf tŏ appeal tŏ bily cultivated readers, if the latter wil take the small trouble of adjusting the focus tŏ their vision." [Nation.] — The book "is amusing and readable; but if this is indeed german middle-class life and these ar the 'hausfrauen' of **Berlin**, ŏne can ŏnly be thankful that he is not a Berliner. President Lincoln's welknŏn commendation is, however, here in order: 'For anybody whŏ likes that sort of thing, it is just the sort of thing he would like,' — and presumably the plaçid Berliner likes women of this sort, for he takes especial pains tŏ train them and compress them and trim them intŏ just this type, and resists with horror any suggestion tŏ make them more interesting or more reasonable." [Overland.

The second series of these sketches "differs tŏ sŏme extent from the first in style and method. Emphasis is laid on the kind and motherly qualities of Frau Buchholz rather than on her unconscious humor, and in the lŏve story of her dauter Betti an attempt is made tŏ suggest a romantic element of serious interest. . . . The author presents an admirable picture of a foppish young 'poet,' whŏ thinks nothing good enuf for him in the writings of the grêat poets of the past, and is always convicting them of plagiarism. At last he is persuaded tŏ read a poem of his ŏn, when he is found practically tŏ have appropriated ŏne of Heine's lyrics." [Athenæum.] For continuation see *FRAU WILHELMINE.* **2349**

BURGOMASTER OF BERLIN (The), in *The Anglo-American*, 4 Nov., 1843. **2350**

BURIED GEM, by AUERBACH, in *Ladies' Repository*, Nov., 1873. **2351**

BUSY HANDS AND PATIENT HEARTS. [by [C:] GUSTAV NIERITZ (†, 1876) : London, *Jackson*, 1863.] "Thêre is no mistake as to the charming style of German tales. . . . The first chapter, in which little Magda cŏmes early in the morning tŏ Master Tanzer, the potter, with a broken cup tŏ be mended, is enuf tŏ seal the character of the rest; and we promis ŏûr young friends that thêy wil not be content until thêy read of the blind boy, the hard landlord, and the merry Christmas, with all the other exciting but instructiv incidents of the volume, which is ŏne we can recommend without hesitation." [London Review.

—, SAME, transl. by HARWOOD, *Lippincott*, 1869. **2352**

BY HIS OWN MIGHT [by WILHELMINE (B.) VON HILLERN : *Lippincott*, 1872.] "is intended tŏ teach the young the advantages of overcŏming all obstacles in the way of good works. As a work of fiction we must say that we found it extremely dul, tho perhaps no duller than most german novels. With all respect for the Germans, it would seem as if thêy thŏt fiction wer a science, and, given a problem, 2 or 3 incarnate

qualities, and sŏme morally sound conversation, the novel must be good." [Nation.] — "The author conducts a frail, crippled lad from infancy tŏ manhood. The tale, which has great variety in its scenes and an interest decidedly abŏve the common run of novels, is abŏve all a study of character. Young Alfred, the child of aristocrats, is delineated at full length in his pampered weakness, with his intelligence shooting forward intŏ unnatural precoçity, and his habits tinged with cowardice and valetudinarianism. Everything is conspiring tŏ make him the despised, spoiled pet of the household ladies, when the discŏvery, just at the turning point of his youth, of a home tragedy, suddenly makes him the judge of his mŏther, the protector and inheritor of the family estates, and the avenger of his father. How he becomes studious and heroic, how he embraces that profession of surgery which has remodeled his on frame intŏ symmetry, how he carries his healing science tŏ the battle-field, and arrives at fame and royal favor, ar told with a most inventiv wealth of detail and with never-flagging spirit." [Lippinc. **2353**

CASTLE [Schloss] AND TOWN. [by F.. M.. PEARD : *Smith*, [rep., *Lippincott*] 1882.] "It is pleasant tŏ think that thêre ar people in the world whŏ, tho commonplace, engrossed in the petty concerns and anxieties of every-day life, and not abŏve occasional small jealousies and squabbles, possess, nevertheless, a genuin heroism which holds itself in reserv til called out by sŏme emergency, and then manifesting itself quietly and spontaneously, as a real and essential element in thêir composition. Schloss and Town affords capital examples of such people, drawn with much quiet humor and fidelity tŏ life, whŏm it is impossible for the reader tŏ help

BY THE ELBE. [by "S.. Tytler," i. e., Henrietta Keddie: *Smith*, 1876.] "An english squire, his wife, and 3 dauters go tŏ **Dresden** in search of opportunities for retrenchment. Dresden is so much frequented by english, that . . . the fact of having spent a vacation in that artistic but dullish capital seems tŏ admit tŏ a kind of Freemasonry. No doubt those whŏ ar thus initiated wil read with interest the adventures of the Carterets : how they went tŏ Prag aŋd Nürnberg; how they attended ' smoking concerts,' and studied picture-galleries; finally, how the maidens, at least, of the family got married (or failed tŏ dŏ so) in the land of thêir exile." [Athenæum. **425 u** liking. The whole representation of the Von Tellenbach family is delightful, with their troubles, manner of life, little jars, individual weaknesses, and strong, mutual affection; it is truthful, amusing, and yet, now and then, touching." [Spectator.] — "Within its modest limits it is singularly wel sustained and harmonious. Thêre is a **Nürnberg** episode, which, without delaying the action of the story, sets before the reader all the charm of that 'quaint old town of art and song.'" [Nation. **2354**

CASTLE HOHENWALD = No. 629.

CHARLOTTE ACKERMAN [by O: Müller: Phil'a, *Porter*, 1874.] "is a bily romantic story, very pleasantly written, and full of the metaphysics of lôve. It begins with a death, and ends with the death of the heroin in the full blaze of youth, beauty, and talent, its termination being, in fact, remarkably infeliçitous. . . . Cnarlotte is very beautiful, very clever, proud, and sensitiv, encouraging nône in particular of her numerous admirers. . . . The style of the novel is occasionally very good, but it is a dismal story. Virtue is not made even its ôn reward, nor is crime adequately punished." [Arcadian. **2355**

CHILDREN OF THE WORLD (The) [by Paul Heyse: *Chapman*, 1882; N.-Y., *Worthington*, 1890.] "is a classic; the most thôtful and philosophic of all Heyse's novels. The pictures of artist life, the mysterious young girl, beautiful and alone, the tender lôve-story of Leah and Edwin, all hold fast the reader's attention. Interspersed with the story ar numerous beautiful reflections and philosophic musings, tôgether with poems, which, tho inadequately rendered, possess sôme

of the charms of their originals." [Writer. **2356**

CHRISTIAN GELLERT by B. Auerbach: *Low*, 1858, 8°. **2357**

CHRISTOPHER'S FIRST JOURNAL, with No. 2471.

CINDERELLA OF THE BLACK FOREST (A) = No. 2455.

CLARA. [by F: W: Hackländer (1816–77): *Harpers*, 1856.] "The author made up his mind that thêre was a slave-life in Europe as wel as in America, and sets himself tô work tô prôve this. He lays his scene amông the loer classes; in the green-rooms of theatres; in the dens of thîeves, and in the wholesale nurseries of children of doubtful birth. His characters belông tô the localities in which he finds them; they ar poor and wretched, and sômetimes villainous. The women ar the slaves of the men; the men the slaves of thêir passions. - . As a mere character the Baron is capitally drawn; but he reminds us of the melodramatic impossibilities of Sue. The author of 'Clara' is indeed a sort of german Sue, and 'Clara' itself is ʌ german 'Mysteries of Paris.' They ar purer, however, than their french originals. The môvement of the story is complicated and brisk; you ar deeply interested, even in its improbabilities. We should judge it to be a fair picture of slave-life in Europe; at any rate, it is an absorbing ône, and the work of a skilful hand." [Albion.

— SAME ("European Slave Life"), *Tinsley*, 1880. **2358**

CLOCKMAKER (The) = EDELWEISS.

CELIA, by " A: Mels," i. e., Martin Cohn: Boston, *Littell*, 1869. **2359**

CLOISTER WENDHAUSEN [by " W. Heimburg," i. e., Bertha Behrens: Chicago, *Rand*, 1890.] "is an

old-fashioned lŏve-tale, separated from
ŏŭr busy life by several centuries, altho
it is presumably written of the present
time. It is a story of women and for
women, dealing more with emotions
than actions, and ending in happiness
and wedding bels. The characters ar
either saints or fiends, in the good old
style of fiction; and the book can be
warranted tŏ please the most romantic
schoolgirl." [Critic.

—, SAME ("Magdalen's Fortune")
N.-Y., *Worthington*, 1889.

CONVICTS AND THEIR CHIL-
DREN (The) by B. AUERBACH: *Holt*,
1877.   **2360**

COQUETTE (The), in *N. Y. Mirror*,
12–19 Sept., 1840.   **2361**

COUNT ERNEST'S HOME, by P.
HEYSE: in *Tales from the German;* also
in Part IV. of *Good Stories, Ticknor*,
1868.   **2362**

COUNT SILVIUS = No. 655.

COUNTESS ANNA, by A. WELLMER
in *Canadian Month.*, Nov., 1874. **2363**

COUNTESS ERIKA'S APPREN-
TICESHIP [by "OSSIP SCHUBIN,"
i. e., Lola Kirschner: *Lippincott*, 1892]
"describes the manners of aristocratic
society in **Berlin.** No ŏne under a
countess figures in her pages, and princesses gro on every bush. Thêre ar, of
course. a few artists whêrewith tŏ stoc
the princesses' bêar-gardens, but even
thêy ar all 'vons.' With few exceptions, the characters ar a wicked and
adulterous generation, and the story
consists of the list of thêir misde-
meanors, either detailed or hinted. The
supreme struggles of the small fry tŏ
associate with the grêat, of the grêat tŏ
keep themselvs supplied with scandals,
subjectiv and objectiv, ar equalled ŏnly
by those of the writer tŏ sho an arm-in-
arm intimacy with human nature, and
more particularly with the aristocracy.

The whirling of the scene from Berlin
tŏ Bayreuth and tŏ Venice changes ŏnly
the sky and not the mind. The Grand
Canal, 'Parsifal,' the Thiergarten, ar
simply pegs on which tŏ hang the same
clever but sballo feats of pen, the same
display of knoingness. Thêre is an
air of cheerful alacrity about the vices
of Ossip Schubin's world which is wanting tŏ its reluctant and perfunctory virtues. Wit and the wish tŏ be caustic ar
not absent, and in a superficial sense the
story is entertaining." [Nation. **2364**

COUNTESS GISELA (The) [by
'E. MARLITT," i. e., Eugenie John (†,
1887): *Macmillan*, 1870.] "carries the
reader tŏ the end without any flagging
of interest. . . . At the beginning a
dark story of crime and death is told,
and many names ar introduced.   . .
This want of distinctness at the outset
throes a mist over the rest of the story,
and makes it like a picture the outlines
of which ar blurred. The countess herself is charming; the gradual grŏth of
her noble nature, in spite of the systematic deceit and heartlessness with
which she is trained, is very interesting." [Athenæum.   **2365**

COUNTESS OF ST. ALBAN (The).
["Namenlose Geschichten" by F: W:
HACKLÄNDER (†, 1877): London, 1854.]
"Description is the author's best
quality. He relates humorous incidents in a manner both festiv and
easy; and can rise intŏ eloquence and
pathos, without offending the modesty
of Nature. The outward aspects of
stil-life at home or abroad, old places,
lonely forests, busy streets, the glitter
of boudoirs and saloons, the squalor of
the rogue's asylum, the starvling tailor's
garret, or the home of decent industry,
ar each in turn exhibited by him in
lively and appropriate pictures. In passages apt for sober color he can glide

maffectedly into a pensiv tone, both
:legant and winning; and be never vio-
ates decorum by tirades unsuited tŏ the
:haracter of his subject; or out of pro-
)ortion with the event which he is
:elating." [Athenæum. **2366**
COUNTRY HOUSE ON THE
RHINE (The). [by BERTHOLD AUER-
3ACH († 1882) : *Bentley*, 1870.] " The
)lot turns on the attempt of a man whŏ
las been a slave-dealer in America tŏ
)ecōme a german noble. He changes
his name, buys a villa on the Rhein,
gets intŏ society, procures more than
jne friend at court, and is then found
jut. . . . ' Das Landhaus am Rhein,'
' Auf der Höhe ' [No. 881]' and ' Waldfried' [No. 2538] ar tedious, diffuse, didactic romances, filled with a sentimental
falsetto of which Auerbach's earlier
works had shŏn sŏme indication, but
which here assumed intolerable shril-
ness. The books met sŏme success in
Germany, whêre their spirit was not antagonistic; but outside the Fatherland
thêy wer accounted failures, and tho
translated intŏ English, hav found few
readers. Auerbach's fame rests, and
wil continue tŏ rest, on his village tales,
and it is tŏ these that he ōes his european reputation, tho out of his nativ
land he is more talked of than read."
[Athenæum.]— . . . " The first twŏ
books of the ' Villa ' ar charming. . ..
But this dōes not continue; wit and
freshness and good sensé ar swallōed in
philosophical inquiry; — lŏve continues.
The people make metaphysical lŏve tŏ
one another. They analyze thêir sensations, and express them in technical
formulary ! Could anything be more
hopelessly german, or tedious, or better
:alculated tŏ make the reader close the
volume with a si? " [Overland.
—, SÁME (" Villa on the Rhine ?"),
Leypoldt, 1869. **2367**

DAME CARE [by HERMANN SUDER-
MAN : *Harper*, 1892] " is very dainty and
with that touch of pathos and trace of
mysticism so common in German tales.
Meyerhofer has met misfortune, and
just as his third son, Paul, is born, his
home falls into the hands of creditors
and is sold. The story which folloes is of
the after life of the little one born at
such a time of distress, a child of whŏm
it was said : ' Care stood at his cradle.'
The story is sad, but it is the story of
ōne whŏ bore a wêight of care, and whŏ
was ever thŏtful of ōthers. The nobility of the character of Paul is at its
climax when he is willing to suffer imprisonment for a technical crime, committed in order to save his father from
the cŏmmission of ōne far worse. The
story, dĕspite the sadness which pervades
it, ends brightly." [Boston Advertiser.]
— " Let not him whŏ begins ' Dame
Care ' be discouraged by its commonplace tone at the outset. . . A
little story at ōuce striking and poetic;
sad with the sadness of Turgénief almost, but blooming with more of the
humanities than usually flourish on Russian soil. Paul Meyerhofer hears the
fairy story of Dame Care from his
mŏther, whŏ, however, wil never tel
him the ending. He spends his life in
learning it, and it is not until it is told in
full on the last page that the completeness and artistic quality of the little
book are wholly revealed. Thêre ar
plenty of Teutonisms tŏ be forgiven,
but it wel stands u searching test for
any work of art, that of retrospect."
[Nation. **2368**
DEAD LAKE, by HEYSE, = No.
669.
DEBIT AND CREDIT [by GUSTAV
FREYTAG : *Bentley*, 1857.] " contains all
the elements of popularity. It is fresh,
rich in incident, vital with character,

thôt, and fancy, and in all respects an uncommon, genuin, interesting book. The humor is not broad, but quiet; the irony glances out in sudden, mild irradiations, and the narrativ is ōne of unbroken strength and consistency. . . The dark characters ar brôt out amid Rembrandt shadōs; thêy appear and vanish like the demons in a mediæval allegory; thêir shapes and voices ar startling, and thêy impress a peculiar moral horror upon certain episodes of the romance. . . . But the chief merit of the book is its reality as a picture of manners, its broad and deep perspectiv, throing open the interior of german life, its faithful illustration of the intercourse between classes, its assortment of representativ characters." [Leader. **2369**

DIANA WENTWORTH [Posen] = No. 434.

DOCTOR CLAUDIUS [Heidelberg] = No. 675.

DIARY OF POOR YOUNG GENTLEWOMAN [by M.. (Scheele) von Nathusius (1817–57) : *Trübner*, 1860.] "givs in autobiographic form the experiences of a wel-born damsel, whōse necessities force her tŏ be a governess in a noble family. The picture of inner german life is extremely wel delineated, and thêre ar touches of pathos and of quiet humor which ar pretty and original." [Albion.

—, SAME ("Louisa von Plettenhaus)," N.-Y., *Francis*, 1857. **2370**

DR. GOETHE'S COURTSHIP. ['Der Stadtschultheiss von Frankfurt,' (1856) by O: Müller: *Routledge*, 1866] "In the quiet, minute german manner the author's characterizations ar admirable. He has combined most successfully a mixture of simplicity and homely wisdom in the worthy couple, thêir honesty and shrewdness and sincerity,

the elephantin playfulness of the worshipful mayor and the matronly dignity of his spouse, whŏ regards him with blended aw and admiration, and has a proclivity for drawing auguries from those incidents of everyday life which popular tradition has invested with a mystic significance. . . . The story is ōne of those quiet, pleasing descriptions of domestic life in a place and age themselvs interesting which ar especially pleasant reading by contrast with the harroing recitals of crime and despair which form the staple of the fiction of the day." [Round Table. **2371**

DOCTOR JACOB [**Frankfurt**] = No. 436.

DOOMED, by Heyse, = No. 669.

DOROTHY'S PICTURE [by "W. Heimburg," i. e., Bertha Behrens: *Worthington*, 1891] "the first of a collection of Christmas Stories, is a sweet, simple little tale of a woman whŏ sacrifices herself for the man she lōves, givs him up tŏ another, takes care of his old mother, and dōes many ōther beautiful things which ar impossible tŏ the average human being. The other stories ar in the same vêin." [Critic. **2372**

DRESDEN ROMANCE (A), by Laura M. Lane: London, *S. P. C. K.*, 1884. **2373**

EBERHARD [by K.. Clive: *Tinsley*, 1883] "describes very wel the life of an english pupil teacher in a small german town." [Athenæum. **2374**

EDELWEISS [by Berthold Auerbach (†, 1882) : *Roberts*, 1869.] "We think the first charm the reader wil find in this most charming book is the fact that the story seems tŏ tel itself. From the beginning it goes alone, and ōne dōes not think of the author til the end, when perhaps ōne's homage is all the more devout in recognition of the genius which could produce so ex-

722

quisit a fiction, and nowhêre in it betray a consciousness of creation. The scene is not among courtly people : but in a little cloc-making district in the **Black Forest,** and the characters of the story ar the cloc-makers and their friends and kinsfolk. It is simply the story of Lenz, whŏ makes musical cloes, and marries Annele, the worldly-minded but not bad-heârted dauter of the innkeeper, whŏ leads him a very miserable life. . . . The glimpses of sweet, simple, refined life in the physician's family, and of the tender esteem in which all Lenz' friends and nêbors hold him, ar almost the only cheerful lights in the picture ; the humorous passages, tho abundant, ar for the most part ŏnly varied expressions of the gloom of the story, for it is, indeed, as the author premises, ' a sad, cruel history,' tho ' the sun of lŏve brêaks throu at¦last.' " [Atlantic.]
— " *Edelweiss, Little Barefoot,* and *Joseph in the Snow* ar 3 stories which form the connecting link between the brief sketches and the novels. The last twŏ ar simpler in form than many of the village stories [No. 2342] ; they ar charming pastorals, full of deep feeling, and appealing tŏ uncomplex emotions. Little Barefoot [No. 2455], indeed, is almost a child's story, and it is not alone the plot of the story which makes it so ; thêre is sŏmething in Auerbach's delight in his simple narration which may be noticed in any ŏne whŏ is entertaining children with a story. Everything is made perfectly clear, thêre is no obscurity ; the passions are far from being a tumultuous ocean, they ar, rather, a placid lake. . . Edelweiss, on the other hand, is a more serious attempt at novel-writing ; it deals with more intricate matters than the repetition of a fairy story in the 19th century, like Little Barefoot ; it is really a very

thŏro and wel-managed study of character. The hero Lenz, a young man of delicate sensibility and loyal feeling but of a sŏmewhat weak, lachrymose character, full of amiability and the gentle virtues but inclined tŏ sentimentality, falls in lŏvc with Annele, a young woman about whŏm the reader is likely tŏ be of twŏ or more minds. Her fascinations ar wel presented, and the reader is very likely tŏ be blinded in the same way that Lenz was. . .
As the novel groes more and more tragic, until the dreadful accident which crushes all wickedness and the memory of it from them both, we ar led on with the keenest sympathy in their sad fate. Their reconçiliation is beautifully told ; and it is not every writer whŏ could carry a novel tŏ so grêat a hit of feeling with so sure a hand. . . .
The whole book is written with admirable strength, and thêre is nŏne which those whŏ ar unfamiliar with Auerbach can be more warmly advised to read." [T: Sergeant Perry.
—, SAME (" The Clockmaker ") with " *JOSEPH,*" London, 1861.   **2375**
EICHHOFS (The). [by " MORITZ VON REICHENBACH," i. e., Valeska Bethusy-Huc : *Lippincott,* 1881.] " How Count Eichhof gets his 3 sŏns married and settled, — the matrimonial afflictions of the eldest, the spendthrift career of the second, and the tribulations of the youngest in choosing a profession, — these afford the warp of the story, and the woof is composed of the plots, plans and sentiments of a fashionable nêborhood." [American.   **2376**
EIGHT DAYS IN THE LIFE OF A PASTOR'S WIFE, by — ESSING, in *Ladies' Repository,* Aug.-Sept., 1871.
EKKEHARD   No. 679.   [**2377**
ELECTIVE AFFINITIES [by J: WOLFGANG VON GOETHE (†, 1832) :

Bohn, 1856] is "elaborate and skilful as a composition. . . . The gradual progress by which a husband's affections ar estranged from his wife, and fixed on her adopted dauter, whŏ is made a most winning character, tho returning the passion felt for her : likewise, the wife's estrangement from the husband and preference for his friend the Captain, ar the central points of the story, wrŏt with consummate tact. Thêre is no guilt in this condition of things; it is the necessary result of those 'affinities' which operate as inevitably in the moral as in the chemical world. The husband and dauter die of grîef for ungratified passion." [Southern Lit. Messenger.

2378

ELEONORE. [by " E. VON ROTHENFELS," i. e., Emilie (von Loga) von Ingersleben, 1822–71 : *Lippincott*, 1872.] "This is a very plotty novel, which recounts in an autobiografical form the adventures of a simple-heârted young lady with an artful step-mŏther and an intrîging 'companion.' What arts these twŏ false women used tŏ entrap the heroin, first intŏ a lo marriage and afterwards intŏ a hi ōne in which her heàrt was not engaged ; how her father was deluded by his beautiful wife; how the stepmother exerted herself tŏ fascinate every man of her circle ; and how they ōne and all deserted her colors for those of the ingenuous narrator of the tale, whŏ is, however, steadily true throuōut — or, at least, with only ōne short interval in which she became engaged tŏ another — tŏ an upright and unsophisticated admirer, whŏ livs in the country and appears rather awkward in the company of those whŏ surround her in her father's house — all these fine things ar told in a rather lively way, and ar put intŏ readable and easy english." [Nation.

2379

ELSIE = No. 2492.

EMERENZ, by HEYSE, in *Cosmopolitan*, Oct.-Nov., 1888.

2380

ERL QUEEN (The). [by NATALY VON ESCHSTRUTH : *Worthington Co.*, 1892] "The old-fashioned novel, which cares little for analysis and is written for the sake of the story rather than as a statement of some problem of life, may stil be found, and ' The Erl Queen' is a good type of this class. There is a certain artlessness about these stories — a pleasant homeliness — that carries even the realist critic along with measurable content throu lengthy descriptiv passages, brief orations in the place of the give-and-take of dialog, and even vêils such a preposterous proceeding as the solitary midnight ramble of a child-Baroness — lightly-clad, at that — throu a clover-del, with a graceful garb of romantic illusion which half-conceals the absurdity. The obsequious deference which noble birth ōnce demanded is anōther survival in these novels which concern themselvs with German nobility. and tho the loly hero wins his hi-born belōved, it is ōnly after he has cōme into his fortune and his relativs hav pardoned his father's ' mésalliance.' All the slanderers ar punished — lightly, all the lovers ar made happy, all debts ar paid, and the comfortable, mildly-exciting story is gracefully concluded." [Commonwealth.

2381

ERLACH COURT = No. 441.

ESTHER'S FORTUNE [**Munich**] = No. 445.

EUROPEAN RELATIONS [by TALMAGE DALIN : *Cassell*, 1892] "is a pleasant little sketch. A count quarrels with his family, changes his name and cōmes tŏ America. Here he marries and dies, leaving a wife and twŏ children — a dauter nearly gron and a boy. The family go abroad in obedience tŏ an invitation reçeived from the head of the family whŏ livs in the old castle in **Tirol.** Before the time for the visit arrives thêy spend weeks wandering over the mountains with twŏ friends — a man and his sister, — the man very much older than the girl whŏse father was his friend, but not too old tŏ fall a complete victim tŏ her fascinations. He looks upon himself as absurd, is persuaded the girl wil lâf at him, and lets her go tŏ the castle without declaring his lŏve for her. No scruples of this kind chec the passionate declaration which her handsōme, dashing cousin makes before he has knŏn her 3 weeks. The girl confesses that she has lŏved her father's old friend, but as he seemed tŏ take ŏnly a paternal interest in her she is willing at least tŏ consider her new lŏver. It happens that this con versation is overheard by the man most concerned in it. When the young couple ar married he writes a new book — his grêatest success — which deals with the vaçillation of the heârt, and the absurdity of a man's not putting his lŏve and his faith tŏ the test. One dŏes not trouble ŏneself about the improbability of the dénoument, but is content tŏ enjoy the mountain atmosphere which pervades the book and the unusual interest which the characters inspire." [Critic. **2382**

EXCHANGE NO ROBBERY = No. 688.

EYE-BLINDNESS AND SOUL-BLINDNESS, by Heyse. = No. 707.

FAIRY OF THE ALPS = *ALPINE FAY.*

FALKENBURG [by Hamilton Murray: *Harper*, 1852.] " is wel worth reading for its piquant delineations of character, apart from the interest of the plot, which is ŏne of grêat power and intensity. The scene is laid in the picturesque regions of the **Rhein.**" [Harper's. **2383**

FAMILY FEUD (A) [by L; Harder: *Lippincott*, 1877.] " Thé action lies between a baron, his seconc wife and a dauter, on the ōne side, and a young kinsman on the ōther, whŏse earlier prospects of inheritance ar destroyed by the birth of the dauter. Otto, the disinherited, is unjustly accused of a plot against the life of his little rival, and groes up under this cloud intŏ a sōmewhat gloomy character. Reconciliation, however, cōmes at last, and the girl becōmes Mrs. Otto. The book is interesting and wholesome.' [Boston " Literary World." **2384**

—, SAME, by J: Gottfried Kinkel, in *Tales from Blackwood*, N. S., 21 ; also in (Boston) *Saturday Rambler*, 18-25 may, 1850. **2385**

FARINA = No. 691.

FATAL PICTURE, in *Ladies' Repository*, Jan. 1868. **2386**

FAUSTINA [by Ida (Hahn) Hahn (†, 1880) : N.-Y., *Carleton*, 1872.] " is the story of a woman whŏ married a man whŏm she did not lŏve; learned tŏ lŏve anōther, and with him left her husband's house ; and ere long, being separated from her protector, gave her heârt, or what was left of it, tŏ a third claimant. The heroin is a Countess, and all the characters ar nobles, Faustina, the heroin, is powerfully drawn, and sōme of the scenes in which she figures ar wōnderfully effectiv. But the book has little tŏ dŏ with life; it is a record of Faustina's meditations and speculations about lŏve, and must be regarded as a vue of that passion from a German sentimental stand-point. As a story it is not interesting; but it is written with boldness and vigor, and sets forth in a brilliant light sōme of the rarest qualities of woman's nature.' [Boston " Literary World." **2387**

FELIX LANZBERG'S EXPIATION.

FAILURE OF ELIZABETH (The)
[by EMMA F., POYNTER: *Bentley*,
1890.] " is a pleasing, wholesŏme story,
and Miss Poynter's carefully drawn,
distinctiv characters can never fail tŏ
arouse interest. Elizabeth belongs tŏ
that charming type of fresh, unspoilt
girlhood which Miss Poynter knoes wel
how tŏ depict. Sent out alone into the
world with the inexperience of 17, it is
scarcely surprising that this much neglected girl with her generous impulses
should fall in lŏve with the first person
whŏ interests himself in her. Unfortunately her hero is an elderly, invalid
clergyman of the worst type of vanity and
sordid egotism. [Compare plot of Nos.
436 & 452 k.] We ar ŏnly glad tŏ think
that this chapter of her history is finally
closed while she is stil young, and, we
hope, wholesŏme-minded enuf tŏ begin
life anew under brighter and more
worthy circumstances. Miss Poynter
givs a humorous description of life in a
German *pension*, with its uncomfortable economies, and petty jealousies."
[Athenæum.   **449 t**

FELICIA. [by Matilda [Barbara]
Betham Edwards, London, 1875.]
"The part of the lady who givs her
name tŏ the book is subordinate tŏ that
of a morbid clergyman whŏ has unfrocked himself on conscientious grounds
and thenceforth is principally occupied
with drifting intŏ sentimental relations
with various friends of the softer sex.
Stickland's moody temperament seems tŏ
becŏme more or less gloomy only under
the annoying or refreshing influence of
these successiv flirtations; but his cold
nature givs him a most unfair advantage
over the ladies, whŏ, ōne and all, fall in
lŏve with him. Felicia, his earliest lŏve,
makes the mistake, when he fails tŏ cŏme
forward as she expects, of marrying
the musical dictator of a little german
court, a graceless but not unamusing
scoundrel, whŏ neglects and cannot appreciate her. The german life is wel
described." [Athenæum. 452 k

[by "Ossip Schubin," i. e., Lola Kirschner: N. Y., *Worthington*, 1892.] "At a watering-place the hero, a man under the shado of an early sin, meets beautiful Linda Harfink, the dauter of a millionaire bourgeois, whŏ, dazzled by his rank, encourages his suit. He believes she knoes his story, and thêy ar married; but the secret has been kept from her by her mŏther, whŏ fears the match wil be broken off. How Felix fared with his frivolous young wife, her discŏvery of her husband's secret, and his final expiation, ar develŏped in a wel-told story of dramatic interest." [Pub. Weekly. **2388**

FICKLE FORTUNE = No. 1011.

FIDDLER OF LOGAU = No. 696.

FIRE AND FLAME [by Levin Schücking (†, 1883): *Appleton*, 1876.] "abounds in exciting incident, the plot is bold and wrŏt with masterly audacity. . . . No mere abstract could giv a just idea of it, and we dismiss the book with the remark that it is exceptionally noble in tone, keen in analysis, vivid in its sketches of character, and cultivated in style." [Boston "Lit. World." **2388 t**

FIRST AND LAST BALL, by Hackländer, in *Ladies' Repository*, June, 1872. **2389**

FIRST TEMPTATION (The). [London, *Newby*, 1863.] "The story ranges within a very narro circle and introduces us tŏ but a smǎll number of characters: the principal persons belonging tŏ the professorial class. The hero is a university professor and ŏne of the greatest lights of the atheistic philosophy; a tall, handsŏme man whŏ has traveled, and studied art and literature, is cold and critical; looking at all things from an æsthetic point of vue, and never so satisfied as when anatomizing conduct and character. His wife Elizabeth, in

whŏm the deepest interest of the story is centred, was the ŏnly dauter of a professor of philology, a friend of Schartel. . . . Associated with Doctor Schartel as fello-professor is the grave, earnest Fischman, whŏse married life is unhappy also. He, devoted tŏ the same philosophy as his friend, has married a simple-minded little woman whŏm he found in a romantic way among the Alps. . . . Poor Susette! She pines for her mountains, and her spouse pines for the sympathy and companionship she can not giv him. [Compare plot of No. 2458.] Then Madeline appears on the scene — a brilliant, beautiful, and intellectual woman, but also bad and unscrupulous. . . Schartel remonstrates with him in a very wise way about his passion for this attractiv woman, but with no further effect than a brief hesitation before he sends away the 'Swiss peasant tŏ her mountains,' and take steps tŏ obtain a divorce. One of the most pathetic passages in the book is that which describes the return of Susette, with her brŏther and child, tŏ see whether the Schartels can dŏ anything for her toards a reunion with her husband. The simplicity and naturalness of her story ar beautiful; and the subsequent scene, when she goes with the child tŏ see her husband, and makes the most touching appeal tŏ his old sympathies, is no less so." [London Review. **2390**

FIRST VIOLIN [**Dusseldorf**] = No. 698.

FIVE ERAS IN A WOMAN'S LIFE, by H: Zschokke: in *Boston Miscellany*, Feb. 1842, and *So. Lit. Messenger*, Oct. 1845. **2390 m**

FLEURANGE [**Heidelberg**]= No. 700.

FLORIAN AND CRESCENZ, by B. Auerbach: *Low*, 1853. **2391**

FLOWER BASKET(The), by Chris-

TOPH VON SCHMID: N.-Y., P. Price, 1842. **2392**

FLOWER, FRUIT AND THORN PIECES, or the marriage, death and wedding of the Poor Lawyer Siebenkäs, by JEAN PAUL F: RICHTER: (1796) Boston, Ticknor, 1859. **2393**

FORBIDDEN FRUIT [by F: W: HACKLÄNDER (†, 1877): Boston, Estes, 1877.] " takes us from France tŏ a german capital, and introduces us tŏ a domestic circle in which a talented artist, his wife, his wife's brŏther, and his pupil-model ar chîef personages. The brŏther is conditional hêir tŏ a large property,the condition being his marriage within a certain period [compare plot of " In Hot Haste"] ; and but twŏ mŏnths of grace remain. He has cŏme tŏ obtain the helpful offices of the sister in finding the desired wife. He finds her in the pupil-model of his brŏther-in-law. Certain peculiar, tho innocent, relations between her and the artist provoke the bitterest jealousy of the latter's wife, grêatly tŏ the complication of the suit in question, but that is of course finally successful. The relation of the title to the book we fail to see." [Boston " Lit. World." **2394**

FORESTER OF ALTENHAIN (The), London, 1852. **2395**

FORESTERS (The), [by BERTHOLD AUERBACH (†, 1880): Appleton, 1880] " These characters make a picturesque and pretty group, set off by the shadŏs and solitudes of the forest, the dash of the mountain brook, the pleasures and excitements of the chase, and the indescribable, indefinable sweetness and simplicity of german character on its rural and domestic sides. Thêre is no badness in the book, either, beyond Schaller's, and his is the badness ŏnly of jealousy and slander and maliçe. The life is pure and peaceful; the very

animals share its joy. . . . It is a sweet and gentle story. One touch more would hav made it a work of power." [Boston " Lit. World." **2396**

FORESTER'S FAREWELL SUPPER (The), in Ladies' Companion (London), vol. 2. **2397**

FORGET-ME-NOT, by G. ZU PUTLITZ, in Lippincott's, Jan. 1868. **2398**

FORTUNE IN MISFORTUNE, in Appleton's, 4 Oct. 1870. **2399**

FORTUNES AND FATE OF LITTLE SPANGLE [by HANS HOPFFEN, in Masterpieces of German Fiction. **2400**

FORTUNES OF MISS FOLLEN [**Baden**] = No. 704.

FOUR PHASES OF LOVE, by HEYSE, = No. 707.

FRANCESCA DA RIMINI. [by ERNST VON WILDENBRUCH: Chicago, Laird, 1891] " Francesca livd in ŏne of the large towns of Prussia. She attracts the attention of the new gŏvernor and soon becŏmes his wife. Tho her husband is much her senior, she admires him grêatly and marriage begins happily. A young officer whŏ secretly admires Francesca is the ŏne tŏ destroy thêir promising future. A picture of her which he paints in the character of Francesca da Rimini is the cause of a tragedy." [Publishers' Weekly. **2401**

FRAU ANTJE, by A. MEINHARDT, in The Modern Age, Mar., 1884. **2402**

FRAU DOMINA [by CLAIRE (v. TOLSTOY) VON GLÜMER: Boston, Lockwood, 1877.] " ushers us intŏ painful scenes; but the sympathies of the author and the heroin ar on the right side, nor is the guilt of a hazy description. And the usual clearness of the story dŏes not lie in the fact that the heroin instinctivly repulses the man whŏ has entrapped her intŏ an illegal marriage from the moment he is discŏvered, but in a certain resolute dealing with herself, which dŏes

not allow her tŏ look bac, dŏes not permit her to brêak the heraldic seal which
closes the letters annually sent her, nor
even tŏ look from a distance on the face
of the man she lŏves, until death has
taken his epileptic wife. Then, perhaps,
she mit hav forgiven him, but the
excitement is too much for her wasted
frame, and her gray-haired lŏver is glad
tŏ fall soon after on the field of battle."
[Boston "Lit. World." **2403**
FRAU VON BERNHARD'S VALET,
by L. SCHÜCKING, in *Every Saturday*,
6–13 apr. 1867. **2405**
FRAU WILHELMINE. [by JULIUS
STINDE : *Scribner*, 1888.] "The fourth
'and last' series of the adventures of
the Buchholz Family resembles the previons volumes, and is wel worth reading
by all whŏ enjoy a book whŏse humor is,
so tŏ say, ŏnly incidentally revealed, but
which, like the perfume in a dress, exhales with every motion of the wêarer.
But perfumes ar sŏmetimes offensiv,
and, without being unduly sensitiv, a
person with a nose less robust than that
of Bismarck might wel fiud too strong
the scent of sŏme of the suggestions in
these volumes. Thêre is little which is
'improper' in the allusions — nothing,
indeed, tŏ recall the typical french novel,
in which vice is supposed to lŏse half its
evil by lŏsing all its grossness. On the
contrary, references tŏ vice ar of the
most distant kind, and ar of such a nature as tŏ imply that it is non existent
in the Landsberger-Strasse. But thêre
is plenty of 'grossness' — that is, allusions tŏ accidents of life which persons
of refinement ignore or keep in the bac
ground, and for the use of which, as
material for exciting a smile, ŏne would
hav to go bac, in english literature, 150
years. Hence the ·comparison of this
book, sŏmetimes made, with *Cranford*
[No. 1175] is most misleading. The

atmosphere of 'Cranford' is of the most
delicate and fastidious refinement; the
air of 'The Buchholz Family' is that
breathed by people whŏ ar good-natured
and wel-meaning, but thŏroly coarse in
grain. Frau Buchholz, in fact, in spite
of her veneer of book-culture, belongs
tŏ the social level of Mr. Howells' 'Manda Greer [No. 315]. The laboring class,
as represented in novels, however unfavorable thêretŏ their life may be, possess a certain innate refinement, as dŏes
also the grisette of the præ-Zola era. It
is ŏnly the middle class in Germany and
England and the loer middle in this country, whŏ appear tŏ be entirely destitute
of it." [Nation, 1887.] — "The comfort
here is, that all these dul, sordid, contracted creatures ar of ŏne nationality.
Since the Germans hav taken Stinde tŏ
their bosoms and proclaimed him the
profet of thêir middle class, far be it
from a foreiner tŏ protest that they ar
in âny respect more attractiv than he has
painted them. Anyŏne in doubt about
the meaning of the word vulgar is commended tŏ 'The Buchholz Family,'
whêre it is amply and exactly defined.
The vulgarity is not only in their customs, which ar disgusting, but in their
thôts and feelings. Their standards ar
lo, their judgments narro, their motivs
mean. They hav no manners, and thêy,
— the women especially, — talk tŏ each
other with brutal coarseness. The civili-
ties of life ar unknŏn tŏ them, the proprieties ignored, ·and the deçençies outraged. They ar envious, spiteful, meddle-
sŏme, and merçenary, and thêy thank
Heaven that thêy belong tŏ the cultivated
classes! If the Buchholz family appeared
tŏ the Germans what they ar, it is natural
tŏ suppose that the family would not
hav been reçeivd with such favor. If
Stinde thôt they wer at all offensiv, he
could not so thŏroly hav identified him-

728

self with thêir vulgarity. Thêrefore an outsider must accept his work for what it seems tŏ be, a close transcript of an actual phase of life of which he is a part. If the author can remotely conceive of the impression on the foreign mind made by Frau Wilhelmine and her tribe, he must write for the purpos of exciting inveterate repugnance for the whole german nation." [Nation, 1888. **2406**

FRERES (The) [**Saxony**] = No. 456.

FRIEDEL [by " W. O. von Horn," i. e., F: W: Oertel, (1798–1867) : N.-Y., *Collins*, 1856.] " is a pleasing story portraying the manners of rural life sŏme hundred years ago. It shŏs the german naïveté of narrativ, and contains an excellent moral beneath its lively pictures." [Harper's. **2407**

FRIEDEMANN BACH, by Albert Emil Brachvogel : (1858), *Tinsley*, 1875. **2407 d**

FRIEND FRITZ [by Emile Erckmann & P: Alex. Chatrian (†, 1890) : *Scribner*, 1877.] " is ŏne of the britest, purest, sunniest stories we hav read for mãny a day. It is just charming in its way. Not that it is a grêat work as respects either plan or execution, except so far as thêre is the grêatness of true art in the simpliçity of the ŏne and the beauty of the ŏther, but that it is a fresh, tuneful, natural, and in every way delightful tale wrŏt of commonplace materials, yet with a consummate skil and that refinement of touch which ŏne so quicly recognizes, but finds it so hard tŏ define. Thêre is the merest thread of a story. ' How cŏmes it that Mr. Kobus, that rich man, that man of position, is going tŏ marry a simple country girl, the dauter of his farm manager, he whŏ for the last 15 years has refused so many fine matches? ' This is a question occurring on ŏne of its pages, tŏ

which the whole book may be set down as the answer. The charm of the work lies in the ease of the dramatic development, the life-likeness with which the characters ar drawn, the absolutely untainted sweetness of its materials, the delicacy with which sentiment and feeling ar portrayed, the amusing turns which ar given here and thêre tŏ the narrativ, and the careful finish which is bestoed upon every part." [Boston " Lit. World."] — " One never wearies of the idyllic pictures of elsatian life presented in the happy and seemingly artless style of these authors. One hears all about the ancestors of Fritz, his intimate friends, his housekeeper, and finally of his farm in Meissenthal. Thêre groes a little maiden whŏ upsets all his cunningly devised and solidly argued theories of bachelor life. She is the dauter of his farmer, a little thing of 16 ; but the jovial gourmand Fritz is slain in his turn, and indeed takes on after a wŏnderful fashion when he finds he is really deep in lŏve. His terror lest she shal not hav him is as grêat as his former philosophic indifference tŏ the fair sex. But not Fritz alone is admirably described ; his friends and boon companions ar alike vividly portrayed. The whole story overruns with good-nature and good cheer." [Scribner's. **2408**

FRIENDSHIP'S TEST. [Zwei Freundinnen by " W. Heimburg," i. e., Bertha Behrens : N. Y., *Ogilvie*, 1889.] " Heimburg's stories ar always pleasing. Simple and pure in tone, fresh in sentiment, with enuf motiv tŏ render the reader unwilling tŏ pause, and with a heroin as sweet and charming as a June rose, the present book bids fair tŏ sustain the reputation of the author's earlier works. The local cŏlor is good ; the scene whêre Hortense tries tŏ kil herself is affecting without being sensational, and the story ends wel. The characters ar live men and women, and the interest of the pretty tale is wel sustained." [Writer.

—, SAME ("Hortense"), Chicago, *Rand*, 1891, 336 pp.

—, SAME ("Lucie's Mistake"), N.-Y., *Worthington*, 1890.

—, SAME ("My Heart's Darling"), *Munro*, 1889.   **2409**

FROM HAND TO HAND [by "Go-LO RAIMUND," i. e., Bertha (Heyn) Frederich (1810-83): *Lippincott*, 1882.] "It is not surprising that Mrs. Wister's heroin should murmur sorrōfully, 'I am passed from hand to hand.' She is separated from her mōther by a divorce suit which adjudged the child tŏ her father; given by her father, when very young, tŏ a husband of whŏm she knew nŏthing, except that he had been her father's friend; entrusted by the bridegroom tŏ a pastor and his wife with whŏm she is to remain til her education is completed; sent bac tŏ her husband in disgraçe by the indignant Frau when the secret marriage is discōvered, only tŏ find that, as she is led tŏ believe, her husband is hers ŏnly in name; flying from him for refuge tŏ her divorced mōther, just in time tŏ discōver that her mōther has repented of her sins, and in the safe seclusion of a convent is quite as indifferent tŏ her dauter's welfare as she had been in the gay world; hastening finally tŏ her grandmother, tŏ be restored at last, in perfeet confidence and lōve, tŏ her husband's side—the young lady certainly dōes seem to be 'passed from hand to hand.' The story is interesting and graçefully told, and the heroin is not passed from hand to hand in any way to imply a lac either of strength or sweetness." [Critic.   **2410**

GEIER WALLEY = No. 1005.

GELLERT, in *Sabbath at Home*, vol. 1.   **2411**

GERMAN LOVE = No. 714.

GERMAN TALES. [by BERTHOLD AUERBACH: *Roberts*, 1869.] "The stories of this collection wil probably be found uninteresting by most readers. They ar, however, full of that homely wisdom which is ōne of Auerbach's most marked characteristics, and which forms a so singular contrast tŏ the half-sentimental sort of transcendentalism which also distinguishes him." [Nation.] The tales in this collection arɔ: *Christian Gellert's Last Christmas* (No. 2357). *The Stepmother, Benigna, Rudolph and Elizabeth, Erdmutha.* See, also, *Black Forest Stories.*   **2412**

GERTRUDE'S MARRIAGE. [by "W. HEIMBURG," i. e., Bertha Behrens: *Worthington*, 1888.] "Gertrude is a proud, tho sincere, young woman, with a large fortune, and is deeply in lōve with a worthy suitor in humbler circumstances. After thêy ar happily married, which it takes about half the book tŏ accomplish, Gertrude unfortunately conceives that Frank married her for mōney, and that he even had the affair arranged by a matrimonial broker. So she goes away and pines for some months, and it takes the other half of the book to get her back tŏ Frank. This is not a bad plot, and thêre ar sŏme rather entertaining side characters." [American.] — Husband and wife "settle their difficulties in the end, and leave ōne thankful, as usual, for that perennial supply of very young people, skirting about the 'terra incognita' of the natural affections whŏ make the production of innocent, unexciting fiction a recognized and, we hope, a paying industry." [Catholic World.   **2413**

GLORIA VICTIS = No. 716.

GOLD ELSIE = No. 717.
GOLDEN DAYS = No. 460.
GOLDEN LION OF GRANPÈRE
(The). [by ANTHONY TROLLOPE (†,
1882): *Tinsley*, 1872.] "In the charming village of Granpère, amŏng the
Vogesen, stands the Lion d'Or, an excellent speçimen of an old-fashioned
inn. . . . The character of Michel
Voss, the real hero of the tale, is developed with all Mr. Trollope's best
skill. The gradations by which the
unexpected obstinacy of his ward and
sŏn, in resisting a 'mariage de conven-
ance' which he has decided upon for the
benefit of the former, infuriates beyond
all bounds the usually good-tempered
gardian, and the stil subtler workings
of natural affection and common sense
which gradually reduce him tŏ a better
state of mind, ar traçed in a way which
leaves nothing tŏ be desired. The true-
hearted, rather strong-minded girl,
whŏse happiness is plaçed in such
jeopardy, is sufficiently charming tŏ
enlist ŏŭr interests in her favor, tho
Master George, her lŏver, has too much
of his father's hasty and imperious character, and is too easily induced tŏ be
hard in his estimate of Marie's conduct,
tŏ cŏme quite up tŏ ŏŭr ideal of fidelity
or tenderness. However, he is perhaps
the more thŏroly a man of his class for
not being altŏgether a model of chivalry,
and Marie is right in preferring him
tŏ the curled and oiled Adonis from
Basel, whŏse successful linendrapery
has seduced all Michel's affections. It
is a very natural proçess in a mind of
Marie's type tŏ estimate these worthies
at thêir proper relativ worth; for with
all her activity and external absence of
sentiment, thêre ar sound depths in her
unpretending character, and nothing vulgar or shallo. Her fondness for her
gardian, even when he is wounding her

most deeply (a fondness which that excellent man reçiprocates with sŏmething
of youthful ardor, unsuspected by him,
but not absolutely unnotiçed by his
wife); her not unnatural indignation
against her old lŏver, struggled against
as heroically as her absolute detestation
of her new ŏne; her devotion tŏ daily
duty; her readiness, when George is
prŏved sincere, tŏ go forth tŏ she
knŏes not what ruf fortune in the world,
satisfied with that knoledge, and content tŏ abandon, for duty's sake, any
further fruition of her hopes; — all
mark her as a heroin of no common mold.
When we add tŏ the conception of twŏ
wel-defined and original characters, a
lifelike rendering of the subordinate
parts, and occasionally, as in the naïve
expedient of the panic, a vêin of humor
more decided than is frequently the case
with Mr. Trollope, we hav indicated the
principal merits of an excellent tale."
[Athenæum. **2414**

GOLDMAKER'S VILLAGE, [by J:
H: ZSCHOKKE: *Appleton*, 1845; also in
New England Family Mag., Aug.–
Sept., 1845; also in *Chambers' Miscel-
lany*, No. 2. **2415**

GOOD LUCK ("Glück Auf") [by
"E. WERNER," i. e., E.. Bürstenbinder:
Boston, *Osgood*, 1874.] "is remarkably good. In delineation of character
it is especially strong. A proud baron
sels his dauter tŏ a rich parvenu. The
young wife despises her husband, whŏ
seems tŏ deserv her contempt. He is
the sŏn of a mine-ŏner whŏ is killed
by an accident, and the management
of the property falls suddenly on the
sŏn, whŏ had been indolent and spirit-
less. The shoc of responsibility makes
a new man of the latter, whŏ displays in
the critical circumstances attending a
strike, the hiest qualities of manhood.
His young wife begins tŏ respect, and

presently tŏ lŏve him, — the vicissitudes of her feelings being described very skilfully. Ulrich Hartmann, a miner, whŏ leads the strike, hating the husband and madly in lŏve with the wife, is a strikingly original character. But the, charm of the story lies in the gradual approximation of husband and wife, the slo crumbling of the barrier which separates them, under the influence of the noble qualities of each." [Boston "Lit. World."] —" However looked at as a romance, no ŏne can deny that the story is, like its title, a ' success,' since it has the unanalysable quality of carrying the reader on with it, without for a moment getting tame or dul. Many stories mit be written embodying a far deeper insight intŏ character, yet without ŏne-half the interest. The incidents ar skilfully woven, the circumstances ar vivid, the sympathics of the reader ar never lost hold of, and thêre is no irritating shifting of the scenes and dropping of the thread tŏ take up another. In fact, whatever the faults in the conception, Herr Werner (sic!) knoes how tŏ narrate, and the freshness of his industrial subject, — which is not overloaded with any sho of economic detail, — lends a new fascination tŏ the story." [Spectator.

—, SAME ("Success and how he won It") transl. by C. TYRRELL, Bentley, 1876.

—, SAME (" She Fell in Love with her Husband ") N. Y., Primrose Series, No. 91 [1892.] **2416**

GRANDIDIERS (The). [by JULIUS RODENBERG: Low, 1881.] " The charm of this book lies in its freshness. The plot is simple, and the characters familiar. The estrangement of a father and sŏn, from the latter's devotion tŏ painting, the sŏn's successful fight tŏ secure his place in the world of art, and their ultimate reconçiliation, hav been the

basis of more novels than we care tŏ specify. But it is in this very point that the writer's superiority is manifest. Dealing with emotions so general that in the hands of ordinary novelists they would be commonplace, the author engages ŏūr attention at ŏnce, and when we lay down the book, ɯe seem tŏ hav parted from old and dear friends. In almost every character the writer's skilful hand has achîevd success. As is natural the hero is the least satisfactory. He is shadŏy. In Mr. Grandidier, the prosperous hatter, with his lŏve for his children, his pride in his ancestry, and his almost religious respect for the Grêat Elector, Mr. Rodenberg has drawn what we think his most striking character. . . . And this is dŏne not by the laborious accumulation of minute detail, but by the force of a delicate imagination, of a quiet humor, and a truthful pathos. Tŏ readers whŏse critical palates can appreciate the finer flavors of the literary table, we commit this novel." [Spectator. **2417**

GREAT UNKNOWN (The) in *Godey's*, july-aug. 1850. **2418**

GREEN GATE (The) [by ERNST WICHERT: *Lippincott*, 1875.] " is a story of unusual interest. The erotic (sic) element in it is handled with exceptional skil, and several of the characters posses an attractiv individuality,— especially the professor, whŏse course ŏne folloes with deep sympathy. Its tone is pure, and its incidental lessons wholesŏme." [Boston " Lit. World." **2419**

GREIFENSTEIN [**Freiburg**] = No. 724.

GRETCHEN'S JOYS AND SORROWS [" Backfischen's Leiden und Freuden"] by CLEMENTINE HELM," i. e., — ( ) Beyrich: Boston, *Williams*, 1877.] " wer, for the most part, such as ar not recorded in fashionable novels. Her sorrŏs wer in good measure the

732

result of her not knōing the use of sponge, soap, etc., and so having tŏ be taut them by a careful ânt. When she had acquired these important rudiments of education she went intŏ the gay world and was married. It is interesting to obsery that the author,˙a german lady, throes the wêight of her authority in favor of helping ōne's self tŏ salt with a knife. It should be said in justiçe, however, that the ōnly ōther alternativ suggested was the employment of the hand." [Nation.] "This is an unpretending little story, which, without much plot, or any subtle study of character, yet manages tŏ interest the reader. It is a picture of home life in ōne of its most attractiv aspects, with the proper admixture of sentiment, without which a tale could hardly claim tŏ hav a raison d'être." [Spectator.

—, SAME ("A Miss in her 'Teens"), London, *Klockmann*, 1878. **2420**

HALLIG (The), a tale of humble life on the coast of Schleswig, by J: Christoph Biernatzki (†, 1850): Boston, *Gould & Lincoln*, 1856. **2420 p**

HAMMER AND ANVIL, by F: Spielhagen : N.-Y., *Holt*, 1870. **2421**

HARD HEART (A) by "Golo Raimund," i. e., Bertha (Heyn) Frederich (†, 1884) : *Lippincott*, 1884.] "is an extremely pleasant and readable story, told with simpliçity of purpos and turning on questions of real heârt and feeling. The character of Frau Sybilla is forcibly presented : strong, and for a time relentless, in bêaring her woes and in making ōthers suffer, she at last listens tŏ the voiçe of conscience, and alters the course of things for those she can make happy. Thêre is no doubt of the popularity of these german stories, and it lies, we believe, in thêir reflection of the simple elementary emotions. The men ar not

dilettanti, whŏ play with ideas until thêy forget the feelings which ôt to lie behind them, and the women limit thêir range of thôt tŏ what lies within thêir reach. Thus thêir hopes and fears, lōves and passions, hav an idyllic effect, which is refreshing tŏ the reader after more elaborate efforts and æsthetically-minded heroes and heroins." [Lippincott's. **2422**

HEAPS OF MONEY, [**Dresden.**] by Norris, = No. 463.

HEAVY RECKONING (A) = *ALPINE FAY.*

HEIDELBERG BROTHERHOQD (The), by Gustav Liston, in *The Crayon*, may–aug., 1856. **2423**

HELEN YOUNG [by Paul Lindau : Chicago, *Rand*, 1892.]"The scene opens in the Royal Theatre, Berlin, during the play of 'Elsa' founded on a noted murder. Prince von Lohenburg is attracted by the entrance of twŏ ladies, and tries tŏ learn thêir identity, but fails. On the next day, however, circumstances favor him, and the unknōn is soon knōn tŏ him as Helen Young; and thêre folloes a story of mystery, lōve and pathos which seems real." [Publisher's Weekly. **2424**

HELOISE, by "Talvi: " *Appleton*, 1850. **2425**

HER ONLY BROTHER [by "W. Heimburg," i. e., Bertha Behrens : N.-Y., *Crowell*, 1888.] "may be sŏmewhat spun out; but is nevertheless an excellent and entertaining story. Here we hav no disregard of the unities of time and place : on the contrary, all the sensational business is transacted in the precincts of a venerable abode on the storm-beaten shores of the Baltic. The various incidents and episodes hav their rise in the ordinary play of feeling or passion ; and any further effects ar tŏ be found only in sketches of old-fashioned manners, or descriptions of half-savage nature. The story sounds true; it is the more impressiv that it is simple. . . . We ar interested from the first in all the inhabitants of the manor-house; they enlist ōur sympathies by their good old-fashioned german kindliness and simpliçity of manners; and we feel personally concerned in the misunderstandings which drove them tŏ infinit trouble, by destroying their domestic harmony. . . . The reader is permitted tŏ hav an insight into the heroin's real character, which is denied tŏ those whŏ ar nearest and dearest tŏ her. We kno her to conceal passionate emotions under an apparently phlegmatic exterior, and tŏ rise unpretentiously tŏ sublime hights of self-denial, while all the time she is the victim of most irritating misconceptions." [Blackwood's.] — " When her only brother was 15, little Anne Marie was laid in his arms by his mother, and at her death-bed, Klaus promisd never to leav his sister. He sternly put aside lōve and marriage for her sake, and when she was 19 she did the same for him. They livd in an old castle with a dear old maiden ânt, whŏse diary furnishes the chief part of the tale. Her only brŏther has reached the ripe age of 35, when a little sprite, — selfish, pleasure-loving, in all things the opposit of his sister, dances and sings her way into his heârt. The story passes over 30 years, and the life of the ōnly brŏther is read by anŏther generation at the cradle of anŏther Klaus." [Publisher's Weekly.] — "Fräulein Anna Maria von Hegewitz calculates thaler and groshen, tels her knoing old ânt that she means never tŏ marry, and that neither wil her brother, whŏ has promised always tŏ care for her. But this, as the reader wel knōes, is as tho a green apple should swear never tŏ turn red in

the rind. He watches the melloing of the acrid juices in the fräulein's character as he might his nêbors' fruit ripening over the wall. In the fullness of time, Anna Maria is married tŏ an old friend of the family, and brŏther Klaus, whŏse brotherly affection she at first held sufficient, tho a good fello enuf, is the ōne from whŏm most of her troubles cōme." [Critic, 1888.] — " It contains the same descriptions of the quaint maiden ânt, the country life of the nobles, and the strong family affection which we find in the numerous novels translated by Mrs. Wister. The author displays fine descriptiv powers in his rendering of country scenes and interiors, so we can almost believe we, too, hav vegetated in a Märkisch house. The 3 women in the story ar the best drawn and most inter-, esting characters; they ar also excellent foils tŏ each other — ânt Rosamunde, anxious and affectionate; Anna Marie, strong, self-controled, and lōving; Susanne, weak, childish, and pleasure-seeking. The power half-consiously wielded by a beautiful, selfish, spoilt girl in the lives of those around her is trenchantly illustrated. Perhaps she may be summed up as lōving pleasure and lōve." [Critic, 1889.

—, SAME (" A Sister's Love"), *Worthington*, 1890. **2426**

HER SON [by " E. WERNER : " *Bentley*, 1887.] = *ST. MICHAEL.*

HERMANN [by " E. WERNER," i. e., E.. Bürstenbinder : *Tinsley*, 1879.] " is a powerful tale, and very readable. The story treats the bane which the sins of the fathers cast upon the children. A cloud of dark crime blights the childhood and youth of a young count, and the same crime has darkened the life of a young girl whŏm he lōves, unconcious that the evil deed of his father has raised a fatal barrier between them. How this

barrier was raised, how overcŏme, is the theme of the story. All ends wel; the crime is expiated, not avenged, and the lŏvers united." [Athenæum. **2427**
HERO OF THE PEN (A) [by " E. WERNER,' i.e., E.' Bürstenbinder : *Low & Co.*, 1878.] " deals with the fortunes of the dauter of a German whŏ, exiled to America in 1848, determind tŏ rear his child as much of a forêiner as he could. The story is simply, naturally, and gracefully told." [Athenæum. **2428**
HIGHER THAN THE CHURCH = No. 737.
HIS WORD OF HONOR = *NORTHERN LIGHT.*
HOHENSTEINS (The) = No. 738.
HOLE IN THE SLEEVE, by H: ZSCHOKKE : in *Godey's*, May, 1844.
HOME SOUNDS [Heimatklang] by " E. WERNER : " Munro, 1888.
—, SAME (" The Spell of Home "), *Lippincott*, 1887. **2429**
HONOR [by CLEMENS BRENTANO (1778–1842) : London, *J: Chapman*, 1848.] is " a little story worthy tŏ take rank with Auerbach's ' Village Tales.' We feel grateful tŏ the translator for having put intŏ an english dress a charming little tale." [Westminster. **2429 k**
HOUSEHOLD IDOL (The). [by MARIE BERNHARD : N. Y., *Worthington*, 1892.] " The story opens in Rome, after the fall of the Casa Borteni. Andrée, an artist, is hastily summoned tŏ the death-bed of a young sculptor, whŏ beseeches him tŏ convêy the news of his death tŏ the belŏved dauter of a Hamburg banker. In fulfilling this commission the artist lŏses his heârt, and there folloes a romance of contradiction and unexpected action." . . . [Publisher's Weekly. **2429 r**
HORTENSE = No. 2409. *FRIEND-SHIP S TEST.*
HOW THE BARON GOT HIM A

WIFE, by L. SCHÜCKING, in *Penn Monthly*, nov., 1878. **2429**
HULDA [by FANNY (LEWALD) STAHR (1811–89) : *Lippincott*, 1874.] " tels the lŏve of the humble pastor's dauter for the Baron Emanuel, and all the suffering which embittered that young woman's path in life. It is not a remarkable novel, but it is readable." [Nation.] " From ŏne of the advertising pages we learn that Mrs. Wister has given tŏ the world sŏme nine volumes of versions of German tales. Thêre would appear tŏ be nothing but want of the time employed in the mere mecbanical writing tŏ prevent her from speedily increasing this number. A tolerable knoledge of German, and the ability tŏ render that language into fair English ar all the qualities we can discern in Mrs. Wister's writings. As they ar stated to be ' after the German,' the reader would be led to believe that the idioms and style of the original text had not been closely adhered to, but that the English adaptation would flo smoothly and naturally. In this, however, he would be disappointed, as many long and involvd sentences sho that the original has been too faithfully folloed. The scene of the early portion of the book is laid on Prussian northern coast, and the time is early in the century. In the opening chapters the reader is introduced tŏ Hulda, the heroin, whŏ is the only child of a pastor of a village. All the inhabitants of this village ar dependents of a noble family, which occasionally occupies the castle. We ar all familiar with the nursery tales in which the poor peasant girl falls in lŏve with a rich noble, and by her silent adoration wins his affection. . . . But in ' Hulda ' we ar asked tŏ believe that a country girl, after ŏnly twŏ months' instruction, can becŏme a

HYPERION. [by H: WADSWORTH
LONGFELLOW: N.-Y., *Coleman*, 1839.]
"The hero, a young American, oppressed
with grief for the loss of a friend, makes
a tour tŏ **Germany.** Here he passes
sŏme time with a young Baron, and then
sets out for Switzerland. He falls in
lŏve thêre and is rejccted — but the tone
of his mind becŏmes, finally, restored,
and the book leaves him on the eve of
returning tŏ his nativ land. This is the
story, but the story is merely the vehi-
cle for beautiful similę, aphorism, thŏt
and description." [Southern Lit. Mes-
sęnger. **467 t**

gr$\hat{e}$at actress, and that a villain, a valet, wh$\breve{o}$ has been horsewhipped and kicked out of his place for his crimes and impudence, could be the grandest tragic actor in Germany. . . . 'Hulda' is concluded by the marriage of the Baron with the actress, so in a true fairy-like manner all ends happily." [Arcadian. **2430**

HUNGER-PASTOR (The) [by W: RAABE: *Chapman*, 1885.] "is by a writer wh$\breve{o}$m Germany claims as its gr$\hat{e}$atest living humorist. His best book is generally acknoledged t$\breve{o}$ be the 'Hunger Pastor,' published s$\bar{o}$me 20 years ago. It is full of merit, and quite deservd the honor of translation; but in putting it int$\breve{o}$ forein dress most of its humor has evaporated, being rather of the superficial nature which deals with curious mistakes of speech and quaint language than of the true pathos which remains under all dis$\breve{g}$uises. The story, which folloes the career of tw$\breve{o}$ village boys, is wel sustained. The best portions of the novel ar the descriptions of life in the seaboard village wh$\hat{e}$re the protagonist is curate." [Athenæum. **2431**

IMMENSEE = 747.

IN EXILE [*Lippincott*, 1871.] "is an agreeable and pleasantly written story. . . . The characters of Elizabeth and her husband, and that of the Prince Alexis, ar very delicately d$\bar{o}$ne, and in a manner not unsuggestiv of work so much better that even t$\breve{o}$ hav recalled them it is no small achievement. The book is very wel translated, also, and may be recommended t$\breve{o}$ the class of novel-readers wh$\breve{o}$ like to be careful in their selections." [Nation. **2432**

IN HOT HASTE [by M.• E. HUL-LAH: *Holt*, 1888.] "is a wel-told, interesting tale. The haste was due t$\breve{o}$ the necessity of the hero's marriage be-

for his 28th birthday, in order not t$\breve{o}$ l$\breve{o}$se an inheritance. . . In the first blush of her indignation she begs permission of her now angry husband t$\breve{o}$ leave him and go t$\breve{o}$ her english relativs, which he grants. That they afterwards c$\bar{o}$me t$\breve{o}$gether in reconciliation and l$\breve{o}$ve is due t$\breve{o}$ a sudden generosity which novelists always implant in the nature of a german hero t$\breve{o}$ be br$\breve{o}$t t$\breve{o}$ light $\bar{o}$nce and $\bar{o}$nce $\bar{o}$nly in the course of the story, and which usually overturns all $\bar{o}$ne's preconçeived idea of character." [Critic. **2433**

IN PARADISE [by PAUL HEYSE: *Appleton*, 1878.] "is a story of artist life, and takes its rather enigmatic title from a club of München artists, which has been formed by a circle of congenial spirits on the theory that it is possible even in the midst of this world t$\breve{o}$ thro off the hypocrisy of society and return $\bar{o}$nce more t$\breve{o}$ a state of innocence— t$\breve{o}$ substitute for the constraint, conventionality, and philistinism of ordinary life a social state in which each man shal act out his individuality, and reveal himself as he is. The opportunity thus afforded for depicting bohemian life is very happily used. . . . The plot of the story is ingenious and intricate without being complicated, and the interest expands and deepens t$\breve{o}$ the end." [Appleton's Journal. **2434**

IN THE COUNSELLOR'S HOUSE = No. 2335.

IN THE SCHILLINGSCOURT [by " E. MARLITT," i. e., Eugenie John (†, 1887): *Lippincott*, 1879.] "has the usual elements of the german novel; the grave stern hero maintains an agreeable and lively game of fençing with the hauty heroin, til it is finished on the last page by a happy marriage. In this instance, a complication results from the circumstance that the hero is already married tŏ a woman selected by his father because of her wealth, but this is easily arranged by means of a divorce. It is notiçeable that discussion of all sorts, from socialism to decorativ art, is beginning to push its way into the regions of such pure romance as Marlitt's stories with the effect of making them more unreal and far less agreeable." [Nation.] — "The story turns upon the frieñdship and ultimate enmity of twŏ nêboring families, ōne of whŏm dwels in a former monastery, while the ōther inhabits the hostelry of the monastic building. A large part of the tale is concerned with the designing interference of priests. It is a sensational story, but the plot is skilfully constructed, and the reader's interest is never allowed tŏ flag. The writing, too, is good, and the descriptions of scenery both graphic and attractiv. The scene is Thüringia, with its woods and streams." [Athenæum. **2435**

IN THE VILLAGE SALON, by CLAIRE VON GLÜMER, in *Ladies' Repository*, Oct., 1870. **2436**

INGEMISCO [**Bavaria**] = No. 472.

INITIALS [**Bavaria**] = No. 473.

INSIGNIFICANT WOMAN (An). [by "W. HEIMBURG," i. e., Bertha Behrens: N. Y., *Bonner*, 1891.] "The insignificant woman is rather too good for human nature's daily food. She is the dauter of rich parents whŏ hav earned mŏney. She marries a selfish, exacting artist, whŏ uses her property tŏ surround himself with luxuries, and traces his lac of success to the prosiness of his wife. He finds a kindred soul in a wild baroness, and his wife puts up with untold insult at the hands of this woman. After many pages the husband groes tired of his old habits and ways and tries being good." [Publishers' Weekly.

—, SAME (" Misjudged"), *Worthington*, 1891. **2437**

INTERESTING TALES [by J: H: JUNG STILLING: London, 1838.] "Altho this is not so beautiful a book as the autobiografy of Stilling, it is stil ōne of grêat and rare merit. The ten short tales, of which it consists, ar, with ōne exception, (The Way to the Throne) narrativs of humble life — not the life of fantastic metaphysicians and poets, but of real homely, honest burgers, and peasants of the better class. We have read the stories of ' *Conrad the Good*,' ' *The Emigrant*,' ' *Blind Leonard and his Guide*,' ' *The Watchman and his Dauter*,' and ōne or twŏ ōthers, with singular satisfaction. Thêre is a bonbommie about them — a simplicity and strait-forwardness which contrasts in a happy manner with the artificiality of modern stories." [Metropolitan. **2438**

IT HAPPENÈD YESTERDAY [by F: Marshall: New York, D. Appleton & Co., 1891.] "is a story the scene of which is laid in **Augsburg.** It is rather a clever picture of society life in that city, and is fairly interesting, but it lacks individuality. It is only a familiar picture in a new frame." [San Fran. Chronicle. **2439**

IT IS THE FASHION [" Modern ") by " ADELHEID VON AUER," i. e., C.. von Cosel: *Lippincott*, 1872.] "is the record of a family given up tŏ worldly ways—tŏ extravagance, and tŏ all manner of pomps and vanities. The story is told in letters from a young woman whŏ is boarding with them, and whŏ having a very keen observation, and a fine talent for gossiping, cŏvers many pages with descriptions of thêir ways of life, and the troubles it brings upon them. Naturally, this is not the sort of novel which wil please the giddy, and even steadier-headed people may find it a trifle dul, but it is by no means unreadable. It is tŏ be remembered that this is a german novel and what german novels generally ar." [Nation. **2440**

IVO. [by BERTIIOLD AUERBACH: London, *Bogue*, 1847.] "This charming little story completes the series of Auerbach's 'Village Tales' [No. 2342]. Ivo is the youngest son of the carpenter and desires tŏ becŏme a priest. In this wish he is encouraged by his parents; and when of proper age, he proceeds tŏ the university. Here his mind becŏmes harassed by numerous doubts and difficulties, which result in a determination tŏ quit the university, and tŏ follo any ŏther vocation than that of the priesthood even at the risk of incurring his father's lasting displeasure. This determination he puts in practiçe, and wanders on he cares not whither: a lucky chance conducts him tŏ the farm of an old servant of his father's, named Naza, tŏ whom he had been warmly attached from childhood, and whŏ now receives him with open arms, and the tale thus concludes." [Westminster. **2441**

JOSEPH IN THE SNOW. [by BERTNOLD AUERBACH: London, *Saunders*, 1861, 3 v.; Boston, *Fuller*, 1867.] "Māny of the best of the *Village Stories* [No. 2342] ar familiar tŏ english readers, indeed ŏur acquaintance with the Black Forest dates from the appearance of *Barfüssle* [No. 2455] or of *Edelweiss* [No. 2375]; but tŏ ŏur mind the crown of them is a little ŏne — *.Joseph in the Snow*, a bit of simple, pathetic, soul-touching village-life, told so vividly and so naturally that we seem tŏ smel the pines of that hilly land and tŏ feel as ours the tender wo of little Joseph and his mŏther. We might wel spare the weak moral tone and the sentimentality of *On the Heights* [No. 881] or the morbid weariness of the *Villa on the Rhein* [No.

2367]; but the man whŏ led us by the hand intŏ the innermost life of the wise and patient peasant of the woods of Baden has earned ŏur heartiest gratitude. We should think it might placate the veriest 'Jew-hater' of Berlin, when he remembers that Germany ŏes sŏme of its sweetest songs tŏ ŏne Jew (Heine) and its very purest, sweetest, and most appealing tales of loly life tŏ anŏther (Auerbach)." [Boston "Lit. World."] — *Joseph* is a "grêat favorit abroad and at home. The plot is simple and touching, and the capital descriptions of country life and country characters make the story stil more interesting. Joseph is the illegitimate child of Martina, the dauter of a wood-turner, whŏ is an old man of unblemished character, and has taken grêat pride in his dauter's good prinçiples and promising talents. The shoe produced by the news of Joseph's birth is terrible, and David is near murdering his child. The parson, however, interferes, and brings the old man round not ŏnly tŏ pardon but even tŏ lŏvc his dauter and her offspring, and tŏ be paternally solicitous for thêir welfare. The struggle between the father's lŏve and his sense of shame is wel depicted. The parson, too, and his wife ar finely-drawn characters and splendid types of thêir class. Joseph's father is faithfully attached tŏ Martina, but neither his father nor, much less, his mŏther wil hear of his marrying the penniless girl; thêy keep him so close a prisoner that he finds it impossible even tŏ see her. By his parents he is betrothed tŏ Tony, the miller's dauter, and is about tŏ be married tŏ her against his wil. In the night preceding this unnatural wedding the complication reaches its climax. Adam is sent tŏ make lŏve tŏ Tony, but, forgetting himself, talks tŏ her of her rival and his faithful attachment tŏ her, and at last wins his 'bride,' whŏ is a good girl at heart, to his scheme of secretly marrying Martina." [Englishwoman's Domestic Mag. **2442**

JUDITH STERN, in *TALES* by HEYSE.

KATHERINE = No. 772.

KICKLEBURYS ON THE RHINE = No. 477.

KLAUS BEWER'S WIFE [by PAUL LINDAU: *Holt*, 1887.] " is worth reading, if it wer only to contemplate the finished portrait of ' Katie Schöne,' whom Bewer so rashly married. Katie's notion of the value of truth was crude, and, being a concert-hall singer, her propensities wer vagabond. Nevertheless, she had no desire to offend her conventional husband, or to outrage the fine society to which she unexpectedly found herself elevated. But the introduction of very respectable relativs into her house, her husband's delight in their company, and her discomfort, quite upset her equanimity, drawing her to the activ antagonism which resulted fatally to Bewer. Katie's character is so completely disclosed by her acts and words, with the smallest amount of description, that misunderstanding is impossible. The rest of the characters ar interesting and life-like, save the Americans, who ar of a kind which Americans never see." [Nation. **2443**

—, SAME (" Mr. & Mrs. Bewer "), *Rand*, 1892.

KNIGHT OF THE BLACK FOREST = No. 480.

LABOR STANDS ON GOLDEN FEET [by [J:] H: [DANIEL] ZSCHOKKE: *Cassell*, 1871.] " illustrates artisan life in the german towns as it was many years ago. The tale is interesting as a picture of life and manners, and it is valuable as embodying the principles which ar the basis of all true and healthy civilization. It is the history of the progress of a family for 3 genera-

tions, — now, beginning with Thadeus the tinker, it groes and prospers by the exerçise of honesty, piety, and good se se. The prosperity of the family is not confined to themselvs, but it works like leaven amöngst the artisans of the town, til the efforts of the old ' Master Girdler,' to giv his sön a good education gradually extend to forming schools and reading-rooms, and delivering lectures for the instruction and cultivation of all the workmen, — a general spread of education and the means of learning." [Athenæum. **2444**

LACE [by PAUL LINDAU: *Appleton*, 1889.] " is a good specimen of the modern german novel, — heavy, as it seems that class of fiction must inevitably be, but full of matter and of fine and conscientious workmanship. The finish and elaboration of the german novelist may wel serv as a model for his fello craftsmen in öther lands. The story is too complicated and full of plot to be easy reading, but from its point of vue it is a meritorious performance. It is chiefly conçerned with the political and hier social life of the Empire, and apart from its literary force wil be found of value by any öne concerned in study of the people and institutions of Germany." [American. **2445**

LADY OF EISENACH .(The), in Temple Bar, 1867, [*Every Saturday*, 21 Sept., 1867.] **2446**

LADY WITH THE RUBIES = No. 779.

LAKE HOUSE. [by FANNY (LEWALD) STAHR (1811–89): Boston, *Ticknor*, 1861.] " A young German of hi aspirations fails to get any acknoledgment from his relativs of his marriage to a most lovely french lady of noble family. And so, throu söme interference of his father and her bröther, the young wife dies, and her miserable husband becomes an exile tŏ America, and a desolated soul for the rest of his days. · The cruelty of such rigid conventionalism adds tŏ the tragical course of events in making the narrativ intensely sad. The opening portion givs a glimpse at the early horrors of the french Revolution, but most of the incidents cluster around a retired country-seat near **Hamburg**. Thêre is little dialog, very little variety, and nŏthing akin tŏ american wedded trials in this touching record of what seems a real experiençe of bliss blasted by the inexorable pride of an old family, the needless embarrassments of a concealed lŏve, and the exaggerated sensibility resulting from misdirected education." [Christian Examiner. **2447**

LANDOLIN. [by BERTHOLD AUERBACH (†, 1882): *Holt*, 1878.] "The inevitable Nemesis bý which crime, unatoned for, wŏrks out its punishment in the soul, even when legal penalties ar evaded is the motif and moral of the book; and the tragic theme is wrŏt with a dramatic forçe and effect which contrast impressivly with the peaceful rural scenes and the simple people amid whŏm the scene is laid." [Appleton's. **2448**

LAST VON RECKENBURG (The). [by LUISE VON FRAŇ‚OIS: transl., Boston, *Cupples*, 1888.] "The noble Fraulein Eberhardine is bound, by what in fairy tales is described as the mysterious laws of her being, tŏ defend the weak and unworthy whŏ depend upon her, no matter how grêat the cost tŏ herself. Then the obligation is increased by a sense of what is due tŏ her ŏn rank when protection is demanded by a plebeian, ŏne whŏm circumstances hav made her companion and, with certain reservations, her friend. The novel in which this heroin displays the nobility of her nature and of her order is thŏroly

romantic. The scene is laid in the early years of the century in a village whêre the Von Reckenburgs subsisted chîefly on the consciousness of their long descent and on the deference accorded it. Their feeling that a Von Reckenburg is neither degraded by poverty nor exalted by riches, that personal dishonor is as impossible tŏ them as personal dishonesty, is so genuin and delightful that a fiery radical could scarcely withhold respectful acquiesçence. The village never dreams of questioning the validity of the poverty-stricken Von Reckenburg's claim tŏ superiority. When Dörl, the common sinner, grovels at the patrician Hardine's feet, and is lifted, comforted, and shîelded from the worst consequences of her sin, thêre is an almost comical recognition of the immeasurable social distance between the twŏ. The beauty of the story is that the reader accepts the situation as naturally as Dorl and the rest of the villagers, and the credit of this effect should be given tŏ the author's unpretentious, sincere literary manner. The interest in Hardine's sorrŏs and Dörl's sins is strong enuf tŏ survive the artistic blunder of telling the end before the beginning." [Nation. **2449**

LEFT-HANDED ELSA [by Ro. E: FRANCILLON: Boston, *Loring*, 1879.] is "a quaint little tale. It is about a young artist, whŏ wins a prize, and is nearly ruined by his success. In his obscurity, he had lŏved the humble maiden, Elsa; in his grêatness he neglects; when he falls he finds consolation in her affection." [Boston "Lit. World." **2450**

LENORE VON TOLLEN [by "W. HEIMBURG," i. e., Bertha Behrens: *Munro*, 1890.] "is a natural, unaffected, and purely domestic story of a sort on which ŏur german kinsmen seem tŏ hav a patent. An unbroken thread of narrativ conducts the reader from ōne incident tŏ anŏther by wel-trodden, homely ways, and throu an atmosphere suffused with sentiment until it brings him contentedly tŏ the most orthodox and prosperons of endings. The good ar rewarded and the evil punished, deaths happen opportunely, and people inconvenient tŏ the villain turn up at the most convenient moment for his trembling victim." [Catholic World.] — "It is a rather tragic story of the sacrifiçe of a young and beautiful girl tŏ pay the debts of a scapegrace brŏther. Her mother and sister connived tŏ sel her tŏ a coarse, brutal husband, and separate her from the lŏver tŏ whŏm she had given her heârt. The girl's despair and her disgust for the man she marries ar very wel pictured. By a happy turn of circumstances she is finally able tŏ thro off her yoke and marry her early lōve. Novels in which matrimonial mistakes ar rectified by divorce ar not always the healthfulest; but in the book before us, Lora has the reader's sympathies throu-ōut. . . . Thêre is a Teutonic simplicity about her which makes her a fascinating heroin." [Boston " Lit. World."] —Lora "is the typical german heroin of the ' Marlitt ' style, ' devoured with the hate of hate, the scorn of scorn, the lōve of lōve.' She carries her little head so very hi that ŏue feels sure the muscles of her nec must oftcn hav ached sadly. Sŏme of the characters ar sufficiently life-like, but the plot is weak and sentimental. The [Worthington] translation is well dŏne and is in easy, colloquial English." [American.] — "The plot is commonplace and badly worked out, the trouble. sŏm characters being either sent tŏ America or killed off by convenient maladies. Sŏme of the dialog, however, is brightly written; and the author has

succeeded in presenting an attractiv heroin of a thōroly german type. ∟Athenæum.

—, SAME ("Lora" Worthington, 1882.
—, SAME (" Was she his Wife?") London, Eden, 1891. **2451**
LIESCHEN = LIZZIE OF THE MILL.
LIFE AND DEATH, in Ladies' Repository, june–july, 1868. **2452**
LINDA TRESSEL. [by ANTHONY TROLLOPE (†, 1882): Littell and Gay, 1868.] " Looking at these short novels candidly, taking the good with the bad and comparing them with the multitudinous host of kindred works, we find ourselvs ready tŏ say that they contain more of the real substance of common life and more natural energy of conception than any of the clever novels now begotten on ōur much tried english speech. . . . Thêre ar many ways by which an effect may be reached. Scott traveled throu romantic gorges and enchanted forests, and scaled the summits of mountains crowned with feudal towers. Mr. Trollope trudges throu crowded city streets and dusty hiways, and level garden-paths. But the twŏ roads converge and meet at a spot whêre a sweet young girl lies dying of a broken heârt. It matters little whether she be called Lucy Ashton or Linda Tressel." [Nation.] — " The same strong character-painting, the same striking contrasts, and remarkable but almost painful reality which distinguished ' Nina Balatka,' ar shŏn with equal power in the present story, altho it affords less scope for variety than did the former. The plot is laid in **Nürnberg** — and while it certainly introduces us tŏ a singularly unattractiv set of people, the exhibition of thêir peculiar modes of thinking and action, and thêir effect upon individual fortunes,

LIKES AND DISLIKES. [Oxford, *Parker*, 1858.] "Two-thirds of this volume ar occupied with an account of a family tour in Germany. . . . Altho the plot is the simplest conceivable — being summed up in the popular phrāse, whŏ would hav thôt it? — an interest is gradually created which is sustained tŏ the last chapter. As tŏ the continental wanderings of the Marsdens and the Digbys, they supp'ly at ŏnce the basis of a charming domestic tale, and of a most intelligent narrativ of travel, for we seldom meet with criticism so suggestiv, or gossip so pleasant, in the diaries of ordinary tourists. . . . The book is full of grace and fascination." [Leader.   **486 h** thêir very strange manners, and the strong claim tŏ ŏūr sympathies which the author bespeaks for poor Linda — whŏ seems tŏ be entirely misplaced amid the picturesque antiquities and besotted prejudices of this Bavarian city, ar decidedly interesting. . . The conversation is particularly good, and servs gradually tŏ develope the peculiar qualities and opinions of the speakers in a manner so natural as tŏ bring each individual before the reader with a degree of distinctness which no mere description could produce." [Round Table. **2453**

LINKED AT LAST [by FANNY E.. BUNNÈTT : London, *King*.] "Mrs. Bunnètt's slight story derives most of its interest from the picture of pleasant life which it contains. Thêre is much which is true and wel described in the simple routîne of the Massengers' homestead at the foot of the **Odenwald.** The fête-days and working days, the 'aussitz' in the gardens of the 'Crown,' the rustic lŏve-making, and the village ambitions which cross its happiness, the simple true-heârtedness of Rosa, the honest worldliness of her hard mistress, the phlegm of the male Massingers, father and son, ar all sketched with an appreciativ and not unskilful pen. [Athenæum. **2454**

LITTLE BAREFOOT. ["Barfüssle") by BERTHOLD AUERBACH : Boston, *Fuller*, 1867, 12° London, 1873, 4°.] "It is rarely that thêre is published anything so simple and naturally delightful in tone and so complete in finish. The common sufferings and pleasures which mark the life of a peasant orphan ar rescued from insipidity by the poetry and humanity with which they ar treated. The thriftiness, cheerfulness and wisdom of Amrei, the little heroin, ar made touching by the circumstances

under which they hav tŏ be exercised. 'Brŏther and sister' is ōne of the most charming combinations of lŏve and confidence, clear of selfishness, — but 'sister and brŏther' is yet more so, and never was woman's self-sacrificing care of the weak boy left alone in the world with her more innocently and naturally displayed than in the career of Amrei and Dauci." [Athenæum.] — "We hav in this story of a shŏeless maiden ōne of those simple yet exquisit fictions which stand unrivaled in their department of romance, the faculty of producing which seems tŏ belong tŏ sŏme peculiar element of the german mind. It is characterized by the rare charm of freshness, a spontaneity, and a purity which renders the perusal, like inhaling the breezes of spring, redolent of mingled perfumes from gardens, meadŏs, and groves. It would be stinted praise tŏ say this little volume has excellence ; for it possesses the many excellences essential tŏ a truly artistic production. In design it is appropriate throuŏūt, ever natural and truthful. A depth of guileless wisdom speaks in the tender, earnest strain of the story, the reflectiv tenor of which is relîevd by the perpetual play of a sparkling fancy, and warmed by irrepressible utterances of the hiest and sweetest intuitions." [Leader.] — "'Little Barefoot,' as she should be called, is a most fascinating creation, and her story is told in an altŏgether charming manner. The picture is taken from the humblest life, the scene is laid in an ordinary german village, the dramatis personæ ar peasants . . . but the beauty and the glory of humanity ar here, encompassed by lŏliness, and yet all the more able tŏ mŏve ŏūr heârts. The book, without making a profession of religion, is religious, — and moral, too, without moralizing, — and withal a charming combination of the real and the ideal, of hard, grasping, mean, grinding village life, under iron conditions, and of that faith and knoledge and sweetness — the gifts of God as manifestly as the flowers and the fruits, the birds and the soft breezes — which create théir ōn world, and that world almost a heaven, out of the most unpromising materials." [Monthly Religious Magazine.

—, SAME ("Cinderella of the Black Forest"), in *SKETCHES*, translated by Georgina Gordon, London, 1861. **2455**

—, SAME ("Barefooted Maiden"), *Low*, 1857; Boston, *Monroe*, 1860.

LITTLE HEATHER-BLOSSOM [by EMILIE VON INGERSLEBEN : *Bonner*, 1891.] is "a pretty and sōmewhat intricate romance of a little watering-place on ōne of the inlets of the Baltic. Erica, the heather-blossom, upon lōsing her mōther, drifts into māny strange surroundings, and eventually discōvers the place which is hers by right of birth as wel as by merit and fitness." [Publisher's Weekly. **2456**

LITTLE MOORLAND PRINCESS = No. 795.

LITTLE WHITE HAT (The) in *Amer. Monthly Mag.*, aug.-oct., 1833.

LIZZIE OF THE MILL ("Lümpenmüller's Lieschen") [by "W. HEIMBURG," i. e., Bertha Behrens: transl. by Tyrrell, *Bentley*, 1880.] "is a pleasant enuf little story. It tels how the hêir of a half-ruined house fel in lōve with an il-tempered and treacherous cousin, whō leavs him in the lurch and in grêat pecuniary difficulties, and how he is rescued thêrefrom by the usual faithful and munificent girl of the people. A wicked italian grandmōther with ruthlessly aristocratic vues is the ōnly ōther person deserving mention." [Athenæum.

—, SAME ("Lottie of the Mill"),

Lippincott, 1882. [In this version, the first chapter is omitted.]

—, SAME ("Lieschen"), N.-Y., *Tribune Co.*, 1882.

—, SAME ("Tale of an Old Castle"), *Munro*, 1889.

—, SAME ("A Maiden's Choice"), *Worthington*, 1891. **2457**

LORA = No. 2451.

LORENZO STARK, by ENGEL, = No. 821.

LORLEY AND REINHARD. [by BERTHOLD AUERBACH (†, 1882) : *Holt*, 1877.] "A painter visiting a village paints as a Madonna the beautiful dauter of the keeper of the village inn. He falls in lōve with her, attracted no less by her unconcealed lōve for him than by her beauty. He takes her tō town with him, a town whêre thêre is a little court, very refined, æsthetic, and very hi dried old manners. The poor girl drives him almost mad with her awkwardness, her ignorance of polished life, and her independence. [Compare plot of No. 2390.] It dōes not matter that in the latter respect she wins the favor of ōthers, even of the Prince. After awhile he avoids her, and cōmes home drunk. She sees her position, and from what he is suffering, and she goes bac tō her parents, leaving behind her an unreproachful, fond, and most touching letter of farewel. . . . After awhile she dies, and he after a long time betroths himself tō another woman whō lōves him, and tō whose lōve he responds with such a feeling as beauty and sweetness and devotion might raise in the breast of a man whōse heârt is really in the grave of his dead wife. He dies before a second marriage from injuries receivd in a dispute with his brōther-in-law. It wil be seen that this simple story of humble life presented temptations tō treatment in the most literal and realistic way. But in Auerbach's hands it is ideal." [Galaxy.

—, SAME ("The Professor's Wife") [No. 2498], Oxford, *Parker*, 1850. This includes, however, only the first part. **2458**

LOST IN THE SNOW, in (N. Y.) *Citizen*, 17–24 Sept., 1870. **2459**

LOST MANUSCRIPT (The) = No. 799.

LOTTIE OF THE MILL = No. 2457.

LOUISA VON PLETTENHAUS = No. 2370.

LOVE AND SILENCE, or the Family of Almstein by K. (v. G.) PICHLER, in Boston *Saturday Rambler*, 18 and 25 may, 1850.

—, SAME ("Silent Love") in *Boston Miscellany*, jan., 1842; also in *Ladies' Repository*, july, 1844; also in "The Passion Flower," N.-Y., *Leavitt & Alden*, 1859 (?). **2460**

LUCIE'S MISTAKE = No. 2409.

LUCY, or Married from Pique, by "E. JUNCKER," i. e., Else ( ) Schmieden: *Loring*, 1868. **2461**

LULU'S NOVEL [by ELISE POLKO: Boston, *Loring*, 1874.] "is a pretty story of family-life. Lulu is ŏne of those wild-flowers of genius, whŏ in stories but not outside, gro, without much training, intŏ the ability tŏ dŏ grĕat things. Scarcely out of childhood, she is betrothed tŏ a grave Herr Doctor, whŏm she reverences more than lŏves, and whŏ has very strict ideas with regard tŏ her education and sphere. A gay and genial young officer is introduced under the right conditions tŏ make trouble, but he, or Lulu, or both, disappoint ŏur expectations in this respect, and she ends rather tamely with her affianced at last. She is scarcely more prominent in the story, however, than all her friends. The gentle Professor,

her father, with his birds and flowers, her over-anxious mother, the romantic ânt Elsbeth, with her worship of female grĕatness afar off, — these make a family circle whŏse life is like a pastoral." [Repository. **2462**

MAGDALEN'S FORTUNES = No. 2360.

MAGIC OF A VOICE (The) [by MARGARET RUSSELL MACFARLANE: *Cassell*, 1886.] "is a charming story of german life, resembling those chosen [see No. 595] by Mrs. Wister for translation, in its bright or pathetic episodes and its clear representation of german customs and modes of thôt." [Critic.]— "The picture of life as it is led by the gentry of **Mecklenburg,** with their narro interests and restricted companionship, is full of local color and realistic touches. . . . Given, a dark man, with close cut hair curling crisply around his open brow, with an eye like a falcon, and ŏther manly attributes, in lŏve with a mysterious voice; the ŏner of the voice, a tall, slender maid, with ash blonde hair, arms like a Psychē, aspirations in music and the gift of their expression, for principal actors, and the wild waters of the Baltic, the woods, and the rockbound shore for a romantic setting, ŏne is somewhat exasperated at having tŏ listen to old women gossiping over thĕir knitting." [Nation. **2463**

MAID, WIFE, OR WIDOW? [by "MRS. ALEXANDER," i. e., Annie (French) Hector: *Chatto*, 1879.] is a "pretty, pathetic, wel-modulated little romance. As a matter of fact, the story cannot be read without pleasure; and it is written with so much delicacy, as wel as correctness, that criticism is disarmed from the outset. 'Maid, Wife or Widow?' is in many respects cast in a different mold from that which produced *The Wooing O't,* [No. 1934] but the twŏ novels hav their best qualities in common. Humanity at its truest and tenderest, youthful affection and faith at their purest and simplest, circumstance and detail in their most natural form — these ar the materials out of which Mrs. Alexander has woven a charming tale. The thŏro ease of the narrativ is ŏne of the best proofs of the fidelity of the pictures which it brings before ŏur eyes.; and no ŏne wil be likely tŏ carp at the delineation of the quiet phases of saxon rural life, set in their bacground of military bustle and excitement. The half-transparent mystery which is created by the title before ŏne dips intŏ the first chapter is maintained without effort tŏ the last; we feel that there is not much tŏ be discŏvered when all is over, and we ar content tŏ lend ŏurselvs to the delusion until it may please the hero and heroin tŏ unravel their silken skein. This is art of a simple kind; but it is true art for all that." [Athen. **2464**

MAIDEN'S CHOICE (A) = No. 2457.

MARGARETHE [by " E. Junker," i. e., Else (   ) Schmieden : *Lippincott*, 1878.] " is the simplest of narrations, a much-used theme; the marriage of the ŏnly son of an aristocratic house and a young girl from a class beneath him — a count with a tradesman's daughter. She is lovely in person and character; but her exacting lŏve and childlikeness weary him, and he is about to give himself up tŏ the influence brŏt to bear upon him by a magnificent but unprincipled woman of his rank, whŏm he had formerly admired, when his wife Margarethe learns the truth and nearly dies of the shoe. Stung with remorse and shame, he strives and waits for restoration of the lŏve and trust he has forfeited, and which now seem to him treasures beyond price; but she, from a confiding, affectionate girl, has becŏme

at ŏnce a woman, self-possessed, reti-çent and unapproachable. The result of his now absorbing passion and patient waiting, and of the disciplin of his truly noble nature, is such as tŏ gratify the reader. Another lŏve story of grêat pathos runs along with the leading ŏne — that of the Count's sister for a lŏver beneath her. The sketches of the home life of a cultivated family of rank ar very graphic, as ar the general scenes and incidents; and the characters ar so clearly drawn that we recognize their fidelity." [Boston " Lit. World." **2465**

MARIA WUZ, by Richter, No. 821.

MARIE AND MARIA, by Ottilie (Ronschütz) Wildermuth : in *Ladies' Repository*, Jan.-May, 1871.   **2466**

MARRIAGE TIE (The). [by "Johannes van Dewall," i. e., A: Kühne : *Remington*, 1879.] " The author makes about as much as is possible of material which an english reader would deem impracticable. The heroin, a miracle of beauty and virtue, is found tŏ hav twŏ husbands. Not all the author's ingenuity can account for the first divorce in a satisfactory way — tŏ lŏve too much seems to be as fatal tŏ the stability of the ' marriage tie ' as tŏ lŏve tŏo little. The tale is wel told, and rises at its climax tŏ a hight of interest which all readers wil acknowledge." [Spectator.   **2467**

MARRIED OR NOT MARRIED in *Imperial Magazine*, 1839, and *Gift of Friendship*, 1852.   **2468**

MARTHA = No. 2514.

MASTER BIELAND AND HIS WORKMEN. [by Berthold Auerbach, († , 1882) : *Holt*, 1883.] " The Philadelphia exhibition figures in its pages, but in it Auerbach returns to the same theme which was long ago the *motif* in ' Edelweiss ' [No. 2375] cooperation in handicraft. Then it was the cloc-makers', here it is the shŏemakers'. Thêre is in it that same comprehension of the significance of all the littleness of the life of a small community which was the success of his first stories, tho thêre is less of picturesque detail such as made us intimate with the Black Forest." [Nation. **2469**

MASTER OF ETTERSBERG (The) = No. 1011.

MASTERPIECES OF GERMAN FICTION : Milwaukee, 1885.

MATRIMONIAL AGENT OF POTSDAM (The) [by ADOLF VON WIN-TERFELD. N.-Y., *T: R. Knox*, 1887.] " is called a 'humoro-social' romance. The recipe for this is a certain propor-tion of sentiment, a certain quantity of sententious discourses on women, lŏve, matrimony, the spirit of the age and a large amount of horse-play. It is in this that the humor consists. A man stands on his feet; therefore a man standing on his head must be irresistibly funny. Wives must obey their hus-bands; thêrefore men afraid of thêir wives ar side-splitting. In the same measure physical defects, such as stam-mering, can convulse the gods. This is a cheap and easy way of raising a lâf, but ŏne with which we confess we are not greatly in sympathy. Otherwise the book professes tŏ illustrate a curious phase of German society, but one which is equally farcical." [Epoch. **2470**

MAX WILD, THE MERCHANT'S SON, Edinburgh, *Nimmo*, 1874. **2471**

MEN AND BOYS, by TH. KÖRNER, in *Amer. Monthly*, Apr. 1836. **2472**

MINNIE'S HOLIDAY [by MATILDA BARBARA BETHAM EDWARDS : London, *M. Ward*, 1875.] " is a fresh and pleasant story. The scene is Vienna, and the little country cousins cŏme from Salz-burg. It is told in a lively, pleasant way, and it shŏs that girls in Austria and England ar much alike." [Athe-næum. **2473**

MISJUDGED = No. 2437.

MISS IN HER 'TEENS = No. 2420.

MISTRESS OF IBICHSTEIN = No. 845.

MONEY, London, 1852. **2474**

MY HEART'S DARLING = No. 2409.

NANNCHEN VON MAINZ [by BER-THOLD AUERBACH : in *Appleton's Jour-nal*, 10 and 17 July, 1875.] " is much like sŏme of the author's earlier work. It tels how a young girl of Mainz fell in lŏve with a prussian soldier, much tŏ the wrath of her father, and how finally they wer married. It is a clever enuf little story, and it is amusing tŏ notice that it has, or rather had, its political meaning, in shoing how much il-feel-ing existed between different sections of Germany." [Atlantic. **2475**

NEW RACE (A) = No. 864.

NINA BALATKA, see No. 2453.

NOBLE NAME (A) [by CLAIRE (VON TOLSTOY) VON GLÜMER : *Lippin-cott*, 1883.] " givs the purposes and cross-purposes of the grandchildren of the aged head of the house of Dönning-hausen, a house 'whŏse members,' ac-cording to his pronouncement, ' ar not in the world solely tŏ enjoy them-selvs, but tŏ dŏ their confounded duty as far as they can, and fulfil their re-sponsibilities.' " [Nation. **2476**

NORA [London, *Burns*. 1877.] " is not an uninteresting novel; it is livelier and more attractiv than most german stories of the sentimental order, and its morality is all which can be de-sired, — it is, indeed, of a hier order than we ar generally fortunate enuf tŏ find in novels of either home or forein man-ufacture. We should hav been pleased tŏ make the acquaintance of the ac-

MY COUSIN MAURICE. [*Low*,
1872] "is a very pleasant, readable
tale, written by sŏme ōne whŏ has evi‡
dently seen a good deal of the world.
We are taken here and thėrę, tŏ Ĭndia,
Ireland, and **Germany**, and the writer
is evidently at home in each land. Sŏme
of the translations of poetry ar particularly wel dŏne." [Westminster. **501 q**

complished scion of a french noble
house [which has espoused the cause of
the Revolution] whŏ found himself
obliged tŏ take tŏ circus riding, and
also of his charming wife and their
dauter Nora." [Spectator. **2477**
NORICA [**Nürnberg**] = No. 870.
NORTHERN LIGHT ["Flammen-
zeichnen"] by "E. WERNER," N.-Y.,
Bonner, 1890.
NOT FOR THE WORLD. [by D.
O. T.. *Newby*, 1872.] "Not til we get tŏ
the last page of D. O. T.'s unpretending story dŏ we find the connexion, a
very slight ŏne after all, between it and
the title; and the enigma which the
latter presents tŏ us is the only perplexity involvd in the simple plot. Thêre
is no doubt as to the general fidelity of
the representation of german life and
character. This is convêyed throu the
medium of a narrativ by an english girl,
whŏ leavs her 'villa at Brompton' tŏ
stay with some german relativs, a good-
tempered, rather sluggish baron, and
his vixenish but affectionate ânt, whŏ
rules her doçile nephew with despotic
sway. By very slo degrees, during
which ŏne frequently gets completely
out of patience with her hero, that gentleman makes up his mind tŏ assert his
right of independent choice in the important question of matrimony. Clara Leybach, the young lady whŏm he wisely
prefers even tŏ the approbation of his
ânt, is, in every way, charming, womanly, and natural. Unfortunately, as
the dauter of a village pastor, she dōes
not boast the patrician Von, and this
defect, when coupled with sŏme early
reminiscences which ânt Minuschka
stil retains of ŏther members of the
Leybach family, prŏves suffiçient tŏ
induce the hi-heârted old baroness tŏ giv
the match her stoutest opposition. Of
course, after much resistance, in the

course of which ânt Minuschka shōs
herself in colors very unworthy of her
better nature, a happy consummation is
arrived at. Thêre is a good deal of skil,
tho no attempt at striving after effect,
in the manner in which the complex but
homely nature of the old lady is revealed tŏ us; much truth in the exposition of the really loering tendency of
misplaced pride, and a good deal of
humor in the description of the final
'coup' on which the gallant old combatant stakes her all, and lŏses. The
younger people, Clara, Fanny, and the
baron, ar tame in comparison with
her — the latter provokingly so; but
thêy all hav thêir merits, and the tone
of the book is lady-like and refined.
Especially notiçeable is the absence of
coquetry in Fanny, whŏm most novelists
would hav instantly placed in rivalry
with the gentle Clara, but whŏ, while
giving us suffiçient indications that her
heârt is not without its susceptibility,
acts and thinks like a modest and a
loyal english lady." [Athenæ. **2478**
NOT IN THEIR SET. [by MARIE
LENZEN: Boston, *Lee*, 1874.] "The
heroin is the illegitimate child of Count
Steinthal, whŏ deçeived her beautiful
mōther Helene, dauter of the proud
Regierungsrath Lorsberg. The Count
lŏves Helene, tŏ whŏm he is betrothed,
and would marry her, but weakly yìelds
tŏ the appeals of his father tŏ save the
tottering fortunes of thêir noble house
by wedding the wealthy Fräulein von
Metelen. The Regierungsrath is furious when he hears of the Count's insult
tŏ his family, altho as yet he dōes nŏt
kno its full extent. Helene becōmes a
listless invalid, and dies. Pretty little
Margarethe, now twŏ years old, is reared
in the cottage of Jost, a poor basket-
maker, on a barren moor, throu which,
at the opening of the story, a survêy is

being made under direction of Mr. Berger, whŏ is accompanied by his sŏn. The boy at ŏnce lŏves Margarethe, and becŏmes her friend. He visits her often, brings her books, and educates her. Thĕy gro up tŏgether and becŏme lŏvers. Herr Berger sees the danger of thĕir intimacy, for he wishes Leo tŏ marry an hĕiress for the benefit of the firm. He sends him tŏ England tŏ learn the trade of a merchant, and in the belief that a few years' stay thêre wil thŏroly cure him of his passion, promises him that if, when he shal return tŏ Germany, he persists in marrying the girl, the paternal sanction shal not be withheld. Leo cŏmes back a thŏro Merchant, but is more anxious than ever tŏ wed Margarethe." [Arcadian. **2479**
NOVEL WITH TWO HEROES [**Leipzig.**] = No. 506.

NUN (The), by K: SPINDLER: N.-Y., *Dewitt*, 1850. **2480**

"O THOU, MY AUSTRIA." [by "OSSIP SCHUBIN," i.e., Lola Kirschner: *Lippincott*, 1890] " We ar carried throu the diary of a young girl, as lively in its way as the ' Neuvaine de Colette ' [No. 2267]; we ar introduced tŏ a sentimental irish gŏverness wĕaring red stockings and flourishing a Gamp umbrella, and tŏ a globe-trotting uncle whŏse ambition it is tŏ be the austrian Canning, and whŏ imports ' his clothes, his soap and his political ideas,' from England. Then folloes the pretty lŏve-affair of the principals Idena and her cousin Harry, interwoven and sŏmewhat overclouded by the tiresome tragedy of a man whŏ has married a rich parvenue tŏ repair his fortunes and commits suicide in consequence. Clever as the story is, ŏne's attention, toard the close, cannot resist straining in vain conjecture as tŏ the meaning of the title in its relation to the book." [Critic. **2481**

ODDS AGAINST HER = No 873.

OLD COUNTESS (The). [by BERNARD HÖFER: *Lippincott*, 1870.] " I all his novels ar as good as this, we hopĕ Bernard Höfer's name wil becŏme familiar one. ' The Old Countess ' is ₓ story of hi life, involving a grave famil) mystery and divers lŏve affairs, whicl ar handled with pleasing effect. Thĕ action is lively, and each ŏne of thĕ characters makes a claim upon the reader's interest. Thêre is no moralizing oi philosophizing in the book, not a tediou page ; the author's single purpos seem: tŏ hav been tŏ make an interesting stor) of natural elements, and without the aic of extravagance or sensationalism.' [Boston " Lit. World." **2482**

OLD MAM'SELL'S SECRET = No 877.

OLD MONASTERY (The). [by F: W: HACKLÄNDER: *Bentley*, 1862. " The ' old monastery ' is not a monastery after all; but a place which ŏncĕ was monastic, and is now inhabited b) washerwomen, receivers of stolen property, etc. Of the personages whŏse good or evil fortunes fil the drama, thĕ most interesting is the heroin, Maria, ar orphan, the dauter of a female lamplighter in a german town and an italiar peer. She is thrŏn upon the mercy oi the world, and the world, personified b) a most sedate and admirable laundress. takes charge of her, and, faithful tŏ hei mother's wish, educates the child for thĕ ballet. Her vicissitudes ar narratec with pleasant simplicity. Other wise the book is entertaining enuf. I is lively, cleverly written, and in sŏmĕ respects, the scheme of the romance i: originally conçeivd." [Leader. **2483**

OLD STORY OF MY FARMING DAYS (An) = No. 2509.

ON GUARD, by AUERBACH, in *Apple*

ton's, 19 june, 1875; also in *Modern Age*, jan., 1884. **2509 t**
ON THE HEIGHTS = No. 881.
ONE HUNDRED SHORT TALES, by CHRISTOPH VON SCHMID: London, 1852. **2484**
OPEN DOOR (The) [by BLANCHE WILLIS (HOWARD) TEUFFEL: *Houghton*, 1889.] "as a story, is very simple. A count meets an accident in early manhood, and becŏmes a cripple. The lady whŏ would probably hav married him is thenceforth the heârtless woman of the world. His mŏther is an old frump, whŏ lavishes all her tenderness on a lap-dog, and this lap-dog is thrust disagreeably upon ŏne at every turn in the story. The mŏther has a way of taking young girls as companions, expending her foolish fondness on them, and then tiring of them and thrŏing them aside. At last cŏmes along the 15th of them, a pure, hispirited girl, a baroness remotely connected with the family, whŏ refuses tŏ be a sycophant, and marches throu the story with uncompromising sturdiness dealing out truth on every hand. Early in the novel it is clear that the crippled count wil marry her, and the reader is not deceivd by the obstacles which spring up. The countess tries tŏ marry her to an officer, but she disdains him, and he sets about sedu̧çing the baroness' maid. Here cŏmes the ŏne notable passage in the book: the baroness at night goes tŏ an outcast's room, whither her silly maid has gŏne tŏ meet the officer, and has thêre a long intellectual and sentimental struggle with the outcast and the maid, finally winning the game. But the passage is ŏnly superficially strong; it is shŏy rather than genuin. Indeed, this is the term to be applied to the entire novel. The manner of the book is forced, exaggerated, with occasional brilliancy, but with the glitter of tin foil rather than of precious metal." [Atlantic.] — It "is bright and sufficiently readable, tho the interest nowhêre becŏmes so absorbing that the volume may not easily be laid down. A certain suspicion of dulness may be accounted for by the lac of actuality in the characters. The story treats of german life; but unlike Mr. Crawford's new book, which is german in its whole warp and woof [see No. 724] 'The Open Door' is not distinctively german at all. Thêre is no forêin bacground, no local color; and as all the lively dialog is carried on in english and american slang and idiom, it is a difficult matter tŏ catch the characteristic Teutonic tendency in any ŏne of the characters." [American. **2485**
OTTILIE = No. 855.
OTTILIE ASTER'S SILENCE ["Eine Lüge"), by IDA ( ) BOYED: N.-Y., *Bonner*, 1891. **2485 t**
OUR DOOR BELL, by "W. HEIMBURG," in *Cosmopol.*, dec., 1886. **2486**
OUR FRÄULEIN. [by W. H. WATTS: *Chapman*, 1877.] "A young english lady, reduced tŏ great difficulties by the death of her father, takes the management of the household of a certain german professor, and reduces tŏ order the chaos in which she first finds it involvd. Her last and grêatest victory is over the Professor himself, whŏ begins with the strongest and most obstinate prejudi̧çes against England and english women in particular, and ends by laying down his arms in a most ignominious subjection. . . . The story is fairly amusing, and the writer has evidently sŏme acquaintance with german life, tho he writes of a time now past, and indeed further away than the mere laps of time would shŏ, — the period of 1848. This suggests the interweaving of politics with the plot.

PARTNERS [by "E. WERNER," i. e..
E.. Bürstenbinder: *Remington*, 1892.]
"deals with the characters and
situations of which the author seems
particularly fond. We hav the usual
strông man, whŏ wins his wife by sheer
strength of wil in her ōn despite. The
partners ar the brothers Sandow, of whŏm
the elder is head of a mercantile house in
America, and the younger a journalist of
grêat brilliancy... They ar tŏ be partners
because the elder wishes his ward Jessie
Clifford tŏ marry the younger, whŏ is tŏ
cōme over and take a wife and a partnership. Miss Clifford's consent is deemed a
very unimportant thing by the elder Sandow, and the young lady shōs a helplessness which is surprising considering that
she is an American citizen with a large
fortune, and is nowise disposed tŏ be
handed over in a business transaction tŏ
Mr. Gustav Sandow. The journalist, however, is not only an Admirable Crichton,
but a fine fello, and has not cōme tŏ America on a fortune-hunting errand. His first
object is tŏ reconcile his brōther tŏ a dauter whŏm he has long refused tŏ recognize
for painful family reasons. This danter
he introduçes intŏ the house as a young
German in search of a place as a gōverness.
He tels Miss Clifford that he has a deep
plot tŏ carry throu, but tels her nothing as
tŏ its details. Hençe the inevitable misunderstandings and surprising situations.
The plot is further complicated by the
efforts of the younger brōther tŏ dissuade
the elder from mixing himself in a promising land swindle. All cōmes right at the
proper time. The hard man surrenders as
soon as his finêr feelings ar properly appealed tŏ, and the virtuous younger brōther
makes everybody else, and himself too,
happy and prosperous." [Saturday Review. **2489**

'Our Fräulein's' patron is a revolutionary thinker, and we hav a somewhat vague account of the Continental movement in that year of disturbance." [Spectator. **2487**

OVER YONDER [by " E. MARLITT " i. e., Eugenie John (†, 1887) : *Lippincott*, 1869.] "is simple and charming, and short enuf to make ōne quite regret its brevity." [Round Table. **2488**

OWL'S NEST = No. 888.

PARTNERS (Egoist), by "E. WERNER," London, *Remington*, 1882. **2489**

PARTY OF FOUR, by E. ECKSTEIN, in *Appleton's*, 21 Aug. 1875. **2490**

PASTOR'S DAUGHTER (The) = No. 2514. **[2491**

PENDULUM OF FORTUNE, by R. LINDAU, in *Lippincott's*, Nov., 1876.

PENNILESS GIRL (A). [" Ein Armes Mädchen " by " W. HEIMBURG," i. e., Bertha Behrens : *Lippincott*, 1884.] " When a german novel is at all good, it is generally very good. Thêre is a simplicity about it, a tenderness, a warmth and radiance of feeling, a familiarity with and fondness for nature, a kindly humor, a bias toard the domestic virtues, and a vindication of truth, honor, and fidelity, which combine intŏ an unusual charm. This story may be read with affectionate interest in the pathetic childhood and youth of Elsie, with heârty sympathy for the suit of her manly lŏver, Bernardi, with lively concern for her deliverance from the bonds which family pride undertakes tŏ weav about her, and with joyful congratulations over the Providence which finally unites twŏ deserving heârts and lives in ŏne. . . . . Altogether a sweet and rewarding story is this of *A Penniless Girl*, full of the briter phases of german life, picturesque with castles, spears, Moravian sisters, and grim old ânts, and alive with the humanities, chastened

with suffering, and sanctified by self-denial." [Boston " Lit. World."] — " We hav becŏme so accustomed tŏ the energetic modern heroin, eager tŏ be a lawyer, physician, author, at least a professor, anything rather than be condemned tŏ the stagnation of the life of a conventional young woman, that Elsie, the ' penniless girl ' is refreshing tŏ us by way of contrast. The accident of her sex cuts her off from the possibility of inheriting the family prosperity, and the ' gray set of life and apathetic end ' of a governess is appointed tŏ be her destiny. Elsie, however, lŏves the freedom and ease of every-day existence; she lŏves society, she is quickened by all a young girl's hopes of a happy marriage. How at first the life of a happy woman seems tŏ hav been denied her, — her temptations tŏ accept grêat wealth without lŏve, — her fidelity tŏ the promptings of her heârt, — all this makes a pleasing and excellent story." [Lippincott's.

—, SAME (" A Penniless Orphan "), *Munro*, 1887. **2492**

—, SAME (" Elsie "), *Rand*, 1891.

PICKED UP [by H. SCHOBERT : *Lippincott*, 1888.] " is undeniably interesting, tho for american taste it may be too sentimental and overburdened with plot. It narrates the history of a waif whŏ prŏves tŏ be the abandoned child of a noble family, and whŏ in the end cŏmes triumphantly tŏ her ŏn." [American. **2493**

PICTURES OF LIFE, by A. STIFTER : London, *Parlor Library*, 1852. **2494**

PLUMWOMAN (The) and CHILD WITH THREE MOTHERS, by G. NIERITZ : N.-Y., *Scribner*, 1854. **2495**

POOR MARGARET, in *Democratic Review*, dec., 1842, and in *Tales* transl. by Greene. **2496**

PRIEST'S COAT (The) by A. von Bulow, in *Amer. Keepsake*, 1851. **2497**

PRINCE OTTO = No. 901.

PRINCESS EVA, by " C. Helm," Boston, *Lee*, 1887. **2497 h**

PROBLEMATIC CHARACTERS [by F: Spielhagen: N.-Y., *Leypoldt*, 1869.] is "a story of dramatic incident, of continuous interest, and displaying a humorous, as wel as keen appreciation of character. One might think that nŏthing less than a miracle could keep the german novelist out of that slŏū of mysticism and metafysics in which he usually lŏscs himself, or, at least, becŏmes unintelligible; but the intervention of humor has, in this case, prŏved as efficacious. . . The author seems tŏ hav nothing tŏ dŏ with the immorality with which certain lŏve passages may justly be charged. One feels that the persons tŏ whom he is introduced ar flesh and blood — not mere heroes and heroins, shaped in a very uncommon, if not unearthly mold. Thêre is tangibility about them, with all their virtues and vices — qualities which ar continually puzzling ŏne tŏ determin on which side of the ' fence ' tŏ put them. The plot is elaborated skilfully and artistically, and the interest is not for a moment allowed tŏ fag. Perhaps the final dénoûment is sŏmewhat vague and unsatisfactory ; and the whole book leaves a slightly bitter taste." [Overland.] — " The scene is laid in a prussian manor-house, the time is that immediately preceding the Revolution of 1848, whŏse oppressiv, electric atmosphere pervades the entire story. Every character is unnatural and stilted, and thêir language is as artificial as their ideas. Disquiet harasses all spirits, evincing itself amŏng the aristocracy in reclessness, and amŏng the burgers and thinkers in utopian or despairing conclu-

sions. The heroes ar of course, problematic characters. It is significant of german life that thêy ar both connected with philosophy, the ŏne as a student, the ŏther as a professor, of Nihilism. This novel, published in 1861, was succeeded by a continuation, ' Durch Nacht Zum Licht,' which, like all continuations, is not so good as its forerunner, but which possesses the curious attraction which renders all Spielhagen's novels, when ŏnce begun, so hard tŏ lay aside. The tenor of the books is similar — they depict the impassible barrier which exists between the aristocracy and the middle class in Germany." [Spectator. **2498**

PROFESSOR'S WIFE (The) [by Berthold Auerbach (†, 1882) : Oxford, *Parker*, 1850.] " is charming. The author endeavors tŏ set off nature against conventional civilisation, and he has succeeded in presenting the world with a composition so truly poetical and original that it is difficult tŏ imagine a reader w hŏm it would not please. Auerbach has in this story got the mastery over his favorit weakness of laying too much stress upon subordinate events and sacrifiçing the necessary perspectiv ; but has, on the contrary, grouped the incidents in a manner setting them off to the grêatest advantage " [Englishwoman's Domestic Mag.] For continuation see No. 2458. **2499**

PYTHIA'S PUPILS [by " Eva Hartner," i. e., Emma von Twardowska (1845–89) : *Routledge*, 1888.] " is a capital story about 4 german girls whŏ had a little cooking school, with the august ' Pythia' for instructor. . .. The cookery forms, however, but a small part of the book. The daily home life of the several households is portrayed, and an insight given intŏ pleasant interiors in a german city. Dr. Stein-

PROUD MAISIE [by BERTHA THOMAS: *Low*, 1877.] "is the autobiography of a fascinating, wayward, lŏvable young lady, whŭ relates in these volumes the story of her life's lŏve. As gay and light-heârted at the beginning of the story as the original of the ballad whŏse name she bĕars, her ultimate fate prŏves more fortunate than that predicted for Scott's heroin. The plot is original in its development, for we ar transported from humdrum, respectable english surroundings tŏ an unconstrained art-student existence in Ludwigsheim [**Munich**]. The heroin portrays herself with ability, her character stands out firmly, and her individuality is wel sustained. The writing of the book is excellent. It is easy and pleasant to perceive that it is the work of a cultivated person: this is shŏn by the references to various literatures; and the thŏro acquaintance with music and art betrayed. The book abounds in touches of quaint humor as wel as in epigrammatic writing. 'Proud Maisie' is a readable, clever novel, which keeps the reader's attention fixed tŏ its close." [Athenæum. **519 k**

QUEEN OF CURDS AND CREAM
(A). [by DOROTHEA GERARD: *Appleton*, 1892] "Glockenau, an Austrian
mountain village, and afterwards London, ar the scenes. In the first, Count
Emil Eldringen dies, leaving his
dauter Ulrica penniless and friendless; a marriage beneath his rank and
a life of dissipation had so estranged
the count's relativs, that nothing was
left tŏ Ulrica but tŏ work with her
hands like a peasant. At Glockenau,
after many vicissitudes, she earns a
living for herself in a large dairy farm.
Here an English cousin discŏvers her,
a lŏve-story of varied interests folloing. Ulrica believes herself the hêir
of a large fortune, and figures for a
time as a fine lady of London." [Pub-
lishers' Weekly.   **519 r**

mann, the father of Dora, gardian of Lotta, and true friend of faithful Eva and Marie, is the typical good physician, always delightful tŏ meet. He makes the way smooth for his sensitiv wife, is the wise adviser for Lotta's nervous mŏther, and almost cures Marie's irascible soldier father. Sŏme of the young people hav serious faults and make mistakes, but they ar teachable and sound at core. Thêre ar mild mysteries and pretty little romances, lŏves, an attempt at authorship, unselfish living, patient waiting, and final reward. Pleasingly written, vivacious, full of the incidents which might naturally happen in so many lives, kindly in spirit, commendable in its tone, it is an excellent book." [Boston "Lit. World." **2500**

QUEEN (A) [N. Y., *Dutton*, 1864.] "is a pleasant story, shŏing how a little girl, whŏ was ever dreaming she was a queen, became a queenly woman. It is very pleasant as shŏing the ways of german children; and its pure lessons of kindness tŏ all make it a gem of a book. It is written with simple, childlike feeling." [Church Monthly. **2501**

QUICKSANDS = No. 909.

QUIET HOUSE (The), in *Ladies' Companion*, oct.–dec. 1852. **2502**

QUISISANA, by F: SPIELHAGEN: N.-Y., *Munro*, 1892. **2503**

QUITS, by TAUTPHÖUS [Bavaria] = No. 521.

RANK AND NOBILITY, by "JEANNE MARIE," in *National Era*, 27 may tŏ 19 aug. 1852. **2504**

RAYMOND'S ATONEMENT = Nos. 600, 683.

REATA = No. 914.

RECTOR OF ST. LUKE'S (The) [by MARIE BERNHARD, N. Y., *Worthington*, 1891.] "is a very unusual and a most lŏvely story. A young girl, beau-tiful and attractiv from every point of

vue, is the idol of the town. The officers of the regiment ar all in lŏve with her, but théy ar distanced by the rector and an artist, both of whŏm ar devoted tŏ the girl. The artist wins her at last, and he and she ar perfectly happy in their betrothal, tho thêre is sŏmething strange about the man which makes everyŏne distrust him and doubt his ability tŏ make his sweethéart happy throu life. The facts of his early life cŏme intŏ the possession of the rector in the most curious manner, and he generously resolvs tŏ say nŏthing about them. Acçident, however, reveals tŏ the artist the fact that his history is knŏn tŏ his rival, and he sees that it wil be impossible for him tŏ marry Annie with this knoledge hanging over him. He leavs without seeing her and writes her that thêre is sŏmething which he can never overcŏme, and that she wil not see him again. Shortly afterwards he dies. It is ŏnly a question of time then as tŏ when the rector shal win the girl for himself. The charm of the story is in the telling, and in the deep interest which the characters, ŏne and all, inspire. The exquisit daintiness of the girl around whŏm the story revolvs; the unusual charm of her elder and invalid sister with whŏm she livs; the beauty and harmony in the development of the rector's character; and the wonderful fascination of the artist, notwithstanding the cloud which seems from the first tŏ envelope him, combine tŏ produce that most uncommon thing — a really charming german novel." [Critic. **2506**

RIVEN BONDS = No. 2348.

ROMANCE OF A GERMAN COURT = No. 923.

ROMANCE OF THE CANONESS (The) [by PAUL HEYSE: *Appleton*, 1887.] "is devoted tŏ descriptions of life in those religious houses, the members of which liv in common, but without taking monastic vows. It is intelligent, even able, but heavy." [American.] — "Romantic enuf, and of course interesting; the situations ar not such as the realists would devise, and a melancholy air pervades the whole as if the narrator did not quite expect tŏ be believed; but it is conceived with poetic thôt, and taken as a lyric of the stage is not without beauty." [Atlantic. **2507**

ROSE OF TANNENBURG, by CHRISTOPH VON SCHMID (1768–1854) Phil'a, *Cunningham*, 1848. **2508**
ROSE OF THE PARSONAGE [by Ro. GISEKE : N.-Y., *Parry*, 1854. **2509**
SACRED VOWS = No. 594.
SACRISTAN'S HOUSEHOLD (The) [by F. . ELINOR (TIERNAN) TROLLOPE : London, *Virtue*, 1869.] "The fidelity tŏ nature with which all these scenes ar sketched, the details of life which ar skilfully woven in, the picturesque bits of architecture, and the descriptions of woodland scenery which form the setting of the story, recommend it tŏ all whŏ hav livd in Germany. It is hardly a fair ground of objection tŏ most of the characters that they ar typical rather than individual. The military men, the wild-haired professors, the stout and plaçid matrons, and the romantic old maids, whŏ form the cream of **Detmold** society,— the small tradesmen and farmers whŏ hold thêir social gatherings at the Pied Lamb, — ar the familiar figures of german life rather than the persons of this particular story. But if we look at the characters which hav been worked out with grêater pains, and notably at the lawyer, we see that thêre is no lac of dramatic force or of life-like painting.
. .. It is for thêir sakes in the first instance that we read the book with such pleasure. As each of them develops new attractions, we rejoice in thinking

that each is becŏming more worthy of the ŏther; and when they confess their mutual lŏve, in a delicious scene of playful happiness, we join with them in forgetting all the ŏther persons of the story. But, after all, the ŏther persons ar not tŏ be forgotten. The plot may be put aside, yet in the course of working it out the author brings us in contact with so much which is pleasant, the chief characters ar so perfect, the minor characters bêar marks of such care and observation, that we can forgiv any of those failings at which we hav hinted, and can ask ŏur readers tŏ take the book on its merits." [Athenæum.] — "In these german stories thêre is always a certain freshness, coming, in the case of translations, in great part from the kind of thôt and speculation with which they ar occupied; and in the case of studies made by foreiners, from the novelty of the manners, the household customs, and the ways of looking at life which thêy describe, which generally makes them interesting. To ŏur taste, ŏne of the pleasantest of the latter class is the ' Sacristan's Household.' It is written with a grêat deal of grace and spirit, the lŏve story is prettily told, the characters ar sketched in cleverly, and the life of a village [?] with its homely heartiness, its petty economies, and its small punctilios, is described in a way which makes the reader understand how carefully the author has studied it, and how thŏroly she has enjoyed it. Then, too, thêre is no dul or irrelevant matter tŏ be skipped; and altho the characters ar not spécially remarkable for originality, nor analyzed with any grêat subtlety, they hav a certain vigor and vitality, and ar uniformly interesting." [Nation. **2510**
ST. MICHAEL [by " E. WERNER," i. e., E.. Bürstenbinder: *Lippincott*, 1887.] is " a strong, enjoyable story

of northern Germany, with a hero of the sort which old-fashioned novel-readers have a partiality for, — ŏne whŏ has been defrauded of his rights in his youth, but rises superior tŏ poverty and il usage and eŏmes to a noble manhood, brave, honorable, and true; asserts him-self, and wins the girl he lŏves. What better hero could ŏne ask than the con-quering Michael Rodenberg? Hans, the artist, is as good in his way, while the old genealogist, Gerlinda, whŏ repeats genealogy like a parrot, is delightful; and the scenes whêre Hans gets the advantage of his father, and whêre the twŏ fathers ar made tŏ accept the situa-tion, ar capital bits of light and whole-sŏme comedy." [Boston "Lit. World."] — "The story is interesting, the plot consistent and wel developed, the dialog natural, and the characterization dis-tinctly good. Hanty, intolerant, domi-neering, but not hard-hearted Count Steinrück and his unacknoledged grand-sŏn, Michael Rodenberg, ar the protag-onists representing intolerable pride and passionate determination conflicting in an eager life drama. The author has sŏt tŏ delineate the power of con-sanguinity — how il-treatment, indiffer-ence, neglect, absençe, and a hundred other ils of life ar incapable of arrest-ing the manifestation of the charac-teristics of a dominant race. By slo degrees Michael Rodenberg forces his way in the world, under the very eyes of his antagonistic grandfather; and in the end he cŏmes to his ŏn again (and anŏther's also) and marries his bẹautiful cousin. A skilful plot has been woven for the evolution of this motiv." [Acad-emy.

—, SAME (" Her Son "), *Bentley*, 1887.   **2511**

SCHLOSS AND TOWN = see No. 2354.

SCULPTOR OF THE BLACK FOREST (The) by SOUVESTRE, in *Southern Lit. Mes.*, Dec., 1854. **2512**

SECOND WIFE (The) [by " E. MARLITT," i. e., Eugenie John (†, 1887) : *Lippincott*, 1874; *Bentley*, 1875.] " is a bright, spirited novel, much more interesting than most German works of fiction, which indeed ar generally dis-tasteful tŏ us, with thêir mixture of silly sentiment and commonness of life and manners, and their resemblance tŏ the lordly-baron and faithful-retainer school which vanished long ago. In this instance, tho there are a rêgning duchess and a ' hof-Marschal,' tho titled people abound, and the flavor of Pumpernickel is everywhêre, stil thêre is a strong human interest in the story, and at least ŏne striking character, that of Frau Lohn. The Second Wife is introduced in the position of a victim, but she makes her exit with flying colors, having conquered her enemies, routed her rival, and wŏn the true lŏve and respect of her husband with a woman's noblest weapons, lŏve, patiençe, gentle-ness, and self-sacrifice; his motiv for marrying her is so unworthy that Baron Mainau inspires us with anything but esteem and interest. A scene in which the baron presents his wife tŏ the duchess, — whŏ has a pleasing conviction that he is about tŏ desert the baroness for her sake, — and utterly disconcerts the royal coquette by the announcement that the contemplated journey is tŏ be made 'à deux' — is very effectiv. The translator [Wood] has dŏne her part ad-mirably; her rendering of the story has no hitches, no blunders, no rawness in it." [Spectator.] — "We hav all the old char-acters with which the ' Old Mam'selle's Secret' [No. 877] and the author's suc-ceeding tales hav familiarized us. Thêre is the wel-knŏn hero, gloomy, sardonic, ŏn cousin tŏ the Stranger, with a tinge of commonplace, not tŏ s.ıy vulgar, scepticism. Like the professor in the 'Old Mam'selle' and the subsequent heroes, he continually poses with bitter smiles and folded arms. He indulges in alternate infinities and worlds of scorn. His passion is revealed by a quite unnecessary intensification of his usual exceedingly bad manners, and his kindness finds expression, according tŏ the time-honored tradition of this family of creations, in increased rudeness and brusqueness. And in spite of his lofty character and spirit, he often finds it necessary, in keeping with the dramatic habits of his kind, tŏ lurk in convenient spots for the purpos of over-hearing private conversations. The heroin is not less like her predecessors, nor less unlike any proper flesh-and-blood heroin. She is ŏne of those personages grĕatly affected by the purvĕyors tŏ the Bowery stage, with supernatural clearness of vision for misty plots and deeply-hidden depths of subtle villany, united tŏ the most extraordinary stupidity as tŏ what is going on under her nose. . . . If the author, however much passing the limits of probability, had given us a number of noble, ideal characters, much might be forgiven the staginess and unreality of her portraiture. But these characters, Raoul von Mainau, Liana, and the rest, ar not noble, and ar very unlŏvely. Thĕir sentiments, when thĕy hav not the false ring of those of a man whŏ is perpetually calculating thĕir effect, ar absurd, vulgar, and tiresom, and thĕir actions, instead of being inspiriting, ar, for the most part, il-brĕd or positivly brutal." [Arcadian. See also No. 936. **2513**

SALTMINER OF HALLSTADT, by A: Silberstein: in *Ladies' Repository*, apr. 1870. **2514**

SEED TIME AND HARVEST

["Ut mine Strombid") by Fritz Reuter (†, 1874): Boston, *Littell & Co.*, 1871.] "Mr. Reuter tels his story with his pipe in his mouth, and his slippers on, his feet on the fender, and the fog outside. The business of life is over, and thĕre is no need for hurry. . . To those whŏ hav leisure tŏ enjoy it, we can promis a quiet treat of an uncommon kind; thĕy shal be made free of half-a-dozen households, and breathe an air of homeliness and simpliçity which shal for the moment carry them out of the tawdry civilisation in which we liv. . . . But no ŏne must imagin this is a story all hŏney-sweet of pleasant parsonages and blooming girls, — far from it. Thĕre is enuf of sorro, and suffering, and sin." [Spectator.

—, SAME (An Old Story of my. Farming Days), *Low*, 1879. **2516**

SEVERA [by "E. Hartner," i. e., Emma von Twardowska, 1845–89: *Lippincott*, 1881.] The story is of "a man deserted by his betrothed, living to see her again, with her child, Severa, by her side; and waiting for Severa tŏ gro up tŏ take the place which the mŏther was tŏ hav had, but which in a moment of infatuation she had abandoned. Such an experience is ŏne of suffering, and the cŏlors in this relation of it ar grave and subdued." [Boston "Lit. World." **2517**

SHE FELL IN LOVE WITH HER HUSBAND = No. 2416.

SHORT STORIES, by "W. Heimburg:" N. Y., *Worthington*, 1890. **2518**

SILENT LOVE = No. 2459.

SISTER'S LOVE (A) = No. 2426.

SKELETON IN THE HOUSE (The) [by F: Spielhagen: N. Y., *Harlan*, 1881.] "is scarcely more than a sketch, but it is admirably told. . . . Every stroke tels, and ŏne hardly knoes which tŏ like best: a plot ingeniously contrived tŏ rivet the reader's attention yet giv him a heârty lâf at the end, or the portraiture of character, which is exceedingly clever, and full of hints for the wise. The moral of the story is that husbands may dare tŏ confess anything 'down tŏ the dot on the i,' tŏ a wife whŏ lōves them; but let them beware of her learning what they hav tŏ confess from the lips of anyŏne else!" [Critic. **2519**

SMOKE, by Turgénief = No. 948 **[Baden].**

SOUGHT AND FOUND. [by "Golo Raimund," i. e., Bertha (Heyn) Frederich (†, 188) : N.-Y., *Funk*, 1888.] "A young German returns tŏ his nativ land from America, wealthy, of course, and in the ruins of his hotel, burned on the night of his arrival, finds the charred leaves of a girl's diary. The diary causes him tŏ wish tŏ find its author, for it is a charming record of a fine character, amid grievous disappointments and misfortunes. He seeks his relativs, and the rest of the narrativ is taken up with the strife between the rival claims of a pretty but designing cousin and a maiden not fair tŏ see but of much modest merit. Modest merit wins, and of course prŏves tŏ be the unknōn writer of the diary, and the story ends with virtue triumphant. Slight enuf for a framework, but sufficient tŏ carry much of the simple and pleasing narrativ often found in german tales." [Overland. **2520**

SPELL OF HOME = No. 2429.

SPRING FLOODS, by Turgénief, ⟂ No. 952.

STORY FOR CHRISTMAS (A) in Graham's Mag., Jan., 1852. **2521**

STORY OF A CLERGYMAN'S DAUGHTER by "W. Heimburg:" N. Y., *Munro*, 1889.

—, SAME ("A pastor's Daughter"), N. Y., *Worthington*, 1890.

—, SAME ("Martha"), N.-Y., *Street*, 1891. **2522**

STORY OF A GENIUS, by "Ossip Schubin," in *Modern Age*, Mar.-Apr., 1884. **2523**

STORY OF A MILLIONAIRE (The). [by "L.. Mühlbach," i. e., Clara (Müller) Mundt (†, 188): *Appleton*, 1872.] "Mrs. Mühlbach, having eŏme tŏ the end of her historical novels, which threw a dark vail of romance over the dry records of history, has written a social novel. Its merit is about that of the works of Mrs. Caroline Lee Hentz, Mrs. Holmes, etc., in this country; so we may suppose it wil be ōne of the most popular works of the year. In Germany Mrs. Mühlbach holds about the same position as a writer that these ladies dŏ here." [Nation. **2521**

STRANGE FOLK. [by Hermann Oelschalager : *Longman*, 1872.] "A pleasant dreaminess pervades 'Strange Folk.' Authors, actresses, and monks ar its chief characters. We alternately exchange the stage for the cloister, and step from the greenroom tŏ the greenwood. Dr. Anselmus is an author whŏ suffers from extreme nervousness. The least noise prevents him from writing. He flies from home with his nĭece tŏ a little town in **Franken.** He finds a house thêre beautifully situated. Everything is charming. His book progresses. He feels the inspiration of the scenery. Summer cōmes. The grass in the meadōs changes from its varying shades of green tŏ its last purple tints. From that moment thêre is no more rest for the doctor. From morn til night sounds the eternal sharpening of the scythes. He flies from his new quarters tŏ the Convent of the 'Fifteen Saints.' His nîece, disguised as a student, aecompanies him as secretary. Here the real story begins. Of the characters, that of the Doctor is, perhaps, the best drawn. Marion is more interesting and less vulgar than most actresses ar. Dr. Breitman is ŏne of those odious hangers-on tŏ be found at every theatre, whŏ sponge upon every ŏne alike. We fancy however that Dora's unconventional habits may prŏve sŏme bar to the popularity of the story." [Westminster.] — "The story is bily amusing. . . . For a time, uncle and niece liv quietly enuf in the monastery, and the romance of the 13th century goes on apace. Dr. Anselmus discŏvers a set of old chessmen, which must date from the time of the Crusades, while Dora becŏmes acquainted with a novîçe, whŏ tels her the history of his early life, and makes an impression on her heârt. Before very long, Dr. Anselmus is roused from his pleasant dream by discŏvering that the novîçe and his niece ar in lŏve, and that the antiquity of the treasured set of chessmen is a delusion. One morning the novîçe calmly walks out of the monastery in the doctor's clothes, as the ŏnly way of bidding farewell tŏ the plaçe without causing an open scandal. The Doctor is furious at this unauthorized use of his garments, and at the relations which hav sprung up between the twŏ young people, but in time he relents, and they ar happy." [Athenæum.] Compare plot of No. 2576. **2522**

STRANGE HEART (A) by HEYSE, in *Cosmopolitan*, Apr., 1886. **2523**

STRUGGLE FOR EXISTENCE (The). [by "ROBERT BYR," i. e., Robert v. Bayer: Chicago(?), *McKinney*, 1874.] "Translations of recent german novels ar chiefly of importance as shŏing how hard put tŏ it for entertainment the

reading public is. Almost without exception they ar dul with a deadly dulnes, considered as stories, and tŏ that thêy add the dulness of the lofty platitudes and long winded abstractions which somehow hav such a charm for the teutonic mind. . . . The book is a thing tŏ be delivered from, but many good souls wil devoutly go throu it, and fancy they ar being amused and ar besides that lîstening tŏ numerous pregnant truths." [Nation. **2525**

SUCCESS = No. 2416.

SUPERFLUITIES OF LIFE, by L: TIECK: in *Blackwood's*, Feb., 1845. [*So. Lit. Mes.*, Oct. 1845.] **2526**

SWALLOWS OF ST. JÜRGENS, by TH. STORM, in *Canadian Monthly*, oct., 1872. **2527**

TALE OF AN OLD CASTLE (A) = No. 2457.

TALES, by TH. KÖRNER, London, 1845. **2528**

TALES by PAUL HEYSE [*Appleton*, 1876.] contains *Count Ernest's Home, The Dead Lake* [also No. 669], *The Fury* (*L'Arrabiata*), *Judith Stern.* **2529**

TALES FROM THE GERMAN: London, *Emily Faithful*, 1863. **2530**

TALES FROM THE GERMAN [by MUSÆUS, SCHILLER, KLEIST, IMMERMANN, HOFFMANN, AND VAN DER VELDE] *Chapman*, 1844, see *FANCIFUL NOVELS*.

TEACHER OF THE VIOLIN (A) = No. 975.

TEMPTED OF THE DEVIL, by A: Becker: London, *A. Gardner*, 1888. **2531**

THEKLA [Vienna] = No. 980.

THROUGH NIGHT TO LIGHT, [by F: SPIELHAGEN: N.-Y., *Holt*, 1869.] See No. 2498. **2533**

TOO RICH. [by ADOLF STRECKFUSS; *Lippincott*, 1878.] "For ingenuity and complication, and for the ease

THREE SISTERS. [*Low*, 1884.]
"Any ŏne whŏ cares to follo the fortunes
of 3 brave Irish girls whŏ ar forced tŏ
support themselvs in a South German
'Residenz' can not fail tŏ be amused.
The Miss Denbighs hav a perfect genius
for making the best of most things, and
extracting the fun out of everything.
But besides the fun thêre ar glimpses
of genuin pathos, and Darry's fate
touches the reader very nearly . . .
That the author knoes german town life
wel, and is alive tŏ the opportunities it
presents for humorous description is
obvious. The book is, moreover, wel
written, and sŏme of the anecdotes ar
wel told." [Athenæum.   **541 p**

TREHERNE'S TEMPTATION. [by ALARIC CARR. *Smith*, 1883] The author has "set himself a very difficult task, and has performed it with skil and power. The story is full of interest from beginning tŏ end — the plot unusually good and thŏroly developed. It would be unfair tŏ the reader even tŏ hint at the unravelment of this romantic novel. One of the chief charms of the book is the description of easy Continental life; whether in Paris, or at Baden-Baden, the author is always equally at home, and evidently fond of his subject. The characters ar remarkably wel drawn, and distinctly defined — the Vicomte a most polished and perfeet specimen of a French noble. His very weaknesses ar charming. Our sympathies ar always with him, and with his nation because of him. The German element in the book is not the least agreeable feature of it. The very servants and dogs add their quota tŏ the enjoyment tŏ be derived from this most agreeable novel. We must not omit tŏ notice that thêre is a great deal of interesting talk about music." [Westminster. **545 h** with which its intricate knots ar untied by the natural development of the story, its plot would dŏ honor tŏ the masters of fiction, while the style has that transparent simpliçity and singular brilliancy which with sŏme french and german writers seem so natural a quality. The story opens in a capital, but is speedily transferred to a village in Tirol. Out of the chîef parties tŏ it, 3 pairs of lŏvers ar curiously evolvd, 2 of the 3 gentlemen being army officers. The first passages ar in the tone of a delightful light comedy, in which an old Uncle Balthasar is a most enlivening figure; but the action speedily takes on a graver character, and in the dismal ruins of Castle Reifenstein sweeps by the verge of a tragedy. The narrativ is compact; the people ar all of an interesting sort, even tŏ the rascal Bertram and the silly Nanette; and while thêre ar ŏne or twŏ glimpses of social impurity, the book is free as a whole from any taint. Its ingenuity wil baffle the best guessing as tŏ the issue and the freshness of its materials and beauty of thêir treatment wil awaken new sensations of pleasure even in the satiated novel-reader." [Boston " Lit. World." **2534**

TOWN STORIES, by Max Ring, London, 1853. **2535**

TRAGIC COMEDIANS = No. 985.

TREE IN THE ODENWALD (A) by O ː Roquette, in *Appleton's*, dec., 1880. **2536**

TRUDEL'S BALL, by Hans Hopfen, in *Masterpieces of German Fiction*, 70 p.

TRUE DAUGHTER OF HARTENSTEIN. [by E. Vely ː N.-Y., *Bonner*, 1892.] "The Castle of Hartenstein, in the Harz Mountains, was entailed; and as circumstances prevented Count Hartenstein from making provision for his ŏnly dauter, on his sudden death Hertha leaves home. Her story after this is

ŏne of romance, revelation, adventure and heroism." [Pub. Weekly. **2538**

TWIXT WIFE AND FATHERLAND [Tirol] = No. 546.

TWO BROTHERS (The) [Eine Familie aus der ersten Gesellschaft) by Mathilde (Beckmann) Raven ː *Bentley*, 1850.] " wil be welcŏme tŏ the many whŏ enjoyed ' The Initials' [No. 473]. Like that book, it contains a faithful picture of german domestic life. This time, moreover, it is a nativ whŏ has ' played the painter.' . Here the general animus is graver and bitterer — the tragedy is longer drawn. In both stories, the lŏve of appearance and establishment is shŏn as uppermost in a german woman's mind, tŏ a degree which wil shoc all whŏ hav given her a blank credit for simpliçity; but in ' The Two Brothers,' the foible is mingled with, and crossed by, class and caste prejudiçes of a force and a folly which justify the sharpest satire because they bring on the saddest consequences. . . So much for the moralists, and for the more superficial reader this tale will be found tŏ possess deep interest and welcŏme freshness. The characters ar capitally marked. We hav never met a better study of fine frivolity than in the person of the noble Mrs. Hattesohl. Poor Amelia, her victim, — and Steinheim her sŏn-in-law, chosen, but not choosing, — ar delicately and clearly drawn, without exaggeration. The good people, of course, ar more strained in thêir proceedings, and less palatable tŏ us." [Athenæum. **2539**

TWO DAUGHTERS OF ONE RACE = No. 993.

TWO DAYS IN THE COUNTRY, in *Leaflets of Memory*, 1848. **2540**

TWO SISTERS, by Heyse, in *Ladies' Repository*, july–aug., 1871. **2541**

TWOFOLD LIFE (A) [byW..(Birch)

UP THE RHINE [by T: Hood : London, 1840 ; N.-Y., *Putnam*. 1852] is "ōne of the pleasantest of Hood's many pleasant books. It is composed of letters, written by the various members of a family traveling up the Rhein, and conceived sōmewhat after the model of Humphrey Clinker. Hood's characters ar a hypochondriac, a wido, a dashing young man, and a maid servant; and it is in exhibiting the oddities and humors of these, rather than in any description of the scenery, that the charm of the book consists. The letters of Martha Penny, the servant, are the gems of the volume. Her spelling and grammar ar so felicitous in thêir infelicities, as tŏ amount tŏ a kind of genius; and the character is ŏne of the best which Hood ever delineated." [Graham's. **552 k** von Hillern: *Lippincott*, 1873.] "treats a great deal more of various forms of profligacy than ŏne cares tŏ see in a book intended for the family circle. He whŏ leads the twŏfold life is Heinrich von Ottmar, whŏ, when on his good behavior, calls himself Heinrich, but when, as is very often the case, he abandons himself tŏ evil ways, translates his name intŏ the more appropriate french, and as Henri imperils the virtue of every woman near him. In general, the german novelist is notorious for stuffing a suit of clothes with sŏme moral quality, and calling the product a human being, but here we hav the clothes — the richest purple court dress — stuffed with all sorts of immoralities, and the result is a bad and tedious representation of a bad life." [Nation. **2542**

ULRICH, by Ida (Hahn) Hahn: London, 1885. **2544**

UNDER THE STORK'S NEST = No. 997.

VAIN FOREBODINGS [by E. Oswald: *Lippincott*, 1885.] "is a domestic tale, quite void of sensationalism or unclean passion of any kind, but which steadily maintains a real if plaçid interest. The writer excels in descriptiv power, and we hav not lately encountered anything more genuinly delightful than the series of sweet pictures of country life tŏ be found in this book. 'Vain forebodings' is a capital summer book — and a good book to keep when summer is over." [The American.] — "It is a pleasant story, but containing a sŏmewhat surprising point: for the story is of a benevolent physician, whŏ first cured of insanity a youth upon whŏm this disaster had fallen, after he had long been predisposed tŏ it, and then allowed his dauter tŏ marry the patient, telling him that his forebodings of in-

sanity as his doom ar folly and his ser023ples about marrying unnecessary since all he needs tŏ be safe is tŏ exercise due mental self-control." [Overland. **2545**

VALENTINE THE COUNTESS [by "Carl Detlef," i. e., Klara Bauer (†, 188-): Phil'a, *Porter*, 1874.] "is a story of remarkable power. The heroin, a young girl of extraordinary beauty and intellectual charms, meets a lŏver, a young man whŏ reçiprocates and seems worthy of her affections. . . After a time she is induced tŏ marry a very wealthy but weak-minded nobleman, tŏ whom she prŏves a tender and faithful wife. . She is ŏne of the lŏveliest women in fiction, tho her look is always sad, and the reader's admiration for her is faithful. The general effect of the story is melancholy, but it is intensely interesting." [Boston "Lit. World." **2546**

VILLA ON RHINE = No. 2368.

VILLAGE ASTRONOMER = London, 1851. **2547**

VINETA = No. 1003.

VILLAGE COQUETTE (The) [by F: Spielhagen: *Chapman*, 1875.] "is a curious study of nature. The beautiful, almost soulless Bertha is brŏt tŏ sŏmething like human steadfastness and feeling by the savage disciplin which may be used tŏ subdue an animal. The cruel wound, which, at the bidding of a wise woman, the lŏver whŏm she is ready tŏ deceive inflicts upon her, works in a strange way on her limited nature, and she is vanquished by that which would hav roused a being of hier faculties intŏ irreconçilable hostility. The plot is wel worked out, and it is founded upon what may be a real, tho a rare phase of nature." [Spect. **2548**

VILLAGE TALES, by Auerbach = No. 2342.

VIOLETTA. [by Ursula Zöge von

MANTEUFFEL : *Lippincott*, 1886.] " The story runs smoothly, and thêre is the agreeable union of homeliness and military glitter which makes the atmosphere of most novels of upper-class german life. The õne unusual situation is the Baroness von Treffenbach's flight from her husband, and the unusualness is not in the fact, but in the underlying reasons. The woman, whŏ had been a grêat singer, was neither inconstant nor unlõving, but the moment came when the monotony of assured rank and respectability pressed on her so heavily that she had tŏ go. [Compare ' Klaus Bewer.'] Thêre is much tŏ be said in behalf of a woman in such a case, but the author has little more charity for the Baroness than has the world, which passes a superficial yet inexorable judgment on the deed. The younger Treffenbach is very wel characterized, but a prig of 30 years' standing is not tŏ be reformed in a day. Even during the hõneymoon he probably drew from his pocket a MS. nicely calculated properly tŏ repress the too volatil and light-hearted Violetta." [Nation. **2549**

VISIT TO THE LOCKUP, by E. ECKSTEIN, in Masterpieces of German Fiction. **2550**

VULTURE MAIDEN (The) = No. 1005.

WALDFRIED. [by BERTHOLD AUERBACH (†, 1882) : N.-Y., *Holt*, 1880.] " The more familiar the reader is with Germany, the more entertaining wil he find this novel; it has not life enuf tŏ force itself upon those whŏ hav not a tolerably keen interest in that country; indeed, such wil find it almost ·unreadable; and it demands a respectable knoledge of all which has been going on in Germany during the last 25 and· especially during the last 10 years, to be fully enjoyed. . Tŏ ôur think-

ing Waldfried is the best of the long novels. It is infinitly more natural than the Villa Eden, [No. 2368] or On the Heights, [No. 881] but it can. hardly be brŏt intŏ fair comparison with them. That many should find it intolerably dul is not surprising, for many readers require for their entertainment more than a disconnected assemblage of incidents; ŏthers, however, wil read it with sŏme pleasure, not with the keen enjoyment õne gets from the few masterpieces of fiction, but with the calm satisfaction õne has in reading about matters which turn out as õne would hav them." [Atlantic. **2552**

WALT & WULT, or the Twins [" Flegeljahre," 1805) by JEAN PAUL F : Richter : Boston, 1845, 2 v. **2553**

WANDA = No. 1006.

WAS SHE HIS WIFE? London, *Eden*, 1891 = No. 2451.

WEDDING UNDER GROUND, in *Brother Jonathan*, 20 aug., 1842. **2554**

WELLFIELDS (The) = No. 1010.

WHAT THE SPRING BROUGHT = No. 1011.

WHITE ROSE (The), in *Canadian Monthly*, Jan., 1874. **2555**

WHY DID HE NOT DIE ? [by ADELHEID VON VOLCKHAUSEN : *Lippincott*, 1871.] " has the same virtues and the same defects as its predecessors. It is sprightly and entertaining, full of all sorts of generous sentiments, and pervaded by that gentle, half-timid radicalism, which contents itself with aiming innocuous blõs at safe objects; at german protestant orthodoxy; at the hypocrisy of the ' rigidly righteous ; ' at the excesses of the agitators of the Woman Question; and at the arrogance of an aristocracy which yet must not resign too many of its pretensions if it would please its fair opponents. We recommend the book tŏ everybody

WHEN ALL WAS YOUNG. [by
CECIL CLARK : London *Stock*, 1885] "is
a very innocent and tender little lŏve
story.   A lōvelorn damsel, dwelling in
Saxon Switzerland, encloses in a
tin canister a despairing letter tŏ her
lŏver, entreating him tŏ cōme bac tŏ her.
This canister she sends floating down the
Elbe, and it is fished up by sōme English
children.   Thêir widqed mōther determins tŏ trace the writer, and bring about
a reconciliation between the lōvers.
In carrying out this purpos, she accidentally falls in with an old friend and
admirer, whŏ co-operates with her so
ardently and effectually, that not ōne,
but twŏ happy marriages ar brŏt aboqt
by the old canister." [Westmin. **558 p**

in search of amusing reading." [Nation. **2556**

WHY FRAU FROHMANN RAISED HER PRICES. [by ANTHONY TROLLOPE (†, 1882): London, *Isbister*, 1882.] " The old hostess of the Brunnenthal, anxious tŏ entertain the old customers of the Peacock at the old rates, ịs driven ' by the cheapness of money,' tŏ raise her prices. The perplexities and mortifications of good Frau Frohmann, whŏ is tormented by her advisers, by her old-world honesty, and by the march of time, ar very wel handled, while the woodland setting of the Tirolese inn makes a pretty picture. ' *The Lady of Launay* ' is a wel-told little. domestic tale of the struggles of an old lady tŏ prevent the union, on hi grounds of family polity, of her sŏn and an adopted dauter whom she dearly loves." [Athenæum. **2557**

WIFE–HUNTER (The), by KAROLINE (VON GREINER) PICHLER : in Omnibus, vol. III., N.-Y., 1844. **2558**

WIFE TO ORDER = No. 1016.

WILD ROSE OF GROSS-STAUFFEN (The), [by NATALY VON ECHSTRUTH : N.-Y., *Worthington*, 1891.] " is ŏne of those novels, made up of an unsophisticated heroin, a too-sophisticated hero, a wicked princess, an injured duchess, hard-hearted cŏurt ladies, and court gentlemen of all degrees of worthlessness. All virtuous persons ar rewarded, and all the bad perish miserably. Thêre is even an element of novelty in this book, in the transformation of the hero by various afflictions intŏ a pattern of virtue. But all such books hav for their major premis a social order in which the regard of a prince is the biest prize a man can win, and in which a woman's sole pro-

fessịon is tŏ be married." [Commonwealth. **2559**

WILHELM MEISTER = No. 1017.

WILL (The) = No. 1018.

WON [**Hamburg**] = No. 563.

WOODCUTTER (The) by C. (v. G.) PICHLER, in *Arthur's Mag.*, Jan., 1845. **2560**

WOODLAND TALES [by JULIUS STINDE : London, *Whittaker*, 1887.] " ar 6 quiet stories. Dr. Stinde here shŏs himself tŏ hav the imagination of a poet ; the romantic element which runs throu the whole volume is made distinctly prominent ; and the treatment is always delicate and discerning. In '*Aunt Juliana* ' we hav unfolded before us the heârt history of a gentlewoman whŏ is lŏved by the count, altho he marries anŏther, and whŏ, lŏving him in return, altho she pities his weakness, ' found her happiness in making the happiness of others.' ' *His Stupid Wife* ' is the story of a marital misunderstanding, and how it was remedied ; ' *Brother Johannes* ' relates the fate of a mŏnk falsely suspected of crime and sustained by the affection of a woman whŏ strives tŏ save him by declaring herself guilty ; ' *Three Times Ten Years* ' is the story of an artist fallen from his youthful ideals by pride and thirst for wealth, but won bac to the road of truth throu lŏve ; in ' *Bello* ' is depicted the life of a noble mind outlawed by conventional prejudiçes, and driven tŏ destruction ; and ' *Princess Goldenhair* ' is a dainty idyl of youth and youthful dreams." [Boston " Lit. World." **2561**

YOUNG WIDOW OF BREMEN, in *Albion*, 22 Sept., 1832. **2562**

YOUNGEST BROTHER, by E. WICHERT : Chicago, *Laird*, 1891. **2563**

PRICE: ONE COPY, ♦ .25; TWO COPIES, ♦ .37; THREE, ♦ .50; FOUR, ♦ .66; FIVE, ♦ .60; TEN, ♦1.25; FIFTEEN, ♦1.70,

A

DESCRIPTIVE LIST

OF

NOVELS AND TALES

DEALING WITH

LIFE IN ITALY.

COMPILED BY
W: M. GRISWOLD.

CAMBRIDGE, MASS.:
W: M. GRISWOLD, PUBLISHER.
1892.

[*From the "School Bulletin," Aug.*, 1892.]

We hope teachers will not fail tŏ recognize the work W. M. Griswold is dŏing in his classified bibliography. He sends us a DESCRIPTIVE LIST OF NOVELS AND TALES DEALING WITH LIFE IN FRANCE (Cambridge, Mass., 1892, 8vo, pp. 94, $1.00), which is of immediate practical use tŏ the teacher of French history as well as of French literature.

[*From the "Central Christian Advocate."*]

Mr. Griswold has dŏne an excellent work, which will be appreciated by all librarians, and by many people of cultivated taste whŏ wish tŏ get on the track of the best French fiction, or at least tŏ secure sŏme guidance and information in regard tŏ its qualities and characteristics. His former "lists" have dealt with American City and Country Life, with Life in England, etc . . . Life in city and country, peasant life and soldier life, the reckless and adventurous career of the free and easy student in Paris, and the rude rustic amōng the mountains,—all these phases of French life pass in review in the books which Mr. Griswold has here catalogued. A guide like this would be invaluable tŏ a student of French literature, telling as well what tŏ avoid, as what tŏ secure and read.

[*From the "Boston Commonwealth,"* 13 *Aug.*, 1892.]

If all libraries wer generously equipped with these Lists, the long-suffering curator of books would find more pleasure in life. The compilation and selection ar made with rare skill. The poor book drops into deservd oblivion, while the worthy but neglected and forgotten good book is restored tŏ the eye of the world.

Sŏme not too busy people make note of the name of a novel recommended by a trustworthy critic, but when the time for use cōmes the note seldom is at hand, and, if ready, generally givs the mere title and no idea of the contents. But here is a series of brochures that contain excerpts from the fairest critical notices, often from several sources, and ōne is enabled tŏ form a sort of judgment of choice without actually glancing at the book itself. Of course, those dealing with foreign lands must for the grēater part be translations, since with few exceptions the most truthful and vivid characterizations cōme from the compatriot whŏ has summered and wintered his fellows. Few people realize the patience, skill, and labor involvd in such an undertaking as the publication of these successiv lists, but those whŏ dŏ should urge upon ōthers the use of so valuable a means of education and pleasure. As a series of 'condensed novels' they ar interesting, too.

NOVELS DESCRIPTIV OF ITALIAN LIFE.

The object of this list is to direct readers, such as would enjoy the kind of books here described, to a number of novels, easily accessible, but which, in many cases, hav been forgotten within a year or two after publication. That the existence of works of fiction is remembered so short a time is a pity, since, for every new book of merit, there ar, in most libraries, a hundred as good or better, unknown to the majority of readers. It is hoped that the publication of this and similar lists will lessen, in some measure, the disposition to read an inferior NEW *book when superior* OLD *books, equally fresh to most readers, ar at hand. It may be observed that the compiler has tried to include only such works as ar well-written, interesting, and free from sensationalism, sentimentality, and pretense.* BUT *in a few cases, books hav been noticed on account of the reputation of their authors, or their great popularity, rather than their merit.*

The selected "notices" ar generally abridged.

This list will be followed by others describing RUSSIAN, NORWEGIAN, SPANISH,—HUMOROUS, ECCENTRIC *and* FANCIFUL *novels and tales.*

AGATHA PAGE = No. 406.

AMAZON (The). [by CARL VOS-
MAER: *Unwin*, 1884.] "The value of
the work depends upon its descriptions of character, and not on the
artistic, æsthetic, and archæological
disquisitions tŏ which we ar unwillingly treated, and in this respect Mr.
Vosmaer has scored a signal success.
Of course, the Amazon abandons her
resolv of remaining mistress of herself, and Aisma finds another mistress
besides Art." [Athenæum. **2565**

AMONG ALIENS = No. 587.

ANDROMEDA = No. 411.

ARIADNE = No. 591.

AT CAPRI = No. 413.

AURORA [by M.. AGNES TINCK-
ER: *Lippincott*. 1886.] "is certainly a
fresh and flowery spot in the midst of

the sŏmewhat rank over-luxuriance of
modern story-telling. It is unique in,
being full of the local cŏlor of a locality not too familiar, and in being a
story without a purpos, ideal: rather
than realistic, aiming at little but being a reproduction, at ŏnce faithful·
and picturesque, of life under picturesque conditions as it may stil be livd
and seen in Italy and Spain . . .
Whether it is a beautiful old garden,
or a woman's lŏvely gown. or sŏme
delightful little boys being tucked
intŏ bed. the thing described livs in,
the memory. And yet the author has
a tremendous catastrophe for the crisis
of her novel. Her use of the earthquake at Ischia is most dramatic and
powerful." [Critic.]—"Miss Tincker's stories of italian life invariably

AGNES TREMORNE [by Isa Blag-
den (†, 1873): *Smith*, 1861] is
"a graceful, tho perhaps over-senti-
mental book. The story, vued as a
story of English life and manners, must
be regarded as fanciful and slight.
The plot is rather unreal, and the
curious connexion subsisting between
the leading characters, is so unworldly
and imaginativ, that ōne feels in reading
it that a pure fancy rather than knoledge
of the world is the wel from which the
author has drawn. But the very unworldliness of the book suits, perhaps,
its Italian dress. When we ar in the
land of statues and of pictures, of olivs
and villas, of a blue sky and a blue sea,
life becōmes invested with brighter
cōlors, and dusty English family histories ar lighted intŏ sŏmething of romance. One of the most charming of
modern novels is a book in which a
simple and elegant plot is almost hidden
in descriptions of Italian life and
scenery — like statuary half lost in
leaves and flowers. The plot, and the
form in which the plot is given tŏ us
in such works as "Transformation"
[No. 817] ar mutually adapted tŏ ōne
anōther. The imaginativ character of
the story, its airy unreality and grace,
suit the region in which its action is
laid." [Saturday Review. **406 d**

BABEL [by Margaret [I..] (Collier) Galetti : *Blackwood*, 1887] " is a
pleasant little tale, dealing with the
fortunes of a young lady born of an
Italian father and an English mŏther.
She is a nativ of a village at no grêat
distance from the line tŏ Brindisi; and
thêre she has passed her youth in the
country house of her father, a count,
with no company but her reservd mother,
a boorish brother, her tutor, a quaint
French professor, and his warm-heârted
and shrewd Russian wife. From this
polyglot society the house has got the
name which it givs tŏ the story. How
the elements of it ar stirred by the
arrival among them of an English
"Milor," and how Giannetta's fate is
affected thêreby, may be read in the
book. Of course, she gets tŏ England
in course of time; and here the story
becŏmes sŏmewhat commonplace, tho
thêre ar amusing touches." [Athe-
næum.   **416 k**

possess points of hǐ charm, ar eloquent in description, and ar pervaded
by a poetic ardor. which she puts intǒ
striking relief by offering in contrast
vivid and realistic pictures of commonplace existence. In 'Aurora,'
which is a sequel tǒ 'The Jewel in the
Lotos,'—thêre ar scandals, falsehoods,
intrigues, and all the machinations of
powerful and unscrupulous workers
in evil." [American.   **2566**
BABYLON = No. 417.
BEAUTY OF AMALFI = No. 603.
BEPPO THE CONSCRIPT. [by
T: ADOLPHUS TROLLOPE: *Chapman*,
1856.] The scene is "the narro strip
of territory shut in between the Apennines and the Hadriatic, whêre Tasso
sang and the dukes of Urbino flour-
ished. But not tǒ revive thêir past
glories ar we beguiled tǒ the decayed
old city of Fano, and the umbrageous
valleys which nestle amid the surrounding hils; it is the normal, primitiv, agricultural life and economy of
the region, and the late political and
social condition of the inhabitants,
which this story illustrates. The
means and methods of rural toil,—the
"wine, corn, and oil" of Scriptural
and Vergilian times; the avariçe, the
pride, the lǒve, the industry, and the
superstition of the peasants of
Romagna; a household of prosperous
rustics, thêir ways and traits; and the
subtil and prevailing agency of
priestcraft in its secret opposition tǒ
the gǒvernment,—ar all exhibited
with a quiet zest and a graphic fidelity
which takes us intǒ the heârt of the
people, and the arcana, as wel as the
spectacle of daily life, as thêre latent
and manifest. The domestic, peasant,
and provincial scenes and characters
ar drawn with fresh and natural cǒlors and faithful outlines."

[Atlantic.   **2567**
BEPPO THE STARGAZER, by
HEYSE, in *Masterpieces of German
Fiction*.   **2568**
BETROTHED (The), by MAN-
ZONI, = No. 608.
BIMBI, by OUIDA, = No. 609.
BRUSHES AND CHISELS [by
TEODORO SERRAO: *Lee*, 1890.] "is a
transcript of artist life in Rome,
which in delicate and poetic phrases
recounts the lǒve-story of Angelica,
a modern Corinne, and Cormoto, a
Roman painter, whǒ for lǒve of the
fair Muse throes away his life in a
duel. Angelica, more happy, marries
a Russian noble." [Critic.   **2569**
BY THE TIBER = No. 622.
CAMILLA'S GIRLHOOD = No.
623.
CAPTAIN MAN:;ANA = No. 427.
CARLINO = No. 428.
CASTELLAMONTE. [by "L.
Mariotti," i. e., ANTONIO [C: NAPO-
LEONE] GALLENGA: London, *Wester-
ton*, 1854.] "One of the grêat charms
of the book is that it is truly what it
is described as being—an illustration of
Italian domestic life in town and
country. We hav, too, sǒme good
sketches of individuals, a specimen of
the now happily almost extinct species of 'cicisbeo,' and the pompous
and penniless marquis, ǒne of the few
lingering remnants of the feudal nobility stil to be found in secluded
nooks of the Apennines." [Westmin-
ster.   **2570**
CASTLE OF OTRANTO = No. 630.
CONSUELO = No. 650.
CORINNA. [by "Rita," i. e.,
ELIZA J. (GOLLAN) BOOTH: *Maxwell*,
1885.] "Thêre is not much substance
in it, but the heroin is graceful and
gracefully described. The lively
little countess, coquettish and world-

BROKEN TROTH (The) [by PHILIP TRETON: *Macmillan*, 1861.] "is a genuin Italian tale — a true picture of the Tuscan peasant population, with all their virtues, faults, weaknesses, follies, and even vices. It is not a tale concocted tŏ meet the popular passion or prejudice of the day; for it dŏes not touch in the remotest degree upon politics, and is completely free from the slightest strain of sectarianism. It is a domestic tale — its hero, a humble, hard-working shŏemaker — its heroin, the rich dauter of a crafty miser, whŏ by his skil and cunning has contrived tŏ amass a large property in houses and vineyards; and its villain is an idling, gambling, town-bred fop — a personification of that worthless class, whŏse numbers and dissoluteness make them the curse of Italy. We recommend 'The Broken Troth' as the best Italian tale which has been published since the appearance of the 'Promessi Sposi' [No. 608]; because, like that work, thêre ar tŏ be found in it genuin pictures of the Italian peasant population. Thêre is no exaggeration in the portraiture of character; and the incidents — even the worst described — ar of constant occurrence — such as the murder of the hero's father, by the hand of a villain who envied the humble man's happiness — such too, as the robbery and attempted murder of the heroin's father by twŏ wretches, whŏse frightful bargain with each ŏther was that he whŏ took life should also becŏme sole possessor of the money and jewels tŏ be found in the house whêre the murder was committed. The records of crime in Italy exhibit the frequency of such deeds of cruelty and atroçity; and the author keeps within the strict lines of probability when introduçing them intŏ his story. The grêat charm, however, of this work is the protraiture of Stefanino — the hero. It is an exquisit picture of virtue struggling against poverty — against the charms of beauty — the passions of youth — the temptations of wealth. And despite of the many difficulties in his way, triumphing over every obstacle, and with a clear conscience, finally winning, with the approbation of his fello-men, all he had wished for. The foil tŏ this character, his cousin Cecco, is a wel-intentioned youth, but with no control over his vehement disposition, and whŏse fiery spirits ar constantly involving him in the most unpleasant scrapes." [London Review. **2568t**

763 h

BUCHHOLZES IN ITALY (The)
[by JULIUS STINDE : London, *Bell,*
1887.] " is not equal to ' the Buchholz
Family.' It has sŏme clever passages,
of course, but the author strains too
much after effect, and in the end ŏne
becŏmes thŏroly tired of Mrs. Buchholz'
comments on the pictures, scenery, and
social life of Italy. It is worth noting,
perhaps, that she is made tŏ express all
the notions current in Germany about
English travelers." [Athenæum. 424 k

CAMORISTI (The) and other
TALES [by Ma. [I..] (Collier) Galetti : London, 1882] " is attractiv and
interesting." [Sat. Review.   426 k

CARA ROMA. [by Maria M. Grant :
Chapman, 1885.] "Life at **Rome,**
both in outside aspect and in the conditions which it excites is described with
considerable power; and the study of
Lady Daring, with its curious strata,
so to speak, — an outside of sentiment,
a deep layer of what may be called
practical or worldly, and underneath all,
again, a capacity for being disinterested,
which can assert itself if ōuly it can be
roused, — is a really successful effort."
[Spectator. **427 k**

CARTOUCHE. [by F.. M.. PEARD : *Smith*, 1879.] "The author prefers good tŏ bad people, likes things tŏ turn out wel, and has a sympathetic acquaintance with a good deal of forêin society. The scene of 'Cartouche' lies chiefly at **Florence** and **Rome,** and the descriptions of scenery and of the life of English residents in those places ar charming, and, what is rarer, ar given withoyt extravagance; but the best point in the author's treatment of her story is her skilful management of twŏ heroins, girls of very different characters, but both of them true and noble-minded." [Athenæum. **428 h**

CONTRADICTIONS. [by F.. M.. PEARD: *Bentley*, 1883.] "The twŏ sisters ar an attra'ctiv pair of fresh, right-thinking, vigorous English girls; and Olivia, with her more conventional and worldly aims, which dŏ not, however, wholy occupy her heârt, forms an effectiv contrast. Life in **Venice,** tpo, is described with sŏme skil, and thêre ar descriptions of scenery and of the effects of light and color in the canals and lagoons which ar wel and forcibly written." [Spectator. **431 d**

CORINNE [by A.. L.. GERMAINE (NECKER), baroness STAEL-HOLSTEIN (†, 1817) : Boston, 1808, 2 v., 12°; Phil'a, Carey, 1836; N. Y., Langley, 1844; London, 1856, Warne, 1884.] " The hero is the son of a Scotch nobleman, whŏ possessed all the excellencies of that region, viz : hī mental cultivation, grêat moral purity, strong religious faith, and a rooted attachment tŏ the quiet, demure habits of his countrymen. . . . His prejudices against Italian women wer melting away as the frost of his nativ hils would hav dŏne under an Italian sun. Passion impelled him tŏ an immediate union with this charming creature ; but the mystery resting on her origin and early history, the recollection of his former imprudence, and of his father's opinions, and an occasional relaps intŏ his old feelings, always made him shrink from that final step. She is nursed by him in sicness; she traverses the peninsula from ōne end tŏ the ōther in his company, and defies even Italian public sentiment in all her intercourse with him. . . With grêat difficulty he têars himself away, and she despairs. The sight of Britain revives his attachment tŏ English manners, and with it his prejudiçe against those of Italy. The appearance of Miss Edgemond, blush-

ing like a young rose, chimed in with this renewal of old prepossessions. He dŏes not cease tŏ lŏve Corinne; but she is fast lŏsing the monopoly of his heârt, and his letters becŏme less frequent and more cold. Altho this ŏnly realized the gloomy anticipations of Corinne, it drove her nearly frantic, and when the intelligence reached her that he was about starting with the army for the West Indies, she returned tŏ England with more impatience than she left it. . . . Corinne returns tŏ Italy tŏ die of a broken heârt. Oswald, in a short time after his marriage, goes tŏ the West Indies, whêre he encounters the toils and perils of war for four years. When he returns, the feelings and tastes which had partially lost thêir hold amid the din of battle and the horrors of pestilence, resumed their power. His conscience is troubled about the unknōn fate of the poor Italian ; he finds that his English wife, with all her lŏveliness and innocent affection, lacs the genius and acquirements, which gave such constant attraetion tŏ the conversation of her sister. This occasions no actual dissension, but a want of perfect sympathy and confidence." [Southern Lit. Messenger] Compare No. 2004.   **431 p** ly, whŏm we meet in her company at the outset of the story, is a good foil tŏ the beautiful, single-heârted, and imaginativ author and poet whŏ is her traveling companion." [Athen. **2571**

DANIELE CORTIS. [by ANTONIO FOGAZZARO: *Remington*, 1890.] "It is not easy tŏ create sympathy for Italian fiction. The obstacle is not so much the forêinness of the "ways" of the people and thêir social customs, as it is the moods of mind, the objects of life, and the curious staccato style in which modern Italian prose is written. That style departs as widely from the floing sentences and rather over-dŏne elegance of the older Italian writers, as the naturalist French style departs from the romantic. In 'Daniele Cortis' we hav a favorable example of the modern Italian novel, ŏne which ŏt tŏ arouse interest, even vivid curiosity, and which not ŏnly tels a clever story in a clever way, but offers sŏme striking types of character. The lŏve-story is not a happy ŏne; the tragic element cŏmes intŏ it, and "its earthly close" is separation; but its interest is pathetic, and the underlying political element is admirably convêyed. Count Leo is an original and entertaining personage. The translation has the charm of ease and gracefulness." [Spectator. **2572**

DAPHNE = No. 667.

DEVIL'S PORTRAIT (The) [by ANTONIO GIULIO BARRILI: *Remington*, 1885.] "is a painful, but yet a rather powerful story of lŏve, vengeance, and tragedy. As in most fictions of the kind, the plot is practically everything,—the incidents and the characters nŏthing. The unfortunate hero is Spinelli, whŏ develops intŏ a grêat artist. But his betrothed, the dauter of his master, is spirited away from him by a rival artist, in a marvellous, and indeed, incredible fashion. Tuccio di Cridi, a confederate of Buonalente, fastens himself upon Spinelli as a friend and admirer, and allows him tŏ drift intŏ a marriage which is nearly, if not quite, lŏveless. At last Spinelli discŏvers that Fiordalisa, whŏm he believes tŏ be dead, has been forced tŏ marry Buonalente. Him he kils, tho not before the villain has had time tŏ strike an Iago's blo at Fiordalisa. Finally, he goes mad, altho, before his death, he retains reason enuf tŏ achieve wŏnders as an artist, and tŏ kil the second villain of the story. Next tŏ the plot, the artistic babble is most tŏ be commended, because it is true tŏ nature.— at least, tŏ nature in Italy." [Spectator. **2573**

DIAMOND CUT DIAMOND [by T: ADOLPHUS TROLLOPE: *Harper*, 1874.] "is a wel-written, excellent, and soporific tale of Tuscan life. The best portion deals with the prîesthood, and the portraitures of the different prîests ar drawn with a firm and masterly hand. The object of the story is tŏ sho the evil results of prîestly interference in the management of the domestic affairs of private families, and if this purpos be held steadily in vue, we must pronounce the novel a success. But it is not til we reach the end that we discŏver the moral, and most people we suspect wil fall asleep by the way." [Arcadian. **2574**

DOCTOR ANTONIO = No. 435.

DREAM NUMBERS [by T: ADOLPHUS TROLLOPE: *Chapman*, 1868.] "is a charming picture of life in Tuscany; the life of wel-tŏ-dŏ farmers and peasants; pictures of life as it is in those little old-world towns and

DON FINIMONDONE. [by E..
(JONES) CAVAZZA: N.-Y., *Webster*, 1892.]
"Don Finimondone was a Calabrian kil-
joy, always prophesying evil and the end
of the world. Hençe his nicname. Whŏever wishes tŏ read a good story, wel
told, quite in the manner of the old 'fab-
liaux,' should read how he disguised himself as the devil and threw a gloom over
the carnival by hinting his intimate knoledge of all his nêbors' pecadilloes, until
his dauter Filomena, recognizing him by
certain patches which she had sewn on
the knees of his trousers, recommended
him tŏ go learn of himself, in his capacity
of head of a household, how to play the
part properly. Mrs. Cavazza, tŏ whŏm
we o ŏur acquaintançe with this delightful old skinflint, introduçes us also tŏ a
proçession of ŏther quaint charaçters,
very real for all their shŏy Italian virtues
and viçes. Thêre is Cirillo, the frog-
catcher, born a baron, and whŏ knoes it,
yet whŏ wil not claim his ŏn because he
has promised his foster-mŏther not tŏ
publish her fraud. Thêre is the Calabrian
Penelope whŏ forçes her husband, returned from South-America, tŏ put a bullet
throu her wedding-ring, held in her hand,
the ŏnly proof that wil convince her of
his identity; thêre ar the women whŏ
carry içe on thêir heads, bound in rush
mats and sheepskins, from the mountains
tŏ the city; the shepherd whŏ suddenly
appears from behind a roç, with his pipe,
tŏ play tŏ them, while thêy lay down thêir
burdens and dançe; and Donna Rosina, a

'grêat piece of a woman' like a purple
cabbage, whŏ in her day was the belle of
the village, and whŏ spoiled her ŏn funeral
in an extraordinary way. Even the tom-
tits and the grasshoppers in these stories
hav charactêr and chirp and wag thêir
tails after a fashion of thêir ŏn. The
Madonna del Carmine, tŏ whŏm the villagers pray for suçços, is able tŏ make
'any ten ŏther Madonnas run away with
lifted legs.' In general, the tales conçern
such humble folk as peasants and thêir
donkeys, priests and proprietors of pup-
pet-shŏs. But, as Theokritos sketched
his Syracusan dames, Mrs. Cavazza paints
the likeness of the Neapolitan grêat folk
in '*Princess Humming-bird*'; and the
same light touch which puts before us
the gypsy, Nastasia, in her tinsel finery,
or Pina weeding in the furrŏs, answers as
wel for thêir superiors, whŏ revile Christ-
ofero Colombo for letting loose on them
the American hêiress with the bodiçe of
humming-bird's feathers. The conclusion
of this last tale reminds ŏne a little of
Hawthorne, but ŏne need not take that
as an injury. In fact, seeing that the
book puts us in mind of what is best ŏnly,
in idyl and story, we ar open tŏ discuss
the question whether its plaçe is not sŏme-
whêre in Hawthorne's nêborhood—
whether, smacking, as it dŏes, of fat
olivs and blac wine, it may not claim
standing-room on the shelf beside Leigh
Hunt's 'Jar of Honey from Mount
Hybla'." [Critic. **2574 m**

DODD FAMILY ABROAD (The). [by C: Lever (1806–72): *Harper*, 1854.] " This is ōne of the gayest, shrewdest, most sparkling and most rollicking of the many works cf Lever. The Dodds, an Irish family of encumbered estate, ar taken tŏ the Continent by the senior member of the concern, in the hope of living more economically abroad than at home. The book is made up of letters, written by the various members of the Dodd connection, and as various in style and sentiment as the characters of their writers. The result is a picture, or series of pictures, of German and Italian life and manners, strongly provocativ of lâfter. The absurdities of the family in their desire tŏ be fashionable and distinguished, and their queer adventures and mishaps, ar exhibited with grêat humor. Dodd, the father, is a splendid specimen of the elderly Irish gentleman, impulsiv, irascible, full of animal spirits, shrewd, and sensible enuf in his mode of thinking, foolish and reɑless in his conduct. His letters ar perhaps the best in the book. Dodd, mŏther, is a vixen of a peculiar stamp, wrông-headed and wrŏng-heârted, whŏ spoils her children, plagues her husband, and worships herself. Dodd, dauter, is a beautiful and sentimental young lady, eager for conquests, a coquette, a jilt, and almost a jade. James Dodd, the son, is a young scapegrace, whŏ gets intŏ all kinds of ridiculous scrapes, but is so good-natured in his good-for-nothingness that he never entirely lŏses the sympathy of the reader. The failures ar Capt. Morris and Carry Dodd, characters in which the author attempts tŏ delineate excellent people, and succeeds ŏnly in describing bores. They fortunately occupy but a small space in the book, and can be easily skipped. We dŏ not kno but that the interposition of their dulness is a contrivance of the author tŏ hav sŏme foil tŏ his brilliancy; if sρ, he has succeeded tŏ a charm." [Graham's Mag. **437 h**

DRIVEN BEFORE THE STORM.
[by GERTRUDE FORDE: *Hurst*, 1887.]
"The early chapters, which take us tŏ
the coast of Italy, and tel us how Barrington de Witt fel in with the traveling
party, with the members of which he
was tŏ becŏme so fatefully allied, ar
full of brisk incident, bright character-
sketching, and quiet humor. The Brere-
tons, father and sŏn, ar solidly executed
portraits, the former being the morĕ
successful, as the churlish irascibility of
the older man is better realized for us
than the brutal caddishness of the
younger, which surely passes the bounds
of credibility. An equally clever and
much pleasanter creation is the pretty
American girl, Blanche Hopkins, with
her piquant grace, her free but always
self-respectful ways, and her wŏnderful
knac of turning lŏvers into permanent
friends. . . . Thêre is no strain, no
exaggeration, no melodrama, but a vividness and intensity after which the dealers
in these things strive in vain. The early
part of the book is admirable, but it is
this later portion which marks out the
writer as ŏne of whŏm grêat expectations may reasonably be indulged."
[Spectator. **438 k**

hamlets, perched in nooks of the mountains, hardly accessible tŏ the dwellers themselvs, and never seen or knōn by ordinary travelers. The state of rude plenty, with its rustic and yet classic grace, its ignorance, shrewdness and beauty; the energy which underlies its laziness; the sense of unbounded leisure, which precludes the possibility of haste or hurry; the charm of glad animal-life, which hardly needs labor tŏ support it; all combine tŏ make the people seem a race set apart from those whŏ dwel under the iron rule of the 19th century, and under the self-conscious laws of political economy. Thêy liv in beauty instead. The lights and shadōs of Italian peasant life ar the subject of, "The Dream Numbers." The hīest social personage is the lawyer Morini, whŏ livs in the city of Lucca, and whōse sŏn Meo, the type of the young provincial "gent," is the lōver of Pegina, the dauter of a rich 'contadino.' " [Athenæum.]—"Be it remembered that in this, as in his ōther sweet and true pictures of Italian life, it is a domestic chronicle he weaves; thêre ar no complex characters—nŏne of the subtlety of analysis and portraiture appropriate tŏ a hīer or more varied culture or stage of civilization; it is with the people he deals, with their simple tastes, thêir harmless gossip. thêir poor superstitions, thêir limited knoledge, thêir local traditions and habitudes. Incident ìs, of course, essential, and incident of a dramatic or picturesque kind, and this he finds in such authentic events as a trìc of prīestcraft which came tŏ light in the records of the local tribunals; in a memorable and destructiv inundation of the Serchio. and the cōurse of a true lōve which

did not run smooth until it had encountered and overcōme numerous obstacles—doubts. fears, meetings and separations—the story whêreof takes the reader pleasantly from the cathedral of Lucca tŏ the mountain path from Pescia. from a funeral tŏ a court-room, from the jewelers' bridge at Florence tŏ the trim little 'bagarino' with its smart pony and scarlet worsted rêins, from a supper of macaroni and Chianti wine tŏ a cemetery. and from a gay 'passeggiata' tŏ a tearful vigil—all minutely true tŏ local life and character, and narrated with a tact. wisdom, ethical justice, and human sympathy alike pleasing and rare." [Round Table. 2575

ELEVENTH COMMANDMENT (The) [by ANTONIO GIULIO BARRILI: N.-Y.. *Gottsberger*, 1882.] "is a gay. sparkling little comedy. The first act passes amid the petty strivings and plottings of the town, with its subprefect and its register-general. Enter a grand personage. a duke, whŏ is seeking a richly-dowered bride. Act. II. In the mountains, abōve the town, in an monastery. is gathered a party of 9 gentlemen whŏ hav voluntarily bound themselvs tŏgether as the "Reformed Order of Saint Bruno." Thêy devote themselvs tŏ archæology— "monks whŏ ar not monks, a craze worthy of an Ariosto," but "the convent of madmen." Tŏ them enter a young novie with "round, fresh face like an archangel out for a holiday," with his uncle, likewise a novie, a portly, cōmfortable man of 50. The young novie brings tŏ the community an eleventh commandment: "Thou shalt stay amōng thy fello-men. liv thêir life, lōve and suffer as thêy dŏ; for thou mayest not escape the common lot." The book ìs so wholy

ELENA. [by L. N. COMYN: *Long-man*, 1873.] "The dauter of an English father and an Italian mother, bred in ignorance of her birth, and in little more than peasant rank, by an il-tempered ' cugina,' Elena meets acci-dentally an officer in the then Piedmontese army, whŏ is thrŏn from his horse close tŏ her home. From her good offices tŏ him, after the accident, an acquaintance arises, and his kindness tŏ the lonely and hardly-used girl wins her heârt. . . After an interval, during which she wŏnders never tŏ hav heard his name, a certain Marquis Montanari appears as suitor for her hand, tŏ her grêat dismay, for her heârt has long been given tŏ Marco. Of course, Mon-tanari and Lorenzini turn out tŏ be the same person; but poor Elena finds that tho tŏ please his father he has under-taken tŏ make a ' mariage de conven-ance,' his affections ar at first wholy given tŏ her beautiful step-sister. Thus, in spite of Marco's kindness, which, how-ever, proceeds from a kind disposition rather than from any affection for her, the first months of Elena's married life pass unhappily enuf. In course of time, however, his eyes ar opened tŏ Pauline's sballo nature (be it understood, he is too honorable a man tŏ hav con-tracted any serious ' liaison ' with her) and tŏ the depths of his wife's lŏve for him. . . . Our readers wil see that the story is a sad one, pitched, so tŏ say, in a minor key throuŏut. It is told, however, with good taste, and avoid-ance of ' sensation,' for which the sub-jcet might offer a favorable opportunity."
[Athenæum. **439 h**

FANTASIA. [by MATILDE ( ) SERAO: 1883; *Lovell*, 1891.] "When we ar introduçed tŏ Lucia Altemare as a schoolgirl in the convent, she thinks she wil find her ideal in ecstatic worship of the Virgin, and faints with exçitement on the tŏld flags of the chapel before her image. She vows she wil hav nōthing tŏ dŏ with earthly lŏve, that she is born tŏ be lonely and sad; vows it tŏ her bosom friend, a quiet, simple, gentle girl, whŏ is devoted tŏ her strange comrade with all the strength of a fond and straitforward nature . . . So the school-life brĕaks up. Lucia at home lŏses herself in religious fervors and in studies conducted under the tuition of the poor Professor, whŏm she at last drives intŏ a mad-house. Caterina marries a handsŏme, athletic cousin, whŏ at first takes a violent dislike tŏ her sicly "athletic" friend; but ŏne evening on being maliçiously left alone with her by his wife, whŏ is anxious tŏ coax the twŏ beings she lŏves best intŏ sŏme kind of sympathy, he falls a prĕy tŏ her subtle fasçination. From this moment the lŏve-duet begins. Lucia deems it a philanthropical duty tŏ marry a despicably selfish, consumptiv cousin, whŏse last years she wishes tŏ briten; but her elaborate display of pitying affection toards this wretched creature is rather repulsiv than the reverse. Even in the last horribly realistic death-bed scene, when the mask has fallen, and the twŏ whŏ hav been betrayed sit side by side looking at thĕir fate, and ŏne after the ōther turning over the leaves of the diary in which Lucia has written her ecstatic lŏve-thŏts tŏ her friend's husband—even in the viçinity of death, the wild and selfish ravings of a poor nature must fil us with disgust; and it is tŏ the silent and patient grief of the outraged young wife that we giv all the pathos, guessing what the lapis-lazuli rosary is tŏ mean for her. The character of Lucia is a clever psychological study, but it is little Caterina whŏ claims ŏur tears as she orders her apartment in Naples, like the methodical little housewife that she is, and goes quietly off tŏ the deserted villa whĕre thĕy all four spent such pleasant summer days, and thĕre lavs herself down in the closed room with the smōldering charcoal tŏ keep her part, according tŏ her simple notion, of the bargain of the lapis-lazuli rosary." [Saturday Review.]—"It would be impossible for the English lady novelist tŏ write such a book. An English woman might kno a Lucia Altimare thŏroly, might depict her perfectly up tŏ the crisis of her career; but just at this point she would certainly succumb tŏ tradition. She would arrange for a Lucia a tĕarful parting from her lŏver, and sanctimonious retirement tŏ the hĕarth she has cŏme so near tŏ desecrating, or she would kil Lucia, or represent her as dŏing anything, everything, except what a Lucia always dŏes when she gets the chançe—bolt with the husband of a dearest friend, leaving behind wild, ejaculatory epistles for *her* husband and *his* wife. The presentation of a nervous, exçitable, sensual woman, whŏse real character is scarçely suspected bv her nearest friends, and whŏ, with occasional spasms of scathing frankness, livs in a state of blissful self-deception, is exçeedingly clever and surpassingly cold . . . Thĕre is much grasp, power, and knoledge in it." [Nation. **2576 k**

ELSA [by E. McQueen Gray:
Harper, 1892] " is ŏne of those delightful old-fashioned novels with a lŏve-
story pure and simple and all the
adjuncts tŏ the furtherance and hindrance of the same. The scene is laid
chiefly in **Venice** Thêre is Elsa,
whŏse mŏther was Italian and whŏse
father is Austrian, pure in spirit and
with a marvelous voice; thêre is the
morose old father; thêre is Somerled
the Englishman, an artist whŏ lŏves
Elsa; thêre is the baroness, an ex-ballet
dancer, whŏ in her vain and silly fashion devotes herself tŏ Elsa's fortunes; thêre is Kramer, the little Munich
artist whŏ sentimentalizes about beer and
lŏve in the same breath; thêre is the
Princess Morini, old and bitter, with the
thirst for vengeance in her heârt, giving
' Wednesday evenings ' tŏ which everyone eŏmes, in spite of her il-humor;
thêre is Francesco Savarni, the villain
of the tale, whŏ oppresses Elsa after her
father dies, and upon whŏm tŏ be
avenged the Princess has livd until she
is 83; and finally thêre is Antonio the
gondolier, silent and discreet. And out
of this material the author has made a
story which is charming in scene and
conversation, absorbing in interest, absolutely true in its premises, even if its
conclusions ar sŏmetimes a trifle exaggerated and theatrical,— artistic in arrangement, and healthful and objectiv
in tone — a story so little modern, so
unlike sŏme of the monstrosities of
realism, as tŏ command ôur genuin admiration." [Critic.   **440 k**

without pretension, and so lightly
told, that ŏne pardons minor faults,
and no more questions probabilities
than ŏne would in the 'The Princess'."
[Nation.]—"It rehearses the history
of certain friars whŏ established a
convent, merely tŏ secure seclusion
from politics and society. Women ar
excluded. not because thêy had found
Woman dangerous, but because thêy
had not felt her charm. Thêy propose. in short. tŏ giv up the world
without renouncing it. But a young
and beautiful girl, in the disguise of a
friar, gains acçess tŏ thêir retreat, and
the processes by which she gradually
brêaks up the lay convent ar admirably described." [Critic.]—Compare
plot of No. 2522.   2576

FIAMMETTA. [by W : WETMORE
STORY : *Houghton.* 1875.] "Its theme
resembles "Guenn" [No. 725.] ; it is
less painstaking and less ambitious
than "Guenn." perhaps less spirited,
but it is gentler and prettier. It is,
we think. both good art and good nature tŏ drop intentional wrŏnging of
each ŏther out of ŏur stories of life
and human relations. and sho more
how fates unavoidably clash. In this
theme—the Elaine theme, we may call
it—it is an open question how far the
Lancelots should be, as thêy usually
ar. held responsible morally for having allowed lŏve tŏ be given which
thêy could not return in kind. The
girl herself should hav sŏme right tŏ
say sŏmething in the matter ; and it is
certain that such a girl as either Guenn
or Fiammetta would choose tŏ hav
had the first lŏve and its consequences,
rather than the lifeless peasant content which would hav ŏtherwise hav
been hers. Whêre thêre has been no
effort tŏ win lŏve, no advantage taken
of the lŏve given, no deception or cre-

ating of expectations which can not
be fulfilled—merely the ŏpportunity
given for the girl's pure and unsolicit-
ed devotion tŏ attach itself—it is a
question whether the novelist should
hold up the result as disastrous. and
the man as a wrong dŏer. It is a fortunate arrangement of fate that the
girl whŏ is not strong-heârted enuf tŏ
prefer. on the whole, the hĭer lŏving
and its consequence of sorro, is also
the girl whŏ gets over such an experience easily, and takes the cheaper
attainable. rather than the costly unattainable." [Overland.   2577

FOREGONE CONCLUSION (A)
[**Venice**] = No. 453.

FROM THE FOAM OF THE SEA
[by SALVATORE FARINA : *Charing
Cross Pub. Co.,* 1880.]—"is written
with quite as much sprightliness as
'Lŏve Blinded' [No. 2591] and with
similar grace ; but it is, on the whole. of
slighter texture, the incidents being
extremely improbable, and thêy belong more tŏ the region of light comedy than that of novel-writing. At
first ŏne's curiosity is agreeably
aroused, and all promises wel ; but
before the end of vol. 1. the mysteries
of the plot becŏme artificial and practically impossible. and from that point
forward ŏne reads on with diminished
zest. tho certainly not with entire dis-
relish." [Athenæum.   2578

GEMMA. [by T : ADOLPHUS
TROLLOPE : *Chapman,* 1866.] "The
scene is Siena ; and, altho the stŏry is
based upon ŏne of those impassioned
tragedies of lŏve and jealousy which
can be found ŏnly in the family chronicles of Italy. the stil-life, social
phases, and local traits of the romance
ar delineated with the same quiet simplicity and graphic truth which constitute the authentiçity of the author's

FORTUNES OF GLENCORE (The)
[by C: LEVER (1806–72): *Chapman*,
1857.] "is a very pleasant book. Thêre
is a flo of hi animal spirits throuõut, ánd
the best characters ar usually the gay,
hot-blooded Irishmen, fond of wild
horses, whisky, duelling, and pretty
girls. The scene of the story changes
from the western coast of Ireland, whêre
the sea dashes against the castle of the
Glencores, tõ the soft skies of Val
d'Arno and the sunny shore of the Bay
of Naples." [Southern Lit. Messenger.
453 k

previous delineations of Italian life. The grave, conservativ, and old-fashioned Tuscan city reappears, with its mediæval aspect and traditional customs. Convent education, the homes of the patrician and the citizen, the little gig of the 'fattore,' with the small, wiry ponies of the region, the local antiquarian and doctor. the letter-carrier, family servant, lady-superior, pharmacist, the noble and plebeian, the costumes, phrases, and natural language characteric of that non-commercial and isolated Tuscan city before the days of railways, ar drawn with emphasis and significant detail. Shades and causes of character ar finely discriminated; the old mediæval 'festa' peculiar tŏ Siena, with all its original features and social phenomena, is vividly enacted in the elaborate description of the "Palio;" while the insalubrious and picturesque Maremma is portrayed, from the Etruscan crypts of the ravines tŏ the desolate streets of Savona, by an artistic and philosophic hand." [Atlantic.   2579

GIANNETTO [by MARGARET [E ..] (LINDSAY) MAJENDIE: Holt, 1876.] "is a prettily-written story, with charming descriptions of sŏme few sides of life in Italy, and a general air of having been studied from nature, while it suffers meanwhile from the introduction of a sort of supernatural flavor which nowadays, when literalness of local cŏlor is so abundant, is as unimpressiv as a ghost would be in a horse-car at midday. The story tels of a singer whŏ, after having been dumb from birth, bursts out intŏ song; and his voice, obtained, it is suggested, by a compact with the Evil One, givs him wealth tŏ the detriment of his moral

character. With that exception, which is an important ŏne, the little book is agreeable reading." [Nation.]—Compare No. 715.   2580

GIULIO MALATESTA. [by T: ADOLPHUS TROLLOPE: Chapman, 1863.] "As the story is, in spite of all its perilous chances and changes, light and pleasant, it was necessary tŏ make the interest hang on the private fortunes of the actors, and not the tragical elements of the struggle for liberty; but the reader is throuŏut made sensible of how much he escapes. for between convents, priests, agents of police and prisons, the dangers and abuses of all kinds make the reader tremble. The influence of convent life is very wel painted; and Stella, the heroin of Giulio. is a brave, hĭ-spirited little creature. tho even she almost succumbs tŏ the treatment, and except in a novel must hav dŏne so. But the author is merciful, and he brings on the scene a charming abbess—we shal not tel the reader whŏ she is, nor shal we hint at the ending of the story; it is enuf tŏ say that poetical justiçe and generosity ar both consulted, and the end is so pleasant that we can ŏnly wish all parties the blessing of continuance." [Athenæum.   2581

HOUSE BY THE MEDLAR TREE. [by GIOVANNI VERGA : Harper, 1890.] "In the beginning, thêre is no family in the Italian fishing village of Trezza so happy and prosberous as the Malavoglia, whŏse home is 'The House by the Medlar Tree.' The Malavoglia ar honest, industrious. pious, and much more addicted tŏ minding thêir ŏn business than ar thêir nêbors ... The sadness of the story—and what in life could be sadder?—is not mitigated by the manner

HARRY JOSCELYN. [by Ma. Oliphant (Wilson) Oliphant : *Hurst*,
1881.] "When Harry, the youngest
son, rushes away intŏ space from the
home which is made so intolerable, a
chapter of Italian life succeeds which is
made as charming and idyllic by the
lŏves of Harry and the young half-English girl he marries, as his first days
wer gloomy and depressing in the grim
mansion on the Fels. By an extraordinary combination of circumstances, aided
by his good conduct, he induces the
jealously affectionate father of Rita tŏ
consent tŏ his dauter's marriage with a
man of whŏse antecedents he knoes
nothing except that he has quarrelled
with his family. Mr. Bonamy's is an
excellent portrait. The union of business-like energy with extreme simplicity
is very fascinating, and the playful tenderness which subsists between father
and dauter is touchingly described. Indeed, the relations between the members
of the little party at **Livorno** ar so
charming that ŏne is vexed when the
inevitable discŏvery takes place, and
Harry's sister Liddy, the "little Liddy"
of his boyhood, unearths him in his retirement, and brings about the reconciliation which no doubt is desirable and
proper. All this is very wel told, and
we fully sympathize with the happiness
of poor Mrs. Joscelyn in the fairer
weather of her declining years ; but in
spite of ŏur pity for her and respect for
her warm-heârted tho undemonstrativ
elder dauter, we prefer Livorno tŏ
Westmoreland, and think Paolo, an
amusing Italian friend of Harry's, was
right in not folloing the later fortunes of
the family." [Athenæum. **462 p**

HOUSE OF THE MUSICIAN
(The). [by VIRGINIA WALES JOHNSON:
Boston, *Ticknor*, 1887.] "The ·title
dŏes not describe a character in the story
but the scene of the narrativ, which is
in **Venice,** whither a young Dutch
artist goes tŏ ply his calling, and by a
strange web of circumstances is carried
deep intŏ the romance of ŏne of the
most entrancĭng of cities. Thêre is a
good deal of merit in this book. It is
rather excessivly sentimental, but it is
written in a good style and especially
givs a charming series of pictures of
life in Venice." [American. **467 h**

HUGH MOORE. [by Evelyn Stone: *Blackwood*, 1885.] " A yacht in the Ionian seas, a golden evening in Corfu, the English ōner of the yacht and his companion, younger sŏn of an Irish lord, a wily consul, and ḫis pretty dauter, with the intrîging spirit of her Levantiné mōther strông1y developed — such is the opening scene and such ar the leading characters of this acceptable story. The impressionable young Irishman is the hero whŏse adventures ar related in terse English, studded with natural incidents and dialogs. Thêre is nothing out of the ordinary beat in Hugh Moore's experiences, and when the reader knoes that thêre ar more heroins than ōne he may make a tolerably confident surmise as tŏ the development of the plot which dates its origin from that aưtumn trip in the Mediterrænean." [Athenæum.

467 p

of its telling. No story could o more of its worth tŏ the author and seem tŏ o less. As we read we ar not conscious of an author, a person whŏ has selected a scene and a group of people, then proceeded tŏ arrange a number of events in which each shares, and tŏ present all in orderly fashion with more or less regard for effect. For the time, we ar actually in the village, an unseen and all-seeing guest, liking or disliking the people whŏ liv thêir lives and ar themselvs, without any reference tŏ us, lâfing, gossiping, and wrangling with them, and with an ever-deepening sense of pain for the Malavoglia which barely stops short of heârtbrêak. For an example of realism in its widest and ŏnly true sense, a sincere rendering of reality which is lasting and universal, and of reality which is transient and local, we hav nŏthing in English comparable with 'The House by the Medlar Tree'." [Nation. 2582

HOUSE DIVIDED AGAINST IT-SELF [**Bordighera**] = No. 467.

IMPROVISATORE (The). [by HANS CHRISTIAN ANDERSEN (1805-76) : Kopenhagen, 1834 ; *Harper*. 1846.] "The talent of Andersen is shŏn here by its sympathetic perception and delicate power of deṣcription. It is ŏne of the books which ar full of Italy, so that as you read it in the Valley of the Connecticut, or whêreever you may be, you ar transported tŏ that far country, and feel and see the very Italy of which. in the land itself, you ar ŏnly sŏmetimes conscious. This is the charm of a few books ŏnly. Beckford's little sketch has it, and so hav parts of Goethe's Italian Journey, and Stendhal. And The 'Improvisatore' has it, with Childe Harold." [Harper's. 2583

IN A WINTER CITY = No. 468.

IN THE GOLDEN SHELL [by LINDA (WHITE) (MAZINI) VILLARI : *Macmillan*, 1873.] "introduces us tŏ a graceful and interesting picture of life and scenes in **Palermo**. It has all the freshness and reality of a sketch from nature, and it is set in a delightful little framework of family life. The characters ar wel drawn, from Ciccio, the funny little nauty boy, tŏ the mŏther of Linda, whŏ has seen and knŏn much sorro, but whŏ is all the gentler and more tender for the experience." [Athenæum. 2584

IN THE RICE-FIELDS. [by the "MARCHESA COLOMBI" : *Chapman*, 1887.] "Simple and rapid almost tŏ a fault and with a certain puerility in the conclusion, this little tale stil contrives tŏ charm by its natural representation of human nature, its unforced and abundant feeling, its gentle, yet irresistible touches of occasional humor . . . The ŏther stories —'Too Late' and the wel-knŏn 'Sunset of an Ideal' [No. 2607]—dŏ not quite equal 'In the Rice-fields.' This dwelling on the monotony of passiv, uneducated, and unmarried women ends by becŏming monotonous itself. Yet a certain likeness tŏ life recommends the narration, altho the critic wil resent his transportation from the rice-marshes, whêre the author holds an unchallenged sway, tŏ cities such as Torino and Milano." [Ath. 2585

INDIAN SUMMER [**Florence**]= No. 471.

IRENE = No. 754.
ITALIAN (The) = No. 756.
JEALOUSY = *TEVERINO*.
JEWEL IN THE LOTUS. ☞ 2566.
JUNIA. [by M.. ALLEN OLNEY : *Blackwood*, 1878.] "The heroin is all which is noble, pure, and unselfish.

She is crushed and broken by what she endures, but not soured nor hardened; and in this, as in many ŏther respects, the narrativ of her life is made tŏ seem thŏroly consistent and natural. The majority of the characters ar clear and life-like, and the reader is not likely tŏ leave the book unfinished, in spite of its monotonous melancholy. The scenes borroed from Italian history ar treated with vigor and success." [Ath. **2586**
KNIGHT ERRANT [**Naples**] = No. 479.
LA BEATA [**Florence**] = No. 481; 𝕏 also *MARIETTA*.
LA MARCHESA = No. 482.
LA RABBIATA, by PAUL HEYSE, in *Chambers' Repos.* [*Living Age*, 22 dec. 1855]; also in *The Crayon*, aug., 1859; also in *The Ladies' Repository*, feb. 1863; also in *Tales by Heyse*. (No. 2521); also in *Masterpieces of German Fiction.* **2587**
LAST ALDINI (The) = No. 782.
LAVINIA = No. 484.
LAZY BEPPO, by HANS HOFFMANN, in *Appleton's*, sept., 1880; also in *Independent*, 5 july, 1885. **2588**
LEONORA CASALONI. [by T: ADOLPHUS TROLLOPE : *Chapman*, 1869.] "The heroin, so proud and noble, unable tŏ understand baseness, or tŏ comprehend that faith can be broken, struc down by her lŏver's worthlessness, is a fine type of character. The little glimps intŏ **Roman** manners and customs given by the relations of the Monsignor and the Marchesa opens possibilities of more tragedies and sins and miseries than hav ever cŏme tŏ light. The curious complications of the Casaloni family arrangements work out a very pleasant and interesting story ; and thêre is, at the last, ŏne moment of supreme

poetical justiçe which the reader wil regret was not more prolonged, ŏnly that the victims ar too contemptible tŏ be even trodden upon." [Athenæum. **2589**
LEONE = No. 789.
LEPER OF AOSTA (The), by XAVIER DE MAISTRE : London, *Williams*, 1872. **2590**
LIKE SHIPS UPON THE SEA [**Rome**] = No. 486.
LORENZO BENONI = No. 797.
LOUISA = No. 804.
LOVE BLINDED [by SALVATORE FARINA : *Charing Cross Pub. Co.*, 1879.] "is a compact little story of a young married couple of the upper middle class settled in **Milan**. Thêy hav married throu whim, and almost immediately afterwards suppose that thêy dŏ not care for ŏne anŏther. Thêy agree tŏ liv apart without any scandal, each taking a spel of town life at a time when the ŏther is in the country. Then the husband lŏses his eyesight by cataract ; his wife stretches a point in his favor so far as tŏ tend him in his blindness ; thêy fall in lŏve with ŏne anŏther during the process, and, on his restoration tŏ sight by an operation, ar the happiest and most tender of lŏvers. The thread of this simple plot is twined with the humors of a materialistic physician, whŏ at first wishes tŏ make lŏve on his ŏn account tŏ the unsatisfied bride, thinking that no real wrong wil be dŏne thêreby tŏ his patient, the chilly Leonardo, but afterwards sacrifiçes his inclination tŏ the pleasure of reconciling the young couple, and gets himself married, willy-nilly, tŏ the wife's ugly cousin. The story is prettily told, with a certain combination of the sentimental, the gallant, and the domestic in tone ; thêre is a

MAID CALLED BARBARA (A).
[by CATHARINE CHILDAR : *Hurst*, 1888.]
" The story is a good õne, and it is wel
told. The scenes in **Florence**, with
the picture of the life of the English
colony, ar particularly good. The
writer, too, givs frequent proof of a gift
of quiet humor." [Spectator. **492 k**

touch of Italian grace throuoūt."
[Athenæum. **2591**
MADAME DE PRESNEL [Rome]
= No. 490.
MADEMOISELLE MORI. [by
MA. ROBERTS: Boston, *Ticknor*,
1860.] "The descriptions of Roman
scenes and places ar full of truth, and
render the common, everyday aspect
of streets and squares, of gardens and
churches, of popular customs and
social habits, with equal spirit and
fidelity." [Atlantic] See No. 812. **2592**
MAE MADDEN [Rome] = No.
492.
MAN'S A MAN FOR A' THAT
[Rome] = No. 490.
MARIA FRANCESCA. by HEYSE.
in *Masterpieces of German Fiction*,
(64 pp.) **2593**
MARBLE FAUN [Rome] = No.
817.
MARIETTA [by T: ADOLPHUS
TROLLOPE: *Chapman*, 1862.] is "a
skilfully-executed and hīly-finished
picture of middle-class life in Florence. The incidents ar so accurately
described that we feel thêy be matter
of every-day occurrence in Tuscany.
Marietta is as different a heroin from
LA BEATA as can be conceived.
Nor dōes this book, like that, contain
the simple, touching story of a woman's wrôngs. Marietta is of quite
anôther nature from the devoted little
model,—a woman with but ōne idea,
which amounts almost tŏ a monomania—relentlessly stern of purpos—
sacrifiçing herself and all about her,
tŏ the accomplishment of her ōne object. viz.. the restoration of the Lunardi family tŏ its hī position."
[Athenæum.]—"In Marietta family
pride is the all-engrossing sentiment.
She is a persevering, but ōtherwise
not remarkable woman; and yet she
rises abōve the level of her surroundings by the force of her character and
the power which has sustained her in
the surrender of all human sympathy
and lōve for the achievement of ōne
grêat object. She is not a lōvable
person, but ōne whŏ commands respect. The same can not be said for
her nephew, the last scion of the
house of Lunardi,—weak, dreamy,
and irresolute—as much in lōve with
Laura as his half-alive nature wil admit, and yet incapable of a lofty or
absorbing passion. We ar at a loss tŏ
see what a charming girl like Laura
can find tŏ admire in such a slo,
nervless lōver, except, perhaps that
his gentle nature yields readily tŏ her
control, and that it is gratifying tŏ
her self-lōve tŏ be the Egeria from
whŏm he draws aid and inspiration.
The old Canonica is ōne of a thousand whŏm we daily meet in the
streets of an Italian city; but the
canon Guido is a more subtle and
dangerous personage. A man of
moderate intellect, no hī standard of
morality, and a dignified and per-
suasiv address, he seems secure in a
position established by history and
tradition, and dating bac tŏ an age tŏ
which Italians refer with unquestion-
ing reverence. The little sketch of
poor Gobbo Bonanera is ōne of the
best in the book; it is short, but full
of vigor, and imparts a degree of life
tŏ the latter'pages of the novel which
is very desirable. No ōne whŏ has
been in Florence can read without
interest the graphic sketches—so satisfactory in thêir fullness of detail—
of this lōvely old town and its surroundings; and those whŏse wanderings hav been more circumscribed wil
feel themselvs transported intŏ the
atmosphere of that beautiful city,

MISS MEREDITH [by AMY LEVY
(†, 1889) : *Hodder*, 1889.] ''is a short
story prettily told; a forlorn young governess, experiences in an aristocratic
Italian family with the brief trial, and —
this time — the entire reward, of a happy
löve. The style is animated, the English pure, and a tone of cheerfulness
prevails. The descriptions of **Pisa,** of
the old palace, and of its inhabitants ar
all equally happy. The atmosphere of
the little town, full of color and sunshine, is wel reproduced; while the different members of the Brogi family ar
humorously sketched with few strokes.
The löve story is extremely slight, but
supplies a sufficient excuse for its bright
and pretty setting.ᵛ [Athenæum. **498 p**

whêre everything, except humanity, may be seen in the grêatest perfection." [Round Table. 2594

MARZIO'S CRUCIFIX. [by FR. MARION CRAWFORD: *Macmillan*, 1887.] "Mr. Crawford has here givén us anòther of his striking pictures of Italian life and character, which yet differs from the rest of his work; since here, instead of taking a large canvas and cõvering it with brilliant, varied, and contrasting groups, he has made a careful study of a few personages, has presented tò us but twò interiors and worked out a single situation. Thêre ar 5 characters: Marzio, a silver-chiseller and an artist of hī merit in his rich designs and the perfection of his work; his wife, Maria Louisa, a handsõme, self-indulgent Roman woman of the loer class, whò spends her time in church-going and visiting, and is afraid of her hauty, severe husband; his dauter; his apprentiçe; and his brõther, a priest and his patron, for it is throu Don Paolo's influence that Marzio reçeives lavish orders for his best work ... Marzio's motiv for killing his brõther seems inadequate, and the characters dò not take hold of the reader tò such a degree that the story, wel conceived and executed tho it is, possesses a deep interest. It is, as all Mr. Crawford's work is, extremely picturęsque in design; and the descriptions of the workshop suggest a series of clever 'genre' pictures. We ar not sure but that the book is Mr. Crawford's concession tò the present fashion for realistic novels. If so, we ar glad that he stopped short of actual crime, and, instead, allowed his imagination tò develop his work with an ennobling idealizing influence which makes it what it is, and a book with a powerful moral." [American. 2595

MOSAIC-WORKERS (The) [Venice] = No. 850.

MOSAIC-WORKER'S DAUGHTER (The) [Rome] = No. 501.

NEPTUNE VASE (The) [Siena] = No. 502.

NINO AND MASO, by HEYSE, in *Modern Age*, June, 1883. 2596

NOBLE KINSMAN (A). [by ANTONIO GIULIO BARRILI : *Unwin*. 1885.] "Those whò lõve a rather old-fashioned story of the complications and intrĩgues which arise from loss of a wil must enjoy 'A Noble Kinsman.' The story, of which the scene is laid in modern **Naples**, deals with the history of a family throu twò generations. Thêre is a most ardent lõvetale, and plots and counterplots innumerable. The characters, which ar mostly pleasant, ar wel delineated, and the occasional descriptions interposed ar graphic." [Athenæ. 2597

ONLY A CORAL GIRL [Capri] = No. 511.

ONWARDS! BUT WHITHER? [by A. E. N. BEWICKE : *Smith*, 1875.] "Thêre is not any resemblance between Onwards and Hawthorne's 'Transformation' [No. 817], beyond the general outlines of a story in which a young girl of exceptional talent and artistic taste, not satisfied tò let the world wag without asking it why. finds herself at **Rome**, surrounded with admirers of various ranks and nationalities, with whòm she dões not flirt but philosophises; but probably no õne wil read the opening chapters of the õne book without being reminded of the õther. ... The 3 young men whò ar types of the 3 modes of thõt which the author traces in thêir influence and action throuõut the story ar all cleverly

771

ONE OF THEM [by C: LEVER
(1806–72) : *Chapman*, 1861.] " is amusing — very amusing. The scene is
placed in Italy, whêre English people of
various kinds, Irish people of Mr.
Lever's infallibly clever kind, and a
Yankee who is ' sui generis,' meet and
make acquaintance — and the present
story. Quackinboss, the Yankee, is,
perhaps, the most successful." [Spec-
tator. **509 p**

drawn; but the third, the cousin, Gaspard, the fiercely orthodox, brave, uncompromising, rather inhuman, yet ardently helpful Lieutenant in the Papal Zouaves, is the most interesting and original . . . Cécile is a most interesting creation, more so, perhaps, by her faults and errors, than throu the fine characteristics with which the author invests the careful, elevated, and suggestiv 'life study'." [Spectator. **2598**

ORCO [**Venice**] = No. 850; also in *Lippincott's Mag.*, Nov. 1873.

PAOLO GIANINI. [by PERICLES TZIKOS: *Tinsley*, 1879.] "Without being particularly wel written, without much plot or striking incident, this is a racy romance of bohemian life. Journalists and actors hold most of the stage, tho a few cheap aristocrats appear in the wings, and a Russian prince emerges from the side scenes and carries off ōne of the subsidiary heroins. In fact, the boards ar crowded with characters of all kinds, sōme of them having ōnly a remote connexion with the leading personages." [Athenæum. **2599**

PASCAREL = No. 890.

PILLONE = No. 899.

PRELATE (The) [**Rome**] = No. 518.

RECLUSE (The), by HEYSE, in *Ladies' Repository*, feb., 1868. [Sorrento.] **2600**

ROBIN [**Venice**] = No. 523.

RODERICK HUDSON [**Rome**]= No. 525.

ROMAN SINGER (A). [by FR. MARION CRAWFORD: *Houghton*, 1884.] "It is hard tŏ say in just what the pure and dignified quality of style here displayed consists : but no fastidious reader can fail tŏ find pleasure in its frank simplicity and its

mature air of having the language entirely in hand and feeling under no anxiety in using it. Professor Grandi seems tŏ us the best thing in it: the principal characters ar very objectiv, and thêre is not much character-drawing about them, ōnly such blocking out in large. simple outline as tŏ giv them distinctivness, whêreas the fact that the good professor is the narrator, and that his narration is kept excellently in character throuóut makes it inevitable that a pretty intimate knoledge of him should be acquired by the reader. We find his economies and generosities, his braveries and cowardiçes, really the most pleasing thing in the book; and his sale of the vineyard he had at last just succeeded in paying for, in order tŏ be able tŏ help his foster-sōn search for his sweetheârt, is a very successful bit of pathos. Yet Professor Grandi is altŏgether too uneventful and too cōlorless tŏ be artistically valuable except as a bacground tŏ the twŏ vivid young figures of the singer and the contessina; as a bacground he is charmingly effectiv. The framework of incident upon which the story is built is old : the plebeian but noble-spirited lōver; the faithful, hī-born maiden imprisoned by a stern father; the attempted compulsion tŏ accept an old and offensiv suitor; the final elopement by way of the secret stairs of a lonely castle. Even the lōver's deviçe of making her acquaintance by masquerading as a tutor. is old. But everything is so freshly handled that the antiquity of the main inçidents seems rather tŏ impròve them. After having said all this. as ōnly a part of what we might say of the pleasantness of the novel. it is almost out of place tŏ add that in spite of the grêat

passions it deals with, it nowhẽre
attains tŏ the hĩer province of art in
rousing emotion. be it ŏnly the excitement of narrativ." [Overland.
[See also, No. 922.   **2601**
ROMOLA = No. 926.
SANT' ILARIO = No. 933.
SARACINESCA. [by FR. MARI-
ON CRAWFORD: *Macmillan*, 1887.]
·'The author has taken for his dramatic personages Romans with
princely titles and long pedigrees, tŏ
whŏm the rich basilicas, the historic
palaces, the splendid church ceremonials,—instead of being a sho,—
belong by inheritance. This stately
life Mr. Crawford describes from the
interior. Few story-tellers could dŏ
this. He is a cosmopolitan. wel
equipped with ready knoledge of men
and things, while he has a floing
style and a brilliant. inçisiv touch.
But the secret of his success lies deeper than this, and consists in the clear
realization of the fact that he is writing about men and women. and that
men and women liv, mŏve. and hav
thêir being in emotions,—in sympathies. lŏves, hates. joys. and fears.
In the present book he has taken a
plot worn threadbare by long use,
but has invested it with new and rich
tints. and offers the reader so splendid
a spectacle, with such dignified and
stately figures for actors against
his magnificent bacground. that the
whole has the effect of novelty. He
never hesitates; his touch is never
crude. He has the insight of a man
of the world intŏ all social machinery.
He recognizes conventionalities and
obêys them, but is sŏ brilliant, so fluent. abãve all so picturesque, that
what is technical, even commonplace,
seems fresh. This is the story : Corona d'Astradenti is the young wife of

a worn-out roué, of grêat fortune and
of hĩ rank. Beautiful as Corona is
she is no less discreet. and no scandal
has sullied her fair name. But however wise she may hav been, the
present drama opens at a moment
when she realizes, with alarm at her
ŏn weakness, that she is under the
sway of a strong feeling for Giovanni
Saracinesca, whŏ is deeply in lŏve
with her. Saracinesca is ãlso the
object of the passionate and ambitious
hopes of Donna Tullia. a rich wido
whŏm Del Felice. the villain of the
story, is scheming tŏ marry. This is
the plot with which we ar over-
familiar, but it is filled in with clever
dialog. spirited action. and scenes
which would carry off with éclat a
much weaker story." [Amer. **2602**
SEALED PACKET (The) = *GIU-
LIO MALATESTA.*
SICILIAN ROMANCE (A) = No.
943.
SIGNA. [by "OUIDA", i. e., L..
de la Ramé: *Lippincott*, 1875.]
" 'Ouida' has taken a new departure.
She has abandoned the sublime alti-
tudes of hĩ society, whêre her heroes
wer Admirable Crichtons, and her
heroins ladies of impossible lŏveliness,
and descended tŏ child-life amõng the
humble ... 'Signa' is a story of remarkable intensity, but overwrŏt and
decidedly painful. It deals with life
in a villàge, describing it with singular vividness. The hero is an orphan
boy whŏ becõmes a grêat composer, a
and dies in the dawn of manhood, a
vietim tŏ the wiles of a woman. The
characters in the story ar drawn with
a stern vigor which is very impressiv.
Bruno, Gemma, Lippo, Signa himself,
ar masterly conceptions. Thêre is no
humor in the book.—which is sad,
intense, hard from the beginning tŏ

its tragical end." [Boston "Literary World." **2603**

SIGNOR I. [by SALVATORE FARINA: London. *Gardner*, 1888.] "A graceful, not uncommon theme is here treated in a decidedly original manner. The story of how Marc Antonio Abate's dauter married without his consent, and how the ultimate reconciliation was brôt about, is told with delicate humor, gentle pathos, and sympathetic observation of human nature, in the playful, suave style which Farina handles with such rare literary skil." [Athenæum.

——, SAME. in *Cosmopolitan Mag.*, Dec. 1886—June, 1887. **2604**

SIGNOR MONALDINI'S NIECE = No. 944.

SILVIA [**Sorrento**] = No. 530.

SIREN (A). [by T: ADOLPHUS TROLLOPE: *Smith*. 1870.] "The novels which best describe the daily life of the Italians of the present day ar written not in Italian but English. The most delightful of them is "Doctor Antonio" [No. 435], next Ruffini's, Mr. Adolphus Trollope's novels ar undoubtedly tô be placed. Thêy ar valuable, not merely because thêy ar wel-constructed and wel-written, but because thêy giv us studies of Italian life and manners painted with the utmost accuracy. The story is told with the skil of an accomplished narrator. In the "Siren" we ar shôn the ancient and secluded city of **Ravenna**; and its streets and suburbs becôme as familiar tô us as tho we knew them by heârt. We ar introduced tô the leaders of fashion, the players, the young men of pleasure, the lawyer. the physician, and the monk of the quaint provinçial town. We learn thêir habits, thêir ways of thôt, thêir crude theories of

politics and science, thêir narro prejudiçes and rapid passions. The carnival, with its wild liçense and its dul and stately ball; the gay, feverish life of the prima-donna, and the lonely vigils of the monk whô watches in the wayside church; the pompous pride of the conceited poet. and the fierce passion of the infatuated nobleman whô rushes intô crime at the bidding of jealousy, all pass before us with the vivedness of the magic-lantern. and the minute faithfulness of the stereoscope." [Round Table. **2605**

STELLA [**Rome**] = No. 955.

SUMMER'S ROMANCE (A) [**Capri**] = No. 536.

TEVERINO. [by "GEORGE SAND", i. e., Amantine Lucile Aurore (Dupin) Dudevant († 1876): N.-Y., *Fetridge*. 1856.] "Within the brief space of 24 hôurs, a whole romance is here comprehended. It is as bright and attractiv as the clime it illustrates, and full of that wisdom which lôses nothing from the sportiv mood in which it sômetimes shôs itself. "Teverino" exhibits but little passion or action, nor is it tô be taken exactly as a portraiture of manners, but the story is admirably told, and givs sôme new and interesting studies of character. The author paints not ônly the hîlyborn, fastidious woman of fashion. sated with pleasure, and seeking relief from ennui in any new adventure which is suggested, but she shôs that her sympathies ar tenderly awakened by the virtues and sorrôs of humble life. She understands the fervor and truth of loly affection. and describes the vicissitudes of toil and penury with close fidelity and touching pathos. Thêre ar likewise indications of common-sense and sagacity, such as ar not generally looked for in a

TALES OF EUROPEAN LIFE.
[Boston, *Loring*,1870.] "So many of ŏŭr countrymen hav been in Italy, and so many travelers hav written about it, that if we ar ignorant of any particular concerning the scenery, climate, or ruins, it is not oing tŏ any scarcity of works on the subject. These simple little stories, which ar entirely free from any pretension, ar tŏ be treated as pictures of manners and customs with which strangers ar not always acquainted. '*St. Cecilia*' is the most interesting, but '*Prato Fiorito*' is, perhaps, more characteristic of Italian feeling, its impulse and passion, its remorse and exaggerated contrition. The sketch entitled, '*Salvi and Cesare,*' is briefly and plainly given, and the '*Adventure in Prag*' wil repay perusal." [Hearth and Home. **538 p**

TWO ENGLISH GIRLS. [by
MABEL HART: *Hurst*, 1890.] "The
heroins ar charming specimens of very
modern English girls. . . . Thêy ar
art students at **Florence,** and their
adventures in the city of flowers ar deftly
and delicately treated. Both liv in a
world which is much more Italian than
ōūr country women usually mǒve in, and
both in their different ways giv as much
as thêy gain from the teachers and fello
pupils whǒ receive them so heârtily and
finally cōme tǒ adore them. About the
best points in this little sketch ar the
easy dialog and the natural manner in
which the passionate old 'maestro,'
his ruffish, masculin sǒn, and the
selfish, unmoral, not immoral, genius
Guido Gindotti, act and ar acted on by
the bright society of twǒ simple-heârted
English gentlewomen. It is obvious
that every member of the little coterie is
the better for the intercourse which is
so vividly described, tho a terrible laps
on Guido's part leads tǒ a tragic end of
the hopes he ōnce shared with Evelyn
Grey." [Athenæum. **546 p**

writer whŏ is supposed tŏ be devoted tŏ the "cloud-land" of imagination, and a power of sketching scenery and incident of a very hĭ order. The lady whŏ resigns herself tŏ the guidance of Leonce, upon condition that she shal be wel amused during the day, has no reason tŏ complain of his efforts for her entertainment, altho her treatment of him shōs little generosity. He is as naturally jealous and unreasonable as most lōvers ar, and she as coquettish and vain as ŏthers of her class. Madeleine, the little bird-tamer, is most captivating." [Hearth and Home. **2606**

——. SAME ("Jealousy"), *Peterson,* 1870.

TO LEEWARD [**Rome**] = No. 543.

TOLLA, Boston. *Whittemore,* 1856, [**Rome**] = No. 983.

TREASURE TOWER (The) [**Malta**] = No. 545.

TWO CORONETS = No. 992.

VERA [**Rome**] = No. 553.

VESTIGIA [**Livorno**] = No. 1000.

VIRGINIA [**Rome**] = No. 556.

WANE OF AN IDEAL (The) [by "the MARCHESA COLOMBI", i. e., Maria Torelli-Torriani : N.-Y., *Gottsberger,* 1885.] is "ŏne of the saddest of stories, sadder than any tale of constancy and death. We dŏ not call it a tragedy in the ordinary sense when the hero is left prosperous and successful, and the heroin peaceful and moderately content with life; yet it is really tragical tŏ trace the decadence of generous and enthusiastic youth tŏ worldly-wise and self-seeking middle age, and tŏ see pure and strong lŏve supplanted by meaner passions. The work in which this is dōne is ŏne of no ordinary ability; the characters ar so forcibly drawn as tŏ bêar the stamp of reality and truth, and ar characteristic both as individuals and as national types. Especially is this true of 'La Matta,' the pathos of whŏse dumb devotion tŏ her young master is tŏ be paralleled ōnly in the pages of Turgénief. Altŏgether, this is a remarkable book, particularly surprising as the work of a feminin hand." [American. **2607**

——, SAME, with No. 2585.

WHIMSICAL WOOING (A). [by ANTONIO GIULIO BARRILI : N.-Y., *Wm. S. Gottsberger,* 1883.] "If 'The Eleventh Commandment' [No. 2576] was a good three-act play, 'A Whimsical Wooing' is a sparkling comedietta. It has ōne situation, a single catastrophē, yet, like a bit of impressionist painting of the finer sort, it reveals in a flash all the possibilities of the scene. The hero, a man of wealth, position, and accomplishments, finds himself at the end of his resources for entertainment or interest. Hopelessly bored, he abandons himself tŏ the drift of chance, and finds himself, in no longer space of time than from midnight tŏ daylight —when and how, the reader will thank us for not forstalling his pleasure in finding out for himself." [Nation. **2608**

WHO BREAKS—PAYS = No. 559.

YOUNG HOSTESS OF TREPPI, by HEYSE, in *Ladies' Repository,* jan.-feb., 1870. **2609**

PRICE: ONE COPY. $.50, TWO COPIES. $.75; THREE. $1 00, FOUR, $1,25; FIVE, $1,50 TEN, $2.50; FIFTEEN, $3.00.

A

DESCRIPTIVE LIST

OF

NOVELS AND TALES

DEALING WITH

LIFE IN RUSSIA.

COMPILED BY
W: M. GRISWOLD.

CAMBRIDGE, MASS.:
W: M. GRISWOLD, PUBLISHER.
NEW-YORK, FOR SALE BY G: P. PUTNAM'S SONS, 27 W. 23D ST.
1892.

[*From the "School Bulletin," Aug.*, 1892.]

We hope teachers will not fail tŏ recognize the work W. M. Griswold is dŏing in his classified bibliography. He sends us a DESCRIPTIVE LIST OF NOVELS AND TALES DEALING WITH LIFE IN FRANCE (Cambridge, Mass., 1892, 8vo, pp. 94, $1.00), which is of immediate practical use tŏ the teacher of French history as well as of French literature.

[*From the "Central Christian Advocate."*]

Mr. Griswold has dōne an excellent work, which will be appreciated by all librarians, and by many people of cultivated taste whŏ wish tŏ get on the track of the best French fiction, or at least tŏ secure sōme guidance and information in regard tŏ its qualities and characteristics. His former "lists" have dealt with American City and Country Life, with Life in England, etc . . . Life in city and country, peasant life and soldier life, the reckless and adventurous career of the free and easy student in Paris, and the rude rustic amōng the mountains,—all these phases of French life pass in review in the books which Mr. Griswold has here catalogued. A guide like this would be invaluable tŏ a student of French literature, telling as well what tŏ avoid, as what tŏ secure and read.

[*From the "Boston Commonwealth,"* 13 *Aug.*, 1892.]

If all libraries wer generously equipped with these Lists, the long-suffering curator of books would find more pleasure in life. The compilation and selection ar made with rare skill. The poor book drops into deservd oblivion, while the worthy but neglected and forgotten good book is restored tŏ the eye of the world.

Sōme not too busy people make note of the name of a novel recommended by a trustworthy critic, but when the time for use cōmes the note seldom is at hand, and, if ready, generally givs the mere title and no idea of the contents. But here is a series of brochures that contain excerpts from the fairest critical notices, often from several sources, and ōne is enabled tŏ form a sort of judgment of choice without actually glancing at the book itself. Of course, those dealing with foreign lands must for the grêater part be translations, since with few exceptions the most truthful and vivid characterizations cōme from the compatriot whŏ has summered and wintered his fellows. Few people realize the patience, skill, and labor involvd in such an undertaking as the publication of these successiv lists, but those whŏ dŏ should urge upon ōthers the use of so valuable a means of education and pleasure. As a series of 'condensed novels' they ar interesting, too.

NOVELS DESCRIPTIV OF RUSSIAN LIFE.

The object of this list is to direct readers, such as would enjoy the kind of books here described, to a number of novels, easily accessible, but which, in many cases, hav been forgotten within a year or two after publication. That the existence of works of fiction is remembered so short a time is a pity, since, for every new book of merit, there ar, in most libraries, a hundred as good or better, unknown to the majority of readers. It is hoped that the publication of this and similar lists will lessen, in some measure, the disposition to read an inferior NEW *book when superior* OLD *books, equally fresh to most readers, ar at hand. It may be observed that the compiler has tried to include only such works as competent critics hav proclaimed to be well-written, interesting, and free from sensationalism, sentimentality, and pretense.* BUT *in a few cases, books hav been noticed on account of the reputation of their authors, or their great popularity, rather than their merit. The selected "notices" ar generally abridged.*

This list will be followed by others describing DANISH, NORWEGIAN, SPANISH,—HUMOROUS, ECCENTRIC *and* FANCIFUL *novels and tales.*

AFTER DEATH, by TURGÉNIEF, in *Modern Age*, july-aug., 1883. **2610**

ANNA KARÉNINA [by LYOF [N.] TOLSTOI: N.-Y., *Crowell*, 1886.] "is the most mature and probably the gréatest of the author's works. Unlike 'War and Peace' [No. 1007] it is purely domestic in its subject matter, but thêre is no lac of variety in its scenes and characters. It is, indeed, a world in itself, so comprehensiv is its grasp, and so intimately dŏes it bring us intŏ relations with the manifold aspects of country and city life in Russia. Wer this work the sole available document, it would be possible tŏ construct from its pages a grêat deal of Russian contemporary civilisation. It is, of course, realistic tŏ the last degree. but its realism is not confined tŏ minute descriptions of material objects;—it is no less made use of in the treatment of emotion. Thêre ar few works of art in which the art is so wel conçealed; few works of fiction which giv so strong a sense of reality as this. We seem tŏ look upon life itself and forget the medium of the novelist's imagination throu which we really vue it. And right here we ar brŏt tŏ compare the methods of Tolstoi with those of his better knŏn and unquestionably grêater countryman, Turgénief. In the marvellous novels of the latter we hav this same feeling of immediate contact with the facts of material existence and of emotional life, and the effect is produçed with much less machinery than

Tolstoi is compelled tŏ use. The work of Turgénief surpasses the work of Tolstoi, in revealing that sublimation of thŏt and imagination which giv tŏ it an artistic value beyond that of almost any ŏther imaginativ prose. Tolstoi lacs this power of concentration and this unerring judgment in the choiçe of word or phrase. He can not sum up a situation in a simple pregnant sentence, but he can present it with grēat force in a chapter. Now that this grēat story of 'Anna Karénina' has been brŏt tŏ the cognizance of the western world, it is not likely tŏ be soon forgotten. It wil be remembered for its minute and unstrained descriptions, for its deep tragedy, unfolded act after act as by the hand of fate, and for its undercurrent of gentle religious feeling, never falling tŏ the offensiv level of dogmatism, yet giving marked character tŏ the book, and revealing unmistakably the spiritual lineaments of the Russian apostle of quietism." [Dial.]—"The free, unconscious mŏvement, and the marvelous vitality of Tolstoi's work, is ŏne of the many impressions left in the reader's mind on laying down "Anna Karénina." The succession of pictures is so natural, the development of the characters apparently so simple, that ŏur idea of the grēatness of the artist is lost in ŏur perception of the absolute truth of his work. The novel seems tŏ be not a creation, but a revelation of sŏmething which exists ... No mere realist could hav written the chapter which describes 'Levin's' long day in the hay-fields, and the birth of Kitty's and Levin's first child. These ar transcriptions from nature,—from life; they giv us, too, that exquisit thril of feeling which it is the province of poetry tŏ stir. ... 'Anna' herself is a more complex creation than either, but she is not less real. It would be impossible tŏ find a more truthful study of a woman, ŏne which better enables us tŏ recognize the struggle in the moral nature. 'Anna' is married tŏ an official, hi in power, whŏ is much older than she. The marriage has not satisfied her, but she has, nevertheless been happy in her life and in her child, and she is startled tŏ find that new and rich sources of enjoyment ar stirred in her whole nature by the mere presence of 'Vronsky', a young officer whŏm she meets while on a visit tŏ Moscow. 'Vronsky' folloes her tŏ Petersburg, and for him gradually she givs up everything— her husband, her social status, and finally even her sŏn. She goes away and livs with her lŏver, and as long as she believes that he lŏves her she is, she believes, completely happy. When she suffers it is not from conscience,—at least she dŏes not believe that it is conscience, but from a jealous dread of sŏme new influence which shal draw 'Vronsky' away from her. This jealousy is a vital and progressiv disease. She tries tŏ fil her lŏver's life so absolutely that he can care for nŏthing else. She interests herself in everything which interests him, she develops all her powers, and studies eve-y art tŏ preserve her beauty, and yet she feels every day an increasing conviction that he is tired of her, that he is cramped, mortified tŏ be excluded from the society he lŏves by his anomalous position ... He lŏves her, but she can not endure it that his lŏve for her is nof the only thing in his life. Her irritability poisons all thēir intercourse. She knoes that she is wrong and that her jealousy overthroes more than she can ever build up again. It is like a madness, —she feels that it wil destroy her, and she finally rushes toards it that it may destroy her. Thére is no sadder story on record and no truer ŏne." [American. 2611

ANNALS OF A SPORTSMAN. [by IVAN TURGÉNIEF: N.-Y., *Holt*, 1885.] "Turgénief's first large work is perhaps his best. The "Recollections" ar thrŏu intŏ the form of short sketches, of which the ablest ar "*Khor and Kalinitsh*," "*The Devil's Dale*," "*The Singers*," "*Kasjan*," "*Two Days in the Forest*," and "*Forest and Steppe*". . . This book contains almost a natural history of the Russian people. Nearly all the sketches ar taken from amŏng the dwellers in the country; Turgénief pictures the houseless serf, shŏs peasant after peasant, givs type after type of land-ŏner and aristocrat. The peasant is, in his pages, an extremely good-natured, easily-satisfied man, clever, ready, and of robust health . . . The aristocrats employed at Court or in the public serviçe liv in his pages as Tartars, with a slight exterior polish of manner. Théy ar all either spendthrifts, whŏ ruin ŏthers as wel as themselvs, or fools honored with servile reverence. Debauchés, tyrants, wild beasts of all sorts hav sat tŏ him for thĕir picture." [Spectator.] — "These simple, quiet stories made no startling revelations of the woes of the serfs, but théy opened the eyes of the masters tŏ thĕir ŏn forlorn, hopeless position . . . These sad, stunted existences ar ŏur brŏthers, ŏurselvs. Tŏ this has ŏur injustiçe brŏt us. Let us save ŏur children from the like . . . 'The Annals of a Sports-

man' is best described as a piece of pure realism all the more remarkable since the Romantics wer stil the rulers. It is realism in that sense which applies not tŏ choice of subject, but tŏ method of treatment. It sets before the reader the scene, the character in so clear white light that he may judge of them with *his* eyes, *his* thŏt. By any such word or phrase as impartial, impersonal, or disinterested curiosity, the same thing is meant. Tŏ set forth the subject not in *our* way, not in ŏur party's way, not tŏ serv a special end, but tŏ represent life perfectly—this is realism." [Nation. 2612

——, SAME ("Russian Life in the Interior"), Edinburgh, *Black.* 1853.

——, SAME (abridged) in *Fraser's Mag.* [*Graham's Mag.*, Nov.] 1854.

ANNOUCHKA, by TURGÉNIEF: Boston, *Cupples.* 1884. [Same as No. 2616?] 2613

ANTCHAR (The), by TURGÉNIEF, in *Galaxy*, mar.-apr 1873. 2614

APOTHECARY'S WIFE (The), by SOLLUGUB, in *Dublin Univ. Mag.* [*Daguerreotype*, 25 mar and 8 apr.] 1848. 2615

ARIADNE. [by "H: GRÉVILLE," i. e., Alice M.. Céleste (Fleury) Durand: *Appleton*, 1878.] "The heroin is lo-born and poor; but the divine gift of song rescues her from companionship with the 'canaille,' and plaçes her in the çircle of the Princess Orlin and ŏther lords and ladies of hi degree . . . But it is due tŏ the author tŏ say that sho apparently delineates hi society simply becauxe she is most familiar with its ways, and is aware of the pictorial and striking effects tŏ be obtained from luxurious surroundings.

'Ariadne' is a simple and affecting löve-story, diversified with a charming picture of school-girl life and a few vivid glimpses of the operatic stage and green-room, the whole written in an exquisitly easy, graçeful, polished style." [Appleton. **2616**

ASSYA. [by IVAN [NIKOLAIVICH] TURGÉNIEF: in *Galaxy*, mar. 1877; also with *AN UNFORTUNATE WOM-AN.*] "The logic of destiny has full sway in determining the conclusion of Assya. The heroin is a creation of extraordinary vitality, a remarkable type of perverted womanhood. She is the dauter of a noble-man, the möther being a peasant. Assya has many fine qualities, but the shame of her origin acts as a continual irritant upon her proud, shy nature; "she was asham-ed,—ashamed of that feeling of shame, and proud of it at the same time." An un-trained mind, given over tö the impulses of the moment, how could she be any-thing but a problem tö öthers as wel as tö herself? When she falls in löve with the vaçillating youth in whöse words the story is told, she is overwhelmed with the fervor of her passion, and when her ad-vances ar repulsed, she is like a wounded animal, seeking a hiding place. Here again Turgénief has aimed tö depict the viçes and shortcömings of the nobility, and tö foretel the results of thêir selfish and ignorant power. But in reading Turgénief öne öt not tö push the allegory too far. The interest of his writings lies in thêir artistic power, and throu that thêy speak tö us in no uncertain way." [Bos-ton "Literary World." **2617**

BLIND MUSICIAN (The) [by VLADI-MIR KOROLENKO: N.-Y., *Lovell*, 1890.] "is a charming, idyllic tale in which the gröth and development of a musical genius is described with grêat insight and delicaçy of feeling. The blind boy, whö gains a wide acquaintance with the ex-ternal world throu hearing sounds inandi-ble tö öthers, and with the inner world of emotion throu his groom's flute-playing, groes tö be a grêat pianist, and every step in the proçess is shön with a singular power." [Critic. **2618**

——, SAME, Boston, *Little & Brown.*

BURIED ALIVE [by FEDOR DOSTOI-EFSKI: *Holt*, 1881.] "is a vivid picture of life in a convict prison in Siberia 30 years ago. It is difficult tö see why it should be bröt forward now, for the supposed nar-rator (he had killed his wife in a fit of jealousy) is at pains tö remark more than önce that even in 1862, many things had been changed for the better. The book has little tö say of political prisoners ... The childish, recless yielding tö momen-tary passion which reappears in every öne of the convicts' stories, and the dumb in-difference tö consequences, sho preçisely the qualities of the men whö use the dag-ger and the bomb. As tö the prison and its disciplin, hideous and cruel as many of the inçidents seem, thêy ar not without parallel." [Nation. **2619**

CAPTAIN'S DAUGHTER, by PUSH-KIN, = No. 625.

CHILDHOOD AND YOUTH [by LYOF [NIKOLAIVICH] TOLSTOI: London, *Bell*, 1862.] "is a very clever and life-like story of childhood and boyhood. The Russian dress dões not disguise the truth of the human nature. It givs a wel-described picture of daily life. Story it can scarcely be called, for it is the ram-bling recollections of a child and youth:

but it givs an insight intŏ the thŏts, perverseness and sorrŏs of a child. The translation [by M. von Meysenbug] is that of a foreiner, and the stif, peculiar English givs it an originality which is quaint and pleasant." [Athenæ. **2620**

CLEMENCE D' ORVILLE, by CARL DETLEF, Boston, *Littell*, 1868. **2621**

CLOAK (The), by GOGOL, in *Short Stories*, Aug., 1891, 29 p.; also with No. 2631, which see, **2622**

CORRESPONDENCE (A), by TURGÉNIEF, = No. 652.

COSSACK TALES, by GOGOL, London, 1860. **2623**

CRIME AND PUNISHMENT, by DOSTOIEVSKI, ☞ *ECCENTRIC NOVELS.*

CRUEL CITY (The). [by DIMITRI GRIGOROVICH, N.-Y., *Cassell*, 1891.] "Grigorovich represents an entirely different school of literature from that of Tolstoi and Gogol, being as cheerful and optimistic as thêy ar gloomy and pessimistic. 'The Cruel City' is an admirable picture of life in St. Petersburg, described with a Balzac minuteness. It is the story of a countryman whŏ came tŏ St. Petersburg with all his savings in his pocket. He had a number of relativs thêre whŏm he believed tŏ be rich and grêat because thêy livd in a city. Thêy wer neither. and the way thêy fleeced the amiable countryman is as amusing as it is pathetic." [Publishers' Weekly. **2624**

DEAD SOULS [by N: [VASILIEVICH] GOGOL: N.-Y., *Crowell*, 1888.] "is not a novel; it is a document in the history of civilization. It is the permanent record, in artistic form, of the life of a nation at an important period of its existence. It shares with Turgénief's 'Annals of a Sportsman' [No. 2612] the distinction of preserving for future students the Russia of Nicholas and the period preceding the emançipation. The art of Gogol is less perfect than that of Turgénief, but the twŏ writers ar equal in the power of minute observation and its interpretation, and thêy combine alike the closest attention tŏ details with the utmost breadth of conception. Just as in ōne book the sportsman whŏ relates his experience cōmes intŏ contact with all sorts of people, so the rascally hero of the ōther, in his quest for dead souls, vues all the typical phases of provincial life, and portrays them with marvellous accuracy. Dead souls, it should be understood, ar souls, or serfs, legally existent and taxable after death, because thêir names ar stil on the census lists. Tchitchikoff purchases dead souls with the extremely discreditable design of mortgaging them as valuable property, and living in opulence upon the il-gotten proceeds. His travels from ōne country tŏ anōther, and the descriptions of the people whŏm he meets, form the substance of Gogol's work. The story of Tchitchikoff and his rascalities is amusing enuf, but it is ōnly a pretext for introduçing the reader tŏ a grêat variety of people, so the fact that the work was left unfinished at Gogol's death dōes not grêatly detract from its value." [Dial.

——, SAME ("Home Life"), London, *Hurst*, 1854. **2625**

DEAD TO THE WORLD. [by "CARL DETLEF," i. c., Klara Bauer (†, 1876): Boston, *Gill*, 1875.] "Prince Ugarin, when more that half his life has been passed in debauchery, marries a woman, young, hĭ-born, and beautiful, but whŏm he dŏes not pretend tŏ lŏve, and whŏm he fails tŏ treat with even common respect. She livs with him for years in the splendid solitude of a home from which truth and trust, lŏve and purity, hav fled. At last, when she can bêar it no longer, she goes away, leaving a letter in which she reveals her knoledge of his past life, and confesses her ŏn sin. "Leo, my favorit child, is not your sŏn." The princess is overtaken with her lŏver and thêir child, both of whŏm disappear, while she is left "dead tŏ the world," a garded prisoner for life, behind the walls of a nunnery in the heârt of Russia. The prince announces his wife's death tŏ his ŏnly legitimate dauter—a mere child,—keeping from her the whole story. This girl, as she groes tŏ womanhood, becŏmes violently in lŏve with the prince's nephew. He again is in lŏve with and secretly marries an illegitimate dauter of the prince, a foundling whŏ had been kept in the manor-house—the fact of her kinship unknŏn tŏ any but herself. By and by the nephew is seized for partiçipation in a conspiracy, and shoots himself rather than be taken. The foundling dauter asserts her kinship tŏ the prince, and confesses the secret marriage with his nephew. Poor Olga, the prince's dauter, is crushed for a time, and is restored ŏnly when she finds the mŏther whŏm all had believed tŏ be dead." [Overland.]—"The tone of the story is singularly stern and sad; thêre is no happiness or light, and thêre is far more sin than atonement. Sŏme of the characters—indeed, we may say, all—ar powerfully drawn. Dina and

Paul Petrovich being especially original. The inçidents ar few; but sŏme of the scenes,—that between Prince Ugarin and his wife, and the arrest of Vladimir, for instance, ar terribly dramatic. The effect of the story is not pleasant,—tho its moral is unexceptionable; but the author's genius exerçises an undeniable fascination in its pages." [Boston "Lit. World." **2626** DEATH OF IVAN ILYITCH [ETC.], (The). [by LYOF [N.] TOLSTOI: N.-Y., Crowell, 1877.] "These short stories may be taken as the fairest expression of the author's philosophy of life. The first story seems tŏ hav been written for educated readers; all the ŏthers as tracts for the instruction of the peasantry. Curious and interesting tho these popular stories ar, we think most readers wil find a deeper impression left upon them by the ŏne in which Tolstoi speaks from *his* mind tŏ *his* class ... In substance, several of the moral tales ar not so very different from those which English and American children ar bred on as the Tolstoi enthusiasts would hav us believe (what a curiously familiar sound, e. g., hav the tales called "If you Neglect the Fire you don't Put it Out," "Whêre Lŏve is, thêre God is also," and "Little Girls Wiser than Old Men") : but the quaint vigor of these, and a sort of inherent originality, an unconscious re-originating of what ŏthers had long-dŏne, make them unique." [Overland.]—It is "most gloomy; here the miserable act of dying is described at length and with full details, the chief actor in the very realistic tragedy being a bily respectable, but unsympathetic judicial officer, whŏse wife and dauter ar a good deal annoyed by his impatience during his sufferings, and the inordinate length tŏ which his dying agony is protracted. Every ŏne must admit that the descriptions ar powerful, the sketches of character excellent, and no ŏne can read the tale without being grêatly depressed." [Athenæum. **2627**

—— SAME, with *MY HUSBAND.*
DESPERATE, by TURGÉNIEF, in *Cosmopolitan*, Aug., 1888. **2628**

DIMITRI ROUDINE. [by IVAN [S.] TURGÉNIEF: N.-Y., *Holt*, 1873.] "We almost forget, in folioing this tender yet keen analysis of a pathetic character, that thêre is really sŏmething of a story in the book. Roudine imagins that he lŏves Natalie, and he wins her brave, inexperieneed heârt; but when thêir lŏve is prematurely discŏvered tŏ her mŏther, and Natalie cŏmes tŏ him ready to fly with him, tŏ be his at any cost, he is paralyzed at the thŏt of Daria's opposition . . . We ar not quite sure whether we like or dislike the carefulness with which Roudine's whole character is kept from us, so that we pass from admiration tŏ despite before we cŏme finally tŏ half-respectful compassion; and yet is not this the way it would be in life? Perhaps, also, if we fully understood him at first, his relations tŏ the ŏthers would not so much interest us. But dŏ we wholly understand him at last? This many be doubted, tho in the meantime we ar taut a merciful distrust of ŏur judgment, and we take Leschnieff's forgiving and remorseful attitude tŏards him. It may be safely surmised that this was the chief effect that Turgénief desired tŏ produce; certainly he treats the story involvd in the portrayal of Roudine's character with almost contemptuous indifference, letting three

epilogs limp in after the first rambling narrativ has spent itself, and seeming tŏ care for these ŏnly as thêy further reveal the hero's traits. But for all this looseness of construction, it is a very grêat novel,—as much grêater than the novel of inçident as Hamlet is grêater than Richard III. It is of the kind of novel which can alone keep the art of fiction from being the weariness and derision of mature readers; and if it is most deeply melancholy, it is also as lenient and thôtful as a just man's experience of men." [Atlantic. **2629**

DOMINION OF DARKNESS (The), by TOLSTOI: *Vizetelly*, 1888. **2630**

DOSIA [by "H: GRÉVILLE," i. e., Alice M.. Céleste (Fleury) Durand; Boston, *Estes*, 1878; London, *Charing Cross Co.*, 1881.] "is a Russian story, but it wil add nŏthing tŏ that mass of sombre lore which we call knoledge of Russian life. The half-dozen personages whŏ talk so wittily and behave so naturally with ŏne anŏther, throu its 260 very open pages, all belong tŏ that bily privileged and triply garded class of society for whŏm life is much the same in every land . . . A wild and wayward, but hî-spirited, warm-heârted, and bewitching little hoyden wins the lŏve of a peculiarly grave and fastidious man. A stately and experienced woman, the sister of the first lŏver, bestoes her oft-sŏt hand on the cousin of the first lady,—a young officer, remarkable for nŏthing previously but simple honor and boyish vivacity. This is the whole story, but it is charmingly told, with an abundançe of odd inçident and sparkling dialog. The fasçinations of the heroin ar nowhêre solemnly proclaimed, but the reader falls under thêir spel the moment she is introduçed." [Atlantic.

——, SAME ("Wayward Dosia"), Chicago, *Laird*, 1891. **2631**

DOURNOF [NIANIA] by "H: Gréville," i. e., Alice M.. Céleste (Fleury) Durand: 1879.] "is a sweet and touching little story, introduçing, tŏ be sure, an unfaithful wife and a disordered home, but presenting in the pure lŏve of Dournof and Antonine a charming picture; in the disillusion of Dournof after his marriage with Marianne, a tender but telling rebuke of inconstancy; in Marianne herself a forçible illustration of a hollo and selfish heàrt: and in the nurse Niania ŏne of the noblest and most impressiv figures which this true artist has drawn. The story is short and sad." [Boston "Literary World." **2632**

DREAM (The), by TURGÉNIEF, in *Home Journal*, Jan.-Feb., 1878. **2633**

EVE OF ST. JOHN (The). [by N: [VASILIEVICH] GOGOL (1808-52): N.-Y., *Crowell*, 1886.] "These 5 stories range ŏver a wide field—" *The Eve of St. John*," a peasant witch story; "*How the Two Ivans Quarreled*," a sŏmewhat broadly humorous tale; "*Old Fashioned Farmers*," a gentle, half-humorous and half-pathetic genre study; "*The Portrait*," which, with a half supernatural machinery, expresses a lofty vue of moral purpos in art; and "*The Cloak*," whŏse motiv is purely pathetic (all the more, perhaps, for its genial style) a pitiful little story, which the tender-heàrted wil dŏ as wel not tŏ read." [Overland. **2634**

EXPIATION, = *SAVELI'S EXPIA.*

FAMILY HAPPINESS = *KATIA.*

FATHERS AND SONS. [by IVAN

[SERGEIVICH] TURGÉNIEF († 1883): N.-Y., *Leypoldt*, 1867.] "What a novel should hav this novel dŏes not lac. Rather it possesses, in large measure, several of the requisits of a really excellent novel, and we feel sure of its taking an honorable place amŏng the more valued contemporary works of fiction. Thêre can, at any rate, be no doubt that novel readers wil thank Mr. Schuyler for a most readable addition tŏ thêir stoc of stories; it is a grêat deal tŏ say nowadays for a novel of any length, but, after beginning "Fathers and Sons," it wil be found easier tŏ go on tŏ the end than tŏ stop. And if it be the end of novels that thêy be readable, as for comedies, açcording tŏ Dr. Johnson, that thêy make people lâf—and certainly a tale which can not be told seems tŏ want the main thing—then what we hav said is praise enuf. But "Fathers and Sons" is not wholy dependent for its interest upon its plot, upon its freshness of inçident, the strangeness of the manners depicted, the rapidity of mŏvement, the dramatic situations, the careful and sŏmetimes poetical painting of natural scenêry, the humor, the pathos—tho these ar amŏng its characteristics; stil less is it wholy dependent upon the glimpses it givs us of the working of various social forces which ar now operating upon Russia—tho these also it offers us. The author is successful in the novelist's biest labor—in conçeiving and delineating his characters. He dŏes not paint with elaboration, but he sketches with a vigorous and accurate pencil; and he has given us real men and real women." [Nation.]—"Thêre ar 3 elderly men in the book, Nicolas Kirsanof, the father of Arcadi,—Paul, his bachelor brŏtber, a sort of Russian *Major Penden-nis*, lŏving neatness and luxury, and the maxims and principles of the "fine old gentleman",—and the father of Basarof, the Nihilist or free-thinker, which last *becŏmes, we scarcely kno how, the most interesting character in the book, tho Tur-génief has resolutely denied bim any charm. He contradicts and criticizes his elders; he lays down the law tŏ the younger con-gregation whŏ sit at his feet; he despises established usages; he has no soul for the things of imagination, he is in sŏme de-gree a sensualist; his very system of negation is inconclusiv, tending tŏ no pos-itiv action for the reconstruction of society, after its superstitions, religious and mor-al, shal hav been abolished. Not the slit-est glimmer of a halo is thrŏu round him; and yet, like every person in the tale, we look for him, we listen tŏ him. Thêre is no difficulty in believing that, rude as he was, and not without a touch of Orson in his ways, he could engage the attention of so refined a woman as Mrs. Odintsof, and as much lŏve as she had tŏ giv. Thêre ar few things in fiction better wrŏt out than the commotion excited by his return tŏ his humble provincial home, and the deferential, oppressiv affection of his parents, which becŏmes too importu-nate tŏ be endured. His mŏther is touch-ed with a master's hand. His death, too (possibly a novelist's necessity, as dispos-ing of ŏne with whŏm everything in life was so much at variance), wil not be read without emotion. The ŏther characters ar sliter, but not less individual. A strong-minded lady, whŏ cultivates science and philosophy in a bewildered way of her ŏn, givs champagne brêakfasts tŏ

students, and goes tŏ a ball in dirty gloves but with a bird of Paradise in her hair, is expressly tŏ be commended tŏ the cu-rious of her sex, whŏ desire tŏ see a Russian variety of the species. Tŏ con-clude, tho the tale, like its predecessors, is a saddening ŏne, it is excellent as a work of Art." [Athenæum, 1863.]—
"The account of the origin of Bazarof in 'Fathers and Sŏns,' is extremely interest-ing. It appears that Turgénief had met, when on a journey, a young physician whŏ gave him his Bazarof. The author began tŏ keep "Bazarof's Diary," that is tŏ say, each time that he read an interest-ing book or met a person whŏ had much tŏ tel him which was new, he criticized the book or the person in his diary, not from his point of vue, but from that which his Bazarof would hav taken. The result was a masterpiece which. has given both a name and a form tŏ a school of thŏt which has, since the appearance of 'Fathers and Sŏns,' pervaded Russian let-ters." [Athenæum, 1889. **2635**
——, SAME (Fathers and Children), *Munro*, 1883.

FAUST, by TURGÉNIEF, in *Galaxy*, may-june, 1872. **2636**

FIRST LOVE, by TURGÉNIEF, Lon-don, *Allen*, 1884. **2637**

FLAMING-FIRE (The), by TOLSTOI, in *Cosmopolitan*, vol. 5. **2638**

FRIEND OF THE FAMILY (The). [by FEDOR [MICHÁIOVICH] DOSTOIEF-SKY († 1881): *Vizetelly*, 1887.] "It is difficult tŏ believe that 'Crime and Punish-ment' and 'The Friend of the Family' ar by the same hand What the former is we kno. Of the latter it need ŏnly be said that it is rather a truculent essay in what may be called the satirical farce of character. The hero, Thomas Tomich, a kind of Russian Pecksniff, is a capital creation; and the characters about him ar not unworthy of their eminent nêbor." [Athenæum.   **2639**

GAMBLER (The). [by FEDOR DOSTOIEFSKY: with No. 2639] "Thêre is more of the true Dostoiefsky—the Dostoiefsky of 'Crime and Punishment' and 'The Brothers Karamasoff'—in 'The Gambler.' Here the humor is sombre, the purpos ruthless, the effect a trifle insane. Slight as it is—and it is but a sketch—the thing is very powerful; it fixes the attention at ônce, and tŏ begin it is tŏ be constrained tŏ read tŏ the bitter end. The twŏ principals, Paulina and Alexis Ivanovich, ar rendered in a fashion nŏthing less than masterly; and the same may be sajd of the extraordinary old maniac Antonída Vassilievna, whŏ côming tŏ Roulettenberg tŏ play the justiciar on her gambling relativ the General, plays for the first time in her life, and lŏses 90,000 roubles or so in a couple of days. The translation, it remains tŏ note, is lively enuf, but so full of slang as tŏ produce an effect of real vulgarity." [Athenæum.   **2640**

HERO OF OUR TIME [by MICHAIL [YURYEWICH] LERMONTOF (1812-41): London, *Warne*, 1888.] "is very short and utterly unconventional, yet fuller of poetic feeling and psychological insight than a score of the novels of the period roled intŏ ône. It, moreover, possesses a weird interest all its ŏn, and is in every way a remarkable romançe. It also givs, inçidentally, sŏme vivid descriptions of Circassian scenery, and the condition of

the country during the long struggle waged against it by Russia. Altŏgether, the book is not ŏnly wel worth reading, but suffiçiently suggestiv tŏ be made the subject of a treatis as long as itself. We regret that we can not compliment Mr. ⁴ Lipman on the feliçity of his translation." [Spectator.   **2641**

——, SAME (transl. by Pulszky) London, *Bogue*, 1854.

——, SAME ("Sketches of Russian Life in the Caucasus") London, *Ingram*, 1853.

HOME LIFE = *DEAD SOULS.*

HOW RUSSIANS MEET DEATH = *SORCERER.*

HOW THE TWO IVANS QUARRELED, by GOGOL, ☞ No. 2631.

IDIOT (The) [by FEDOR DOSTOIEFSKY: *Vizetelly*, 1887.] "may bê deemed tedious by ordinary readers; but it wil exerçise a weird fasçination upon those minds tŏ which its author's ŏther writings appeal with irresistible forçe. It is as unconventional as 'Crime and Punishment' and 'Injury and Insult,' and as rich as thêy ar in minute studies of moral disease. It is easy tŏ understand the immense charm which such works possess for Russian readers, whŏ ar terribly in earnest in thêir study of vexed social problems, and whŏ find ŏnly in fiction the free discussion of questions of that nature. It is more difficult tŏ explain the remarkable influençe which thêy hav recently exerçised in France and, tŏ a certain extent, amŏng us. However this may be, 'The Idiot' undoubtedly deservs tŏ be carefully studied. The hero of the story, a pauper prince, whŏ suffers from epileptic attacs and inçipient softening of the brain, is at first sight an unattractiv personage; but the author, of whŏse opinions he is apparently the mouth-piece, has endowed him with so noble aspirations and so tender a sympathy with all forms of suffering and distress, that his material weaknesses ar forgotten by those whŏ can rightly appreçiate his spiritual perfection." [Athenæum. **2642**

IDIOT (The), by TURGÉNIEF, in *Temple-Bar*, may, 1870. **2643**

IN TWO MOODS [by VLADIMIR KOROLENKO: N.-Y., *Lovell Co.*, 1891.] "was written in circumstances which required on the part of the author considerable retiçençe and many vailed allusions, and ŏne must in many instançes read between the lines. In this story Korolenko has graphically portrayed the typical young Russian of 1873-5, a period which marked the beginning of militant Nihilism. The first part is a song of youth, lŏve, enthusiasm and exuberant life, dyeing rose cŏlor everything which it touches. The second half of the story abounds in psychologic analysis, and it is possible that sŏme readers may think it heavy." [Critic. **2644**

INJURY AND INSULT, by DOSTOIEVSKY, ☞ No. 2639.

INVADERS (The), by TOLSTOI, N.-Y., *Crowell*, 1887. **2645**

IVAN CZAROWITZ, or The Rose without prickles that stings not, by CATHERINE II., London, *Robinson & Sons*, 1793. **2646**

IVAN ILYITCH, ☞ *DEATH* ——

IVAN VEJEEGHAN [by THADDEUS BULGARIN (†, 1859): London, *Whittaker*, [Phil'a, rep. *Carey*, 1832] 1831.] "affords a striking picture of the domestic habits that prevail amŏngst those classes

of Muscovites whŏ ar a little abŏve the rank of boors. The hero is an orphan, whŏ rises in the world, of the interior of which, like Gil Blas, he happens tŏ see a good deal. The story is, however, not wel put tŏgether. Here and thêre we hav sŏme good sketches of locr social life; but the work is rather too full of petty details." [Monthly Review. **2647**

JOURNAL OF A SUPERFLUOUS MAN, by TURGÉNIEF, with *MOU-MOU*. **2648**

KATIA [by LYOF [N.] TOLSTOI: *Gottsberger*, 1887.] "is an attempt by Count Tolstoi tŏ tel simply the lŏve-story of a young girl, and it is dŏne with grêat fidelity and graçe. The author whŏ has worked so skilfully on grêat problems with a much larger canvas, here enters intŏ the ordinary details of family life, and intŏ the happiness, the tragedy, and the pathos of very simple surroundings. Katia is represented as telling the story of her lŏve and suffering herself, and you would never imagin that ŏne of the grêat thinkers of Europe was holding the pen for her. She falls in lŏve with her gardian, and is in turn belŏved. The pretty romance is told with taste and feeling; but by and by life becŏmes at ŏnce prosaic and dangerous. Katia longs for the city, her husband gratifies her, apparent estrangement is the result of widening Katia's horizon, ŏnly tŏ end in final reconçiliation, and the settling of romantic passion intŏ excellent but calm family affection. The ŏnly flaw in the story is in this ending. Tolstoi seems tŏ imply that you must not expect dramatic passion tŏ last in all its fervor; but passion tried as was that of Katia and her husband either dŏes last with a good deal of its first power, or is killed entirely. Romance may melt away, unsuspected and unmissed, intŏ placid domestic affection; but if ŏnce interrupted by a crisis, it either doubles in intensity, or is lost forever. Stil, the story is a pretty ŏne, and the moral virtuous, if not lofty." [Critic.]— "The story of 'My Husband and I' is of a most simple nature, so far as its plot is conçerned, but it is rendered remarkable by the skil with which the character of its leading personage is made tŏ unfold itself as the unsensational narrativ proceeds. Count Tolstoi is at his best when he is analyzing and describing the fitful currents of feeling which stir a girl's heårt, and he has seldom written anything better than the account of Katia's quiet affection before marriage for the sŏmewhat unromantic wooer whŏ becŏmes her husband, and of her temporary waywardness afterward. That the tone of the tale is not gloomy may be inferred from its final lines:—"Thus ended my romance with my husband. The old passionate emotion remained a dear memory; but a new feeling of lŏve for my children and thĕir father laid the foundation for anŏther life, happier in a different sense tŏ that which had gone before. And this existence stil lasts, and has an endless charm for me, for I hav learnt that true happiness can be found ŏnly at ŏne's fireside, amid the pure delights of family life." [Athenæum.]—"Katia is a young orphan married tŏ her gardian. Thêre ar misunderstandings which cŏme from her inexperiençe and his peculiar scheme of letting her hav her ŏn way and then suffering for it. Thêre ar fine analyses of

character and motiv in Katia, and the story is almost idyllic in its purity and simpliçity." [Catholic World. **2649**

——, SAME ("My Husband and I"), *Vizetelly*, 1887.

——, SAME ("Family Happiness"), *Crowell*, 1888.

——, SAME ("Romance of Marriage") *Laird*, 1890.

LEAR OF THE STEPPES (A), by TURGÉNIEF, in *London Society* [*Living Age*, jan. 1873.] **2650**

——, SAME, with No. 952.

LITTLE RUSSIAN SERVANT (The), by "H: GRÉVILLE": in *Modern Age*, feb., 1884; also in *Romance*, sept., 1892, 15 p. **2651**

LIVING MUMMY (The), by TURGÉNIEF, in *Scribner's Monthly*, aug., 1876. **2652**

LIZA [by IVAN [S.] TURGÉNIEF: N.-Y., *Holt*, 1872; London, *Ward*, 1884.] "is the story of Fedor Ivanovich Lavretsky, whŏse handsŏm wife, after his discŏvery of her unfaithfulness, is left tŏ lead the life which pleases her ... Lizaveta Mikhailovna is his distant relativ, a young girl of 19 when he cŏmes tŏ live on his estate near the town whêre her family dwels. She is of a pure, hĭ, religious nature. sensitivly conscientious, and of a reservd and thŏtful temperament. Before either is aware thĕy ar in lŏve. A paper cŏmes tŏ Lavretsky with the announcement of his wife's death; and he shŏs it tŏ Liza. That night thĕy meet by aççident in her mother's garden, and ar suprised intŏ the acknoledgement of thĕir lŏve. It is a moment of rapture tŏ him and of doubt and trouble tŏ her; and the next night Lavretsky's wife, whŏ is not dead, returns. Then all is over; he rids himself of her, but Liza goes intŏ a convent; old friends die, children gro intŏ men and women; Lavretsky's wife leads her old life in Paris; Lavretsky becŏmes 45: Liza remains in her convent; and that is the way the story ends." [Atlantic.]—"It may be an inevitable consequence of its truth tŏ nationality that it should be melancholy, even as Russian music is ... Turgénief's hero Lavretsky, had, at all events, no chance of a happy life. Curbed, cramped, neglected in his boyhood, with ŏnly rude and ecçentric kinsfolk tŏ lean on, the world opened for him too late. When the passions of a man began tŏ urge him he had stil the inexperience of a child; and so, in his lŏve-time, he stumbled intŏ a fatal marriage with a mercenary, cold-heârted coquette, whŏ used him, grasped his substance, fooled him, deceived him." [Athenæum. **2653**

MAD LOVE, by V. Garshinski: London, *Blackett*, 1890. **2654**

MAKAR'S DREAM, by Korolenko, in *Cosmopolitan*, vol. 6, pp 147-158. **2655**

MARIE = No. 625.

MARKOF [by "H: Gréville," i. e., Alice M.. Céleste (Fleury) Durand: *Peterson*, 1879.] "is a story of home and artist life; simple, and yet dramatic; deeply disçerning, yet unfailingly delicate, a little sad, and not a little drŏll; a serupulously fair and faithful, yet friendly and hopeful study ... Twŏ honest lŏves, in fervid alliance, fight gallantly for the soul in danger, and effect its rescue: the touching, self-annihilating lŏve of the artist's hunchbac brŏther; the more sorroing and disçerning, but ever pure and

purifying, passion of the gentle but admirably hī-spirited Helen. We grumble, when the fight is wŏn, that Helen is too good for Demiane, but the author's skil has suffiçed tŏ sho us in the latter just ŏne of those men whŏ wil be good themselvs under the influence of a better woman, and not ŏtherwise. And it is tŏ be observed that, in life, such unions appear tŏ be, of all ŏthers, those in which a woman is most sure tŏ be humbly and profoundly happy,—whêreby aliens ar certainly cheated of thêir right tŏ complain." [Atlantic.]—"In 'Markof' Mrs. Durand has given us ŏne of her largest and most carefully elaborated works. In sŏme respects we think it is her strongest and best ... Markof is a young violinist, whŏse passion for his instrument defeats his father's purpos of educating him for the priesthood, and whŏ afterwards barely escapes ruin under the seductions of a modern Kleopatra. His good angel is a young girl, whŏ servs him in the capaçity of an accŏmpanist; ŏne of those sweet and lŏvely creatures whŏm this author knoes so wel how tŏ create." [Boston "Literary World." **2656**

MARPHA, by Lydia Paschkof, in *Romance*, june, 1892, 9 p. **2657**

MAY EVENING (A), by Gogol, in *Cosmopolitan*, vol. 3, p 186. **2658**

MOUMOU, by Turgénief, = No. 851.

MUST IT BE? [by "Carl Detlef," i. e., Klara Bauer (†, 1876): *Lippincott*, 1873.] "The heroin is the charming dauter of evil-behaving, quarreling parents; her lŏver is poor in worldly goods, but rich in all which makes heroes admirable. Thêre is much more melodrama in the plot than is needed, but the novel wil be

found not unreadable by those who care tŏ find out anything about the country which is described in it." [Nation. **2659**
NADIA. [by R. ORLOFFSKY: *Son-nenschein*, 1888.] "The heroin is a charming girl, full of sympathy and enthusiasm, whŏ is induced tŏ join a secret society by the influence of a Nihilist, and whŏ spends sōme time at Zürich in the company of fello enthusiasts eternally engaged in the discussion of "the question whether ōne ŏt tŏ rebuild society after having destroyed it, or simply destroy it without rebuilding it." But before long she begins tŏ perceive that she has made a mistake, and she tries tŏ extricate herself from the toils which hav been woven about her by the cunning of Neradovitch, whŏ is represented as a type of all which is mean and odious. The story of her struggles, ultimately crowned with suçcess, toards a hier and a nobler life is told with much power. The author's style is excellent throuóŭt, and the moral tone of his work irreproachable." [Athenæum.]—"*Nadia* is marked by the melancholy which seems the characteristic note of Russian fiction . . . Thêre is a liter and more cheerful story mixed with that of the heroin. Jenny Gregorievna is a very sprightly maiden, and never fails tŏ amuse and charm." [Spectator. **2660**
NARKA = No. 860.
NEGLECTED QUESTION (The), [by B. MARKEWICH: London, *King*, 1874.] "The plot is coarse, sōme of the situations ar revolting, and the poetical justiçe meted out tŏ the female offender—tŏ her only— in the end, as a homage tŏ conventional propriety, by no means atones for the offenses of the book." [Spectator. **2661**

NIKANOR, by "H: GRÉVILLE," *Chatto*, 1889. **2662**
NOBLEMAN OF THE STEPPE, by TURGÉNIEF, in *Scribner's*, july, 1877. **2663**
OLD-FASHIONED FARMERS, by GOGOL, ☞ No. 2631.
ON THE EVE [by IVAN [S.] TURGÉNIEF: N.-Y., *Holt*, 1873.] "is of a simpler plan than Liza [No. 2653], and its merits ar in loer relief; but the careful reader wil find it no less opulent in evidences of the author's genius. It is a story of lōve, meagre in incident and inexpressibly sad in its dénoument. Its principal personages ar not striking or winning, save as lōve dignifies and beautifies them; and, indeed, thêre ar no features in the book, which, under ordinary manipulation, would stand out either conspicuous or fasçinating. But beneath the hand of a master thêy take on a beauty and a significance which it is impossible fairly tŏ characterize, and on which the appreçiativ reader wil never weary of dwelling . . . We kno few novels which ar better worth reading than this; it instructs throu its sketches of Russian life; it pleases and charms by its manifestations of genius in narration and description, and its marvellous insight intŏ the operations of human passions; and elevates and cheers by its exhibition of noble ideals brŏt down tŏ the level of ordinary life, and mōving before us as stimulating examples." [Boston "Literary World."]—"The book is full of Turgénief's peculiar power, that by which he givs us again the fresh, abruptly fractured surfaces of ordinary life, tōgether with the immeasurable depth of thêir sugges-

tions. It abounds in touches of hǐ power and pathos ... The style is marked by that studied independence of mere literarv graçes which appears in his ŏther novels. We observ, also, his clear painter's eye for nature; and his fine, artistic impartialitv, which enables his characters tŏ stand apart from him, and be themselvs; ŏnly, thêre is the all-pervading, grim sarcasm of the Russians ... For the rest, too much can not be said, in urging a faithful studv and careful record, by all readers, of his keen poetic sensibility and his finished and forcible method." [Atlantic.]—"Not that Turgénief is all gloom and despair. In "On the Eve" we see the lŏve of Helena outlasting everything, and, in spite of its unhappy termination, the reader is left in presençe of the sublimity of a woman's lŏve, rather than wêighed down by an unneçessarily painful reminder of the truth that man is mortal." [Nation. **2664**

PISTOL-SHOT (The), by PUSHKIN, in *Albion*, 28 dec., 1861. **2665**

PHILOSOPHY AT HOME, by TCHEKOF, in *Short Stories*, oct., 1891, 9 p. **2666**

POLIKUSHKA. [by LYOF [N.] TOLSTOI: (with *THE INVADERS*, also with *MY HUSBAND*.] "Polikushka" has a social or domestic interior, relating the melancholy suiçide of a servant whŏ had lost a rŏll of money, and feared tŏ façe the consequences, which wer averted by the discŏvery of the mŏuey by a later traveler, almost before the poor fello's body was cold." [Boston "Literary World." **2667**

PORTRAIT (The), by GOGOL, in *Blackwood's* [*Living Age*, 13 nov.] 1847; also with No. 2631, which see. **2668**

PRETTY LITTLE COUNTESS ZINA [Les Koumassine) by "H: GRÉVILLE," i. e., Alice M.. Céleste (Fleury) Durand: *Peterson*, 1879.] is "a cheerful, interesting, and thŏroly pleasant story. Count Koumassine is a good-natured and verv wealthy gentleman, wedded tŏ a selfish but fasçinating woman of the world. Early in her married life, when thêre seemed tŏ be no prospect of her having children, she had adopted a niece, the dauter of a poor sister. But soon after a dauter is born, and eventually a sŏn also. The niece, whŏ is pretty and charming, is now supposed by the countess tŏ stand in her dauter's way, espeçially as she early attracts the attention of a nêboring nobleman, by marrying whŏm she would outrank her patroness. A skilful stratagem of the latter prevents "Prince Charming" from declaring himself, but she sees that at ŏnce her niece must be gotten out of the way. Twŏ marriages, in succession, with disreputable persons, ar arranged, ŏnly tŏ be thwarted by the perversity of the girl, whŏ meanwhile has fallen in lŏve with ŏne Maritzky, a good fello, but poor. The Countess thêreupon confines her niece tŏ her room until she shal promis tŏ marry the man of her ânt's choice. With the aid of her twŏ cousins, whŏ hav remained true tŏ her throu all, and of the Prince, an escape is effected. The Prince was not very seriously in lŏve, and his devotion tŏ the girl is now that of a merely chivalrous friend. But in the close intercourse with the cousin "Zina," rendered neçessary by the escape plot, he learns tŏ appreciate her excellent qualities, and becŏmes finally her most devoted lŏver. Thus everything ends tŏ the satisfaction of all concerned. [Boston "Literary World."]— "In a word, this is just the novel that those people want whŏ ar always looking after a story in French which shal not deal directly or by implication with evildŏing. It is not tŏ be put on the shelf with Mrs. Craven's bily religious stories, [Nos. 440, 700.] but it may be safely commended tŏ those whŏ care for a really entertaining French novel treating of society, and, ever and abŏve, of society of an unfamiliar kind in which everyŏne is interested." [Atlantic. **2669**

PRIEST'S SON (The), by TURGÉNIEF, in *Lippincott's*, june, 1877. **2670**

PRINCE AND JEW (The), in *Modern Age*, apr., 1883. **2671**

PRINCESS OGHÉROF (The). [by "H : GRÉVILLE," i. e., Alice M.. Céleste (Fleury) Durand : tran. by T. H., N.-Y., *C: F. Roper*, 1879; *Peterson*, 1880.] "What could be finer than this, either in power or spirit? We defy any reader with any sensibilities at all tŏ take the passage in its connection without sharing both in the pain and the joy of the renunçiation which it describes—pain at the seeming annihilation of as just a lŏve as heârts ever felt, joy at the victory of consçience and principle after a hard conflict. Thêre is the hïest art, too, in the skil with which the outward scene is fitted tŏ the play of passion, and every tint made tŏ contribute tŏ the beautiful harmony which rules the picture. The tragic intensity of the story of Michel and Martha is skilfully relieved by the parallel fortunes of Serge and Nastia, which ar related in a very amusing vêin, not however so as tŏ introduçe any element of

incongruity. The whole charming episode of the courtship and marriage of these young people we must leave tŏ the reader tŏ take for himself." [Boston "Literary World." **2672**

PRINCESS ROUBINE (The) [by "H : GRÉVILLE," i. e., Alice M.. Céleste (Fleury) Durand : *Peterson*, 1887.] "is ŏne of Henry Gréville's most charming stories. It is free from any of the disagreeable elements tŏ be classified as 'Frenchy'; and it is not merely an interesting story, but ŏne which deals with a problem. Moreover, it dŏes not end with the heroin's marriage; that takes place early in the book, and we ar permitted tŏ observ an entire life run its course tŏ the end, instead of merely seeing a young girl's life merged in her married identity. The heroin is a spirited and beautiful enthusiast, whŏ is anxious about the social problems of the day, and whŏ solvs them in her case very picturesquely, uniquely and touchingly. What she livs tŏ see her children reap from her ideas, how she herself outgroes sŏme of them, is admirably shŏn ; the effect of heredity, of age, of çircumstançe, all cŏming tŏ giv wêight and dignity tŏ a very pretty lŏve story." [Critic. **2673**

PUNIN & BARBURIN, by TURGÉNIEF, with No. 2637. **2674**

QUEEN OF SPADES, by PUSHKIN, [in *Chambers' Papers*, 1850 [*Living Age*, 30 nov. 1850] ; also in *Gift of Friendship*, 1854; also in *Lippincotts' Mag.*, sept., 1876; also in *Modern Age*, jan., 1884] = No. 908. **2675**

ROMANCE OF MARRIAGE (The) = *KATIA.*

RUSSIAN COUNTRY-HOUSE, (A),

by "CARL DETLEF": N.-Y., *Worthington*, 1890. **2676**
RUSSIAN LIFE IN THE INTERIOR
= No. 2612.
RUSSIAN MARRIAGE (A), by Turgénief, in *Modern Age*, may, 1884. **2677**
RUSSIAN PRIEST (A) by N. H. Hotahehko: *Cassell*, 1891.] "throes a certain amount of light upon the habits and condition of the peasants whŏ form the grĉat mass of the nation, and the influençe of the clergy upon them.'· [Critic. **2678**
RUSSIAN PROPRIETOR (A), ETC. [by Lyof [N.] Tolstoi: N.-Y., *Crowell*, 1888.] "In *"Albert,"* a musician's tale, and *"Recollections of a Scorer,"* a gambling history, we hav evidently leaves out of Tolstoi's earlier experiençes, the days of his wild and irregular life; and the story of *"The Two Hussars"* belongs tŏ the same category. The teaching here —so far as thêre is any teaching—is hardly more than that of the cruelty of fate, the pitilessness of retribution. Thêy ar powerfųl cartoons of the working passions. In *"Three Deaths*," again, and in *"A Prisoner in the Caucasus,"* we hav a simpler and quieter realism, not less effectiv, but less intense. Throu the scenes here depicted the reader wil pass with a sense of relief, as if emerging from a sombre wood intŏ a clearing, tŏ which sŏme sunshine has acçess, and whêre an occasional flower groes." [Boston "Literary World." **2679**
RUSTY LINCHPIN (The). [by —— (   ) Kokhanovsky: *Lothrop*, 1887.] These tales "picture the uncventful life of the provinces with what seems tŏ be a delicate and a faithful touch.

Thêv bring us very close tŏ that strange civilization which has lately becŏme so fasçinating tŏ western readers and help us tŏ realize how truly the aims and the emotions of common life ar the same in all lands." [Dial. **2680**
SAVÉLI'S EXPIATION [by "H: Gréville," i. e., Alice M.. Célesste (Fleury) Durand: *Peterson*, 1878.] "is a story of the days of serfdom. The lord of the manor sends his serfs tŏ Siberia, or tŏ the army, or treats them even worse. A young girl, his victim, drowns herself. Savéli—her lŏver—and her father. with thêir friends, kil the lord in his bed and burn him with his house, but save the lives of his wife and dauter, whŏ, with the general public, ar kept ignorant of the bloody facts. Mrs. Bagrianof frees her serfs, and, impoverished, remŏves tŏ Moscow. Years after she returns, with her beautiful grauddauter, whŏ is wooed by Savéli's accomplished sŏn. Savéli's and the priest's superstition brêaks the young lŏvers asunder forever, and in grêat agony Saveli dies cŏmforted by Catherine. The cruelty of the lord, the nobility of the priest, the sufferings of the serfs, the despair of Fedotia, the lŏve and reverençe of Philip for his father and his agony at the discŏvery of the murder, the pathetic trust of Catherine—ar amŏng the grandest triumphs in fictional literature." [South-Atlantic.]—"George Eliot never wrote anything so intensely dramatic in its situations, so thrillingly tragic in its course, so infinitlý pathetic in its sorro, as this remarkable tale. But it is inexpressibly painful, and we should advise no ŏne tŏ begin it whŏ has not the heârt tŏ façe the direst sorro which human experi-

ençe can be made tŏ endure. So life-like ar the people and thêir action tnat, incredible as ar sŏme of the harroing details, it is impossible not tŏ feel that the author had a basis of fact for her imagination tŏ play upon. It is hard tŏ say in which her power is most skilfully exercised;—in the delineation of the cruelties of Bagrianof, the heroism of Father Vladimir, the stern consecration of Savéli, or the spiritual beauty and lŏveliness of little Fedotia, whŏse fate was too terribly sad tŏ be rehearsed here." [Boston "Lit. World."] —" It is a true tragedy. Not an element is wanting. Thêre is the insolent tyrant, provoker tŏ wrath—the incarnation of irresponsible power; then the groing tolerance of wrong which rouses the oppressed tŏ meet crime with crime; then the slo, inevitable proçess whêreby the consequences of crime reach the criminal, and the innoçent suffer for the guilty. It is complete, and rouses in us a lively curiosity tŏ kno whether the story is a record of facts or a construction by the author." [Nation. **2681**

——, SAME ("Expiation") N.-Y., Tousey, 1886.

SEBASTOPOL IN 1855, by TOLSTOI, in Hours at Home, feb., 1869. **2682**

SERGE PANIN, by G: OHNET: Manchester, Tubbs, 1883. **2683**

SMOKE. [by IVAN [S.] TURGÉNIEF: N.-Y., Holt, 1872.] "A hasty summary of the plot would rather mar the enjoyment which so largely consists in its surprises, and would giv after all but a very unsatisfactory notion of the real merit of the story, which dŏes not lie in the machinery, but in the marvellous way in which the innermost secrets of character

ar revealed. This much may be said, however, that it tels of the lŏve of a young man for a married woman, whŏm he had formerly lŏved, and whŏ had lŏved him in the days of thêir early youth. The problem is further complicated by the fact that the man, Litvinof, is engaged tŏ anŏther girl. In the hero we see a man of a pleasing nature, honest, modest, and sinçere, in spite of the position in which he is plaçed. He is neither exalted as a model of manhood nor yet denounced as a disgraçe tŏ humanity. Here, as everywhêre, Turgénief understands perfectly how tŏ keep his characters in the proper perspectiv. The heroin, Irene, is a much more complicated character. She is a fascinating woman whŏ interests us most, however, by reason of the incongruity between what she seems tŏ be and what she really is. She is a cŏquette, but no flirt, that is tŏ say, she possesses that charm of coquetry which consists in suggestivness, in arousing wŏnder and admiration, without the heârt which alone can make a woman admirable. She is dishonest from weakness and not from wickedness; she can not be ŏther than she is. Julian Schmidt has spoken of the difference of the author's treatment of Irene and of heroins like Helen in "On the Eve," [No. 2664] whŏ hide the richness of her natures just as Irene hides the poverty of hers, and so both kinds remain a problem tŏ the reader. This is true, and it is of especial interest tŏ observ the gradual way in which this complexity of Irene's character is set before us. It is not analyzed for us. We see her in different circumstances, and hav tŏ make up ŏur minds for ŏurselvs; and it is ŏnly later in the story that a full-perçeption of it begins tŏ dawn upon us. The most touching part of this very sad novel is the account of Litvinof's relation tŏ his betrothed, Tatiana. She is a simple-minded, transparent girl; no heroin, bedecked with every charm, tŏ whŏm Irene is tŏ serv as a rival." [Nation.] ☞ No. 948. **2684**

SONIA [by "H: GRÉVILLE," i. e., Alice M.. Céleste (Fleury) Durand: *Peterson*, 1879.] "is good reading. It is very simple and not wŏnderfully impressiv, but it shŏs the author's intelligençe and ready wit. ' The story of the young man's lŏve for the girl whŏ dŏes not care for him, and of her subsequent fate, makes the book bright and noteworthy." [Atlantic. **2685**

SORCERER (The), by TURGÉNIEF, in *Appleton's*, 22 jan., 1870. **2686**

——, SAME ("How Russians meet Death") in *Temple Bar* [*Living Age*, jan., 1887.]

SPRING FLOODS, by TURGÉNIEF, = No. 952.

STRANGE ADVENTURE OF LIEUT. YERGUNOF, by TURGÉNIEF, in *Galaxy*, oct., 1877. **2687**

TANIA'S PERIL [by "H: GRÉVILLE," i. e., Alice M.. Céleste (Fleury) Durand: *Peterson*, 1882.] "is good; short, sweet, and wholesŏme. The "peril" is that of a pure and noble wife, with a noble and trustful husband on the ŏne side, and an old friend of herself and her husband on the ŏther, whŏ drifts, in spite of himself, intŏ a hopeless passion which both he and its innoçent subject ar strong enuf tŏ put beneath their feet in a spirit of true heroism ... The whole thing is told with light. graçeful. delicate touches.

Thêre ar ŏnly the 3 characters. The situation is simple. The style is simple. The ŏnly excitement is a thunder tempest, and almost a runaway aççident. The book is like a fair and gentle woman, dressed in white muslin, with violets at her throat." [Boston "Literary World." **2688**

TARANTASS (The), by SOLLOGUB, London, 1850. **2689**

TATIANA. [by JOSEPH LUBOMIRSKI: *Tinsley*, 1877.] "The object of 'Tatiana' the preface says, is "tŏ portray certain phases of Russian society during the years which immediately preceeded the Crimean War." It may be described as a historico-social novel, and is fresh and attractiv. It should seem that the story before us is, tŏ sŏme extent, founded on facts. Officials ar not spared, but the system rather than the individual is blamed. The Czar is tenderly treated, and represented as a man of a kind and noble nature, unable tŏ prevent the villany of sŏme of his chief servants, and forçed by çircumstances tŏ adopt measures of severity abhorrent tŏ his disposition. Several ŏther characters ar depicted in pleasing cŏlors, and thêre is internal evidence of an absence of exaggeration. The most unpleasant feature of the system during the last years of Nicholas was the arbitrary power, unscrupulously used, of the police. Sŏme ghastly stories of Siberian life and corporal punishment ar powerfully told." [Athenæum. **2690**

THREE MEETINGS, by TURGÉNIEF, in *Lippincott's*, july, 1875. **2691**

TRIALS OF RAISSA (The). [by "H: GRÉVILLE," i. e., Alice M.. Céleste (Fleury) Durand: *Peterson*, 1880.] "A pure and lŏvely Russian maiden, of the middle class, is abducted by 3 half-drunken officers, is carried tŏ a house of bad reputation, and thêre in a darkened room is forçed by ŏne of them tŏ undergo "the grêatest outrage which can be offered tŏ͵a woman." Late in the evening she makes her escape, and re-enters her home with so tragic a wêaring of her involuntary shame that her mŏther dies of the shoe. Hençeforth, her old father has but ŏne object—tŏ ferret out the villains whŏ hav wrŏt this wrong ... But which is the guiltiest of the guilty? Thêir lips ar silent on this point, and ŏnly by chance, as it seems, is the chief crime fixed upon Valerien Gretsky. The Czar directs that he marry Raissa, and the marriage ceremony takes place dramatically in the cathedral. From this point on the work of the novel is tŏ join as true and lŏving husband and wife the man and woman whŏm çircumstances hav thus put asunder. The barrier of external separation, wide tho it be, seems nŏthing as compared with the cruel uncertainty in which Raissa is left as tŏ whether it really wer Gretsky whŏ should hav married her, and with the repugnance which Gretsky feels toards her tŏ whŏm he has been compelled tŏ giv his name. But the author is equal tŏ the exigency, and succeeds in transforming this unhappy alliance intŏ a true wedloc. The consummation is effected throu a heroic journey of Raissa tŏ Siberia for the purpos of nursing her husband. Her character is a noble ŏne, and sustains her unfalteringly throu all her "trials"." [Boston "Literary World." **2692**

TSAR'S WINDOW (The). [by LUCY HAMILTON (JONES) HOOPER: *Roberts*, 1881.] "It wer ungracious tŏ surmise that the mise-en-scène of 'The Tsar's Window' was made up from Gautier, eked out by the 'Court Circular.' Yet assuredly, if the author has veritably seen St. Petersburg and Moscow, then never had the famous pussy-cat whŏ went tŏ London tŏ see the queen a worthier rival in scant narroness of vue. If the city and its life wer crowded out by the development of a plot or the portrayal of character, wel and good, but thêre is neither of these. Six or êight people go in and out, not ŏne of whŏm says a beautiful or clever thing; the heroin lŏves ŏne man and dŏes not lŏve anŏther; the wrong man takes himself conveniently out of the way—and that is all. It might just as wel hav been quite the reverse, for any logic in the book.' [Nation. **2693**

TWO GENERATIONS. [by TOLSTOI, with *MY HUSBAND.*] "The least attractiv features of young military aristocrats ar here made disagreeably conspicuous. Thêy ar not pleasing persons with whŏm the twŏ stories make us acquainted — but thêy ar thŏroly Russian, and thêy deserv attention as wel on account of thêir singularity as of the undoubted skil with which thêy ar portrayed." [Ath. **2694**

UNCLE'S DREAM (The), by DOSTOIEVSKI: *Vizetelly*, 1888. **2695**

UNFORTUNATE WOMAN (An). [by IVAN [SERGEIVICH] TURGÉNIEF: *Funk & Wagnalls*, 1887.] "These stories ar both masterpieces of the faultless realism, the pitiless analysis, of which Turgénief alone comprehended the possibilities. The first is unspeakably tragic. Susanna Ivanovna, the offspring of an alliance between a nobleman and a Jewess, becŏmes step-dauter tŏ a brutal foreiner, a German, whŏ has wŏn a title by the meanest services; and in the sordid and debasing atmosphere of her home she famishes for companionship. By the schemes of her uncle she has been separated from the man she lŏves, and her step-father uses all the means in his power tŏ isolate her and make her existence a torture. From this she escapes by death, which may hav been suiçide or murder. The funeral scenes ar portrayed with Rembrandtesque touches which leave no phase of horror unexpressed. The whole effect is oppressivly somber. In its representation of the condition of the Russian nobility of a generation ago the work is a revelation." [Boston "Literary World."]—"The translation is evidently very bad—even the reader unacquainted with Russian can see that. No translation, however, can altŏgether destroy the simple force and beauty of Turgénief's style, or conceal the grĕatness of his thŏt. All the Russian novelists tŏ whŏm we hav been introduçed ar writers of power, and, in varying degree, of grĕatness, but it wil not dŏ, in enthusiasm over Tolstoi, or Gogol or Dostoievsky, tŏ gro forgetful of the grĕatest Russian of all. For we cannot read him beside these ŏthers without being impressed with his surpassing grĕatness. In a calm and masterly grasp of life, in nobility of spirit and motiv, in both intellect and emotion, he towers abŏve them all. In the poet's vividness of external beauty and picturesqueness, in freshness and humor, Gogol alone equals, and perhaps surpasses, him. The trueness of Turgénief's moral insight is sŏmething wŏnderful, when ŏne considers how often it was self-attained, counter tŏ all the influençes of his environment." [Overland. **2696**

——, SAME (trans. by Thompson), *Trubner*, 1888.

VAGRANT (The) ETC. [by VLADIMIR KOROLENKO: N.-Y., *Crowell*, 1888.] "tels of the escape of a band of exiles in a hily interesting way. The '*Sketches of a Siberian Tourist*' ar quite as graphic and hardly less interesting. The remaining sketches ar worth a place in the volume. Thêy ar full of the 'Russian melancholy' and full also of that vague poetic sentiment which natural scenes inspire in the Russian writers." [Dial. **2697**

VASSILISSA, by TURGÉNIEF, in *Romance*, mar., 1892. **2698**

VIRGIN SOIL. [by IVAN [SERGEIVICH] TURGÉNIEF: N.-Y., *Holt*, (transl. by T: S. Perry) 1878; London, *Macmillan*, (transl. by A. W. Dilke), 1879.] "Nejdanof is a Hamlet on a small scale, adapted tŏ the sphere of Socialist life. But Marianna is unlike anything which English readers ar likely tŏ be acquainted with. Generous, self-sacrifiçing, pure-minded, true-heârted, full of sympathy with all whŏ suffer and ar oppressed, she is at the same time utterly devoid of religious feeling and totally defiçient in respect for all existing laws. And so, in spite of her position, her beauty, her graçe, and her culture, she is ready tŏ brĕak with society, tŏ abandon her home and her relativs, and tŏ giv up all which women of her class most prize, for the sake of an idea. It is not easy for us tŏ conçeive the possibility of such a sacrifiçe being made by a lady like Marianna, tho it dŏes not seem so incredible in the case of the ŏther female conspirator of the story, the humble and hard-working Machourina, whŏse unconfessed lŏve for Nejdanof, most delicately made manifest by means of a few stray hints, lends the solitary touch of romançe tŏ her homely features." [Spectator. **2699**

VISIONS, by TURGÉNIEF, in *Galaxy*, july, 1872; also in *Cornhill* [*Living Age*, apr.] 1880. **2700**

VITAL QUESTION (A). [by TCHERNYCHEWSKY: N.-Y., *Crowell*, 1886.] "Whatever the novel may be in the Russian, it is inexpressibly tedious in English." [Atlantic. **2701**

——, SAME ("What's tŏ be Dŏne?") Boston, *Tucker*, 1886.

WAR AND PEACE, by TOLSTOI, = No. 1007.

WATCH (The), by TURGÉNIEF, in *Lippincott's*, may, 1876. **2702**

WAYWARD DOSIA = *DOSIA*.

WHAT'S TO BE DONE? = *VITAL*.

WHITE SLAVE (The), or the Russian Peasant Girl, *Harper*, 1845. **2703**

WILD DOVE'S NEST, in *Appleton's*, apr., 1877. **2704**

XÉNIE'S INHERITANCE. [by "H:

GRÉVILLE," i. e., Alice M.. Céleste (Fleury) Durand: *Peterson*, 1881.] "H: Gréville" has written no briter, tender-er, purer story than this. The old tones and harmonies ar in it; its key-note, as so often before, is· self-renunçiation; but the composition is fresh, and its effect is that of a symphony, based upon a plaintiv strain, with deeply minor passages in it, and the whole brŏt tŏ a gently modulated close, which leaves the mind content and at peace. Xénie is a hï-spirited, noble-minded girl, the only dauter of parents whŏ hav separated. When the father dies the dauter cleaves tŏ the mŏther beyond the power of lŏvers tŏ têar her away. Tŏ dŏ her duty tŏ this mŏther she sacrifiçes everything, even the true and worthy affection of Paul Rabof, whŏm, tŏ cure of his grief for her, she persuades tŏ marry her little cousin Anna. Paul and Anna prŏve tŏ be mismated, and the 3 chief parties in the drama ar not long in dis-cŏvering thêir mutual relations. Then ensues a sturn and noble consecration tŏ thêir several parts in the loftiest spirit." [Boston "Literary World." **2705**

The translations of forêin fiction, which increase in number and variety every year, ar generally more interesting than the average novels written originally in the english tung. One reason of this obvious superiority is that an author almost always has made a reputation in *his* language before his work is deemed worth translating, but a wêightier, reason is that in the literature which deals directly with life, that in the English language, more than any ŏther, is conventional and unimpassioned; thêrefore, weak, dry, ineffectiv. [Nation.

PRICE: ONE COPY, $.25; TWO COPIES, $.37; THREE, $.50; FOUR, $.60; FIVE, $.80; TEN, $1.20; FIFTEEN, $1.75.

A

DESCRIPTIVE LIST

OF

NOVELS AND TALES

DEALING WITH

LIFE IN NORWAY.

COMPILED BY
W: M. GRISWOLD.

CAMBRIDGE, MASS.:
W: M. GRISWOLD, PUBLISHER.
NEW-YORK. FOR SALE BY G: P. PUTNAM'S SONS, 27 W. 23D ST.
1892.

[*From the "School Bulletin," Aug.*, 1892.]

We hope teachers will not fail tŏ recognize the work W. M. Griswold is dŏing in his classified bibliography. He sends us a DESCRIPTIVE LIST OF NOVELS AND TALES DEALING WITH LIFE IN FRANCE (Cambridge, Mass., 1892, 8vo, pp. 94, $1.00), which is of immediate practical use tŏ the teacher of French history as well as of French literature.

[*From the "Central Christian Advocate."*]

Mr. Griswold has dŏne an excellent work, which will be appreciated by all librarians, and by many people of cultivated taste whŏ wish tŏ get on the track of the best French fiction, or at least tŏ secure sŏme guidance and information in regard tŏ its qualities and characteristics. His former "lists" have dealt with American City and Country Life, with Life in England, etc . . . Life in city and country, peasant life and soldier life, the reckless and adventurous career of the free and easy student in Paris, and the rude rustic amŏng the mountains,—all these phases of French life pass in review in the books which Mr. Griswold has here catalogued. A guide like this would be invaluable tŏ a student of French literature, telling as well what tŏ avoid, as what tŏ secure and read.

[*From the "Boston Commonwealth,"* 13 *Aug.*, 1892.]

If all libraries wer generously equipped with these Lists, the long-suffering curator of books would find more pleasure in life. The compilation and selection ar made with rare skill. The poor book drops into deservd oblivion, while the worthy but neglected and forgotten good book is restored tŏ the eye of the world.

Sŏme not too busy people make note of the name of a novel recommended by a trustworthy critic, but when the time for use cŏmes the note seldom is at hand, and, if ready, generally givs the mere title and no idea of the contents. But here is a series of brochures that contain excerpts from the fairest critical notices, often from several sources, and ŏne is enabled tŏ form a sort of judgment of choice without actually glancing at the book itself. Of course, those dealing with foreign lands must for the grēater part be translations, since with few exceptions the most truthful and vivid characterizations cŏme from the compatriot whŏ has summered and wintered his fellows. Few people realize the patience, skill, and labor involvd in such an undertaking as the publication of these successiv lists, but those whŏ dŏ should urge upon ŏthers the use of so valuable a means of education and pleasure. As a series of 'condensed novels' they ar interesting, too.

NOVELS DESCRIPTIV OF NORWEGIAN LIFE

The object of this list is to direct readers, such as would enjoy the kind of books here described, to a number of novels, easily accessible, but which, in many cases, hav been forgotten within a year or two after publication. That the existence of works of fiction is remembered so short a time is a pity, since, for every new book of merit, there ar, in most libraries, a hundred as good or better, unknown to the majority of readers. It is hoped that the publication of this and similar lists will lessen, in some measure, the disposition to read an inferior NEW *book when superior* OLD *books, equally fresh to most readers, ar at hand. It may be observed that the compiler has tried to include only such works as competent critics hav proclaimed to be well-written, interesting, and free from sensationalism, sentimentality, and pretense.* BUT *in a few cases, books hav been noticed on account of the reputation of their authors, or their great popularity, rather than their merit.*

The selected "notices" ar generally abridged.

This list will be followed by others describing DANISH, DUTCH, SPANISH,— HUMOROUS, ECCENTRIC *and* FANCIFUL *novels and tales.*

AFRAJA, ☞ *HISTORICAL NOVELS.*

AMERICAN IN NORWAY (An). [by J : F. VICARY : London, *Allen*, 1886.] "A young Norse-American goes tŏ the land of his forefathers tŏ fish, shoot and bring bac a norwegian wife. He stays with an old friend of his father, and his daily fishing, sporting, and walking excursions, and the narrativ of his wooing and winning a wife from amŏng the 3 dauters of his host, form the framework upon which Mr. Vicary has built his book." [Athenæum.   2706

ARNE. [by BJÖRNSTJERNE BJÖRNSON: Cambridge, Mass., *Sever*, 1869.] "At first, the reader of these stories is so charmed that he can ŏnly enjoy; and if

he begins tŏ think of the sources of his pleasure, he very likely says that sŏme books ar simply tŏ be enjoyed and not critically examind. "Arne," in particular, so nearly perfect and so purely delightful, affects ŏne as any beautiful appearance in nature dŏes,—a brook, the first green, a lŏvely sunset—and for a while analysis of the charm seems impertinent. But the books which disarm criticism, even if it be that thêy dŏ not best repay it, ar those which best endure it. So, while we can in no way so wel fulfil ŏne of the critic's most important duties as by indulging ŏŭrselvs in ŏne of his chief pleasures—as by heàrtily advising all lŏvers of stories, and all lŏvers of poetry, and all lŏvers of nature in her sunny aspects, and all whŏ get pleasure from the quickening of thêir best and kindliest sympathies, tŏ make the acquaintance of this captivating poet of nature and the affections—stil, it may be as wel tŏ say a word or twŏ of less undiscriminating comment on works upon which it is so easy tŏ lavish praise—which it is so impossible not tŏ praise." [Athenæum.]—"Thêre is in the way the tales ar told a singular simpliçity, or a retiçence and self-control which pass for this virtue, and which take the æsthetic sense as winningly as thêir sentiment touches the heârt. The author has entire confidençe in his reader's intelligençe. He believes, it seems, that we can be fully satisfied with a few distinct touches in representing a situation or a character; he is the reverse, in a word, of all which is Trollopian in literary art. He dŏes not conçern himself with detail, nor with general statement, but he makes sŏme ŏne expressiv particular serv for all introduction and explanation of a fact. The life he portrays is that, for the most part, of humble but deçent folk; and this choiçe of subject is also novel and refreshing ... With people in anŏther rank, C: Reade [see No. 639] would hav managed this as charmingly, tho he would hav thrŏu lutŏ it sŏmewhat too much of the brilliancy of the footlights; and Auerbach [See Nos. 2342, 2375, 2442] would hav dŏne it with equal naturalness; but neither could hav cast about it that poetic atmosphere which is so peculiarly the gift of Björnson and of the Northern mind, and which is felt in its creations, as if the glamor of the long summer days had got intŏ literature. ... In that region of novel characters,

wholesŏm sympathies, and simple interests tŏ which he transports us, we hav not ŏnly a blissful sense of escape from the jejune inventions and stoc repetitions of what seems a failing art with us, but ar aware of ŏùr contact with an exçellent and enviable civilization. Of course the reader sees the Norwegians and thêir surroundings throu Björnson's poetic eyes, and is aware that he is reading romançe, yet he feels that thêre must be truth tŏ the real as wel as the ideal in these stories." [Atlantic.]—"In Arne we hav a Norwegian drama-idyl wrŏt of many bits of landscape, dialog, description, but pursued and penetrated by such an Imp of the Perverse, such a plenitude of provoking and jerky inçident, so brusque and explosiv in its manner, and so incomprehensible in its ever-changing motivs, that we no more follo it than we follo a capriccio of Liszt, even tho we ar entrançed with its vocal melody and spritelike changefulness. In 'The Fisher Lassie' [No. 2713] it is different: the tale has the same changeable charm of word which 'Arne' has, and yet it is harmonious and intelligible in evolution and end." [Critic. **2707**

——, SAME, London, *Bell*, 1890. **2708**

BARQUE FUTURE (The). [by JONAS LIE: Chicago, *Griggs*, 1879.] "A fresher, sweeter story than this we hav not read for many a day. Its interest lies not in intricaçy of plot, nor harroing tragedy, nor brilliant dialog; but in the faithful and vivid presentation of new and strange scenery, the development of a quiet but tender domestic history, and the presentation of the biest vues of character and dùty. Thêre is no villainy, no taint in inçident or conversation; but throu all the charm of a pure imagination and a refined and refining purpos. The story opens with storm and ship-wrec . . . In this outline we hav given the reader no idea of the real depths of the story, which has its mystery and its counterplot as wel as its romançe; nor hav we more than barely hinted at the novel and picturesque materials of which it is wrôt, but we hav said enuf tŏ indicate the grounds on which we base ôŭr judgment of it. Its pictures of life in the north—the fishermen of Norway, the lonely trading-posts on the fjord, the habits of the peo-ple—ar full of a simple and rare beauty." [Boston "Literary World." **2709**

BRIDAL MARCH (The) [by BJÖRN-STJERNE BJÖRNSON : *Houghton*, 1882; also in "Life by the Fells." London, *Strahan*, 1879.] "Björnson here dŏes for Norway what Auerbach did for the Black Forest [See Nos. 2342, 2375 and 2442] or Daudet for Elsass [sic! See No. 2100]. Half pas-toral, half idyl, these tales hav the true poetic charm, and ŏne finds in them the whole range of experiençe of a stil primitiv people. The sketch of the horse Blakken, and the little story of "A Dangerous Woo-ing" ar, in a way, parallel passages. Leif, whŏ dies in his attempt tŏ reach the Eagle's Nest, in spite of the elder brŏther of Thorvald, the priest's sŏn, whŏ carries ôff with him the whole school tŏ meet the victorious bêar-hunter and his booty." [Athenæum. **2710**

COMMODORE'S DAUGHTERS (The). [by JONAS [LAURITZ EDEMIL] LIE: Lon-don, *Heinemann*, 1892.] "Jonas Lie is chiefly, if not solely [? see Nos. 2709 & 2718] knŏn tŏ English readers by "The

Pilot and his Wife" [No. 2720]. "The Commodore's Dauters" is a much stronger book . . . Of the Commodore's 3 children, the sŏn is a selfish fribble, spoilt by his mŏther, and stranded in a marriage for mŏney and without lŏve, which secures him neither lŏve nor mŏney. The elder dauter is sharp of tung, and lŏses such happiness as she might hav enjoyed. The younger, baulked of a marriage with a cousin whŏm she lŏves, "throes the bon-net over the mil," and lŏses her lŏver by a death at sea. It is all perfectly true; but it is not relieved as it should be, and it is not suffiçiently tinged by that more universal knoledge of human nature which the grêat novelists hav, and which puts things in proportion as wel as in relief. Yet the book is wel worth read-ing, and is on the whole about the best Norwegian novel we kno." [Manchester Guardian. **2711**

DUST. [with "Captain Mansana") by BJÖRNSTJERNE BJÖRNSON: *Houghton*, 1882.] "Its literary style is admirable, and as a singular mingling of pathetic child-life with the most solemn questions which can engage the mind, it is an ex-ample of the coldest and clearest intellec-tual judgment touched by poetic fire and thrilled, if not warmed, by sympathy. The story is that of twŏ children whŏse father is coldly radical, but whŏse mŏther and gŏverness ar 'religious' tŏ the point of seeing an answer tŏ prayer in a sno-storm or a dangerous illness. The effect of thêir teaching on the imaginativ tem-peraments of the children is tŏ lead them in thêir first perplexity in life tŏ seek the heaven which thêy hav been assured is better than earth; and the 'dust' is the clogging superstition which the mŏther has allowed tŏ settle on her children's souls when, instead of inspiring them 'tŏ vue life properly—tŏ lōve life, tŏ gain courage for life, vigor for work, and patriotism,' she has tant them 'that life here belo is nōthing tŏ the life abōve; that tŏ be a human being is far inferior tŏ being an angel; that tŏ liv is not by any means as wel as being dead'." [Critic. 2712

FISHER MAIDEN (The). [by BJÖRNSTJERNE BJÖRNSON: N.-Y., Leypoldt, 1869.] "It would be difficult tŏ conceive a more delicately inflected piece of dramatic reçital than this. It is the history of an ingenuous, healthy, bily imaginativ girl, whŏse gloing impulses involv her in a curious inconsisteucy and faithlessness with a pair of lōvers, and bring temporary disgraçe upon her mŏther. But at last her imagination makes an escape intŏ art, and she becŏmes an actress. In the prejndiçed community she livs in she can not dŏ this without a struggle; and the climax of the tale is in her ultimate triumph." [G: P. Lathrop.]—"The heroin has a mystery in her character from childhood. Indeed, the author is careful tŏ put the proper amount of odness intŏ her ançestry for twŏ generations bac, so that no ŏne can dispute her right tŏ be peculiar. The mystery is solvd when Petra has an opportunity tŏ witness a theatrical performance. Tŏ be an actress becŏmes her grĕat passion. This is the career for which, by the constitution of her nature, she is destind. She had had her lōve |affairs, but the 'grand passion' is now subordinate tŏ anŏther. Her lōver, too, with far

more observation than that class ar generally presumed tŏ hav, sees the propriety of her decision. He recŏvers from his despair and gets ŏther 'filling' for the aching void with a çelerity sŏmetimes witnessed in life, but seldom seen in a novel." [Southern Review.

——, SAME, transl. by Plesner, Cassell, 1870; by Hjerleid, Trübner, 1871; by Low, Bell, 1890. 2713

GARMAN AND WORSE [by ALEXANDER L. KIELLAND: London, Paul, 1885.] "is charming reading. A grĕat variety of characters ar introduçed, and ar admirably treated. The twŏ old brŏthers Garman—"The Consul" and "the Attaché," remind ŏne of Mr. Shandy and Uncle Toby, not in themselvs, but in thĕir touching relations tŏ each ŏther. Everything in the book is very real, the talk, the physical features of the country, its varying atmospheric conditions, and the way events often fritter ŏff and dwindle away tŏ nŏthing, just as thĕy dŏ in life. In fact Mr. Kielland's work is not so much an artistic picture as a striking realistic study." [Westminster Review.] See, also, SKIPPER WORSE. 2714

GUNNAR. [by HJALMAR HJORTH BOYESEN: Boston, Osgood, 1874.] "The plot is of the simplest, being what might be termd the primal plot. A lo-born youth lōves abŏve him, is lōved again, and leaves his village tŏ return as a successful artist and demand the fair ŏne from her cruel parents. This being the old, old story, we look tŏ the aççessories of the lōve of Gunnar and of the yellohaired Ragnhild for the requisit amount of novelty, and if the by-play and the setting hav nŏthing startling about them, thêy ar, at least, fresh and charming as nature is charming. It is impossible tŏ read "Gunnar" without feeling that the author is a poet." [Scribner's. **2715**

HAPPY BOY (The) [by BJÖRN-STJERNE BJÖRNSON: Cambridge, Mass., *Sever*, 1870.] "is a charming story, beautifully told; thêre is a freshness and novelty given tŏ the "old, old story" of a true lŏve which did not run smooth,—the lŏve of a peasant boy for ŏne abŏve him in position and riches, tho both belŏng tŏ the peasant class; and the story tels how the little boy lŏved the girl; and the youth, the maiden; how the young man went out and worked for her sake, and how he sucçeeded; and how stil the obstacles continued, but thêy wer both faithful, and at last wer made happy; tho for the matter of that, thêy had never been miserable, for thêy had never mistrusted each ŏther. Thêre is a schoolmaster, whŏ is as much belŏved by the reader as by the children in the story. Oeyvind's father and mŏther ar wel sketched. Marit, the young girl, is like a young girl all over the world, but her little coquetries and vaçillations ar charming, for she makes all she says and dŏes seem delightful tŏ ŏthers besides Oeyvind, and tŏ the reader espeçially! Thêre is a charm of simpliçity, a fragrance from the pine-woods, over the whole tale. It is also full of sweet and tender wisdom,—and no ŏne can read it without feeling the better for its unpretending words of help and counsel." [Athenæum.]—"It is a trifle, judged by the present standard of plot and elaboration of character, but it is such a trifle as ŏnly a man of genius could hav

produçed. What distinguishes Björnson beyond any writer of his class with whŏm we ar familiar is his intuitiv knoledge of the heârt in thc first flush of virginal lŏve. It was that which made "Arne" so delightful, aud it is that which makes "The Happy Boy" so enchanting. It has no plot tŏ speak of ... but then how exquisit this is, as Björnson has handled it, and how life-like ar his characters!" [Putnam's.]—"A village in which the schoolmaster watches the lŏve-affairs, reçeives the confidençes, reprŏves the sins, and invests the mŏney of the floc; in which the first grêat ambition of a youth's life is tŏ pass brilliantly an examination for confirmation: while the grêatest temptation of the hero's life is tŏ pass this same examination and by his subsequent course at an agricultural school, with a mind full of determination, tŏ "spite," by his sucçess, an older and wealthier rival for the affections of his little sweetheârt. Such is the bacground on which the sweet, natural, hopeful, ardent boy livs out his simple drama of lŏve and work. The affectionate good sense of his parents; the pretty Marit, always so much more loyal than she seems; the goodness and shrewdness of the schoolmaster; the boy's industry, perseverançe and doçility —all make the tale idyllic." [Californian. **2716**

—, SAME ("The Happy Lad"), London, *Blackie*, 1882, 118 p.

—. SAME ("Ovind"), London, *Simpkin*, 1869.

HARDY NORSEMAN (A) [by EDNA LYALL," i. e., Ada Ellen Bayley: London, *Hurst*, 1889.] "is a remarkably wel constructed and pleasant story ... Frithiof's disçiplinary misfortunes ar of an ordinary kind. He learns what English flirtation, snobbishness, and selfishness ar, with the help of Blanche Morgan, whŏ jilts him, and her father, whŏ, after using him and his relativs for holidav purposes, has no abjection tŏ letting ruin descend upon them. He makes the acquaintance of English vulgarity in the shape of James Horner, the partner of Bonifaçe the music-seller. His troubles bring him tŏ death's door. He is even suspected of a petty theft. Then, of course, when things ar at thêir blackest, Frithiof's prospects begin tŏ mend, and finally fortune smiles upon him. This is as it should be, and as it has been a thousand times. But a variety of essentially fresh scenes and characters ar mixed with the evolution of this familiar story." [Academy. **2717**

LAILA, by J. A. FRIIS, London, *S. P. C. K.*, 1883 = No. 780.

LIFE BY THE FELLS AND FIORDS, by BJÖRNSON [London, *Strahan*, 1879], contains "Arne" [No. 2607] and "The Happy Boy" [No. 2715.] **2718**

LITTLE GREY, the Pony of Nordfjord, by JONAS LIE: London, *Hamilton*, 1873. **2719**

LOVE AND LIFE IN NORWAY = *SYNNOVE SOLBAKKEN.*

NEWLY-MARRIED COUPLE (The) [by BJÖRNSTJERNE BJÖRNSON: London, *Simpkin*, 1871.] "is a comedy, very slight in its construction, but indicating a whole drama of hopes, and fears, and passions beneath the surfaçe. A young man has married a girl, the ōnly child of rich parents; the young people ar tŏ dwel with them, as the dauter can not and wil not be separated from them. Laura has

lōved Axel, and the parents hav consented tŏ the marriage as thêy would hav given thêir dauter any new toy she might hav wished for. She is quite contented and happy, but Axel finds himself little more than a supernumerary footman. Laura lōves her parents, and can not understand that any change has taken place in her relations tōards them. Thêre is a good deal of humor in the picture of the household, and the immutable laws which rule even the position of the tables and chairs. Axel, in a fit of disgust, determins tŏ go away and take his wife with him, and, after a painful struggle, he carries his point. A vear is supposed tŏ elapse, and the scene shōs Axel's home, which he has furnished and arranged exactly like the home from which he had taken his wife. He has dōne all in his power tŏ win Laura's forgivness; but the wife is a spoiled child, and keeps up a feeling of sullen resentment. Matilde, a humble friend, whŏse relations with the family ar very delicately indicated, accompanied the wife when she was taken from her parents. When Axel was trying tŏ win Laura for his wife, he had, with a lōver's selfishness, made use of Matilde as a stepping-stone tŏ reach her. Matilde had believed that Axel lōved her. The event has undeçeived her; but she stil lōves him with a noble, unselfish lōve, and she is loyal tŏ Laura and tŏ the family. It is in the indication of Matilde's position and character that Björnson shōs his dramatic ability: it is charmingly dōne. Laura continues so long perverse and estranged, that the husband is almost alienated. Matilde might win him for herself. Laura has grōn jealous; Matilde continues loyal. At this critical moment the parents côme tŏ visit thêir child; and Matilde contrives tŏ smooth the way tŏ an explanation between Laura and her husband. The parents ar charmed with all thêy see. Axel is raised tŏ the summit of feliçity, and says, with the sublime egoism of a happy man, "Now you can go, Matilde;" but Laura has a sense of childlike gratitude, and says, "Without you I should never hav got Axel." [Athenæum. **2720**

NILS JENSEN [with "A Man of His Word") by W: E: NORRIS: *Smith*, 1885.] "is much the best story of the series. Thêre is a touch of real pathos in the way in which this noble Norwegian sacrifiçes himself when he finds that the woman of his hêart is in lŏve with a German painter. The descriptions of scenery also ar exceedingly good." [Academy. **2721**

OVIND = *THE HAPPY BOY.*

PILOT AND HIS WIFE (The). [by JONAS LIE: Chicago, *Griggs*, 1876; Edin., *Blackwood*, 1877.] "No ŏne can read this book without feeling the breath of a civilization which is simpler and purer than ŏurs. And stil, we would not hav it inferred that the chief attraction of this beautiful tale lies in its strangeness. Those touches which make the world akin ar suffiçiently abundant tŏ render the emotions of the prinçipal actors not ŏnly intelligible, but by very reason of thêir kinship tŏ ŏur ŏn, most absorbingly interesting." [Scribner's.]—"The characters ar as forçible and as strong as the wild scenery amŏng which thêy ar plaçed. The Pilot's wife is a rare character; at first appearançe she seems mismated tŏ

the weatherbeaten sailor whŏ seems more of a taskmaster than a husband, but as we follo thêir fortunes we gro tŏ appreçiate the rare influençe which she exerts over him, and tŏ understand that ŏne of its chief powers lies in her inherent gentleness and apparent submission. The The book dŏes not deal with an elaborate plot; on the contrary the forte of the author seems tŏ lie in his power of characterization." [Library Table.]—"The scene is now in Norway, now in America; we follo the hero tŏ Pernambuco, the hero-in tŏ Amsterdam, and the scenes of South American life ar very vivid. This constant variety adds considerably tŏ the life of the story, and thêre is no point slurred over or carelessly treated. But the psychological interest is felt tŏ be grêatest when Elizabeth and Salve ar married, and return tŏ Norway, whêre he becŏmes a pilot. The natural jealousy of his nature, nurtured by early misadventure and hardship, deepens tŏ a mania, and the figure of Elizabeth, under this terrible moral torture, attains a noble strength and beauty. The story, as a mere novel, is extremely skilful and vivaçious, and wil everywhêre be read with interest; but it belongs tŏ literature in the polish of style and delicacy of observation which remind the reader of the preçise, almost mannered, writing of the author of 'Madame Bovary' [No. 2122] and LIE is as fresh and wholesŏme as the grêat Frenchman is morbid and over-subtle ... It is difficult tŏ guess why the translator has taken the liberty of omitting all the first 22 pages, as it destroys an effect evidently planned by the author." [Athenæum. **2722**

RAILROAD AND THE CHURCH-YARD (The). [by BJÖRNSTJERNE BJÖRNSON: (with "The Flying Mail." Cambridge, Mass., *Sever*, 1870.] "The third story is by Björnson. It is not so characteristic as Arne, but is a simple tale of village life, the main feature of which is the quarrel of twŏ ŏnce dear friends. One supplants the ŏther in popular favor, and becŏmes the chief man of the village, and the title is derived from the projection of a railroad, which it is proposed tŏ carry throu the churchyard. The story is very quiet and pleasing, but it lacs the beauties which distinguish the author's ŏther tales." [Boston "Literary World." **2723**

SARTAROE [by JAMES A. MAIT-LAND: *Peterson*, 1858.] "is an interesting story, and inspires us with a hī respect for Mr. Maitland's talents ... But small defects of this kind wêigh nŏthing against the obvious merits of the book." [Southern Literary Messenger. **2724**

SIGNE'S HISTORY. [by ANNA MAG-DALENE (KRAGH) THORESEN: *Chapman*, 1865.] "The scene is laid in a primitiv village situated on a fiord, a village lying amidst mountain passes and glaçiers. The clergyman is the grêatest man knŏn tŏ the inhabitants, and even the prinçipal yeoman is a kind of local aristocrat. But if he is aristocratic in the eyes of the villagers, he is but a peasant in the estimation of the pastor, whŏ has been educated at a university and has passed his early days in the society of Copenhagen. The latter, in fact, is hauty and disdainful, and givs himself airs which even in England would scarçely be assumed by anybody under a Canon. The interest of the story turns upon an attachment which arises between Signe, the rich peasant's danter, and Gudmund the sŏn of the clergyman. The result of this unhappy intimaçy (which dŏes not meet the apprŏval of the parents of either) is very melancholy, and the tale must.be deemed rather didactic than pleasing." [Athenæum. **2725**

SKIPPER WORSE [by ALEXANDER L. KIELLAND: *Low*, 1886.] "is a sad tale, but lifelike and natural; the several characters and incidents ar developed with the ease and power which can dispense with the sensational, and the whole picture is continually lited with quiet humor and kindly wit, no less than with a keen and penetrating observation." [Spectator.] See *GARMAN*. **2726**

SPELLBOUND FIDDLER (The). [by KRISTOFER JANSON: Chicago, *Griggs*, 1880.] "The title of this book is not very clear, but the book itself is as clear as can be; pelluçid and sparkling and fresh, like a mountain stream. It is a romançe founded on fact, and we ar able tŏ say that the part which Ole Bull is made tŏ take in it is told with substantial truthfulness. The story is a very pretty and touching ŏne of a Norse boy whŏ grew up with a genius for the violin, which brŏt him both good and evil fortune,—told with that simpliçity and sweetness which attach tŏ the best Norse stories. Between his gift for music and his appetite for drink poor Torgeir has a hard time of it, and many a wrench; but throu all his trial the faithful and lŏvable Kari stands by him with the fervor and courage of the true wife, and the picture of her devotion is very tenderly drawn."

[Boston "Literary World." 2727 STORY OF ULLA, by E. L. ARNOLD, in *Short Stories*, mar., 1892, 22 p. 2728 SYNNOVE SOLBAKKEN. [by BJÒRNSTJERNE BJÖRNSON: transl. by Julie Sutter, *Macmillan*, 1882; *Houghton*, 1882.] "It is refreshing tŏ light upon anything so healthy and natural as this primitiv tale of peasant life. The 19th century, with its noisy politics and its complex society, had, until very recently, no existence in the remote mountain valleys of Norway, and thêre was a patriarchal simplicity in the manners and speech of the people which seemed tŏ offer but the slenderest resources tŏ the novelist. It is in the way he has used these slender resources that Björnson has shōn that he has the true artistic instinct." [Century.]—It "is a picture of peasant life, shōing thêir piety, thêir lŏve of home and of religion, thêir Church serviçes,—which tŏ a primitiv people take the plaçe of amusements,—and thêir family life. Thorbjörn, the eldest sŏn, is a grêat, ruf lad, whŏ means no il, but whŏ has the faculty of always seeming tŏ be a ruf and nanty boy, with a strong, stubborn wil, which his father, whŏ belongs tŏ a strict religious sect, tries tŏ beat out of him; the mŏther, a sweet, gentle woman, endeavors tŏ soften things; the little sister lōves her ruf, strong brŏther; and thêre is a beautiful young maiden, the dauter of a rich nêbor, with whŏm Thorbjörn falls in lōve when thêy ar both little children. The influençe of this lōve upon him is delicately described. The characteristic of Björnson's writing is his faculty for shōing the beautiful soul which may underlie the rude and contradictory outward seeming; and for delineating the efforts by which it is striving tŏ work itself clear, and tŏ make the outward seeming and the inward intention gro intŏ harmony. He exçels in painting the pathetic indication of the difficulties and contradictions of a fine character in a state of grŏth, and in shōing the struggles tŏ dŏ right. The grêat simpliçity of Björnson almost conçeals the dramatic faculty evinçed in his stories, which givs them thêir freshness and thêir charm. Of all his works which we hav seen, we prefer the first by which he was introduçed tŏ the English reader—the story of Ovind, 'The Happy Boy'." [Athenæum.]— "Readers whŏse administration for Björnson, kindled by the charming story of "Arne," was perhaps a little cooled by what seemed the inferior merit of the "Fisher Maiden," wil be glad tŏ find in this book a work which is nearly as delightful as "Arne" itself, the (Power) translation of which was an almost perfect piece of literary workmanship, in which the English-speaking reader lost nōne of the meaning, and wōnderfully little of the beauty and vigor, of the original ... The story of "Synnöve Solbakken," or, as the translators for sōme incomprehensible reason hav renamed it, "Love and Life in Norway," is in itself so charming that nŏthing but the clumsiest manipulation could hav made it less than attractiv, and tŏ such a charge this translation is by no means open ... The story itself, for beauty and picturesqueness, hardly suffers by comparison with "Arne." Synnŏve is perhaps hardly so charming as Eli Baardsdatter, and thêre is no scene in this book which makes so unique an impression as that in which Arne's mŏther displays tŏ Eli her sŏn's hidden treasures, and with timid maternal cunning tries tŏ secure for him a prize which is already his without his kuŏing it. In this story the interest centres on the hero, Thorbjörn, whŏse impetuous temper, a little aggravated by the mistaken harshness of a father whŏ stil lŏves him passionately, is finally brŏt under control by the grêat influençe which his lŏve for Syunöve has over him. It is the way in which the story is told, and the beauty of isolated scenes, such as that in which Thorbjörn and his father cŏme tŏ Synnöve's parents tŏ beg for her hand, or that in which the pair of lŏvers first acknoledge thêir passion, which make the book so charming." [Athenæum. **2729**

——, SAME ("Love and Life in Norway"), *Cassell*, 187Q.

TALES OF TWO COUNTRIES [by ALEX. L. KIELLAND: London, *Osgood*, 1891.] "excel in vividness of presentment and keen appreciatiqn of nature; but we demur to the author's claims tŏ be deemed a humorist or a story-teller. He can be sympathetic, but he is seldom genial; his prevailing bent is toards pessimism, and his satire is uniformly mordant. A story is generally supposed tŏ hav a beginning and an end; but thêre is no rounding ŏff or reading up in Kielland's work. These "tales" ar rather episodes or transcripts of a fragment of life, and in spite of thêir poetical feeling and pathos the resultant impression left by thêir perusal is singularly tantalizing and unsatisfying." [Athenæum.]—"The intellectual power is unmistakable, and thêre is in the literary manner a reservd irony which is very effectiv as a means tŏards the desired ends of impression; but the pertinacious turning-up of the seamy side of life deprives the stories of all charm ŏther than that given by a sort of relentless cleverness. Notwithstanding this, however, there ar 2 or 3 short sketches, which in their sombre beauty prŏve that Mr. Archer dŏes not miss the mark in speaking of Kielland as a poet." [Academy. **2730**

INDEX TO AUTHORS.*

*PART I., Novels of American Country Life (Numbers 1-178),
II., Novels of American City Life (Nos. 179-0413), III., International
Novels (Nos. 401-564),—price: $ .50 each; IV., Romantic Novels (Nos.
579-1024), $1.00; V., British Novels (1025-1941), $2.00; VI., Novels
descriptive of Life in France (Nos. 1943-2322), $1.00; —— of Germany
(Nos. 2323-2563), $1.00; —— of Italy (Nos. 2565-2609), $ .25; —— of
Russia (Nos. 2610-2705), $ .50; —— of Norway (Nos. 2706-30), $ .25.

9

11

TRAVEL. A Series of Narratives of Personal Visits to places famous for Natural Beauty and Historical Association.

This publication is not an easy one to describe and is wholly beyond criticism. It is made up from the contents of Travel, an interesting and unique semi-monthly periodical published by W: M. Griswold, which consists of select narratives of personal visits to famous places. These selections, indexed in a thoroughly scientific manner, compose the two volumes before us. They are a museum of miscellanea, interesting to the traveler who is endowed with intellectual curiosity. The only drawback on their use en route is their miscellaneous character, a drawback which disappears when the journey is done and the well seasoned traveler, at home by his family fireplace, wishes to refresh his memories, renew his experiences, or to add to his own personal discoveries. Readers of both classes will find this publication, especially as bound in a permanent form, an invaluable aid in bringing to their notice the best, freshest, and most interesting illustrations which have been published on the field of travel, whether at home or abroad.—[The Independent, 18 Dec. 1890.

A serial of which two volumes have been published, composed of reprints, either in full or abridged, of papers which have appeared in a variety of periodicals and books. The personal element gives a special flavor to this serial, and the editor, who is also the publisher, has a keen scent for the interesting, as well as a good faculty for leaving out the superfluous. The English Lakes, Vallombrosa, the Engadine, Lake George, Quebec, the Black Forest, the Pyrenees, Heidelberg, the White Mountains, are among the subjects treated. The editor has annotated the text judiciously and sparingly.—[The Atlantic Monthly, March, 1891.

LIST OF NUMBERS ISSUED. Riviera, Lago-Maggiore, Montafon, Franconian-Switzerland, Wengern Alp, English Lakes, Ardennes, Neckar, Rouen to Metz (by Oscar Browning), Quebec (by H : James), Vallombrosa, Lakes George and Champlain (by H : James), Leuk, Tirol, Holland, Killarney, Dauphiné, Salzkammergut, Brienz and Thun, Harz (by H : Blackburn), Hyères (by Grant Allen), Scotch Highlands, Black Forest, Pyrenees, Tarasp, Ravenna, Mosel, Engelberg, Venice (by E. (L.) Linton), Monaco (by Grant Allen), Zermatt, Mountains near Nice, Spanish Travel, Bay of Naples (by E. (L.) Linton), Vogesen, Sabine Mountains, Arcachon, Devonshire, Lake of Zurich, Eastern Pyrenees, Heidelberg, Etretat, Schaffloch, Badenweiler, Sicily, Bavarian Highlands, Wiesen, Oybin, Val Maggia, Pegnitz Valley, Uriage, Eifel, Albenga, Weimar (by "Geo. Eliot"), Lake Leman, Bohemian Forest, Heiden, Environs of Dresden, Environs of Florence, Lakes of Savoie, Locarno to Rhone, Thüringen, Headwaters of Rhein, Riesengebirge, White Mountains (by Grant Allen), Normandie and Brétagne, Varese, Herculesbad, Fontainebleau, Channel Islands, Odenwald, Mont Dore, Stelvio, Cap d'Antibes (by Allen), Urbino, Along the Seine, Birkenfield and Idar, Along the Eastern Apennines (by Theo. Bacon), Niagara, Rheinland, Heidelberg to Nürnberg (by Taylor), etc.

PRICE, POST PAID, IN LIGHT GRAY CLOTH, $2.25 PER [SMALL 8VO.] VOLUME. IN SHEETS, $2.00 PER VOL. OF 30 NUMBERS. EACH NUMBER SOLD SEPARATELY AT 10 CENTS A COPY.—ADDRESS :

W: M. Griswold, 25 Craigie St., Cambridge, Mass.

CPSIA information can be obtained
at www.ICGtesting.com
Printed in the USA
BVHW07*1000180918
527708BV00025B/206/P